D1287090

Bibliography on the Colonial Germans of North America

Bibliography on the Colonial Germans of North America

Especially the Pennsylvania Germans and Their Descendants

Compiled and Edited by

Emil Meynen

Baltimore

GENEALOGICAL PUBLISHING CO., INC.

1982

Originally published as *Bibliography on German
Settlements in Colonial North America*, Leipzig,
Germany, 1937. Reprinted, under a new title, by
Genealogical Publishing Co., Inc., Baltimore, 1982.
Library of Congress Catalogue Card Number 81-84186
International Standard Book Number 0-8063-0964-4
Made in the United States of America

Address

delivered on the occasion of presenting the bibliography at the annual meeting of the Pennsylvania-German Society at Pennsburg, Pa., on October 21, 1932.

I have great pleasure in presenting to your Society the bibliography I have compiled during the last three years. Your decision to promote the publication of this bibliography is most encouraging. Allow me to use this opportunity to give you a brief outline of the origin and character of the bibliography.

The bibliography is not a check list of Pennsylvania-German writings or a collection of all the titles of books written by Pennsylvania-Germans. It is a compilation of printed source material which bears upon the history of that people. It is a bibliography on the German settlements in colonial North America in general, and especially a compilation of all books and papers which "set forth the part, belonging to the Pennsylvania-German in the growth and development of American character, institutions and progress."

It is not four decades since the state historian William H. EGLE ended an obituary with the remarks: "He was a good representative of a grand, unflinching God-fearing ancestry, the story of whose descendants has not yet been told because they were 'Pennsylvania-German'." This statement is no longer true. The tremendous amount of material I have filed here in this bibliography is an eloquent proof.

That I, as a young student among you, have compiled this index is but an incidental fact. The eldest among you have seen almost the whole evolution of the writing of the Pennsylvania-German history. Three-quarters of all the items listed have been written or edited within the last fifty years. Your Society, founded in 1891, was a centre of the development. Looking over the bibliography you can trace very clearly the stimulating effect of your publications. A great number of the authors were members of your Society. In short, most of the writers and editors were and are your contemporaries and personal acquaintances. I, on the other hand, came to this country three years ago. The Rockefeller Foundation granted me a fellowship for a cultural-geographic survey of the Pennsylvania-German habitat. Early studies of mine centered on Western Germany. My attention was called to the great exodus of thousands of German men and women who left their war ridden frontier homes on the border of the Rhine in the 18th century to become the pioneers of the frontier inlands of the British colonies in America, or others to build up in the Danube lowlands of Banat and Batschka Europe's frontier defence against the Turks; and again others to become tillers of soil on the border of the far off Volga.

Were these re-locations of such great masses of German people only of temporary character or were they of lasting significance? This question puts itself by no means only to the historian, but also to the student of economics, sociology, folk-lore and last but not least to the student of cultural geography. As such I shall approach in my special research the facts of migration and settlement. The geographic investigation deals with the Pennsylvania-German lands in their present conditions as a result of enviroment and of people reacting upon it. The undertaking has asked for extensive fieldwork and a broad study of literature. That was what led me to the compilation of this bibliography.

At the outset the work was merely intended for personal orientation. I found myself confronted with a mass of literature I had not known in Germany. Soon, however, I noticed that the American student also had difficulties in finding and in becoming acquainted with the material existing in print. The materials—and very often the most valuable papers-are widely scattered over numerous magazines. As modern historians have recognized the significance of the Pennsylvania-German pioneers and their descendants in the upbuilding of the American people and her cultural habitat, nation-wide attention has been paid to their history and to their ways and manners. On the other hand I saw a tremendous task before me when I came to realize the great amount of local literature. This, however, was not discouraging; on the contrary, I was fully aware that only by the help of such a bibliography the various detailed studies of mere local character could be made use of when the Pennsylvania German phenomena were to be treated in their entity. If I have succeeded in this my intention I shall regard the many hours I have spent on it as justified.

The bibliography attempts to bring out in the fullest manner all information attainable, incident to the subject. It, however, is not a bibliophile investigation. Its primary intention is to serve research purposes. The arrangement of it is made according to a subject-system, and, under the heading of a special subject, alphabetically according to the author. Local history is arranged according to the county divisions of the states. An author index will be added, and, it is expected that the index will be helpful with its references to throw light on the character of the authors. The many listed papers are naturally unequal in their character and merit. Some are colored by the consciousness of group feelings; some are the expression of historical rivalries. Although any critical student will recognize and freely concede this fact, the compiler of a bibliography should not advance any judgement or give rise to prejudice.

All in all the bibliography is a compilation of about 8000 items, 8000 titles of books and papers. Articles issued in magazines, exhaustive essays as well as shorter communications form a distinct group within the bibliography.

Addresses and pamphlets as far as they represent printed source-material bearing upon the Pennsylvania-German question are also included. Of course, numerous difficulties appear in the attempt to be complete in all the various fields of research.

This is by no means the first bibliography on the Pennsylvania-Germans. I should like to give credit to the bibliographical work done by various students in their particular fields. But beside them we might speak of 4 or 5 predecessors in general bibliography.

(1) A bibliography on "The Germans in the United States", issued by the Library of Congress in the year 1904, is the oldest one. It is a list of ca. 200 items.

(2) Also of general character, considering the entire German emigration to America, is the comprehensive compilation of A. B. FAUST in his outstanding work "The German Element in the United States", first published in 1909, revised with many bibliographical addenda in 1927.

(3) A selected list of 170 books, directly called "Bibliography on the Pennsylvania-Germans" is that which Miss H. Catherine LONG compiled in partial fulfilment of the degree: Bachelor of Library Science, New York State Library School in 1910. It was printed in the XIth volume of "The Pennsylvania-German," as well as issued separately.

(4) Because since 1910 the literature has been enriched by original and essential publications and the interest of the public is still increasing, the Library of Congress compiled a reference list of 148 items on the special topic in 1929.

(5) Finally, I should like to mention the Harrisburg publication "The Pennsylvania German Library" which Monroe AURAND printed in 1928, with a preface of personal reminiscences, as a catalogue for customers of his bookstore as well as other book collectors.

All these named are selective lists. They are valuable as introductions; as such they were compiled and edited. The present bibliography, however, attempts to give as complete an account of the existing printed resource material as possible.

For this reason it includes many titles which deal only partly with the more special Pennsylvania-German subjects. One will find listed the outstanding books of general character on Pennsylvania and Maryland and the various county histories of these states as far as they touch Pennsylvania-German settlements. A few references of the comprehensive works on the neighbors of the Pennsylvania-Germans, the Swedish and Dutch, the English, the Welsh and Scotch-Irish are also included. A few titles of modern, outstanding works of American history with relation to the Pennsylvania-German part will be given at the beginning of the list. My attitude in my own research as well as in the compilation of the bibliography is that the Pennsylvania-Germans are a distinct group, but not an isolated body in a closed area by itself; they are a part of the American people and their land is a part of Pennsylvania as well as the United Staates as a whole.

I have almost exclusively listed the books which I have personally examined. I may say with truth that I went through the catalogues of all greater libraries in Pennsylvania and over the shelves of many local institutions. Philadelphia was the starting point of my research. The various libraries of the Quaker City, especially the rich collections of the Historical Society of Pennsylvania and the University Library contain a great amount of Pennsylvania Germaniana. The State Library in Harrisburg, the Public Library in New York and especially the Library of Congress in Washington, where I had direct access to the shelves, have enabled me to present to you this bibliography to-day. Alongside with my research at these centrally located libraries, I followed the expansion of the Pennsylvania-German people as far *south* as North and South Carolina and into Tennessee, *north* to Ontario, Canada and *west* through Ohio, Indiana and Illinois as far as into Iowa. The collected items dealing with the share of the Pennsylvania-Germans in the intermigration amount to about 500.

Furthermore, I visited the main denominational libraries and archives as far as they are related to my task. The early development of the Pennsylvania-German people was very largely influenced by their religious faith, and still to-day the churches among the Pennsylvania-Germans are such important factors from the cultural as well as social aspect that it has been deemed necessary to include for each of the denominations and sects the full account of its growth and development. Of course, theological writings are not included.

I have already pointed out that this is not a bibliography of German imprints published in America. Such work has been done by Oswald SEIDENSTICKER in his Book "The First Century of German Printing in America 1723-1830." In relation to it I should like also to call your attention to research studies in the denominational field such as Harold BENDER's "Bibliography of Mennonitica Americana 1727-1928," or I may mention the work of John S. FLORY on the "Literary Activities of the German Baptist Brethren in the Eighteenth Century."

The Pennsylvania-German dialect writings are also omitted. Your Society has only recently published the comprehensive compilation of "Pennsylvania-German Writings and their Writers" by Harry Hess REICHARD. All literature, however, bearing upon the use of the German language, dialect writing, authors and printers among Pennsylvania-Germans are collected under special headings.

For a check list of German newspapers, published in this country, I am able to refer to Daniel MILLER's publication in Vol. XIX of the Proceedings of your Society. I only give a list of the historical literature bearing upon them.

I should have liked to include in the bibliography a list of the historical romances and novels about Pennsylvania-German life because these numerous publications have painted a rich picture of Pennsylvania-German land, people, homes and traditions, and are a most interesting focus of their sentiments and attitudes, although they should not be taken as scientific resource material. Due to the limited time, however, I had to give up the original plan to add such a list on "Pennsylvania-Germans in American fiction." I should like to voice it as a suggestion for a future paper of your Society.

Considerable attention has been given by authors to the attitude to education, the history of schools and colleges among the Pennsylvania-Germans, which forms a division of the work. Another section lists books dealing with the participation of the Pennsylvania-Germans in the wars of the country, in politics and in local and state administration. Though the bibliography gives numerous papers held on these subjects, it is astonishing how few books give reliable material on the economic side of the Pennsylvania-German history. The bibliography shows not only what has been written, but points out also the gaps in our literature. With special regard to the cultural and social history it offers a list of the early narratives, accounts and diaries of travellers through the Pennsylvania-German county. The most informative diaries of the Moravian Brethren are arranged as a special group. It is needless to say that all diaries, notes and letters written by Pennsylvania-Germans as far as they appeared as special publications in print have been listed.

Biography and genealogy are the most exploited field of local American history. I have collected about 1700 items within this group. William H. Egle in his "Notes and Queries" called attention to the generally unknown fact that the first family record published in America is believed to be a Pennsylvania-German genealogy, a broad side record of a Bollinger Family, printed at Ephrata in 1764. But it is not until within the last decades of the last century that the interest in compiling genealogica became general, and family reunions a typical feature of Pennsylvania-German social gatherings. I am aware of the fact that my compilation of genealogical material is not complete. Books, papers, and pamphlets relating to genealogical data are often printed privately, issued in a limited number and distributed only among family members. Furthermore, it is to be considered that the Pennsylvania-Germans, like the descendants of other early settlers of the thirteen colonies, have scattered over the whole United States. The list may prove to be a good cross section through the subject.

The largest section is that dealing with local history. County histories, accounts of settlements of local extent, histories of cities and towns, church records of single congregations, printed tax lists of early days constitute a list of 2200 items. This bibliography, I believe, is the first attempt of a list of all Pennsylvania-German records and tombstone inscriptions as far as they appeared in print.

A proposal of the compiler is to illustrate the bibliography with the portraits of authors outstanding in the writing on the Pennsylvania-Germans and typical as representatives of their times. I should think of Henry Melchior MÜHLENBERG, and Michael SCHLATTER, the church fathers; of Johann David SCHÖPF and Theophile CAZENOVE, whose travel accounts are most informative sources on Pennsylvania-German farm life in the 18th century; of Benjamin RUSH, the author of the well-known vindication of the Pennsylvania-Germans; Franz von LÖHER, whose "History and Conditions of the Germans in America" (1847) is an early manifestation of interest in the fate of the emigrants on the part of European historians. I should like to name Samuel KERCHEVAL and Israel Daniel RUPP, diligent students of local history; Friederich KAPP to whome we owe the first history on the Palatines in New York, and G. D. BERNHARD, the historian of the Germans in North and South Carolina; Samuel S. SCHMUCKER and Henry HARBAUGH, the outstanding figures of Lutheran and Reformed church history in the second half of the last century, both of Pennsylvania-German ancestry; S. S. HALDEMAN who gave us the first critical study on the Pennsylvania-German dialect; Oswald SEIDENSTICKER and H. A. RATTERMANN, pioneers in search for historical records of the Germans in the United States. I am thinking of the founders of this Society, men such as William H. EGLE, the state historian at Harrisburg and genealogist of many Scotch-Irish and Pennsylvania-German families; Samuel Whitaker PENNYPACKER, the historian of Germantown and advocate of "the plain people"; Julius F. SACHSE, author and editor of many illustrious publications; Morton L. MONTGOMERY, the painstaking recorder of Berks county history; and John W. JORDAN, the archivist, and at a time the vice-president of the Historical Society of Pennsylvania, author of many papers relating to the Moravians. Again I should like to call your attention to writers on ecclesiastical matters as well as Pennsylvania-German topics: Joseph Henry DUBBS and James Isaac GOOD on the Reformed side, Henry Eyster JACOBS and Th. Emmanuel SCHMAUCK on the Lutheran side. Oscar KUHNS, by his lively account of the "German and Swiss settlement of Colonial Pennsylvania," has acquired a unique place among the many writers. I have to mention W. J. HOFFMAN and H. C. MERCER, pioneer students of Pennsylvania-German folk-lore and Pennsylvania-German art respectively; or Marion Dexter LEARNED, professor in the University of Pennsylvania and the author of the comprehensive study on Franz Daniel Pastorius, founder of Germantown. Nathan C. SCHAEFER and Martin Grove BRUMBAUGH have called the attention to the progress of education among the Pennsylvania Germans. Henry Melchior Muhlenberg RICHARDS and Wilhelm KAUFMANN have given us the history of the share of the Germans in the American wars.

The list of writers is a very long one. George Bancroft's remark that neither the Germans nor their descendants "have laid claim to all that is their due," is not true anymore.

There is, however, still a wide field of research and collection open to the student of Pennsylvania-German people and things, a field in which new discoveries of old material still wait for the diligent student. An outstanding trend of the present phase of the writings on Pennsylvania-German topics is illustrated in a systematic approach, though undertaken quite independently by individual students. Descriptive guides to archive material, publications of original source material, works of bibliographical nature give a new basis for future studies.

Let me conclude with an appreciation of the local history. The tendency of the Pennsylvania-Germans to cling to the abode of their fathers and mothers, to the family homestead, and the way in which a large part of them still observe with pious care and unquestioning faith the ideals of their ancestors has made local research peculiarly Pennsylvania-German. Almost two-thirds of the listed authors are Pennsylvania-Germans themselves. I wonder if there is any other group of men among the descendants of colonial emigrants who in honor of their inheritance and in love of their native surroundings have given such effective contributions to the cultural and social history of their own as well as to that of their adopted country, as have the Pennsylvania-Germans to Pennsylvania and to the American nation far beyond the boundaries of the commonwealth. Allow me to dedicate the bibliography to your Society on behalf of the long tradition of the native Pennsylvania-German history, which began with the letters of Franz Daniel PASTORIUS to his father 250 years ago and is represented to-day in the work of this Society.

Table of Contents of the Bibliography

Benutzte Bibliotheken und Archive

Libraries and Archives consulted

Vereinigte Staaten von Amerika

United States

Library of Congress. Washington, D. C.
New York Public Library, 476 5th Ave. New York City, N. Y.
Pennsylvania State Library. Harrisburg, Pa.
Library and Archives of the Historical Society of Pennsylvania. Philadelphia, Pa.
Library of the University of Pennsylvania. Philadelphia, Pa.
Library and Archives of the German Society of Philadelphia. Philadelphia, Pa.
Carnegie Library of Pittsburgh. Pittsburgh, Pa.
Virginia State Library. Richmond, Va.
North Carolina State Library. Raleigh, N. C.
New York State Library. Albany, N. Y.
Ohio State Library. Columbus, O.
Library of the Ohio State Archaeological and Historical Society. Columbus, O.
Library of the University of Illinois. Chicago, Ill.
Library of the American Antiquarian Society. Worcester, Mass.
Krauth Memorial Library and Archives of the Evangelical Lutheran Ministerium of
    Pennsylvania, Lutheran Theological Seminary Mt. Airy. Philadelphia, Pa.
Library and Archives of the Lutheran Historical Society, Lutheran Theological Seminary.
    Gettysburg, Pa.
Smith Library, Columbia Theological Seminary. Columbia, S. C.
College Library of the Wittenberg College. Springfield, O.
Seminary Library and Archives of the Historical Society of the Reformed Church in the
    United States, Theological Seminary of the Reformed Church in the United States.
    Lancaster, Pa.
College Library of the Franklin and Marshall College. Lancaster, Pa.
Seminary Library, Auburn Theological Seminary. Auburn, N. Y.
Library and Archives of the Presbyterian Historical Society. Philadelphia, Pa.
Library of the Juniata College and Archives of the Church of the Brethren, Juniata
    College. Huntingdon, Pa.
Archives of the Unitas Fratrum or Moravian Church in the United States of America.
    Bethlehem, Pa.
College Library, Moravian College and Theological Seminary. Bethlehem, Pa.
Moravian Archives at Salem. Winston-Salem, N. C.
Schwenkfelder Historical Library and Archives. Pennsburg, Pa.
Library and Archives of the Mennonite Historical Society, Goshen College. Goshen, Ind.
Library and Archives of the Historical Society of the United Brethren in Christ, Bonebrake
    Seminary. Dayton, O.
Library of the School of Theology and Archives of the Historical Society of the Evangelical
    Church, School of Theology. Reading, Pa.
The Library and Archives of the American Catholic Historical Society of Philadelphia.
    Philadelphia, Pa.

County Historical Libraries and Archives:
    Bucks County Historical Society. Doylestown, Pa.
    Hamilton Library Association and Cumberland County Historical Association.
        Carlisle, Pa.
    Historical Society of Bucks County. Reading, Pa.
    Historical Society of Montgomery County. Norristown, Pa.
    Historical Society of Schuylkill County. Pottsville, Pa.
    Historical Society of York County. York, Pa.
    Kittochtinny Historical Society. Chambersburg, Pa.
    Lancaster County Historical Society. Lancaster, Pa.
    Lebanon County Historical Society. Lebanon, Pa.
    Lehigh County Historical Society. Allentown, Pa.
    Wyoming Historical and Geological Society. Wilkes-Barre, Pa.
    Handley Library. Winchester, Pa.
United Lutheran Publication House. Philadelphia, Pa.
Central Office of the Board of Christian Education of the Reformed Church in the United
    States, Schaff Building. Philadelphia, Pa.
Mennonite Publishing House. Scottdale, Pa.
Brethren Publishing House. Elgin, Ill.
Brethren Publishing House. Ashland, O.
E. V. Publishing House of the Brethren in Christ Church. Nappanee, Ind.
"The Otterbein Press", United Brethren Publishing House. Dayton, O.
The Publishing House of the Evangelical Church. Harrisburg, Pa.
The Central Publishing House of the Churches of God. Harrisburg, Pa.

Europa

Europe

British Museum Library. London, England.
Preußische Staatsbibliothek. Berlin, Deutsches Reich.
Bibliothèque Nationale. Paris, Frankreich.
Bibliothek des Deutschen Ausland-Instituts. Stuttgart, Deutsches Reich.
Bibliothek der Georg-August-Universität. Göttingen, Deutsches Reich.
Bibliothek der Universität Heidelberg. Heidelberg, Deutsches Reich.
Bibliothek des Theologischen Seminars der evangelischen Brüder-Unität. Herrenhut,
    Deutsches Reich.
Badische Landesbibliothek. Karlsruhe, Deutsches Reich.
Pfälzische Landesbibliothek. Speyer, Deutsches Reich.
Württembergische Landesbibliothek. Stuttgart, Deutsches Reich.
Zentralbibliotheken. Zürich, Schweiz.
Universitätsbibliothek. Basel, Schweiz.
Reichsdeutsche, schweizer und österreichische Archive vgl. M. D. Learned [= Nr. 7834]
    und A. B. Faust [= Nr. 7831] — German, Swiss and Austrian archives see M. D.
    Learned [= no. 7834] and A. B. Faust [= no. 7831].
Public Record Office. London, England.
Synodal-Archiv der Niederländisch-Reformierten Kirche. 's Gravenhage, Niederlande.
Klassikal-Archiv der Niederländisch-Reformierten Kirche. Amsterdam, Niederlande.

Amerika allgemein
The American Background

Adams, James Truslow: Provincial society, 1690—1763. *New York, N. Y.: The Macmillan Co. 1927. pp. XVII, 374, ill.*
= *A history of American life. Edited by Arthur M. Schlesinger and Dixon Ryan Fox. Vol. III.* [1

Beard, Charles A. and **Beard, Mary R.:** The rise of American civilization. *2 vols. New York, N. Y.: The Macmillan Co. 1929. Vol. I. „The agricultural era." pp. 824, ill.; Vol. II. „The industrial era." pp. 828, ill.* [2

Beverly, W. Bond: The quit-rent system in the American colonies. *By . . . With an introduction by Charles M. Andrews. New Haven, N. Y.: Yale University Press; London: Humphrey Milford; Oxford: University Press 1919. pp. 492.* [3

Bidwell, Percy Wells and **Falconer, John I.:** History of agriculture in the northern United States, 1620—1860. *Washington, D. C.: The Carnegie Institution of Washington 1925. pp. XII, 512, ill., maps.*
= *Carnegie Institution of Washington, Publication no. 358.* [4

Bishop, J. Leander: A history of American manufactures from 1608 to 1860: *exhibiting the origin and growth of the principal mechanic arts and manufactures, from the earliest colonial period to the adoption of the constitution and comprising annals of the industry of the United States in machinery, manufactures and useful arts, with a notice of the important inventions, tariffs and the result of each decennial census. By . . . With an appendix, containing statistics of the principal manufacturing centres and descriptions of remarkable manufactories at the present time. 3 vols.* *Philadelphia Pa.: Edward Young & Co.; London: Sampson Low, Son & Co. 1866, 1868. pp. (1), 7—642; 13—654; V, 14—574, ill.* [5

Bogart, Ernest Ludlow: Economic history of the American people. *New York, N. Y.; London; Toronto: Longmans, Green and Co. 1930. pp. XII, 797, maps.* [6

Bolton, Herbert Eugene and **Marshall, Thomas Maitland:** The colonization of North America 1492—1783. *New York, N. Y.: The Macmillan Co. 1927. pp. XVI, 609, ill., maps.* [7

Cambridge History of the British Empire: „The old empire from the beginning to 1783." *New York, N. Y.: The Macmillan Co.; Cambridge, England: The University Press 1929. pp. XXI, 931.*
= *Vol. I. of The Cambridge History of the British Empire. General editors: J. Holland Rose, A. P. Newton, E. A. Benians.*
[Bibliography pp. 823—888.] [8

Channing, Edward: A history of the United States. *New York, N. Y.: The Macmillan Co. 1905ff. Vol. II. A century of colonial history. 1660—1760. New York, N. Y. 1908 pp. VII, 614, maps; Vol. III. The American Revolution 1761—1789. New York, N. Y. 1912 pp. VII, 585, maps.* [9

Cheyney, Edward Potts: European background of American history 1300—1600. *New York, N. Y. and London: Harper & Brothers 1904. pp. XXVIII, 343, ill., maps.*
= *The American Nation: A history. Edited by A. B. Hart. Vol. I.* [10

Chitwood, Oliver Perry: A history of colonial America. *New York, N. Y. and London: Harper and Brothers Publishers 1931 pp. XIII, 811, maps.* [11

Clark, Victor S.: History of manufactures in the United States. *Vol. I.* 1607 — 1860. *With an introductory note by Henry W. Farnam. 1929 edition. Published for the Carnegie Institution of Washington. New York, N. Y.: McGraw-Hill Book Co., Inc. 1929. pp. XI, 607, maps.* [12

Faulkner, Harold Underwood: American economic history. *Revised edition. New York, N. Y. and London: Harper & Brothers 1931. pp. XIV, 795, maps.* [13

Fish, Carl Russell: The rise of the common man . . . *New York, N. Y.: The Macmillan Co. 1927. pp. XIX, 391, ill.* = *A history of American life. Edited by Arthur M. Schlesinger; Dixon · Ryan Fox. Vol. VI.* [14

Friederici, Georg: Der Charakter der Entdeckung und Eroberung Amerikas durch die Europäer. *Einleitung zur Geschichte der Besiedlung Amerikas durch die Völker der alten Welt. Herausgegeben mit Unterstützung durch die Preußische Akademie der Wissenschaften. Bd. III. Stuttgart: Verlag Friedrich Andreas Perthes A.G. 1936. S. XVI, 520.* = *Allgemeine Staatengeschichte. Herausgegeben von Hermann Oncken. Zweite Abteilung: Geschichte der Außereuropäischen Staaten. Zweites Werk, Bd. III.* [14a

Gray, Lewis Cecil: History of agriculture in the southern United States to 1860. *By . . ., assisted by Esther Katharine Thompson. With an introductory note by Henry Charles Taylor. 2 vols. Washington, D. C.: Published by the Carnegie Institution of Washington 1933. pp. XIX, 567; IX, 571—1086, maps* = *Carnegie Institution of Washington, Publication no. 430. [Bibliography pp. 951—1016.]* [14b

Greene, Evarts Boutell: Provincial America 1690—1740. *New York, N. Y. and London: Harper & Brothers 1905. pp. XXI, 356, ill., maps.* = *The American Nation: A history. Edited by A. B. Hart. Vol. VI.* [15

— The foundation of American nationality. *New York, N. Y.; Cincinnati, O.; Chicago, Ill.; Boston, Mass.; Altanta, Ga.: American Book Co 1922. pp. XII, 614, XIII—XL, ill., maps.* [16

MacGill, Caroline E.: History of transportation in the United States before 1860 *Prepared under the direction of Bal-*

thasar Henry Meyer by . . . and a staff of collaborators. Published by the Carnegie Institution of Washington. Washington, D. C.: Press of Gibson Brothers, Inc. 1917. pp. XI, 678, maps. = *Carnegie Institution of Washington. Publication no. 215 c.* [17

Pfeifer, Gottfried: Die Bedeutung der „Frontier" für die Ausbreitung der Vereinigten Staaten bis zum Mississippi. *In: Geographische Zeitschrift. Begründet von Alfred Hettner, herausgegeben von Heinr. Schmitthenner. Jg. XLI. Leipzig-Berlin 1935. S. 138—158.* [17a

Osgood, Herbert L.: The American colonies in the seventeenth century. *2 vols. New York, N. Y.: Columbia University Press 1904. Reprinted 1930. Vol. I:* The proprietary province in its earliest form, the corporate colonies of New England. *pp. XXXII, 578; Vol. II:* The proprietary province in its later forms. *pp. XIX, 490.* [18

Ratzel, Friedrich: Politische Geographie der Vereinigten Staaten von Amerika unter besonderer Berücksichtigung der natürlichen Bedingungen und wirtschaftlichen Verhältnisse. *2. Aufl. München: R. Oldenbourg 1893. XIV (2) 763 S., Karten.* = *Die Vereinigten Staaten von Amerika. Von Friedrich Ratzel. Bd. II.* [18a

Rossiter, W. S.: A century of population growth from the first census of the United States to the twelfth 1790—1900. *[Editor: U. S.] Department of Commerce and Labor. Bureau of the Census. Washington, D. C.: Government Printing Office. pp. X, 303, maps.* [19

Schmieder, Oscar: Länderkunde Nordamerikas. Vereinigte Staaten und Kanada. *Leipzig und Wien: Franz Deuticke 1933. S. XI, 453 S., ill., Karten.* = *Enzyklopädie der Erdkunde. Herausgegeben von Oscar Kende. Vol. XXVII.* [20

Schönemann, Friedrich: Die Vereinigten Staaten von Amerika. *2 Bde. Stuttgart-Berlin: Deutsche Verlagsanstalt 1932. Bd. I:* Von der Kolonie zum Weltreich. *XV, 338 S.; Bd. II:* Die amerikanische Demokratie von heute. *XII, 556 S.; [Bibliographie in Bd. I, S. 465—522].* [21

Schultze-Gaevernitz, G. v.: Die geistigen Grundlagen der angelsächsischen Weltherrschaft: Vorbemerkung; *(I).* Die drei Wellen der angelsächsischen Kirchenreformation. *In: Archiv für Sozial-*

wissenschaft und Sozialpolitik. Bd. LVI. Tübingen 1926. S. 26—65; Die geistesgeschichtlichen Grundlagen der anglo-amerikanischen Weltsuprematie: *(II). Die Wurzel der Demokratie.* In: *Bd. LVIII. Tübingen 1927. S. 60—112.* [22

Semple, Ellen Churchill: American history and its geographic conditions. *Boston, Mass. and New York, N. Y.: Houghton, Mifflin and Co. 1903. pp. (5), 466, ill., maps.* [23

Smith, J. Russell: North America. *Its people and the resources, development, and prospects of the continent as an agricultural, industrial, and commercial area. London: G. Bell and Sons, Ltd. 1925. pp. VIII, 849, ill., maps.* [24

Turner, Frederick Jackson: The significance of the frontier in American history. *Paper in: The Annual Report of the American Historical Association for the* *year 1893. Washington, D. C.: Governement Printing Office 1894. pp. 199—227.* [25

Turner, Frederick Jackson: The frontier in American history. *New York, N. Y.: H. Holt and Co. 1921. Reprinted 1926. pp. (4), 375.* [26

Baker, O. E.: A graphic summary of American agriculture, based largely on the census. *Compiled by . . . Washington, D. C. 1931. pp. 228; figures & maps 360.* = *United States Department of Agriculture. Miscellaneous publication, No. 105.* [27

Paullin, Charles O.: Atlas of the historical geography of the United States. *Compiled by . . . Published jointly by the Carnegie Institution of Washington, and the American Geographical Society of New York. Washington, D. C. 1932. pp. 145; maps 620.* [28

Das Deutschtum in den Vereinigten Staaten

Germans in the United States

Allgemein

General

Angerstein, George W.: Unrolling the scroll. Authentic historical and educational articles, dealing with vitally important phases of American civilization . . . *Compiled by* . . . *Edited by* Helen E. **Brenneman;** *Art direction by* William Miller. *Vol. I (only published).* Chicago, Ill.: *Published by National Historical Society. 1928. pp. 230, ill.* [29

Bosse, Georg von: Das deutsche Element in den Vereinigten Staaten unter besonderer Berücksichtigung seines politischen, ethischen, sozialen und erzieherischen Einflusses. *Stuttgart: Chr. Belsersche Verlagsbuchhandlung 1908. XIII, 480 S., ill.* [30

Brauns, E.: Practische Belehrungen und Rathschläge für Reisende und Auswanderer nach Amerika. *Braunschweig: Herzogl. Waisenhaus Buchdruckerei 1829. IV, 5—492 S.* [„Die Landwirtschaft der Deutschen in Nordamerika." *S. 169—187; „Geschichte der Deutschen Einwanderung" S. 188—209; „Wird die deutsche Sprache in Amerika bestehen oder untergehen?" S 210—222.]* [31

Brauns, Ernst Ludwig: „Kolonisierungen der Deutschen." *In: Amerika und die moderne Völkerwanderung. Nebst einer Darstellung der gegenwärtig zu Ökonomie — Economy — am Ohio angesiedelten Harmonie-Gesellschaft, von E. L. Brauns. Potsdam: H. Voglersche Buchhandlung 1833. Teil II. S. 152—307.* [32

Bromme, Traugott: „Die Deutschen in Nord-Amerika". *In: Gemälde von Nord-Amerika in allen Beziehungen von der Entdeckung an bis auf die neueste Zeit. Eine pittoreske Geographie für Alle, welche unterhaltende Belehrung suchen und ein umfassendes Reise-Handbuch*

für Jene, welche in diesem Lande wandern wollen, von Traugott Bromme. Bd. I. Stuttgart: J. Scheible's Buchhandlung 1842. S. 257—284.* [33

Cronau, Rudolf: Drei Jahrhunderte deutschen Lebens in Amerika. Eine Geschichte der Deutschen in den Vereinigten Staaten. *Berlin: Dietrich Reimer (Ernst Vohsen) 1909. XIII, 640 S. ill; 2. Auflage Berlin 1924. XIII, 696 S., ill. [Quellen z. Gesch. d. deutschen Elements in den Vereinigten Staaten. S. 613—632; 2. Aufl. 1924 S. 664—683.]* [34

— The German element in the United States. *In: The Forum. Vol. XLVI. London and New York 1911. pp. 257—267.* [35

— German achievments in America. *A tribute to the memory of the men and women, who worked, fought and died for the welfare of this country; and a recognition of the living who with equal enterprise, genius and patriotism helped in the making of our United States. New York, N. Y: Rudolf Cronau 1916. pp. (2) 9—233.* [36

— Die Deutschen als Gründer von Neu-Amsterdam — New York und als Träger der amerikanischen Freiheitsbestrebungen. *Eine Denkschrift zur Erinnerung an die vor 300 Jahren erfolgte Erwerbung der Insel Manhattan durch Peter Minuit, und an die 150jährige Feier des amerikanischen Unabhängigkeitskrieges. New York, N. Y.: Heiß Verlag 1926. 70 S.* [37

Dubbs, J. H.: German life and culture in America. *In: The Reformed Quarterly Review. Vol. XXXV. = New series, vol. X. Philadelphia, Pa. 1888. pp. 453 —471.* [38

Eickhoff, Anton: In der neuen Heimath. Geschichtliche Mittheilungen über die deutschen Einwanderer in allen Theilen der Union. *Herausgegeben von . . . New York, N. Y.: E. Steiger & Co. 1884. VII, 398 S.; Anhang: Die Deutsche Gesellschaft der Stadt New York. S. 1—164.* [39

Eiselmeier, J.: Das Deutschtum in Anglo-Amerika. *Berlin: Deutscher Schutzbund Verlag 1926. 35 S.*
= *Taschenbücher des Grenz- und Auslanddeutschtums. Heft 36—37.* [40

Everett, E.: German immigration to America. *[Review of]: Der Deutsche in Nord-Amerika — The Germans in North America: Stuttgart und Tübingen 1818 [= no. 53]. In: North American Review and Miscellaneous Journal (No. XXVIII, New series, no. III.) Vol. XI. New series — Vol. II. Boston, Mass., July, 1820. pp. 1—19.* [41

Faust, Albert Bernhardt: The German element in the United States. With special reference to its political, moral, social and educational influence. *2 vols. Boston, Mass. and New York, N. Y.: Houghton Mifflin Co.: The Riverside Press Cambridge 1909. pp. XXVI, 591, ill., maps; pp. XVI, 605, ill.*
[Bibliography: Vol. II. pp. 479—562.] Second enlarged edition. Both vols. bound as one. New York, N. Y.: The Steuben Society of America. [Printed: Kingsport, Tenn. (Kingsport Press)] 1927. pp. XXVIII, 591; XIV, 730, ill., maps.
[Additional bibliographical material see: Appendix to both volumes. In: Vol. II. pp. 607—730.] [42

— Übersicht über die Geschichte der Deutschen in Amerika. *In: Das Buch der Deutschen in Amerika. Philadelphia, Pa. 1909. [= Nr. 59] S. 49—82.* [43

— Das Deutschtum in den Vereinigten Staaten in seiner geschichtlichen Entwicklung. *Berechtigte deutsche Ausgabe. Leipzig: B. G. Teubner 1912. VIII, 504 S., Karten.* [44

— Das Deutschtum in den Vereinigten Staaten in seiner Bedeutung für die amerikanische Kultur. *Berechtigte deutsche Ausgabe. Leipzig: B. G. Teubner 1912. XII, 447 S., ill.* [45

— The Germans in the United States. *An address delivered before the German University League. New York, N. Y., Jan. 14, 1916. pp. (14).* [46

[—] [Striking facts about] the Germans in the United States. *Extracts from the book of . . .: The German element in the United States. In: The Concord Society of America. Historical Bulletin 5. [Hoboken, N. J.] 1916. pp. 3—16.* [47

Faust, Albert Bernhardt: Swiss emigration to the American colonies in the 18th century. *In: The American Historical Review. Vol. XXII, no. 1. Oct., 1916. pp. 21—44.* [48

— German cultural influence in American life. *In: The Concord Society of America. Year book 1928. Detroit, Mich.: Herold Printing Co. 1929. pp. 6—16.* [49

— Das Deutschtum in den Vereinigten Staaten *(Festrede auf der Jahresversammlung des Deutschen Ausland-Instituts, Stuttgart, 10. Mai 1929). In: Der Auslanddeutsche. Halbmonatsschrift für Auslanddeutschtum und Auslandkunde. Mitteilungen des Deutschen Ausland-Instituts, Stuttgart. Jg. XII, No. 12. Stuttgart, 1929. S. 388—392.* [50

Fehling, August Wilhelm: Die Deutschamerikaner. *In: Die Vereinigten Staaten von Amerika. Land und Menschen unter dem Sternenbanner. Von A. W. Fehling. Berlin: Deutsche Buch-Gemeinschaft 1933. S. 55—63.* [50a

Fischer, P. D.: Die Anfänge der deutschen Auswanderung nach Amerika. *Vortrag, gehalten im Berliner Unions-Verein am 1. April 1870. Berlin: F. Henschel 1870. 36 S.* [51

Fulda, Ludwig: Die Deutschen in Amerika. Ein Kulturproblem. *Vortrag, gehalten im Hotel Astor, New York, den 31. Oktober 1913. In: Germanistic Society Quarterly. Published by the Germanistic Society of America. Vol. I, no. 1. Lancaster, Pa. March, 1914. pp. 10—35* [52

[Fürstenwärther, Moritz]: Der Deutsche in Nord-Amerika. *Edited by* **H. Chr. E. von Gagern**. *Stuttgart und Tübingen: J. G. Cotta'schen Buchhandlung 1818. 124 S.*
[Vgl. Everett, E.: German immigration to America = Nr. 41; Huch, C. F.: Der Deutsche in Nord-Amerika im Jahre 1817 = Nr. 66 und Kohler, Max J.: An important European mission to investigate American conditions 1817—1818 = Nr. 73] [53

G., F. J.: Über den Germanismus in den Vereinigten Staaten von Amerika. *In: Deutsche Vierteljahrs-Schrift. Erstes Heft 1839. Stuttgart und Tübingen 1839. S. 33—73.* [54

Gehring, Albert: German-American achievements. *[Cleveland, O. (?) 19 . . .] pp. (8).* [55

Goebel, Julius: Das Deutschtum in den Vereinigten Staaten von Nord-Amerika. *München: J. F. Lehmanns Verlag 1904. 88, (2) S. = Der Kampf um das Deutschtum, Nr. 16. Herausgegeben vom Alldeutschen Verband. [Bibliographisches S. 85—88.]* [56

— Die Deutschen in der amerikanischen Geschichtsschreibung. *Nach einem Vortrag, gehalten bei der 25. Jahresversammlung der American Historical Society. In: Deutsche Erde. Zeitschrift für Deutschkunde. Herausgegeben von Paul Langhans. Jg. X. Gotha, 1911. S. 176—182.* [57

Grothe, Hugo: Die Deutschen in Übersee. *Eine Skizze ihres Werdens, ihrer Verbreitung und kulturellen Arbeit. Berlin: Zentralverlag 1932. VIII, 315 S., Karten. [Kanada. S. 125—165; Das Deutschtum in den Vereinigten Staaten von Amerika und ihre Einwanderungspolitik. S. 166—194.]* [57a

Handelmann, Heinrich: Geschichte der Vereinigten Staaten. *Erster Theil: Die historische Entwicklung des Landes, des Volkes und der Verfassung. Kiel: Verlag der Schwersschen Buchhandlung 1856. XVI, 688 S. = Geschichte der amerikanischen Kolonisation und Unabhängigkeit. Erster Band. Die Staaten der weißen und schwarzen Race. Erste Hälfte. Buch I. Vereinigte Staaten. [Kap. III: Die Bevölkerung der Vereinigten Staaten. Die Weißen, ihre Einwanderung. S. 311 ff.: . . . Die deutschen Amerikaner der älteren Einwanderung (Pennsylvania-Deutsche) S. 321 f, und der neueren Einwanderung, S. 335—337; der Kampf um die Nationalität im Neuen Niederland und Nordwesten zwischen Englischen und Deutschen bis zum Rückzug der Pennsylvanier. S. 353 f.; der neue Aufschwung des Deutschtums. S. 364—367.]* 58

[Heinrici, Max]: Das Buch der Deutschen in Amerika. *Herausgegeben unter den Auspicien des Deutsch-Amerikanischen National-Bundes. Philadelphia, Pa.: Walther's Buchdruckerei 1909. VII, 974 S., ill.* [59

Hennighausen, Louis P.: The first German immigrants to North-America. *In:*

Seventh Annual Report of the Society for the History of the Germans in Maryland Baltimore, Md. 1893. pp. 13—25. [60

Hermann, Friedrich: Die Deutschen in Nordamerika. *In drey Schilderungen. [Teil II: „Character und Lebensweise der in Nord-Amerika angesessenen Deutschen".] In: Minerva. Ein Journal historischen und politischen Inhalts. Herausgegeben von J. W. v. Archenholz. Dritter Band für das Jahr 1804. Hamburg 1804. S. 440—485; vierter Band für das Jahr 1804. S. 142—162; erster Band für das Jahr 1805. S. 83—100; 317—337; 487—509; zweiter Band für das Jahr 1805. S. 36—64; dritter Band für das Jahr 1805. S. 117—142; 267 — 315.* [61

— Die Deutschen in Nordamerika. *In drey Schilderungen entworfen von . . . Lüben: Christian Traugott Gotsch; Wittenberg: gedruckt bey Friedrich Immanuel Seibt 1806. (4), 191 S.* [62

Hexamer, C. J.: Address . . . *delivered at the celebration of „German Day" at Washington Park, 26th Street and Allegheny Avenue, Philadelphia, Pa., July 25, 1898. pp. 12.* [63

— German achievement in America. *Address delivered at the German Day Celebration, Madison Square Garden, New York, November 9, 1902. In: German American Annals. New series, vol. I. Philadelphia, Pa. 1903. pp 46—53.* [64

— Die Bedeutung der deutschen Einwanderung. *In: Das Buch der Deutschen in Amerika. Philadelphia, Pa. 1909 [= Nr. 59]. S. 9—17.* [65

Huch, C. F.: Der Deutsche in Nordamerika im Jahre 1817. *In: Mitteilungen des Deutschen Pionier Vereins von Philadelphia, Pa. Heft 22, 1911. [Philadelphia, Pa. 1911.] 13 S. [Auf Grund der Berichte und Briefe von Moritz von Fürstenwärther; vgl. Nr. 53]* [66

Kapp, Friedrich: Deutsch-amerikanische Wechselbeziehungen. *In: Deutsche Rundschau. Herausgegeben von Julius Rodenberg. Bd. XXV. Berlin 1880. S. 88—123.* [68

Kaufmann, Wilhelm: Die Bedeutung des deutschen Elements in Amerika. *Festrede zur Einweihung der Germania-Halle in Cleveland am 15. Januar 1888. In: Der Auslanddeutsche. Halbmonatsschrift für Auslanddeutschtum und Aus-*

landkunde. Mitteilungen des Deutschen Ausland-Instituts, Stuttgart. Jg. IV. Stuttgart 1921. S. 38—40; 70—74. [69

Klenze, Camillo von: Das deutsche Element in den Vereinigten Staaten. *In: Süddeutsche Monatshefte. Jg. XXVI, Heft 9. München 1929. S. 650—655.* [70

Kloß, Heinz: Übersehenes Deutschtum in Amerika. *In: Jungnationale Stimmen. Jg. IV. Berlin 1930. S. 49—53.* [71

Knortz, Karl: Das Deutschtum der Vereinigten Staaten. *Hamburg: Verlagsanstalt und Druckerei A.G. (vormals J. F. Richter) 1898. 83 S.* [72

Kohler, Max J.: An important European mission to investigation, American immigration conditions, and John Quincy Adams' relations thereto (1817—1818). *In: Deutsch-Amerikanische Geschichtsblätter. Jahrbuch der Deutsch-Amerikanischen Historischen Gesellschaft von Illinois. Jg. 1917. Vol. XVII. Chicago, Ill. 1917. S. 393—415;* Aus Moritz von Fürstenwärthers Schrift. Der Deutsche in Nordamerika. *Mit einer Vorbemerkung des Herausgebers. S. 416—458. [Vgl. Nr. 53]* [73

Körner, Gustav: Das deutsche Element in den Vereinigten Staaten von Nordamerika, 1818—1848. *Cincinnati, O.: A. E. Wilde & Co. 1880. 461 S. [Pennsylvanien. S. 19—92; Maryland-Virginia. S. 393—420.]* [74

Learned, Marion Dexter: „Deutsche Ideale in Amerika." *In: Das Buch der Deutschen in Amerika. Philadelphia, Pa. 1909 [= Nr. 59]. S. 19—30.* [75

— The early German immigrant and the immigration question of to-day. *Address delivered at the annual meeting of the American Philosophical Society. In: The Pennsylvania-German. Vol. XII. Lititz, Pa. 1911. pp. 356—361.* [76

Levan, F. K.: The Germans in the United States. *In: The Mercersburg Review. Vol. XVII. Philadelphia, Pa. 1870. pp. 523—537.* [77

Lohan, Oswald: Das Deutschtum in den Vereinigten Staaten von Amerika. *Berlin: Carl Heymanns Verlag — New York, N. Y.: E. Steiger & Co. 1913. (1) 56 S.* [77a

Löffler, Eugenie: Vereinigte Staaten v. Amerika: Deutschtum. *In: Staatslexikon im Auftrage der Görres-Gesellschaft herausgegeben von Herman Sacher. Bd. V. Freiburg i. Br. 1932. Sp. 726—734.* [77b

Löher, Franz: Geschichte und Zustände der Deutschen in Amerika. *Cincinnati, O.: Eggers und Wulkop; Leipzig: K. F. Köhler 1847. XII, 544 S.; Zweite Auflage. Göttingen: Georg H. Wigand 1855. X, 544 S.* [78

Löher, Franz: Die Deutsche Auswanderung und ihre Bedeutung in der Kulturgeschichte. *(Aus einem Vortrag, im Februar 1847 vor dem deutschen Lese- und Bildungsverein in Cincinnati gehalten). In: Der Deutsche Pionier. Jg. VII. Cincinnati, O. 1875—1876. S. 47—53; 105—108; 136—140.* [79

Lohr, Otto: The first Germans in North-America, and the German element of New Netherland. *New York, N. Y.: G. E. Stechert & Co. 1912. pp. 15.* [80

— Die Anfänge deutscher Einwanderung in Nordamerika. *In: Deutsch-Amerikanische Geschichtsblätter. Jahrbuch der Deutsch-Amerikanischen Historischen Gesellschaft von Illinois. Jg. 1912. Vol. XII. Chicago, Ill. 1912. S. 499—509.*[81

— Die Anfänge deutscher Einwanderung in Nordamerika. *(Vgl.: Deutsch-Amerikanische Geschichtsblätter . . . Jg. 1912. Chicago, Ill. 1912). In: Deutsche Erde. Zeitschrift für Deutschkunde. Herausgegeben von Paul Langhans. Jg. XII. Gotha 1913. S. 99—104.* [82

— Das Deutschamerikanertum vor hundert Jahren und der Krieg von 1812—1815. *In: Deutsch-Amerikanische Geschichtsblätter. Jahrbuch der Deutsch-Amerikanischen Historischen Gesellschaft von Illinois. Jg. 1914. Vol. XIV. Chicago, Ill. 1915. S. 392—450; Seperatabdruck 1915. 59 S.* [83

— A brief historical review of the achievements of German nationals in the early days of American colonization. The period from 1564 to 1682 inclusive. *New York, N. Y.; Hoboken, N. J. 1923. pp. 8. = Historical Bulletin no. 1. of the Concord Society of America.* [84

— Die deutsche Sprache in Nordamerika im 17. Jahrhundert. *In: Mitteilungen der Akademie zur wissenschaftlichen Erforschung und zur Pflege des Deutschtums. Deutsche Akademie. Jg. 1933. No. 1. München 1933. S. 90—103.* [85

Meyer, Geo.: The German American. *Dedicated to the celebration of the „German American Day" held in Milwaukee, Oct. 6, 1890. Milwaukee: Hake & Stirn Prtg. Co. 1890. pp. 41, (1), ill.* [86

Meynen, Emil: Das Deutschtum in Nord-
amerika. *In: Das Buch vom deutschen
Volkstum. Wesen — Lebensraum —
Schicksal. Herausgegeben von P. Gauss.
Leipzig: F. A. Brockhaus 1935. S. 332
—339, ill., Karten.* [87
Mönckmeier, Wilhelm: Die deutsche über-
seeische Auswanderung. *Ein Beitrag zur
deutschen Wanderungsgeschichte. Jena:
Verlag von Gustav Fischer 1912. X, 269 S.
[Insbesondere: ,,Die geschichtliche Ent-
wicklung der deutschen Auswanderung".
(1) Vorläufer und Anfänge. = Abschnitt I.
S. 5—14.]* [88
Münch, Fr.: Welchen Einfluß auf das sitt-
liche Leben unserer hiesigen deutschen
Landbevölkerung hat deren Versetzung
aus der alten in die neue Welt bisher
gezeigt? *In: Der Deutsche Pionier.
Jg. III. Cincinnati, O. 1871—1872.
S. 338—342.* [89
Myers, Jacob W.: The beginning of the
German immigration in the Middle West
*In: Journal of the Illinois State Histo-
rical Society. Springfield, Ill. 1922/23.
pp. 592—599.* [90
Nath, Dorethea: German American records.
*(Gathered from Niles' Weekly Register,
published in Baltimore from 1811 to 1849,
76 volumes, founded, edited and printed
by Hezekiah Niles, since 1836 by his
son, W. O. Niles). In: German American
Annals. New series, vol. II. Philadel-
phia, Pa. 1904. pp. 83—105.* [91
Oncken, Hermann: Die deutsche Auswande-
rung nach Amerika und das Deutsch-
amerikanertum vom 17. Jahrhundert
bis zur Gegenwart. *Auszug aus 5 Vor-
trägen, gehalten im Freien Deutschen
Hochstift zu Frankfurt am Main 1911.
In: Historisch-politische Aufsätze und
Reden von Hermann Oncken. Bd. I.
München-Berlin: Druck und Verlag von
R. Oldenbourg 1914. S. 95—119.* [92
Petersen, Carl und andere: Handwörterbuch
des Grenz- und Auslanddeutschtums.
*Unter Mitwirkung von etwa 800 Mit-
arbeitern herausgegeben von Carl Petersen,
Otto Scheel, Paul Hermann, Ruth und
Hans Schwalm. Breslau: Ferdinand
Hirt 1933ff. Bd. 1 in 9 Lieferungen
Breslau 1933—35. XIV, 746 S.; Bd. II
und folgende im Erscheinen.
[Bd. I u. a.: Akron, O. S. 74—75;
Alabama S. 75—77; Albany S. 82—83;
Allentown S. 89; Astor, Johann Jacob
S. 161—163; Baltimore, Md. S. 205—
207; Berlin, Ont. S. 389—390; Bethlehem*

*Pa. S. 422—425; Boston, Mass. S. 503
—504.
Bd. II: Chicago, Ill. S. 5—10; Cin-
cinnati, O. S. 58—62; Cleveland, O.
S. 62—63; . . .]* [93
Rattermann, H. A.: Die Deutschen in der
amerikanischen Geschichte. *Festrede
auf dem 8. Stiftungsfest des Deutschen
Pionier-Vereins, 30. Mai 1876. In: Der
Deutsche Pionier. Jg. VIII. Cincinnati,
O. 1876—1877. S. 109—123.* [94
— Gesammelte ausgewählte Werke.
*Bd. XVI. Cincinnati, O.: Selbstverlag
des Verfassers 1912 = Abhandlungen,
Verträge und Reden. Bilder aus
Deutsch-Amerikanischer Geschichte.
Vermischte Schriften. Erster Theil. Cin-
cinnati, O. 1912. 462 S.
Aus dem Inhalt u. a.: Der Kampf um die
Geistesfreiheit in den Vereinigten Staa-
ten von Nord-Amerika. Vortrag gehalten
beim Stiftungsfest der ,,Freien Deutschen
Gemeinde" von Sauk City, Wisconsin
22. Oktober 1893. S. 69—98.
Die Ursachen der Massenauswanderung
aus Deutschland im 18. Jahrhundert.
Vortrag gehalten im ,,Deutschen Litterarischen Klub von Cincinnati" am
1. Nov. 1882 S. 99—144.
Die deutsche Sprache in der amerikanischen Schule. Vortrag gehalten in der
öffentlichen Versammlung des ,,Deutsch-
Amerikanischen Lehrertages" in Davenport, Ia. am 4. Aug. 1881. S. 266—290.
Ein Leitfaden der deutsch-amerikanischen Geschichte. Vortrag gehalten
vor dem Deutsch-Amerikanischen Lehrer-
tag in Chicago, am 2. August 1883.
S. 291—304.
Eröffnungsrede bei Gelegenheit der
Feier des Jubiläums der deutschen Einwanderung in Amerika. Gehalten in
Cincinnati am 17. Okt. 1883. S. 381—
384.
[Deutsche Einwanderung, deutsche Ar-
beit, deutsche Kultur in Amerika.]
Festrede gehalten bei Gelegenheit der Feier
des ,,Ersten Deutschen Tages" in Cin-
cinnati, O., am 13. Sept. 1896. S. 421—
430.* [95
Ratzel, Friedrich: ,,Die Weißen oder die
Europäo-Aemrikaner." *In: Politische
Geographie der Vereinigten Staaten von
Amerika . . . Von Friedrich Ratzel.
2. Aufl. München 1893 [= Nr. 18a].
S. 235—260.
[Die Stellung der Deutschen in den
V. St. S. 247—251. Einige Bemerkungen*

über die deutschen, französischen und spanischen Elemente. S. 253ff.] [96

Reynolds, William M.: German emigration to North America. *Introductory to the history of the Lutheran Church among the Germans and their descendants in the United States. In: The Evangelical Review. Vol. XIII. Gettysburg, Pa. 1861 —1862. pp. 1—27.* [97

Rohrbach, Paul: „Das Deutschtum in Nordamerika." *In: Das Deutschtum über See. Von P. Rohrbach. Karlsruhe: Wilhelm Schille 1931. S. 13—136, ill. [Das Deutschtum in Nordamerika. (I) Bis zum Jahre 1783. S. 14—58, ill.]* [97a

[Roosevelt, Theodore]: President Roosevelt's opinion of our German-American population. 1904. *In: The Pennsylvania-German. Vol. V. Lebanon, Pa. 1904. pp. 43—44.* [98

Ross, Colin: Unser Amerika. Der deutsche Anteil an den Vereinigten Staaten. *Leipzig: F. A. Brockhaus 1936. 317 S., Karten* [98 a

Ross, Edward Alsworth: The Germans in America. *In: The Century. Illustrated monthly magazine. Vol. LXXXVIII. = New series, vol. LXVI. New York, N.Y., May, 1914. pp. 98—104, map.* [99

Roßnagel, Paul: Die Stadtbevölkerung der Vereinigten Staaten von Amerika nach Herkunft und Verteilung. *Mit besonderer Berücksichtigung des deutschen Elements. Ein siedlungsgeographischer Versuch. Stuttgart: Ausland und Heimat Verlags-Aktiengesellschaft 1930. VI, 103 S., ill. Karten. = Schriften des Deutschen Ausland-Instituts, Stuttgart. A. Kulturhistorische Reihe. Bd. XXV.* [100

[Ruetenik, Hermann Julius]: Berühmte deutsche Vorkämpfer für Fortschritt, Freiheit und Friede in Nord Amerika. *Von 1626—1888. Einhundert und fünfzig Biographien. Cleveland, O.: Forest City Bookbinding Co. 1888. 500 S., ill.* [101

[—] Deutsche Amerikaner in Kirche und Staat von 1626 bis zur Gegenwart. *Cleveland, O.: Lauer & Mattil 1892. (6), 15—316. S., ill. [Auszug aus: (Ruetenik, Hermann J.): Berühmte deutsche Vorkämpfer . . . 1888.]* [102

Russell, George B.: Anglo-German life in America. *In: The Mercersburg Review. Vol. XI. Chambersburg, Pa. 1859. pp. 536—556.* [103

S., G.: Die Deutschen in Amerika. *In: Atlantische Studien. Von Deutschen in Amerika. Bd. VII. Göttingen: George Heinrich Wigand 1855. S. 190—200.* [104

Schem, Alexander Jacob: Deutsch-Amerikanisches Conversations-Lexicon. *Mit specieller Rücksicht auf das Bedürfniß der in Amerika lebenden Deutschen, mit Benutzung aller deutschen, amerikanischen, englischen und französischen Quellen, und unter Mitwirkung vieler hervorragender deutschen Schriftsteller Amerika's, bearbeitet von Alexander J. Schem . . . New York, N. Y.: E. Steiger 1869—1874. 11 Bde. [Bd. I—II, IV—V haben den Aufdruck New York, N. Y.: F. Gerhard, agt.; Bd. III: New York, N. Y.: German cyclopedia; etc.] [u. a. vgl.: Pennsylvania S. 552—573; Pennsylvanisch-Deutsch S. 573—579.]* [105

Schönemann, Friedrich: „Die Deutschen in Amerika." *In: Die Vereinigten Staaten von Amerika. Von Friedrich Schönemann. Bd. I. Stuttgart-Berlin 1932 [= Nr. 21]. = Kapitel XII. S. 286—315.* [105a

Schönfeldt, H.: Geschichte der Deutschen in Amerika. *In: Seventh Annual Report of the Society for the History of the Germans in Maryland. Baltimore, Md. 1893 pp. 63—69.* [106

Schrader, Frederick Franklin: The Germans in the making of America *Boston, Mass.: The Stratford Co. 1924. pp. (5), 274. [Bibliography pp. 259—264.]* [107

Seibel, George: The hyphen in American history. *Address delivered on „German Day" Aug. 31, 1916, at Johnstown, Pa. Reprint from the: „New Yorker Staats Zeitung" of Sept. 4, 1916. Pittsburgh, Pa. Neeb Hirsch Publishing Co. 1916. pp. 15.* [108

Skal, Geo. von: History of German immigration in the United States and successful German-Americans and their descendants. *New York City, N.Y. F. T. & J. C. Smiley 1908. pp. 277, ill. [The Pennsylvania Germans. pp. 13—18; The Germans during the Revolution. pp. 18—25.]* [111

Smalley, E. V.: The German element in the United States. *In: Lippincotts's Magazine of Popular Literature and Science. Old series, vol. XXXI. = New series, vol. V. Philadelphia, Pa. 1883. pp. 355 —363.* [112

Smith, Rufus B.: The influence of the Germans of the United States on its life and institutions. *An address before the German Societies of Cincinnati, O., on „German Day", Sept. 3, 1905. [Cincinnati, O.] 1905. pp. 12.*   [113

Spiess, Edmund: The Germans in the United States, — their duty and destiny. *(Über Aufgabe und Zukunft der Deutschen in den Vereinigten Staaten von Amerika. An address delivered before the Literary Society of Jena by Edmund Spiess, 1873). Translated from the German by* J. B. Bittinger. *In: The Quarterly Review of the Evangelical Lutheran Church-New series, vol. V. Gettysburg, Pa. 1875,. pp. 335—376.*   [114

Steiner, Edward A.: The German immigrant in Amerika. *In: The Outlook. A weekly newspaper. Vol. LXXIII. New York. N. Y., Jan. 1903. pp. 260—264.*   [115

Stricker, Wilhelm: Die Verbreitung des deutschen Volkes über die Erde. Ein Versuch. *Leipzig: Gustav Mayer 1845. Insbesondere: Bd. III. Die Deutschen in Afrika, Amerika und Australien. S. 89 —131.*   [116

[—] Die Deutschen in Nordamerika. *In: Germania. Archiv zur Kenntniß des deutschen Elements in allen Ländern der Erde. Herausgegeben von Wilhelm Stricker. Bd. I. Frankfurt a. M.: H. Ludwig Brönner 1847. S. 28—45.* [117

Ten Brook, Andrew: Our German immigrations. *In: Historical Collections. Collections and researches made by Michigan Pioneer and Historical Society. Vol. XXVI. Lansing, Mich. 1896. pp. 241—255.*   [118

Turner, Frederick, J.: German immigration in the colonial period. *In: The Record-Herald's Current Topics Club. Chicago, Ill.: Record Herald, Aug. 28, 1901. = Studies of American immigration. Chapter XI.*   [119

Young, William W.: What our Germanic population is doing for America. *In: The PennGermania. New series, vol. III, = Old series, vol. XV. Cleona, Pa. 1914. pp. 27—32.*   [120

Die Zukunft der Vereinigten Staaten und der Deutschen in Amerika. *In: Deutsche Vierteljahrs Schrift 1844. Zweites Heft. Stuttgart-Tübingen 1844. S. 299—348.*   [121

The Germans. *Remarks to Herman Ridder's address in Charleston, S. C., Jan. 15, 1908. Reprint from: The Hartford Courant of January 16, 1908. In: The Pennsylvania-German. Vol. IX. Cleona, Pa. 1908. pp. 180—181.*   [122

1683 — October 6 — 1908. German Day of Founder's Week. (Announcement.) *Two hundred and twenty-fifth anniversary of the arrival of the first German settlers of Germantown. — Laying of the cornerstone of a monument to Francis Daniel Pastorius, their leader. Under the auspices of the National German American Alliance and the German Society of Pennsylvania. In: German American Annals. New series, vol. VI Philadelphia, Pa. 1908. pp. 341—368.*   [123

1683—1933 German Day — Deutscher Tag. *In commemoration of the 250th anniversary of the arrival in America of the first group of German settlers under the leadership of Franz Daniel Pastorius and of the 200th anniversary of the valiant fight made by John Peter Zenger for the freedom of the press. Under the auspices of the Steuben Society of America and with the cooperation of the United German Societies and other organized groups of German Americans. Madison Square Garden Wednesday, Dec. 6, 1933 pp. 144, ill.*

[It contains a. o.:

The 250th anniversary of the first German settlement in the United States. Taken from on article of Paul Schwarz, *supplemented by extracts from A. B. Faust's „The German element in the U. St." p. 3ff.*

Theo Huebner: Deutschamerikanertum. p. 5ff.

John Peter Zenger. Extract from A. B. Faust's „The German element in the U. St.".]   [124

Die Auswanderung aus der Heimat

The European Background

Allgemeines

General

Cheney, Edward Potts: European background of American history 1300—1600. *New York, N. Y. and London: Harper & Brothers 1904. pp. XXVIII, 343, ill. maps.* = The American Nation: A, history. Edited by. A. B. Hart. Vol. I. [125

Faust, A. B.: „Increase in German immigration in the eighteenth century and its causes." *In: The German element in the United States. By A. B. Faust. Second edition. Vol. I. New York, N. Y. 1927 [= no. 42]. = Chapter III. pp. 53—72.* [126

Freeden, Hermann von und Smolka, Georg: Auswanderer. Bilder und Skizzen aus der Geschichte der deutschen Auswanderung. *Leipzig: Bibliographisches Institut AG. 1937. 182 S., ill.* [126a

Hubben, Wilhelm: Die Quäker in der Deutschen Vergangenheit. *Leipzig: Quäker-Verlag 1929. 202 S.* [127

Hull, William J.: William Penn and the Dutch Quaker migration to Pennsylvania. *Swarthmore, Pa. Swarthmore College 1935. pp. XIII, 445, ill.* = Swarthmore College Monographs on Quaker History. No. 2. [127a

Mellick, Andrew D.: German emigration to the American colonies, its cause, and the distribution of the emigrants. *In: The Pennsylvania Magazine of History and Biography. Vol. X. Philadelphia, Pa. 1886. pp. 241—250; 375—391.* [128

Penn, William: An account of W. Penn's travails in Holland and Germany. Anno MDCLXXVII. *For the service of the gospel of Christ, by way of journal. Containing also divers letters and epistles writ to several great and eminent persons whilst there. London: Printed and sold by T. Sowle 1694 pp. (8), 295.* [129

Rattermann, H. A.: Die Ursachen der Massenauswanderung aus Deutschland im 18. Jahrhundert. *Vortrag gehalten im „Deutschen Litterarischen Klub von Cincinnati", am 1. Nov. 1882. In: Abhandlungen, Vorträge und Reden. Bilder aus Deutsch-Amerikanischer Geschichte. Vermischte Schriften. Ertser Teil. =* H. A. Rattermann. Gesammelte ausgewählte Werke. Bd. XVI. *Cincinnati, O.: Selbstverlag des Verfassers 1912 S. 99—144.* [129a

Sachse, Julius Friedrich: Benjamin Furley. *In: The Pennsylvania Magazine of History and Biography. Vol. XIX. Philadelphia, Pa. 1895. pp. 277—296.* [130

— The fatherland: (1450—1700) showing the part it bore in the discovery, exploration and development of the western continent, with special reference to the Commonwealth of Pennsylvania. *Philadelphia, Pa. 1897.* = Part I. „A narrative and critical history", prepared at the request of the Pennsylvania-German Society. In: The Pennsylvania-German Society. Proceedings and Addresses. Vol. VII. Reading, Pa. 1897. pp. 33—198, ill., maps; Appendix. Title pages of book and pamphlets that influenced German emigration to Pennsylvania. Reproduced in facsimile for the Pennsylvania-German Society. pp. 201—256. [131

Scheben, Joseph: Die Frage nach der Geschichte der deutschen Auswanderung. Eine Aufgabe für die geschichtl. Landeskunde. In: Rheinische Vierteljahrsblätter. Mitteilungen des Instituts für geschichtliche Landeskunde der Rheinlande an der Universität Bonn. Jg. V. Bonn 1935. S. 175—190. [131a

Seidensticker, Oswald: William Penn's Reisen in Deutschland. In: Der Deutsche Pionier. Jg. III. Cincinnati, O. 1871—1872. S. 262—267; 305—310; 366—374. [132

— William Penn's travels in Holland and Germany in 1677. Paper read before

*the Historical Society of Pennsylvania,
Dec. 10, 1877. In: The Pennsylvania
Magazine of History and Biography.
Vol. II. Philadelphia, Pa. 1878. pp. 237
—282.* [133
Causes of migration to America. *Extracts
from various books. In: The Pennsylvania-German. Vol. XI. Lititz, Pa. 1910.
pp. 536—542.* [134
Anfrage, das Auswandern der Teutschen
nach Amerika betreffend. *[Gezeichnet:
Medicus.] Abdruck aus: ,,Fränkischer
Merkur''. In: Kaiserliche privilegirter
Reichsanzeiger. Nr. 107. Mittwochs, den
11. Mai 1796. Jg. 1796. Bd. I. Spalte
2024—2028.* [135
Über Auswanderung, eine Bemerkung zu
der in R.A.N. 107 Sp. 2024 d. J. ge-
schehene Anfrage, die Auswanderung
der Deutschen nach Amerika betreffend.
*[Gezeichnet: D.] In: Kaiserlich privile-
girter Reichsanzeiger. Nr. 215. Freitags,
den 16. Sept. 1796. Jg. 1796, Bd. II.
Spalte 5903—5905.* [136

Goebel, Max: *Geschichte des christlichen
Lebens in der rheinisch westphälischen
evangelischen Kirche. 3 Bde. Koblenz:
in Commission bei Karl Bädeker. 1849
—1852—1860. Bd. I. (bis 1609). Die
Reformationszeit oder die Kirchen unter
dem Kreuz. 1849. XVI, 478 f.; Bd. II.
Das siebenzehnte Jahrhundert oder die
herrschende Kirche und die Sekten.
1852. X, 880 S.; Bd. III. Die niederrheinische reformierte Kirche und der
Separatismus in Wittgenstein und am
Niederrhein im achtzehnten Jahrhundert. Aus den hinterlassenen Papieren des Verfassers herausgegeben von*
Theodor Link. *1860. XIII, 616 S.* [137
Die Taufgesinnten-Gemeinden. *Eine kurz-
gefaßte Darstellung der wichtigsten Er-
eignisse des Täufertums. Herausgegeben im Auftrag der Konferenz der Altevangelischen Taufgesinnten-Gemeinden
(Mennoniten) der Schweiz. Karlsruhe
(Baden): Druck und Verlag: Heinrich
Schneider; Bern: Im Kommissionsverlag
bei der Buchhandlung der Freien Evang.
Gemeinden 1931. VIII, 9—496 S.* [138
Correll, Ernst H.: *Das schweizerische Täu-
fermennonitentum. Ein soziologischer
Bericht. Tübingen: J. C. B. Mohr (Paul
Siebeck). 1925. X, 145 S., ill.
[Allgemeine bibliographische Vorbe-
merkung (S. 1—2) und reiche Text-Lite-
raturangaben in den einzelnen Abschnit-
ten: Allgemeine historisch-soziologische
Kennzeichnung des Täufertums. S. 3—9;
Ausbreitung und ökonomisch-sozialer
Charakter des Täufer-Mennonitentums.
S. 10—23; Die täuferische Art in der
Schweiz. S. 24—53; Die schweizerischen
Täufer im 17. und 18. Jahrhundert.
S. 54—74; Die Täuferemigranten im
Elsaß, in Baden und der Kurpfalz (der
,,elsässische'' und ,,pfälzische'' Mennonit
im besonderen). S. 75—143: Die Rechts-
verhältnisse und ihre Wirkungen. S. 79
—99; Die Mennonitische Musterwirt-
schaft. S. 100—134.]* [139
Hamm, Johann Jacob: *Die Gemeinschafts-
bewegung in der Pfalz. Ein Beitrag zur
Geschichte des Pietismus. Herausgegeben
mit Unterstützung der Pfälzischen Gesellschaft zur Förderung der Wissenschaften.
Eisenberg, (Pfalz): Gedruckt bei J. Heil-
mann, Buchdruckerei 1928. 366 S.* [140
Müller, Ernst: *Geschichte der Bernischen
Täufer. Nach den Urkunden dargestellt.
Frauenfeld. J. Hubers Verlag. 1895.
411 S.* [140a
[Nafziger, Johannes]: An Amish church
discipline of 1781. *Letter of the Amish
bishop Johannes Nafziger of Essingen in
the Palatinate to the Swiss emigrant
churches in the Netherlands. Translated
and printed in: The Mennonite Quarterly Review. Vol. IV, Goshen, Ind. —
Scottdale, Pa. 1930. pp. 140—148.* [141
Stuckey, Joseph: *Eine Begebenheit, die
sich in der Mennoniten-Gemeinde in
Deutschland und in der Schweiz von 1693
bis 1700 zugetragen hat. Elkhart, Ind.:
John F. Funk und Brud. 1871. 54 S.;
Abdruck: Elkhart, Ind. 1883, 1906.* [142
The discipline adopted by the Strasburg
Conference of 1568. *Edited by* **H. S.
Bender.** *Translated by* **D. B. Swar-
zendruber.** *In: The Mennonite Quar-
terly Review. Vol. I, no. 1. Goshen, Ind.
1927. pp. 57—66.* [143
Artikel und Ordnungen der Christlichen Ge-
meinde in Christo Jesu. *Elkhart, Ind.:
Mennonite Publishing Co. 1905. 16 S.
[Enthält die altüberlieferten Ordnungen
eingehalten von den Alt-Amischen (Old
Order Amish of America) und beginnt
mit einer 1568 zu Strassburg angenom-
menen.]* [144

Auswanderungsgebiete
Districts of Emigration

Hartnack, Karl: Ein Beitrag zur Geschichte der bergischen Auswanderung nach Nordamerika. *In: Zeitschrift des Bergischen Geschichtsvereins. Jg. 1930. Bd. LIX. Wuppertal-Elberfeld 1930. S. 150—212.*
[„Ältere Zeit". S. 151—174.] [145

Hubben, Wilhelm: Labadisten, Mennoniten und Quäker am Niederrhein. Kirchengeschichtliches aus der Zeit von 1670—1683. *In: Die Heimat. Mitteilungen des Vereins für Heimatkunde in Krefeld. Jg. V., Heft 4. Krefeld 1926 S. 268—273.*
[146

[Keussen, Herman]: Ein Aktenstück über die erste Einwanderung der Mennoniten im Jahre 1655 und über die damit verknüpften Vorgänge. *Abdruck aus: Krefelder Zeitung, 1894, No. 421 in: Die Heimat. Mitteilungen der Vereine für Heimatkunde in Krefeld-Uerdingen. Herausgegeben von K. Rembert. Jg. X. Heft 2. Krefeld 1931. S. 96—98.* [147

Rembert, Karl: Die „Wiedertäufer" im Herzogtum Jülich. *Studien zur Geschichte der Reformation, besonders am Niederrhein. Berlin: R. Gaertners Verlagsbuchhandlung, Herman Heyfelder 1899. XI, 637 S.*
[„Zur Geschichte der Mennoniten Gemeinde in Krefeld". S. 571—575.] [148

Zur Feier der Übernahme des Pastorius Denkmals im Krefelder Heimatmuseum, 27. Mai 1931. *In: Die Heimat. Mitteilungen der Vereine für Heimatkunde in Krefeld-Uerdingen Jg. X, Heft 2. Krefeld, 15. Juli 1931. S. 73—88.* [149

Neu, Heinrich: Beiträge zur Geschichte der rheinischen Amerika-Auswanderung im 18. Jahrhundert. *In: Rheinische Vierteljahrsblätter. Mitteilungen des Instituts für geschichtliche Landeskunde der Rheinlande an der Universität Bonn. Jg. VI. Bonn 1936. S. 176—185.* [149a

Hartnack, Karl: Wittgensteiner in den Vereinigten Staaten von Nordamerika. *In: Mitteilungen des Vereins für Geschichte und Volkskunde Wittgensteins. Jg. VII, Heft 1. Laasphe, Deutsches Reich 1926 S. 9ff.* [150

Hartnack, Karl: Über Auswanderung von Wittgensteinern nach den Vereinigten Staaten von Nordamerika. *In: Das schöne Wittgenstein. Seine Bewohner und Freunde in Gegenwart und Vergangenheit, mit den „Mitteilungen des Vereins für Geschichte und Heimatkunde Wittgensteins", Jg. 1928, Heft 3/4. Laasphe, Deutsches Reich 1928. S. 89—93.* [150a

Hiester, Isaac: The Hiester homestead in Germany. *A paper read March 12, 1907. In: Transactions of the Historical Society of Berks County. Vol. II. 1905—1909. Reading, Pa. 1910. pp. 180—188, ill. Reprint in: The Pennsylvania-German. Vol. IX. Cleona, Pa. 1908. pp. 496—499.*
[the village of Elsoff in the Grafschaft of Wittgenstein, in the Province of Westphalia, Germany.] [150b

Gerber, Adolf: Die Nassau-Dillenburger-Auswanderung nach Amerika im 18. Jahrhundert. Das Verhalten der Regierungen dazu und die späteren Schicksale der Auswanderer. *Flensburg: Flensburger Nachrichten, Deutscher Verlag 1930. 51 S., ill.* [151

Goebel, Julius: Briefe deutscher Auswanderer aus dem Jahre 1709. *In: Deutsch-Amerikanische Geschichtsblätter. Jahrbuch der Deutsch-Amerikanischen Historischen Gesellschaft von Illinois. Jg. 1912. Vol. XII. Chicago, Ill. 1912. S. 124—189.*
[Material zur Auswanderung aus dem Herzogtum Nassau-Dillenburg.] [152

Hartnack, Karl: Die erste Niederlassung von Siegerlandern in den Vereinigten Staaten [Germanna, Va.] *In: Siegerland. Blätter des Vereins für Heimatkunde und Heimatschutz im Siegerlande samt Nachbargebieten. Bd. VIII. Siegen 1926. S. 49—52. Nachtrag der Schriftleitung von* **Hans Kruse.** *S. 52—57.* [152a

Becker, Albert: Pfälzer Auswanderer. *In: Pfälzisches Museum. Jg. XXXIX — Pfälzische Heimatkunde. Jg. XVIII. Kaiserslautern 1922. Heft 11/12. S. 292—293.* [153

Becker, Albert: Zur Geschichte der pfälzisch-amerikanischen Auswanderung. *In: Pfälzisches Museum. Jg. XXXIX — Pfälzische Heimatkunde. Jg. XVIII. Kaiserslautern 1922. Heft 11/12. S. 293.*   [154

Gothein, Eberhard: Bilder aus der Kulturgeschichte der Pfalz nach dem dreißigjährigen Kriege. *Karlsruhe: G. Braunsche Hofbuchhandlung 1895. 63 S. = Badische Neujahrsblätter herausgegeben von der Badischen Historischen Kommission. Fünftes Blatt. 1895.*   [155

Haas, Rudolf: Die Pfälzer in Nordamerika. *In: Mannheimer Geschichtsblätter. Monatsschrift für die Geschichte, Altertums- und Volkskunde Mannheims und der Pfalz. Herausgegeben vom Mannheimer Altertumsverein, E. V. Bd. XXVII. Mannheim 1926. Spalte 5—13; 27—32;* **Antz, E. L.,** Nachtrag *Spalte 52—55.*   [155a

Häberle, Daniel: Auswanderung und Kolonialgründung der Pfälzer im 18. Jahrhundert. *Zur Zweihundert-Erinnerung an die Massenauswanderung der Pfälzer (1709) und an den pfälzischen Bauerngeneral Nicholaus Herchheimer, den Helden von Oriskany (6. August 1777). Kaiserslautern: Kgl. bayer. Hofbuchdruckerei H. Kayser 1909. XIX, 263 S., Karten.*   [156

— Die Auswanderung aus der Pfalz im 18. Jahrhundert. *In: Der Auslanddeutsche. Halbmonatsschrift für Auslanddeutschtum und Auslandkunde. Mitteilungen des Deutschen Ausland-Instituts. Jg. VII, No. 8. Stuttgart 1924. S. 228 —232.*   [157

— Pfarrer aus der Pfalz bzw. Kurpfalz während des 18. Jahrhunderts in Nordamerika. *In: Pfälzisches Museum. Monatsschrift für heimatliche Altertumskunde, Geschichte, Kunst, Volkskunde und Literatur. Herausgegeben vom Historischen Verein der Pfalz und vom Verein ,,Historisches Museum der Pfalz." Jg. XXVII. Kaiserslautern 1910. S. 9—10.*   [157a

Hartmann, Gabriel: Amerikafahrer von Dossenheim im 18. Jahrhundert. Nach dem Familienbuch der dortigen reformierten Gemeinde. *In: Mannheimer Geschichtsblätter. Monatsschrift für Geschichte, Altertums- und Volkskunde Mannheims und der Pfalz. Herausgegeben vom Mannheimer Altertumsverein, E. V. Bd. XXVII. Jg. 1926. Spalte 55—58.*   [158

Häusser, Ludwig: Geschichte der Rheinischen Pfalz nach ihren politischen, kirchlichen und literarischen Verhältnissen. *Unveränderter Neudruck der Erstausgabe von 1845. 2 Bde. Heidelberg: Carl Winters Verlagsbuchhandlung 1924. XXIV, 652 S.; VIII, 1002 S.*   [159

Learned, Marion Dexter: Francis Daniel Pastorius. The founder of Germantown. *In: German American Annals. New series, vol. V. Philadelphia, Pa. 1907. pp. 131—171; 195—234; 259—293; 323—356; Vol. VI. 1908. pp. 3—31; 65—101; 121—156; 187—237, ill., maps.*   [160

— The life of Francis Daniel Pastorius, the founder of Germantown. *With an appreciation of Pastorius by Samuel Pennypacker. Philadelphia, Pa.: William J. Campbell 1908. pp. X, 324, ill., maps. [Separate reprint of no. 157]. [,,Ancestors"; ,,Early years and education"; ,,Years of practice and travel." = Chapter I—III. pp. 1—115.]* [161

Lutz, Ralph Haswell: A recent visit to Kriegsheim. *In: The Pennsylvania-German. Vol. XII. Lititz, Pa. 1911. pp. 85—86.*   [162

Macco, Hermann Friedrich: The church visitations of the deanery of Kusel in the Palatinate 1609. *Philadelphia, Pa. 1930. pp. 136. = Publications of the Genealogical Society of Pennsylvania. Special number.*   [163

Metz, Friedrich: Das Oberrheinland als Ein- und Auswanderungsgebiet. *In: Verhandlungen und wissenschaftliche Abhandlungen des 22. Deutschen Geographentages zu Karlsruhe 7. bis 9. Juni 1927. Breslau: Ferdinand Hirt 1928. S. 222—237.*   [164

Müller, Bernhard und **Heilbrunn, Ludwig:** Frankfurt/Amerika. *Teil I. Alte und neue Beziehungen von Bernhard Müller; Teil II. Frankfurt im Sezessionskrieg von Ludwig Heilbrunn. Frankfurt am Main: Herausgegeben vom Wirtschaftsamt der Stadt Frankfurt am Main, Abteilung für Werbe- und Ausstellungswesen, anläßlich der Ausstellung Frankfurt-Amerika. 1926. 91 S. ill. [,,Frankfurter Landkompagnie, Pastorius und Germantown. S. 14—32.]* [165

Raschen, J. T. L.: The ancestral home of the Pennsylvania-Germans. *Read before the Northampton County Historical Society, Easton, Pa., June 6th, 1908.*

In: The Pennsylvania-German. Vol. IX. Cleona, Pa. 1908. pp. 387—395. [166

Raumer, Kurt von: Die Zerstörung der Pfalz von 1689 im Zusammenhang der französischen Rheinpolitik. *München und Berlin: R. Oldenburg 1930. VII, (1), 335 S., ill., Karten.* [167

Riehl, W. H.: Die Pfälzer. Ein rheinisches Volksbild. *Stuttgart und Augsburg: J. G. Cotta'scher Verlag 1857. VI, 408 S.* [168

Schwerz, J. N.: Beobachtungen über den Ackerbau der Pfälzer. *Berlin: G. Reimer 1816. XVI, 285 S.* [169

An account of the present condition of the Protestants in the Palatinate. *In two letters to an English gentleman . . . London: Printed for Richard Parker . . . sold by A. Baldwin . . . 1699.*

Pamphlet in the British Museum, London, transcribed and contributed by **Wm. J. Hinke.** *In: Ecclesiastical Records. State of New York, N. Y.: Published by the state under the supervision of Hugh Hastings. Vol. III. Albany, N. Y. 1902. [= No. 436] pp. 1453—1459.* [170

The state of the Palatines for fifty years past to this present time *containing*

I. An account of the principality of the Palatinate; and the barbarities and ravages committed by order of the french king upon the inhabitants . . .

II. The case of the Palatines, published by themselves, and humbly offered to the tradesmen of England . . . . London Printed for J. Baker 1710.

Pamphlet in the British Museum, contributed by **Wm. J. Hinke.** *Reprint in: Ecclesiastical Records. State of New York. Published by the state under the supervision of Hugh Hastings. Vol. III. Albany, N. Y. 1902 [= no. 436]. pp. 1820—1832.* [171

Pfälzische Auswanderung nach Amerika Palatine emigration to North America. *(1)* Aus dem Herzogtum Zweibrücken 1724 bis 1749. *(Aus dem Staatsarchiv Speier, Abt. Zweibrücken III, 2025). [Im Druck.]* [172

Amerika-Nummer der „Pfalz am Rhein". *Pfälz. Verkehrs- und Touristenzeitung. Pfälzer Illustrierte. Jg. XIV. Nr. 16. Neustadt a. d. Haardt 1931: S. 411—440.*

Klug, Hermann: Die Rheinpfalz und ihre Auswanierer, eine Selbstbesinnung und eine Anregung. *S. 410.*

Häberle, Daniel: Die Auswanderung aus der Pfalz nach den Vereinigten Staaten. *S. 411—412.*

Klug, Hermann: Die Pfalz und die nach Europa reisenden Amerikaner. *S. 413—414.*

Antz, E. L.: Pfälzische Biografien: Namhafte Pioniere und Auswanderer. *S. 414 —415.*

Zink, Th.: Pfälzer in Amerika. *S. 415 —416.*

Becker, Albert: Pfälzisch-amerikanische Kulturströmungen. *S. 416—419, ill.*

— Pfälzer Dichterstimmen aus Amerika. *S. 420—421.*

Merk, Ernst: Ellerstadt. Die Heimat der Vorfahren des Präsidenten Herbert Hoover. *S. 423.*

Antz, E. L.: 250 Jahre Auswanderung und Siedlung der Pfälzer in Amerika. *S. 426—428.* [172a
—————

L.[äugin], Th.[eodore]: Das Schrifttum über Badener im Ausland. *Von der Badischen Landesbibliothek in Karlsruhe. In: Der Auslanddeutsche. Halbmonatsschrift für Auslanddeutschtum und Auslandkunde. Mitteilungen des Deutschen Ausland-Instituts, Stuttgart. Jg. VI, No. 12. Stuttgart 1923. 339—342.* [173

Schnabele, Franz: Badische Auswanderer. *In: Der Auslanddeutsche. Halbmonatsschrift für Auslanddeutschtum und Auslandkunde. Mitteilungen des Deutschen Ausland-Instituts, Stuttgart. Jg. VI, No. 12. Stuttgart 1923. S. 321—324.* [174
—————

Gerber, Adolf: Beiträge zur Auswanderung nach Amerika im 18. Jahrhundert aus altwürttembergischen Kirchenbüchern. *Stuttgart: J. F. Steinkopf [1928] 32 S.* [175

— Neue Beiträge zur Auswanderung nach Amerika im 18. Jahrhundert aus altwürttembergischen Kirchenbüchern unter Hinzuziehung anderer Quellen. *Stuttgart: J. F. Steinkopf 1928. 44 S.* [175a

Kapff, Paul: Schwaben in Amerika, seit der Entdeckung des Weltteils. *Stuttgart: D. Gundert 1893. 48 S. ill. = Württembergische Neujahrsblätter, herausgegeben von J. Hartmann. Blatt X, 1893.* [176

— Anteil der Württemberger an der Kolonisation Amerikas. *Vortrag vor dem XIV. Amerikanisten-Kongreß, Stuttgart 1904. In: Internationaler Amerikanisten-Kongreß. Vierzehnte Tagung, Stuttgart 1904. Stuttgart: Druck und Verlag von W. Kohlhammer 1906. S. XLVIII— LVII.* [177

Neu, Heinrich: Elsässer und Lothringer als Ansiedler in Nordamerika. *In: Jahrbuch der Elsaß-Lothringischen wissenschaftlichen Gesellschaft zu Straßburg. Bd. III. Heidelberg: Carl Winter's Universitätsbuchhandlung 1930. S. 98—127.* [178

Dotterer, Henry S.: Goetschy's colony. *In: Historical Notes, relating to the Pennsylvania Reformed Church. Vol. I. Philadelphia, Pa. 1900. pp. 171—173; 179—186.* [179
— Days devoted to research abroad. *In: The Perkiomen Region, Past and Present. Vol. II. Philadelphia, Pa. 1900. pp. 5—7; 20—21; 36—38; 55—57; 71—72; p. 87; pp. 103—105; 121—122; 136—137; 167—168; p. 184. Vol. III. 1901. pp. 99—102; 115—116; 131—133; 148—149; p. 165; pp. 181—184.* [180
Faust, Albert Bernhardt: Swiss emigration to the American colonies in the 18th century. *In: The American Historical Rewiew. Vol. XXII, no. 1. Oct., 1916. pp. 21—44.* [181
— List of Swiss emigrants in the eighteenth century to the American colonies. *Vol. I. Zurich, 1734—1744 from the archives of Switzerland. Washington, D. C.: Published by the National Genealogical Society. 1920. pp. XI, 122, ill.* [182
— and **Brumbaugh, Gajus Marcus:** List of Swiss emigrants in the eighteenth century to the American colonies. *Vol. II. From the state archives of Bern and Basel, Switzerland. Compiled and edited by A. B. Faust and G. M. Brumbaugh. Washington, D. C.: The National Genealogical Society. 1925. pp. IX, 243.* [183
Hinke, William J.: Early Swiss settlers. *(List of Swiss emigrants to Pennsylvania as found in a pamphlet entitled ,,The description of a journey from Zurich to Rotterdam by Ludwig Weber from Wallisellen, etc.", Zurich, 1735 [= no. 195]). In: Notes and Queries. Edited by W. H. Egle. Annual vol. 1900. Harrisburg, Pa. 1901. pp 121—122.* [184
Kuhns, Oscar: A genealogical trip to Switzerland. *In: The Pennsylvania-German. Vol. VII. Lebanon, Pa. 1906. pp. 311—312.* [185
— The Emmenthal. Canton Berne, Switzerland. *In: The Pennsylvania-German. Vol. XI. Lititz, Pa. 1910. pp. 372—376, ill.* [186

Kuhns, Oscar: Lancaster County families from the Canton Zurich, Switzerland. *In: The Pennsylvania-German. Vol. XI. Lititz, Pa. 1910. pp. 608—610. Reprint in: The National Genealogical Society Quarterly. Vol. VIII, no. 3. Washington, D. C. 1919. pp. 36—38.* [187
— Some Lancaster County families from the Canton of Berne Switzerland. *In: The Pennsylvania-German. Vol. XI. Lititz, Pa. 1910. pp. 733—735. Reprint in: The National Genealogical Society Quarterly. Vol. VIII. no. 3. Washington, D. C. 1919. pp. 39—41.* [188
— The homeland of the first settlers in Lancaster County. *In Papers and Addresses of the Lancaster County Historical Society. Vol. XXI. Lancaster, Pa. 1917. pp. 23—28, map.* [189
— Switzerland plays a part in the founding of the American nation. *In: The National Genealogical Society Quarterly. Vol. VIII, no. 3. Washington, D. C. 1919. pp. 33—34.* [190
Lerch, E.: Die bernische Auswanderung nach Amerika im 18ten Jahrhundert. *In: Blätter für bernische Geschichte, Kunst und Altertumskunde. Herausgegeben von Gustav Grunau. Jg. V, Heft 4. Bern, 1909. S. 294—325.* [191
Moetteli, Hans: Die schweizerische Auswanderung nach Nord-Amerika, mit besonderer Berücksichtigung der Kolonie Glarus und der Auswanderungspropaganda von Nat.-Rat. Dr. Joos, *Thesis of Doctor Rerum Cameralium, Rechts- und Staatswissenschaftliche Fakultät, Universität, Zürich. 21. Febr. 1920. Langansalza: Hermann Beyer u. Söhne (Beyer & Mann) 1921. VIII, 148 S. [,,Die Auswanderung vor 1800." S. 4—21.]* [192
Sieveking, H.: Die Verflechtung der Schweiz in die Law'sche Krise (1720). *In: Festgabe zur Einweihung der Neubauten der Universität Zürich. Zürich 1914. Teil II, S. 75—105.* [193
Steinemann, Ernst: Die schaffhauserische Auswanderung und ihre Ursachen. *Ein Beitrag zur Wirtschaftsgeschichte. In: Zeitschrift für Schweizerische Geschichte Jg. XIV, Zürich 1934. S. 310—359; 401—450. Sonderdruck: Zürich, Verlag von A. G. Gebr. Leemann, 1934. 106 S.* [194
Weber, Ludwig: Der hinckende Bott von Carolina, oder Ludwig Webers von Wallisellen Beschreibung seiner Reise

von Zürich gen Rotterdam, mit derjenigen Gesellschaft *[194 Personen unter der Führung des Pfarrers Götschi von Zürich],* welche neulich aus dem Schweizerland in Carolinam zu ziehen gedacht. *Zürich 1735. 32 S.* [195

Auswanderungen *[aus dem Kanton Bern]. In: Berner Monatsschrift. Jg. I. Bern 1825. S. 77—89; 101—103; 131—136; 165—167. [Fragment: vgl.; Guide to the materials for American history in Swiss and Austrian Archives. By A. B. Faust. Washington, D. C. 1916 [= Nr. 7830]. p. 73.]* [196

Bechler, Theodor: Ortsgeschichte von Herrnhut mit besonderer Berücksichtigung der älteren Zeit. *Zum 200 jährigen Jubiläum Herrnhuts am 17. Juni 1922. Herrnhut: Verlag der Missionsbuchhandlung 1922. 228 S., ill., Karten.* [197

Korschelt, G.: Geschichte von Herrnhut, *bearbeitet und herausgegeben . . . Berthelsdorf: Selbstverlag des Herausgebers; in Commission bei E. Kummer; Zittau: Gedruckt bei J. G. Seyfert 1853. 167 S.* [198

— Geschichte von Berthelsdorf, *bearbeitet und herausgegeben . . . Berthelsdorf bei Herrnhut: Selbstverlag des Herausgebers; Leipzig: in Commission bei E. Kummer; Löbau: Gedruckt in der Hohlfeld'schen Offizin 1852. 131 S.* [199

Uttendörfer, O.: Alt-Herrnhut. Wirtschaftsgeschichte und Religionssoziologie Herrnhuts während seiner ersten zwanzig Jahre (1722—1742). *Herrnhut i. Sa.: Verlag Missionsbuchhandlung 1925. 185 S.* [199 a

— Wirtschaftsgeist und Wirtschaftsorganisation Herrnhuts und der Brüdergemeine von 1743 bis zum Ende des Jahrhunderts *[Alt-Herrnhut, 2. Teil]. Herrnhut i. S.: Verlag der Missionsbuchhandlg. 1926. (1), (1). 7 — 486 S.* [199 b

Kadelbach, Oswald: Ausführliche Geschichte Caspar von Schwenkfelds und der Schwenkfelder in Schlesien, der Ober-Lausitz und Amerika, *nebst ihren Glaubensschriften von 1524—1860 nach*

den vorhandenen Quellen bearbeitet von . . . Lauban: M. Baumeister 1860. (1), (1), (2), 254, (1) S. [200

Schultz, Elmer: The Jesuits among the Schwenkfelders. *In: The Pennsylvania-German. Vol. XI. Lititz, Pa. 1910. pp. 645—649.* [201

Obstfelder, Joh. Carl Friedr.: Die Evangelischen Salzburger, ihre Auswanderung nach Preußen und ihr Durchzug durch Naumburg 1732. *Ein kirchengeschichtliches Lebensbild für das evangelische Christenvolk. Naumburg: Verlag von Louis Garcke 1857. (4) 148 S.* [202

Ochsenfcrd, S. E.: Salzburg and the Salzburg Lutherans. *In: The Lutheran Church Review. Vol. VII. Philadelphia, Pa. 1888. pp. 294—311.* [203

Panse, Karl: Geschichte der Auswanderung der evangelischen Salzburger im Jahre 1732. *Beitrag zur Kirchengeschichte. Nach Quellen bearbeitet von . . . Leipzig: Leopold Voss 1827. LVI, 191 S.* [204

Ausführliche Historie derer Emigranten oder Vertriebenen Lutheraner aus dem Ertz-Bißthum Saltzburg (und anderen Römisch-Catholischen Ländern). *4 Theile. Leipzig: Teubners Buchladen 1732—1734.* [205

[Koehler, Andreas Rudolf]: Beschreibung des Hallischen Waisenhauses und der übrigen damit verbundenen Frankischen Stiftungen nebst der Geschichte ihres ersten Jahrhunderts. *Zum Besten der Vaterlosen. Halle: Waisenhaus-Buchhandlung 1799. XVI, 214, (4) S., ill., Karte.* [206

Wotschke, . . .: Das pietistische Halle und die Auslandsdeutschen. *In: Neue kirchliche Zeitschrift. Jg. XLIII. Leipzig 1932. S. 428—434; 475—492.* [206a

Farewell address to „Christoph Immanuel Schulze, beruffenen Prediger der christlichen Gemeinde zu Philadelphia, in Pennsylvanien," 22 June, 1765 by his friends in Halle. *(German original and English translation). In: The Pennsylvania-German. Vol. II. Lebanon, Pa. 1901. pp. 118—121.* [207

England

Boyer, Abel: History of the reign of Queen Anne, digested into annals. *11 vols. London 1703—1712.*
> *Vol. VIII. London: Printed for T. Ward 1710.*
> *[1709. Poor Palatines and other Germans come over in great numbers. pp. 166 —167; They encamp on Blackheath and near Camberwell. pp. 167—168; The German Popists sent back. p. 168; The Palatines disposed of. p. 168; Appendix. No. III. containing several authentic pieces relating to the support and settlement of the distress'd Palatines. pp. 34—57.]*
> *Vol. IX. London: Printed for T. Ward 1710.*
> *[1710/11. Petition against the poor Palatines. p. 304; Address for papers realting to the Palatines, Jan. 16. p. 305; Febr. 1 st, papers about the Palatines. p. 310. Reports about the Palatines. p. 323; 1711. Resolutions about the bringing over the poor Palatines, April 14. p. 361.]* [208

— The history of Queen Anne wherein all the civil military transactions of that memorable reign are faithfully compiled from the best authorities and impartially related . . . *London: Printed and sold by T. Woodward 1735. pp. XII, 722, 65, (15).*
> *[,,Palatines, Poor, come over into Great Britain." pp. 399—400; ,,Votes in their favour in Ireland." p. 402. ,,Resolutions against bringing them over." p. 496.]* [209

Sachse, Julius Friedrich: The Lutheran clergy of London, and how they aided German immigration during the XVIII century. *In: The Lutheran Church Review. Vol. XXII. Philadelphia, Pa. 1903. pp. 14—28; 313—321; 565—573, ill.* [210

A view of the queen's and kingdom's enemies in the case of the poor Palatines. *To which is added a list of the persons appointed commissioners and trustees of that charity, by her majesty's letters patent: as also of those members of the late parliament that voted for the naturalization bill. In a letter from a gentleman in London to his friend in the country. Sold by the Booksellers (1711) Guildhall Library, London.*
> *Pamphlet in the British Museum, copied, 1898, by* **Wm. J. Hinke** *and contributed*

by him. *In: Ecclesiastical Records. State of New York. Published by the state under the supervision of Hugh Hastings. Vol. III. Albany, N.Y. 1902 [= no. 436]. pp. 1752—1755.* [211

A brief history of the poor Palatine refugees lately arrived in England. *July 18, 1709. London: Printed, and sold by J. Baker . . . 1709.*
> *Pamphlet in the British Museum, copied by* **Wm. J. Hinke,** *and contributed by him. In: Ecclesiastical Records. State of New York. Published by the state under the supervision of Hugh Hastings. Vol. III. Albany, N. Y. 1902 [= no. 436]. pp. 1774—1794.* [212

The Palatines catechism or a true description of their camps at Black Heath and Camberwell. *In a pleasant dialogue between an English tradesman and a High-Dutchman. London: Printed for P. Hase . . . 1709.*
> *Pamphlet in the British Museum, contributed by* **Wm. J. Hinke.** *Reprint in: Ecclesiastical Records. State of New York. Published by the state under the supervision of Hugh Hastings. Vol. III. Albany, N. Y. 1902 [= no. 436]. pp. 1817—1820.* [213

The state of the Palatines for fifty years past to this present time containing
> *I. An account of the principality of the Palatinate; and the barbarities and ravages committed by order of the french king upon the inhabitants; . .*
> *II. The case of the Palatines, published by themselves, and humbly offered to the tradesmen of England . . .*
> *III. The humble petition of the Justices of Middlesex . . . on their behalf . . .*
> *IV. A letter about settling and employing them in other countries.*
> *V. A proclamation of the States General for naturalizing all strangers . . .*
> *VI. Lastly their present encamping at Camberwell and Black-heath.*
> *London: Printed for J. Baker 1710*
> *Pamphlet in the British Museum, contributed by* **Wm. J. Hinke.** *Reprint in: Ecclesiastical Records. State of New York. Published by the state under the supervision of Hugh Hastings. Vol. III. Albany, N. Y. 1902 [= no. 436]. pp. 1820—1832.* [213a

Die ersten Deutschen in den nordamerikanischen Kolonien, insbesondere die Deutschen in Neu Niederland[1])

The first Germans in North America especially the German Element of New Netherland[2])

[Broadhead, John Romeyn]: Documents relative to the colonial history of the State of New York; *procured in Holland, England and France. By John Romeyn Broadhead. Edited by E. B. O'Callaghan. 11 vols. Albany, N. Y.: Weed Parsons and Co. 1855—1858.* [214

O'Callaghan, E. B.: History of New Netherland or, New York under the Dutch. *2 vols. New York, N. Y.: D. Appleton & Co. 1855. pp. 493, map.; pp. 608 ill.* [214a

Hastings, Hugh: Ecclesiastical records. State of New York. *Published by the state under the supervision of . . ., state historian. 6 vols, and index vol. Albany, N. Y.: James B. Lyon 1901—1905/1916. pp. XXXV, 744; XXVIII, 745—1442; XL, 1443—2308; LIX, 2309—3146; XLIX, 3147—3800; LIX, 3801—4413. Vol. VII. Index. Prepared by E. T. Corwin under the auspices of the state historian James A. Holdan. Albany, N. Y.: The University of the State of New York 1916. pp. 382.* [214b

Fernow, Berthold: New Amsterdam family names and their origin. *New York-London: 1898 pp. . . .* [214c

Innes, J. H.: New Amsterdam and ist people. *Studies, social and topographical of the town under Dutch and early English rule. New York, N. Y.: Charles Scribners 1902. pp. XIV, 365 ill. map.* [214d

Jameson, J. Franklin: Narratives of New Netherland 1609—1664. *Edited by J. Fr. Jameson. New York, N. Y.: Charles Scribner's Sons 1909. pp. XX, (1), 478, ill.*

= Original narratives od early American history. Reproduced under the auspices of the American Historical Association. [214e

Cronau, Rudolf: ,,Die ersten Deutschen in den amerikanischen Kolonien. Die deutschen Gouverneure von Neu-Niederland und Neu-Schweden." *In: Drei Jahrhunderte deutschen Lebens in Amerika. Eine Geschichte der Deutschen in den Vereinigten Staaten. Von R. Cronau. Berlin 1909 [= Nr. 34]. S. 15—25, ill; 2. Aufl. 1928. S. 10—24, ill.* [214f

— Die Deutschen als Gründer von New Amsterdam-New York und als Urheber der amerikanischen Freiheitsbestrebungen. *Eine Denkschrift zur Erinnerung an die vor 300 Jahren erfolgte Erwerbung der Insel Manhattan durch Peter Minuit, und an die 150jährige Feier des amerikanischen Unabhängigkeitskrieges. New York, N. Y.: Heiss Verlag 1926. 70 S., ill.* [214g

Eickhoff, Anton: ,,Die Deutschen in New York. Neu Niederland." *In: In der neuen Heimath. Geschichtliche Mittheilungen über die deutschen Einwanderer in allen Theilen der Union. Herausgegeben von . . . New York, N. Y. 1884 [= Nr. 39]. = Erster Abschnitt. S. 29—47 ff.* [214h

Faust, A. B.: ,,The earliest Germans in the Anglo-American colonies." *In: The German element in the United States. By A. B. Faust. Second edition. Part I. New York, N. Y. 1927 [= no. 42]. = Chapter I. pp. 1—29.* [214i

Kaufmann, Wilhelm: Die ersten deutschen Einwanderer. *In: Deutsch-Amerikanische Geschichtsblätter. Jg. VII, Nr. 2. Chicago, Ill. 1907. S. 107—112.* [214k

— The Pastorius protest and real beginning of the German immigration

---

[1]) Siehe auch unter: New York Stadt Nr. 540ff.

[2]) See also City of New York, no. 540ff.

A reply to H. A. Rattermann. *In: The Penn Germania. Vol. I. = Old series, vol. XIII. Lititz, Pa. 1912. pp. 529—533.*
[See: Rattermann, H. A.: A vindication of Francis Daniel Pastorius [= nos. 5093a and 5093b] and Rattermann, H. A.: Pastorius und die Gründung von Germantown, Pa., Replik [= no. 5093c].]   [214 l

Lohr, Otto: Die ersten Deutschen im Staate Neu York. *In: Sonntagsblatt der Neu Yorker Staatszeitung, New York, N. Y. Nr. 28. 3. 1909 und Nr. 4. 4. 1909.*   [214 m

— The first Germans in North America, and the German element of New Netherland. *New York, N. Y.: G. E. Stechert & Co. 1912. pp. 15.*   [214 n

— Die Anfänge deutscher Einwanderung in Nordamerika. *In: Deutsch-Amerikanische Geschichtsblätter. Jahrbuch der Deutsch-Amerikanischen Historischen Gesellschaft von Illinois. Jg. 1912. Vol. XII. Chicago. Ill. 1912. S. 499—509.*   [214 o

— Die Anfänge deutscher Einwanderung in Nordamerika. *(Vgl.: Deutsch-Amerikanische Geschichtsblätter . . . Jg. 1912. Chicago, Ill. 1912). In: Deutsche Erde. Zeitschrift für Deutschkunde. Herausgegeben von Paul Langhans. Jg. XII. Gotha 1913. S. 99—104.*   [214 p

— A brief historical review of the achievements of German nationals in the early days of American colonization. The period from 1564 to 1682 inclusive. *New York, N. Y.; Hoboken, N. Y. 1923. pp. 8.*
=Historical Bulletin no. 1 of the Concord Society of America.   [214 q

— Die deutsche Sprache in Nordamerika im 17. Jahrhundert. *In: Mitteilungen der Akademie zur wissenschaftlichen Erforschung und zur Pflege des Deutschtums, Deutsche Akademie. Nr. 1. München 1933. S. 90—103.*   [214 r

— Das früheste Überseedeutschtum in seinen Ahnen und Enkeln. *In: Der Auslanddeutsche. Jg. 19. Stuttgart 1936. S. 93—96.*   [214 rr

— Amerikanische Familien des 17. Jahrhunderts. *In: Jahrbuch für auslanddeutsche Sippenkunde. Herausgegeben aus Anlaß der ersten Tagung für auslanddeutsche Sippenkunde 24.—25. August 1936 vom Deutschen Ausland-Institut, Hauptstelle für auslanddeutsche Sippenkunde. Stuttgart: Verlag Karl Weinbrenner & Söhne 1936. S. 44—54. [Deutsche Einzeleinwanderer und Familien in Neu-Niederland. S.45—53.]*   [214 s

Kretzmann, Karl: The oldest Lutheran Church in America. A brief chronicle of events in the history of the Evangelical Lutheran Church of Saint Matthew in the City of New York 1664—1914. *Compiled for the 250th anniversary of the church, December 6th 1914. New York, N. Y.: Published by the Evangelical Lutheran Church of St. Matthew in the City of New York, Convent Ave. and W 145th Str. 1914. pp. 47, ill.*   [214 ss

Nicum, John: The beginning of the Lutheran Church on Manhattan Island. *In: Papers of the American Society of Church History. Second series, vol. II. New York, N. Y. 1910. pp. 85—101.*   [214 t

Precht, Victor: New York im Siebzehnten Jahrhundert. *Vortrag, gehalten vor dem Deutschen Gesellig-Wissenschaftlichen Verein von New York, am 19. März 1884. New York, N. Y.: Druck der Cherouny Printing and Publishing Co. 1884. pp. 35.*   [214 u

Remensnyder, J. B.: Early history of the Reformed and Lutheran Churches in New York City. *In: The Lutheran Church Review. Vol. XV. Philadelphia, Pa. 1896. pp. 382—386.*   [214 v

Schmucker, B. M.: The Lutheran Church in the City of New York, during the first century of its history. *In: The Lutheran Church Review. Vol. III. Philadelphia. Pa. 1884. pp. 204—222.*   [214 w

---

Barnouw, Adriaan J.: Minuit Peter (1580—1638) director general of New Netherland and governor of New Sweden. *In: Dictionary of American biography. Under the auspices of the American Council of Learned Societies. Vol. XIII. Edited by Dumas Malone. London-New York 1934. pp. 33—35.*   [215

De Boer, L. P.: Peter Minuit. *In: The New York Genealogical and Biographical Record. Vol. LIX. New York, N. Y. 1928, Jan. pp. 58—60.*   [215 a

Faust, A. B.: Peter Minuit, purchaser and governor of Manhattan Island (1626) founder of New Sweden. *In: The German element in the United States. By A. B. Faust. Second edition. New York, N. Y. 1927 [= no. 42]. Part I. pp. 9—13; appendix in part II. pp. 609—610.*   [215 b

Hauff, Walter v.: Peter Minnewit, der erste führende Deutsche in Nordamerika. *Nach New York eingewandert im Jahre 1626. Der deutsche Spiegel. Politische Wochenschrift. Herausgegeben von E. Haeuber, Otto Kriegk. Jg. III, Heft 39. Berlin 1926. S. 1856—57.* [215c

Fernow, Berthold: Minuit. — *Contributed by . . . In: The New York Genealogical and Biographical Record. Vol. XVI. New York, N.Y.Oct.,1895. p. 202.* [215d

Kapp, Friedrich: ,,Peter Minnewit aus Wesel am Rhein." *In: Die Deutschen im Staate New York bis zum Anfang des neunzehnten Jahrhunderts. VonFriedrich Kapp. Leipzig 1868 [= Nr. 440]. = Kapitel II. S. 11—33.* [215e

Moore, Jacob B.: Notes for a memoir of Peter Minuit, one of the early directors of New Netherland *presented by . . . In: Proceedings of New York Historical Society, February, 1849. pp. 73—82.* [215f

Muckley, Joseph J.: Some account of William Usselinx and Peter Minuit, two individuals who were instrumental in establishing the first permanent colony in Delaware. *Wilmington, Del.: The Historical Society of Delaware. 1881. pp. 27.* = *Papers of the Historical Society of Delaware, III.* [215g

Muckley, Joseph J.: Peter Minnewit aus Wesel am Rhein. *In: Der Deutsche Pionier. Jg. I. Cincinnati, O. 1869— 1870. S. 169—181.* [215h

Leisler. *Documentary materials see: The documentary history of the State of New York. By E. O'Callaghan [= no. 446]. Vol. II. pp. 1—438; Documents relative to the colonial history of the State of New York. By John Romeyn Broadhead [= no. 427]. pp. 585—875.* [215i

Cronau, Rudolf: ,,Jacob Leisler; die stürmischste Periode in der Geschichte der Kolonie New York." *In: Drei Jahrhunderte deutschen Lebens in Amerika. Eine Geschichte der Deutschen in den Vereinigten Staaten. Von R. Cronau. Berlin 1909 [= Nr. 34]. S. 26—40; 2. Aufl. 1924. S. 25—40.* [215k

Faust, A. B.: ,,Jacob Leisler, governor of New York, defender of the people's cause, his martyrdom (1691), and services to the colonies." *In: The German element in the United States. By A. B. Faust. Second edition. New York, N. Y.*

1927 [= no. 42]. Part I. pp. 13—26; Note relating to his racial ancestry. In: Appendix in part II. pp. 610—611. [215l

Hoffmann, Chas. F.: The administration of Jacob Leisler, a chapter in American history. *In: Jared Spark's Library of American Biography. Second series, vol. III. Boston 1844. pp. 179—238.* [215m

Kern, J. W.: Jacob Leisler. *Weiterführung der Festrede, gehalten am 23. April 1911 im City Hall Park. In: Deutsch-Amerikanische Geschichtsblätter. Jahrbuch der Deutsch-Amerikanischen Historischen Gesellschaft von Illinois. Vol. XIII. Chicago, Ill. 1913. S.149—179. [Bibliographie.]* [215n

Lessing, O. E.: Jacob Leisler. *Vortrag. Berlin: P. Schmidt 1931. 17 S.* = *Der Austausch Heft 5.* [215o

Pargellis, Stanley M.: Leisler, Jacob (1640— 1691) de facto lieutenant-governor of New York. *In: Dictionary of American biography. Under the auspices of the American Council of Learned Societies. Vol. XI. Edited by Dumas Malone. London-New York 1933. pp. 91—92. [born at Frankfurt, Germany and came to New Amsterdam 1660 a soldier of the Dutch West India Company.* [215p

Purple, Edwin R.: Genealogical notes relating to Lieut. — Gov. Jacob Leisler and his family connections in New York. *New York, N. Y.: Privately printed 1887. pp. 5—24.* = *Reprint from the New York Genealogical and Biographical Record; with additions.* [215q

Vermilye, A. G.: The Leisler troubles of 1689. *An address delivered before the Oneida Historical Society. Reprinted from Old New York, March, 1891. pp. 35.* [215r

A modest and impartial narrative of several grievances and great oppressions that the peaceable and most considerable inhabitants of their majesties Province of New York in America lye under by the extravagant and arbitary proceedings of Jacob Leisler and his accomplices. *Printed at New York . . . Reprinted at London 1690. Reprinted in: Colonial history of the State of New York, procured in Holland, England and France. By John Romeyn Brodhead. Vol. III. Albany, N. Y. 1853 pp. 665—684.* [215s

Jacob Leisler: The first German governor. A martyr to the cause of civil liberty and selfgovernment. *Two German oak trees planted in his memory. Reprint from: ,,New York Sun." In: The Pennsylvania-German. Vol. XII. Lititz, Pa. 1911. pp. 343—346.*   [215 t

---

Munsey, Creighton Spencer: The Carmer family of New York. Abraham Kermer and some of his descendants. *Contributed by ... In: The New York Genealogical and Biographical Record. Vol. LXI New York, N. Y. 1930. pp. 356—373.*
[Came from Hamburg to New Amsterdam in or before 1656, and died there after Dec. 13, 1685, or before 1686.]
   [215 u

Heck, Earl L. W.: Hack, George (c. 1623—c. 1665) merchant, physician, colonist. *In: Dictionary of American Biography. Under the auspices of the American Council of Learned Societies. Vol. VIII. Edited by Allen Johnson and Dumas Malone. London-New York 1932. S. 70—71.*
[b. in Cologne, Germany of a Schleswig-Holstein family, emigrated to New Amsterdam and 1651 to Virginia.]   [215 v

Hoffman, Eug. A.: Genealogy of the Hoffman family, descendants of Martin Hoffman. *With biographical notes. New York, N. Y.: Dodd Mead & Co. 1899.* [215 w
Hoffman . . . *[descendants from Martin Hoffman, born at Reval, on the Gulf of Finland, who emigrated to New York in 1657]. In: Dictionary of American biography. Under the auspices of the American Council of Learned Societies. Vol. IX. Edited by Dumas Malone. London-New York 1932:*

Hoffman, David Murray (1791—1878) jurist. *By* **Richard B. Morris** *p. 112.*
Hoffman, Eugene Augustus (1829—1902) Protestant Espiscopal clergyman, educator. *By* **Albert M. Farr** *pp. 112—113.*
Hoffman, John Thompson (1828—1888) lawyer, politician, mayor and governor of New York. *By* **Lucius H. Holt.** *pp. 113—114.*
Hoffmann, Josiah Ogden (1766—1837) lawyer. *By* **Richard B. Morris** *pp.114—115.*
Hoffman, Ogden (1793—1856) lawyer, member of Congress. *By* **Richard B. Morris.** *pp. 115—117.*
[Bibliography].   [215 x

Schoonmaker, L. E.: Lineage of the Schoonmaker family. *Contributed by ... In: Olde Vlster. An historical and genealogical magazine. Vol. II. Kingston, N. Y. 1906. pp. 81—85; 121—125; 151—158; 183—188; Vol. III, Kingston, N. Y. 1907. pp. 242—246.*
[Hendrick Jochemsen Schoonmaker, the progenitor of the Schoonmaker family in America, was according to an old diary yet in existence, a native of Hamburgh, Germany. He came to America in the military service of Holland and settled at Albany previous to 1654.]   [215 y

Lanza, Conrad H.: Sickles, Daniel Edgar (1825—1914) congressman, Union soldier, diplomat. *In: Dictionary of American biography. Under the auspices of the American Council of Learned Societies. Vol. XVIII. Edited by Dumas Malone. London-New York 1935. pp. 150—151.*
[Descendant of Zacharias Sickels, of Vienna, Austria, who entred the service of the Dutch West India Company and settled in America about 1656.]   [215 z

Deutsche Flugblätter zur Auswanderung nach Amerika

German Pamphlets, which influenced German Immigration

[Penn, William]: Eine Nachricht wegen der Landschaft Pennsylvania in America: *Welche Jüngstens unter dem Großen Siegel in Engelland an William Penn, &c. Sambt den Freyheiten und der Macht, so zu behöriger guten Regierung derselben nötig übergeben worden, und zum Unterricht derer, so etwan bereits bewogen, oder noch möchten bewogen werden, ümb sich selbsten darhin zu begeben, oder einige Bediente und Gesinde an diesem Ort zu senden, hiermit kund gethan wird. Aus dem in London gedrucktem und alldar bey Benjamin Clarck, Buchhändlern in George-Yard Lombard-street befindlichem Englischen übergesetzet. Nebenst beygefügtem ehemaligem im 1675. Jahr gedrucktem Schreiben des obererwehnten Will. Penns. In Amsterdam: gedruckt bey Christoff Cunraden. 1681. 31 S. [Englische Ausgabe = Nr. 3312.]* [216

[—] Kurtze Nachricht von der Americanischen Landschafft Pennsilvania. *... [Übersetzt und veröffentlicht von* **Benjamin Furley.**] *Amsterdam 1682. ... S. [Englische Ausgabe = Nr. 3313.]* [216a

[—] German translation of William Penn's letter to the Free Society of Merchants in London, 1683. *[Transcription of a copy at the Royal Privy Archives in Munich.] Edited by* **M. D. Learned.** *In: German American Annals. New series, vol. VIII. Philadelphia, Pa. 1910. pp. 51—75, fac-similes. [Englische Ausgabe = Nr. 3314.]* [217

[—] Beschreibung der in America neuerfundenen Provinz Pensylvanien. *Derer Inwohner, Gesetz, Arth, Sitten und Gebrauch: auch sämtlicher Reviren des Landes, sonderlich der Haupt-Stadt Philadelphia. Alles glaubwurdigst auß des Gouverneurs darinnen erstatteten Nachricht. In Verlegung bey Henrich Heuss an der Banco, im Jahr 1684. 32 S. Karte.* [218

[Pastorius, Franz Daniel]: Copia, eines von einem Sohn an seine Eltern auß America abgelassenen Briefes, sub dato Philadelphia, d. 7. Martii, 1684. *1. S. Facsimile reproduction of a printed copy at the City Library of Zürich, Switzerland in: The life of Francis Daniel Pastorius, the founder of Germantown. By M. D. Learned. Philadelphia, Pa. 1908 [= no. 158], between pp. 124 and 125.* [219

[—] Sichere Nachricht auß America, wegen der Landschafft Pennsylvania, von einem dorthin gereißten Teutschen, de dato Philadelphia, den 7. Martii 1684. 8 S. *Facsimile reproduction of a original copy at the City Library of Zürich in: The life of Francis Daniel Pastorius, the founder of Germantown. By M. D. Learned. Philadelphia, Pa. 1908 [= no. 158], between pp. 128—129.* [220

[—] Positive information from America, concerning the Country of Pennsylvania, from a German who has migrated thither; dated Philadelphia March 7, 1684. *[Full version of the Zürich imprint „Sichere Nachricht ...“ = no. 220] Translated by* **A. Cook Myers.** *In: Narratives of early Pennsylvania, West New Jersey and Delaware 1630—1707. Edited by A. Cook Myers. New York, N. Y. 1912 [= no. 3310]. pp. 392—411.* [221

Wertmüller, Joris: „Missive uyt German Town in Pennsylvania". *In: Twee missiven geschreven uyt Pensilvania d'Eene door een Hollander, woonachtig in Philadelphia, d'Ander door en Switzer, woonachtig in German Town. Dat is Hoogduytse Stadt. Von den 16 en 26 Maert 1684. Nieuwe Stijl. Tot Rotterdam: by Pieter van Alphen. Anno 1684. pp. (2). English translation of the two missives see: Hendrick Pannebecker, surveyor of lands for the Penns. 1674—1754. By S. W. Pennypacker. Philadelphia, Pa. 1894 [= no. 7183]. pp. 27—39.* [222

[Pastorius, Franz Daniel]: Beschreibung von Pennsylvanien, Epistola ad [Georgium Leonhardium] Modelium, rectorem scholae Windsheimensis. *Datiert: Germanopoli, 1. Dec. 1688. In: W. E. Tenzel's Monatliche Unterredungen einiger guten Freunde von allerhand Büchern und anderen annehmlichen Geschichten. Leipzig, Aprilis 1691. S. 278—288.* [223

[—] Auszug aus einem Briefe an seinen Vater in Windsheim, datiert 20. Junii 1692. *In: W. E. Tenzel's Monatliche Unterredungen einiger guten Freunde. Leipzig, Februarius 1693. S. 162—164.* [223a

[—] Zwei unbekannte Briefe von Pastorius. *Reprints from Tentzel's „Monatlichen Unterredungen einiger guten Freunde von allerhand Buechern und anderen annehmlichen Geschichten." April 1691, resp. Februar 1693 [= no. 223]. Herausgegeben von* Julius Goebel. *In: German American Annals. New series, vol. II. Philadelphia, Pa. 1904. pp. 492—503.* [224

[—] Pastorii Kurtze Geographische Beschreibung von der allerneulichst erfundenen Americanischen Landschafft Pennsylvanien. *[Auszug und Inhaltsangabe der hernach in Druck erschienenen Arbeit = Nr. 225]. In: W. E. Tentzel's Monatliche Unterredungen einiger guten Freunden von allerhand Büchern und anderen annehmlichen Geschichten. Leipzig, December 1691. S. 1038—1041.* [224a

[—] Francisci Danielis Pastorii Sommerhusano-Franci. Kurtze Geographische Beschreibung der letztmahls erfundenen Americanischen Landschafft Pennsylvania, *mit angehenckten einigen notablen Begebenheiten und Bericht Schreiben an dessen Hrn. Vattern, Patrioten und gute Freunde. [Nurmberg in 1692.] 33 S. Veröffentlicht als Anhang zu „Kurtze Beschreibung des H. R. Reichs Stadt Windsheim . . . in den Druck gegeben durch Melchiorem Adamum Pastorium, ältern Burgemeistern und Ober-Richtern in besagter Stadt. Nürnberg: Christian Sigmund Froberg 1692.* [225

[—] Geographisch-Statistische Beschreibung der Provinz Pensylvanien von Fr. Daniel Pastorius. *Im Auszug mit Anmerkungen. Memmingen: bey Andreas Sevler 1792. . . . S.* [226

Seelig, Johann Gottfried: Copia eines Send-Schreibens aus der neuen Welt, *betreffend, die Erzehlung einer gefährlichen*

Schiffarth, und glücklichen Anländung etlicher Christlichen Reisegefehrten, welche zu dem Ende diese Wallfahrt angetretten, den Glauben an Jesum Christum allda außzu breiten. [s. l.; Halle oder Frankfort?] 1695. . . . S. Bericht an August Herman Francke, zu Halle; datiert „Germandom in Pennsylvania, America d. 7. August 1694". [227

[Pastorius, Franz Daniel]: Umständige geographische Beschreibung der zu allerletzt erfundenen Provintz Pennsylvania in denen End-Gräntzen Americae in der West-Welt gelegen, *durch Franciscum Danielem Pastorium, J. V. Lic. und Friedens-Richtern daselbsten. Worbey angekencket sind einige notable Begebenheiten, und Bericht-Schreiben an dessen Herrn Vattern Melchiorem Adamum Pastorium, und andere gute Freunde. Franckfurt und Leipzig: Zu finden bey Andreas Otto 1700. (1), (12), 140 S. Abdruck: . . . 1704. pp. (12), 140 [vgl. Nr. 237].*

Auszug vgl. in: Monatlicher Auszug aus allerhand neu-herausgegebenen, nützlichen und artigen Büchern. Dezember MDCC. Hannover: Zu finden bey Nicol. Förstern, Buchhändl. 1700. S. 895—902. [228

[Pastorius, Franz Daniel]: A particular geographical description of the lately discovered Province of Pennsylvania, situated on the frontiers of the western world, America. *By Francis Daniel Pastorius [= no. 228]. Translated from the original German by* Lewis H. Weiss. *In: Memoirs of the Historical Society of Pennsylvania. Vol. IV. = Part II. Philadelphia, Pa.: Henry C. Baird 1850. pp. 83—104.* [229

— Franz Daniel Pastorius' Beschreibung von Pennsylvanien. *Nachbildung der in Frankfurt a./M. im Jahre 1700 erschienenen Original-Ausgabe [= Nr. 228]. Herausgegeben vom Crefelder Verein für wissenschaftliche Vorträge. Mit einer Einleitung von Friedrich Kapp. Crefeld: Kramer & Baum 1884. (1), XXIII, (1), (10), 140 S.* [230

[—] Pastorius's description of Pennsylvania. 1700. A particular geographical description of the lately discovered Province of Pennsylvania, situated on the frontiers of this western world. *Translated from the original German by* Lewis H. Weiss *[= no. 229]. (With introductory note to "The Pennsylvania Pilgrim" by*

John G. Whittier.) [Boston, Directors of the Old South work. 1898.] = Old South Leaflets. Vol. IV, no. 95. [231
Pastorius, Franz Daniel: Circumstantial geographical description of Pennsylvania ..., 1700. *English translation of „Umständige geographische Beschreibung ..."* [= no. 228] *made under the direction of Dr. J. F. Jameson by* **A. Cook Myers.** *In: Naratives of early Pennsylvania, West Jersey and Delaware 1630—1707. Edited by A. Cook Myers. New York, N. Y. 1912 [= no. 3310]. pp. 353—448.*

[232
Wahrhafftiger Bericht des in derer Schwärmer und gute Tage wehler Hertzen fest-stehenden gelobten Landes Pennsylvanien in America, ein Land, darinnen Zucker und Holtz wächset, *abgefasset von zweyen gelahrten Männern, als treuen und wahrhafftigen Zeugen, deren der erste, von obgedachter Einbildung, der andere, von Gewissens-Bedrängung, hineingejaget worden; Jener, sich betrogen gesehen, bald wieder nach Teutschland kommen; Dieser, nachdem er 2 Jahr drinnen gewesen, und sein Gewissen unruhig geblieben, wieder herauseilen müssen. Allen denen mit gleicher phantastischen Schwärmer-Einbildung besessenen Geistern zur Warnung mitgetheilet im Jahr, da Babels Gefängnis in Pensylvanien noch hefftiger als in Deutschland war, wie aus diesem Bericht kund und offenbar. [s. l.] 1701. (32) S.*

[233
Falckner, Daniel: Curieuse Nachricht von Pensylvania in Norden-America *welche, auf Begehren guter Freunde, uber vorgelegte 103. Fragen, bey seiner Abreiß aus Teutschland nach obigem Lande Anno 1700. ertheilet, und nun Anno 1702 in den Druck gegeben worden. Von ... Professore, Burgern und Pilgrim allda. Franckfurt und Leipzig: Zu finden bey Andreas Otto, Buchhändlern 1702. (1), (4), 58 S.* [234
[—] Daniel Falckner's Curieuse Nachricht from Pennsylvania, the book that stimulated the great German immigration to Pennsylvania in the early years of the XVIII century *[= no. 234]. Translated and annoted by* **Julius Friedrich Sachse.** *Lancaster, Pa.: New Era Printing Co. 1905. = Part XIV. "A narrative and critical history", prepared at the request of the Pennsylvania-German Society. In: The Pennsylvania-German Society.*

Proceedings and Adresses ... 1903. Vol. XIV. Lancaster, Pa. 1905. Separate pagination. pp. IX, 5—256, ill., maps.
[235
Falckner, Justus: Abdruck eines Schreibens an Tit. Herrn D. Henr. Muhlen, aus Germanton, in der Americanischen Province Pensylvania, sonst Nova Suecia, den ersten Augusti, im Jahr unsers-Heyls eintausend siebenhundert und eins, den Zustand der Kirchen in America betreffend. *[s. l.] 1702. ... S.* [236
[Pastorius, Franz Daniel]: Umständige geographische Beschreibung der zu allerletzt erfundenen Provintz Pensylvaniae, *... [Abdruck von Nr. 228] und Leipzig: Zu finden bey Andreas Otto 1704. (12), 140 S.*
[Angefügt]: Continuatio der Beschreibung der Landschafft Pensylvaniae an denen End - Gräntzen Americae. *Uber vorige des Herrn Pastorii Relationes. In sich haltend: Die Situation, und Fruchtbarkeit des Erdbodens. Die Schiffreiche und andere Flüsse. Die Anzahl derer bißhero gebauten Städte. Die seltsame Creaturen an Thieren, Vögeln und Fischen. Die Mineralien und Edelgesteine. Deren eingebohrnen wilden Völker Sprachen, Religion und Gebräuche. Und die ersten Christlichen Pflanzer und Anbauer dieses Landes. Beschrieben von* **Gabriel Thomas,** *15. jährigen Inwohner dieses Landes [= Deutsche Übersetzung von Nr. 3318]. Welchem Tractätlein noch beygefüget sind: Des Hn.* **Daniel Falckners,** Burgers und Pilgrims in Pensylvania 103. Beantwortungen uff vorgelegte Fragen von guten Freunden *[= Curieuse Nachricht von Pensylvania. ... 1702. = Nr. 234]. Franckfurt und Leipzig: Zu finden bey Andreas Otto, Buchhändlern 1702.(1),(2),40 S.;(1),(4), 58 S.* [237
Königl. Englisch in Teutschland verschickte Erklärung oder Abmahnungs-Schreiben. *Datiert: London, den 31. December 1709. (1) S.*
Reprinted in: The German exodus to England in 1709. (Massenauswanderung der Pfälzer). By Fr. R. Diffenderffer. Lancaster, Pa. 1897 [= no. 296]. p. 271.
[238
Kocherthal, Joshua: Außführlich und umständlicher Bericht von der berühmten Landschafft Carolina in dem Engelländischen America gelegen. *An den Tag gegeben von ... Zweyter Druck. Franck-*

furt am Mayn: Zu finden bey Georg
Heinrich Oehrling 1709.
. . . . Vierter Druck. Mit Anhängen
zweyer Engelischen Authoren gethanen
Beschreibung, und eines auff der Reyse
dahin begriffenen Hochteutschen auß
London. Benachrichtigung; Nebst einer
Land-Carte von Carolina vermehrt.
Franckfurt am Mayn: Georg Heinrich
Oehrling 1709. 80 S.
[Gegenschrift zu Nr. 238.]　　　[239
Boehme, Anton Wilhelm [unter dem Pseudonym: Hoen, Moritz Wilhelm]: Das
verlangte, nicht erlangte Canaan bey
den Lust-Gräbern; oder Ausführliche Beschreibung von der unglücklichen Reise
derer jüngsthin aus Teutschland nach dem
Engländischen in America gelegenen Carolina und Pennsylvanien wallenden Pilgrim, absonderlich dem einseitigen übel-
gegründeten Kochenthalerischen Bericht
wohlbedächtigt entgegen gesetzt . . . Franckfurt und Leipzig: (Andreä) 1711. (12),
127 S.　　　[240
Ochs, Joh. Rudolff: Amerikanischer Wegweiser oder kurtze und eigentliche Beschreibung der englischen Provintzen
in Nord-Amerika, sonderlich aber der
Landschafft Carolina, mit großem Fleiß
zusammen getragen und an den Tag gegeben durch . . . neben einer neuen und
correcten Land-Karten von Nord- und
Süd-Carolina. Bern: 1711. 102 S.
[Stadt. Bibliothek Bern, Schweiz]　　[241
[Lawson, John]: Allerneueste Beschreibung
der Provintz Carolina in West-Indien.
Samt einem Reise-Journal von mehr als
Tausend Meilen unter allerhand Indianischen Reisen. Auch einer accuraten
Land-Carte und andere Kupfer-Stichen.
Aus dem Englischen übersetzt durch
M. Visher. Hamburg: Gedruckt und verlegt durch seel. Thomas von Wierings
Erben . . . Anno 1712. (7), 365, (3) S.,
ill., Karte.　　　[242
Simmendinger, Ulrich: Wahrhafte und
glaubwürdige Verzeichnueß, jeniger,
durch die Gnade Gottes, annoch im
Leben sich befindenden Personen, welche
sich Anno 1709 unter des Herrn wunderbarer Führung aus Teutschland in Americam oder neue Welt begeben, und allda
an verschiedenen Orten ihr Stuecklein
Brods suchen. Allen Liebhabern, insonderheit aber deroselben Familien
und nahen Freunden zur freudigen Nachricht gestellet. Von . . ., siebenjährigen
Nord-Americanern, in der Provintz Neu-

York, anjetzo aber in seiner Vatter-Stad
Reuttlingen. Daselbst gedruckt. Bey Joh.
G. Fuesing [1717]. 22 S.　　　[243
Simmendinger, Ulrich: True and authentic
register of persons still living, by God's
grace, who in the year 1709, under the
wonderful providences of the Lord
journeyed from Germany to America
or the new world, and there seek their
piece of bread at various places.
Reported with joy to all admirers, especially to their families and close friends
by Ulrich Simmendinger, a North
American, seven years in the province of
New York but now returned to his native
Reutlingen. Printed there by John G. Fuesing. Translated from the German [=
no. 243] by Herman F. Vesper. Reprinted
by the Enterprise and News, St. Johnsville, N. Y. 1934. 20 p.　　　[243a
Ausführliche historische und geographische
Beschreibung des an dem großen Flusse
Mississippi in Nord-Amerika gelegenen
herrlichen Landes Louisiana. Leipzig:
Bei dem Sohn des verstorbenen J. Fried.
Gledetschen 1720. . . . S.　　　[244
Auszug einiger Send-Schreiben aus Philadelphia in Pennsylvanien, worinnen
die gantze Reise, von Rotterdam nach
Pensylvanien, fleißig aufgezeichnet, und
dieses Landes Clima, dessen Bewohner
Handlung, andere Gewerbe, Ordnung, etc.
entdecket ist; Samt Benennung dasiger
zahmen und wilden Thiere, Gevögel,
Fische, Feld- und Garten-Früchte, etc.
Auch wird zugleich von vielen merkwürdigen Umständen, die uns bisher un-
bekandt geblieben, aufrichtiger Bericht
abgestattet. Dem Nächsten zur nöthigen
Nachricht durch den Druck mitgetheilet.
[s. l.] Im Jahre Christi 1729. 12 S.
English translation: Diary of a voyage
from Rotterdam to Philadelphia in 1728.
Translated by Julius F. Sachse. Lancaster, Pa. 1909. In: The Pennsylvania-
German Society. Proceedings and Addresses. Vol. XVIII. Lancaster, Pa. 1909.
Separate pagination. pp. 25, ill.　[245
L., J. K.: Der nunmehro in der Neuen Welt
vergnügt und ohne Heim-Wehe lebende
Schweitzer. Oder: Kurtze und eigent-
liche Beschreibung des gegenwärtigen
Zustandes der königlichen englischen
Provinz Carolina, aus den neulich an-
gekommenen Briefen der Alldorten sich
befindenden Schweizeren, zusammen-
getragen von J. K. L. Bern: getruckt bey
Joh. Bondeli 1734. 46 S.

[Gibt an, die Eindrücke von Schweizer Siedlern in Süd-Karolina, besonders in Purysburg, aus Briefen wiederzugeben.] [246
Neue Nachricht alter und neuer Merkwürdigkeiten, enthaltend ein vertrautes Gespräch und sichere Briefe von der Landschaft Carolina und übrigen Englischen Pflantz-Städten in Amerika. *Zu finden zu Zürich, Bern, Basel, Schaffhausen und St. Gallen in den Gericht-Häusern gegen Ende des Jahres 1734. 80 S.*
[Gegenschrift zu Nr. 246] [247
Nöthigste Nachricht, betreffend Carolina, aus den Weitläuffigern kurtz gefasset, für den gemeinen Mann. *[s.l.] 1734. 2. S.*
[Warnung.] [248
Weber, Ludwig: Der hinckende Bott von Carolina, Oder Ludwig Webers von Wallissellen Beschreibung seiner Reise von Zürich gen Rotterdam, mit derjenigen Gesellschaft, welche neulich aus dem Schweizerland in Carolinam zu ziehen gedachte. *Zürich: bey Joh. Jac. Lindinner. 1835. 32 S.*
[betrifft die Gruppe von 194 personen unter der Führung des Pfarrers Götschi von Züirch; vgl. Nr. 184] [249
Byrd, William: Neu gefundenes Eden. Oder ausführlicher Bericht von Süd- und Nord-Carolina, Pensilphania, Mary-Land & Virginia. *Entworffen durch zwey in dise Provintzen gemachten Reisen, Reiß-Journal, und ville Brieffen, dadurch der gegenwärtige Zustand diser Ländern warhafftig entdecket und dem Nebenmenschen zu guten an Tag gelegt wird. Samt beygefügtem Anhang, oder freye Unterweisung zu dem verlohrnen, nun aber wieder gefundenen Lapide Philosophorum, dadurch man bald zur Vergnügung, und wahrer Reichthum gelangen kan. In Truck verfertigt durch Befelch der Helvetischen Societät. 1737. 288 S. 2 Karten.*
Abgedruckt in: Der Westen. Chicago, Ill., 6, Nov. 1892 u. 29, Jan. 1893. [250
Trachsler, Hans W.: Kurtz verfaßte Reiß-Beschreibung eines neulich aus Carolina in sein Vaterland zurückgekommenen Lands-Angehörigen. *Zürich: Bürkli 1738. 13 S.*
[Ungünstiger Bericht.] [251
Wahrhafftige und gantz zuverlässige gute Zeitung von der Königlich-Englischen Provintz Carolina, *hergebracht von glaubwürdigen Männern, die vor 4 Jahren hineingereiset, anjetzo glücklich wiederum zurück gekommen und aufs neue dahin*

sich zuverfügen entschlossen. *St. Gallen: Gedruckt bey Ruprecht Weniger 1740. 15 S.*
[Gezeichnet von 31 Siedlern in Sachse-Gotha, S. C. in 1740.] [252
[Ziegler, Joh. Rud.]: Christholds Gedanken, bey Anlaß der Bewegung, welche die bekannte Beschreibung von Carolina, in Amerika, in unserem Land verursacht, und der vor etlichen Tagen dahin geschehenen Abreiß verschiedener von unserem Volck. *[s. l. Schweizer Druck; s. d.] 12 S.* [253
Translation of General Waldo's circular . . . 1753. *With an introduction by John L. Locke. In: Collections of the Maine Historical Society. Vol. VI. Portland, Me. 1859. pp. 321—332.* [254
Kurtze Beschreibung derer Landschafft Massachusetts-Bay, in Neu Engellandt. *Absonderlich des Landstrichs an der Breyten Bay, so dem Königlichen Britischen Obersten, Samuel Waldo, Erbherrn des Breyten Bay, zugehörig, sampt denen Hauptbedingungen nach welchen sich fremde Protestanten daselbsten, ansiedeln mögen. Speyer, 1741.*
[Vgl. Der deutsche Pionier, Vol. XIV, S. 10.] [255
,,Historische und geographische Beschreibung von Neu-Schottland, *wie auch von den Sitten und Gewohnheiten der Indianer, und von den merkwürdigen Begebenheiten, die sich zwischen den Cronen Frankreich und England seit der Besitznehmung zugetragen, hinlängliche Nachricht ertheilet wird.`` Frankfurt und Leipzig: H. L. Brömer 1750. 216 S.*
[Werblatt aus dem Englischen ins Deutsche übersetzt von dem Agenten Köhler.] [256
[Tobler, Joh.]: ,,Beschreibung von Süd Carolina``. *In: Alter und verbesserter Schreib-Calender, auf das . . . Christ-Jahr MDCCLIV . . . mit einer merkwürdigen Beschreibung von Süd-Carolina versehen, verfaßt . . . von Herr Joh. Tobler, St. Gallen: Verlegt und zu haben bei Hans Jacob Hochreutener 1754. S. [32—42].* [257
Eine leyder wahrhaffte traurige Geschicht und Beschreibung, wie im nächst abgewichenen Monat Julii, 1754, ein großes Schiff nach West-Indien mit 468 Personen, . . . ein lamentes Ende genommen. *(1754). 4 S.* [258
Mittelberger, Gottlieb: Gottlieb Mittelbergers Reise nach Pennsylvanien im Jahre 1750 und Rückreise nach Teutsch-

land im Jahr 1754. *Enthaltend nicht nur eine Beschreibung des Landes nach seinem gegenwärtigen Zustande, sondern auch eine ausführliche Nachricht von den unglückseligen und betrübten Umständen der meisten Teutschen, die in dieses Land gezogen sind, und dahinziehen. Frankfurth und Leipzig 1756. (6), 120 S.* [259
[Mittelberger, Gottlieb]: Gottlieb Mittelberger's journey to Pennsylvania in the year 1750 and return to Germany in the year 1754, *containing not only a description of the country according to its present condition, but also a detailed account of the sad and unfortunate circumstances of most of the Germans that have emigrated, and are emigrating to that country. Translated from the German by* **Carl Theo Eben.** *Philadelphia, Pa.: Privately printed for Joseph Y. Jeanes 1898. pp. 129, 1 fac-simile.*
[Translation of no. 259.]   [260
Nachricht von der Provinz Virginien in Nord-America, *nebst ausführlichen Beschreibung der entsetzlichen Wasser-Fluth so gedachte Provinz im Jahr 1771, Monaths May erlitten. Als auch Beschreibung von der Schlacht und gänzlichen Ausrottung der Regulatorn in Nord-Carolina in America. Deme annoch beygefueget eine ausfuerliche und accurate geographische Beschreibung der Provinz Pennsylvanien in Nord-America. Frankfurt am Mayn: Joh. Georg Fleichers Buchhandlung 1772. 16 S.*   [261

Freyheiten welche die Regierung von Süd-Carolina unter Protection Sr. Königlichen Groß-Britannischen Majestät denen dorthin von Hamburg kommenden und sich selbst daselbst niederlassenden Personen vermöge eines auf 5 Jahre von 1773 vestgesetzten und von Höchst-Deroselben confirmirten Rath-Schlusses oder Acte, allergnädigst angedeyhen lasset. *[Am Ende] ,,Dieses Avertissement wird von Herrn Hofrath Bodo Wilhelm Stöckeen auf der Bockenheimergaß Lit. E. Nr. 104 umsonst ausgegeben, wobey auch einem jeden allernöthiger Unterricht freundlichst ertheilt wird.“ [s. l.; s. d. wahrscheinlich Frankfurt 1773.] 4 S.*
[Stadtarchiv Frankfurt am Main.]   [262
Berichte über den Genesee-District in dem Staate von New York der vereinigten Staaten von Nord-Amerika nach der im Jahr 1791 Englischen herausgegeb. Ausgabe übersetzt. *[s.l.] Dezember 1791. 32 S.*
[Steht in Zusammenhang mit den Bemühungen von ,,William Berczy, Bevollmächtigter der Genesee Association“, Siedler für das Genessee-Gebiet in New York zu werben.]
[Preußisches Geheimes Staatsarchiv, Berlin]   [263
Auszug der Anmerkungen zum Unterricht derjenigen Europäer, die sich in Amerika niederzulassen gesonnen sind, *von dem letzlich verstorbenen berühmten* **Dr. Franklin.** *[s. l.; s. d.] 8 S.*   [264

Die Frankfurter Landkompagnie, gegründet 12. Nov. 1686

The Frankfort Company, Founded Nov. 12, 1686

Learned, Marion Dexter: The life of Francis Daniel Pastorius, the founder of Germantown. *With an appreciation of Pastorius by Samuel Whitaker Pennypacker. Philadelphia, Pa.: William J. Campbell 1908. pp. X, 324, ill., maps. [Separate print of no. 157]* [„Agent of the German Company." = Chapter IV. pp. 116—155.] [265

Müller, Bernhard: „Frankfurter Landkompagnie Pastorius und Germantown." *In: Frankfurt / Amerika. Frankfurt am Main: Herausgegeben vom Wirtschaftsamt der Stadt Frankfurt am Main, Abteilung für Werbe- und Ausstellungswesen, anläßlich der Ausstellung Frankfurt-Amerika. 1926 [= Nr. 162]. S. 14—32.* [266

[Pastorius, Francis Daniel]: Exemplum sine exemplo. *[Paper of Francis Daniel Pastorius relating to the case of John Henry Sprogel vs. The Frankfort Company.] In: S. W. Pennypacker: „Pennsylvania colonial cases." Philadelphia, Pa. 1892. pp. 171—178.* Reprint in: *The life of Francis Daniel Pastorius, the founder of Germantown. By M. D. Learned. Philadelphia, Pa. 1908 [= no. 265]. = Appendix B. pp. 294—297.* [267

Pennypacker, Samuel Whitaker: Richard Heather, demise of John Henry Sprogel vs. The Frankfort Company. *In: S. W. Pennypacker: „Pennsylvania colonial cases. „Philadelphia, Pa. 1892. pp. 142 —170, resp. —178.* [268

Vertrag der Frankfurter Gesellschaft. *[„Frankfurt am Mayn, den 12. November anno 1686."] In: Der Deutsche Pionier. Jg. XII. Cincinnati, O. 1880—1881. „Alte deutsch-amerikanische Dokumente." S. 317—321.* [269

Articles of an agreement between the members of the Frankfurt Company, 1686. *In: The Pennsylvania Magazine of History and Biography. Vol. XV. Philadelphia, Pa. 1891. pp. 205—211.* [270

„Diplomatic print of the agreement of the German Company of Frankfurt, [signed Franckfurt am Mayn, den 12. Novemb. anno 1686."] Reprint in: *The life of Francis Daniel Pastorius, the founder of Germantown. By M. D. Learned. Philadelphia, Pa. 1908 [= no. 265]. Appendix A. pp. 288—293.* [271

„Petition subscribed by ffr. Danl. Pastorius, by order and in behalf of the German Corporation," *[Frankfort Co.] read at the council held in Philadelphia, 5, 1 mo. 1700—1. See: Colonial records of Pennsylvania [= no. 3139]. Vol. II. 1852. pp. 13—14.* [272

The patent to the Frankfort Company *[dated 25th of October, 1701, concerning the land variously named in early deeds: The German tract, The Manatawny tract, The Frankfort Company's land and The Great tract of 22377 acres.] In: The Perkiomen Region, Past and Present. Vol. I. Philadelphia, Pa. 1895. pp. 98 —101.* [273

„Letter of Attorney to Falkner, Kelpius and Jawert." Reprint in: *The life of Francis Daniel Pastorius, the founder of Germantown. By M. D. Learned. Philadelphia, Pa. 1908 [= no. 265]. Appendix D. pp. 299—300.* [274

Two several petitions, concerning the administration of the affairs of the Frankfort Company *(petition for an ejectment of Jno Henry Sproegel and Daniel Falkner, presented by F. D. Pastorius & Johannes Jawert, attending the Board) at Council at Philadelphia, March 1, 1708—09. See: Colonial records of Pennsylvania [= no. 3139]. Vol. II. 1852. pp. 429—432.* [275

Ejectment of the Frankfort Company. *In: The Perkiomen Region, Past and Present. Vol. I. Philadelphia, Pa. 1895. pp. 121 —123.* [276

„The German tract" *[known variously as the Frankfort, the Manatawny, the German, the Sproegell tract, or even as Falkner Swamp in Philadelphia County, but what is now Montgomery County, Pa.] In: The Perkiomen Region. Vol. VI, no. 1. Pennsburg, Pa. 1928. pp. 2— 21.* [277

Die Pennsylvanien-Deutschen
The Pennsylvania Germans

Allgemein[1])
General[2])

Pennsylvania: The German influence in its settlement and development. A narrative and critical history. *Prepared by authority at the request of the Pennsylvania German Society. Published by the Society in: The Pennsylvania-German Society. Proceedings and Addresses. (Vol. VII. 1897ff.); also issued as separate publications.*

Part. I. **Sachse, J. F.**: The fatherland: (1450—1750) showing the part it bore in discovery, exploration and development of the western continent, with special reference to the Commonwealth of Pennsylania. *Philadelphia, Pa. 1897. In: Vol. VII. Reading, Pa. 1897. pp. 32—256, ill., maps.*

Part II. **Diffenderffer Frank Ried:** The German exodus to England in 1709. (Massen-Auswanderung der Pfälzer.) *Lancaster, Pa. 1897. In: Vol. VII. Reading, Pa. 1897. pp. 257—413, ill.*

Part III. **Jacobs, Henry Eyster:** The German emigration to America 1709—1740. *Lancaster, Pa. 1898. In: Vol. VIII. Lancaster, Pa. 1898. pp. (1), 31—150, ill.*

Part IV. **Pennypacker. Samuel Withacker:** The settlement of Germantown, Pa. and the beginning of German immigration to North America. *Lancaster, Pa. 1899. In: Vol. IX. Lancaster, Pa. 1899. pp. 51—345, ill., map.*

Part V. **Richards, Mathias Henry:** The German emigration from New York Province into Pennsylvania. *Lancaster, Pa. 1899. In: Vol. IX. Lancaster, Pa. 1899. pp. 351—447, ill.*

Part VI. **Schantz, F. J. F.:** The domestic life and characteristics of the Pennsylvania-German pioneer. *Lancaster, Pa. 1900. In: Vol. X. Lancaster, Pa. 1900. Separate pagination. pp. 97, ill.*

Part VII. **Diffenderffer, Frank Ried:** The German immigration into Pennsylvania. *[Part I.]* Through the port of Philadelphia from 1700 to 1775; *[Part II.]* The redemptioners. *Lancaster, Pa. 1900. In: Vol. X. Lancaster, Pa. 1900. Separate pagination. pp. IX, 138; 141—328, ill.*

Part VIII. **Falkenstein, Georg N.:** The German Baptist Brethren or Dunkers. *Lancaster, Pa. 1900. In: Vol. X. Lancaster, Pa. 1900. Separate pagination. pp. 148, ill.*

Part IX. **Schmauk, Theodore Emanuel:** A history of the Lutheran Church in Pennsylvania (1638—1820). *From the original sources. Lancaster, Pa. 1902—03. In: Vol. XI. Lancaster, Pa. 1902. Separate pagination. pp. VIII, 355, ill.; Vol. XII. Lancaster, Pa. 1903. Separate pagination. pp. XXIII, 357—588.*

Part X. **Dubbs, Joseph Henry:** The Reformed Church in Pennsylvania. *Lancaster, Pa. 1902. In: Vol. XI. Lancaster, Pa. 1902. Separate pagination. pp. X, 375, ill.*

Part. XI. **Sachse, Julius Friedrich:** The music of the Ephrata cloister also Conrad Beissel's treatise on music as set forth in a preface to the ,,Turtel Taube" of 1747. Amplified with fac-simile reproductions of parts of the text and some original, Ephrata music of the Weyrauchs Hügel, 1739; Rosen und Lilien, 1745; Turtel Taube, 1747. Choralbuch, 1754, etc. *Lancaster, Pa. 1903. In: Vol. XII. Lancaster, Pa. 1903. Separate pagination pp. 108.*

Part XII. **Kriebel, Howard Wiegner:** The Schwenkfelders in Pennsylvania. A historical sketch. *Lancaster, Pa. 1904. In: Vol. XIII. Lancaster, Pa. 1904. Separate pagination. pp. XIV, 232, ill., map.*

Part XIII. **Rosengarten, J. G.:** American history from German archives with reference to the German soldiers in the Revolution and Franklin's visit to Germany. *Lancaster, Pa. 1904. In: Vol. XIII. Lancaster, Pa. 1904. Separate pagination. pp. VII, 93, ill., maps.*

[1]) Vgl. Deutschtum in den Vereinigten Staaten, Allgemein, und Die pfälzische Einwanderung in New York Provinz.

[2]) See also: Germans in the United States, general, and The Palatine emigration in New York Province.

Part XIV. **Daniel Falckner's** Curieuse Nachricht from Pennsylvania, the book that simulated the great German immigration to Pennsylvania in the early years of the XVIII century. *Translated and annoted by* Julius Friedrich Sachse, *Lancaster, Pa. 1905. In: Vol. XIV. Lancaster, Pa. 1905. Separate pagination. pp. IX, 256, ill., maps.*

Part XV. **Richards, Henry Melchior Muhlenberg:** The Pennsylvania-German in the French and Indian War. A historical sketch. *Lancaster, Pa. 1905. In: Vol. XV. Lancastre Pa. 1906. Separate pagination. pp. 559 ill., maps.*

Part XVI. **Sachse, Julius Friedrich:** The wreck of the ship New Era upon New Jersey coast November 13, 1854. *Lancaster, Pa. 1907. In: Vol. XVI. Lancaster, Pa. 1907. Separate pagination pp. V, 55, ill.*

Part XVII. **Richards, Henry Melchior Muhlenberg:** Governor Joseph Hiester. A historical sketch. *Lancaster, Pa. 1907. In: Vol. XVI. Lancaster, Pa. 1907. Separate pagination. pp. 51, ill.*

Part XVIII. **Richards, Henry Melchior Muhlenberg:** The Pennsylvania-German in the Revolutionary War. 1775—1783. *Lancaster, Pa. 1908. In: Vol. XVII. Lancaster, Pa. 1908. Separate pagination. pp. XI, 542, ill.*

Part XIX. Diary of a voyage from Rotterdam to Philadelphia in 1728. *[„Auszug einiger Send-Schreiben aus Philadelphia in Pennsylvanien, worinnen die gantze Reise, von Rotterdam nach Pennsylvanien, fleißig aufgezeichnet, und dieses Landes Clima, dessen Bewohner Handlung, andere Gewerbe, Ordnung, etc. entdecket ist; . . . Dem Nächsten zur nöhtigen Nachricht durch den Druck mitgetheilet. In Jahr Christi 1729“.] Translated by* Julius F. Sachse. *Lancaster, Pa. 1909. In: Vol. XVIII. Lancaster, Pa. 1909. Separate pagination. pp. 25, ill.*

Part. XX. A brief history of the colony of New Sweden *which, by the kind permission of the Faculty of Philosophy at Upsala, . . .* Carolus David Arfwedson *of West Goth, the author publicly presented in the Gustivianeum, on the 19th day of November, 1825 . . . Upsala (Set up by the Typographers of the Royal Academy). Translation of the Swedish text by* K. W. Granlund; *of the Latin text by* Edward T. Horn. *Edited by* Julius F. Sachse. *Lancaster, Pa. 1909. In: Vol. XVIII. Lancaster, Pa. 1909. Separate pagination. pp. 44, ill., map.*

Part XXI. An account of the manners of the German inhabitants of Pennsylvania *by* Benjamin Rush. *With an introduction and annotations by* Theodore E. Schmauck *and with the notes of* I. D.

Rupp *revised. Lancaster, Pa. 1910. In: Vol. XIX. Lancaster, Pa. 1910. Separate pagination. pp. 128, ill.*

Part XXII. **Miller, Daniel:** Early German American newspapers. *Lancaster, Pa. 1911. In: Vol. XIX. Lancaster, Pa. 1910. Separate pagination. pp. 107, ill., fac-similes.*

Part XXIII. The Lutheran Church in New Hannovor, (Falckner Swamp), Montgomery Co., Pa. *Lancaster, Pa. 1911. In: Vol. XX. Lancaster, Pa. 1911. Separate pagination pp. VI, 5—444, ill.*

Part XXIV. **Sachse, Julius Friedrich:** The wayside inns on the Lancaster roadside between Philadelphia and Lancaster. *Lancaster, Pa. 1912—1914. In: Vol. XXI. Lancaster, Pa. 1912. Separate pagination. pp. 77, ill.; Vol. XXII. Lancaster, Pa. 1913. Separate Pagination pp. 109, ill.*

Part XXV. **Nead, Daniel Wunderlich:** The Pennsylvania-German in the settlement of Maryland. *Lancaster, Pa. 1914. In: Vol. XXII. Lancaster, Pa. 1913. Separate pagination. pp XII, 304, ill., maps.*

Part XXVI. **Wentz, Abdel Ross:** The beginnings of the German element in York County, Pa. *Lancaster, Pa. 1916. In: Vol. XXIV. Lancaster, Pa. 1916. Separate pagination. pp. 217, ill.*

Part XXVII. The diarium of Magister Johannes Kelpius, *with annotations by* Julius Friedrich Sachse. *Lancaster, Pa. 1917. In: Vol. XXV. Lancaster, Pa. 1917. Separate pagination. pp. 100, ill.*

Part XXVIII. **Reichard, Harry Hess:** Pennsylvania-German dialect writings and their writers. *Lancaster, Pa. 1918. In: Vol. XXVI. Lancaster, Pa. 1918. Separate pagination. pp. XI, 13—400, ill.*

Part XXIX. **Hinke, William John:** A history of the Goshenhoppen Reformed charge, Montgomery County, Pa. (1727—1819). *Lancaster, Pa. 1920. In: Vol. XXVII. Lancaster, Pa. 1920. Separate pagination. pp. XVII, 271, ill.; Church records of the Goshenhoppen Reformed charge 1731—1833. In: Vol. XXVIII. Lancaster, Pa. 1922. Separate pagination. pp. 272—490.*

Part XXX. **Knauss, James Owen:** Social conditions among the Pennsylvania Germans in the eighteenth century, as revealed in the German newspapers published in America. *Lancaster, Pa. 1922. In: Vol. XXIX. Lancaster, Pa. 1922. Separate pagination. pp. X, 217.*

Part XXXI. **Richards, Henry Melchior Muhlenberg:** The Pennsylvania-German in the British military prisons of the Revolutionary War. An historical sketch. *Lancaster, Pa. 1924. In: Vol. XXXII. Lancaster, Pa. 1924. Separate pagination. pp. 33.*

Part XXXII. **Dapp, Charles Frederick:** The evolution of an American patriot. Being an intimate study of the patriotic activities of John Henry Miller, German printer, publisher and editor of the American Revolution. *Lancaster, Pa. 1924. In: Vol. XXXII. Lancaster, Pa. 1924. Separate pagination. pp. 68, ill.*

Part XXXIII. **Smith, C. Henry:** The Mennonite immigration to Pennsylvania in the eighteenth century. *Norristown, Pa. 1929. In: Vol. XXXV. Norristown, Pa. 1929. Separate pagination. pp.412, ill.*

Part. XXXIV. **Fogel, Edwin M.:** Proverbs of the Pennsylvania Germans. *Lancaster, Pa. 1929. In: Vol. XXXVI. Lancaster, Pa. 1929. Seperate pagination. pp.122.*

Part XXXV. **Livingood, Frederick George:** Eighteenth century Reformed Church schools. *Norristown, Pa. 1930. In: Vol. XXXVIII. Norristown, Pa. 1930. Separate pagination. pp. XIX, (2), 313, ill. [Bibliography. pp. 299—313.]*

Part. XXXVI. **Maurer, Charles Lewis:** Early Lutheran education in Pennsylvania. *Philadelphia, Pa. 1932. In: Vol. XL Norristown, Pa. 1932. Separate pagination pp. XII, (1) 284, ill.* [278

The Pennsylvania-Germans who they are and what they have done. A. symposium of short sketches. *In: The Pennsylvania German. Vol. VII. Lebanon, Pa. 1906. pp. 147—207, ill.:*

Schantz, F. J. F.: The Pennsylvania-German as pioneer and home-builder. *pp. 147—150.*

Mays, G. F.: The Pennsylvania-German as farmer. *pp. 151—154.*

Harley, L. R.: The Pennsylvania-German manufacturer and merchant. *pp. 154—156.*

Bergey, D. H.: The Pennsylvania-German as scientist. *pp. 157—159.*

Jordan, J. W.: The Pennsylvania-German as artist. *pp. 160—161.*

Rosengarten, J. G.: The Pennsylvania-German as patriot and soldier. *pp. 161—164.*

The Pennsylvania-German in law. *pp. 164—166.*

Jones, G. M.: The Pennsylvania-German as statesman and legislator. *pp. 166—169.*

Koons, U. S.: The Pennsylvania-German as governor. *pp. 169—173.*

Schuler, H. A.: The Pennsylvania-German as printer and publisher. *p. 174.*

Stapleton, A.: Early German musical publications in Pennsylvania. *pp. 174—176.*

— Gustav Sigismund Peters, pioneer stereotyper and color-printer. *pp. 177—178.*

Schuler, H. A.: The Pennsylvania-German in literature. *pp. 178—180.*

Kauffmann, R. W.: Some Pennsylvania-German storywriters. *pp. 180—183.*

Schuler, H. A.: Education among the Pennsylvania-German. *pp. 183—186.*

Bittinger, L. F.: The Pennsylvania-German as churchman. *pp. 186—188.*

Dubbs, J. H.: German church life in Pennsylvania. *pp. 188—191.*

Kriebel, H. W.: The Pennsylvania-German as champion of religious liberty. *pp. 191—193.*

Fisher, S. G.: Characteristics of the Pennsylvania-German. *pp. 194—195.*

Schuler, H. A.: Some Pennsylvania-German statistics. *pp. 196—198.*

Where the Pennsylvania-German has been first. *pp. 198—200.*

Croll, P. C.: The Pennsylvania chautauqua: Mount Gretna. *pp. 201—205.*

Zimmerman, T. C.: The Pennsylvania-German as American citizen. *pp. 205—207.* [279

Baer, George Frederick: The Pennsylvania Germans. *An address delivered at the dedication of the Palatinate College, Myerstown, Pa. December 23, 1875. In: The Mercersburg Review. Vol. XXIII. Philadelphia, Pa. 1876. pp. 248—267. Reprint in: Addresses and writings (1916) [= no. 283] pp. 163—183.* [280

— „The Germans in Pennsylvania". *Address before Teacher's Institute of Berks County, Reading, Pa., September, 26, 1895. pp. 15. Reprint in: Addresses and writings (1916) [= no. 283] pp. 203—218.* [281

[—] The Germans in the State of Pennsylvania. *[Address of George F. Baer before the Teachers' Institute of Berks County, at Reading, Pa., September 26, 1895. Reported stenographically by Geo W. Delaney.] In: The Pennsylvania School Journal. Organ of the Department of Public Instruction and the State Teachers' Association. Vol. XLIV. Lancaster, Pa. 1895. pp. 239—245.* [282

[—] Addresses and writtings of George F. Baer, *including his argument before the Anthracite Coal Strike Commission. Collected by his son-in-law William N. Appel. [Lancaster, Pa.] Privately printed: [Wickersham Press] 1916. pp. VI, 365* [283

Beidelman, William: The story of the Pennsylvania, Germans. Embracing an account of their origin, their history, and their dialect. *Easton, Pa.: Express Book Print 1898. pp. VIII, 254, map.* [284

Beobachter *(Pseudonym):* Deutsches Leben in Pennsylvanien. *In: Der Deutsche Pionier. Jg. VII. Cincinnati, Ohio. 1875—1876. S. 175—178.* [285

Berlin, Alfred Franklin: The German immigrant in Pennsylvania before and during the Revolution. *In: Proceedings and Papers read before the Lehigh County Historical Society. Allentown. Pa. 1921. pp. 3—29.* [286

Bierbower, Austin: Pennsylvania Germans in the Susquehanna Islands and surroundings. *In: The Pennsylvania-German. Vol. XII. Lititz, Pa. 1911. pp. 527 —532.* [287

Bittinger, Lucy Forney: The Germans in colonial times. *Philadelphia, Pa. and London: J. B. Lippincott Co. 1901. pp. 314, map.* [288

— The Pennsylvania Germans. *In: New England Magazine. An illustrated monthly. New series, vol. XXVI. Boston, Mass. 1902. No. 3, (May), pp. 366—384; No. 4, (June), pp. 498—512; No. 5, (July), pp. 617—624.* [289

Bokum, Hermann: The stranger's gift. A Christmas and New Years' present. *Edited by . . . Boston, Mass. Light and Horton 1836. pp. (1), 9—103, ill. [Includes: „The American Germans". (Paper taken partly from matter laid before the American Institute of Instruction, partly from a review written by the author, and published in the seventh volume of the „Christian Spectator".) pp. 23—41.]* [290

Bolenius, R. M.: Germans in Pennsylvania. *In: Papers and Addresses of the Lancaster County Historical Society. Vol. X. Lancaster, Pa. 1906. pp. 325—349, ill.* [291

Brumbaugh, M. G.: The Pennsylvania German. *Address delivered to the twenty-seventh annual meeting of the Teachers' Institute, of Berks county, Pa., held in the Opera House, at Reading, Pa., on Oct. 23, 1899. Reprint from „Reading Eagle" 1899. pp. 7.* [292

— Rose Day address. *Delivered on the tenth anniversary of the Feast of Roses, held in Zion Lutheran Church, at Manheim, Pa., on June 11, 1899. Reprint*

from „The New Era" 1899. pp. 9. [293

Channing, Edward: „The comming of the Foreigners." *In: „A history of the United States" by Edward Channing. Vol. II. A century of colonial history. 1660—1760. New York, N. Y.: The Macmillan Co. 1908. = Chapter XIV. pp. 401—422.* [294

Croll, P. C. and others: Historical pilgrimages into Pennsylvania-Germandom. *In: The Pennsylvania-German. Vol. I —VI. Lebanon, Pa. 1900—1905. All installments ill.*

A trip over the Horse-shoe pike. *Vol. I. no. 1. 1900. pp. 22—36.*

Croll, P. C. and Redsecker, J. H.: Through the state's garden county. *Vol. I. no. 2. 1900. pp. 22—42.*

Up the historic Susquehanna. *Vol. I. no. 3. 1900. pp. 21—39.*

Historic Harrisburg. *Vol. I. no. 4. 1900. pp. 35—43.*

Over an old state road from the Susquehanna to the Swatara. *Vol. II. 1901. pp. 73—85.*

Down the Lebanon Valley. *Vol. II. 1901. pp. 123—132; 165—183.*

Mohr, Howard C.: Down the Schuylkill Valley. *Vol. II. 1901. pp. 27—43.*

A trip over the old Easton road. *Vol. III. 1902. pp. 67—86.*

Over the Oley pike to Boyertown and back. *Vol. III. 1902. pp. 113—132.*

From the Reading to York. *Vol. III. 1902. pp. 163—174.*

Betz, I. H.: A town and county of the olden time. Historic York, Pa. *Vol. IV. 1903. pp. 215—228; 265—286.*

Betz, I. H.: From York, Pa. to Harper's Ferry, W. Va. *Vol. IV. 1903. pp. 355—374.*

. . . into Pennsylvania-Germandom and Scotch-Irishdom. **Betz, I. H.:** From Winchester to Harrisburg. *Vol. V. 1904. pp. 8—22; 61—72.*

A detour on the Forks of the Delaware. *Vol. V. 1904. pp. 121—143.*

Moravian headquaters, old Bethlehem. *Vol. V. 1904. pp. 166—181; Appendix pp. 182.*

A stroll through modern Bethlehem. *Vol. VI. 1905. pp. 210—229.*

Fishing along two Lehigh county streams. *Vol. VI. 1905. pp. 310—327.*

Down the Little Lehigh from source to mouth. *Vol. VI. 1905. pp. 366—378.* [295

Diffenderffer, Frank Ried: The German exodus to England in 1709. (Massenauswanderung der Pfälzer.) *Lancaster, Pa. 1897. = Part II. „A narrative and critical history", prepared at the request of the Pennsylvania-German Society. In: The Pennsylvania-German Society. Proceedings and Addresses . . . 1896. Vol. VII. Reading, Pa. 1897. pp. 257 —413, ill.* [296

— The Palatine and Quaker as commonwealth builders. *Address delivered before the Pennsylvania Historical Society at Philadelphia, Pa., March 14, 1898. Lancaster. Pa. 1899. pp. 30.* [297

— The Quaker and Palatine as commonwealth builders. *In: The Reformed Church Review. Fourth series, vol. III. Philadelphia, Pa. 1899. pp. 145—172.* [298

— „The Pennsylvania Dutch." A few observations. *Reply to the article of Albert Bushnell Hart [= no. 322]. Paper read before the Lancaster County Historical Society, Febr. 7, 1908. In: The Pennsylvania-German. Vol. IX. Cleona, Pa. 1908. pp. 370—372.* [299

E.[gle], W. H.: „Dutchland in America." *In: Notes and Queries. Edited by W. H. Egle. First series, part III. Harrisburg, Pa. 1881 pp. 81—85; Reprint in: First & Second series, vol. I. Harrisburg, Pa. 1894. pp. 391—396.* [300

— The Pennsylvania-German. His place in the history of the Commonwealth. *In: The Pennsylvania-German Society. Proceedings and Addresses at . . .; Mount Gretna, July 14, 1892. Vol. II. Lancaster, Pa. 1892. pp. 118—130.* [301

Ermentrout, Daniel: Our people in American history. *An oration delivered at the German Centennial Jubilee, at Reading, Pa., June 19, 1876. Reading, Pa.: Daniel Miller 1876. pp. 34.* [302

— Das Deutsche in Ost-Pennsylvanien. *Vortrag, gehalten vor den Schülern der „Oley Academy" in Oley, Berks Co., Pa., am 14. Februar 1880. In: Der Deutsche Pionier. Jg. XII. Cincinnati, Ohio 1880—1881. S. 25—33.* [303

Eshleman, H. Frank: Historic background and annals of the Swiss and German pioneer settlers of South Eastern Pennsylvania, and of their remote ancesters, from the middle of the dark ages, down to the time of the Revolutionary War. *An authentic history, from original sources, of their suffering during several* centuries before and especially during the two centuries following the Protestant Reformation, and of their slow migration, moved by those causes, during the last mentioned two hundred years, westward in quest of religious freedom and their happy relief in the Susquehanna and Schuylkill Valleys in the New World; with particular reference to the German-Swiss Mennonites or Anabaptists, the Amish and other non-resistance sects. *Lancaster, Pa. 1917. pp. (2), 386.* [304

Faust, A. B.: „The Germans in Pennsylvania." *In: The German element in the United States. By A. B. Faust. Second edition. New York 1927 [= no. 42]. Vol. I. = Chapter V. pp. 111—148.* [305

Fisher, H. L.: An historical sketch of the Pennsylvania Germans, their ancestry, character, manners, customs, dialect, etc. *Chicago, Ill.: F. A. Battey Publishing Co. 1885. pp. 59, ill. Reprint from: History of York Co. Edited by John Gibson. Chicago, Ill. 1886 [= no. 5250]. pp. 219—277.* [306

Fisher, Sydney George: Characteristics of the Pennsylvania-German. *In: The Pennsylvania-German. Vol. VII. Lebanon, Pa. 1906. pp. 194—195.* [307

Focht, Benjamin: German immigration to Pennsylvania. *Address delivered . . . at the Hummel family reunion held at Packer's Island, Northumberland Co., Aug. 28, 1907. Washington, D. C.: Press of Judd & Detweiler, Inc. 1908. pp. 38, ill.* [308

Focht, B. K.: The Pennsylvania-Germans. *In: The Penn Germania. New series, vol. III. = Old series, vol. XV. Cleona, Pa. 1914. pp. 19—26. Address delivered in the House of Representatives, Washington, D. C., Saturday 14, 1912. See: Congressional Record, January 29, 1913. p. 2277.* [309

[Franklin, Benjamin]: [Franklin's opinion on the Germans in Pennsylvania:] *Letter to Richard Jackson, Philadelphia, Pa., May 5, 1753. In: The writings of Benjamin Franklin. Collected and edited by Albert Henry Smith. Vol. III. New York, N. Y.: Macmillan Co. 1905. pp. 133—141.* [310

[—] Franklin's knowledge of things German. *(a) At home. [Letter to (Edward Jackson, see: The writings of Benjamin Franklin. By A. H. Smith. Vol. III. 1905 [= no. 310]. pp. 133ff.) Philadelphia, Pa., May 9 (5), 1753 and answer*

*of Peter Collinson, August, 12 1752].
In: Benjamin Franklin and Germany. By
Victory Beatrice Marquerite. Philadelphia, Pa.: Publications of the University of Pennsylvania 1915. = American Germanica Monographs no. 21. pp. 57
—59.* [311

Gibbons, Phebe Earle: Pennsylvania Dutch.
*In: The Atlantic Monthly. A magazine
of literature, science, art, and politics.
Vol. XXIV. Boston, Mass.: Fields,
Osgood & Co. 1869. pp. 473—487.
[Particularly relating to the Mennonites
and Amishs of Lancaster County, Pa.]
Netherlandish translation: Kerleijk en
huiselijk leven der Doopsgezinden hier te
lande en die in Pennsylvanie. Translated
by J. G. de Hoop Scheffer. In; Doopsgezinde Bijdragen. Uitgegeven onder redactive van D. Harting en P. Cool. New
series, vol. III. Leeuwarden: H. Kuipers
1869. pp. 129—147.* [312

[—] Pennsylvania Dutch and other essays.
*Philadelphia, Pa.: J. B. Lippincott &
Co. 1872. pp. VII, 9—207; second edition, with additions 1874. pp. 318; Third
edition, revised and enlarged 1882.
pp. 427.* [313

Giorg, Kara *[Pseudonym of* **Georg Brühl]:**
Die deutschen Ansiedlungen in Pennsylvanien. *In: Der Deutsche Pionier.
Jg. I, Cincinnati, O. 1869—1870. S. 238
—241; 261—268.* [314

Goebel, Julius: Neue Dokumente zur Geschichte der Massenauswanderung im
Jahre 1709. *In: Deutsch-Amerikanische
Geschichtsblätter, Jahrbuch der Deutsch-
Amerikanischen Historischen Gesellschaft
von Illinois. Jg. 1913. Vol. XIII. Chicago, Ill. 1913. S. 181—201.* [315

[Gordon, P.]: Remarks to the assembly concerning petition of several Germans to
be naturalized. Jan. 13th, 1730. *In:
Pennsylvaina Archives. Fourth series.
Edited by G. E. Reed. Vol. I. Papers of
the governors 1681—1747. Harrisburg,
Pa. 1900. p. 471.* [316

[—] Remarks to the assembly concerning
a petition of several Germans for naturalization. Jan. 9th, 1731. *In: Pennsylvania Archives. Fourth series. Edited
by G. E. Reed. Vol. I. Papers of the
governors 1681—1747. Harrisburg, Pa.
1900. p. 477.* [317

Gotwald, Frederick Gebhart: The Teutonic
factor in American history. *In: The
Lutheran Church Review. Vol. XXI. Philadelphia, Pa. 1902. pp. 398—423.* [318

Greene, Evarts Boutell: ,,Expansion in the
middle provinces." *In: The foundations
of American nationality. By E. B.
Greene. New York etc.: American
Book Co. 1922. = Chapter XIII. pp. 281
—310.* [319

Gruber, M. A.: The Pennsylvania-Germans.
A reply to Professor Albert Buchnell
Hart *[see no. 322]. In: The Pennsylvania-German. Vol. IX. Cleona, Pa.
1908. pp. 21—26.* [320

Haring, C. H.: The Pennsylvania Germans.
*In: The London Quarterly Review.
No 227. July 1910. = Vol. CXIV —
Fourth series, no. 23. London 1910.
pp. 72—83.* [321

[Hart, Albert Bushnell]: The Pennsylvania-
Dutch. *By . . . Reprint from: Boston
Evening Transcript. In: The Pennsylvania-German. Vol. VIII. Lebanon, Pa.
1907. pp. 539—543.
[See: Diffenderffer, F. R. [= no. 323];
and Gruber, M. A. [= no. 320]* [322

[—]- Diffenderffer, Frank Ried: The Pennsylvania-Dutch. *By Albert Bushnell
Hart. With notes by F. R. Diffenderffer. In: Papers and Addresses of
the Lancaster County Historical Society.
Vol. XII. Lancaster, Pa. 1908. pp. 82—
100.
[See also no. 299]* [323

Heiderich, Wilhelm: Ein deutsches Schicksal
in Pennsylvanien. *In: Volk und Rasse.
Illustrierte Vierteljahrsschrift für deutsches Volkstum. Jg. VI. Heft 4. München 1931. S. 220—230.* [324

Hennighausen, L. P.: General Washington
and the German-Americans. *In: Eighth-
Tenth Annual Reports of the Society for
the History of the Germans in Maryland.
Baltimore, Md. 1896. pp. 43—44.* [325

Henry, Granville: The Pennsylvania Germans. Personal and social characteristics. *Read before the Wyoming Historical and Geological Society May 14, 1909.
In: Proceedings and Collections of the
Wyoming Historical and Geological Society 1910. Vol. XI. Wilkes-Barre, Pa.
1910. pp. 201—210.
Reprint in: The Pennsylvania-German.
Vol. XII. Lititz, Pa. 1911. pp. 288—292.* [326

Hensel, W. U.: Picturesque character of
Pennsylvania-Germans. *Address. In:
The Pennsylvania-German. Vol. XI.
Lititz, Pa. 1910. pp. 418—420.* [327

Hocker, E. W.: Traits and characteristics.
[Extracts from the ,,Germantown Inde-

3*

*pendence-Gazette", Sept.—Oct., 1910.] In:
The Pennsylvania-German. Vol. XII.
Lititz, Pa. 1911. pp. 24—27.* The Penn-
sylvania-Germans once more. *By* E.
Schultz. *[Reply to the articles of E. H.
Hocker in the: „Germantown Indepen-
dence-Gazette", Sept.—Oct., 1910.] In:
The Pennsylvania-German. Vol. XII.
Lititz, Pa. 1911. pp. 28—32.*   [328

Horne, A. R.: The Pennsylvania Germans.
*In: History of the Counties of Lehigh and
Carbon, in the Commonwealth of Penn-
sylvania. By A. Mathews and A. N.
Hungerford. Philadelphia, Pa.: Everts
& Richards 1884. = Chapter VI. pp. 23
—42.*   [329

— The worth and character of the Pennsylvania-Germans. *Read at Durham
Cave meeting, July 28, 1885. In: A Collection of Papers read before the Bucks
County Historical Society. Vol. I. Easton, Pa. 1908. pp. 333—349.*   [330

Jacobs, Henry Eyster: The German emigration to America 1709—1740. *Lancaster, Pa. 1898. = Part. III. „A narrative and critical history", prepared at
the request of the Pennsylvania-German
Society. In: The Pennsylvania-German
Society. Proceedings and Addresses . . .
1897. Vol. VIII. Lancaster, Pa. 1898.
pp. 31—150, ill.*   [331

Kapp, Friedrich: Die deutschen Pilgerväter.
*In: Deutsche Rundschau. Herausgegeben
von Julius Rodenberg. Vol. XXXVIII.
Berlin 1884. S. 130—138.*   [332

Keith, Charles P.: „The Germans." *In:
Chronicles of Pennsylvania from the
English Revolution to the peace of Aix-
La- Chapelle 1688—1748. Vol. II. Philadelphia, Pa.: Patterson & White Co.
1917 [= no. 3169]. = Chapter XVII.
pp. 511—551.*   [333

Kloß, Heinz: Ein unbekannter Stamm: Die
Pennsylvania-Deutschen. *In: Der Aus-
landdeutsche. Halbmonatsschrift für
Auslanddeutschtum und Auslandkunde.
Mitteilungen des Deutschen Ausland-
Institutes, Stuttgart. Jg. XI, No. 4.
Stuttgart 1928. S. 96—99.*   [334

— Nationalität und Boden in Pennsyl-
vania. *In: Petermanns Mitteilungen.
(Dr. A. Petermanns Mitteilungen aus
Justus Perthes Geograph. Anstalt.) Vol.
LXXVII. Gotha 1931. S. 21—22,
Karten.*   [335

— Fünf Stationen einer Reise in Pennsylvanien. *In: Der Auslanddeutsche. Halbmonatsschrift für Auslanddeutschtum und*

*Auslandkunde. Mitteilungen des Deut-
schen Ausland-Instituts, Stuttgart.
Jg. XIV. No. 1. Stuttgrat 1931. S. 2—4.*
                                       [336

Kloß, Heinz: Karten zur pfälzischen Aus-
wanderung I—II. *Nach Unterlagen von
H. Kloß. In: Pfälzischer Geschichtsatlas.
Im Auftrag der Pfälzischen Gesellschaft zur
Förderung der Wissenschaften und des
Vereins zur Herausgabe eines historischen
Atlasses von Bayern herausgegeben von
Wilhelm Winkler. Neustadt a. d. Haardt:
Verlag der Pfälzischen Gesellschaft zur
Förderung der Wissenschaften. 1935.
Blatt 15 u. 16, Textbeilage S. 10—11.*
   *Kt. I. Oberdeutsche, überwiegend
pfälzische Einwanderung nach Pennsyl-
vanien und Südwanderung dieser „Penn-
sylvaniendeutschen".*   [336 a
   *Kt. II. Siedlungsnamen deutschen Ur-
sprungs in Pennsylvanien.*

Knauss, James Owen: Social conditions
among the Pennsylvania Germans in the
eighteenth century, as revealed in the
German newspapers published in America. *Lancaster, Pa.: The New Era
Printing Co. 1922. = Part XXX. „A
narrative and critical history", prepared
at the request of the Pennsylvania-German
Society. In: The Pennsylvania-German
Society. Proceedings and Addresses . . .
1918. Vol. XXIX. Lancaster, Pa. 1922.
Separate pagination. pp. X, 217.*   [337

Krenkel, F. P.: Lob der deutsch-amerika-
nischen Ansiedler am Anfang des
19. Jahrhunderts aus französischem
Gelehrtenmunde. *[F. A. Michaux.] In:
Deutsch-Amerikanische Geschichtsblätter.
Jg. IV. Chicago, Ill. S. 51—58.*   [338

Kuhns, Oscar: The German and Swiss settlement of colonial Pennsylvania. *A
study of the so-called Pennsylvania
Dutch. New York, N. Y.: Henry Holt
and Co. 1901. pp. V, 268.
Reprinted in: The PennGermania. Vol.I.
= Old series, vol. XIII. Lititz, Pa. 1912.
pp. 289—320; 385—416; 481—509;
577—583.
New edition New York, N. Y. — Cincinnati, O.: The Abingdon Press 1914.
pp. V. 268.*   [339

— Ethnical origin of the Pennsylvania
Germans. *Paper read at the celebration
of the 200th anniversary of first permanent
white settlement in Lancaster County, Pa.,
Sept. 8, 1910. In: The Pennsylvania-
German. Vol. XII. Lititz, Pa. 1911.
pp. 81—84.*   [340

Kurth, Hans: Friedhof in Pennsylvanien. *In: Der Auslanddeutsche. Halbmonatsschrift für Auslanddeutschtum und Auslandkunde. Mitteilungen des Deutschen Ausland Instituts, Stuttgart. Jg. XI. No. 4. Stuttgart 1928. S. 99—101, ill.* [341

Lacher, J. H. A.: Traits and characteristics of Pennsylvania Germans. *In: The Pennsylvania-German. Vol. XII. Lititz, Pa. 1911. pp. 96—97.* [342

— The Germans of colonial Pennsylvania. *In: The Concord Society, Yearbook 1929. New York City, N. Y.: Rosswaag's Stuyvesant Press 1930. pp. 6—28.* [343

Learned, M. D.: Die Anfänge der deutschen Kultur in Amerika. *In: Sixth Annual Report of the Society for the History of the Germans in Maryland. Baltimore, Md. 1892. pp. 53—73.* [344

Lincoln, Charles H.: ,,The influence of the German and Irish immigration." *In: The Revolutionary movement in Pennsylvania, 1760—1776. By Charles H. Lincoln. Published by the University Philadelphia: Ginn & Co., Boston, Mass. 1901. pp. 23—39.* [345

Lohman, Martin: Die Bedeutung der deutschen Ansiedlungen in Pennsylvanien. *Stuttgart: Ausland und Heimat Verlags-Aktiengesellschaft 1923. 153 S.; Anhang: Schrifttum S. I—V.* = *Schriften des Deutschen Ausland-Instituts, Stuttgart, A. Kulturhistorische Reihe, Band 12.* [346

Lohr, Otto: Amerikadeutsche Familien des 17. Jahrhunderts: Einwanderer in Pennsylvanien vor 1700. *In: Jahrbuch für auslanddeutsche Sippenkunde. Herausgegeben aus Anlaß der ersten Tagung für auslanddeutsche Sippenkunde 24.—25. August 1936 vom Deutschen Ausland Institut, Hauptstelle für auslanddeutsche Sippenkunde. Stuttgart: Verlag Karl Weinbrenner & Söhne 1936. S. 53—54.* [346a

Lutynes, Gotthilff Nicolas: Etwas über den gegenwärtigen Zustand der Auswanderungen und Ansiedlungen im Staate von Pennsylvanien in Nord-Amerika, besonders in Ansehung der Deutschen. *Hamburg: Carl Ernst Bohn 1796. 23 S.* [346b

— Über den gegenwärtigen Zustand der Auswanderungen, und Ansiedlungen im Staate von Pensylvanien in Nord-Amerika, besonders in Ansehung der Deutschen. *In: Amerikanisches Magazin oder authentische Beiträge zur Erdbeschreibung, Staatskunde und Geschichte von Amerika, besonders aber der vereinten Staaten. Herausgegeben von Hegewisch-Kiel und Ebeling-Hamburg. Erster Band. Zweites Stück. Hamburg: Carl Ernst Bohn 1796. S. 25—40.* [346c

Lutz, Henry F.: The Germans, Hessians and Pennsylvania Germans. *A paper read at the Lutz family re-union, Aug. 10, 1909. In: The Pennsylvania-German. Vol. X. Lititz, Pa. 1909. pp. 435—443.* [347

McMinn, Edwin: A German hero of the colonial times of Pennsylvania; or the life and times of Henry Antes. *Moorestown, Burlington Co., N. J.: William J. Lovell 1886. pp. 305, ill.* [348

Mays, George: Why the Pennsylvania German still prevails in the eastern section of the state. *Reading, Pa.: Daniel Miller 1904. pp. 16.* [349

Mellick, Andrew D.: German emigration to the American colonies, its cause, and the distribution of the emigrants. *In: The Pennsylvania. Magazine of History and Biography. Vol. X. Philadelphia, Pa. 1886. pp. 241—250; 375—391.* [350

Metzger, H. D.: The Pennsylvania Germans. *A treatise, setting forth an account of their immigration with reasons for coming, their settlement, and their influence upon state and national history also their present characteristics. Salemville, Pa.: Publishing House, November, 1896. pp. 37.* [351

Meyer, T. P.: The Germans of Pennsylvania, their coming and conflicts with the Irish. *In: The Pennsylvania-German. Vol. XI. Lititz, Pa. 1910. pp. 38—47. Reviewed and corrected by Martin I. J. Gfiffen, ibid. pp. 124—126.* [352

Meynen, Emil: Das deutschpennsylvanische Bauernland. *[The Pennsylvania-Dutch country side]. Eine kulturgeographische Studie auf Grund eigener Forschung in den Jahren 1930—1932. [In Vorbereitung.]* [352a

Nead, Benjamin M.: The Pennsylvania-German in history. *In: The Pennsylvania-German Society. Proceedings and Addresses at Lebanon, Pa., Oct. 12, 1892. Vol. III. Lancaster, Pa. 1893. pp. 34—51.* [353

Omwake, Geo Leslie: The heroism of our immigrant ancestors. *Address delivered at the annual reunion of the Hunsicker family, on the grounds of Ursinus College, at Collegeville, Pa., August 17, 1912*

In: The Penn Germania. Vol. I. = Old series, vol. XIII. Lititz, Pa. 1912. pp. 718—724. [354

Osgood, Herbert L.: Immigration into the American colonies during the first half of the eighteenth century. *In: The American colonies in the eighteenth century. By H. L. Osgood. Vol. II. New York, N. Y.: Columbia University Press 1924. = Chapter VI. pp. 483—529. [The influx of Germans after 1700. pp. 490—498; German immigration to Pennsylvania. pp. 498—499; Emigration favored by Pietism in Germany and the Netherlands. pp. 499—505; The economic basis of the German emigration. pp. 506; German emigration from Pennsylvania southward through the valley. pp. 507—508.]* [355

Pennypacker, Samuel Whitaker: Historical and biographical sketches. *Philadelphia, Pa.: Robert A. Tripple 1883. pp. 416. It contains among other papers:*
(1) The settlement of Germantown, Pa. and the causes which led to it. (From: The Pennsylvania Magazine of History and Biography. Vol. IV.) [= no. 5088]. pp. 9—58.
(2) David Rittenhouse, the American astronomer. (From: Harper's Monthly, for May 1882) [= no. 7261]. pp. 61—88.
(3) Christopher Dock, the pious schoolmaster on the Skippack, and his works. pp. 91—153.
(4) Der Blutige Schau-platz oder Martyrer Spiegel, Ephrata, Pa. 1748. A noteworthy book. (From: The Pennsylvania Magazine of History and Biography. Vol. V. pp. 276 [= no. 2054]. pp. 157—173.
(5) Mennonite emigration to Pennsylvania. By Dr. J. G. De Hoop Scheffer, of Amsterdam. Translated from the Dutch by S. W. Pennypacker. (From: The Pennsylvania Magazine Vol. II. pp. 117 [= no. 933]. pp. 177—199;
(6) Abraham and Dirck op den Graeff. (From: The Penn Monthly, Sept. 1875 [= no. 7153]. pp. 203—221.
(7) Zionitischer Weyrauchs Hügel oder Myrrhen Berg. Germantown, 1739. (From: The Bulletin of the Library Company of Philadelphia, January, 1882 [= no. 2055]. pp. 225—228. [356
— German immigration. *(An address at the Bi-Centennial celebration of the settlement of Germantown, Pa., and the beginning of German immigration to Ame-*

rica, in the Philadelphia Academy of Music, on the evening of October 6, 1883.) Reprint in: Pennsylvania in American history. By S. W. Pennypacker. Philadelphia, Pa.: William J. Campbell 1910 [no. 3175]. pp. 195—207. [357

Pennypacker, Samuel Whitaker: The Germans in Pennsylvania. *An address before the Deutsche Pionier-Verein, April 27, 1893. Philadelphia, Pa.: Schaefer & Koradi 1895. pp. 20.* [358
— The Pennsylvania Dutchman, and wherein he has excelled. *In: The Pennsylvania Magazine of History and Biography. Vol. XXII. Philadelphia, Pa. 1898. pp. 452—457.* [359
— The Pennsylvania Dutchman. *Address delivered before the second annual festival. In: Year Book of the Pennsylvania Society of New York. New York, N. Y. 1901. pp. 29—32.* [360
— The Pennsylvania Dutchman in Philadelphia. *Address at the annual meeting of the Pennsylvania-German Society in 1896, held in Philadelphia, Pa. Philadelphia, Pa. 1907. pp. 12.* [361

Richards, George W.: The German pioneers in Pennsylvania. *An essay read before the Cliosophic Society of Lancaster, Pa., and the Reformed Ministerial Association of Philadelphia. Philadelphia, Pa.: Reformed Church Publication Board 1905. pp. 32.* [362
— The German pioneers in Pennsylvania. *In: History of the Lehigh County, Pa., and a genealogical and biographical record of its families. Edited by Ch. Rhoads Roberts — J. Baer Stoudt — Th. H. Krick — William J. Dietrich. Allentown, Pa.: Lehigh Valley Publishing Co. 1914 [= no. 4477]. Vol. I. pp. 41—53.* [363

Richards, Henry Melchior Muhlenberg: The German leaven in the Pennsylvania loaf. *A paper read before the Wyoming Historical and Geological Society, May 21, 1897. Wilkes-Barre, Pa.: Printed for the Society 1897. pp. 5—27.* [364
— The heroic laying of a noble foundation. *Address, July 2, 1904. In: Publications of the Historical Society of Schuylkill County. Vol. I. Pottsville, Pa. 1907. pp. 23.* [365

Richards, Matthias Henry: The German emigration from New York Province into Pennsylvania. *Lancaster, Pa. 1899. = Part V. „A narrative and critical history, prepared at the request of the Pennsylvania-German Society. In: The*

*Pennsylvania-German Society. Procee-
dings and Addresses . . . 1898. Vol. IX.
Lancaster, Pa. 1899. pp. 351—447, ill.*
[366
Richardson, William H.: The picturesque
quality of the Pennsylvania German.
*An address, with illustrations presented
at the eleventh annual meeting. In: The
Pennsylvania-German Society. Procee-
dings and Addresses . . . 1902. Vol. XIII.
Pa. 1904. Separate pagination. pp. 27,
ill.* [367
Roberts, Charles R.: The first Swiss settle-
ments in America. *In: Proceedings.
Lehigh County Historical Society. An-
nual publication for the year 1923. Allen-
town, Pa. 1923. pp. 9—13.* [368
R.[odenberg], J.[ulius]: Die Deutschen in
Pennsylvanien. *[Auszug aus] ,,The
German and Swiss settlement of colonial
Pennsylvania. A study of the so-called
Pennsylvania-Dutch. Von Oscar Kuhn
New York, N. Y. 1901 [= Nr. 339]. In:
Deutsche Rundschau. Herausgegeben von
Julius Rodenberg. Jg. XXVIII—Bd.
CXII. Berlin 1902. S. 462—468.* [369
Rohrbach, Paul: ,,Die Deutschen in Penn-
sylvanien." *In: Das Deutschtum über
See. Von P. Rohrbach. Karlsruhe
1931 [= Nr. 97a]. S. 61—66, ill.* [369a
Rosenberger, Jesse Leonard: The Pennsyl-
vania-Germans. A sketch of their hi-
story, and life of the Mennonites, and of
side lights from the Rosenberger family.
*Chicago, Ill.: The University of Chicago
Press 1923. pp. X, 173, ill.* [370
— In Pennsylvania-German land. *Chicago,
Ill.: The University of Chicago Press
1929. pp. XIII, 91, ill.* [371
Rosengarten, Joseph G.: The German side
of Pennsylvania history. *A paper read
before a joint meeting of the Pennsylvania
Library Club and the New Jersey Association, at Atlantic City, March 25, 1898.
Philadelphia, Pa.: Edward Stern & Co.
1899. pp. 6.
= Pennsylvania Library Club. Occasional Papers. No. 4.* [372
R.[osengarten], Joseph G.: The Palatines
in New York and Pennsylvania. *In:
German American Annals. New series,
vol. VI. Philadelphia, Pa. 1908. pp. 251
— 256.* [373
Roßnagel, Paul: ,,Die pennsylvanisch-
deutsche Region". *In: Die Stadtbevölkerung der Vereinigten Staaten von Amerika nach Herkunft und Verteilung. Mit
besonderer Berücksichtigung des deutschen*

*Elements. Ein siedlungsgeographischer
Versuch. Stuttgart 1930 [= Nr. 100].
S. 66—68.* [373a
Rupp, I. Daniel: Die Leiden und Bedrük-
kungen der ersten deutschen Einwanderer. *In: Der Deutsche Pionier. Jg. I.
Cincinnati, O. 1869—1870. S. 329—335;
362—367.* [374
[Rush, Benjamin]: An account of the
manners of the German inhabitants of
Pennsylvania. *In: The Columbian Ma-
gazine, or Monthly Miscellany . . . for
January, 1789. Vol. III. Philadelphia,
Pa. 1789. pp. 22—30.* [375
[Rush, Benjamin]-Rupp, I. Daniel: An
account of the manners of the German
inhabitants of Pennsylvania, written
1789, by Benjamin Rush, M. D. Notes
added by I. Daniel Rupp. *Philadelphia,
Pa.: Samuel P. Town 1875. pp. 72;
Reprint in: The Pennsylvania-German.
Vol. X. Lititz, Pa. 1909. pp. 157—161;
220—224.* [376
[— —]-Rattermann, H. A. R.: Eine Darstellung der Sitten und Lebensweise der
deutschen Einwanderer von Pennsylvanien. *Geschrieben im 1789 von Benjamin Rush, M. D., mit hinzugefügten
Noten und Erklärungen von Prof. I. Daniel Rupp. Edited by [H. A.] R.[atter-
mann.] In: Der Deutsche Pionier.
Jg. VII. Cincinnati, O. 1875—1876.
S. 267—280; 326—340; 368—373; 410
—414. Abdruck in: H. A. Rattermann.
Gesammelte ausgewählte Werke. Bd. XVI.
Cincinnati, O.: Selbstverlag des Verfassers 1912. = Abhandlungen, Vorträge
und Reden. Bilder aus Deutsch-Amerikanischer Geschichte. Vermischte Schriften. Erster Theil. S. 155—195.* [377
[— —]-Schmauk, Theodore E.: An account
of the manners of the German inhabitants of Pennsylvania, by Benjamin
Rush. *With an introduction and annotations by Theodore E. Schmauk, and
with notes of I. D. Rupp revised. Lancaster, Pa.: New Era Printing Co. 1910.
= Part XXI. ,,A narrative and critical
history", prepared by the authority of the
Pennsylvania-German Society. In: The
Pennsylvania-German Society. Proceedings and Addresses . . . 1908. Vol. XIX.
Lancaster Pa. 1910. Separate pagination.
pp. 128, ill.* [378
S., H. B.: The first two German settlers in
Pennsylvania. *[Henry Frey of Heilbronn and Joseph Plattenbach of Bruchsal.] Reprint from ,,Familien Freund"*

of Milford Square, Pa. in 1893. In: The
Pennsylvania-German. Vol. VIII. Le-
banon, Pa. 1907. pp. 477—479.
[See: Wollenweber, nos. 407 and 408.]
[379
Sachse, Julius F.: True heroes of provincial
Pennsylvania. *In: The Pennsylvania-*
German Society. Proceedings and Ad-
dresses at . . .; Mount Gretna, July 14,
1892. Vol. II. Lancaster, Pa. 1892.
pp. 106—118. [380
Sandt, George W.: Are the Pennsylvania-
Germans a „peculiar people?" *After-*
dinner address delivered before the Penn-
sylvania-German Society at Allentwon,
Pa., Nov. 2, 1906. In: Pennsylvania-
German. Vol. VII. Lebanon, Pa. 1906.
pp. 419—422. [381
Schantz, F. J. F.: The domestic life and
characteristics of the Pennsylvania-
German pioneer. *Lancaster, Pa. 1900.*
= Part VI. „A narrative and critical
history", prepared at the request of the
Pennsylvania-German Society. In: The
Pennsylvania-German Society. Procee-
dings and Addresses . . . 1899. Vol. X.
Lancaster, Pa. 1900. Separate pagina-
tion. pp. 97, ill. [382
— The Pennsylvania-German as pioneer
and homebuilder. *In: The Pennsyl-*
vania-German. Vol. VII. Lebanon, Pa.
1906. pp. 147—150, ill. [383
Schlatter, Michael: Wahrhafte Erzehlung
von dem wahren Zustand der meist
Hirtenlosen Gemeinden in Pennsylvanien und denen angrenzenden Provinzen . . .
A true history of the real condition
of the destitute congregation in Pennsylvania . . .
[See nos. 1531—1533.] [384
Schmucker, Samuel C.: The racial composition of Pennsylvania Germans. *Address.*
In: The Pennsylvania-German Society.
Proceedings and Addresses. Vol. XXXIII.
1923. Part II. pp. 15—19. [385
Schuler, H. A.: Some Pennsylvania-German statistics. *In: The Pennsylvania-*
German. Vol. VII. Lebanon, Pa. 1906.
pp. 196—198. [386
[—] Where the Pennsylvania-German has
been first. *(Compiled chiefly from:*
Samuel W. Pennypacker: „The Penn-
sylvania-Dutchman and wherein he has
excelled" in: Pa. Mag. of Hist. a. Biogr.,
Jan. 1899 and G. G. Groff: „Pennsyl-
vania's proud record" in: Lewisburg
Saturday News, April 13, 1906.) In:

The Pennsylvania-German. Vol. VII.
Lebanon, Pa. 1906. pp. 198—200. [387
Seidensticker, Oswald: Geschichte der
Deutschen Gesellschaft von Pennsyl-
vanien. Von der Zeit der Gründung
1764 bis zum Jahre 1876. *Festgabe zum*
Jubeljahre der Republik. Verfaßt auf
Veranlassung der Deutschen Gesellschaft.
Philadelphia, Pa.: Verlag von Jg.
Kohler 1876. 336 S. [388
— Die erste deutsche Einwanderung in
Amerika und die Gründung von German-
town, im Jahre 1683. *Philadelphia, Pa.:*
Globe Printing House 1883. 92, (2) S.
= Festschrift zum deutsch-amerikanischen
Pionier-Jubiläum am 6. Okt. 1883. [388a
— „Die Deutschen in Pennsylvanien." *In:*
In der neuen Heimath. Geschichtliche
Mittheilungen über die deutschen Ein-
wanderer in allen Theilen der Union.
Herausgegeben von A. Eickhoff. New
York, N. Y. 1884. [= Nr. 39] = Dritter
Abschnitt. S. 115—190. [388b
— Bilder aus der Deutsch-pennsylvani-
schen Geschichte. *New York: E. Steiger*
& Co. 1885. VIII, 276 S.
= Geschichtsblätter. Bilder und Mit-
theilungen aus dem Leben der Deutschen
in Amerika. Herausgegeben von Carl
Schurz. Band II.
2. Auflage. New York, N. Y.: E. Steiger
& Co. 1886. VIII, 276 S. [389
[—] Synopsis of Prof. O. Seidensticker's
address. *In: Third Annual Report of*
the Society for the History of the Ger-
mans in Maryland. Baltimore, Md. 1889.
pp. 11—17. [390
[—] German Day 1892. *Memorial volume*
published to celebrate the 209th anniver-
sary of the landing of the first German
settlers in America. Thursday, Oct. 6,
1892 [Philadelphia, Pa. 1892]. pp.
106. [391
— German-American events, principally
of Pennsylvania, up to 1870. *In: German*
Day 1892 [= no. 391]. pp. 8—32. [392
Sherk, M. G.: The Pennsylvania-German in
history. *Address. In: Fourteenth Annual*
Report of the Waterloo Historical Society,
Kitchner, Ont. 1926. pp. 237—246. [393
Smith, Edgar Fahs: Eminent Pennsylvania
Germans. *(Prepared for his address as*
president to the Society at the annual mee-
ting in Bethlehem, October 5, 1924, but
read at the meeting in Lancaster, October 7,
1925.) In: The Pennsylvania-German
Society. Proceedings and Addresses.
Vol. XXXIV. 1929. pp. 39—52. [394

[Sol, Uncle] *(Pseudonym)*: The Pennsylvania Dutch. *[Signed] Uncle Sol. In: Our Home: A monthly magazine of original articles, historical, biographical, scientific and miscellaneous, mostly by Somerset and Hunterdon county writers, and on subjects largely pertaining to these counties. Edited by A. V. D. Honeyman. Vol. I. Somerville, N. J. 1873. pp. 33—36.* [395

Stall, Sylvanus: The relation of the Lutheran Church in the United States to the limestone districts. *In: The Lutheran Quarterly. New series, vol. XIII. Gettysburg, Pa. 1883. pp. 509—515.* [396

Stoudt, John Baer: The liberty bells of Pennsylvania. *Presented to the Pennsylvania German Society at the annual meeting in the Pennsylvania building at the Sesqui-Centennial on Friday, October 8, 1926. Norristown, Pa.: Norristown Press 1930. In: The Pennsylvanja German Society. Proceedings and Addresses . . . . 1926. Vol. XXXVII. Norristown, Pa. 1930. Separate pagination. pp. XVI, 204, (1), ill.* [397

[Thomas, George]: Introductory address to the assembly. Jan. 3, 1739. *[Remarks on the German immigrants in Pennsylvania.] In: Pennsylvania Archives. Fourth series. Edited by G. E. Reed. Vol. I. Papers of the governors, 1681—1747. Harrisburg, Pa. 1900. pp. 673—675.* [398

[—] To the assembly concerning the rights of the Germans of the province. May 14, 1739. *In: Pennsylvania Archives. Fourth series. Edited by G. E. Reed. Vol. I. Papers of the governors. 1681—1747. Harrisburg, Pa. 1900. pp. 681—682.* [399

[—] To the assembly with regard to the provision of suitable quarters for immigrants to the province [set forth in a petition of "several of the most substantial Germans now inhabitants of this province"] Jan. 5th, 1741; *Further to the assembly concerning the provision of proper quarters for German immigrants. In: Pennsylvania Archives. Fourth series. Edited by G. E. Reed. Vol. I. Papers of the governors 1681—1747. Harrisburg, Pa. 1900. pp. 767—771.* [400

[—] Governor Thomas to the bishop of Exeter. *[,,Turnville Park, near Henly, April 23, 1748." — Relating to the Palatines settled in Pennsylvania.] In: Historical collections relating to the American colonial church. Edited by William Thomas Perry. Vol. II. Pennsylvania,*

Pa. 1871 [= no. 3276]. pp. 256—257. [401

Vollmer, Ph.: The Germans as a factor in our national life. *In: The Pennsylvania-German. Vol. III. Lebanon, Pa. 1902. pp. 180—185.* [402

Wanamaker, John: The German colonist. *President's annual address before the Pennsylvania-German Society, Lancaster, Pa. October 6, 1908. In: The Pennsylvania-German. Vol. X. Lititz, Pa. 1909. pp. 31—34.* [403

Wannamaker, William H.: The German element in the settlement of the South. *In: The South Atlantic Quarterly. Vol. IX. Durham, N. C. 1910. pp. 144—155.* [404

Wellnitz, Hermann: Zur Deutsch-Amerikanischen Geschichte. *In: Fest-Programm zur Feier des Deutschen Tages am 5. Oktober 1902 in der Ost-Denver Turnhalle. Herausgegeben von Ludwig Schmitz Denver, Colo: Druck des Colorado Herold 1902. S. 5, 7, 9, 11, 13, 17, 19, 21, 23.* [405

Weygandt, Cornelius: The red hills. A record of good days outdoors and in, with things Pennsylvania Dutch. *Philadelphia, Pa.: University of Pennsylvania Press, Nov. 1929. pp. XI, (1), (1) 251, ill; Second printing. Jan. 1930.* [406

Wollenweber, L. A.: Zwei treue Kameraden. *Die beiden ersten Deutschen Ansiedler in Pennsylvanien. [Heinrich Frey und Joseph Plattenbach] Historische Erzählung aus der ersten Epoche der deutschen Einwanderer in Pennsylvanien im Jahre 1680. Philadelphia, Pa.: Jg. Köhler 1880. 72 S., ill.* [407

— Die beiden ersten deutschen Ansiedler in Pennsylvanien. *Philadelphia, Pa.: 1882. S. . . .* [408

Wuchter, Astor C.: En bissel vun de Pennsylvania-Deitsche. *In: Lewendische Schtimme aus Pennsylveni. Schreiwes von Charles R. Robert, Astor C. Wuchter rausgewwe un eigeleided vum Heinz Kloß. Stuttgart und New York 1929. S. 5—11.* [409

Zimmerman, Thomas C.: Ancestral virtues of the Pennsylvania-Germans. *In: The Pennsylvania-German Society. Proceedings and Addresses at . . .; Mount Gretna, July 19, 1894. Vol. IV. Lancaster, Pa. 1894. pp. 133—150. [Reprinted in no. 413]* [410

— The Pennsylvania German as a formative influence in the upbuilding of our commonwealth and in the development of eastern Pennsylvania. *An address delivered before the faculty and students of Muhlenberg College, Allentown, Pa., October 14, 1904. In: The Pennsylvania-German. Vol. VI. Lebanon, Pa. 1905, pp. 271—285.* [411

Zimmerman, Thomas C.: German influence on our state and nation. *Extract from an address delivered before the Pennsylvania-German Society at Allentown, Pa., November 2, 1906. In: The Pennsylvania German. Vol. VIII. Lebanon, Pa. 1907. pp. 57—59.* [412

— *Olla Podrida, consisting of addresses, translations poems, hymes and sketches of out-door life. Reading, Pa.: Times Publishing Co. 1908. pp. (1), 7—220, ill.*

It includes the following papers:

(1) 'Our German ancestry. Address delivered at the banquet of the Cannstatter-Verein, Jan. 15, 1890. pp. 63—75

(2) The story of earliest migration. Address at the celebration of „German Day", Oct. 7, 1890, before the Harmonie-Männerchor of Reading. pp. 91—98.

(3) Puritan and cavalier — Why not the Pennsylvania-German? Address in the Court House at Lancaster on the formation of the Pennsylvania-German Society, April 15, 1891. pp. 107—123.

(4) Lebanon: A bit of retrospect, reminiscence and sentiment. Address delivered before the Historical Society of Lebanon Co., Oct. 21, 1898, pp. 139—167.

(5) Ancestral virtues of the Pennsylvania-Germans. Address delivered before the Pennsylvania Chautauqua at Mount Gretna as the representative of the Pennsylvania-German Society, July 17, 1893. pp. 191—215. [413

Zimmerman, Thomas C.: German character — An appriciation. *President's annual address delivered at the meeting of the Pennsylvania-German Society, Bethlehem, Oct. 29, 1909. In: The Pennsylvania-German. Vol. X. Lititz, Pa. 1909. pp. 585—594.* [414

The English settlers' contempt for the Germans. — *Extract of a letter, dated Philadelphia, 27th Sept., 1747, written by one of the early English settlers. In: Notes and Queries. Edited by W. H. Egle. Third series, vol. II. 1887—1890. Harrisburg, Pa. 1891. pp. 534—535. Reprint in: Third series, vol. III. Harrisburg, Pa. 1896. pp. 552—553.*

[Compare: Pennsylvania Magazine of History and Biography. Vol. XVI. 1892. p. 120 = no. 416.] [415

English versus Germans. — *Extracts from the letter of a German gentleman visiting relatives in Philadelphia in the autumn of 1747, translated. In: The Pennsylvania Magazine of History and Biography. Vol. XVI. Philadelphia, Pa. 1892. p. 120.* [416

Pennsylvania and the Pennsylvania-Germans. *In: The Pennsylvania-German. Vol. II, no. 1. Lebanon, Pa. 1901. pp. 18—22.* [417

Significance of Pennsylvania Germans: Testimonials. *In: The Penn Germania. New series, vol. III. = Old series, vol. XV. Cleona, Pa. 1914. pp. 57—60.* [418

„Pennsylvania-Dutch" oder „Pennsylvania-German"[1])

Brendle, A. S.: Pennsylvania Dutch or German? *In: The Pennsylvania-German. Vol. IX. Cleona, Pa. 1908. p. 573.* [419

Bruncken, Ernest: Dutch or German? *In: The Pennsylvania-German. Vol. XI. Lititz, Pa. 1910, pp. 744—745.* [420

[1]) Der Gegenstand ist häufig in Werken allgemeiner Art berührt.
The topic is frequently touched in works of general character.

Buehrle, R. K.: Pennsylvania-German or Pennsylvania-Dutch. *In: Papers and Addresses of the Lancaster County Historical Society. Vol. X. Lancaster, Pa. 1906. pp. 216—221.* [421

Diller, Theodore: Pennsylvania Dutch or German? *In: The Pennsylvania-German. Vol. IX. Cleona, Pa. 1908. pp. 458—461.* [422

Die pfälzische Einwanderung und die deutschen Siedlungen in der Provinz Neu York

The Palatine Emigration and German Settlements in New York Province

Allgemeines[1])
General[2])

Matthews, Albert: The word Palatine in America. *Read at December meeting, 1903. In: Publications of the Colonial Society of Massachusetts. Vol. VIII. Transactions 1902—1904. Boston, Mass. 1906. pp. 203—224. Reprint: Cambridge: John Wilson and Son 1905. pp. 24.* [423

Antz, E. L.: Die Pfälzer in Nordamerika. *In: Mannheimer Geschichtsblätter. Monatsschrift für Geschichte, Altertums- und Volkskunde Mannheims und der Pfalz. Herausgegeben vom Mannheimer Altertumsverein, E. V. Bd. XXVII. Mannheim 1926. Sp. 52—55.* [424

Benheim, W. Hamilton: The churches and clergy of colonial New York. *In: Proceedings of the New York State Historical Association. The eighteenth annual meeting. Vol. XVI. 1917. pp. 82—102. [Includes the story of the Palatines.]* [425

Brink, Benjamin Myer: The Palatine settlements. *In: Proceedings of the New York State Historical Association. The thirteenth annual meeting . . . Vol. XI. 1912. pp. 136—143.* [426

[Broadhead, John Romeyn]: Documents relative to the colonial history of the State of New York; *procured in Holland, England and France. By John Romeyn Broadhead. Edited by E. B. O'Callaghan. 11 vols. Albany, N. Y.: Weed Parsons and Co. 1855—1858.*
Vol. V. Transcripts of documents in the Queens State Paper Office, in the Office of the Privy Council, in the British Museum and the Library of the Archbishop of

Canterbury of Lambeth, *in London. London documents XVII—XXIV. 1707—1733. Albany, N. Y. 1855. pp. XIX, 985. Vol. VI. . . . London documents XXV—XXXII. 1734—1755. Albany, N. Y. 1855. pp. XX, 1028. [Contents as far as pertaining to the German [Palatine] settlements see appendix S. 45—47.]* [427

Cobb, Sanford H.: The story of the Palatines An episode in colonial history. *New York & London: G. P. Putnams' Sons: The Knickerbocker Press 1897. pp. IX, 319, 3 maps.* [428

— The Palatine or German immigration to New York and Pennsylvania. *A paper read before the Wyoming Historical and Geological Society. Wilkes-Barre, Pa.: Printed for the Society 1897. pp. 30.* [429

Eickhoff, Anton: ,,Die Deutschen in New York." *In: In der neuen Heimath. Geschichtliche Mittheilungen über die deutschen Einwanderer in allen Theilen der Union. Herausgegeben von A. Eickhoff. New York 1884 [= Nr. 39]. = Erster Abschnitt. S. 29—100.* [430

Faust, A. B.: ,,The first exodus — The Palatinate immigration to New York." *In: The German element in the United States. By A. B. Faust. Second edition New York, N. Y. 1927 [= no. 42]. Vol. I. = Chapter IV. pp. 73—110.* [431

Fischer, P. D.: Die Anfänge der deutschen Auswanderung nach Amerika. *Vortrag gehalten im Berliner Unions-Verein am 1. April 1870. Berlin: F. Henschel 1870. S. 36.* [432

Genzmer, George Harvey: Kocherthal, Josua von (1669—1719) Lutheran clergyman, the leader of the Palatine emigration to New York. *In: Dictionary of American biography. Under the auspices of the American Council of Learned Societies. Vol. X. Edited by Dumas Malone. London-New York 1933. p. 484.* [432a

---

[1]) Vgl. die Abschnitte: Die Pennsylvanien-Deutschen, Allgemein, und Das Deutschtum in den Vereinigten Staaten, Allgemein.

[2]) See also: The Pennsylvania Germans, General, and Germans in the United States, General.

Haas, Rudolf: Die Pfälzer in Nordamerika. *In: Mannheimer Geschichtsblätter. Monatsschrift für Geschichte, Altertums- und Volkskunde Mannheims und der Pfalz. Herausgegeben vom Mannheimer Altertumsverein E. V. Bd. XXVII. Mannheim 1926. Sp. 5—13; 27—31.* [433

Häberle, Daniel: Auswanderung und Koloniegründungen der Pfälzer im 18. Jahrhundert. *Zur zweihundertjährigen Erinnerung an die Massenauswanderung der Pfälzer (1709) und an den pfälzischen Bauerngeneral Nicholaus Herchheimer, den Helden von Oriskany (6. August 1777). Kaiserslautern: Kgl. bayer. Hofdruckerei H. Kayser 1909. XIX, 263 S., ill., Karten.* [434

— Die Auswanderung aus der Pfalz im 18. Jahrhundert *In: Der Auslanddeutsche. Halbmonatsschrift für Auslanddeutschtum u. Auslandkunde. Mitteilung. des Deutschen Ausland-Instituts. Jg. VII, no. 8. Stuttgart 1924. S. 228—232.* [435

Hastings, Hugh: Ecclesiastical records. State of New York. *Published by the state under the supervision of . . ., state historian. 6 vols. and index vol. Albany, N. Y.: James B. Lyon 1901—1905/1916. pp. XXXV, 744; XXVIII, 745—1442; XL, 1443—2308; LIX, 2309—3146; XLIX, 3147—3800; LIX, 3801—4413. Vol. VII. Index. Prepared by E. T. Corwin under the auspices of the state historian James A. Holdan. Albany, N. Y.: The University of the State of New York 1916. pp. 382.*
[Contents as far as pertaining to the early German [Palatine] settlements see appendix S. 47—52.] [436

Hill, C. F.: The Palatines of 1723. The first fleet of white men that ever traversed the North Branch of the Susquehanna River — Who they were, from whence they came and their destination — A brief history of the course of the expedition. *In: The Historical Record. A quarterly publication devoted principally to the early history of Wyoming Valley and contiguous territory with notes and queries. Vol. V. Wilkes-Barre, Pa. 1895. pp. 89—90.* [437

Hofmann, Joseph: Pfälzer Kolonisten in Nordamerika. *In: Rheinpfalz. Ein Heimatbuch. By Roland Betsch und Lorenz Wingerter. Leipzig: Friedrich Brandstetter 1928. S. 115—121.* [438

Honeyman, A. van Doren: The early Palatine immigrations. *Address delivered before the New Brunswick Historical Society. Febr. 19, 1925. In: Proceedings of the New Jersey Historical Society. New series, vol. X. Newark, N. J. 1925. pp. 256—273.* [439

Kapp, Friedrich: Geschichte der Deutschen im Staate New York bis zum Anfange des neuzehnten Jahrhunderts. *New York, N. Y.: Verlag von E. Steiger 1867. VII, 410 S., Karte.*
= Geschichte der deutschen Einwanderung in Amerika. Von Friedrich Kapp. Bd. I. Deutschländische Auflage: Leipzig: Verlag von Quandt & Händel 1868. VIII, 370; XXVII S. Karte. Dritte vermehrte und mit einem Vorworte versehene Auflage. New York, N. Y.: Steiger 1869. XXVIII, 416 pp. [440

— Die Deutschen im Staate New York während des achtzehnten Jahrhunderts. *New York, N. Y.: E. Steiger & Co. 1884. IV, 229 S.*
= Geschichtsblätter. Bilder und Mittheilungen aus dem Leben der Deutschen in Amerika. Herausgegeben von Carl Schurz. Band I. [441

Knittle, Walter Allen: The early 18th century Palatine emigration. A British government redemptioner project to manufacture naval stores. *A dissertation submitted to the Faculty of the University of Pennsylvania . . . Doctor of Philosophy. June 1931. Typewritten pp. IV, 215.* [442

— Early eigteenth century Palatine emigration. *Introduction by Dixon Ryan Fox. Philadelphia, Pa.: Dorrance 8 Co. 1937. pp. XIX, 320, ill.* [442 a

Laux, James B.: The Palatines of the Hudson and Schoharie, A tragic story of colonial times. *In: The Pennsylvania-German. Vol. X. Lititz, Pa. 1909. pp. 103—107.* [443

Maar, Charles: The High Dutch and the Low Dutch in New York. 1624—1924. *In: The Quarterly Journal of the New York Historical Association. Vol. V. (Proceedings . . . Vol. XXII) Albany, N. Y. 1924. pp. 317—329.* [444

MacWethy, Lou D.: The book of names especially relating to the early Palatines and the first settlers in the Mohawk valley. *Compiled and arranged by Lou D. Macwethy. Published by the Enterprise and News, St. Johnsville N. Y. 1933. 209 p.*
[It contains among other (1) The Kocherthal records, pp. 15—50; (2) Pala-

tine heads of families from Hunter's ration lists, pp. 65—72; (3) Four lists of Palatines in London, 1709, pp. 75—110, and other important lists of Germans in New York State.] [444a

O'Callaghan, E. B.: „Papers relating to the Palatines and to the first settlement of Newburgh, Orange County." *In: The documentary history of the State of New York arranged under direction of Christopher Morgan by E. B. O'Callaghan ... Vol. III. Albany, N. Y.: Weed, Parsons & Co. 1850. = Chapter IX. pp. 327 —364; small edition: pp. 541—607.* [445

— „Papers relating to Manor of Livingston. Including the first settlement of Schoharie. 1680—1795." *In: The documentary history of the State of New York arranged under direction of Christopher Morgan by E. B. O'Callaghan . . . Vol. III. Albany, N. Y.: Weed, Parsons & Co. 1850. = Chapter X. pp. 367—502, maps; small edition. pp. 611—841, maps.* [446

Rohrbach, Paul: „Die Pfälzer in New York." *In: Das Deutschtum über See. Von P. Rohrbach. Karlsruhe 1931 [= Nr. 97a]. S. 39—53.* [446a

Spitzhoff, Heinrich: Mitteilungen aus Amerika. *In: Leininger Geschichtsblätter. Jg. XII, No. 2. Grünstadt, Febr. 1913. S. 11—13.* [447

Todd, Charles Burr: The story of the Palatines. *In: Lippincott's Magazine of Popular Literature and Science. Old series, vol. XXXI. = New series, vol. V. Philadelphia, Pa. 1883. pp. 242—252.* [448

Walter, F. K.: The Germans in eastern New York. *In: The Pennsylvania-German. Vol. VIII. Lebanon, Pa. 1907. pp. 9— 12, ill.* [449

[Weiser, Conrad]: Family register and journal of . . . *[see nos. 3429—3432.]*

Palatine pamphlet, *no title. [General letter written by the Comissioners for Settling the Palatines to prospective landlords.] Dublin: Printed by Andrew Crooke 1710. pp. 4.*
[Copy at Harvard Library, Cambridge, Mass.] [451

List of Germans from the Palatinate who came to England in 1709 *(Copied from the original documents preserved in the British Museum Library, London, England.) In: The New York Genealogical and Biographical Record. Vol. XL. New York, N. Y.: 1909. pp. 49—54; 93—100; 160—167; 241—248; Vol. XLI. New York, N. Y.: 1910. pp. 10— 19.*
[The same is to find in no. 444a.] [452

Vosburgh, R. W.: Early New York church records. *In: New York Genealogical and Biographical Record. Vol. XLIX New York, N. Y. 1918. pp. 11—16.* [452a

---

Hiller, A.: History of the first ten years of the Synod of New York. *In: The Lutheran Quarterly. Vol. XLIX. Gettysburg, Pa. 1919. pp. 247—268.* [453

Lintner, G. A.: The early history of the Lutheran Church in the State of New York. *A discourse delivered before the Hartwick Synod in the Lutheran Church of Richmondville, N. Y., Sept. 21, 1867. Published by resolution of Synod. Albany, N. Y.: J. Munsell 1867. pp. 24.* [454

Tercentenary studies. 1928. Reformed Church in America. A. record of beginnings. *Compiled by the Tercentenary Committee on Research and Publication. Published by the Church 1928. pp. VI, 515.*
[„The church in Passaic Valley"; „Mohawk Valley"; „Columbia Co." etc. ff.] [455

Anhang

Appendix

Brodhead, John Romeyn: Documents relative to the Colonial History of the State of New York; *procured in Holland, England and France. By . . . Edited by E. B. O'Callaghan [= no. 427]. Vol. V. Albany N. Y.: Weed, Parsons and Co. 1855. pp. XIX, 985.*

1708

June 22. Letter of Secretary Boyle to the Lords of Trade — distressed Protestants from Holland desirous to be transported to America. *p. 44.*

June 25. Petition of the Reverend Joshua Kocherthal to the Queen. *p. 44.*

June 28. Names, trades etc. of the German Protestants going to New York. *pp. 52—53.*

June 29. Letter of the Lords of Trade to Secretary Boyle — German emigrants to New York. *pp. 53—54.*

July 7. Petition of Rev. Mr. Kocherthal to the Queen for a salary. *p. 62.*

July 13. Letter of the Lords of Trade to Secretary Boyle, recommending that Mr. Kocherthaler have a grant of land and a gratuity. *pp. 62—63.*

1709

March 28. Letter of the Lords of Trade to Lord Lovelace, encouraging the production of naval stores in the provinces. *p. 72.*

Nov. 30. Letter of Colonel Hunter to the Lords of Trade, relating to the Palatines from Jamaica. *pp. 112—113.*

Dec. 1. Letter of Colonel Hunter to the Lordsof Trade — Palatines from Jamaica. *pp. 113—114.*

Dec. 5. Report of the Lords of Trade upon Colonel Hunter's proposals for settling the Palatines. *pp. 117—120.*

Dec. 21. Letter of Attorney-General Mountague to Secretary Popple — Convenants of the Palatines. *p. 121.*

Dec. 21. Draught of covenants for the Palatines' residence and employment in New York. *pp. 121—222.*

1710

Jan. 7. Letter of the Earl of Sunderland to the Lords of Trade — matter of the Palatines. *p. 158.*

Jan. 20. Letter of the Lords of Trade to the Earl of Sunderland with instructions to employ Palatines in manufacturing naval stores. *pp. 160—161.*

June 16. Letter of Governor Hunter to Secretary Popple — arrival of Palatine ships etc. *p. 165.*

July 26. Letter of Mr. Bridger to Secretary Popple — instruction of the Palatines in raising naval stores. *pp. 168—169.*

Oct. 3. Letter of Governor Hunter to the Lords of Trade — settling of the Palatines on Hudson River. *p. 170.*

Oct. 4. Letter of Secretary Du Pré to Mr. Vernon — Colonel Hunter's proceedings in settling the Palatines. *pp. 171—172.*

Nov. 10. Letter of Mr. Bridger to the Lords of Trade — naval stores raised by the Palatines. *pp. 174—175.*

Nov. 13. Letter of Mr. Bridger to the Lords of Trade — salary for instructing the Palatines. *p. 176.*

1711

Febr. 8. Representation of the Lords of Trade to the Queen about naval stores and settling the Palatines. *pp. 188—190.*

March 8. Letter of Lord Clarendon to Lord Dartmouth — matter of the Palatines — character of Robt. Livingston. *pp. 195—197.*

May 7. Letter of the Governor Hunter to the Lords of Trade — . . . Palatines. *pp. (199), 210—212.*

May 30. Letter of Mr. Clarke to the Lords of Trade — Palatines refuse to work, etc. *pp. 238—242.*

May 31. Letter of Mr. Clarke to the Lords of Trade — submission of the Palatines. *pp. 249—250.*

June 7. Letter of Mr. Clarke to the Lords of Trade — Palatines. *pp. 250—251.*

Sept. 12. Letter of Governor Hunter to the Lords of Trade — . . . Palatines. *p. (262), 263—265.*

Nov. 26. Letter of Mr. Lownders to Secretary Popple — matter of the Palatines. *pp. 288—289.*

Dec. 6. Letter of Mr. Du Pré to the Lords of Trade — support of the Palatines. *p. 289.*

Dec. 11. Letter of Messrs. Perry, Keill and Du Pré to the Lords of Trade — settlement of the Palatines in New York. *pp. 292—296.*

1712

Jan. 1. Governor Hunter to the Lords of Trade — . . . 300 of the Palatines in the land forces, under Coll. Nicholsons. *p. 301.*

Febr. 1. Letter of the Lords of Trade to the Lord High Treasurer — Palatines in New York. *pp. 303—304.*

March 1. Letter of Governor Hunter to the Lords of Trade — naval stores — money bills, etc. *pp. 304—305.*

Oct. 31. Letter of Governor Hunter to the Lords of Trade — proceedings of the Palatines — Schoharie. *pp. 347—349.*

1713

May 11. Letter of Governor Hunter to Secretary Popple — . . . Palatines. *p. 364.*

1714

Nov. 8. Letter of Governor Hunter to Secretary Popple — Palatine accounts. *p. 389.*

1715

June 22. Letters of the Lords of Trade to Governor Hunter — Palatines — queries. *pp. 412—414.*

Oct. 10. Letter of Governor Hunter to Secretary Popple — Palatines, etc. *pp. 447—450.*

Nov. 12. Letter of Governor Hunter to the Lords of Trade — naval stores. *pp. 457—463.*

1716

Nov. 12. Letter of Governor Hunter to the Lords of Trade — Palatines. *p 481.*

1718

July 7. Letter of Governor Hunter to the Lords of Trade — . . . Palatines, the greater part of the . . . remain upon the lands on the Hudson River — Weiser gone to England . . . .*pp. (509—510).*

1720

July 26. Letter of Brigardier Hunter to Secretary Popple relating to the Palatines *pp. 552—553.*

Aug. 2. Petition, or case, of the Palatines in New York, praying that their lands may be secured to them (with marginal remarks). *pp. 553—555.*

Sept. 6. Minute of General Nicholson's and Mr. Long's attendance upon the Lords of Trade, about the Palatines, etc. *p. 570.*

Nov. 1. Petition of Wilhelm Schefs, in behalf of the Palatines, to the Lords of Trade, praying that they might be confirmed in the possession of lands in the valley of the Schoharie. *pp. 574—576.*

Nov. 29. Letter of Secretary Popple to Governor Burnet — Palatines. *pp. 581—582.*

1721

June 18. Letter of Governor Burnet to the Lords of Trade — Palatines. *pp. 585—586.*

1722

Nov. 21. Letter of Governor Burnet to the Lords of Trade — . . . settlement of the Palatines. *p. (656).* [456

Hastings, Hugh: Ecclesiastical records. State of New York. *Published by the State under the supervision of . . ., state historian. 6 vols. and index vol. Albany, N. Y.: James B. Lyon 1901—1905/1906. pp. XXXV, 744; XXVIII, 745—1442; XL, 1443—2308; LIX, 2309—3146; XLIX, 3147—3800; LIX, 3801—4413. Vol. VII. Index. Prepared by E. T. Corwin under the auspices of the state historian James A. Holdan. Albany, N. Y.: The University of the State of New York 1916. pp. 382.*

Items pertaining to the German-[Palatine] settlements:

In Vol. III:

An account of the present condition of the Protestants in the Palatinate In two letters to an English gentleman. London: Printed for Richard Parker at the Unicorn under the Royal Exchange and sold by A. Baldwin. 1699. *[Contributed by* **Wm. J. Hinke.]** *pp. 1453—1459.*

The records of the Board of Trade. List of items relating to the Palatines.

[Vol. 20. Journal M. Jan. 2, 1707/08 to Jan. 28, 1708/09.] *[Contributed by* **Wm. J. Hinke.]** *pp. 1691—1695.*

Order of Council for naturalizing and sending certain Palatines to New York. [At the Court of Kensington ye 10th of May 1708.] *pp. 1702—1703.*
[In: Doc. Hist., N. Y. Vol. III. pp. 327—328.]

Second petition of the Reverend Joshua Kocherthal to the Queen. [June 22, 1708.] *p. 1705.*
[In: Col. Hist., N. Y. Vol. V. p. 44.]

Petion of the Reverend Mr. Kocherthal to the Queen [July 7, 1908]. *p. 1708.*
[In: Col. Hist., N. Y. Vol. V. p. 62.]

Report of the Board of Trade on the preceding petition of (Reverend Joshua Kocherthal) [July 13th, 1708.] *pp. 1708—1709.*
[In: Col. Hist., N. Y. Vol. V. pp. 62, 63.]

Extract of a letter from the Lord Lovelace, dated March 4, 1708/09, 1709. The Palatines. *pp. 1720—1721.*

Extracts from the Journal of the House of Commons concerning the Palatines. Vol. XVI. 1709—1711. *pp. 1724—1732.*

Sunderland to the Board of Trade — The Palatines. [May 3, 1709.] *p. 1733.*

Letter of Sunderland to the Board to inquire into the condition and number of Palatines. [White Hall, May 5, 1709.] *p. 1734.*

Memorial of Lutheran ministers about the Palatines. [May 12, 1709.] *pp. 1735—1737.*

Letter from Earl of Sunderland to the Lords of Trade about the Palatines. [White Hall, May 15, 1709.] *p. 1738.*

Extracts from the Journal of Society for Propagating the Gospel. About the Palatines. [Vol. I. May 20, 1709. p. 164, § 7.] . . . [June 3, 1709. p. 170, § 3.] *pp. 1738—1739.*

Letter of Mr. Chamberlain whit account what has been done for the Palatines. [May 20, 1709; May 23, 1709; May 24, 1709.] *pp. 1739—1742.*

Rumors that certain Palatines turn Pietists. Petition of Rev. Joshua Kocherthal for food. Committee to report. Rumors are true. To be supplied. [Council Minutes, May 26, — June 21, 1709.] *pp. 1742—1743.*
[In: Doc. Hist., N. Y. Vol. III. p. 329.]

Governor Hunter to the Lords of Trade. [London, May 30, 1709.] — The Palatines. *p. 1744.*

Letter of Mr. Chamberlayne. [June 1st, 1709.] The Palatines. *pp. 1745—1748.*

Number of arrival of Palatines in England. [Second list 1193 Palatines . . . taken at Walworth the 27th of May, 1709; Third list . . . June 2, 1709; Fourth list . . . arrived at St. Cath, June 11, 1709.] *pp. 1747—1749.*

Memorial of Mr. Tribbeko. [June 23, 1709.] — The Palatines. *pp. 1749—1750.*
A view of the queen's and kingdom's enemies in the case of the poor Palatines. To which is added a list of the persons appointed commissioners and trustees of that charity, by her majesty's letters patent: as also of those members of the late parliament that voted for the Naturalization Bill. In a letter from a gentleman in London to his friend in the country sold by the booksellers (1711) Guildhall Library, London. *[Copied, 1898 by* **Wm. J. Hinke.** *in British Museum, London.] pp. 1752—1755.*
A brief history of the poor Palatine refugees lately arrived in England. July 18, 1709. London, printed; and sold by J. Baker . . . 1709. *[Copied from a pamphlet in the British Museum, London. By* **Wm. J. Hinke.]** *pp. 1774—1794.*
Report of Board of Trade respecting the Palatines. [Aug. 30, 1709.] *pp. 1796 —1797.*
[In: Col. Hist., N. Y. Vol. V. pp. 87—88.]
Petition of the German Company at Quassaick Creek and Thanskamir (for assistance). [New York, 7ber 23rd, 1709.] *p. 1800.*
[In: Doc. Hist., N. Y. Vol. III. pp. 330 —331.]
Petition of Rev. Joshua Kocherthal. (Desires to go to London to seek help from the Queen for the Palatines.) [Sept. ?, 1709?] *pp. 1801—1802.*
[In: Doc. Hist., N. Y. Vol. III. p. 330.]
Another petition in behalf of the Germans by J. C. Codweis (to borrow money for the Palatines in New York, upon the pledge of the Governor) [Oct. 10, 1709.]; granted in Council, [Oct. 10, 1709.] *pp. 1804—1805.*
[In: Doc. Hist., N. Y. Vol. III. pp. 331, 332.]
Letter of Sunderland to President of Council of New York [White Hall, Nov. 10, 1709.] The Palatines. *p. 1808.*
Society for Propagating the Gospel (to seek out a German minister for the Palatines in New York) [Dec. 2, 1709. pp. 205. § 4.] *p. 1811.*
Report of the Board of Trade on the plans for settling the Palatines. [Dec. 5, 1709]. *pp. 1811—1812.*
[In: Col. Hist., N. Y. Vol. V. pp. 117, 118. Also Doc. Hist., N. Y. III. 382—386.]
Petition of the Palatines to retain Mr. Haeger as their minister. [Appendix to Journal B. 1701—1711. No. 133.] *p. 1813.*
Letter from Mr. Attorney General returning draught of an instrument for obliging the Palatines to the terms of Dec. 5, 1709, read Dec. 22, 1709. (Covenant for the Palatines residence and employment in New York.) *pp. 1814—1816.*

Society for Propagating the Gospel (Rev. John Frederick Haeger to be sent to New York) [Dec. 16, 1709. p. 211. § 5; Dec. 30, 1709. p. 217. § 7.] *pp. 1816—1817.*
The Palatines Catechism or a true description of their camps at Black Heath and Camberwell. In a pleasant dialogue between an English tradesman and a High-Dutchman. — (A representation of their Camp.) — London, Printed for P. Hase in Holborn, 1709. *[Contributed by* **Wm. J. Hinke.]** *pp. 1817—1820.*
The state of the Palatines for fifty years past to this present time containing . . . [An account of the Palatinate and the destructive French War. The case of the Palatines, published by themselves, and sent to the Tradesman of England. Petition of the Justices of Middlesex in their behalf, with her Majesty's answer. A letter about settling and employing them in other countries. A proclamation of the States-General for naturalizing all strangers. Their present camps at Black Heath and Camberwell, England; their support; and the kindness their ancestors showed the English in the times of Queen Mary] . . . London, printed for J. Baker at the Black Bay in Pater Noster Row, 1710. *[Contributed by* **Wm. J. Hinke.]** *pp. 1820—1832.*
Extracts from the Journal of the House of Commons concerning the Palatines. [Vol. XVI, 1709—1711.] *pp. 1832—1841.*
Letter of the Earl of Sunderland of the 7th instant signifying her Majesty's approbation of report of the 5th of last Month about the Palatines to be sent to New York read Jan. 11, [1710]. *p. 1841.*
Second immigration of Palatines, and arrangements for their welfare. [Council minutes, 13 June, — June 16, — June 17 1710.] *pp. 1854—1855.*
Letter of Col. Hunter to the Lords of Trade, dated June 16, 1710. — The Palatines. *p. 1855.*
Extract from letter of Col. Quary to Mr. Pulteney, dated July 5, 1710. — The Palatines. *p. 1855.*
Letter of Col. Hunter to the Lords of Trade, dated July 24, 1710. The Palatines. *p. 1861.*
Rev. J. F. Haeger to the Secretary of the Society for Propagating the Gospel. [July 25, 1710.] — *[This and all the following Haeger letters were contributed by* **Wm. J. Hinke.]** *pp. 1861—1863.*
Journal of Society of Propagating the Gospel. (Arrival of Rev. John Frederick Haeger in New York. [Oct. 20, 1710. p. 295. § 14.] *p. 1871.*
Letter of Rev. John Frederick Haeger, Oct. 28, 1710, to the Secretary for Propagating the Gospel in Foreign Parts, at

London. *[Translated by* **Wm. J. Hinke.**] *pp. 1871—1872.*
Contract with R. Livingston to victual the Palatines; Nov. 13, Anno 1710. *pp. 1872—1873.*
[In: Doc. Hist., N. Y. Vol. III. pp. 391, 392.]
Palatine school house (an acknowledgement of receipt of building-material) By Joh. Fr. Haeyer (Haeger). *p. 1877.*
[In: Doc. Hist., N. Y. Vol. III. p. 400.]
Mr. Cast to Gov. Hunter. [March 27, 1711.] Palatines on Livingston lands. Contentment and expectations. Rev. Kocherthal. *pp. 1877—1878.*
[In: Doc. Hist., N. Y. Vol. III. p. 394.]
Bill to naturalize foreign Protestants. Council Journal, New York. [1711, April 11.] *p. 1878.*
Journal of Society for Propagating the Gospel. (Letter from Rev. Haeger received. Condition of his Palatine church. German prayer-books to be sent.) [May 18, 1711. Vol. II. p. 39. § 14.] *p. 1880.*
Journal of Society for Propagating the Gospel. (Rev. Boehm asks for a minister for Palatines in Carolina) [July 20, 1711. Vol. II. p. 80. § 14.] *p. 1884.*
Letter of John Frederick Haeger, to the Society for Propagating the Gospel in Foreign Parts, at London, Aug. 15, 1711. (Lives in the woods. Palatine services under the open sky. Going with 300 Palatines to war with Canada. Indian baptized. Small vocabulary of Indian words). *[Contributed and translated by* **Wm. J. Hinke.**] *p. 1886.*
Journal of Society for Propagating the Gospel. (Receives letter of Aug. 15, from Rev. J. F. Haeger.) [Nov. 29, 1711. p. 127. § 12.] *p. 1896.*
John Conrad Weiser. — The Palatines. 1711—1760. (Abridged from „Collections of the Historical Society of Pennsylvania." I. 1—6.) *p. 1898.*
[In: Col. Hist., N. Y. Vol. V. p. 575.]
Rev. John F. Haeger to Society for Propagating the Gospel. [Vol. 7. p. 223. No. 38.] Translation of Mr. Haeger's letter to Mr. Chamberlayne [New York, the 12th July, 1712.] (His chaplaincy in the army going to Canada. Copies of German „Common Prayers" not yet received. Thanks for £ 10 received. His missionary journeys. Baptisms. Number of communicants.) *[Translated by* **Wm. J. Hinke.**] *pp. 1960—1963.*
Bill for naturalizing foreign Protestants, passed. Council Journal, New York [1712, Oct. 29.] *p. 1964.*
Gov. Hunter to the Lords of Trade. (His fortune exhausted in subsisting the Palatines. Must sustain themselves during the winter, Palatines left for Schoharie. The Assembly demands the right

of fixing salaries, and of keeping custody of the public money . . .) [Oct. 31, 1712.] *pp. 1965—1967.*
[In: Col. Hist., N. Y. Vol. V. pp. 347 —349.]
Rev. F. Haeger to Society for Propagating the Gospel. [Vol. 8. p. 121. No. 12.] (About 139 communicants at Queensbury, [near Germantown, N. Y.; same as Kingsbury]) [Nov. 1st, 1712.] *Translated. pp. 1967—1968.*
Governor Hunter to the Lords of Trade. (. . . The Palatines on the Mohawk . . .) [Dec. 6, 1712.] *pp. 1969—1970.*
[In: Col. Hist., N. Y. Vol. V. pp. 350 —351.]
Governor Hunter to the Lords of Trade. (. . . The Palatines remain within the province . . .) [March 14, 1713.] *p. 1993.*
[In: Col. Hist., N. Y. Vol. V. pp. 356, 358.]
Warrant of survey for the German [Palatines] at Quassaick Creek. [April 30, 1713.] *p. 1998.*
[In: Doc. Hist., N. Y. Vol. III. p. 344.]
Governor Hunter to Secretary Popple. (. . . The Palatines . . .) [May 11, 1713.] *p. 2000.*
[In: Doc. Hist., N. Y. Vol. V. p. 364.]
Rev. John F. Haeger to Society for Propagating the Gospel. [Vol. 8. p. 189. No. 53.] written to Mr. Chamberlayne, July 6, 1713. (Famine among the Palatines. Appeal for help.) *pp. 2001—2002.*
Letters from the Consistory at Albany to Schenectady in relation to distributing food to the Palatines. Albany, July 7, 1713. *pp. 2002—2003.*
[In: Munsell's Annals of Albany. Vol. VII. pp. 236—237.]
Rev. John F. Haeger to the Society for Propagating the Gospel. [Vol. 8. p. 158. No. 31.] written to the Secretary, July 8, 1713. (Reception of liturgies in German. Census of catechumens, of marriages, of christinings, of communicants.) *pp. 2003 —2006.*
Governor Hunter to the Lords of Trade. [July 18, 1713.] (. . . The Palatines . . .) *p. 2006.*
[In: Col. Hist., N. Y. Vol. V. pp. 365, 366.]
Journal of Society of Propagating the Gospel. (Letters received from Rev. J. F. Haeger.) [Oct. 2, 1713. p. 314. § 3; Oct. 9, 1713. p. 319. § 5; Oct. 16, 1713. p. 330. § 7.]. *p. 2011.*
Bill in Council for support of Government, and payment of certain debts incurred by the Governor. (Debts for feeding the Palatines.) Journal of the New-York Council. [1715, June 14.] *pp.2050 —2051.*
Petition of the Germans at Quasseck [Quassaick] Creek (for better land.) to

Governor Hunter [17th June 1714.] *pp. 2051—2052.*
[In: Doc. Hist., N. Y. Vol. III. p. 345.
Letter of Mr. Haeger to the Secretary of the Society for Propagating the Gospel. (His itinerant life. His endeavors to locate them together. His need of liturgies in German. Instructions from the Society awaited . . . Statistics.) [New York, July 19, 1714.] — [Vol. 9. p. 139. No. 26. New York letters; Vol. 9. p. 230. No. 23. New York letters.] *pp. 2059—2063.*
Journal of Society for Propagating the Gospel. (Letter from Rev. J. F. Haeger — Copies of the German translation of the „Common Prayer" submitted to the Bishop for his approval.) [Nov. 19, 1714. Vol. III. p. 18. § 13; Dec. 17, 1714. Vol. III. p. 24. § 12.] *pp. 2074—2076.*
Rev. J. F. Haeger to the Society for Propagating the Gospel. (Palatines gradually conforming to Church of England. Need of German „Common Prayer" Books. — Three different settlements. Statistic) [May 19, 1715. Vol. 10. p. 181.] *pp. 2093—2094.*
An act for naturalizing all Protestants of foreign birth. — Passed July 5, 1715. *pp. 2094—2095.*
[see Colonial Laws of New York. Vol. I. pp. 858—863.].
Journal of Society for Propagating the Gospel. [Oct. 7, 1715, Vol. III. p. 92. § 16.] Letter from Rev. J. F. Haeger of May 19. *pp. 2097—2098.*
Petition of J. F. Haeger and others to erect a church at Kingsbury, Dutchess Co., N. Y. [East Camp.] *p. 2098.*
[In: Doc. Hist., N. Y. Vol. III. p. 42.]
Rev. John F. Haeger to the Society for Propagating the Gospel. [Vol. II. p. 275.] (reporting the grant of a license to build a church [Oct. 24, 1715.]) *p. 2102.*
Society for Propagating the Gospel [March 6, 1716. Vol. III. p. 127. § 20.] Application to grant a salary of 50 pounds, paid by the Society to Mr. Haeger among the Palatines at New York.) *p. 2106.*
Society for Propagating the Gospel. [April 20, 1716. Vol. III. p. 136. § 10.] (Concerning salary to the missionary among the Palatines.) *p. 2107.*
Rev. John F. Haeger to the Society for Propagating the Gospel. [Vol. II. p. 341.] (Church begun for the Palatines on Hudson river, . . ., Schoharie, Many communicants, statistics.) [Sept. 14, 1716.] *pp. 2109—2110.*
Society for Propagating the Gospel. [Dec. 21, 1716. Vol. III. p. 189. § 5.] Letter of Rev. J. F. Haeger, dated New York 14th of Sept. 1716. *pp. 2111—2112.*
Rev. J. F. Haeger to the Secretary of the Society for Propagating the Gospel. [Vol. 12. p. 341.] (The building of his

church. His former hardships. Kingsbury, only church between Kingston and Albany. Hears his salary is to be discontinued. His sad circumstances; appeal for help. Necessity of a schoolmaster. [Kingsbury on the East side of Hudson River . . . 20, Oct. 1717.] *pp. 2116—2118.*
Petition of Joshua Kocherthal. [June 28, 1718.] (about the manner of making out the Patents for land for the Palatines and for Rev. Kocherthal, at Quaseck Creek, [near Newburgh, N, Y.]) *p. 2122.*
Number of Palatine families remaining in the Province of New York, Anno 1718. „An account of the families of Germans settled on Hudson's river . . . by Joshua Kocherthal and John Fred. Haeger." *p. 2123.*
[In: Col. Hist., N. Y. Vol. V. p. 515.]
Petition of certain Palatines for the disposal of the glebe, at Quassaick creek. [Oct. 8, 1718.] *p. 2124.*
[In: Doc. Hist., N. Y. Vol. III. pp. 346, 347.]
Society for Propagating the Gospel. [Oct. 24, 1718. Vol. III. p. 407f. § 10.] (recieves letter from Rev. J. F. Haeger of Oct. 26, 1717.) *pp. 2124—2126.*
Report of the Committee of Council upon the petition of certain Palatines. The Glebe Land. [Dec. 18, 1719.] (Action of Lord Lovelace, 1708. Survey of land at Quassaick, and 500 acres laid out for a Lutheran minister. Rev. Kocherthal's lot. Description of the lots. The Glebe land. — Exhibits accompanying the preceding petitions.) *pp. 2143—2146.*
[In: Doc. Hist., N. Y. Vol. III. pp. 347, 348.]
Governor Hunter to Secretary Poppel. Letter dated London ye 26 July, 1720. — The Palatines. *p. 2146.*
[In: Col. Hist., N. Y. Vol. V. pp. 552—553.]
Petition of the New York Palatines to the Lords of Trade. [Aug. 2, 1720.] (Setting forth their history, their numbers, voyage, first settlement, removal of some to Schoharie, and the attempts to oppress them; appeal to the King for justice.) *pp. 2147—2148.*
[In: Col. Hist., N. Y. Vol. V. pp. 553—555.]
The condition, grievances and oppressions of the Germans in his Majesty's Province of New York in America, Aug. 20, 1720. (Pledges to them unfulfilled — John Conrad Weiser — Children taken and bount out — Removal to Livingston Manor — Failure of the enterprise to make naval stores — Request to be permitted to go to Schoharie — Furnished men to go on expedition to Canada; never paid for it — Helped to garrison Al-

bany; never paid — Commission sent to the Governor; no relief — Lamentations of the people — Seek help from Indians, who invite them to settle in Schoharie — but their way thither, forbidden by the Governor to settle there — Obliged to disobey — Next spring, other Germans came to Schoharie — Bougth more land of the Indians in that vicinity — Opposition of the Governor, and parties in Albany — Protection by the Indians — Governor visits Albany, and orders a delegation of these Germans to meet him, especially Captain Weiser — The conference — The Governor's orders to them — Obliged to disobey.) *pp. 2168—2172.*
[In: Doc. Hist., N. Y. Vol. III. pp. 423—427.]

Journal of Society for Propagating the Gospel. [Aug. 18, 1721. Vol. IV. p. 167. § 1.] Rev. J. F. Haeger and the Palatines. *p. 2185.*

Journal of Society for Propagating the Gospel. [Nov. 17, 1721. Vol. IX. p. 179. § 14.] Rev. John F. Haeger. *p. 2187.*

Journal of Society for Propagating the Gospel. [July 20, 1722. Vol. IV. p 225.] Rev. J. F. Haeger dead; Widow to be paid. *p. 2191.*

. . . [Aug. 17, 1722. Vol. IV. p. 227. § 5.] More Palatines en route to New York; a German minister to follow. *p. 2191.*

Third immigration of Palatines. — Sanitary orders. [In Council, Oct. 27, 1722.] *p. 2195.*
[In: Doc. Hist., N. Y. Vol. III. p. 428.]

Gov. Burnet to the Board. — The Palatines. [New York 21st Nov. 1722.] *pp. 2195—2196.*
[In: Doc. Hist., N. Y. Vol. III. pp. 428—429.]

Petition of Jacob Sharp etc., in behalf of the Palatines in the Manor of Livingston. [June 13, 1724.] (Ask for the tract afterward known as Germantown. Report on same.) *pp. 2218—2219.*
[In: Doc. Hist., N. Y. Vol. III. pp. 430, 431.]

Journal of Society for Propagating the Gospel. [Aug. 21, 1724. Vol. IV. p. 319.] (Rev. Jas. Ogilvie has married Mrs. Haeger; moneys due Mrs. Haeger.) *p. 2221.*

Report in favor of issuing letters patent to the Palatines in Germantown, N. Y. [Aug. 7, 1724.] *p. 2222.*
[In: Doc. Hist., N. Y. Vol. III. pp. 434, 435.]

Journal of Society for Propagating the Gospel. [Oct. 16, 1724. Vol. V. p. 10. § 11.] Rev. John James Ehlig [Ehle, Oehl], a Palatine minister in New York. . . . [Nov. 20, 1724. Vol. V. p. 13. § 7.] (Report of a letter from John James Ehlig, dated 29th of June 1724, advising that it is about 2 years since he went over

from Germany to New York, suceeding Rev. Haeger, now administering among the Palatines of Schoharie; Agreed to make him a gratuity.) *p. 2232.*

In Vol. IV:

Rev. John Jacob Ehe (Ehle, Oehl) to the Society for Propagating the Gospel. [Schoharie, Oct. 5, 1725.] — *[Contributed by Wm. J. Hinke as all the letters from the S. P. G. volumes]. p. 2332.*

Rev. Wm. C. Berkenmeyer at Quassaick, occasionally, 1725—1731. *p. 2335.*

Gov. Burnet to Rev. Mr. Berkenmyer as to his rigth to the profits of the glebe at Quassaick, N. Y. March 1, 1726. *pp. 2344—2345.*

The Palatine Lutheran Church of Quassaick call Rev. C. Berkenmyer to officiate twice a year. March 30, 1727. [Newburgh.] *pp. 2380—2381.*

Society for Propagating the Gospel receive a letter dated June 15, 1730, from Rev. John Ehlig (Ehle, Oehl) [Feb. 19, 1731. Vol. V. p. 285, § 18.] — Consideration of Mr. Ehlig's letter — His poor circumstances. [March 19, 1731. Vol. V. p. 290, § 6.] *p. 2535.*

Lt. Gov. George Clarke on Mohawk Flatts. — Settlers to be sought from Germany (Palatines) and from Irland [May 17, 18, 28, 1736.] *pp. 2670—2672.*
[In: Col. Hist., N. Y. Vol. VI. pp. 57 ff.]

Lt. Gov. G. Clarke to the Lords of Trade. — Mohack Flatts-Protestant settlers. [New York, April 9, 1737.] *p. 2680.*
[In: Col. Hist., N. Y. Vol. VI. pp. 89—90.]

The Lutherans at Newburgh, N. Y., 1749. *pp. 3046—3047.*
[In: Col. Hist., N. Y. Vol. III. p. 356.]

Petition of Rev. Michael C. Knoll, Lutheran minister at Newburgh and others, to Governor Clinton, for a patent for the glebe lands there. — Brief review of the Palatine settlement there . . . [May 12, 1749.] *p. 3078.*
[In: Doc. Hist., N. Y. Vol. III. pp. 350—351.]

Petition of Rev. Michael C. Knoll, Lutheran minister at Newburgh, etc., against the intrusion of Rev. J. L, Hoofgood, who is unauthorized to preach. and is dividing the flock. — Certificates against Hoofgood. [June 5, 1749.] *pp. 3082—3084.*
[In: Doc. Hist., N. Y. Vol. III. pp. 592—594.]

Lutheran Church of New York petitions the Governor. — Further explanation of their settlement at Newburgh and their church possessions and services there. — Wants protection from unauthorized preachers. [Oct. 29, 1749.] *p. 3095.*
[In: Doc. Hist., N. Y. Vol. III. p. 352.]

4*

German Lutherans petition Gov. Clinton for a brief to build a Lutheran meeting house in New York. — Cannot worship with Holland Lutherans on account of language. [April 4, 1750.] *pp. 3106—3107.*

In Vol. V:

The Lutheran Church of Newburgh, N. Y., succeeded by the Church of England. Petition of Colden, Alberton and others for the Palatine lands at Newburgh. Sept. 6, 23, 1751. *pp. 3171—3173.*

[In: Doc. Hist., N. Y. Vol. III. pp. 357 —359.]
Order to the Attorney General to prepare patent conveying the Palatine Glebe at Newburgh to the Church of England. March 3, 1752. *p. 3218.*
[In: Doc. Hist., N. Y. Vol. III. pp. 359 —360.]
Rev. John Aemilius Wernig, (or Wernich) of Stone Arabia, to his patron, Sept. 14, 1752. *pp. 3285—3287.*   [457

Hudson-Tal

Hudson Valley

Barnett, J. N.: History of Gilead Evangelical Lutheran Church, Centre Brunswick, Rensselaer County, N. Y. and the vicinity. *Fort Wayne, Ind.: Gazette Co. Book Printers 1881. pp. 181, ill.*   [458
Brink, Benjamin Myer: The early history of Saugerties, 1660—1825. *Kingston, N. Y.: R. W. Anderson & Sons 1902. pp. IX, 365, ill.*   [459
— The Palatines at Newburgh. *In: Olde Vlster. An historical and genealogical magazine. Edited by . . . Vol. III. Kingston. N. Y. 1907. pp. 65—71.* [460
— The Newburgh Palatines. *In: Olde Vlster. An historical and genealogical magazine. Vol. III. Kingston, N. Y. 1907. pp. 97—102.*   [461
— Names and occupations of Newburgh Palatines. *In: Olde Vlster. An historical and genealogical magazine. Vol. VIII. Kingston, N. Y. 1913. pp. 102— 103.*   [462
— The Palatine exodus. *In: Olde Vlster. An historical and genealogical magazine. Vol. III. Kingston, N. Y. 1907. pp. 129 —136.*   [463
— The Palatines at „the Camp". *In: Olde Vlster. An historical and genealogical magazine. Vol. III. Kingston, N. Y. 1907. pp. 161—166.*   [464
— The naval stores project. *In: Olde Vlster. An historical and genealogical magazine. Vol. III. Kingston, N. Y. 1907. pp. 193—200.*   [465
— The West Camp Palatines. *In: Olde Vlster. An historical and genealogical magazine. Vol. III. Kingston, N. Y. 1907. pp. 225—234, ill.*   [466
[—] Palatine families at West Camp in 1710—11. „*Statement of heads of Pa-*

laten famileys and number of Persons in both Towns on ye west side of Hudson River." *Taken from Documentary History of the State of New York, vol. III. [see no. 445] In: Olde Vlster. An historical and genealogical magazine. Vol. VII VII. Kingston, N. Y. 1911. pp. 269— 271.*   [467
Curry, Kate S.: The minutes of the Committee of Safety of the Manor Livingston, Columbia County, New York in 1776. *Contributed by . . . Transcribed by* H. S. F. R.[andolph.] *In: The New York Genealogical and Biographical Record. Vol. LX. New York, N. Y. 1929. pp. 239—243; 325—341, ill.*   [468
[Ellis, Franklin]: History of Columbia County, N. Y. with . . . biographical sketches of some of its prominent men and pioneers. *Philadelphia, Pa.: Everts and Ensign 1878. pp. 447, ill., map.*
[Settlements on the Livingston lands — the Palatines pp. 24—27; Germantown. pp. 264—277.]   [469
Hasbrouck, Frank: The history of Dutchess County, N. Y. *Edited by . . . Poughkeepsie, N. Y.: S. A. Matthieu 1909. pp. 791, XXXII, ill., maps.*   [470
Hull, William: The Lutheran Church in Columbia County, N. Y. *In: The Quarterly Review of the Lutheran Church. New series, vol. X. Gettysburg, Pa. 1880. pp. 33—55.*   [471
— The Palatine parish by Quassaick. *In: The Quarterly Review of the Evangelical Lutheran Church. New series, vol. X. Gettysburg, Pa. 1880. pp. 438—455.*[472
— The Lutheran Church in Dutchess County, N. Y. *In: The Quarterly Review of the Evangelical Lutheran Church. New*

series, vol. XI. Gettysburg, Pa. 1881.
pp. 381—397.   [473
Hull, William: The Lutheran Church in
Ulster County, N. Y. *In: The Quarterly
Review of the Evangelical Lutheran
Church. New series, vol. XII. Gettysburg, Pa. 1882. pp. 539—548.* [474
— The Lutheran Church in the courts. A
congregation's agreement with its pastor. *(Rev. John Frederick Ernst's suit
against the Lutheran congregation of St.
Thomas, at Churchtown, Columbia County, N. Y.) In: The Lutheran Church Review. Vol. XVIII. Philadelphia, Pa.
1899. pp. 35—41.*   [475
Ketner, Geo J. M.: Two hundredth anniversary. St. Paul's Evangelical Lutheran Church, West Camp, N. Y. *Wednesday, May 25th, 1910. pp. (6).*
*[At the archive of the Lutheran Church,
Gettysburg, Pa.]*   [476
[Kocherthal, Joshua]: The Kocherthal records. *(A translation of the early records
of St. Paul's Evangelical Lutheran
Church of West Camp, N. Y., kept by
the Revs. Joshua Kocherthal, Justus
Falckner and William Christian Ber-
kenheimer and others). Translated by*
Christian Krahmer. *In: Olde Vlster.
An historical and genealogical magazine.
Vol. III. Kingston, N. Y. 1907. pp. 51—
57; 83—92; 119—124; 156—158; 183—
188; 217—223; 247—254; 281—286;
314—318; 341—351; 377—382; Vol. IV.
Kingston, N. Y. 1908. pp. 24—27; 56—
59; 86—89.*
[The same is to find in no. 444a.] [477
[—] A translation of the Kocherthal records of the West Camp Lutheran
Church. *By* **Christian Krahmer.** *October
1926. [Together with an] introduction
by G. L. Kieffer and a preface by
J. Christian Krahmer. In: The Lutheran Quarterly. Vol. LVII. Gettysburg,
Pa. 1927. pp. 90—117; 270—280;
416—419.*   [478
[—] Das älteste deutsch-amerikanische
Kirchenbuch (1708—1719) *[Abschrift
von Kocherthals Trauregister S. 138—
153.] Mit einer Vorbemerkung von* **Otto
Lohr.** *In: Jahrbuch für auslanddeutsche Sippenkunde. Herausgegeben
aus Anlaß der ersten Tagung für auslanddeutsche Sippenkunde 24.—25. Aug. 1936
vom Deutschen Ausland Institut, Hauptstelle für auslanddeutsche Sippenkunde.
Stuttgart: Verlag Karl Weinbrenner &
Söhne 1936. S. 54—60.*   [478a

Lefevre, Ralph: History of New Paltz, New
York and its old families (from 1678 to
1820), including the Huguenot pioneers
and others who settled in New Paltz
previous to the Revolution. *Albany,
N. Y.: Fort Orange Press — Brandow
Printing Co. 1903. pp. XIV, 593, ill.,
maps.*   [479
[Mancius, G. W. - Ronde, Lambertus De]: The
Katsbaan church records (1730—1801).
*[„Church records of the (Reformed) con-
gregation on the Kaats baan which are begun in the year 1730, November 8, by its
pastor at that time G. W. Mancius, comprising the register of baptised children
. . . and that of marriages"; „which is
continued in the year 1780 by the, at that
time, settled pastor, Lambertus De Ronde".
Translated from the Dutch of the records by* **Sarah Crispell Bernard** *and*
Mary Swart (Hoes) Burhans] *In:
Olde Vlster. An historical and genealogical magazine. Vol. VII. Kingston,
N. Y. 1911. pp. 111—116; 151—156;
184—190; 215—221; 245—255; 272—
285; 310—319; 342—350; 372—382;
Vol. VIII. 1912. pp. 23—31; 56—63;
81—93; 118—126; 148—158; 180—190;
211—222; 245—253; 280—287; 305—
318; 342—351; 372—382; Vol. IX.
1913. pp. 20—30; 51—62; 83—95;
112—126; 153—159; 182—189; 218—
222.*   [480
Morse, Howard H.: Historic old Rhinebeck.
Echoes of two centuries. *A Hudson river
and post road colonial town. When;
Where; By whom settled and named; the
Whys and the Wherefores, Who's, Who,
and Was. Historical; genealogical; bio-
graphical; traditional. Rhinebeck, N. Y.:
Published by the author 1908. pp. (4),
448, ill.*   [481
O'Callaghan, E. B.: „Papers relating to the
Palatinate and the first settlement of
Newburgh, Orange County." *In: The
documentary history of the State of New
York arranged under direction of the
Hon. Christopher Morgan by E. B.
O'Callaghan . . . Vol. III, Albany,
N. Y.: Weed, Parsons & Co. 1850. =
Chapter IX. pp. 327—364; small edi-
tion: pp. 541—607.*   [482
— „Papers relating to Manor of Livingston.
Including the first settlement of Scho-
harie. 1680—1795." *In: The documen-
tary history of the State of New York
arranged under direction of the Hon.
Christopher Morgan by E. B. O'Calla-*

ghan. . . . Vol. III. Albany, N. Y.:
Weed, Parsons & Co. 1850. = Chapter
X. pp. 367—502, maps; small edition.
pp. 611—841, maps.   [483
Poucher, J. Wilson - Reynolds, Helen Wil-
kinson: Old gravestones of Dutchess
County, N. Y. Nineteen thousand in-
scriptions collected and edited by . . .
Poughkeepsie, N. Y. 1924. pp. XI, 401,
ill.
= Collections of the Dutchess County
Historical Society. Vol. II.   [484
Reynolds, Helen Wilkinson: Notices of
marriages and deaths about 4,000 in
number, published in newspapers printed at Poughkeepsie, N. Y. 1778—1825.
Compiled and edited by . . . Poughkeepsie,
N. Y.: Frank B. Howard 1930. pp. XII,
140.
= Collections of the Dutchess County
Historical Society. Vol. IV.   [485
Simmendinger, Ulrich: Wahrhaffte und
glaubwürdige Verzeichnüß, jeniger,
durch die Gnade Gottes, annoch in
Leben sich befindenden Personen. Welche sich Anno 1709 unter des Herrn
wunderbarer Führung aus Teutschland
in Americam oder Neue Welt begeben,
und allda an verschiedenen Orten ihr
Stücklein Brods suchen. Allen Liebhabern, insonderheit aber deroselben
Familien und nahen Freunden zur freudigen Nachricht gestellet. Von . . . ,
siebenjährigen Nord-Americanern, in der
Provintz Neu-York, anjetzo aber in
seiner Vatter-Stadt Reutlingen. Daselbst gedruckt [Reutlingen, Deutsches
Reich]: bey Joh. G. Füsing [1717] 22 S.
                                      [486
— True and authentic register of persons
still living, by God's grace, who in the
year 1709, under the wonderful providences of the Lord journeyed from
Germany to America or the new world,
and there seek their piece of bread at
various places. Reported with joy to all
admirers, especially to their families and

close friends by Ulrich Simmendinger,
a North American, seven years in the
province of New York but now returned
to his native Reutlingen. Printed there
by John G. Fuesing. Translated from the
German [=no. 486] by Herman F. Vesper.
Reprinted by the Enterprise and News,
St. Johnsville. N. Y. 1934. 20 p. [486a
Simms, Jeptha Root: The frontiersmen of
New York: showing customs of the
Indians, vicissitudes of the pioneer
white settlers, and border strife in two
years war . . . 2 vols. Albany. N. Y.:
G. C. Riggs 1882—1883. pp. 712; 759.
                                      [487
Smith, James H.: 1683 History of Dutchess
County, N. Y. with . . . biographical
sketches of some of its prominent men
and pioneers. By . . ., assisted by Hume
H. Cale and William E. Roscoe. Syracuse,
N. Y.: D. Mason & Co. 1882. pp. 562,
XXX.   [488
Smith, Philip H.: General history of Dut-
chess County, from 1609 to 1876 in-
clusive. Pawling, N. Y.: Published by
the author. Armenia, N. Y.: De Lacey
& Walsh 1877. pp. 507, ill., map.   [489
Traver, Chester H.: Historical sketch of
St. Paul's Lutheran Church, Rhinebeck,
N. Y. In: The Lutheran Quarterly Re-
view. Vo. XLVI. Gettysburg, Pa. 1916.
pp. 382—398.   [490
Commemorative biographical record of
Dutchess County, N. Y., containing
biographical sketches of prominent and
representative citizens, and of many of
the early settled families. Chicago, Ill.:
J. H. Beers & Co. 1897. pp. 950, ill.
                                      [491
The Palatines' church at Newburg, N. Y.
In: The Pennsylvania-German. Vol. III.
Lebanon, Pa. 1902. pp. 87—89, ill.
                                      [492
Pioneers of Newburgh, N. Y. In: Ge-
nealogy. Journal of American ancestry.
Vol. I. New York, N. Y. 1912. pp. 27—
28.   [493

Schoharie-Tal

Schoharie Valley

Abrams, Alfred W.: Schoharie in the border
warfare of the Revolution. In: Proceedings of the New York State Historical
Association. The eighth annual meeting
. . . Vol. VII. 1907. pp. 30—41.   [494

Beekmann, Dow: History of the Mark's
Evangelical Lutheran Church, Middleburgh; also treating of „Weiser's Dorf"
and the early churches of the Schoharie
valley. Being an address . . . at the cen-

tenary of St. Mark's Evangelical Luthe-
ran Church, May 15, 1924. Middle-
burgh, N. Y.: Published by the Middle-
burgh News Publishing Co. [1924.]
pp. [24].   [495
Belfour, Edmund: Historical sketch of St.
Paul's Evangelical Lutheran Church, in
Schoharie, New York. *Delivered at the*
Centennial celebration of the building of
the present church edifice. Nov. 22, 1896.
Pittsburgh, Pa.: Foster, Dick & Co. 1896.
pp. 43, ill.   [496
Brown, John M.: Brief sketch of the first
settlement of the County of Schoharie,
by the Germans: *Being an answer to a*
circular letter, addresses to the author by
,,The Historical and Philosophical So-
ciety of the State of New York". Scho-
harie, N. Y.: Printed for the author, by
L. Cuthbert 1823. pp. 23.   [497
[Cady, Henry]: Deaths and burials in Schoharie County, N. Y. *Collected by . . .,*
edited by **Charlotte Taylor.** *Luckhurst,*
Albany 1921. Typewritten copy. pp. (197).
[At the Library of Congress, Washing-
ton, D. C.]   [498
O'Callaghan, E. B.: ,,Papers relating to
Manor of Livingston. Including the

first settlement of Schoharie. 1680—
1795. *In: The documentary history of*
the State of New York arranged under
direction of the Hon. Christopher Mor-
gan by E. B. O'Callaghan. . . . Vol. III.
Albany, N. Y.: Weed, Parsons & Co.
1850. = Chapter X. pp. 367—502,
maps; small edition. pp. 611—841,
maps.   [499
Roscoe, William E.: 1713. History of Schoharie County, New York with . . . biographical sketches of some of its prominent men and pioneers. *Syracuse,*
N. Y.: Published by D. Mason & Co.
1882. pp. 470, XXVIII, ill.   [500
Simms, Jeptha R.: History of Schoharie
County, N. Y. and border wars of New
York; *containing also a sketch of the*
causes which led to the American Revo-
lution; and interesting memoranda of the
Mohawk Valley; together with much other
historical and miscellaneous matter, never
before published. Albany, N. Y.: Mun-
sell & Tamer 1845. pp. 21—672, ill. [501
Warner, George H.: Military records of
Schoharie County veterans of four wars.
Compiled by . . . Albany, N. Y.: Weed,
Parsons & Co. 1891. pp. 428.   [502

Mohawk-Tal

Mohawk Valley

Benton, Nathaniel S.: A history of Herkimer County, including the upper Mohawk Valley, from the earliest period to
the present time: *with a brief notice of*
the Iroquois Indians, the early German
tribes, the Palatine immigrations into
the colony of New York, and biogra-
phical sketches of the Palatine families,
the patentees of Burnetsfield in the year
1725. Also biographical notices of the
most prominent public men of the
county: with important statistical in-
formation. Albany, N. Y.: J. Munsell
1856. pp. V, 497, ill., maps.   [503
Cox, Henry M.[iller]: History of the Reformed Church of Herkimer, N. Y. from
the settlement of Herkimer County in
1723. *By the pastor . . . Herkimer, N. Y.:*
Press of L. C. Childs & Son 1886.
pp. VIII, 77.   [504
Dailey, W. N. P.: History of Montgomery Classis R.[eformed] C.[urch]
[of] A.[merica.] *To which is added*
sketches of Mohawk Valley men and

events of early days . . . Amsterdam,
N. Y.: Recorder Press [1916]. pp. 197,
ill.   [505
Dailey, W. N. P.: German Flatts Reformed
Protestant Dutch Church. Fort Herkimer,
New York. Organized in 1723, land given
for the church in 1730 and 1733, present
church begun about 1730. *Historical*
sketch. Amsterdam, N. Y.: Amsterdam
Evening Recorder 1916. pp. 12, ill. [506
— Earliest Herkimer and Fort Herkimer
history. *In: Papers read before the*
Herkimer County Society, covering the
period from May, 1914 to November,
1922. Vol. V. [s. l. 1922.] pp. 94—98.
                                        [507
— Bi – centenary of the Reformed (Dutch)
churches of Herkimer and Fort Herkimer 1723—1923. *Historical brochure.*
[Herkimer, N. Y.]: Herkimer Telegram
Publishing Co. Oct. 1923. pp. 86, (4),
ill.   [508
— History of the old Fort Herkimer Church
German Flatts Reformed Church 1723

St. Johnsville, N. Y.: Published by the St. Johnsville Enterprise and News [1927 (?)] pp. 31.   [509

Diefendorf, Mary Riggs: The historic Mohawk. *New York & London: G. P. Putnam's Sons 1910. pp. XIV, 331, ill.* [510

Dillenbeck, Andrew L.: Early Stone Arabia. *Paper read before the New York State Historical Association at Canajoharie on the historical tour of Sept. 24, 1931. In: New York History. Published by the New York State Historical Association, vol. XIII. Geneva, N. Y. 1932. pp. 276 —283.*   [511

Earl, Robert: Fort Herkimer. *In: Papers read before the Herkimer County Historical Society during the year 1898. Vol. I. Herkimer and Ilion 1899. pp. 47—49.*   [512

— The Mohawk Valley and the Palatines. *In: Papers read before the Herkimer County Historical Society during the year 1898. Vol. I. Herkimer and Ilion 1899. pp. 57—62.*   [513

— John Frank, his contempories and his account book. *[Beginning with entries bearing the date of 1774]. In: Papers read before the Herkimer County Historical Society, during the years 1899, 1900, 1901, to July 1, 1902. Vol. II. Herkimer and Ilion, N. Y. 1902. pp. 347 —354.*   [514

Earl, Samuel: The Palatines and their settlement in the valley of the upper Mohawk. *Delivered before the Oneida Historical Society, May 11, 1880. In: Transactions of the Oneida Historical Society, at Utica, with the annual addresses and reports for 1881 . . . Utica, N. Y. 1881. pp. 31—51.*   [515

Ehle, Boyd: Dominie John Jacob Ehle and his descendants. *By Boyd Ehle, C. E. St. Johnsville, N. Y. Published by Enterprise and News 1930. 51 p.*
[Contains the life of the Rev. John Jacob Oehl, sent to New York by the Society for the Propagating of the Gospel, in 1722. He came from Hachenburg and studied at Herborn.]   [515 a

Ellsworth, Wolcott Webster: The Palatines in the Mohawk Valley. *In: Proceedings of New York State Historical Association. Vol. XIV. 1915. pp. 295—311.* [516

Greene, Nelson: The story of old Fort Plain and the middle Mohawk Valley. *A review of Mohawk Valley history from 1609 to the time of the writing of this book (1912—1914), treating particularly of*

the central region comprised in the present Counties of Herkimer, Montgomery and Fulton. Especial attention is given to western Montygomery County and the region within a twenty mile radius of the Revolutionary fortification of old Fort Plain, including the Canajoharie and Palatine Districts of the Tryon County. Written, compiled and edited by . . . Fort Plain: O'Connor Brothers 1915. pp. XV, 399, maps.*   [517

Greene, Nelson: The old Mohawk turnpike book. *[First edition of this book was issued for the Mohawk Valley Historical Association.] Little Falls, N. Y.: Press of the Journal and Courier 1924. pp. 291, ill, maps.*   [518

— History of the Mohawk Valley, gateway to the West 1614—1925, covering the six Counties of Schenectady, Schoharie, Montgomery, Fulton, Herkimer and Oneida. *4 vols. Chicago, Ill.: The S. J. Clarke Publishing Co. 1925. pp. 954, ill., maps; pp. 955—1898, ill., maps; vol. III—IV: Biographical. pp. 816—916.*   [519

Halsey, Francis Whiting: The old New York frontier. Its wars with Indians and Tories, its missionary schools and land titles. 1614—1800. *New York, N. Y.: Charles Scribner's Sons 1901. pp. XIII, 432, ill., maps.* [520

Hardin, George A.-Willard, Frank H.: History of Herkimer County, N. Y. *Syracuse, N. Y.: D. Mason & Co. 1893. pp. 11 —550; 276, ill.*   [521

Johns, Wm. A historical discourse of Fort Herkimer Reformed Church. *Preached by . . . Nov. 15th 1874. pp. 7.*   [522

Kapp, Friedrich: „Die Revolution. General Nicolaus Herckheimer." *In: Die Deutschen im Staate New York bis zum Anfang des neunzehnten Jahrhunderts. Von Friedrich Kapp. Leipzig 1868. = Kapitel XI. S. 229—252.*   [523

Koetteritz, John, B.: The Town of Manheim. *In: Papers read before the Herkimer County Historical Society during the years 1899, 1900, 1901 to July 1, 1902. Vol. II. Herkimer and Ilion, N. Y. 1902. pp. 392—419.*   [524

Reid, W. Max: The Mohawk Valley. Its legend and its history. *New York and London: G. P. Putnam's Sons. The Knickerbocker Press 1901. pp. VII, 455, ill.*   [525

Scisco, L. D.: Mohawk Valley householder in 1800. *(Transcript of the original cen-*

sus returns for the County of Montgomery,
N. Y. 1800). Contributed by . . . In: The
New York Genealogical and Biographical
Record. Vol. XLIX. New York, N. Y.
1918. pp. 51—62; 107—116; 280—291;
330—343; Vol. L. New York, N. Y. 1919.
pp. 26—33; 274—284; 307—316.   [526
Simms, Edward: The Town of Danube. *In:*
Papers read before the Herkimer County
Historical Society during the year 1898.
Vol. I. Herkimer and Ilion 1899. pp. 42
—46.   [527
Teall, E. H.: A brief history of the Town of
Fairfield. *In: Papers read before the Her-*
kimer County Historical Society covering
the period from May 1914 to Nov. 1922.
Vol. V. [s. l. 1922.] pp. 134—138.   [528
Tyron County, Committee of Safety: The
minute book of the Committee of Sa-
fety of Tyron County, the old New York
frontier, now printed verbatim for the
first time. *With an introduction by*
J. Howard H a n s o n and notes by Samuel
Ludlow F r e y. New York, N. Y. Dodd
Mead & Co. 1905. pp. XV, 151, ill.   [529
Vrooman, John W.: 1807—1907. Centennial celebration of the Village of Herkimer, August 6—8, 1907. *Address by*
. . . on the churches of Herkimer. [s. l., s. d.
(1907)]. pp. (16).   [530
Walter, William Irving: The Lutheran
Church in Herkimer County. *In: Papers*
read before the Herkimer County Historical
Society during the years 1899, 1900, 1901
to July 1, 1902. Vol. II. Herkimer and
Ilion, N. Y. 1902. pp. 333—346.   [531
— A sketch of some of the prominent families of the Town of Danube. *In: Papers*
read before the Herkimer County Histo-
rical Society, covering the period from
Sept. 1902 to May 1914. Vol. III. Her-
kimer, N. Y. 1914. pp. 55—70.   [532
Warren, Mary Shepard: The first settlers of
the Mohawk Valley. *In: Papers read*
before the Herkimer County Historcical
Society during the years 1896, 1897, 1898.

Vol. I. Herkimer and Ilion, N. Y. 1899.
pp. 36—43.   [533
White, W. Pievrepont: An ancient trail in
central New York. *Reprint from Ameri-*
can Motorist, June 1912. In: The Penn
Germania. Vol. I. = Old series, vol. XIII.
Lititz, Pa. 1912. pp. 617—624.   [534
Following the old Mohawk turnpike. The
old Palatine church. Together with
a description of the Gen. John Cochran
House; also an article on the early Nellis
pioneers by Milo Nellis. *St. Johnsville,*
N. Y.: Published by the Enterprise and
News 1927. pp. 27, ill. maps.   [535

Dedication of the Oriskany monument,
Aug. 6th 1884. *Addresses by John F.*
S e y m o u r, Ellis H. R o b e r t s, William
D o r s h e i m e r, Otto E. G u e l i c h.
Utica, N. Y.: Ellis H. Roberts' & Co.
1885. pp. 5—29, ill.
= *Reprint from: Transcations of the*
Oneida Historical Society at Utica, N. Y.
1881—1884. Utica, N. Y. 1885. pp. 190
—225, ill.   [536
Daughters of the American Revolution:
Unveiling of markers under auspices of
the Daughters of the American Revolution of the Mohawk Valley, Flag Day,
June 14, 1912. Commemorate of General Herkimer's march to the Oriskany
battlefield. Aug. 3—6, 1777. *[s. l.*
(1912)] pp. 24, ill.   [537
Holden, James A.: A bibliography of Oriskany and Herkimer. *In: Proceedings*
of the State Historical Association. The
thirteenth annual meeting . . . Vol. XI.
1912. pp. 42—45.   [538
Klock, Max Otto von: The battle of Oriskany
Aug. 6, 1777. *Issued in commemoration*
of the 150th anniversary of the Battle by
Oriskany Unit Boston Branch of the
Steuben Society in America. Compiled
and edited by . . . [s. l.] 1927. pp. 24.
Also published as: Concord Society of
America. Historical Bulletin, no. 8.   [539

New York — Stadt
City of New York

Kretzmann, Karl: The oldest Lutheran
Church in America. A brief chronicle of
events in the history of the Evangelical
Lutheran Church of Saint Matthew in
the City of New York 1664—1914.
Compiled for the 250th anniversary

of the church, December 6th 1914. New
York, N. Y.: Published by the Evan-
gelical Lutheran Church of St. Matt-
hew in the City of New York, Convent
Ave. and W 145th Str. 1914. pp. 47, ill.
    [540

Nicum, John: The beginning of the Lutheran Church on Manhattan Island. *In: Papers of the American Society of Church History. Second series, vol. II. New York. N. Y. 1910. pp. 85—101.* [541

Precht, Victor: New York im Siebzehnten Jahrhundert. *Vortrag, gehalten vor dem Deutschen Gesellig-Wissenschaftlichen Verein von New York, am 19. März 1884. New York, N. Y.: Druck der Cherouny Printing and Publishing Co. 1884. pp. 35.* [542

Remensnyder, J. B.: Early history of the Reformed and Lutheran Churches in New York City. *In: The Lutheran Church Review. Vol. XV. Philadelphia, Pa. 1896. pp. 382—386.* [543

Schmucker, B. M.: The Lutheran Church in the City of New York, during the first century of its history. *In: The Lutheran Church Review. Vol. III. Philadelphia, Pa. 1884, pp. 204—222;* . . . during the second century of its history. *pp. 276—295; Vol. IV. 1885. pp. 127—151; 187—209.* [544

Wenner, George U.: The Lutherans of New York. Their story and their problems. *New York, N. Y.: The Petersfield Press 1918. pp. XVII, 160, ill. [Bibliography pp. 154—156.]* [545

Johann Peter Zenger

John Peter Zenger

[Zenger, John Peter]: A brief narrative of the case and tryal of John Peter Zenger, printer of the New York weekly Journal. *New York: Printed and sold by John Peter Zenger. MDCCXXXVI 20 leaves.*
Literal reprint of the first edition 1736 in: John Peter Zenger. His press, his trial and a bibliography. By Livingston Rutherford. New York, N. Y. 1904 [= no. 548]. pp. 171—246. [546

Rutherford, Livingston: Bibliography of the trial of John Peter Zenger. [1736—1816]. *In: John Peter Zenger. His press, his trial and a bibliography of Zenger imprints. New York, N. Y. 1904. By Livingston Rutherford [= no. 548]. pp. 247—255.* [546a

Kapp, Friedrich: „Johann Peter Zenger, der deutsche Drucker. Ein Preßprozeß aus dem Jahre 1735." *In: Die Deutschen im Staate New York bis zum Anfang des neunzehnten Jahrhunderts. Von Friedrich Kapp. Leipzig 1868 [= Nr. 440]. = Kapitel IX. pp. 170—198.* [547

Rutherford, Livingston: John Peter Zenger: His press, his trial and a bibliography of Zenger imprints. *New York, N. Y.: Dodd, Mead & Co. 1904. pp. 275, ill., facsimiles.*
[born in Germany, the name of the place is unknown, in 1697. He was one of a large company of Palatines who were sent to America in 1710 by Queen Anna.] [548

— Bibliography of the issues of the Zenger press, 1725—1751. *In: John Peter Zenger. His press, his trial and a bibliography of Zenger imprints. By Livingston Rutherford, New York, N. Y.: 1904 [= no. 548]. pp. 133—169.* [549

Steiner, Bernard C.: Andrew Hamilton and John Peter Zenger. *In: The Pennsylvania Magazine of History and Biography. Vol. XX. Philadelphia, Pa. 1896. pp. 405—408.* [550

Auswanderer der zweiten Hälfte des 18. Jahrhunderts

Emigrants of the Later Half of the 18th Century

Anthon, Charles Edward: Narrative of the settlement of George Christian Anthon in America, and of the removal of the family from Detroit, and its establishment in New York City. *New York: A small number of copies printed for the family by the Bradstreet Press, April 1872. pp. 22.*
[born Aug. 25, 1734, at Salzungen in the Duchy of Saxe-Meiningen, a surgeon in the Dutch West Indian trade having been captured by a British

privateer was landed in New York 1753.
[551

Drisler, Henry: Charles Anthon. *A commemorative discourse, prepared and delivered at the request of the trustees and alumin of the College . . . 1868.* [552
Anthon . . . *In: Dictionary of American biography. Under the auspices of the American Council of Learned Societies. Vol. I. Edited by Allen Johnson. London-New York 1928:*
Anthon Charles (1797—1867) classical scholar. *By* **Harold North Fowler.** *pp. 313—314.*
Anthon, Charles Edward (1823—1883) educator, numismatist. *By* **Harris Elwood Starr** *p. 314.*
Anthon, John (1784—1863) lawyer. *By* **H. W. Howard Knott.** *pp. 314—315.*
[Bibliography.] [553

Gebhard, Elizabeth L.: The life and ventures of the original Jacob Astor. *Hudson, N. Y.: Bryan Printing Co. 1915. pp. XI—XIX, 321, ill.*
[bom July 17, 1763 at Walldorf, near Heidelberg, Germany, emigrated to America 1783 and settled in New York City, N. Y.] [554

Ghent, W. J.: Astor . . . *In: Dictionary of American biography. Under the auspices of the American Council of Learned Societies. Vol. I. Edited by Allen Johnson. London-New York 1928:*
Astor, John Jacob (1763—1848) fur trader, capitalist. *pp. 397—398;*
Astor, John Jacob (1822—1890) capitalist. *pp. 399—400;*
Astor, John Jacob (1864—1912) capitalist, inventor. *pp. 400—401;*
Astor, William Backhouse (1792—1875) capitalist. *p. 401;*
Astor, William Waldorf (1848—1919) capitalist, journalist. *p. 402.*
[555

Kapp, Friedrich: „Johann Jakob Astor." *In: Die Deutschen im Staate New York bis zum Anfang des neunzehnten Jahrhunderts. Von Friedrich Kapp. Leipzig 1868. [= Nr. 440] = Kapitel XV. S. 339—361.* [556

Kern, Albert J. W.: Johann Jakob Astor und die Astor Bibliothek. *In: German American Annals. New series, vol. II. Philadelphia, Pa. 1904. pp. 147—174.*
[Bibliography pp. 173—174.] [557

Niemeier, Otto: Johann Jakob Astor. *In: Der deutsche Pionier. Jg. III Cincinneti, O. 1871¹/₂. S. 277ff.* [558

Parton, James: Life of John Jacob Astor to which is appended a copy of his last will. *New York: The American News Co. 1865. pp. VI, 13—121.* [560

Porter, Kenneth Wiggins: John Jacob Astor, business man. *2 vols. Cambridge, Mass.: Harvard University Press 1931. pp. XXVII, 585; pp. XIII, 589—1353, ill.*
= Harvard Studies in Business History.
[561

Schilling, F.: Astor, Johann Jakob. *In: Handwörterbuch des Grenz- und Ausland-deutschtums. Bd. I. Breslau 1933 [= Nr. 93]. S. 161—163.* [562

Weech, Friedrich von: Johann Jakob Astor. *In: Badische Biographien. Hrsg. von F. v. Weech. Teil I. Heidelberg 1875. S. 13—14. Ders. in: Allgemeine deutsche Biographie. Bd. I. Leipzig 1875. S. 628—629.* [563

Dix, Morgan: Mr. John Jacob Astor and his American ancestry. *In: New York Genealogical and Biographical Record. Vol. XII. New York, N. Y. 1891, July. pp. . . .* [564

Greene, Richard Henry: Colonel John Jacob Astor. *In: The New York Genealogical and Biographical Record. Vol. XLIV. New York, N. Y. 1913. pp.1—5, ill.* [565

William Waldorf Astor, Baron Astor of Hever, Viscount Astor. Necrology, 1919. *In: The New York Genealogical and Biographical Record. Vol. LI. New York, N. Y. 1920. pp. 118—119.* [566

Fairchild, Mary C. Doll: Memoirs of Colonel Sebastian Beauman and his descendants. *Edited by . . . [s. l.] 1900. pp. (2), 137, ill.*
[Sebastian Beauman — Major, N. Y. Artillery, born at Frankfort-on-the-Main in Germany on the 6th of April 1739, and died in New York City, on the 19th of Oct. 1803.] [567

Robinson, William A.: Gallinger, Jacob Harold (1837—1918) physician and politician. *In: Dictionary of American biography. Under the auspices of the American Council of Learned Societies. Vol. VII. Edited by Allen Johnston and Dumas Malone. London-New York 1931. pp. 112—113.*
[he was descended from Michael Gallinger, a German, who settled in New York in 1754. [568

Gebhard, Elizabeth L.: The parsonage between two manors, annals of Clovereach. *Third edition. Hudson, N. Y. The Hudson press 1925. 330 p.* [*Contains the life of Rev. John Gabriel Gebhard, a German minister, who preached to the Dutch Reformed people at Claverack, N. Y. He came from Walldorf in the Palatinate.*] [569

The remarkable case of Peter Hasenclever, merchant; formerly one of the proprietors of the Iron Works Pot-Ash Manufactory, &c. established, and successfully carried on under his direction, in the Provinces of New York, and New Jersey, in North America, 'till November 1766. *In which the conduct of the trustees of that undertaking, in the dismission of the said Peter Hasenclever, and their unpresedented proceedings against him in America, and in the Court of Chancery, since his return to England, are exposed. This case is humbly submitted to the consideration of the king, and both Houses of Parliament, to whome the much-injured complainant looks up for redress. [Double rule.] London: Printed in the year 1773. pp. [13], 2—97.* [570

Day, Richard E.: Hasenclever, Peter (1716—1793) iron manufacturer. *In: Dictionary of American biography. Under the auspices of the American Council of Learned Societies. Vol. VIII. Edited by Allen Johnson and Dumas Malone. London-New York 1932. pp. 379—380.* [571

Hasenclever, Adolf: Peter Hasenclever aus Remscheid-Ehringhausen, ein deutscher Kaufmann des 18. Jahrhunderts. Seine Biographie, Briefe und Denkschriften *im Auftrage der Familie Hasenclever herausgegeben von . . . Gotha: Verlag*

Friedrich Andreas Perthes, A. G. 1922. VII, 252 S. ill.

Teils auch erschienen in: Deutsch-Amerikanische Geschichtsblätter. Jahrbuch der Deutsch-Amerikanischen Historischen Gesellschaft von Illinois. Jg.1920 —1921. Vol. XX. Chicago, Ill. 1922. S. 314—337. [572

Homes, Henry A.: Notice of Peter Hasenclever, an iron manufacturer from *1764—1769. Read before the Albany Institute, April 7, 1874. Albany, N. Y. 1875. pp. 8.* [573

R.[attermann], H. A.: Ein Pionier der Industrie im Staate New York. Peter Hasenclever aus Remscheid. *In: Der Deutsche Pionier. Jg. XV. Cincinnati, O. 1883—1884. S. 258—267.* [574

Shaw, William Bristol: Havemeyer ... *In: Dictionary of American Biography. Under the auspices of the American Council of Learned Societies. Vol. VIII. Edited by Allen Johnson and Dumas Malone. London-New York 1932.*

Havemeyer, William Frederick (1804 —1874) sugar refiner, capitalist, mayor of New York City. *pp. 405—406.*

Havemeyer, Henry Osborne (1847— 1907) sugar refiner, capitalist. *pp. 404 —405.*

[*William Havemeyer born in New York, descendant of a family of Bückeburg in the principality of Schaumburg-Lippe, son of William Havemeyer, who had emigrated from England, where he had learned the trade of sugar refining.*] [575

Loth, C. W.: Ein deutscher Pionier. Johann Schwerdkopf, Brooklyn, N. Y. *In: Der Deutsche Pionier. Jg. III. Cincinnati, O. 1871—1872. S. 143—146.* [576

Herrnhuter in Neu York[1])

Moravians in New York[2])

[**Brink, Benjamin Myer**]: Count Zinzendorf in Old Ulster. *In: Olde Vlster. An historical and genealogical magazine. Vol. III. Kingston, N. Y. 1907. pp. 201—208.* [581

---

[1]) Vgl. auch Reisetagebücher von Mährischen Missionaren und Brüdern, Nr. 1752—1795.
[2]) See also: Moravian Itineraries, nos. 1752 —1795.

Hastings, Hugh: Ecclesiastical records. State of New York. *Published by the state under the supervision of . . . 6 vols. and index vol. Albany, N. Y. 1901—1905 [= no. 436].*

[*Items relating to the Moravians see vol. IV and V.*] [582

Jordan, John W.: Proposed Moravian settlement in Ulster Connty. *Copied from*

„The Moravian" Sept. 16, and 23, 1896. In: Olde Vlster. An historical and genealogical magazine. Vol. VII. Kingston, N.Y. 1911. pp. 297—306; 360—366. [583

Kapp, Friedrich: „Die Herrnhuter in Schekomeko." In: Die Deutschen im Staate New York bis zum Anfang des neunzehnten Jahrhunderts. Von Friedrich Kapp. Leipzig 1868 [= Nr. 440]. = Kapitel X. S. 199—228. [584

Leibert, Eugene: Sketch of the history of the congregation on Staten Island, N. Y. In: Transactions of the Moravian Historical Society. Vol. I. Nazareth, Pa. 1858—1876. pp. 57—63; Appendix. pp. 78. [585

O'Callaghan, E. B.: „Papers relating to Quakers and Moravians". In: The documentary history of the State of New York arranged under direction of Christopher Morgan by E. B. O'Callaghan . . . Vol. III. Albany, N. Y.: Weed, Parsons & Co. 1850. = Chapter XV. pp. 603—624; small edition pp. 999—1030. [586

Stocker, Harry Emilius: A history of the Moravian Church in New York City. New York City, N. Y. 1922. pp. 389, ill. [587

Records of the United Brethren congregation (commonly called Moravian), Staten Island, N. Y. Baptisms and births. In: The New York Genealogical and Biographical Record. Vol. XXXVIII New York, N. Y. 1907. pp. 39—54; 113—128; 117—192; 257—272. Vol. XXXIX. 1908 pp. 17—32; 93—108; Marriages: 167—178; 253—268. Marriages [1835—1862]. In: Vol. XL. 1909. pp. 33—45. [588

Die kolonialzeitlichen deutschen Siedlungen in Neu Jersey

German Settlements in Colonial New Jersey

Acton, R. M.: A short history of the glass manufacture in Salem County, N. Y. *Paper read before the Salem County Historical Society. In: The Pennsylvania Magazine of History and Biography. Vol. IX. Philadelphia, Pa. 1885. pp. 343—346.* [589

Berg, Alex: History of Evangelical Lutheran Christ Church. Trenton, N. J. 1869—1911. [s. l.] pp. 12. [590

[Binder, Clarence Kunkel]: A brief history of Epiphany Evangelical Lutheran Church of Camden, New Jersey. *(1914) pp. 22, ill.* [591

Chambers, Theodore Frelinghuysen: The early Germans of New Jersey, their history, churches and genealogies. *Dover, N. J.: The Dover Printing Co. 1895. pp. V—XIII, (1), 667, ill., maps.* [592

Faris, John T.: „With the Moravians at Hope, N. J." *In: The Romance of forgotten towns. By John T. Faris. New York and London: Harper & Brothers 1924. pp. 95—98.* [593

Faust, Albert B.: „The early Germans of New Jersey . . . ." *In: The German element in the United States. By. A. B. Faust. Second edition. New York 1927 [= no. 42]. Vol. I. = Chapter VI. pp. 149—161.* [594

Fisher, Ben van D.: Records of the corporation of Zion in New Germantown in West Jersey. — Births and baptisms. *Contributed by . . . In: The New York Genealogical and Biographical Record. Vol. XXXI. New York, N. Y. 1900. pp. 107—110; 139—142; 232—235; Vol. XXXII. New York, N. Y. 1901. pp. 36—39; 97—100; 138—141; 200—203; Vol. XXXIII. New York, N. Y. 1902. pp. 27—31; 108—113; 141—144; 220—222; Vol. XXXIV. New York, N. Y. 1903. pp. 56—59; 100—102; 197—200; 248—250.* [595

Genzmer, George Harvey: Frelinghuysen, Theodorus Jacobus (1691—1748) Reformed Dutch clergyman. *In: Dictionary of American biography. Under the auspices of the American Council of Learned Societies. Vol. VII. Edited by Allen Johnson and Dumas Malone. London-New York 1931. pp. 17—18. [born in Germany at Lingen on the Ems, son of the local Reformed Pastor, Johannes Hendricus Frielinghausen — See Nr. 6481 a—d; 7763.]* [595 a

Hamilton, J. Taylor: A sketch of the Moravian activity in New Sweden and its vicinity. *In: Transactions of the Moravian Historical Society. Vol. IV. 1891—1895. Nazareth, Pa. 1895. pp. 165—186.* [596

Hiller, Alfred: History of the Lutheran Church in New Jersey. From the earliest settlement of the state to the year 1893. *In: The Quarterly Review of the Evangelical Lutheran Church. Vol. XXVIII. Gettysburg, Pa. 1898. pp. 98—130; 165—169.* [597

Honeyman, A. van Doren: The Lutheran Church of „Raritan in the Hills". *In: Somerset County Historical Quarterly. Vol. II. Somerville, N. J. 1913. pp. 87—98; 161—172.* [598

Honeyman, John C.: Zion [at New Germantown] (now Oldwick) Hunterdon County, N. J., St. Paul [at Pluckemin, N. J.] and other early Lutheran churches in central New Jersey. *In: Proceedings of the New Jersey Historical Society. New series, vol. IX. Newark, N. J. 1924. pp. 255—273; Vol. X. 1925. pp. 41—56; 294—306; 395—409; Vol. XI. 1926. pp. 57—70; 191—198; 378—396; 532—542; Vol. XII. 1927. pp. 67—78; 214—224; 326—335; 462—471; Vol. XIII. 1928. pp. 209—223; 330—347; 433—446; Vol. XIV. 1929. pp. 55—69; 336—350; 466—475; Vol. XV. 1930. pp. 95—108; 250—261; 392—401; 503—508; Vol. XVI. 1931. pp. 34—50; 180—185; 441—451.* [599

63

Honeyman, R. R.: More local history —
New Germantown, [Hunterdon County
N. J.]. *In: Our Home: A monthly
magazine of original articles, historical,
biographical, scientific and miscellaneous,
mostly Somerset and Hunterdon County
writers, and on subjects largely pertaining to these counties. Edited by A. V. D.
Honeyman. Vol. I. Somerville, N. J.
1873. pp. 116—130.* [600

Kluge, Charles F.: Sketch of the settlement
of Hope, N. J. *In: Transactions of the
Moravian Historical Society. Vol. I.
Nazareth, Pa. 1858—1876. pp. 51—56.*
[601

Kretzman, Karl: The earliest Germans in
New Jersey. *In: The Concordia Society of America. Year book 1928. Detroit, Mich.: Herold Printing Co. 1929.
pp. 54—57.* [602

Mellick, Andrew D.: The story of an old
farm or life in New Jersey in the eighteenth century. *With a genealogical
appendix. Somerville, N. J.: The Unio-
nist-Gazette 1889. pp. XXIV, (2),* 743,
ill. [603

Race, Henry: The Moravians of New Jersey. *In: The early Germans of New
Jersey, their history, churches and genealogies. By Theodore Frelinghuysen
Chambers. Dover, N. J. 1895 [= no.
592]. = Chapter III. pp. 16—24.* [604

Wack, Mr.: Our older churches — German
Reformed of Lebanon, [Hunterdon
County, N. J.]. *In: Our Home: A
monthly magazine of original articles,
historical, biographical, scientific and
miscellaneous, mostly by Somerset and
Hunterdon County writers, and on subjects largely pertaining to these counties.
Edited by A. V. D. Honeman. Vol. I.*

Somerville, N. J. 1873. pp. 389—393.
[605

Die Anfänge der lutherischen Kirche im
südlichen New Jersey. *Abdruck aus
,,Herold und Zeitschrift". In: Der Deutsche Pionier. Jg. XIV. Cincinnati,
Ohio. 1882—1883. S. 234—235.* [606

A forgotten Moravian settlement [Hope,
Hunterdon County] in New Jersey. *In:
The Pennsylvania Magazine of History
and Biography. Vol. XXXVI. Philadelphia, Pa. 1913. pp. 248—252.* [607

Moravian register of the Moravian con-
gregation of Oldman's Creek and vi-
cinity, in West Jersey, 1743—1790.
*Note in: The Pennsylvania Magazine of
History and Biography. Vol. XII.
Philadelphia, Pa. 1888. p. 383.* [608

Extracts from the diary of the Moravian
congregation at Oldmans Creek, N. J.,
1777—78. Rev. Frederick Schmidt,
pastor. *In: The Pennsylvania Magazine
of History and Biography. Vol. XXXV.
Philadelphia, Pa. 1911. pp. 378—379.*
[609

_____

Cummins, Georg Wyckoff: History of
Warren County, N. J. *New York,
N. Y.: Lewis Historical Publishing Co.
1911. pp. VII, 433, ill.* [610

Snell, James P.: History of Sussex and
Warren Counties, N. J. with . . . biographical sketches of its prominent men
and pioneers. *Compiled by . . . Philadelphia, Pa.: Everts & Peck 1881. pp.
XI, 9—748, ill., maps.* [611

A history of Morris County, N. J. Embracing upwards of two centuries. 1710
bis 1913. 2 vols. *New York, N. Y.;
Chicago, Ill.: Lewis Publishing Co.
1914. pp. 509; 503, VI, ill.* [612

Die kolonialzeitlichen deutschen Siedlungen im Süden, die Siedlungen der deutschpennsylvanischen Weiterwanderung ausgenommen

Colonial Settlements of Germans in the South, exclusive the Pennsylvania German Expansion

Augustin Herman und Bohemia Manor, Grafschaft Cecil, Md.

Augustine Herman and Bohemia Manor, Cecil County, Md.

Beck, Herbert H.: Augustine Herman, Lancaster County's first map maker. *In: Papers and Addresses of the Lancaster County Historical Society. Vol. XXXV. Lancaster, Pa. 1931. pp. 261—266, map.* [613

Čapek, Thomas: Augustine Herrman of Bohemia Manor. *Monography by . . . Prague: State Printing Office in Praha Czechoslovakia. 1930. pp. 36, ill.* [614

Cronau, Rudolf: „Augustin Herrman, der erste deutsche Kartograph". *In: Drei Jahrhunderte deutschen Lebens in Amerika. Eine Geschichte der Deutschen in den Vereinigten Staaten. Von R. Cronau. Berlin 1909 [= Nr. 34]. S. 41—43.* [614a

Heck, Earl L. W.: Herrman, Augustine (c. 1605—1686) colonial cartographer merchant, landholder. *In: Dictionary of American biography. Under the auspices of the American Council of Learned Societies. Vol. VIII. Edited by Dumas Malone. London-New York 1932 pp. 592—593.* *[born in Prag c. 1605 son of Augustin Ephraim Herrman, merchant and councilor of Prague and Beatrix Herrman, daughter of Kaspar Redel.]* [614b

Rattermann, H. A.: Augustus Herrman. Eine Charakterfigur aus der Begründungsgeschichte von New York and Maryland. *In: Deutsch-Amerikanisches Magazin. Vierteljahrsschrift für Geschichte, Literatur, Wissenschaft, Kunst, Schule und Volksleben der Deutschen in Amerika . . . herausgegeben von H. A. Rattermann. Vol. I. Cincinnati, O. 1887. pp. 202—225; 524—538.* [615

Stump, H. Arthur: Augustine 1606—1686, founder of Bohemia Manor 1661. *Baltimore, Md.: Alrams Printing Co. 1929. pp. (7), 28, ill.* [616

Ward, Townsend: Augustine Herman and John Thompson. *In: The Pennsylvania Magazine of History and Biography. Vol. VII. Philadelphia, Pa. 1883. pp. 88—93.* [617

Weishaar, J. A.: The German element in Maryland up to the year 1700. *In: Fifteenth Annual Report of the Society for the History of the Germans in Maryland. Baltimore, Md. 1900—1901. pp. 13—34.* Reprint in: *The Pennsylvania-German. Vol. XII. Lititz, Pa. 1911. pp. 486—491.* [618

Copy of the will of Augustine Herman of Bohemia Manor. *Edited by* Gilbert **Cope.** *In: The Pennsylvania Magazine of History and Biography. Vol. XV. Philadelphia, Pa. 1891. pp. 321—326.* [619

Wilson, James Grant: Augustine Herman, Bohemian 1605—1686. *Paper read May 15, 1890. In: Proceedings of New Jersey Historical Society. Vol. XI. No. 2. Newark, N. J. 1890. pp. [21—22], 23—34.* [620

Die Labadist-Kolonie in Maryland

The Labadist Colony in Maryland

Bartlett, B. J.: The labadist colony in Maryland. *Baltimore, Md.: The Johns Hopkins Press 1899. pp. (1), 7—45.* = *Johns Hopkins University Studies in Historical and Political Science, Series XVII, no. 6.* *[Bibliography. pp. 43—45.]* [621

Lohr, Otto: Peter Schlüter, Leiter der Labadistenkolonie in Maryland: Amerikaner deutschen Stammes. *In: Deutsch Amerika. The illustrated weekly. Vol. IX, Nr. 5. New York, N. Y. 1923. S. 5.* [622

Mallery, Charles Payson: Ancient families of Bohemia Manor; their homes and their graves. *Paper prepared at the request, and published under the super-* vision of the Delaware Historical Society 1888. pp. 74. = *Papers of the Historical Society of Delaware VII.* [623

[Schluter, Peter-Danckers, Jasper]: Journal of . . . . *Translated and edited by* **Henry C. Murphy.** *In: Memoirs of the Long Island Historical Society. Vol. I. Brooklyn, N. Y. 1867. pp. 440, 12 pl.* [624

Wilson, James Grant: An old Maryland manor. *Paper read before the Maryland Historical Society March 11 th, 1889 . . . . Baltimore, Md.: J. Murphy & Co. 1890. pp. 37.* [625

— Bohemia manor. . . . . *In: Dutch-American Magazine for 1886. [?]* [626

Die Forscher Johannes Lederer und Franz Ludwig Michel

The Explorers Johannes Lederer and Franz Ludwig Michel

[Lederer, Johannes]: The discoveries of John Lederer, in three several marches from Virginia, to the west of Carolina and other parts of the continent; begun in March, 1669, and ended in September, 1670. *Collected and translated out of Latin from his discourse and writings by Sir* **William Talbot.** *London: J. C. for Samuel Heydrick 1672. pp. (6), 27, map.* *Reprint: Charleston, S. C.: Walker, Evans & Cogswell Co. 1891. pp. 47, map.* *Reprint: Rochester, N. Y.: Reprinted for G. P. Humphrey 1902. pp. 30, map.* [627

— Die Entdeckungen von Johannes Lederer auf seinen drei verschiedenen Reisen von Virginien nach dem Westen von Carolina und anderen Theilen des Continents: Begonnen im März 1669, und vollendet im September 1670. *[Gesammelt und übersetzt aus dem Lateinischen . . . durch* **William Talbot,** *London 1672.] Deutsche Übertragung des englischen Textes. Herausgegeben von* **H. A. R.[attermann].** *In: Der Deutsche Pionier. Jg. VIII. Cincinnati, O. 1876 —1877. S. 403—407; 456—460; 484— 495, Karte.* [628

[Lederer, Johannnes]: Johann Lederer's book of travels in Virginia, North and South Carolina and Georgia in 1669 and 1670. *In: Third Annual Report of the Society for the History of the Germans in Maryland, Baltimore, Md. 1889. pp. 21—23.* [629

R.[attermann, H. A.]: Der erste Erforscher des Alleghany-Gebirges. — Johannes Lederer. *In: Der Deutsche Pionier. Jg. VIII. Cincinnati, O. 1876—1877. S. 399—402.* [630

Starck, Ch.: [Johann Lederer]. *In: Berichte der Deutschen historischen Gesellschaft für den Distrikt Columbia. Washington, D. C. 1906.* [630a

Cronau, Rudolf: ,,Johann Lederer, der erste deutsche Forschungsreisende". *In: Drei Jahrhunderte deutschen Lebens in Amerika. Eine Geschichte der Deutschen in den Vereinigten Staaten. Von R. Cronau. Berlin 1909 [= Nr. 34]. S. 43—45 ill.; 2. Aufl. Berlin 1924. S. 43—45, ill.* [630b

Shipman, Fred W.: Lederer, John (fl. 1669 —1670) traveler and explorer. *In: Dictionary of American biography. Under the auspices of the American Council of Learned Societis. Vol. XI. Edited by*

Dumas Malone. London-New York 1933.
pp. 91—92. _____ [630c]

[Michel, Franz Ludwig]: Kurzer Bericht
Über die Amerikanische Reiß, so Von
2te Weinmonat deß Verwichenen, biß
den ersten Christmonat deß nun Lau-
fenden 1702te Jahrs Vollbracht worden...
[Herausgegeben von J. H. *Graf].* *In:*
Neues Berner Taschenbuch auf das Jahr
1898. Bern 1897. S. 63—127, Kt.
[Teil von Nr. 633]. [631
— Report of the journey of Francis Louis
Michel, from Berne, Switzerland, to

Virginia, October 2, 1701 — December 1,
1702. *Translated and edited by* Wm. J.
Hinke. *In: The Virginia Magazine of*
History and Biography. Vol. XXIV.
Richmond, Va. 1916. pp. 1—43, 113—
141, 275—303, ill. [632
Graf, J. H.: Franz Michel von Bern und
seine ersten Reisen nach Amerika
1701—1704. *Ein Beitrag zur Vor-*
geschichte der Gründung von New-Berne,
herausgegeben von J. H. Graf. *In: Neues*
Berner Taschenbuch auf das Jahr 1898.
Herausgegeben von Heinrich Türler.
Bern 1897. S. 59—144, Karte. [633

Die Siedlungen in Virginia, östlich der Blue Ridge
Settlements in Virginia, east of the Blue Ridge

Gehman, L. H.: Hebron Lutheran Church.
In: The Pennsylvania-German. Vol. XI.
Lititz, Pa. 1910. pp. 173—175. [634
Green, Raleigh Travers: Genealogical and
historical notes on Culpeper County,
Virginia. *Embracing a revised and en-*
larged edition of Dr. Philip Slaughter's
History of St. Mark's Parish. Compiled
and published by . . . Culpeper, Va.:
Exponent Printing Office 1900. pp. (1),
VIII, 160, XXVI, (1). [635
Hartnack, Karl: Die erste Niederlassung
von Siegerländern in den Vereinigten
Staaten *[Germanna, Va.]. In: Sieger-*
land. Blätter des Vereins für Heimat-
kunde und Heimatschutz im Siegerlande
samt Nachbargebieten. Bd. VIII. Siegen
1926. S. 49—52; Nachtrag *der Schrift-*
leitung von Hans Kruse. *S. 52—57.* [635a
Hinke, William J.: The first German Reformed colony in Virginia. 1714—1750
In: Journal of the Presbyterian Historical
Society. Vol. II. Philadelphia, Pa. 1904.
pp. 1—17; 98—110; 140—150. [636
— The Germans in Madison County, Virginia. Documents bearing on their history. *Translated and annotated by . . .*
In: The Virginia Magazine of History
and Biography. Vol. XIV. Richmond,
Va. 1906—1907. pp. 136—170. [637
— The 1714 colony ot Germanna, Virginia.
In: the Virginia Magazine of History
and Biography. Vol. XL. Richmond,
Va. 1932. pp. 317—327; Vol. XLI.
pp. 41—49; also issued separately.
Richmond, Va. 1933. pp. 22. [638
Huddle, W. P.: History of the Hebron Lu-
theran Church, Madison County, Vir-

ginia, from 1717 to 1907. *New Market,*
Va.: Henkel & Co. 1908. pp. XI, 115,
ill. [639
Kemper, Charles E.: The history of Germantown. *In: Bulletin. Fauquier Hi-*
storical Society, Warrenton, Va. No. 2.
Richmond, Va.: Old Dominion Press,
Inc. July 1922. pp. 125—133, ill. [640
Kemper, Willis Miller: Genealogy of the
Kemper family in the United States,
descendants of John Kemper of Virginia, with a short historical sketch of
his family and of the German Colony
at Germanna and Germantown, Va.
Chicago: Geo. K. Hazlitt & Co., printers
1899. pp. 248, XIX.
[sketch of the Germanna Colony.
pp. 5—53.]
[See also no. 7763.] [640a
— Genealogy of the Fishback family in
America. *The descendants of John Fish-*
back, the emigrant, with an historical
sketch of his family and of the colony at
Germanna and Germantown, Virginia,
1714—1914. New York, N. Y. Thomas
Madison Taylor 1914. pp. V, 359.
[See also no. 6437, 7763.] [640b
Mannhardt, Emil: Der Ursprung German-
na's, der ersten deutschen Niederlassung
in Virginien. Der erste Hochofen. —
Die Familie Kemper. *In: Deutsch-*
Amerikanische Geschichtsblätter. Jg. II.
Chicago, Ill. 1902. Heft 4. S. 28—32. [641
Scott, W. W.: A history of Orange County,
Virginia. From its formation in 1734
(O. S.) to the end of reconstruction in
1870; *compiled mainly from original re-*
cords. With a brief sketch of the be-

ginnings of Virginia, a summary of local
events to 1907, and a map. Richmond,
Va.: Everett Waddey Co. 1907. pp. 252,
ill., map.   [642
Stöver, Johann Caspar: Kurtze Nachricht
von einer Evangelisch-Lutherischen
Deutschen Gemeinde in dem Amerikanischen Virginien, und zwar an den
eußersten Grentzen des Ammts Spotsilvanien wohnend, aufgesetzt von . . .
ersteren Prediger dieser Gemeinde. [s. l.]
Anno 1736. (4) S. Abdruck: Hannover:
gedruckt bey L. C. Holwein 1737. (4) S.
                                    [643
Yowell, Claude Lindsay: A history of Madison County, Va. Strasburg, Va.: Shenandoah Publishing House 1926. pp. 203
ill., map.   [644
Complaint by Germans against Governor
Spotswood. (From Virginia State Archives.) In. The Virginia Magazine
of History and Biography. Vol. VI.
Richmond, Va.1898. pp. 385—386. [645
North Virginia church history. [Reprint
of an appeal for funds for the support of a congregation at Germantown in

North Virginia, which is printed in the
Extraordinaire Kayserliche Reichs-Post-
Zeitung, Anno 1720, den 15. Junij] in:
The Perkiomen Region, Past and Present. Vol. II. Philadelphia, Pa. 1900.
pp. 14—16.   [646
„Court orders from Orange County naturalizing Germans. 1742." In: Moravian
diaries of travels through Virginia. Edited
by Wm. Hinke and E. Kemper.
In: The Virginia Magazine of History
and Biography. Vol. XII. 1904—1905
[= no. 5584]. pp. 76—77.   [647

Catterell, Louise Fontaine: Mettauer, John
Peter (1787—1875) physician and surgeon. In: Dictionary of American biography. Under the auspices of the American Council of Learned Societies.
Vol. XII. Edited by Dumas Malone.
London-New York 1933. pp. 585—586.
[son of Francis Joseph Mettauer, an
Alsatian, who came to America under
Rochambeau and after the Revolution
settled in Prince Edward County, Va.,
near Farmville.]   [647a

Neu-Bern, Grafschaft Craven, Nordkarolina
New Bern Settlement, Craven County, North Carolina

Boyd, William K.: Graffenried, Christopher,
Baron de (1661—1743) Swiss adven-
turer and colonizer. In: Dictionary of
American biography. Under the auspices
of the American Council of Learned Societies. Vol. VII. Edited by Allen Johnson and Dumas Malone. London-New
York 1931. p. 468.   [647b
Brinson: The early history of Craven Coun-
ty. In: The North Carolina Booklet. Vol.
X. No. 4. Raleigh, N. C. 1911. pp. 176
—195.   [648
Goebel, Julius: Die Gründung von Neu-
Bern in Nord Carolina. Festrede, ge-
halten bei der Zweijahrhundertfeier der
Gründung von Neu Bern, N. C., am
25. Juli 1910. In: Internationale Wo-
chenschrift für Wissenschaft, Kunst und
Technik. Jg. IV, Nr. 40. 1. Okt. 1910.
Berlin 1910. Sp. 1257—1268.   [649
— The Bi-Centennial of New Bern, N. C.
In: The Pennsylvania-German. Vol.
XII. Lititz, Pa. 1911. pp. 403—407.
                                    [650
[Graffenried, Christoph von]: De Graffen-
ried's manuscript, copied for the Colo-

nial Records of North Carolina from the
original Mss. in the Public Library at
Yverdon, Switzerland, and translated by
M. Du Four. In: The Colonial Records
of North Carolina, published under the
supervision of the trustees of the public
libraries, by order of the General Assembly.
Collected and edited by William L. Saun-
ders. Vol. I. 1662—1712. Raleigh:
P. M. Hole 1886. pp. 905—990.   [651
[Graffenried, Christoph von]: Extract of a
letter from Baron De Graffenried to
Edward Hyde, Esq. governor of North
Carolina. Reprinted from Williamson's
History of North Carolina. Vol. II.
p. 283. In: The Colonial Records of
North Carolina. Vol. I. 1662 to 1712.
Raleigh, N. C. 1886. pp. 990—992. [652
[—] The Graffenried manuscripts. [Tran-
scription of] The German manuscript of
Graffenried on the New Bern settlement.
Letters of Swiss-German colonists in
Carolina, 1711; a French letter of Graf-
fenried to Governor Hyde, relating to his
capture by the Indians, and his escape.
Edited by Albert B. Faust. In: Ger*

man American Annals.   New Series,
vol. XI. Philadelphia, Pa. 1913. pp. 205
—312.   [653
[Graffenried, Christoph von]: The Graffenried manuscript C. [Transcription of]
„Relation du voyage d'Amerique que le B.
de Graffenried a fait, en y amenant une
Colonie Palatine et Suisse; et son retour
en Europe." Edited by Albert B. Faust.
In: German American Annals.   New
series, vol. XII. Philadelphia, Pa. 1914.
pp. 63—190, ill., maps.   [654
Graffenried, Thomas P. De: History of the
De Graffenried family 1191 A. D. to
1925.   Published by the author.   Bing-
hampton and New York: The Vail Bal-
lou Press 1925. pp. (1), 282.   [655
Landry, John: New Berne. In: Revue histo-
rique voudoise. Jg. XV. Lausanne 1907.
pp. 83—94.   [656
Mülinen, Wolfgang Friedrich von: Christoph Graffenried, Landgraf von Carolina, Gründer von Neu-Bern. Zumeist
nach Familienpapieren und Copien seiner
amtlichen Berichte von . . . Bern: Druck
und Verlag K. J. Wyss 1896. 43 S.,
Karten.
= Neujahrsblatt herausgegeben vom Historischen Verein des Kantons Bern für
1897.   [657
O'neall, John Belton: The annals of Newberry, historical, biographical and anecdotical.   Charleston, S. C.: S. G. Cour-
tenay and Co. 1859. pp. 413, VIII. [658
R.[attermann, H. A.]: Beitrag zur Geschichte der Deutschen in Nord- und
Süd-Carolina. In: Der Deutsche Pionier.
Jg. X. Cincinnati, O. 1878—1879.
S. 188—190.   [659
Todd, Vincent Hollis: Baron Christoph von
Graffenried's New Bern adventures.
Thesis: University of Illinois, Urbana,

Ill. [s. l.] 1912. pp. (5), 124, maps
[= no. 661].   [660
Todd, Vincent Hollis: Christoph von Graffenried and the founding of New Bern,
N. C. In: Deutsch-Amerikanische Geschichtsblätter. Jahrbuch der Deutsch-Amerikanischen Historischen Gesellschaft von
Illinois. Jg. 1912. Bd. XII. Chicago,
Ill. 1912. S. 1—123.
Sonderdruck: Baron Christoph von Graffenried's New Bern adventures.   Chicago, Ill.: Deutsch-Amerikanische Historische Gesellschaft von Illinois. 1913.
(1), (4), 124 S., Karten.   [661
— Christoph von Graffenrieds account of
the founding of New Bern. Edited with
an historical introduction and an English
translation by . . . in cooperation with
Julius Goebel. Raleigh, N. C.: Edwards
& Broughton Printing Co. 1920. pp. 434,
map.
= Publications of the North Carolina
Historical Commission.   [662
Vass, L. C.: History of the Presbyterian
Church in New Bern, N. C., with a ré-
sumé of early ecclesiastical affairs in
eastern North Carolina, and a sketch of
the early days of New Bern, N. C.. Richmond, Va.: Whittet & Shepperson 1886.
pp. 196, ill.   [663
Waters, Mary Louise: A short historical
sketch. New Bern, N. C. Published under
the direction of the Craven County Committee North Carolina Society Colonial
Dames of America. New Bern, N. C.:
Owen G. Dunn. 1924. pp. 19, ill.   [664
Presentation of a flag, Febr. 27th, 1896,
from the City of Bern, Switzerland,
founded in 1191 to the City of New
Bern, N. C., U. S. A., founded in 1710.
New Bern: N. S. Richardson & Son
1896. pp. 12.   [665

Die Siedlungen in Südkarolina
Settlements in South Carolina

Bernheim, G. D.: History of the German
settlements and of the Lutheran Church
in North and South Carolina from the
earliest period of the colonization of the
Dutch, German and Swiss settlers to the
close of the first half of the present century. Philadelphia, Pa.: The Lutheran
Book Store 1872. pp. XVI, 25—557. [666
Chapman, John A.: History of Edgefield
County from the earliest settlements to

1897.   Biographical and anecdotical;
with sketches of the Seminole War; nulli-
fication; secession, reconstruction, churches and literature; with rolls of all the
companies from Edgefield in the War of
the Secession, war with Mexico and with
the Seminole Indians. Newberry, S. C.:
Elbert H. Aull 1897. pp. 521, VI. [667
Faust, Albert B.: „The Germans in North
and South Carolina during the eigh-

teenth century. *In: The German element in the United States. By A. B. Faust. Second edition. New York, N. Y. 1927 [= no. 42]. Vol. I. = Chapter VIII. pp. 212—233.* [668

Hinke, William J.: The origin of the Reformed Church in South Carolina. *In: Journal of the Presbyterian Historical Society. Vol. III. Philadelphia, Pa. 1906. pp. 367—389, map.* [669

Johnston, J.: Decree of chancellor Johnston in the church case: ,,Jacob Harmon & others, vs. Godfrey Dreher & others", tried in the court of equity for Lexington District, June term, 1841. *Columbus, S. C.: I. C. Morgan 1842. pp. 34.* [670

Mills, Robert: Statistics of South Carolina including a view of the natural, civil, and military history, general and particular. *Charleston, S. C.: Hurlbut and Lloyd 1826. pp. VII, 17—782; 47, map. [Purrysburg settlement p. 369.]* [671

R.[attermann, H. A.]: Das hundertjährige Stiftungsfest der deutschen Füsiliere von Charleston, S. C. *In: Der Deutsche Pionier. Jg. VI. Cincinnati, O. 1875—1876. S. 103—105.* [672

— Beitrag zur Geschichte der Deutschen in Nord- und Süd-Carolina. *In: Der Deutsche Pionier. Jg. X. Cincinnati, O. 1878—1879. S. 188—190.* [673

Ridder, Hermann: Speech *delivered by . . . at the one hundred and forty-second anniversary dinner, German Friendly Society, Charleston, S. C., January 15th, 1908. Charleston, S. C.: Press of Walker, Evans & Cogswell Co. 1908. pp. 18.* [674

Salley, A. S.: The history of Orangeburg County, South Carolina from its first settlement to the close of the Revolutionary War. *Orangeburg, S. C.: R. Lewis Berry 1898. pp. VIII, 572, maps.* [675

Voigt, Gilbert P.: The German and German-Swiss element in South Carolina 1732—1752. *Columbia, S. C. September, 1922. pp. 60. = Bulletin of the University of South Carolina. Nr. 113.* [676

— A history of Ebenezer Lutheran Church, Columbia, S. C. *Columbia, S. C. 1930. pp. V, 152, ill.* [677

Wagener, J. A.: Die Deutschen in Süd-Carolina. *In: Der Deutsche Pionier. Jg. II und III. Cincinnati, O. 1870—1871; 1871—1872.*

I. Johann Peter Purry. *Jg. II. S. 327 — 334.*

II. Michael Kalteisen. *Jg. III. S. 2—8; 36—40; ill.*

III. ,,Die Stadt am Meere." *Jg. III. S. 120—124; 152—155; 165—169; 212 — 214.*

IV. Walhalla. *Jg. III. S. 234—239; 268—272; 295—298; 342—344.* [678

St. John's Lutheran Church, Charleston, S. C. *Services commemorating the Centennial of the consecration of the present edifice. Palm Sunday, March 24, 1918. pp. 47, ill.* [679

Bachman, John: The funeral discourse of the Rev. John G. Schwartz. *Delivered Sept. 11, 1831. Charleston, S. C.: James S. Burges 1831, pp. 23. [Born in Charleston, S. C. 6th of July, 1807, son of a German immigrant.]* [680

Ficken, John T.: Michael Kalteisen. Captain of United States artillery. *A historical address delivered . . . on 17th January, 1909, being the occasion of the unveiling of the monument erected by the German Friendly Society of Charleston, S. C. In memory of Michael Kalteisen. Charleston, S. C.: Walker, Evans & Cooswell Co. 1910. pp. 14.* [681

M., E. H.: Der dritte deutsche Mayor in Charleston, S. C. [John A. Wagener]. *In: Der Deutsche Pionier. Jg. III. Cincinnati, O. 1871—1872. S. 184—185. [geb. 1816, in Sievern, Amt Lehe, Hannover, Deutsches Reich.]* [682

Freyheiten welche die Regierung von Süd-Carolina unter Protection Sr. Königlichen Groß-Britannischen Majestät denen dorthin von Hamburg kommenden und sich selbst daselbst niederlassenden Personen vermöge eines auf 5 Jahre vom 1773 vestgesetzten und von Höchst-Deroselben confirmirten Rath-Schlusses oder Acte, allergnädigst angedeyhen lasset. *[Am Ende] ,,Dieses Avertissement wird von Herrn Hofrath Bodo Wilhelm Stöckeen auf der Bockenheimergass Lit. E. Nr. 104 umsonst ausgegeben, wobey auch einem jeden allernötiger Unterricht freundlichst ertheilt wird." [s. l., s.d., wahrscheinlich Frankfurt 1773.] 4 S. [Stadtarchiv Frankfurt am Main.]* [683

Die Salzburger Siedlungen und die Herrnhuter in Georgia
The Salzburger Settlements and the Moravians in Georgia

Brantley, R. L.: The Salzburger in Georgia.
    In: The Georgia Historical Quarterly.
    Vol. XIV. Savannah, Ga. 1930. pp. 214
    —224.   [684
Brühl, G.: Wann ließen sich die Herrnhuter
    in Georgia nieder? *In: Der Deutsche*
    Pionier. Jg. VI. Cincinnati, O. 1874
    —1875. S. 248—250.   [685
Cronau, Rudolf: „Die Salzburger in Ge-
    orgia." *In: Drei Jahrhunderte deutschen*
    Lebens in Amerika. Eine Geschichte der
    Deutschen in den Vereinigten Staaten.
    Von R. Cronau. Berlin 1909 [= Nr. 34].
    S. 81—84, ill.; 2. Aufl. 1924. S. 81—84.
                                           [685a
Faris, John T.: „The story of Ebenezer."
    In: The romance of forgotten towns. By
    John T. Faris. New York and London:
    Harper & Brothers 1924. pp. 28—34.
                                           [686
Finck, William J.: St. Matthew's history
    Augusta, Georgia. A brief sketch of
    St. Matthew's Evangelical Lutheran
    Church, *prepared for the golden jubilee,*
    Jan. 29, 1910. Columbia, S. C.: Lu-
    theran Board of Publication 1911. pp. 90,
    ill.   [687
— The orphan house in the Salzburger Co-
    lony. America's first Protestant orpha-
    nage. *In: The Lutheran Church Review.*
    Vol. XXXIII. Philadelphia, Pa. 1914.
    pp. 91—101.   [688
Fries, Adelaide: The Moravians in Georgia
    1735—1740. *Raleigh, N. C.: Edwards*
    & Broughton 1905. pp. 252, ill.   [689
Genzmer, George Harvey: Boltzius, Johann
    Martin (1703—1765) Lutheran clergy-
    man. *In: Dictionary of American bio-*
    graphy. Under the auspices of the
    American Council of Learned Societies.
    Vol. II. Edited by Allen Johnson.
    London-New York 1929. pp. 425—426.
                                           [689a
Gilbert, D. M.: Early history of the Lutheran
    Church in Georgia. *In: The Quarterly*
    Review of the Evangelical Lutheran
    Church. Vol. XXVII. Gettysburg 1897.
    pp. 155—174.   [690
Harden, William: The Moravians of Georgia
    and Pennsylvania as educatores. *By the*
    editor . . . In: The Georgia Historical
    Quarterly. Vol. II. Savannah, Georgia
    1918. pp. 47—56.   [691

Jones, Charles C.: „Old and new Ebenezer,"
    In: The dead towns of Georgia. Savan-
    nah, Ga.: Morning News Steam Printing
    House 1878. = Chapter I. pp. 11—44,
    map.   [692
— The history of Georgia. *Vol. I.* Abori-
    ginal and colonial epochs. *Boston:*
    Houghton, Mifflin and Company. The
    Riverside Press, Cambridge 1883. pp.
    XIV, (1), 556, ill. with map showing
    the Town of Ebenezer. Vol. II. Revo-
    lutionary epoch. *Boston, Mass. 1883.*
    pp. XIV, (1), 540, ill.   [693
Knight, Lucian Lamar: Georgia's land-
    marks, memorials and legends. *Vol. II.*
    Atlanta, Ga.: Printed for the author by the
    Byrd Printing Co. 1914.
    [Ebenezer: The story of the Salzburgers.
    pp. 179—214; The Moravians in Georgia.
    pp. 211—214.]   [694
Kretzmann, Karl: Johann Adam Treutlein
    1733—1782. *The first governor of Ge-*
    orgia whom America should remember
    in the Sesqui-Centennial year of his ad-
    ministration. A tribute to a noble hero
    of the Revolution. In: The Concord So-
    ciety of America. Historical Bulletin no. 7.
    pp. 3—7.
    [Born 1733 of Salzburger parentage.]
                                           [695
Linn, Charles Adolphus: The Georgia colony
    of Salzburgers. *Thesis of Ph. D. Hart-*
    ford Theological Seminary Hartford Se-
    minary Foundation. Hartford, Conn.
    1931. Typwritten. pp. (9), 186.
    [Bibliography pp. (6)]   [696
McKinstry, Mary Thomas: Silk culture in
    the Colony of Georgia. *In: The Georgia*
    Historical Quarterly. Vol. XIV. Sa-
    vannah, Ga. 1930. pp. 225—235.   [697
Prinzinger, A.: Die Ansiedlung der Salz-
    burger im Staate Georgien in Nord-
    amerika. *In: Mitteilungen der Gesell-*
    schaft für Salzburger Landeskunde, Ver-
    einsjahr XXII. Salzburg, Österreich 1882.
    S. 1—36, ill.   [698
R.[attermann, H. A.]: Die Ansiedlung der
    Salzburger in Georgia. *In: Der Deut-*
    sche Pionier. Jg. VI. Cincinnati, O.
    1874—1875. S. 207—214.   [699
— Der erste Volksgovernör vom Staate
    Georgia. Johann Adam Treutlen. *In:*

Der Deutsche Pionier. *Jg. VII Cincinnati, O. 1875—1876.* *S. 303—318.*
[700
[Reck, Frederick von — Bolzius, Martin]: An extract of the journals of Mr. Commissary von Reck, who conducted the first transport of Saltzburgers to Georgia: and of the Reverend Mr. Bolzius, one of their ministers. Giving an account of their voyage to, and happy settlement in that province. *Published by the Direction of the Society for Promoting Christian Knowledge. London: M. Downing 1734. pp. (2), 72.* [701
Reprinted in: Peter Force. Tracts. Washington, D. C. 1836—1846. Vol. IV. 1846, no. 5. [701
Strobel, P. A.: The Salzburgers and their descendants: being the history of a colony of German (Lutheran) Protestants, who emigrated to Georgia in 1734, and settled at Ebenezer, twenty-five miles above the City of Savannah. *Baltimore Md.: T. Newton Kurtz 1855. pp. 308.*
[702
Urlsperger, Samuel: Ausführliche Historie derer Emigranten oder Vertriebenen Lutheraner aus dem Ertz-Bißtum Saltzburg und anderen Römisch-Catholischen Ländern.
Vierdter Teil. Leipzig: Teubners Buchladen 1734.
[„Das V. Capitel meldet von den Emigranten, welche nach Georgien in America gereiset seyn." *S. 109—117.]* [703
— Zuverlässiges Sendschreiben von den geist- und leiblichen Umständen der saltzburgischen Emigranten, die sich in America niedergelassen haben, wie sich solche bis den 1 ten September 1735, befunden, und von denen Predigern in Ebenezer und einigen Saltzburgern selbst nach Teutschland überschicket worden. *Halle: In Verlegung des Waysenhauses 1736. 17 S., Karten. (Mit seiner ausführlichen Nachricht, Halle, 1744.)* [704
— Ausführliche Nachricht von den Saltzburgischen Emigranten, die sich in America niedergelassen haben. *Worin, nebst einem historischen Vorbericht von dem ersten und andern Transport derselben, die Reise Diaria des Königlichen Groß-Britannischen Commissarii und der beyden Saltzburgischen Prediger, wie auch eine Beschreibung von Georgien ingleichen verschiedene hierzu gehörige Briefe enthalten. Herausgegeben von*

. . . *Halle: In Verlegung des Waysenhauses 1735. (6), (6), 242 S., Karten.*
[705
Urlsperger, Samuel: Erste Continuation der ausführlichen Nachricht von denen Saltzburgischen Emigranten, die sich in America niedergelassen haben. *Worin die Tage-Register der beyden Saltzburgischen Prediger zu Eben Ezer in Georgien vom 17. Jul. 1734 bis 1735 zu Ende, mit einigen hierzu gehörigen Briefen enthalten sind: Nebst einem gedoppelten Anhang. Bestehend: (1) In einer im August 1735 zwischen Ihro Excellentz Herrn Jonathan Belcher, Ritter, General Capitain und Gouverneur ein Chef in Neu-England und einigen Indianischen Nationen zu Deerfield gehaltenen Conferentz; So denn. (2) In M. Nathan. Appelletons, bey der Ordination des Herrn Johann Sargent, unter den Indianern von Houssatonoe bestellten ersten Dieners des Evangelii zu Deerfield in Neu-Engeland den 31. August 1735 gehaltenen Predigt, und einer Vorrede herausgegeben von . . . Halle: In Verlegung des Waysenhauses 1738. (18), 243—574 S.* [706
— Zweyte Continuation der ausführlichen Nachricht von denen Saltzburgischen Emigranten, die sich in America niedergelassen haben. *Worin enthalten sind: (I) Das Tage-Register der beyden Prediger zu Eben Ezer in Georgien vom Jahr 1736. (II) Des Herrn Reck Reise-Diarium, als derselbe anno 1735 mit dem dritten Transport Evangelischer Emigranten nach America gegangen, nebst zweyen Briefen aus Neu-England. (III) Der Prediger in Eben Ezer Briefe vom Jahre 1735 und 1736. (IV) Einige Briefe der Saltzburger in Eben Ezer vom Jahr 1735, 1737 und 1738. Nebst einer Vorrede herausgegeben von . . . Halle: In Verlegung des Waysen-Hauses 1739. (14), 575—980 S.* [707
— Die Sammlung und Führung des IV ten Transports Saltzburgischer Emigranten und nach Eben-Ezer in dem Americanischen Georgien von den Hn. Hn. Trustees in London gnädig beruffenen Groß-Brittanischen Colonisten: *Das ist: Eine ausführliche Nachricht: Wie sie zu diesem Beruf gekommen, was ihnen bey ihrem Aufbruch, auf dem March bis nach Canstatt, und vor, bey und nach ihrer Embarqirung daselbst auf dem Nekkar, vor vieles Gute, sonderlich von*

dem Hertzogthum Würtemberg wieder-
fahren; als ein Beweis des noch lebenden
alten guten Gottes, zu seinem Preis, und
zur Stärkung des Glaubens in diesen
Zeiten, auch aus Danckbarkeit gegen die
respective höchste, hohe, und andere
Christliche Wohlthäter dieses Transports
und der Ebenezerischen Gemeine, besonders ediret von ... Halle: In Verlegung
des Waysenhauses 1741. 174 S. [708
Urlsperger, Samuel: Americanisches Ackerwerk Gottes oder zuverlässige Nachrichten, den Zustand der americanisch englischen und von saltzburgischen Emigranten erbauten Pflanzstadt Ebenezer in
Georgien betreffend, aus dorther einge-
schickten glaubwürdigen Diarien genommen, und mit Briefen der dasigen Herrn
Prediger noch weiter bestättiget. 4 Teile.
Augsburg 1754—1767. Erstes Stück. Augsburg 1754. (12), 174 S.; Zweytes Stück.
Augsburg 1755. (26), 175—390, (23) S.;
Drittes Stück. Augsburg 1756. (4),
335—525 S.; Samuel Urlspergers in
seinem 82sten Jahre durch Gottes Gnade
noch lebenden resignirten Senioris eines
evangelischen Predigtamts in Augsburg
Americanisches Ackerwerk .... Viertes
Stück herausgegeben von Johann August

Urlsperger. Augsburg 1767. (58),
286 S. [709
Urlsperger, Samuel: Americanisches Ackerwerk Gottes oder zuverlässige Nachrichten, den Zustand der americanischen, und
von saltzburgischen Emigranten erbauten, Pflanzstadt Ebenezer, und was dazu
gehört, in Georgien betreffend, aus dorther eingeschichteten glaubwürdigen Diarien vom 1sten Jenner 1759 bis den
31sten May selbigen Jahres genommen
und mit Briefen der dasigen Herren Prediger, auch anderer, noch weiter bestättiget; heraus gegeben von . . . Augsburg
1760. (10), 84 S., ill. [710
Voigt, A. G.: John Wesley and the Salzburgers. In: The Quarterly Review of
the Evangelical Lutheran Church. New
series. Vol. XXVII. Gettysburg, Pa.
1897. pp. 370—376. [711
— Ebenezer record book containing early
records of Jerusalem Evangelical Lutheran Church, Effingham, Ga., more
commonly known as Ebenezer Church.
Translated by . . . Edited and published by C. A. Linn. Evangelical
Lutheran Synod of Georgia and Adjacent
States. Savannah, Ga.: Braid & Hutton,
Inc. 1929. pp. (1), 112; XIX, ill. [712

Die Siedlungen in Louisiana, die deutsche Küste am Mississippi

Settlements in Louisiana, the German Coast of the Mississippi Delta

Deiler, J. Hanno: Geschichte der Deutschen
Gesellschaft von New Orleans. Mit
einer Einleitung: Die europäische Ein-
wanderung nach den Vereinigten Staa-
ten von 1820—1896, New Orleans.
Festschrift zum Goldenen Jubiläum der
Gesellschaft. New Orleans, La.: Im
Selbstverlage 1897. 136 S. [713
— Die ersten Deutschen am unteren
Mississippi und die Creolen deutscher
Abstammung. Vortrag gehalten am
16. September 1904 vor dem „Germani-
stischen Congress" in der Congresshalle
der St. Louiser Weltausstellung. New
Orleans, La. Im Selbstverlage des Verfassers 1904. 31 S. [714
— The settlement of the German Coast of
Louisiana and the Creoles of German
descent. In: German American Annals.
New series, vol. VII. Philadelphia, Pa.
1909. pp. 34—63; 67—102; 123—163;
179—207, ill., map.

[Also published separately as Americana Germanica Monograph no. 8.
Philadelphia, Pa. 1909. pp. 136.] [715
Deiler J. Hanno: Die ersten Deutschen
am unteren Mississippi. In: Das Buch
der Deutschen in Amerika. Philadelphia, Pa. 1909 [= Nr. 59]. S. 195
—210. [716
— The German language and family
names among the Creoles of Louisiana.
(Reprint of the concluding paragraphs of
a series of papers by the author on „The
settlement of the German Coast of Louisiana", published in „German American
Annals".) In: The Pennsylvania-German. Vol. X. Lititz, Pa. 1909. pp.
448—453. [717
Franz, Alexander: Die erste deutsche Einwanderung in das Mississippital. Eine
kritische Würdigung. In: Deutsch-Amerikanische Geschichtsblätter. Jahrbuch der
Deutsch-Amerikanischen Historischen

Gesellschaft von Illinois. Jg. 1912. Vol. XII. Chicago, Ill. 1912. S. 190—282. [718

Heinz, Jacob: Kurpfälzisches Blut in Louisiana. *In: Pfälzisches Museum. Jg. XLIII. — Pfälzische Heimatkunde. Jg. XXII. Kaiserslautern 1926. S. 12—16.* [719

Le Conte, René: Les Allemands a la Louisiane au XVIIIᵉ siècle. *In: Journal de la Société des Americanistes de Paris. Nouvelle serie. Vol. XVI. Paris 1924. pp. 1—17.*
[Bibliography. p. 17.] [720

Lehnhart, John M.: German Catholics in colonial Louisiana (1721—1803). *In: Central-Blatt and Social Justice Vol. XXV. St. Louis: Central Bureau, Catholic Central Verein of America 1932, pp. 17—19, 53—55, 89—91, 127—129.* [721

Voss, Louis: History of the German Society of New Orleans. *With an introduction giving a synopsis of the history of the Germans in the United States, with special reference to those in Louisiana. Written at the request of the German Society and published by it on the occasion of its eightieth anniversary celebrated on December 6, 1927. New Orleans, Louisiana: Sendker Printing Service, Inc. 1927. pp. 92, (3), ill.*
From the contents:
Voss, Louis: The German element in the national life of America. *p. 6ff.*
Newton, C. A.: German pilgrim fathers. *p. 16ff.*

Vollmer, Philip: What Germans have contributed to our national life. *p. 38ff.*
Elder, S. B.: The Germans in Louisiana history — their splendid work in colonization. *p. 48ff.*
Voss, Louis: What Germans have done for Louisiana. *p. 56ff.*
A visit to the German colonies in Louisiana. *p. 66ff.*
Two splendid Germans in Louisiana. *Reprint from the Illinois Staatszeitung of Chicago. Sept. 25, 1926. pp. 72—73.*
History of the German Society. *pp. 74—92.* [722

Voss, Louis: The German coast of Louisiana. *Hoboken, N. J. 1928. pp. 24, ill. = The Concord Society. Historical Bulletin no. 9.* [723

Ausführliche historische und geographische Beschreibung des an dem großen Flusse Mississippi in Nord Amerika gelegenen herrlichen Lande Louisiana; *In welches die neu-aufgerichtete Frantzösische große Indianische Compagnie Colonien zu schicken angefangen; Worbey zugleich einige Reflexionen über die weit-hinaus sehende Desseins gedachter Compagnie, und des darüber entstandenen Actien-Handels eröffnet; Auch über dieses noch einige curiöse Beylagen, So zu der Historie dieser Angelegenheit gehören, mitgetheilet werden. Leipziger Neu-Jahrs-Messe. 1720. (6), 83 S., Karte.* [724

Die kolonialzeitlichen deutschen Siedlungen in Neu-England

German Settlements in Colonial New England

Bolton, Ethel Stanwood: Immigrants to New England 1700—1775. *Compiled by . . . Salem, Mass. 1931. pp. 235.* [725

Faust, A. B.: ,,German settlements before the Revolution . . . in New England.'' *In: The German element in the United States. By A. B. Faust. Second edition New York 1927 [= no. 42]. Vol. I. = Chapter IX. pp. 247—262; Vol. II. Appendix pp. 619—620.* [726

Schoff, Wilfred H.: The German immigration into colonial New England. *In: The Pennsylvania-German. Vol. XII. Lititz, Pa. 1911. pp. 395—402; 517—522.* [727

Maine

Allen, Charles E.: Leaves from the early history of Dresden. *Read before the Maine Historical Society, March 27, 1880. In: Collections and Proceedings of the Maine Historical Society. Second series, vol. I. Portland, Me. 1890. pp. 313—320.* [728

— History of Dresden, Maine. Formerly a part of the old Town of Pownalborough from its earliest settlement to the year 1900. *Augusta, Me.: Kennebec Journal Print Shop 1931. pp. (5), (4), 894, ill.* [729

Bliss, George: The Centennial celebration of the incorporation of Waldoboro', Maine. *July 4, 1873. Published by . . . Bangor, Me.: Benj. A. Burr 1873. pp. 3—52.* [730

Brown, Gilbert Patten: New England's oldest Lutheran Church. *In: The Pennsylvania-German. Vol. XI. Lititz, Pa. 1910. pp. 731—733.* [731

Drummond, R. R.: The Centennial of Lubec, Maine. *In: The Penn Germania, Vol. II. = Old series, vol. XIV. Lititz, Pa. 1913. pp. 215—216.* [732

Jordan, John W.: Sketch of the Moravian settlement at Broadbay, Maine 1760—1770. *In: Transactions of the Moravian Historical Society. Vol. IV. 1891—1895. Nazareth, Pa. 1895. pp. 3—12.* [733

Miller, Samuel L.: History of the Town of Waldoboro, Maine. *Wiscasset: Emerson 1910. pp. 281, ill.* [734

Mitchell, [H. E.], Daggett, Sawyer and Lawton: The town register Waldoboro, Nobleboro and Jefferson. 1906. *Compiled by . . . Brunswick, Me.: The H. E. Mitchell Co. 1906. pp. 264.* [735

Neu, Heinrich: Beiträge zur Geschichte der rheinischen Amerika-Auswanderung im 18. Jahrhundert. *In: Rheinische Vierteljahrsblätter. Mitteilungen des Instituts für geschichtliche Landeskunde der Rheinlande an der Universität Bonn. Jg. VI. Bonn 1936. S. 176—185.* [735a

Patterson, William D.: An old Waldoborough muster roll. *Contributed by . . . In: Sprague's Journal of Maine History, Vol. XII. Dover, Me. 1924. pp. 221—222.* [736

Pohlman, H.: The German colony and the Lutheran Church in Maine. *Gettysburg 1869.* [736a

Rattermann, H. A.: Geschichte des deutschen Elements im Staate Maine. Dessen Ursprung, Entwicklung und Verfall vom Jahre 1739 bis zur Gegenwart. *In: Der Deutsche Pionier. Jg. XIV. Cincinnati, O. 1882—1883. S. 7—13; 53—62; 90—98; 141—150; 174—188; 217—233; 266—276; 292—303; 338—361; 425—434; 464—468; Jg. XV. 1883—1884. S. 74—82; 104—114; 201—210; 226—235; 267—283; 358—375; Jg. XVI. 1884—1885. S. 11—18; 71—77; 98—102; 195—204; 227—238; 276—281; 302—311; 349—359. Sonderdruck: New York, N. Y.: Steiger & Co. 1884. 160 S.* [737

[Starman, John W.]: Some account of the German settlement, in Waldoborough.

By Rev. Mr. Starman . . . And a biographical sketch of Mr. Starman by Nath'l Groton. In: Collection of the Maine Historical Society. Vol. V. Portland, Me. 1857. pp. 403—406; 407—411. [738

Thompson, Garret W.: The Germans in Maine. In: The Pennsylvania-German. Vol. XII. Lititz, Pa. 1911. pp. 595—601; 684—690; 724—734.

— The Germans in Maine. In: The Penn-Germania. Vol. I. = Old series, vol. XIII. Lititz, Pa. 1912. The religious development of the Broad Bay settlement. pp. 36—44. The settlement in Frankfort. pp. 106—112. The religions development of the Frankfort community. pp. 161—166. The settlements at other places. pp. 166—169. [739

Thompson, Garret W.: The Germans in Maine. In: Sprague's Journal of Maine History. Vol. V. Dover, Me. 1917. pp. 3—7; 140—146. [740

Williamson, Jos ph: General Samuel Waldo. (Read at Portand, March 30, 1876.) In: Collections of the Maine Historical Society. Vol. IX. Portland, Me. 1887. pp. 75—93, ill. [741

Translation of General Waldo's circular . . . 1753. With an introduction by John L. Locke. In: Collections of the Maine Historical Society. Vol. VI. Portland, Me. 1859. pp. 321—332. [742

A Moravian colony in Maine. In: Collections and Proceedings of the Maine Historica Society. Second series, vol. II. Portland, Me. 1891. p. 333. [743

Massachusetts

Baensch, Emil: A Boston boy, the first martyr to American liberty. [Theophilus Lillie.] Manitowoc, Wisc.: Published by the author; Menasha, Wisc.: Printed by George Banta Publishing Co. 1924. pp. 44. [744

Davis, Andrew McFarland: Palatines at Martha's vineyard, Massachusetts, 1731. In: The Pennsylvania Magazine of History and Biography. Vol. XXI. Philadelphia, Pa. 1897. pp. 124—125. [745

Heldt, A.: „Boston." In: Handwörterbuch des Grenz- und Auslanddeutschtums. Bd. I. Breslau 1933 [= Nr. 93]. S. 503 —505. [745a

K.: Die Deutschen in Massachusetts. (Aus Steiger's „Literarischer Monatsbericht".) In: Der Deutsche Pionier. Jg. II. Cincinnati, O. 1870—1871. S. 101—106; 143—147. [746

Pattee, William S.: A history of old Braintree and Quincy, with a sketch of Randolph and Holbrook. Quincy: Green & Prescott 1878. pp. XIV, 660, ill. [See especially chapter: „Glass works" (at Braintree, in that part of Quincy now called Germantown.) pp. 473—492.] [747

Schoff, Wilfred H.: The descendants of Jacob Schoff who came to Boston in 1752 and settled in Ashburnham in 1757 with an account of the German immigration into colonial New England. Philadelphia, Pa. 1910. pp. 5—163, ill. [See also no. 7763.] [748

(Germans at Plymouth.) See: Plymouth Church Records 1620—1859. Part II. = Publications of the Colonial Society of Massachusetts. Vol. XXIII. Collections. Boston 1923. pp. 614—620; 705—710. [749

Connecticut

Vollmann, Charles F.: Zur Geschichte des Deutschtums von New Haven, Conn. In: Deutsch-Amerikanische Geschichtsblätter. (German-American Historical Review.) Jahrbuch der Deutsch-Ameri-kanischen Historischen Gesellschaft von Illinois. Jg. 1927—28. Vol. XXVII—XXVIII. Chicago, Ill. 1928. S. 211—236. [750

Das Deutschtum in den kanadischen See-Provinzen
Germans in the Canadian Maritime Provinces

Kanada, allgemein
Canada, general

Bryce, George: A short history of the Canadian people. *Second edition. London: Samson Low, Marston & Co. 1914. pp. 621.* [751

Lucas, Sir C. P.: Canada. *Oxford: The Clarendon Press 1901—1911. pp. 364. = Vol. V. A historical geography of the British colonies.*
[Especially part III: Geographical. By J. D. Rogers.] [752

Shortt, Adam and **Doughty, Arthur G.:** Canada and its provinces. *A history of the Canadian people and their institutions. By one hundred associates. General editors: . . . 22 vols and index, vol. XXIII. Toronto, Ont.: Glasgow, Brook & Co. 1914—1917. ill., map.*
[Especially Vol. XIII, XIV, XVII. (see nos. 779, 780 and 5838), Vol. XXIII, section XII. Manuscript sources. pp. 224—232; Bibliography. pp. 233—283.] [753

Canada, Dominion of, Department of Trade and Commerce: Census, reports of: 1870—1871; 1880—1881; 1890—1891; 1901; 1911; 1921; 1931. [754

Gourlay, Robert F.: Statistical account of Upper Canada. *3 vols. London . . . . . . 1822.* [755

Kloß, Heinz: Materialien zur Geschichte der deutschkanadischen Presse. *In: Der Auslanddeutsche. Halbmonatsschrift für Auslanddeutschtum und Auslandkunde. Mitteilungen des Deutschen Ausland-Instituts. Jg. XI, No. 12. 1928. S. 382—384.* [756

Lehmann, Heinz: Zur Geschichte des Deutschtums in Kanada. *Band I: Das Deutschtum in Ostkanada. Stuttgart: Ausland und Heimat Verlags-Aktiengesellschaft 1931. (3), 125 S., Karten. = Schriften des Deutschen Ausland-Instituts Stuttgart. A. Kulturhistorische Reihe. Bd. XXXI.* [757

— Das Deutschtum in Ost-Kanada. *In: Deutsche Arbeit. Jg. XXXIV. Berlin 1934. S. 610—613; Jg. XXXV, 1935, S. 12—18.* [757a

Lehmann, Heinz: Das evangelische Deutschtum in Kanada. *In: Auslanddeutschtum und evangelische Kirche. Jahrbuch 1935. München 1935. S. 218—252.* [757b

— „Deutsche Zeitung für Canada". *Zur Geschichte der deutschkanadischen Presse. In: Deutsche Arbeit. Jg. XXXV. Berlin 1935. S. 482—487.* [757c

Miller, H. H.: Die Deutschen in Canada. *(Auszug einer Rede, gehalten im canadischen Parlament in Ottawa von dem Mitglied des Unterhauses für Süd-Grey). In: Deutsch-Amerikanische Geschichtsblätter. Jg. VIII, Nr. 3. Chicago, Ill. 1908. S. 118—124.* [758

[Müller-Grote, Karl]: Onkel Karl. Deutschkanadische Lebensbilder. *Bremen: Angelsachsen-Verlag 1924. 320 S.* [759

Oppel, Alwin: Kanada und die Deutschen. *Dresden: Heimat und Welt-Verlag 1916. 160 S. = Heimat und Welt-Bücher: Das Deutschtum im Ausland: Band III.* [760

Tuckermann, Walther: Das Deutschtum in Kanada. *In: Social- und Wirtschaftsgeschichte. Gedächtnisschrift für Georg von Below. Stuttgart: W. Kohlhammer 1928. S. 299—322, Karte.* [761

Zeitschriften:

Periodicals:

Royal Society of Canada, Proceedings and Transactions of the . . . *Second series, vol. I. Ottawa, Toronto, London, 1895ff.* [762

The Canadian Historical Review. *Vol. I. Toronto, Ont. 1920ff.* [763

Lennox and Addington Historical Society Papers and Records. *Vol. I. Nappanee, Ont. 1909. Annually ff.* [764

Missisquoi County Historical Society, Reports of the . . . *Vol. I. St. Johns, Que. 1906ff.* [765

New Brunswick Historical Society, Collections of the . . . *Vol. I. Saint John, N. B. 1894ff.* [766

Niagara Historical Society, Transactions. *Vol. I. Niagara, Ont. 1896 ff.* [767
Nova Scotia Historical Society, Collections of the . . . *Vol. I. Halifax, Nova Scotia 1878 ff.* [768

Ontario Historical Society. Papers and Records. *Vol. I. Toronto, Ont. 1899 ff.* [769
Waterloo Historical Society, Annual Reports of the . . . *Vol. I. Berlin; Kitchener, Ont. 1913 ff.* [770

Die Siedlungen in Neu-Schottland und Neu-Braunschweig

Settlements in Nova Scotia and New Brunswick

Bourinot, Sir John G.: Builders of Nova Scotia. *In: Proceedings and Transactions of the Royal Society of Canada, Second series, vol. V. Ottawa and Toronto, May, 1899. Section 2. pp. 1—198.* [771
Creighton, Agnes: A plea for remembrance. *In: Acadiensis. Ed. by D. R. Jack. Vol. VII. St. John, N. B. January 1907. pp. 3—8.* [772
— Relics of the history of Lunenburg. *Paper read before the Canadian Historical Society. pp. . . .* [773
Des Brisay, M. B.: History of the County of Lunenburg. *Second edition. Toronto, Ont. 1895. pp. . . .* [774
Fisher, Peter: First history of New Brunswick (1825). *New print St. John, N. B. 1921. pp. . . .* [775
Ganong, W. F.: A monograph of the origins of the settlements in the Province of New Brunswick. *In: Proceedings and Transactions of the Royal Society of Canada. Second series, vol. X. Ottawa, Toronto and London, June, 1904. Section 2. pp. 3—185.* [776
Haliburton, T. C.: Historical and statistical account of Nova Scotia. *2 vols. Halifax, Nova Scotia 1829. pp. 340; pp. 453.* [777
Lehmann, Heinz: ,,Das Deuschtum in den kanadischen Seeprovinzen." *In: Zur Geschichte des Deutschtums in Kanada. Band I. Das Deutschtum in Ostkanada. Von H. Lehmann. Stuttgart 1931 [= Nr. 757]. = Kapitel II. S. 21—40.* [778
MacMechan, Archibald: ,,The founding of Halifax." *In: Canada and its provinces . . . Vol. XIII. Section VII. The Atlantic provinces. Toronto, Ont. 1914 [= no. 753]. pp. 81—84.* [779
— and **[Cunning, M.]:** ,,The Lunenburg settlement." *In: Canada and its provinces . . . Vol. XIII. Section VII. The Atlantic provinces. Toronto, Ont. 1914 [= no. 753]. pp. 84—85; see also* ,,Agriculture in Nova Scotia'' *(by M.*

Cunning). In: Vol. XIV. Section XII. pp. 647—648. [780
Patridge, Francis: Notes on the early history of St. George's Church, Halifax. *A paper read May 7th, 1885. In: Nova Scotia Historical Society Collections. Vol. VI. Halifax, Nova Scotia 1888. pp. 137—154;* The early history of the parish of St. George. *A paper read March 3rd, 1887. In: Vol. VII. 1891. pp. 73—87.* [781
Raymond, W. O.: Colonel McNutt and the pre-loyalist settlement of Nova Scotia. *In: Proceedings and Transactions of the Royal Society of Canada. Third series, vol. V. Ottawa, Toronto and London 1911. Section 2. pp. 23—115.* [782
Scheffer, J. A.: The Germans in Nova Scotia. *In: The Pennsylvania-German. Vol. VIII. Lebanon, Pa. 1907. pp. 104—105; 151—153; 201—203; 248—251.* [783
Seccombe, John: Eine Predigt gehalten zu Halifax, den 31ten July, 1770, an die Hochteutsch-Reformirte Gemeine zu Lüneburg, bey der Einsetzung des Ehrw. Hern. Bruin Romcas Comingoe, durch John Seccombe, von Chester. *Welche die erste ist, die in der Provinz Nova Scotia bey einer solchen Gelegenheit abgelegt worden. Nebst einem Anhange . . . Aus dem Englischen übersetzt, nach der zu Halifax gedruckten Ausgabe. Philadelphia, Gedruckt bey Henrich Miller 1771. 40 S.* [783a
Historische und geographische Beschreibung von Neuschottland, *wie auch von den Sitten und Gewohnheiten der Indianer, und von den merkwürdigen Begebenheiten, die sich zwischen den Cronen Frankreich und England seit deren Besitznehmung zugetragen, hinlängliche Nachricht ertheilet wird. Frankfurt und Leipzig: H. L. Brömer 1750. 216 S.*
[Werbeblatt, aus dem Englischen ins Deutsche übersetzt von dem Agenten Köhler.] [784

Die pfälzischen Siedlungen in Irland
The Palatine Colonies in Ireland

Crookshank, C. H.: History of Methodism in Ireland. *3 vols. Belfast: R. S. Allen, Son & Allen-University House; London: T. Woolmer 1885—1886—1888.* [On the Palatines. Vol. I. pp. 56—57.] [785

Diffenderffer, Frank Ried: ,,The German colony in Ireland. *In: The German exodus to England in 1709. (Massen-auswanderung der Pfälzer.) Lancaster, Pa. 1897. = Part II. ,,A narrative and critical history" prepared at the request of the Pennsylvania-German Society. In: The Pennsylvania-German Society. Proceedings and Addresses . . . 1896. Vol. VII. Reading, Pa. 1897 [= no. 296]. pp. 328—339, map.* [786

Ferrar, John: The history of Limerick, ecclesiastical, civil and military, from the earliest records to the year 1787. *Limerick: A. Watson & Co. 1787. pp. XVIII, 492, ill., map.* [Palatines brought over by Lord Southwell. p. 409. Palatines, their manners and customs. pp. 411—413.] [787

Hall, Mr. & Mrs. S. C.: Ireland: its scenery, character &c. *A new edition. London: Hall, Virtue and Co. 1841—1843.* [The German Palatines in the vicinity of Adare. Vol. I. pp. 346—349; 353 ff.; 372 ff] Übersetzung in: Bran's Miscellen der ausländischen Literatur 1842. Heft 5, und in: Die Verbreitung des deutschen Volkes über die Erde. Von Wilhelm Stricker. Leipzig 1845. S. 83—85. [788

Hasenkamp, S.: Das Deutschtum in Irland. *In: Festschrift für Carl Uhlig. Oehringen: Verlag der Hohenloheschen Buchhandlung F. Rau. 1932. S. 141—150.* [789

Helfferich, A.: Skizzen und Erzählungen aus Irland. *Berlin: Verlag von Julius Springer 1858. XII, (1), 322 S.* [Über die Pfälzer. S. 77—88.] [790

Kohl, J. K.: Reisen in Irland. *Bd. I. Dresden und Leipzig: Arnoldische Buchhandlung 1843. VIII, 436 S.* [Deutsche Colonisten in Irland. S. 152—154.] [791

Lecky, William Edward Hartpole: A history of Ireland in the 18th century. *5 vols.*

New edition. *London: Longmans, Green & Co. 1892.* [German Palatine colony. Vol. I. p. 183 and pp. 35ᵻ—352.] [792

Matheson, Robert E.: Special report on surnames in Ireland. *Dublin 1909. pp. 29 f.* [793

Schultze Ernst: Irland und Deutschland. *In: Irische Blätter, im Auftrage der Deutsch-Irischen Gesellschaft herausgegeben von Georges Chatterton Hill. Jg. II. Nr. 6. Berlin 1918. S. 559—580.* [16.—18. Jahrhundert. Deutsche als Einwanderer und Soldaten. = Teil II. S. 569—576.] [794

[Wesley, John]: The journal of the Rev. John Wesley, A. M. . . . Edited by Nehemiah Curnock. *Standart edition. 8 vols. London: Charles H. Kelly 1909—1916.* [For the Palatines see especially vol. IV. pp. 168—169; 275—276; 396—397. Reprints of the notes of John Wesley's pertaining to his visits among the Palatines are to be found also in: Geschichte des Methodismus von seinen Anfängen bis zur Gegenwart. Von John L. Nuelsen, Theophilmann und J. J. Sommer. Zweite Auflage Bremen: Verlagshaus der Methodistenkirche, G.m.b.H., 1929. S. 139—141; erneut abgedruckt in: Die Gemeinschaftsbewegung in der Pfalz. Von Johann Jacob Hamm. Eisenberg 1928 (= Nr. 140). S. 309—311.] [795

Young, Arthur: A tour in Ireland with general observations on the present state of that kingdom: made in the years 1776, 1777, and 1778. And brought down to the end of 1779. *2 vols. Second edition. London: Printed by H. Goldney for T. Cadell 1780. pp. 539, (1), ill.; p. 416, ill.* [Colonies of Palatines. Vol. I. p. 468; pp. 480—482.] New edition. Edited by **C. Maxwell.** *Cambridge 1925. pp. 124 ff..; 181 f.; 230, (Note p. 145).* [796

Neues von den Pfälzer Auswanderern des Jahres 1709 in Irland. *In: Pfälzisches Museum. Jg. XLVII. — Pfälzische Heimatkunde. Jg. XXVI. Heft 9/10. Kaiserslautern 1930. S. 219—220.* [797

Die irland-pfälzischen Weiterwanderer

Palatine-Irish-Americans

Starr, Harris Elwood: Heck, Barbara (1734
—1804) mother of Methodism in Ame-
rica. *In: Dictionary of American Coun-
cil of Learned Societies. Vol. VIII.
Edited by Allen Johnson and Dumas
Malone. London-New York 1932.
p. 493.
[Bibliography.]* [797a
Tucker, W. Bowman: The Camden Colony
of the seed of the righteous. A story of
the United Empire Loyalists. *With genea-
logical tables. Montreal, Can.: John
Lovell & Son, Limited 1908. pp. (1).
XVI, 216 (9), ill.* [798
Tucker, W. Bowman: The romance of the
Palatine Millers. A tale of Palatine Irish-
Americans and United Empire Loyalists.
*Second edition of ,,The Camden Colony"
revised and enlarged. Montreal, Que.:
Published by the author; Southam Press
Montreal Limited 1929. pp. (1), (1),
XXXIV, 369, ill.* [799

Die Pfälzer von Block Island

Palatines of Block Island

Davis, Andrew McFarland: The Palatines of
Block Island. *In: The Pennsylvania
Magazine of History and Biography.
Vol. XI. Philadelphia, Pa. 1887.
pp. 243—244. See also Replies: Vol. XI.
1887. p. 248; Queries: Vol. XI. 1887.
pp. 506—507; Replies: Vol. XIX. 1895.
p. 274.* [800
Matthews, Albert: ,,The traditions of the
Palatine Light and of the shipwreck of
a Palatine vessel at Block Island" *see:
The word Palatine in America. Paper
read by Albert Matthews. In: Publications of the Colonial Society of Massa-
chusettes. Vol. VIII. Transactions 1902
—1904. Boston, Mass. 1906. pp. (217)
—224.* [801

Einwanderer-, Eides- und Schiffslisten

Lists of Emigrants and Ship Registers

Brumbaugh, G. M.: Unpublished Revolutionary records of Maryland. List of citizens who took the oath of fidelity and support to the government, March, 1778. *Edited by . . . [,,A List of Persons in Frederick County who have taken the following Oath before the different Magistrates as mentioned below and returned them to Frederick Court.''] In: The National Genealogical Society Quarterly. Vol. VI, no. 2. Washington, D. C. 1917. pp. 33—34.* [802

Egle, William Henry: Names of foreigners who took the Oath of Allegiance to the Province and State of Pennsylvania 1727—1775, with the foreign arrivals, 1786—1808. *Edited by . . . Harrisburg, Pa.: Edwin K. Meyers 1892. p. 787. = Pennsylvania Archives. Second series. Edited by Wm. H. Egle. Vol. XVII. Harrisburg, Pa. 1890.* [803

Faust, Albert Bernhardt: List of Swiss emigrants in the eighteenth century to the American colonies. *Vol. I. Zürich. 1734—1744 from the archives of Switzerland. Washington, D. C.: Published by The National Genealogical Society. 1920. pp. XI, 122, ill.* [804

— and **Brumbaugh, Gajus Marcus:** List of Swiss emigrants in the eighteenth century to the American colonies. *Vol. II.* From the State Archives of Bern and Basel, Switzerland. *Compiled and edited by A. B. Faust and G. M. Brumbaugh. Washington, D. C.: The National Genealogical Society. 1925. pp. IX, 243.* [805

Gerber, Adolf: Beiträge zur Auswanderung nach Amerika im 18. Jahrhundert aus altwürttembergischen Kirchenbüchern. *Stuttgart: J. F. Steinkopf [1928]. 32 S. [Liste der Auswanderer, alphabetisch unter der Stadt aus der sie kamen.]* [806

— Neue Beiträge zur Auswanderung nach Amerika im 18. Jahrhundert aus Altwürttembergischen Kirchenbüchern unter Hinzuziehung anderer Quellen. *Stuttgart: J. F. Steinkopf 1928. 44 S. [Familiennamen der Auswanderer].* [807

Gerber, Adolf: Die Nassau-Dillenburger Auswanderung nach Amerika im 18. Jahrhundert. *Das Verhalten der Regierungen dazu und die späteren Schicksale der Auswanderer. Flensburg: Flensburger Nachrichten, Deutscher Verlag G.m.b.H. 1930. 51 S. ill. [Familiennamen der Auswanderer.]* [808

Hinke, William J.: Early Swiss settlers. *(List of Swiss emigrants to Pennsylvania as found in a pamphlet entitled ,,The description of a journey from Zurich to Rotterdam by Ludwig Weber from Wallisellen, etc.; Zurich, 1735. 8 vo. pp. 32.'') In: Notes and Queries. Edited by W. H. Egle. Annual vol. 1900. Harrisburg, Pa. 1901. pp. 121—122.* [809

— The lists of immigrants entering Pennsylvania from 1727 to 1808. *In: The Pennsylvania-German Society. Proceedings and Addresses at Harrisburg, Pa., October 18, 1929. Vol. XL. Norristown, Pa. 1932. pp. 15—32.* [810

Jordan John W.: A register of members of the Moravian Church who emigrated to Pennsylvania, 1742 to 1767. *In: Notes and Queries. Edited by W. H. Egle. Fourth series, vol. I. 1891—1893. Harrisburg, Pa. 1893. pp. 241—242; 247—248; 249—251; 255—257; 294—296; 400—402. 1747 (1761)—1799. In: Fourth series, vol. II. 1894—1895. Harrisburg, Pa. 1895. pp. 1—3.* [811

Lohr, Otto: Amerikadeutsche Familien des 17. Jahrhunderts: Deutsche Einzeleinwanderer und Familien in Neu-Niederland. — Einwanderer in Pennsylvanien vor 1700. *In: Jahrbuch für auslanddeutsche Sippenkunde. Herausgegeben aus Anlaß der ersten Tagung für auslanddeutsche Sippenkunde 24. und 25. August 1936 vom Deutschen Ausland Institut, Hauptstelle für auslanddeutsche Sippenkunde. Stuttgart: Verlag Karl Weinbrenner & Söhne 1936. S. 44—54.* [811a

MacWethy, Lou D.: The book of names especially relating to the early Palatines and the first settlers in the Mohawk valley. *Compiled and arranged by*

Lou D. MacWethy. Published by the Enterprise and News, St. Johnsville, N.Y. *1933. 209 p.*

[It contains among other (1) The Kocherthal records, pp. 15—50; (2) Palatine heads of families from Hunter's ration lists, pp. 65—72; (3) Four lists of Palatines in London, 1709, pp. 75—110, and other important lists of Germans in New York State.] [811 b

Meynen, Emil: Die deutschen Pioniere Pennsylvaniens. *In: Die Westmark. Monatsschrift für deutsche Kultur. Jg. III. Heft 2. Heidelberg-Saarbrücken 1935. S. 383—386.* [812

Roberts, Charles R.: Germanic immigrants named in early Pennsylvania ship lists. *In: The Pennsylvania-German Society. Proceedings and Addresses . . . at Easton, Pa., October 12, 1928. Vol. XXXIX. Norristown, Pa. 1930. Separate pagination. pp. 5—20.* [813

Rupp, I. Daniel: A collection of thirty thousand names of German, Swiss, Dutch, French, Portuguese and other immigrants in Pennsylvania; chronologically arranged from 1727 to 1776; *the names of ships in which these immigrants were transported, whence they sailed, and their arrival at Philadelphia, to which is prefixed a general introduction containing brief notices of the principal German, Swiss and French settlements in North America, during the colonial era, with an appendix. Harrisburg, Pa.: Theo F. Scheffer 1856. [Originally issued in monthly serials of p. 24.] pp. XXIV, 368. General remarks on the origin of surnames; interpretation of baptismal names which occur in the collection of thirty thousand names of German, Swiss and other immigrants; to which are added other baptismal names, both of males and femals, collected by I. D. Rupp. Harrisburg, Pa.: Theo F. Scheffer 1856. p. 37.* [814

— A collection of upwards of thirty thousand names of German, Swiss, Dutch, French and other immigrants in Pennsylvania from 1727 to 1776, *with a statement of the names of ships, whence they sailed and the date of their arrival in Philadelphia, chronologically arranged, together with the nescessary historical and other notes, also an appendix containing lists of more than thousand German and French names in New York prior to 1712. Second revised and enlarged edition with German translation. Philadelphia, Pa.: Jg. Köhler 1876. pp. X, 495, ill.*

Reprint: Philadelphia, Pa.: Leary. Stuart Co. 1927. pp. X, 495. [815

[Rupp, I. Daniel]: Chronologisch geordnete Sammlung von mehr als 30000 Namen von Einwanderern in Pennsylvania aus Deutschland, der Schweiz, Holland, Frankreich und anderen Staaten von 1727 —1776, *mit Angabe der Namen der Schiffe, des Einschiffungsortes und Datums der Ankunft in Philadelphia nebst geschichtlichen und anderen Bemerkungen . . . (Unveränderter Abdruck des im Verlage von Jg. Köhler in Philadelphia 1880 erschienenen Werkes, vermehrt um ein Personenverzeichnis. [Mit] Namensregister. Angefertigt nach der Ausgabe von 1880 durch Ernst Wecken). Leipzig: Degener & Co. 1931. pp. VIII, 478, 89.*

[Deutscher und Englischer Text.] [816

Simmendinger, Ulrich: Wahrhaffte und glaubwürdige Verzeichnüss, jeniger, durch die Gnade Gottes, annoch im Leben sich befindenden Personen. Welche sich Anno 1709 unter des Herren wunderbarer Führung aus Teutschland in Americam oder Neue Welt begeben, und allda an verschiedenen Orten ihr Stücklein Brods suchen. Allen Liebhabern, insonderheit aber deroselben Familien und nahen Freunden zur freudigen Nachricht gestellet. Von . . ., siebenjährigen Nord-Americanern, in der Provintz Neu-York, anjetzo aber wieder in seiner Vatter-Stadt Reuttlingen. Daselbst gedruckt.

[Reutlingen, Deutsches Reich] bey Joh. G. Füsing [1717 ?]. 22 S. [817

— True and authentic register of persons still living, by God's grace, who in the year 1709, under the wonderful providences of the Lord journeyed from Germany to America or the new world, and there seek their piece of bread at various places. *Reported with joy to all admirers, especially to their families and close friends by Ulrich Simmendinger, a North American, seven years in the province of New York but now returned to his native Reutlingen. Printed there by John G. Fuesing. Translated from the German [= no. 817] by Herman F. Vesper. Reprinted by the Enterprise and News, St. Johnsville, N. Y. 1934. 20 p.* [817a

Strassburger, Ralph Beaver and **Hinke, William John:** Pennsylvania German pioneers. *A publication of the originally lists of arrivals in the Port of Philadelphia from 1727 to 1808. By Ralph*

6

Beaver Strassburger. Edited by *William John Hinke. 3 vols Norristown, Pa.: Pennsylvania German Society 1934. Vol. I: 1727—1775. pp. LV, 776, ill., maps; Vol. II: Facsimiles 1727—1775. pp. XV, (1). 893, ill.; Vol. III: 1785 —1808. Indexes pp. XXIX, 709, ill. = Pennsylvania-German Society Proceedings and Addresses ... Vol. XLII— XLIV.* [818

Westcott, Thompson: Names of persons who took the Oath of Allegiance to the State of Pennsylvania between the years 1777 and 1789. *With a history of the ,,Test Laws" of Pennsylvania. Philadelphia, Pa.: John Campbell 1865. pp. V—XLII, 145.* [819

A partial list of the families who arrived at Philadelphia between 1682 and 1687 with the dates of their arrival. *From the original in the possession of the Historical Society. In: The Pennsylvania Magazine of History and Biography. Vol. VIII. Philadelphia, Pa. 1884. pp. 328 —340.* [820

Lists of Germans from the Palatinate who came to England in 1709. *(Copied from the original documents preserved in the British Museum Library, London, England.) In: The New York Genealogical and Biographical Record. Vol. XL. New York, N. Y. 1909. pp. 49—54; 93—100; 160—167; 241—248; Vol. XLI. New York, N. Y. 1910. pp. 10—19.* [821

Pfälzische Auswanderung nach Amerika, Palatine emigration to North America. *(I) Aus dem Herzogtum Zweibrücken 1724—1749. (Aus dem Staatsarchiv Speier, Abt. Zweibrücken III, 2025). [In Druck.]* [821a

Names of foreigners who took the Oath of Allegiance to the Province and State of Pennsylvania 1727—1775, with the foreign arrivals, 1786—1808. *Edited by* **William H. Egle.** *Harrisburg, Pa.: Edwin K. Meyers 1892. pp. 787. = Pennsylvania Archives. Second series. Edited by Wm. H. Egle. Vol. XVII. Harrisburg, Pa. 1890.* [822

Persons naturalized in the Province of Pennsylvania 1740—1773. *In: Pennsylvania Archives. Second series. Edited by John B. Linn and Wm. H. Egle. Vol. II. Harrisburg, Pa. 1896. pp. 293—415.* [823

Names of persons who took the Oath of Allegiance to the State of Pennsylvania between the years 1776 and 1794. *In: Pennsylvania Archives. Second series.*

Edited by John B. Linn and Wm. H. Egle. Vol. III. Harrisburg, Pa. 1896. pp. 1—86. [824

List of foreigners who arrived at Philadelphia, 1791—1792. *[The lists are additional to those printed in Pennsylvania Archives, Second series, vol. XVII.] Contributed by* Luther R. Kelker. *In: The Pennsylvania Magazine of History and Biography. Vol.XXIV. Philadelphia, Pa. 1900. pp. 187—194; 334—342.* [825

Extract from the naturalization paper of Rev. Joshua Kocherthal. *In: The Pennsylvania Magazine of History and Biography. Vol. XXV. Philadelphia, Pa. 1901. p. 588.* [826

German families: — *(Lists of German families, arrived at Philadelphia, which appears in an advertisement in Henry Miller's Staats Bote of February 9, 1758). Contributed by* **R. G. Swift.** *In: The Pennsylvania Magazine of History and Biography. Vol. XXXIII. Philadelphia, Pa. 1909. pp. 501—502.* [827

A list of German emigrants, 1773. *In: The Pennsylvania Magazine of History and Biography. Vol. XIII. Philadelphia, Pa. 1889. pp. 113—115.* [828

Passenger list of the ,,Pennsylvania Packet", 1773. *In: The Pennsylvania Magazine of History and Biography. Vol. XIII. Philadelphia, Pa. 1889. pp. 485—486.* [829

Passenger list of the ship ,,Elizabeth" which arrived at Philadelphia in 1819. *(Copied from the original in the Library of the Historical Society of Pennsylvania. In: The Pennsylvania Magazine of History and Biography. Vol. XXV. Philadelphia, Pa. 1901. pp. 255—258.* [830

The register of the Port of Philadelphia, 1726—1775. *In: The Pennsylvania Magazine of History and Biography. Vol. XXIII. Philadelphia, Pa. 1899. pp. 254 —264; 370—385; 498—515; Vol. XXIV 1900. pp. 108—115; 212—223; 348— 366; 500—519; Vol. XXV. 1901. pp. 118—131; 266—281; 400—416; 560— 574; Vol. XXVI. 1902. pp. 126—143; 280—284; 390—400; 470—475; Vol. XXVII. 1903. pp. 94—107; 238—247; 346—370; 482—498; Vol. XXVIII. 1904. pp. 84—100; 218—235; 346— 374; 470—507.* [831

Ships registers 1762—1776. *In: Pennsylvania Archives. Second series. Edited by John B. Linn and Wm. H. Egle. Vol. II. Harrisburg 1896. pp. 542—577.* [832

Käuflinge und Hörige

Redemptioners and Indentured Servants

Bushong, Robert G.: Pennsylvania's old apprenticeship-law. *In: The Pennsylvania-German. Vol. VIII. Lebanon, Pa. 1907. pp. 536—538, ill.* [833

Cronau, Rudolf: „Die Käuflinge oder Redemptionisten und das Entstehen der Deutschen Gesellschaften". *In: Drei Jahrhunderte deutschen Lebens in Amerika. Eine Geschichte der Deutschen in den Vereinigten Staaten. Von R. Cronau. Berlin 1909 [= Nr. 34]. S. 116—123; 2. Aufl. 1924. S. 116—123.* [833a

Diffenderffer, Frank Ried: The German immigration into Pennsylvania. *[Part I.]* Through the Port of Philadelphia from 1700 to 1775; *Part II.* The Redemptioners. *Lancaster, Pa. 1900. = Part VII. „A narrative and critical history", prepared at the request of the Pennsylvania-German Society. In: The Pennsylvania-German Society, Proceedings and Addresses . . . 1899. Vol. X. Lancaster, Pa. 1900. Separate pagination pp. IX, 5—138; 141—328, ill.* [834

Geiser, Karl Frederick: Redemptioners and indentured servants in the Colony and Commonwealth of Pennsylvania. *New Haven, Conn.: The Tuttle, Moorehouse & Taylor Co. 1901. pp. (1), (1), 5—125. = Supplement of the Yale Review, vol. X, no. 2. August, 1901.* [835

Harley, Lewis R.: The redemptioners. *In: Historical Sketches. A Collection of Papers prepared for the Historical Society of Montgomery County, Pa. Vol. I. Norristown, Pa. 1895. pp. 209—218.* [836

Herrick, Cheesman A.: White servitude in Pennsylvania indentured and redemption labor in colony and commonwealth. *Philadelphia, Pa.: Published by John Joseph McVey 1926. pp. IX, 330, ill.* [837

Myers, Albert Cook: A runaway redemptioner. *In: The Perkiomen Region, Past and Present. Vol. III. Philadelphia, Pa. 1901. p. 146.* [838

[Redsecker, J. H.]: Indentures ot apprenticeship. *[Copy of the indenture of Bernard Stahl to „John Slotterbeck of the Town of Lebanon.] I · x Notes and Queries. Edited by W. H. Egle. Fourth series vol. I. 1891—1893. Harrisburg, Pa. 1893. pp. 272—273.* [839

Weiser, R.: The new-landers and German redemptioners. *In: The Evangelical Review. Vol. XXI. Gettysburg, Pa. 1870. pp. 290—299.* [840

Vom Deutschen-Handel in N. Amerika. *(I) Aus der XIten Fortsetzung der Nachricht von einigen Evangelischen Gemeinen in Amerika, absonderlich in Pennsylvanien. Halle 1769. S. 997—1000. (II) Aus Hrn. Franklins Aussagen über den gegenwärtigen Zustand der Englischen Kolonien in Nord-Amerika. S. 162 —164. In: August Wilhelm Schlözers Briefwechsel, meist historischen und politischen Inhalts. 1776—1782 [= Nr. 2969]. = Theil I. Heft IV. No. 40. S. 217— 226.* [841

Account of servants and apprentices bound and assigned before James Hamilton, mayor of Philadelphia, 1745." *Contributed by George W. Neible. In: The Pennsylvania Magazine of History and Biography. Vol. XXX. Phildelphia, Pa. 1906. pp. 348—352; 427—436; Vol. XXXI. Philadelphia, Pa. 1907. pp. 83—102; [1746] pp. 195—206; 351 —367; 461—473; Vol. XXXII. 1908. pp. 88—103; 237—249; 351—370.* [842

Record of indentures of individuals bound out as apprentices, servants, etc., and of German and other redemptioners in the office of the mayor of the City of Philadelphia, October 3, 1771 to October 5, 1773. *Copied under the direction of the Publication Committee of the Pennsylvania-German Society from the original volume in possession of the American Philosophical Society held at Philadelphia for Promoting Useful*

Knowledge. Lancaster, Pa.: New Era Printing Co. 1907. In: The Pennsylvania-German Society. Proceedings and Addresses . . . 1905. Vol. XVI. Lancaster, Pa. 1907. pp. (1), 4—325.
[843

Record of servants and apprentices bound and assigned before Hon. John Gibson, mayor of Philadelphia, December 5th, 1772 — May 21, 1773. *In: The Pennsylvania Magazine of History and Biography. Vol. XXXIII. Philadelphia, Pa. 1909. pp. 475—491; Vol. XXXIV. 1910. pp. 99—121; 213—228.*
[844

Palatines — *(Note relating to the passage money of Philip Kaas, sold on the ship „Crawford", at Philadelphia, Pa.,*

Oct. 23, 1773; and for the daughter of Johann Martin Furni, on the ship „Minerva", paid Oct. 10, 1772.) In: The Pennsylvania Magazine of History and Biography. Vol. XXVIII. Philadelphia, Pa. 1904. p. 105.
[845

„125 German redemptioners." *[„on board the Hamburg ship Anna, Capt. John Jurgens"; advertisement of Jacob Sperry & Co.] Cuttings from the „Gazette of the United States", of Friday evening, September 12, 1800. In: The Pennsylvania Magazine of History and Biography. Vol. XXXIX. Philadelphia, Pa. 1915. p. 239.*
[846

Copy of an old indenture. *(1803). In: The Perkiomen Region. Vol. II, no. 1. Pennsburg, Pa. 1923. pp. 2—3.* [847

Kolonialzeitliche Abgaben- und Steuerlisten von Pennsylvanien

Proprietary and other Tax Lists of Provincial Pennsylvania

Pennsylvania Archives. *Third series. Edited by* **William H. Egle**. *Vol. XI. Harrisburg, Pa. 1897.*
Provincial papers: Proprietary tax lists of the County of Chester for the years 1765, 1766, 1767, 1768, 1769, 1771. *Ed. by* **W. H. Egle**. *Harrisburg, Pa.: Wm. Stanley Ray 1897. (map.) p. XIII; 783.*
— *Vol. XII. Harrisburg, Pa. 1897:*
Provincial papers: Proprietary and other tax lists of the County of Chester for the years 1774, 1779, 1780, 1781, 1785. *Ed. by* **W. H. Egle**, *Harrisburg, Pa.: Wm. Stanley Ray 1897. (map.) p. XI; 823.*
— *Vol. XIII. Harrisburg, Pa. 1897:*
Provincial papers: Proprietary and other tax lists of Bucks for the years 1779, 1781, 1782, 1783, 1784, 1785, 1786. *Ed. by* **W. H. Egle**. *Harrisburg, Pa.: Wm. Stanley Ray 1897. p. XIII; 820.*
— *Vol. XIV. Harrisburg, Pa. 1897:*
Provincial papers: Proprietary, supply, and state tax lists of the City and County of Philadelphia for the years 1769, 1774 and 1779. *Ed. by* **W. H. Egle**. *Harrisburg, Pa.: Wm. Stanley Ray 1897. p. VIII; 838.*
— *Vol. XV. Harrisburg, Pa. 1897:*
Provincial papers: Supply, and state tax lists of the City and County of Philadelphia for the years 1779, 1780 and 1781. *Ed. by* **W. H. Egle**. *Harrisburg, Pa.: Wm. Stanley Ray 1897. pp. VI; 789.*
— *Vol. XVI. Harrisburg, Pa. 1897:*
Provincial papers: Supply, and state tax lists of the City and County of Philadelphia for the years 1781, 1782 and 1783. *Ed. by* **W. H. Egle**. *Harrisburg, Pa.: Wm. Stanley Ray 1898. p. VI; 837.*
— *Vol. XVII. Harrisburg, Pa. 1897:*
Provincial papers: Proprietary and state tax lists of the County of Lancaster, for the years 1771, 1772, 1773, 1779 and 1782. *Ed. by* **W. H. Egle**. *Harrisburg.*

Pa.: Wm. Stanley Ray 1898. p. VIII; 896.
Pennsylvania Archives. *Vol. XVIII. Harrisburg, Pa. 1897:*
Provincial papers: Proprietary and state tax lists of the County of Berks for the years 1767, 1768, 1779, 1780, 1781, 1784, 1785. *Ed. by* **W. H. Egle**. *Harrisburg, Pa.: Wm. Stanley Ray 1898. p. XI; 814.*
— *Vol. XIX. Harrisburg, Pa. 1897:*
Provincial papers: Proprietary, supply, and state tax lists of the Counties of Northampton and Northumberland, for the years 1772 to 1787. *Ed. by* **W. H. Egle**. *Harrisburg, Pa.: Wm. Stanley Ray 1898. p. XII; 805.*
— *Vol. XX. Harrisburg, Pa. 1897:*
Provincial papers: State and supply transcripts of the County of Cumberland for the years 1778, 1779, 1780, 1781, 1782 and 1785. *Ed. by* **W. H. Egle**. *Harrisburg, Pa.: Wm. Stanley Ray 1898. p. IX; 781.*
— *Vol. XXI. Harrisburg, Pa. 1897:*
Provincial papers: Returns of taxables of the County of York, for the years 1779 1780, 1781, 1782 and 1783. *Ed. by* **W. H. Egle**. *Harrisburg, Pa.: Wm. Stanley Ray 1898. p. VIII; 820.*
— *Vol. XXII. Harrisburg, Pa. 1897:*
Provincial papers: Returns of taxables for the Counties of Bedford (1773 to 1784), Huntingdon (1788), Westmoreland (1783, 1786), Fayette (1785, 1786), Allegheny (1791), Washington (1786) and Census of Bedford (1784) and Westmoreland (1783). *Ed. by* **W. H. Egle**. *Harrisburg, Pa. 1898. p. XI; 782.*
— *Vol. XXVII—XXX. Harrisburg, Pa. 18 ..*
General index to volumes *XI—XXVI. Ed. by* **Geo Edward Reed**.
A—Cost. = Vol. XXVII; Co—Jo. = Vol. XXVIII; K—Ref. = Vol. XXIX; Ref.—Zy. = Vol. XXX. pp. 333—790.

[848

Die Volkszählung von 1790

Census 1790

United States, Department of Commerce and Labor, Bureau of the Census: Heads of families at the first census of the United States taken in the year 1790. Pennsylvania *Washington, D. C. Government Printing Office 1908. pp. 426, map.* [849

— Heads of families at the first census of the United States taken in the year 1790. Maryland. *Washington, D. C.: Government Printing Office 1907. pp. 189, map.* [850

— Heads of families at the first census of the United States taken in the year 1790. Records of the state enumerations: 1782 to 1865. Virginia. *Washington, D. C.: Government Printing Office 1908. pp. 189, map.* [851

— Heads of families at the first census of the United States taken in the year 1790. North Carolina. *Washington, D. C.: Government Printing Office 1908. pp. 292, map.* [852

— Heads of families at the first census of the United States taken in the year 1790. South Carolina. *Washington, D. C.: Government Printing Office 1908. pp. 150, map.* [853

— Heads of families at the first census of the United States taken in the year 1790. New York. *Washington, D. C.: Government Printing Office 1908. pp. 308, map.* [854

United States, Department of Commerce and Labor, Bureau of the Census: Heads of families at the first census of the United States taken in the year 1790. Maine. *Washington, D. C.: Government Printing Office 1908. pp. 105.* [855

American Council of Learned Societies: Report of committee on linguistic and national stocks in the population of the United States. *In: Annual Report of the American Historical Association for the year 1931. Vol. I. — Proceedings. Washington, D. C.: United States Government Printing Office 1932 pp. 103—452.*

Report . . . *pp. 107—125 (,,Proportion of German Descent" pp. 118—119); Annex A.:* National stocks in the population of the United States as indicated by surnames in the census of 1790. *By* Howard F. Barker. *pp. 126—359 (Chapter VII. ,,German contributions to 1790 America". pp. 271—305; ,,Bibliography". pp. 325—359); Annex B:* The minor stocks in the American population of 1790. *By* Marcus L. Hansen *pp. 360—397.* [855a

Kirchengruppen und religiöses Leben
Denominations and Religious Life

Baird, Robert: Religion in the United States of America. Or an account of the origin, progress, relations to the state, and present condition of the Evangelical churches in the United States with notices of the unevangelical denominations. *Glasgow and Edinburgh: Blackie and Son 1844. pp. XIX, 736, maps; edited New York, N. Y.: Harper & Brothers 1856. pp. XVII, 19—696.* [856

Belcher, Joseph: The religious denominations in the United States: their history, doctrine, government and statistics. *With a preliminary sketch of Judaism, Paganism and Mohammedanism. Philadelphia, Pa.: J. E. Potter 1854. pp. XII, 13—1024, ill.* [857

Bittinger, Lucy Forney: German religious life in colonial times. *Philadelphia and London: J. B. Lippincott Company 1906. pp. (1), 11—145.* [858

— The Pennsylvania German as churchman. *In: The Pennsylvania-German. Vol. VII. Lebanon, Pa. 1906. pp. 186—188, ill.* [859

— Johann Arndt and his ,,True Christianity." *In: The Pennsylvania-German. Vol. X. Lititz, Pa. 1909. pp. 249—261.* [860

Carroll, H. K.: The religious forces of the United States enumerated, classified, and described on the basis of the Government Census of 1890. *With an introduction on the condition and character of American Christianity. New York, N.Y.: The Christian Literature Co. 1893. pp. LXVII, 478. = The American church history series Vol. I.* [861

— *Revised edition and brought down to 1910. Returns for 1900 and 1910 compared with the Government Census of 1890. New York, N. Y.: Charles Scribner's Sons 1912. pp. LXXXVIII, 488.* [861 a

Conzett, Jacob und **Launitz, Johann:** Rundschau auf dem Gebiete der deutschen Evangelischen Kirche in Nord-Amerika ..., *Herausgegeben von Jakob Conzett und Johann Launitz. unter Mitwir-*

kung mehrerer angesehener Prediger der verschiedenen ev. Benennungen dieses Landes. Pittsburgh, Pa. Verlag von Ernst Luft, No. 135. Smithfield Straße. [1877] 270 S. [861 b

Dubbs, Joseph Henry: The founding of the German churches of Pennsylvania. *An address delivered before the Historical Society of Pennsylvania, April 17, 1893. In: The Pennsylvania Magazine of History and Biography. Vol. XVII. Philadelphia, Pa. 1893. pp. 241—262.* [862

— German church life in Pennsylvania. *In: The Pennsylvania-German. Vol. VII. Lebanon, Pa. 1906. pp. 188—191, ill.;* [863

Falckner, Justus: The missive of Justus Falckner of Germantown, concerning the religious condition of Pennsylvania in the year 1701. — ,,*Imprint of a missive to Tit: Lord D. Henr. Muhlen, from Germantown in the American Province of Pennsylvania, otherwise New Sweden, the first of August, in the year of our salvation one thousand, seven hundred and one concerning the condition of the churches in America 1702.*" — *Translated by* **Julius Sachse.** *In: The Pennsylvania Magazine of History and Biography. Vol. XXI. Philadelphia, Pa. 1897. pp. 216—224.* [864

Faris, John T.: Old churches and meeting houses in and around Philadelphia. *Philadelphia, Pa. and London: J. B. Lippincott Co. 1926. pp. XVI, 261, ill. [Three old churches in Germantown. pp. 35—38; How the Moravians came to have a church in Philadelphia. pp. 112—118; The brilliant career of St. Michael's and Zion Lutheran Churches. pp. 137—144; Ten Evangelical Lutheran churches. pp. 158—163; Trappe, the oldest Lutheran Church in America. pp. 168—170; Intimate glimpses of Germantown meeting. pp. 178—184; In Germantown and Frankford. pp. 193—196.]* [865

Fry, Harold Curtis: Union churches in Lancaster, County, Pa. *Thesis of Master of Sacred Theology. Lutheran Theological*

Seminary, Gettysburg, Pa. 1930. Type-written. pp. 278, (5). [866

Gohdes, C. B.: Puritan or Palatine. *In: The Lutheran Quarterly. Vol. XLVII. Gettysburg, Pa. 1917. pp. 241—259.* [867

Good, James Isaac: Early attempts at church union in America. *Paper read Dec. 29, 1908. In: Papers of the American Society of Church History. Second series, vol. II. New York, N. Y. 1910. pp. 105—114.* [868

Graeff, I. E.: The tendency to individualism in the German churches in America. *In: The Mercersburg Review. Vol. XX. Philadelphia, Pa. 1873. pp. 302—316.* [869

Hennighausen, L. P.: Die ersten deutschen Sekten in Amerika. *In: Fifth Annual Report of the Society for the History of the Germans in Maryland Baltimore, Md. 1891. pp. 75—88. Sixth . . . 1892. pp. 29—39.* [870

Hiester, Anselm V.: Religious liberty in Pennsylvania and the other American colonies. *In: The Reformed Church Review. Fourth series, vol. IX. Philadelphia, Pa. 1905. pp. 81—96.* [871

Hinke, William, J.: Diaries of missionary travels among the German settlers in the American colonies 1743—1748. *Read before the Pennsylvania-German Society at Bethlehem, Oct. 5, 1923. In: The Pennsylvania-German Society. Proceedings and Addresses. Vol. XXXIV. . . . Pa. 1929. pp. 69—82. ill.* [872

Hocker, Edward W.: The lottery as a religious institution. *In: Historical Sketches. A collection of papers prepared for the Historical Society of Montgomery Co., Pa. Vol. VI. Norristown, Pa. 1929. pp. 280—285.* [873

Hoskins, John Preston: German influence on religious life and thought in America during the colonial period. *In: The Princeton Theological Review Vol. V. Princeton, N. J.: Published quarterly for the Princeton Theological Review Association by the Princeton University Press 1907. pp. 48—79; 210—241.* [874

— German influence on religious life and thought in America. *In: The Lutheran Church Review. Vol. XXVI. Philadelphia, Pa. 1907. pp. 276—284.*

[See: Prof. Hoskins on the Lutheran Church and the Reformation. In: The Lutheran Quarterly. Vol. XXXVII. Gettysburg, Pa. 1907. pp. 572—591.] [875

Kloß, Heinz: Zur Entwicklung des Protestantismus im Überseedeutschtum. *In Mitteilungen der Akademie zur wissenschaftlichen Erforschung und zur Pflege des Deutschtums — Deutsche Akademie. Jg. 1930. No. 4. München 1930. S. 173 —214.* [876

Kriebel, H. W.: The Pennsylvania-German as champion of religious liberty. *In: The Pennsylvania-German. Vol. VII. Lebanon, Pa. 1906. pp. 191—193.* [877

L., J. B.: Dr. Doddridge's tribute to the Penna Germans. *In: The Pennsylvania-German. Vol. XII. Lititz, Pa. 1911. pp. 306—307.* [878

Maxson, Charles Hartshorn: The great awakening in the middle colonies. *Chicago, Ill.: The University Press 1920. pp. VII, 158.*

[Introduction, and Pietism in Pennsylvania. pp. 1—10.] [879

Mode, Peter G.: The frontier spirit in American Christianity. *New York, N. Y.: The Macmillan Co. 1923. pp. X, 196.* [880

Mühlenberg, Henry Melchior: Alte Kirchengeschichte in Pennsylvanien. Etwas vom Kirchenbau im Jahre 1743. *[Auszug aus: ,,Halle'sche Nachrichten."] In: Der Deutsche Pionier. Jg. V. Cincinnati, O. 1873—1874. S. 209—210.* [881

Müller, Wilhelm: Der deutsche Protestantismus in Amerika. *In: Deutsch-Amerikanische Geschichtsblätter. Jg. IX. No. 3. Chicago, Ill. 1909. S. 65—80.* [882

N.[evin,] J. W.: The sect system. *[Review of:] History of all the religious denominations in the United States: containing authentic accounts of the rise, progress, faith and practice, localities and statistics, of the different persuasions: written expressly for the work, by fifty-three eminent authors belonging to the respective denominations. Second improved and portrait edition of Rupp's work, published by John Winebrenner. Harrisburg, Pa. 1848 [= no. 886]. In: The Mercersburg Review. Vol. I. Mercersburg, Pa. 1849. pp. 482—507; 521—539.* [883

Pennypacker, Isaac R.: The Quaker origins. *In: American Speech. Vol. II. no. 9. 1927. pp. 395—402.* [884

[Rupp, I. Daniel]: He Pasa Ekklesia. An original history of the religious denominations at present existing in the United States. Containing authentic accounts of their rise, progress, statistics and doctrines. *Written expressly for the work by eminent theological professors, ministers, and lay-members of the respective denominations. Projected, compiled and arranged by I. D. Rupp. Philadelphia, Pa.: Published by J. Y. Humphreys. Harrisburg, Pa: Clyde and Williams 1844. pp. VIII, 734.* [Second edition, see no. 886] [885

[—] History of all the religious denominations in the United States: containig authentic accounts of the rise and progress, faith and practice, localities and statistics, of the different persuasions: *written expressly for the work, by fifty-three eminent authors, belonging to the respective denominations. Second, improved and portrait edition. Harrisburg, Pa.: Published by John Winebrenner. Philadelphia, Pa. Stereotyped by R. P. Mogridge 1848—1849. pp. 598.* [886

[—] The religious denominations in the United States: their past history, present condition and doctrines, *accurately set forth in fifty carefully-prepared articles, written by eminent clerical and lay-authors connected with the respective persuasions, together with complete and well-digested statistics, to which is added, a historically summary of religious denominations in England and Scottland. Philadelphia, Pa.: Charles Desilver 1859. pp. 621; 208, ill.* [887

Schaff, Philipp: Geschichte der deutschen Kirche in Amerika. *In: Deutscher Kirchenfreund, Vol. II, 1849 S. 1—21; 129—148; 161—186.* [887a

— Amerika. Die politischen, socialen und kirchlich-religiösen Zustände der Vereinigten Staaten von Nordamerika mit besonderer Rücksicht auf die Deutschen, *aus eigener Anschauung dargestellt. . . . Berlin: Wiegandt und Grieben 1854. XXI, (2), 278 S. Zweite Auflage: Berlin 1858. XXIV, 366S.* [,,Die deutschen Kirchen in Amerika." = Teil III. S. 165—278.] [888

— America. A. sketch of the political, social and religious character of the United States of North America. *In 2 lectures. Delivered at Berlin with a report read before the German Church Diet at Frankfort on-the-Main. Sept. 1854. Translated from the German. New York, N. Y.: C. Scribner 1855. pp. XXIV, 25—291.* [889

Schneder, Charles B.: The Pennsylvania German clergy during the Revolutionary period. *Read before the Pennsylvania-German Society at Sesqui-Centennial Exposition at Philadelphia, Pa., October 8, 1926. In: The Pennsylvania-German Society. Proceedings and Addresses at Philadelphia, Pa., Oct. 8, 1926. Vol. XXXVII. Norristown, Pa. 1930. pp. 17—21.* [890

Stille, Charles J.: Religious tests in Provincial Pennsylvania. *Paper read Nov. 9, 1885. In: The Pennsylvania Magazine of History and Biography. Vol. IX. Philadelphia, Pa. 1885. pp. 365—406.* [891

Sweet, William Warren: The story of religions in America. *New York, N. Y. and London: Harper & Brothers. 1930 pp. VII, 571, ill.* [Religious diversity in the middle colonies: German sectaries. = Chapter VII. pp. 150—171. Bibliography. pp. 524—542.] [892

Thompson, Charles Lemuel: The religious foundations of America. *A study in national origins. New York, N. Y.: Fleming H. Revell Co. 1917. pp. 7—307.* [893

United States Department of Commerce, Bureau of the Census: Special reports. Religious bodies: 1906. *Part I.* Summary and general tables. *Part II.* Separate denominations: History, description and statistics, *2 vols. Washington, D. C.: Government Printing Office. 1910. pp. 576; 670.* [894

— Religious bodies: 1916. *Part I. and II. 2 vols. Washington, D. C. 1919. pp. 594; 727.* [894a

— Religious bodies: 1926. *2 vols. Washington, D. C. 1929—1930. Vol. I.* Summary and detailed tables. *1930. pp. VI, 769; Vol. II.* Separate denominations. Statistics, history, doctrine, organization, and work. *1929. pp. XIII, 1405.* [894b

Gestalt des Reichs Gottes unter den Deutschen in Amerika. *In: Evangelisches Magazin, unter der Aufsicht der Deutschen Evangelisch-Lutherischen Synode. Bd. III. Philadelphia, Pa. 1814. S. 22—24; 65—70; 129—138.* [895

Penn and religious liberty. *Interpreted by representatives of sixteen denominations. Founder's Week. Philadelphia, Pa., Oct. 6, 1908. Philadelphia, Pa.: Keterlinus [1908 ?] pp. 81.* [896

Deutsche Pietisten der frühen Einwanderung nach Pennsylvanien
The German Pietists of Early Pennsylvania

Cassel, Abraham H.: John Kelpius, the hermit of the Wissahickon. *[n. p. 1897.] Typewritten pp. 19.*
[Library of the University of Pennsylvania, Philadelphia, Pa.] [897

Cronau, Rudolf: „Die Labadisten und Rosenkreuzer". *In: Drei Jahrhunderte deutschen Lebens in Amerika. Eine Geschichte der Deutschen in den Vereinigten Staaten. Von R. Cronau. Berlin 1909 [= Nr. 34]. S. 70—74, ill.; 2. Aufl. 1924. S. 70—74, ill.* [897 a

Genzmer, George Harvey: Kelpius, Johann (1673—1708) mystic. *In: Dictionary of American biography. Under the auspices of the American Council of Learned Societies. Vol. X. Edited by Dumas Malone. London-New York 1933. pp. 312—313.*
[born near Schässburg in Transsylvania (Siebenbürgen) probably at Halwegen, son of Georg Kelp. [897 b

Klein, K. K.: Magister Johannes Kelpius Transsylvanus, der Heilige und Dichter vom Wissahickon in Pennsylvanien. *In: Festschrift Seiner Hochwürden D. Dr. Friedrich Teutsch gewidmet zu seinem 25jährigen Bischofs-Jubiläum vom Ausschuß des Vereins für Siebenbürgische Landeskunde. Hermannstadt: Honterus-Buchdr. und Verlagsanstalt d. ev. Landeskunde 1931. S. 57—77.* 897 c

Rupp, I. D.: Defunct German sects in Pennsylvania. *In: Notes and Queries. Edited by W. H. Egle. Annual vol. 1896. Harrisburg, Pa. 1897. pp. 166—170; 172—174; 177—179.* [898

Sachse, Julius Friedrich: The German pietists of Provincial Pennsylvania 1694—1708. *Philadelphia, Pa.: Printed for the author by P. C. Stockhausen 1895. pp. XVIII, 504, ill., 2 maps.* [899

Seidensticker, Oswald: Johannes Kelpius, der Einsiedler am Wissahickon. *In: Der Deutsche Pionier. Jg. II. Cincinnati, O. 1870—1871. S. 35—42; 67—75, ill.* [900

— The hermits of the Wissahickon. *In: The Pennsylvania Magazine of History and Biography. Vol. XI. Philadelphia, Pa. 1887. pp. 427—441.* [901

Stamp, v.: Die Protestanten Klöster der Siebentäger in Pennsylvanien. *In: Third Annual Report of the Society for the History of the Germans in Maryland. Baltimore, Md. 1889. pp. 27—41.* [902

[Kelpius, Johannes]: The diarium of Magister Johannes Kelpius, *with annotations by Julius Friedrich Sachse. Lancaster, Pa.: The New Era Printing Co. 1917. = Part XXVII. „A narrative and critical history", prepared by authority of the Pennsylvania-German Society. In: The Pennsylvania-German Society. Proceedings and Addresses . . . 1914. Vol. XXV. Lancaster, Pa. 1917. Separate pagination. pp. 100, ill.* [903

[Kelpius, John]: Extract of a letter from John Kelpius to Esther Palmer. *Philadelphia, Pa.: Printed for C. C. C. by Paul C. Stockhausen 1886. pp. 16.* [904

Weiss, George Michael: Der in der Amerikanischen Wildnuß Unter Menschen von verschiedenen Nationen und Religionen Hin und wieder herum Wandelte und verschiedentlich Angefochtene Prediger, Abgemacht und vorgestellt In einem Gespraech mit Einem Politico und Neugeborenem, Verschiedene Stuck insonderheit Die Neugeburt betreffende, *Verfertiget, und zur Beforderung der Ehre Jesu Selbst aus eigener Erfahrung an das Licht gebracht von Georg Michael Weiss, V. D. M. Philadelphia, Pa.: Andrew Bradfordt 1729. S. 34.*
[Printed in the original German and in an English translation, made by **William Edwin Weisgerber,** *edited by* M. A. Gruber, *in: The PennGermania. Vol. I. Cleona, Pa. 1912. pp. 338—360.]* [905

— The Newborn. *[An obsolete sect, known as „Die Neugeborene," that appears to have been in existence in Pennsylvania, especially in Oley, Berks County, from 1718—1769.](A copy of a certain tract, or pamphlet, of 34 pages, written by George Michael Weiss, V. D. M., and printed at Philadelphia, Pa. in 1729, by Andrew Bradfordt [= no. 905]; and copy of a sketch of the sect and its founder, from a translation by* **J. Max Hark,** *published in 1889, at Lancaster, by S. H. Zahm & Co., of Chronicon Ephratense [= no. 1150].) Introductory note by* **M. A. Gruber.** *In: The Penn Germania. Vol. I. = Old series, vol. XIII. Lititz, Pa. 1912. pp. 336—364.* [906

Mennoniten

Mennonites

Alt-Mennoniten: Mennoniten-Kirche
Old-Mennonites: Mennonite Church

United States, Department of Commerce, Bureau of Census: Mennonite bodies. History, descriptions and statistics. *In:* *Religious bodies: Part II. Separate denominations. Washington, D. C. 1910* [= no. 894]. *pp. 404—428.*
— *In: Religious bodies: 1916. Part II. Washington, D. C. 1919. pp. 416—445.*
— *In: Religious bodies: 1926. Part II. Washington, D. C. 1929. pp. 842—913.* [907
— Mennonite Church. History, descriptions and statistics. *In: Religious bodies: Part II. Separate denominations. Washington, D. C. 1910* [= no. 894]. *pp. 407—410.*
— *In: Religious bodies: 1916. Part II. Washington, D. C. 1919. pp. 419—422.*
— Statistics. History, doctrine and organization. *In: Religious bodies: 1926. Part II. Washington, D. C. 1929. pp. 848—854.* [908
Bender, Harold S.: Two centuries of American Mennonite literature. A bibliography of Mennonitica Americana. *In: The Mennonite Quarterly Review. Vol. I. Goshen, Ind. 1927. No. 1. pp. 34—53; No. 2. pp. 46—72; No. 4. pp. 61—79; Vol. II. 1928. No. 1. pp. 16—55; No. 2. pp. 124—150; No. 3. pp. 206—224.*
Revised reprint. . . . 1727—1928. Goshen, Ind.: Goshen Printery 1929. pp. XII, (2), 181, ill.
= Studies in Anabaptist and Mennonite History . . . Published by the Mennonite Historical Society. Goshen College, Goshen, Ind., No. 1. [909
— Was William Rittenhouse the first bishop in America? *In: The Mennonite Quarterly Review. Vol. VII. Goshen, Ind. — Scottdale, Pa. 1933. pp. 42—47.* [910
— William Rittenhouse, 1644—1708: First Mennonite minister in America. *In:*

The Mennonite Quaterly Review. Vol. VIII. Goshen, Ind. -Scottdale, Pa. 1934. pp. 58—61. [911
Bender, Wilbur J.: Pacificism among the Mennonites, Amish Mennonites and Schwenkfelders of Pennsylvania to 1783. *[Abstract of thesis submitted in candidacy for honors at Harvard College, 1927.] In: The Mennonite Quarterly Review. Vol. I, no. 3. Goshen, Ind. July, 1227. pp. 23—40; No. 4. October, 1927. pp. 21—48.* [912
Brons, A.: Ursprung, Entwicklung und Schicksale der Taufgesinnten oder Mennoniten in kurzen Zügen übersichtlich dargestellt. *Norden: Diedr. Soltau. 1884. XX, 447 S.; Zweite Auflage 1891. 447 S. Dritte Auflage 1912.*
[Die Anfänge der Mennoniten Gemeinden in Amerika. Nachtrag zur Geschichte der Pfälzer Gemeinden. = Teil V. S. 220—241.] [913
Cassel, Daniel K.: History of the Mennonites. Historically and biographically arranged from the time of the Reformation; more particularly from the time of their emigration to America. *Containing sketches of the oldest meeting houses and prominent ministers. Also their confession of faith, adopted at Dortrecht, in 1632. Philadelphia, Pa.: Daniel K. Cassel 1888. pp. VIII, 450, ill.* [914
[—] Geschichte der Mennoniten. Von Menno Simon's Austritt aus der Römisch-Katholischen Kirche in 1536 bis zu deren Auswanderung nach Amerika in 1683. Mehr speciell ihre Ansiedlung und Ausbreitung in Amerika. *Enthaltend: Kurze Skizzen der einzelnen Gemeinden mit dem Namen ihrer Prediger vom Jahre 1683 bis zur gegenwärtigen Zeit. Zusammengetragen und geordnet von Daniel K. Cassel. Philadelphia, Pa.: J. Kohler 1890. XV, 545 S., ill.* [915
Conyngham, Redmond: History of the Mennonites and Aymenists or Amish. *In: Hazard's Register of Pennsylvania. Vol.*

VII. Philadelphia, Pa. 1831. pp. 128—
132; 150—153.   [916
Eby, Benjamin: Kurzgefaßte Kirchengeschichte und Glaubenslehre der Tauf-
gesinnten-Christen oder Mennoniten.
Verfaßt und herausgegeben von . . .
Berlin, Can.: Heinrich Eby 1841. VII,
9—240 S.
Neudruck: Lancaster, Pa.: Johann Bär
1853. 238 S.; Elkhart, Ind.: John F.
Funk 1868. 177 S.; Elkhart, Ind.:
Druck von der Mennonitischen Verlags-
buchhandlung 1879. 211 S.; . . . 1901.
IV, 5—228 S.; Kitchener, Ont. 1919.
[917

Edwards, Morgan: Materials towards a
history of the Baptists in Pennsylvania
both British and German, distinguished
into Firstday Baptists Keithian Baptists, Seventh-day Baptists, Tunker
Baptists, Mennonist Baptists. *Philadel-*
phia, Pa.: Joseph Crukshank and
Isaac Collins 1770. pp. (1), IV, 5—134.
= Vol. I. Materials towards a history of
the American Baptists.
[,,Treats of the Mennonist Baptists
in Pennsylvania." = Part V. pp. 90
—98.]   [918
Eshelman, Cyrus H.: The ordination: a
story of the Mennonites. *In: The Penn*
Germania. Vol. I. = Old series, vol.
XIII. Lititz, Pa. 1912. pp. 245—453.
[919
Eshleman, H. Frank: Historic background
and annals of the Swiss and German
pioneer settlers of South Eastern Pennsylvania, and of their remote ancestors,
from the middle of the dark ages, down
to the time of the Revolutionary War.
An authentic history, from original
sources, of their suffering during several
centuries before and especially during
the two centuries following the Protestant
Reformation, and of their slow migration,
moved by those causes, during the last
mentioned two·hundred years, westward
in quest of religious freedom and their
happy relief in the Susquehanna and
Schuylkill Valleys in the New World;
with particular reference to the German-
Swiss Mennonites or Anabaptists, the
Amish and other non-resistance sects.
Lancaster, Pa. 1917. pp. (2), 386.
[919a
Funk, John F.: The Mennonite Church and
her accusers. *A vindication of the cha-*
racter of the Mennonite Church of Ame-
rica from her first organization in this

country to the present time. Elkhart
Ind.: Mennonite Publishing Co. 1878.
pp. 210.   [920
Gibbons, Phebe Earle: *[See no. 312]*
Gottschall, W. S.: Mennonite history.
(Household edition). Bluffton, O.: News
Print 1921. pp. 84.   [922
Hartzler, J. S. and **Kauffman, Daniel:** Men-
nonite church history. *Scottdale, Pa.:*
Published by Mennonite Book and Tract
Society 1905. pp. 422.   [923
Hartzler, Jonas S.: Mennonites in the World
War or Nonresistance under test. *By . . .*
assisted by a committee appointed by
Mennonite General Conference. Scottdale,
Pa.: Mennonite Publishing House 1921.
pp. 246.   [924
— Nonresistance in practice. *Written at the*
request of the Peace Problems Committee.
Scottdale, Pa.: Mennonite Publishing
House 1930. pp. 5—47.   [925
Hartzler, John Ellsworth: Education among
the Mennonites of America with intro-
duction *by Elmer E. S. Johnson. Dan-*
vers, Ill.: The Central Mennonite Pu-
blishing Board 1925. pp. 195.
[Bibliography. pp. 189—195.]   [926
Heatwole, L. J.: Mennonite handbook of
information. *Issued by authority of the*
Mennonite General Conference through
its Historical Committee. Scottdale, Pa.:
Published by Mennonite Publishing
House 1925. pp. 187, ill.   [927
Hege, Christine: Kurze Geschichte der Mennoniten. *Frankfurt am Main: Herman*
Minjou 1909. VIII, 126 S.   [928
Hege, Christian und **Neff, Christian:** Menno-
nitisches Lexikon. *Herausgegeben von*
. . . Frankfurt am Main und Weierhof
(Pfalz): Im Selbstverlag der Heraus-
geber. Bd. I. 1913/14. (2), 717, (2) S.,
ill.; Bd. II, im Erscheinen ff.   [929
Hertzler, Silas: Early Mennonite Sunday
schools. *In: The Mennonite Quarterly*
Review. Vol. II. Goshen, Ind. 1928.
pp. 123—124; 205—206.   [930
— Attendence in Mennonite schools and
colleges, 1928. *In: The Mennonite*
Quarterly Review. Vol. III. Goshen, Ind.
1929. pp. 197—202; . . ., 1929—1930. In:
Vol. IV. 1930. pp. 166—177; . . ., 1930
—1931. In: Vol. V. 1931. pp. 272—283;
. . ., in 1932—1933. In: Vol. VII. 1933.
pp. 251—260; . . ., in 1933—1934. In:
Vol. VIII. 1934. pp. 180—191.   [931
Hoop Scheffer, J. G. de: Vriendschaps-
betrekkingen tusschen de Doopsgezinden
hier te lande en die in Pensylvanie. *In:*

Doopsgezinde Bijdragen. Uitgeven onder redactie van D. Harting en P. Cool. New series, Vol. III Leeuwarden: H. Kuipers. 1869. pp. 1—26. [932

[Hoop Scheffer, J. G. de]: Mennonite emigration to Pennsylvania. Friendly relations between the Mennonites in Holland and those in Pennsylvania. *Translation of an article of J. G. Hoop Scheffer, of Amsterdam, ,,Vriendschapsbetrekkingen tusschen de Doopsgezinden hier te land en die in Pensylvanie", appeared in the ,,Doopsgezinde Bijdragen" for 1869. Translated from the Dutch, with notes, by* Samuel W. Pennypacker. *In: The Pennsylvania Magazine of History and Biography. Vol. II. Philadelphia, Pa. 1878. pp. 117—138. Reprint in: S. W. Pennypacker: Historical and biographical sketches. Philadelphia, Pa. 1883 [= no. 356]. pp. 177—199.* [933

Hoover, Jonas Wagner: Social attitudes among the Mennonites. *Thesis of M. A., University of Chicago, Ill. 1915. Typewritten. pp. III, 82, III.* [934

Horsch, Johannes: Kurzgefaßte Geschichte der Mennoniten-Gemeinden. *Nebst einem Abriß der Grundsaetze und Lehren sowie einem Verzeichnis der Literatur der Taufgesinnten. Elkhart, Ind.: Mennonite Publishing Co. 1890. (1), (1), 146 S. [Bibliographie. S. 107—146.]* [935

Horsch, John: The Mennonites, their history faith and practice. *Elkhart, Ind.: Mennonite Publishing Co. 1893. pp. 40.* [936

— Wordly conformity in dress. *Scottdale, Pa.: Mennonite Publishing House 1925. pp. 48. Second edition 1926. pp. 48.* [937

Kauffman, Daniel: Mennonite history. *Including a brief sketch of the church from the time of Christ. Scottdale, Pa.: Mennonite Publishing House 1927. pp. 147.* [938

Kaufman, Edmund George: The development of the missionary and philanthropic interest among the Mennonites of North America. *With introduction by Archibald Gillies Baker. Berne, Ind.: The Mennonite Book Concerne 1931. pp. VII—XIX, 416, ill., maps.* [939

Krehbiel, H. P.: Mennonite churches of North-America; a statistical compilation collected and arranged under the auspices of the Mennonite General Conference of North America. *Berne, Ind.: The Mennonite Book Concern. Newton,* *Kan.: Herold Book & Publishing Co. [1911.] pp. 92.* [940

Krehbiel, H. P.: Mennonites of America. *A paper prepared for and read at the Bible Course at Bethel College, Jan., 1925. Newton, Kan.: Herold Publishing Co. 1926. pp. 21.* [941

[Krehbiel, Jacob]: A few words about the Mennonites in America in 1841: A contemporary document by Jacob Krehbiel. *Translated and edited by* Harold S. Bender. *In: The Mennonite Quarterly Review. Vol. VI. Scottdale, Pa. — Goshen, Ind. 1932, pp. 43—57.* [942

Langenwalter, J. H.: The immigration of Mennonites into North America. *Newton, Kan: Bethel College Library, Publishers. 1914. pp. 100.* [943

Lutz, John J.: Boehm's chapel and the Pennsylvania Mennonites. An unfamiliar chapter in early Methodist history. *In: The Pennsylvania-German. Vol. XI. Lititz, Pa. 1910. pp. 340—343.* [944

Lyman, Richard M.: Mennonites or German Friends, *[with reference to their settlement in Bucks Co., Pa. Read July 18, 1882.] In: A Collection of Papers read before the Bucks County Historical Society. Vol. I. Easton, Pa. 1908. pp. 39—44.* [945

Martin, E. K.: The Mennonites. *Philadelphia, Pa.: Everts & Peck 1883. pp. 17.* [946

Miller, Louis L.: Religious education in Mennonite preparatory schools and colleges. *Thesis of M. A., Department of Religious Education, Divinity School. Chicago, Ill. 1918. pp. 36.* [947

Smissen, Carl H. A. van der: Kurzgefaßte Geschichte und Glaubenslehre der Altevangelischen Taufgesinnten oder Mennoniten. *St. Louis, Mo.: Im Selbstverlag des Verfassers; (A. Wiebusch & Son, Prtg. Co.) XIV, 251 S., ill. Die Mennoniten in Amerika. S. 131—154.* [948

Smith, C. Henry: Mennonites in history. *Scottdale, Pa.: Published by the Mennonite Book and Tract Society 1907. pp. 5—41.* [949

— Mennonites of America. *Dissertation Ph. D. The University of Chicago, Department of History. Scottdale, Pa.: Mennonite Publishing House 1909. pp. 147, ill. [Bibliography. pp. 131—147.]* [950

— The Mennonites of America. *Goshen, Ind.: Published by the author; Scottdale,*

Pa.: Mennonite Publishing House Press 1909. pp. 484, ill.
[Bibliography. pp. 456—478.] [951
[**Smith, C. Henry**]: The Mennonites as pioneers. *(Extracts from: The Mennonites in America. By C. H. Smith [= no. 951]).* In: *The Pennsylvania-German. Vol. X. Lititz, Pa. 1909. pp. 387—390.* [952
— Die Mennoniten während des neunzehnten Jahrhunderts. Niederlassungen in Ohio, Indiana, Illinois und den westlichen Staaten. *Aus seinem Buche: Die Mennoniten in Amerika. [Englisch] Scottdale, Pa. 1909.*
[= Nr. 951] In: Deutsch-Amerikanische Geschichtsblätter. Jg. IX. Chicago, Ill. 1909. S. 113—121. [953
— The Mennonites. A brief history of their origin and later development in both Europe and America. *Berne, Ind.: Mennonite Book Concerne 1920. pp. 340.*
[Bibliography. pp. 335—340.] [954
— The Mennonite immigration to Pennsylvania in the eighteenth century. *Norristown, Pa.: The Norristown Press 1929. = Part XXXIII. ,,A narrative and critical history", prepared at the request of the Pennsylvania-German Society.* In: *The Pennsylvania-German Society. Proceedings and Addresses . . . 1924. Vol. XXXV. Norristown, Pa. 1929. Separate pagination. pp. 412, ill.*
[955
Souder, John D.: Early churches in the First Mennonite Conference District. *In: Christian Monitor. A monthly magazine for the home. Vol. XXV, no. 2. Scottdale, Pa. 1933. pp. 46—47.* [956
Umble, John: Seventy years of progress in Sunday school work among the Mennonites of the Middle West. *In: The Mennonite Quaterly Review. Vol. VIII. Goshen, Ind. —Scottdale, Pa. 1934. pp. 166—179.* [957
Wedel, C. H.: Bilder aus der Kirchengeschichte für mennonitische Gemeindeschulen. *Newton, Kan.: Schulverlag von Bethel-College; St. Louis, Mo.: A. Wiebusch & Son Prtg. 1899. 86 S.* [958
— Abriß der Geschichte der Mennoniten. *4 Bde. Newton, Kan.: Schulverlag von Bethel College; St. Louis, Mo.: A. Wiebusch & Son Prtg. 1900/1904. 153 S.; 180 S.; 190 S.; 212 S.*
Die Geschichte der Täufer und Mennoniten in der Schweiz, in Maehren, in Süddeutschland, am Niederrhein, und in Amerika. = Vol. IV. 1904. 211 S. [959

Wedel, C. H.: Kurzgefaßte Kirchengeschichte fuer Schulen und Familien. *Newton, Kan.: Schulverlag von Bethel College. 1905. 262 S.* [960
[—] Sketches from church history for Mennonite schools. *Translated by* **Gustav A. Haury**. *Newton, Kan.: The Western District Conference of Mennonites of North-America 1920. pp. 134.* [961
Yoder, Edward: The Christian's attitude toward participation in war activities. *Paper read at the Mennonite Conference on Peace and War, held at Goshen College under the auspices of the Peace Problems Committee of the Mennonite General Conference, February 15 to 17, 1935.* In: *Mennonite Quaterly Review. Vol. IX. Goshen, Ind.-Scottdale, Pa. 1935. pp. 5—19.* [962
Zook, Ephraim Jacob: Social tendencies of Mennonits in America. *Thesis of M. A., University of Chicago. 1905. Typewritten. pp. III, 32.* [963
[Several papers bearing on the early history of the (Mennonite) Church in America] *secured by N. B. Grubb, from the Librarian of the Mennonite Church at Amsterdam.* In: *The Mennonite Year Book and Almanac for 1910. Quakertown, Pa. 1910. pp. 17—27.* [964
An interesting document on the early history of Germantown. *[Reply of the ministers and elders of the Mennonite Church in Altona, Germany to an appeal to send a delegate to Germantown, Pa. to ordain a bishop in the regular way. (Letter to Claes Beerends, op Pennsylvanien. Ao. 1702: Martio.)] Edited by* **Harold S. Bender**. In: *The Mennonite Quarterly Review. Vol. V. Goshen, Ind. — Scottdale, Pa. 1931. pp. 284—285.* [965
A letter from Pennsylvania Mennonites to Holland in 1773. *[Composed and signed by* **Andrew Ziegler, Isaac Kolb** and **Christian Funk**, *three Mennonite bishops, the former at Skippack, and the latter two at what is now Franconia; dated ,,Schippak, Indian Krik, and Blen, Philadelphia County, March 1, 1773"] Reprint from: Hendrick Pannebecker, surveyor of lands for the Penns, 1674—1754. By Samuel W. Pennypacker. Philadelphia, Pa. 1894 [= no. 7183]. pp. 46—63.* In: *The Mennonite Quarterly Review. Vol. III. Goshen, Ind. 1929. pp. 225—234.* [966
Dress. *A brief treatise prepared by a committee appointed by Mennonite General*

Conference. Second edition. Scottdale, Pa.: Mennonite Publishing House 1921. pp. 47. [967
Will there be a union of Mennonite churches? *Reprint from: ,,Gospel Herold". In: The Penn Germania. Vol. I. = Old series, vol XIII. Lititz, Pa. 1912. pp. 728—730.* [968

Report of the General Conference of Mennonites in France in Reconstruction Work held at Clermont-en-Argonne, Meuse, France, June, 20—22, 1919. *[s. l. 1912.] pp. 77.* [969

Fisher, H. H.: The famine in Soviet Russia, 1919—1923. The operations of the Relief Administration. *New York, N. Y.: The Macmillan Co. 1927. pp. X, 609.* [970

Hiebert, P. C. and **Miller, Orie O.:** Feeding the hungry, Russia famine 1919—1925. American Mennonite relief operations under the auspices of Mennonite Central Committee. *P. C. Hiebert, A. M., chairman of the Mennonite Central Committee, author, editor. Orie, O. Miller, assistant secretary of the Mennonite Central Committee and relief worker, associate editor. Scottdale, Pa.: Mennonite Central Committee 1928. pp. 450.* [971

Alt-Mennonitische Konferenzen
Old-Mennonite Church Conferences

Weaver, Martin G.: Mennonites of Lancaster Conference, *containing biographical sketches of Mennonite leaders, histories of congregations, missions, and Sunday schools; record of ordinations; and other interesting historical data. Scottdale, Pa.: Published by the Mennonite Publishing House 1931. pp. XVI, 496, ill.* [972
Proceedings of the Mennonite Conference in the Valley of Virginia. *Elkhart, Ind.: Mennonite Publishing Co. 1884. pp. 37. [Contains the minutes of Conference proceedings beginning with the Spring Conference, 1860 and including the Spring Conference of 1884. Minutes of a Conference of 1835 are also given translated from the German.]* [973
A history of the Mennonite Conference of Virginia and its work. *With a brief biographical sketch of its founders and organizers. As arranged and formulated by a committee appointed especially for the work by the Conference session held at the Warwick River Church, May 13th, and 14th, 1910. Scottdale, Pa.: Mennonite Publishing House 1910. pp. 117.* [974
History of the Southwestern Pennsylvania Conference. *[s. l.] 1923. pp. 228. [a compilation of conference minutes and statistical data.]* [975
Calender fuer die Versammlungen der Mennoniten Gemeinden in (Ontario?) *Berlin, Ober Canada: H. Peterson 1836. pp. ....*

Since 1836 annually ff., first in German, since 1890 in English; current issue 1930—1931: Calender of appointments of the Mennonite Church of Ontario for the year, July 1st, 1930 to June 30th. 1931. *= 96th issue, 41st English- and reports of the Annual Conference and Rural Mission Board. [s. l. 1930.] pp. (26).* [976
A manual of the Conference resolutions of the Mennonite Church of the Canada Conference District 1904. *Berlin, Ont.: E. S. Hallman 1904. pp. 15.* [977
Bericht der Conferenz, gehalten am 11. Oktober 1872, in Yellow Creek Versammlungshause, in Elkhart County, Ind. *[s. l. 1872.] 4 S. [Die ersten gedruckten Verhandlungen der Indiana Konferenz.]* [978
Conference in Indiana held at Yellow Creek, on Thursday and Friday, Oct. 9th and 10 th, 1873. *[s. l. 1873.] pp. 4. [Contains also minutes of the first Missouri Conference, October 24, 1873.]* [979
Conference in Indiana. Gehalten Donnerstags und Freitags den 9. und 10. October 1873. *[s. l. 1873.] 4. S.* [980
Conference in Elkhart County, Indiana held at Yellow Creek on Thursday and Friday, Oct. 8th and 9th, 1874. *[s. l. 1874.] pp. 4.* [981
Conference report. Report of the Conference held at the Olive Church in Elkhart County, Ind., Oct. 9th, 1891. *Elkhart, Ind.: Mennonite Publishing Co. 1891. pp. 12.*

[Appeared in German at the same time under the title Bericht der Indiana Conferenz . . .] [982

Mennonite church history of Howard and Miami Counties, Indiana, *By the Y. P. C. A. Historical Committee,* **Glen L. Troyer, John W. Horner, Sadie Miller Mishler, Kathryn King, Melvin Myers.** *Scottdale, Pa.: Mennonite Publishing House 1916. pp. 189.* [983

Minutes of the Indiana — Michigan Mennonite Conference 1864—1929. *Compiled by Order of Conference. Compiling Committee,* **Ira S. Johns, J. S. Hartzler, Amos Hostetler,** *Scottdale, Pa.: Mennonite Publishing House 1929. pp. 356.* [984

Verhandlungen der ersten Zusammenkunft in Illinois. Gehalten den 24. Mai in Whiteside County. *[s. l. 1872.] Kleinfolioblatt.* [985

Conference record containing the proceedings of the Kansas-Nebraska Mennonite Conference 1876—1914. *Compiled by a committee appointed by Conference.* **L. O. King, T. M. Erb, D. H. Bender,** *committee. [s. l. 1914.] pp. 207.* [986

Shetler, S. G.: History of the Pacific Coast Mennonite Conference. *In: The Mennonite Year-Book and Directory. 1926. Scottdale, Pa. 1916. pp. 25—34, ill.* [987

— Church history of the Pacific Coast Mennonite Conference District. *Scottdale, Pa.: Press of the Mennonite Publishing House. [1931.] pp. 102.* [988

Report of preliminary General Conference meeting. *[s. l. 1897.] pp. 12.* [989

Minutes of General Conference (held at the Holdeman M. H., Wakarusa, Ind., Nov. 2, 1898.) *[s. l., 1898.] pp. 19.* [990

Bericht der Allgemeinen Konferenz . . . 1898. *[s. l., 1898.] 22 S.* [991

Proceedings of the Second Mennonite General Conference. Held at Sterling,

Ill., Oct. 31 and Nov. 1, 1900. *[s. l. 1900.] pp. 36.* [992

Minutes of the third General Conference held at the Pike meeting house near Elida, Ohio, Nov., 1902. *[s. l., 1902.] pp. 32.* [993

Proceedings of the preliminary, 1897; the first, 1898 to the eleventh, 1919 Mennonite General Conference including discussions leading to its organization. *Scottdale, Pa.: Mennonite Publishing House 1921. pp. 231.* [994

Mennonite General Conference, held near Garden City, Mo., Aug. 24—26, 1921. *(Inside: Report of the twelfth Mennonite General Conference . . .) [s. l., 1921.] pp. 28. Since 1921 biennially ff.* [995

Umble, John: Early conditions leading to General Conference. *In: The Mennonite Quarterly Review. Vol. III. Goshen, Ind. 1929. pp. 13—25.*
Reprint in: Christian Monitor. A monthly magazine for the home. Vol. XXI, no. 8. Scottdale, Pa. 1929. pp. 244—246; 253—254. [996

Meeting calender of a part of the Mennonite churches in the Unites States. For the year of our Lord 1872. With a list of ministers' names and addresses. *Elkhart, Ind.: J. F. Funk & Bro., Publishers 1872. pp. 28.* [997

Names and addresses of Mennonite ministers. *Elkhart, Ind.: Mennonite Publishing Co. 1901. pp. 26. [An annual printed for a number of years 1901ff.—1905.]* [998

Mennonite yearbook and directory. A. D. 1905. *Published by the Mennonite Board of the Charitable Homes and Missions. [s. l. 1905.] pp. 72. Annually published 1905ff., except 1910 and 1913; since 1909 published by the Mennonite Publishing House at Scottdale, Pa. Edited by* **J. A. Ressler,** *1913—1924,* **J. L. Horst,** *1924ff.* [999

Amische Mennoniten

Amish Mennonites

United States, Department of Commerce, Bureau of Census: Amish Mennonite Church. *In: Religious bodies 1906. Part II. Separate denominations: History, description and statistics. Washing-*

ton, D. C. 1910 *[= no. 894]. pp. 411—413.* [1000

— Conservative Amish Mennonite Church. History, description and statistics. *In: Religious bodies: 1916. Part II. Sepa-*

rate denominations. Washington, D. C. 1919. pp. 424—425.
— Statistics. History, doctrine, and organization. *In: Religious bodies: 1926. Part II. Washington, D. C. 1929. pp. 858 —860.* [1001
— Old Amish Mennonite Church. History, description and statistics. *In: Religious bodies: 1906. Part II. Separate denominations. Washington, D. C. 1910. pp. 414—415.*
— *In: Religious bodies: 1916. Part II. Washington, D. C. 1919. pp. 425—426.*
— Statistics. History, doctrine and organization. *In: Religious bodies: 1926. Part II. Washington, D. C. 1929. pp. 861—864.* [1002
Bachmann, Calvin George: Old Order Amish of Lancaster County, Pa. *Thesis of M. A., University of Pennsylvania, Philadelphia, Pa. 1929. Typewritten. pp. (1), 68.* [1003
Bender, Harold S.: Some early American Amish Mennonite disciplines. *Translated and edited by . . . In: The Mennonite Quaterly Review. Vol. VIII. Goshen, Ind.-Scottdale, Pa. 1934 pp. 90—98.*
[The discipline of 1809; . . . of 1837; . . . of 1865.] [1004
Borntreger, Hans E.: Eine Geschichte der ersten Ansiedlung der Amischen Mennoniten und die Gründung ihrer ersten Gemeinde im Staate Indiana, nebst einer kurzen Erklärung über die Spaltung die in dieser Gemeinde geschehen ist. *Elkhart, Ind.: Mennonite Publishing Co. 1907. 24 S.* [1005
Conyngham, Redmond: Further information relative to the Amish or Aymenist sect. *(Obtained from a member of the Society). In: Hazard's Register of Pennsylvania. Vol. VII. Philadelphia, Pa. 1831. pp. 161—163.* [1006
Guengerich, S. D.: Settlement of the Amish Mennonites in America. *In: The Mennonite Year Book and Directory 1918. Scottdale, Pa. 1918. pp. 26—32.* [1007
Hard, William: Your Amish Mennonite. *Reprint from the ,,New Republic", Febr. 1, 1919. New York City, N. Y.: National Civil Liberties Bureau [1919]. pp. 11. [Relative to the principle of nonresistance.]* [1008
Hartzler, Jonathan K.: Fifty years in the Amish Mennonite churches of Pennsylvania. *In: Herald of Truth. Vol. XXXIV, no. 11. Elkhart, Ind.: Mennonite Publishing Co. 1902. pp. 163—164.* [1009

Horsch, John: The Amish of Mifflin County, Pa. *[Remarks on the article ,,The Amish of Lancaster County, Pa." in ,,The Pennsylvania-German". Vol. XII, 1911. pp. 330ff.] In: The Pennsylvania-German. Vol. XII. Lititz, Pa. 1911. p. 446.* [1010
— Reply to the sensational accusations recently preferred against members of the Amish Mennonite Church at Berne, Indiana. *Berne, Ind.: Jacob J. Schwarz. pp. 32.* [1011
Jutzi, Georg (und **Zook, Sam**): Ermahnungen von Georg Jutzi in Stark County, Ohio, an seine Hinterbliebenen, *nebst einem Anhange über die Entstehung der amischen Gemeinde, von Sam Zook, Mifflin County, Pennsylvania. Somerset, Pa. Herausgegeben von Alexander Stutzman, Somerset Co., Pa.; Gedruckt von G. Voegtly in Somerset. 1853. 336 S.* [1012
[Miller, Christ L.]: Glimpses of Amish-Mennonite homes and some plain talks to the inmates. *By a friend Humanity. With an introduction by S. D. Guengerich. Scottdale, Pa.: Mennonite Book and Tract Society. 1907. pp. 341.* [1013
Miller, Daniel D.: Die altamischen Mennoniten Gemeinden. *In: Herald der Wahrheit. Jg. XXX, No. 3. Elkhart, Ind. 1893. S. 34—35.* [1014
Peachey, Samuel W.: Amisch of Kishacoquillas Valley, Mifflin County, Pa. *Scottdale, Pa.: Mennonite Publishing House 1930. pp. 48.* [1015
Smith, Clyde: The Amishman. *Toronto, Can.: William Briggs 1912. pp. 132.* [1016
Treyer, David A.: Ein unparteiischer Bericht von den Hauptumständen, welche sich ereigneten in den sogenannten Alt-Amischen Gemeinden in Ohio, vom Jahre 1850 bis ungefähr 1861, wodurch endlich eine vollkommne Spaltung entstand. *Abgeschrieben, den 11. August 1898. 16 S.* [1017
Umble, John: The Amish Mennonites of Union County, Pa. *In: The Mennonite Quarterly Review. Vol. VII. Goshen, Ind. — Scottdale, Pa. 1933. pp. 71—96.* [1018
Zook, Shem: Eine wahre Darstellung von Dem, welches uns das Evangelium in der Reinheit lehrt, so wie auch ein unparteiischer Bericht von den Haupt-Umständen, welche sich in unterschiedlichen Gemeinden ereigneten, woraus endlich

die unchristlichen Spaltungen entstanden sind. *Herausgegeben von . . . Mattawana, Mifflin Co., Pa.: Shem Zook 1880; Lancaster, Pa.: Gedruckt von John Baer's Sons 1880. 31 S.* [1019

The Amish of Lancaster county, Pa. *In: The Pennsylvania-German. Vol. XII. Lititz, Pa. 1911. pp. 330—337, ill.*

[Reviewed by John Horsch, see no. 1010.] [1020

[Wie die Alte Amische Gemein gebaut und fortgepflanzet worden ist durch die Nachkommende von Nicholas Stoltzfuß und Jacob Mast.] *Kutztown, Pa.: Kutztown Publishing Co., Inc. 1928. 32 S., Karte von den Amischen Gemeinen in Lancaster County.* [1021

Amische Konferenzen

Amish Conferences

Verhandlungen der Diener-Versammlung der Deutschen Taeufer oder Amischen Mennoniten gehalten in Wayne County, O. im Juny 1862. *Wie auch ein kurzer Bericht von der Herkunft der Mennoniten. Von S.[am] Z.[ook.] Lancaster, Pa.: Johann Baers Soehnen 1862. 23 S.* [1022

Verhandlungen der [zweiten] jährlichen Diener Versammlung der Deutschen Täufer oder Amischen Mennoniten . . .; *seit 1866: Bericht der Verhandlungen der . . . jährlichen Zusammenkunft der Amischen Mennoniten-Diener und Brüderschaft . . .; seit 1868: . . . der Amischen Mennoniten Bruderschaft . . . [s. l.]. Jährlich 1863—1878.* [1023

Report of the Eastern Amish Mennonite Conference from the time of its organization to the year 1911 *with Conference constitution and appendix. Arranged by* **C. Z. Yoder,** *by order of Conference held in 1910. Sugarcreek, O.: J. C. Miller 1911. pp. 63.* [1024

Report of the Eastern Amish Mennonite Conference, 1912—1919. *Arranged by* **C. Z. Yoder,** *secretary of Conference. Sugarcreek, O.: Budget Publishing Co., Febr. 1920. 48.* [1025

Report of the Eastern Amish Mennonite Conference 1920—1924, *arranged by a committee appointed by Conference held in 1923. Scottdale, Pa.: Mennonite Publishing House 1924. pp. 235.* [1026

Bericht der Westlichen District Konferenz der Amischen Mennoniten, abgehalten am 26. September 1901 mit der Gemeinde nahe Gridley, Livingston County, Ill. *[s. l. 1901.] 8 S.* [1027

Western District Amish Mennonite Conference. Record of Conference proceedings from the date of its organization. *[1890 to 1912 inclusive.] Arranged and formulated by a committee appointed especially for this work by the Conference held at Tiskilwa, Ill., Sept. 6—7, 1911. Scottdale, Pa.: Mennonite Publishing House 1912. pp. 71.* [1028

Bericht der ersten Amisch Mennoniten (Conservative) Ratsversammlung, gehalten in dem Pigeon River Versammlungshaus zu Pigeon, Michigan, den 24, 25. Nov. 1911. *[s. l. 1911.] . . . S. Jährlich 1911ff.* [1029

History of the Amish Mennonite Conference (Conservative). *Scottdale, Pa.: Mennonite Publishing House 1925. pp. 137.*

[Compilation of conference minutes.] [1030

Funk-Leute[1])

Funkites[2])

Funk, Christian: Ein Aufsatz oder Vertheidigung von Christian Funk gegen seine Mitdiener der Mennonisten Gemeinschaft, *Germantown, Pa.: Leibert & Billmeyer 1785. 16 S.* [1031

Funk, Christian: Spiegel fuer alle Menschen; oder Nutzanwendung aus dem Leben und Wandel Christel Funk's, eines in seinem

---

[1]) Anhänger von Christian Funk, der 1777 von seinen Mitbrüdern ausgeschlossen wurde.

[2]) Followers of Christian Funk, who was excluded by his fellow minister 1777.

Leben treu gewesenen Mennonisten-Predigers des gottlichen Worts durch und viele Jahre nach der amerikanischen Revolution. *(,,Written by me, Christian Funk, the 10th day of November 1809 in the 76th year of my age'' Endbemerkung). Reading, Pa.: Gedruckt bey Johann Ritter & Co. fuer die Verleger 1813. 54 S.* [1032

Funk, Christian: A mirror for all mankind or instructive examples from the life and conduct of Christian Funk, a faithful minister of the Word of God among the Mennonites during and many years after the American Revolution. *Translated from the German. Norristown, Pa.: J. Winnard 1814. pp. 47.* [1033

Rosenberger, Elizabeth D.: The Funkites *[or followers of the Mennonite preacher Christian Funk, of Bechtel's Mill on the Indian Creek, Montgomery Co., Pa.] In: The Penn Germania. Vol. I. = Old series, vol. XIII. Lititz, Pa. 1912. pp. 829—830.* [1034

Reformierte Mennoniten-Kirche, gegründet 1812

Reformed Mennonite Church, founded 1812

United States, Department of Commerce, Bureau of Census: Reformed Mennonite Church. History, description and statistics. *In: Religious bodies: 1906. Part II. Separate denominations. Washington, D. C. 1910 [= no. 894]. pp. 415—416.*
— *In: Religious bodies: 1916. Part II. Washington, D. C. 1919. p. 429.*
— Statistics. History, doctrine and organization. *In: Religious bodies: 1926. Part II. Washington, D. C. 1929. pp. 873—875.* [1035

Herr, John: John Herr's complete works *comprising The Way to Heaven, The Illustrating Mirror, An Appendix relating to John Herr's Life, A Few Facts concerning John Herr, A Brief and Apostolic Answer, A Remarkable Vision, and A Letter to Erie County, N.Y. Buffalo, N.Y.: Peter Paul & Bro. 1890. pp. 520.* [1036

Moser, Johannes: Eine Verantwortung gegen Daniel Musser's Meidungs-Erklaerung, welche er gemacht hat in seinem Buch, betitelt: ,,Reformirte Mennoniten.'' *Geschrieben von . . ., zu Bluffton, Ohio. Lancaster, Pa.: Samuel Ernst, in der Druckerei des ,,Waffenlosen Wächter'' 1876. 83 S.*
[Vgl. Nr. 1038] [1037

Musser, Daniel: The Reformed Mennonite Church, its rise and progress, with its principles and doctrines. *Lancaster, Pa.: Inquirer Printing & Publishing Co. 1873. pp. 608; Second edition Lancaster, Pa. 1878. pp. IV, 5—608.* [1038

The Reformed Mennonites. Some of their views, principles and peculiarities. *Williamsville, N. Y.: Published by D. N. Long 1886. pp. 14.* [1039

Herr, John. *In: The National Cyclopaedia of American Biography. Vol. VII. New York, N. Y. 1897. p. 498.* [1040

Ostpennsylvanische Konferenz der Mennonitischen Gemeinschaft 1848 gebildet und 1860 vereinigt mit der Allgemeinen Mennonitischen Gemeinschaft in Nord-Amerika

Eastern Mennonite Conference, organized 1848 and merged with the General Conference of Mennonites of North Amerika, 1860

United States, Department of Commerce, Bureau of Census: General Conference of Mennonites of North America. History description and statistics. *In: Religious bodies: 1906. Part II. Sepa-rate denominations. Washington, D. C. 1910 [= no. 894]. pp. 416—419.*
— *In: Religious bodies: 1916. Part II. Washington, D. C. 1919. pp. 430—433.*
— Statistics. History, doctrine and

organization. *In: Religious bodies: 1926. Part II. Washington, D. C. 1929. pp. 876—882.* [1041

Oberholtzer, John H.: Der wahre Character von J. H. Oberholtzer, Prediger und Bishof über mehrere Gemeinden in Ost-Pennsylvanien nebst Einsicht und Erkenntnis ueber verschiedene Staende sammt anderen Verhaeltnissen die Christl. Kirche ueberhaupt, so wie die Menn. Gemeinschaft besonders betreffend. *(Außentitel: Verantwortung und Erlaeuterung) Milford Square, Bucks County, Pa.: Herausgegeben vom Verfasser, 1860. 115 S.* [1042

[—(?)] Die Geschichte der Trennung in 1847 und 1848 der Mennoniten in Ost-Pennsylvanien. *(Wahrscheinlich von ...) [s. l. 1865.] Folioblatt mit 4 Spalten* [1043

[Schuler, H. A.]: Rev. John H. Oberholtzer, teacher, locksmith, preacher and publisher. *Compiled from material, furnished by N. B. Grubb, and by H. P. Krehbiel's History of the General Conference of the Mennonites of North America". St. Louis, Mo. 1898 [= no. 1055]. In: The Mennonite Year-book and Almanac for 1908. Quakertown, Pa. 1908. pp. 34—38, ill. Reprint in: The Pennsylvania-German. Vol. VIII. Lebanon, Pa. 1907. pp. 420—423, ill.* [1044

Rev. John H. Oberholtzer. Sketch of the founder of the New Mennonites. *From: The Reading Eagle, Nov. 2, 1891. In: The Perkiomen Region. Vol. IX, no. 2. Pennsburg, Pa. 1931. pp. 39—40.* [1045

The Eastern District Conference. *In: The Mennonite Year Book and Almanac for 1898. Quakertown, Pa. 1898. p. 18.* [1046

Historical sketches of Mennonite congregations. *In: The Mennonite Year Book and Almanac. Quakertown, Pa. 1896 ff.* The Mennonite Church and congregation of Schwenksville, Pa. By W. S. **Gottschall**, *1896. pp. 33, ill.;* Swamp congregations. *1898. pp. 26—27, ill.;* Wadsworth congregation, O. *1898. p. 28, ill.:* First Mennonite congregation of Philadelphia, Pa. *1898. pp. 29—30, ill.;* Sketch of Deep Run (General Conference) congregation. *1899. pp. 26—27, ill.* Sketch of Zion Mennonite Church, Souderton, Pa. *1899. pp. 27—28, ill.* Flaatland Mennonite Church. *1899. p. 28—29, ill.;* The Herford Mennonite congregation *1899. pp. 29—31, ill.;* The Zionsville Mennonite congregation. *1899. pp. 31—32, ill.;* Pottstown Mennonite Church *1900. p. 24, ill.;* Second Mennonite Church of Philadelphia. *1900 p. 28, ill.;* Sketch of the Goshen, Ind., Mennonite Church. *1900. p. 29;* Bethany Mennonite Church, Quakertown, Pa. *1902. p. 37, ill.;* The Springfield Mennonite Church *1903. p. 36, ill.;* The work in Allentown, Pa. *1906. p. 22, 24, ill.;* Zion Mennonite Church, Souderton. *1910. pp. 38—39, ill.;* Napier Mennonite Church. *1914. p. 19, ill.;* The Settlement-meeting house and churchyard. *1914. pp. 19—20, ill. with:* Interments in the Settlement graveyard. *pp. 21—22.* How the separation of 1848 worked out in one locality *[Hereford meeting house.] 1914. pp. 29—32, ill.;* Rothrock Mennonite congregation *1915. p. 31, ill.,* Eden Mennonite congregation of Schwenksville, Pa. *1919. pp. 29—30, ill.;* Zion Mennonite Church, Souderton, Pa. *pp. 30—32, ill.;* Historical sketch of the Mennonite churches in Blair and Bedford Counties, Pa. *1921. pp. 26—27.* How the Bowmansville congregation *[Lancaster Co., Pa.]* came to be 1921. *pp. 27—28;* History of the. first Mennonite Church, Nappanee, Ind *(by* E. S. **Mullett.)** *1929. pp. 32—34, ill.* [1047

Verhandlungen des Hohen Rathes der Mennoniten Gemeinschaft. *Abraham Hunsicker, Vorsitzer, Johannes H. Oberholtzer, Schreiber. [s. l.] Gedruckt bey Johann H. Oberholtzer 1848. [Bericht der ersten Konferenz der Oberholtzer Gruppe.]* [1048

Verhandlungen der Ost-Pennsylvanischen Conferenz der Mennoniten Gemeinschaft, 1847—1872. *(Ohne Titelblatt). [1872.] 55 S.* [1049

Verhandlungen der Ost-Pennsylvanischen Conferenz der Mennoniten Gemeinschaft, 1872—1884. *[s. l. 1884.] 79 S.* [1050

Die Confeienzverhandlungen der Allgemeinen Mennoniten Gemeinschaft in Nord-Amerika. Abgehalten in West Point, Lee County, Iowa, den 28 ten und 29ten Mai, 1860. *[s. l. 1863.] 24 S. [Officielle Berichte der ersten drei Hauptkonferenzen.]* [1051

Allgemeine Conferenz Verhandlungen der 7ten Allgemeinen Conferenz der Mennoniten von Nord-Amerika. Gehalten vom 15 ten bis 26 ten Nov. 1875. *[s. l. 1875.] 28 S. [Seit 1875 dreijährlich ff.]* [1052

Verhandlungen der Allgemeinen Konferenz der Mennoniten von Nord-Amerika. *Erste bis elfte Sitzung, Berne, Ind.: Verlag der Christlichen Central-Buchhandlung der Allgemeinen Konferenz der Mennoniten 1887. 108 S.* [1053
Jubilaeums-Fest der Allgemeinen Konferenz der Mennoniten von Nord-Amerika. Gefeiert in Beatrice, Nebraska, den 7. September 1908, in Verbindung mit der achtzehnten Sitzung der Allgemeinen Konferenz. *Herausgegeben auf Verordnung der Konferenz. Berne, Ind.: Mennonite Book Concern 1909. 95 S.* [1054

Krehbiel, H. P.: The history of the General Conference of the Mennonites of North-America. *St. Louis, Mo.: The author 1898. pp. XX, 504, ill.* [1055
Mennonite yearbook and almanac for 1895. *Published under resolution of Conference adopted May 1, 1894 at Souderton, Pa. Quakertown, Pa.: U. S. Stauffer 1895. pp. 40.*
Annually published by the Eastern District Mennonite Conference with N. B. Grubb as chief editor up to 1924; ... by the Mennonite Book Concern, Berne, Ind. 1925ff. [1056

Unabhängige

Independent Men

Hunsicker, Abraham: A statement of facts, and summary of views on morals and religion, as related with suspension from the Mennonite meeting 1851. *Philadelphia, Pa.: G. S. Harris 1851. pp. 15.* [1057
— Eine Darstellung der Ereignisse und Summarium von Ansichten ueber Moral und Religion wie dieselben mit einer gewissen Ausschließung aus der Mennoniten-Gemeine verbunden sind. *Geschrieben zu Trappe, Montgomery County, Pa. Philadelphia, Pa.: George S. Harris 1851. 15 S.* [1058
G.[rater], A.[braham]: An explanation of incidents that took place among the socalled Mennonites. *Skippack, Pa.: J. M. Schünemann & Co. 1885. pp. 8.* [1059

G.[rater], A.[braham]: Vertheidigung. *[Deutsche Ausgabe von Nr. 1059] Schippach, Pa.: J. M. Schuenemann 1855. 8 S.* [1060
— A brief church history concerning the origin and progress of the socalled Trinity Christian Church, Freeland, Montgomery County, Pa. Also, somewhat in relation to the church in general. *[s. l.] Dec. 22, 1864. pp. 4.* [1061
— Eine kurze Kirchen-Geschichte. Etwas vom Anfang und Fortgang von der sogenannten „Trinity Christian Church" in Freeland, Montgomery County, Pa., wie auch etwas über die Kirche im Allgemeinen. *[Am Ende.] Skippackville, Montgomery County, Pa., Dec. 22, 1864. [s. l. 1864.] 4 S.* [1062

Stauffer-Gemeinde, gegründet um 1840—1850

Stauffer Mennonite Church, organized about 1840—1850

United States, Department of Commerce, Bureau of Census: Stauffer Mennonites. History, description and statistics. *In: Religious bodies: 1916. Part II. Separate denominations. Washington, D. C. 1919 [= no. 894]. p. 445.*
—Statistics. History, doctrine and organization. *In: Religious bodies: 1926. Part II. Washington, D. C. 1929. pp. 910—911.* [1063
St.[aufer], J.[acob]: Eine Chronik oder Geschicht-Buechlein von der sogenannten

Mennonisten Gemeinde. *Zum Dienst und Lehre fuer alle Liebhaber der Wahrheit, durch Gnade und Segen Gottes. Aus Geschichten, Vorfaellen, Begebenheiten oder Exempeln, und aus heiliger Schrift zusammengezogen. Durch J. St. geschrieben im Jahre 1850. Lancaster, Pa.: Gedruckt für den Verleger, von Johann Bär und Söhnen 1855. 439 S.; Zweiter Druck. Lancaster, Pa. 1859. 439 S.; zweite Auflage durch* Joh. D. Hochstettler. *Scottdale, Pa.: Mennonite Publishing House 1922.* [1064

Vereinigte Mennonitenbrüder in Christo

Ursprünglich in Pennsylvanien genannt Evangelische Mennoniten-Gemeinschaft von
Ostpennsylvanien „(Gehman Spaltung) 1858''; nach Verschmelzung mit anderen seit
1882 unter obigem Namen.

The Mennonite Brethren in Christ Church

In Pennsylvania originally called „Evangelical Mennonites (Gehman faction), 1858'';
after mergers with other bodies under present name since 1882.

United States, Department of Commerce,
Bureau of Census: Mennonite Brethren
in Christ. History, description and
statistics. *In: Religious bodies: Part II.
Separate denominations. Washington,
D. C. 1910 [= no. 894]. pp. 422—424.*
— *In: Religious bodies: 1916. Part II.
Washington, D. C. 1919. pp. 435—438.*
— Statistics. History doctrine, organization, work. *In: Religious bodies:
1926. Part II. Washington, D. C. 1929.
pp. 886—891.*   [1065
Glaubenslehre und Kirchenzucht-Ordnung
der Evang. Mennoniten Gemeinschaft
von Ost-Pennsylvanien. *Mit beyge-
fuegter Constitution der Missions-Gesell-
schaft. Skippackville, Pa.: Druck von
A. E. Dambly 1866. 48 S.*   [1066
Constitution and discipline of the Reformed Church. *Skippackville, Pa.:
A. E. Dambly 1867. pp. 36.*

[Edited newly at different times.]
                                       [1067
Huffmann, Jasper Abraham: History of the
Mennonite Brethren in Christ Church.
*Editor-in-chief . . . New Carlisle, O.:
The Bethel Publishing Co. 1920. pp. 283,
ill., map.*
[Bibliography. pp. 279—281.] [1068
General Conference journal containing
the proceedings of the Mennonite Bre-
thren in Christ Church, held in Berlin,
Ont., October 10th, 1900. *Berlin, Ont.:
Gospel Banner Print 1900.*
  *Since 1900 printed regularly for each
quadriennial conference 1900ff.* [1069
Mennonite Brethren in Christ, Pennsylvania Conference. Year-book for
1928. *Editor:* **C. H. Brunner.** *Published by order of the Conference. Allentown, Pa.; Bethlehem, Pa.: Times Publishing Co. 1928.*   [1070

Gemeinde Gottes in Christo, 1858

The Church of God in Christ (Mennonite), 1858

United States, Department of Commerce,
Bureau of Census: Church of God in
Christ (Mennonite). History, descrip-
tion and statistics. *In: Religious bodies:
1906. Part II. Separate denominations.
Washington, D. C. 1910 [= no. 894].
pp. 419—420.*
— *In: Religious bodies: 1916. Part II.
Washington, D. C. 1919. pp. 426—472.*
— Statistics. History, doctrine and
organization. *In: Religious bodies: 1926.
Part II. Washington, D. C. 1929. pp.
865—868.*   [1071
Holdeman, Johannes: Eine Geschichte der
Gemeinde Gottes, wie sie von Anfang
gewesen ist, wobei sie erkannt mag
werden, und wie sie fortgepflanzt worden
ist bis auf diese gegenwartige Zeit.

*Lancaster, Pa.: Johann Bär's Söhnen
1875. VI, 7—152 S.
Erweiterte Ausgabe, fortgeführt bis zum
28. November 1879. Lancaster, Pa.
1879. pp. 203. Gebunden mit* Ein Spiegel
der Wahrheit. *Ein Lehrbuch, den From-
men zum Trost, und den Sündern zur
Buße. Geschrieben durch* **Johannes Holdeman.** *Lancaster, Pa.: Johann Bär's
Söhnen 1878. 408 S.*   [1072
Holdeman, Johannes: A history of the
Church of God as it existed from the
beginning, whereby it may be known,
and how it was propagated until the
present time . . . *Written by . . .
Lancaster, Pa.: John Baer's Sons 1876.
pp. 303.*   [1073

Wisler-Gemeinschaft, 1870

Old (Wisler) Mennonite Church, 1870

United States, Department of Commerce, Bureau of Census: Old (Wisler) Mennonite Church. History, description and statistics. *In: Religious bodies: 1906. Part II. Separate denominations. Washington, D. C. 1910 [= no. 894]. pp. 420—421.*

— *In: Religious bodies: 1916. Part II. Washington, D. C. 1919. pp. 427—428.*
— Statistics. History, doctrine and organization. *In: Religions bodies: 1926. Part II. Washington, D. C. 1929. pp. 869—872.*   [1074

Allgemeine Mennoniten-Gemeinschaft (Allgemeine Konferenz), 1872 (1898)

Central Conference Mennonite Church, 1872 (1898)

United States, Department of Commerce, Bureau of Census: Central Conference of Mennonites. History, description and statistics. *In: Religious bodies: 1906. Part II. Separate denominations. Washington, D. C. 1910 [= no. 894]. pp. 426—427.*
— *In: Religious bodies: 1916. Part II. Washington, D. C. 1919. pp. 442—445.*
— Statistics. History, doctrine and organization. *In: Religious bodies: 1926. Part II. Washington, D. C. 1929. pp. 903—906.*   [1075

Weaver, William B.: History of the Central Conference Mennonite Church. *Danvers, Ill.: Published by the author 1926. pp. 254, ill.*
   [Bibliography. pp. 252—254.] [1076
Year-book of the Central Conference of Mennonites for the year of Our Lord 1922. *First year of the publication. Published by resolution of Conference; s. l. 1922.] pp. 36.*
   Annually issued 1924ff. Editors: W. H. Grubb, *1922—25;* H. E. Nunemaker, *1926;* W. B. Weaver, *1927ff.*   [1077

Deutsche Baptisten-Brüder, Täufer oder Dunker

German Baptist Brethren (Dunkers)

United States, Department of Commerce, Bureau of Census: Dunkers or German Baptist Brethren. *In: Religious bodies: 1906. Part II. Separate denominations: History, description and statistics. Washington, D. C. 1910 [= nol 894]. pp. 244—257.*

— German Baptist Brethren (Dunkers). *In: Religious bodies: 1916. Part II. 1919. pp. 153—166.*

— *In: Religious bodies: 1926. Part II 1929. pp. 228—254.* [1078

Brumbaugh, Martin Grove: A history of the German Baptist Brethren in Europe and America. *Mount Morris, Ill.: Brethren Publishing House 1899. pp. XXII, 559, ill. Second edition. 1906. pp. XXII, 559, ill.* [1079

— Alexander Mack. *Address delivered at the unveiling of the Alexander Mack memorial tablet, Germantown Church, Pa., April 9, 1911. Reprint from: The Gospel Messenger. In: The Penn Germania. Vol. I. = Old series, vol. XIII. Lititz, Pa. 1912. pp. 254—259.* [1080

Busch, Moritz: „Ein Tunkermeeting." *In: Wanderungen zwischen Hudson und Mississippi 1851 und 1852. Von Moritz Busch. Bd. I. Stuttgart u. Tübingen: J. G. Cotta'scher Verlag 1854. S. 151 —169.* [1080a

D.[iffenderffer, Frank Ried]: The Taufers or the German Baptist Brethren. The origin, history, religious beliefs and achievements of one of the prominent religious denominations in the United States. *Reprinted from: „The New Era." Lancaster, Pa. 1899. pp. 23.* [1081

Dove, Frederick Denton: Cultural changes in the Church of the Brethren. *Elgin, Ill.: Brethren Publishing House 1932. pp. 256.*

[Bibliography pp. 240—246.] [1082

Edwards, Morgan: Materials towards a history of the Baptists in Jersey; distinguished into First-day Baptists, Seventhday Baptists, Tunker Baptists, Rogerene Baptists. *Philadelphia, Pa.:*

Thomas Dobson 1792. pp. VII; 9—155. = Vol. II. Materials towards a history of the American Baptists. „Treats of the Tunker Baptists." *= Part III. pp. 144—146.* [1083

Flory, John S.: Literary activity of the German Baptist Brethren in the eighteenth century. *Elgin, Ill.: Brethren Publishing House 1908. pp. XII, 335.*

[Bibliography pp. 291—327.] [1084

Gillin, John Lewis: The Dunkers. A sociological interpretation. *Thesis of Ph. D., Columbia University, New York City, N. Y. 1906. pp. 238.*

[Bibliography pp. 233—238.] [1085

Holsinger, H. R.: Holsinger's history of the Tunkers and the Brethren Church. . . . *1901 see no. 1136.* [1086

Horst, Melvin Clyde: Government in the Church of the Brethren. (Historical and critical). *A thesis presented for graduation from the School of Theology of Juniata College, Huntingdon, Pa. May 1924. Typewritten. pp. 131, (2).* [1087

Kurtz, Daniel Webster: Nineteen centuries of the Christian Church. *Published by the General Sunday School Board of the Church of the Brethren. Elgin, Ill.: Brethren Publishing House 1914. pp. 197.* [1088

Llyod, Nelson: Among the Dunkers. *In: Scribner's Magazine. Vol. XXX, no. 5. New York, N. Y. 1901. pp. 513—528. Illustrations by G. W. Peters* [1089

[—] Among the Dunkers. *Reprint from Scribner's Magazine. Vol. XXX, no. 5. Yearbook of the Pennsylvania Society of New York 1902. pp. 101—107.* [1090

Sanger, Samuel F. and Hays, D.: The olive branch of peace and good will to men; anti-war history of the Brethren and Mennonites, the peace-people of the South during the Civil War 1861—1865. *Elgin, Ill.: Brethren Publishing House 1907. pp. XX. 23—232, ill.* [1091

Swigart, M. C.: 200th anniversary of the first Baptism and Love Feast held in the Mother Church Germantown, Philadelphia, Pa., December 23rd, and Christmas Day, December 25th, 1923. *Edited by . . . Rockton, Pa.: Keystone Printing Office 1924. pp. 28, ill.*   [1092

Winger, Otho: History and doctrines of the Church of the Brethren. *Second edition. Elgin, Ill.: Brethren Publishing House 1920. pp. 320.*
[Bibliography pp. 295—304.]   [1093

Two centuries of the Church of the Brethren of the beginnings of the brotherhood. *Bicentennial address at the annual conference, held at Des Moines, Iowa, June 3—11, 1908. Published by the authority of Conference. Elgin, Ill.: Brethren Publishing House 1908. pp. 398.*
[See no. 1118]   [1094

Church of the Brethren (Conservative Dunkers)

United States, Department of Commerce, Bureau of Census: German Baptist Brethren Church (Conservative). *History, description and statistics. In: Religious bodies: 1906. Part II. Separate denominations. Washington, D. C. 1910 [= no. 894]. pp. 245—252.*
— Church of the Brethren (Conservative Dunkers) . . . *In: Religious bodies: 1916. Part II. 1919. pp. 153—160.*
— Statistics. History, doctrine and organization. *In: Religious bodies: 1926. Part II. 1929. pp. 229—238.*   [1095

Kurtz, Henry: The Brethren's Encyclopedia *containing The United Counsels and Conclusions of the Brethren at their annual meetings, carefully collected, translated (from the original German in part) and arranged in alphabetical and chronological order, accompanied with necessary and explanatory notes etc. Columbia, O.: Published by the author; Pittsburgh: W. S. Haven 1867. pp. VIII, 200, (2).*
                    [1096

[Davy, H. D.-Quinter, J.]: Minutes of the annual meetings of the Brethren. *Designed for the promotion of the peace and harmony of the Brotherhood. Published by authority of the annual meeting, May 26—27, 1874. Dayton, O.: Christian Publishing Association 1876. pp. . . .*
                    [1097

Classified minutes of the annual meetings of the Brethren. A history of the General Councils of the Church from 1778 to 1885. *Designed for the use of the churches. Mt. Morris, Ill. and Huntingdon, Pa.: The Brethren's Publishing Co. 1886. pp. VI, 7—398.*   [1098

The minutes of annual meeting 1886—1892. *Arranged and indexed, with a new index of the Classified minutes of annual meeting. Mt. Morris, Ill.: The Brethren's Publishing Co. 1892. pp. 76.*   [1099

Revised minutes of the annual meetings of the German Baptist Brethren. *Revised by* **D. L. Miller, D. E. Price** *and* **Daniel Hays,** *Committee appointed by the Annual Conference, 1898. Designed for the use of the churches. Mt. Morris, Ill.: The Brethren Publishing House 1899. pp. VII, 206.*   [1100

Revised minutes of the annual meetings of the German Baptist Brethren. *Revised by* **D. L. Miller, D. E. Price** *and* **Daniel Hays,** . *Committee appointed by the Annual Conference, 1898. With appendix giving minutes from 1897 to 1907. Elgin, Ill.: Brethren Publishing House 1908. pp. VI, 90.*   [1101

Minutes of the annual meetings of the Church of the Brethren. Containing all available minutes from 1778—1909. *Published by the General Mission Board under authority of the Annual Conference, June 1—3, 1909. Elgin, Ill.: Thre Brethren Publishing House 1909. pp. 944.*
                    [1102

Revised minutes of the annual meetings of the Church of the Brethren from 1778 to 1922. *Revised by* **Otho Winger, J. H. Longenecker** *and* **George L. Studebaker,** *Committee appointed by the annual conference of 1917. Elgin, Ill.: Brethren Publishing House 1922. pp.226*
                    [1103

Proceedings of the annual meeting of the Brethren for 1876 . . . *Huntingdon, Pa.: J. R. Durborrow & Co. 1876. Annually ff. Since 1880:* Report of the Proceedings of the Brethren's annual meeting; *since 1903:* Full report of the proceedings of the Brethren's annual meeting. *Huntingdon, Pa.: Quinter & Brumbach Bros. 1877—1880; [Huntingdon, Pa., Mt. Morris, Ill.; Elgin, Ill.: Brethren Publishing House [1881. ff.]*   [1104

Miller, Howard: The record of the faithful for the use of the Brethren. Being a statistical record and a complete directory of the Brethren Church, for the years 1881—1882. *Arranged according to the most authentic information attainable. Lewisburgh, Pa.: J. R. Cornelius 1882. pp. 100.* [1105

The Brethren's Almanac for the United States for the year of Lord and Saviour, Jesus Christ, 1871 . . . *Tyrone, Pa.: H. R. Holsinger 1871. Annually ff. Since 1873:* Pilgrim Almanac; *since 1875:* The Brethren's family almanac; *since 1918:* Yearbook of the Church of the Brethren. *[Published at different places] since 1874: Huntingdon, Pa.: Quinter & Brumbach Bros; since 1881: Brethren Publishing House; since 1891: Mt. Morris, Ill.: Brethrens' Publishing Co.; since 1900: Elgin, Ill.: Brethren Publishing House.* [1106

Calbe, W. Arthur-Sanger, Homer F.: Educational bluebook and directory of the Church of the Brethren 1708—1923. *With biographies. Compiled and edited by W. Arthur Calbe [and] Homer F. Sanger. Elgin, Ill.: The General Educational Board of the Church of the Brethren [1923]. pp. 656.* [1107

Davis, C. Ernest: Our church. *Elgin, Ill.: General Christian Worker's Board 1923. pp. 100.* [1108

Falkenstein, George N.: The German Baptist Brethren or Dunkers. *Lancaster, Pa. 1900. = Part VIII. „A narrative and critical history", prepared at the request of the Pennsylvania-German Society. In: The Pennsylvania-German Society, Proceedings and Addresses . . . 1899. Vol. X. Lancaster, Pa. 1900. Separate pagination. pp. 148, ill.* [1109

Flory, John S.: Builders of the Church of the Brethren. *Elgin, Ill.: The Elgin Press 1925. pp. 137, ill.* [1110

Francis, J. G.: The General Conference of the Church of the Brethren of 1912. *In: The Penn Germania. Vol. I. = Old series, vol. XIII. Lititz, Pa. 1912. pp. 641—649.* [1111

Miller, D. L.-Royer, Galen B.: Some who led our fathers in the Church of the Brethren who have passed over. *Written and compiled by ...Elgin, Ill.: Brethren Publishing House 1912. pp. 223, ill.* [1112

Moore, J. H.: Some Brethren pathfinders. *Elgin, Ill.: Brethren Publishing House 1929. pp. 366, ill.* [1113

Moyer, Elgin S.: Missions of the Church of the Brethren. Their development and effect upon the denomination. *[Thesis of Ph. D., Yale University, Newhaven, Conn.] Elgin, Ill.: Brethren Publishing House 1931. pp. 301.* [1114

Noffsinger, John Samuel: A program for higher education in the Church of the Brethren with special reference to the number and distribution of colleges. *New York City, N. Y.: Published by Teachers College, Columbia University 1925. pp. VI, 80. = Teachers College, Columbia University, Contributions to Education, no. 172.* [1115

Royer, Galen, B.: Thirty-three years of missions in the Church of the Brethren. *Second edition. Elgin, Ill.: Brethren Publishing House 1914. pp. 448, ill.* [1116

Sharp, S. Z.: The educational history of the Church of the Brethren. *Elgin, Ill.: Brethren Publishing House 1923. pp. 383, ill.* [1117

Two centuries of the Church of the Brethren or the beginnings of the brotherhood. *Bicentennial addresses at the annual conference, held at Des Moines, Iowa, June 3—11, 1908. Published by the authority of Conference. Elgin, Ill.: Brethren Publishing House 1908. pp. 398, ill. Second edition. Elgin, Ill. 1909. pp. 398, ill. It includes among the historical papers of general character:*

Brumbaugh, M. C.: The conditions in Germany about 1708. *pp. 17—26.*

Myers, T. T.: The birth of the Schwarzenau Church and its activity. *pp. 27—39.*

Falkenstein, G. N.: The mother church at Germantown and her children. The settlement of Germantown. *pp. 43—54.*

Wayland, J. W.: The church before the Revolution. *pp. 55—68.*

Royer, J. G.: The growth to the Mississippi. *pp. 71—85.*

Frantz, Edward: The growth to the Pacific. *pp. 87—100.*

Myer, Elizabeth: The growth of the Sunday-school movement in the Brethren Church. *pp. 249—269.*

Royer, Galen B.: The development of missions in the church. *pp. 273—290.*

Sharp, S. Z.: Early educational activities. *pp. 307—329.*

Flory, John S.: Present educational activities. *pp. 331—339.*

Brumbaugh, H. B.: The publications of the church. History of growth and development. *pp. 343—360.* [1118

[Falkenstein, G. N.-Reber, D. C.]: History of the Church of the Brethren of the Eastern District of Pennsylvania. *By the Committee appointed by District Conference. Lancaster, Pa.: Press of the New Era Printing Co. 1915. pp. XVII, 670, ill.* [1119

Minutes of District Meetings of the German Baptist Brethren of the Eastern District of Pennsylvania from 1867 to 1896. *Lansdale, Pa.: Press of Lansdale „Republican" [s. a.] pp. 135.* [1120

[Royen, Galen B.]: A history of the Church of the Brethren in the Middle District of Pennsylvania. *Prepared and published under the supervision of the District Conference through its Home Mission Board. [1924.] pp. 561.* [1121

Blough, Jerome E.: History of the Church of the Brethren of the Western District. *Elgin, Ill.: Brethren Publishing House 1916. pp. 600, ill.* [1122

Zigler, D. H.: History of the Brethren in Virginia. *Elgin, Ill.: Brethren Publishing House 1908. pp. XVI, 278, ill., map. Second edition. Elgin, Ill. 1914. pp. XVI, 17—340, ill., map.* [1123

Moherman T. S. and **Harrold, A. W.:** A history of the Church of the Brethren. Northeastern Ohio. *Elgin, Ill.: Brethren Publishing House 1914. pp. 366, ill.* [1124

Garst, Jesse O.: History of the Church of the Brethren of the Southern District of Ohio. *By the Historical Committee . . .*

Editorial Supervision by **Jesse O. Garst.** *Dayton, O.: The Otterbein Press 1920. pp. 605, ill.* [1125

Winger, Otho: History of the Church of the Brethren in Indiana. *Elgin, Ill.: Brethren Publishing House 1917. pp. 479, ill.* [1126

[Gibson, D. B.]: Compiled minutes and history of the Church of the Brethren of the Southern District of Illinois. *Published by authority of the District meeting of Southern Illinois, held at Astoria, Oct. 1907. Committee on publication. D. B. Gibson, J. H. Brubaker, J. W. Lear. [s. l., s. d.] pp. 253.* [1127

Compiled minutes of the German Baptist Brethren Church (called Dunkers) of the Middle District of Iowa 1867 to 1906. *Published by authority of the District meeting of Iowa, held at Garrison, Iowa, September 26, 1906. Committee on publication:* **J. S. Synder [Jno. Zuck,** *selected on the stead of former.]* **J. D. Haughtelin, S. B. Miller.** *Elgin, Ill.: Brethren Publishing House 1907. pp. 88.* [1128

Craik, Elmer Le Roy: A history of the Church of the Brethren in Kansas. *McPherson, Kansas: Published by the author; Press of Daily Republican 1922. pp. 397.* [1129

A history of the Church of the Brethren. *Published by authority of District meeting of Southern California and Arizona through the following Committee:* **M. M. Eshleman,** *chairman . . . Los Angeles 1917. pp. 184, ill.* [1130

Morris, James H.: Thirty-one years of organized work in Oklahoma, Texas, New Mexico and Louisiana by the Church of the Brethren from 1891 to 1922. *Editor-in-chief . . . Butler, Ind.: The Highley Printing Co. [1922.] pp. 531.* [1131

Old (Order) German Baptist Brethren

United States, Department of Commerce, Bureau of Census: Old [Order] German Baptist Brethren. History description and statistics. *In: Religious bodies: 1906 Part II. Separate denominations. Washington, D. C. 1910 [= no. 894]. pp. 252—253.*

— *In: Religious bodies: 1916. Part II. Washington, D. C. 1919. pp. 160—161.*

— Statistics. History, doctrine and organization. *In: Religious bodies: 1926.*

Part II. Washington, D. C. 1929. pp. 239—242. [1132

The Brethren's reasons for producing and adopting the resolutions of August 24th [1881]. *Consisting of a collection of petitions made to the annual meeting from year to year, but without grant and the accomplishment of the much desired ends prayed for. Kinsey, O. (near Dayton): Office of the Vindicator 1883. pp. 53.* [1133

The Brethren Church (Progressive Dunkers)

United States, Department of Commerce, Bureau of Census: The Brethren Church (Progressive Dunkers). History description and statistics. *In: Religious bodies: 1906. Part II. Separate denominations. Washington, D. C. 1910 [= no. 894]. pp. 253—256.*
— *In: Religious bodies: 1916. Part II. Washington, D. C. 1919. pp. 162—164.*
— Statistics. History doctrine and organization. *In: Religious bodies: 1926. Washington, D. C. 1929. pp. 243—248.* [1134

The Brethren annual. *[Since 1892 containing the proceedings of the General Conference], Ashland, O.: H. R. Holsinger & Co. 1883 annually ff.* [1135

Holsinger, H. R.: Holsinger's history of the Tunkers and the Brethren Church embracing The Church of the Brethren, The Tunkers, The Seventh-Day German Baptist Church, The Old German Baptist Church, The Old German Baptists and the Brethren Church, including their origin, doctrine, biography and literature. *Lathrop, Cal.: Printed for the author by Pacific Publishing Co., Oakland, Cal. 1901. pp. 826, ill.* [1136
The Church: retrospective and prospective: How the path was found again. *By* J. Allen Miller; Two hundred years of Brethren history. *By* Charles A. Bame; The Brethren plea in the new day. *By* J. A. Garber. *[Ashland, O.: Brethren Publishing House 1908.] pp. (8).* [1137

Siebentäger-Baptisten und Ephrata Kloster, Grafschaft Lancaster, Pa.

Seventh Day Baptists (German 1728) — Ephrata Cloister, Lancaster County, Pa.

United States, Department of Commerce, Bureau of Census: German Seventh-Day Baptists. History, description and statistics. *In: Religious bodies: 1906. Part II. Separate denominations. Washington, D. C. 1910 [= no. 894]. pp. 256—257.*
—*In: Religious bodies: 1916. Part II. Washington, D. C. 1919. pp. 165—166.*
— Seventh-Day Baptists (German 1728) Statistics. History, doctrine and organization. *In: Religious bodies. Part II. Washington, D. C. 1829. pp. 249—252.* [1138
Brumbaugh, Martin G.: The Ephrata Society, and its relation to the German Baptist Brethren. *In: A history of the German Baptist Brethren in Europe and America. Mount Morris, Ill. 1899 [= no. 1079]. Chapter XI. pp. 438—470.* [1138a
— An outline for historical romance. *In: The Pennsylvania-German Society. Proceedings and Addresses at Easton, Oct. 12, 1928. Vol. XXXIX. Norristown, Pa. 1930. Separate pagination. pp. 12, ill.* [1139
[Conyngham, Redmond]: An account of the settlement of the Dunkers at Ephrata,

in Lancaster County, Pa. *By . . . To which is added a short history of that religious society. By the late Rev.* Christian Endress. *Read at a meeting of the Council, October 18th, 1826. In: Memoirs of the Historical Society of Pennsylvania. Vol. II. Part I. Philadelphia, Pa. 1827. pp. 135—153.* [1140
Conyngham, Redmond: An account of the settlement of the Dunkers, ta Ephrata. *Reprint from: Memoirs of the Historical Society of Pennsylvania. Vol. II. Part I. Philadelphia, Pa. 1827. In: Hazards' Register of Pennsylvania. pp. 331—334.* [1141
Correll, Ernst: Ephrata am Cocalico in Pennsylvanien. *In: Mennonitisches Lexikon. Bd. I. 1913/14 [= Nr. 929]. S. 595—596.* [1141a
[Croll, P. C.]: Famous Pennsylvania-Germans: John Peter Miller, the scholarly mystic of Ephrata. *In: The Pennsylvania-German. Vol. I, no. 2. Lebanon, Pa. 1900. pp. 3—17, ill.* [1142
Cronau, Rudolf: ,,Die Tunker und das Kloster Ephrata". *In: Drei Jahrhunderte deutschen Lebens in Amerika. Eine Geschichte der Deutschen in den Vereinigten Staaten. Von R. Cronau. Berlin 1909*

[= Nr. 34]. S. 75—80, ill.; 2. Aufl. 1924 S. 75—80, ill. [1142a

Diffenderffer, Frank Ried: Ephrata community 125 years ago. *In: Papers and Addresses of the Lancaster County Historical Society. Vol. III. Lancaster, Pa. 1899. pp. 3—13, ill.* [1143

— The Ephrata community 120 years ago, as described by an Englishman. *In: Papers and Addresses of the Lancaster County Historical Society. Vol. IX. Lancaster Pa. 1905. pp. 127—146.* [1144

Dubbs, Joseph Henry: Ephrata hymns and hymn books. *In: Papers and Addresses of the Lancaster County Historical Society. Vol. XIII. Lancaster, Pa. 1909. pp. 21—37, ill.* [1145

Fahnestock, William M.: Historical sketch of Ephrata; together with a concise account of the Seventh-Day Baptist Society of Pennsylvania. *(Written for the Portraiture of Pennsylvania, and communicated in a letter to Thomas F. Gorden, Esq. — By him furnished for the Register.) In: Hazard's Register of Pennsylvania. Vol. XV Philadelphia, Pa. 1835. pp. 161—167.* [1146

Genzmer, George Harvey: Miller, John Peter (1709—1796) German Reformed clergyman, later head of the Ephrata Commuinty of Seventh Day Baptists. *In: Dictionary of American biography. Under the auspices of the American Council of Learned Societies Vol. XII. Edited by Dumas Malone. London-New York 1933. p. 632.* [1146a

Hantzsch, Viktor: Beissel, Johann Konrad B. *In: Allgemeine deutsche Biographie. Bd. XLVI. Leipzig 1902. S. 341—344.* [1146b

J.[ordan, J. W.]: The Sharon house at Ephrata. An interesting note in the history of the Brethren. *In: Notes and Queries. Edited by W. H. Egle. Third series, vol. II. 1887—1890. Harrisburg, Pa. 1891. pp. 8—9. Reprint in: Third series, vol. II. Harrisburg, Pa. 1896. pp. 390—391.* [1147

[K.]: Drei Briefe aus Pennsylvanien — 1784. *[,,Nachricht von einer kleinen wiedertäuferischen Gemeine in Nordamerika. Ephrata in der Grafschaft Lankaster in Pennsylvanien, den 29. April 1784." . . . Gedruckt in der ,,Berlinischen Monatsschrift", Mai, 1785.] Neudruck mit Vorwort in: Der Deutsche Pionier. Jg. XIII. Cincinnati, O. 1881—1882. S. 10—15.* [1148

Kriebel, H. W.: Henry Sangmeister, the Ephrata chronicler. *In: Papers and Addresses of the Lancaster County Historical Society. Vol. XVI. Lancaster, Pa. 1912. pp. 127—132.* [1149

[Lamech and Agrippa] *(Pseudonym):* Chronicon Ephratense. A history of the community of Seventh Day Baptists at Ephrata, Lancaster County, Penn'a, by ,,Lamech and Agrippa." *Translated from the original German by* **Max J. Hark,** *D. D. Lancaster, Pa.: S. H. Zahm & Co. 1889. pp. XVI, 288.* [1150

Leinbach, Paul S.: Beissel, Johann Conrad (1690—1798) founder of the Solitary Brethren of the community of Seventh Day Baptists at Ephrata. *In: Dictionary of American biography. Under the auspices of the American Council of Learned Societies. Vol. II. Edited by Allen Johnson. London-New York 1929. pp. 142—143.* *[born in Eberbach, Germany, started for America in 1720, arriving in Boston.]* [1150a

[Miller, Peter]: A unique manuscript by Rev. Peter Miller (Brother Jabez), Prior of the Ephrata community, in Lancaster County. Pa. written for Benjamin Franklin, together with a fac-simile and translation of Beissel's 99 mystical proverbs, originally printed by Benjamin Franklin in 1730. *Compiled at the request of the Excutive Committee of the Pennsylvania-German Society by* **Julius F. Sachse.** *Lancaster, Pa.: The New Era Printing Co. 1912. In: The Pennsylvania-German Society. Proceedings and Addresses . . . 1910. Vol. XXI. Lancaster, Pa. 1912. Separate pagination. pp. 44, ill.* [1151

[—] Original letters of Peter Miller. *In: Hazard's Register of Pennsylvania. Vol. XVI. Philadelphia, Pa. 1835. pp. 253 —256.* [1152

P.[arthemore, E. W. S.]: The Ephrata Brethren. *(Some tombstone rerords). In: Notes and Queries. Edited by W. H. Egle. Annual vol. 1896. Harrisburg, Pa. 1897. p. 67.* [1153

— The Ephrata community. *(Transcript of the tombstone record of this ancient burial place). In: Notes and Queries. Edited by W. H. Egle. Annual vol. 1899. Harrisburg, Pa. 1900. pp. 173—176.* [1154

Pyle, Howard: A peculiar people. *In: Harper's New Monthly Magazine. Vol.*

LXXIX. October Number 1889. New New York, N. Y. 1889. pp. 776—785, ill. [*Speaks of the Dunkers and describes a visit to the cloister of Ephrata of the Seventh Day German Baptists.*] [1155

R.[attermann, H. A.]: Die alte Ephrata Presse. *In: Der Deutsche Pionier. Jg. VIII. Cincinnati, O. 1876—1877. S. 45 —48.* [1156

Reiter, A. O.: A visit to the Ephrata cloister. *In: The Penn Germania. Vol. I. = Old series, vol. XIII. Lititz, Pa. 1912. pp. 534—537.* [1157

Richards, H. M. M.: The Ephrata cloister and ist music. *Paper read Nov. 17, 1922. In: Papers read before the Lebanon County Historical Society. Vol. VIII. 1921— 1924. Lebanon, Pa. 1924. pp. 279—299, ill.* [1158

Russel, William: ,,Secte der Dumpler. Ihre Colonie . . .`` *In: Geschichte von Amerika von dessen Entdeckung an bis auf das Ende des vorigen Krieges. Bd. III. Leipzig: im Schwickertschen Verlage 1780 [= Nr. 3353a]. S. 380—384.* [1158a

Sachse, Julius Friedrich: The registers of the Ephrata community. *In: Pennsylvania Magazine of History and Biography. Vol. XIV. Philadelphia, Pa. 1890. pp. 297—312, ill., 387—402.* [1159

— The Ephrata papermill. *In: Papers and Addresses of the Lancaster County Historical Society. Vol. I. Lancaster, Pa. 1897. pp. 323—341.* [1160

— The German sectarians of Pennsylvania 1708—1742; 1742—1800. A critical and legendary history of the Ephrata cloister and the Dunkers. *2 vols. Philadelphia, Pa.: Printed for the author by P. C. Stockhausen 1899; 1900. pp. XXI, 506, ill.; XVI, 535, ill.* [1161

— The music of the Ephrata cloister also Conrad Beissel's treatise on music as set forth in a preface to the ,,Turtel Taube`` of 1747. Amplified with facsimile reproductions of parts of the text and some original Ephrata music of the Weyrauchs Hügel, 1739; Rosen and Lilien, 1745; Turtel Taube, 1747; Choral Buch 1754 etc. *Lancaster, Pa.: New Era Printing Co. 1903. = Part XI. ,,A narrative and critical history,`` prepared at the request of the Pennsylvania German Society. In: The Pennsylvania-German Society. Proceedings and Addresses . . . 1901. Vol. XII. Lancaster, Pa. 1903. Separate pagination. pp. 108, ill.* [1162

Sangmeister, Ezechiel: Das Leben und Wandel des in Gott ruhenten und seligen Br. Ezechiel Sangmeisters; Weiland ein Einwohner von Ephrata. *Dessen höchst sonderbare, und bemerkungswürdige Laufbahn, unter der Leitung und Führung Göttlicher Vorsehung! Mit allen Merckwürdigkeiten, womit seine Laufbahn begleitet, bis zu seiner Seligen Vollendung; Von ihm selbst beschrieben. Bestehend in 6 Theile. Welchem vorangeht, ein kurzer Entwurf einer Chronick, von der Stiftung und Grundlegung des Ephrataner-Wercks; bis auf des seligen Autores Ankunft daselbst: Wo alsdann die Chronick nebst seiner Laufbahn, gelegentlich mit fortgeführt, und aus dem Grunde der Wahrheit, mit unverfälschter Treue, ohne einige Partheylichkeit; Frey und offen ans Licht gestellt wird. Ephrata: Joseph Bauman 1825. 96 S.* Dieses Folgende ist der zweite Theil und der Anfang meiner armen Lebens-Beschreibung und nimmt seinen Anfang im Jahre 1752. *Erste treu nach dem Original bearbeitete Ausgabe. Zweiter Theil. Erste Auflage. Ephrata: Joseph Baumann 1825. 158, (2) S.* Dieses Folgende ist der dritte Theil von meiner armen und elenden Lebens-Beschreibung im Jahr 1764. *Erste treu nach dem Original bearbeitete Ausgabe. Dritter Theil. Erste Auflage. Ephrata: Joseph Baumann 1826. 88 S.* Folgendes ist der vierte Theil von meinem armen Lebens-Lauf; nimmt seinen Anfang im Jahr 1766. *Erste Auflage. Ephrata: Joseph Baumann 1827. 72 S.* [1163

— Mystische Theologie, . . . *Bestehend in 3 Theilen. Erste Auflage. Ephrata, Pa.: Joseph Baumann 1819 und 20. 142 S.* [*Angefügt*]: Kurze Lebens-Beschreibung des seligen Ezechiel Sangmeister. *Worinnen zu sehen, wie ihn Gott durch die dunkle Leidens-Nacht, bis zum hellen Mittage der Frohen Ewigkeit, so wunderbarlich geführet! Zweite Auflage. Ephrata: Joseph Bauman 1820. S. 143—168.* [1164

Seidensticker, Oswald W.: A colonial monastery [Ephrata]. *In: The Century Illustrated Monthly Magazine. Vol. XXIII. = New series, vol. I. New York, N. Y. 1881/2. pp. 209—223, ill.* [1165

— Ephrata, eine amerikanische Klostergeschichte. *In: Der Deutsche Pionier.*

*Jg. XIV. Cincinnati, O. 1882—1883.
S. 310—316; 362—371; 388—395; 418
—422; 449—455; Jg. XV. 1883—1884.
S. 8—14; 65—69; 98—102; 145—151;
190—195; 350—355; 396—408; 435—
446; 481—488; Jg. XVI. 1884—1885.
S. 54—62; 88—96; 134—142; 180—188.*
[1166

— Ephrata, eine amerikanische Klostergeschichte. *Sonderdruck des ,,Deutschen
Pionier". Cincinnati, O.: Druck von
Mecklenburg und Rosenthal 1883. 141 S.*
[1167

Yeager, Chas. S. and **Yeager, Arthur M.:** Brief
story of historic Ephrata. *Data gathered,
compiled and published by . . . Ephrata,
Pa.: ,,Review" Book Store 192 . . . pp.
48. Addenda.* Our early sectarians. *By
S. G. Zerfass. Read before the Berks
County Historical Society, April 13, 1920.
pp. 43—48.* [1168

Zerfass, S. G.: Souvenir book of the Ephrata cloister. Complete history from its
settlement in 1728 to the present time.
Included is the organization of Ephrata
Borough and other information of Ephrata connected with the cloister. *Lititz,
Pa.: John G. Zook 1921. pp. 84, ill.*
[1169

Account of the society of Dunkards in
Pennsylvania. *Communicated by a Bri-
tish officer to the editor of the Edinburgh
Magazine. (Date of letter): Edinburgh,
April 27, 1786. Edited with notes. In:
The American Museum or Repository of
ancient and modern fugitive pieces, &c.
Vol. VI. Philadelphia, Pa.: Mattew
Carey 1789. pp. 35—40.* [1170

Beissel, Johann Conrad. *In: The National Cyclopaedia of American Biography. Vol. VII. New York, N. Y.
1897. p. 497.* [1171

Lutheraner: Vereinigte Lutherische Kirche in Amerika

Lutherans: United Lutheran Church in America

Allgemeines

General

United States, Department of Commerce, Bureau of Census: Lutheran bodies. History, descriptions and statistics. *In: Religious bodies: 1906. Part II. Separate denominations. Washington, D. C. 1910 [= no. 894]. pp. 340—404.* — *In: Religious bodies: 1916. Part II. Washington, D. C. 1919. pp. 348—415.* Lutherans. *In: Religious bodies: 1926. Part II. Washington, D. C. 1929. pp. 698—841.* [1172

— United Lutheran Church in America. Statistics. History, doctrine, and organization. *In: Religious bodies: America. Statistics. History, doctrine, and organization. In: Religious bodies: 1926. Part II. Separate denominations. Washington, D. C. 1929 [= no. 894]. pp. 708—719.* [1173

Andersen, R.: Den Evangelisk-Lutherske Kirkes Historie i Amerika. *Fra dens Begyndelse til Nutiden Brooklyn, New York: Forfatterens Forlag 1889. pp. XVI, 672.* [1174

Aughey, Samuel: Course and character of emigration and what per cent. is available to the Lutheran Church. *In: The Quarterly Review of the Lutheran Church. New series, vol. VIII. Gettysburg, Pa. 1878. pp. 382—395.* [1175

B.[augher, H. Louis]: Theological education in the Lutheran Church in the United States. *In: The Evangelical Review, Vol. I. Gettysburg, Pa. 1849/50. pp. 19—39.* [1176

Bente, F.: American Lutheranism. *Vol. I.* Early history of American Lutheranism and the Tennesee Synod. *St. Louis, Mo: Concordia Publishing House 1919. pp. X, 237; Vol. II:* The General Synod of the General Council and the United Synod in the South. *St. Louis, Mo.: Concordia Publ. House 1919. pp. . . . .* [1177

Benze, C. F.: The Foreign Mission Board of the United Lutheran Church. *In: The Lutheran Church Review. Vol. XXXVIII. Philadelphia, Pa. 1919. pp. 110—115.* [1178

Berkemeier, G. C.: German Lutherans and American patriotism. *In: The Lutheran Church Review. Vol. XXVII. Philadelphia, Pa. 1908. pp. 72—78.* [1179

Brown, J. A.: The Evangelical Lutheran Church in the United States. *Reprint from: „The Bibliotheca sacra", July 1868. Andover: Warren F. Draper 1868. pp. 435—500.* [1180

Bushnell, J. E.: Some items of Lutheran Church history. *In: The Quarterly Review of the Evangelical Lutheran Church. New series, vol. XVII. Gettysburg, Pa. 1887. pp. 296—301.* [1181

Clutz, J. A.: The United Lutheran Church in America. *In: The Lutheran Quarterly. Vol. XLIX. Gettysburg, Pa. 1919. pp. 1—22; 313—329.* [1182

Conrad, Victor L.: The Press in the Lutheran Church. *In: The Lutheran Quarterly. Vol. XXVIII. Gettysburg, Pa. 1898. pp. 532—544.* [1183

Drach, George and Kuder, Calvin F.: The beginning of foreign mission work in the Lutheran Church in America. *In: The Lutheran Church Review. Vol. XXVII. Philadelphia, Pa. 1908. pp. 288—293; 438—445; 647—659; Vol. XXVIII. 1909. pp. 29—35; 216—224; 375—383; Vol. XXIX. 1910. pp. 76—86; 397—408; 603—615; 828—834; Vol. XXX. 1911. pp. 113—119; 374—385; 558—565; 739—751.* [1184

Early, J. W.: Rev. J. Nicholas Kurtz' account of the doings of the Synod, 1749—1750. As contained in the church record of Christ Church, Stouchsburg, Pa. *In: The Lutheran Church Review. Vol.*

XVIII. Philadelphia, Pa. 1899. pp. 675—677. [1185

Fandrey, G. A.: German Lutheranism. *In: The Lutheran Church Review. Vol. XXII. Philadelphia, Pa. 1903. pp. 520—534.* [1186

Finck, William J.: Lutheran landmarks and pioneers in America. A series of sketches of colonial times. *With an introduction by Elmer J. Krauss. Philadelphia, Pa.: General Council Publication House 1913. pp. 200.* [1187

— Lutheranism south of the Potomac. *A Sesqui-Centennial review. In: The Lutheran Quarterly. Vol. LVI. Gettysburg, Pa. 1926. pp. 268—286.* [1188

Fortenbaugh, Robert: The development of the syndical polity of the Lutheran Church in America, to 1829. *Thesis of Ph. D., the Graduate School, University of Pennsylvania, Philadelphia, Pa. 1926. pp. (8), 5—252. [Bibliography: pp. 231—252.]* [1189

Fritschel, Georg I.: Geschichte der Lutherischen Kirche in Amerika auf Grund von Prof. Dr. H. E. Jacobs History of the Evangelical Lutheran Church in the United States. *1. Teil:* Geschichte der Entwicklung der lutherischen Kirche in Amerika bis zu Mühlenbergs Tode. *Gütersloh: C. Bertelsmann 1896. XIV, 211 S. ill., Karten; 2. Teil:* Geschichte der Entwicklung der lutherischen Kirche von Mühlenbergs Tode bis zur Gegenwart . . . *1897. XVI, 432 S. ill., Karten.* [1190

Gerberding, G. H.: The Lutheran Church in the country. A study, an explanation, an attemped solution. *Philadelphia, Pa.: General Council Publication Board 1916. pp. 212.* [1191

Gilbert, D. M.: A chapter of colonial Luthero-Episcopal Church history. *(An address delivered at the laying of the corner stone of Emanuel Evangelical Lutheran Church, Woodstock, Va., Friday, Aug. 8, 1884.) In: The Quarterly Review of the Evangelical Lutheran Church. New series, vol. XIV. Gettysburg, Pa. 1884. pp. 479—500. Separate print: Gettysburg, Pa.: J. E. Wible 1884. pp. 24.* [1192

Gotwald, Frederick, Gebhart: Pioneer American Lutheran journalism, 1812—1850. *In: The Lutheran Quarterly. Vol. XLII. Gettysburg, Pa. 1912. pp. 161—204, ill.* [1193

Gräbner, A. L.: Geschichte der Lutherischen Kirche in Amerika. *Erster Teil. St.*

Louis, Mo.: Concordia Publishing House 1892. XI, 726 S. [1194

[Hallische Nachrichten]: Nachrichten von den vereinigten Deutschen Evangelisch-Lutherischen Gemeinen in Nord-America, absonderlich in Pennsylvanien. *Erster Band mit einer Vorrede von D. Johann Ludewig Schulze. Halle: In Verlegung des Waisenhauses 1787. Fortsetzung I—XVI. (7), 808, (9), 809—1518, (10) S.* [1195

[—] Reports of the United German Evangelical Lutheran congregation in North America, especially in Pennsylvania, with a preface by D. John Ludwig Schulze. *Published in the Orphan House, Halle, A. D. 1750. Translated from the German by Jonathan Oswald. No. 1. Philadelphia, Pa.: Lutheran Publication Society. 1880. pp. XVI, 17—356.* [1196

[—] Nachrichten von den vereinigten Deutschen Evangelisch-Lutherischen Gemeinen in Nord-America, absonderlich in Pennsylvanien. *Mit einer Vorrede von Dr. Johann Ludewig Schulze. Halle: In Verlegung des Waisenhauses 1787. Neu Herausgegeben mit historischen Erläuterungen und Mittheilungen aus dem Archiv der Franckeschen Stiftungen zu Halle von W. J. Mann, B. M. Schmucker, W. Germann. Bd. I. Allentown, Pa.: Brobst, Diehl & Co. 1881. 672 S.; Zweite Auflage 1886. XI, 724 S.; Bd. II. Philadelphia, Pa.: P. G. C. Eisenhardt 1895. X, VI, 821 S.* [1197

[—] Reports of the United German Evangelical Lutheran congregations in North America, especially in Pennsylvania; *with a preface by Dr. John Ludwig Schulze. Vol. I. [Halle reports.]. New edition, with extensive historical, critical and literary annotations and numerous documents, copied from the manuscripts in the archives of the Francke institutions at Halle. By W. J. Mann; B. M. Schmucker; W. Germann. Translated from the German by C. W. Schaeffer. Reading, Pa.: Pilger Book-store 1882. Vol. I. pp. (2), 220, ill.* [1198

Hashinger, W. Roy: What shall be the distinctive contribution of the Lutheran Church to the religious life of America. *In: The Lutheran Church Review. Vol. XXXVII. Philadelphia, Pa. 1918, pp. 39—47.* [1199

Hassler, J. W.: Our American Lutheran Church. *In: The Lutheran Church Re-*

view. Vol. XIII. Philadelphia, Pa. 1894. pp. 142—150. [1200

Hazelius, Ernest L.: History of the American Lutheran Church, from its commencement in the year of our Lord 1685, to the year 1842. *To which several appendices are added, containing the constitution of the first Synod, and statistical tables of the number of churches and members in connexion with the different acknowledged Lutheran Synods; the theological seminaries and other institutions under the care of the American Lutheran Church as also the Constitution of the General Synod. Zanesville, O.: Edwin C. Church. 1846. pp. VII, 9—300.* [1201

Heathcote, Charles William: The Lutheran Church and the Civil War. *Burlington, Iowa: The Lutheran Literary Board 1919. New York, N. Y.: Fleming H. Revell Co. 1919. pp. 160.* [1202

Heilman, Lee M.: Lutheranism in America liberty vindicated. *In: The Quarterly Review of the Evangelical Lutheran Church. Vol. XXIV. Gettysburg, Pa. 1894. pp. 81—100.* [1203

Herbst, Johann: Geschichte der Lutherischen Kirche in den Vereinigten Staaten von Nord-Amerika. *In: Das Evangelische Magazin der Ev. Lutherischen Kirche in den Freistaaten von Nordamerika. Herausgegeben unter der Aufsicht eines Ausschusses von der Westpennsylvanischen Synode dazu ernannt. Redakteur: Johann Herbst. Bd. I. Gettysburg, Pa. 1829. S. 3—7; 33—38; 65—69; 97—100; 129—132; 161—164.* [1204

Hoffmann, J. N.: The Evangelical Lutheran Church, or Historical reminiscenses, designed to meet the antagonistic tendencies of our age and country. *In: The Evangelical Review. Vol. II. Gettysburg, Pa. 1850—1851. pp. 265—281.* [1205

Hubert, E.: The Lutheran Church between the Potomac and the Rio Grande. *In: The Quarterly Review of the Evangelical Lutheran Church. New series, vol. IX. Gettysburg, Pa. 1879. pp. 245—261.* [1206

Jacobs, Henry Eyster: A history of the Evangelical Lutheran Church in the United States. *New York, N. Y.: The Christian Literature Co. 1893. pp. XVI, 539. = The American Church History Series. Vol. IV. Second edition. New York, N. Y. 1919. pp. XVI, 539.* [1207

Jacobs, Henry Eyster: Beginnings of the foreign mission work of the Lutheran Church in America. From an unpublished narrative of Father Heyer. *In: The Lutheran Church Review. Vol. XIX. Philadelphia, Pa. 1900. pp. 50—62.* [1208

— The confessional problem in the Lutheran Church of America in 1742. *In: The Lutheran Church Review. Vol. XXXI. Philadelphia, Pa. 1912. pp. 245—252.* [1209

— Three Lutheran Synods in eastern Pennsylvania. *In: The Lutheran Church Quarterly. Vol. I. Gettysburg, Pa. 1928. pp. 320—335.* [1210

Jensson, J. C.: American Lutheran biographies; or, historical notices of over three hundred and fifty leading men of the American Lutheran Church from its establishment to the year 1890 with an historical introduction and numerous portrait engravings. *Milwaukee, Wis. Press of Houtkamp & Son 1890. pp. XVI, 17—901, ill.* [1211

Johnson, Roy H.: The Lutheran Church and the western frontier, 1789—1830. *In: The Lutheran Church Quarterly. Vol. III. Gettysburg, Pa. 1930. pp. 225—248.* [1212

Kieffer, G. L.: The Lutherans in America 1923. *In: The Lutheran Quarterly. Vol. LIV. Gettysburg, Pa. 1924. pp. 366—373.* [1213

Kraeling, Carl H.: In quest of the Muhlenbergiana. *In: The Lutheran Church Quarterly. Vol. II. Gettysburg, Pa. 1929. pp. 180—189.* [1214

Kraushaar, Chr. Otto: Verfassungsformen der Lutherischen Kirche Amerikas. *Gütersloh: C. Bertelsmann 1911. XI, 496 S.* [1215

Krauth, C. P.: The Lutheran Church in the United States. *In: The Evangelical Review. Vol. II. Gettysburg, Pa. 1850—51. pp. 1—16.* [1216

Kunzmann, J. C.: The hindrance to our church's growth in the United States. *In: The Lutheran Church Review. Vol. XV. Philadelphia, Pa. 1896. pp. 34—50.* [1217

— The Lutherans in America. Their heroic past and their promising future. *[s. l., s. d.] pp. 34.* [1218

Lenker, J. N.: Lutherans in all lands, the wonderful works of God. *Milwaukee, Wis.: Lutherans in all Lands Co. 1896. Fifth revised and enlarged edition. pp. 830, (10), ill.* [1219

Mann, W. Julius: Lutheranism in America: An essay on the present condition of the Lutheran Church in the United States. *Philadelphia, Pa.: Lindsay & Blakiston 1857. pp. XII, 13—152.* [1220

— Vergangene Tage. Aus den Zeiten des Patriarchen Dr. H. M. Mühlenbergs. *Vortrag, gehalten bei der Reformationsfeier des Theol. Luth. Seminars, am 31. Oktober. 1879, in der Evang. Luth. Zions-Kirche. Reading, Pa.: Pilger Buchhandlung; Allentown, Pa.: Brobst, Diehl & Co. 1879. 23 S.* [1221

— Lutherans in America before Mühlenberg. *In: The Lutheran Church Review. Vol. VI. Philadelphia, Pa. 1887. pp. 93—114.* [1222

— Life and times of Henry Melchior Mühlenberg. *Philadelphia, Pa.: G. W. Frederick 1887. pp. XVI. 547; Second edition Philadelphia, Pa.: General Council Publication Board 1911. pp. XVI, 547, ill.* [1223

— The conservatism of Henry Melchior Mühlenberg. *In: The Lutheran Church Review. Vol. VII. Philadelphia, Pa. 1888. pp. 18—46* [1223a

— Ordination pledges in the time of Mühlenberg. *In: The Lutheran Church Review. Vol. X. Philadelphia, Pa. 1891. pp. 164—168.* [1224

— Heinrich Melchior Mühlenbergs Leben und Wirken. *Zum 150. Jahrestag von Mühlenbergs Ankunft in der Neuen Welt. Philadelphia, Pa.: A. Hellwege, Roxborough 1891. pp. 77 ill.* [1225

— und **Wischan, F.**: Die lutherische Kirche in Amerika. *Teil I. Heinr. Melch. Mühlenbergs Leben. Zum 150. Jahrestag von Mühlenbergs Ankunft in der Neuen Welt. Von W. J. Mann. [Neudruck von Nr. 1225] Teil II. Kurze Geschichte der deutschen evangel. luther. Gemeinde in und um Philadelphia und der lutherischen Synoden Amerikas. Von F. Wischan. (1892). 2. Bde. in einem. Leipzig: Theodor Rother 1893. 77 S. ill.; (1), 79—240 S., ill.* [1226

Maurer, Heinrich H.: Studies in the sociology of religion. *Part II. Religion and American Sectionalism. The Pennsylvania German. In: The American Journal of Sociology. Vol. XXX, no. 4. Chicago, Ill.: The University of Chicago Press. 1925. pp. 408—438.* [1227

Morris, John G.: The literature of the Lutheran Church in the United States. *In:*

The Evangelical Review. Vol. XV. Gettysburg, Pa. 1864. pp. 416—428. [1228

Morris, John G.: Bibliotheca Lutherana: a complete list of the publications of all the Lutheran ministers in the United States. *Philadelphia, Pa.: Lutheran Board of Publication 1876. pp....* [1229

Muhlenberg, F. A.: Educational efforts of the Pennsylvania Synod. *In: The Evangelical Review. Vol. X. Gettysburg, Pa. 1858—59. pp. 269—290; 530—563.* [1230

Mühlenberg, Henry Melch or: Vgl. *Hallische Nachrichten [= Nr. 1195f.].* [1231

— Heinrich Melchior Mühlenberg, Patriarch der Lutherischen Kirche Nordamerika's. *Selbstbiographie, 1711—1743. Aus dem Missionsarchive der Fränkischen Stiftungen zu Halle. Mit Zusätzen und Erläuterungen von W. Germann. Allentown, Pa. Brobst, Diehl & Co.; Halle a. S.: Waisenhausbuchhandlung 1881. X, (2), 256 S.* [1232

Neve, J. L.: Kurzgefaßte Geschichte der Lutherischen Kirche. *Burlington, Ia.: German Literary Board; Für Deutschland: Leipzig: H. G. Wallmann 1904. 205 S. Zweite verbesserte und erweiterte Auflage. Burlington, Ia.: German Literary Board 1915. 391 S.* [1233

[—] A brief history of the Lutheran Church in America. *By ... Translated from the German by* **Joseph Stump**. *Burlington, Ia.: German Literary Board 1904. pp. 203. Second revised and enlarged edition. Burlington, Ia.: The German Literary Board 1916. pp. V, 469.* [1234

Nicum, John: The confessional history of the Evangelical Lutheran Church in the United States. *In: Papers of the American Society of Church History. Vol. IV. New York, N. Y. — London: G. P. Putnam's Sons. The Knickerbocker Press 1892. pp. 93—109.* [1235

Nothstein, Ira Oliver: Lutheran makers of America. *Brief sketches of sixty-eight notable early Americans. Philadelphia, Pa.: The United Lutheran Publication House. 1930. pp. 232, ill.* [1236

Ochsenford, S. E.: The Lutheran Church in America. *In: The Lutheran Church Review. Vol. IV. Philadelphia, Pa. 1885. 12—28.* [1237

Sachse, Julius Friedrich: The genesis of the German Lutheran Church in the land of Penn. *In: The Lutheran Church Review. Vol. XVI. Philadelphia, Pa. 1897. pp. 60—76; 283—301; 435—452; 521—539,*

8*

ill.; Vol. XVII. 1898. pp. 723—727; Vol. XVIII. 1899. pp. 118—120.   [1238

Sachse, Julius Friedrich: The influence of the Halle pietism in the provincial development of Pennsylvania. *In: The Lutheran Quarterly. Vol.XXXI. Gettysburg, Pa. 1901. p. 170—176.*   [1239

— Pennsylvania, a Lutheran colony. *Paper read before the Philadelphia. Theological Seminary at Mt. Airy. In: The Lutheran Church Review. Vol. XX. Philadelphia, Pa. 1901. pp. 277—292.*   [1240

Sandt, George W.: Lutheran adjustment to American environment. *In: The Lutheran Church Review. Vol. XIV. Philadelphia, Pa.1895. pp.262—270.* [1241

Schaeffer, C. F.: The present transition state of the Evangelical Lutheran Church in the United States. *Read May 26, 1853, at Winchester, Va., before the Historical Society of the General Synod. In: The Lutheran Church Review. Vol. VII. Philadelphia, Pa. 1888. pp. 185—210.*   [1242

Schaeffer, C. W.: Early history of the Lutheran Church in America from the settlement of the Swedes on the Delaware, to the middle of the eighteenth century. *Philadelphia, Pa.: Lutheran Board of Publication 1857. pp. 143. View and reprint of part of fifth chapter. In: The Evangelical Review. Vol. IX. Gettysburg, Pa. 1857—58. pp.115—129. New edition . . . Philadelphia, Pa.: The Lutheran Book Store 1868. pp. 142.*   [1243

Schierenbeck, Joh. Heinr. Con.: Lebens-Beschreibungen, oder Nachrichten von dem Leben und den Schriften aller evangelisch-lutherischen Prediger, welche seit Dr. Heinr. Melchior Mühlenberg's Zeit im Staate Pennsylvanien Gemeinden bedient haben oder noch bedienen, ingleichen von denen welche in andern Staaten ihre Versorgung gefunden, aber mit den ev.-luth. Synoden Pennsylvaniens in Verbindung gestanden haben oder noch stehen. *Zusammengetragen von . . . ev.-luth. Prediger in New-Castle, Lawrence Co., Pa. Se-lins-Grove, Pa. In der Druckerei des ,,American Lutheran". 1865. Vier Hefte. 128 S.*   [1243a

Schmauk, Theodore Emanuel: A history of the Lutheran Church in Pennsylvania (1638—1820). From the original sources. *Lancaster, Pa.: New Era Printing Co. 1902—1903. = Part IX. ,,A narrative*

and critical history", prepared at the request of the Pennsylvania-German Society. In: The Pennsylvania-German Society. Proceedings and Addresses. 1900. Vol. XI. Lancaster, Pa. Separate pagination. pp. (1), VIII, (1), 355, ill.; . . . 1901. Vol. XII. Lancaster, Pa. 1903. Separate Pagination. pp. (1), VII—XXIII, 357—588.   [1244

Schmauk, Theodore Emmanuel: The confessional situation in the Lutheran Church in America in 1827. The period from 1792—1831. *In: The Lutheran Church Review. Vol. XXXI. Philadelphia, Pa. 1912. pp. 253—263.*   [1245

Schmucker, Beale M.: The organization of the congregation in the early Lutheran churches in America. *In: The Lutheran Church Review. Vol. VI. Philadelphia, Pa. 1887. pp. 188—226.*   [1246

Schmucker, S. S.: The patriarchs of American Lutheranism, *being a discourse, delivered before the Historical Society of the Lutheran Church in the United States, at its first meeting, held during the Session of the General Synod in Philadelphia, May 17, 1845. Baltimore, Md.: Publication Rooms 1845. pp. 55.*   [1247

— The American Lutheran Church, historically, doctrinally and practically delineated, in several occasional discourses: *Springfield, O.: Harbaugh & Butler 1851. pp. X, 11—280, ill.; Second edition. 1851. pp. X, 11—280, ill.; Third edition. 185.. pp. X, 11—280, ill.; Fourth edition. 1852. pp. X, 11—280, ill.*   [1248

Späth, Adolph: Amerikanische Beleuchtung der ,,Amerikanischen Reisebilder" des Herrn Prof. J. G. Pfeiderer. Mit besonderer Rücksicht auf württembergische Leser. *Philadelphia, Pa.: C. G. Fischer 1882. 24 S.*   [1249

Sprague, William B.: Annals of the American Lutheran pulpit; or commemorative notices of distinguished clergymen of the Lutheran denomination in the United States, from its commencement to the close of the year 1855 with an historical introduction. *New York, N. Y.: Robert Carter & Brothers 1869. pp. XII, 216, (3), ill.*   [1250

Stall, Sylvanus: The relation of the Lutheran Church in the United States to the lime-stone districts. *In: The Quarterly Review of the Evangelical Lutheran Church. New series, vol. XIII. Gettysburg, Pa. 1883. pp. 509—515.* [1251

Stoever, M. L.: A brief sketch of the Evangelical Lutheran Church in the United States of America. *Philadelphia, Pa.: Issued by the Lutheran Board of Publications [s. d.] pp. 12.*
= No. 2. *pp. 21—32.* [1252
— Memoir of the life. and times of Henry Melchior Mühlenberg, D. D., patriarch of the Evangelical Lutheran Church in America. *For the Board of Publication. Philadelphia, Pa.: Lindsay & Blakiston 1856. pp. XII, 13—120.* [1253
[—] The patriarchs of the Lutheran Church from Halle. *Delivered by appointment of the Historical Society of the Evangelical Lutheran Church at the meeting of the General Synod in Lancaster, May 7th, 1862. In: The Evangelical Review. Vol. XV. Gettysburg, Pa. 1864. pp. 159—190.* [1254
— Reminiscences of Lutheran clergymen. *In: The Evangelical Review. Gettysburg, Pa. Vol. V. 1853/4 — Vol. XXI. 1870.* John C. Kunze, D. D. *In: Vol. V. pp. 515—520;* Henry Ernst Mühlenberg, D. D. *In: Vol. V. pp. 520—527;* John Nicolas Kurtz. *In: Vol. VI. pp. 261—268;* Jacob Goering. *In: Vol. VI. pp. 268—275;* Frederick David Schaeffer, D. D. *In: Vol. VI. pp. 275 287;* J. George Schmucker, D. D. *In: Vol. VI. pp. (412)—425;* John W. Richards. *In: Vol. VI. pp. 425—434;* John G. Schwartz. *In: Vol. VI. pp. 542—553;* Christopher F. Bergman. *In: Vol. VI. pp. 553—562;* Ezra Keller. *In: Vol. VII. pp. 63—73;* Walter Gun. *In: Vol. VII. pp. 74—85;* Peter Brunholtz. *In: Vol. VII. pp. (151)—159;* John Frederick Handschuh. *In: Vol. VII. pp. 159—168;* John Christopher Hartwig. *In: Vol. VII. pp. 168—173;* John Helfrich Schaum. *In: Vol. VII. pp. 527—538;* Christopher Emanuel Schultze. *In: Vol. VII. pp. 538—544;* Michael J. Steck. *In: Vol. VIII. pp. 105—112;* Michael Eyster. *In: Vol. VIII. pp. 113—123;* John Peter Goertner. *In: Vol. VIII. pp. 186—199;* Frederick Christian Schaeffer, D. D. *In: Vol. VIII. pp. 200—210;* Jacob Berger. *Vol. VIII. pp. 210—218;* Charles Augustus Gottlieb Storch. *In: Vol. VIII. pp. 398—404;* Gottlieb Shober. *In: Vol. VIII. pp. 404—415;* Frederick William Geissenhainer, D. D. *In: Vol. VIII. pp. 501—519;* John Daniel Kurtz, D. D. *In: Vol.*

VIII. pp. 519—532; John Martin Bolzius. *In: Vol. IX. pp. 1—12;* John Ernest Bergman. *In: Vol. IX. pp. 13 —18;* Henry Moeller. *In: Vol. IX. pp. 273—277;* Christian Streit. *In: Vol. IX. pp. 378—384;* John Ruthrauff. *In: Vol. IX. pp. 384—390;* Frederick Jonathan Ruthrauff. *In: Vol. IX. pp. 390—400;* Nicholas G. Sharretts.*Vol. IX.pp. 511—515;* Emanuel Keller. In: *Vol. IX. pp. 515—522;* Frederick Henry Quitman, D. D. *In: Vol. X. pp. 183—190;* Philip Frederick Mayer, D. D. *In: Vol. X. pp. 190— 214;* William Schmidt. *In: Vol. X. pp. 386—392;* Charles Henkel. *In: Vol. X. 392—399.* John George Butler. *Vol. X. pp. 564—572;* George Daniel Flohr. *In: Vol. X. pp. 573—579.* John Christopher Baker, D. D. *In: Vol. XI. pp. 202—225;* John Dietrich Mathias Heintzelman. *In: Vol. XI. pp. (428) —432;* John Lewis Voigt. *In: Vol. XI. pp. 432—435;* John Andrew Krug. *In: Vol. XI. pp. 435—438;* [Swedish Lutheran Church. *Vol. XI. pp. 585— 593];* William Christopher Berkenmeyer. *In: Vol. XIII. pp. 362—370;* Peter Nicholas Mayer. *In: Vol. XIII. pp. 370—375;* Lewis Eichelberger, D. D. *In: Vol. XIV. pp. 293—298;* John Ulrich. *In: Vol. XIV. pp. 299— 306;* William Carpenter. *In: Vol. XV. pp. 129—135;* John Christian William Yeager. *In: Vol. XV. pp. 135—140;* Charles Rudolph Demme, D. D. *In: Vol. XV. pp. 428—448;* Charles Alfred Baer. *In: Vol. XV. pp. 534—544;* Benjamin Keller. *In: Vol. XVI. pp. 470—476;* Frederick August Muhlenberg Keller. *In: Vol. XVI. pp. 476— 480;* John Samuel Crumbaugh. *In: Vol. XVII. pp. (391)—396;* Thomas William Kemp. *In: Vol. XVII. pp. 396—402;* Augustus Wackerhagen, D. D. *In: Vol. XVII. pp. 485—493;* Benjamin Kuntz, D. D. L. L. D. *In: Vol. XVIII. pp. 25—46;* Daniel Garver. *In: Vol. XVIII. pp. 232—240;* William Henry Harrison, D. D. *In: Vol. XVIII. pp. 240—249;* William Beates. *In: Vol. XIX. pp. 405—424;* John Caspar Stoever. *In: Vol. XIX. pp. 622—625;* Lucas Raus. *In: Vol. XIX. pp. 625—627;* John Nicholas Martin. *In: Vol. XX. pp. 381—387;* Paul Henkel. *In: Vol. XX. pp. 387— 392;* Jacob Wingard. *In: Vol. XX.*

pp. 392—396; Araon Jacob Karn. *In: Vol. XX. pp. 396—400;* George Benjamin Miller. *In: Vol. XXI. pp. 24—44;* John Heck. *In: Vol. XXI. pp. 171—177;* Michael Diehl. *In: Vol. XXI. pp. 177—182;* Charles Frederick Edward Stohlman, *D. D. In: Vol. XXI. pp. 334—339;* Abraham Beck. *In: Vol. XXI. pp. 339—450.* [1255

Stump, Adam: The living issue before the Lutheran Church in America. *In: The Quarterly Review of the Evangelical Lutheran Church. Vol. XIX. Gettysburg, Pa. 1889. pp. 347—363.* [1256

Trabert, George H.: Inner mission work of the Evangelical Lutheran Church in America. *In: The Lutheran Church Review. Vol. XXVII. Philadelphia, Pa. 1908. pp. 305—311; 407—414.* [1257

[Washington, George]: Washington to the German — Lutherans. *Letter of George Washington ,,To the Ministers, Church Council, and members of the German Lutheran congregations in and near Philadelphia." Contributed by* H. C. Salem. *In: The Pennsylvania-German. Vol. X. Lititz, Pa. 1909. pp. 152—153.* [1258

Weller, H. A.: Pioneer Lutheranism beyond the frontier of early civilization in Pennsylvania. *A paper read before, the Historical Academy of the Lutheran Church at Harrisburg, Pa., Dec., 1911. In: The Lutheran Quarterly. Vol. XLII. Gettysburg, Pa. 1912. pp. 337—354.* [1259

Wentz, Abdel Ross: The Lutheran Church im American history. *With an introduction by Henry Eyster Jacobs. Philadelphia, Pa.: The United Lutheran Publication House. 1923. pp. 355, ill.; Second edition, revised and enlarged Philadelphia, Pa. 1933. pp. 465.* [1260

— The Lutheran Church in the foundations of America. *In: The Lutheran Quarterly. Vol. LVI. Gettysburg, Pa. 1926. pp. 257—267.* [1261

Wolf, Edmund Jacob: The Lutheran Church in this country one hundred years ago. *In: The Quarterly Review of the Evangelical Lutheran Church. Vol. XIX. Gettysburg, Pa. 1889. pp. 242—280.* [1262

— The Lutherans in America. A story of struggle, progress, influence and marvelous growth. *With an introduction by Henry Eyster Jacobs. New York, N. Y.: J. A. Hill & Co. 1889. pp. XX, 544, ill.; Second edition 1890. pp. XX, 544.* [1263

[Wolf, Edmund Jakob]: Die Lutheraner in Amerika. Eine Geschichte ihres Kampfes, Fortschritts, Einflusses und ihres staunenswerten Wachstums. *Mit einer Einleitung von Henry Eyster Jacobs. Deutsch bearbeitet von* Joh. Nicum. *New York, N. Y.: J. A. Hill & Co. 1891. XX, 21—542 S., ill.* [1264

Zahn, Adolf: Abriß einer Geschichte der Evangelischen Kirche in Amerika im neunzehnten Jahrhundert. *Stuttgart: F. J. Steinkopf. 1889. 127 S.* [1265

Zundel, W. A.: Lutheran influence in America affairs. *Rochester, Pa.: C. W. Retzer. Printing Co. 1914. pp. 23.* [1266

In memoriam. Henry Melchior Mühlenberg 1711, 1742, 1787. *Commemorative exercises held by the Susquehanna Synod of the Evangelical Lutheran Church, at Selinsgrove, Pa., Oct. 18 and 19, 1887. Published for the Synod's Committee. Philadelphia, Pa.: Lutheran Publication Society 1888. pp. 61.*

Ochsenford, S. E.: Lutheranism in America prior to the coming of Mühlenberg. *pp. 3—20.*

Focht, John B.: Pietsm and Halle. *pp. 21—27.*

Wolf, E. J.: Heinrich Melchior Mühlenberg. *pp. 28—41.*

Morris, J. G.: Brief synopsis of the remarks on the Muehlenberg family. *pp. 42—50.*

Cressman, Mark S.: Lutheranism in America since the death of Mühlenberg. *pp. 51—61.* [1267

Lutherans in colonial days. *Edited by* Nathan Raymond Melhorn. *Philadelphia, Pa.: The Board of Publication of the United Lutheran Church in America (1926). pp. 93*
[Collective reprint of papers written at the occasion of the 150th anniversary of the Declaration of American Independence and originally printed in: The Lutheran. Special issue July 1, 1926.]

Wentz, Abdel Ross: Spiritual freedom produces civil liberty. *The Religion of Lutheran colonists in relation to the achievement of American independence pp. 9—22, ill.*

Sandt, G. W.: Early Lutheran footprints on American soil. *pp. 25—37, ill.*

Fortenbaugh, Robert: Inland Lutheran migrations in colonial times. *pp. 39—57, ill.*

Horine, John W., A tale of two cities. Our church in the South in colonial times. *pp. 59—69, ill.*

Kieffer, G. L.: They helped erect the government. *An analysis of colonial enumerations which finds Lutherans a considerable percentage of the population. pp. 71—79, ill.*

Kieffer, G. L.: Congregations listed in the minutes of the various synods for the year 1925, organized prior to 1800. *pp. 81—92.* [1268

Kurzer Bericht von den Anstalten in den Deutsch Evangelisch-Lutherischen Gemeinden in Pennsylvanien und einigen benachbarten Staaten. Die Reise Prediger; Erziehung junger Lehrer, und Fürsorge für arme Prediger, Witwen be-

treffend. *Philadelphia, Pa.: Conrad Zentler 1808. 24 S.* [1269

The Evangelical Lutheran Church in the United States of America. *In: The Evangelical Review. Vol. XX. Gettysburg, Pa. 1869. pp. 113—125.* [1270

First free Lutheran diet in America. Philadelphia, December, 27—28, 1877. The essays, debates and proceedings. *Edited by H. E. Jacobs Philadelphia, Pa.: J. Frederick Smith 1878. pp. VIII, 9—346. . . . Philadelphia, November 5—7, 1878. Edited by W. M. Baum and J. A. Kunkelmann. Philadelphia, Pa.: Lutheran Publication Society; Lutheran Bookstore 1879. pp. VI, 7—282.* [1271

Synoden

Synods

Ministerium von Pennsylvanien, 1748 errichtet

Ministerium of Pennsylvania, org. 1748

Verhandlungen der Deutschen Evangelisch-Lutherischen Synode von Pennsylvanien und den benachbarten Staaten, gehalten zu Yorktaun, den 2ten Juny, 1817. *Philadelphia, Pa.: Conrad Zentler 1818. 16 S.*

[Verhandlungen der 69sten Versammlung.] [1272

Verhandlungen . . . der . . . jährlichen (Jahres)Versammlung . . . Deutsche Evangelisch-Lutherische Synode; *seit 1844:* Deutsches Evangelisch-Lutherisches Ministerium von Pennsylvanien und den benachbarten Staaten; *seit 1883:* Evangelisch-Lutherisches Ministerium . . .; *seit 1909:* Protocoll der Verhandlungen. *Jährlich veröffentlicht. 1818ff.—1918.* [1273

Proceedings of the German Evangelical Synod of Pennsylvania held at Harrisburg, in Trinity week, 1826. *Easton, Pa.: Henry and William Hutter 1826. pp. 20.*

[= Minutes of the 78th convention 1826 and at the same time first minutes in English.] [1274

Proceedings of the . . . German Evangelical Synod of Pennsylvania; *since 1844:* German Evangelical-Lutheran Ministe-

rium of Pennsylvania and adjacent states; *since 1883;* Evangelical Lutheran Ministerium . . .; *since 1830:* Minutes . . .; *since 1903:* Minutes of proceedings . . . of . . . annual convention. *Annually published. [English edition since the 78th convention 1826.] 1826ff.* [1275

Documentary history of the Evangelical Lutheran Ministerium of Pennsylvania and adjacent states. Proceedings of the annual conventions from 1748 to 1821. *Compiled and translated from records in the archives and from the written protocols. Philadelphia, Pa.: Board of Publication of the General Council of the Evangelical Lutheran Church in North America. 1898. pp. IV, 619.* [1276

The first convention of the Ministerium of Pennsylvania. *Reprint from: Documentary history pp. 3ff. In: The Lutheran Church Review. Vol. XLII. Philadelphia, Pa. 1923. pp. 97—109.* [1277

Minutes of the proceedings of the 100th annual meeting of the German Evangelical Lutheran Ministerium of Pennsylvania and the adjacent states, held in Philadelphia, Pa. on Trinity Sunday, May the 30th, A. D. 1847. *Reading, Pa.: C. W. Guenther 1847. pp. 48.* [1278

Jubilee services in commemoration of the 150th anniversary of the Evangelical Lutheran Ministerium of Pennsylvania and adjacent states. June 2—4, 1898.

*Philadelphia, Pa.: Published by order of
the Ministerium 1898. pp. 77, ill.* [1279
175th anniversary. The Evangelical Lutheran Ministerium of Pennsylvania
and adjacent states. Held at Trinity
Church, Reading, Pa. The Rev. E. P.
Pfatteicher, Ph. D. D. D., Pastor.
June 4—5, 1923 . . . . *1923. pp.* . . .
                                          [1280
Early, J. W.: Constitution of the Ministerium
of the Evangelical Lutheran Chruch of
North America, in force in 1781. *Edited
by . . . In: The Lutheran Church Review. Vol. IX. Philadelphia, Pa. 1890.
pp. 254—269.*   [1281
— The Ministerium of Pennsylvania and
the organization of the General Synod.
*In: The Lutheran Church Review. Vol.
XI. Philadelphia, Pa. 1892. pp. 61—
70; 172—186.*   [1282
— History of the Sunday school in the Ministerium of Pennsylvania. *In: The
Lutheran Church Review. Vol. XV.
Philadelphia, Pa. 1896. pp. 413—419.*
                                          [1283
Horn, Edward T.: Committee to prepare a
sketch of the history of the Synod, etc.
Report of Sub-Committee on minutes
of 1781—1821. *[Chronological summary
of the acts of the Synod of Pennsylvania,
recorded in the minutes of 1781—1821.]
pp. 28, (1).*   [1284
Jacobs, Henry Eyster: In commemoration of
the 150th anniversary of the Ministerium
of Pennsylvania, 1748—1898. *Reprint
from: The Lutheran Church Review,
Jan. and April, 1898. pp. 65.*   [1285
— The ideals of 1748 and their realization.
*Address at the 175th anniversary of the
Ministerium of Pennsylvania. Reading,
Pa., June 5, 1923. In: The Lutheran
Church Review. Vol. XLII. Philadel-
phia, Pa. 1923. pp. 209—228.* [1286
Krotel, G. F.: The mother synod. *In: The
Lutheran Church Review. Vol. XVII. Philadelphia, Pa. 1898. pp. 82—92.* [1287
Ochsenford, S. E.: In commemoration of the
150th anniversary of the Ministerium
of Pennsylvania: Leading characte-
ristics of the Pennsylvania Ministerium
*In:The Lutheran Church Review. Vol.
XVII. Philadelphia, Pa. 1898. pp. (64),
67—81.*   [1288
Offermann, Henry: Historical development
of the Lutheran Ministerium of Pennsylvania and adjacent states. *Prepared
for the committee on celebration of the 175th
anniversary. pp. (3).*   [1289

Offermann, Henry: The Ministerium of
Pennsylvania and Lutheranism in Ame-
rica. *Address delivered at the meeting of
the Norristown Conference in Augustus
Lutheran Church, Trappe, Pa., April 30th,
1923. In: The Lutheran Church Review.
Vol. XLII. Philadelphia, Pa. 1923.
pp. 110—118.*   [1290
[Spaeth, A.]: Our jubilee. *Edited by . . .
Published quarterly, for free distribution,
by the Central Jubilee Committee of the
Evangelical Lutheran Ministerium of
Pennsylvania and adjacent states, in the
interest of the 150th anniversary of the
Ministerium. No. 1—8. Allentown, Pa.
1896. pp. 64; Unser Jubiläum. Deutsche
Ausgabe. Allentown, Pa. 1896. 64 S.,
ill.*   [1291
Laury, Preston A.: The history of the Allen-
town Conference of the Ministerium of
Pennsylvania. *Kutztown, Pa.: Kutztown
Publishing Co., 1926. pp. 387, ill.*
                                          [1292
[Ochsenford S. E. and Pflueger, O. E.]:
Jubilee memorial volume of the Dan-
ville Conference of the Evangelical
Lutheran Ministerium of Pennsylvania
and adjacent states. *Published by the
Danville Conference, Lebanon, Pa.:
Report Print 1898. pp. 372, ill., map.*
                                          [1293
[Kline, J. Jacob and others]: 1517—1917.
Jubilee volume. Norristown Conference
of the Ministerium of Pennsylvania and
adjacent states. Reformation Quadri-
Centennial. *Published by the Conference.
Lebanon, Pa.: Sowers Printing Co. 1917.
pp. 312, ill.*   [1294
Fisher, Allen S.: Lutheranism in Bucks
County, 1734—1934. *With a restudy of the
Indians of Eastern United States to more
definitely prove Lutheran Missions among
the Lenape of the Delaware vallay, 1638—
1740, Tinicum, Pa., 1935. pp. 208. ill.*
                                          [1294a
[Trabert, G. H. and others]: History of the
Wilkes-Barre Conference. *Prepared by
its pastors as a memorial in honor of the
one hundred and fiftieth anniversary of
the Ministerium of Pennsylvania and
adjacent states. Published under the
auspices of the Conference. 1898. Lebanon, Pa.: Press of Report Publishing
Co. 1898. pp. 250, ill.*   [1295
— Geschichte der Wilkes-Barre Konferenz.
*Dargestellt von deren Pastoren zur Er-
innerung an das 150. Jubiläum des Evangelisch-Lutherischen Ministeriums von*

*Pennsylvanien and angrenzenden Staaten.
Herausgegeben auf Beschluß der Kon-
ferenz, 1898. Wilkes-Baare, Pa.: Robt.
Baur & Sohn 1898. 240 S., ill.*   [1296

Evangelisch-Lutherische Synode von West-
pennsylvanien, 1825 errichtet

Evangelical Lutheran Synod of West Pennsylvania, org. 1825

Minutes of the Synod & Ministerium of the
Evangelical Lutheran Church, West of
the Susquehannah in the State of Pennsylvania. Convened at Chambersburg,
on the 4 th of September, 1825. *York, Pa.
1825. pp. 16, 8.*
[= Proceedings. Vol. I.]   [1297
Minutes . . .; *since 1849:* Proceedings . . . of
annual convention of the Evangelical
Lutheran Church of West Pennsylvania.
Annually published. 1825ff.
*[1828, 1838, 1844 printed in Lutheran
Observer.]*   [1298
Stump, Adam and **Anstadt, Henry:** History
of the Evangelical Lutheran Synod of
West Pennsylvania of the United Lu-
theran Church in America, 1825—1925.
*Edited by . . . Published by action of the
Synod in celebration of its centennial.
Chambersburg, Pa.: J. R. Kerr & Bro.
1925. pp. 696, ill.*   [1299

Evangelisch-Lutherische Alleghany Synode,
1842 errichtet

Evangelical Lutheran Alleghany Synod,
org. 1842

Proceedings of a convention and of the first
session of the Evangelical Lutheran
Alleghany Synod of Pennsylvania, held
at Hollidaysburg, Huntingdon County,
Sept. 8 et seq. A. D., 1842. *Baltimore,
Md.: Printed at Publication Rooms
1842. pp. 30.*
[= Proceedings. Vol. I.]   [1300
Proceedings . . . of . . . annual convention of
the Alleghany Evangelical Lutheran
Synod of Pennsylvania of the [United]
Lutheran Church in America. *Annually
published. 1842ff.*
[1845 not printed.]   [1301
Carney, W. H. Bruce: History of the Alle-
ghany Evangelical Lutheran Synod of
Pennsylvania. *Together with a topical
handbook of the Evangelical Lutheran
Church, its ancestry, origin and develop-
ment. 2 vols. Published by the autho-*

*rity of the Alleghany Synod in comme-
moration of its seventh-fifth anniversary,
and of the Quadricentennial of the Reformation. Philadelphia, Pa.: The Lutheran
Publishing Co. 1918. pp. XII, 454; 455
—871, ill.*   [1302

Evangelisch-Lutherische Synode von Mittel-
pennsylvanien, 1855 errichtet

Evangelical Lutheran Synod of Central
Pennsylvania, org. 1855

Minutes of the first annual convention of
the Synod of Central Pennsylvania convened at Mifflintown, Juniata County,
June 10, A. D. 1855. *Containing also
the constitution of said Synod. Lewisburg, Pa.: Worden and Cornelius 1855.
pp. 22.*
[= Proceedings. Vol. I.]   [1303
Minutes of the annual convention of the
Synod of Central Pennsylvania . . . .;
since 1856: Proceedings of the . . . annual [session] convention of Evangelical
Lutheran Synod of Central Pennsylvania . . .; *since 1881:* Minutes of the . . .
annual convention . . .; *since 1903:* Minutes of the regular convention . . .
Annually published 1855ff.   [1304

Susquehanna Synode der Evangelisch-
Lutherischen Kirche, 1867 errichtet

Susquehanna Synod of the Evangelical
Lutheran Church, org. 1867

Proceedings of the organization of the Susquehanna Synod at Montoursville, Pa.,
on Nov. 5th anf 6th, 1867, and first
annual convention of the Synod at
Sunbury, Pa., from April 23 d to April 27,
1868. *Sunbury, Pa.: J. E. Eichholtz
1868.*
[= Proceedings. Vol. I.]   [1305
Proceedings . . . of . . . annual convention of
the Susquehanna Synod of the Evangelical Church. *Annually published,
1868ff. to 1923.*   [1306
— Susquehanna Synod of the Evangelical
Lutheran Church. — Commemorative
exercises at Selinsgrove, Pa., — Oct. 18,
19, 1887. *Philadelphia, Pa. 1888. pp 61.*   [1307
[Manhart, Franklin Pierce]: The Susquehanna Synod of the Evangelical Lutheran Church in the United States. A
history 1867—1917. *[Edited by . . .]
Published by the Synod on its fiftieth anniversary. [s. l.] 1917. pp. 340, ill.*   [1308

Susquehanna Synode von Mittelpennsyl-
vanien der Evangelisch - Lutherischen
Kirche, 1924 durch Verschmelzung errichtet

Susquehanna Synod of Central Pennsylvania of the Evangelical Lutheran Church,
org. 1924 by merger

1924. The Susquehanna Synod of Central
Pennsylvania of the Evangelical Luthe-
ran Church. The merger conventions.
The first annual convention. *Milton,
Pa.: Dentler Print Shop 1924.*
[= Minutes. Vol. I.]   [1309
Minutes . . . of . . . annual convention of the
Susquehanna Synod of Central Penn-
sylvania of the Evangelical Lutheran
Church. *Annually published 1924 ff.*
[1310

Evangelisch-Lutherische Synode von Ost-
pennsylvanien, 1842 errichtet

Evangelical Lutheran Synod of East Pennsylvania, org. 1842

Proceedings of the Evangelical Lutheran
Synod of East Pennsylvania convened
in St. Peter's Church, Chester County,
Pa. on the 15th of October, 1842. To-
gether with the preliminary proceedings
in the formation of said Synod, at Lan-
caster, in May, 1842. *Gettysburg, Pa.:
H. C. Neinstedt 1842. pp. 24.*
[= Proceedings. Vol. I.]   [1311
Proceedings . . . *[1848 to 1853:* Minutes] . . .
of annual convention of the Evangelical
Lutheran Synod of East Pennsylvania.
Annually published 1842 ff.   [1312
Verhandlungen der Evangelisch-Luthe-
rischen Synode von Ost-Pennsylvanien.
Gehalten in der St. Peter's Kirche,
Chester County, Pa., den 15 ten Okt.
1842. Samt den Preliminar Verhand-
lungen bei der Bildung besagter Synode,
in Lancaster, im Mai, 1842. *Gettysburg,
Pa.: Heinrich C. Neinstedt 1843. 29 S.*
|[1313
History of the Evangelical Lutheran
Synod of East Pennsylvania, with brief
sketches of its congregations. *Published
by the Synod in commemoration of its
Semi-Centennial anniversary. 1842—
1892. Philadelphia, Pa.: Lutheran Publication Society. 1892. pp. 383, ill.*
[1314
Henry, E. S.: History of Lebanon Conference of the East Pennsylvania Synod.
*Harrisburg, Pa.: W. P. Swartz & Bro.
1878. pp. 14.*   [1315

Evangelisch-Lutherische Synode von
Maryland, 1820 errichtet

Evangelical Lutheran Synod of Maryland,
org. 1820

Proceedings of the Evangelical Lutheran
Synod of Maryland, Virginia &c. at
Winchester, Va. for the year 1820.
*Baltimore, Md.: Frederick G. Schaeffer
1820. pp. 16.*
[= Proceedings. Vol. I.]   [1316
Proceedings . . .; *since 1823:* Minutes of
the session . . .; *since 1831:* Minutes of
the proceedings . . .; *since 1834:* Proceedings . . .; *1838:* Journal . . .; *since
1839:* Proceedings . . . of . . . annual
session (convention) of the Evangelical
Lutheran Synod of Maryland. *Annually
published 1820 ff.*   [1317
Reinewald, Charles: Ministerial education
in the Maryland Synod. *In: The Lutheran Quarterly. Vol. XXXIII. Gettysburg, Pa. 1903. pp. 117—125.*   [1318
Wentz, Abdel Ross: History of the Evangelical Lutheran Synod of Maryland of
the United Lutheran Church in America
1820—1920 together with a brief sketch
of each congregation of the Synod and
biographies of the living sons of the
Synod in the ministry. *Edited by the
same author. Harrisburg, Pa.: Printed
for the Synod by the Evangelical Press
1920. pp. 641, ill.*   [1319

Evangelisch-Lutherische Synode von
Virginia, 1829 errichtet

Evangelical Lutheran Synod of Virginia,
org. 1829

Verrichtung der Special Conferenz der
Evangelisch-Lutherischen Prediger und
Abgeordneten im Staate Virginien, gehalten in der Neuen Röders-Kirche,
Rockingham County, den 6 ten October,
1806. *Mit zugesetzter Ermahnung an alle
Glieder der Kirche, auf besserem Kirchen-
gang; und etliche Verse die bey der Einweihung besagter Kirche gesungen wurden,
wie auch eine kurze Nachricht von den
deutschen Kirchen und ihre gegenwärtigen
Lage in Nord-Carolina. New-Market,
Va.: Ambrosius Henkel 1806, 24 S.*
[1320
Die Verrichtungen der Special Conferenz
der Evangelisch Lutherischen Prediger
und Abgeordneten in der Salomons-
Kirche Schenandoah County, Va., ge-

halten den ersten und zweyten October, 1809. *New-Market, Va. 1810. 24 S.* [1321
The proceedings of a special conference, held in Madison County, Va. in the Lutheran congregation of said county, on the 14th day of September, 1817, together with a letter by a travelling Jew. *1818. pp. 18.* [1322
Proceedings of the Evangelical Lutheran Conference held at Woodstock, Virginia. August 10 & 11, 1829.
[= Minutes. No. 1.] [1323
Proceedings . . .; *1830:* Minutes . . .; *1831:* An extract from the minutes . . .; *since 1832:* Minutes of the proceedings . . .; *since 1838:* Minutes . . . of . . . annual convention of the Evangelical Lutheran Synod of Virginia. *Annually published (except 1836 and 1837 when no minutes were printed.) . 1829ff. — the ninety-second convention 1921.* [1324

Lutherische Synode von Virginia der Vereinigten Lutherischen Kirche von Amerika, 1920 durch Verschmelzung errichtet

Lutheran Synod of Virginia of the United Lutheran Church of America, org. 1920 by merger

Minutes of the merger convention and annual convention of the Lutheran Synod of Virginia, held in St. Marks Evangelical Lutheran Church, Roanoke, Va., March 17, and September 6, and September 7 to 11, 1922, together with minutes of the special and annual conventions of the merging Synods. *pp. 156, 35, 13, (17).*
[= Minutes. Vol. 1]. [1325
Minutes . . . of . . . annual convention of the Lutheran Synod of Virginia. *Annually published. 1922ff.* [1326
Cassell, C. W., Finck, W. J. and Henkel, Elon O.: History of the Lutheran Church in Virginia and East Tennessee. *Edited by . . . Published by the authority of the Lutheran Synod of Virginia. Strasburg, Va.: Shenandoah Publishing House, Inc. 1930. pp. XVII, 401, ill.* [1327

Evangelisch-Lutherische Synode von Nordkarolina, 1803 errichtet

Evangelical Lutheran Synod of North Carolina, org. 1803

Kurzer Bericht von den Conferenzen der Vereinigten Evangelisch Lutherischen Predigern, und Abgeordneten, in dem Staat Nord-Carolina, vom Jahr 1803, bis zum Jahr 1810. *New Market, Va.: Ambrosius Henkel und Co. Shenandoah County, Va. 1811. 34 S.* [1328
Minutes of the Evangelical Lutheran Synod of North Carolina. From 1803—1826, twenty-three conventions. *Translated from the German protocol by F. W. E. Peschau, 1898. Newberry, S. C.: Aul & Houseal 1894. pp. 67.* [1329
Principal translation of the Synod of the Lutheran Ministry in North Carolina, from 1811 to 1812. *New Market, Shenandoah Co., Va.: Ambrose Henkel 1812. pp. 38.* [1330
Principal transactions of the Lutheran Gospel Ministry of North Carolina, in Synod assembled in the month of October, 1812. To which is added a circular letter to the clergy of said church. *Salisbury, N. C.: Couppee and Crider, 1813. pp. . . .* [1331
Report of the transactions during the Synod of the Lutheran ministry: begun and held in the State of North-Carolina, in the year of our Lord, 1813. *Together with an appendix. Raleigh, N. C.: Minerva Press, by Alexander Lucas 1814. pp. 52.* [1332
Succinct information of the transactions of the German and English Lutheran Synod for North-Carolina and adjacent states: begun and held at Buffaloe Creek Church, Cabarrus County, on the second Sunday after Easter, April 25th, A. D. 1819. *Baltimore, Md.: Schaeffer & Maund. 1819. pp. 21, (1).* [1333
Extract from the transactions of the German and English Lutheran Synod for North-Carolina and adjacent states, in the year of our Lord 1820. *Raleigh, N. C.: Lucas & Harvey 1820. pp. 19.* [1334
Extracts from the minutes of the Evangelical Lutheran Synod for North Carolina and adjacent states: Begun and held at the Pilgrim's Church, Rowan Co., on Trinity Sunday, June 2 d. A. D., 1822. *Hillsborough: Dennis Heartt 1822. pp. 10.* [1335
Minutes of the proceedings of the Evangelical Lutheran Synod of North Carolina and adjacent states . . .; *since 1828* Minutes of the Lutheran . . .; *1831:* Ex-

tract from the minutes . . .; *1832:* Minutes of the Evangelical Lutheran Synod and Ministerium of the State of North Carolina and adjacent parts . . .; *1833:* Minutes of the Evangelical Lutheran Synod of North Carolina and adjacent states . . .; *1834:* Proceedings of the . . .; *1835:* Proeedings of the . . . Synod and Ministerium . . .; *1836:* Minutes of the Synod and Ministerium of the Evangelical Lutheran Church in the State of North Carolina and adjacent parts . . .; *since 1837:* Minutes of the Evangelical Lutheran Synod and Ministerium of North Carolina and adjacent parts . . .; *1841:* Proceedings . . .; *[1842 not printed]; since 1843:* Minutes of the Evangelical Lutheran Synod and Ministerium of North Carolina . . .; *since 1873;* Minutes of the . . . (annual) convention (meeting) of the Evangelical Lutheran Synod (and Ministerium) of North Carolina . . .; *1921:* Minutes of the 118th annual convention of the United Evangelical Lutheran Synod of North Carolina. Together with the minutes of the called conventions of the Evangelical Tennessee Synod held in connection with the merger. Salisbury, N. C., March 1—2, 1921; Burlington, N. C., June 7—10, 1921 . . . ; *since 1922:* Minutes of the . . . annual convention of the United Evangelical Lutheran Synod of North Carolina . . . *Since 1826 annually published ff.*   [1336

Bernheim, G. D. and **Cox, George H.:** The history of the Evangelical Lutheran Synod and Ministerium of North Carolina, in commemoration of the completion of the first century of its existence. *Philadelphia, Pa.: Published for the Synod by the Lutheran Publication Society. 1902. pp. VIII, 9—191.*   [1337

Henkel, Paul: Eine Reisebeschreibung von Pfr. Paulus Henkel; Vom 28sten May bis zum 18ten August, im Jahr 1811. *New Market, Va.: Ambrosius Henkel & Co. Shenandoah Caunty, Va. 1812. 24 S.*   [1338

Ansprache an die gesammten Glieder der Deutsch Evangelisch Lutherischen Gemeinen in Pennsylvanien und den benachbarten Staaten. *Philadelphia, Pa.: Conrad Zentler 1811. 12(?) S.*
Mit Auszug des Reiseberichtes des Herrn J. Paul Hinkel vom 21sten August, bis 13ten November 1810.   [1339

Evangelisch-Lutherische Synode von Tennessee. 1820—1920

Evangelical Lutheran Tennessee Synod. 1820—1920

Kurtze Nachricht von den Verrichtungen der ersten Conferenz, der Deutschen, Evangelisch Lutherischen Prediger, gehalten in dem Staate Tennessee, den 17ten Julius 1820. Samt einem Bericht von der Spaltung der Evangelisch Lutherischen Synode, welche hat sollen gehalten werden den 31sten May, 1820, in Lincolnton, N. C. *Wie auch der Plan-Entwurf der General-Synode und die bedenklichen Einwendungen dagegen. Also auch die unveränderte Augsburgische Confession, und etliche Anmerkungen wegen der Heiligen Taufe etc. Neu-Market, Va.: S. Henkel's Druckerey 1821. pp. 68. Die Augsburgische Confession 50 S.*
[= Minutes. Vol. I.]   [1340

Bericht von den Verrichtungen . . .; *1836:* Verhandlungen der . . .; *seit* 1837: Bericht von den Verrichtungen . . .; *seit 1853:* Verhandlungen der . . . Sitzung, der Evangelisch Lutherischen Tennessee Synod. *1820 jährlich ff.*   [1341

Report of transactions, of the second Evangelical Lutheran Conference: held in Zion's Church, Sullivan County, Tennessee, the 22d of Oct., 1821, also two letters; and the objections against the Constitution of the General Synod. *New Market, Va.: S. Henkel Printing Office, 1821. pp. 36.*
[= First English minutes and at the same time = Minutes. Vol. II.]   [1342

Report of the transaction . . .; *since 1839;* Report of proceedings . . .; *since 1850:* Proceedings . . .; *since 1852:* Minutes . . . of . . . annual convention of the Evangelical Lutheran Tennessee Synod. *Annually published. [1820 only in German] 1821 ff. to 1919. — Centennial Convention 1920.*   [1343

1820—1920. Centennial convention. Minutes of the annual meeting of the Evangelical Lutheran Tennessee Synod held in Emmanuel Church, Lincolnton, N. C., October 12—16, 1920. *New Market, Va.: Henkel & Company's 1920. pp. 123, ill.*   [1344

Fox, L. A.: Origin and early history of the Tennessee Synod. *In: The Quarterly Review of the Evangelical Lutheran*

Church. Vol. XIX, Gettysburg, Pa. 1889. pp. 45—68. [1345

Fox L. A.: The origin of the Tennessee Synod. *An address delivered at its Centennial celebration. In Lincolnton, N. C., Oct. 14, 1920. pp. 10.* [1346

Henkel, Socrates: History of the Evangelical Lutheran Tennessee Synod embracing an account of the causes, which gave rise to its organization; its organization and name; its position and confessional basis; object of its organization; work, development and various sessions; its policy; and its future. *New Market, Va.: Henkel & Co. 1890. pp. V, 275, ill.* [1347

Stirewalt, J. P.: The pioneers of the Tennessee Synod. *An address delivered at its Centennial celebration in Lincolnton, N. C., Oct. 14, 1920. pp. 9.* [1348

Wessinger, B. D.: The work of the pioneers of the Tennessee Synod. *An address delivered at its Centennial celebration in Lincolnton, N. C., Oct. 14, 1920. pp. 17.* [1349

Lutherische Synode von Tennessee, 1848 erneuert

Lutheran Tennessee Synod, re-organized 1848

Ecclesiastical annals. Report of transactions of the Lutheran Tennessee Synod, reorganized. Held in St. John's Church, Catawba County, N. C., from the 12th to the 17th October, A. D., 1850. — *To which is appended the Augsburg Confession of Faith.* — *Also an obituary notice of the death of Rev. George Easterly. Greenville, Tenn.: Printed at the „Spy" Office 1851. pp. 56.* [1350

Evangelisch-Lutherische Holston-Synode, 1860—1922

Evangelical Lutheran Holston Synod, 1860—1922

Minutes of the first annual meeting of the Evangelical Lutheran Holston Synod, held in Zion's Church, Sullivan County, Tenn. from December 29th, 1860 to January, 2nd, 1861. *Knoxville, Tenn.: Beckett, Haws & Co. 1861. pp. 12.*
[= Minutes. Vol. I.] [1351

Minutes . . . of . . annual [meeting] convention of the Evangelical Lutheran Holston Synod. *Annually 1861 ff. to 1921.* [1352

Evangelisch-Lutherische Concordia-Synode von Virginia, 1868—1920.

Evangelical Lutheran Concordia Synod of Virginia, 1868—1920.

Minutes of the Evangelical Lutheran Concordia Synod of Virginia, held in Probst Church, Pendelton County, W.-Va., November 3d—5th, 1868. *Staunton, Va.: „Spectator" Job Printing Office 1868. pp. 11.* [1353

Minutes . . .; *since 1875:* Transactions of the Evangelical Lutheran Concordia Synod of Virginia . . . *1868 annually ff. — 1920.* [1354

Evangelisch-Lutherische Synode von Südwest-Virginia, 1842—1922

Evangelical Lutheran Synod of South Western Virginia, 1842—1922

Minutes of the Evangelical Lutheran Synod and Ministerium of Western Virginia and adjacent parts. Convened at Zion's Church, Floyd County, Virginia, on the 21st of May, 1842, and continued its sessions until the 26th. *Baltimore, Md.: Publication Rooms 1842. pp. 21.*
[= Minutes. Vol. I.] [1355

Minutes of the . . . session . . .; *since 1873:* . . . convention . . .; *since 1907:* . . . annual convention . . . of the Evangelical Lutheran Synod of Western Virginia and adjacent parts; *since 1867:* . . . South Western Virginia; *since 1910:* . . . of the Evangelical Lutheran Synod and Ministerium of South Western Virginia. *1842 annually ff. — 1921.* [1356

Greiner, J. B.: Synod of Southwest Virginia. *In: The Quarterly Review of the Evangelical Lutheran Church. Vol. XXII. Gettysburg, Pa. 1892. pp. 98—109.* [1357

Evangelisch-Lutherische Synode von Mittel-Tennessee, 1878—1894

Evangelical Lutheran Synod of Middle Tennessee, 1878—1894

Organization and proceedings of the first convention and a special session of the Evangelical Lutheran Synod of Middle Tennessee held respectively at Ebenezer Lutheran Church, Moore County, Tenn., Nov. 7—11, 1878, and Shofner Lutheran Church, Bedford County, Tenn., May 3,

1879. *Philadelphia, Pa.: Lutheran Publication House. 1879. pp. 24.*   [1358
Organization and proceedings of the first convention and special session of the Evangelical Lutheran Synod of Middle Tennessee . . .; *since 1879:* Minutes of the . . . annual convention . . .; *since 1890:* Proceedings . . . *1879 annually ff.* — *1894.*   [1359

Pittsburg-Synode der Evangelisch-Lutherischen Kirche, 1845—1867

Pittsburgh Synod of the Evangelical Lutheran Church, 1845—1867

Proceedings of a convention and of the first and second sessions of the Pittsburgh Synod of the Evangelical Lutheran Church, convened in the First English Lutheran Church, Pittsburg, Pa., on the 15th of January, 1845 and in the Evangelical Lutheran Church in Shippensville, Clarion County, Pa., on the 5th of June 1845. *Baltimore, Md.: The Publication Rooms 1845. pp. 44.* [= *Proceedings. Vol. I.]*   [1360
Minutes of the third session of the Pittsburg Synod of the Evangelical Lutheran Church. *Baltimore, Md.: Publication Rooms 1846. pp. 50.*   [1361
Fourth, fifth, sixth and seventh conventions and extra session. Pittsburgh Synod 1846 to 1850. Lechburg, Pa., May 27—June 3, 1847; Brush Creek, Pa., October 14—18, 1847; Middle Lancaster, Pa., May 25—30, 1848; Klecknerville, Pa., May 24—30, 1849; Pittsburgh, Pa., May 23—29, 1850. *[s. l., s. d.] pp. 152.*   [1362
Minutes of the (eighth) annual convention of the Evangelical Lutheran Synod of Pittsburg . . .; *since 1855:* Proceedings of the . . . annual session . . .; *since 1856* . . . Pittsburgh . . .; *since 1860:* . . . Pittsburgh Synod of the Evangelical Lutheran Church . . .; *since 1864:* . . . convention . . . *1851 annually ff.* — *twenty-fourth convention 1866.*   [1363

Evangelisch-Lutherische Pittsburg-Synode (Generalsynode), 1867—1919

Evangelical Lutheran Pittsburgh Synod (General Synod), 1867—1919

The Pittsburgh Synod of the Evangelical Lutheran Church: Proceedings of the adjourned meeting of the twenty-fifth

convention. Worthington, Armstrong County, Pa., December 4th to 7th, 1867. *Wheeling, W. Va. Campbell, Frew & Co. 1868. pp. 24.*
[= *Minutes of Pittsburgh Synod (General Synod). Vol. I.]*   [1364
Proceedings of the adjourned meeting of the 25th convention . . .; *since 1868:* Proceedings of convention of the Pittsburgh Synod of the Evangelical Lutheran Church of the United States of America . . .; *since 1869:* . . . of the Evangelical Lutheran Synod of Pittsburgh . . .; *since 1880:* . . . of the Pittsburgh Synod of the Evangelical Lutheran Church . . .; *since 1906:* . . . of the Pittsburgh Synod of the Evangelical Lutheran Church in the United States of America . . . *1867 annually ff.* — . . . *convention 1919.*   [1365
Burgess, Ellis B.: History of the Pittsburgh Synod of the General Synod of the Evangelical Lutheran Church 1748—1845—1904. Together with a brief sketch of each congregation of the Synod. *Published by the authority of the Synod. Philadelphia, Pa.: Lutheran Publication Society. 1904. pp. 488, ill.*   [1366

Evangelisch-Lutherische Pittsburg-Synode (Generalkonzil), 1867—1919

Evangelical Lutheran Pittsburgh Synod (General Council), 1867—1919

The Pittsburgh Synod of the Evangelical Lutheran Church: Sessions and action of the twenty-fifth convention, Greenville, Mercer County, Pa., October 10th to 17th, 1867. *Pittsburgh, Pa.: Bakewell & Marthens 1867. pp. 64.*
[= *Minutes of Pittsburgh Synod (General Council. Vol. I.]*   [1367
The Pittsburgh Synod of the Evangelical Lutheran Church: Sessions and action of the . . . convention . . .; *since 1886:* . . . : . . annual convention . . .; *since 1902:* The Proceedings of the . . . annual . . .; *1911:* . . . of the special convention and sixty-ninth annual convention . . .; *1912:* . . . of the special and seventieth convention . . .; *1913:* . . . of the eleven sessions of the seventy-first convention . . .; *1913:* . . . of the 12th—15th sessions of the seventy-first convention . . .; *since 1914:* . . .; Proceedings of the . . . convention . . .; *1919:* . . . of the special convention held in the First

Church, Pittsburgh, Pa., February 6th, 1919, and the seventy-seventh convention of the Pittsburgh Synod of the Evangelical Lutheran Church held in Grace Lutheran Church, Youngstown, O., June 19th to 23rd, 1919. *1867 annually ff. — 1919.*   [1368

Ulery, William F. and Youndt, A. L.: History of the Southern Conference of the Pittsburgh Synod of the Evangelical Lutheran Church. *By . . . Edited and published by W. F. Ulery and A. L. Youndt, Committee of Conference. Greensburg, Pa.: Church Register Co. 1902. pp. XV, (1), 416, ill., map.; Second and enlarged edition. 1903. pp. XV, 431, ill., map.*   [1369

Pittsburg-Synode der Evangelisch-Lutherischen Kirche, 1919 durch Verschmelzung errichtet

Pittsburgh Synod of the Evangelical Lutheran Church, org. 1919 by merger

The Pittsburgh Synod. Merger convention 1919 and minutes of adjourned sessions of the Pittsburgh Synod, formerly General Council and the Pittsburgh Synod, formerly General Synod, . . . *Pittsburgh, Pa., Nov. 18—21. pp. 176, (4).*   [1370

Proceedings of the (seventy-eighth) annual convention of the Pittsburgh Synod of the Evangelical Lutheran Church . . . *1920 annually ff.*   [1371

Burgess, Ellis Beaver: Memorial history of the Pittsburgh Synod of the Evangelical Lutheran Church 1748—1845—1924. Together with a sketch of each of the 317 congregations found in the fellowship of the Synod in the year of the merger. *Greenville, Pa.: Published for the Synod by the Beaver Co. 1925. pp. 814, ill.*   [1372

Synode und Ministerium der Evangelisch-Lutherischen Kirche von Ohio, 1818—1832

Synod and Ministerium of the Evangelical Lutheran Church, in the State of Ohio, 1818—1832

Verrichtung der 6ten Special Conferenz der Evangelisch-Lutherischen Prediger im Staate Ohio, und dem westlichen Theil von Pennsylvanien. *Lancaster, Ohio: Johann Herman 1816. 24 S.*   [1373

Verrichtungen der ersten General Conferenz der Evangelischen-Lutherischen Prediger in Ohio, und den angrenzenden Staaten [1818]. *Lancaster, O.: Johann Herman 1819. 32 S.*
[= Minutes. Vol. I.]   [1374

Verrichtungen der . . . General Conferenz der Evangelisch-Lutherischen Prediger in Ohio, und den angrenzenden Staaten; *seit 1825:* . . . der Evangelisch Lutherischen Synod von Ohio und, . . .; *seit 1826:* . . . der Synodal Versammlung, der Evangelisch-Lutherischen Prediger von Ohio und den angrenzenden Staaten . . . ; *seit 1828:* Verhandlungen . . .; *seit 1831:* Protokoll der . . . Sitzung der Synode und des Ministeriums der Evangelischen Lutherischen Kirche in dem Staate Ohio . . . *1819 jährlich ff. bis (15ten Sitzung) 1832.*   [1375

Minutes of the proceedings of the thirteenth session of the Synod and Ministerium of the Evangelical Lutheran Church, in the State of Ohio, convened at Zanesville, Ohio, in Trinity week. A. D., 1830. *pp. 20.*
[First minute in English.]   [1376

Minutes of the proceedings of the . . . session of the Synod and Ministerium of the Evangelical Lutheran Church, in the State of Ohio . . . *1830 annually ff. to (15th session) 1832.*   [1377

Ost-Ohio-Synode der Evangelisch-Lutherischen Kirche, 1836—1920

East Ohio Synod of the Evangelical Lutheran Church, 1836—1920

Minutes of the proceedings of the first session of the Synod and Ministerium of the English Evangelical Lutheran churches in Ohio and adjacent states. Convened at Somerset, O., on the sixth of November, and following days, A. D., 1836. *Steubenville, O.: James Wilson 1836. pp. 24.*
[= Minutes of the East Ohio Synod. Vol. I.]   [1378

Minutes (of the proceedings) of the . . . session of the Synod and Ministerium of the English Evangelical Lutheran churches in Ohio and adjacent states . . .; *since 1838* . . . of the Synod and Ministerium of the English Evangelical Lutheran Church . . .; *since 1842;* . . . of the English Evangelical Lutheran Synod of

Ohio and adjacent states . . .; *since 1845 [published 1846]* . . . convention . . .; *since 1857:* Proceedings of . . . annual convention . . .; *since 1858:* . . . of the East Ohio Synod of the Evangelical Lutheran Church . . .; *since 1917:* Proceedings . . . of the East Ohio Synod of the General Synod of the Evangelical Lutheran Church in the United States of America . . .; *since 1919:* . . . of the East Ohio Synod of the United Lutheran Church in America . . . *1836 annually ff. (with exception of 1844 when there was no convention convened) to (85th annual convention) 1920.*   [1379

Smith, Arthur Harms: A history of the East Ohio Synod of the General Synod of the Evangelical Lutheran Church 1836—1920. Together with a brief sketch of each congregation of the Synod. *Prepared and edited by... Published by the authority of the Synod. Columbus, O.: Lutheran Book Concern 1924. pp. 250, ill.*   [1380

Evangelisch-Lutherische Synode von Miami, 1844—1920

Evangelical Lutheran Synod of Miami, 1844—1920

Proceedings of a convention and of the first and second sessions of the Evangelical Lutheran Synod of Miami, together with the Constitution of the same. Convened in Xenia, O., Oct. 16th, 1844, — and in Dayton, O., April 19th, 1845. *Baltimore, Md.: The Publication Rooms of the Evangelical Lutheran Church 1845. pp. 39.*
[= Minutes. Vol. I.]   [1381
Proceedings of a convention of the first and second session in 1844 and 1845...; *1847:* . . . of the third and fourth session in 1846 and 1847 . . .; *various titles between 1849—1888:* Minutes (Proceedings) of the . . . annual convention (session; meeting) . . .; *since: 1880:* Proceedings of the . . . annual convention . . . of the Evangelical Lutheran Synod of Miami; *since 1848 annually published, 1845ff. — 1920.*   [1382

[Imhoff, A. J.:] History of the Evangelical Lutheran Synod of Miami. *Published by the Synod. Philadelphia, Pa.: Lutheran Publication Society. [s. d.; 1893/94?] pp. 117, ill.*   [1383

Wittenberg-Synode der Evangelisch-Lutherischen Kirche von Ohio, 1847—1920

Wittenberg Synod of the Evangelical Lutheran Church of Ohio, 1847—1920

Minutes of the . . . session of the Wittenberg Synod of the Evangelical Lutheran Church of Ohio . . .; *since 1851:* Proceedings of the . . . annual convention . . .; *since 1856:* . . . of the Wittenberg Synod of the Evangelical Lutheran Church . . .; *since 1861:* . . . Wittenberg Synod; Lutheran Church . . .; *since 1867:* . . . Wittenberg Synod of Evangelical Lutheran Church . . .; *since 1872:* Minutes . . .; *since 1914:* Proceedings of . . . of the Wittenberg Synod of the Evangelical Lutheran Church in Ohio. *1847 annually ff. — 73rd annual convention 1919.*   [1384

Ernsberger, C. S.: A history of the Wittenberg Synod of the General Synod of the Evangelical Lutheran Church 1847—1916. Together with a brief sketch of each congregation of the Synod. *Edited by the same author. Published by the authority of the Synod. Columbus, O.: Lutheran Book Concern. 1917. pp. 582, ill.* [1385

Evangelisch-Lutherischer Distrikt der Ohio-Synode (Generalkonzil), 1857—1920

Evangelical Lutheran District of Synod of Ohio (General Council), 1857—1920

Minutes of the English District of the Joint Synod of Ohio and adjoining states. At the first and second meetings, held in Circleville, Aug. 26—28, 1857, and in Lima, Aug. 26—30, 1858. *Columbus, O.: Osgood & Pearce 1858. pp. 24.*
[= Minutes. Vol. I.]   [1386

Mechling, G. W.: History of the Evangelical Lutheran District Synod of Ohio, covering fifty-three years 1857—1910. *Dayton, O.: Press of The Giele & Pelaum Co. 1911. pp. 208.*   [1388

The Evangelical Lutheran Synod of Ohio. *In: The Penn Germania. Vol. I.=Old series, vol. XIII. Lititz, Pa. 1912. pp. 826—828.*   [1389

Synode von Ohio der Vereinigten Lutherischen Kirche in Amerika, 1920 durch Verschmelzung errichtet

Synod of Ohio of the United Lutheran Church in America, org. 1920 by merger

The minutes of the special convention of the East Ohio Synod, Wittenberg

Synod, Miami Synod and the District of Ohio and the minutes of the merger convention of the Synod of Ohio, held in the Fourth Lutheran Church, Springfield, O., Nov. 3rd and 4th, 1920. *pp. 72.*
[= Minutes. Vol. I.] [1390
Minutes (of . . . annual conventions) . . of the Synod of Ohio of the United Lutheran Church in America. *1920 annually ff.* [1391

Allgemeine Evangelisch-Lutherische Synode von Ohio und anderen Staaten, 1818 errichtet

Joint Synod of Ohio and other states, org. 1818

Sheatsley, C. V.: History of the Evangelical Lutheran Joint Synod of Ohio and other states. From the earliest beginnings to 1919. Century memorial edition. *Columbus, O.: Book Concern 1919. pp. 312, ill.* [1392
Peter, P. A. - Schmidt, Wm.: Geschichte der Allgemeinen Evangelisch-Lutherischen Synode von Ohio und anderen Staaten. *Im Auftrage der Publikations-Behörde verfaßt . . . Columbus, O.: Verlagshandlung der Synode 1900. V, 415 S.* [1393
Spielmann, C.: Abriß der Geschichte der evangelisch-lutherischen Synode von Ohio und anderen Staaten, in einfacher Darstellung, von ihren ersten Anfängen bis zum Jahre 1846; *Nebst einem Anhang. Columbus, O.: Ohio Synodal-Druckerei 1880. 197 S.* [1394

Evangelisch-Lutherisches Ministerium von Neu York und umliegenden Staaten und Grafschaften, 1786—1929

Evangelical Lutheran Ministerium of New York and adjacent states and countries, org. 1786—1929

Proceedings of the Evangelical Lutheran Synod of the State of New York etc., convened in St. Peter's Church in the Town of Rhinebeck, Dutchess County, on the fourth day of September, A. D., 1819. *Albany, N. Y.: G. J. Loomis 1819. pp. 15.*
[= Minutes, first printed volume.] [1395
Proceedings of the Evangelical Lutheran Synod of the State of New York &c. . . .; *since 1821:* Extracts from the minutes of the Synod of the Lutheran Church

. . .; *since 1823:* . . . in the State of New York and adjacent parts . . .; *1824:* . . . of the Synod and Ministerium of . . .; *since 1825:* Extracts from the minutes of the . . . session . . .; *since 1828:* . . . of the Evangelical Lutheran Ministerium of the State of New York and adjacent parts . . .; *since 1831:* Minutes of the . . . Synod . . .; *since 1840:* . . . of the State of New York, adjacent states and countries . . .; *1847—1849, 1851—1853:* . . . Session of the Evangelical Lutheran Ministerium . . .; *since 1854:* . . . Synod . . .; *since 1872:* Minutes . . .; *since (1894):* Minutes of the . . . annual convention of the Evangelical Lutheran Ministerium of New York and adjacent states and countries; *since 1919:* Extract from . . . (of) the Minutes . . . *1819 annually ff.* — *1929.* [1396

Hartwick-Synode und Ministerium der Evangelisch-Lutherischen Kirche im Staate Neu York, 1830—1908

Hartwick Synod and Ministerium of the Evangelical Lutheran Church in the State of New York, 1830—1908

Verhandlungen der . . . Synode des Evangelisch Lutherischen Ministeriums des Staates New York und der benachbarten Staaten . . .; *seit 1864:* . . . Staaten und Länder . . .; *1926:* Evangelisch-Lutherisches Ministerium des Staates New York und angrenzender Staaten und Länder. Gegründet 1786 Extra Syndical-Versammlung . . . 10. bis 11. Nov. 1925 und 136. Versammlung 1926 . . .; *seit 1927:* . . . (137.) Versammlung . . . *1831 jährlich ff.* — *1929.* [1397
Extracts from the first session of the Hartwick Synod and Ministerium of the Evangelical Lutheran Church in the State of New York; convened at St. Paul's Church, Johnstown, Montgomery County, Pa., Sept. 24, 1831. *Troy, N. Y.: F. Adancourt 1831. pp. 24.*
[= Minutes. Vol. I.] [1398
Extracts from the . . . session of the Hartwick Synod and Ministerium of the Evangelical Lutheran Church in the State of New York . . .; *since 1834:* Minutes (Proceedings) of the annual session. *(Since 1857:* . . . convention) . . .; *since 1884:* Proceedings . . . *1831 annually ff.* — *77th convention 1907.* [1399

Nicum, J.: Geschichte des Evangelisch-Lutherischen Ministeriums vom Staate New York und angrenzenden Staaten und Ländern. *New York, N. Y.: Verlag des New York Ministeriums [Reading, Pa.]: Druck: Theodore Wischau 1888. VII. 636 S., ill.* [1400

Strobel, P. A.: Memorial volume to commemorate the Semi-Centennial anniversary of the Hartwick Lutheran Synod, of the State of New York. Containing the historical address, written by P. A. Strobel, a list of all the ministers who have belonged to the Synod, sketches of many of the churches, brief biographies of some of the pastors, and a sketch of the Hartwick seminary. *Compiled and edited by . . . Philadelphia, Pa.: The Lutheran Publication Society. 1881. pp. XIV, 15—424, ill.* [1401

Franck-Synode der Evangelisch-Lutherischen Kirche, 1837—1908

Franckean Synod of the Evangelic (since 1874: Evangelical) Lutheran Church, 1837—1908

Proceedings of a convention of ministers and delegates from Evangelical Lutheran churches, in the State of New York. Convened in the chapel, in Fordsbush, Montgomery County, May 24, 1837. *Albany, N. Y.: Hoffman & White 1837. pp. 16.* [1402

Journal of the special meeting of the Franckean Synod of the Evangelic Lutheran Church, convened at Richmondville, Schoharie County, N. Y., October 5th, 1837. *Albany, N. Y.: Hoffman & White 1837. pp. 40.* [1403

Journal of the first annual session of the Franckean Synod of the Evangelic Lutheran Church, convened at Clay, Onondaga County, N. Y., June 7th, 1838. *Albany, N. Y.: Hoffman & White 1838. pp. 32.* [1404

Journal of the . . . annual session of the Evangelic Lutheran Church . . .; *since 1834:* . . . of the Franckean Evangelic Synod . . .; *since 1872:* . . . convention . . .; *since 1874:* . . . Evangelical . . .; *since 1889:* Proceedings of the . . . annual convention . . . *1838 annually ff. — 71st convention 1908.* [1405

Alstine, N. van: Historical review of the Franckean Evangelical Lutheran Synod of New York. *Read at the convention of Synod, held at Manheim, N. Y., June 9,*

1893. Philadelphia, Pa.: Lutheran Publication Society. 1893. pp. 24. [1406

A reunion of ministers and churches, held at Gardnersville, May 14—17, 1881. *Published for the compilers. Philadelphia, Pa.: Lutheran Publication Society. 1881. pp. IV, 5—211.* [1407

Evangelisch-Lutherische Synode von Neu Jersey, 1859—1872

Evangelical Lutheran Synod of New Jersey, 1859—1872

Minutes of the convention held at German Valley, Morris County, N. J., on 19th and 20th February, 1861, which resulted in the formation of the Evangelical Lutheran Synod of New Jersey. Also minutes of the first annual meeting of the New Jersey Synod — held at Spruce Run, Hunterdon County, N. J., from 12th to 15th Oct., 1861, together with the constitution of said Synod. *Easton, Pa.: William H. Hutter 1861. pp. 23; 18.*
[= Minutes. Vol. I.] [1408

Minutes (Proceedings) of the . . . annual meeting (convention) of the Evangelical Lutheran Synod of New Jersey. *1861 annually published ff. — convention 1872.* [1409

Evangelisch-Lutherische Synode im Staat Neu York, 1867—1871

Evangelical Lutheran Synod of the State of New York, 1867—1871

Proceedings of the convention and minutes of the first session of the Evangelical Lutheran Synod of the State of New York. Held in St. Paul's Church, Red Hook, from Friday, Oct. 18th, to Tuesday, Oct. 22d, 1867. *Albany, N. Y.: J. Munsell 1867. pp. 23.*
[= Minutes. Vol. I.] [1410

Minutes of the . . . annual session of the Evangelical Lutheran Synod of the State of New York . . . *1867 annually ff. — 5th session 1871.* [1411

Evangelisch-Lutherische Synode von New York und New Jersey, 1872—1907

Evangelical Lutheran Synod of New York and New Jersey, 1872—1907.

Minutes of the Synod of New York and New Jersey. Held at St. John's Church,

Hudson, N. Y. From Thursday, Oct. 3 d, to Tuesday evening, Oct. 8th, 1872. Combining the minutes of the sixth annual session of the Evangelical Lutheran Synod of the State of New York, and the minutes of the twelfth annual session of the Evangelical Lutheran Synod of the State of New Jersey. *Oswego, N. Y.: Printed at the „Lutheran Kirchenfreund" Office 1872. pp. 37.*
[= Minutes of first annual session, 1872.] [1412

Minutes of the . . . annual session of the Evangelical Lutheran Synod of New York and New Jersey . . .; *since 1877:* . . . convention . . .; *1881—1884:* Proceedings . . .; *since 1885:* Minutes of the New York and New Jersey Synod of the Evangelical Lutheran Church . . . annual session (convention) . . .; *since 1895:* Minutes of the . . . annual convention of the Evangelical Lutheran Synod of New York and New Jersey. *1872 annually ff. — 36th annual convention 1907.* [1413

Synode von Neu York der Evangelisch-Lutherischen Kirche, 1908 errichtet

Synod of New York of the Evangelical Lutheran Church, org. 1908

Proceedings of the first annual convention of the Synod of New York of the Evangelical Lutheran Church, held in the First Lutheran Church, Albany, N. Y., Oct. 7—9, 1908. Proceedings of the seventy-eighth annual convention of the Hartwick Synod, held in the First English Lutheran Church, Albany, N.Y., Oct. 5—7, 1908. . . . Proceedings of the thirty-seventh annual convention of the Lutheran Synod of New York, and New Jersey, held in the First Lutheran Church, New York, Oct. 6—7, 1908. . . . Also the proceedings of the adjourned session of the seventy-first annual convention of the Franckean Synod, held in St. Paul's English Lutheran Church, Rensselaer, N. Y., Oct. 7, 1908. *Philadelphia, Pa.: Printed for the Synod by the Lutheran Publication Society 1908. pp. 207.*
[= Minutes. Vol. I.] [1414

Proceedings of the . . . annual convention of the Synod of New York of the

Evangelical Lutheran Church . . . *1908 annually ff. — 21th annual convention 1928.* [1415

Evangelisch-Lutherische Synode von Neu York und Neu England, 1902—1929

Evangelical Lutheran Synod of New York and New England, 1902—1929

Minutes of the twelfth semi-annual convention of the English conference of the Evangelical Lutheran Ministerium of New York and adjacent states and countries. Held in the Church of the Holy Trinity, Elizabeth, N. J., June 3 and 4, 1902. *pp. 18.* [1416

Minutes of the first annual convention. (Meeting for permanent organization) of the Evangelical Lutheran Synod of New York and New England. Utica, N. Y., Church of the Reedemer, Sept. 23—25, 1902. *Newark, N. J.: Baker Printing Co. 1902. pp. 47.*
[= Minutes. Vol. I.] [1417

Minutes of the . . . annual convention of the Evangelical Lutheran Synod of New York and New England. *1902 annually ff. — 28th convention 1929.* [1418

Vereinigte Lutherische Synode von Neu York der Vereinigten Lutherischen Kirche in Amerika, 1929 durch Verschmelzung errichtet

United Lutheran Synod of New York of the United Lutheran Church in America, org. 1929 by merger

The United Lutheran Synod of New York of the United Lutheran Church in America. Minutes of the first annual convention, also the special act of incorporation. Minutes of the incorporators' meetings held January 15th and June 5th, 1929, the constitution and the certificate of merger. St. John's Evangelical Lutheran Church, Albany, N. Y. *pp. 107.*
[= Minutes. Vol. I.] [1419

The United Lutheran Synod of New York. Minutes of the . . . annual convention. *1929 annually ff.* [1420

Pre-convention bulletin. The United Lutheran Synod of New York. Second annual convention, June 16, 17, 18, 19, 1930. Evangelical Lutheran Church of the Reformation, Rochester, N. Y. *Meridian, Conn.: Journal Press 1930. pp. 110, (1).* [1421

Evangelisch-Lutherische Synode von Süd-karolina, 1824 errichtet

Evangelical Lutheran Synod of South Carolina, org. 1824

Proceedings of the Evangelical Lutheran Synod of South Carolina and adjacent states convened in Lexington District, S. C., A. D. 1824. *Charleston, S. C.: Wm. Riley 1825. pp. 25.*
    [= Minutes. Vol. I.]   [1422

Proceedings of the Evangelical Lutheran Synod of South Carolina and adjacent states . . .; *since 1832:* Extracts from the minutes of the . . . session of the . . .; *since 1835:* . . . Evangelical Lutheran Synod and Ministerium of South Carolina and adjacent states . . .; *since 1836:* . . . meeting . . .; *since 1859:* Minutes of the Evangelical . . .; *1867:* Minutes of the extra session of the Synod of South Carolina, held in Luther Chapel, New-berry, S. C., Sept. 24 th and 25 th, 1867 and of the 43 rd annual convention of the Evangelical Lutheran Synod and Ministerium of South Carolina and adjacent states convened . . . Charleston, S. C. Nov. 14—19, 1897 . . .; *since 1868:* Minutes of the annual convention of the Evangelical Lutheran Synod and Ministerium of South Carolina and adjacent states . . . *1824 annually ff. published except 1925,when no meeting was called.* [1423

Hallman, S. T.: History of the Evangelical Lutheran Synod of South Carolina 1824—1924. *Prepared by a Committee of the Synod. Rev. S. T. Hallman, editor. Published by authority of the Synod. Printed for the Synod. Columbia, S. C.: Press of Farrell Printing Co., Inc. 1924. pp. 318, ill.*   [1424

Schirmer, Jacob: Historical sketches of the Evangelical Lutheran Synod of South Carolina, from its formation in 1824, also, a brief history of the church in the State of South Carolina, with other important statistics. *Published by request of the Synod. Charleston, S. C.: A. J. Burke 1875. pp. 50.*   [1425

Evangelisch-Lutherische Synode vom Staate Georgia, 1860 errichtet. Seit 1930: Georgia-Alabama-Synode.

Evangelical Lutheran Synod of the State of Georgia, org. 1860. Since 1930: Georgia-Alabama-Synod.

Minutes of the . . . th annual convention of the Evangelical Lutheran Synod of the State of Georgia; *since 1869:* Minutes of the Evangelical Lutheran Synod and Ministerium of Georgia . . .; *since 1870:* Minutes of the . . . convention . . .; *since 1873:* . . . the . . annual convention of the Evangelical Lutheran Synod and Ministerium of Georgia and adjacent states . . .; *1929:* Minutes of the . . . annual convention of the Evangelical Lutheran Synod and Ministerium of Georgia and adjacent states and the first annual convention of the Florida Synod of the United Lutheran Church . . .; *since 1930:* Proceedings of the . . . annual convention of the Georgia-Alabama Synod . . . *1860 annually ff. published, except 1924, when no meeting was called.*   [1426

Generalsynode der Evangelisch-Lutherischen Kirche in den Vereinigten Staaten von America, 1819—1918

General Synod of the Evangelical Lutheran Church in the United States of America, 1819—1918

Plan-Entwurf zu einer Central Verbindung der Evangelisch-Lutherischen Kirche in den Vereinigten Staaten von Nord-Amerika. *Baltimore, Md.: Schäffer und Maund 1819. 7 S.*   [1427

Grundverfassung der Evangelisch-Lutherischen General Synode in den Vereinigten Staaten von Nord-Amerika, nebst dem Protokoll der Versammlung, die sie entworfen. *[Okt., 1820.] Baltimore, Md.: F. G. Schäffer [1820]. 16 S.*   [1428

Verhandlungen . . . (der . . . [alle 2 Jahre zusammentretenden] Versammlung) der Evangelisch-Lutherischen Kirche in den Vereinigten Staaten. *Zweijährig veröffentlicht. [In deutscher Ausgabe erschienen: 1821 — 44ten Versammlung... 1889; seit 1862 mit dem Vermerk: Aus dem Englischen übersetzt; seit 1887: „Im Auszug."] 1821ff.—1889.*   [1429

Minutes of the General Synod of the Evangelical Lutheran Church in the United States, convened at Fredericktown, Md., Oct. 21, 22, 23, 1821. *Lancaster, Pa.: J. Schnee 1821. pp. 12.*
    [= (Minutes) Proceedings. Vol. 1.]   [1430

Minutes . . . General Synod of the Evangelical Lutheran Church . . .; *since 1823:* Minutes of proceedings . . .; *since 1831:*

Proceedings . . . of [biennial] convention. *Biennially published 1821 ff. — 48th convention, Chicago, Ill. 1917.* [1431

Dunbar, W. H.: The centenary of the General Synod. *In: The Lutheran Quarterly. Vol. XLVIII. Gettysburg, Pa. 1918. pp. 271—274.* [1432

Giese, E. F.: The chasm between the German and English in the General Synod. *In: The Quarterly Review of the Evangelical Lutheran Church. New series, vol. VII. Gettysburg, Pa. 1877. pp. 409—440.* [1433

Kline, Marion J.: The Genesis of the General Synod. *In: The Lutheran Quarterly. Vol. XLIX. Gettysburg, Pa. 1919. pp. 44—60.* [1434

Krueger, J. F.: The history of the English catechism of the General Synod. *In: The Lutheran Quarterly. Vol. XLIII. Gettysburg, Pa. 1913. pp. 181—199.* [1435

Lambert, W. A.: The General Synod and the General Council in history. *In: The Lutheran Quarterly. Vol. XLIV. Gettysburg, Pa. 1914. pp. 218—226.* [1436

Singmaster, J. A.: The General Synod. *In: The Lutheran Quarterly. Vol. XLIV. Gettysburg, Pa. 1914. pp. 341—361.* [1437

Sparks, C. E.: The development of the General Synod Lutheran Church in America. *In: The Lutheran Quarterly. Vol. XXXVI. Gettysburg, Pa. 1906. pp. 566—584.* [1438

Stump, Adam: The General Synod — its place and mission. *In: The Lutheran Quarterly. Vol. XXXII. Gettysburg, Pa. 1902. pp. 550—564.* [1439

Wolf, E. J.: History of the General Synod. *In: The Quarterly Review of the Evangelical Lutheran Church. Vol. XIX. Gettysburg, Pa. 1889. pp. 420—458.* [1440

Evangelisch-Lutherische Generalsynode im Süden (ursprünglich genannt . . . . . in den Konföderierten Staaten von Amerika), 1863—1918

Evangelical Lutheran General Synod in the South (first called . . . . . in the Confederate States of America), 1863—1918

Minutes of the first convention of the General Synod of the Evangelical Lutheran Church in the Confederate States of America. Held at Concord, N. C., May 20—26, 1863. *Columbia, S. C.: Steam Power Presses of Evans & Cogswell 1864. pp. 36.*
[= Minutes. Vol. I.] [1441

Minutes of the first convention . . . General Synod of the Evangelical Lutheran Church in the Confederate States of America; *since 1867:* Evangelical Lutheran General Synod in North America; *since 1878:* Evangelical Lutheran General Synod South . . . *1863ff. (1864; 1866; 1867; 1868; 1870; 1873; 1874; (Ninth and tenth convention); 1878; biennially published ff.) — 14th and second last convention 1884.* [1442

Minutes of the Diet of the Evangelical Lutheran Church in the South, held at the Court House, Salisbury, N. C., November 12th and 13th, 1884. *New Market, Va.: Henkel & Co. 1884. pp. 14.* [1443

Minutes of the last convention of the Evangelical Lutheran General Synod South, of the second convention of the Evangelical Lutheran Diet, and of the first convention of the United Synod of the Evangelical Lutheran Church in the South, held in St. Mark's Church, Roanoke, Va., June 23—28, 1886. *New Market, Va.: Henkel & Co. 1886. pp. 73.* [1444

Minutes of the last convention of the Evangelical Lutheran General Synod South, of the second convention of the Evangelical Lutheran Diet, and of the first convention of the United Synod of the Evangelical Lutheran Church in the South . . . ; *since 1887:* Minutes of the . . . convention of the United Synod of the Evangelical Lutheran Church in the South . . . ; *since 1917* . . . biennial convention . . . *Biennially published since 1887. 1886ff.—1918.* [1445

Jacobs, H. E.: The problem of the Lutheran Church in the South, *delivered by . . . at the third annual Lutheran reunion, held at Hickory, N. C., Aug. 7, 1902. Hickory, N. C.: A. L. Course & Son. 1902. pp. 22.* [1446

(Allgemeine Kirchenversammlung) Generalkonzil der Evangelisch-Lutherischen Kirche in Amerika, 1867—1918

General Council of the Evangelical Lutheran Church in America, 1867—1918

Verhandlungen der Kirchenversammlung bestehend aus Delegaten verschiedener

Evangelisch Lutherischen Synoden in
den Staaten und Canada, welche sich
zur ungeänderten Augsburgischen Confession bekennen. Gehalten in Reading,
Pa., vom 12. bis 14. Dez., 1866. *Allentown, Pa.: Gedruckt und zu haben bei
Pastor S. K. Brobst 1867. 32 S.* [1447

Proceedings of the convention held by
representatives from various Evangelical Lutheran Synods in the United
States and Canada accepting the unal-
tered Augsburg Confession, at Reading,
Pa., Dec. 12, 13 and 14, A. D. 1866.
*Pittsburgh, Pa.: Bakewell & Marthens
1867. pp. 31.* [1448

Allgemeine Versammlung der Evangelisch-
Lutherischen Kirche in Amerika.
Zweite Convention, gehalten zu Pitts-
burg, Pennsylvanien vom 12.—18. No-
vember 1868. Mit einem Auszug aus den
Verhandlungen der ersten Convention
zu Fort Wayne, 20—26 November 1867.
*Philadelphia, Pa.: G. P. Lippe. 1869.
51 S.*
[= Verhandlungen. Bd. I.] [1449

Allgemeine Versammlung der Evangelisch-
Lutherischen Kirche in Amerika. Zweite
Convention. . . . *(Mit einem Auszug aus
den Verhandlungen der ersten Convention) . . .; seit 1877:* Verhandlungen der
. . . Convention des Generalkonzils der
Evangelisch-Lutherischen Kirche in
Nord-Amerika. *Jährlich 1869—1891,
einschließlich; zweijährig seit 1893 —
31. Versammlung 1907. (Erschienen
1908.)* [1450

General Council of the Evangelical Lutheran Church in America. First convention, Fort Wayne, Indiana, November
20 to 26, A. D. 1867. *Pittsburgh, Pa.:
Bakewell & Marthens 1867. pp. 36.*
[= Minutes. Vol. I.] [1451

Minutes . . . of the General Council of the
Evangelical Lutheran Church in America. *Annually; since 1889 biennially
published. 1867ff. — the 36th convention, Philadelphia, Pa. 1917.* [1452

Jacobs, Henry E.: The historical antecedents of the General Council. *In: The
Lutheran Church Review. Vol. XXXI.
Philadelphia, Pa. 1912. pp. 221—227.*
[1453

Jacobs, C. M.: Address for the fiftieth anniversary of the General Council. *Philadelphia, Pa., October, 24th, 1917. In:
The Lutheran Church Review. Vol.
XXXVII. Philadelphia, Pa. 1918.
pp. 1—14.* [1454

Krauth, C. P.: The General Council before
its first anniversary. *In: The Lutheran
Church Review. Vol. XXVI. Philadelphia, Pa. 1907. pp. 656—665.*
[1455

Ochsenford, S. E.: Causes leading to the
organization of the General Council. *In:
The Lutheran Church Review. Vol. V.
Philadelphia, Pa. 1886. pp. 217—243.*
[1456

— Documentary history of the General
Council of the Evangelical Lutheran
Church in North America. *Philadelphia,
Pa.: General Council Publication House.
1912. pp. IX, 578.* [1457

Schmauk, Theodore E.: The General
Council in view of its approaching 14th
anniversary. *In: The Lutheran Church
Review. Vol. XXVI. Philadelphia, Pa.
1907. pp. 651—655.* [1458

Spaeth, Adolph: The General Council of the
Evangelical Lutheran Church in North
America. *In: The Lutheran Church
Review. Vol. IV. Philadelphia, Pa.
1885. pp. 81—126.* [1459

— The General Council of the Evangelical
Lutheran Church in North America.
*Philadelphia, Pa.: The Pastorial Asso-
ciation 1885. pp. 51.* [1460

Die lutherischen Diäten von 1877 und 1878,
und die Generalkonferenzen,
1898—1902—1904

The Lutheran Diets of 1877 and 1878, and
the General Conferences, 1898—1902—1904

First free Lutheran Diet in America,
Philadelphia, December 27, 28, 1877.
*The essays, debates and proceedings.
Philadelphia, Pa.: J. Frederick Smith
1878. pp. 346.* [1461

Second free Lutheran Diet in America,
Philadelphia, November 5 to 7, 1878.
*The essays, debates and proceedings.
Philadelphia, Pa.: Lutheran Book Store,
The Lutheran Publication Society, 1879
pp. 282.* [1462

The first General Conference of Lutherans
in America, held in Philadelphia, December 27 to 29, 1898. *Proceedings,
essays and debates. Philadelphia, Pa.:
Lutheran Publication Society and General
Council Publication Board 1899. pp. 339.*
[1463

The second General Conference of Lutherans in America, held in Philadelphia
April 1 to 3, 1902. *Proceedings, essays*

and debates. Newberry, S. C.: Lutheran Publication Board 1904. pp. 292.
[1464

The third General Conference of Lutherans in America, held in Pittsburgh, Pa., April 5 to 7, 1904. *Proceedings, essays and debates. Columbia S. C.: United Synod Publishing Co. 1905. pp. 382.*
[1465

Nicum, John: The third General Conference of Lutherans, held in Pittsburg, Pa., April 5—7, 1904. *In: The Lutheran Church Review. Vol. XXIII. Philadelphia, Pa. 1904. pp. 597—613.* [1466

Vereinigte Lutherische Kirche in Amerika, 1918 durch Verschmelzung errichtet

United Lutheran Church in America, organized 1918 by merger

Minutes of the first convention of the United Lutheran Church in America together with minutes of the conventions of the General Synod, the General Council and the United Synod, held in connection with the merger. Nov. 10—18, 1918. *[Philadelphia, Pa.: Board of Publication of the United Lutheran Church in America. 1919.];* Minutes of the second biennial convention of the United Lutheran Church in America, Washington, D. C., Oct. 19, to 27, 1920. *Biennially 1920ff.* [1467

Minutes . . . of . . . biennial convention of the United Lutheran Church in America. *Biennially published 1920. ff.* [1468

The United Lutheran Church in America. Souvenir of the first convention. New York, Nov. 12—18, 1918. *pp. 32, ill.* [1469

Carroll, H. K.: Great Lutheran Union accomplished. *In: The Lutheran Church Review. Vol. XXXVIII. Philadelphia, Pa. 1919. pp. 125—131.* [1470

[Hochdeutsche] Reformierte Kirche in den Vereinigten Staaten

[German] Reformed Church in the United States

Allgemein

General

United States, Department of Commerce, Bureau of Census: Reformed Church in the United States. History, description and statistics. *In: Religious bodies: 1906. Part II. Separate denominations. Washington, D. C. 1910 [= no. 894]. pp. 585—591.*

.... *In: Religious bodies: 1916. Part II. Washington, D. C. 1919. pp. 629—634.*

... Statistics. History, doctrine, organization. *In: Religious bodies; 1926. Part II. Washington, D. C. 1929. pp. 1227—1236.* [1471

Boehm, Johann Philipp: Der Reformierten Kirchen in Pennsylvanien Kirchen-Ordnung, *welche im Jahr 1725 von D. Johann Philipp B ö h m, damahls von den versammelten Gliedern der Reformierten Kirchen einhellig erwählten Prediger aufgestellet, und vor der Menge der Glieder vorgelesen, welche alle Glieder vor nützlich und gut gehalten, und auch willig angenommen haben. Nach Erwählung der nöthig geachteten Aeltesten aber und mit gesammtlichen Rath derselben an die Wohlehrwürdige und Hochgelehrte Herren, der Hoch-Ehrwürdigen Classe von Amsterdam correspondirende Predicanten, Gualterus Du Bois, and Henricus Boel zu New-York, und Vincentius Antonides von Langen Eyland zur Censur übergeben. Welche dieselbe an gedachte Hochwürdige Classe von Amsterdam überschickt, von dieser Hochansehnlichen Versammlung vor gut und stifftlich erkennet und erlaubt. Und darauf auch bey denen aufgerichteten Gemeinden fest gestellet worden. Und wurden bis hieher verschiedene unter dieser Ordnung sich submittirte Reformierte Gemeinden in gutem Frieden regieret. Weilen aber das von denen Hoch-Ehrwürdigen und Christlichen Synoden von Süd- und Nord-Holland verwilligte Coetus der Reform. Kirchen in Pennsylvanien, den letzt verwichenen 28. Sept. diss 1748sten Jahrs in Philadelphia seinen ordentlich- und jährlichen Sitz gehalten, und diese Ihme bekannt gemachte Kirchen-Ordnung vor nützlich und heylsam angemercket, so hat dieses E. Coetus einstimmig beschlossen, dieselbe zu eines jeden Gliedes der Reformierten Kirchen nützlichen Nachricht öffentlich im Druck zu befördern; welches zu bewerkstelligen das gantze Ehrwürdige Coetus überlassen, an D. Johann Philipp B ö h m, Prediger zum Falckner Schwamm, Providenz und Witpen, p. t. Coetus Praeses. Philadelphia, Pa.: gedruckt bey Gotthard Armbriester 1748. (7), 14 S.*

[Die erste Verfassung der Reformierten Kirche in Pennsylvanien.] [1472

[Boehm, John Philip]: The writings of the Rev. John Philip Boehm, founder of the Reformed Church in Pennsylvania. *Translated and edited by W. J. Hinke. In: The Journal of the Presbyterian Historical Society. Vol. VI. Philadelphia, Pa. 1912. ff. — Vol. VIII. 1916. Part I.* Letters and reports of the Rev. John Philip Boehm. *In: Vol. VI. 1912. pp. 295—324. Part II.* Letters of the year 1730. *In: Vol. VII. 1914. pp. 24—60; Part III.* Letters and reports of the year 1734. *In: Vol. VII. pp. 113—141; Part IV.* Letters and reports of the years 1738—1740. *In: Vol. VII. pp.274—303; Part V.* Letters and reports of the years 1740—1741. *In: Vol. VII. pp. 305—333; Part VI.* Letters and reports of the year 1741. *In: Vol. VII. pp. 353—384; Part VII.* Letters and reports of the years 1742—1744. *In: Vol. VIII. 1916. pp. 70—89; Part VIII.* Letters of the year 1744. *In: Vol. VIII. pp. 97—113; Part IX.* Letters of the year 1744. *In: Vol. VIII. pp. 162—183; Part X.* Letters of the years 1746—1748. *In: Vol. VIII. pp. 210—225; Part XI.* Letter of the year 1748 and obituary notices. *In: Vol. VIII. pp. 258—281.* [1473

[Boehm, John Philip]: Life and letters of the Rev. John Philip Boehm. Founder of the Reformed Church in Pennsylvania 1683 —1749. *Edited by* **W. J. Hinke.** *Philadelphia, Pa.: Publication and Sunday School Board of the Reformed Church in the United States. 1916. pp. XXVI, 501, ill., map.* [1474

Büttner, J. G.: Die hochdeutsche reformirte Kirche in den Vereinigten Staaten von Nordamerika, von ihrer Gründung bis auf die neueste Zeit. Nebst vier Beilagen: Versuche, die lutherische und die hochdeutsche reformierte Synode im Osten der Vereinigten Staaten zu vereinigen. *(u. a.)* . . . *Schleiz: O Bockelmann's Hof-Buchhandlung 1846. IV, 5—154 S.* [1475

Clever, C.: The benevolent work of the past century in the Reformed Church. *In: The Reformed Quarterly Review. Vol. XLI. New series, vol. XVI. Philadelphia, Pa. 1894. pp. 89—108.* [1476

Crawford, James: History and characteristics of the Reformed Church in the United States. *A paper read before the Presbyterian Historical Society, Febr. 19, 1895. In: The Journal of the Presbyterian Historical Society. Vol. I. Philadelphia, Pa. 1902. pp. 32—40.* [1477

Dengler, J. G.: Early trying days of the Reformed Church in America. *Read July 18, 1893. In: A Collection of Papers read before the Bucks County Historical Society. Vol. II. Easton, Pa. 1909. pp. 132—136.* [1478

Dotterer, Henry S.: The ill started collecting tour. *The journey of Elder Jacob Reiff and Pastor George Michael Weiss to Holland and Germany in 1730. In: Historical Notes, relating to the Pennsylvania Reformed Church. Vol. I. Philadelphia, Pa. 1900. pp. 5—7.* [1479

[—] Holland and Pennsylvania. *In: Historical Notes, relating to the Pennsylvania Reformed Church. Vol. I. Philadelphia, Pa. 1900. pp. 18—19; p. 52; pp. 67—68; p. 83; pp. 120—122; 137—139; p. 158; pp. 174—175; p. 197.* [1480

Dubbs, Joseph Henry: Otterbein and the Reformed Church. *In: The Reformed Quarterly Review. Vol. XXXI. =New series, vol. VI. Philadelphia, Pa. 1884. pp. 110—133.* [1481

[—] Historic manual of the Reformed Church in the United States. *Lancaster, Pa. Inquirer Printing Co. 1885. pp. VI, 9—433, ill.* [1482

Dubbs, Joseph Henry: Reformed Church archives. Papers in Reiff case. 1730 —1749. *Edited by . . . In: The Reformed Church Quarterly Review. Vol. XL. =New series, vol. XV. Philadelphia, Pa. 1893. pp. 55—70.* [1483

— The progress of a century, 1793—1893. *In: The Reformed Quarterly Review. Vol. XLII. =New series, vol. XVII. Philadelphia, Pa. 1895. pp. 28—38.* [1484

— History of the Reformed Church, German. *In: A history of the Reformed Church, Dutch, the Reformed Church, German, and the Moravian Church in the United States. New York. N. Y.: The Christian Literature Co. 1895. =The American Church History Series. Vol. VIII. pp. 213—423.*
[=Bibliography. pp. 214—220.] [1485

— The Reformed Church in Pennsylvania. *Lancaster, Pa.: New Era Printing Co. 1902. =Part X. „A narrative and critical history", prepared at the request of the Pennsylvania-German Society. In: The Pennsylvania-German Society. Proceedings and Addresses . . . 1900. Vol. XI. Lancaster, Pa. 1902. Separate pagination. pp. X, 357, ill.*
[Bibliography of the Reformed Church of the United States by **W. J. Hinke.** *pp. 341—380, only given in full in the separate reprints.]* [1486

Fackenthal, B. F., jr.: List of deceased ministers of the Reformed Church in the United States. 1710—1929. *Compiled by . . . Riegelsville, Pa. [1929]. pp. 33.* [1487

Fischer, S. R.: History of the publication efforts of the German Reformed Church. *Paper prepared and read before the Historical Society of the Reformed Church at the anniversary held in Baltimore, Md. in Oct., 1867. In: The Reformed Quarterly Review. Vol. XXXII. =New series, vol. VII. Philadelphia, Pa. 1885. pp. 67—93; also published separately. pp. 27.* [1488

Gerhart, E. V.: The life and labors of Michael Schlatter. *[Review of: „The life and labors of Rev. Michael Schlatter . . . 1716—1790." By H. Harbaugh. Philadelphia, Pa. 1857 [=no. 1497]. In: The Mercersburg Quarterly Review. Vol. IX. Chambersburg, Pa. 1857. pp. 466—485.* [1489

Gerhart, E. V.: The German Reformed Church. *A monograph. Andover: Warren F. Draper 1863. pp. 78.*

Reprint from the Bibliotheca Sacra. No. LXXVII and Biblical Repository. No. CXXIX. Jan., 1863.   [1490

Good, James I.: The early fathers of the Reformed Church in the United States. Reading, Pa.: Daniel Miller 1897. pp. 75.   [1491

— Historical hand-book of the Reformed Church in the United States. (Coetus edition) Philadelphia, Pa.: Reformed Church Publication Board 1897. pp. 90, V.   [1492

— History of the Reformed Church in the United States, 1725—1792. Reading, Pa.: Daniel Miller 1899. pp. VII, 701, ill.   [1493

— Famous women of the Reformed Church. Philadelphia, Pa.: The Sunday-School Board of the Reformed Church in the United States. 1901. pp. 295, (3), ill.   [1494

— History of the Reformed Church in the United States in the nineteenth century. New York, N. Y.: The Board of Publication of the Reformed Church in America. 1911. pp. XIII, 662.   [1495

— Union of the Dutch and German Reformed churches. Adopted by the Reformed Ministerial Association of Philadelphia, Pa. [s. l.; s. d.] pp. 12.   [1496

Harbaugh, H.: The life of Rev. Michael Schlatter, with a full account of his travels and labors among the Germans in Pennsylvania, New Jersey, Maryland and Virginia, including his services as chaplain in the French and Indian War and in the War of the Revolution. 1716—1790. Philadelphia, Pa.: Lindsay & Blackiston 1857. pp. XXXI, 27—375, ill.   [1497

—-**Heisler, D. Y.**: The fathers of the (German) Reformed Church in Europe and in America. 6 vols. Vol. I and II by H. Harbaugh; Vol. III by H. Harbaugh, edited by D. Y. Heisler; Vol. IV—V continued by D. Y. Heisler; Vol. VI edited by Wm. M. Deatrick. Lancaster, Pa.: Sprenger & Westhaeffer 1857. Vol. I. pp. XXIX, 21—394; vol. II. pp. 12, 13—408; vol. III. Lancaster, Pa.: J. M. Westhaeffer 1872. pp. XXIII, 15—493; vol. IV. 1872. pp. XII, 13—504; vol. V. Reading, Pa.: Daniel Miller 1881. pp. XII, 15—427; vol. VI. 1888. pp. XI, 15—415. [1498

Harner, Nevin C.: Factors related to Sunday school growth and decline in the Eastern Synod of the Reformed Church in the United States. New York City,

N. Y.: Bureau of Publications. Teachers College, Columbia University. 1931 pp. VI, 101.

= Teachers College, Columbia University. Contributions to Education. No. 479.   [1499

Hastings, Hugh: Ecclesiastical records. State of New York. Published by the state under the supervision of . . . 6 vols, and index vol. Albany, N. Y. 1901—1905, 1906 [= no. 436]·

[Vols. IV and V bring numerous items pertaining to the Reformed churches of Pennsylvania and the church of Holland.]   [1500

Hinke, William J.: Famous Pennsylvania-Germans: Michael Schlatter, the organizer of the Reformed Church in the United States. In: The Pennsylvania-German. Vol. I., no. 4. Lebanon, Pa. 1900. pp. 3—21, ill.   [1501

— The protest against the ordination of Rev. Boehm, May 10, 1730. In: Historical Notes, relating to the Pennsylvania Reformed Church. Vol. I. Philadelphia, Pa. 1900. pp. 102—103.   [1502

— History to the Reiff case. In: Historical Notes, relating to the Pennsylvania Reformed Church. Vol. I. Philadelphia, Pa. 1900. pp. 133—137; 150—157; 164—166; 187—197.   [1503

— The origin of the Union of the Reformed Church of Pennsylvania with the Reformed Church of Holland. In: The Perkiomen Region, Past and Present. Vol. III. Philadelphia, Pa. 1901. pp. 69—71; 85—88.   [1504

— Philip William Otterbein and the Reformed Church. In: The Presbyterian and Reformed Review. Vol. XII. 1901. pp. 437—452.   [1505

— Diaries of early missionaries travelling among the German Reformed churches. 1743—1749. In: The Journal of the Presbyterian Historical Society. Vol. III. Philadelphia, Pa. 1906. pp. 219—223. [1506

— The early catechisms of the Reformed Church in the United States. In: The Reformed Church Review. Fourth series, vol. XII. Philadelphia, Pa. 1908. pp. 473—512.   [1507

— The sources of Reformed Church history in Pennsylvania. Address delivered before the Historical Society of the Reformed Church at Lancaster, Pa., May 13, 1920. In: The Reformed Church Review. Fourth series, vol. XXIV. Philadelphia, Pa. 1920. pp. 251—264. [1508

Hinke, William J.: History of the Reformed Church in Eastern Pennsylvania. *An address before East Pennsylvania Classis of the Reformed Church, in session at Bethlehem, Pa., May 19, 1925. Easton, Pa.: Printed and distributed with the compliments of Geo A. Laubach First Reformed Church 1925. pp. 9.* [1509

— The contribution of the Reformed Church in the 18th century. *Address delivered before Eastern Synod . . . October 13, 1925. In: Reformed Church in the United States, Synod of the East. Acts and proceedings . . . 1925. pp. 131 —138.* [1510

— The Bi-Centennial of the Reformed Church in the United States. *In: The Journal of the Presbyterian Historical Society. Vol. XII. Philadelphia, Pa. 1926. pp. 325—338.* [1511

Koplin, A. B.: The history of missions of the Reformed Church in the United States. *In: The Reformed Quarterly Review. Vol. XXVIII. = New series, vol. III. Philadelphia, Pa. 1881. pp. 325—343.* [1512

Krampe, A. W.: Our German work in the Reformed Church in the United States. *Address before the Historical Society of the Reformed Church in the United States. Lancaster, Pa., May 11, 1922 . . . In: The Reformed Church Review. Fifth series, vol. I. 1922. Lancaster, Pa. 1922. pp. 388—403.* [1513

[Lischy, Jacob and Rauch, Christian Henry]: Diary of Lischy's and Rauch's journey among the Reformed congregations in Pennsylvania, in the month of February, 1745. *Translated and edited by Wm. J. Hinke. In: The Reformed Church Review. Fourth series, vol. IX. Philadelphia, Pa. 1905. pp. 74—90.* [1514

[Lischy, Jacob]: Report of the Rev. Jacob Lischy to Bishop Augustus G. Spangenberg. *Translated and edited by Wm. J. Hinke. In: The Reformed Church Review. Fourth series, vol. IX. Philadelphia, Pa. 1905. pp. 517—534; Vol. X. Philadelphia, Pa. 1906. pp. 85— 98.* [1515

Mayer, Lewis: The history of the German Reformed Church. *To which is prefixed a memoir of his life by Elias Heiner. Vol. I. Second edition. Philadelphia, Pa.: Lippincott, Grambo & Co. 1851. pp. XVI, 461, ill.*

[The second volume never printed is as manuscript in possession of the Historical Society of the Reformed Church, Lancaster, Pa.] [1516

Miller, Daniel: Early history of the Reformed Church in Pennsylvania. *With an introduction by Wm. J. Hinke. Reading, Pa.: Daniel Miller 1906. pp. VIII, 9—280, ill.* [1517

Nevin, J. W.: „The enterprise of the German Reformed Church." *In: Address delivered at the inauguration of Rev. J. W. Nevin, D. D., as Professor of Theology in the Theological Seminary of the German Reformed Church, Mercersburg, Pa., May 20th, 1840. Published by order of the Board of Visitors. Chambersburg, Pa.: Office of Publication of the German Reformed Church. 1840. pp. 17—28.* [1518

— Our relations to Germany. *In: The Mercersburg Review. Vol. XIV. Philadelphia, Pa. 1867. pp. 627—633.* [1519

Omwake, George L.: Reformed Church in the United States. *Forward movement handbook. Philadelphia, Pa.: The Forward Movement, Reformed Church in the United States. 1920. pp. 189, 6 maps.* [1520

[Rauch, Christian Henry]: Diary of Lischey's and Rauch's journey among the Reformed congregations in Pennsylvania. *In the month of February, 1745. Translated and edited by Wm. J. Hinke. In: The Reformed Church Review. Fourth series, vol. XI. Philadelphia, Pa. 1907. pp. 74—90.* [1521

Richards, George Warren: Reformed what? *Philadelphia, Pa.: Publication and Sunday School Board of the Reformed Church in the United States. Philadelphia, Pa. [s. d.] pp. 28.* [1522

— The contribution of the Reformed Church in the 19th century. *Address delivered before Eastern Synod . . . October 13, 1925. In: Reformed Church in the United States, Synod of the East: Acts and proceedings . . . 1925. pp. 139— 153.* [1523

Roentgen, J. H. C.: Comparative statistics of the Reformed Church in the United States. 1891—1900. *Compiled by . . . Cleveland, O.: Central Publishing House. pp. 13.* [1524

Ruetenik, Herman, J.: The pioneers of the Reformed Church in the United States of North America. *Cleveland, O.: Central Publishing House 1901. pp. 123, ill.* [1525

— Bahnbrecher der Deutsch-Reformierten Kirche in den Vereinigten Staaten von

Nord-Amerika. *Cleveland, O.: Central Publishing House. 1901. VI, 7—113 S.* [1526

Rupp, William: Our relation to German theology. *Paper read as an address at the Centennial Convention of the Pittsburgh Synod held in Grace Reformed Church, Pittsburgh, Pa., April 27, 1893. In: The Reformed Quarterly Review. Vol. XL. = New series, vol. XV. Philadelphia, Pa. 1893. pp. 473—492.* [1527

Schaeffer, Charles E.: Our home mission work. An outline study of the home mission work of the Reformed Church in the United States. *Philadelphia, Pa.: Publication and Sunday School Board of the Reformed Church in the United States. 1914. pp. 263, ill.* [1528

Schaeffer, William C.: The Reformed Church in the United States. *In: The Reformed Church Review. Fourth series, vol. XXI. Philadelphia, Pa. 1917. pp. 354—371.* [1529

Schlatter, Michael: Diary of the Rev. Michael Schlatter, June 1—Dec. 15, 1746. *Edited by W. J. Hinke. In: Journal of the Presbyterian Historical Society. Vol. III. Philadelphia, Pa. 1906. pp. 105—121; 158—176.* [1530

— Getrouw Verhaal van den waren toestant der meest herderloze gemeentens in Pennsylvanien en aangrensende Provintien, *voorgestelt en opgedragen met nedrig verzoek om hulpe en bystand, a an de H. Eerw. Christelyke Synodens van Nederland, en voorts aan all milddadige Christenen door . . . predikant te Philadelphia. Met eene aanpryzende voorrede van de Gecommitteerde des Classis van Amsteldam. T'Amsteldam: Jacobus Loveringh 1751. pp. XXII, 56.* [1531

— Wahrhafte Erzehlung von dem wahren Zustand der meist Hirtenlosen Gemeinden in Pensilvanien und denen angrenzenden Provinzen, *von . . . Evangelisch Reformirter Prediger zu Philadelphia, denen Hoch-Ehrw. Christlichen Synoden in den Niederlanden, wie auch andern mildthätigen Christen in holländischer Sprache vorgestellet. Nunmehro aber von dem Verfasser selbst in deutscher Sprache übersetzt, und zugleich an die löbliche Reformirte Eidgenossschaften und Ministeria in der Schweiz dediciret. Nebst einem Vorbericht der Verordneten von der Classe Amsterdam. In: Johann Philip Fresenii Pastoral Sammlungen. Zwölfter Theil. Frankfurt und Leipzig:*

bey Johann Gottlieb Garbe 1752. S. 181 —408. [1532

[Schlatter, Michael]: A true history of the real condition of the destitute congregations in Pennsylvania. *By M i c h a e l S c h l a t t e r, Evangelical Reformed minister in Philadelphia. Addresses, in the Dutch language, to the very Reverend Christian Synods in the Netherlands and other Christians: and now translated into the German language by the author, and dedicated to the Honorable Reformed Magistrates and Ministers of the Swiss Confederacy, together with an introduction by the commissioners of the Classis of Amsterdam. English translation. In: The life of Rev. Michael Schlatter; with a full account of his travels and labors among the Germans in Pennsylvania, New Jersey, Maryland and Virginia . . . 1716—1790. By H. Harbaugh. Philadelphia, Pa. 1857 [= no. 1497]. pp. 87—234.* [1533

Swander, John I.: The Reformed Church. A sketch of its history together with a statement of its doctrines, government, cultus and customs. *Dayton, O.: Reformed Publishing Co. 1889. pp. 172.* [1534

Truxal, A. E.: The Reformed Church in the United States. 1793—1893. *In: The Reformed Quarterly Review. Vol. XL. = New series, vol. XV. Philadelphia, Pa. 1893. pp. 366—382.* [1535

Weiser, C. Z.: The Reformed Church in America. *In: The Reformed Quarterly Review. Vol. XXVII. = New series, vol. II. Philadelphia, Pa. 1880. pp. 577 —601.* [1536

Whitmer, A. C.: Forty years in forty minutes. A brief outline of the history of the Reformed Church in the United States from 1854 to 1894. *Philadelphia, Pa.: Reformed Church Publication House. 1895. pp. 32.* [1537

— One hundred and fifty years of home missionary activity. An outline history of the home missionary work of the Reformed Church in the United States. *Lancaster, Pa.: The New Era Print. 1897. pp. 128.* [1538

Whithmer, A. C.: Address on the occasion of the visit of the Synod of the Potomac to the Birthplace of the Rev. Professor Henry Harbaugh, D. D. Oct. 25, 1917. *In: Addresses on the life and the theology of the Rev. H. Harbaugh, and Rev. E. Vogel Gerhart (1917) [= no. 1497]. pp. 3—6.* [1539

Yost, Francis C.: 100 questions and answers of the history, government and usages of the Reformed Church in the United States. *Arranged by . . . Reading, Pa.: Daniel Miller 1891. pp. 16.* [1540
Addresses delivered on the occasion of the one hundred and fiftieth anniversary of the founding of the Eastern Synod of the Reformed Church in the United States. *Carried out during the sessions of Synod at Bethlehem, October 7—11, 1896. pp. 131.* [1541
Sesqui-Centennial services of the Evangelical Reformed Church, Frederick, Maryland, May 9, 14, and 16, 1897. *Rev.* **E. R. Eschbach,** *pastor. Frederick, Md. 1897. pp. 91.* [1542
Michael Schlatter memorial addresses at the Sesqui-Centennial services held in Hagerstown, Md., by the Synod of the Potomac, October 20, A. D., 1897, in honor of the pioneer organizer of Reformed churches in America. *Prepared for the occasion by* **Cyrus Cort, John E. Roller** *and* **E. R. Eschbach,** *and published by request of Synod, Jan. 1900. Reading, Pa.: Daniel Miller 1900. pp. 61, ill.* [1543
Addresses in commemoration of the one hundredth anniversary of the birth of the Reverend Henry Harbaugh, D. D. and of the Reverend Emanuel Vogel Gerhart, D. D., LL. D. *Delivered respectively at the annual sessions of the Synod of the Potomac Zion's Reformed Church, Hagerstown, Md. and of the St. Paul's Reformed Church, Lancaster, Pa. Held in the month of Oct., 1917. Published by direction of the two Synods and printed by the Publication and Sunday School Board of the Reformed Church in the United States. Philadelphia, Pa. 1918. pp. IV, 82.* [1544
Berigt en onderrigtinge, nopens en aan de Colonie en Kerke van Pensylvanien. *Opgestelt en uytgegeven door de Gedeputeerden van de E. Christelyke Synodus van Zuyd-Holland, benevens de Gecommitteerden van de E. Classis van Delft en Delfsland en Schieland. [1731.] pp. 18.* [1545
Circular Schreiben der Vereinigten Reformierten Prediger in Pennsylvanien an dasige sämtliche nach Gottes Wort Reformirte Gemeinen; Darin sie kürzlich darlegen, wie der Große Jehova die von Sr. Ehrw. Michael Slatter, V. D. M. an unsere Hochw. Christl. Kirchenväter

übernommene Commissions zu ihrer Rettung und Hülfe, in Gnaden gesegnet: Wie solches von sothanen Gemeinen solle gebührend erkannt, mit Danksagung angenommen, und recht gebraucht, ja, zum Lobe Gottes und dem Heil ihrer unsterblichen Seelen angewandt werden. *Zu allgemeiner Nachricht herausgegeben von* **Georg Michael Weiß, Joh. Phil. Leydich, Jacob Lischy.** *Lancaster, Pa.: H. Müller und S. Holland 1752. 14 S.* [1546
Verschuldigt Dank-Adres aan de Edele Groot Mogende Heeren Staaten van Holland en West-Vriesland aan de correspondere Christelyke Synoden, Classen en Kerkenraden der Vereendige Provintien en aan alle Liefdadige Weldoenders, die zich, zeer tederhartig, der zaak van de Gereformeerde Gemeenten in Pennsylvanien, voor het meerdere gedeelte uit Hoogduitsche Emigranten bestaande, hebben aangenomen, en der zelver welstand, door hune zeer Edelmoedige en milde Liefdegaven, helpen bevorderen: streckende met een tot nodig Bericht, hoe, tot welke eindens, en met welk gevolg, de ruime giften der Edelmoedige Weldoendern besteedt zyn, en wat' er van het geen' er zedert enige Jaren in deze zaak gedaan is, en om de Liefdadigheid verder op te wakkeren. *Opgestelt door de Deputation der Zuid-en Noord-Hollandsche Synoden, en de Gecomitteerden van de Classis van Amsterdam. Te Amsterdam: By Jacobus Loveringh, Boekverkooper voor aan op den Nieuwendyk 1758. 24 S.* [1547
Letters from Holland connected with the first organization of the German Reformed Church in the United States *Chambersburg, Pa.: Publication Office of the Reformed Church. 1841. pp. 24.* [1548
An old document relating to the early planting of the German Reformed Church in Pennsylvania. *In: The Evangelical Quarterly devoted to Christian Literature and Theology. Edited by J. F. Berg. Vol. II. Philadelphia, Pa. 1861. pp.495—504.* [1549
Reformirte Prediger für Pennsylvanien. = *Erlasse des Kurpfälzischen Kirchenrats. Mitgetheilt von* **Hrch. Lützel.** *No. 3. In: Blätter für Pfälzische Kirchengeschichte. Jg. V. Grünstadt 1929. S. 18—19.* [1550
To the president of the United States. the address of the ministers and elders of the

German Reformed congregations in the United States, at their general meeting, held at Philadelphia, on the 10th day of June, 1789. *(Signed by order of the meeting, W. Hendel . . . F. Delliker . . .)* and answer of George Washington. *Reprint in: The American Museum. For repository of ancient and modern fugitive pieces etc. Vol. VI. Philadelphia, Pa. 1789. pp. 222. Republished in: Bulletin, Theological Seminary of the Reformed Church in U. S. Lancaster, Pa. January 1932. pp. 55—56.* [1551
Conference on union between the Reformed Church in America and the Reformed Church in the United States. Held in Philadelphia, April 3d and 4th, 1888.

Published by the authority of the conference, and under the auspices of the joint committee appointed by the general synods of the two churches. Philadelphia, Pa.: Reformed Church Publication House. 1888. pp. 144. [1552
A survey of the Reformed Church in the United States. *Under the auspices of the Laymen's Missionary Movement. By 4 commissions. Second edition [Philadelphia, Pa.]: Laymen's Missionary Movement of the Reformed Church in the United States. 1914. pp. 212, 6 maps.* [1553
The great advance. The story of the Forward Movement 1919—1926. *Philadelphia, Pa.: Forward Movement Commission of the Reformed Church in the United States Schaff Building 1926. pp. 196.* [1554

Synoden
Synods

Ost-Synode der [Hochdeutschen] Reformierten Kirche in den Vereinigten Staaten (ursprünglich Synode der Hochdeutschen Reformierten Kirche in den Vereinigten Staaten genannt), 1793

Eastern Synod of the [German] Reformed Church in the United States (originally called: Synod of the German Reformed Church in the United States), 1793

Minutes and letters of the coetus of the German Reformed congregations in Pennsylvania 1747—1792 together with three preliminary reports of Rev. John Philip Boehm, 1734—1744. *Edited by* **W. J. Hinke.** *Published by authority of the Eastern Synod of the Reformed Church in the United States. Philadelphia, Pa.: Reformed Church Publication Board 1903. pp. XXII, 463.* [1555
Acts and proceedings of the Coetus and Synod of the German Reformed Church in the United States, from 1791 to 1816 inclusive. *Translated from the German. Chambersburg, Pa.: M. Kieffer & Co. 1854. pp. 4—74. Reprinted by Synod 1930. pp. 80.* [1556
Synodal-Ordnung des Hochdeutschen Reformirten Synods und der mit ihr verbundenen Gemeinden in den Vereinigten Staaten von Nord-Amerika. *Lancaster, Pa.: Henrich und Benjamin Grimler, In ihrer Neuen English und Deutschen Buchdruckerey 1805. pp. 20.* [1557

Verhandlungen der Synode der Hoch-Deutschen Reformirten Kirche in den Vereinigten Staaten von Nord Amerika, gehalten zu Yorktaun, Pennsylvanien, September, 1817. *Philadelphia, Pa.: Conrad Zentler 1818. 20 S.* [1558
Verhandlungen der Synode der Hochdeutschen Reformirten Kirche in den Vereinigten Staaten von Nord-Amerika . . .; *1818:* Verrichtungen des Synodes . . .; *1825—1829, 1831:* Synodal Verhandlungen . . . *Jährlich 1818 ff.—1887.* [1559
Synodal-Proceedings of the German Reformed Church in the United States of North America. Held at Philadelphia from the 25th to the 30th September 1825. *(Translated from the German). Philadelphia: Printed by John George Ritter. 1825. pp. 27. (These are the first minutes of the Synod in English..)* [1559a
The proceedings of the Synod of the German Reformed Church in North America, at York, Pa., Sept., 1827. *With an appendix. Hagers Town, Md.: Gruber and May 1828. pp. 56.* [1560
The proceedings of the Synod of the German Reformed Church in North America . . .; *since 1828:* . . . of the Synod of the United States of North America . . .; *1828 and since 1835:* The acts and proceedings . . .; *since 1845:* . . . in the United States . . .; *since 1870:* . . . Reformed

Church in the United States . . .; *since 1889*: . . . of the Eastern Synod of the Reformed . . . *Annually published 1827ff.* [1561

Gerhard, D. W.: History of Lancaster Classis, Eastern Synod of the Reformed Church in the United States. For the first 50 years of its existence 1852—1902. *Lancaster, Pa.: Rider & Snyder 1902. pp. 47.* [1562

Hinke, William J.: The Reformed Church within the bounds of Lebanon Classis during the eighteenth century. *Address delivered before Lebanon Classis at its 100th annual session, June 1, 1920. In: The Reformed Church Review. Fourth series, vol. XXV. Philadelphia, Pa. 1921. pp. 46—64.* [1563

— Early History of Philadelphia Classis, 1820—1840, together with the Minutes of the old Philadelphia Classis, 1820—1825. *In: Acts and Proceedings of the Classis of Philadelphia, Monday and Tuesday, January 21st and 22nd 1935. pp. 123—140.* [1563a

Stein, Thos S.: Centennial history of Lebanon Classis of the Reformed Church in the United States, together with brief sketches of various churches, congregations and prominent workers in the kingdom. 1820—1920. *Compiled by . . . Lebanon, Pa.: Sowers Printing Co. [1920]. pp. XIV, 473, ill., map.* [1564

Wolff, D. U., Sechler, J. H., Hoover, H. C. and **Detwiler, Jones:** Philadelphia Classis 1836—1897. Facts and figures. *Prepared by . . . Collegeville, Pa.: Tompson Bros. 1897. pp. 17, and 3 charts.* [1565

Freie unabhängige deutsche Reformierte Gemeinden von Pennsylvanien, 1822—1836

Synod of the Free Independent German Reformed Congregations of Pennsylvania, 1822—1836

Proceedings of the Synod of the Free Indepaendant German Reformed congregations of Pennsylvania, held at Middletown, Dauphin County, Pa. the 6th, 7th and 8th of September, 1829. *Reading, Pa.: John Ritter & Co. 1829. pp. 11.* [1566

Proceedings of the Synod of the Free Indepaendant German Reformed congregations of Pennsylvania . . .; *since: 1831* . . . of the German Reformed Synod of Pennsylvania and adjacent states . . . *Annually 1822 to 1836.* [1567

Synodal-Verhandlungen der unabhängigen reformirten Gemeinen in Pennsylvanien; gehalten in der Stadt Riehmstaun, Lancaster County, den 4ten und 5ten September, 1826. *Fünfte Jahres-Versammlung. Reading, Pa.: Heinrich B. Sage 1826. 12 S.* [1568

Synodal-Verhandlungen der freyen unabhängigen deutschen Reformirten Gemeinen von Pennsylvanien, gehalten in Jackson Taunschip, Libanon County, den 14ten, 15ten und 16ten October, 1827. *Reading, Pa.: Johann Ritter und Co. 1828. 10 S.* [1569

Potomac Synode der Reformierten Kirche in den Vereinigten Staaten, 1873

Synod of the Potomac of the Reformed Church in the United States, 1873

Acts and proceedings of the Synod of the Potomac convened in the Reformed Church of Frederick, Md., April 18. A. D., 1873. *For the purpose of organization. Philadelphia, Pa.: Reformed Church Publication Board 1873. pp. 14.* [1570

First annual meeting. Acts and proceedings of the Synod of the Potomac of the Reformed Church in the United States, convened in convention, Chambersburg, Pa., October, 1873. *Philadelphia, Pa.: Reformed Church Publication Board 1873. pp. . . . [= Minutes. Vol. I.]* [1571

First annual meeting. Acts and proceedings of the Synod of the Potomac of the Reformed Church in the United States. *Annually 1873ff.* [1572

Clapp, Jacob C.: Historic sketch of the Reformed Church in North Carolina. *By a Board of editors, under the Classis of North Carolina. Edited by . . . With an introduction by the late Geo. Welker, D. D. Philadelphia, Pa.: Publication Board of the Reformed Church in the United States [1908]. pp. 327.* [1573

Welker, George William and **Murphy, Joseph L.**: A historical sketch of the Classis of North Carolina, *by the late George Wm. Welker, D. D., with notes and introduction by Joseph L. Murphy. Hickory, N. C.: A. L. Grouse 1895. pp. 35.* [1574

Pittsburg Synode der Reformierten Kirche in den Vereinigten Staaten, 1870

Pittsburgh Synod of the Reformed Church in the United States, 1870

Preliminary meeting. Pittsburgh Synod of the Reformed Church in the United States. Held in Pittsburgh, Pa., February, 1870. *[s. l., 1870.] pp. 12.* [1575

First annual meeting. Pittsburgh Synod of the Reformed Church in the United States 1870. *[s. l., 1870.] pp. 36, (1).* [1576

(First) annual meeting. Pittsburgh Synod of the Reformed Church in the United States . . .; *since 1875:* (Sixth) annual sessions. Acts and proceedings of the Pittsburgh Synod of the Reformed Church in the United States . . . *Annually 1870* ff. [1577

Truxal, A. E.: Pittsburgh Synod — its twenty-fifth anniversary. *In: The Reformed Quarterly Review. Vol. XLII. = New series, vol. XVII. Philadelphia, Pa. 1895. pp. 203—224.* [1578

— Pittsburgh Synod, 1870—1920. *In: The Reformed Church Review. Fourth series, vol. XXV. Philadelphia, Pa. 1921. pp. 21—26.* [1579

A history of the Reformed Church within the bounds of the Westmoreland Classis. *Edited by a committee of the Classis. Philadelphia, Pa.: Reformed Church Publication Board 1877. pp. VI, 232.* [1580

Ohio-Synode der Reformierten Kirche in den Vereinigten Staaten (ursprünglich Hochdeutsche Evangelische Reformierte Synode von Ohio), 1824—1922.

Ohio Synod of the Reformed Church in the United States (originally called: German Evangelical Reformed Synod of Ohio), 1824—1922

Verhandlungen der Classical Synode des sechsten Districts der Hochdeutschen Reformirten Kirche in den Vereinigten Staaten von Nord Amerika, gehalten zu Neu Lancaster, im Jahre 1823 zu Neu Lancaster, den 20sten, 21sten und 22sten April 1823. *Lancaster, O.: Johann Herman 1823. 11 S.* *[= Minutes. Vol. I.]* [1581

Verhandlungen der Classical Synode des sechsten Districts der Hochdeutschen Reformirten Kirche in den Vereinigten

Staaten von Nord-Amerika; *seit 1824:* Verhandlungen der Hochdeutschen Evangelisch Reformirten Synode in Ohio; *seit 1826:* . . . der Synode der Reformirten Kirche von Ohio; *1828:* . . . der Hochdeutschen Evangelisch Reformirten Synode in Ohio . . .; *seit 1829:* . . . der Reformirten Synode von Ohio; *1831:* . . . der hochteutschen reformirten Synode, von Ohio; *seit 1832:* . . . der . . . Sitzung der hochdeutschen . . .; *1836:* . . . der hochdeutsch-Reformirten . . . *seit 1847:* . . . der Synode der Hochdeutschen Reformirten Kirche von Ohio und den angrenzenden Staaten . . . *Jährlich 1823* ff.—*1872.* *[Bis 1843 als Original verbindlich, seither die englische Ausgabe.]* [1582

Proceedings of the Synod of the High German Reformed Church, of Ohio, held in New Lancaster the 21st, 22d, and 23d days of May, 1826. *[s. l., 1826.] pp. 10.* *[First translation of the minutes into English.]* [1583

Proceedings of the Synod of the High German-Reformed Church, of Ohio; *since 1830(?)* . . . of the Synod of the Reformed Church of Ohio . . .; *since 1832:* . . . of the . . . session of the German Reformed Synod of Ohio, and the congregations in connexion with it in other states; *1837:* Minutes of the . . . session of the German Reformed Synod of Ohio; *1838:* Minutes of the German Reformed Synod . . .; *1843:* Acts and proceedings of the delegate Synod of the German Reformed Church of Ohio and adjacent states . . .; *since 1844:* The acts and proceedings of the Synod of the German Reformed Church of Ohio and adjacent states; *since 1870:* . . . of the Reformed Church . . .; *since 1871:* . . . of the Reformed Synod of Ohio and the congregations in connection with it in other states . . .; *since 1874:* . . . Ohio Synod of the Reformed Church in the United States. *Annually 1826* ff. to *1922.* [1584

Die drei Distrikte der Hochdeutsch-Evangelisch-Reformierten Synode von Ohio, 1840—1842

The three districts of the German Synod of Ohio, 1840—1842

Verhandlungen der ersten Hochdeutschen Evangelisch-Reformierten District-Synode von Ohio, und der mit ihr verbundenen Gemeinden in anderen Staaten. Gehalten in Somerset, Somerset County, Pennsylvania, vom 23sten bis 25sten Mai, im Jahr unsers Herrn, 1841. *Chambersburg, Pa.: Druckerei der hochdeutsch-reformirten Kirche 1841. 20 S.* [1585

Verhandlungen der ersten Hochdeutschen Evangelisch-Reformirten District-Synode von Ohio und der mit ihr verbundenen Gemeinden in andern Staaten. Gehalten in der Brusch Creek Kirche, bei Adamsburg, Westmoreland County, Pennsylvania, vom 23sten bis zum 25sten Mai, im Jahr unsers Herrn, 1842. *Chambersburg, Pa.: ,,Christlichen Zeitschrift "Druckerei 1842. 16 S.* [1585a

Proceedings of the Second District of the German Reformed Synod of Ohio and the adjoining states; held at Canfield, Trumbull County, Ohio, from the 16th to the 18th of May, A. D. 1841. *Canton, O.: Peter Kaufmann & Co. 1841. pp. 16.* [1585b

Verhandlung des dritten Districts, der Hochdeutsch-Evangelisch-Reformirten Synode von Ohio und der mit ihr verbundenen Gemeinden in anderen Staaten. Gehalten in Dayton, Montgomery County, Ohio, vom 7ten bis 10ten Juny, im Jahre unseres Herrn 1840. *Columbus, O.: J. S. Wiestling 1840. 16 S.* [1586

Minutes of the Third District of the German Reformed Synod of Ohio, and congregations in connexion with it in other states. Held at Farlton, Pickaway County, Ohio, from May 30th to June 3d, 1841. *Columbus, O.: J. S. Wiestling 1841. pp. 15.* [1587

Verhandlungen der dritten Sitzung der dritten Distrikts-Synode der Hochdeutsch-Reformirten Kirche von Ohio, gehalten zu Delaware, Delaware County, O. . . . 16ten bis zum 18ten Mai, im Jahre unseres Herrn, 1842. *Cincinnati, O.: St. Molitor, in der Druckerei des Volksblattes 1842. 19 S.* [1588

Minutes of the Third District, of the German Reformed Synod of Ohio, and congregations in connexion in other states. Held in Delaware, Delaware County, O. From May 16, to 18, 1842. *Rossville, O.: J. M. Christy 1842. pp. 13.* [1589

Reiter, I. H.: History of the Ohio Synod. *In: The Reformed Quarterly Review.*

Meynen, Bibliographie

Vol. XXVI. = New series, vol. I Philadelphia, Pa. 1879. pp. 143—168. [1590

Zerbe, A. S.: The seventy-fifth anniversary of the organization of the Ohio Synod of the Reformed Church. *A historical review. Read during the sessions of Ohio Synod of the Reformed Church in Warren, O., October 11—16, 1899. Published as an appendix to: Acts and proceedings of the Ohio Synod of the Reformed Church in the United States convened in Zion's Reformed Church, in Warren, Trumpull County, O., Oct. 11th to 16th, 1899. pp. 19.* [1591

Souvenir booklet. Centennial. One hundred years of Reformed Church history in Ohio and adjacent states. *Program. Merger Meeting and Central Synods. Ohio and Central Synodical Womans Missionary Societies. The Centennial and Merger Meetings were held 1923, in First and Trinity Reformed Churches, Canton, O. [s. l.] 1923. pp. 133, ill.* [1592

Ohio Synode der Reformierten Kirche in den Vereinigten Staaten, 1923
Ohio Synod of the Reformed Church in the United States, 1923

Acts and proceedings of the Ohio Synod of the Reformed Church in the United States. First annual meeting held in Trinity Reformed Church, Canton, O., September 28th to October 2nd, 1923. *Containing also minutes of the special meeting of Ohio Synod. Held in Central Reformed Church, Dayton, O., May 2nd, 1923; Minutes of the one hundredth annual meeting of Ohio Synod, held in Trinity Reformed Church, Canton, O., Sept. 28th, 1923; Minutes of the forty-second annual meeting of Central Synod. Held in First Reformed Church, Canton, O., Sept. 28th, 1923. Cleveland, O.: Central Publishing House. pp. 155, tables.* [1593

Acts and proceedings of the Ohio Synod of the Reformed Church in the United States. *(First) annual meeting in . . . Annually 1923ff.* [1594

Nordwestliche Distrikt-Synode der Deutsch-Reformierten Kirche von Nordamerika (in den Vereinigten Staaten), 1867
Synod of the Northwest of the Reformed Church in the United States, 1867

Verhandlungen der nordwestlichen Distrikt-Synode der Deutsch-Reformirten

10

Kirche von Nord-Amerika, erste jährliche Sitzung gehalten in Fort-Wayne, Indiana, vom 28 sten Mai bis 1 sten Juni 1867. *Cleveland, O.: Druckerei der evang. reformirten Buch-Anstalt 1867. 30, (6) S.* [1595

Verhandlungen der nordwestlichen District-Synode der Deutsch-Reformirten Kirche von Nord-Amerika, (Erste) jährliche Sitzung; *seit 1870:* ... in den Vereinigten Staaten ...; *seit 1873:* ... der Deutsch-Reformirten Synode des Nordwestens der Reformirten Kirche in den Vereinigten Staaten ...; *seit 1902:* ... der Deutschen Synode ...; *seit 1918:* Beschlüsse und Verhandlungen der Synode des Nordwesten der Reformirten Kirche in den Vereinigten Staaten. *Jährlich 1867ff.* [1596

„Synod of the Interior" der Reformierten Kirche in den Vereinigten Staaten, 1887—1921

Synod of the Interior of the Reformed Church in the United States, 1887—1921

Preliminary and first annual meeting. Synod of the Interior of the Reformed Church in the United States. Held in St. Paul's Reformed Church, Kansas City, Mo., from September 29 th to October 3 d, 1887. *Abilene, Kan.: The Gazette Printing Co. 1888. pp. 26.* [1597

Preliminary and first annual meeting. Synod of the Interior of the Reformed Church in the United States; *since 1888:* (Second) annual sessions. Acts and proceedings of ... *Annually 1887ff. — 1921.* [1598

„Synod of the Mid-West" der Reformierten Kirche in den Vereinigten Staaten, 1921

Synod of the Mid-West of the Reformed Church in the United States, 1921

First annual sessions. Acts and proceedings of the Synod of the Mid-West of the Reformed Church in the United States. Held in the Zion's Reformed Church, Freeport, Ill., Oct. 18 th to 21 st, 1921. — Eighth annual sessions. Acts and proceedings of the Southwest of the Reformed Church in the United States. Held in the Zion's Reformed Church, Freeport, Ill., Oct. 18 th, 1921. — Thirty-fifth annual sessions. Acts and procee

dings of the Synod of the Interior of the Reformed Church in the United States. Held in the First English Reformed Church, Freeport, Ill., Oct. 18 th, 1921. *Cleveland, O.: Central Publishing House 1921. pp. 253.* [1599

(First) annual sessions. Acts and proceedings of the Synod of the Mid-West of the Reformed Church in the United States. *Annually 1921ff.* [1600

General-Synode der (Deutsch) Reformierten Kirche in den Vereinigten Staaten, 1863

General Synod of the (German) Reformed Church in the United States, 1863

The acts and proceedings of the General Synod of the German Reformed Church in the United States of America, at Pittsburgh, Pa., November 18 th to 25 th, 1863. *Chambersburg, Pa.: S. R. Fisher & Co.'s 1864. pp. 40. [= Minutes. Vol. I.]* [1601

The acts and proceedings of the first General Synod of the German Reformed Church in the United States of America ...; *since 1869:* ... Reformed Church in the United States ... *Triennially 1863ff.* [1602

Protokoll der ersten General-Synode der Deutsch Reformirten Kirche in Nord-Amerika, gehalten in der Gnaden-Kirche in Pittsburg, Pa., von Mittwoch den 18. Oct. bis zum Mittwoch den 25. Oct. 1863. *[Statt Oktober müßte November stehen, vgl. S. 3.] Amtlicher Deutscher Abdruck. Cleveland, O.: Druckerei des Evangelist. 1863. pp. 24. [= Minutes. Vol. I.]* [1603

Protokoll der ersten General-Synode der Deutsch Reformirten Kirche in Nord Amerika ...; *seit 1866:* Verhandlungen ... Kirche in den Vereinigten Staaten Nord-Amerikas ...; *seit 1869:* ... der Reformirten Kirche in den Vereinigten Staaten ... *Alle drei Jahre 1863ff.* [1604

Cort, Cyrus and others: Digest of acts and decisions of the General Synod of the Reformed Church in the United States. *Prepared by* Cyrus Cort, John H. Sechler, Joseph H. Apple, Ambrose Cort, John W. Bickel, *a committee appointed by the General Synod at Tiffin, Ohio, May, 1899. Published by authority of the General Synod. Philadelphia, Pa.: Reformed Church Publication Board 1902. pp. VIII, 176.* [1605

Schwenkfelder

Schwenkfelders

United States, Department of Commerce, Bureau of Census: Schwenkfelders. History, description and statistics. *In: Religious bodies: 1906. Part II. Separate denominations. Washington, D. C. 1910 [= no. 894]. pp. 622—624.*
. . . *In: Religious bodies: 1916. Part II. Washington, D. C. 1919. pp. 673—674.*
. . . Statistics. History, doctrine and organization. *In: Religious bodies; 1926. Part II. Washington, D. C. 1929. pp. 1307—1310.* [1606

The Schwenkfeldian. *Published by the first Schwenkfeldian church, 30th & Cumberland Streets. Philadelphia, Pa. Since. Vol. II. No. 7, 1905 published by the General Conference of the Schwenkfeldian (-der) Churches. Vol. I, no. 1. December 1903. Philadelphia, Pa. 1903, monthly ff.*
[Includes annual statistical reports.] [1607

Anders, Asher A.: The Schwenkfelders. *Read January 19, 1892. In: A Collection of Papers read before the Bucks County Historical Society. Vol. II. Easton, Pa. 1909. pp. 35—42.* [1608

Brecht, Samuel Kriebel: The genealogical record of the Schwenkfelder families, seekers of religious liberty who fled from Silesia to Saxony and thence to Pennsylvania in the years 1731 to 1737. *Edited by . . . Printed for the Board of Publication of the Schwenkfelder Church, Pennsburg, Pa. New York, N. Y.-Chicago, Ill.: Rand Mc Nally & Co. 1923. pp. (1), VII—XX; 1752, ill., maps.*
[Bibliography. pp. XIX—XX.] [1609

Hartranft, John F.: The Schwenkfelders. *Read June 10, 1886. In: A Collection of Papers read before the Bucks County Historical Society. Vol. I. Easton, Pa. 1908. pp. 404—408.* [1610

[Heebner, Balthasar] - Kriebel, Reuben: Genealogical record of the descendants of the Schwenkfelders, who arrived in Pennsylvania in 1733, 1734, 1736, 1737 *from the German of the Rev. Balthasar Heebner and from other sources. By Reuben Kriebel. With an historical sketch by C. Heydrick. Manayunk: Josephus Yeakel 1879. pp. XXXII, 339.* [1611

Hinke, William J.: Caspar Schwenkfeld and the Schwenkfelders in Pennsylvania. *Address before the Schwenkfeldian Exiles, at Pennsburg, Pa., May 23, 1925. In: The Exile Herold. Published by the Society of the Descendants of the Schwenkfeldian Exiles. Vol. II, no. 3. Philadelphia, Pa. 1925. pp. 9—18.* [1612

Jähne, Christoph Gottlieb: Dankbare Erinnerung an die Gemeinde der Schwenkfelder zu Philadelphia in Nordamerika. *Görlitz: C. G. Anton 1816. 64 S.* [1613

Johnson, Elmer E. S.: The Schwenkfelders and Perkazie Manor. *In: The Perkiomen Region. Vol. II, no. 1. Pennsburg, Pa. 1923. pp. 11.* [1614

Kadelbach, Oswald: Ausführliche Geschichte Caspar v. Schwenkfelds und der Schwenkfelder in Schlesien, der Ober-Lausitz und Amerika, *nebst ihren Glaubensschriften von 1524—1860 nach den vorhandenen Quellen bearbeitet von . . . Lauban: M. Baumeister 1860. (1), (1), (2), 254, (1) S.* [1615

Kriebel, Howard Wiegner: The Schwenkfelders in Pennsylvania. A historical sketch. *Lancaster, Pa.: New Era Printing Co. 1904. = Part XII. „A narrative and critical history", prepared at the request of the Pennsylvania-German Society. In: The Pennsylvania-German Society. Proceedings and Addresses . . . 1902. Vol. XIII. Lancaster, Pa. 1904. Separate pagination. pp. XIV, 232.* [1616

— The Schwenkfelders. *In: Historical Sketches. A Collection of Papers prepared for the Historical Society of Montgomery County, Pa. Vol. III. Norristown, Pa. 1905. pp. 189—196.* [1617

R.[attermann, H. A.]: Die Einwanderung der Schwenkfelder. *In: Der Deutsche*

*Pionier. Jg. XII. Cincinnati, O. 1880
—1881. S. 381—389.* [1618
[**Schultze, David**]: Narrative of the journey
of the Schwenkfelders to Pennsylvania,
1733. *[A translation of a German MS, in
the Library of the Historical Society of
Pennsylvania, — ,,Reise Beschreibung,''
— and is supposed to have been written
by David Schultze.] In: The Pennsylvania Magazine of History and Biography. Vol. X. Philadelphia, Pa. 1866.
pp. 167—179.* [1619
Weiser, C. Z.: Caspar Schwenkfeld and the
Schwenkfelders. *In: The Mercersburg
Review. Vol. XVII. Philadelphia, Pa.
1870. pp. 347—373.* [1620
Erläuterung für Herrn Caspar Schwenkfeld,
und die Zugethanen, seiner Lehre, wegen
vieler Stücke, beydes aus der Historie
und Theologie, welche insgemein un-
richtig vorgestellt, oder gar übergangen
werden. *Deroselben Historie bis 1740
kürzlich entworffen; Ihre Glaubens-Be-
känntnisse summarisch verfaßt; und der
eigentliche Zustand der Streitigkeiten,
über dem heiligen Predigt-Amt, dem heiligen Sacramenten, und der Gloria der
Menschheit Jesu Christi entdecket ist.
Alles aus bewährten, glaubhaften und
vielen niemahls an Tag gekommenen,
richtigen Documenten, und eigener Erfahrung, treulich und einfältig beschrieben und allen aufrichtigen Nachforschern
und Liebhabern der Wahrheit zu Dienste,
ans Licht zu stellen bedacht, durch Etliche
der ehmahligen Emigranten aus Schlesien, und nunmehro eingesessene Inn-
wohner in Pennsylvanien in Nord-
Amerika. Auf eigene Kosten. Breslau u.
Leipzig: In Commission bey Gottfr.
Wilh. Seidel; Jauer: Heinr. Christ.
Müllern 1771. (14), 468, (4) S.* [1621
Erläuterung für Herrn Caspar Schwenkfeld, und die Zugethanen seiner Lehre,
wegen vielen Stücken, beydes aus der
Historie und Theologie; *allen aufrichtigen Nachforschungen und Liebhabern*

*der Wahrheit zum Dienste ans Licht zu
stellen, beabsichtigt und verfaßt worden,
durch Etliche der ehemahligen gottseligen
Auswanderer aus Schlesien nach Pennsylvanien in Nord-Amerika. Zweite Auflage. Von einer dazu angestellten Committee revidirt, und unter der unmittel-
baren Aufsicht derselben, auf Kosten der
Subscribten, gedruckt. Sumnytown, Pa.:
E. Brenner 1830. (2), XIV, 507,
(2). S.* [1622
The Schwenkfeldians of Montgomery County, Pa. *In: Hazard's Register of Pennsylvania. Vol. IV. Philadelphia, Pa. 1829.
pp. 127.*
*[Includes a reprint of the ,,Edict'' of
Frederick II, King of Prussia, ,,Con-
cerning the re-establishment of the so
called Schwenkfeldians in Silesia, and
other Provinces of his Royal Majesty;
De datto Selowitz, the 8th March, 1742.'']*
[1623
Historische Anmerkungen. A Schwenkfelder chronicle. *Edited and prefaced
by* **M. D. Learned.** *[(I) Historische Anmerkungen was sich von Anno 1750 an,
folgentlich biß 1775 mit den Schwenkfeldern, Merkliches verlauffen; (II.)
Historische Anmerkungen was sich Anno
1775 an folgentlich mit den Schwenkfeldern Merkliches zugetragen. etc.] In:
Americana Germanica. A quarterly.
Vol. II. Philadelphia, Pa. 1898. No. 1.
pp. 43—69.* [1624
Schwenkfelder-Marriages in Pennsylvania,
1735—1804. *Original letters and documents. In: The Pennsylvania Magazine
of History and Biography. Vol. V. Philadelphia, Pa. 1881. pp. 470—475.* [1625
Schwenkfelder school documents. *Edited
by* **M. D. Learned.** *In: Americana Germanica. A quarterly. Vol. II. Philadelphia, Pa. 1898. No. 1. pp. 70—86.* [1626
The conduct of the Schwenkfelders during
the Revolutionary War. *In: The Pennsylvania-German. Vol. XI. Lititz, Pa.
1910. pp. 659—663.* [1627

Die Unitas Fratrum oder Mährische Brüderkirche
Unitas Fratrum or Moravian Church

Allgemeines
General

Cranz, David: Alte und neue Brüder-Historie oder kurz gefaßte Geschichte der Evangelischen Brüder Unität in den älteren Zeiten und insonderheit in dem gegenwärtigen Jahrhundert. *Barby: Heinrich Detlef Ebers; in Leipzig in Commission bey Weidmans Erben und Reich 1771. (14), 808, (57) S.* [1628

Fortsetzung von David Cranzens Brüder-Historie. *Barby 1791. (6), 390, (42) S.* [1629

Fortsetzung von David Cranzens Brüder-Historie. *Dritte Abschnitt.* Von Synodo 1782 bis zum Synodo 1789. *Barby: Conrad Schilling 1804. (8), 339 S.* [1630

Fortsetzung von David Cranzens Brüder-Historie. *Vierter Abschnitt.* Von Synodo 1789 bis zum Synodo 1801. *Gnadan 1816. 3—752 S.* [1631

[Cranz, David]: The ancient and modern history of the Brethren: or a succinct narrative of the Protestant Church of the United Brethren, or, Unitas Fratrum, in the remoter ages, and particulary in the present century. *Written in German by David Cranz; now translated into English, with emendations; and published with some additional notes, by* Benjamin La Trobe. *London: W. and A. Strahan 1780. pp. (14), XII, 13—621; index pp. (85).* [1632

Erbe, H. W.: „Brüdergemeine". *In: Handwörterbuch des Grenz- und Auslanddeutschtums. Bd. I. Breslau 1933 [= Nr. 93]. S. 547—550.* [1632a

Hamilton, J. Taylor: The recognition of the Unitas Fratrum as an old Episcopal Church by the parliament of Great Britain in 1749. *Bethlehem, Pa.: Times Publishing Co. 1925. pp. 27.*
Reprint from: Transactions of the Moravian Historical Society. [1633

Holmes, John: History of the Protestant Church of the United Brethren. 2 vols.

London: Printed by the author 1825— 1830. pp. 430; XXI, 396. [1634

Hutton, J. E.: A short history of the Moravian Church. *London: Moravian Publication Office 1905. pp. VII, 280.* [1635

— A history of the Moravian Church. *Second edition, revised and enlarged, London, E. C.: Moravian Publication Office 1909. pp. 520.* [1636

Leibert, Morris W.: The government of the Moravian Church. *Bethlehem, Pa.: Keystone Printing Co. 1905. pp. 23, ill.* [1637

Reichel, William Cornelius: Memorials of the Moravian Church. *Printed for the Association: The Moravian Book Association, instituted 1870, for the issuing of documents and papers illustrating the history of the Moravian Church. Vol. I. Philadelphia, Pa.: J. B. Lippincott & Co. 1870. pp. XV, 11—366.* [1638

Romig, W. H.: The Moravian Church. *A treatise giving information in regard to the history, doctrine, government, discipline, strength and general character of the Moravian Church, in a brief and concise form.*
Bethlehem, Pa.: The Comenius Press 1895. pp. 24. [1639

Schweinitz, Edmund de: The history of the Church known as the Unitas Fratrum or the Unity of the Brethren, founded by the followers of John Hus, the Bohemian reformer and martyr. *Bethlehem, Pa.: Moravian Publication Office 1885. pp. XXV, 693, ill.* [1640

Steinberg, Hermann: Die Brüderkirche in ihrem Werden und Sein. *Eine Jubelgabe, zum 200jährigen Gedenkfest des Bestehens der Brüdergemeine ihren Mitgliedern und Freunden gewidmet. Herrnhut: Verlag der Missionsbuchhandlung 1921. 194 S., ill.* [1641

Uttendörfer, O. Alt-Herrnhut. Wirtschafts-geschichte und Religionssoziologie Herrnhuts während seiner ersten zwanzig Jahre (1722—1742). *Herrnhut i. Sa.: Verlag Missionsbuchhandlg. 1925. 185 S.*
[1641 a
— Wirtschaftsgeist und Wirtschaftsorganisation Herrnhuts und der Brüdergemeine von 1743 bis zum Ende des Jahrhunderts *[Alt-Herrnhut, 2. Teil] Herrnhut Verlag der Missionsbuch-*

handlung 1926. (1), (1), 7 — 486 S.
[1641 b
Neisser, George: A list of the Bohemian and Moravian emigrants to Saxony. *Collected from various sources in print and manuscript; begun and completed at New York, from June 2. to July 20, 1772. Translated and edited by* Albert G. Rau: *In: Transactions of the Moravian Historical Society. Vol. IX. Nazareth, Pa. 1913. pp. 37—39.*
[1642

Mährische Brüderkirche in Amerika [Herrnhuter]

The Moravian Church in America

United States, Department of Commerce, Bureau of Census Moravian Church (Unitas Fratrum). History, description and statistics. *In: Religious bodies: 1906. Part II. Separate denominations. Washington, D. C. 1910 [= no. 894]. pp. 494—499.*
. . . *In: Religious bodies: 1916. Part II. Washington, D. C. 1919. pp. 522—527.*
[1643
— Moravian Church in America. Statistics. History, doctrine and organization. *In: Religious bodies. 1926. Part II. Washington, D. C. 1929. pp. 1048—1056.* [1643 a
Benham, Daniel: Memoirs of James Hutton; comprising the annals of his life and connection with the United Brethren. *London: Hamilton, Adams & Co. 1856. pp. IV, 639.*
[Referring to Pennsylvania and especially to Salem, N. C.] [1644
[Berg, J. F.]: Moravian life and character. *[Review of:] Sketches of Moravian life and character. Comprising a general view of the history, life, character, and religious and educational institutions of the Unitas Fratrum. By James Henry. Philadelphia, Pa.: J. B. Lippincott & Co, 1859 [= no. 1653]. In: The Evangelical Quarterly devoted to Christian Literature and Theology. Edited by J. F. Berg. Vol. I. Philadelphia, Pa. 1860. pp. 84 —101.* [1645
Brickenstein, John C.: The first „Sea congregation." A. D. 1742. *In: Transactions of the Moravian Historical Society. Vol. I. Nazareth, Pa. 1858—1876. pp. 33 —50.* [1646
— The second „Sea congregation" 1743. *In: Transactions of the Moravian*

Historical Society. Vol. I. Nazareth, Pa. 1858—1876. pp. 107—124. [1647
Cronau, Rudolf: „Die Mährischen Brüder oder Herrnhuter." *In: Drei Jahrhunderte deutschen Lebens in Amerika. Eine Geschichte der Deutschen in den Vereinigten Staaten. Von R. Cronau. Berlin 1909 [= Nr. 34]. S. 85—100, ill.; 2. Aufl. 1924. S. 85—100, ill.* [1647 a
Ettwein, John: Fragments from the papers of Bishop John Ettwein. *Edited by the Publication Committee. First collection:* Miscellaneous correspondence and sraps of history. *In: Transactions of the Moravian Historical Society. Vol. IV. 1891 —1895. Nazareth, Pa. 1895. pp. 39— 99; Second collection:* Correspondence with Henry Laurens and related matter, referring chiefly to a proposed Moravian settlement in South Carolina. *In: Transactions . . . Vol. IV. pp. 189—234.*
[1648
Hamilton, J. Taylor: A history of the Unitas Fratrum, or Moravian Church, in the United States of America. *In: A history of the Reformed Church, Dutch, the Reformed Church, German and the Moravian Church in the United States. New York, N. Y. The Christian Literature Co. 1895. = The American Church History Series. Vol. VIII. pp. 425—508. [Bibliography. pp. 426—428.]* [1649
— A sketch of the Moravian activity in New Sweden and its vicinity. *In: Transactions of the Moravian Historical Society. Vol. IV. Nazareth, Pa. 1895. pp. 165—186.* [1650
— A history of the Church known as the Moravian Church or the Unitas Fratrum or the Unity of the Brethren,

during the eighteenth and nineteenth centuries. *Bethlehem, Pa.: Times Publishing Co. 1900. pp. XI, (1), 631, (1), ill.*
= *Transactions of the Moravian Historical Society. Vol. VI.*
[Bibliography pp. V—VIII.] [1651

[Heckewelder, Christian — Ettwein, John]: Three letters written at Bethlehem, Pennsylvania in 1778 [of Christian R. Heckewelder and John Ettwein]. *In: The Pennsylvania Magazine of History and Biography. Vol. XXXVI. Philadelphia, Pa. 1912. pp. 293—302. [Relating to the enforcement of the „Test oath", see also no. 1684.]* [1652

Henry, James: Sketches of Moravian life and character comprising a general view of the history, life, character, and religious and educational institutions of the Unitas Fratrum. *Philadelphia, Pa.: J. B. Lippincott & Co. 1859. pp. 316, ill.*
[See no. 1645] [1653

Hermann, F.: Die Deutschen in Nordamerica. *In: Minerva. Ein Journal historischen und politischen Inhalts. 1804 —1805 [= Nr. 61].* Dritte Schilderung, besonders in Betreff der Herrenhuter-Colonien. *Vol. III of 1805. S. 118— 142; 267—315.* [1654

J.[ordan], J. W.: Moravian ordinations 1742—92. (List of a few Moravian ordinations, between 1742—1792, administered in congregations without the County of Philadelphia, Pa.) *In: Notes and Queries. Edited by W. H. Egle. Fourth series, vol. I. 1891—1893. Harrisburg, Pa. 1893. pp. 130—131.* [1655

Jordan, John W.: A register of members of the Moravian Church who emigrated to Pennsylvania, 1742 to 1767. *In: Notes and Queries. Edited by W. H. Egle. Fourth series, vol. I. 1891—1893. Harrisburg, Pa. 1893. pp. 241—242; 247—248; 249—251; 255—257; 294—296; 400— 402; [1747 (1761)—1799]. In: Fourth series, vol. II. 1894—1895. Harrisburg, Pa. 1895. pp. 1—3.* [1656
— Moravian immigration to Pennsylvania, 1734—1767, with some account of the transport vessels. *In: Transactions of the Moravian Historical Society. Vol. V. Nazareth, Pa. 1899. pp. 51—90.* [1657
— Moravian notes. *Communicated by . . . In: Historical Notes, relating to the Pennsylvania Reformed Church. Vol. I. Philadelphia, Pa. 1900. pp. 95—96.* [1658

Jordan, John W.: Moravian immigration to Pennsylvania 1734—1765. *In: The Pennsylvania Magazine of History and Biography. Vol. XXXIII. Philadelphia, Pa. 1909. pp. 228—248.* [1659

K.: Über die Brüdergemeinen in Nordamerika. *[Bethlehem in Pennsylvanien, den 2ten Mai 1784]. In: Berlinische Monatsschrift. Herausgegeben von F. Gedike u. J. E. Biester. Bd. VI. Julius bis December 1785. Berlin: Bei Haude und Spener 1785. S. 223—233.* [1659a

Lockwood, J. P.: Memorials of the life of Peter Boehler. *London 1868 pp. . . .* [1659b

Myers, Elizabeth Lehman: A century of Moravian sisters. A record of Christian community life. *New York, N. Y.: Fleming H. Revell Co. 1918. pp. 243, ill.* [1660

Nagel, Charles: Our church literature. *A paper read at the fifth Synod of Second District of the Moravian Church, convened at York, Penn'a. May 7th to 9th, 1901. York, Pa.: Gazette Print 1901. pp. (1), 5—18.* [1661

Nitzsche, George E.: Moravian towns in Pennsylvania. — *Exceptional field for modern writers of fiction. Peculiar early customs of the Moravians — Their historical monuments — Their early interest in education — Marriage by lot — Their aversion to war — Their love for music — Their Christmas and Easter festivals, etc. In: The Pennsylvania-German. Vol. XII. Lititz, Pa. 1911. pp. 321— 329, ill.* [1662

[Reichel, Eduard H.]: Historical sketch of the church and missions of the United Brethren, commonly called Moravians. *Bethlehem, Pa.: J. and W. Held 1848. pp. 104.* [1663

Reichel, Levin Theodore: The early history of the Church of the United Brethren (Unitas Fratrum) commonly called Moravians, in North America, A. D. 1734—1748. *Nazareth, Pa.: Published for the Moravian Historical Society 1888. pp. 241.*
= *Transactions of the Moravian Historical Society. Vol. III.* [1664
— Des Grafen Zinzendorf Wirksamkeit in Pennsylvanien und deren Folgen, 1742 —1748. *In Deutscher Kirchenfreund, Jg. II, 1849. S. 93—107.* [1664a

[Reincke, Abraham]: A register of members of the Moravian Church and of persons attached to said church in this country and abroad, between 1727 and 1754. *Transcribed from M. S. in the handwriting of the Rev. Abraham Reincke to be found in the archives of the Moravian Church at Bethlehem, Pa. and illustrated with historical annotations by* W. C. Reichel. *Nazareth, Pa. 1873.* In: *Transactions of the Moravian Historical Society. Vol. I. Nazareth, Pa. 1858 —1876. pp. 285—426.* [1665

Rondthaler, Edward: The use of the lot in the Moravian Church. *Paper read before the Wachovia Historical Society, Oct. 21, 1901. Winston-Salem, N. C. pp. 8.* [1666

Schneider, Carl F.: Goethe-Herrnhut-Amerika. In: *Deutsch-Amerikanische Geschichtsblätter. Jahrbuch der Deutsch-Amerikanischen Gesellschaft von Illinois. Jg. 1920/21. Vol. XX—XXI. Chicago, Ill. 1922. S. 305—313.* [1666a

Schwarze, William Nathaniel: The American section of the Unity. In: *Moravian Bicentenary pamphlets. No. V. Bethlehem, Pa.: Published by the Committee on Popular Moravian Literature. 1922. pp. 93—118, ill.* [1667

— Early Moravian settlements in America. *Presidential address, read Dec. 26, 1922.* In: *Papers of the American Society of Church History. Second series, vol. VII. New York, N. Y. 1923. pp. 71—88.* [1668

Schweinitz, Edmund de: The Moravian manual: containing an account of the Protestant Church of the Moravian United Brethren, or Unitas Fratrum. *Published by authority of the Synod, and sanctioned by the Provincial Synod. Philadelphia, Pa.: Luidsay & Blakiston 1859. pp. XII, 13—178.* [Present condition of the Church. Section I. The American Province. pp. 51—61.] *Second enlarged edition. Bethlehem, Pa. A. C. and H. T. Clander 1869. pp. ... Third edition. Edited by J. Taylor Hamilton. Published by authority of the Provincial Synod of the American Moravian Church, North. Bethlehem, Pa.: Times Publishing Co. 1901. pp. VII, 117.* [1669

— The historic character of the American Moravian Church. *A discourse preached, by appointment, before the Moravian Provincial Synod. Published by order of the Synod. Bethlehem, Pa.: Moravian Publication Office. 1867. pp. 15.* [1670

Schweinitz, Edmund de: The financial history of the American Province of the Unitas Fratrum and of its Sustentation Fund. *Bethlehem, Pa.: Moravian Publication Office 1877. pp. 29.* [1671

— Some of the fathers of the American Moravian Church. A series of brief biographies. In: *Transactions of the Moravian Historical Society. Vol. II. Nazareth, Pa. 1886. pp. 147—269. Separate reprint: Bethlehem, Pa.: Henry T. Clander 1881. pp. 125.* [1672

Schweinitz, Paul de: The German Moravian settlements in Pennsylvania 1735—1800. In: *The Pennsylvania-German Society. Proceedings and Addresses at York, Oct. 11, 1893. Vol. IV. Lancaster, Pa. 1894. pp. 54—72, ill.* [1673

Sessler, Jacob John: Communal pietism among early American Moravians. *New York: Henry Holt and Co. 1933. pp. 265.* = *American Religion Series VIII.* [1674

[Spangenberg, August Gottlieb]: Kurzgefaßte historische Nachricht von der gegenwärtigen Verfassung der evangelischen Brüderunität augspurgischer Confeßion. *Frankfurt und Leipzig 1774. 84 S.* [Verzeichnis der Orte, wo sich die Brüdergemeinen und ihre Mißionen dermalen befinden = Abschnitt I S. 5ff. [1675

— Kurzgefaßte historische Nachricht von der gegenwärtigen Verfassung der evangelischen Brüder-Unität augsburgischer Confession. *Dritte Auflage. Barby 1793. 78 S.* [1675a

[—] A concise historical account of the present condition of the Unitas Fratrum, or Unity of the Evangelical Brethren, who adhere to the Augustan Confession. *Translated from the German, with a preface by* B. La Trobe. *London: M. Lewis (1784) pp. VIII, 72.* [In America, and first in the Province of Pensilfania, are the following congregations of the Brethren ... pp. 15—(18) —22.] [1675b

Stocker, Harry Emilius: Moravian customs and other matters of interest. *Bethlehem, Pa.: Times Publishing Co. 1918. pp. 128; Second edition pp. 131.* [1676

— A home mission history of the Moravian Church in the United States and Canada (Northern Province). *Published by the Special Publication Committee of the Moravian Church. 1924. pp. 256.* [1677

Ward, A. Gertrude: John Ettwein and the Moravians in the Revolution. In:

Pennsylvania History, Official organ of the Pennsylvania Historical Association. Vol. I. Philadelphia, Pa. 1934. pp. 191—201. [1678

Weitzel, Louisa A.: How Christmas is observed by the Moravians. *In: The Pennsylvania-German. Vol. IX. Cleona, Pa. 1908. pp. 531—534.* [1679

— How New Year is observed by the Moravians. *In: The Pennsylvania-German. Vol. X. Lititz, Pa. 1909. pp. 11—12.* [1680

— How Easter is observed by the Moravians. *In: The Pennsylvania-German. Vol. X. Lititz, Pa. 1909. pp. 150—152.* [1681

Westphal, Milton C.: Early Moravian pietism. *In: Pennsylvania History. Official organ of the Pennsylvania Historical Association. Vol. III. Philadelphia, Pa 1936. pp. 164—181.* [1681a

A brief history of the Moravian Church. *Prepared by teachers and friends of the Salem Home Sunday School. Winston-Salem, N. C. January, 1909. Raleigh, N. C.: Edwards & Broughton Printing Co. 1909. pp. 146. Appendix:* Funeral chorals of the Unitas Fratrum, or Moravian Church. *pp. 23.* [1682

Historische Nachrichten über die Herrenhuter-Sekte in Amerika. *In: Der Deutsche Pionier. Jg. VIII. Cincinnati, O. 1876—1877. S. 205—206.* [1683

A petition by the Moravians during the American Revolution, *[presented in 1778 by Bishop Ettwein to Congress in session at York and to the Assembly of Pennsylvania, at Lancaster asking to have the Moravians excepted from the requirements of the Test Act of 1777.] Copied from a manuscript found in a Schwenkfelder home by* H. W. Kriebel. *In: The Pennsylvania-German. Vol. XII. Lititz, Pa. 1911. pp. 43—45. [See no. 652.]* [1684

Marriage by lot among Moravians. *[Correcting the statement in: „The pictorial sketch book of Pennsylvania" by Eli Bowen. Eighth edition 1854.] In: The Penn Germania. Vol. II. = Old series, vol. XIV. Lititz, Pa. 1913. pp. 114—116.* [1685

Journals of the Provincial Synods of the American Moravian Church North. *Bethlehem, Pa. 1847* ff. [1686

Zinzendorfs Versuche einer Kirchen-Union
Zinzendorf's Attempts at Church Union

[Zinzendorf, Nicholas Ludwig von]: Pennsylvanische Nachrichten. Von dem Reiche Christi. Anno 1742: B. Ludwigs *[d. i. N. L. von Zinzendorf]* Wahrer Bericht de dato Germantown, den 20. Febr. 1741/42 an seine liebe Teutsche und wen es sonst nützlich zu wissen ist, wegen Sein und seiner Brüder Zusammenhanges mit Pennsylvania, zu Prüfung der Zeit und Umstände ausgefertiget; *Nebst einem P. S. de dato Philadelphia den 5. Martii und einigen unsere Lehre überhaupt, und dieses Schrifftgen insonderheit, erläuternden Beylagen. [Büdingen]: Gedruckt bey Johann Christoph Stöhr 1742. 191 S. [Sonderteil der Büdingische Sammlung einer in die Kirchen Historie einschlagenden Schriften, beigeheftet Bd. II.]* [1687

[—] Authentische relation von dem Anlaß, Fortgang und Schlusse der am 1sten und 2ten Januarii Anno 1741/42 in Germantown gehaltenen Versammlung einiger Arbeiter derer meisten Christlichen Religionen und vieler vor sich selbst Gott-dienenden Christen-Menschen in Pennsylvania; *Aufgesetzt in Germantown am Abend des 2ten obigen Monats. Philadelphia, Pa.: B. Franklin 1742. 16 S.* [1688

[Zinzendorf, Nicholas Ludwig von]: Authentische Nachricht von der Verhandlung und dem Verlaß der am 14den und 15den Januarii Anno 1741/42 im sogenannten Falckner-Schwamm an Georg Hübners Hause gehaltenen zweyten Versammlung sowol einiger Teutschen Arbeiter der Evangelischen Religionen als verschiedener einzeln treuen Gezeugen und gottsfürchtiger Nachbarn. *Nebst einigen Beylagen. Philadelphia, Pa.: B. Franklin [1742.] S. 17—40.* [1689

[—] Zuverlässige Beschreibung der dritten Conferenz der Evangelischen Religionen

Teutscher Nation in Pennsylvania, welche am 9. 10. und 11ten Februarii 1741/42 in Oley an Johann De Türcks Hause gehalten worden; samt denen dieses mahl verfassten Gemein-Schlüssen. *Philadelphia, Pa.: B. Franklin [1742]. S. 41—58.* [1690

[Zinzendorf, Nicholas Ludwig von]: The Oley conference. *A rare pamphlet, published by Benjamin Franklin in 1742. [Translation of]: Zuverlässige Beschreibung der dritten Conferenz der Evangelischen Religionen Teutscher Nation in Pennsylvania, welche am 9. 10. und 11ten Februarii 1741/42 in Oley an Johann De Türcks Hause gehalten worden; Samt denen dieses mahl verfaßten Gemein-Schlüssen. Philadelphia, Pa. [1742] [= no. 1690]. Edited by* P. C. Croll. *In: The Lutheran Quarterly. Vol. LVI. Gettysburg, Pa. 1926. pp. 84— 108.* [1691

[—] Vierte General-Versammlung der Kirche Gottes aus allen Evangelischen Religionen in Pennsylvania, Teutscher Nation; Gehalten zu Germantown am 10. 11. und 12ten Martii im Jahr 1741/42 an Mr. Ashmeads Hause. *Philadelphia, Pa.: B. Franklin [1742]. S. 59—76.* [1692

Gründliche An- und aufforderung an die ehmahlig erweckte hier und dar zerstreute Seelen dieses Landes, in und außer Parteyen, zur neuen Umfassung, gliedlicher Vereinigung, und Gebets-Gemeinschaft; *Dargelegt aus dringendem Herzen eines um Heilung der Brüche Zions ängstlich bekümmerten Gemüths, im jahr 1736. Philadelphia, Pa.: B. Franklin 1742. 14 S.* [1693

Extract aus unsers Conferenz-Schreibers Johann Jacob Müllers geführten Protocoll bey der fünften Versammlung der Gemeine Gottes im Geist, Gehalten in Germantown 1742, den 6ten April und folgende Tage: *Nebst einer Vorrede an die ehrwürdige Conferenz aller Arbeiter bey der Kirche Jesu Christi in Pennsylvania. Philadelphia, Pa.: B. Franklin 1742. S. 93—102.* [1694

Extract aus des Conferenz-Schreibers Johann Jacob Müllers Registratur von der sechsten Versammlung der Evangelischen Arbeiter in Pennsylvania, und der Gemeine Gottes im Geist siebender General-Synodus zu Philadelphia am 2ten und 3ten Junii 1742. st. v. *[Phila-*

delphia, Pa.]: B. Franklin [1742]. S. 105—120. [1695

Etliche zu dieser Zeit nicht unütze Fragen über einige Schrift-Stellen, welche von den Liebhabern der lauteren Wahrheit deutlich erörtert zu werden gewünschet hat. Ein Wahrheit-Forschender in America im Jahr 1742: *So deutlich und einfältig erörtert als es ihm möglich gewesen ist; und in folgender klaren und bequemen Form herausgegeben. Von einem Knecht Jesu Christi. Philadelphia, Pa.: B. Franklin 1742. 14 S.* [1696

Diejenigen Anmerkungen, welche der Herr Autor des kurzen Extracts, &c. von dem Herrn v. Thurnstein, d. z. Pastore der Evangelischen Lutherischen Gemeine Jesu Christi zu Philadelphia, in einer Vorrede seiner Schrift freundlich begehret hat. *Philadelphia, Pa.: Isaias Warner 1742. 24 S.* [1697

Jacob Lischys Reformirten Predigers zweyte Declaration seines Sinnes an seine Reformirte Religions-Genossen in Pennsylvanien. *Auf Begehren guter Freunde heraus gegeben. Germantown, Pa.: Christoph Saur 1748. 20 S.* [1698

[Weiser, Conrad (?)]: Old Tulpehocken Church. Interesting facts in Pennsylvania church history. *(Following document is contributed by John Blair Linn, who found it among papers of Peter Spyker; it is evidently drawn up by Conrad Weiser. „The state of the case between the Lutherans and Moravians at Tulpehocken, in the County of Berks, with the opinion thereon by Tench Francis, Esq., dated 26th April, 1755." In: Notes and Queries. Edited by W. H. Egle. Fourth series, vol. I. 1891—1893. Harrisburg, Pa. 1893. pp. 3—4.* [1699

Die Büdingische Sammlung einiger in die Kirchen Historie einschlagender sonderlich neuerer Schriften. *3 Bde. Büdingen: Joh. Christ. Stöhr; Leipzig: In Commission bey D. Korte 1742—1745. (32), 820, (22) S.; (2), 940, (20), 1042, (20) S.* [Inhaltsangabe s. Anhang S. 155—157.] [1700

Fresenius, Johann Philip: Johann Philip Fresenius bewährte Nachrichten von Herrnhutischen Sachen. *Dritter Band. Worin die fünfte und sechste Samlung nebst einem Register enthalten. Frankfurt und Leipzig: Heinrich Ludwig Brömer 1748. (16), 999, (1) S. Das dritte Stück.* Americanische Nachrichten von Herrnhutischen Sachen. S. 87—872. [Inhaltsangabe s. Anhang S. 157—160].

[1701
Hamilton, J. Taylor: The confusion at Tulpehocken. In Transactions of the Moravian Historical Society. Vol. IV. Nazareth, Pa. 1895. pp. 237—273.   [1702

Keith, Charles P.: „Unitas Fratrum and attempted church unity." In: Chronicles of Pennsylvania from the English revolution to the peace of Aix-La-Chapelle 1688—1748. By Ch. P. Keith. Vol. II. Philadelphia, Pa. 1917 [= no. 3169]. pp. 813—847.   [1703

Anhang:

Appendix:

Die Büdingische Sammlung einiger in die Kirchen Historie einschlagender sonderlich neuerer Schriften. 3. Bde. Büdingen: Joh. Christ. Stöhr; Leipzig: in Commission bey D. Korte 1742—1745. (32), 820, (22); (2), 940, (20), 1042, (20) S.
Bd. I. Stück II:
Nr. VI. Schreiben im Nahmen der Directoren in Georgien, an den Herrn Grafen L. v. Zinzendorf wegen einiger daselbst vorgefallenen Irrungen. Gezeichnet von Benj. Martin. [Datiert „de l'Office de la Georgie à Westmunster", Sept. 23, 1737.] S. 174—176.
Bd. I. Stück III:
Nr. VIII. Instruction für die Georgische Colonie. Von L. v. Zinzendorf. [Datiert 27. Nov. 1734.] S. 351—353.
Nr. XX. Schreiben der Mährischen Brüder an Mr. Causton in Georgia. S. 374—376.
Bd. II. Stück VII:
Nr. IV. Herrn Ed. Iac. Ogletorps Brieff an Herrn Gr. N. L. von Zinzendorf. [In Latein] S. 19—24.
Nr. XV. Brieff aus Georgien vom 19. Junii 1740. Von Johann Hagen. S. 136—140.
Bd. II. Stück VIII:
Nr. V. Brieff aus Savanna Anno 1740, 5 Oct. Von Johann Hagen. S. 173—178
Nr. VI f. Brief aus Georgien Anno 1740, 9 Jul. Von Johann Hagen. S. 194—196.
Bd. II. Stück XI:
Nr. XXI. Ernstliche Erklärung an die vernünfftigen Einwohner von Pensylvania über dem Bezeigen derer übrigen. [In Latein.] Von Ludwig Thürenstein. [Datiert Sept., 1742.] S. 672—677.
Bd. II. Stück XII:
Nr. I. Wörtliche Extracte aus den 7. General-Synodis von Pennsylvania, als ein Supplementum zu dem XIten Stück der Büdingischen Sammlungen mitgetheilet. S. 722—825.
Nr. II. Schreiben des Governeurs der freyen Provintz Pennsylvanien und deren drey vereinigten Graffschafften, Ritter G. Thomas an den Gr[afen von Zinzen-

dorf]. [Datiert Philadelphia, 24. Dez. 1741.] S. 825—827.
Nr. III. Extract aus des Ehrwürdigen Herrn von Thürnsteins Fragen an die Lutheraner in und um Philadelphia. S. 827—828.
Nr. IVa. Vocation zum Pastorat der Lutherischen Kirche in Philadelphia. [Philadelphia, 19. Mai 1742.]. S. 828—830.
Nr. IVb. Vocation zum Pastorat in Tulpehokin. [4. Jul. 1742.] S. 830—832.
Nr. V. Pfarrers J. Ph. Meurers von Tulpehockin Bericht ans Consistorium in Philadelphia. [5/6. Nov. 1742.] S. 832—845
Nr. VI. Vorschlag zu einer Teutschen Land-Schule in Pensylvania. [Datiert Germantown, 22. März 1742.] S. 845—846.
Nr. VII. Abermaliger Vorschlag wegen gedachter Schule. [Datiert 25. Mai 1742.] S. 846—847.
Nr. VIII. Circular-Schreiben an alle Justices wegen Bekanntmachung des zweyten Vorschlags. [Gezeichnet Thürnstein.] S. 847.
Nr. XI. Anerbietungs-Schreiben an das gantze Land Pennsylvania, aus dem Pennsylvanischen Geschicht-Schreiber 19. Stück 1742. [Von L. v. Zinzendorf; datiert Philadelphia, 2. Febr. 1742.] S. 851.
Nr. XII. Schönfelds Beschwerung über gedachtes Schreiben, als das in Harlemischen Zeitungen angeführte Haupt-Document, aus gedachten Geschicht-Schreibers, 20. Stück 1742. S. 854—859.
Nr. XIII. Brief an den Pennsylvanischen Gazetier aus Nro. 692. The Pennsylvania Gazette. Antwort an Schönfeld im Pennsylvanischen Geschicht-Schreiber, 20. Stück 1742 von L. v. Zinzendorf. S. 860—862.
Nr. XIV. Schreiben wegen des letztern Briefes, aus Nro. 693. The Pennsylvania Gazette. [Von J. W.; datiert 22. März 1742.] S. 862—863.
Nr. XV. Brief an des Proprietors Secretarium, in dieser Materie. [Von L. v. Zinzendorf, datiert Philadelphia, 27. März 1742.] S. 864.

Nr. XVI. Privat-Erinnerung an Schönfelden und Consorten. [Von L. v. Zinzendorf; datiert Philadelphia, 27. März 1742.] *S. 865—867.*

Nr. XVII. Die Haupt-Schrifft gegen die Brüder Unternehmungen in Pennsylvania zuerst in Fragen verfaßt, nebst den darauf gegebenen Antworten. [Vorwort datiert 21. April 1742.] *S. 868—887.*
[vgl. Nr. 1705 (Bd. III, Drittes Stück, VIII.)]

Nr. XVIII. Extract aus einer aufrichtigen Nachricht ans Publicum, über eine von dem Holländischen Pfarrer Joh. Phil. Böhmen bey Mr. Andr. Bradford edirte Lästerschrift gegen die sogenannten Herrenhuter, das ist, die Evangelischen Brüder aus Böhmen, Mähren usf., welche jetzo in den Forks von Delaware wohnen. Herausgegeben von Georg Neisser aus Sehlem in Mähren, Schulmeister zu Bethlehem. *S. 888—906.*
[vgl. Nr. 1705 (Bd. III, Drittes Stück, XXXIII.)]

Nr. XIX. Die von dem Herrn von Thürenstein, auf Verlangen eines Gegners verfaßte Anmerkungen zu dessen Gegenschrifft. Von Thürenstein. (Extract aus einer Schrifft genannt diejenigen Anmerkkungen, welche der Herr Autor des kurtzen Extracts, etc. von dem Herrn von Thurnstein, d. z. Pastore der Evangelisch-Lutherischen Gemeine Jesu Christi zu Philadelphia. In der Vorrede seiner Schrifft freundlich begehret hat.) *S. 906—922.*

Nr. XX. Hrn. von Thurensteins Hand-Schreiben an denselben. [Datiert Nov. 1741.] *S. 922—923.*

Nr. XXIII. Heinrich Antes Avertissement an diejenigen, so den Bruder Ludewig noch gerne predigen hörten. [Datiert Friedrichs-Township in Philadelphia County, 15. Sept. 1742.] *S. 927—929.*

Nr. XXIV. Revers einer in einem Township [Sackenheim] erweckten Seelen, die mit der Gemeine wolten geschlossen seyn, als ein Modell in allen gleichen Fällen. *S. 929—930.*

Nr. XXV. Bericht ans Gouvernement wegen der Indianischen Irruption auf Nazareth. [Gezeichnet: Louis de Thurenstein; datiert 12. Jun. 1742.] *S. 930—931.*

Nr. XXVI. Brief an Justus Irisch aus dem Englischen Original. *S. 931—933.*

Nr. XXVII. Privat-Vergleich der Gemeine mit den Indianern m. Dez. 1742. Dem Indianer Detamy zu Handen gestellt. *S. 933—936.*

Nr. XXVIII. Plan, wie sich Herr M. Spangenberg mit denen Herren Proprietors in Ansehung des Kauffs zu vernehmen habe, (Ecrit de la Main du L. de Zinzendorff, le 15. Mars 1743. a Gravesande). *S. 937—938.*

Bd. III. Stück XIII:
Nr. V. Joh. Adam Grubers An- und Aufforderung an die ehmalig erweckte hier

und dar zerstreute Seelen in Pensylvania, in oder außer Partheyen, zur neuen Umfassung, gliedlicher Vereinigung, und Gebets-Gemeinschaft, dargelegt, aus dringendem Hertzen eines um Heilung der Brüche Zions ängstlich, bekümmerten Gemüths, im Jahr 1736. *S. 13—39.*

Nr. XIII. Extract aus den Pensylvanischen Landes-Gesetzen. *S. 58—60.*

Nr. XIV. Contract zwischen den Reformirten und Lutheranern in Philadelphia wegen einer gemeinschaftlichen Kirche. [Datiert Philadelphia, 1. Jan. 1740/1.] *S. 60—61.*

Nr. XV. Anfrage an den Reformirten Inspector der Holländischen Conferentz in Philadelphia, J. Ph. Böhme. [Gezeichnet Ludwig, Herr zu Thürnstein; datiert Philadelphia, 7/18. Jan. 1741/2.] *S. 62—63.*

Nr. XVI. Antwort [von John Ph. Böhme.] [Philadelphia, 8. Jan. 1742.] *S. 63—64.*

Nr. XVII. Des sogenannten Vaters in Zion [= Conrad Beissel] Schreiben an den Grafen von Zinzendorf. [Datiert Ephrata, 9. Nov. 1741.] *S. 64—67.*

Nr. XVIII. An die Versammlung auf Zion in Ephrata. *S. 68.*

Nr. XX. Etliche Plane von Gemeinen in Pensylvanien. (a) Im Falckner-Schwamm; (b) Philadelphia (c) Der Arbeiter bey der Gemeine Jesu in Germantown. *S. 71—76.*

Nr. XXI. Instruction an Pfarrer Büttner in Tulpehockin [Philadelphia, März, 1742.] *S. 76—77.*

Nr. XXII. Desselben Schrifft so er am Sonntage Palmarum abgelesen. *S. 78—79.*

Nr. XXIII. Praesentations-Schreiben des Brieffs an die General-Assemblée der Quäker 2 te Band XII. St. n. 9. [Gezeichnet: Louis; Germantown, 18. Mai 1742.] *S. 79—80.*

Nr. XXIV. Extract aus der Species Facti wegen des Philadelphischen Tumults. [Datiert Philadelphia, 5. Aug. 1742.] *S. 80—86.*

Nr. XXV. Eine Relation aus America. [Von Anna Nitschmann; New York, 30. Juli 1742.] *S. 86—88.*

Nr. XXVI. Ein Lied des Missionarii Gottlob Büttners am 6. Oct. 1742. *S. 88—90.*

Nr. XXVII. Methodus der Wilden Bekehrung. *S. 90—91.*

Nr. XXVIII. Die Abolitions-Schrifft wegen des Mr. Böhms. [Datiert Philadelphia, Dez., 1742; Nota von Peter Böhler, datiert Bethlehem, 18/29. Dez. 1742.] *S. 91—95.*

Nr. XXIX. Catalogus des Synodi generalis in Pennsylvanien. Ordinaire Raths-Glieder des Teutschen General-Synodi in Pennsylvania nach Joh. 17. aus allen Evang. Christl. Religionen. *S. 95—97.*

Nr. XXXI a. An eine Pennsylvanische Mutter, wegen des Mitgehens ihrer Tochter. [Von Graf von Zinzendorf.] *S. 100—101.*
Nr. XXXI b. An eine andere Art Eltern. [Von Graf von Zinzendorf; datiert Philadelphia, 26. Dez. 1742.] *S. 101—102.*
Nr. XXXII. Schreiben des Ältesten in Pensylvanien, an die Gemeine in Europa. Am Bord des Schiffes den 20. Jan. 1743. *S. 103—104.*
Nr. XXXIII. M. Sp. Brief an A. G. *S. 104—109.*
Nr. XXXIV. Vocation der Reformirten Vorsteher an Br. Jac. Lischy zu dero Lehrer. [Datiert Conventry Township, 10. April 1743.] *S. 109—110.*
Bd. III. Stück XIV:
Nr. VIII. An das Gouvernement in Pensylvanien wegen der letzten Zeitungs-Notel [Gezeichnet Lewis of Thurnstein born Count Zinzendorf; datiert Wratislavia in Silesia, Nov., 1743.] *S. 183—184.*
Nr. XI. Bruder Ludwigs [von Thürnstein] Rede zum Abschied und Verlaß mit den einländischen und Europäischen in Pennsylvanien zurückgelassenen Arbeitern, gehalten in Herrn Stephan Bennezets Hause in Philadelphia am 29 Dez. / 9 Jan. 1742/3. *S. 188—252.*
Nr. XII. Diarium der Heyden-Boten unter den Indianern in Schecomeko. [Gezeichnet B. M. S. P.; datiert Schecomeko, den 8/19 Aug. 1743.] *S. 252—282.*
Nr. XIII. Eines Königl. Richters Schreiben an einen Bruder in Schecomeko. [Gezeichnet C. W.] *S. 282—283.*
Bd. III. Stück XV:
Nr. X. Des Herrn Grafens Erklärung an einen Quaeker, warum er mit keiner Convoy nach America gehen wolle. [A. Josias Martin.] *S. 307—308.*
Nr. XI. Desaveu des Herrn Gilbert Tennents Pfarrers in Neu-Braunschweig, inserirt in die Philadelphischen Zeitungen. *S. 308—309.*
Nr. XII. Erste Erklärung des Herrn Grafen [L. v. Zinzendorf] an die Schwenckfelder. [Datiert Germantown, 20. März 1741/2.] *S. 311—312.*
Nr. XIII. Zweyte Final-Erklärung. [Datiert Germantown, 12. April 1742.] *S. 313—314.*
Nr. XIV. Abschied mit der Gemeine zu Oley vor ihrer neuen Anfassung. *S. 314—315.*
Nr. XV. Antwort an den Hohenpriester in Zion, welcher den Brief in der 13. Sammlung No. XVII an den Herrn Grafen geschrieben. [Von L. v. Zinzendorf; datiert Philadelphia, 27. März 1742.] *S. 316—326.*
Nr. XVI. Des Herrn Grafens [L. v. Zinzendorf] Erklärung an die sämmtl. Alt-Täufer-Gemeinen in Pensylvanien. [Datiert Germantown, 27. Mai 1742.] *S. 326—330.*

Nr. XVIII. Relation von des Herrn Grafen und seiner Tochter arretirung von den Pesbyterianern in New York. *S. 332—336.*
Bd. III. Stück XVI:
Nr. XV. Extrait de la lettre des Trustées à Mr. Causton à Savannah en Georgie dattée le 3 d' Aôut 1737. *S. 479—480.*
Nr. XVII. Herr G. Neumanns Abschieds-Brief an den Grafen [L. v. Zinzendorf] bey der zweyten Reise nach America. [Datiert Marienborn, 4. Aug. 1741.] *S. 481—483.*
Bd. III. Stück XVII:
Nr. XV. Attestat der Gemeine, welches sie einer nach Pensylvanien gehenden Gesellschaft mitgegeben. [Datiert Herrnhuth, 23. April 1731.] *S. 650—651.*
Nr. XLI. Die entworffene und approbirte Lutherische Kirchen-Ordnung von Philadelphia. *S. 702—708.*
Nr. XLIII. Der Lutherischen Vorsteher in Philadelphia Schreiben an Herrn Mühlenberg. [Datiert Philadelphia, 31. May 1743.]. *S. 712—716.* [1704

Fresenius, Johann Philip: Johann Philip Fresenius bewährte Nachrichten von Herrnhutischen Sachen. *Dritter Band. Worin die fünfte und sechste Samlung nebst einem Register enthalten. Frankfurt und Leipzig: Heinrich Ludwig Brömer 1748. (16), 999 (1) S.*
Das Dritte Stück. Americanische Nachrichten von Herrnhutischen Sachen. *S. 87—872.*

I Ausführliche Nachricht von den Unternehmungen des Herrn Grafen von Zinzendorf in Pensilvanien. (Ausführliche Nachricht, welchergestalt die Herrnhutische Sache in diesen Americanischen Landen, sonderlich in Pensilvanien, Eingang und Aufnahm gesucht und gefunden: Soviel man selbst davon erfahren, aus ihren hier herausgegebenen Schriften, und durch glaubhafte Menschen, davon vernommen, anno 1742 und 1743). *S. 97—237.*
II Händel des Herrn Grafen von Zinzendorfs mit denen Schwenkfeldern in Pennsilvanien [1742]. Siehe die vorhergehende Nachricht, § 47. *S. 237—261.*
III Bericht des Geringen, [eines ungenanten in Pensilvanien,] was sich zwischen ihm und Herrn Ludwigen, [oder Herrn Grafen von Zinzendorf] und andern seiner Zugehörigen in der Herrnhuter Sache in Jahr und Tag begeben 1743, samt denen nöthigen Belegen. *S. 262—297.*
IV Einfältige Warnungs- und Wächter-Stimme an die gerufene Seelen dieser Zeit. Verfaßt im Jahr 1741 von einem Geringen. *S. 297—303.*
V Heinrich Antes Einladungs-Schreiben zur Conferenz, so er an die Germantowner Freunde gesandt und an J. A. Gruber ad-

dressiert. [15. Dez. 1741]; J. A. Gruber Antwort [25. Dez. 1741]. *S. 303—314.*
VI Des Geringen Klage von Bethulia aus einem in Germantown gedruckten halben Bogen hieher gesetzet. *S. 314—323.*
VII Eben deselben 32. Fragen, an etliche sehr eingenommene Freunde. (Einige zu dieser Zeit nicht unnütze Fragen über einige Schriftstellen, welche von den Liebhabern der lautern Warheit deutlich erörtert zu werden wünschet, ein Warheit Forschender in America 1742.) *S. 323—329.*
VIII Zergliederung und Beantwortung dieser Fragen, von Herrn Grafen von Zinzendorf. (Etliche zu dieser Zeit nicht unnütze Fragen über einige Schrift-Stellen, welche von den Liebhabern der lauteren Wahrheit deutlich erörtert zu werden gewünschet hat ein Wahrheit-Forschender in America im Jahr 1724, so deutlich und einfältig erörtert, als es ihm möglich gewesen ist; und in folgender klaren und bequemen Form herausgegeben von einem Knecht Jesu Christi.) *S. 329—351.*
[Auch abgedruckt in: Büdingische Nachrichten Bd. II, Nr. XVII. pp. 869—887.]
IX Aufforderung zur gliedlichen Gemeinschaft, von dem Geringen aufgesetz A. 1736 und nach seinem eigenen Aufsatz abgedruckt. (Johann Adam Grubers gründliche An- und Aufforderung an die ehmalig erweckte hier und da zerstreute Seelen dieses Landes, in und außer Parteyen, zur neuen Umfassung, gliedlicher Vereinigung, und Gebets-Gemeinschaft; . . . 1736) *S. 351—380.*
X Kurtzer doch nöthiger Bericht, wegen der vor sechs Jahren verfasseten, und nun ohne mein Wissen, Befragen und Willen, (und das mit Beysetzung meines Namens, wie auch sonst ungantz,) von andern heraus gegebenen Schrift; Aufforderung zur gliedlichen Gemeinschaft genannt. Anno 1742. *S. 381—391.*
XI Herrn Grafen von Zinzendorfs Banden-Aufforderung an vier seiner Nachbarn in Germantown, Johann Bechteln, Theobald Endt, Johann Eckstein, und Johann Adam Grubern [14. April 1742.] *S. 391—393.*
XII Johann Adam Grubers Antwort auf voriges [15. April 1742.] *S. 393—394.*
XIII Ferner erforderter Bericht des Geringen wegen der sogenannten letzten Privat-Erklärung so ohnlängst über seinen kurtzen Bericht (Num. X) heraus gekommen, zum Nachdencken abgefaßt im Sept. 1742. *S. 393—400.*
XIV Etliche Schriften, die Sache der Täufer und Siebentäger betreffend, welche sich mit dem Herrn Grafen Zinzendorf eingelassen haben. (Copia Herrn Zinzendorfs Schreiben an Joseph Müller, den er aus den Pensilvanischen Taufs-Gesinnten bekommen hat, Germantown, den 11. Mertz 1742). *S. 400—401.*

XV Copia Herrn Zinzendorfs Schreiben, an die General-Versamlung derer, im vorigen gemeldeten, Swartzenauer Täufer, welche geschahe den 16. May 1742. *S. 401—410.*
XVI Eine gedruckte Schrift der sogenannten Siebentäger in Pensilvanien, auf Veranlassung der Herrnhutischen Bewegungen herausgegeben, unter folgendem Titul: Mystisches und kirchliches Zeugnis der Brüderschaft in Zion, von den wichtigsten Puncten des Christenthums, nebst einem Anhang, darinnen dieselbe ihr unpartheyisches Bedencken an Tag gibt von dem Bekehrungs-Werck der sogenannten Herrnhutischen Gemeine in Pensilvanien, und warum man ihnen keine Kirche zustehen könne. Germantown, [Pa.] gedruckt und zu finden bey C. Sauer 1743. *S. 410—446.*
XVII (Derselben) Unpartheyisches Bedencken über das Bekehrungs-Werck der Herrnhutischen Gemeine in Pensylvanien. *S. 446—462.*
XVIII Ein Kurtzer Bericht von den Ursachen, warum die Gemeinschaft in Ephrata sich mit dem Grafen Zinzendorf und seinen Leuten eingelassen. Und wie sich eine so große Ungleichheit im Ausgang der Sachen auf beyden Seiten befunden. *S. 462—474.*
XIX Johannes Hildebrands, eines Siebentägers, Schrift gegen die Herrnhuter, vom Ehestande: Schriftmäsiges Zeugnis von dem himlischen und jungfräulichen Gebährungs-Werck, wie es an dem ersten Adam ist mit Fleisch zugeschlossen, aber an dem zweyten Adam by seiner Creutzigung durch einen Speer wiederum geöfnet worden. Entgegen gesetzt dem gantz ungegründeten Vorgeben der Herrnhutischen Gemeine von einem heiligen Ehestand, daraus sie das Ebenbild Gottes auszugebähren vorgeben. Ans Licht gegeben durch Johannes Hildebrand, einem Mitglied der Gemeine Jesu Christi in Ephrata, hausväterlicher Seite. *[Schlußbemerkung von J. P. F. S. 503.] S. 474—503.*
XX Copia eines Berichts von J. H., der zu Oly von Herrn Zinzendorf und Eschenbach zu einen Ältesten aufgefordert worden nebst noch zwey andern, gegen ihnen Sinn und Willen. A. 1742. *S. 504—510.*
XXI Handel des Grafen mit Schönfelden. Aufforderung des Grafen in der Teutschen Pensilvanischen Zeitung, ob jemand etwas wieder ihn zu klagen habe? [Febr. 1741/2.] *S. 511—515.*
XXII Schönfelds Bericht. *S. 515—521.*
XXIII Des Herrn Grafen Ablehnung [16. März 1741/2.] *S. 521—524.*
XXIV Johann Weisen Certificat vor Schönfelds Sache. *S. 524—525.*
XXV Brief des Herrn Grafen an den Secretarium des Proprietors [27. März 1742.] *S. 526.*

XXVI Brief des Herrn Grafen an den Drucker der deutschen Zeitung, Schönfelden und andere [Philadelphia, Pa., 27. März 1742]. *S. 527—530.*

XXVII Deutsche Verse, welche ein Verfechter des Herrn Grafen von Zinzendorf, wegen des Schönfeldischen Handels, in die englische Zeitung des Herrn Franklins setzen lassen. [28. März 1742.] *S. 530—533.*

XXVIII Des Buchdrucker Sauers Privat Antwort auf den Brief Num. XXVI des Grafen. [8. April 1742.] *S. 534—540.*

XXIX Kurtze Unterschrift des Herrn Grafen, so unter des Sauers vorstehenden Brief gesetzet, den ihm acht Tage hernach wieder zurücksandte. [8. April 1742.] *S. 540—541.*

XXX. XXXI Etliche Briefe, den von den Herrnhuter abgesetzten Lutherischen Pfarrer Stiefer in Pensilvanien betreffend:

XXX Büttners Schreiben an den Pfarrer Stiefer [Tulpehaken, den 17. April 1742.] *S. 541—547.*

XXXI Des Herrnhutischen Pfarrers Joh. Ph. Meurers von Tulpohockin Bericht wegen Caspar Stiefers, an das Consistorium zu Philadelphia [Tulpohokin, den 5./16. Nov. 1742.] *S. 548—561.*

XXXII Einige Auszüge, aus des hochdeutschen Reformirten Predigers in Pensilvanien, John Phil. Böhmen, sogenannten getreuen Warnungs-Brief an die Reformirte Gemeine gegen die Herrnhuter. (Philadelphia gedruckt bey A. Bradford 1742. mense Jun. Jul. & Augusto in 8 vo. p. 96). Wider welchen sich die Herrnhuter, in der unten Num. XXXIII folgenden Nachricht in ein und anderen Puncten verantwortet haben. [„Auf Witpens Township, in Philadelphia County," 23. Aug. 1742.] *S. 562—677.*

XXXIII Herrnhutische Gegenschrift wider den Warnungsbrief Joh. Phil. Böhmen [unter Neissers Namen von Herrn Graf von Zinzendorf verfaßt]: Aufrichtige Nachricht ans Publicum, über eine von dem Holländischen Pfarrer Joh. Phil. Böhmen bey Monsr. Andr. Bradford edirte Lästerschrift gegen die sogenanten Herrnhuter, das ist, die Evangelischen Brüder aus Böhmen, Mähren, usf. welche jetzo in den Forcks von Delaware wohnen. Herausgegeben von Georg Neisser, aus Sehlen in Mähren, Schulmeister zu Bethlehem. Cum Approbatione Superiorum. Philadelphia, Gedruckt und zu haben bey B. Fräncklin 1742. Imprimatur. Johann Brandmüller. Bethlehem, am 31. Julii 1742. *S. 678—715.*

[Auszug in: Büdingische Nachrichten Bd. II, Stück XII, Nr. XVIII. S. 888—906.]

XXXIV Herrn Pryläi [eines studirten herrnhutischen Lehrers] Aufruf-Zeddel [Advertissement] an die Einwohner in Pensilvanien, daß diejenige, so Herrn Grafen

von Zinzendorf noch einmal wolten predigen hören, sich melden solten. Unter Heinrich Antes Namen geschrieben, und in Pensilvanien gedruckt. 15. Sept. 1742.] *S. 715—718.*

XXXV Brief einer Sieben-Tägerin an eine ihrer Verwandten, betreffend den Besuch, welchen des Herrn Grafen von Zinzendorf Comtesse Tochter bey ihnen abgelegt, und den Eingang, den sie unter diesen Sieben-Täger Nonnen gehabt haben soll. [1743.] *S. 718—722.*

XXXVI Schröcklicher Brief des Herrn Grafen von Zinzendorf an Friedrich Vende, Kiefer in Germantown, und seine Hausfrau, wegen ihrer Tochter. [Dez. 1742.] *S. 722—728.*

XXXVII Postscript der Pensilvanischen Englischen Zeitung, darin dieser, und der Bannbrief wider Neumannen, mit Anmerckungen übersetzt worden. *S. 728—730.*

XXXVIII Herrn Lischy, Declaration und Erbieten an die Reformirte, ihnen umsonst zu predigen [Philadelphia, 12. März 1743.] *S. 730—739.*

XXXIX Herrn Grafen von Zinzendorfs Vorschlag zu einer deutschen Landschule in Pensilvanien. [Germantown, 22. März 1742.] *S. 740.*

XL Abermaliger Vorschlag deselben wegen gedachter Schule. [Philadelphia, 25. Mai 1742.] *S. 740—742.*

XLI Herrn Grafen von Zinzendorfs Zircular-Schreiben an alle Justices, wegen Bekanntmachung des zweyten Vorschlages. *S. 742.*

XLII Heinrich Antes historischer Bericht, an Johann Adam Gruber, wegen der Gemeine der Herrnhuter alhier in Pensilvanien. [15. März 1743.] *S. 742—746.*

XLIII Bericht eines (ungenannten) in Neu-Yorck, von denen Herrnhutischen Erweckungen daselbst. [10. Febr. 1743.] *S. 747—748.*

XLIV Herrn Magister Spangenbergs Recipisse über das Bundes-Zeichen der fünf Nationen [1743.] *S. 748—749.*

XLV Abschrift eines Berichts [von Christian Sauer] aus Germantown, vom 1. November 1740. *S. 749—762.*

XLVI J. C. Schreiben wegen des Herrn Grafen von Zinzendorf [Germantown, 22. Jan. 1742.] *S. 762—764.*

XLVII Copia Schreibens von Christian Sauern [Germantown, 26. März 1742.] *S. 765—769.*

XLVIII Copia Schreibens, von Gruber aus Pensylvanien. [Germantown, 27. März 1742.] *S. 769—773.*

XLIX Copia Andreas Eschenbachs Schreiben an einen Mann in Oly, so sich zu ihm und den Herrnhutern gehalten [1742.] *S. 773—781.*

L Schreiben eines Unparteyischen [J. H.] an etliche seiner Freunde, wegen

der Herrnhutischen Sache. [Juli, 1742.]
S. 781—783.
LI Ein anderer Bericht, aus German-
town, vom 3. Nov. 1742. S. 784—785.
LII Schreiben eines Taufs-Gesinnten,
die Herrnhuter betreffend. Germantown,
den 15. Nov. 1742. S. 785—788.
LIII Auszug eines Briefes aus German-
town auch die Herrnhuter betreffend.
[16. Nov. 1742.] S. 788—790.
LIV Auszug aus Grubers Schreiben,
vom 19ten Nov. 1744 in Germantown.
S. 791—793.
LV Ein Postscriptum von J. A. Gruber,
ad. A. G. dd. 5. Dez. 1744. S. 793—794.
LVI Spangenbergs Schreiben an C. Sauer,
Regniers Schrift betreffend, Bethlehem den
27. Apr. 1745. S. 794—795.
LVII Sauers Antwort darauf [German-
town, 2. Mai 1745.] S. 795—798.
LVIII Auszug aus Grubers Schreiben
an Herrn Gross, Germantown, den 18. Nov.
1745. S. 798—799.
LIX Auszug aus M. G. Schreiben an
Herrn G., Pfarrer in Würtenbergischen,
15. Mai 1746. S. 799—806.
LX Schreiben von N. an A. G. aus Ger-
mantown den 24. Jul. 1746. S. 806—809.

LXI Auszug eines Schreiben von C.
Sauer in Germantown an A. G. [20. Nov.
1744.] S. 809—818.
LXII Extract Schreibens von einem un-
gelehrten einfältigen Mann, übersetzt von
C. Sauer. S. 819—822.
LXIII Schreiben von Conrad Weiser im
September 1747. S. 822—830.
LXIV Schreiben von Johann Frantz
Regnier. Bey der Bermudien Krick, den
22sten September 1747. S. 830—837.
LXV Auszug aus C. Sauers Schreiben,
Germantown, den 16. Nov. 1747. S. 837
—839.
LXVI Auszug aus Grubers Schreiben
an Herrn Gros, Germantown vom 29ten
Nov. 1747. S. 839—842.
LXVII Joh. Christian Sieberbergs
Schreiben an Herrn Gros, Germantown
vom 30. Nov. 1747. S. 842—843.
LXVIII Herrn Conrad Weisers, einer
obrigkeitlichen Person in Pennsilvanien,
Schreiben an Herrn Pastor Brunholtz in
Philadelphia, vom [Tulpehockin 16. Fe-
bruarii 1747.] S. 844—872.
[Abdruck aus Dr. Baumgartens Theolo-
gischen Bedenken. VI. Sammlung S. 673ff.]
[1705

Die Missionen der Brüdergemeinde[1])
Moravian Missions[2])

Blumhardt: Vie de D. Zeisberger, missio-
naire de l'église des Frères de Moravie.
Publié par la société pour traduction
d'ouvrage chrétiens allemands. Neuchatel
Jean Pierre Michaud 1844. pp. VII,
8—184   [1706
Bowman, Earl J.: Efforts to christianize the
Indians of Pennsylvania in colonial
times. (I. By the Swedish Lutherans
pp. 21—25; II. By the Quakers. pp. 25
—32; III. David Brainerd. pp. 32—41;
IV. By the Moravians. pp. 190—219;
V. By the Catholics. p. 219). In: The
Lutheran Church Quarterly. Vol. II.
Gettysburg, Pa. 1929. pp. 21—41;
190—222.   [1707
Dahlinger, Charles W.: The Moravians and
their missions among the Indians of the
Ohio Valley. In: Western Pennsylvania
Historical Magazine. Vol. III. Pitts-
burgh, Pa. 1920. pp. 45—67.
[Bibliography. pp. 96—97.]   [1708

Frey, August Emil: Eliot, Brainerd und
Zeisberger. Drei Glaubenszeugen unter
den Indianern. Allentown, Pa.: Brobst,
Diehl u. Co. 1883. pp. IV, 5—139, ill.
= Missions-Bibliothek für Jung und
Alt. Vol. V.   [1709
Fritschel, Gottfried: ,,Die Mission der Brü-
dergemeinde." In: Geschichte der christ-
lichen Missionen unter den Indianern
Nordamerikas im 17. und 18. Jahrhun-
dert. Nebst einer Beschreibung der Reli-
gion der Indianer. Für Freunde der
Mission aus den Quellen erzählt von
Gottfried Fritschel. Nürnberg: Verlag
von Gottfr. Löhe 1870. = Kapitel IV.
S. 149—175.   [1710
Greenfield, John: Moravian educational
labors among the Indians. In: The
Pennsylvania-German. Vol. VIII. Le-
banon, Pa. 1907. pp. 415—420, ill.
                                    [1711
— David Zeisberger. Memorial delivered
Sunday, Nov. 15, 1908, in Nazareth, Pa.
In: Ohio Archaeological and Historical
Quarterly. Vol. XVIII. Columbus, O.
1909. pp. 189—198.   [1712

---

[1]) Vgl. auch unter Ohio, Die Brüder-
missionen, Nr. 5956—5972.
[2]) See also: Ohio, Moravian missions, nos.
5956—5972.

Hamilton, J. Taylor: A history of the missions of the Moravian Church during the eighteenth and nineteenth centuries. *Bethlehem, Pa.: Times Publishing Co. 1901. pp. XV, 235, ill., maps.* [1713

Heckewelder, John: Sketch of the report to be laid before the president of the United States by the President and Directors of the Society for Propagating the Gospel among the Heathen. *[Bethlehem, Pa., June, 1822.] In: Transactions of the Moravian Historical Society. Vol. IV. 1891—1895. Nazareth, Pa. 1895. pp. 277—314.* [1714

Heim, J. J.: David Zeisberger, der Apostel der Indianer in Nord-Amerika, wie er unter denselben 67 Jahre lebte, wirkte und starb. *Bielefeld: Druck von Velhagen und Klasing 1849. 83 S.* [1715

Holmes, John: Historical sketches of the missions of the United Brethren for propagating the gospel among the Heathen, from their commencement to the year 1817. *Second improved edition. London: Printed for the author 1827. pp. (6), 470.* [1716

Humrichhouse, Harry H.: Rev. Christian Post and Peter Humrichhouse, and some of the latter's family. *[s. l.] 1913. pp. (1), 7—51.* [1717

Hutton, J. E.: A history of Moravian missions. *London, E. C.: Moravian Publication Office. Printers: William Walker & Son (Otley) Ltd. 1922. pp. (5), 550, maps.* [1718

Jacobson, Henry A.: Narrative of the attempt to establish a mission among the Chippewa Indians of Canada, between the years 1800 and 1806. *Compiled by ... In: Transactions of the Moravian Historical Society. Vol. V. Nazareth, Pa. 1899. pp. 3—24.* [1719

— Dispersion and flight of the missionaries and Indians living at Fairfield. Canada, in October 1813. *Compiled by ... In: Transactions of the Moravian Historical Society. Vol. V. Nazareth, Pa. 1899. pp. 27—47.* [1720

Johnson, Edward Payson: Christian work among the North American Indians during the eighteenth century. *In: Papers of the American Society of Church History, Second series, vol. VI. New York, N. Y. 1921. pp. 3—41.* [1721

Johnson, F. C.: Early Moravian missions. Reprint from: Daily Record, May 19, 1894. *In: Historical Record. A quar-*terly publication devoted principally to the early history of Wyoming Valley ... *Vol. V. Wilkes-Barre, Pa. 1895. pp. 122 —123.* [1722

Jordan, John W.: Annals of Friedenshütten on the Susquehanna, 1765—1772. *In: Notes and Queries. Edited by W. H. Egle. Annual vol. 1897. Harrisburg, Pa. 1898. pp. 199—200; 205—206; 211— 214; 216—218; 221—223; 227—230; 233—235;* Notes to the Annals of Friedenshütten. *pp. 235—238. [Wyalusing.]* [1723

Levering, J. M.: The first Moravian missionary society in America. *Read Sept. 5, 1895. In: Transactions of the Moravian Historical Society. Vol. V. 1895—1899. Nazareth, Pa. 1899. pp. 311—355.* [1724

Loskiel, Georg Heinrich: Geschichte der Mission der evangelischen Brüder unter den Indianern in Nordamerika. *Barby: zu finden in den Brüdergemeinen und in Leipzig in Commission bey Paul Gotthelf Kummer 1789. (12), (1), 783 S.* [1725

[—]-La Trobe, Christian Ignatius: History of the mission of the United Brethren among the Indians in North America. *In three parts. By George Henry Loskiel. Translated from the German by Christian Ignatius La Trobe. London: Printed for the Brethren's Society for the Furtherance of the Gospel. 1794. pp. XII, 159; 234; 233; 21, map.* [1726

[Meginness, John F.]: The grave of Zeisberger. *By John of Lancaster. In: Notes and Queries. Edited by W. H. Egle. Fourth series, vol. I. 1891—1893. Harrisburg, Pa. 1893. pp. 355—356.* [1727

Müller, Karl: 200 Jahre Brüdergemeine. *2 Bde. Herrnhut: Verlag der Missionsbuchhandlung 1931—1932. VIII, 380 S., Karten; XII, 715 S., Karten. [Die Indianermission in Nordamerika. = Vierter Abschnitt. S. 197—246, Kart.]* [1727a

Randell, E. O.: David Zeisberger Centennial. *November 20, 1908. In: Ohio Archaeological and Historical Quarterly. Vol. XVIII. Columbus, O. 1909. pp. 157—181, ill.* [1728

[Reichelt, G. Th.]: The literature of the mission among the North American Indians. *= Chapter III of: The literary works of the foreign missionaries of the Moravian Church. By G. Th. Reichelt. Translated and annotated by Edmund de Schweinitz. In: Transactions of the Moravian Historical Society. Vol. II.*

Nazareth, Pa. 1886. pp. 382—386.
[1729
Rice, Wm. H.: David Zeisberger and his
brown brethren. *Bethlehem, Pa.: Spe-
cial Moravian Publication Fund Com-
mittee 1897. pp. (1), 5—57, ill.* [1730
— The Rev. John Heckewelder. *Born at
Bedford, Eng., March 12, 1743. Died at
Bethlehem, Pa., January 21, 1823.
Aged 80 years, less 50 days. In: Ohio
Archaeological and Historical Publi-
cations. Vol. VII. Columbus, O. 1899.
pp. 314—348, ill.* [1731
Römer, H.: Die Indianer und ihr Freund
David Zeisberger. *Gütersloh: C. Ber-
telsmann 1890. 109 S.* [1732
Romig, W. H.-(Schultze, A.): The first
American missionaries. *Paper pre-
pared by . . . Reprint from: „The Mora-
vian" Sept. 12, 1912; Addenda by
A. Schultze. Reprint from: „The Mora-
vian" Sept. 19. In: The Penn Germania.
Vol. I. = Old series, vol. XIII. Lititz,
Pa. 1912. pp. 884—886.* [1733
Ronthaler, Edward: Life of John Hecke-
welder. *By . . . Edited by B. H. Coates.
Philadelphia, Pa.: Townsend Ward
1847. pp. XXV, (1), 29—149, ill.*
[1734
Schultze, A.: Die Missionsfelder der Er-
neuerten Brüderkirche, *dargestellt von
. . . Bethlehem, Pa. 1890. VI, 257 S.,
ill., Karten.* [1735
Schwarze, William N.: Characteristics and
achievements of David Zeisberger. *In:
Ohio Archaeological and Historical
Quarterly. Vol. XVIII. Columbus, O.
1909. pp. 182—188.* [1736
Schwarze, Edmund: History of the Mora-
vian missions among southern Indian
tribes of the United States. *Bethlehem,
Pa.: Times Publishing Co. 1923. pp.
XVII, 331, ill.
= Transactions of the Moravian Historical Society, Special Series, vol. I.*
[1737
— Missions of the Moravians in North Carolina among the southern Indian tribes.
*In: Proceedings of the 22nd annual ses-
sion of the State Library and Historical
Assoziation of North Carolina. Raleigh,
Dec. 7—8, 1922. Raleigh, N. C.: Bynum
Printing Co. 1923. pp. 53—69.* [1738
Schweinitz, Edmund de: The life and times
of David Zeisberger, the western pioneer
and apostle of the Indians. *Philadelphia, Pa.: J. B. Lippincott & Co. 1870.
pp. XII, 13—747.* [1739

Schweinitz, Paul de: „Which is the first
American Foreign Mission Board?" and
a list of the first American foreign missionaries. *In: The Pennsylvania-German Society. Proceedings and Addresses
at Ephrata, Oct. 8, 1920. Vol. XXXI.
Meadville, Pa. 1925. = Annual address
of the president. pp. 7—20.* [1740
Spangenberg, August Gottlieb: Von der
Arbeit der evangelischen Brüder unter
den Heiden. *Barby 1782. 168 S.* [1740a
Stocker, Harry Emilius: A history of the
Moravian mission among the Indians
on the White River in Indiana. *Bethlehem, Pa.: Times Publishing Co. 1917.
In: Transactions of the Moravian Historical Society. Vol. X. 1913—1917.
Nazareth, Pa. 1917. pp. 233—408,
map.* [1741
— A history of the Moravian mission
among the Indians on the White River
in Indiana. *Bethlehem, Pa.: Times
Publishing Co. 1917. pp. 180, map.*
[1742
Thompson, Augustus C.: Moravian missions. *Twelve lectures. New York,
N. Y.: Charles Scribner's Sons 1886.
pp. IX, 516.* [1743
Willett, William M.: Scenes in the wilderness: an authentic narrative of the la-
bours and sufferings of the Moravian
missionaries among the North American
Indians. *New York, N. Y.: G. Lane
& P. P. Sanford; J. Collard, printer,
1842. pp. 208.* [1744
Vormbaum, Reinhold: David Zeisberger,
Missionar der Brüdergemeinde unter
den Indianern Nordamerika's und seine
Mitarbeiter. *Düsseldorf: W. H. Scheller
1853. 187 S.* [1745
Missions of the Moravians among the North
American Indians inhabiting the middle
states of the Union. *Written for the
American Sunday School Union 1831.
pp. VIII, 9—162, ill.* [1746
Übersicht der Missions-Geschichte der evan-
gelischen Brüderkirche in ihrem ersten
Jahrhundert. *Erste Abtheilung. Vom
Jahr 1732 bis 1760. Gnadau 1832: im
Verlag der Buchhandlung der Evange-
lischen Brüder Unität bey Hans Franz
Burkhard 1832. (4), 103 S.; . . . Zweyte
Abtheilung. Vom Jahr 1760 bis 1801.
Gnadau 1833. (2), 142 S.; . . . Dritte Ab-
theilung. Vom Jahr 1801 bis 1832.
Gnadau 1833. (2), 182 S.* [1747
The history of the Moravian mission among
the Indians in North America from its

commencement to the present time. *With a preliminary account of the Indians. Compiled from authentic sources by a member of the Brethren's Church. London: T. Allman 1838. pp. VI, 316.* [1748

Annals of Wekquitank, (one of the Moravian missions) 1760—1763. (,,Extracts from the Diaries" by John W. Jordan). *In Notes and Queries. Edited by W. H. Egle. Annual vol. 1899. Harrisburg, Pa. 1900. pp. 123—126; 129—132; 134—138; 140—142;* Notes to the

,,Annals of Wekquitank." *pp. 142—143.* [1749

First American missionaries. *Reprint from:* ,,Easton Argus." *In: The Penn Germania. Vol. I. = Old series, vol. XII. Lititz, Pa. 1912. p. 425.* [1750

An old fathom of wampun. *[Given by the Five Nations to Count Zinzendorf in 1742 and handed over to Bishop A. G. Spangenberg whose receipt is given.] In: The Pennsylvania Magazine of History and Biography. Vol. XXXIX. Philadelphia, Pa. 1915. pp. 2️⃣—232.* [1751

Reise-Tagebücher von Mährischen Missionaren und Brüdern

Moravian Itineraries

,,Personal material. Diaries, Journals" *in:* ,,*The Archives of the Unitas Fratrum or Moravian Church in the United States of America", Bethlehem, Pa. Part of: Inventory of unpublished material for American religious history in Protestant church archives and other repositories by William Henry Allison. Washington, D. C. 1910 [= no. 7822]. pp. 158—161.* [1752

[Cammerhoff]: Interior Pennsylvania in 1748. Extracts from Bishop Cammerhoff's Narrative of a Journey to Shamokin in the Winter of 1748. *Contributed by Aug. H. Leibert. In: Notes and Queries. Edited by W. H. Egle. Second series. Harrisburg, Pa. 1883. pp. 138—141; 142—144. Reprint in: First and second series, vol. II. Harrisburg, Pa. 1895. pp. 237—241; 243—246.* [1753

[Ettwein, John]: Rev. John Ettwein's notes of travel from the North Branch of the Susquehanna to the Beaver River, Pa., 1772. *Contributed by John W. Jordan. In: The Pennsylvania Magazine of History and Biography. Vol. XXV. Philadelphia, Pa. 1901. pp. 208—219.* [1754

[—] Rev. John Ettwein's journal of the removal of the Christian Indians from Friedenshütten on the Susquehanna to Friedenstadt on the Big Beaver in 1772. *Furnished by John W. Jordan. In: Notes and Queries. Edited by W. H. Egle. Annual vol. 1898. Harrisburg 1899. pp. 49—51; 58—59; 68—70; 77—79.* [1755

[Gottschalk, Mathias Gottlieb]: Report and observations of Bro. Gottschalk on his journey through Virginia and Maryland, undertaken in March and April, 1748. *Part of: Moravian diaries of travels through Virginia. Edited by Wm. J. Hinke and Ch. E. Kemper. In: The Virginia Magazine of History and Biography. Vol. XI. Richmond, Va. 1903—04. pp. 225—234.* [1756

[—] Extracts from the diary of Bro. Gottschalk's journey through Maryland and Virginia, March 5—April 20, 1748. *Part of: Moravian diaries of travels through Virginia. Edited by Wm. J. Hinke and E. Kemper. In: The Virginia Magazine of History and Biography. Vol. XII. Richmond, Va. 1904—1905. pp. 62—76.* [1757

[—] The places in Maryland and Virginia where our Brethren have an open door. *Part of: Moravian diaries of travels through Virginia. Edited by Wm. J. Hinke and E. Kemper. In: The Virginia Magazine of History and Biography. Vol. XII. Richmond, Va. 1904—1905. pp. 77—80.* [1758

[Grube, Bernhard Adam (?)]: Diary of the journey of the first colony of single Brethren to North Carolina, October 8, — November 17, 1753. *Part of: Moravian diaries of travels through Virginia. Edited by Wm. J. Hinke and Ch. E. Kemper. In: The Virginia Magazine of History and Biography. Vol. XII. Richmond, Va. 1904—1905. pp. 134—153; 271—281.* [1759

[**Grube, Bernhard Adam (?)**]: Diarium einer Reise von Bethlehem, Pa., nach Betharaba, N. C. Von October 8 bis November 23, 1753. *[„Reisse Diarium der ersten Colonne led.(iger) Brüder nach Nord Carolina, 1753", geschrieben wahrscheinlich von Bernhard Adam Grube, dem ersten Prediger der Colonie.] Herausgegeben von* **Wm. J. Hinke.** *In: German American Annals. New series, vol. III. Philadelphia, Pa. 1905. pp. 342—356; 369—379; Vol. IV. 1906. pp. 16—32.*
[English translation published partly by the same editor in: The Virginia Magazine of History and Biography. Vol. XII. Richmond, Va. 1904—1905. pp. 134—153; 271—281.] [1760

[—] Diary of a journey of Moravians from Bethlehem, Pennsylvania, to Bethabara in Wachovia, North Carolina, 1753. *[Travel diary of the First Company of Single Brethren going to North Carolina, 1753.] Reprint in: Travels in the American colonies. Edited by Newton D. Mereness, under the auspices of the National Society of the Colonial Dames of America. New York, N. Y.: The Macmillan Co. 1916. pp. 325—356.* [1761

[—] A missionary's tour to Shamokin and the West Branch of the Susquehanna, 1753. *In: The Pennsylvania Magazine of History and Biography. Vol. XXXIX. Philadelphia, Pa. 1915. pp. 440—444.* [1762

[**Heckewälder, Johann**]: Johann Heckewälder's Reise von Bethlehem in Pennsylvanien bis zum Wabashfluß im Nordwestlichen Gebiet der vereinigten Staaten von Nordamerika. *Mit Anmerkungen herausgegeben von* **M. C. Sprengel.** *Halle: in der Rengerschen Buchhandlung 1797. 94 S.* [1763

[**Heckewelder, Johann**]: Narrative of John Heckewelder's journey to the Wabash in 1792. *[Translation of „Johann Heckewälder's Reise von Bethlehem in Pennsylvania bis zum Wabash Fluß im Nordwestlichen Gebiet der Vereinigten Staaten von Nordamerika. Mit Anmerkungen herausgegeben von* **M. C. Sprengel.** *" printed at Halle, 1797.] Translated by* **Henry B. Luckenbach.** *Annotated and edited by* **J. W. Jordan.** *In: The Pennsylvania Magazine of History and Biography. Vol. XI. Philadelphia, Pa. 1887. pp. 466—475; Vol. XII. 1888. pp. 34—54; 165—184.* [1764

[**Heckewelder, Johann**]: Narrative of John Heckewelder's journey to the Wabash in 1792. *In: Heckewelder's narrative, Heckewelder's journal 1797. Edited by* **William Elsey Conneley** *[= no 1771]. pp. 58—95.* [1765

[—] Notes of travel of William Henry, John Heckewelder, John Rothrock and Christian Clewell, to Gnadenhütten on the Muskingum, in the early summer of 1797. *Translated by* **Robert W. Henry.** *Edited by* **John W. Jordan.** *In: The Pennsylvania Magazines of History and Biography. Vol. X. Philadelphia, Pa. 1886. pp. 125—157.* [1766

[—] Notes of travel of William Henry, John Heckewelder, John Rothrock and Christian Clewell, to Gnadenhütten in the early summer of 1797. *Edited by* **John Jordan.** *In: Heckewelder's narrative, Heckewelder's journal 1797. Edited by* **William Elsey Conneley** *[= no. 1771]. pp. 34—57.* [1767

— A narrative of the mission of the United Brethren among the Delaware and Mohegan Indians, from its commencement in the year 1740, to the close of the year 1808. Comprising all the remarkable incidents which took place at their missionary stations during that period. *Interspersed with anecdotes, historical facts, speeches of Indians, and other interesting matters. Philadelphia, Pa.: M'Carty & Davis 1820. pp. XII, 17—429, portr.* [1768

[—] Johann Heckewelder's Evangelischen Predigers zu Bethlehem Nachricht von der Geschichte, den Sitten und Gebräuchen der Indianischen Völkerschaften, welche ehemals Pennsylvanien und die benachbarten Staaten bewohnten. *Aus dem Englischen übersetzt und mit den Angaben anderer Schriftsteller über eben dieselben Gegenstände (Carver, Loskiel, Long, Volney) vermehrt von* **Fr. Hesse.** *Nebst einem die Glaubwürdigkeit und den anthropologischen Werth der Nachrichten Heckewelder's betreffenden Zusatze von* **G. E. Schulze.** *Göttingen: Vandenhoek und Ruprecht. 1821. XLVIII, 582 S.* [1769

— History, manners and customs of the Indian nations who once inhabited Pennsylvania and the neighboring states. *By the Rev.* **John Heckewelder,** *of Bethlehem, Pa. New and revised edition, with an introduction and notes by* **William C. Reichel.** *Philadelphia, Pa.:*

Publication Fund of the Historical Society of Pennsylvania 1876. pp. VII—XLVI, 47—465, ill. = Memoirs of the Historical Society of Pennsylvania. Vol. XII. [1770

[Heckewelder, John]: A narrative of the missions of the United Brethren among the Delaware and Mohegan Indians, from its commencement in the year 1740 to the close of the year 1808 by John Heckewelder, who was many years in service of the mission . . . 1820; new edition edited by William Elsey Conneley. Cleveland, O.: The Burrows Brothers Company 1907. pp. XII, 429. [1771

[Loskiel, George Henry]: Extempore on a wagon; a metrical narrative of a journey from Bethlehem, Pa. to the Indian town of Goshen, Ohio, in the autumn of 1803. Translated with notes by J. Max Hark. Lancaster, Pa. Published by Samuel H. Zahm & Co. 1887. pp. V, 7—45, ill. [1772

[Mack, John Martin]: John Martin Mack's journal of a visit to Onondaga in 1752. Contributed by John W. Jordan. In: Notes and Queries. Edited by W. H. Egle. Third series, vol. I. 1884—1887. Harrisburg, Pa. 1887. pp. 345—350; 351—355; 361—364; Reprint in: Third series, vol. II. Harrisburg, Pa. 1896. pp. 50—58; 58—63; 64—69. [1773

[—] Journal of John Martin Mack. Contributed by John W. Jordan. In: The Historical Journal. Vol. I. Williamsport, Pa. 1888. pp. 92—97. [1774

[—] Rev. John Martin Mack's narrative of a visit to Onondaga, in 1752. Contributed by John W. Jordan. In: The Pennsylvania Magazine of History and Biography. Vol. XXIX. Philadelphia, Pa. 1905. pp. 343—358. [1775

[Reichel, Gotthold Benjamin]: A journey to Bethlehem and Nazareth, in September and October, 1815. Described by . . . Translated from the original German M. S. by Helen Bell. In: Tranactions of the Moravian Historical Society. Vol. IV. 1891—1895. Nazareth, Pa. 1895. pp. 127—161. [1776

[Reichel, John Frederick]: Travel diary of Bishop and Mrs. Reichel and their company from Lititz, Pennsylvania, to Salem in Wachovia, North Carolina, 1780. Reprint in: Travels in the American colonies. Edited by Newton D. Mereness, under the auspices of the National Society of the Colonial Dames of America.

New York, N. Y.: The Macmillan Company 1916. pp. 585—599. [1777

[Reichel, John Frederik]: Extract from the travel diary of the beloved Br. and Sr. Reichel and the single Br. Christ Heckewalder from Salem to Lititz. Reprint in: Travels in the American colonies. Edited by Newton D. Mereness under the auspices of the National Society of the Colonial Dames of America. New York, N. Y.: The Macmillan Company 1916. pp. 603—613. [1778

[Rice, Owen]: Four hundred miles overland for Salome Heckewelder. [A father's (Owen Rice 2nd) Journal of his son's (Joseph Rice) wedding journey from Bethlehem, Northampton County, Pa. to Gnadenhütten, Ohio and how they brought home the bride.] Translated from the original German manuscript by William H. Rice. In The Pennsylvania-German. Vol. IX. Cleona, Pa. 1908. pp. 450—455. [1779

[Schnell, Leonhard-Hussey, Robert]: Extracts from the diary of Leonhard Schnell and Robert Hussey, of their journey to Georgia, Nov. 6, 1743, — April 10, 1744. Part of: Moravian diaries of travels through Virginia. Edited by Wm. J. Hinke and Ch. E. Kemper. In: The Virginia Magazine of History and Biography. Vol. XI. Richmond, Va. 1903—1904. pp. 370—393. [1780

[——Handrup, Vitus]: Diary of the journey of Rev. L. Schnell and V. Handrup, to Maryland and Virginia, May 29th to August 4, 1747. Part of: Moravian diaries of travels through Virginia. Edited by Wm. J. Hinke and Ch. E. Kemper. In: The Virginia Magazine of History and Biography. Vol. XII. Richmond, Va. 1904—1905. pp. 55—61. [1781

[——Brandmüller, J.]: Extracts from the diary of Leonhard Schnell and John Brandmueller of their journey to Virginia, Oct. 12—Dec. 12, 1749. Part of: Moravian diaries of travels through Virginia. Edited by Wm. J. Hinke and Ch. E. Kemper. In: The Virginia Magazine of History and Biography. Vol. XI. Richmond, Va. 1903—1904. pp. 115—131;

[Bro. Schnell's journey to Va., from Oct. 12—Dec. 24, 1749. In: Vol. XII. 1904—1905. pp. 81—82.] [1782

[Schweinitz, Ludwig, David von]: Übers Weltmeer. Die Reise des Bruders Ludwig von Schweinitz von Herrnhut nach

Bethlehem in Pennsylvanien im Jahre 1812, *von ihm selbst erzählt. Bearbeitet und herausgegeben von* Ernst Graeber. *Herrnhut: Verlag der Missionsbuchhandlung 1927. 44 S.* [1783

[Schweinitz, Ludwig von]: Account of the journey of Br. and Sr. Ludwig von Schweinitz from Herrenhut to Bethlehem in Pennsylvania. [1812.] *Translated from the Moravian Church Archives by* Adelaide L. Fries. *In: The Pennsylvania Magazine of History and Biography. Vol. XLVI. Philadelphia, Pa. 1922. pp. 312—333.* [1784

[—] The journey of Lewis David von Schweinitz to Goshen, Bartholomew County, in 1831. *Translated by* Adolf Gerber. *Indianopolis, Ind.: Published for the Society. Greenfield, Ind.: The Wm. Mitchell Printing Co. 1927. pp. 205 —285.*
= *Indiana Historical Society Publications. Vol. VIII, no. 5.* [1784a

[Spangenberg, Joseph]: Extracts from the diary of the journey of Bros. Joseph Spangenberg and Mattew Reutz through Maryland and Virginia in July and August, 1748. *Part of:* Moravian diaries of travels through Virginia. *Edited by* Wm. J. Hinke *and* Ch. E. Kemper. *In: The Virginia Magazine of History and Biography. Vol. XI. Richmond, Va. 1903—04. pp. 235—242.* [1785

[Spangenberg, A. G.]: Spangenberg's notes of travel to Onondaga in 1745. *Contributed by* John W. Jordan. *In: The Pennsylvania Magazine of History and Biography. Vol. II. Philadelphia, Pa. 1878. pp. 424—432; Vol. III. 1879. pp. 56—64.* [1786

[Zeisberger, David]: Auszüge aus dem Tagebuche David Zeisbergers. *Nach dem einzigen, im Besitz der Ohio Historical and Philosophical Society befindlichen, bisher ungedruckten Manuscripte mitgetheilt von* Karl Knortz. *In: Der Deutsche Pionier. Jg. V. Cincinnati, O. 1873—1874. S. 284—290; 306—311; 364 —367; Jg. VI. 1874—1875, S. 58—61.* [1787

[—] Diary of David Zeisberger, a Moravian missionary among the Indians of Ohio. *Translated from the original German manuscript and edited by* Eugene F. Bliss. *2 vols. Cincinnati, O.: Robert Clarke & Co. For the Historical and*

Philosophical Society of Ohio. 1885. pp. V—XXXII, 464; 535. [1788

[Zeisberger, David]: The Cowanesque Valley in 1767. Tour of Rev. David Zeisberger, the Moravian missionary. *[Extracts from his diary; contributed by* Charles Tübbs.] *In: Notes and Queries. Edited by W. H. Egle. Fourth series, vol. I. 1891—1893. Harrisburg, Pa. 1893. pp. 351—352.* (Continuation of:) *Zeisberger's diary of 1767. pp. 356—357.* [1789

[—] A Moravian diary of 1768. „Diary of the journey of David Zeisberger and Gottlob Sensemann to Goschgoschunk on the Allegena and their arrival, May, 1768." *In: Notes and Queries. Edited by* W. H. Egle. *Fourth series, vol. I. 1891—1893. Harrisburg, Pa. 1893. pp. 362—365.* [1790

Clark, John S.: The Zeisberger diaries. *In: Notes and Queries. Edited by W. H. Egle. Fourth series, vol. I. 1891—1893. Harrisburg, Pa. 1893. pp. 372—374.* [1791

[Zeisberger, David]: The Moravian records. *Volume two. The diaries of Zeisberger relating to the first missions in the Ohio basin. Edited by* Archer Butler Hulbert *and* William Nathaniel Schwarze. *In: Ohio Archaeological and Historical Quarterly. Vol. XXI. Columbus, O. 1912. pp. 1—125.* [1792

[—] David Zeisberger's history of northern American Indians. *Edited by* Archer Butler Hulbert *and* William Nathaniel Schwarze. *Columbus, O. 1910. pp. II, 189.*
= *Ohio Archaeological and Historical Quarterly. Vol. XIX. Jan. & April, 1910. No. 1—2.* [1793

[Zinzendorf, N. L. von]: Extracts from Zinzendorf's diary of his second, and in part of his third journey among the Indians, the former to Shekomeko, and the other among the Shawanese, on the Susquehanna. *Translated from a German M. S. in the Bethlehem Archives, by* Eugene Schaeffer. *In: Transactions of the Moravian Historical Society. Vol. I. 1858—1876. Nazareth, Pa. 1876. pp. 81—89.* [1794

Moravian journals relating to Central New York 1745—66. *Arranged and edited by* Wm. M. Beauchamp *for the Onondaga Historical Association 1916. Syracuse, N. Y.: The Dehler Press 1916. pp. 243.* [1795

Fluß-Brüder
River Brethren

United States, Department of Commerce, Bureau of Census: River Brethren. History description and statistics. *In: Religious bodies: 1906. Part II. Separate denominations: Washington, D. C. 1910 [= no. 894]. pp. 169—174;*
. . . In: Religious bodies: 1916. Part II. Washington, D. C. 1919. pp. 177—182.
. . . In: Religious bodies: 1926. Part II.

Washington, D. C. 1929. pp. 286 —296.
[See: Brethren in Christ, Old Order or Yorker Brethren, United Zion's Children.] [1799
Miller, John K.: The River Brethren. A historical sketch. *In: The Pennsylvania-German. Vol. VII. Lebanon, Pa. 1906. pp. 17—22, ill.* [1797

Brüder in Christo
Brethren in Christ

United States, Department of Commerce, Bureau of Census: Brethren in Christ. History, description and statistics. *In: Religious bodies. 1906. Part II. Separate denominations. Washington, D. C. 1910 [= no. 894]. pp. 170 —172.*
. . . In: Religious bodies: 1916. Part II. Washington, D. C. 1919. pp. 178—180.
. . . Statistics. History, doctrine and organization. In: Religious bodies: 1926. Part II. Washington, D. C. 1929. pp. 288—292. [1798
Minutes of the General Conference of the Brethren in Christ known as „Tunkers" in Canada. *1926. Fairland Church near Cleona, Pa. pp. 91.* [1799

Hand book of missions home and foreign of the Brethren in Christ Church. *Nappanee: E. V. Publishing House. 1920 annually ff.* [1800
Engle, Morris M.: History of the Engle family in America 1754—1927. The Engle history and family records of Dauphin and Lancaster counties. The numerous lineal descendants of Ulrich Engle. Short sketches of Engle families not related. A sketch of the arrival and record of the origin of the Brethren in Christ Church of which a large, number of these descendants are members. *Compiled, arranged, indexed and published by . . . Mt. Joy, Pa.: The Bulletin Press. 1927. pp. 161, ill.* [1801

Brüder alter Ordnung oder Yorker Brüder
Old Order or Yorker Brethren

United States, Department of Commerce, Bureau of Census: Yorker, or Old Order Brethren. History, descriptions and statistics. *In: Religious bodies: 1906. Part II. Separate denominations. Washington, D. C. 1910 [= no. 894]. p. 173.*

. . . In: Religious bodies: 1916. Part II. Washington, D. C. 1919. pp. 180—181.
. . . Statistics. History, doctrine and organization. In: Religious bodies: 1926. Part II. Washington, D. C. 1929. pp. 293—294. [1802

Vereinigte Zions-Kinder

United Zions Children

United States, Department of Commerce, Bureau of Census: United Zion's Children. History, description and statistics. *In: Religious bodies: 1906. Part II. Separate denominations. Washington, D. C. 1910 [=no. 894]. pp. 173—174.* ... *In: Religious bodies: 1916. Part II. Washington, D. C. 1919. pp. 181—182.* ... Statistics. History, doctrine and organization. *In: Religious bodies:* *1926. Oart II. Washington, D. C. 1929. pp. 295—296.* [1803

Brinser, H. S.: Bishop Brinser and the Brinser meeting house. *In: The Pennsylvania-German. Vol. II. Lebanon, Pa. 1901. pp. 23—31, ill.*

[Rev. Mathias Brinser, founder and first bishop of the United Zion's Children.] [1804

Anfänge des Methodismus
Early Methodism

Nuelsen, John L.: „Die deutschen Methodisten in Amerika". *In: Kurzgefaßte Geschichte des Methodismus von seinen Anfängen bis zur Gegenwart. Von John L. Nuelsen, Theophil Mann und J. J. Sommer. Zweite Auflage. Bremen: Verlagshaus der Methodistenkirche, G.m.b.H. 1929. S. 500—518.* [1805

Starr, Harris Elwood: Heck, Barbara (1734—1804) mother of Methodism in America. *In: Dictionary of American biography. Under the auspices of the American Council of Learned Societies. Vol. VIII. Edited by Allen Johnson and Dumas Malone. London-New York 1932. p. 493.*
[Bibliography.] [1805a

Good, J. B.: „Henry Boehm (1775—1875)". *In: A biographical history of Lancaster County. By Alex. Harris. Lancaster, Pa. 1872 [= no. 4084]. pp. 49—62.* [1805b

Lutz, John J.: Boehm's chapel and the Pennsylvania Mennonites. An unfamiliar chapter in early Methodist history. *In: The Pennsylvania-German. Vol. XI. Lititz, Pa. 1910. pp. 340—343.* [1806

R.[attermann], H. A.: Ein deutsch-amerikanischer Patriarch. [Heinrich Böhm.] *In: Der Deutsche Pionier. Jg. VIII. Cincinnati, O. 1876—1877. S. 25—35. ill.* [1807

Tipple, Ezra Squier: Boehm, Henry (1775—1875) Methodist iteneraut preacher. *In: Dictionary of American biography. Under the auspices of the American Council of Learned Societies edited by Allen Johnson. Vol. II. London-New York 1929. pp. 402—403.* [1807a

Wakeley, J. B.: The Patriarch of one hundred years; being reminiscences, historical and biographical, of Rev. Henry Boehm. *With several additional chapters, containing an account of the exercises on his one hundredth birthday; his sermon before the Newark Conference and the addresses then delivered; his centennial sermon in Trinity Church, Jersey City, and in Johnstreet Church, New York, and the addresses made on those occasions. Phonographically reported. New York, N. Y.: Nelson & Phillips 1875. pp. 587, ill.* [1808

Kriebel, H. W.: Reverend Jacob Gruber, Methodist preacher. *In: The Pennsylvania-German. Vol. VIII. Lebanon 1907. pp. 154—160, ill.*
[Condensed account from the „Life of Jacob Gruber" by W. P. Strickland. = no. 1810.] [1809

Strickland, W. P.: The life of Jacob Gruber. *New York, N. Y.: Published by Carnot & Porter 1860. pp. 384, ill.* [1810

Vereinigte Brüder-Gruppen
United Brethren bodies

United States, Department of Commerce, Bureau of Census: United Brethren bodies. History, description, and statistics. *In: Religious bodies: 1906. Part II. Separate denominations. Washington, D. C. 1910 [= no. 894]. pp. 643—653.*

... In: Religious bodies: 1916. Part. II. Washington, D. C. 1919 pp. 694—705.
... In: Religious bodies: 1926. Part II. Washington, D. C. 1929. pp. 1358—1373. *[See: Church of the United Brethren in Christ Church; Church of the United Brethren in Christ (Old Constitution.)]* [1811

Kirche der Vereinigten Brüder in Christo
Church of the United Brethtren in Christ

United States, Department of Commerce, Bureau of Census: Church of the United Brethren in Christ. History, description, and statistics. *In: Religious bodies: 1906. Part II. Separate denominations. Washington, D. C. 1910 [= no. 894]. pp. 644—650.*
... In: Religious bodies: 1916. Part II. Washington, D. C. 1919. pp. 701—705.
... Statistics. History, doctrine and organization. In: Religious bodies. 1926. Part II. Washington, D. C. 1929. pp. 1359—1366. [1812
Minutes of the Annual and General Conference of the Church of the Brethren in Christ, 1800—1818. *Translated and edited by* A. W. Drury, Dayton, O.: *Published for the United Brethren Historical Society by the United Brethren Publishing House 1897. pp. VII, 9—90.* [1813
Disciplines of the United Brethren in Christ. *Part I. In English, 1814—1841. Part II. In German, 1814—1841. Translated and reprinted from the originals. Edited by* A. W. Drury. Dayton, O.: *United Brethren Publishing House 1895. pp. X, 232; 109.* [1814
Minutes of early conferences. *See: Religious Telescope (Church of the United Brethren in Christ.) Vol. I. No. 1. Circleville, O., Dec. 31, 1834. Twoweekly ff.; since 1845: weekly ff. Since 1853: Dayton, O. See also: Die geschäftige Martha Jg. II. No. 1. Baltimore, Md., 1. July 1841; since 1846: Das deutsche Telescop; since 1851: Die fröhliche Botschaft.* [1815
Proceedings of the General Conference of the United Brethren in Christ *held in western Linn County, Iowa from the 11th to 12th May, 1865, inclusive. Dayton, O.: United Brethren Printing*

Establishment 1865: since 1865 always separately printed. ff. [1816
Separate pamphlet minutes of all the annual conferences exist beginning with 1885, of the Sandusky conference since 1861, of the Miami Conference since 1864. *[Hist. Soc., Library of Bonebrake Seminary, Dayton, O.]*
The following of the eastern annual conferences are especially relating to the Pennsylvania German history:
Allegheny 1839.
Auglaize 1853—1901.
Central Ohio 1878—1901.
East Ohio (by union of Muskingham, 1818 and Western Reserve, 1861—1886.
East Pennsylvania 1846.
Erie 1852.
Maryland 1887—1901.
Miami 1810.
Pennsylvania (by division of Hagerstown 1800) 1831.
Sanduski 1834.
South East Ohio (formerly Scioto, 1825) 1901.
Virginia (by division of Hagerstown 1800) 1831.
West Virginia (formerly Parkersburg) 1857. [1817
The United Brethren almanac for the year 1867. Dayton, O.: *Published by* W. J. Shuey, *Tellescope Office 1867. Annually ff.; since 1871: Dayton, O.: United Brethren Publishing House; since 1883:* Year book. [1818
Albright, Raymond W.: The common heritage of the Church of the United Brethren in Christ and the Evangelical Church. *In: The Christian Union Quarterly. Baltimore, Md. July 1931. pp. 55—65.* [1819
Berger, D.[aniel]: History of the Church of the United Brethren in Christ. *In: A*

history of the' Disciples of Christ, the Society of Friends, the United Brethren in Christ and the Evangelical Association. New York, N. Y.: The Christian Literature Co. 1894. = The American Church Series. Vol. XII. pp. 309—382. [Bibliography pp. 310—314.] [1820

Berger, D.[aniel]: History of the Church of the United Brethren in Christ. Dayton, O.: United Brethren Publishing House 1897. pp. XV, 17—682, ill. New print: 1904. pp. XVI, 17—682, ill. [1821

Brane, C. I. B.: An old time camp-meeting. In: The United Brethren Review. Vol. XIII. Dayton, O. 1902. pp. 1—4, ill. [1822

— Landmark history of United Brethrenism in Pennsylvania. In: The Pennsylvania-German. Vol. IV. Lebanon, Pa. 1903. pp. 322—336, ill. [1823

Cowden, Col. R.: A century of Sabbathschool work in the United Brethren Church. In: Quarterly Review of the United Brethren Church. Vol. IV. Dayton, O. 1893. pp. 135—149. [1824

Drury, A.[ugustus] W.[aldo]: History of the Church of the United Brethren in Christ. Dayton, Ohio: The Otterbein Press 1924. pp. 821, ill. Supplement to preceding parts. 1931. pp. 783—832. [Supplement also issued separately: Supplement with enlarged index. Dayton, O.: The Otterbein Press. 1931. pp. 783—832.] [1825

Hough, S. S. - Shupe, H. F.: Partners in the conquering cause. Dayton, O.: Board of Administration United Brethren in Christ 1924. pp. 144, ill. [1826

Lawrence, John: The history of the Church of the United Brethren in Christ. 2 vols. Dayton, O.: United Brethren Printing Establishment 1868. pp. XIV, 17—416; XIII, 17—431. [1827

[—] Die Kirchengeschichte der Ver. Brüder in Christo. Verfaßt von J. Lawrence. Frei aus dem Englischen übersetzt von Wilhelm Mittendorf. Dayton, O.: Druck-Anstalt der Vereinigten Brüder in Christo 1871. S. 288. [1828

Mills, J. S.: Polity of the United Brethren in Christ. In: Quarterly Review of the United Brethren in Christ. Vol. V. Dayton, O. 1894. pp. 52—58. [1829

— The United Brethren in Christ. The rise, growth, and present characteristics of one of the bodies with which union is suggested. In: The United Brethren Review. Vol. XV. Dayton, O. 1904. pp. 129—134. [1830

P.[arthemore], E. W. S.: The first U. B. conference. Where it was held in the year 1791. In: Notes and Queries. Edited by W. H. Egle. Third series, vol. II. 1887—1890. Harrisburg, Pa. 1891. pp. 321—323, ill. Reprint in Third series, vol. III. Harrisburg, Pa. 1896. pp. 374—375. [1831

Sanders, T. J.: The educational work of the Church. In: Quarterly Review of the United Brethren in Christ. Vol. V. Dayton, O. 1894. pp. 59—65. [1832

Shuey, E. L.: A hand-book of the United Brethren in Christ. Prepared by . . . Dayton, O.: U. Br. Publishing House 1885. pp. 72; second edition: 1889. pp. V, 7—64. Advertisements pp. 42; Third edition 1897. pp. V, 7—82. Advertisements 22; Fourth edition 1901 pp. V, 7—66. Advert. 67—80; Revised to date by H. F. Shupe. Dayton, O. 1911. pp. V, 7—97. [1833

Shuey, William A.: Manual of the United Brethren Publishing House. Historical and descriptive. With an introduction by A. W. Drury. Dayton, O.: United Brethren Publishing House 1893. pp. XX, 371, ill. [1834

Spayth, Henry-[Hanby, William]: History of the Church of the United Brethren in Christ. Circleville, O.: Published at the Conference office of the United Brethren in Christ 1851. pp. 344, ill. Including: Hanby, William: History of the United Brethren in Christ. From the year 1825, to the year 1850. pp. 201—344. [1835

Thompson, H. A.: Our bishops, a sketch of the origin and growth of the Church of the U. Br. in Christ as shown in the lives of its distinguished leaders. With an introduction by Colonel Robert Cowden. Chicago, Ill.: Elder Publishing Co. 1889. pp. 631, ill.; New edition revised to date. Dayton, O.: U. B. Publishing House 1904. pp. 668, ill. [1836

Weekly, W. M. — Fout, H. H.: Denominational mission study course. Our heroes or United Brethren home missionaries. Introduction by J. P. Landis. 2 vols. Dayton, O.: U. Br. Home Missionary Society 1908. pp. X, 11—340, ill. Vol. II. 1911. pp. 267, ill. [1837

Lehre und Zucht-Ordnung der Vereinigten Brüder in Christo. — Doctrine and discipline of the United Brethren in Christ. [Including: Von dem Ursprung der Vereinigten Brüder in Christo. — Of the origin of the United Brethren in

Christ. S. 6—17.] Hagerstown: Gruber & May 1819. 77 S.
[Erste Ausgabe 1814.] [1838
The Church of the United Brethren in Christ represented at the World's Columbian exposition. *Chicago, Ill. 1893. Dayton, O.: United Brethren Publishing House 1893. pp. (1), 7—50.* [1839
A century. Addresses delivered at the Centennial celebration of the Church of the United Brethren in Christ. *Edited by G. M. Mathews. Dayton, O.: U. B. Publishing House 1901. pp. VIII, 203, ill.* [1840

Eberly, Daniel; Albright, Isaiah H. and Brane, C. I. B.: Landmark history of the United Brethren Church. Treating of the early history of the church in Cumberland, Lancaster, York, and Lebanon Counties, Pa., and giving the history of the denomination in the original territory. *Reading, Pa.: Behney & Bright 1911. pp. VIII (1), 15—292, ill.* [1841
Fulton, J. S.: History of the Allegheny Conference of the Church of the United Brethren in Christ. Telling of the origin, growth, and development of the ,conference and its attitude toward great issues and its part in their solution. *[Dayton, O.: United Brethren Publishing House]1931. pp. XIV, 279, ill.* [1842
[Funkhouser, A. P.] and Morton, Oren F.: History of the Church of the United Brethren in Christ, Virginia Conference. *By A. P. Funkhouser. Compiled by Oren F. Morton. Dayton, Va.: Ruebush-Kieffer Co. 1921. pp. 315.* [1843
Condo, Adam Byron: History of the Indiana Conference of the Church of the United Brethren in Christ. With a brief review of the events leading up to the organization of the Conference in 1830. *Published by order of the Indiana Conference. [Dayton, O.] 1926. pp. 422, ill.* [1844
Luttrell, J. L.: History of the Auglaize Annual Conference of the United Brethren Church from 1853—1891. *Dayton, O.:*

U. Br. Publishing House 1892. pp. XV, 17—475, ill. [1845
Mathes, Wm. M.: History of the Sandusky Conference. *Toledo, O.: Toledo Commercial Book and Job Printing 1887. pp. 100.* [1846
Wilmore, Augustus Cleland: History of the White River Conference of the Church of the United Brethren in Christ, containing an account of the anticedent annual conferences. *Dayton, O.: United Brethren Publishing House 1925. pp. IX, 504; XVI, ill.* [1847
Becker, H. J.: History of the United Brethren in Christ of California, for a period of thirty years, together with an article on the Chinese question. *Sacramento, Cal.: Valley Press, Book and Job Printing Office 1879. pp. II, 67.* [1848
Funk, W. R.: Life of Bishop J. S. Mills. D. D. *Introduction by S. S. Hough. Dayton, O.: The Otterbein Press 1913. pp. 271, ill.* [1849
Warner, Z.: The life and labors of Rev. Jacob Bachtel of the Parkersburg Annual Conference, United Brethren in Christ. *Dayton, O.: United Brethren in Christ 1868. pp. VII, 224.* [1850
Thompson, H. A.: John Wesley Etter. *In: Quarterly Review of the United Brethren in Christ. Vol. VI. Dayton, O. 1895. pp. 239—246, ill.* [1851
Drury, Marion R.: The life and career of James William Hott, D. D., LL. D. Late bishop of the United Brethren in Christ. *With an introduction by Lewis Bookwalter. Dayton, O.: United Brethren Publishing House 1902. pp. XIX, 21—214, ill.* [1852
Curtis, E. W.: Philip William Otterbein. *In: Quarterly Review of the United Brethren in Christ. Vol. VIII. Dayton, O. 1897. pp. 245—251.* [1853
Drury, A. W.: The life of Rev. Philip Otterbein, founder of the United Brethren in Christ. *With an introduction by bishop Weaver, D. D. Dayton, Ohio: United Brethren Publishing House. 1893. pp. XVII, 21—384.* [1853a

Kirche der Vereinigten Brüder in Christo (Alte Verfassung)
Church of the United Brethren in Christ (Old Constitution)

Church of the United Brethren in Christ. (Old Constitution.) History, description and statistics. *In: Religious bodies: 1906. Part II. Separate denominations: Washington, D. C. 1910 [= no. 894].*

pp. 650—653; . . . In: Religious bodies: 1916. Part II. 1919. pp. 694—701; . . . Statistics. History, doctrine and organization. In: Religious bodies: 1926. Part II. 1929. pp. 1367—1373. [1854

Evangelische Gruppen
Evangelical bodies

United States, Department of Commerce, Bureau of Census: Evangelical bodies. *In: Religious bodies. 1906. Part II. Separate denominations: History, description and statistics. Washington,* D. C. *1910 [= no. 894]. pp. 268—277.*
[See: Evangelical (Association) Church (no. 1856) and Evangelical Congregational Church (no. 1891).] [1855

Evangelische Kirche (ursprünglich Evangelische Gemeinschaft)
Evangelical Church (formerly Evangelical Assoziation)

United States, Department of Commerce, Bureau of Census: Evangelical Association. History, description and statistics. *In: Religious bodies: 1906. Part II. Separate denominations. Washington,* D. C. *1910 [= no. 894]. pp. 269—274.* . . . *In: Religious bodies: 1916. Part II. Washington,* D. C. *1919. pp. 265—270.* [1856
— Evangelical Church. Statistics. History, doctrine and organization. *In: Religious bodies: 1926. Part II. Washington,* D.C. *1929. pp. 522—531.* [1856a
Verhandlungen der General Conferenz der Evangelischen Gemeinschaft, gehalten zu Pittsburg, Pa. 1867. *Cleveland, O.: Buchanstalt der Evangelischen Gemeinschaft, alle vier Jahre 1867ff.—1915. English edition since 1879: Proceedings of the General Conference of the Evangelical Church* . . . [1857
Proceedings of the General Conference of the Evangelical Church. October 7—21, 1926. *Harrisburg, Pa.: The Eastern Publishing House of the Evangelical Church 1926. pp. 334.* [1858
East Pennsylvania Conference Journal, Evangelical Church, 1840—1931. Official minutes. Ninety-second session East Pennsylvania annual conference, Evangelical Church. *Vol. VII, no. 1.* Convened in First Church, Sunbury, Pa., February 26, 1931. *Published by order of the Conference . . . Harrisburg, Pa.: The Evangelical Publishing House 1931. pp. 116.* [1859

Minutes of the ninety-first annual session of the Central Pennsylvania Conference of the Evangelical Church, held in First Church, Carlisle, Pa., March 5—9, 1931. *Official record published by order of Conference . . . Harrisburg, Pa.: Publishing House of the Evangelical Church 1931. pp. 150.* [1860
Journal of the Pittsburgh Conference, Evangelical Church 1851—1931. Proceedings of the eightieth annual session Pittsburgh Conference, Evangelical Church. Held in First Evangelical Church, Johnstown, Pa. Sept. 8—13, 1931. *Published by order of Conference.* . . . *[s. l.] 1931. pp. 90.* [1861
The year book of the Evangelical Church. *Cleveland, O. — Harrisburg, Pa.: Evangelical Publishing House. 1893a Annually ff.* [1862
Albright, Raymond W.: The common heritage of the Church of the United Brethren in Christ and the Evangelical Church. *In: The Christian Union Quarterly. Baltimore, Md. July 1931. pp. 55—65.* [1863
Bowman, Thomas: Historical review of the disturbance in the Evangelical Association. *Published by authority of the Board of Publication and approved by the Boards of Bishops. Cleveland, O.: Thomas & Mattill 1894. pp. 207.* [1864
Breyfogel, S. C.: Landmarks of the Evangelical Association, *containing all the official records of the annual and general*

conferences from the days of Jacob Albright to the year 1840; and the proceedings of the East Pennsylvania Conference together with important extracts from the transactions of the General Conference from 1840 to the present time. A. D. 1800—1887. Reading, Pa.: Eagle Book Print 1888. pp. 423. [1865

Jäckel, R.: Jacob Albrecht und seine Mitarbeiter. Auf Anordnung der General-Conference der Evangelischen Gemeinschaft verfaßt. Cleveland, O.: Verlag der Evangelischen Gemeinschaft 1879. S. 335. [1866

Yeackel, R.: Jacob Albright and his colaborers. Compiled, according to the direction of the General Conference of the Evangelical Association. Translated from the German. Cleveland, O.: Publishing House of the Evangelical Association 1883. pp. 329, ill. [1867

Jäckel, R.: Geschichte der Evangelischen Gemeinschaft. Bd. I. 1750—1850. Cleveland, O.: Lauer & Mattill 1890. 475 S. Bd. II. 1850—1875. Cleveland, O.: Thomas & Mattill 1895. 368 S. [1868

Yeackel, R.: History of the Evangelical Association. Vol. 1750—1850. Cleveland, O. — Harrisburg, Pa.: Evangelical Publishing House 1894. New Print: 1924. pp. 468. [1869

— History of the Evangelical Association. 2 vols. 1750—1850; 1850—1875. Cleveland, O.: J. H. Lamb 1909. pp. 468; 344. [1870

Knobel, G. C.: The Congress of the Evangelical Association. A complete edition of the papers presented at its sessions held at the Art Institute of Chicago, Sept. 19—21, 1893. Compiled and edited by G. C. Knobel. With an introduction by S. P. Spreng. Cleveland, O.: Thomas & Mattill 1894. pp. 333, ill. [1871

[Miller, Georg]: Leben, Erfahrung und Amtsführung zweyer Evangelischer Prediger, Jacob Albrecht und Georg Miller. Sammt einem Anhang, enthaltend eine Übersicht der Lehre des Antinomianismus und der Endlichen Beharrlichkeit. Zusammen getragen und zum Druck befördert durch eine Committee ernannt von der jährlichen Conferenz Neu-Berlin: gedruckt für die Evangelische Gemeinschaft: G. Miller 1834. 176 S. [1872

Orwig, W. W.: Geschichte der Evangelischen Gemeinschaft. Erster Band: Vom Ursprung der Gemeinschaft bis zu Ende des Jahres 1845. Cleveland, O.: Carl Hammer für die Evang. Gemeinschaft 1857. 456 S., ill. [Nur Bd. I erschienen.] [1873

Orwig, W. W.: History of the Evangelical Association. Vol. I. Cleveland, O.: Chas. Hammer 1858. pp. . . . [Only vol I. issued.] [1874

The Evangelical Centennial celebration, September 26—27, 1916, observed jointly by the Evangelical Association and the United Evangelical Church under the auspices of the Historical Society of the United Evangelical Church . . . held at Dreisbach's, Lewisburg, Winfield, and New Berlin, Pa. Commemorative of the following events: (1) At Dreisbach's the holding of the First General Conference and the permanent organization of the Evangelical Association. (2) At Lewisburg, the establishing of Evangelical work in the State of New York and Canada by pioneers from the Lewisburg Class. (3) At Winfield, the organization of the Evangelical printing business, and the sending out of the first missionaries from the Eyer barn. (4) At New Berlin, the building of the First Church and first printing house in the Evangelical Association. Published by order of the Historical Society of the United Evangelical Church. John D. Shortess and A. D. Gramley, editors and publishers. Harrisburg, Pa.: Publishing House of the United Evangelical Church 1917. pp. 178, ill., map. [1875

Spreng, Samuel P.: History of the Evangelical Association. In: A history of the Disciples of Christ, the Society of Friends, the United Brethren in Christ and the Evangelical Association. New York, N. Y. The Christian Literature Co. 1894. = The American Church History Series. Vol. XII. pp. 383—439. [Bibliography p. 384.] [1876

— History of the Evangelical Association. Cleveland, O.: Publishing House of the Evangelical Association: C. Hausser 1913. pp. 120. [1877

— History of the Evangelical Church. For the use of young people, members of the Evangelical League of Christian Endeavor, brotherhoods and other groups. Revised and brought down to date, first edition in 1913 under the title „History of the Evangelical Association" [=no. 1877]. Cleveland, O. — Harrisburg, Pa.: Pub-

lishing House of the Evangelical Church. 1927. pp. 189. [1878

Stapleton, A.: Annals of the Evangelical Association of North America and history of the United Evangelical Church. *Harrisburg, Penna: Published by Publishing House of the United Evangelical Church 1900. pp. V, 9—665, ill.* [1879

— Flashlights on Evangelical history. *A volume of entertaining narratives, anecdotes and incidents, illustrative of the Evangelical work founded by Rev. Jacob Albright in A. D. 1800. Also Evangelical daughters of song. York, Pa.: Published by the Author 1908. pp. VI, 193, ill.* [1880

— „Old time Evangelical Evangelism". The life and time of Jacob Albright, founder of the Evangelical Association. *Harrisburg, Pa.: Evangelical Press 1917. pp. 143.* [1881

1800—1900 Centennial Programm. — Jubiläumsfeier der Evangelischen Gemeinschaft 1800—1900. *Linnwood Park, O. (August 7—9, 1900). Cleveland, O.: Verlegt für die Evangelische Gemeinschaft von Thomas & Mattill 1900. 64 S., ill.* [1882

1800—1900. Programm of the celebration of the Centennial of the Evangelical Association held by order of the General Conference at Linnwood Park, O., August 7—9, 1900. *Cleveland, O. Published for the Evangelical Association by Thomas & Mattill 1900. pp. 61, ill.* [1883

Shirey, J. H.-Wiest, S. L.: Centennial celebration of the organization of the first

conference of the Evangelical Church. *Held at Kleinfeltersville, Pa., Sept. 25—26, 1907. Harrisburg, Pa.: United Evangelical Press 1907. pp. 104.* [1884

Höhn, M.: Fünfzig Jahre im Predigtamte. Freud' und Leid aus dem Leben der fünfzigjährigen Dienstzeit eines Evangelischen Predigers in America. *Von ihm selbst geschrieben. Chicago, Ill. 1913. Cleveland, O.: C. Hauser 1913. 271 S., ill.* [1885

Horn, W.: Leben und Wirken von Bischof John Jakob Escher. *Cleveland, O.: Verlagshaus der Evangelischen Gemeinschaft 1907. 438 S.* [1886

Spreng, S. P.: The life and labors of John Seybert, first bishop of the Evangelical Association. *Cleveland, O,: Evangelical Publishing House 1888. pp. 439, ill.* [1887

Horn, W.: Bischof Seybert. Ein Mann nach dem Herzen Gottes. *Dargestellt von W. Horn. Stuttgart: Buchdruckerei und Verlag der Ev. Gemeinschaft. IV, 293 S.* [1888

Yost, William: Erinnerungen von Rev. William Yost, Prediger der Evangelischen Gemeinschaft. *Zweite erweiterte Auflage. Cleveland, O.: Verlagshaus der Evang. Gemeinschaft 1911. X, 310 S.* [1889

— Reminiscences by Rev. William Yost, preacher of the Evangelical Association. *Second revised edition. Cleveland, O.: Publishing House of the Evangelical Association 1911. pp. IX, 304.* [1890

Evangelische Kongregations-Kirche (ursprünglich Vereinigte Evangelische Kirche)

Evangelical Congregational Church (formerly United Evangelical Church)

United States, Department of Commerce, Bureau of Census: United Evangelical Church. History, description and statistics. *In: Religious bodies: 1906. Part II. Separate denominations. Washington, D. C. 1910 [= no. 894]. pp. 274—277. ... In: Religious bodies: 1916. Part II. Washington, D. C. 1919. pp. 705—708.* [1891

— Evangelical Congregational Church. Statistics. History, doctrine and orga-

nization. *In: Religious bodies: 1926. Part II. Washington, D. C. 1929. pp. 532—537.* [1891a

Stapleton, A.: Annals of the Evangelical Association and history of the United Evangelical Church. *Harrisburg, Pa.: Published by Publishing House of the United Evangelical Church 1900. pp. V, 9—665, ill.* [1892

Allgemeines Ältestenamt der „Churches of God"
General Eldership of the Churches of God

United States, Department of Commerce, Bureau of Census: Churches of God in North America, General Eldership of the . . . History, description and statistics. *In: Religious bodies: 1906. Part II. Separate denominations. Washington, D. C. 1910 [= no. 894]. pp. 203—207.* . . . *In: Religious bodies: 1916. Part II. Washington, D. C. 1919. pp. 212—216.* . . . Statistics. History, doctrine and organization. *In: Religious bodies: 1926. Part II. Washington, D. C. 1929. pp. 405—411.* [1893

Egle, William Henry: Ordination of Rev. John Winebrenner. *In: Notes and Queries. Edited by W. H. Egle. First series, part V. Harrisburg, Pa. 1881. pp. 199—202. Reprint in: First and second series, vol. II. Harrisburg, Pa. 1895. pp. 50—52.* [1894

Forney, C. H.: History of the Churches of God in the United States of North America. *Authorized by the General Eldership of the Churches of God, in* session at Fort Scott, Kansas, in 1909; read and approved by the Book Committee of the Board of Directors. *Published by the Board of Directors of the Publishing House and Book Rooms of the Churches of God. Harrisburg, Pa.: Publishing House of the Churches of God. 1914. pp. XIV, 933, ill.* [Bibliography pp. 913—918.] [1895

Hamilton, Hugh: Some Remarks. Made upon presentation of the Historical Society of Dauphin County, Penn. of a „History of the Churches of God in the United States of North America." by Rev. Christian Henry Forney, DD. LL. D., of Harrisburg, Pa. [= no. 1895]. Also about John Winnebrenner, of Harrisburg, Pa., the Founder of the Churches of God. *[s. l.; s. d.] pp. 6.* [1896

Yahn, S. G.: History of the Churches of God in America. *Third edition. Harrisburg, Pa.: Central Publishing House 1926. pp. 149, ill.* [1897

Deutsche Katholiken

German Catholics

The official Catholic directory for the year of our Lord 1930. *Containing ecclesiastical statistics of the United States, Alaska, Philippine Islands, the Canal Zone . . . Complete Edition. New York: P. J. Kenedy & Sons 1930. pp. 136 (4), 1118; 221; 204, ill.* [1898

Bernt, Joseph: Deutsche Katholiken in Amerika. *In: Das Buch der Deutschen in Amerika. Philadelphia, Pa., 1909 [= Nr. 59]. S. 249—259.* [1899

[Bonenkamp, W.-Jessing, J.-Müller, J. B.]: Schematismus der deutschen und der deutsch-sprechenden Priester, sowie der deutschen Katholiken Gemeinden in den Vereinigten Staaten Nord-Amerika's, nebst einer Statistik der deutschen Pfarrschulen, der Wirkungskreise der deutschen Katholiken und genauen Verzeichnissen aller römisch-katholischen Diöcesen, Bischöfe, höheren Unterrichts- und Wohltätigkeits Anstalten in der nordamerikanischen Union. *Begonnen von W. Bonenkamp, fortgesetzt von J. Jessing, vollendet von J. B. Müller. St. Louis, Mo.: B. Herder 1882. XV, 447 S.* [1900

[Carroll, John]: Rev. John Carroll to German Catholics in Philadelphia, 1788. *From original draft in Archives at Baltimore. In: The American Catholic Historical Researches. Vol. VII. Parkesburg, Pa. 1890. pp. 180—183.* [1901

Conner, Philip S. P.: The early register of the Catholic Church in Pennsylvania. *In: Records of the American Catholic Historical Society of Philadelphia. Vol. II. Philadelphia, Pa. 1886—88, pp. 22—28.* [1902

[Doerfler, Bruno]: Sources of information about early German priests. *In: American Catholic Historical Researches. New series, vol. I. Parkesburg, Pa. 1905. pp. 151—153.* [1903

Guilddy, Peter: The life and times of John Carroll, Archbishop of Baltimore (1735—1815.) *New York, N. Y. The Encyclopedia Press 1922. pp. XI—XIV, (1), 864, ill.*

[Germans in Pensylvania. pp. 244—245; in Philadelphia, Pa. pp. 292—295; in New York. p. 628; in Baltimore, Md. pp. 723—728.] [1904

Hasset, M. M.: A historical sketch of the Diocese of Harrisburg. *In: Records of the American Catholic Historical Society of Philadelphia, Pa. Vol. XXIX. Philadelphia, Pa. 1918. pp. 194—218.* [1905

Hertkorn, Francis J.: Our Catholic German forefathers in Pennsylvania. *In: Official Souvenir. 68th Convention German Roman Catholic Central Verein, U. S. A., 31st Convention German Roman Catholic Staats-Verband of Pennsylvania. . . . Allentown, Penna. — Aug. 23—27, 1924. pp. [(80)] (17), ill.* [1906

[Kenrick, Peter R.]: Report of the situation and condition of the Diocese of Philadelphia, 'given by the Rev. Peter R. Kenrick, Vicar-general of the same diocese, from Rome, November 21, 1838. *In: The American Catholic Historical Researches. New series, vol. I. No. 2. Parkersburg, Pa. 1905. pp. 144—146.* [1907

[Kohlmann, Anthony]: Rev. Anthony Kohlman's, S. J. visitation of Germans of Pennsylvania in 1807. *[Catholic Almanac 1842.] Reprint in: The American Catholic Historical Researches. New series, vol. I. No. 2. Parkesburg, Pa. 1905. pp. 130—131.* [1908

Lambuig, A. A.: A history of the Catholic Church in the Dioceses of Pittsburg and Allegheny from its establishment to the present time. *New York, N. Y., Cincinnati, O., St. Louis, N. W.,: Benzinger Brothers. 1880. pp. 531, ill.* [1909

Pekari, Matthew Anthony: The German Catholics in the United States of America. *In: Records of the American Catholic Historical Society. Vol. XXXVI, no. 4. Philadelphia, Pa. 1925. pp. 305—358.* [1910

Schrott, Lambert: Pioneer German Catholics in the American colonies (1734—1784). *New York City, N. Y.: The United States Catholic Historical Society 1933. pp. 139.*

= *United States Catholic Historical Society. Monograph Series 13. (Part I).*
[1911

Shea, John Gilmary: The Catholic Church in colonial days. The thirteen colonies, the Ottowa and Illinois country, Louisiana, Florida, Texas, New Mexico and Arizona 1521—1763. *New York, N. Y. John G. Shea; Rahway, N. J.: The Mershon Co. Press 1886. pp. XXIX, 9—663, ill., maps.* [1912

— Life and times of the most Rev. John Carroll, bishop and first archbishop of Baltimore. Embracing the history of the Catholic Church in the United States. 1763—1815. *New York, N. Y. John G. Shea; Rahway, N. J.: The Mershon Co. Press 1888. pp. 15—695. ill.* [1913

— History of the Catholic Church in the United States. From the division of the Diocese of Baltimore, 1808, and death of Archbishop Carroll, 1815, to the fifth Provincial Council of Baltimore, 1843. *New York, N. Y. John G. Shea; Rahway, N. J.: The Mershon Co. Press 1890. pp. XVI, 25—734, ill.; . . . From the fifth Provincial Council of Baltimore, 1843 to the second Plenary Council of Baltimore, 1866. New York, N. Y. . . . 1892. pp. XXIX, 23—727.* [1914

Weber, N. A.: The rise of national Catholic churches in the United States. *In: The Catholic Historical Review. Vol. I. Washington, D. C. 1916. pp. 422—434.* [1915

German Catholic history. *[Note] In: The American Catholic Historical Researches. Vol. XXIV. Parkesburg, Pa. 1907. p. 185.* [1916

The Germans of Pennsylvania not „passing to the camps of the priests". 1755—56. *In: The American Catholic Historical Researches. Vol. XXI. Parkesburg, Pa. 1904. p. 140.* [1917

German Catholics in Pennsylvania. *In: The American Catholic Historical Researches. New series, vol I. Parkesburg 1905. pp. 80—81.* [1918

Seeking German priests for Pennsylvania in 1785. *In: The American Historical Researches. Vol. VIII. Parkesburg, Pa. 1891. pp. 131—132.* [1919

Schuyler, William Bishop: Memoirs of the Rev. Augustin Bally, S. J. *In: Records of the American Catholic Historical Society of Philadelphia. Vol. XX. Philadelphia, Pa. 1909. pp. 209—249, ill.* [Born: March 8, 1706 in Merxplas, Belgium.] [1920

Foin, Julius C.: Rev. Louis Barth, a pioneer missionary in Pennsylvania and administrator of the Diocese of Philadelphia. *In: Records of the American Catholic Historcial Society. Vol. II. Philadelphia, Pa. 1886—88. pp. 29—37.* [Louis Barth de Walbach, born of noble parentage in Alsace at Münster, Nov. 1, 1764.] [1921

Molyneux, Robert: Funeral sermon on the death of the Rev. Ferdinand Farmer, who departed this life the 17th of August, 1786, in the 66th year of his age. *Philadelphia, Pa.: C. Talbot 1786. pp. 8. Reprint in: The American Catholic Historical Researches. Vol. VII. Philadelphia, Pa. 1890, pp. 124—128.* [Born, in Swabia, Germany, Oct. 13, 1720.] [1922

The Rev. Lawrence Graessel, one of the first German pioneer priests in the United States and chosen first coadjutorbishop of Baltimore. *[Annexed documents translated by J. F. Meifuss.] In: The American Catholic Historical Researches. Vol. XXI. Parkesburg, Pa. 1904. pp. 49—58.* [Born Aug. 18, 1753, Ruhmannsfelden in the Bavarian Forest, arrived in Philadelphia 1786.] [1923

Paul Miller, the sacristan of Conewago, and one of the first of the congregation of old St. Joseph's, Philadelphia. A deed of trust in his favor by Father Greaton as foreign born Catholics could not hold in provincial Pennsylvania. *In: The American Catholic Historical Researches. Vol. XVI. Parkesburg, Pa. 1899. pp. 128—133.* [1924

Die hochdeutsche Sprache und die pennsylvanischdeutsche Mundart

German Language and Pennsylvania-German Dialect

Brauer, E.: „Wird die deutsche Sprache in Amerika bestehen oder untergehen?" *In: Practische Belehrungen und Ratschläge für Reisende und Auswanderer nach Amerika. Von E. Brauns. Braunschweig 1829 [= Nr. 31]. S. 210—222.* [1924a

Eiselmeier, J.: Die deutsche Sprache als Staatssprache in den Vereinigten Staaten. *In: Die neue Zeit (The New Era) Wochenschrift für Politik, Kunst und Literatur. XI. Jahr Nr. 53. New Ulm, Minn. 31. Mai 1930. S. 5; s. a. Bd. XIII, Nr. 6, 11. Juli 1932. S. 15—16.* [1925

— Mühlenberg und die deutsche Sprache. *In: Die Neue Zeit (The New Era), Wochenschrift für Politik, Kunst und Literatur. Bd. XIII, Nr. 23. New Ulm, Minn. 7. Nov. 1932. S. 6—7.* [1926

Faust, A. B.: „German language" its application as official language in the United States and especially in Pennsylvania. *In: The German element in the United States. By A. B. Faust. Second edition. New York, N. Y. 1927 [= no. 42]. Appendix. pp. 652—656.* [1927

Gehrke, William H.: The transition from the German to the English language in North Carolina. *In: The North Carolina Historical Review. Vol. XII. Boston, Mass.: 1935. pp. 1—19.* [1927a

Harbaugh, Linn: The language question as it confronted old Marshall. *In: The Reformed Church Review. Fourth series, vol. X. Philadelphia, Pa. 1906. pp. 448—463.* [1928

Kloß, Heinz: Deutsch als Gottesdienstsprache in den Vereinigten Staaten von Amerika. *In: Der Auslanddeutsche. Halbmonatsschrift für Auslanddeutschtum und Auslandkunde. Mitteilungen des Deutschen Ausland-Instituts, Stuttgart. Jg. XIV. Stuttgart, 1931. S. 630—634; 689—692; 715—721.* [1929

— Die deutsche Sprache in der pennsylvanischen Schule. *In: Die Westmark.*

Monatsschrift für deutsche Kultur. Jg. III, Heft 2. Heidelberg-Saarbrücken S. 386—395. [1929a

Learned, Marion Dexter: German as a culture element in American education. *A lecture delivered before the National German American Teachers' Association at Cincinnati, O., on July 8, 1898. Milwaukee, Wis.: Freidenker Publishing Co., printers. 1898. pp. 24.* [1930

Lohr, Otto: Deutsch als „Landessprache" der Vereinigten Staaten? *In: Mitteilungen der Akademie zur wissenschaftlichen Erforschung und zur Pflege des Deutschtums. Deutsche Akademie. Jg. 1931. Heft 4. München, 1931. S. 283—290.* [1931

— Die deutsche Sprache in Nordamerika im 17. Jahrhundert. *In: Mitteilungen der Akademie zur wissenschaftlichen Erforschung und zur Pflege des Deutschtums. Deutsche Akademie. Jg. 1933. Nr. 1. München 1933. S. 90—103.* [1932

Mühlenberg, Frederick August Conrad: Rede vor der incorporirten Deutschen Gesellschaft in Philadelphia, im Staat Pennsylvanien, am 20sten September, 1794, von *Friedrich August Mühlenberg, dermaligen Präsident der Gesellschaft. Auf Order derselben zum Druck befördert. Philadelphia, Pa.: Steiner und Kämmerer 1795. 15 S. [Über die deutschen Schulen, die deutsche Sprache in Pennsylvanien und die Notwendigkeit der Erlernung des Englischen.]* [1933

Rattermann, H. A.: Die deutsche Sprache in der amerikanischen Schule. *Vortrag gehalten in der öffentlichen Versammlung des „Deutsch-Amerikanischen Lehrertages" in Davenport, Ia. am 4. Aug. 1881. In: Abhandlungen, Vorträge und Reden. Bilder aus Deutsch-Amerikanischer Geschichte. Vermischte Schriften. Erster Teil = H. A. Rattermann. Gesammelte ausgewählte Werke. Bd. XVI.*

Cincinnati, O.: Selbstverlag des Verfassers 1912. S. 266—290. [1933a
Severinghaus, J. D.: The German language in the educational institutions of the Lutheran Church in the United States. *In: The Quarterly Review of the Evangelical Lutheran Church. New series, vol. III. Gettysburg, Pa. 1873. pp. 228—253.* [1934
Spieckermann, A.: The language question in the Lutheran Church of America. *In: The Lutheran Quarterly. Vol. XXXVI. Gettysburg, Pa. 1906. pp. 83—92.* [1935
Deutsch oder Englisch. Ein Gespräch zwischen zwei Nachbarn, Sebastian and Jacob, über die deutsche Sprache in Nordamerika. *Allentown, Pa.: Druck und Verlag von Trexler, Harlacher & Weiser 1862. 11 S.* [1936
Die deutsche Sprache in Pennsylvania. *In: Der Deutsche Pionier. Jg. I. Cincinnati, O. 1869—1870. S. 208—212.* [1937
Die deutsche Sprache in den deutschen Kirchen. *In: Mitteilungen des Deutschen Pionier Vereins von Philadelphia. Heft 20, 1911. [Philadelphia, Pa.] 1911. S. 23—26.* [1938
Deutsch in den Schulen von Allentown, Pa. *Reprint from: „Allentown Lecha Bote" Febr. 1, 1876. In: Der Deutsche Pionier. Jg. VIII. Cincinnati, O. 1876—1877. S. 66—67.* [1939

Bender, Ruth: A study of the Pennsylvania-German dialect as spoken in Johnson County Iowa. *Thesis of M. A., State University of Iowa, Iowa City, Ia. 1929. (Typewritten) pp. 72.* [1940
Bonneheur, Armin de: Pennsylvania Dutch. *In: The Nation. A weeckly journal devoted to politics, literature, science & art. Vol. LXVII. New York, N. Y. The Evening Post Publishing Co. 1898. Correspondence to the editor. p. 482.* [1941
Ellis, Alexander J.: „Pennsylvania German the analogue of Chaucer's English." *In: On early English pronounciation, with especial reference to Shakspere and Chaucer . . . By Alexander J. Ellis. Part III. London: Published for the Early English Text Society by Kegan Paul Trench, Trübner & Co. 1871. [Reprint 1910.] — Early English Text Society. Extra series, XIV. pp. 652—663.* [1942
Fisher, H. L.: Kurzweil un Zeitfertreib odder Pennsylfaanisch Deutsche Folks

Lieder fon . . . *York, Pa.: Ferlaag fon Fischer Brüder 1882. 186 S. [Glossary S. 156—186.]* [1943
Götz, Karl: Pennsylvanisch Dutch. Ein pfälzisch-englischer Dialekt. *In: Pfälzisches Museum. Jg. XLVI — Pfälzische Heimatkunde. Jg. XXV. Speyer 1929. Heft 5/6. S. 162—164.* [1944
Grumbine, Lee L.: The Pennsylvania-German dialect. *A study of its status as a spoken dialect and form of literary expression, with reference to its capabilities and limitations, and lines illustrating same. Written for the Pennsylvania-German Society. In: The Pennsylvania-German Society. Proceedings and Addresses . . . 1901. Vol. XII. Lancaster, Pa. 1903. Separate pagination. pp. (1), 37—99, ill.* [1945
Haldeman, Samuel S.: On the German vernacular of Pennsylvania. *In: Transactions of the American Philological Association. 1869—70. Hartford: Published by the Association, printed by Case, Lockwood & Brainard 1871. pp. 80—83.* [1946
— Pennsylvania Dutch: A dialect of South German with an infusion of English. *Philadelphia, Pa.: Reformed Church Publication Board 1872. pp. VIII, 69.* [1947
Hark, J. Max: En hondfull Färsh: Experiments in Pennsylvania-German verse, with an introduction on „The capability of the Pennsylvania-German for poetic expression." *In: The Pennsylvania-German Society, Proceedings and Addresses at Ephrata, Oct. 20, 1899. Vol. X. Lancaster, Pa. 1900. Separate pagination. pp. 31.* [1948
Hays, H. M.: On the German dialect spoken in the Valley of Virginia. *In: Dialect notes. Publication of the American Dialect Society. Vol. III. Part IV. New Haven, Conn.: Published by the Society; printed by The Tuttle, Morehouse & Taylor Co. 1908. pp. 263—278. Reprint in: The Pennsylvania-German. Vol. X. Lititz, Pa. 1909. pp. 510—520.* [1949
Heydrick, B. A.: Provincialism of southeastern Pennsylvania. A list of dialect expressions, chiefly of Pennsylvania-German origin, found in Lancaster and adjoining counties. *In: German American Annals. New series, vol. V. Philadelphia, Pa. 1907. pp. 307—313; 370—381; Vol. VI. 1908. pp. 32—52.* [1950

Hoffman, W. J.: Grammatic notes and vocabulary of the Pennsylvania German dialect. *Read before the American Philosophical Society, Dec. 21, 1888. In: Proceedings of the American Philosophical Society held at Philadelphia for promoting useful knowledge. Vol. XXVI. Philadelphia, Pa. 1889. pp. 187—285. [Vocabulary: pp. 200—285.]* [1951

Horne, Abraham R.: Pennsylvania German manual, for pronouncing, speaking and writing English. A guide book for schools and families. *In 3 parts: Part I. Pronouncing exercises. Part II. Pennsylvania German reader. Part III. Pennsylvania German dictionary. Kutztown, Pa.: Urik & Gehring 1875. pp. 170, ill.*
Revised and enlarged edition. Allentown, Pa.: National Educator Print. 1896. pp. 415, ill., maps.
Horn's Pennsylvania German manual. How Pennsylvania German is spoken and written for pronouncing speaking and writing English. *Third edition. Enlarged and profusely illustrated. Allentown, Pa.: T. K. Horne 1905. pp. 192; 146, ill.*
Fourth edition. Allentown, Pa.: Press of Democrat Publishing Co. 1910. pp. 372, ill. [1952

Kloß, Heinz: Nebensprachen — Niederländisch, Deutsch, Jiddisch, Africans, Friesisch, Pennsylvania-Deutsch —. *Eine sprachliche Studie über die Beziehungen eng verwandter Sprachgemeinschaften. Wien—Leipzig: Wilhelm Braumüller, Universitäts-Verlagsbuchhandlung 1929. 60 S.* [1953
— Varianten der pennsylvaniadeutschen Sprache. *In: Monatshefte für deutschen Unterricht. Formerly Monatshefte für deutsche Sprache und Pädagogik. A journal devoted to the teaching of German in the schools and colleges of America. Vol. XXI, no. 8. Madison, Wisc: Published at the University of Wisconsin 1929. S. 225—230.* [1954
— Etwas von der pennsylvaniadeutschen Sprache. *In: Hamburg-Amerika-Post. Bd. II, Heft 9. Hamburg 1930. S. 286 —292.* [1954a

Knortz, Karl: Deutsch-Pennsylvanisch. *In: Der Deutsche Pionier. Jg. V. Cincinnati, O. 1873—1874. S. 66—70.* [1955

[Kriebel, H. W.]: The spelling of our dialect. *[By the editor of the Pennsylvania-German and its literary department.] In:*

The Pennsylvania-German. Vol. X. Lititz, Pa. 1919. pp. 235—237. [1956

Lambert, Marcus Bachman: A dictionary of the non — English words of the Pennsylvania-German dialect. *With an appendix. Published by the Pennsylvania-German Society. Lancaster, Pa.: Lancaster Press, Inc. 1924. In: The Pennsylvania-German Society. Proceedings and Addresses ... 1919. Vol. XXX. Lancaster, Pa. 1924. Separate pagination. pp. XXXI, 193.* [1957

Learned, Marion Dexter: The Pennsylvania German dialect. *In: The American Journal of Philology. Vol. IX. Baltimore, Md. 1888. pp. 64—83; 178—197; 326—339; 424—456; Vol. X. 1889. pp. 288—315.* [1958
— The Pennsylvania German dialect. *Baltimore, Md.: Press of Isaac Friedenwald 1889. pp. (4), 114.* [1959
— Application of the phonetic system of the American Dialect Society to Pennsylvania German. *In: Modern Language Notes. Vol. V. Baltimore Md. 1890. [Col. 238—241] pp. 119—121.* [1960

[Leisenring, Edmund Daniel]: Pennsylvanichs-Deutsch. Brief an „der deutsch Pionier" von „N'alter Pennsylvanier". *In: Der Deutsche Pionier. Jg. XIV. Cincinnati, O. 1882—1883. S. 70—71. Reprint in: The Pennsylvania-German. Vol. IX. Cleona, Pa. 1908. p. 325.* [1961

Lins, James C.: Common sence Pennsylvania German dictionary, containing nearly all the Pennsylvania German words in common use, with their English equivalents. *Kempton, Pa.: Published by James C. Lins 1887. pp. (2), 80.*
Revised and enlarged edition. Reading, Pa.: James C. Lins 1895. pp. (2), 9—170. [1962

Long, F. A.: Is the dialect dying out? *In: The Pennsylvania-German. Vol. IX. Cleona, Pa. 1908. p. 85.* [1963

Mencken, H. L.: „Non — English dialects in America. (1) German." *In: The American language. An inquiry into the development of English in the United States. By H. L. Mencken. New York, N. Y.: Alfred A. Knopf 1929. pp. 407 —410.* [1964

Prettyman, William: Dialect peculiarities in the Carlisle vernacular. *In: German American Annals. New series, vol. V. Philadelphia, Pa. 1907. pp. 67—79.* [1965

Rauch, Edward H.: The Pennsylvania Dutchman. *Published by Edward H. Rauch, author of the Pit Schweffelbrenner" papers etc. Vol. I, no. 1—3. Lancaster, Pa.: Wylie & Griest, printers, January, 1873 — March, 1873.* [1966
— Rauch's Pennsylvania Dutch handbook. A book for instruction. — Rauch's Pennsylvania Deitsh Hand-Booch. En Booch for Inshtructa. *By E. H. Rauch (,,Pit Schweffelbrenner"). Mauch Chunk, Pa.: E. H. Rauch 1879. pp. VIII, 9—238.* [1967

Rupp, I. D.: Eppes über Pennsylvanisch-Deutsch. *In: Der Deutsche Pionier. Jg. II. Cincinnati, O. 1870—1871. S. 307—309.
Reprint in: The Pennsylvania-German. Vol. IX. Cleona, Pa. 1908. pp. 230—231.* [1968

[Schoepf, Johann David]: The Pennsylvania German dialect in 1783. *Quoted from ,,German American Annals, Sept.-Dec., 1910. In: The Pennsylvania-German. Vol. XII. Lititz, Pa. 1911. pp. 368—369.* [1969

Schuler, H. A.: The spelling of our dialect. *In: The Pennsylvania-German. Vol. VII. Lebanon, Pa. 1906. pp. 31—35.* [1970

Spieker, G. F.: Is Pennsylvania-German used in the pulpit? *In: The Pennsylvania-German. Vol. XI. Lititz, Pa. 1910. pp. 252—253.* [1971

Stahr, J. S.: Pennsylvania German. *Delivered before the students of Franklin and Marshall College, at the opening of the Spring Term, 1870. In: The Mercersburg Review. Vol. XVII. Philadelphia, Pa. 1870. pp. 618—463.* [1972

Stibitz: ,,Pure German" and ,,Pennsylvania-Dutch." *In: The Pennsylvania-German. Vol. IX. Cleona, Pa. 1908. p. 36.* [1973

Wood, Ralph: Das Pennsylvaniendeutschtum und seine Mundart. *In: Mein Heimatland. Jg. XXIV. Freiburg i. Br. 1937. S. 13—23.* [1973a

Yoder, Edward: The study of the Pennsylvania-German dialect. *In: The Mennonite Quarterly Review. Vol. VI. — Goshen, Ind. Scottdale, Pa., 1932. pp. 59—62.* [1974

Ziegler, Charles Calvin: Is Pennsylvania-German a dialect? *In: The Pennsylvania-German. Vol. IX. Cleona, Pa. 1908. pp. 66—68.* [1975

Pennsylvania Dutch. *[Ausführungen über die pennsylvanisch-deutsche Mundart, veranlaßt durch Bemerkungen von Ph. H. Earle Gibbon in ihrem Buche ,,Pennsylvania Dutch and other essays", Philadelphia, Pa. 1872.] In: Der Deutsche Pionier. Jg. IV. Cincinnati, O. 1872—1873. S. 218—220; 249—251; 272—277; see also: Schreiben an den ,,Deutschen Pionier" von ,,Der alta Kunradt". S. 298—300.* [1976

Pennsylvanisch-Deutsch. *In: Deutsch-Amerikanisches Conservations-Lexicon... bearbeitet von Alexander J. Schem. Bd. VIII. New York, N. Y.: 1873. S. 573—579.* [1977

Deutsch-Pennsylvanisch. *Abdruck aus ,,Philadelphia Demokrat". In: Der Deutsche Pionier. Jg. XVI. Cincinnati, O. 1884—1885. S. 225—227.* [1978

Wörterbücher und Verzeichnisse von pennsylvanischdeutschen Wörtern

Dictionaries and Lists of Pennsylvania-German Words

Bender, Ruth: A study of the Pennsylvania-German dialect as spoken in Johnson County, Iowa. *Thesis of M. A., State University of Iowa, Iowa City, Ia. 1929. (Typewritten) pp. 72.* *[gives more than 200 words taken from the oral speech of the community.]* [1979

Fisher, H. L.: „Glossery". *In: Kurzweil un Zeitfertreib odder Pennsylfaanisch Deutsche Folks Lieder fon . . . York, Pa. 1882 [= no. 1943]. S. 156—186.* [1980

Harbaugh, H.: „Wortverzeichniß". *In: Harbaugh's Harfe. Gedichte in Pennsylvanisch-Deutscher Mundart. Herausgegeben von B. Bausman. Phildelphia, Pa.: Reformed Church Publication Board 1870. S. 111—121.* [1981

Heydrick, B. A.: Provincialism of southeastern Pennsylvania. A list of dialect expressions, chiefly of Pennsylvania-German origin, found in Lancaster and adjoining counties. *In: German American. Annals. New series, vol. V. Philadelphia, Pa. 1907. pp. 307—381; Vol. VI. 1908. pp. 32—52.* [1982

Hoffman, W. J.: „Vocabulary". *In: Grammatic notes and vocabulary of the Pennsylvania-German dialect. By W. J. Hoffman. In: Proceedings of the American Philosophical Society held at Philadelphia for promoting useful knowledge. Vol. XXVI. Philadelphia, Pa. 1889 [= no. 1951]. pp. 200—285.* [1983

Horne, Abraham R.: Pennsylvania German dictionary. *In: Pennsylvania German manual, for pronouncing, speaking and writing English. A guide-book for schools and families. In 3 parts. By A. R. Horne. Kutztown, Pa. 1875 [=no. 1952]. pp. 95—169; In: Revised and enlarged edition. Allentown, Pa. 1896. pp. . . . .; In: Third edition. Allentown, Pa. 1905. pp. . . . .; 1—146; In: Fourth edition. Allentown, Pa. 1910. pp. 226—371.* [1984

King, Wilbur L.: Pennsylvania German plant names. *In: The Pennsylvania-German. Vol. XII. Lititz, Pa. 1911. pp. 98—109.* [1985

Lambert, Marcus Bachman: A dictionary of the non-English words of the Pennsylvania-German dialect. *With an appendix. Published by the Pennsylvania-German Society. Lancaster, Pa.: Lancaster Press, Inc. 1924. In: The Pennsylvania-German Society. Proceedings and Addresses . . . 1919. Vol. XXX. Lancaster, Pa. 1924. Separate pagination. pp. XXXI, 193.* [1986

A number of Pennsylvania-German names which seemingly are not listed by Lambert *[see no. 1986]. In: The Perkiomen Region. Vol. III, no. 3. Pennsburg, Pa. 1925. pp. 42—43.* [1987

Learned, Marion Dexter: „Character of English mixture in Pennsylvania-German words." *Word list of the article: The Pennsylvania-German dialect [= no. 1959]. In: The American Journal of Philology. Vol. X. Baltimore, Md. 1889. pp. 295—304. In: Separate print . . . Baltimore, Md. 1889 [= no. 1958]. pp. 94—103.* [1988

Lick, David E.-Brendle, Thomas R.: Plant names and plant lore among the Pennsylvania Germans. *In: The Pennsylvania-German Society. Proceedings and Addresses . . . Vol. XXXIII. Lancaster, Pa. 1923. Separate pagination pp. XIX, 21—300.* [1989

Lins, James C.: Common sence Pennsylvania German dictionary, *containing nearly all the Pennsylvania-German words in common use, with their English equivalents. Kempton, Pa.: Published by James C. Lins. 1887. pp. (2), 80; Revised and enlarged edition. Reading, Pa.: James C. Lins 1895. pp. (2), 9—170.* [1990

Mell, C. D.: Pennsylvania German plant names. *In: The Pennsylvania-German. Vol. XI. Lititz, Pa. 1910. pp. 543—546; Addenda see: p. 636; pp. 701—702.*
[1991
— Pennsylvania German names of trees. *In: The Pennsylvania-German. Vol. XI. Lititz, Pa. 1910. pp. 706—708.* [1992
Mercer, Henry C.: Tools of the nation maker. *A description catalogue of objects in the Museum of the Historical Society of Bucks County, Pa. Collected and arranged by . . . Doylestown, Pa. 1897 [= no. 2675].* With Pennsylvania German index. *pp. 85—87.* [1993

Rauch, Edward H.:Rauch's Pennsylvania Dutch hand-book. A book for instruction. — Rauch's Pennsylvania Deitsch Hand-Booch. En Booch for Inshructa. *By . . . („Pit Schweffelbrenner"). Mauch Chunk, Pa.: E. H. Rauch 1879. pp. VIII, 9—238.* [1994
Saur's „Kleines Kräuterbuch". *In: The Pennsylvania-German. Vol. XII. Lititz, Pa. 1911. pp. 105—109.* [1995
A list of Pennsylvania-German names of birds. *In: The Perkiomen Region. Vol. II, no. 4. Pennsburg, Pa. 1923. pp. 64—65; More names for the birds. Vol. III, no. 1. 1924. p. 17.* [1996

Deutsche Drucke, Verfasser und Drucker

German Printings, Authors and Printers

Bausman, Lottie M.: A bibliography of Lancaster County, Pa. 1745—1912. Publication of the Pennsylvania Federation of Historical Societies. Philadelphia, Pa.: Patterson & White Co. 1916. pp. IV, 460. [1997

Bender, Harold S.: Two centuries of American Mennonite literature. A critical bibliography of Mennonitica Americana. . . . 1727—1927. In: The Mennonite Quarterly Review. Vol. I. Goshen, Ind. 1927. No. 1. pp. 34—53; No. 2. pp. 46 —72; No. 4. pp. 61—79. Vol. II. 1928. No. 1. pp. 16—55; No. 2. pp. 124—150; No. 3. pp. 206—224.
Revised reprint: . . . 1727—1928. Published by the Mennonite Historical Society, Goshen College, Goshen, Indiana. Goshen, Ind.: Goshen Printery 1929. pp. XII, (2), 181, ill.
= Studies in Anabaptist and Mennonite History. . . . Published by the Mennonite Historical ⸺ Society, Goshen College, Goshen, Ind.
[Review see no. 2006] [1998

— A brief summary of American Mennonite literature. In: Christian Monitor. A monthly magazine for the home. Vol. XX. Scottdale, Pa. 1928. pp. 50—52. [1999

— The literature and hymnology of the Mennonites of Lancaster County, Pa. In: The Mennonite Quarterly Review. Vol. VI. Goshen, Ind. — Scottdale, Pa. 1932. pp. 156—168. [2000

Benner, Edwin B.: Enos Benner, printer. In: The Perkiomen Region. Vol. IV, no. 1. Pennsburg, Pa. 1926. pp. 19—26, ill. [2001

Bittinger, Lucy Forney: German-American literature. In: The Lutheran Quarterly. Vol. XLIII. Gettysburg, Pa. 1913. pp. 375—388. [2002

Brumbaugh, Martin G.: Famous Pennsylvania-Germans. Christopher Sower, jr. In: The Pennsylvania-German. Vol. II. Lebanon, Pa. 1901. pp. 51—65, ill. [2003

Cassel, Abraham H.: The German almanac of Christopher Sauer. In: The Pennsyl-

vania Magazine of History and Biography. Vol. VI. Philadelphia, Pa. 1882. pp. 58—68. [2004

Coffman, Magdalena: Mennonite authors past and present. In: Christian Monitor. A monthly magazine for the home. Vol. XVII, no. 5. Scottdale, Pa. 1925. pp. 147—148. [2005

Correll, Ernst: Two centuries of American Mennonite literature: an appraisal [Review of no. 1998]. In: The Mennonite Quarterly Review. Vol. IV. Goshen, Ind. — Scottdale, Pa. 1930. pp. 291— 302. [2006

Croll, P. C.: Lebanon County, Pa, imprints and bibliography. In: Papers read before the Lebanon County Historical Society. Vol. IV. 1906—1909. Lebanon, Pa. 1909. pp. 153—199. [2007

Dapp, Charles Frederick: Johann Heinrich Miller. In: German American Annals. New series, vol. XIV. Philadelphia, Pa. 1916. pp. 118—136. [2008

— The evolution of an American patriot. Being an intimate study of the patriotic activities of John Henry Miller, German printer, publisher and editor of the American Revolution. Lancaster, Pa.: Lancaster Press, Inc. 1924. = Part XXXII. „A narrative and critical history," prepared at the request of the Pennsylvania-German Society. In: The Pennsylvania-German Society. Proceedings and Addresses . . . 1921. Vol. XXXII. Lancaster, Pa. 1924. Separate pagination. pp. 5—68, ill. [2009

Diffenderffer, F. R.: Early German printers of Lancaster and the issues of their press. In: Papers and Addresses of the Lancaster County Historical Society. Vol. VIII. Lancaster, Pa. 1904. pp. 53—83, ill. [2010

Dubbs, Jos. Henry: The pioneers of German literature in America. In: The Mercersburg Review. Vol. XXV. Philadelphia, Pa. 1878. pp. 371—385. [2011

Faust, Albert Bernhardt: „German." In: The Cambridge History of American Literature. Edited by William Peterfield

Trent, John Erskine, Stuart P. Sherman, Carl van Doren. Vol. IV. ,,Later national literature: part III." New York, N. Y.: G. P. Putnam's Sons 1921. Part of the chapter XXXI. ,,Non-English writings. I. German, French, Yiddish." pp. 572—590.
[Bibliography. pp. 813—820]. [2012

Fick, H. H.: Die Dialectdichtung in der deutsch-amerikanischen Literatur. [s. l.; s. d.] . S. 5—30. [2013

Flory, John S.: Literary activity of the German Baptist Brethren in the eighteenth century. Elgin, Ill.: Brethren Publishing House 1908. pp. XII, 335.
[Bibliography. pp. 291—327.] [2014
— Literary activities of the Brethren in the nineteenth century. In: Yearbook of the Church of the Brethren 1919. Elgin, Ill. 1919. pp. 39—45. [2015
— Our literary activity in the twentieth century. In: The Gospel Messenger. Vol. LXXIII, no. 38. Elgin, Ill. Brethren Publishing House 1924. pp. 598—599. [2016

Frick, W. K.: Notes on the Penna.-German literature. 5 installments, dated May 31, 1887. In: The Mühlenberg Monthly. Allentown, Pa. Vol. IV, No. 10. Juni 1887; Vol. V. No. 2. Oct. 1887; No. 6. Feb. 1888; No. 8. April 1888; No. 10. Juni 1888.
[Bibliography. 3rd to 5th installment.] [2017

Harbaugh, Linn: Some of our native poets. Read at March meeting, April 7, 1904. In: The Kittochtinny Historical Society. Papers read before the Society from March, 1903 to February, 1905. Vol. IV. Chambersburg, Pa. 1906. pp. 204—229. [2018
— Introductory to bibliography of Franklin County. Read Febr. 24, 1911. In: The Kittochtinny Historical Society. Papers read before the Society, Febr., 1910 to Febr., 1912. Vol. VII. Chambersburg, Pa. 1912. pp. 90—99. [2019

Heckman, Samuel B.: The religious poetry of Alexander Mack, jr. Elgin, Ill.: Brethren Publishing House 1912. pp. 268. [2020

Heilman, A. Henry: The genesis of ,,Der Pihwie" with reminiscences of its author the Rev. Henry Harbaugh, D. D. Paper read Febr. 28, 1919. In: Papers read before the Lebanon County Historical Society. Vol. VII. 1916—1919. Lebanon, Pa. 1919. pp. 377—385, ill. [2021

Hildeburn, Charles R.: A century of printing. The issues of the press in Pennsylvania. 1685—1784. Philadelphia, Pa.: Press of Matlack & Harvey 1885/6. 2 vols. Vol. I. 1685—1763. pp. XV, 392; Vol. II. 1764—1784. pp. 516. [2022

Hinke, William J.: The early German hymn books of the Reformed Church in the United States. In: Journal of the Presbyterian Historical Society. Vol. IV. Philadelphia, Pa. 1908. pp. 147—161. [2023
— The early catechismus of the Reformed Church in the United States. In: The Reformed Church Review. Fourth series, vol. XII. Philadelphia, Pa. 1908. pp. 473—512, with bibliography. [2023a

Hocker, Edward W.: Pennsylvania German literature. Paper read before the Historical Society of Montgomery County. In: Historical Sketches. A Collection of Papers prepared for the Historical Society of Montgomery County, Pa. Vol. IV, Norristown, Pa. 1910. pp. 150—157; also published in the Books News Monthly, August, 1910. [2024
— Christopher Sower and his publications.
[In the making.] [2025

Honeyman, A. van Doren: The author of ,,The story of an old farm. Andrew D. Mellick [= no. 603]. In: Somerset County Historical Quarterly. Vol. I. Somerville, N. J. 1912. pp. 23—34. [2026

Huch, C. F.: Die erste Schriftgießerei in den Vereinigten Staaten von Nordamerika. In: Deutsch-Amerikanische Geschichtsblätter. Jg. IX, Nr. 3. Chicago, Ill. 1909. S. 101—103. [2027

Jackson: Outlines of the literary history of colonial Pennsylvania. Thesis of Ph. D., Columbia University, New York City, N. Y. Lancaster, Pa.: Press of the New Era Printing Co. 1906. pp. VII, 177.
[Bibliography. pp. 164—172.] [2028

Jockers, Ernst: Deutschamerikanische Dichtung. In: Der Auslanddeutsche. Halbmonatsschrift für Auslanddeutschtum und Auslandkunde. Mitteilungen des Deutschen Ausland-Instituts, Stuttgart. Jg. XII, Nr. 10. Stuttgart 1929. S. 321—326. [2029

Jordan, John W.: Early Northampton County printing. In: The Pennsylvania Magazine of History and Biography. Vol. V. Philadelphia, Pa. 1881. pp. 116—117. [2030

Jordan, John W.: Rev. John Brandmiller, the Moravian printer. *In: The Pennsylvania Magazine of History and Biography. Vol. VI. Philadelphia, Pa. 1882. pp. 249—250.*
[born Nov., 1704, in Basel, Switzerland.] [2031

Kapp, Friedrich: Biblia, that is the Holy Bible of Old and New Testaments. *After the German translation of Dr. Martin Luther . . . Germantown, Pa.: Printed by Christopher Saur. 1743. [s. l.] (1902). Typewritten. pp. 17—75.*
[At the Library of the University of Pennsylvania.] [2032

Kleemeier, Friedrich: Die deutschamerikanische Literatur. *In: Deutsche Erde. Zeitschrift für Deutschkunde. Herausgegeben von Paul Langhaus. Jg. VIII. Gotha 1909. S. 243—250.* [2033

Kloß, Heinz: Proben aus dem pennsylvaniadeutschen Schrifttum. *In: Die Neue Zeit. (The New Era.) Wochenschrift für Politik, Kunst und Literatur. Bd. XI, Nr. 14. New Ulm, Minn. 31. Aug. 1929. S. 6—8; Nr. 15. 7. Sept. 1929. S. 9—10.* [2034

— Rauch und Horne. Ein Abschnitt des pennsylvanisch-deutschen Volkes. *In: Deutsch-Amerikanische Geschichtsblätter. German-American Review. Jahrbuch der Deutsch-Amerikanischen Historischen Gesellschaft von Illinois. Jg. 1929. Vol. XXIX. Chicago, Ill. 1929. S. 221—242. [Bibliographie S. 242.]* [2035

— Drei pennsylvaniadeutsche Biographien. (Edward Henry Rauch, Lee Light Grumbine, Samuel Kistler Brobst.) *In: Die Neue Zeit. (The New Era.) Wochenschrift für Politik, Kunst und Literatur. Bd. XI, Nr. 41. New Ulm, Minn. 8. März 1930. S. 6—7; Nr. 42. 15. März 1930. S. 7—9; Nr. 43. 22. März 1930. S. 7—9.* [2036

— Die pennsylvania deutsche Literatur. *In: Mitteilungen der Akademie zur wissenschaftlichen Erforschung und zur Pflege des Deutschtums. Deutsche Akademie. Jg. 1931. Heft 4. München 1931. S. 230—272.* [2037

Knauß, James O.: Christopher Saur the third. *In: Proceedings of the American Antiquarian Society at the semi-annual meeting held in Boston. April 15, 1931. New series, vol. XLI, part I. Worcester, Mass. 1931. pp. 235—253* [2037a

Knauß, O. P.: Printers I have met. References to colleagues in the business during a long active career. *In: Annual Proceedings of the Lehigh County Historical Society. Allentown, Pa. 1930. pp. 31—38.* [2038

Koons, Ulysses Sidney: Harbaugh's Harfe. (Harbaugh's Harp.) *In: The Pennsylvania-German Society. Proceedings and Addresses at Philadelphia, Dec. 8, 1907. Vol. XVIII. Lancaster, Pa. 1909. Separate pagination. pp. 5—17, ill.* [2039

[Kriebel, Howard W.]: Benner prints. *[Transcription of title pages of Enos Benner prints as far as they are in possession of the Schwenkfelder Historical Library.] In: The Perkiomen Region. Vol. VI, no. 4. Pennsburg, Pa. 1928. pp. 117—124.*
[See no. 2001] [2040

[—] Ciphering books. *(Partial list of . . . in the Schwenkfelder Historical Society.) In: The Perkiomen Region. Vol. VII, no. 3. 1929. pp. 95—96.* [2041

— Philadelphia prints in Schwenkfelder Historical Library, *[not listed in: The first century of German printing in America, 1728[2]—1830. By O. Seidensticker. Philadelphia, Pa. 1893 [= no. 2072]]. In: The Perkiomen Region. Vol. IX, no. 2. Pennsburg, Pa. 1931. pp. 42—48.* [2042

Kron, Gretchen: America's first bible in a European language. *In: ,,Unrolling the scroll.'' Published by the National Historical Society. Vol. I. Chicago, Ill. 1928 [= no 29]. pp. 67—71, ill.* [2043

Learned, Marion Dexter: From Pastorius' Bee-Hive or Bee-Stock. *In: Americana Germanica. A quarterly. Vol. I. Philadelphia, Pa. 1897. No. 4. pp. 66—110; Vol. II. 1898. No. 1. pp. 32—42; No. 2. pp. 59—70; No. 4. pp. 65—79.* [2044

Long, Henry G.: Some early printers. *In: Papers and Addresses of the Lancaster County Historical Society. Vol. III Lancaster, Pa. 1899. pp. 203—212.* [2045

McCreary, George W.: The first book printed in Baltimore-Town. Nicholas Hasselbach, printer. *The book reprinted with a sketch of Hasselbach's life and work. Baltimore, Md.: Press of Kohn & Pollock 1903. pp. XIII, 48, ill.* [2046

McCreary, Nancy H.: Pennsylvania literature of the colonial period. *In: The Pennsylvania Magazine of History and Biography. Vol. LII. Philadelphia, Pa. 1928. pp. 289—316.*
[Bibliography. pp. 313—316.] [2047

Mechter, Charles K.: Christopher Sower. An account of what happened to him during American the Revolution. *In: The Perkiomen Region, Past and Present. Vol. I. Philadelphia, Pa. 1895. pp. 182—184.*   [2048

Miller, Daniel: Early German American bibles. *In: The Pennsylvania-German. Vol. XI. Lititz, Pa. 1910. pp. 302 —303.*   [2049

Morris, J. G.: Christopher Saur and his first German bible. *In: Eight-Tenth Annual Report of the Society for the History of the Germans in Maryland. Baltimore, Md. 1896. pp. 47—49.*   [2050

Nolan, J. Bennett: The first decade of printing in Reading, Pennsylvania. *Published and distributed by Reading National Bank and Trust Company. Reading, Pa.: Reading Eagle Press 1930. pp. 64, ill.*   [2051

O'Callaghan, E. B.: A list of editions of the Holy Scriptures and parts thereof, printed in America previous to 1860: *with introduction and biographical notes. Albany, N. Y.: Munsell & Rowland 1861. pp. V-LIV, (6), 415, ill. with facsimiles.*

[Lists of the early German bibles printed and published in America.]   [2052

Oerter, A. L.: Specimes of old Moravian poetry. *In: Transactions of the Moravian Historical Society. Vol. X. Nazareth, Pa. 1917. pp. 7—35, ill.*   [2053

Pennypacker, Samuel Whitaker: A noteworthy book: Der Blutige Schau-platz oder Martyrer Spiegel. Ephrata, Pa. *In: The Pennsylvania Magazine of History and Biography. Vol. V. Philadelphia, Pa. 1881. pp. 276—289. Reprindet in: S. W. Pennypacker: Historical and biographical sketches. Philadelphia, Pa. 1883 [= no. 356]. pp. 157 —173.*   [2054

— Ziontischer Weyrauchs Hügel oder Myrrhen Berg. Germantown, 1739. *In: Bulletin of the Library Company of Philadelphia. New series, no. 8. Philadelphia, Pa. 1882. pp. 41—43. Reprinted in: S. W. Pennypacker: Historical and biographical sketches. Philadelphia, Pa. 1883 [= no. 356]. pp. 225—228.*   [2055

— The quarrel between Christopher Sower, the Germantown printer, and Conrad Beissel, founder and vorsteher of the cloister at Ephrata. *In: The Pennsyl-*

vania Magazine of History and Biography. Vol. XII. Philadelphia, Pa. 1888. pp. 76—96.   [2056

Pennypacker, Samuel Whitaker: The early literature of the Pennsylvania-German. *In: The Pennsylvania-German Society. Proceedings and Addresses at Harrisburg, Oct. 14, 1891; ... Vol. II. Lancaster, Pa. 1892. pp. 33—46.*   [2057

R.[attermann, H. A.]: Die alte Ephrata Presse. *In: Der Deutsche Pionier. Jg. VIII. Cincinnati, O. 1876—1877. S. 45—48.*   [2058

— Deutsch-Amerikanische Dichter und Dichtungen des 17ten und 18ten Jahrhunderts. (Eine Anthologie.) *In: Deutsch-Amerikanische Geschichtsblätter. Jahrbuch der Deutsch-Amerikanischen Historischen Gesellschaft von Illionois. Jg. 1914. Vol. XIV. Chicago, Ill. 1915. S. 84—316.*   [2059

Reichard, Harry Hess: Pennsylvania-German dialect writings and their writers. *Lancaster, Pa.: The New Era Printing Co. 1918. = Part XXVIII. „A narrative and critical history", prepared at the request of the Pennsylvania-German Society. In: The Pennsylvania-German Society. Proceedings and Addresses ... 1915. Vol. XXVI. Lancaster, Pa. 1918. Separate pagination. pp. XI, 13—400, ill.*   [2060

S.: The Saur New Testaments. *[Reproductions of the title pages of the seven editions.] In: Year Book of the Pennsylvania Society. 1911. New York, N. Y. 1911. pp. 122—135.*   [2061

Sachse, Julius Friedrich: A German poem by Frederick Augustus Mühlenberg. *In: Americana Germanica. A quarterly. Vol. I, no. 2. Philadelphia, Pa. 1897. pp. 1—6.*   [2062

Schuler, H. A.: The first printed Pennsylvania-German poem. *In: The Pennsylvania-German. Vol. VII. Lebanon, Pa. 1906. pp. 120—122.*   [2063

— The Pennsylvania-German as printer and publisher. *In: The Pennsylvania-German. Vol. VII. Lebanon, Pa. 1906. p. 174.*   [2064

— The Pennsylvania-German in literature. *In: The Pennsylvania-German. Vol. VII. Lebanon, Pa. 1906. pp. 178— 180, ill.*   [2065

Schuricht, Hermann: The first school-book printed in Virginia. *Extracts from Schuricht's „History of the German element in Virginia," 1898/1900. In: The*

Pennsylvania-German. Vol. XII. Lititz, Pa. 1911. pp. 300—301.   [2066
Seidensticker, Oswald: Welches ist das erste deutsche in Amerika gedruckte Buch? *In: Der Deutsche Pionier. Jg. II. Cincinnati, O. 1870—71. S. 62—63.*   [2067
— Die deutsch-amerikanischen Incunabelen. *In: Der Deutsche Pionier. Jg. VIII. Cincinnati, O. 1876—1877. S. 475—484.*   [2068
— Die beiden Christoph Saur in Germantown. *In: Der Deutsche Pionier. Jg. XII. Cincinnati, O. 1880—1881. S. 10—15; 47—51; 89—92; 178—182; 305—310; 350—357; 389—393; 437—444; Jg. XIII. 1881—1882. S. 63—67; 114—118; 138—142.*   [2069
— Francis Daniel Pastorius. Pennsylvania's first poet. *In: „German Day 1892." Memorial volume. [Philadelphia, Pa. 1892.] pp. 62—65, ill.*   [2070
— Deutsch-amerikanische Bibliographie bis zum Schlusse des letzten Jahrhunderts. *In: Der Deutsche Pionier. Jg. IX. Cincinnati, O. 1877—1878. S. 178—183; 241—245; 264—268; 324—328; 348—351; Jg. X. 1878—1879. S. 22—28; 62—66; 94—101; 133—136; 158—161; 194—199; 224—230; 264—270; 309—316; 374; 384—389; 422—429; 466—472. Nachtrag Jg. XII. 1880—81. S. 220—224.*   [2071
— The first century of German printing in America 1728—1830. *Proceded by a notice of the literary work of F. D. Postorius. Published by the German Pionier-Verein of Philadelphia, Pa.: Schaefer & Koradi 1893. pp. X, 253, (1), fac-simile.*
[Supplements see nos. 2042, 2075 and 2077.]   [2072
Sower, Charles G.: Genealogical chart of the descendants of Christopher Sower, printer of Germantown, Philadelphia, Pa. *Philadelphia, Pa.: C. G. Sower 1887.*
[Gives biographical sketches of Christopher Sower 1693—1758; and of Christopher Sower 1721—1784; and a list of their publications.]   [2073
— The Sower publications. *[List of the publications of both the two Christopher Sowers, father and son, taken from the Sower chart.] In: The Pennsylvania-German. Vol. II. Lebanon, Pa. 1901. pp. 89—93.*   [2074
Stapleton, A.: Researches in the first century of printing in America. 1728—1830.

(Issues of the German press omitted in: The first century of German printing in America 1728—1830. By O. Seidensticker. Philadelphia, Pa. 1893 [= no. 2072].) In: The Pennsylvania-German. Vol. V. Lebanon, Pa. 1904. pp. 81—89; p. 183; pp. 262—263.   [2075
Stapleton, A.: Gustav Sigismund Peters, pioneer, sterotyper and color-printer. *In: The Pennsylvania-German. Vol. VII. Lebanon, Pa. 1906. pp. 177—178.*   [2076
Wayland, John W.: „Literary activities and associations" *[of the Shenandoah County, Va.] — „Henkel press bibliography." In: A history of Shenandoah County, Va. By John W. Wayland. Strasburg, Va. 1927 [= no. 5626].*
pp. 481—497.
[Gives a number of items, which are not listed in: The first century of American printing in America. 1728—1830. By O. Seidensticker. Philadelphia, Pa. 1893 [= no. 2972].].   [2077
Welfley, W. H.: Early printing in Somerset, Pa. *In: The Pennsylvania-German. Vol. XI. Lititz, Pa. 1910. pp. 148—149.*   [2078
Wright, John: The Saur bible. *In: Early bibles of America. By John Wright. New York, N. Y.: Thomas Whittaker 1892. pp. 28—54; Appendix F.: List of owners of the Saur bibles as far as known. pp. 163—164. Third edition. 1894.*   [2079
Lutheran bibles at the Historical Society of Pennsylvania. *Note in: The Pennsylvania Magazine of History and Biography. Vol. LIV. Philadelphia, Pa. 1930. pp. 383—384.*   [2080
First German almanac. *Note in: The Pennsylvania Magazine of History and Biography. Vol. VI. Philadelphia, Pa. 1882. p. 370.*   [2081
Der deutsche Buchdruck in Nord-Amerika im letzten und im Anfang dieses Jahrhunderts *[Bemerkungen zu der „Liste der vom Archivcommittee seit 1867 gesammelten Bücher" in: 108ter Jahresbericht der Deutschen Gesellschaft von Pennsylvanien, für das Jahr 1872. Philadelphia, Pa. 1873. S. 32—38]. In: Der Deutsche Pionier. Jg. V. Cincinnati, O. 1873—1874. S. 160—163.*   [2082
Lee L. Grumbine. *In: The Pennsylvania-German. Vol. V. Lebanon, Pa. 1904. pp. 145—148, ill.*   [2083
John Peter Zenger *[See nos. 546—9].*

Deutschsprachige Zeitungen

German Newspapers

A., H. F.: Einige Notizen über die ersten deutschen Zeitungen Philadelphia's. *In: Der Deutsche Pionier. Jg. VI. Cincinnati, O. 1874—1875. S. 318—319.* [2085

Breithaupt, W. H.: Waterloo County newspaper. *In: Ninth Annual Report of the Waterloo Historical Society. Kitchener, Ont. 1921. pp. 152—159.* [2086

Brigham, Clarence S.: Bibliography of American newspapers, 1690—1820. *In: Proceedings of the American Antiquarian Society at the semi-annual meeting held in Boston April 9, 1919. New series, vol. XXIX. Part I.* [2087

Conrad, Victor L.: The press of the Lutheran Church. *In: The Lutheran Quarterly. Vol. XXVIII. Gettysburg, Pa. 1898. pp. 532—544.* [2088

[Crevecœur, St. John de]: Verzeichnis der Zeitungen und Magazine, welche in den vereinten Staaten von Nordamerika gedruckt werden, *nebst Berechnung der jährlichen Summen der ersten. Verfertiget den 1. Julius 1789. In: Amerikanisches Magazin oder authentische Beiträge zur Erdbeschreibung, Staatskunde und Geschichte von Amerika, besonders aber der vereinten Staaten. Herausgegeben von Hegewisch-Kiel und Ebeling-Hamburg. Erster Band. Zweites Stück. Hamburg: Carl Ernst Bohn 1776. S. 118—123.* [2088a

Dampman, John B.: A short history of the newspapers of Reading, Pa. *Compiled by . . . Presented by* **John D. Mishler** *to the Reading Press Club. Reading, Pa.: Press of Pengelly & Bro. . . . pp. 55.* [2089

Diffenderffer, F. R.: The oldest daily paper in Lancaster County. *[Lancaster Gazette, 1752ff.] In: Papers and Addresses of the Lancaster County Historical Society. Vol. I. Lancaster, Pa. 1897. pp. 72—84.* [2090

— The newspapers of Lancaster County. *In: Papers and Addresses of the Lancaster County Historical Society. Vol. VI. Lancaster, Pa. 1902. pp. 103—113, ill.* [2091

— An early newspaper. *[Neue Unparteyische Lancaster Zeitung.] In: Papers and Addresses of the Lancaster County Historical Society. Vol. XI. Lancaster, Pa. 1907. pp. 175—194, ill.* [2092

Gotwald, Frederick Gebhart: Pioneer American Lutheran journalism, 1812—1850. *In: The Lutheran Quarterly. Vol. XLII. Gettysburg, Pa. 1912. pp. 161—204, ill.* [2093

Hostetter, A. K.: A newspaper relic. *[„Neue Unpartheiische Lancaster Zeitung und Anzeige Nachrichten".] In: Papers and Addresses of the Lancaster County Historical Society. Vol. XXII. Lancaster, Pa. 1918. pp. 77—86.* [2094

Huch, C. F.: Die erste deutsche Zeitung in Philadelphia. *In: Mitteilungen des Deutschen Pionier-Vereins von Philadelphia. Heft 7. Philadelphia, 1908. Pa. S. 20—27.* [2095

— Die erste deutsche Zeitung in America. *In: Mitteilungen des Deutschen Pionier-Vereins von Philadelphia. Heft 8. Philadelphia, Pa. 1908. S. 29—32.* [2096

— Deutsche Zeitungen in Philadelphia während der ersten Hälfte des neunzehnten Jahrhunderts. *In: Mitteilungen des Deutschen Pionier-Vereins von Philadelphia. Heft 9. Philadelphia, Pa. 1908. pp. 1—11. Abdruck in: Deutsch-Amerikanische Geschichtsblätter Jg. IX. Chicago, Ill. 1909. S. 23—27; 56—58.* [2097

Jockisch, Hermann: Die deutschsprachige Presse in den Vereinigten Staaten. *In: Hamburg-Amerika-Post. Bd. V, Heft 3/5 Hamburg 1933. S. 60—71.* [2097a

Keidel, George C.: The earliest German newspapers of Baltimore. An essay. I. The eighteenth century. *Washington, D. C.: Privately printed 1927. pp. 12. facsimile.* [2098

Kriebel, H. W.: The people's Instructor. *(First copy of weekly . . ., issued Aug. 8, 1810). In: The Pennsylvania-German. Vol. XI. Lititz, Pa. 1910. pp. 603—606.* [2099

Kloß, Heinz: Materialien zur Geschichte der deutschkanadischen Presse. *In: Der Auslanddeutsche. Halbmonatsschrift für Auslanddeutschtum und Auslandkunde. Mitteilungen des Deutschen Ausland Instituts. Jg. XI, Nr. 12. Stuttgart 1928. S. 382—384.* [2100

Miller, Daniel: In ye olden times. *[Notes on old newspapers, viz Reading Adler, Welt Bote and others.] In: The Pennsylvania-German. Vol. X. Lititz, Pa. 1909. pp. 557—564.* [2101

— Early German American newspapers. *Lancaster, Pa.: The Era Printing Co. 1911 = Part XXIII. „A narrative and critical history", prepared by authority of the Pennsylvania-German Society. In: The Pennsylvania-German Society. Proceedings and Addresses . . . 1908. Vol. XIX. Lancaster, Pa. 1910. Separate pagination. pp. 5—107, ill., facsimiles.* [2102

R.[attermann, H.]: Die älteste bestehende deutsche religiöse Zeitung in den Vereinigten Staaten. *In: Der Deutsche Pionier. Jg. VI. Cincinnati, O. 1874— 1875. S. 382—385.* [2103

— Der Deutsch-amerikanische Journalismus und seine Verbreitung von 1800 bis zur Einwanderung der sogenannten „Dreißiger". *In: Deutsch-Amerikanische Geschichtsblätter. Jahrbuch der Deutsch-Amerikanischen Historischen Gesellschaft von Illinois. Jg. 1912. Vol. XII. Chicago, Ill. 1912. S. 283—305.* [2104

Sachse, Julius F.: The first German newspaper published in America. *[Philadelphische Zeitung. (Philadelphia Gazette) June 10, 1732.] In: The Pennsylvania-German Society. Proceedings and Addresses at Ephrata, Oct. 20, 1899. Vol. X. Lancaster, Pa. 1900. pp. 41—46; facsimile of no. II, Philadelphische Zeitung, 24. Jun. 1732. pp. (4).* [2105

Seidensticker, Oswald: Die Entstehung der deutschen Zeitungs-Presse in Amerika. *(Aus einer handschriftlichen biographischen Skizze über die beiden Christoph Saur.) In: Der Deutsche Pionier. Jg. VI. Cincinnati, O. 1874—1875. S. 143 —149.* [2106

— und **Rattermann, H. A.:** Geschichte der Deutsch-amerikanischen Zeitungspresse von ihrem Anfange bis zum Jahr 1850. *Mit einer Einleitung von H. A. Rattermann. In: Deutsch-Amerikanisches Magazin. Vierteljahrsschrift für Geschichte, Literatur, Wissenschaft, Kunst, Schule und Volksleben der Deutschen in Amerika . . . herausgegeben von H. A. Rattermann. Bd. I. Cincinnati, O. 1887. S. 269—289; 405—434; 568—588; Faksimile.* [2107

Weaver, Ethan Allen: Centennial of journalism in Northampton County. *In: The Pennsylvania Magazine of History and Biography. Vol. XVIII. Philadelphia, Pa. 1894. pp. 121—122.* [2108

— „The American Eagle": The first English newspaper printed in Northampton County, Pa. *In: The Pennsylvania Magazine of History and Biography. Vol. XXIII. Philadelphia, Pa. 1899. pp. 69—76.* [2109

Worner, William Frederic: The Times or Weekly Porcupine *[a German weekly newspaper in Lancaster Borough, established by Johann Albrecht & Co. Jan. 3, 1798.] In: Papers and Addresses of the Lancaster County Historical Society. Vol. XXXV. Lancaster, Pa. 1931. pp. 257—258.* [2110

Newspapers published in Pennsylvania prior to the Revolution. *Extracted from Thomas's History of Printing, 1810.* German newspapers, printed in Philadelphia previously to the year 1775. *Reprint in: Hazard's Register of Pennsylvania. Vol. I. Philadelphia, Pa. 1828. pp. 177—179.* [2111

Deutsche Zeitungen in den Vereinigten Staaten im Jahre 1848. *In: Mitteilungen des Deutschen Pionier-Vereins von Philadelphia. Heft 16. Philadelphia, Pa. 1910. S. 38—39.* [2112

Die deutsche Presse in den Vereinigten Staaten. *[Liste deutscher Zeitschriften, zusammengestellt auf Grund der von Herren Geo. P. Rowell & Co. veranstalteten Ausstellung aller in den Vereinigten Staaten erscheinenden Zeitungen.] In: Der Deutsche Pionier. Jg. VIII. Cincinnati, O. 1876—1877. S. 289—320.* [2113

The first German newspaper published in America: Philadelphische Zeitung, published by Benjamin Franklin. *In: The Pennsylvania Magazine of History and Biography. Vol. XXIV. Philadelphia, Pa. 1900. pp. 306—307; fac-simile of no. II., Sonnabend, den 24. Jun. 1734. pp. 4.* [2114

Philadelphische Zeitung: the first German newspaper published in America. *In: The Pennsylvania Magazine of History and Biography. Vol. XXVI. Philadelphia, P. a 1902. p. 91; fac-simile of no. I. Philadelphische Zeitung. Sambstag, den 6. May 1732. pp. 4.* [2115

Allentown Unabhängiger Republikaner. Established 1810. *In: The Pennsylvania-German. Vol. VI. Lititz, Pa. 1910. pp. 510—511.* [2116

Deutschpennsylvanisches Leben in der Erzählung

The Pennsylvania German in Fiction

Brumbaugh, Martin G.: An outline for historical romance. *In: The Pennsylvania-German Society. Proceedings and Addresses at Easton, Oct. 12, 1928. Vol. XXXIV. Norristown, Pa. 1930. Separate pagination. pp. 12, ill.* [2117

Eastburn, Iola Kay: Whittier's relation to German life and thought. *Thesis: of Ph. D. University of Pa. Philadelphia, Pa.: Publications of the University of Pa. 1915. pp. 5—161, ill. = Americana Germanica. No. 20.* [2118

Fogel, E. M.: Review of ,,Tillie, a Mennonite maid, A story of the Pennsylvania Dutch". By Helen Reimensnyder Martin. *New York. N. Y. The Century Co. 1904. In: German American Annals. New series, vol. III. Philadelphia, Pa. 1905. pp. 27—31.* [2119

Hocker, Edward W.: A defiant dialect. Pennsylvania German in fiction. *In: The Bookly News Monthly. Vol. XXVIII, No. 12. Philadelphia, Pa., Aug., 1912. pp. 894—895; p. 904. Reprint in: The Pennsylvania-German. Vol. XI. Lititz, Pa. 1910. pp. 598—602.* [2120

Kauffman, Reginald Wright: Some Pennsylvania-German story-writers. *In: The Pennsylvania-German. Vol. VII. Lebanon, Pa. 1906. pp. 180—183, ill.* [2121

Keyser, N. H.: Fiction dealing with Pennsylvania-Germans. *[List of works of fiction relating to the Pennsylvania-Germans.] In: The Pennsylvania-German. Vol. VII. Lebanon, Pa. 1906. p. 272.* [2122

Richardson, W. H.: Literary opportunities in Pennsylvania-Germany. *In: The Pennsylvania-German. Vol. IX. Cleona, Pa. 1908. pp. 243—248.* [2123

Roberts, Ellwood: The Pennsylvania-German in fiction. *In: The Pennsylvania-German. Vol. VII. Lebanon, Pa. 1906. pp. 68—70. [A vindication and regret for Helen R. Martin: ,,Tillie, a Mennonite maid."]* [2124

Shoemaker, Henry W.: True stories of the Pennsylvania mountains. *An address at meeting of the Story Telling League. Girl's High School, Reading, Pa., May 2, 1923. Altoona, Pa.: Altoona Tribune Press (s. d.) pp. 10.* [2125

Deutschpennsylvanische Volkskunde

Pennsylvania German Things and Folk-lore

Aurand, A. Monroe: The „Pow-Wow" book. *A treatise on the art of „Healing by Prayer" and Laying on of Hands", etc., practised by the Pennsylvania-Germans and others; testimonials; remarkable recoveries; popular superstitions; etc. Including an account of the famous „witch" murder trial, at York, Pa. Containing also the complete collection of remedies and cures in John George Hohman's „Pow-Wows, or long lost friend"; in popular use since 1820.* Harrisburg, Pa.: Privately printed by the Aurand Press. 1929. pp. X, 85; 31, XI, 13—64. [2126

— An account of the „witch murder trial" York, Pa., January 7—9, 1929. Commonwealth of Pennsylvania vs. John Blymyer, et al. *Harrisburg, Pa.: Privately printed by The Aurand Press 1929. pp. 31.* [2127

Berlin, Alfred F.: Introduction of the Christmas tree in the United States. *Read June 1, 1915. In: A Collection of Papers read before the Bucks County Historical Society. Vol. IV. Easton, Pa. 1917. pp. 552—553.* [2128

Bittinger, Lucy Forney: Pennsylvania German folklore. *In: The Pennsylvania-German. Vol. IX. Cleona, Pa. 1908. pp. 171—173.* [2129

Bornemann, Henry: Illuminative writings among Pennsylvania Germans. . . . *[In press].* [2130

Brendle, Thomas R. and Unger, Claude W.: Folk medicine of the Pennsylvania Germans. *The non-occult cures. Norristown, Pa. 1935. In: The Pennsylvania-German Society. Proceedings and Addresses . . . 1931, 1932, 1933, 1934. Vol. XLV. Norristown, Pa. 1935. Separate pagination. pp. 304, facsimiles. [Bibliography of recipes in manuscript. pp. 289—303.]* [2130a

Croll, P. C.: Quaint and humorous epitaphs. *In: The Pennsylvania-German. Vol. I., no. 4. Lebanon, Pa. 1900. pp. 29—34.* [2131

Daugherty, G. Earl: Grandmother's old blue historical china and its makers. *Paper read before the Lebanon, County Historical Society. Oct. 28, 1927. Vol. IX. no. 8. Lebanon, Pa. 1927. pp. 271—287, ill.* [2132

Diffenderffer, F. R.: The Red Rose question. *In: Papers and Addresses of Lancaster County Historical Society. Vol. VI. 1901—1902. Lancaster, Pa. 1902. pp. 3—7.* [2133

Downs, Joseph: A Pennsylvania-German house. *In: The Pennsylvania Museum Bulletin. Vol. XXII., no. 108. December 1926. Philadelphia. Pa. 1926. pp. 265—275, ill.* [2134

— The house of the Miller at Millbach. The architecture, arts, and crafts of the Pennsylvania Germans. *[s. l.]: Published by the Pennsylvania Museum of Art, Philadelphia, Pa. 1929. pp. (31), ill.* [2135

Dubbs, J. H.: Christmas among Pennsylvania Germans. *Reprint from „Public Ledger", Philadelphia, Pa. In: The Pennsylvania-German. Vol. XII. Lititz, Pa. 1911. pp. 705—707.* [2136

Dutch Recipe Co., The . . . Easton, Pa.: Pennsylvania-Dutch recipes. *Issued by . . . Easton, Pa. 1908. pp. . . .* [2137

„Pennsylvania-Dutch" recipes. *From a booklet of this name, issued by the Dutch Recipe Co., Easton, Pa. In: The Pennsylvania-German. Vol. IX. Cleona, Pa. 1908. p. 134.* [2138

E., J. W.: Funerals in Pennsylvania and Massachusetts. — A contrast. *In: The Pennsylvania-German. Vol. XII, Lititz, Pa. 1911. pp. 479—485* [2139

Fisher, H. L.: Olden times: or, Pennsylvania rural life, some fifty years ago, and other poems. *York Pa. Fisher Bros. 1888. pp. XIV, 472, (1), ill.* [2140

— 'S alt Marik-Haus Mittes. In D'r Schtadt, un Die Alte' Zeite'. *En centennial poem in Pennsylfanisch Deutsch, in zwe Dhel. York, Pa.: The York Republican 1879. (English preface: pp.*

*VII—XVIII) S. XIX—XXII, 24—
218 S.;* Glossary *S. 221—273, (1), ill.*
                                    [2141
Fogel, Edwin M.: The Himmelsbrief. *In:
German American Annals. New series,
vol. VI. Philadelphia, Pa. 1908. pp.
286—311.*   [2142
— Beliefs and superstitions of the Pennsylvania Germans. *Philadelphia, Pa.:
American Germanica Press; Harrisburg,
Pa.: J. J. Nungesser 1915. pp. V, 387.
= Americana Germanica. Monographs
devoted to the comparative study of the
literary, linguistic and other cultural
relations of Germany and America. Edited by Marion Dexter Learned. No. 18.
Supplement: Sex. For private distribution, not for public perusal. Philadelphia, Pa.: American Germanica Press.
1915. pp. 345—357.*   [2143
— Proverbs of the Pennsylvania Germans.
*Lancaster, Pa.: Lancaster Press, Inc.
1929. In: The Pennsylvania-German
Society. Proceedings and Addresses . . .
1925. Vol. XXXVI. Lancaster, Pa.
1929. Separate pagination. pp. 122.*
    *Supplement. For private distribution,
not for public perusal. Fogelsville, Pa.:
Americana Germanica Press. 1929.
pp. 10.*   [2144
Franklin, Walter M.: Impress of early
names and traits. *In: Papers and Addresses of the Lancaster County Historical
Society. Vol. III. Lancaster, Pa. 1899.
pp. 45—53.*   [2145
Funk, H. H.: Some oldtime breakfast-cakes.
*In: The Pennsylvania-German. Vol. IX.
Cleona, Pa. 1908. p. 37.*   [2146
— Marriage superstitions. *In: The Pennsylvania-German. Vol. IX. Cleona 1908.
pp. 372—373.*   [2147
Gerhard, Emer S.: Pennsylvania German
folk lore. *Read before the Montgomery
County Historical Society, November 17,
1928. In: The Perkiomen Region. Vol.
IX, no. 3. Pennsburg, Pa. 1931.
pp. 87—96.*   [2148
[Gernerd, Jeremiah M. M.]: Pioneer home
life. *Quoted from: The Gernhardt fa-
mily history. In: The Pennsylvania-
German. Vol. IX. Cleona. Pa. 1908.
pp. 323—324.*   [2149
Gibbons, Phebe Earle: Pennsylvania Dutch.
*In: The Atlantic Monthly. A magazine
of literature, science, art and politics.
Vol. XXIV. Boston, Mass.: Fields,
Osgood & Co. 1869. pp. 473—487.*

Netherlandish translation: Kerlelijk en
huiselijk leven der Doopsgezinden hier
te lande en die in Pennsylvanie. *Translated by.* J. G. de Hoop Scheffer. *In:
Doopsgezinde Bijdragen. Uitgegeven
onder redactive van D. Harting en P.
Cool. New series, vol. III. Leeuwarden
H. Kuipers 1869. pp. 129—147.*
    [See also no. 313]   [2150
Gift, Aaron Kern: Glimpses of pioneer life.
*[Extracts from Gift's ,,Genealogical hi-
story of the Gift, Kern and Royer families." 1908.] In: The Pennsylvania-
German. Vol. XI. Lititz, Pa. 1910.
pp. 684—686.*   [2151
Graham, Wm. A.: New Year's shooting, an
ancient German custom. *In: The North
Carolina Booklet. Vol. XIII, no. 3.
Raleigh, N. C. 1914. pp. 147—151.*
                                    [2152
Gummere, Amelia Mott: The Quaker. A
study in costume. *Philadelphia, Pa.:
Ferris & Leach 1901. pp. VI, (1), (3),
(3), 232, ill.*
    *[Not directly dealing with Pennsyl-
vania-German, but informative in general
way on ,,the plain dress" in Pennsyl-
vania; Chapter V.: The evolution of the
Quaker Bonnet. pp. 187—228.]*   [2153
H., E. W.: An old time scrivener August
Bauman. *In: The Magazine of History,
with notes and queries. Vol. IV. July
—Dec. 1906. New York, N. Y. 1906.
pp. 321—323.*   [2154
Harbaugh, Linn: Truth and traditions of
early times. *(Read Jan. 30, 1908.) In:
The Kittochtinny Historical Society.
Papers read before the Society from
March, 1905 to Febr., 1908. Vol. V.
Chambersburg, Pa. 1908. pp. 315—319.*
                                    [2155
Hark, J. Max: Cooking utensils and coo-
kery of our grandmothers. *In: Papers
read before the Lebanon County Historical Society. Vol. VI. 1912—1916. Lebanon, Pa. 1916. pp. 225—231, ill.* [2156
[Helffrich, W. A.]: An old-fashioned witch
story. *Extract from Dr. W. A. Helffrich's autobiography, translated by* **W. U.
Helffrich.** *In: The Pennsylvania-German. Vol. VIII. Lebanon, Pa. 1907.
pp. 379—380.*   [2157
[—] An oldtime country frolic. *Extract
from Dr. W. A. Helffrich's Autobiography, translated by* **W. U. Helffrich.**
*In: The Pennsylvania-German. Vol.
VIII. Lebanon, Pa. 1907. pp. 486—
488.*   [2158

[Helffrich, W. A.]: A Blue Mountain funeral sixty years ago. *Extract from Dr. W. A. Helffrich's Autobiogarphy, translated by* W. U. Helffrich. *In: The Pennsylvania-German. Vol. VIII. Lebanon, Pa. 1907. pp. 599—600.* [2159

[—] Spinning in the oldtime winter nights. *Extract from Dr. W. A. Helffrich's Autobiography, translated by* W. U. Helffrich. *In: The Pennsylvania-German. Vol. IX. Cleona, Pa. 1908. p. 83.* [2160

Hoffman, W. J.: Folk-medicine of the Pennsylvania Germans. *Read before the American Philosophical Society, May 3, 1889. In: Proceedings of the American Philosophical Society held at Philadelphia for promoting useful knowledge. Vol. XXVI. Philadelphia, Pa. 1889. pp. 329—352.* [2161

— Folk-lore of the Pennsylvania Germans. *In: The Journal of American Folk-Lore. Vol. I. Boston, Mass. and New York, N. Y. Published for the American Folk-Lore Society by Houghton, Mifflin & Co. 1888. pp. 125—135; Vol. iI. 1889. pp. 23—35; 191—202.* [2162

— Gshicht fun dä al'tä tsai'tä in Pensilfani. *[Sketch of the olden times in Pennsylvania.] In: Proceedings of the American Philosophical Society held at Philadelphia for the promotion of useful knowledge. Vol. XXXII. May, 1893. Philadelphia, Pa. 1894. pp. 325—331.* [2163

The Pennsylvania Germans. *From Harrisburg Telegraph. In: The Historical Record. A quarterly publication devoted principally to the early history of Wyoming Valley . . . Vol. I. Wilkes-Barre, Pa. 1886/87. p. 95.*
[Review of an ethnological and philological history of the Pennsylvania Germans. By W. J. Hoffman.] [2164

Hoffman, W. J.: Popular superstitions. *In: The Pennsylvania-German Society. Proceedings and Addresses at Reading, Oct. 3, 1894. Vol. V. Reading, Pa. 1895. pp. 70—81.* [2165

Hohman, Johann Georg: Der lange Verborgene Freund, oder: Getreuer und Christlicher Unterricht für Jedermann, Enthaltend: Wunderbare und probmäßige Mittel und Künste, sowohl für die Menschen als das Vieh. *Mit vielen Zeugen bewiesen in diesem Buch, und wovon das Mehrste noch wenig bekannt ist, und zum allerersten Mal in Amerika im*

Druck erscheint. Herausgegeben von . . , Nahe bey Reading, in Elsaß Taunship, Berks County. Zweite und verbesserte Auflage. [1819.] 87 S. [2166

Hohman, Johann Georg: The long hidden friend. *By John George Hohman. With introduction and notes by* Carletod F. Brown. *In: The Journal of American Folk-Lore. Vol. XVII. (No. LXV.) Boston, Mass. and New York, N. Y. April-June 1904 pp. 89—152.* [2167

— John George Hohman's Long Lost Friend; or Book of Pow-Wows. *A collection of mysterious and invaluable arts and remedies; For man as well as animals; with many proofs of their virtue and efficacy in healing diseases, etc., the greater part of which was newer published until they appeared in print for the first time in the U. S. in the year 1820. With a historical foreword by* A. Monroe Aurand, jr. *Privately printed. Harrisburg, Pa.: The Aurand Press 1930. pp. 94.* [2168

Horne, A. R.: Proverbs and sayings of the Pennsylvania-Germans. *In: The Pennsylvania-German Society. Proceedings and Addresses at Harrisburg, Oct. 14, 1891; . . . Vol. II. Lancaster, Pa. 1892. pp. 47—54.* [2169

Johaneson, Bland: Victualry among the Pennsylvania Germans. *The Society of Pennsylvania German Gastronomes. [Cedar Rapid, Iowa: Torch press.] 1928. pp. 8.* [2170

[Johnson, Elmer E. S.]: Hunting ,,Elbetriches". A popular story in two versions. *In: The Pennsylvania-German. Vol. VII. Lebanon, Pa. 1906. pp. 35—37.* More about ,,elbetritches". *In: Vol. VII. pp. 122—123.* [2171

Keller, J. A.: The Pennsylvania German cook book. *Revised and enlarged. Containing 560 excellent recipes compiled by . . . Alliance, O. The R. M. Scranton printing co. 1902. pp. 71.* [2172

Knortz, Karl: Streifzüge auf dem Gebiete amerikanischer Volkskunde. Altes und Neues. *Leipzig: Ed. Wartigs Verlag Ernst Hoppe 1902. (1), 284 S.* [2173

Laatz, Eugene: German games and plays. *In: A Collection of Papers read before the Bucks County Historical Society. Vol. IV. Easton, Pa. 1917. pp. 30—34.* [2174

Learned, M. D.: Ethnographical data. Pennsylvania. *In: Americana Germanica. A quarterly. Philadelphia, Pa.*

13*

No. 1. Preliminary circular. *Vol. I No. 3. pp. 107—108;* Circular No. 2. — Ballads and rimes. *Vol. II. 1898. No. 1. pp. 107—108;* Circular No. 3. — Sentence accent. *Vol. II. 1898. No. 2. pp. 108—109.* [2175

Learned, M. D.: The American ethnographical survey. Conestoga expedition 1902. **Marion Dexter Learned,** Director. *Publication of the University of Pennsylvania. New York, N. Y.: D. Appleton & Co. 1911. = Americana Germanica. Monographs devoted to the comparative study of the literary, linguistic and other cultural relations of Germany and America. No. 12. [Various papers which appeared in ,,German American Annals," Philadelphia]:*
Learned, Marion Dexter: The American ethnographical survey. The Conestoga expedition, summer 1902. *Preliminary report. Separate pagination. pp. 7.*
— An American ethnographical survey. *Separate pagination. pp. 24, map. [Includes: List of surveys and chart made by the late* **Jacob Hildebrand,** *Esq., of Stosberg. pp. 21—24, map.]*
An old German midwife's record. *(Kept by* **Susanna Müller,** *of Providence township, Lancaster, Co., Pa., during the years 1791—1815.) Edited by* **M. D. Learned** *and* **C. F. Brede.** *Separate pagination. pp. 46.*
Benj. Herr's journal 1830. *Separate pagination pp. 24.* **Luetscher, G. D.:** Industries of Pennsylvania after the adoption of the federal constitution, *with special reference to Lancaster and York counties. Separate pagination pp. 33, maps.* [2176

Leonard, J. C.: The ghosts of Abbott's creek, North Carolina. *In: The Penn Germania. Vol. I. = Old series, vol XIII. Lititz, Pa. 1912. pp. 198—203.* [2177

Mercer, Henry C.: The survival of the mediaeval art of illuminative writing among Pennsylvania Germans. *Read September 17, 1897. In: Proceedings of the American Philosophical Society held at Philadelphia for promoting useful knowledge. Vol. XXXVI. Philadelphia, Pa. 1897. pp. 424—433, ill.*
Separate print: [Doylestown, Pa., s. d.] pp. 423—432, ill.
= Contributions to American History by the Bucks County Hist. Society, no. 2. [2178

Mercer, Henry C.: Folk-lore, notes taken at random. *Read July 21, 1896. In: A Collection of Papers read before the Bucks County Historical Society. Vol. II. Easton, Pa. 1909. pp. 406—416.* [2179
— and others: Remarks on the Christmas tree. *In: A Collection of Papers read before the Bucks County Historical Society. Vol. IV. Easton, Pa. 1917. pp. 554—557.* [2180

Mercer, William R.: Origin and customs of Christmas festivals. *Read Dec. 20, 1907. In: A Collection of Papers read before the Bucks County Historical Society. Vol. III. Easton, Pa. 1909. pp. 493—504.* [2181

Mercer, William: Bucks County samplers. *Read June 18, 1921. In: A Collection of Papers read before the Bucks County Historical Society. Vol. V. Meadville, Pa. 1926. pp. 347—356, ill.* [2182

Meyer, T. P.: Grandmother home remedies. *In: The Pennsylvania-German. Vol. X. Lititz, Pa. 1909. pp. 272—278.* [2183
— Country funerals and mortuary customs of long ago. *In: The Pennsylvania-German. Vol. IX. Cleona, Pa. 1908. pp. 403—407.* [2184

Neifert, William N.: Witchcraft. *In: The Pennsylvania-German. Vol. IX. Cleona, Pa. 1908. pp. 114—121.* [2185

North American, Philadelphia: Trial of lawsuit against this paper. Dr. J. H. Hageman's action based on article that appeared in The North American, May 22, 1900 [= no. 2191]. *In: The North American Daily Newspaper 132d year. Philadelphia, Pa. 1903. No. 169. March 7, p. 1, col. 4; p. 4, col. 1—4; p. 5, col. 1—5; No. 173. March 11, p. 1, col. 2; p. 4, col. 1—3; p. 5, col. 1—7; p. 9, col. 2—5; p. 11, col. 1—5; No. 174. March 12, p. 1, col. 4, p. 6, col. 1—7; p. 11, col. 1—7; p. 13, col. 1—3; No. 175. March 13, p. 1, col. 1; p. 12, col. 1—7; p. 13, col. 1—7; No. 176. March 14,* ,,Witch doctor's case against North American withdrawn by counsel." *p. 1, col. 1; p. 3, col. 3; p. 6, col. 1—6.* [2186

Owens, J. G.: Folk-lore from Buffalo valley, Central-Pennsylvania. *In: The Journal of American Folk-Lore. Vol. IV. (No. XIII.) Boston, Mass. — New York, N. Y. 1891. pp. 115—128.* [2187

Raschen, J. F. L.: The may-tree, a relic of antiquity. *In: The Penn Germania. Vol. I. = Old series, vol. XIII. Lititz, Pa. 1912. pp. 448—451.* [2188

Reichard, H. H.: Doctor Johann Andreas Eisenbart. *In: The Penn Germania. Vol. II. = Old series, vol. XIV. Cleona, Pa. 1913. pp. 119—122.* [2189

Ritter, H. B.: Witchcraft trial in Northampton County. *In: The Pennsylvania-German. Vol. XI. Lititz, Pa. 1910. p. 575.* [2190

Rix, Alice: The Reading witch Doctor's sway over the trusting and ignorant. He sells potions, charms, forbiddings and blessings, his clientele is large and his fees are extortionate. — Belief in spells and in necromatic means of undoing them prevails astonishing in parts of Pennsylvania. *In: The North American 129th year No. 208. [Daily newspaper] Philadelphia, Tuesday, May 22, 1900. pp. 16, ill.* [2191

Rupp, I. D.: Pennsylvänisch-deutsche Hochzeiten vor 100 Jahren. *[In Pennsylvania-German dialect written.] In: Der Deutsche Pionier. O. 1872—1873. S. 88—91.* [2192

Rutherford, W. F.: The ghosts of Swatara and the region round about. *In: Notes and Queries. Edited by W. H. Egle. Second series. Harrisburg. Pa. 1883. pp. 265—268. Reprint in: First and second series, vol. II. Harrisburg, Pa. 1895. pp. 367—372.* [2193

Sachse, Julius F.: Popular beliefs and superstitions. *In: Papers and Addresses of the Lancaster County Historical Society. Vol. VII. Lancaster Pa. 1903. pp. 75—101, ill.* [2194

[—] Old-time home superstitions. *Extract from ,,Prognostics and superstitions" by Julius F. Sachse. In: The Pennsylvania-German. Vol. VIII. Lebanon, Pa. 1907. pp. 389—399.* [2195

Schneider, Karl: Südwestdeutschland in Nordamerika. *[Review of ,,The American ethnographical survey. The Conestoga expedition 1902. By Marion Dexter Learned (= no. 2176).] In: Deutsche Erde. Zeitschrift für Deutschkunde. Herausgegeben von Paul Langhans. Jg. VI. Gotha 1907. S. 140—141.* [2196

Schuler, H. A.: The old-time Pennsylvania-German Christmas. *In: The Pennsylvania-German. Vol. VII. Lebanon, Pa. 1906. pp. 411—419, ill.* [2197

— Shooting — in the new year. A peculiar Pennsylvania-German custom. *In: The*

Pennsylvania-German. Vol. VIII. Lebanon, Pa. 1907. pp. 15—18. [2198

Seip, Elisabeth Cloud: Witch-finding in western Maryland. *Paper read at the 12th annual meeting of the American Folk-Lore Society, Baltimore, Dec. 28, 1900. In: The Journal of American Folk-Lore. Vol. XIV. (No. LII.) Boston, Mass. — New York, N. Y. 1901. pp. 39—44.* [2199

Shoemaker, Henry W.: Mountain minstrelsy of Pennsylvania. *Compiled by . . . Being a third edition of North Pennsylvania minstrelsy. Revised and enlarged. Philadelphia, Pa.: Newman F. McGirr 1931. pp. (2), 319.* [2200

Smith, Frances Elizabeth: The colonial medecine chest. *In: Papers read before Lebanon County Historical Society. Vol. IX. No. 11. Lebanon, Pa. 1929. pp. 339—356.* [2201

Stahr, John S.: The Pennsylvania-Germans at home. *In: The Pennsylvania-German Society. Proceedings and Addresses at Reading, Oct. 3, 1894. Vol. V. Reading, Pa. 1895. pp. 53—70.* [2202

Starr, Frederick: Some Pennsylvania German lore. *In: The Journal of American Folk-Lore. Vol. IV. (No. XV.) Boston Mass. — New York, N. Y. 1891. pp. 321—326.* [2203

Stephen, Walker Lewis: Catalogue of Pennsylvania German and Huguenot antiques. Pensilfawnish Deitcha olda Housrad. *A list of articles giving ,,Dutch" and English names and uses as employed by ancestors of many living folk. Compiled as a reference for antiquarians and collectors of elaborate and crude antiques for Henry W. Shoemaker, chairman Pennsylvania Historical Commission by Walker Lewis Stephen. Second edition revised. Reading, Pa.: Reading Eagle 1925. pp. 32, ill.* [2204

[Stiles, Henry Reed]-Aurand, A. Monroe: Bundling: i. e., ,,A man and a woman lying on the same bed with their clothes on". — Grose, Dictionary. Its origin, progress and decline in America. *By H. R. Stiles. Reprinted from the scarce edition of 1871. Part II. More about bundling. By A. Monroe Aurand, jr. Harrisburg, Pa.: Privately printed by The Aurand Press. Harrisburg, Pa. 1928. pp. VIII, 97.* [2205

Stoudt, John Baer: Weather prognostications and superstitions among the Pennsylvania Germans. *In: The Pennsyl-*

vania-German. Vol. VI. Lebanon, Pa. 1905. pp. 328—335; Vol. VII. 1906. pp. 242—243. [2206

Stoud, John Baer: The rooster weather vane. *In: The Pennsylvania-German. Vol. VI. Lebanon, Pa. 1905. pp. 364—365.* [2207

— Pennsylvania German riddles and nursery rhymes. *In: The Journal of American Folk-Lore. Vol. XIX. Boston, Mass. and New York, N. Y. 1906. pp. 113—121.* [2208

— Some Palatine riddles. *In: Olde Vlster. A historical and genealogical magazine. Vol. VIII. Kingston, N. Y. 1913. pp. 285—286.* [2209

— The folklore of the Pennsylvania-German. *A paper read at the annual meeting York, Pa., October 14, 1910. Lancaster, Pa.: The New Era Printing Co. 1915. Issued as supplement of: The Pennsylvania-German Society. Proceedings and Addresses . . . 1910. Vol. XXIII. Lancaster, Pa. 1915. pp. 155.* [2210

— Some Pennsylvania German counting-out rhymes. *In: Annual Proceedings of the Lehigh County Historical Society. Allentown, Pa. 1924. pp. 67—73.* [2211

— House mottoes in eastern Pennsylvania. *Paper read January 15, 1927. In: A Collection of Papers read before the Bucks County Historical Society. Vol. VI. Allentown, Pa. 1932. pp. 65—78.* [2212

Thomas, Edith M. Mary at the farm and cook recipes compiled during her visit among the ,,Pennsylvania Germans". *Norristown, Pa.: H. Hartenstein 1915. pp. 440 Second edition. Harrisburg, Pa.: Evangelical Press 1928. pp. 423, ill.* [2213

Thomas, Nettie Allen and others: Pages from old Salem cook books. *Compiled by the Dorcas Co.-Workers of the Salem Home. Winston-Salem, N. C. 1931: Children's Home Printshop 1931. pp. 96.* [2214

Weygandt, Cornelius: The red hills. A record of good days outdoors and in, with things Pennsylvania Dutch. *Philadelphia, Pa.: University of Pennsylvania Press, Nov. 1929. pp. XI, (1), 251, ill.* [2215

White, Emma Gertrude: Folk-medicine among Pennsylvania Germans. *In: The Journal of American Folk-Lore. Vol. X. (No. XXXVI.) Boston, Mass. — New York, N. Y. 1897. pp. 78—80.* [2216

Wintemberg, W. J.: Items of German-Canadian folk-lore. *In: The Journal of American Folk-Lore. Vol. XII. (No. XLIV.) Boston, Mass. — New York, N. Y. 1899. pp. 45—50.* [2217

Wrenshall, Letitia Humphreys: Incantations and popular healing in Maryland and Pennsylvania. *Paper read before the Maryland Folk-Lore Society. In: The Journal of American Folk-Lore. Vol. XV. (No. LIX.) Boston, Mass. — New York, N. Y. 1902. pp. 268—274.* [2218

Pennsylvania-Dutch cooking. *Extract from a Pennsylvania woman's letter in the New York Evening Post. In: The Pennsylvania-German. Vol. VIII. Lebanon, Pa. 1907. pp. 332—333.* [2219

Early cheese-making. *In: The Pennsylvania-German. Vol. VIII. Lebanon, Pa. 1907. pp. 133—134.* [2220

Die ersten Salz-Bretzeln. *In: Deutsch-Amerikanische Geschichtsblätter. Jg. IX. Chicago, Ill. 1909. S. 121.* [2221

Himmelsbrief. *[Several communications bearing on the subject.] In: The Pennsylvania-German. Vol. IX. Cleona, Pa. 1908. pp. 217—222.* [2222

Hexerei. *Press comments. In: The Pennsylvania-German. Vol. XII. Lititz, Pa. 1911. pp. 619—621.* [2223

A Cumberland county, Pa. mystery. *(Cumberland County ss; Examination of George Cover [Jerg Kobers] and Adam Crytzer [Adam Krietze.] [Note of affirmation Febr. 5, 1787] in: The Pennsylvania Magazine of History and Biography. Vol. XXXIX. Philadelphia, Pa. 1915. p. 111.* [2224

Planting time. *Clippings from the ,,Register", Norristown, Pa. In: The Pennsylvania-German. Vol. XI. Litiz, Pa. 1910. p. 178.* [2225

The Red Rose Rental custom. *In: The Penn Germania. Vol. I. Old series, vol. XIII. Lititz, Pa. 1912. pp. 819—823.* [2226

Hausbau

Architecture

Chandler, Joseph Everett: The colonial house. *New York, N. Y.: R. M. McBride and Co. 1924. pp. 222.* [2227

Kimball, Fiske: Architecture in the history of the colonies and of the republic. *In: American Historical Review. Vol. XXVII. New York, N. Y. 1921/22. pp. 47—57.* [2228

Archanbault, A. Margaretta: A guide book of art, architecture, and historic interests in Pennsylvania. *Philadelphia, Pa.: The John Winston Co. 1924. pp. XIV, 509, ill.* [2229

Boggs, John C.: Colonial architecture in Montgomery County. *In: Historical Sketches. A Collection of Papers prepared for the Historical Society of Montgomery County, Pa. Vol. III. Norristown, Pa. 1929. pp. 39—46.* [2230

Brumbaugh, G. Edwin: Colonial architecture of the Pennsylvania Germans. *Originally delivered as an address before the forty-first annual meeting of the Pennsylvania German Society at Reading. October 23, 1931. In: The Pennsylvania-German Society. Proceedings and Addresses . . . 1930. Vol. XLI. Norristown, Pa.: Norristown Herald. 1933. Separate pagination. pp. 60, III, plates 105.* [2231

Cabeen, Francis von A.: An old Dutch oven in New Britain. *In: A Collection of Papers read before the Bucks County Historical Society. Vol. IV. Easton, Pa. 1917. pp. 574—576.* [2232

Collins, Alden M.: Octagonal or so-called „eight square" school-houses. *In: A Collection of Papers read before the Bucks County Historical Society. Vol. V. Meadville, Pa. 1926. pp. 252—260, ill.* [2233

Crews, Hall: Old Salem, now a part of Winston-Salem, N. C. *Photographs by Kenneth Clark. Measured drawings from the George F. Lindsay collection. In: The monograph series recording the architecture of the American Colonies and the early Republic. Vol. XV, no. 2.*

Edited and published by Russel F. Whitehead. New York City, N. Y.: Russel F. Whitehead, 1929. pp. 31—44, plates XVI—XXX. [2234

Dempwolf, Frederick G.: Lutheran Church architecture. *In: The Lutheran Quarterly. Vol. XLVI. Gettysburg, Pa. 1916. pp. 412—429.* [2235

Diffenderffer, Frank Reed: The story of a picture *[Lancaster City, Pa.] In: Papers and Addresses of the Lancaster County Historical Society. Vol. IX. Lancaster, Pa. 1905. pp. 182—230, ill.* [2236

Downs, Joseph: A Pennsylvania-German house. *In: The Pennsylvania Museum Bulletin. Vol. XXII, no. 108. December, 1926. Philadelphia, Pa. 1926. pp. 265—275, ill.* [2237

— The house of the Miller at Millbach. The architecture, arts, and crafts of the Pennsylvania Germans. *[s. l.] Published by the Pennsylvania Museum of Art, Philadelphia, Pa. 1929. pp. (31), ill.* [2238

Ely, Warren S.: Octogonal or so-called „eight-square" school-houses. *In: A Collection of Papers read before the Bucks County Historical Society. Vol. V. Meadville, Pa. 1926. pp. 290—307, ill.* [2239

Groß, A. Haller: The old spring-houses of Bucks County, *[Pa.] In: A Collection of Papers read before the Bucks County Historical Society. Vol. IV. Easton, Pa. 1917. pp. 396—397, ill.* [2240

Jaekel, Frederic B.: Squirrel-tailed bake-oven in Bucks County. *Read Jan. 25, 1916. In: A Collection of Papers read before the Bucks County Historical Society. Vol. IV. Easton, Pa. 1917. pp. 579—586.* [2241

Keyser, Naaman Henry: Old historic Germantown. *An address with illustrations presented at the fourteenth annual meeting. Lancaster, Pa.: The New Era Printing Co. 1916. In: The Pennsylvania-German Society. Proceedings and*

Addresses at Germantown, Oct. 25, 1904. Vol. XV. Lancaster, Pa. 1906. Separate pagination. pp. 78, ill.
[See also other items listed under Germantown, Pa.: No. 5030ff.]   [2242

Leatherman, J. Kirk: An old bakeoven in Plumstead Township, *[Bucks Co., Pa.] Read Jan. 25, 1916. In: A Collection of Papers read before the Bucks County Historical Society. Vol. IV. Easton, Pa. 1917. pp. 572—574.*   [2243

Mercer, Henry C.: The origin of log houses in the United States. *Read Jan. 19, 1924. In: A Collection of Papers read before the Bucks County Historical Society. Vol. V. Easton, Pa. 1926. pp. 568—583, ill.*   [2244

Nutting, Wallace: Pennsylvania beautiful (Eastern). *Illustrated by the author with many examples of landscapes and old houses in all the counties herein described. Framingham, Mass.: Old America Co. 1924. pp. 302, ill.*   [2245

Raymond, Eleanor: Early domestic architecture of Pennsylvania. *Photographys and measured drawings by Eleanor Raymond with an introduction by R. Brognard Okie. New York, N. Y.:*

William Helburn, Inc.; Baltimore, Md.: Garamond Press 1931. pp. (4), (9), 158, plates.   [2246

Reed, Luther D.: Church architecture in America. *In: The Lutheran Church Review. Vol. XLIV. Philadelphia, Pa. 1925. pp. 14—33.*   [2247

Sachse, Julius Friedrich: Quaint old Germantown in Pennsylvania. *Paper read at the annual meeting. Illustrated with 60 copies of the original sketches of John Richard. Lancaster, Pa.: The New Era Printing Co. 1915. In: The Pennsylvania-German Society. Procceedings and Addresses at Riegelsville, Pa., Oct. 4, 1912. Vol. XXIII. Lancaster, Pa. 1915. Separate pagination. pp. 7; 60 plates.* [2248

Thomas, Edith M.: Old Dutch bakeovens. *In: A Collection of Papers read before the Bucks County Historical Society. Vol. IV. Easton, Pa. 1917. pp. 574—576.*   [2249

Watson, John F. Notes of the early history of Germantown. *In: Hazard's Register of Pennsylvania. Vol. I. Philadelphia, Pa. 1828. pp. 279—284; 289—293.*
[Old stile of buildings in Germantown.]   [2250

Ländliches Gemeinschaftsleben
Rural Community Life

Brunner, Edmund de S.: Cooperation in Coopersburg. *Lehigh County, Pa. New York, N. Y.: Missionary Education Movement of the United States and Canada 1916. pp. XVI, 95, ill.* = *Library of Christian Progress.* [2251

Dennis, W. V.: Organization affecting farm youth in Locust Township, Columbus County. *State College, Pa. 1931. pp. 43, ill.* = *Bulletin 265 (June, 1931) of the Pennsylvania State College, School of Agriculture and Experiment Station, State College.* [2252

Fry, C. Luther: A census analysis of American villages, being a study of the 1920 census data for 177 villages scattered over the United States. *New York, N. Y.: Institute of Social and Religious Research 1925. pp. VII—XVI, 165, charts, maps.* = *Institute of Social and Religious Research, American Village Studies. Edmund de S. Brunner, Director.*

[Among other villages: Centre Hall, Centre Co.; Halifax, Dauphin Co.; Martinsburg, Blair Co.; Mc Connellsburg, Fulton Co.; Mercersburg, Franklin Co.; Middleburg, Snyder Co.; Millville, Columbia Co.; Spring Grove, York Co., all in Pennsylvania; Thurmont, Frederick Co., Md.] [2253

Heisey, Paul Harold: The Lutheran Church and the rural problem. *In: The Lutheran Quarterly. Vol. XLIV. Gettysburg, Pa. 1914. pp. 539—570.* [2254

Hill, William Free: A brief history of the Grange movement in Pennsylvania. *Chambersburg, Pa.: Printed by Pennsylvania Grange News 1923. pp. 48, ill.* [2255

Kirkpatrick, Ellis L.: The English River congregation of the Church of the Brethren. *Iowa City, Ia.: Published by the State Historical Society of Iowa; Athens Press 1930. pp. 107.* = *Iowa Monograph Series: No. 2. Edited by Benj. T. Shambaugh.* [2256

Nason, C. Wayne: Rural community fire departments. *Washington, D. C.: United States Government Printing Office 1931. pp. 46, ill.* = *U. S. Department of Agriculture. Farmer's Bulletin no. 1667.*

[A rural fire department at Bernville, Pa. pp. 25—28, ill.] [2257

Rissinger, C. M.: The rural problem. *In: The Reformed Church Review. Fifth series, vol. II. Lancaster, Pa. 1923. pp. 354—368.* [2258

Super, Charles William: A study of a rural community. *In: The Pennsylvania-German. Vol. XII. Lititz, Pa. 1911. pp. 15—23; 65—76; 129—137; 193—201.* [2259

Stump, Adam: Problem of the rural pastorate. *In: The Lutheran Quarterly. Vol. XXXIV. Gettysburg, Pa. 1904. pp. 363—382.* [2260

Tungeln, H. von: A rural survey of Orange Township, Blackhawk County, Iowa. *By . . ., assisted in the field work by* W. A. Brindley *and* H. B. Hawthorn. *Ames, Ia. 1918. pp. 397—450, ill., map.* = *Agricultural Experiment Station Iowa State College of Agriculture and Mechanic Arts. (Rural Sociology Section.) Bulletin no. 184.* [2261

Yoder, Paul D.: The soul of the rural community. *In: The Reformed Review. Fifth series, vol. II. Lancaster, Pa. 1923. pp. 39—55.* [2262

The Country Church number. *Editor* G. H. Gerberding. = *The Lutheran Church Review. Vol. XXXV. Philadelphia, Pa. 1916 no. 2, Febr. pp. 50* [2263

„Inner Mission" number. *Editor* J. F. Ohl. = *The Lutheran Church Review. Vol. XXXV. Philadelphia, Pa. 1916. no. 4, May. pp. 67.* [2264

County and state agricultural organizations, *with dates and places of fairs 1929. Harrisburg, Pa. 1929. pp. 30.* = *Bulletin. Pennsylvania Department of Agriculture. Harrisburg, Pa. Vol. XII, no. 13. Harrisburg, Pa., July 1, 1929* = *General Bulletin No. 482.* [2265

Erziehung und Unterricht

Education and Schools

Allgemeines

General

Albright, R. W. and Leedy, R. B.: A century's progress. A story of religious education in the Evangelical Church 1832—1932. *Cleveland, O. and Harrisburg, Pa.: Evangelical Press 1932. pp. X, 101, ill.* [2266

Bedenbaugh, Z. W.: Sunday school work in the south. *In: The Lutheran Church Review. Vol. XV. Philadelphia, Pa. 1896. pp. 485—489.* [2267

Bell, Sadie: The church, the state, and the education in Virginia. *Thesis of Ph. D. University of Pennsylvania. Philadelphia, Pa. 1930. pp. VII—XII, 796. [The German Protestants. pp. 51—55; Educational activities and tendencies of minor Evangelical groups. pp. 572—579.* [2268

Betz, I. H.: The origin of Sunday schools. *In: The Pennsylvania-German. Vol. X. Lititz, Pa. 1909. pp. 145—149.* [2269

Brane, C. I. B.: United Brethren „church schools". *In: The Pennsylvania-German Vol. VIII. Lebanon, Pa. 1907. pp. 312—317, ill.* [2270

Brecht, Samuel K.: The Hosensack academy. *In: The Pennsylvania-German. Vol. XI. Lititz, Pa. 1910. pp. 664—669. [Schwenkfelder and education.]* [2271

Brumbaugh, Martin G.: An educational struggle in colonial Pennsylvania. *Inaugural address as president of the Pennsylvania State Teachers' Association, Bellefonte, Pa., July 5, 1898. Lancaster, Pa.: Wickersham Press 1898. pp. 20.* [2272

— The life and works of Christopher Dock, America's pioneer writer on education, *with a translation of his works into the English language. With an introduction by Samuel W. Pennypacker. Philadelphia, Pa. & London: J. B. Lippincott Co. 1908. pp. 272, ill.* [2273

Buehrle, R. K.: The educational position of the Pennsylvania-Germans. *In: The Pennsylvania-German Society. Proceedings and Addresses at . . .; Mt. Gretna, July 19, 1894. Vol. IV, Lancaster, Pa. 1894. pp. 121—132.* [2274

— Pennsylvania-German educators. *In: The Pennsylvania-German. Vol. VIII. Lebanon, Pa. 1907. pp. 577—581, ill.* [2275

Cable, W. Arthur - Sauger, Homer F.: Educational blue book and directory of the Church of the Brethren 1708—1923. *With biographies . . . Compiled and edited by . . . Elgin, Ill.: Published by the General Educational Board of the Church of the Brethren 1923. pp. 656, ill.* [2276

Cavell, Jean Moore: Religious education among people of Germanic origin in colonial Pennsylvania. *Read before the Pennsylvania-German Society at Lancaster, Pa., October 9, 1925. In: The Pennsylvania-German Society. Proceedings and Addresses at Lancaster, October 9, 1925. Vol. XXXVI. Lancaster, Pa. 1929. pp. 31—45, ill.* [2277

[Chandler, Samuel]: A memorial in the case of the German emigrants settling in the British Colonies of Pennsylvania and the back part of Maryland, Virginia etc. *London: Printed in the year 1754. pp. 20.* [2278

Collins, Alden M.: Octagonal or so-called „eight square" school-houses. *In: A Collection of Papers read before the Bucks County Historical Society. Vol. V. Meadville, Pa. 1926. pp. 252—260, ill.* [2279

[Crevecœur, St. John de]: Verzeichnis der Universitäten und anderer Lehranstalten, *ingleichen der gelehrten Gesellschaften & in den vereinten Staaten von*

Nordamerika, verfertigt den 1. Julius 1789. In: Amerikanisches Magazin oder authentische Beiträge zur Erdbeschreibung, Staatskunde und Geschichte von Amerika, besonders aber der vereinten Staaten. Herausgegeben von Hegewisch-Kiel und Ebeling-Hamburg. Erster Band. Zweites Stück. Hamburg: Carl Ernst Bohn 1796. S. 109—117. [2279a

Early, J. W.: German Lutheran ,,church-schools". *In: The Pennsylvania-German. Vol. VIII. Lebanon, Pa. 1907. pp. 347—350.* [2280

[Ehman, Heinrich]: Wie es kam, daß ich in Amerika Schulmeister wurde. *Auf Veranlassung Strohm's für das Archiv der Deutschen Gesellschaft geschrieben. 6. April 1903. In: German American Annals. New series, vol. I. Philadelphia, Pa. 1903. pp. 601—610.* [2281

[—] How I became a schoolmaster in America. *(Free translation of a paper prepared in 1903 for the archives of the Deutsche Gesellschaft of Philadelphia, and published in: German American Annals, Oct., 1903 [= no. 2281].) In: The Pennsylvania-German. Vol. X. Lititz, Pa. 1909. pp. 443—448.* [2282

Eiselmeier, J.: Christoph Dock, der Verfasser der ersten Schulkunde in Amerika. *In: Die Neue Zeit (The New Era). Wochenschrift für Politik, Kunst unp Literatur. Bd. XIV, Nr. 39. New Ulm, Minn., 27. Febr. 1932. S. 4—5.* [2283

Ely, Warren S.: Octogonal or so-called ,,eight-square" school-houses. *In: A Collection of Papers read before the Bucks County Historical Society. Vol. V. Meadville, Pa. 1926. pp. 290—307, ill.* [2284

Evjen, John O.: The Berkemeyer library. A two hundred years old church library found at Wittenberg College. *In: The Lutheran Quarterly. Vol. LV. Gettysburg, Pa. 1925. pp. 132—147.* [2285

Falkenstein, G. N.: The German Baptist Brethren's ,,church-school". *In: The Pennsylvania-German. Vol. VIII. Lebanon, Pa. 1907. pp. 470—473, ill.* [2286

Gardner, George Christian: The German Sunday-school. *In: The Lutheran Church Review. Vol. XV. Philadelphia, Pa. 1896. pp. 438—441.* [2287

Good, James I.: Early schools of the German Reformed Church. *In: The Penn-*

sylvania-German. Vol. VIII. Lebanon, Pa. 1907. pp. 358—359. [2288

Gotwald, Frederic G.: Pennsylvania German Lutherans and higher education. *In: The Lutheran Quarterly. Vol. XXXVII. Gettysburg, Pa. 1907. pp. 404—421.* [2289

— Lutheran secondary schools and colleges. *In: The Pennsylvania-German. Vol. VIII. Lebanon, Pa. 1907. pp. 403—415, ill.* [2290

Hamilton, J. Taylor: The early Moravian contribution to liberal education in Eastern Pennsylvania. *An address delivered at Lafayette College on Founder's Day, Oct. 23, 1901. [s. l.] [1915.] pp. (15).* [2291

Hark, J. Max: The ,,church-schools" of the Moravians. *In: The Pennsylvania-German. Vol. VIII. Lebanon, Pa. 1907. pp. 299—304, ill.* [2292

Hartzler, John Ellsworth: Education among the Mennonites of America *with introduction by Elmer E. S. Johnson. Danvers, Ill.: The Central Mennonite Publishing Board 1925. pp. 195. [Bibliography. pp. 189—195.]* [2293

Haussmann, Carl Frederick: Kunze's Seminarium and the Society for the Propagation of Christianity and Useful Knowledge among the Germans in America. *Philadelphia, Pa.: Americana Germanica Press 1917. pp. 141, ill. = Americana Germanica. Monographs devoted to the comparative study of the literary, linguistic and other cultural relations of Germany and America. Edited by Marion Dexter Learned. No. 27.* [2294

Heilman, U. Henry: The early schools and teachers among our German ancestors. *Papers read before the Lebanon County Historical Society, April 19, 1928. In: Papers . . . of the Lebanon County Historical Society. Vol. IX, no. 9. Lebanon, Pa. 1928. pp. 291—307, ill.* [2295

Hertzler, Silas: Mennonite schools in colonial times. *In: Christian Monitor. A, monthly magazine for the home. Vol. XVII, no. 1. Scottdale, Pa. 1925. p. 793; p. 797.* [2296.

— Early Mennonite Sunday schools. *In: The Mennonite Quarterly Review. Vol. II. Goshen, Ind. 1928. pp. 123—124; 205—206.* [2297

— Attendance at Mennonite schools and colleges, 1928. *In: The Mennonite Quarterly Review. Vol. III. Goshen, Ind.*

*1929. pp. 197—202; . . . 1929—1930.
In: Vol. IV, 1930. pp. 166—177; . . .
1930—1931. In: Vol. V, 1931. pp. 272
—283; . . . in 1931—1932. In: Vol. VI,
1932. pp. 264—275; . . . in 1932—33.
In: Vol. VII, 1933. pp. 251—260; . . . in
1933—1934. In: Vol. VIII, 1934, pp.
180—191.*   [2298
Hewitt, Warren F.: Samuel Breck and the
Pennsylvania School Law of 1834. *In:
Pennsylvania History. Official organ
of the Pennsylvania Historical Association. Vol. I. Philadelphia, Pa. 1934.
pp. 63—75.*   [2299
Heydrick, Christopher: Genesis, evolution
and adoption of the public school sy-
stem of Pennsylvania. *In: The Penn
Germania. Vol. I. = Old series, vol.
XIII. Lititz, Pa. 1912. pp. 12—16;
50—57; 81—93.*   [2300
Knauss, James O.: The Pennsylvania-German as school-superintendent. *In: The
Pennsylvania-German. Vol. VIII. Lebanon, Pa. 1907. pp. 581—583.*   [2301
Kriebel, H. W.: Education among the
Schwenkfelders. *In: The Pennsylvania-
German. Vol. VIII. Lebanon, Pa. 1907.
pp. 355—358, ill.*   [2302
**Leonard, R. J. - Evenden, E. S. - O'Rear,
F. B.:** Survey of higher education for
the United Lutheran Church in Ame-
rica. *3 vols. By . . . with the cooperation
of mother members of the staff and gra-
duate students. [School of Education,
Teachers College, Columbia University,
New York City, N. Y.] New York City,
N. Y. Bureau of Publications Teachers
College, Columbia University 1929. pp.
XXXIII, 623, maps; pp. XVII, 612;
XII, 389.*   [2303
Levan, Franklin K.: The beginnigs of our
literary institutions. *In: The Reformed
Quarterly Review. Vol. XXX. = New
series, vol. V. Philadelphia, Pa. 1883.
pp. 380—390; 518—534.*   [2304
Livingood, Frederick George: Eighteenth
century Reformed church schools. *Nor-
ristown, Pa.: Norristown Press 1930. =
Part XXXV. „Narrative and critical
history" prepared at the request of the
Pennsylvania-German Society. In: The
Pennsylvania-German Society, Proceedings and Addresses . . . 1927. Vol.
XXXVIII. Norristown, Pa. 1930. Separate pagination. pp. XIX, (3), 313,
ill.*   [2305
Lohr, Otto: Aus der Frühgeschichte des
deutschen Schulwesens in Nordamerika

(1694—1742). *In: Der Auslanddeutsche.
Zeitschrift für die Kunde vom Auslanddeutschtum. Herausgegeben vom Deutschen Ausland-Institut Stuttgart. Jg.XIX.
Stuttgart 1936. S. 551—554.*   [2305a
Maurer, Charles Lewis: Early Lutheran
education in Pennsylvania. *In: The
Pennsylvania-German Society. Proceedings and Addresses at Harrisburg, Pa.,
Pa., Oct. 18, 1929. Vol. XL. Norristown, Pa. 1932. Separate pagination.
pp. XII, (1), 284, ill.*   [2306
Mays, George: A German schoolmaster of
„ye olden time". *In: The Pennsylvania-German. Vol. IX. Cleona, Pa.
1908. pp. 3—6.*   [2307
Messinger, S. L.: Reformed secondary
schools and colleges. *In: The Pennsylvania-German. Vol. VIII. Lebanon,
Pa. 1907. pp. 459—466, ill.*   [2308
Mulhern, James: A history of secondary
education in Pennsylvania. *Philadelphia, Pa. School of Education, University of Pennsylvania 1933. 714 pp., ill.*
                                       [2309
Nerz, J. J.: Early German Catholic parochial schools. *In: The Pennsylvania-
German. Vol. VIII Lebanon, Pa. 1907.
pp. 292—299, ill.*   [2310
Nitzsche, George E.: Moravian influence in
founding the University of Pennsyl-
vania. *In: The Pennsylvania-German.
Vol. VIII. Lebanon, Pa. 1907. pp.
304—305.*   [2311
Noffsinger, John Samuel: A programm for
higher education in the Church of the
Brethren with special reference to the
number and distribution of colleges.
*New York City, N. Y.: Published by
Teachers College, Columbia University
1925. pp. VI, 80.
= Teachers College, Columbia University,
Contributions to Education, no. 172.* [2312
Nowlan, Ivan Seymour: „The educational
work of the German Reformed and
Lutheran churches in Pennsylvania during the colonial period." *Thesis of M.
A. University of Chicago, Chicago, Ill.
1916. Typewritten. pp. VI, 74.
[Bibliography. pp. I—III.]*   [2313
Pennypacker, Samuel Whitaker: Christopher Dock, the pious schoolmaster on
the Skippack and his works. *In: Historical and biographical sketches. Philadelphia, Pa. 1883 [= no. 356].
pp. 91—153.*   [2314
Richards, H. M. M.: Our educational system in its growth. *Paper read Sept. 26,*

*1930. In: Papers read before the Le-
banon County Historical Society. Vol.
X, no. 2. Lebanon, Pa. 1932. pp. 65—
98, ill.* [2315
Richards, Louis: „The old school and the
new". *An address delivered before the
Berks County Teachers' Institute, in the
Academy of Music, Reading, Pa., Oct. 26,
1908. pp. 19.* [2316
Robarts, J. O. K.: A quintet of notable
Pennsylvanians who were valiant and
successful champions of the Common-
School system. *In: The Pennsylvania-
German. Vol. VIII. Lebanon, Pa. 1907.
pp. 195—198, ill.*
*[Joseph Hiester, John Andrew Schulze;
Georg Wolf; Joseph Ritner, Thaddeus
Stevens.]* [2317
Schantz, F. J. F.: The history of the Sunday
school. *In: The Lutheran Church Review. Vol. XV. Philadelphia, Pa. 1896.
pp. 403—412.* [2318
Schuler, H. A.: Education among the Pennsylvania-Germans. *In: The Pennsylvania-German. Vol. VII. Lebanon, Pa.
1906. pp. 183—186, ill.* [2319
— Reminiscences of a former Hereford
schoolboy. *In: The Pennsylvania-German. Vol. IX. Cleona, Pa. 1908. pp.
11—15, ill.* [2320
[Seilhammer, G. O.]: Education among the
Pennsylvania Germans. *In: The Kittochtinny Magazine. Vol. I. Chambersburg, Pa.: G. O. Seilhamer 1905. p. 108.*
[2321
Seyfert, A. G.: How I became a schoolmaster in Brecknock *[Lancaster Co.,
Pa.] In: The Pennsylvania-German.
Vol. X. Lititz, Pa. 1909. pp. 567—569.*
[2322
Sharp, S. Z.: The educational history of the
Church of the Brethren. *Elgin, Ill.:
Brethren Publishing House 1923. pp.
383, ill.* [2323
Shelly, A. S.: The schools of the Mennonite
settlers. *In: The Pennsylvania-German.
Vol. VIII. Lebanon, Pa. 1907. pp. 466
—470.* [2324
Shimmell, L. S.: The Pennsylvania-German
in his relation to education. *A symposium of historical and descriptive articles.
Edited by . . . In: The Pennsylvania-
German. Vol. VIII. Lebanon, Pa.
1907. pp. 292ff.; 347ff.; 403ff.; 459ff.;
515ff.; 571ff.; Vol. IX. 1908. pp. 3ff.*
[2325
— The Pennsylvania-Germans and the
common-school law of 1834. *In: The*

*Pennsylvania-German. Vol. VIII. Le-
banon, Pa. 1907. pp. 571—577.* [2326
[Smith, Geo]: How the public school system was established in Pennsylvania.
*(Letter of Geo Smith to J. P. Wichersham,
Febr. 15, 1882.) In: The Pennsylvania
Magazine of History and Biography.
Vol. XXXVII. Philadelphia, Pa. 1913.
pp. 76—82.* [2327
Eine kurtze Nachricht, von der Christlichen
und liebreichen Anstalt, welche zum
Besten und zur Unterweisung der
armen Teutschen, und ihrer Nachkommen in Pennsylvanien, und andern
daran gräntzenden Englischen Pro-
vinzien in Nord-America errichtet
worden ist. *Herausgegeben auf Befehl
derer, zu Ausführung dieser Sache, bestimmten Herren General Trustees. Philadelphia, Gedruckt durch Anton Arm-
brüster, in der Dritten-Straß, 1755.
16 S.* [2328
A brief history of the rise and progress
of the charitable scheme, carrying on
by a society of noblemen and gentlemen in London, for the relief and instruction of poor Germans, and their
descendants, settled in Pennsylvania,
and the adjacent British Colonies in
North-America. *([inside:] published for
the information of those whome it may concern, by* James Hamilton, William Allen,
Richard Peters, Benjamin Franklin *and*
Conrad Weiser, *Esquires, and the Reverend
Mr.* William Smith. *Trustees-General,
appointed for the management of the
said Charitable Scheme.) Published by
order of the Gentlemen appointed Trustees-
General, for the Management of the said
Charitable Scheme. Philadelphia, Pa.:
B. Franklin and D. Hall. 1755. pp. 18.*
[2329
Stapleton, A.: Education in the Evangelical
Church. *In: The Pennsylvania-German.
Vol. VIII. Lebanon, Pa. 1907. pp. 350
—355, ill.* [2330
Steiner, Bernard C.: Education among the
early Lutherans of America. *In: The
Lutheran Quarterly. Vol. XXIX. Gettysburg, Pa. 1899. pp. 273—276.* [2331
Sypher, J. R.: School history of Pennsylvania from the earliest settlements to
the present time. *Designed for common
schools, academies, colleges, families, and
libraries. Philadelphia, Pa.: J. B. Lippincott & Co. 1868. pp. VIII, 9—344,
ill.* [2332

Tyson, H. W.: Lutheran education in Pennsylvania 1638—1834. *Thesis of M. A., University of Pennsylvania, Philadelphia, Pa. 1923. Typewritten. pp. 146.* [2333

Umble, John: Seventy years of progress in Sunday school work among the Mennonites of the Middle West. *In: The Mennonite Quarterly Review. Vol. VIII. Goshen, Ind.-Scottdale, Pa. 1934, pp. 166—179.* [2334

Viereck, L.: Zwei Jahrhunderte Deutschen Unterrichts in den Vereinigten Staaten. *Braunschweig: Friedrich Vieweg und Sohn 1903. XVI, 293 S. [Bibliographie. S. XI—XVI.]* [2335

Walsh, Louise Gilchriese - Walsh, Matthew John: History and organization of education in Pennsylvania. *Published by the author. Indiana, Pa.: R. S. Grosse Print shop 1930. pp. XVI, 412, ill.* [2336

Weber, Samuel Edwin: The charity school movement in colonial Pennsylvania. *Thesis of Ph. D.: University of Pennsylvania, Philadelphia. Philadelphia, Pa.: Press of George F. Lasher 1905. pp. 74. [Bibliography. pp. 65—74.]*
Second print. The charity school movement in colonial Pennsylvania 1754—1763. *A history of the educational struggle between the colonial authorities and the German inhabitants of Pennsylvania. Philadelphia, Pa.: William J. Campbell 1905. pp. 74. [Bibliography. pp. 64—74.]* [2337

— The Germans and the charity-school movement. *In: The Pennsylvania-German. Vol. VIII. Lebanon, Pa. 1907. pp. 305—312.* [2338

Wickersham, James Pyle: A history of education in Pennsylvania, private and public, elementary and higher, from the time of the Swedes settled on the Delaware to the present time. *Lancaster, Pa.: Inquirer Publishing Co. 1886. pp. XXIII, 683, ill.* [2339

[—] Neighborhood-schools or pay-schools. *Extract from Dr. James P. Wickersham's History of Education in Pennsylvania. In: The Pennsylvania-German, Vol. VIII. Lebanon, Pa. 1907. pp. 473—474.* [2340

Schwenkfelder school documents. *Edited by M. D. Learned. In: Americana Germanica. A quarterly. Vol. II. Philadelphia, Pa. 1898. No. 1. pp. 70—86.* [2341

To the friends and patrons of schools and of the improvement of youth. *[Circular letter prepared by the trustees of the Latin school conducted in the so-called Hosensack Academy. ,,Philadelphia County, March, 1791."] Reprint in: The Pennsylvania-German. Vol. X. Lititz, Pa. 1909. pp. 133.* [2342

Sunday schools 50 years ago. *Reprint from: The Reformed Church Record. In: The Pennsylvania-German. Vol. XII. Lititz, Pa. 1911. p. 664.* [2343

The first Moravian boarding-school for boys in Pennsylvania, *(in the house of Henry Antes, Frederick Township, in the present Montgomery County, Pa. — Register of the scholars: 1745—1749). In: The Pennsylvania-Magazine of History and Biography. Vol. XXVII. Philadelphia, Pa. 1903. pp. 502—503.* [2344

Geschichte der Colleges
History of Colleges

Vereinigte Lutherische Kirche in Amerika:
United Lutheran Church in America:

Pennsylvania College, Gettysburg, Pa. 1827

Breidenbach, E. S.: The Pennsylvania College book. 1832—1882. *Published for the Alumni Association of Pennsylvania College. Philadelphia, Pa.: Lutheran Publication Society. 1882. pp. X, 475, ill.* [2345

Alumni directory of Pennsylvania College of Gettysburg, 1832—1918. *Gettysburg, Pa. 1918. pp. 256.*

= *Pennsylvania College of Gettysburg Bulletin. Gettysburg, Pa.: Published by the College Quarterly. Vol. VIII, no. 3. June, 1918.* [2346

Gettysburg, Lincoln's address and our educational institutions. *Published by the Board of education of the General Synod of the Evangelical Lutheran Church in the United States. [s. l.] 1907. pp. 31, ill.* [2347

R.[eynolds, W. M.]: Pennsylvania College. *In: The Evangelical Review. Vol. II.*

Gettysburg, Pa. 1850—51. p. 539. [2348
Pennsylvania College. *In: The Evangelical
Review. Vol. XVI. Gettysburg, Pa.
1865. pp. 103—117.* [2349
The remarkable record of Pennsylvania
College, Gettysburg, Pa. *In: The Penn-
sylvania-German. Vol. XII. Lititz, Pa.
1911. pp. 190.* [2350

Wittenberg College, Springfield, O. 1845

Clark, G. Gerlaw: History of Wittenberg
College, Springfield, O. *With portraits
and sketches of the lives of her most pro-
minent men, compiled and written by
G. G. Clark. Introduction by S. A. Ort.
Springfield, O.: J. A. Work 1887. pp.
201, ill.* [2351
[Howard, Elmer Gray]: The Semi-Centen-
nial souvenir of Wittenberg College.
*Published by the Class of Ninety-Six.
Springfield, O., May. 1895. Springfield,
O. — Chicago, Ill.: The Winter's Art
Litho Co. 1895. 136 ls.; XXVII: Ad-
vertisements. ill.* [2352
Alumni and former students of Wittenberg
College [1846—]1922. = *The Wittenberg
Bulletin. Published monthly in Spring-
field, O. By Wittenberg College. Vol.
XIX, no. 3. March, 1922. pp. 22.*
[2353

Roanoke College, Salem, Va. (1853), 1892

Celebration. 1853—1928. Diamond jubilee
and 75th commencement of Roanoke
College. *pp. 42.*
= *Roanoke College Bulletin. Published
quarterly by the College. Salem, Va. Vol.
XVII, no. 4. Dec. 1928.*
Including Dreher, William C.: *Historical
address. pp. 14—24.* [2354
Welsh, Dennis B. - Cronk, Vivian: The
alumni directory of Roanoke College.
*1853—1927. Prepared by ... Salem, Va.
1927. pp. 172, ill.*
= *Roanoke College Bulletin. Published
quarterly, by the College. Salem, Va.
Vol. XVI, no. 2. March, 1927.* [2355

Newberry College, Newberry S. C. 1856

— — —

Susquehanna University, Selinsgrove, Pa. 1858

— — —

Mühlenberg College, Allentown, Pa. 1867

Ochsenford, S. E.: 1867—1892. Muhlenberg
College. *A quarter-centennial memorial
volume being a history of the college and
a record of its men. Published by authority of the Board of Trustees of the College. Allentown, Pa.: Muhlenberg College 1892. pp. 584, ill.* [2356
Schantz, F. J. F.: Semi-centennial celebration of the historical origin of Mühlenberg College, on the college campus,
June 23rd, 1898. *Historical Address
by ... Allentown, Pa.: Published by
Muhlenberg College 1898. pp. (1), 7—15.*
[2357
Seip, Theodore L.: Mühlenberg College and
the University of Halle. *In: The Lutheran Church Review. Vol. XIV. Philadelphia, Pa. 1895. pp. 48—53.* [2358

Reformierte Kirche in den Ver. St.:
Reformed Church in the U. S.:

Franklin College, Lancaster, Pa. 1787— 1853; Marshall College, Mercersburg, Pa. 1836—1853; Franklin and Marshall College, Lancaster, Pa. 1853

Appel, Theodore: Recollection of college life
at Marshall College, Mercersburg, Pa.
From 1839 to 1845. *A narrative with
reflections. Reading, Pa.: Daniel Miller
1886. pp. VIII. 348.* [2359
Dubbs, Joseph Henry: The founding of
Franklin College 1787. *[From the „Reformed Quarterly Review" (= no. 2374).]
Philadelphia, Pa.: Reformed Church
Publication Board 1887. pp. 31.* [2360
— Old Franklin College. *In: Papers and
Addresses of the Lancaster County Hi-
storical Society. Vol. II. Lancaster, Pa.
1898. pp. 163—178, ill.* [2361
— History of Franklin and Marshall Col-
lege. Franklin College 1787—1853;
Marshall College 1836—1853; Franklin
and Marshall College 1853—1903. *Lan-
caster, Pa.: Published by the Franklin
and Marshall Alumni Association; Press
of the New Era Printing Co. 1903. pp.
XV, 402, ill.*
[Bibliography. pp. 382—394.] [2362
Gerhart, E. V.: Franklin and Marshall College and the New endowment scheme.
*Chambersburg, Pa.: M. Kieffer & Co.
1856. pp. 96.* [2363
Hoffman, Frank K.: Franklin and Marshall
College and the war. *Address delivered*

at the commencement of Franklin and Marshall College, at Lancaster, Pa., June 18, 1919. In: The Reformed Church Review. Fourth series, vol. XXIII. Philadelphia, Pa. 1919. pp. 370—383. [2364

Klein, H. M. J.: The beginnings of Franklin College and its first president. *In: The Lutheran Church Review. Vol. XXXII. Philadelphia, Pa. 1913. pp. 244—268.* [2365

— Historical sketch of the beginning of Franklin and Marshall College. *Note and reprint of the article from: The Reformed Church Rewiew. In: The Lutheran Quarterly. Vol. XLIII. Gettysburg, Pa. 1913. pp. 40—58.* [2366

Levan, Franklin K.: The significance of the centennial of Franklin and Marshall College. *In: The Reformed Quarterly Review. Vol. XXXIV. = New series, vol. IX. Philadelphia, Pa. 1887. pp. 248—256.* [2367

Nevin, J. W.: Franklin and Marshall College. *(Address delivered in Lancaster at the celebration of the union of the two colleges, June 7, 1853.) In: The Mercersburg Quarterly Review. Vol. V. Chambersburg, Pa. 1853. pp. 395—418.* [2368

Schiedt, Richard Conrad: On the threshold of a new century; a critical review of ,,Franklin and Marshall's" contribution to one hundred years of American thought. *Philadelphia, Pa.: Publication Board of the Reformed Church in the United States 1900. pp. 71.* [2369

— A tribute to Dr. Frederick Augustus Rauch, first president of Marshall College. Eminent educator and philosopher. *In commemoration of the 125th anniversary of his birth. 1805—1931. Milwaukee 1931. 24 S.* [2369a

Freiheitsbrief der Deutschen Hohen Schule (College) der Stadt Lancaster in dem Staate Pennsylvanien, *nebst einer Anrede an die Deutschen dieses Staats von den Trusties der besagten Hohen Schule. Philadelphia, Melchior Steiner. 1787. 16 S.* [2369b

Freibrief der Deutschen Hochschule (College) in der Stadt Lancaster in dem Staate Pennsylvanien; *nebst einer Anrede an die Deutschen dieses Staats, von der Ost-Pennsylvanischen Synode, welche sich am Dreieinigkeitsfeste A. D. 1830 in Lancaster versammelte. Baltimore, Md.: Gedruckt bei Johann F. Hanzsche 1830. 14 S.* [2370

Freibrief der deutschen Hochschule zu Lancaster, Pa. 1787, und Aufruf der Vorsteher an die deutschen Bewohner Pennsylvaniens. *Neudruck in: Der Deutsche Pionier. Jg. XV. Cincinnati, O. 1883—1884. Deutsch-amerikanische Dokumente. S. 14—27.* [2371

Formal opening of Franklin and Marshall College in the City of Lancaster, June 7, 1853, *together with addresses delivered on the occasion by* **A. L. Hayes,** Rev. **J. W. Nevin** *and* Rev. **Alonzo Potter.** *Lancaster, Pa.: Published by order of the Board of Trustees 1853. pp. 44.* [2372

Dedication of Franklin and Marshall College, Lancaster, Pa., May 16th, 1856. *Introductory by* **E. V. Gerhart,** *President; Address by* **Emlen Franklin.** *Chambersburg, Pa.: M. Kieffer & Co. 1856. pp. 24.* [2373

The centennial of Franklin and Marshall College. *In: The Reformed Quarterly Review. Vol. XXXIV. = New series, vol. IX. Philadelphia, Pa. 1887. pp. 411—547.*

  Pepper, William: An address on Benjamin Franklin.

  Hughes, Robert W.: Chief justice, Marshall and his work.

  Kieffer, J. S.: The claims of the college on the church.

  Steiner, Lewis, H.: The college and college curriculum.

  Dubbs, J. H.: The founding of Franklin College.

  Appel, Th.: A sketch of Marshall College, Mercersburg, Pa. from 1836 to 1841 under the presidency of Dr. Rauch. [2374

The charter anniversary of Franklin and Marshall College. *Extracts from: The Reformed Church Review. October, 1912. In: The Penn Germania. Vol. I. = Old series, vol. XIII. Lititz, Pa. 1912. pp. 863—870.* [2375

Franklin and Marshall College. Obituary record. *(Issued annually). A record of the lives of the deceased alumni of Marshall College and of Franklin and Marshall College. Edited for the Alumni Association. Lancaster, Pa.: Press of the Friedenwald Co., Baltimore, Md. Vol. I. 1897—1900. pp. IV; XI; 319. Vol. II. 1901—1909. pp. 287.* [2376

Franklin and Marshall College. Catalogue of officers and students, 1787—1903 ... *Edited by the Publishing Committee,* **Samuel H. Ranck,** *chairman . . . Lan-*

caster, Pa.: Franklin and Marshall College Alumni Association 1903. pp. XII, 224. [2377

Directory of living alumni of Franklin and Marshall College, arranged in classes, geographically and alphabetically. Published by direction of the Alumni Association of Franklin and Marshall College, Lancaster 1933. pp. 158.
= The Franklin and Marshall Alumnus, vol. IX, no. 2. February 1933. [2378

Catawba College, Sallisbury, N. C. 1851

Leonard, Jacob Calvin: History of Catawba College. Formerly located at Newton, now at Salisbury, N. C.: Published by the College 1927. pp. 352, ill. [2379

Cedar Crest College, Allentown Pa. 1866

— — —

Ursinus College, Collegeville, Pa. 1870

Snyder, S. Emma Price: Reminiscences of Penna. Female college. In: The Pennsylvania-German. Vol. XI. Lititz, Pa. 1910. pp. 321—332. ill. [2380
Weinberger, J. S.: History of Freeland Seminary. In: Historical Sketches. A Collection of Papers prepared for the Historical Society of Montgomery County, Pa. Vol. III. Norristown, Pa. 1905. pp. 44—51. [2381

Deutsche Baptisten-Brüder:
Church of the Brethren:

Cable, W. Arthur and Sanger, Homer F.: Educational blue book and directory of the Church of the Brethren 1708—1923. With biographies . . . Compiled and edited by . . . Elgin, Ill.: Published by the General Educational Board of the Church of the Brethren. 1923. pp. 656, ill. [2382
Sharp, S. Z.: The educational history of the Church of the Brethren. Elgin, Ill.: Brethren Publishing House 1923. pp. 383, ill. [2383

Mount Morris College, Mount Morris Ill. 1840

Culler, David D.: Memoirs of Old Sandstone. Wherein will be found something concerning the happenings within and about the gray pile of stone Old Sandstone.

Contributed to by a loyal host of Mt. Morris College's sons and daughters. Edited by . . . Elgin, Ill.: Brethren Publishing House 1912. pp. 202, ill. [2384

Juniata College, Huntingdon, Pa. 1876

Emmert, David: Reminiscences of Juniata College. Quarter century 1876—1901. Huntingdon, Pa.: Published by the author; Harrisburg, Pa.: Mount Plesant Printery, J. Horace McFarland Co. 1901. pp. VII, 183, ill. [2385
Juniata College, alumni register. Huntingdon, Pa.: Published by the Juniata College. 1932. pp. 76.
= Juniata College Bulletin. Vol. XXIX, no. 1 B. March, 1932. [2386

Bridgewater College, Bridgewater, Va. 1880

Wayland, John Walter: Bridgewater College: its past and present. A tribute of the alumni. Editor-in-chief: . . . Elgin, Ill.: The Brethren Publishing House 1905. pp. 298, ill. [2387
Fifty years of educational endeavor. Bridgewater College 1880—1930; Daleville College 1890—1930. By a staff of alumni. Staunton, Va.: The McClure Co. 1930. pp. (5), (1), 414, ill. [2388
Bridgewater — Daleville College. Alumni register. Bridgewater, Va.: Published by the College 1930. pp. 89.
= Bridgewater — Daleville College Bulletin. Vol. V, no. 6. Bridgewater, Va.: April, 1930. [2389

Schulen und Colleges der Mährischen Brüderkirche:
Moravian Church Schools and Colleges:

Moravian Seminary and College for Women, Bethlehem, Pa. (1742), 1785

Reichel, William C.: A history of the rise, progress, and present condition of the Bethlehem Female Seminary, with a catalogue of its pupils. 1785—1858. Philadelphia, Pa.: J. B. Lippincott & Co. 1858. pp. IX, 17—468, ill. [2390
[—] Historical sketch of the Moravian Seminary for Young Ladies at Bethlehem, Northampton County, Pa. Founded 1785. Bethlehem, Pa.: Moravian Publication Office 1876. pp. 32.
In: Appendix of the Transactions of the Moravian Historical Society. Vol. I. Nazareth, Pa. 1858—1876. [2391

Meynen, Bibliographie

14

[Reichel, William C.]: A history of the rise, progress, and present condition of the Moravian Seminary for Young Ladies, at Bethlehem, Pa. With a catalogue of its pupils. 1785—1858. *Revised and enlarged with a continuation of the history and catalogue to the year 1870. By* William H. Bibler. *Third edition, with continuation of the catalogue to 1880. Philadelphia, Pa.: J. B. Lippincott & Co. 1881. pp. XI, 17—608, ill.*   [2392

Nazareth Hall, Nazareth, Pa. (1775) 1785

Reichel, Levin T.: A history of Nazareth Hall from 1755 to 1855: and of the reunions of its former pupils ih 1854 and 1855. *Philadelphia, Pa.: J. B. Lippincott & Co. 1855. pp. (1), VI, 7—162, ill.*   [2393

Reichel, William C.: Historical sketc h of Nazareth Hall from 1755 to 1869; with an account of the reunions of former pupils and of the inauguration of a monument at Nazarath on the 11th of June, 1868, erected in memory of alumni who fell in the late rebellion. *Philadelphia, Pa.: J. B. Lippincott & Co. 1869. pp. 7—47.* Catalogues. *pp. 51—62; 57;* Historical sketch of the Moravian Theological Seminary of the American Province, founded October 3, 1807, at Nazareth, Pa. *pp. 20.* Reunions at Nazareth Hall. *pp. 118;* The military and naval record of alumni who were enrolled in the service of the United States. *pp. 74.* Appendix *pp. 25.* *[All bound as one volume.]*   [2394

— Historical sketch of Nazareth Hall, a Moravian boarding school for boys, located at Nazareth, Northampton County, Pa. Founded 1785. *Bethlehem, Pa.: Moravian Publication Office. 1876. pp. 27. In: Appendix of the Transactions of the Moravian Historical Society. Vol. I. Nazareth, Pa. 1858—1876.*   [2395

Hacker, H. H.: Nazareth Hall an historical sketch and roster of principals, teachers and pupils. *Bethlehem, Pa.: Times Publishing Co. 1910. pp. 5—191, ill.*   [2396

Reminiscences and letters of Nazareth Hall alumni. *Nazareth, Pa. 1901. pp. 38, ill.*   [2397

Nazareth Hall. *In: The Pennsylvania Magazine of History and Biography. Vol. XXIX. Philadelphia, Pa. 1905. p. 374.*   [2398

Salem College, Winston-Salem, N. C. 1772
— — —

Moravian College and Theological Seminary, Bethlehem, Pa. 1807

Schwarze, William Nathaniel: History of the Moravian College and Theological Seminary, founded at Nazareth, Pa., Oct. 2, 1807, reorganized at Bethlehem Pa., Aug. 30, 1858. *Bethlehem, Pa. In: Transactions of the Moravian Historical Society. Vol. VIII. Nazareth, Pa. 1909. pp. 59—356, ill.*   [2399

Schweinitz, Edmund de: Address delivered at the dedication of the cenotaph, erected in memory of the former pupils of Nazareth Hall who fell in defence of their country, in the War of Rebellion, June 11, 1868. *Bethlehem, Pa.: A. C. & H. H. T. Clauder 1868. pp. 13.* [2400

Moravian College and Theological Seminary, Bethlehem, Pa. A. souvenir of the Centennial celebration, October 2, 3, 1907. *Bethlehem, Pa. Times: Publishing Co. 1908. pp. 94, ill.*   [2401

Proceedings of the first annual meeting of the Moravian Educational Association. April 28—29, 1911. *Bethlehem, Pa. pp. 33.*   [2402

Kirche der Vereinigten Brüder:
United Brethren Church:

Lebanon Valley College, Annville, Pa. 1866

Bierman, E. Benjamin: The first twenty-five years of Lebanon Valley College. *In: Papers read before the Lebanon County Historical Society. Vol. III. Lebanon, Pa. 1905—1906. pp. 114—136, ill.*   [2403

Otterbein College, Westerville, O. 1847

Garst, Henry: Otterbein University 1847—1907. *With an introduction by T. J. Sanders. Dayton, O.: United Brethren Publishing House 1907. pp. 316, ill.*   [2404

Evangelische Kirche:
Evangelical Church:

Albright College, Reading, Pa. 1895

Albright, R. W. and Leedy, R. B.: A century of progress. A study of religious education in the Evangelical Church 1832

— 1932. *Cleveland, O.: Evangelical Press 1932. pp. X, 101, ill.*
[The history of Albright College together with the other educational institutions being set forth in Chap. X. pp. 95—99.]   [2405
The Alumni Association of Albright College. *Directory arranged by classes, including the class of 1932. = Bulletin, vol. XVIII, no. 2. Reading, Pa. 1931. pp. 56.*   [2406

Churches of God:

Findlay College, Findlay, O. 1882

— — —

Mennoniten-Kirche:
Mennonite Church:

Goshen College, Goshen, In. 1903

Hertzler, Silas: A statistical study of Goshen College alumni. *In: The Mennonite Quarterly Review. Vol. V. Goshen, Ind.*
— *Scottdale, Pa. 1932. pp. 286—291.*   [2407
Umble, John: The Elkhart Institute moves to Goshen. *Paper read at the January, 1935, meeting of the Mennonite Historical Society of Goshen College, Goshen, Ind. In: The Mennonite Quarterly Review. Vol. IX. Goshen, Ind.-Scottdale, Pa. 1935. pp. 37—59.*   [2408
Alumni directory of Goshen College and of Elkhart Institute. *Goshen, Ind. 1930. pp. 62.*
= Goshen College Bulletin. Vol. XXIV. Goshen College, Goshen, Ind., October, 1930.   [2409

Hesston College and Bible School, Hesston, Kan. 1919

— — —

Theologische Seminare
Theological Seminaries

Vereinigte Lutherische Kirche in Amerika:
United Lutheran Church in America:

Gotwald, Frederick G.: Theological education in the Lutheran Church in the United States prior to the founding of Wittenberg College and Seminary in 1845. *In: The Lutheran Quarterly. Vol. XLVI. Gettysburg, Pa. 1916. pp. 82—100.*   [2410
Heisey, Paul Harold: The story of Lutheran theological education in America. *In: The Lutheran Church Review. Vol. XLVI. Mt. Airy, Philadelphia, Pa. 1927. pp. 27—49.*   [2411
Sadtler, B.: The education of ministers by private tutore, before the establishment of theological seminaries. *In: The Lutheran Church Review. Vol. XIII. Philadelphia, Pa. 1894. pp. 167—183.* [2412

Hartwick Seminary, Brooklyn, N. Y. 1797

Hull, W.: Hartwick Seminary. *In: The Lutheran Quarterly Review. Vol. VIII. pp. 592ff.*   [2413

Lutheran Theological Seminary, Gettysburg, Pa. 1826

Twesten, A. D. Ch.: Nachricht von dem zu Gettysburg in Pennsylvanien zu errichtenden theologischen Seminare der Evangelisch-Lutherischen Kirche in den Nordamerikanischen Freystaaten, nebst einer Übersetzung seiner Statuten. *Hamburg: gedruckt in der Langhoffschen Buchdruckerey; zu haben bey Perthes & Besser 1826. XII, 72 S.*   [2414

Gettysburg Seminary centennial number 1826—1926. Sept. 21, 22 and 23, 1926. *In: The Lutheran Quarterly. October, 1926. Vol. LVI. Gettysburg, Pa. 1926. pp. 353—534.*

Alleman, H. C.: The sermon.

Byers, J. E.: The prayer.

Lewars, Elsie Singmaster: The hymn.

Delk, Edwin Heyl: Charge of the Board of Directors: The function of a modern theological teacher.

Hoover, H. D.: Inaugural address: A prelude to the teaching of pastorale theology.

14*

Aberly, John: Inaugural address: The new task of the Seminary at the beginning of the new century.

Knebel, F. H.: The Seminary and the church.

Jacobs, Henry E.: The Seminary and the Lutheran faith.

Markward, J. B.: The Seminary and the work of the home field.

Wolf, L. B.: The Seminary and foreign missions.

Greetings from Princeton Theological Seminary, from Drew Theological Seminary, from Yale Divinity School, from Gettysburg College; *Review:* History of the Gettysburg Theological Seminary. [2415

Wentz, Abdel Roß: History of the Gettysburg Theological Seminary of the General Synod of the Evangelical Lutheran Church in the United States and of the United Lutheran Church in America. Gettysburg, Pennsylvania 1826—1926. *Published by the authority of the directors. Philadelphia, Pa.: Printed for the Seminary by the United Lutheran Publication House 1926. pp. 624, ill.* [2416

Lutheran Theological Southern Seminary, Columbia, S. C. 1830

Voigt, A. G.: The centenary of the Southern Seminary. *In: The Lutheran Church Quarterly. Vol. IV. Gettysburg, Pa. 1931. pp. 56—62.* [2417

Hamma Divinity School, Springfield, O. 1845

— — —

Lutheran Theological Seminary Mt. Airy, Philadelphia, Pa. 1864

Jacobs, H. E.: The Philadelphia Seminary. *An address at its fiftieth anniversary commencement by the Dean. In: The Lutheran Church Review. Vol. XXXIII. Philadelphia, Pa. 1914. pp. 450—462.* [2418

Krotel, G. F.: The beginnings of the Seminary [of the Evangelical Lutheran Church, at Mt. Airy, Philadelphia, Pa.] *In: The Lutheran Church Review. Vol. XV. Philadelphia, Pa. 1896. pp. 255—267; Vol. XVI. 1897. pp. 1—14; 368—385; 658—668; Vol. XVII. 1898. pp. 294—311; 441—453.* [2419

Reed, Luther Dotterer: Philadelphia Seminary biographical record, 1864—1923. *Philadelphia, Pa.: Alumni Association 1923. pp. . . .* [2420

Schmauk, Theodore E.: A brief historical summary of the beginning of the Philadelphia Theological Seminary at Mt. Airy and Muhlenberg College at Allentown, Pa. *Being a reprint of a part of the report of the Board of Directors of the Philadelphia Theological Seminary at Mt. Airy, presented to the Evangelical Lutheran Ministerium of Pennsylvania and adjacent states at the 167th annual convention, in St. John's Church, Easton, Pa., June 4 to 9, 1914, and published by the ministerium. pp. 12.* [2421

The Lutheran Theological Seminary at Philadelphia. Fiftieth anniversary 1914. *Annual catalogue. Fifty-first year 1914 —15. pp. 5—71, (1), ill.* [2422

Dedication of the Krauth Memorial Library. Lutheran Theological Seminary, Mt. Airy, Philadelphia, Wednesday, June 3, 1908. *[s. l. 1808] pp. 75, ill.* [2423

Theological Seminary of the Evangelical Lutheran Soint Synod of Ohio

Sheatsley, Clarence V: History of the first Lutheran seminary of the West, 1830 —1930; *historical sketch of the Theological Seminary of the Evangelical Lutheran Joint Synod of Ohio. Columbus, O.: Lutheran Book Concern 1930. pp. . . .* [2424

Reformierte Kirche in den Vereinigten Staaten:

Reformed Church in the United States:

Theological Seminary of the Reformed Church, Lancaster, Pa. 1825

Apple, Thos. G.: The internal history of the Seminary. *In: The Mercersburg Review. Vol. XXIII. Philadelphia, Pa. 1876. pp. 59—87.* [2425

Appel, Theodore: A chapter on the beginnings of the Theological Seminary of the Reformed Church. *In: The Reformed Quarterly Review. Vol. XXXIII. = New series, vol. VIII. Philadelphia, Pa. 1886. pp. 388—414; 454—498.* [2426

— The beginnings of the Theological Seminary of the Reformed Church in the United States from 1817 to 1832. *Phi-*

ladelphia, Pa.: Reformed Church Publication Board 1896. pp. VIII, (2), 11— 116. [2427

[Mayer, John L.]: Geschichte des Theologischen Seminars der Reformirten Kirche in den Vereinigten Staaten; nebst Beantwortung einer kürzlich erschienenen Schmähschrift des Herrn J. S. Ebaugh gegen diese Lehranstalt, den Professor derselben und die Reformirte Kirche überhaupt. Hanover, Pa.: Daniel Philipp Lange 1831. 64 S. [2428

Weiser, C. Z.: The external history of the Theological Seminary of the Reformed Church in the United States, Lancaster, Pa. In: The Mercersburg Review. Vol. XXIII. Philadelphia, Pa. 1876. pp. 5—58. [2429

Addresses at the semi-centennial celebration of the founding of the Theological Seminary of the Reformed Church in the United States, held at Lancaster, Pa., Nov. 5th, 1875. Philadelphia, Pa.: Reformed Church Publication Board 1876. pp. 85. [2430

Richards, George Warren: The Mercersburg Theology historically considered. In: Papers of the American Society of Church History. Second series, vol. II. New York, N. Y. and London: G. P. Putnam's Sons. The Knickerbocker Press 1912. pp. 119—149. [2431

Central Theological Seminary, Dayton, O. 1848

An historical sketch of the Central Theological Seminary of the Reformed Church in the United States. Seventyfifth anniversary. Dayton, O. 1925. pp. 83, ill.
= The Central Theological Seminary Quarterly, Vol. II, nos. 5—6. Dayton, O., Sept., 1925. [2432

The Central Theological Seminary. Alumni register. Dayton, O. 1928. pp. 34.
= The Central Theological Seminary Quarterly. Vol. VI, no. 2. Dayton, O., October, 1928. [2433

Mährische Brüderkirche:
Moravian Church:

Moravian Theological Seminary, Bethlehem, Pa. 1820

Siehe Nr. (See nos.) 2399—2402.

Wissenschaft

Science

Bergey, D. H.: The Pennsylvania-German as scientist. *In: The Pennsylvania-German. Vol. VII. Lebanon, Pa. 1906. pp. 157—159, ill.* [2434

Harshberger, John W.: The botanists of Philadelphia and their work. *Philadelphia, Pa.: T. C. Davis & Sons 1899. pp. XII, 457, ill.*
[Contains bibliographies of a number of Pennsylvania-German men, such as: Gotthilf H. E. Muhlenberg. *pp. 92—97, ill.;* Solomon White Conrad. *pp. 125—126;* Lewis David de Schweinitz. *pp. 127—132, ill.;* John P. Heister. *p. 186;* William Wynne Wister. *pp. 196—197;* J. K. Eshleman. *p. 208;* George W. Fahnestock. *p. 245;* Joseph Trimble Rothrock. *pp. 305—313, ill.;* C. D. Fretz. *pp. 340—342;* Eugene A. Rau. *p. 352;* Elias Diffenbach. *p. 353;* John W. Eckfeldt. *pp. 356—358, ill.;* Charles S. Boyer. *pp. 372—374;* A. Arthur Heller. *pp. 382—388;* John William Harshberger. *pp. 391—399.]* [2435

Fetterolf, D. W.: The Pennsylvania Germans in the field of chemistry. *In: The Pennsylvania-German. Vol. XI. Lititz, Pa. 1910. pp. 77—86.* [2436

Jordan, H. E.: The Pennsylvania-German as biologist. *In: The Pennsylvania-German. Vol. IX. Cleona, Pa. 1908. pp. 60—66.* [2437

Kuhns, Oscar: Pennsylvania-Germans as teachers of science in colleges and universities. *In: The Pennsylvania-German. Vol. IX. Cleona, Pa. 1908. pp. 121—125.* [2438

Porter, Thomas Conrad: The Pennsylvania-German in the field of the natural science. *In: The Pennsylvania-German Society. Proceedings and Addresses at Bethlehem, Oct. 16, 1895. Vol. VI. Reading, Pa. 1896. pp. 22—37, ill.* [2439

Shimer, H. W.: The Pennsylvania-German as geologist and paleontologist. *In: The Pennsylvania-German. Vol. IX. Cleona, Pa. 1908. pp. 411—415.* [2440

Walter, Frank K.: Pennsylvania-Germans as teachers of science in private secondary schools. *In: The Pennsylvania-German. Vol. IX. Cleona, Pa. 1908. pp. 262—266.* [2441

Kunst

Fine Arts

Brandenburg, O. D.: Additional Eichholtz paintings. *In: Papers and Addresses of the Lancaster County Historical Society. Vol. XXVII. Lancaster, Pa. 1923. p. 102.* [2442

Hensel, W. U.: Jacob Eichholtz, painter. *Some „loose leaves" from the ledger of an early Lancaster artist. An address delivered at the opening of an exposition of „The evolution of portraiture in Lancaster County, Pa." under the auspices of the Lancaster Historical Society and the Iris Club, Woolworth Building Lancaster,* Pa. Nov. 22, 1912. (Revised Catalog of Eichholtz's Work) pp. 38, ill.
Reprint in: The Penn Germania. Vol. II = Old series, vol. XIV. 1913. pp. 81—96; 161—175. [2443

Hensel, W. U.: Jacob Eichholtz, painter. *In: The Pennsylvania Magazine of History and Biography. Vol. XXXVII. Philadelphia, Pa. 1913. pp. 48—75.* [2444

Hostetter, Ida L. K.: A short preface to a copy of a memorandum of Jacob Eichholtz, the artist. *In: Papers and Addresses of the Lancaster County Histo-*

rical Society. Vol. XXIX. Lancaster, Pa. 1925. pp. 107—110. [2445

Jordan, John W.: The Pennsylvania-German as artist. *In: The Pennsylvania-German. Vol. VII. Lebanon, Pa. 1906. pp. 160—161.* [2446

Macmurchy, Marjory: Mrs. G. A. Reid, painter. *Reprint from: The Globe, (Toronto, Canada). In: The Pennsylvania-German. Vol. XI. Lititz, Pa. 1910. pp. 709—711.* [2447

Romiger, Charles H. and Bornman, Charles J.: Noah Weis, wood carver. *An unappreciated genius. In: The Pennsylvania-German. Vol. XI. Lititz, Pa. 1910. pp. 673—676, ill.* [2448

Early Lancaster artists. *[Ferdinand Huck; Adam Mortimer Lightner.] In: Papers and Addresses of the Lancaster County Historical Society. Vol. XVII. Lancaster, Pa. 1913. pp. 92—93.* [2449

Loan exhibition of historical and contemporary portraits illustrating the evolution of protraiture in Lancaster County, Pa., *under the auspices of the Iris Club and the Lancaster County Historical Society. Woolworth Building, Lancaster County, Nov. 23, to Dec. 13, 1912. Lancaster, Pa.: Press of the New Era Printing Co. 1912. pp. VIII, 142.* [2450

Musik[1])

Musical Life[2])

Alderfer, David: Life and works of Joseph Funk and his descendants. *In: Christian Monitor. A monthly magazine for the home. Vol. XXII. Scottdale, Pa. 1930. No. 5. pp. 149—150; 159; No. 6. p. 181, p. 187, ill.* [2451

Beck, Herbert H.: Lititz as an early musical centre. *In: Papers and Addresses of the Lancaster County Historical Society. Vol. XIX. Lancaster, Pa. 1915. pp. 71—81.* [2452

Bender, Harold S.: ,,A classified chronological list of American Mennonite hymnals.`` *In: Two centuries of American Mennonite literature. A bibliography of Mennonite Americana 1727—1928. By H. S. Bender. Goshen, Ind. 1929 [= no. 909].* = *Appendix V. pp. 157—158.* [2453

Benson, Louis F.: The common service book and hymnal of the Lutheran Church. *Reprint from Princeton Review, July 1918. In: The Lutheran Church Review. Vol. XXXVII. Philadelphia, Pa. 1918. pp. 298—303.* [2454

Bird, Frederick M.: Lutheran hymnology. *In: The Evangelical Review. Vol. XVI.*

Gettysburg, Pa. 1865. pp. 23—46; 193—225; 328—351. [2455

Drummond, Robert Rutherford: Alexander Reinagle, and his connection with the musical life of Philadelphia. *(May 25, 1907) In: German American Annals. New series vol. V. Philadelphia, Pa. 1907. pp. 294—306.* [2456

— Early music in Philadelphia with special reference to German music. *In: German American Annals. New series, vol. VI. Philadelphia, Pa. 1908, pp. 157—179.* [2457

— Early German music in Philadelphia. *Publications of the University of Pennsylvania. New York, N. Y.: D. Appleton & Co. 1910. pp. XIII—XIV, (1), 88.* = *Americana Germanica, Monographs devoted to the comparative study of the literary, linguistic and other cultural relations of Germany and America. No. 9.* [2458

— The early Pennsylvania German music. *In: The Pennsylvania-German. Vol. XII. Lititz, Pa. 1911. pp. 171—172.* [2459

Dubbs, Joseph Henry: Early German hymnology of Pennsylvania. *In: The Reformed Quarterly Review. Vol. XXIX. New series, vol. IV. Philadelphia, Pa. 1882. pp. 584—610.* [2460

— Ephrata hymns and hymn books. *In: Papers and Addresses of the Lancaster*

---

[1]) Siehe auch: Orgel-, Uhr- und Instrumentenbau, Nr. 2640ff.

[2]) See also: Organ-, clock- and instrument-making, no. 2640ff.

County Historical Society. Vol. XIII.
Lancaster, Pa. 1909. pp. 21—37, ill.
[2461

Engel, Carl: Views and reviews: ,,Church
music and musical life in Pennsylvania
in the eighteenth century," issued by
the Pennsylvania Society of the Colonial
Dames of America. Philadelphia, Pa.
1926/27. In: The Musical Quarterly.
Vol. XIV, no. 2. New York, N. Y. 1928.
pp. 300—305, ill.   [2462

Funk, John F.: A biographical sketch of
Bish. Christian Herr. Also a collection
of hymns written by him in the German
language. Compiled by . . . Elkhart,
Ind.: Mennonite Publishing Co. 1887.
pp. 50.   [2463

Grider, Rufus A.: Historical notes on music
in Bethlehem, Pennsylvania from 1741
1871. (250 copies only printed for
J. Hill Martin). Philadelphia, Pa.:John
L. Pile 1873. pp. 41.   [2464

Haussmann, William A.: German-Ameri-
can hymnology, 1683—1800. In: Ame-
ricana Germanica. A Quarterly. Vol. II.
Philadelphia, Pa. 1898. No. 3. pp. 1—
61. Appendix: A. — Names of German-
American hymn-writers. p. 52; B. —
Prints of hymn-books, 1730—1830.
[Bibliography. pp. 52—61.)   [2465

Hinke, William John: The early German
hymn books of the Reformed Church in
the United States. In: Journal of the
Presbyterian Historical Society. Vol. IV.
Philadelphia, Pa. 1907. pp. 147—161.
[2466

[Hoban, C. F.]: Pennsylvania in music.
Harrisburg, Pa., April, 1926. pp. 24.
= Educational monographs. A presentation of accomplishments and objectives
in education in Pennsylvania. Vol. I.,
no. 1. Edited by Commonwealth of Pennsylvania, Department of Public instruction.   [2467

Jacobs, Henry Eyster: The common hymnal. In: The Lutheran Church Review.
Vol. XXIX. Philadelphia, Pa. 1910.
pp. 250—275.   [2468

Jordan, John W.: Erinnerungsblätter an
Jedidiah Weiß, Karl F. Beckel und
Jacob C. Till, Posaunisten. In: Deutsch-
Amerikanisches Magazin. Vierteljahrsschrift für Geschichte, Literatur, Wissenschaft, Kunst, Schule und Volksleben
der Deutschen in Amerika . . . herausgegeben von H. A. Rattermann. Bd. I.
Cincinnati, O. 1887. S. 108—112.
[2469

Landis, D. B.: The musical and literary organization and their leaders of Landisville
and vicinity. In: Papers and Addresses
of the Lancaster County Historical Society. Vol. X. Lancaster, Pa. 1906. pp.
3—27.   [2470

Lewars, Elsie Singmaster: The common
service book and hymnal. Reprint from
the Lutheran Quarterly in: The Lutheran
Church Review. Vol. XXXVII. Philadelphia, Pa. 1918. pp. 289—297. [2471

Mercer, Henry C.: The zithers of the Pennsylvania Germans. Read January 20,
1923. In: A Collection of Papers read
before the Bucks County Historical Society. Vol. V. Easton, Pa. 1926. pp.
482—497, ill.   [2472

**[National] Society of the Colonial Dames of
America, Pennsylvania:** Church music
and musical life in Pennsylvania in the
eighteenth century. Prepared by the
Committee on historical research. 2 vols.
Philadelphia, Pa.: Printed for the So-
ciety-Press of the Wickersham Printing
Co., Lancaster, Pa. 1926; 1927. Vol. I.
1926. pp. XIII, 261, ill. [Bibliography
pp. 251—255]; Vol. II. 1927. pp. XII,
291, ill. [Bibliography pp. 273—278.]
= Publication of the Pennsylvania Society of the Colonial Dames of America
IV.   [2473

Orr, Sylvester H.: Country singing schools
and social functions. In: Historical
Sketches. A Collection of Papers prepared for the Historical Society of Montgomery County, Pa. Vol. VI. Norristown,
Pa. 1929. pp. 390—397.   [2474

Pennypacker, Samuel W.: Johann Gott-
fried Seelig and the hymn-book of the
hermits of the Wissahickon. In: The
Pennsylvania Magazine of History and
Biography. Vol. XXV. Philadelphia,
Pa. 1901. pp. 336—340.   [2475

Prottengeier: Das deutsche Kirchenlied,
das Kirchenbuch und das Church Book.
Two articles constituting a comparative
hymnological study. (Translated from
the ,,Kirchliche Zeitschrift" by Chas. F.
Dapp. In: The Lutheran Church Review. Vol. XXX. Philadelphia, Pa.
1911. pp. 275—292.   [2476

Ramsey, Alfred: Hymn translating, and
some attemps. In: The Lutheran Church
Review. Vol. XXIX. Philadelphia, Pa.
1910. pp. 229—249.   [2477

Reed, Luther D.: The Common Service
Book and the United Lutheran Church.
In: The Lutheran Church Review. Vol.

XLII. *Philadelphia, Pa. 1923. pp. 30
—38.* [2478
Reichel, W. C.: Posaunen. Ein Beitrag zur
Musikgeschichte der Deutschen in Amerika. *In: Deutsch-Amerikanisches Magazin. Vierteljahrsschrift für Geschichte,
Literatur, Wissenschaft, Kunst, Schule
und Volksleben der Deutschen in Amerika . . . herausgegeben von H. A. Rattermann. Bd. I. Cincinnati, O. 1887.
S. 104—108.* [2479
Richards, H. M. M.: The Ephrata cloister
and its music. *Paper read Nov. 17,
1922. In: Papers read before the Lebanon County Historical Society. Vol.
VIII. 1921—1924. Lebanon, Pa. 1924.
pp. 279—299, ill.* [2480
Rose, H. C.: The new Common Service
Book and Hymnal. *Reprint from: Lutheran Church Work and Observer, June
13, 1918. In: The Lutheran Church
Review. Vol. XXXVII. Philadelphia,
Pa. 1918. pp. 304—315.* [2481
Rosenberry, M. Claude: The Pennsylvania
German in music. *Address delivered before
the Pennsylvania-German Society at
Harrisburg, October 17, 1930. With a pre-
liminary statement by Henry S. B o r n e -
m a n. In: The Pennsylvania-German
Society. Proceedings and Addresses . . .
1930. Vol. XLI. Norristown, Pa.:
Norristown Herald. 1933. pp. 27—44.*
[2481a
Sachse, Julius Friedrich: The music of the
Ephrata cloister also Conrad Beissel's
treatise on music as set forth in a preface to the „Turtel Taube" of 1747.
*Amplified with fac-simile reproductions
of parts of the text and some original
Ephrata music of the Weyrauch's Hügel,
1739; Rosen and Lilien, 1745; Turtel
Taube, 1747; Choral Buch, 1754 etc.
Lancaster, Pa.: New. Era Printing Co.
1903. = Part XI. „A narrative and
critical history," prepared at the request
of the Pennsylvania-German Society. In:
The Pennsylvania-German Society. Proceedings and Addresses . . . 1901. Vol.
XII. Lancaster, Pa. 1903. Separate
pagination. pp. 108, ill.* [2482

Schmauk, Theodore E.: The true hymnological treasury of the Evangelical Lutheran Church. *In: The Lutheran Church
Review. Vol. XXX. Philadelphia, Pa.
1911. pp. 260—274.* [2483
Seipt, Allen Anders: Schwenkfelder hymnology and the sources of the first Schwenkfelder hymn-book printed in America,
Philadelphia, Pa.: Americana Germanica
Press 1909. *pp. VII—IX, 11—112, ill.
= Americana Germanica. Monographs
devoted to the comparative study of the
literary, linguistic and other cultural
relations of Germany and America, Edited by M. Dexter Learnerd. No. 7.
[Bibliography pp. 111—112.]* [2484
Stapleton, A.: Early German musical publications in Pennsylvania. *In: The
Pennsylvania-German. Vol. VII. Lebanon, Pa. 1906. pp. 174—180.* [2485
Walters, Raymond: The Bethlehem Bach
choir. An historical and interpretative
sketch. *Boston, Mass. and New York,
N. Y.: Houghton Mifflin Co. 1918. pp.
XI, 290, ill.* [2486
— The Bethlehem Bach choir. A history
and a critical compendium. *Silver
anniversary edition. Boston, Mass. and
New York, N. Y.: Houghton Mifflin Co.
— The Riverside Press Cambridge 1923.
pp. XIX, 344, ill.* [2487
Warrington, James: A bibliography of
church music books issued in Pennsyl-
vania, with annotations. *In: The Penn
Germania. Vol. I. Old series, vol. XIII.
— Lititz, Pa. 1912. pp. 170—177; 262
—268; 371—374; 460—465; 627—631;
755—759.* [2488
Wayland, John W.: Joseph Funk. Father
of song in northern Virginia. *In: The
Pennsylvania-German. Vol. XII. Li-
titz, Pa. 1911. pp. 580—594, ill.* [2489
English Lutheran hymn books. *In: The
Evangelical Review. Vol. XI. Gettysburg
1859—60. pp. 175—194; 401—414.*
[The Importance of language.] [2490
William Augustus Muhlenberg's famous
hymn. *In: The Pennsylvania-German.
Vol. XII. Lititz, Pa. 1911. pp. 298—299.*
[2491

Landwirtschaft und Gartenbau

Farming and Horticulture

Baker, Oliver E.: Agricultural regions of North America. *Series of installments in: Economic Geography. Vol. II. Worcester, Mass.: Clark University 1926ff.*

[The middle country, where South and North meet. = Part III. In: Vol. III. 1927. pp. 309—339; The hay and dairing belt. = Part IV. In: Vol. IV. 1928. pp. 44—73.] [2492

Berger, A. C.: Agricultural production and marketing in Lebanon County, Pa. *A report of the results of a survey of agricultural conditions in Lebanon County, Pa., for the purpose of furnishing an economic basis for a production and marketing program. By . . . and* **P. R. Taylor, B. H. Critchfield** *and* **R. S. Kiefer.** *State College, Pa., 1925. pp. 47, ill., maps.*

= Pennsylvania State College, School of Agriculture and Experiment Station. Bulletin no. 198. [2493.

Bosse, Georg von: The Germans as farmers *In: The Pennsylvania-German. Vol. XII. Lititz, Pa. 1911. pp. 533—534.* [2494

Carrier, Lyman: The beginnings of agriculture in America. *New York, N. Y.: McGraw-Hill Book Co. 1923. pp. 323, ill.*

[See particularly pp. 173—181 which pertain to agriculture in colonial Pennsylvania.] [2495

[Cazenove, Theophile]: Cazenove Journal 1794. A record of the journey of Theophile Cazenove through New Jersey and Pennsylvania. *(Translated from the French.) Edited by* **Rayner Wickersham Kelsey.** *Haverford, Pa.: Published by the Pennsylvania History Press; Lancaster, Pa.: Press of the New Era Printing Co. 1922. pp. XVII, 103, ill., map. = Haverford College Studies, no. 13.* [2496

Druckerman, Benjamin: An ecological survey of Pennsylvania with particular reference to its limestone soils. *In: The Bulletin of the Geographical Society of Philadelphia. Vol. XXIV, no. 3. Philadelphia, Pa. 1926. pp. 135—150.* [2497

Ellis, Franklin and **Evans, Samuel:** History of Lancaster County, Pennsylvania, *with biographical sketches of many of its pioneers and prominent men. Philadelphia, Pa.: Everts & Peck 1883. pp. VIII, 1101, ill., map.*

[See especially: Chap. XXVIII „Agriculture" pp. 344—358] [2498

Fearon, Hy. Bradshaw: Sketches of America. *A narrative of a journey of 5000 miles through the eastern and western states of America; contained in eight reports addresses to the 39 English families by whom the author was deputed in June, 1817, to ascertain whether any, and what part of the United States would be suitable for their residence. With remarks on Mr. Birbeck's „Notes" and „Letters". London: Printed by Strahan and Spottiswoode for Longman, Hurst, Rees, Orme, and Brown 1819. pp. XXV, 454.*

[Fifth report: Leave Philadelphia for the western country; Pennsylvania farms etc. pp. 181ff.] [2499

Huber, Levi B.: Two hundred years of farming in Lancaster County. *In: Papers and Addresses of the Lancaster County Historical Society. Vol. XXXV. Lancaster, Pa. 1931. pp. 97—110.* [2500

James, Henry F. The agricultural industry of southeastern Pennsylvania. *In: The Bulletin of the Geographical Society of Philadelphia. Vol. XXVI. Philadelphia, Pa. 1928. pp. 29—59; 123—147; 208—229; 305—322; Vol. XXVII. 1929. pp. 87—126; 167—197, maps. Separate print: . . . A study in economic geography. Philadelphia, Pa. 1928. pp. XI, 168, maps.* [2501

Johnson, George Fiske: Agriculture in Pennsylvania. A study of trends, county and state, since 1840. *Harrisburg, Pa. 1929. pp. 94, ill., maps.*

= Pennsylvania Department of Agriculture. Bulletin. Vol. XII, no. 15.

= General Bulletin no. 484. [2502

Kelsey, Rayner: Description and travel as source material for the history of early agriculture in Pennsylvania. *In: Annual report of the American Historical Association for the year 1920. Washington, D. C. 1925. pp. 283—292.* [2503

Mays, George: The early Pennsylvania-German farmer. *In: The Pennsylvania-German. Vol. II. Lebanon, Pa. 1901. pp. 184—188, ill.* [2504

— The Pennsylvania-German as farmer. *In: The Pennsylvania-German. Vol. VII. Lebanon, Pa. 1906. pp. 151—154, ill.* [2505

Miller, Frederic K.: The farmer at work in colonial Pennsylvania. *In: Pennsylvania History. Official organ of the Pennylvania Historical Association. Vol. III, Philadelphia, Pa. 1936. pp. 115—123.* [2505a

Rothrock, Lewis Frederick: Forty-five years of agriculture in Perry County. *Thesis of M. Sc., University of Wisconsin, Madison, Wis. 1929. Typewritten. pp. 70, (2), map.* [2506

Rupp, I. D.: Eppes wege de deutsche Baure *In: Der Deutsche Pionier. Jg. II. Cincinnati, O. 1870—1871. S. 269—272.* [2507

Rush, Benjamin: An account of the progress of population, agriculture, manners, and government in Pennsylvania. *In a letter from . . ., M. D., and professor of chemistry in the University of Pensylvania, to Thomas Percival, M. D. F. R. S. etc., (Read December 6, 1786). In: Memoirs of the Literary and Philosophical Society of Manchester. Vol. III. Warrington. 1790. pp. 183—197.*
Also appeared in: The Columbian Magazine or Monthly Miscellany . . . of the year 1787. Vol. I. Philadelphia, Pa. 1786/87. No.: November, 1786. pp. 117—122. [2508

[—] An account of the manners of the German inhabitants of Pennsylvania. *In: The Columbian Magazine, or Monthly Miscellany . . . for January, 1789. Vol. III. Philadelphia, Pa. 1789. pp. 22—30.* [2509

[—]-Rupp, I, D.: An account of the German inhabitants of Pennsylvania, written 1789, *by Benjamin Rush, M. D. Notes added by J. Daniel Rupp. Philadelphia, Pa.: Samuel P. Town 1875. pp. 72;*
Reprint in: The Pennsylvania-German. Vol. X. Lititz, Pa. 1909. pp. 157—161; 220—224. [2510

Rush, Benjamin - Rupp, I, D. - Rattermann, H. A.: Eine Darstellung der Sitten und Lebensweise der deutschen Einwanderer von Pennsylvanien. *Geschrieben in 1789 von Benjamin Rush. M. D., mit hinzugefügten Noten und Erklärungen von Prof. I. Daniel Rupp. Edited by [H. A.] R.[atterman]. In: Der Deutsche Pionier. Jg. VII. Cincinnati, O. 1875—1876. S. 267—280; 326—340; 368—373; 410—414.*
Abdruck in H. A. Rattermann. Gesammelte ausgewählte Werke. Bd. XVI. Cincinnati, O.: Selbstverlag des Verfassers 1912 = Abhandlungen, Vorträge und Reden. Bilder aus Deutsch-Amerikanischer Geschichte. Vermischte Schriften. Erster Teil. S. 155—195. [2511

[——]- Schmauk, Theodore E.: An account of the manners of the German inhabitants of Pennsylvania, *by Benjamin Rush. With an introduction and annotations by Theodore E. Schmauk, and with the notes of I. D. Rupp revised. Lancaster, Pa.: New Era Printing Co. 1910. = Part XXI. „A narrative and critical history", prepared by the authority of the Pennsylvania-German Society. In: The Pennsylvania-German Society. Proceedings and Addresses . . . 1908. Vol. XIX. Lancaster, Pa. 1910. Separate pagination. pp. 128, ill.* [2512

Schantz, F. J. F.: The domestic life and characteristics of the Pennsylvania-German pioneer. *Lancaster, Pa. 1900. = Part VI. „A narrative and critical history, prepared at the request of the Pennsylvania-German Society. In: The Pennsylvania-German Society. Proceedings and Addresses . . . 1899. Vol. X. Lancaster, Pa. 1900. Separate pagination. pp. 97, ill.* [2513

[Schultze, David]: David Schultze's journal. *In: The Perkiomen Region, Past and Present. Vol. II. Philadelphia, Pa. 1900. p. 165; (David Schultze's coming to America): pp. 181—182; 187—189; Journal of 1752: In: Vol. III. 1901. p. 2: pp. 10—15; Journal of 1757. pp. 81—82; 90—93; p. 98; pp. 106—110; Journal of 1759. pp. 124—127; 140—144; Journal of 1768. p. 146; pp. 155—159; p. 164; pp. 169—174 Continued:*
The David Schultz diary for 1769. *With notes of the editor, H. W. Kriebel. In: The Perkiomen Region. Vol. VI, no. 4.*

Pennsburg, Pa. 1928. pp. 109—113;
113—115; . . . for 1774. *In: Vol. VII,*
no. 1. 1929. pp. 8—15; . . . for 1780. *In:*
Vol. VII, no. 2. 1929. pp. 34—47; . . .
for 1782. *In: Vol. VII, no. 3. 1929. pp.*
66—73; . . . for 1786. *In: Vol. VII, no.*
4. 1929. pp. 106—111; . . . for 1790.
In: Vol. VIII, no. 1. 1930. pp. 3—9.
                                        [2514
Smith, J. Russel: North America. *Its*
people and the resources, development,
and prospects of the continent as an agri-
cultural, industrial, and commercial area.
London 1924 [= no. 24].
[Of particular interest: General far-
ming and dairysection [of the northern
Piedmont.] pp. 187—188; Lancaster
County Germans. pp. 188—189; The
influences of limestone (of the valley
region.) pp. 198—200.]   [2515
Sohn, Friedrich: Farmer oder Bauer ? *Eine*
Betrachtung über den amerikanischen
Farmer. In: Odal, Monatsschrift für
Blut und Boden. Herausgeber R. Walther
Darré. Jg. III. Detmold 1935. Heft 12,
S. 969—978.
[Insbesondere: Die bäuerliche Ein-
stellung der Pennsylvania-Dutch. S.
975f.]   [2516
Spillman, W. J., Dixon, H.M. and **Billings,**
G. A.: Farm management pratice of
Chester County, Pa. *Washington, D. C.*
1916. pp. 99, ill., maps.
= United States Department of Agricul-
ture. Bulletin no. 341. Professional
Papers.   [2517
Strickland, William: Observations on the
agriculture of the United States of Ame-
rica. *London: W. Bulmer and Co. 1801.*
pp. (1), (1), 3—74.   [2518
Taylor, R. S.: Restoring a worn-out farm.
Reprint from: Tennessee Sun. In: The
Pennsylvania-German. Vol. XI. Lititz,
Pa. 1910. p. 638.   [2519
Vanderslice, J. M.: A land prosperous far-
mers. *[Montgomery Co., Pa.] Reprint*
from: The Country Gentlement. In: The
Pennsylvania-German. Vol. VIII. Le-
banon, Pa. 1907. p. 493.   [2520
Watts, Ralph L.: Rural Pennsylvania.
New York, N. Y.: The Macmillan Co.
1925. pp. XVII, 331.
= Rural State and Province Series.
Edited by L. H. Baily.   [2521

Ballinger, Roy A.: Stock share renting in
Virginia. *Blacksburg, Va. 1930. pp. 54.*
= Virginia Polytechnic Institute. Vir-

ginia Agricultural Experiment Station.
Bulletin no. 271.   [2522
Ezekiel, Mordecai: Factors affecting farmers' earnings in southeastern Pennsylvania. *Washington, D. C. 1926. pp. 62,*
ill., maps.
= United States Department of Agricul-
ture. Department Bulletin no. 1400.
                                    [2523
McCord, J. E.: Farm tenancy and lease
forms in Pennsylvania. *A study of types*
of contracts in use between landlords and
tenants in Pennsylvania and suggestions
for adapting these to present day farming
conditions. State College, Pa.1929. pp.46.
= The Pennsylvania State College,
School of Agriculture and Experiment
Station. Bulletin no. 232.   [2524
Weaver, F. P.: Some phases of taxation in
Pennsylvania. Rural taxation in Penn-
sylvania. *In: Pennsylvania Department*
of Agriculture. Bulletin. Vol. IX, no. 24.
Harrisburg, Pa., Dec. 15, 1926. = Gene-
ral Order no. 437. Part I. pp. 7—43.
                                    [2525
County and state agricultural organizations,
with dates and places of fairs 1929.
Harrisburg, Pa. 1929. pp. 30.
= Pennsylvania Department of Agri-
culture. Bulletin. Vol. XII, no. 13. =
General Bulletin no. 482.   [2526

Pennsylvania's farms, crops and livestock
1926. *Annual statistical review of agri-*
culture by the Pennsylvania Federal-
State Crop Reporting Service. The United
States Department of Agriculture, Divi-
sion of Crop and Livestock estimates co-
operating with the Pennsylvania Depart-
ment of Agriculture, Bureau of Statistics.
Harrisburg, Pa. 1927. pp. 250, maps.
= Pennsylvania Department of Agri-
culture. Bulletin. Vol. X, no. 9. = Ge-
neral Bulletin no. 445.   [2527

Clark, J. A., Martin, J. H. and **Ball, C. R.:**
Classification of American wheat varie-
ties. *Washington, D. C. 1922. pp. 238,*
ill., maps.
= United States Department of Agri-
culture. Department Bulletin no. 1074.
[See particularly: Fulcaster wheat. pp.
135—139; Fultz wheat. pp. 83—85;
Mediterranean wheat (Lehigh, Lancaster,
Miller). pp. 166—168.
See also the later bulletin: Distribution
of the classes and varieties of wheat in the
United States. Washington, D. C. 1929.

= *United States Department of Agriculture. Department Bulletin no. 1498. maps.]* [2528

Hacker, A. L.: The potato industry in Lehigh County. *In: The Guide Post. Published bimonthly by the Pennsylvania Cooperative Potato Growers, Inc. Vol. VIII, no. 6. Harrisburg, Pa., Dec., 1931. p. 1 and p. 3.* [2529

Lynn, W. C. and **James, D. M.:** Pennsylvania as a market for potatoes. *Harrisburg, Pa. 1926. pp. 21. = Pennsylvania Department of Agriculture. Bulletin Vol. IX, no. 10. = General Bulletin no. 428.* [2530

Houston, J. W.: Flax culture in Lancaster County. *In: Papers and Addresses of the Lancaster County Historical Society. Vol. IV. Lancaster, Pa. 1900. pp. 155—168.* [2531

Keller, Eli: Flax culture and its utility. *In: The Pennsylvania-German. Vol. IX. Cleona, Pa. 1908. pp. 266—273, ill.* [2532

[—]: Flax culture. *Penn picture in the Pennsylvania-German dialect. By . . ., with preface and translation by Howard W. Kriebel. In: The Perkiomen Region. Vol. IX, no. 3. Pennsburg, Pa. 1931. pp. 78—86.* [2533

Kriebel, H. W.: A change in the farm industry. *(Recollections relating to flax culture.) In: The Perkiomen Region. Vol. IX, no. 1 Pennsburg, Pa. 1931. p. 24.* [2534

[—] Reminiscences of the old oil mill. *In: The Perkiomen Region. Vol. V, no. 1. Pennsburg, Pa. 1927. pp. 14—16.* [2535

Scheetz, Grier: Flax and its culture. *In: A Collection of Papers read before the Bucks County Historical Society. Vol. III. Easton, Pa. 1909. pp. 482—486, ill.* [2536

— Flax seed mills. *In: A Collection of Papers read before the Bucks County Historical Society. Vol. IV. Easton, Pa. 1917. pp. 725—729.* [2537

Frear, William and **Hibshman, E. K.:** The production of cigar-leaf tobacco in Pennsylvania. *Washington, D. C. 1921. pp. 20, ill.*
= *United States Department of Agriculture. Farmers Bulletin no. 416.* [2538

— - — and **Olson, Otto:** The cigar tobacco industry in Pennsylvania. *Harrisburg, Pa. 1922. pp. 90, ill.*

= *Pennsylvania Department of Agriculture. Bulletin. Vol. V, no. 8. = General Bulletin no. 371.* [2539

Hanemann, H. Andrew: The Pennsylvania tobacco situation. *Harrisburg, Pa. 1927. pp. 16, ill.*
= *Pennsylvania Department of Agriculture. Bulletin. Vol. X, no. 1. = General Bulletin no. 435.* [2540

Olson, Otto: Cigar-tobacco production in Pennsylvania. *Washington, D. C. 1929. pp. 22, ill.*
= *United States Department of Agriculture. Farmers Bulletin no. 1580.* [2541

Scheerz, Greer: Tobacco and its culture in Bucks County. *In: A Collection of Papers read before the Bucks County Historical Society. Vol. V. Meadville, Pa. 1926. pp. 612—623.* [2542

Bartlett, R. W.: Milk marketing in Pennsylvania. *State College, Pa. 1926. pp. 39, maps.*
= *The Pennsylvania State College, School of Agriculture and Experiment Station. Bulletin no. 208.* [2543

Lininger, F. F.: The relation of the basic-surplus marketing plan to milk production in the Philadelphia milk shed. *State College, Pa. 1928. pp. 63, maps.*
= *The Pennsylvania State College, School of Agriculture and Experiment Station. Bulletin no. 231.* [2544

The Interstate Milk Producers' Association, Philadelphia, Pa. *Washington, D. C. Oct. 1, 1932 Typewritten. pp. 53, map.*
= *The National Cooperative Milk Producers' Federation. History series, no. 3.* [2545

Maryland State Dairymen's Association, Inc. *Washington, D. C. July 1, 1932. Typewritten. pp. 47, map.*
= *The National Cooperative Milk Producers' Federation. History series no. 2.* [2546

The Maryland and Virginia Milk Producers' Association, Inc. *Washington, D. C., March 1, 1932. Typewritten. pp. 12, (20), map.*
= *The National Cooperative Milk Producers' Federation. History series no. 1.* [2547

Vernon, J. J., Holdaway, C. W., Ezekiel, Mordecai and **Kiefer, R. S.:** Factors affecting returns from the dairy enterprise in the Shenandoah Valley. *Blacksburg, Va. 1927. pp. 87, ill., map.*

= *Virginia Polytechnic Institute. Virginia Agricultural Experiment Station. Bulletin no. 257.*   [2548
Bayard, E. S.: Beef production. *(Reprint) Harrisburg, Pa. 1917. pp. 249, ill.*
= *Commonwealth of Pennsylvania. Department of Agriculture. Bulletin no. 235.*
———   [2549

Bordie, D. A.: Handling barnyard manure in eastern Pennsylvania. *Washington, D. C. 1918. pp. 24, ill.*
= *United States Department of Agriculture. Farmers Bulletin no. 978.*   [2550
Frear, William, Goodling, C. L. and **Kern, C. A.:** (I.) Cost of burning lime in the stack. (II.) Supplementary report upon the limestone resources of Pennsylvania. *State College, Pa. 1919. pp. 23, ill.*
= *The Pennsylvania State College, School of Agriculture. Agricultural Experiment Station. Bulletin no. 157.* [2551

———

Mercer, Henry C.: Ancient methods of threshing in Bucks County. *In: A Collection of Papers read before the Bucks County Historical Society. Vol. V. Meadville, Pa. 1926, pp. 315—323, ill.*   [2552
Heilman, U. Henry: „Deng'lshtuk." *In: Papers read before the Lebanon County Historical Society. Vol. I. Lebanon, Pa. 1902. pp. 47—52;* Der alt Dengelstock. E'n Gedicht nach der Pennsylvanisch-Deutscher Mundart *von* Lee L. Grumbine. *pp. 53—56.*   [2553
Josephson, H. B. and **Blasingame, R. U.:** Farm power and labor. *State College, Pa. 1929. pp. 20, ill.*
= *The Pennsylvania State College, School of Agriculture. Agricultural Experiment Station. Bulletin no. 238.*
                                                     [2554
Steinmetz, Charles, K.: The farm electrified. *Harrisburg, Pa. 1925. pp. 37, ill.*
= *Pennsylvania Department of Agriculture. Bulletin. Vol. VIII, no. 11.*
= *General Bulletin no. 407.*   [2555
Commercial poultry farms in Pennsylvania. *Harrisburg, Pa.: Pennsylvania Department of Agricultural 1929. pp. 46.*
                                                     [2556

Lininger, F. F.: Egg marketing by farmers in Pennsylvania. *A study of prices and costs by various methods of marketing. State College, Pa. 1927. pp. 20.*

= *The Pennsylvania State College, School of Agriculture. Agricultural Experiment Station. Bulletin no. 214.* [2557
— and **Charles, T. B.:** A study of egg and poultry consumption in Pennsylvania. *State College, Pa. 1928. pp. 23.*
= *The Pennsylvania State College, School of Agriculture. Agricultural Experiment Station. Bulletin no. 222* [2558
Wampler, Chas. W.: Wampler's practical turkey methods. *A text giving the essentials for successful turkey managment told in a brief and simple manner. Harrisonburg, Va., Dec., 1929. pp. 61, ill.*
                                                     [2559

———

Nissley, W. B. and **Huffingtin, J. M.:** The family vegetable garden. *State College, Pa. 1929. pp. 49, ill.*
= *The Pennsylvania State College, School of Agriculture and Experiment Station. Division of Agricultural Extension. Circular 120.*   [2560
Mason, C. R.: The vegetable industry of Pennsylvania. *Harrisburg, Pa. 1925. pp. 142, ill.*
= *Pennsylvania Department of Agriculture. Bulletin. Vol. VII, no. 12.* = *General Bulletin no. 408.*   [2561

Anthony, R. D. and **Waring, J. H.:** The apple industry of Pennsylvania. *The results of an orchard survey conducted by the Department of Horticulture, Pennsylvania State College and the Pennsylvania State Department of Agriculture. Compiled by . . . Harrisburg, Pa. 1922. pp. 205, ill., maps.*
= *Pennsylvania Department of Agriculture. Bulletin. Vol. V, no. 6.* = *General Bulletin no. 369.*   [2562
Fletcher, S. W.: A history of fruit growing in Pennsylvania. (I.) The colonial period (1623—1827). *Reprint from the Proceedings of the 72nd annual meeting of the State Horticultural Association of Pennsylvania, Jan., 1931. pp. 26;* (II.) . . .
                                                     [2563
Heilman, S. P.: The old cider mill. *In: Papers read before the Lebanon County Historical Society. Vol. I. Lebanon, Pa. 1902. p. 207, pp. 209—242, ill.*   [2564
Heilman, U. Henry: The premier among our edible fruits. *In: Papers read before the Lebanon County Historical Society. Vol. VIII. Lebanon, Pa. 1921—1924. pp. 303—315.*   [2565

Hance, Anthony M.: Our quest for the Seckel pear tree. *In: A Collection of Papers read before the Bucks County Historical Society. Vol. IV. Easton, Pa. 1917. pp. 256—268. ill.* [2566

James, D. M. and McFeely, H. F.: The market for Pennsylvania fruit. *Harrisburg, Pa. 1927. pp. 35, maps. = Pennsylvania Department of Agriculture. Bulletin. Vol. X, no. 10. = General Bulletin no. 446.* [2567

Commercial orchards in Pennsylvania. *Harrisburg, Pa.: Pennsylvania Department of Agriculture 1929. pp. 36.* [2568

Beck, Clara A.: A „wheat market" of colonial days. *In: The Pennsylvania-German. Vol. XII. Lititz, Pa. 1911. pp. 177—179, ill.* [2569

Frantz, J. Andrew: History of cattle and stock yards in Lancaster County prior to 1800. *In: Papers and Addresses of the Lancaster County Historical Society. Vol. XXVIII. Lancaster, Pa. 1924. pp. 41—46.* [2570

Taylor, P. R. and Hanemann, H. A.: Direct marketing of farm products in Pennsylvania. *Harrisburg, Pa. 1927, pp. 35, ill. = Pennsylvania Department of Agriculture. Bulletin. Vol. X, no. 18. = General Bulletin no. 454.* [2571

Waldwirtschaft
Forestry

Baare, Friedrich: Die Deutschen in der Försterei von Nord-Amerika. *Nach Regierungsakten von Bund und Staaten dargestellt. In: Das Buch der Deutschen in Amerika. Philadelphia, Pa. 1909 [Nr. 59]. S. 657—672.* [2572

Illick, Joseph S.: Joseph Trimble Rothrock, father of Pennsylvania forestry. *Read before the Pennsylvania-German Society at Bethlehem, Oct. 7, 1923. In: The Pennsylvania-German Society. Proceedings and Addresses. Vol. XXXIV. 1929. pp. 85—94, ill.* [2573

Paxon, Henry D.: Forestry in Pennsylvania. *Read July 27, 1886. In: A Collection of Papers read before the Bucks County Historical Society. Vol. I. Easton, Pa. 1908. pp. 408—416.* [2574

Rothrock, J. T.: On the growth of the forestry idea in Pennsylvania. *In: Proceedings of the American Philosophical Society held at Philadelphia for the promotion of useful knowledge. Vol. XXXII. May, 1893. Philadelphia, Pa. 1894. pp. 332—342.* [2575

Dr. Joseph Trimble Rothrock. *In: The Pennsylvania Magazine of History and Biography. Vol. XLVII. Philadelphia, Pa. 1923. pp. 143—145.* [2576

Handwerk, Gewerbe und Industrie

Handicrafts and Industries

Pennsylvanien, allgemein

Pennsylvania, general

Luetscher, G. D.: Industries of Pennsylvania after the adoption of the Federal Constitution, with special reference to Lancaster and York Counties. *In: German American Annals. New series, vol. I. Philadelphia, Pa. 1903. pp. 135—155; 197—208, ill., maps.* [2577

Swank, James M.: Progressive Pennsylvania. *A record of the remarkable industrial development of the Keystone State with some account of its early and its later transportation systems, its early settlers, and its prominent men. Philadelphia, Pa.: J. B. Lippincott Co. 1908. pp. VII, 360.* [2578

Whidden, Guy C. and **Schoff, Wilfred H.:** Pennsylvania and its manifold activities. *Prepared by . . . for the 12th International Congress of Navigation. Philadelphia, Pa.: Published by the local Organizing Commission of the Congress, May 1912. pp. 287, ill., map.* [2579

Wyer, Samuel S.: The Smithonian Institution's study of natural resources applied to Pennsylvania's resources based on latest governmental data. *Columbus, O. 1922. pp. 150, ill., maps. Second edition 1925. pp. 182, ill. maps.* [2580

The manufactories and manufacturers of Pennsylvania of the nineteenth century. *Philadelphia, Pa.: Galaxy Publishing Co. 1875. pp. 533, ill.* [2581

Pennsylvania, Commonwealth of . . ., Department of Internal Affairs: . . . industrial directory of the Commonwealth of Pennsylvania. *Compiled by the* **Bureau of Statistics.** *Harrisburg. Pa. Triennial publication issued regulary since the first edition of 1913.* [2582

Müller und Mühlen

Millers and Mills

Breithaupt, W. H.: Waterloo County millers. *In: Sixteenth Annual Report of the Waterloo Historical Society. Waterloo, Ont. 1928. pp. 78—80.* [2583

Fegley, H. Winslow: Among some of the older mills in eastern Pennsylvania. *In: The Pennsylvania-German Society. Proceedings and Addresses at Easton, October 12, 1928. Vol. XXXIX. Norristown, Pa. 1930. pp. (2), 7—76, ill.* [2584

Kriebel, Howard W.: Perkiomen Valley water power. *(A list compiled from the records of Montgomery County, Pa. showing the mills with names of owners in the various townships of the Perkiomen region at various periods.) In: The Per-kiomen Region. Vol. VIII, no. 1. Pennsburg, Pa. 1930. pp. 10—13.* [2585

Luetscher, G. D.: Industries of Pennsylvania after the adoption of the Federal Constitution, with special reference to Lancaster and York Counties. *In: German American Annals. New series, vol. I. Philadelphia, Pa. 1903. pp. 135—155; 197—208, ill., maps.* [2586

Munro, Ross: The Snider flour mills, Waterloo. *Reprint from: „Saturday Night", Sept. 10, 1927. In: Fifteenth Annual Report of theWaterloo Historical Society. Kitchener, Ont. 1927. pp. 383—384, ill.* [2587

[Richardson, W. H.]: How they made millers a century ago. *A facsimile of a* record of indenture from the docket of Justice of the Peace, Peter Michael Croll, Jan. 12, 1792. — Comments of W. H. Richardson in the Millers' Review of Philadelphia. In: The Perkiomen Region, Past and Present. Vol. I. Philadelphia, Pa. 1895. p. 139.   [2588

Old mills in the vicinity of Sumneytown, 1865. (Edwin Benner's record.) In: The Perkiomen Region. Vol. II, no. 3. Pennsburg, Pa. 1923. p. 51; Persons killed in mills, 1790—1867. (Edwin Benner's record) p. 52.   [2589

Preston mill historical tablet. In: Sixteenth Annual Report of the Waterloo Historical Society. Waterloo, Ont. 1928. p. 77 ill.   [2590

The Millers Review. Vol. I. Philadelphia, Pa.: H. L. Everett, 1882ff. — (with various subtitles) to Vol. XLIII. 1882—1924; now (jointly with Dixie Miller). The Millers Review and Feed Forum. Vol. XCIV, no. 6. Atlanta, Ga., June 1930ff.

[Contains a number of historical sketches relating to Pennsylvania-German mills and millers.]   [2591

Papiermühlen
Paper Mills

Jones, Horatio Gates: Historical sketch of the Rittenhouse papermill; the first erected in America, A. D. 1690. Paper read before the Historical Society of Pennsylvania, May 11, 1863. In: The Pennsylvania Magazine of History and Biography. Vol. XX. Phi-ladelphia, Pa. 1896. pp. 315—333, ill.   [2592

Sachse, Julius Friedrich: The Ephrata paper mill. In: Papers and Addresses of the Lancaster County Historical Society. Vol. I. Lancaster, Pa. 1897. pp. 323—341, ill.   [2593

Grobschmiede, Wagnerei und Schiffsbau
Blacksmiths, Wagon Makers and Shipbuilders

Beck, Clara A.: Manufacturing scythes and sickles in colonial days. Reprint from: ,,The Millers' Review" (The official organ of the State Millers' Association), March 15, 1912. In: Historical Sketches. A Collection of Papers prepared for the Historical Society of Montgomery County, Pa. Vol. V. Norristown, Pa. 1925. pp. 155—158, ill.   [2594

Betz, I. H.: The Studebaker brothers. The wagon builders of South Bend, Indiana. In: The Pennsylvania-German. Vol. XI. Lititz, Pa. 1910. pp. 194—204, ill.   [2595

Erskine, Albert Russel: History of the Studebaker Corporation. Chicago, Ill.: The Studebaker Corporation. Printed by R. R. Donnelly & Sons Co. 1924. pp. XXVII, 229, ill.   [2596

Frey, H. C.: The Conestoga wagon. In: Papers and Addresses of the Lancaster County Historical Society. Vol. XXXIV Lancaster, Pa. 1930. pp. 289—312.   [2597

— Moses Hartz — A Conestoga wagon teamster. (Information furnished by H. H. Stoltzfus). In: Papers and Addresses of the Lancaster County Historical Society. Vol. XXXIV. Lancaster, Pa. 1930. pp. 313—315.   [2598

Hamilton, Bryan: The Conestoga wagon. In: Proceedings of the New Jersey Historical Society. New Series, vol. XIV. 1929. pp. 405—411.   [2599

Lacher, J. H. A.: The Conestoga wagon. In: Unrolling the scroll. Published by the National Historical Society. Vol. I. Chicago, Ill. 1928 [= no. 29]. pp. 212—216.   [2600

Omwake, John: The Conestoga six-horse bell teams. Published by . . . for private distribution. Cincinnati, O.: The Ebbert & Richardson Co. 1930. pp. 128, (8), ill.   [2601

Buell, A. C.: The memoirs of Charles H. Cramp. *Philadelphia, Pa.: J. B. Lippincott Co. 1906.* [2601 a
Hobart, S. Perry: Cramp William [descendant of Johannes Krampf of Baden] (1807—1879) shipbuilder. *In: Dictionary of American biography. Under the* auspices of the American Council of Learned Societies. Vol. IV. Edited by Allen Johnson and Dumas Malone. London-New York 1930. pp. 500—501.* [2601 b
History of Cramp's shipyard, 1830—1902. *Philadelphia, Pa.: Cramp & Sons 1910. pp. . . .* [2601 c

Büchsenmacherei und Grobschmiede

Rifle- and Gunmakers

Diffenderffer, Frank Ried: The Lancaster rifles. *In: Papers and Addresses of the Lancaster County Historical Society. Vol. IX. Lancaster, Pa. 1905. pp. 67—73.* [2602
Heller, William J.: The gunmakers of old Northampton. *In: The Pennsylvania-German Society. Proceedings and Addresses at Allentown, November 2, 1906. Vol. XVII. Lancaster, Pa. 1908. Separate pagination. pp. 14, ill. Reprint in: The Pennsylvania-German. Vol. IX. Cleona, Pa. 1908. pp. 100—114.* [2603
Hensel, W. U.: The American rifle. *In: Papers and Addresses of the Lancaster County Historical Society. Vol. IX. Lancaster, Pa. 1905. pp. 59—66.* [2604
Lacher, J. H. A.: The long rifle or yager in American history. *In: The Concord Society of America. Year book 1928. Detroit, Mich.: Herold Printing Co. 1929. pp. 27—34.* [2605
Lindsay, Cora A. Weber: First riflemaker in America an Ulster Huguenot. *[Philip Le Fevre of Strassburg Twp., Lancaster Co., Pa.] Reprint from: ,,Shooting and Fishing, New York, February 18,* 1897. Contributed by Chaplain **Roswell Randall Hoes.** *In: Olde Vlster. An historical and genealogical magazine. Vol. VII. Kingston, N. Y. 1911. pp. 13—20.* [2606
Kriebel, H. W.: Elias Brey, the gunmaker. *In: The Perkiomen Region. Vol. VII, no. 3. Pennsburg, Pa. 1929. pp. 76—80.* [2607
Magee, D. F.: The so called ,,Kentucky Rifle", as made in Lancaster County. *In: Papers and Addresses of the Lancaster County Historical Society. Vol. XXX. Lancaster, Pa. 1926. pp. 47—60.* [2608
First manufaturer of rifles in Pennsylvania. *In: The Pennsylvania Magazine of History and Biography. Vol. XIV. Philadelphia, Pa. 1890. p. 333.* [2609
Sawyer, Charles Winthrop: Firearms in American history. Vol. I. 1600—1800. *Boston, Mass.: Plimpton Press 1910. pp. (1), 237, ill.; . . . Vol. III. Our Rifles. Boston, Mass.: The Cornhill Co. 1921. pp. 409.* [2610
The first wrought-iron cannon. *Reprint from ,,Der Deutsche Pionier", June, 1876. In: The Pennsylvania-German. Vol. VIII. Lebanon, Pa. 1907. p. 273.* [2611

Gusseiserner Ofenbau

Iron Stoveplates

Fackenthal, B. F., Jr.: Classification and analyses of stoveplates. *Read October 5, 1909. In: A Collection of Papers read before the Bucks County Historical Society. Vol. IV. Easton, Pa. 1917. pp. 55—61.* [2612
Mercer, Henry C.: The decorated stove plates of the Pennsylvania Germans. *Doylestown, Pa.: McGinty's Job Peess 1899. pp. 26, ill. = Contributed to American History by the Bucks County Historical Society, no. 6.* [2613
Mercer, Henry C.: The bible in iron or the pictured stoves and stove plates of the Pennsylvania Germans, *with notes on*

colonial firebacks in the United States, the ten-plate stove, Franklin's fireplace and the tile stoves of the Moravians in Pennsylvania and North-Carolina, together with a list of colonial furnaces in the United States and Canada. Published for the Bucks County Historical Society. Doylestown, Pa.: McGinty 1914. pp. IV. 174, ill. [2614

Mercer, Henry C.: A lost stoveplate inscription. In: A Collection of Papers read before the Bucks County Historical Society. Vol. V. Easton, Pa. 1926. pp. 388—400, ill. [2615
— The decorated stove plates of Durham. [Doylestown, s. d.] pp. (4).

= Contributions to American History by the Bucks County Historical Society, no. 3. [2616

Montague, Wm. E.: Stove plates and textiles of the early Pennsylvania Germans. In: Historical Sketches. A Collection of Papers prepared for the Historical Society of Montgomery County, Pa. Vol. V. Norristown, Pa. 1925. pp. 257—261. [2617

Owen, B. F.: Pennsylvania German stoveplates in Berks County. Read October 5, 1909. In: A Collection of Papers read before the Bucks County Historical Society. Vol. IV. Easton, Pa. 1917. pp. 50—54. [2618

Töpferei

Pottery

Barber, Edwin Atlee: Tulip ware of the Pennsylvania-German potters. An historical sketch of the art of slip-decoration in the United States. Philadelphia, Pa.: Printed for the Museum Memorial Hall, Fairmont Park 1903. pp. 233, ill.
= Art Handbook of the Pennsylvania Museum and School of Industrial Art. [2619
— Salt glazed stone ware. Germany, Flanders, England, and the United States. New York, N. Y.: Doubleday, Page & Co. 1807. pp. 32, ill.
= Publ. of: Art Primer Pennsylvania Museum and School of Industrial Art, Philadelphia. [2620
— Lead glazed pottery. Part first (Common clays) Plain glazed, sgraffite and slip-decorated wares. New York, N. Y.: Doubleday, Page & Co. 1907. pp. 34, ill.
= Publ.: Art Primer Pennsylvania Museum and School of Industrial Art Philadelphia. [2621
— The pottery and porcelain of the United States. An historical review of American ceramic art from the earliest times to the present day. First edition. New York, N. Y. — London: G. P. Putnam's Sons — The Knickerbocker Press 1893. pp. XVII, 466, ill. Third edition. 1909. pp. XXVIII, 621, ill. [2622

:ruger, Eliza: Tulip ware. Paper read on the occasion of an loan exhibition of pottery of the Historical Society of Mont-

gomery County, April 24, 1909. In: Historical Sketches. A Collection of Papers prepared for the Historical Society of Montgomery County, Pa. Vol. IV. Norristown, Pa. 1910. p. 134. [2623

Mercer, Henry C.: The pottery of the Pennsylvania-Germans. In: The Pennsylvania-German. Vol. II. Lebanon, Pa. 1901. pp. 86—88, ill. [2624
— Pottery of the Pennsylvania-Germans. In: A Collection of Papers read before the Bucks County Historical Society. Vol. IV. Easton, Pa. 1917. pp. 187—191. [2625
— Notes on the „Moravian pottery of Doylestown". Read Febr. 10, 1914. In: A Collection of Papers read before the Bucks County Historical Society. Vol. IV. Easton, Pa. 1917. pp. 482—487. [2626

Montague, William E.: Early Pennsylvania pottery. In: A Collection of Papers read before the Bucks County Historical Society. Vol. V. Meadville, Pa. 1926. pp. 197—202. [2627

Müller, Ida: Von deutscher Volkskunst in Pennsylvanien. In: Der Auslanddeutsche. Mitteilungen des Deutschen Ausland-Instituts. Jg. XI. Nr. 21. Stuttgart 1928. S. 664—666.
[Nach Tulip ware of the Pennsylvania-German potters. By E. A. Barber. Philadelphia, Pa. 1903 [= no. 2619].] [2628

15*

Scheetz, Grier: Bucks County potters. *In:* A Collection of Papers read before the Bucks County Historical Society. *Vol. IV. Easton, Pa. 1917. pp. 192—197.* [2629

Stoudt, John Baer: Inscriptions on the pottery of the Pennsylvania Germans. *In:* A Collection of Papers read before the Bucks County Historical Society. *Vol. IV. Easton, Pa. 1917. pp. 587—599.* [2630

Rice, A. H.-—: The Shenandoah pottery. *Strassburg, Va.: Shenandoah Publishing House, Inc. 1929. pp. XII, 277, ill.* [2631

Weygandt, Cornelius: The red hills. A record of good days outdoors and in, with things Pennsylvania Dutch. *Philadelphia, Pa.: University of Pennsylvania Press, Nov. 1929. pp. XI, (1,) 251, ill.* [2632

Kachelofenbau der Herrnhuter

Moravian Tile Stoves

Fries, Adelaide L.: Moravian tile stoves of Salem, North Carolina. *Read, February 10, 1914. In: A Collection of Papers read before the Bucks County Historical Society. Vol. IV. Easton, Pa. 1917. pp. 477—479.* [2633

Mercer, Henry C.: The bible in iron or the pictured stoves and stove plates of the Pennsylvania Germans, with notes on . . . the tile stoves of the Moravians in Pennsylvania and North Carolina . . .

Doylestown, Pa.: McGinty 1914. pp. IV, 174, ill. [See no. 2614]. [2634

Oerter, Albert L.: Tile Stoves of the Moravians at Bethlehem, Pa. *In: A Collection of Papers read before the Bucks County Historical Society. Vol. IV. Easton, Pa. 1917. pp. 479—481.* [2635

Rights, T. M.: Remarks on tile stoves. *In: A Collection of Papers read before the Bucks County Historical Society. Vol. IV. Easton, Pa. 1917. pp. 481—482.* [2636

Glasbläserei[1])

Glassmaking[2])

Daugherty, Harvey Peter: Henry William Stiegel and Stiegel glass. *Read (with exhibit) Dec. 12, 1924. In: Papers . . . read before the Lebanon County Historical Society. Vol. IX, no. 3. Lebanon, Pa. 1924. pp. 79—89, ill.* [2637

Hunter, Frederick William: Stiegel glass. *Illustrated with 12 plats in color from*

----

[1]) Siehe auch Nr. 7548—7558.
[2]) See also nos. 7548—7558.

autochromes by J. B. Kerfoot and with 159 half-tones. Boston, Mass. and New York, N. Y.: Houghton Mifflin Co., The Riverside Press, Cambridge 1914. pp. XVI, 272, ill., maps. [Bibliography. pp. 263—265.] [2638

An interesting relic. Discovery of part of one of Baron Stiegle's stoves. *In: Papers and Addresses of the Lancaster County Historical Society. Vol. XIX. Lancaster, Pa. 1915. pp. 153—155.* [2639

Orgel-, Uhr- und Instrumentenbau

Organ-, Clock- and Instrumentmaking

Auge, M.: Clock and watchmakers of Montgomery County. *In: Historical Sketches. A Collection of Papers prepared for the Historical Society of Montgomery County, Pa. Vol. I. 1895. pp. 187—196.* [2640

Beck, A. R.: David Tannenberg. *In: The Pennsylvania-German. Vol. X. Lititz, Pa. 1909. pp. 339—341.* [2641

Beck, Paul E.: David Tannenberger, organ builder. *In: Papers and Addresses of the Lancaster County Historical Society*

Vol. XXX. Lancaster, Pa. 1926. pp. 3
—11.   [2642
Funk, H. H.: Grandfather's clocks. In:
The Pennsylvania-German. Vol. VIII.
Lebanon, Pa. 1907. pp. 545—546. [2643
Gillingham, Harrold E.: Some early Phila-
delphia instrument makers. In: The
Pennsylvania Magazine of History and
Biography. Vol. LI. Philadelphia, Pa.
1927. pp. 289—308.
[David Rittenhouse. pp. 296—299.]
                                                        [2644
Jordan, John W.: Early colonial organ-
builders of Pennsylvania. In: The Penn-
sylvania Magazine of History and Bio-
graphy. Vol. XXII. Philadelphia, Pa.
1898. pp. 231—233.   [2645
Kistler, William U.: Early organ builders
in northern Montgomery County. In:
Historical Sketches. A Collection of
Papers prepared for the Historical Society of Montgomery County, Pa. Vol.
IV. 1910. pp. 112—117.   [2646
Kriebel, H. W.: The successor to David
Schultze. John Kraus, Esq., the surveyor, scrivener, conveyancer, organ
builder, machinist and mathematician.
In: The Perkiomen Region. Vol. VIII,
no. 1. Pennsburg, Pa. 1930. pp. 29—31.
                                                        [2647
Magee, D. F.: Grandfather's clocks: Their
making and their makers in Lancaster
County. In: Papers and Addresses of
the Lancaster County Historical Society.
Vol. XXI. Lancaster, Pa. 1917. pp.
63—77.   [2648
Miller, H. E.: Old clocks. Read at a joint
meeting of Lebanon Chapter, Daughters
of the American Revolution and Lebanon
County Historical Society, March 18,
1926. In: Papers . . . read before the
Lebanon County Historical Society. Vol.
IX, no. 5. Lebanon, Pa. 1926. pp. 146—
162, ill.   [2649
Moore, N. Hudson: „Pennsylvania clock-
makers." In: The old clock book. By
N. Hudson Moore. New York, N. Y.:
Frederick A. Stockes Co. 1911. pp. 154—
158; see also: List of American clock
makers. pp. 297—330.   [2650
Richardson, W. H.: The birthplace of the
telephone. [The shops of the inventor,
Daniel Drawbaugh, of Eberly's Mills,
Cumberland County, Pa.] Reprint from:
„The Millers' Review", of Philadelphia
in: The Pennsylvania-German. Vol. III.
Lebanon, Pa. 1902. pp. 178—179, ill.
[See nos. 2660—2662.]   [2651

Roberts, Charles R.: Grandfathers clocks.
In: Proceedings and Papers read before
the Lehigh County Historical Society.
Allentown, Pa. 1922. pp. 29—33. [2652
Stockley, James: The Rittenhouse exhibition. In: The Pennsylvania Magazine
of History and Biography. Vol. LVI.
Philadelphia, Pa. 1932. pp. 236—248,
ill.   [2653
Strech, Carolyn Wood: Early colonial clock-
makers in Philadelphia. An address delivered at the Rittenhouse bicentenary
dinner, April 8, 1932. In: The Pennsylvania Magazine of History and Biography. Vol. LVI. Philadelphia, Pa.
1932. pp. 225—235, ill.   [2654
Worner, William Frederic: Ingenious inven-
tions of Martin Shreiner. [Note on in-
vention of an astronomical instrument,
1832.] In: Papers and Addresses of the
Lancaster County Historical Society.
Vol. XXXIV. Lancaster, Pa. 1930. pp.
199—200.   [2655
Ancient home of old organ builders, [the
Krauss home, near the Village of Palm,
Montgomery Co., Pa.] From: Daily Re-
gister. In: The Pennsylvania-German.
Vol. X. Lititz, Pa. 1909. pp. 174—175.
                                                        [2656
Neisser, the clockmaker of Germantown,
Pa. In: The Pennsylvania Magazine of
History and Biography. Vol. XXIII.
Philadelphia, Pa. 1899. p. 126. [2657
The maker of the original state-house clock:
Joseph Stretch. Note in: The Pennsyl-
vania Magazine of History and Biogra-
phy. Vol. XXIV. Philadelphia, Pa.
1900. p. 526.   [2658
An old timepiece, [completed by John
Fisher, Sr., Yorktown, Pa., May 23d,
1790.] In: Notes and Queries. Edited by
W. H. Egle. Annual vol. 1899. Harrisburg, Pa. 1900. pp. 92—93.   [2659
„The telephon cases", wherein a Pennsylvania-German, Daniel Drawbaugh of
Cumberland County claimed the prior in-
vention of the telephone . . .:
The American Bell Telephone Company and The Metropolitan Telephone
and Telegraph Company vs. The
People's Telephone Company and others.
In Equity. Before Wallace, J., Southern District of New York, December
1st, 1884. In: Reports of cases argued
and determined in the Circuit Court of
the United States for the Second Circuit.

By Samuel Blatchford. Vol. XXII. New York, N. Y. 1885. pp. 531—574. [2660 American Bell Telephone Company v. People's Telephone Company and others. Circuit Court, S. D. New York 1885. Reported by Charles C. Linthicum. In: The Federal Reporter. Vol. XXV. Cases argued and determined in the Circuit and District Courts of the United States. Saint Paul 1886. pp. 725—726. [2661 „The telephone cases." In: United States Reports. Vol. CXXVI. Cases adjudged in the Supreme Court at October term, 1887. J. C. Bancraft Davis, reporter. New York, N. Y. — Albany, N. Y. 1888. [2662

Tischlerei

Cabinetmaking

Gillingham, Harrold E.: Benjamin Lehman, a Germantown cabinetmaker. In: The Pennsylvania Magazine of History and Biography. Vol. LIV. Philadelphia, Pa. 1930. pp. 289—306, ill. [2663 Jacob Brandt, canteenmaker [on Vine Str., Philadelphia, Pa.] Note in: The Pennsylvania Magazine of History and Bio- graphy. Vol. XXIV. Philadelphia, Pa. 1900. p. 526. [2664 The furniture of our ancestors. (A catalogue of the cabinetware manufactured by Benjamin Lehman, in the year 1786.) In: The Pennsylvania Magazine of History and Biography. Vol. XXVIII. Philadelphia, Pa. 1904. pp. 78—83; 199—200. [2665

Seilerei und Korbmacherei

Rope and Basketmaking

Erisman, George F. K.: Rope making in Lancaster, Pa. at the Martin rope walk. In: Papers and Addresses of the Lancaster County Historical Society. Vol. XXXI. Lancaster, Pa. 1927. pp. 47—52. [2666 Mercer, Henry C.: Notes on basket making. In: A Collection of Papers read before the Bucks County Historical Society. Vol. V. Meadville, Pa. 1926. pp. 192—196. [2667 Scheetz, Grier: Basket making. In: A Collection of Papers read before the Bucks County Historical Society. Vol. V. Meadville, Pa. 1926. pp. 190—192. [2668

Werkzeuge

Tools

Mercer, Henry C.: Tools of the nation maker. A description catalogue of objects in the Museum of the Historical Society of Bucks County, Pa. Collected and arranged by . . . Doylestown, Pa.: Printed for the Society at the office of the Bucks County Intelligencer 1897. pp. (2), 5—87. With Pennsylvania-German index. pp. 85—87. = Contributions to American History by the Bucks County Historical Society, no. 1. [2669 — Address: (The tools of the nation maker). In: A Collection of Papers read before the Bucks County Historical Society. Vol. II. Easton, Pa. 1909. pp. 486—489, ill. [2670 Mercer, Henry C.: The tools of the nation maker. Read May 28, 1907. In: A Collection of Papers read before the Bucks County Historical Society. Vol. III. Easton, Pa. 1909. pp. 469—481, ill. [2671 — Light and fire making. With 45 illustrations explaining the rubbing of fire from wood, the striking of flint and steel and some of the lamps, candles, torches and laterns of the American pioneer. Ex tracts from an address for the Bucks County Historical Society, at Teachers' Institute, Doylestown, Pa., October 25; at Franklin Institute, Philadelphia, Pa., December 3, 1897, and at the Southampton Farmers' Club at Somerton, Pa., Jan. 5, 1898. Philadelphia, Pa: Press of MacCalla & Co. 1898. pp. 29, ill.

= Contributions to American History by the Bucks County Historical Society, no. 4.   [2672

Roedel, Mary L.: Lard dips, candle sticks and lamps or the light of other days. In: Papers read before the Lebanon County Historical Society. Vol. VI. Lebanon, Pa. 1912—1916. pp. 232—241, ill. [2673

Textil-Industrie[1])
Textile Industries[2])

Bagnall, William R. The textile industries of the United States, including sketches and notices of cotton, woolen, silk, and linnen manufactures in the colonial period. Vol. I. 1639—1810. Cambridge: The Riverside Press 1893.
[Linnen manufacture at Germantown; decline of Germantown hosiery. pp. 9—11, resp. 362—363; Textile industries of the

Moravians at Bethlehem, Pa. 1749—1814—1862. pp. 25—27.]   [2674

Hostetter, Albert K.: The early silk industry of Lancaster County. In: Papers and Addresses of the Lancaster County Historical Society. Vol. XXIII. Lancaster, Pa. 1919. pp. 27—37.   [2675

K., F. P.: Vom Webstuhl. Zum Kapitel deutsch-amerikanischer Hausindustrie. In: Deutsch-Amerikanische Geschichtsblätter. Bd. I. Chicago, Ill. 1901. S. 48—49.   [2676

[1]) Siehe auch unter Germantown, Allentown u a.
[2]) Smaller items see within local literature as Germantown, Allentown etc.

Zigarren-Industrie
Cigar Industries

1892. Historical review of the industrial and commercial growth of York County, including McSherrystown, Adams County. [s. l. 1892.] pp. 130, ill.; Added: Complete gazetteer and shipers' guide of the state, containing a list of all the express, telegraph, money order and post offices in Pennsylvania. pp. 16.   [2677

[Ehehalt, „Rudi" C. M.]: Official souvenir year book 1927. Dedicated to no less noble and honorable a class of people than the thousands of cigar merchants and friends of tobacco of the USA. for their information and guidance in the great battle of cigars. By The York County Cigar Manufacturers Association. Headquarters: Red Lion, Pa.; York, Pa.: Trimmer Printing Co. 1927. pp. 120. From the contents, articles of C. M. Ehehalt:

(1) The cigar industry of York County, an historical study.

(2) The glorious record of the York County Cigar Manufacturers Association.
(3) Statistics of the York County cigar industry.
(4) Sidelights and intimate pictures of York County.
(5) Directory of cigar factories in York County, belonging to the first district of Pennsylvania.   [2678

Tobacco. Weekly trade review. Established 1886. Published by the Trade Journal Company. [Pennsylvania number.] Issued annually in May. East Stroudsburg, Pa.

Schettel, James W.: York and Adams Counties prove right to title „Home of 5c Cigar". In: Vol. LXXXIV, no. 5. 1927. pp. 20—24, 49—50, ill.
— York County cigar production sets a fast pace for the entire country. In: Vol. LXXXVI, no. 6. 1928. pp. 19—21; 32—34.

Schettel, James W.: York County maintains its famed position in the cigar industry. *In: Vol. XC, no. 6. 1930. pp. 15—21, ill.*
Red Lion, the cigar city, celebrating golden jubilee of progress. *In: Vol. XC, no. 6. 1930. p. 22, pp. 31—35, ill.*

Laughton, Herbert J.: How cigar industry has made history in the Borough of Dallastown. *In: Vol. XC, no. 6. 1930. p. 37; pp. 39—40, ill.*
Cigar industry foundation of the Borough of East Prospect, Pa. *In: Vol. XCII, no. 6. 1931. pp. 33—35; 38—40, ill.* [2679

Bergbau und Eisen-Industrie

Mining and Iron Industries

Bining, Arthur Cecil: The iron plantation of early Pennsylvania. *In: The Pennsylvania Magazine of History and Biography. Vol. LVII. Philadelphia, Pa. 1933. pp. 117—137.* [2680

Derr, Chas. F.: The Derr foundry. *Paper. May 28, 1913. In: Publications of the Historical Society of Schuylkill County. Vol. IV. Pottsville, Pa. pp. 213—232.* [2681

Geist, Georg W.: The story of the first Pennsylvania copper mine. *Reprinted from ,,The Mineral Collector''. Vol. XIV, no. 6. Aug., 1907. In: The Perkiomen Region. Vol. II, no. 1. Pennsburg, Pa. 1923. pp. 3—7.* [2682

Grittinger, Henry C.: The iron industries of Lebanon County. *In: Papers read before the Lebanon County Historical Society. Vol. III. 1905—1906. pp. 3—30.* [2683

Keefer, Horace Andrew: Early iron industries of Dauphin County. *Harrisburg, Pa.: Telegraph Press 1927. = Publications of the Dauphin County Historical Society. pp. 35, ill.* [2684

Montgomery, Morton L.: Early furnaces and forges of Berks County, Pa. *In: The Pennsylvania Magazine. Vol. VIII. Philadelphia, Pa. 1884. pp. 56—81.* [2685

Peters, Richard: Two centuries of iron smelting in Pennsylvania. *Second printing. Chester, Pa.: Press of Chester Times 1921. pp. 83.* [2686

Haldeman, Horace L.: The Chickies furnace. *The first furnace using coal. In: Papers and Addresses of the Lancaster County Historical Society. Vol. I. Lancaster, Pa. 1897. pp. 14—23.* [2687

Richards, H. M. M.: American Iron and Steel Manufacturing Company, Lebanon's great iron works. *In: Papers read before the Lebanon County Historical Society. Vol. VI. pp. 442—467, ill.* [2688

Schmidt, N. F.: The old Perkiomen copper mine. *In: The Perkiomen Region. Vol. I, no. 2. Pennsburg, Pa. 1922. pp. 30—32; no. 6. 1922. pp. 101—103.* [2690

Schuler, H. A.: The Hampton furnace. *Reminiscences of an important industry and its old time owner. In: The Pennsylvania-German. Vol. VII. Lebanon, Pa. 1908. pp. 223—240, ill.* [2691

Swank, James M.: Introduction to a history of ironmaking and coalmining in Pennsylvania. *Contributed to the final report of the Pennsylvania Board of Centennial Managers. Philadelphia, Pa.: Published by the author; Philadelphia: Allen, Lane & Scott 1878. pp. VIII, 9—125.* [2692

— History of the manufactures of iron in all ages, and particularly in the United States for three hundred years from 1585 to 1885. *Philadelphia, Pa.: Published by the author; Philadelphia: Allen, Lane & Scott 1884. pp. VII, 428.* [2693

Wiestling, Edward B.: Old iron works of the Cumberland Valley. *Paper read before the Kittochtinny Historical Society, May 25th, 1922. Vol. X, no. 1. Chambersburg, Pa. 1922. pp. 3—14.* [2694

Deutsche die ersten Eisenfabrikanten in Pennsylvanien. *In: Der Deutsche Pionier. Jg. XVI. Cincinnati, O. 1884—1885. S. 191—194.* [2695

Forges and furnaces in the Province of Pennsylvania. *Prepared by the Committee on Historical Research. Philadelphia, Pa.: Printed for the Society; Lancaster, Pa.: The New Era Printing Co. 1914. pp. VII, 204, ill.*

= *Publications of the Pennsylvania So-*
ciety of the Colonial Dames of America
III.   [2696
The first coal mining company of the Le-
high region. *The Lehigh Coal Mining*
Company, formed in Febr., 1792 by Col.
Jacob Weiß and Judge William Henry,
of Northampton; Charles Cist and Mi-
chael Hillegas, of Philadelphia, and
others. In: The Pennsylvania Magazine
of History and Biography. Vol. XXXIX.
Philadelphia, Pa. 1915. pp. 170—175.
(Contains a copy of the prospectus, dated:
Philadelphia, Febr. 13, 1792.)   [2697

Portland Zement-Industrie
Portland Cement Industry

Miller, Benjamin L.: Contribution of David
O. Saylor to early history of the Portland cement industry in America. *In:*
The Pennsylvania-German Society. Pro-
ceedings and Addresses at Easton, Oct. 12,
1928. Vol. XXXIX. Norristown, Pa.
1930. Separate pagination. pp. 5—19.
                                        [2698

Handel

Commerce

Harley, Lewis R.: The Pennsylvania-German as manufacturer and merchant. *In: The Pennsylvania-German. Vol. VII. Lebanon, Pa. 1906. pp. 154—156, ill.* [2699

Griest, W. W.: Banks in Lancaster County, Pa. *[Extract of a speech in the House of Representations, June 9, 1910.] In: The Pennsylvania-German. Vol. XI. Lititz, Pa. 1910. p. 701.* [2700

[Hocker, Edward W.]: A century of the National Bank of Germantown. *Philadelphia, Pennsylvania 1814—1914. Dedicated to the former presidents and cashiers by the directors. Philadelphia, Pa.: Innes & Sons 1914. pp. 66.* [2701

Diffenderffer, Frank Ried: A history of the Farmers Bank of Lancaster, the Farmers National Bank and the Farmers Trust Company of Lancaster. 1810—1910. *Compiled by . . . Lancaster, Pa.: Published by the Farmers Trust Co. of Lancaster 1910. pp. 228.* [2702

McDermott, William: Banks and banking. *In: Historical Sketches. A Collection of Papers prepared for the Historical Society of Montgomery County. Vol. I. Norristown, Pa. 1895. pp, 94—121.* [2703

Landreth, Burnet: Centennial firms in Pennsylvania. *In: Notes and Queries.* *Edited by W. H. Egle. Fourth series, vol. I. 1891—1893. Harrisburg, Pa. 1893. pp. 260—261.* [2704

Schaeffer, Charles H.: The Berks County banking institutions. *A paper read Jan. 14, 1902. In: Trancactions of the Historical Society of Berks County. Vol. I. Reading, Pa. 1904. No. 22. pp. 8.* [2705

Apple, Joseph H.: The business biography of John Wanamaker, founder and builder. *America's merchant pioneer 1861 to 1922. With glimpses of Rodman Wanamaker and Thomas B. Wanamaker. New York, N. Y.: The Macmillan Co. 1930. pp. XXVI, (1), 471.* [2706

Stephenson, Gilbert Thomas: The life story of a trust man being that of Francis Henry Fries, president of the Wachovia Bank and Trust Company, Winston-Salem, N. C. since February 16, 1893. *New York, N. Y.: F. S. Crofts & Co. 1930. pp. 7—267, ill.* [2707

Martin, Asa Earl: Lotteries in Pennsylvania prior to 1833. *In: The Pennsylvania Magazine of History and Biography. Vol. XLVII. Philadelphia, Pa. 1923. pp. 307—327; vol. XLVIII. 1924. pp. 66—93; 159—180, ill.* [2708

Öffentliches und politisches Leben
Civil and Political Life

Ashman, William N.: An address on the life and servives of John F. Hartranft. *Published by the committee on political education. Philadelphia, Pa.: The Pennsylvania Club 1890. pp. 3—44.* = *Pennsylvania Club Lectures, course of 1889—90.* [2709]

Biddle, Edward W.: Governor Joseph Ritner. *Historical address. Read before the Hamilton Library Association, Carlisle, Pa., on Friday evening, Oct. 17, 1919. [s. l. (1919).] pp. 10, ill.* [2710]

Bosse, Georg von: The German as politician. *In: The Penn Germania. Vol. I.* = *Old series, vol. XIII. Lititz, Pa. 1912. pp. 115—117.* [2711]

Burr, Frank A.: Life and achievements of James Addams Beaver. *Early life, military services and public career. Philadelphia, Pa.: Ferguson Bros. & Co. 1882. pp. 224, ill.* [2712]

De Peyster, John Watts: John Frederic Hartranft, governor of Pennsylvania. *[s. l., 1877 (?)] Printed on one side of leaf only. pp. 20.* [2713]

De Witt, W. R.: A discourse on the life and character of Francis R. Shunk. *Harrisburg, Pa. 1848. pp. 30.* [2714]

E.[gle], William Henry: A century of governors. The executives of the commonwealth from 1790 to 1890. *Brief but not comprehensive sketches of Pennsylvania's chief magistrates from Thomas Mifflin to James A. Beaver. In: Notes and Queries. Edited by W. H. Egle. Third series, vol. I. 1884—1887. Harrisburg, Pa. 1887. pp. 550—558. Reprint in: Third series, vol. II. Harrisburg, Pa. 1896. pp. 329—341.* [2715]

Fretz, A. J.: A patriot's fiery speach. *[Speach of Isaac Funk in the Illinois senate in favor of an appropriation for the Sanitary Commission.] In: The Pennsylvania-German. Vol. VIII. Lebanon, Pa. 1907. pp. 270—272, ill.* [2716]

Gerhard, Herm.: Das Deutschtum in der amerikanischen Politik. *Leipzig-Reudnitz: Nationale Kanzlei. Verlag: Leipziger Verlags- und Kommissions-Buchhandlung. Druck: Leipzig, Louis Seidel Nachf. 1915. 21 S.* = *Deutsch-nationaler Volksbund. Volksschriften. Heft 81.* [2716a]

Jones, George M.: The Pennsylvania-German as statesman and legislator. *In: The Pennsylvania-German Vol. VII. Lebanon, Pa. 1906. pp. 166—169, ill.* [2717]

Kenkel, F. P.: Eine Streitfrage der Geschichtsforschung und das Bildnis Michael Hillegas auf dem neuen Zehndollarschein. *In: Deutsch-Amerikanische Geschichtsblätter. Jg. VII. Nr. 4. Chicago, Ill. 1907. S. 173—175.* [2718]

Koons, Ulysses S.: The Pennsylvania-German as governor. *In: The Pennsylvania-German. Vol. VII. Lebanon, Pa. 1906. pp. 169—173, ill.* [2719]

Lincoln, Charles H.: The Revolutionary movement in Pennsylvania. 1760—1776. *Published by the University. Philadelphia, Pa.: Boston, Mass.: Ginn & Co. 1901. pp. 300.* = *Publications of the University of Pennsylvania. Series in history. No. 1. [Chapter II.: The influence of the German and Irish immigration. pp. 23—39.]* [2720]

[Long, Thomas]: Political facts addressed, more especially, to the German citizens of Bucks County, and their descendants. *By a meeting held at Rock Hill, August 30, 1800. (Signed): Thomas Long, chairman. Reprint in: The Pennsylvania-German. Vol. X. East-Greenville, Pa. 1909. pp. 6—10.* [2721]

Mauch, Russell C.: Pennsylvania-German patriotism. *German oration delivered at the commencement of Muhlenberg College, June 20, 1907. Translated by J. A. Scheffer. In: The Pennsylvania-Ger-*

man. Vol. IX. Cleona, Pa. 1908. pp. 34—36. [2722

Nead, Benjamin Matthias: The Pennsylvania-German in civil life. *Address delivered at the annual meeting at Reading, Pa., Oct. 15, 1915. Lancaster, Pa.: The New Era Printing Co. 1918. In: The Pennsylvania-German Society. Proceedings and Addresses ... 1915. Vol. XXVI. Lancaster, Pa. 1918. pp. 25—36.* [2723

[Rahn, George]: Democratic meeting. *Original minutes and resolutions in the handwriting of George Rahn, one of the secretaries, and signed by the officiers in their proper handwriting. Presented by* **A. B. Cochran.** *— May 2, 1907. In: Publications of the Historical Society of Schuylkill County. Vol. II. Pottsville, Pa. 1910. pp. 46—49.* [2724

Richards, Henry Melchior Muhlenberg: Governor Joseph Hiester. A historical sketch. *Lancaster, Pa.: New Era/Printing Co. 1907. = Part XVII. „A narrative and critical history,“ prepared at the request of the Pennsylvania-German Society. In: The Pennsylvania-German Society. Proceedings and Addresses ... 1905. Vol. XVI. Lancaster, Pa. 1907. Separate pagination. pp. 51, ill.* [2725

— Some of our patriots in public life. *In: The Pennsylvania-German in the Revolutionary War. 1775—1783. Lancaster, Pa. 1908 [= no. 2810]. Chapter XVI. pp. 427—445.* [2726

Roberts, Charles R.: Pennsylvania Germans in public life during the colonial period. *In: The Pennsylvania-German. Vol. X. Lititz, Pa. 1909. pp. 153—157.* [2727

— Pennsylvania Germans in public life during the colonial period. *In: Proceedings and papers read before the Lehigh County Historical Society. Vol. II. Allentown, Pa. 1910. pp. 54—59.* [2728

[Shoemaker, Samuel]: A Pennsylvania loyalist's interview with George III. *Extract from M. S. diary of Samuel Shoemaker. In: The Pennsylvania Magazine of History and Biography. Vol. II. Philadelphia, Pa. 1878. pp. 35—39.* [2729

Steele, Henry J.: The life and public services of Governor Georg Wolf. *In: The*

Pennsylvania-German Society. Proceedings and Addresses . . . Easton, Pa., October 12, 1928. Vol. XXXIX. Norristown, Pa. 1930. Separate pagination. pp. 25, ill. [2730

Vaux, Richard: Sketch of the life of Joseph Hiester, governor of Pennsylvania. *Read before the Historical Society of Pennsylvania on the presentation of his portrait to that institution, June 13th, 1887. Philadelphia, Pa.: Allen, Lane & Scott [1887.] pp. 23.* [2731

[Weiser, Conrad]: Die älteste deutsch-amerikanische Wahl-Flugschrift. *„Ernsthaffter und zeitgemäßer Rath an unsere Landsleute, die Teutschen in Pennsylvanien.“ [Unterzeichnet von Conrad Weiser, 20. Sept. 1741.] Von einer englischen Übersetzung in den MS.-Archives of Pennsylvania, Harrisburg, Pa. ins Deutsche zurückübertragen. In: Der Deutsche Pionier. Jg. X. Cincinnati O. 1878—1879. S. 230—232.* [2732

[—] Serious and seasonable advice to our countrymen the Germans of Pennsylvania. *[Circular letter signed by Conrad Weiser and published by order of the Proprietary Government, 20th of Sept., 1741.] In: Notes and Queries. Edited by W. H. Egle. Fourth series, vol. I. 1891—1893. Harrisburg, Pa. 1893. pp. 65—67.* [2733

[—] Two addresses of Conrad Weiser to the German voters of Pennsylvania. *(Manuscript in collection of the Historical Society of Pennsylvania) In: The Pennsylvania Magazine of History and Biography. Vol. XXIII. Philadelphia, Pa. 1899. pp. 516—521.* [2734

Zimmerman, T. C.: The Pennsylvania-German as American settlers. *In: The Pennsylvania-German. Vol. VII. Lebanon, Pa. 1906. pp. 205—207.* [2735

Papers of the governors. *Edited by George Edward Reed. 12 vols. Harrisburg, Pa.: The State of Pennsylvania, 1900—1902. = Pennsylvania Archives. Fourth series, vol. I—XII.* *[Contents see no. 3218.]* [2736

Lebensgeschichte, oder kurzer Entwurf von dem Leben, dem Character, und den öffentlichen Diensten Joseph Ritners. *Von einem Bürger von Lancaster Caunty. [s. l., s. d.] 8 S.* [2737

Public services of Brvt. Maj. Gen. John F. Hartranft, Union candidate for auditor general. *Norristown, Pa.: Wills, Iredell & Jenkins, 1865. pp. 15. (Pamphlet).* [2738

Opinions and acts of Joseph Ritner on all measured on public importance since his inauguration exemplified by copies of, and extracts from his addresses, messages, vetoes and proclamations. *[s. l.] 1838. pp. 31.* [2739

The Pennsylvania-German in law. *By a well known member of the Lancaster County Bar. In: The Pennsylvania-German. Vol. VII. Lebanon, Pa. 1906. pp. 164—166.* [2740

German governors. *Note. In: The Pennsylvania-German. Vol. IX. Cleona, Pa. 1908. p. 573.* [2741

Proceedings of the convention which nominated Joseph Hiester for governor of Pennsylvania. *In: The Pennsylvania Magazine of History and Biography. Vol. XXXIV. Philadelphia, Pa. 1910. pp. 247—251.* [2742

Schreiben des Evangelisch-Lutherisch und Reformirten Kirchen Raths, wie auch der Beamten der Teutschen Gesellschaft in der Stadt Philadelphia, an die Teutschen Einwohner der Provinzen von Neuyork und Nord-Carolina. *Philadelphia, Pa.: Heinrich Miller 1775. 40 S.*

[Eine politische Flugschrift für die Amerikanische Erhebung.] [2743

Der Fries-Aufstand

Fries Rebellion

Davis, W. W. H.: The Fries rebellion 1798 —99. An armed resistance to the House Tax Law, passed by congress, July 9, 1798, in Bucks and Northampton Counties, Pa. *Doylestown, Pa.: Doylestown Publishing Co. 1899. pp. XI, (1), 143; Appendix. pp. 14.* [2745

Dorland, W. A. Newman: „Fries' rebellion of 1798—99." = *Chapter XIII in: The Second Troop Philadelphia City Cavalry. By W. A. Newman Dorland. Reprint in: The Pennsylvania Magazine of History and Biography. Vol. XLVIII. Philadelphia, Pa. 1924. pp. 273—284; 372—376.* [2746

Eastman, Frank M.: The Fries rebellion. *In: „Americana". American Historical Magazine. Vol. XVI. New York, N. Y. 1922. pp. 71—82.* = *Reprint from: Courts and lawyers of Pennsylvania by Frank M. Eastman. 3 vols.* [2747

Harley, Lewis R.: Fries rebellion. *In: Historical Sketches. A Collection of Papers prepared for the Historical Society of Montgomery County, Pa. Vol. I. Norristown, Pa. 1895. pp. 313—326.* [2748

Hauser, J. J.: The Fries rebellion. *In: The Penn Germania. Vol. I. = Old series, vol. XIII. Lititz, Pa. 1912. pp. 703—710.* [2749

Hensel, W. U.: Window tax and Fries' treason trial. *In: Papers and Addresses of the Lancaster County Historical Society. Vol. XVIII. Lancaster, Pa. 1914. pp. 87—89.* [2750

The two trials of the John Fries on an indictment for treason; *together with a brief report of the trials of several other persons, for treason and insurrection in the Counties of Bucks, Northampton and Montgomery, in the Circuit Court of the United States, begun at the City of Philadelphia, April 11, 1799; continued at Norristown, October 11, 1799; and concluded at Philadelphia, April 11, 1800; before the judges Iredell, Peters, Washington and Chase. To which is added, a copious appendix, containing the evidences and arguments of the counsel on both sides, on the motion for a new trial; the arguments on the motion for removing the case to the county, where the crime was committed, and the argument holding the jurisdiction at Norristown. Taken in short hand by* Thomas Carpenter. *Philadelphia, Pa.: William W. Woodward 1800. pp. 226; 51.* [2751

Das erste und zweite Verhör von John Fries, welcher auf die Anklage für Hochverrath, in der Vereinigten Staaten Circuit-Court, verhört wurde. *Nebst den Verhören von einigen anderen Personen für Hochverrath und Aufstand, in den Counties Bucks, Northampton und Montgomery, in den Jahren 1799 und 1800. Vor den Richtern Iredell, Peters, Washington und Chase. Worin sich das Zeugen-Verhör, die Argumente der Advocaten und die Reden der Richter an die Jury befinden. Aus dem Englischen übersetzt. Mit einem Anhange der Constitution der Vereinigten Staaten und die der neuen Constitution von Pennsylvanien. Allentaun: Gedruckt für den Verleger und Übersetzer . . . 1839. 324 S.* [2752

Sklavenhandel und Antisklaverei-Bewegung

Slaveholding and Anti-Slavery Movement

Basset, John Spencer: Anti-slavery leaders of North Carolina. *Baltimore, Md.: The Johns Hopkins Press 1898. pp. 74.*
= *Johns Hopkins University Studies in Historical and Political Science. Series XVI, no. 6.*
[Includes sketches of Hinton Rowan Helper. pp. 11—29; of Benjamin Sherwood Hedrick. pp. 29—47.] [2753

Bausman, Lottie M.: The general position of Lancaster County in negro slavery. *In: Papers and Addresses of the Lancaster County Historical Society. Vol. XV. Lancaster, Pa. 1911. pp. 5—21.* [2754

Bettle, Edward: Notices of negro slavery as connected with Pennsylvania. *Read before the Historical Society of Pennsylvania, 8th mo. 7th, 1826. In: Memoirs of the Historical Society of Pennsylvania. Vol. I. — Part II. Philadelphia, Pa. pp. 353—388.* [2755

Betz, I. H.: The underground railroad. *In: The Pennsylvania-German. Vol. IX. Cleona, Pa. 1908. pp. 361—364.* [2756

Braun, (Brown) Johannes: Circular Schreiben an die Deutschen Einwohner von Rockingham und Augusta, und den benachbarten Counties. *Harrisonburg, Va.: Laurentz Wartmann 1818. 419 S.*
[Die erste Flugschrift über Sklaverei veröffentlicht von einem Mitglied der Deutschen Reformierten Kirche der Vereinigten Staaten.] [2757

Brubacker, Marianna G.: The underground railroad. *In: Papers and Addresses of the Lancaster County Historical Society. Vol. XV. Lancaster, Pa. 1911. pp. 95—119.* [2758

Clark, Martha B.: Who was Jacob Hibshman, the congressman from Lancaster County. *In: Papers and Addresses of the Lancaster County Historical Society. Vol. XV. Lancaster, Pa. 1911. pp. 219—221.* [2759

Eshleman, H. Frank: The position of Lancaster County on the Missouri compromise. *In: Papers and Addresses of the Lancaster County Historical Society. Vol. XV. Lancaster, Pa. 1911. pp. 215—218.*
[Antislavery-movement: J. Hibshman.] [2760

Fortenbaugh, Robert: American Lutheran synods and slavery, 1830—1860. *In: The Journal of Religion. Vol. XIII. Chicago, Ill. Jan., 1933. pp. 72—92.* [2761

Hamilton, J. G. de R.: Helper, Hinton Rowan (1829—1909) Author. *In: Dictionary of American biography. Under the auspices of the American Council of Learned Societies. Vol. VIII. Edited by Dumas Malone. London-New York 1932. pp. 517—518.* [2761a

Harris, Thomas L.: Deitzler, George Washington (1826—1884). Anti-slavery leader in Kansas. *In: Dictionary of American biography. Under the auspices of the American Council of Learned Societies. Vol. V. Edited by Allen Johnson and Dumas Malone. London-New York 1930. pp. 201—202.* [2761b

Hensel, W. U.: An anti-slavery reminiscence. *In: Papers and Addresses of the Lancaster County Historical Society. Vol. XV. Lancaster, Pa. 1911. pp. 123—127.* [2762

Huber, F. F.: A slave. *[Documents about a negro slave of John Adam Hillegass.] In: The Perkiomen Region. Vol. II, no. 1. 1923. pp. 13—14.* [2763

Niemeier, Otto: Deutsche Sklavenhalter und germanisierte Neger. *In: Der Deutsche Pionier. Jg. II. Cincinnati, O. 1870—1871. S. 280—284.* [2764

Seidensticker, Oswald: The first anti-slavery protest. *In: The Penn Monthly, devoted to literature, science, art and politics. July, 1874. Philadelphia, Pa. 1874. pp. 496—503.* [2765

Smedley, R. C.: History of the underground railroad in Chester and the neighboring Counties of Pennsylvania. *Lancaster, Pa.: Office of the Journal 1883. pp. (1), XXIV, 25—407, ill.* [2766

Swank, James M.: Protest against slavery. *In: The Pennsylvania-German. Vol. XI. Lititz, Pa. 1910. pp. 746—748.* [2767

Turner, Edward Raymond: Slavery in colonial Pennsylvania. *In: The Pennsylvania Magazine of History and Biography. Vol. XXXV. Philadelphia, Pa. 1911. pp. 141—151.* [2768

— The underground railroad in Pennsylvania. *In: The Pennsylvania Magazine of History and Biography. Vol. XXXVI Philadelphia, Pa. 1912. pp. 309—318.* [2769

Weeke, Stepben, B.: Hinton Rowan Helper. *In: Biographical History of North Carolina. Edited by S. A. Ashe. Vol. VIII. Greensboro, N. C. 1917. pp. 204—214. [Author of: ,,The Impending Crisis"; grandson of a German emigrant (Helfer) from the vicinity of Heidelberg, Germany who came to N. C. in 1752.]* [2770

Whitson, Thomas: The early Abolionists of Lancaster County. *In: Papers and Addresses of the Lancaster County Historical Society. Vol. XV. Lancaster, Pa. 1911. pp. 69—85.* [2771

Worner, William Frederic: Meetings in Lancaster County to oppose slavery in District of Columbia. *In: Papers and Addresses of the Lancaster County Historical Society. Vol. XXXIV. Lancaster, Pa. 1930. pp. 183—185.* [2772

Early anti-slavery protest. *In: The Mennonite Year Book and Almanac for 1898. Quakertown, Pa. 1898. p. 16.* [2773

Sketches of several Northampton County, Pa. slaves. *In: The Pennsylvania Magazine of History and Biography. Vol. XXII. Philadelphia, Pa. 1898. pp. 503—504.* [2774

Gideon Moor: Slave, freedom and litigant. *[Letters relating to the trouble of the Reformed congregation in Goshenhoppen, Montgomery Co., Pa., with the slave of their late minister, Geo. M. Weiss. 1776.] In: The Penn Germania. Vol. I. = Old series, vol. XIII. Lititz, Pa. 1912. pp. 364—368.* [2775

Address and constitution of the Lancaster County Colonization Society. (1837). *Copied from an original imprint. In: The Pennsylvania-German. Vol. XII. Lititz, Pa. 1911. pp. 721—723.* [2776

Slaves and slavery. *In: The Perkiomen Region. Vol. V, no. 2. Pennsburg, Pa. 1927. pp. 37—39.* [2777

Drewes, Christopher F.: Half a century of Lutheranism among our colored people. *A jubilee book. 1877—1927. St. Louis, Mo.: Concordia Publishing House Print 1927. pp. 111, ill.* [2778

Weaver, Martin G.: ,,Welch Mountain Industrial Mission." *In: Mennonites of Lancaster Conference. By M. G. Weaver. Scottdale, Pa. 1931 [= no. 972]. pp. 298—305.* [2779

Beteiligung an amerikanischen Kriegen[1])

Participation in American Wars[2])

[Bacon, J. Barnitz]: Penn' a-German heroes buried in New York Trinity churchyard. *Noble appeal of J. Barnitz Bacon, asking for the repeal of the ordinate relative to the extension of a street though the Hallowed Spot. From the People's Advocate (York), February 21, 1854. In: The Pennsylvania-German. Vol. IV. Lebanon. Pa. 1903. pp. 235—237.* [2780

Bicker, John W.: Orderly book of the Second Pennsylvania Continental Line Col. Henry Bicker. *Edited by* John W. Jordan. *In: The Pennsylvania Magazine of History and Biography. Vol. XXXV. Philadelphia, Pa. 1911. pp. 333—342; 463—496; Vol. XXXVI, 1912. pp. 30—59; 236—253; 329—345.* [2781

Biddle, Edward W.: Historical address at the unveiling of Molly Pitcher monument in Carlisle, Pa., June 28, 1916. *In: Historical Addresses at Carlisle, Pa. Published under the auspices of the Hamilton Library Association. 1916. pp. 11, ill.* [2782

Bosse, Georg von: The German as soldier. *In: The Pennsylvania-German. Vol. XII. Lititz, Pa. 1911. pp. 602—604; 691—693; 747—748.* [2783

Cronau, Rudolf: Der Deutsche in den Kriegen der Kolonial-Zeit und der Union. *In: Das Buch der Deutschen in Amerika. Philadelphia, Pa. 1909 [= Nr. 59]. S. 85—121.* [2784

Faust, A. B.: „The Germans as patriots and soldiers, during the War of the Revolution, 1775—1783." *In: The German element in the United States. By A. B. Faust. Second edition. New York 1927 [= no. 42]. Vol. I. = Chapter XI. pp. 286—356.* [2785

Fox, Luther A.: Patriotismus of the Germans in the Colonial South. *In: The Lutheran Church Review. Vol. XXXVIII.*

Philadelphia, Pa. 1919. pp. 10—17; 160—166. [2786

Greene, George Washington: The German element in the War of American Independence. *New York, N. Y.: Hurd and Houghton; Cambridge: The Riverside Press 1876. pp. VIII, (1), (1), 13—211.* [2787

Heckman, George C.: Pennsylvania-Germans at the battle of Long Island. *In: The Pennsylvania-German Society. Proceedings and Addresses at Lebanon, Oct. 12, 1892. Vol. III. Lancaster, Pa. 1893. pp. 61—80.* [2788

Heller, William Jacob: The gun makers of old Northampton. *Paper read at the 16th annual meeting. In: The Pennsylvania-German Society. Proceedings and Addresses at Allentown, Nov. 2, 1906. Vol. XVII. Lancaster, Pa. 1908. Separate pagination. pp. 14, ill.* [2789

Hess, Asher L.: Old time battalion drills. *In: The Pennsylvania-German. Vol. IX. Cleona, Pa. 1908. pp. 106—109, ill.* [2790

Hiester, William M.: The place of the Ringgold Light Artillery of Reading among the first five companies from Pennsylvania which marched to the defense of Washington, April, 1861. *Read June 14, 1870. Printed by order of the Society, 1870. Reprint in: Trancactions of the Historical Society of Berks County, Vol. I. Reading, Pa. 1904. No. 1. pp. 13.* [2791

Jordan, John Wolf: The military hospitals at Bethlehem and Lititz during the Revolution. *In: The Pennsylvania Magazine of History and Biography. Vol. XX. Philadelphia, Pa. 1896. pp. 137 157.* [2792

— The military hospitals at Bethlehem and Lititz, Penn'a, during the Revolutionary War. *A paper read before the Wyoming Historical and Geological Society, April 10, 1896, and before the Historical Society of Pennsylvania, May, 1896. Reprinted from: The Pennsylvania Maga-*

---

[1]) Zum Französich-Indianischen Kriege siehe Nr. 3219—3263.
[2]) See also nos. 3219—3263 relating to the French and Indian war.

242 Beteiligung an amerikanischen Kriegen

zine of History and Biography, July, 1896. Wilkes Barre, Pa. 1896. pp. 23, ill. [2793
Jordan, John Wolf: Continental hospital returns, 1777—1780. In: The Pennsylvania Magazine of History and Biography. Vol. XXIII. Philadelphia, Pa. 1899. pp. 35—50; 210—223. [2794
— Return of the sick at Lititz hospital, August 23, 1778. In: The Pennsylvania Magazine of History and Biography. Vol. XXXVI. Philadelphia, Pa. 1912. pp. 379—381. [2795
Kaufmann, Wilhelm: Der deutsche Soldat im Bürgerkriege. In: Das Buch der Deutschen in Amerika. Philadelphia, Pa. 1909 [= Nr. 59]. S. 123—152. [2796
— Die Deutschen im Bürgerkrieg. In: Deutsch-Amerikanische Geschichtsblätter. Vierteljahrsschrift herausgegeben von der Deutsch-Amerikanischen Gesellschaft von Illinois. Jg. VIII. Chicago, Ill. 1908. S. 107—115. [2797
— Die Deutschen im amerkanischen Bürgerkriege (Sezessionskrieg 1861—1865). München und Berlin: R. Oldenbourg 1911. XIII, 588, 36 S. Karten. [2798
Knipe, Irvin P.: The Pennsylvania-German in the Civil War. Address delivered at the annual meeting at Norristown, Pa., Nov. 2, 1916. Lancaster, Pa.: The New Era Printing Co. 1917. In: The Pennsylvania-German Society. Proceedings and Addresses . . . 1916. Vol. XXVII. Lancaster, Pa. 1920. Separate pagination. pp. 12. [2799
Lohr, Otto: Das Deutschamerikanertum vor hundert Jahren und der Krieg von 1812—1815. In: Deutsch-Amerikanische Geschichtsblätter. Jahrbuch der Deutsch-Amerikanischen Historischen Gesellschaft von Illinois. Jg. 1914. Bd. XIV. Chicago, Ill. 1914. S. 392—450. [2800
Metcalf, Frank J.: List of 591 persons who were paid for forage furishing for the magazine at Lancaster, Pa. 1778—1779. In: The National Genealogical Society Quarterly. Vol. XVI, no. 2. Washington, D. C. 1928. pp. 28—32; No. 3. pp. 41—42. [2801
— List of 164 persons who were paid for forage furnished the magazine at Lebanon, Lebanon County, Pa. In: The National Genealogical Society Quarterly. Vol. XVI. No. 3. Washington, D. C. 1928. pp. 42—43. [2802
Meyer, J.[ohn] F.: The German element in two great crisis of American history.

1776—1861. [Columbus, O.] 1915. pp. 29. [2803
Montgomery, Thomas Lynch: Muster rolls [of officers and soldiers of the French and Indian War and the War of the Revolution,] Edited by . . . 8 vols. Harrisburg, Pa.: Harrisburg Publishing Co. 1906. = Pennsylvania Archives. Fifth series. Edited by Thomas Lynch Montgomery. Vol. I—VIII. Index to Pennsylvania Archives, fifth series, 2 vols. Harrisburg, Pa. 1907. = Pennsylvania Archives. Sixth series. Harrisburg, Pa. 1907. Vol. XV [A-Lear.] Vol. XVI. [Leard—Z.] [2804
[Muhlenberg, Peter Gabriel]: Orderly book of Gen. John Peter Gabriel Muhlenberg, March 26—December 20, 1777. In: The Pennsylvania Magazine of History and Biography. Vol. XXXIII. Philadelphia, Pa. 1909. pp. 257—278; 454—474; Vol. XXXIV. 1910. pp. 21—40; 166 —189; 336—360; 438—477; Vol. XXXV. 1911. pp. 59—89; 156—187; 290—303. [2805
R.[attermann, H. A.]: John Rose. Ein deutscher Held während des Unabhängigkeitskrieges im amerikanischen Westen. In: Der Deutsche Pionier. Jg. VII. Cincinnati, O. 1875—1876. S. 83. [2806
— Die Leibgarde Washington's. In: Der Deutsche Pionier. Jg. VII. Cincinnati, O. 1875—1876. S. 215—221; 469—485. [2807
— Die Betheiligung der Deutschen am Unabhängigkeitskriege. In: Der Deutsche Pionier. Jg. VIII. Cincinnati, O. 1876—1877. S. 17ff. I. Christopher Ludwig, der Armeebäcker Washington's. S. 18—25; Nachtrag zur Biographie Christopher Ludwigs. S. 73—74; II. Hauptmann Johann Paul Schott und seine deutschen Dragoner. S. 49—57; III. Gen. Joseph Hiester und die Deutschen von Reading, Pa. S. 98—103; IV. Deutsche Offiziere und Waffensendung. S. 103—104; V. Die erste schmiedeeiserne Kanone. S. 104; VI. Die deutschen Revolutionssoldaten und Pensionäre. S. 132—142; 181—187; 274— 282; 333—336; 496—499; Jg. IX. 1877—1878. S. 276—278; 329—333; VII. Eine deutsche Heldin: Moll Pitcher. Jg. VIII. 1876—1877. S. 187— 190; VIII. Armand's Legion. S. 436 —456; IX. Ein deutscher Kaufmann. Jg. IX. 1877—1878. S. 52—58; 109— 118; 201—212; X. Die·Deutschen in

Fredericktown, Maryland, zur Zeit der Revolution von O. S.[eidensticker.] *S. 157—158. XI.* Gen. Herckheimer und die Deutschen im Mohawk-Thale. *S. 232—240; XII.* Der Fouragemeister Washingtons. [Heinrich Emanuel Lutterloh.] *S. 278—282; XIII.* Ein Helfer in der Noth. [Hayman Salomon.] *S. 410—413.* [2808

Richards, Henry Melchior Muhlenberg: The Pennsylvania-German in the Revolutionary War. 1775—1783. *Lancaster, Pa.: New Era Printing Co. 1908. = Part XVIII. „A narrative and critical history", prepared at the request of the Pennsylvania-German Society. In: The Pennsylvania-German Society. Proceedings and Addresses . . . 1906. Vol. XVII. Lancaster, Pa. 1908. Separate pagination. pp. XI, 542, ill.* [2809

— The Pennsylvania-German in the Revolutionary War. *In: The Pennsylvania-German. Vol. IX. Cleona, Pa. 1908. pp. 407—411.* [2810

— Valley Forge and the Pennsylvania-Germans. *Address delivered at Valley Forge at the annual meeting of the Society, Nov. 2, 1916. Lancaster, Pa.: The New Era Printing Co. 1917. In: The Pennsylvania-German Society. Proceedings and Addresses . . . 1915. Vol. XXVI. Lancaster, Pa. 1918. Separate pagination. pp. 32, ill., map.* [2811

— The Pennsylvania-German in the British military prisons of the Revolutionary War. *An historical sketch. Lancaster, Pa.: Lancaster Press, Inc. 1924. = Part XXXI. „A narrative and critical history", prepared at the request of the Pennsylvania-German Society. In: The Pennsylvania-German Society. Proceedings and Addresses . . . 1921. Vol. XXXII. Lancaster, Pa. Separate pagination. pp. 5—33.* [2812

Richards, John Wm. 150 years ago or how Lutherans helped win liberty. *Columbus, O.: The Lutheran Book Concern 1926. pp. 133.* [2813

Richter, V. W.: General Washington's body guards. *In: The Concord Society Historical Bulletin no. 3. Detroit, Mich., Aug., 1924. pp. 7—24.* [2814

Rohrbach, Paul: „Die Deutschen im Unabhängigkeitskrieg 1775—1783. Friedrich Wilhelm v. Steuben und die deutschen Mietstruppen in Amerika." *In: Das Deutschtum über See Von P. Rohrbach.*

Karlsruhe: 1931 [= Nr. 97a]. S. 39 —58. [2814a

Rosengarten, J. G.: The German soldier in the wars of the United States. *In: The United Service Magazine. New York, N. Y., June—August, 1885. pp. . . .; Second edition. Printed for the Pionierverein. Philadelphia, Pa.: J. B. Lippincott Co. 1890. pp. 49.* [2815

[—] Der deutsche Soldat in den Kriegen der Vereinigten Staaten von Nordamerika. *Übersetzt von C. Große. Kassel: Verlag von Theodor Kay 1890. IV, 97 S.* [2816

— The Pennsylvania-German as patriot and soldier. *In: The Pennsylvania-German. Vol. VII. Lebanon, Pa. 1906. pp. 161—164, ill.* [2817

Schneder, Charles B.: The Pennsylvania-German clergy during the Revolutionary period. *Read before the Pennsylvania-German Society at Sesqui-Centennial Exposition at Philadelphia, October 8, 1926. Norristown, Pa. 1930. In: The Pennsylvania-German Society. Proceedings and Addresses at Philadelphia, Oct. 8, 1926. Vol. XXXVII. Norristown, Pa. 1930. pp. 17—21.* [2818

Schrader, Frederick Franklin: „The Germans in the Revolution . . ." *In: The Germans in the making of America. Boston, Mass. 1924 [= no. 107]. pp. 115 — 141.* [2818a

Shenk, Hiram H.: Pennsylvania women in the Revolution. *Read before a joint meeting of Lebanon Chapter D. A. R. and Lebanon County Historical Society, March 17, 1927. In: Papers read before the Lebanon County Historical Society. Vol. IX, no. 7. Lebanon, Pa. 1927. pp. 229—237.* [2819

Steinmetz, Mary Owen: Revolutionary soldiers not contained in Pennsylvania archives: Muster Roll of Capt. Reif — Pay Roll of a Detachment of 6th Battn., Berks County, (Pa.) Militia, Guarding Convention Prisoners of War, Reading, 1781 — Men's Names of Capt. Jacob Bower's Co., 6th Penna. Regt., Aug. 11, 1778. *Copied by . . . In: The National Genealogical Society Quarterly. Vol. XII, no. 1. Washington, D. C. 1923. pp. 1—3.* [2820

Lefferts, Charles W. - Wall, Alexander J.: Uniforms of the American, British, French and German armies in the War of American Revolution 1775—1783.

16*

Painted and described by the late Lt. Charles W. Lefferts, edited by Alexander J. Wall. New York, N. Y.: Historical Society New York 1926. pp. 286. [2821

Pennsylvania soldiers of the Revolution entitled to depreciation pay. *(A number of pay-rolls on Depreciation Pay account found in the Department of the Auditor-General, at Harrisburg.) In: The Pennsylvania Magazine of History and Biography. Vol. XXVII. Philadelphia, Pa. 1903. pp. 449—471; Vol. XXVIII. 1904. pp. 45—59; 201—203.* [2822

Pennsylvania Revolutionary soldiers. *In: Genealogy. Journal of American ancestry. Vol. I. New York, N. Y. 1912. pp. 3—4; p. 13.* [2823

Pennsylvania pensioners. *(Names, rank, and other details concerning the persons residing in the State of Pennsylvania who were inscribed on the pension list under the act of Congress passed March 18, 1818. In: Genealogy. Journal of American ancestry. Vol. I. New York, N. Y. 1912. p. 45; 52; 76; 117; 147; 189; 205; Vol. II. p. 227; 277; 283; 295; 309; 316; 323; 333; 342; 367; Vol. III. 1913. p. 3; 32; 43; 102.* [2824

Letters to William Henry, of Lancaster, Pennsylvania, 1777—1783. *In: The Pennsylvania Magazine of History and Biography. Vol. XXII. Philadelphia, Pa. 1898. pp. 106—115.*

[Relating to army supplies.] [2825

Sub-Lieutenant Peter Richards. A batch of vouchers for the disbursement made by him in 1781. *In: The Perkiomen Region, Past and Present. Vol. II. Philadelphia, Pa. 1900. pp. 98—99.* [2826

Kriegsverweigerung aus religiösen Grundsätzen

Conscientious Objectors to Participation in War

Bender, Wilbur J.: Pacifism among the Mennonites, Amish Mennonites and Schwenkfelders of Pennsylvania to 1783. *In: The Mennonite Quarterly Review. Vol. I. Goshen, Ind. 1927. No. 3, July. pp. 23—40; no. 4, October. pp. 21—48; p. 80.* [2827

Byler, Joseph N.: Migrations due to nonresistant principles: with especial reference to the Mennonites. *Thesis of M. A. University of Nebraska, Department of Sociology, Lincoln, Nebr., 1925 Typewritten. pp. IX, 159. [Bibliography. pp. 154—159.]* [2828

Hard, William: Your Amish Mennonite. *Reprint from the „New Republic," Febr. I, 1919. New York City, N. Y.: National Civil Liberties Bureau [1919]. pp. 11.* [2829

Hartman, Peter S.: Civil war reminiscences. *In: The Mennonite Quarterly Review. Vol. III. Goshen, Ind. 1929. pp. 203—219.* [2830

Hartzler, Jonas S.: Mennonites in the World War or non-resistance under test. *By J. S. Hartzler assisted by a committee appointed by Mennonite General Conference. Scottdale, Pa.: Mennonite Publishing House 1921. pp. 246; Second edition 1922.* [2831

[Heckewelder, Christian R. and Ettwein, John]: Three letters written at Bethlehem, Pennsylvania, in 1778. *[of Christian R. Heckewelder and John Ettwein.] In: The Pennsylvania Magazine of History and Biography. Vol. XXXVI. Philadelphia, Pa. 1912. pp. 293—302. [Relating to the enforcement of the „Test Oath".]* [2832

Horsch, John: The principle of nonresistance as held by the Mennonite Church. A historical survey. *Scottdale, Pa.: Mennnonite Publishing House 1927. pp. 60. Reprint from: The Mennonite Quarterly Review. Vol. I. Goshen, Ind., July, 1927. pp. 5—22; Oct. 1927. pp. 3—20.* [2833

Johnson, Elmer E. S.: The test act of June 13, 1777. *Read before the Pennsylvania German Society at York, October 21, 1927. Norristown, Pa.: Norristown Press 1930. In: The Pennsylvania-German Society. Proceedings and Addresses . . . 1927. Vol. XXXVIII. Norristown, Pa. 1930. pp. 11—22.* [2834

Kellog, Walter Guest: The conscientious objector. *Introduction by Newton D. Baker. New York, N. Y.: Boni and Liveright. 1919. pp. XVIII,141.* [2835

Lloyd, Thomas: A report of the whole trial of Gen. Michael Bright and others; before Washington & Peters in the circuit court of the United States in and for the District of Pennsylvania in the Third Circuit on an Indictment for obstructing, resisting and opposing the execution of the writ of arrest issued out of the District of Pennsylvania in the case of Gideon Olmstead and others, against the surviving executrices of David Rittenhouse, deceased. *Philadelphia, Pa.: P. Byrne. 1809.* [2836

Miller, Orie O.: Our peace pilicy. *An address delivered at a reunion of Conscious Objectors at Blue Ridge College, New Windsor, Md., Nov. 12, 1928. In: The Mennonite Quarterly Review. Vol. III. Goshen, Ind. 1929. pp. 26—32.* [2837

Sanger, Samuel F. and Hays, D.: The olive branch of peace and good will to men; anti-war history of the Brethren and Mennonites, the peace-people of the south during the Civil War 1861—1865. *Elgin, Ill.: Brethren Publishing House 1907. pp. XX, 23—232, ill.* [2838

Yoder, Edward: The Christian's attitude toward participation in war activities. *Paper read at the Mennonite Conference on Peace and War, held at Goshen College under the auspices of the Peace Problems Committee of the Mennonite General Conference, February 15 to 17, 1935. In: Mennonite Quaterly Review. Vol. IX. Goshen, Ind.-Scottdale, Pa. 1935. pp. 5—19.* [2839

A short and sincere declaration, to our honorable assembly, and all others in high or low station of administration, and to all friends and inhabitants of this country, to whose sight this may come, be they English or Germans. *Philadelphia, Pa.: Printed by Henry Miller, November 7, 1775. Folio broadside.* [2840

Eine kurze und aufrichtige Erklärung, an unsere Wohl Meinende Assembly und alle andere Hohe und Niedrige in der Regierung und alle andere Freunde und Einwohner dieses Landes, denen dies zu Gesicht kommen mag, sowohl Englische als Deutsche. *Den 7. November, 1775. Philadelphia, Pa.: Gedruckt bey Heinrich Miller 1775. Folio Breitseite. Neudruck: Berlin 1840.* [2841

A plea for toleration. *[A document in the possession of the Dunkers or Baptist Brethren and Mennonites in Lancaster County, (Pa. dated) Nov. 7, 1775.] Reprint in: The Penn Germania. Vol. II. = Old series, vol. XIV. Lititz, Pa. 1913. pp. 111—113.* [2842

An address by Mennonites and German Baptists. *(Recorded p. 645 of Vol. VI of the Votes of the Assembly, 1767—1776 of Pennsylvania under the date of November 7, 1775). In: The Perkiomen Region. Vol. IX, no. 2. Pennsburg, Pa. 1931. pp. 62—63.* [2843

A declaration of non-resistance and loyality to the government. *[Reprint of the Declaration signed by a number of Elders and Teachers of the Society of Mennonites, and some of the German Baptists, presented to the Honorable House of Assembly on the 7th day of November, 1775.] In: The Mennonite Year Book and Almanac for 1919. Quakertown, Pa. 1919. pp. 22—23.* [2844

A petition by the Moravians during the American Revolution *[Copy of a petition presented in 1778 by Bishop Ettwein to congress in session at York, and to the Assembly of Pennsylvania, at Lancaster, asking to have the Moravians excepted from the requirements of the Test Act of 1777.] Copied from a manuscript found in a Schwenkfelder home by* **H. W. Kriebel.** *In: The Pennsylvania-German. Vol. XII. Lititz, Pa. 1911. pp. 43—45.* [2845

The conduct of the Schwenkfelders during the Revolutionary War. *In: The Pennsylvania-German. Vol. XI. Lititz, Pa. 1910. pp. 659—663.* [2846

Trials of a Mennonite minister Henry Funck: *In: The Mennonite Year Book and Almanac for 1919. Quakertown, Pa. 1919. p. 24.* [2847

Militia exemption fines *[paid by Abraham Bechtel, a Mennonite minister, of Bally, Berks County. 1801—1819.] In: The Perkiomen Region, Past and Present. Vol. I. Philadelphia, Pa. 1895. pp. 114—115.* [2848

A petition *[of over 7,500 signers, which was presented to the Congress of the United States in 1917.] Believing all war to be a violation of the teachings of Christ whose life and precepts we hold as our supreme law, we feel that we must also avoid having any part in Military Training, therefore we, the undersigned, humbly plead your Honorable body that it pass no laws which will force militarism upon those who have religious convictions against it. We are confident that the passing of Military Laws which would not excuse non-resistant Christians would mean to send thousands of young men to Military Prisons and no good government desires this. [1917.] pp. 141.* [2849

Deutschamerikanische und deutsche Offiziere im Unabhängigkeitskampf

German-American and German Officers in the Revolutionary Army

Heß, Abram: The life and services of General John Philip de Haas 1735—1786. *In: Papers read before the Lebanon Historical Society. Vol. VII. Lebanon, Pa. 1916—1919. pp. 69—124, ill.* *[born in Holland, the son of John Nicholas De Haas of Brandenburg, Prussia and later of Strasburg; the parents emigrated to America about 1737.]* [2849a

Kapp, Friedrich, „Die Revolution. General Nicolaus Herckheimer." *In: Die Deutschen im Staate New York bis zum Anfang des neunzehnten Jahrhunderts. Von Friedrich Kapp. Leipzig 1868 [= no. 441]. = Kapital XI. S. 229—252.* [2850

R.[attermann, H. A.:] General Herckheimer und die Deutschen im Mohawk-Thale. *In: Der Deutsche Pionier. Jg. VIII. Cincinnati, O. 1876—1877. S. 232—240.* [2851

Lyttle, Eugene W.: Nicholas Herkimer. *In: Proceedings of the New York State Historical Association. Fifth annual meeting. Vol. IV. Albany, N. Y. 1904. pp. 19—29.* [2852

Cronau, Rudolf: „Nicholas Herchheimer und die Helden von Oriskany". *In: Drei Jahrhunderte deutschen Lebens in Amerika. Eine Geschichte der Deutschen in den Vereinigten Staaten. Von R. Cronau. Berlin 1909 [= Nr. 34]. S. 196—204, ill.; 2. Aufl. 1924. S. 195—203, ill.* [2852 a

Greene, Nelson: The home and name of General Herkimer. With notes and comments on the Americanism of Herkimer and his troops, the Americanism of the Revolutionary Mohawk Valley and the present American ideal. *In: Proceedings of the New York State Historical Association. The sixteenth mee-*

ting. Vol. XIV. Albany, N. Y. 1915. pp. 365—402. [2853

Hadcock, De Witt C.: Last hours of General Herkimer. An intensly interesting article from the pen of . . . over 90 years of age. *In: Papers read before the Herkimer County Historical Society, covering the period from May, 1914 to November, 1922. Vol. V. [s. l., 1922] pp. 199—200.* [2854

R.[attermann, H. A.]: General Joseph Hiester und die Deutschen von Reading. *In: Der Deutsche Pionier. Jg. VIII. Cincinnati, O. 1876—1877. S. 98—103.* [2855

Egle, William Henry: Prominent Pennsylvanians: General Gabriel Hiester. *In: Historical Register: Notes and Queries, historical and genealogical relating to interior Pennsylvania for the year 1883. Vol. I. Harrisburg, Pa. 1883. p. 156.* [2856

Dotterer, Henry S.: General Daniel Hiester. *In: The Perkiomen Region, Past and Present. Vol. I. Philadelphia, Pa. 1895. pp. 78—79; 82—84; 106—109; 124—126; 148—150; 163—165.* [2857

Häberle, D.: Oberst Johannes Jacob Klock aus Sobernheim. *(Führer der Pfälzer im Mohawktal im Unabhängigkeitskrieg.) In: Pfälzisches Museum. Jg. XLI. — Pfälzische Heimatkunde. Jg. XX. Kaiserslautern 1924. S. 124—125.* [2858

Rush, Benjamin: An account of the life and character of Christopher Ludwick, late citizen of Philadelphia, and Baker-General of the Army of the United States during the Revolutionary War. *Philadelphia, Pa. 1801. pp. . . .* [2859

[—]: An account of the life and character of Christopher Ludwick, late citizen of

Philadelphia, and Baker-General of the Army of the United States during the Revolutionary War. *First published in the year 1801. Revised and republished by direction of the Philadelphia Society for the Establishment and Support of Charity Schools. To which is added, an account of the origin, progress and present condition of that institution. Philadelphia, Pa.: Printed for the Society by Garden and Thompson 1831. pp. 61.* [2860

[Rush, Benjamin]: Life and character of Christopher Ludwick, late citizen of Philadelphia and Baker-General of the Army of the United States during the Revolutionary War. *First published in the year 1801.. Reprint in: Hazard's Register of Pennsylvania. Vol. IX. Philadelphia, Pa. 1832. pp. 161—164.* [2861

R.[attermann, H. A.]: Christopher Ludwig, der Armeebäcker Washington's *In: Der Deutsche Pionier. Jg. VIII. Cincinnati, O. 1876—1877. S. 18—25;* Nachtrag zur Biographie Christopher Ludwigs. *S. 73—74.* [2862

Christopher Ludwig, Baker-General in the Army of the United States during the Revolutionary War. *In: The Pennsylvania Magazine of History and Biography. Vol. XVI. Philadelphia, Pa. 1892. pp. 343—348.* [2863

Huch, C. F.: Christoph Ludwig, der Bäcker-General. *In: Mitteilungen des Deutschen Pionier-Vereins von Philadelphia. Heft 7. Philadelphia, Pa. 1908. 9 S.* [2864

Finck, William J.: Christopher Ludwig. *In: The Lutheran Church Review. Vol. Vol. XLVI. Mt. Airy, Philadelphia, Pa. 1927, pp. 361—372.* [2865

[Muhlenberg, Peter Gabriel]: Orderly book of Gen. John Peter Gabriel Muhlenberg, March 26—December 20, 1777. *In: The Pennsylvania Magazine of History and Biography. Vol. XXXIII. Philadelphia, Pa. 1909. pp. 257—278; 454—474; Vol. XXXIV. 1910. pp. 21—40; 166—189; 336—360; 438—477; Vol. XXXV. 1911. pp. 59—89; 156—197; 290—303.* [2866

Muhlenberg, Henry A.: The life of Major-General Peter Muhlenberg of the Revolutionary army. *Philadelphia, Pa.: Carey and Hart 1849. pp. XII, 13—456, ill.* [2867

Wollenweber, L. A.: General Peter Mühlenberg und seine deutschen Soldaten im

amerikanischen Freiheitskampf. Eine historische Novelle. *In: Der Deutsche Pionier. Jg. I. Cincinnati, O. 1869. S. 343—347; 378—383; Jg. II. 1870. S. 26—29; 58—62; 92—95; 122—126; 153—157; 186—189; 252—255; 285—287; 316—318; 348—351; Jg. III. 1871. S. 23—29; 42—49.* [2868

Ermentrout, Daniel: Remarks of Hon. Daniel Ermentrout, senator from Berks County, on the bill making appropriations for statues of Muhlenberg and Fulton. *The Pennsylvania Statuary Commission. Harrisburg, Pa.: Lane & Hart. 1879. pp. 32.* [2869

Stricker, Wilhelm: Mühlenberg, Peter M. *In: Allgemeine deutsche Biographie. Bd. XLVI. Leipzig 1885. S. 461—463* [2869a

Wright, Marcus J.: A sketch of the life of General Peter Gabriel Muhlenberg. *Read before the District of Columbia Society of the Sons of the American Revolution, Jan. 16, 1901. In: Publications of the Southern History Association. Vol. V, no. 3. Washington, D. C. 1901. pp. 181—187.* [2870

Famous Pennsylvania-Germans. Gen. John Peter G. Muhlenberg. *In: The Pennsylvania-German. Vol. III. Lebanon, Pa. 1902. pp. 3—21, ill.* [2871

Cronau, Rudolf: ,,Generalmajor Peter Mühlenberg.'' *In: Drei Jahrhunderte deutschen Lebens in Amerika. Eine Geschichte der Deutschen in den Vereinigten Staaten. Von R. Cronau. Berlin 1909 [= Nr. 34]. S. 205—207, ill.; 2. Aufl. 1924. S. 204—207, ill.* [2871a

A statue of General Peter Muhlenberg. *[Sculptor: J. Otto Schweizer.] Reprint from: ,,The Lutheran,'' In: The Pennsylvania-German. Vol. XI. Lititz, Pa. 1910. pp. 677—680.* [2872

Staake, William H.: Address at the unveiling of the monument of General Peter Muhlenberg on German Day, October 6, 1910 at the City Hall, Philadelphia. *[Published by] The German Society of Pennsylvania. [Philadelphia, Pa. 1910.] pp. 18.* [2873

Huch, C. F.: General Peter Mühlenberg. *In: Mitteilungen des Deutschen Pionier-Vereins von Philadelphia. Heft 2. Philadelphia, Pa. 1906. S. 2—26.* [2874

Löher, Franz: ,,Kalbs Leben und Charakter.'' *In: Geschichte und Zustände der Deutschen in Amerika. Von Franz Löher.*

Cincinnati, O.-Leipzig 1847 [= Nr. 78].
S. 172—174.   [2874 a
[**Kapp, Friedrich**]: Generalmajor **v. Kalb.**
In: Atlantische Studien. Von Deutschen in
Amerika. Bd. III. Göttingen: Heinrich
Wigand. 1853. S. 32—37.   [2875
— Leben des Amerikanischen Generals
Johann Kalb. *Stuttgart: Cotta'scher*
Verlag 1862. XIV, 306 S., ill.   [2876
— The life of **John Kalb,** Major General in
the Revolutionary Army. *New York,*
N. Y.: H. Holt & Co. 1884. pp. 337.
                                    [2877
Giorg, Kara: Baron de **Kalb.** *In: Der Deut-*
sche Pionier. Jg. II. Cincinnati, O.
1870—1871. S. 162—169, ill.   [2878
Cronau, Rudolf: „General-Major **Kalb** und
seine Heldentaten in der Schlacht bei
Camden." *In: Das Buch der Deutschen*
in Amerika. Herausgegeben unter dem
Auspicien des Deutsch-Amerikanischen

National-Bundes von [Max Henrici].
Philadelphia, Pa. 1909 [= Nr. 59].
S. 102—105, ill.   [2878 a
Cronau, Rudolf: „Generalmajor **Johann von**
Kalb." *In: Drei Jahrhunderte deutschen*
Lebens in Amerika. Eine Geschichte der
Deutschen in den Vereinigten Staaten.
2. Aufl. Berlin 1909 [= Nr. 34]. S. 223
—226.   [2878 b
Monaghan, Frank: Kalb, Johann (1721,
Hüttendorf, Germany — 1780) Revo-
lutionary general, known as „Baron de
Kalb". *In: Dictionary of American*
Council of Learned Societies. Vol. X.
Edited by Dumas Malone. London-
New York 1933. pp. 253—254. [2878 c

Schücking, A.: Oberst von **Weißenfels.** *Eine*
deutsche Revolutions-Reminiscenz. In:
Der Deutsche Pionier. Jg. III. Cincin-
nati, O. 1871—1872. S. 185—188. [2879

Steuben

Meyer, H. H. B.: Bibliography of Baron von Steuben. *In: Proceedings upon the unveiling of the statue of Baron von Steuben . . . Washington, D. C., December 7, 1910 and upon the replica to His Majesty the German Emperor and the German nation in Potsdam, September 2, 1911 . . . Washington, D. C. 1911* [= no. 2885d]. pp. 217—226. [2880

Krey, H.: Das wichtigste Schrifttum über F. W. von Steuben. *In: Der Auslanddeutsche. Halbmonatsschrift für Auslanddeutschtum und Auslandkunde. Mitteilungen des Deutschen Ausland-Instituts. Jg. X. Stuttgart 1927. S. 788—799.* [2880a

Von dem N[ord]Amerikan. General von Steuben. *In: Schlözer's Staatsanzeigen Bd. V. Nr. 17. Göttingen 1783. S. 59—60.* [2880b

Canitz, - (von Steuben) Hauptmannin von: Authentische Familien-Nachrichten von dem N. A. Generalmajor Fr. Wilh. von Steuben. *In: Hausen, K. R. Staatsmaterialien Dessau 1783—1784. St. 6. S. 635—640.* [2880c

Zuverlässige Nachrichten von dem Amerikanischen General von Steuben. *Journal von und für Deutschland. Herausgegeben von Siegmund Freyherrn von Bibra. Jg. II. August/September 1784. S. 84—88.* [2880d

[Steuben, Wilhelm Augustin von]: Zuverlässige Nachrichten von dem Geschlecht und Herkommen des Nordamerikanischen Generals, Friedrich Wilhelm Ludolf Gerhard Augustin von Steuben. *Vom Vater aufgesetzt und eingesandt von J. F. Seyfert. In: Historisches Portefeuille. Zur Kenntnis der gegenwärtigen und vergangenen Zeit. Viertes Stück, April 1785. Wien, Breslau, Leipzig, Berlin, Hamburg 1785. S. 447—453.* [2880e

Ebeling, C. D.: Nachrichten von den Lebensumständen des Baron von Steuben, Generalmajors in Diensten der vereinten Staaten von Nordamerika. *In: Amerikanisches Magazin oder authentische Beiträge zur Erdbeschreibung, Staatskunde und Geschichte von Amerika, besonders aber der vereinten Staaten. Herausgegeben von Hegewisch-Kiel und Ebeling-Hamburg. Erster Band. Drittes Stück. Hamburg: Carl Ernst Bohn 1796. S. 148—163.* [Abdruck siehe Nr. 2887m] [2880f

Bowen, Francis: Life of Baron Steuben. *In: The Library of American Biography. Conducted by Jared Sparks. Vol. IX. New York, N. Y.: Harper & Brothers 1814. pp. 1—88.* [2881

Rogers, Thomas J.: A new American biographical dictionary; or, remembrancer of the departed heroes, sages, and statesmen of America. *2nd edition. Easton, Pa.: T. J. Rogers 1823. pp. 352.* [„Frederick William Steuben" pp. 427—428.] [2881a

Thacher, James: A military journal during the American revolutionary war, from 1775 to 1783. *Boston, Mass.: Richardson & Lord 1823. pp. 603.* [„Frederick William Augustus Baron de Steuben". pp. 517—531.] [2881b

„Baron Steuben". *In: American Military biography; containing the lives and characters of the officiers of the revolution, who were most destinguished in achieving our national independence . . . Published for E. S. Johnson. Cincinnati, O.: Chronicle Office 1834. pp. 606—615* [2881c

[North, William]: Memoir of the Baron Steuben. *In: New York Commercial Adversiter. New York, N. Y. Jan. 4, 1836. (An editorial of this paper).* [2881d

[—] Baron Steuben. *In: Magazine of American history. Vol. VIII. 1882. pp. 187—199.* [2881e

[—] Memoir of the Baron Steuben. *With a prefatory note by Julius Goebel. In: Deutsch-Amerikanische Geschichtsblätter. German-American Historical Review. Jahrbuch der Deutsch-Amerikanischen Historischen Gesellschaft von Illinois. Jg. 1929. Vol. XXIX. Chicago, Ill. 1929. pp. 188—206.* [2881f

Bowen, Francis: Life of Baron Steuben. *In: Library of American biography. Edited by Jared Sparks. Vol. IX. Boston, Mass. 1838. pp. 5—88.* [2881g

Löher, Franz: Geschichte und Zustände der Deutschen in Amerika. *Cincinnati, O.:*

Eggers und Wulkop; Leipzig: K. F. Köhler 1847. XII, 544 S.

[„Steuben" = Zehntes Blatt. S. 175—179.] [2882

Frost, John: The American generals. Philadelphia, Pa.: J. W. Bradley 1848. pp. 912.

[„Major general Steuben". pp. 88—98.] [2882a

Petersen, Charles J.: The military heroes of the revolution; with a narrative of the war of independence. Philadelphia, Pa.: W. A. Leary 1848. pp. 487.

[„Baron Steuben". pp. 359—364.] [2882b

K.[app], Fr.[iedrich]: General von Steuben. Ein Character aus dem amerikanischen Revolutionskriege. In: Atlantische Studien. Deutschen in Amerika. Bd. II. Göttingen: Heinrich Wigand 1853. S. 88—89. Neudruck in Chr. Esseleus „Atlantis" Neue Folge. Bd. IV. S. 106. [2882c

Schröder, Johann Friedrich: Washington und die Helden der Revolution. Bd. II. Neu York: Johnson, Fry & Co. [1857].

[Der General von Steuben. S. 607—637.] 2882d

Schmitt, Nikolaus: Leben und Wirken von Friedrich Wilhelm von Steuben. Vortrag gehalten in dem Künstlerverein von Philadelphia . . . Zum Besten des Steuben-Denkmals. Philadelphia, Pa.: John Weik und Co. 1858. pp. 42, ill. [2882f

Kapp, Friedrich: Leben des Amerikanischen Generals Friedrich Wilhelm von Steuben. Berlin: Duncker & Humblot 1858. XXXII, 667 S., ill. [2882g

— Life of Baron Friedrich Wilhelm von Steuben, Major General in the Revolutionary Army. New York, N. Y.: Mason Bros. 1859. pp. 735.

[Reviewed in North American Review. Vol. XCIX. Oct. 1864. p. 321—364.] [2882h

Holland, F. W.: Baron von Steuben. Livnig age Apr. 21, 1860. Vol. LXV. pp. 173—174. [2882i

Where Baron Steuben was buried. In: New England Historical and Genealogical register. Vol. XVI. Albany, N. Y. 1862. pp. 201—202. [2882k

Greene, George W.: Historical view of the American revolution. Boston, Mass.: Ticknor & Fields 1865. pp. 459.

[Baron von Steuben. p. 233—235; 282—319.] 2882l

— Baron von Steuben. In: The German element in the war of American independence. New York, N. Y.: Hurd &

Houghton, Cambridge, Mass.: The Riverside Press 1876. pp. 211.

[„Baron von Steuben". pp. 13—87.] [2882m

Drake, Francis S.: Dictionary of American biography, including men of the time . . Boston, Mass.: J. R. Osgood & Co. 1872. pp. . . .

[„Baron Frederick William Augustus von Steuben". pp. 865—866.] [2882n

General Friedrich von Steuben. In: Der deutsche Pionier. Jg. VII. Cincinnati,O. 1875. S. 379—380. [2882o

Das Steubenfest und das Steubendenkmal in Baltimore. Baltimore, Md. 1878. pp. . . . [2883

Buttre, Lillian C.: The American portrait gallery. New York, N. Y.: J. C. Buttre 1879. 2 vols.

[„Frederick William von Steuben. Vol. II. pp. 81—82.] [2883a

[Neef, G. L.]: Steuben-Reminiszenzen. In: Der deutsche Pionier. Jg. XIII. Cincinnati, O. 1881. S. 405—406. [2883b

Hopp, Ernst Otto: Geschichte der Vereinigten Staaten von Nordamerika. Teil 2. Leipzig: Freytag; Prag: Tempsky 1884. = Das Wissen der Gegenwart. Bd. 26. S. 224.

[Friedrich Wilhelm von Steuben. S. 206—208.] [2883c

Stone, Edwin M.: Our French allies . . . Providence, Printed by the Providence Press Co. 1884. pp. XXXI, 632.

[Baron Steuben. pp. 138—144.] [2883d

Ruetenik, Herman J.: Berühmte deutsche Vorkämpfer für Fortschritt, Freiheit und Friede in Nord-Amerika. Von 1626—1888. Cleveland. O.: Forest City Bookbinding Co. 1888. pp. 500.

[„Baron Steuben". pp. 70—87.] [2883e

Leister, Mary T.: Biographical sketches of the generals of the Continental army of the revolution. Cambridge, Mass.: University Press 1889. pp. 167.

[„Baron Steuben". pp. 64—67.] [2883f

Poten, B.: Steuben, Friedrich Wilhelm von. In: Allgemeine deutsche Biographie. Bd. XXXVI. Leipzig 1893. S. 142—148. [2883g

Headley, Joel T.: Frederick William Augustus Henry Ferdinand von Steuben. In: Appleton's cyclopaedia of American biography. Vol. V. New York, N. Y. 1898. pp. 668—670. [2883h

Bolton, Charles K.: The private soldier under Washington. *New York, N. Y.: Charles Scribner's Sons 1902. pp. 258.*
[2884

Bremen, W. v.: Friedrich Wilhelm von Steuben. Ein preußischer Offizier und amerikanischer General. *In: Daheim Jg. 38. Nr. 22. Leipzig: Daheim Expedition 1902. S. 20—23.* [2884a

Zingeler, K. Th.: Friedrich Wilhelm von Steuben. *In: Mitteilungen des Vereins für Geschichte und Altertumskunde von Hohenzollern. Jg. XXXVI. 1902—1903. S. 25—92.* [2884b

Bosse, Georg von: Das deutsche Element in den Vereinigten Staaten unter besonderer Berücksichtigung seines politischen, ethischen, sozialen und erzieherischen Einflusses. *Stuttgart: Chr. Belsersche Verlagsbuchhandlung 1908. XIII, 480 S., ill.*
[Friedrich Wilhelm von Steuben. S. 90 —95.] [2884c

Cronau, Rudolf: Drei Jahrhunderte deutschen Lebens in Amerika. Eine Geschichte der Deutschen in den Vereinigten Staaten. *Berlin: Dietrich Reimer (Ernst Vohsen) 1909. XIII, 640 S., ill. 2. Auflage Berlin 1924. XIII, 696 S., ill.*
[„Generalmajor Friedrich Wilhelm von Steuben, der Schöpfer des amerikanischen Heeres." S. 228—241. [S. 227—245].]
2884d

Cronau, Rudolf: „Friedrich Wilhelm von Steuben, der Organisator und General-Inspektor der amerikanischen Armee". *In: Das Buch der Deutschen in Amerika. Herausgegeben unter den Auspicien des Deutsch-Amerikanischen National-Bundes von [Max Henrici] Philadelphia, Pa. 1909 [= Nr. 59]. S. 105—118, ill.* [2884e

Bremen, [W.] v.: Friedrich Wilhelm von Steuben. Ein Preußischer Offizier und Reorganisator des Amerikanischen Heeres. *In: Militär-Wochenblatt. Jg. XCV, Nr. 154. Berlin 1910. Sp. 3589—3593.* [2885

Bigelow, Dana W.: Baron Steuben, an address before the Oneida Historical Society. *April 11, 1910. In: Oneida Historical Society Year book. No. 11. Ottica, N. Y. 1910. pp. XV—XXV.* [2885a

Zingeler, Karl Theodor: Friedrich Wilhelm von Steuben. *In: Hochland. Monatsschrift für alle Gebiete des Wissens, der Literatur und Kunst. Herausgegeben von*

Karl Muth. Jg. VII. Bd. 2. Kempten und München 1910. S. 78—86. [2885b

United German societies of the District of Columbia. Souvenir program, unveiling of the Steuben monument. *Washington, D. C., December 7, 1910. Washington D. C.: The Carnahan Press 1910. pp. 19.* [2885c

Proceedings upon the unveiling of the statue of Baron von Steuben, major general and inspector general in the continental army during the Revolutionary war in Washington, D. C., Dezember 7, 1910 and upon the presentation of the replica to his majesty the German emperor and the German nation in Potsdam, September 2, 1911. Erected by the Congress of the United States. *Compiled by George H. Carter and printed under the direction of the joint committee on printing. Washington, D. C.: United States of America Government Printing Office 1911. pp. 234, ill.*
[It contains among others:
Washington and Steuben letters Dec. 23, 1783—Jan. 1784. p. 6.
Unveiling ceremonies, Washington, D. C. Dezember 7, 1910. p. 15ff.
Presentation of the replica, Potsdam, Germany September 2, 1911. p. 69ff.
Proceedings in the Continental Congress and the Congress of the United States relating to Baron Steuben. pp. 85—198.
Memorials of Steuben: Steuben' burial place, town of Steuben, N. Y. pp. 201— 207, ill. Portraits and relics S. 209f., ill.
Bibliography of Baron von Steuben. By H. H. B. Meyer. pp. 217—226.] [2885d

Addresses delivered at the unveiling of the Steuben statue, Washington, D. C. December 7th, 1910. *In: German American Annals. New series. Vol. VIII. Philadelphia, Pa. 1910. pp. 273—282.*
[Address of Hon. Richard Bartholdt, of Missouri. pp. 265—272.
Address of C. J. Hexamer, president of the National German American Alliance. pp. 273—282.
Address delivered by the German Ambassador, Count Heinrich von Bernstorff. pp. 283—284.
Address of the President of the United States. pp. 285—287.] [2885e

Hexamer, C. J.: Rede bei der Enthüllung des Steubendenkmals [i. Washington]. *In: Mitteilungen des Deutschen Pionier-Vereins von Philadelphia. Heft 20. Phila-*

delphia, Pa.: Deutscher Pionier-Verein 1911. S. 3—12. [2885 f
M., G. A. v.: „Steuben." *In: Der deutsche Herold. Zeitschrift für Wappen-, Siegel- und Familienkunde Jg. LII. Berlin 1911. S. 40—41.* [2885 g
Greeven, Paul: Lebensbild des General v. Steuben. *In: Deutsche Erde. Zeitschrift für Deutschkunde. Herausgegeben von Paul Langhans. Jg. X. Gotha 1911. S. 133—138, ill.* [2885 h
Doyle, Joseph Beatty: Frederick William von Steuben and the American revolution. Aide to Washington and inspector general of the army. *With an account of posthumous honors at various places. Steubenville, O.: Cook 1913. pp. XVIII, 399, ill.* [2885 i
Bigelow, Danna W.: Baron Steuben, at home, at rest, in Oneida County. *In: Proceedings of the New York State Historical Association. The sixteenth annual meeting. Vol. XIV. Albany, N. Y. 1915. pp. 91—100.* [2885 k
Cronau, Rudolf: The army of the American revolution and its organizer. *A thrilling story of the times that tried men's souls. New York, N.Y.: Cronau 1923. pp. III, 150, ill.* [2886
Kalkhorst, Anton B. C.: Auf den Irrwegen der Genealogie. Zu Friedrich Wilhelm Steubens Abstammung. *In: Die Neue Zeit. The New Times. Wochenschrift für Politik, Kunst und Literatur. Jg. V., Vol. V. Nr. 36 und 37. Chicago, Ill. 1923, September. Nr. 36. S. 9—10, 11—13.* [2886 a
[Dettmann, F. O.]: The grave of general von Steuben. *In: The Progressive. Vol. IX, no. 9. New York: Steuben Magazine Corporation 1926. pp. 520—521.* [2886 c
Maring, H.: Von Steuben and the sesquicentennial of American independence. *Historical compendium. Philadelphia, Pa.: Graf u. Breuninger 1926. 32 S.* [2886 d
Steuben, Arndt von: Generalmajor Friedrich Wilhelm v. Steuben, der Schöpfer des amerikanischen Heeres. Ein Amerikaner deutschen Stammes. *In: Deutsche Akademiker-Zeitung. Einheitsblatt der Arbeitsgemeinschaft der völkischen Akademikerverbände des deutschen Sprachgebietes. Jg. XVIII. Berlin-München-Brünn-Wien 1926. Folge 28. S. 1—2; Folge 29 S. 4, S. 6.* [2886 e
Souvenir Steuben Sesqui-Centennial 1777 —1927. *New York: Steuben Society of America 1927. pp. 85.*

Ditfurth, v.: General v. Steuben. *In: Militär-Wochenblatt. Unabhängige Zeitschrift für deutsche Wehrmacht. Jg. 112. Berlin 1927. Nr. 21. Sp. 761—765.* [2886 f
Faust, Albert Bernhardt: Inspector General Frederick William von Steuben. *A sketch of his career and personality. [s. l.] Privately printed by the Steuben Society of America. December, 1927. pp. 7—39, ill.* [2886 h
Kloß, H.: Friedrich Wilhelm von Steubens Bedeutung. *Zur Erinnerung an seine am 1. Dezember 1777 erfolgte Landung in Amerika. In: Der Auslanddeutsche. Halbmonatsschrift für Auslanddeutschtum und Auslandkunde. Mitteilungen des Deutschen Ausland-Instituts, Stuttgart. Jg. X. Stuttgart 1927. S. 788.* [2886 i
Krauß, Ingo: Beiträge zur Geschichte des amerikanischen Generals Friedrich Wilhelm von Steuben und seiner Familie. *In: Familiengeschichtliche Blätter. Herausgegeben von der Zentralstelle für Deutsche Personen- und Familiengeschichte E. V., in Leipzig. Jg. XXV. Leipzig 1927. Sp. 33—38; 73—76.* [2886 k
Selmer C.: More facts on General von Steuben. *In: American Monthly. Vol. XX, no. 8. New York 1927. pp. 23—24.* [2886 l
Stoybe, H. and Seuberlich, E.: Die Herkunft des amerikanischen Generals Steuben. *In: Familiengeschichtliche Blätter. Herausgegeben von der Zentralstelle für Deutsche Personen- und Familiengeschichte E. V. in Leipzig. Jg. XXV. Leipzig 1927. Sp. 181—184.* [2886 m
Steuben, Berndt von: Was die Familie von Steuben über die Abstammung des amerikanischen Generals Friedrich Wilhelm von Steuben weiß. *Entgegnung auf den Artikel im Februar- und März-heft der Familiengeschichtlichen Blätter [= Nr. 2886 k]. In: Familiengeschichtliche Blätter. Herausgegeben von der Zentralstelle für Deutsche Personen- und Familiengeschichte E. V. in Leipzig. Jg. XXV. Leipzig 1927. Sp. 349—352.* [2886 n
Palmer, John McAuley: America's debt to a German soldier. Baron von Steuben and what he taught us. *In: Harper's Magazine. Vol. CLVII. New York, N.Y. Sept. 1928. pp. 456—466.* [2886 o
Steuben, Berndt v.: Gen. v. Steubens Abstammung. *Abdruck aus der „California Presse". In: Eiserne Blätter. Wochen-*

schrift für deutsche Politik und Kultur.
Jg. X. Berlin 1928. S. 595—599. [2886p
Kekule von Stradowitz, Stephan: Zur Frage
der Abstammung Steubens. *In: Fami-*
liengeschichtliche Blätter. Herausgegeben
von der Zentralstelle für Deutsche Per-
sonen- und Familiengeschichte E. V. in
Leipzig. Jg. XXVI. Leipzig 1928. Sp.
35—38.
[Vgl. Nr. 2888.] [2886q
[Stresemann, Gustav]: Rede des Reichs-
außenministers Dr. Gustav Stresemann †
über Friedrich den Großen und Steuben,
gehalten am 1. Dezember 1927 in Berlin
anläßlich der von der ,,Vereinigung Carl
Schurz'' veranstalteten Gedenkfeier des
Tages, an dem vor 150 Jahren Steuben in
New York eintraf. In: S-O-S. Die See.
Deutschlands See- und Kolonialgeltung in
Vergangenheit und Zukunft. Köln a. Rh.:
Hoursch & Bechstedt 1930. S. 16—18.
[2886r
— u. a.: General von Steuben, ein deutscher Pionier in den Vereinigten
Staaten. *Von Reichsminister Dr. S t r e s e -*
m a n n , Botschafter S c h u r m a n , A n t o n
E r k e l e n z , Mitglied des Reichstages,
Prof. S c h r e i b e r , Yale Universität, Ame-
rikanischer Botschaftsrat P o o l e , Baron
v o n S t e u b e n . Berlin: Sieben Stäbe-
Verlags- und Druckereiges. m.b. H. 1928.
48 S.
= Heft II der Schriftenreihe ,,Der Aus-
tausch'' herausgegeben von der Vereini-
gung Carl Schurz, Berlin. [2886s
Stoybe, H.: General Steubens Schicksale.
In: Zeitschrift für Sexualwissenschaft und
Sexualpolitik. Bd. XVI, H. 5. Berlin
und Köln 1929. S. 305—317. [2886t
Kühnemann, E. u. a.: Zum 200. Geburtstage von F. W. v. Steuben. *Festreden*
bei Gelegenheit der Feier im Reichstage
zu Berlin am 19. Oktober 1930. Berlin:
Sieben Stäbe-Verlags- und Druckereiges.
m. b. H. 1930. 31 S.
= Heft IV der Schriftenreihe ,,Der Aus-
tausch'' herausgegeben von der Vereini-
gung Carl Schurz, Berlin. [2886u
Palmer, John McAuley: Washington. Lincoln. Wilson. Three war statemen. *With*
an introduction of General John J.
P e r s h i n g . Garden City, N. Y.: Double-
day, Doran & Comp. Inc. 1930. pp. XV,
417, ill.
[,,Baron von Steuben'' = Chapter I V.
pp. 41—54; ,,How Baron Steuben inven-
ted the National Guard'' = Chapter VII.
pp. 72—83.] [2886v

Schaffer, Michel: Steuben — der deutsche
Idealist. *In: Deutsche Arbeit. Führer-*
zeitschrift des Vereins für das Deutschtum
im Ausland. Jg. XXIX. Dresden 1929
—1930. S. 319—323. [2886w
Bloem, Walter: Das Steuben-Jahr. *In:*
Hochschule und Ausland. Monatsschrift
für Wissenschaft und kulturelles Leben.
Jg. VIII, H. 4. Berlin 1930. S. 7—10.
[2887
— General Steuben. *In: Auslandswarte.*
Zeitschrift zur Förderung der wirtschaft-
lichen und kulturellen Beziehungen von
Heimat und Ausland. Jg. X, Nr. 20.
Berlin 1930. S. 279—280. [2887a
Borries, v.: Steuben. — *Zum 200. Geburts-*
tage am 17. September 1930. In: Deutsche
Wehr. Zeitschrift für Heer und Flotte.
(Früher Deutsches Offizierblatt Jg.
XXXIV.) Jg. III, Nr. 35. Berlin 1930.
S. 901—902. [2887b
Conring, Friedrich Franz v.: Friedrich Wil-
helm v. Steuben. *In: Militär-Wochen-*
blatt. Jg. 115, Nr. 10. Berlin Sept. 1930.
S. 371. [2887c
Draeger, Hans: Friedrich Wilhelm von
Steuben. *Zu seinem 200. Geburtstage.*
In: Hamburg-Amerika-Post Bd. II,
H. 9. Hamburg 1930. S. 265—276, ill.
[2887d
Gudde, Erwin Gustav: Der Organisator des
amerikanischen Revolutionsheeres. *Zur*
200. Wiederkehr des Geburtstages Friedrich
Wilhelm v. Steubens. In: Illustrierte Zei-
tung. Nr. 4469. Leipzig: Verlag J. J.
Weber. 9. Nov. 1930. S. 634, ill.
[2887e
O., K. v.: General Friedrich Wilhelm von
Steuben. *Zu seinem 200. Geburtstage.*
In: Wissen und Wehr. Monatshefte.
Jg. XI. Berlin 1930. S. 564—570.
[2887f
Paul, Alwin: Friedrich Wilhelm von Steu-
ben. *Seine Leistung für die Vereinigten*
Staaten. In: Europäische Gespräche.
Hamburger Monatshefte für auswärtige
Politik. Herausgegeben v. A. Mendelssohn-
Bartholdy. Jg. VIII. Stuttgart, Berlin u.
Leipzig 1930. S. 491—497. [2887g
Rein, A.: Friedrich Wilhelm von Steuben
zum 200. Geburtstage. *Hamburg 1930.*
14 S.
Erschienen auch in: Hamburg-Ame-
rika Post. Beilage z. Bd. 2., Heft 10.
Hamburg 1930. [2887h
Schurman, Jacob Gould: Rede des Bot-
schafters der Vereinigten Staaten in
Berlin, *gehalten in der Halle von Madison*

*Square Gardens in New York zur Feier
der 150jährigen Wiederkehr des Tages der
Landung Friedrichs von Steuben auf
amerikanischem Boden.* In: S-O-S. Die
See. *Deutschlands See- und Kolonial-
geltung in Vergangenheit und Zukunft.
Köln a. Rh.: Hoursch & Bechstedt 1930.
S. 19—24.* [2887i

Steuben, Arndt von: Worte der Erinnerung
an General von Steuben. *Zum 1. Dezember 1927. In: S-O-S. Die See.
Deutschlands See- und Kolonialgeltung in
Vergangenheit und Zukunft. Köln a. Rh.:
Hoursch & Bechstedt 1930. S. 24—26.*
[2887k

Studnitz, P. E. von: Der Exerziermeister
Altamerikas. *Zum 200. Geburtstage Frie-
derich Wilhelms von Steuben. In: Daheim
Jg. LXVII, Nr. 7. Leipzig: Verlag der
Daheim Expedition; Bielefeld: Velhagen
und Klasing 1930. S. 3—4, ill.* [2887l

Festschrift zur Feier des zweihundert-
jährigen Geburtstages von Baron Frie-
drich Wilhelm von Steuben. = *Deutsch-
Amerikanische Geschichtsblätter. German
American Historical Review. Jahrbuch
der Deutsch-Amerikanischen Historischen
Gesellschaft von Illinois. Jg. 1930. Vol.
XXX. Chicago, ill. 1930. S. 5—165, ill.
Inhalt:*

Goebel, Julius: Vorwort. *S. 5—8;*
— Baron von Steubens Geburtstag.
S. 9—15;
Bartholdt, Richard: Steuben. *An address
delivered at Chicago, December 3, 1927.
S. 16—27;*
Palmer, John McAuley: Steuben as a
military statesman. *S. 28—44;*
Hexamer, Charles J.: Baron von Steu-
ben, father of the American army.
*Address delivered at the unveiling cere-
monies of the Steuben monument. S. 45
—55.*
Ebeling, Christoph David: Nachrichten
von den Lebensumständen des Baron
von Steuben, Generalmajors in
Diensten der vereinten Staaten von
Nordamerika. *S. 56—67.*
[Steuben, Fr. W. v. Steuben]: Copie eines
Schreibens von dem General Major
von Steuben an den Geheimrat von
Frank in Hechingen: im Lager zu
Neuwindsor am Nord Fluß, den
4. Jul. 1779. *S. 68—76.*
Memorials of Baron von Steuben. *Un-
published and forgotten papers. Edited
by Julius Goebel. S. 77—164:*

I. Memorandum
II. Letter to the Board of War
III. Abstract of a System of Military
Discipline
IV. List of German Officers taken Prisoners at Yorktown
V. Plan for the establishment of a
military acadmy
VI. Steuben to Baron von Gaudy
VII. The best possible military establishment for the United States
VIII. A letter on the subject of an es-
tablissed militia and military ar-
rangments, addressed to the inhabitants of the United States.
[2887m
Stöbe, Hermann: General Steubens Herkunft. *In: Sachsen und Anhalt. Jahrbuch der Historischen Kommission für
die Provinzen Sachsen und für Anhalt
herausgegeben von R. Holtzmann und
W. Mühlenberg. Bd. VII. Magdeburg:
Selbstverlag der Historischen Kommission
1931. S. 360—448.*
*[Entgegnung auf Nr. 2886q, vgl. Be-
sprechung von F. Schönemann in: Jahresberichte für deutsche Geschichte. 8. Jg.
1932 [= Nr. 7781a]. S. 702ff.]*
[2888
Schäfer, Karl Heinrich: General Steubens
Herkunft. *In: Der deutsche Herold.
Zeitschrift für Wappen-, Siegel- und
Familienkunde. Herausgegeben vom Verein Herold in Berlin. Jg. LXII. Berlin
1931. S. 75—76. Zu "General Steubens
Herkunft". S. 94.* [2888a
Kekule von Stradonitz, Stephan: Zu "Ge-
neral Steubens Herkunft". *In: Der
deutsche Herold. Zeitschrift für Wappen-,
Siegel- und Familienkunde. Heraus-
gegeben vom Verein Herold in Berlin.
Jg. LXII. Berlin 1931. S. 94—95.*
[2888b
Conring, Friedrich Franz v.: Ein Offizier
Friedrich des Großen unter dem Sternen-
banner. *Steubens amerikanische Sendung.
Berlin: Wegweiser Verlag 1931. 266 S.,
ill.*
*= Volksverband der Bücherfreunde.
Auswahlreihe.* [2888c
Rohrbach, Paul: "Das Deutschtum in Nord-
amerika." *In: Das Deutschtum über See.
Von P. Rohrbach. Karlsruhe 1931
[= 97a]. S. 13—136, ill.*
*["Friedrich Wilhelm von Steuben . . ."
S. 53ff.]* [2888cc
Gedanken über die Person und das Werk
Friedrich Wilhelms v. Steuben. *Zur
Verfügung gestellt von der Deutschen*

Steuben Gesellschaft. In: Deutsches Adelsblatt. Jg. XLIX. Berlin 1931. S. 84—86.
[2888d

Deutschland und Amerika. Germany and USA. The Steuben memorial. *Herausgegeben im Auftrage der Deutschen Steuben Gesellschaft E. V. [Potsdam] Schriftleiter: Kurt Schomburg. Berlin, SW 68: Steuben-Verlag 1932. XII, 287 S., ill. (Deutsch und Englisch) u. a. (a. o.):*
Schomburg, Kurt [Pseudonym für K. L. Walter]: Gedanken über die Persönlichkeit und das Werk Friedrich Wilhelm von Steuben. — Something about Friedrich Wilhelm von Steuben's personality and work. *S. 3—27.*

Steuben, Arndt von: Friedrich Wilhelm von Steuben und die Bedeutung der Kapitulation von Yorktown für die Befreiung der Vereinigten Staaten von Amerika, *mit Orginaldokumenten aus dem Unabhängigkeitskrieg („Journal" der hessischen Söldnertruppen).* — Friedrich Wilhelm von Steuben and the importance of the capitulation of Yorktown to the liberation of USA. *S. 27—44.*

Die Steuben-Feier des Stahlhelms in Magdeburg 1930. — The commemoration of Steuben by the Stahlhelm in Magdeburg 1930. *S. 107—110.*

Steuben-Gedenkfeier in Bad Mergentheim anläßlich des 200. Geburtstages des Generals von Steuben (17. Sept. 1930). — Steuben commemoration on occasion of the 200 th birthday of General von Steuben on the 17th of September 1930 at Mergentheim. *S. 146—149.*

Steuben-Anekdoten — Steuben-anecdotes. *S. 284—285.*   [2888e

Losch, Philipp: General Steuben's hessische Herkunft. *In: Hessenland. Illustrierte Monatsblätter für Heimatforschung, Kunst und Literatur. Jg. XLIII. Kassel 1932. S. 114—115.*   [2888f

Tommek: Friedrich Wilhelm von Steuben. *In: 40. Bericht der wissenschaftlichen Gesellschaft Philomathie in Neiße. Herausgegeben vom Sekretär der Gesellschaft, Studienrat Schmalz, Neiße: J. Graveurs' Verlag Rudolf Wuttke 1932. S. 69—70.*
[2888g

Moos, Heinz: Wer ist Steuben? *In: Steuben-Presse. Illustrierte Monatsschrift der Deutschen Steuben Gesellschaft E. V. [Potsdam]. Jg. 1933. Nr. 2—3. S. 1—4; Nr. 4. S. 1—3, ill.*   [2888h

Palmer, John McAuley: Steuben, Friedrich Wilhelm Ludolf Gerhard Augustin, Baron von (1730—1794). *In: Dictionary of American biography. Under the auspices of the American Council of Learned Societies. Vol. XVII. Edited by Dumas Malone. London-New York 1935. pp. 601—604.*   [2888i

[Steuben, Friedrich Wilhelm von]: Correspondence of the American revolution; being letters of eminent men to George Washington from the time of his taking command of the army to the end of his presidency. *Edited by Jared Sparks. Boston, Mass.: Little, Brown and Co. 1853. 4 vol.*
[Letters by Baron Steuben: Vol. II. pp. 420—422; vol. III. pp. 126—129, 203—205, 290—294; vol. IV. pp. 41—43.]   [2889

[—] Copia eines Schreibens von dem General Major von Steuben, an den Geheimen Rat . . . in Hechingen: im Lager zu Neu-Windsor am Nord Fluß, den 4. Jul. 1779. *In: August Ludwig Schlözers Briefwechsel meist historischen und politischen Inhalts. Theil VII. Heft XLI. Nr. 63. Göttingen 1780. S. 327—337.*
[Abdruck siehe Nr. 2887m.]   [2889a

[—] Letter of Baron Steuben to Richard Peters, of the Board of War; 1779. *In: The Pennsylvania Magazine of History and Biography. Vol. XL. Philadelphia, Pa. 1916. p. 374.*   [2889b

[—] Translation of Steuben's letter to Walker *[dated „Schuylkill, Dec. 27, (1782)]. In: The Pennsylvania Magazine of History and Biography. Vol. XLVII. Philadelphia, Pa. 1923. pp. 278—279.*   [2889c

— Letter of General Baron Steuben to the officers of the New Jersey line, July 19th, 1783. *In: New Jersey Historical Society. Proceedings 1850—1851. Vol. V. Newark, N. J. pp. 14—15.*   [2889d

— Baron Steuben's account of his transactions in Virginia [to Richard Peters]. *In: Historical Magazine. Vol. IV. New York, N. Y. Okt., 1860. pp. 301—303.*   [2889e

— Baron von Steuben's appeal to President Washington for justice. *With a prefatory note by Julius Goebel. In: Deutsch-Amerikanische Geschichtsblätter. German-American Historical Review. Jahrbuch der Deutsch-Amerikanischen Historischen Gesellschaft von Illinois. Jg. 1929. Vol. XXIX. Chicago, Ill. 1929. pp. 188—206.*   [2889f

Steuben, Friedrich Wilhelm von: Washington and Steuben letters. *(Letters from the „Steuben paper" in the New York Historical Society.) [Go. Washington to Steuben, dated Annapolis decr. 23d. 1783. — Steuben to Washington, Jan. 1784.]* In: *Proceedings upon the unveiling of the statue of Baron von Steuben. Washington, D. C. 1911 [= no. 2885d]. p. 6.*   [2889g

— [Letter relative to the New York society of the Cincinnati to General van Cortlandt, dated New York, March 16, 1789.] In: *Magazine of American History. Vol. X. New York, NY.-Chicago, Ill. 1883, Sept. p. 253.*   [2889h

Two bills of Baron von Steuben. In: *The Pennsylvania Magazine of History and Biography. Vol. XLIV. Philadelphia, Pa. 1920. p. 92.*   [2889i

Steuben, Friedrich Wilhelm von: A letter on the subject of an established militia, and military arrangements, addressed to the inhabitants of the United States, *by Baron De Steuben. New York, N. Y.: Printed by J. M'Lean & Co. 1784. pp. 16 [Cf. Bibliography of Steuben by H. B. Meyer. p. 223.*   [2889k

— Regulations for the order and discipline of the troops of the United States. *Part I. Philadelphia, Pa.: Printed by Styner & Cist 1779. pp. 154, plates. 8.*   [2889l

— For the use of the Militia of Pennsylvania. An abstract of a system of military discipline: *Framed by the Hon.*

the Baron Steuben, Major General and Inspector General of the Armies of these United States. Approved by His Excellency General Washington. Confirmed by the Hon. the Congress. Philadelphia, Pa.: Francis Bailey 1779. pp. 38.   [2889m

Steuben, Friedrich Wilhelm von: Regulations for the order and discipline of the troops of the United States. *Part. I. Hartford, Conn.: Hudson and Goodwin 1779. pp. 138, plates. 6.*   [2889n

— Regulations for the order and discipline of the troops of the United States. *Part I. Hartford, Printed and sold by Nathaniel Patten. 1780. pp. 107, plates 8.*   [2889o

— Regulations for the order and discipline of the troops of the United States. *Part I. Hartford, Conn.: Printed by Hudson & Goodwin 1782. pp. 89, plates 8.* [2889p

— Regulations for the order and discipline of the troops of the United States. *Part I. Philadelphia, Pa.: Printed by Charles Cist 1785. pp. 151.*   [2889q

— Regeln für die Ordnung und Disciplin der Truppen der Vereinigten Staaten. *Erster Theil. Aus dem Englischen übersetzt. Philadelphia, Pa.: Gedruckt bey Carl Cist 1793. pp. 84. plates 8.* [2889r

— The military assistant: being a collection of company discipline, principally selected from the writings of Frederick W. Steuben ... *By Emery Russel. Springfield, Mass.: T. Dickman [1812]. pp. 48.*   [2889s

---

Friedrich der Große und die Vereinigten Staaten
Frederick the Great and the United States

Kapp, Friedrich: Friedrich der Große und die Vereinigten Staaten von Nordamerika. *Mit einem Anhang: Die Vereinigten Staaten und das Seekriegsgericht. Leipzig: Quandt & Händel 1871. IV, 202, XXX S.*   [2890

Rosengarten, J. G.: Frederick the Great and the United States. In: *The Pennsylvania-German Society. Proceedings and Addresses . . . at Germantown, Pa.,*

October 25, 1904 . . . Vol. XV. Lancaster, Pa. 1906. Separate pagination. pp. 29.   [2891

Schrader, Frederick Franklin: Prussia and the United States. Frederick the Greats' influence on the American Revolution. *Historical sketch. [s. l.] Second printing 1923. pp. 16. = The Conrad Society. Historical Bulletin no. 2.*   [2892

Die deutschen Söldnertruppen im Unabhängigkeitskriege
The German Mercenary Troops in the War of the Revolution

Allgemeines
General

Die drey vollständigen Subsidien-Tractaten, welche zwischen Sr. Großbritt. Majestät einer Seits und dem durchl. Landgrafen von Hessen-Cassel, dem durchl. Herzog von Braunschweig-Lüneburg und dem durchl. Erb-Prinzen v. Hessen-Cassel, als regier. Grafen v. Hanau anderer Seits abgeschlossen sind. *Englisch und Teutsch. Frankfurt und Leipzig 1776. 4⁰.* [2893

Bauer, Max: Deutscher Fürstenspiegel. *Bilder aus deutscher Vergangenheit nach den Quellen geschildert. Dresden: Kaden 1928. 352 S. [Menschenhandel deutscher Fürsten S. 307—329.]* [2894

Cronau, Rudolf: „Der Soldatenhandel deutscher Fürsten und die deutschen Söldlinge im englischen Heer." *In: Drei Jahrhunderte deutschen Lebens in Amerika. Eine Geschichte der Deutschen in den Vereinigten Staaten. Berlin 1909 [= Nr. 34]. S. 208—215, ill.; 2. Aufl. 1924. S. 212—216, ill.* [2895

Davis, Gherardi: Colors carried by the German mercenary troops in the War of the Revolution. *In: German American Annals. New series, vol. VI. Philadelphia, Pa. 1908. pp. 102—110.* [2896

Eelking, Max von: Die deutschen Hülfstruppen im nordamerikanischen Befreiungskriege, 1776—1783. *2 Bde. Hannover 1863. XII, 397 S.; 271 S.* [2897

— The German allied troops in the North America War of Independence, 1776—1783. *Translated and abridged from the German of* Max von Eelking *by* J. G. Rosengarten. *Albany, N. Y.: Joel Munsell's Sons, Publ. 1893. pp. (1), 7—360.* [2897a

Fritsch, W. A.: Stimmen deutscher Zeitgenossen über den Soldatenhandel deutscher Fürsten nach Amerika. *In: Deutsch-Amerikanisches Magazin. Vier-*

teljahrsschrift für Geschichte, Literatur-Wissenschaft, Kunst, Schule und Volksleben der Deutschen in Amerika . . . her, ausgegeben von H. A. Rattermann. Bd. I. Cincinnati, O. 1887. S. 589—593. [2898

Geisler, A. Friedrich: Kurze Charakter- und Tatenschilderung von 157 . . . britischen Offizieren wie auch einiger Offiziere von den deutschen Hilfstruppen. *Dresden 1784.* [2899

Greene, George Washington: „German mercenaries." *In: The German element in the War of American Independence. By* George Washington Greene. *New York, N. Y. 1876 [= no. 2787]. = Chapter III. pp. 171—211.* [2900

Kapp, Friedrich: Der Soldatenhandel deutscher Fürsten nach Amerika, 1775—1783. *Ein Beitrag zur Kulturgeschichte des achtzehnten Jahrhunderts. Berlin: Franz Duncker 1864. XIX, 299 S.; Zweite vermehrte und umgearbeitete Aufl. Berlin: Julius Springer 1874. XVI, 259 S.* [2901

— Anzeige von „Friedrich II. und die Neuere Geschichtsschreibung. Melsungen 1879 [= Nr. 2928d]. *In: Historische Zeitschrift. Herausgegeben von Heinrich von Sybel. Der ganzen Reihe Bd. XLII. Neue Folge Bd. VI. München 1879. S. 304—330.* [2901a

Lezius, M.: Deutsche Kämpfer für fremde Fahnen. Heldentaten und Schicksale deutscher Soldaten. *Berlin: Hensius 1934. 224 S.*
[Mit einem langen Kapitel: „an die Engländer verkauft, hauptsächlich nach Kapp und Seune. Vgl. Hessenland Jg. XLV. Kassel 1933. S. 127. [2902

Löher, F.: „Deutsche Söldlinge". *In: Geschichte und Zustände der Deutschen in Amerika. Cincinnati, O. 1847 [= Nr. 78]. S. 179—182.]*
[Vgl. Nr. 2969c] [2903

Losch, Philipp: Soldatenhandel. *Mit einem Verzeichnis der Hessen-Kasselischen Subsidienverträge und einer Bibliographie. Kassel: Im Bärenreiter-Verlag 1933. 110 S.*

[Bibliographie des Subsidienwesens, insbesondere des hessischen mit besonderer Berücksichtigung der Hessen in Amerika. S. 61—110.] [2904

Lowell, Edward J.: German manuscript sources for the history of the Revolutionary War. *Communicated by . . .In: Proceedings of the Massachusetts Historical Society. Vol. III. Second series, 1886—1887. Boston, Mass. 1888. pp. 219—221.* [2905

Ochs, A. L. v.: Betrachtungen über die neuere Kriegskunst, über ihre Fortschritte und Veränderungen und über die wahrscheinlichen Folgen, welche für die Zukunft daraus entstehen werden. *Cassel; bey Krieger in Commission 1817. IV, 227, (1) S.*

[Strategisch-historische Übersicht des Nordamerikanischen Krieges. = Erster Abschnitt. S. 5—60.] [2906

Pfister, F.: Der Nordamerikanische Unabhängigkeits-Krieg. *Als Beitrag zur Heeresgeschichte deutscher Truppen. Bd. I: Übersicht und Beurtheilung des Abfalles, des Krieges, der Mitstreiter, der Meinungs- und Zeitbewegung. Zugleich als Einleitung in die ausführliche Geschichte dieses Krieges. Bearbeitet von . . . Kassel. J. C. Kriegersche Buchhandlung 1864. XII, 360 S.* [2907

Rattermann, H. A.: Die deutschen Truppen im französischen Hülfsheere des amerikanischen Unabhängigkeitskrieges. *In: Der Deutsche Pionier. Jg. XIII. Cincinnati, O. 1881—1882. S. 317—325; 360—367; 428—440.* [2908

Richards, H. M. M.: Our ancestors in the British prisons of the Revolution. *In: Papers read before the Lebanon County Historical Society. Vol. VI. Lebanon, Pa. 1912—1916. pp. 3—22.* [2909

Rohrbach, Paul: „Die Deutschen im Unabhängigkeitskrieg 1775—1783. *Friedrich Wilhelm v. Steuben und die deutschen Mietstruppen in Amerika." In: Das Deutschtum über See. Von P. Rohrbach. Karlsruhe 1931 [= Nr. 97a]. S. 39—58, ill.* [2910

Rosengarten, J. G.: Sources of history. *A paper read before the German American Historical Society of New York and the Pionier-Verein of Philadelphia. Philadelphia, Pa.: Press of Wm. F. Fell & Co. 1892. pp. 32.*

[Relating to the Hessian troops in the War of the Revolution.] [2911

Rosengarten, J. G.: American history from German archives. *(Read April 6, 1900) In: Proceedings of the American Philosophical Society, held at Philadelphia for promoting useful knowledge. Vol. XXXIX. Philadelphia, Pa. 1900. pp. 129—154; 638—639.*

[No. 1—4 relating especially to the Hessian troops in the war of the Revolution.]

Reprint in: American history from German archives with reference to the German soldiers in the Revolution and Franklin's visit to Germany. By J. G. Rosengarten. In: The Pennsylvania-German Society. Proceedings and Addresses . . . 1902. Vol. XIII. Lancaster, Pa. 1904. [= no. 7838] Nos. 1—4. pp. 5—42. [2911a

— German archives as sources of German-American history. *Paper read before the Pennsylvania-German Society, October, 1907. In:German American Annals. New series, vol. V. Philadelphia, Pa. 1907. pp. 357—369. Vgl. auch Nr. (see also nos.) 2815—2816.* [2911b

M., F. W.: Schreiben eines englischen Werbeoffiziers [G. Schneider] aus dem Jahre 1780. *In: Hessenland. Zeitschrift für hessische Geschichte und Literatur. Jg. XVII. Kassel 1903. S. 82.* [2912

Rainsford, Charles: Transactions as commissary for embarking foreign troops in the English service from Germany with copies of letters relative to it for the years 1776—1777. *By Charles Rainsford, Colonel and Aide de Camp to His Majesty George III., and Major General, August, 1777. In: Collections of the New York Historical Society for the year 1879. Publication Fund Series, vol. XII. New York, N. Y. 1880. pp. 317—543.* [2913

Englische Zahlungen an die deutschen Fürsten. *Neudruck in: Der Soldatenhandel deutscher Fürsten nach Amerika (1775 bis 1783). Von Fr. Kapp. Berlin 1864. [= Nr. 2901] Anhang Nr. XXX—LI. S. 268—299.* [2914

17*

Hessen

Clark, Martha B.: The Hessians: *In: Papers and Addresses of the Lancaster County Historical Society. Vol. IV. Lancaster, Pa. 1900. pp. 119—137.*   [2915

Cochenhausen, von: Vor 150 Jahren. An der Wiege neuzeitlicher Infanterietaktik. *In: Wissen und Wehr. Monatshefte. Jg. XIV. Berlin 1933. S. 210—221.* [2916

Collins, V. L.: A brief narrative of the ravages of the British and Hessians at Princeton 1776—1777. *Princeton: Princeton. Historical Association, Extra pubs. 1906.*   [2917

Danckelman, L. v.: Die Einschiffung und Überfahrt der hessischen Brigarde v. Mirbach nach Nord-Amerika 1776. *In: Mitteilungen an die Mitglieder des Vereins für hessische Geschichte und Landeskunde. Kassel 1881. I. S. 1ff. und II. S. 1ff.*   [2918

— Die ersten Kriegserlebnisse der hessischen Division v. Heister auf amerikanischem Boden. *In: Mitteilungen an die Mitglieder des Vereins für hessische Geschichte und Landeskunde. Kassel 1881, II.*   [2918a

[Du Ry, S. L.]: [Über den Subsidien-Vertrag von 1776. Aufgezeichnet von . . . am 15. Februar 1776.] *Mitgetheilt von* Otto Gerland *unter dem Titel: Kasseler Neuigkeiten aus dem 18. Jahrhundert. In: Hessenland. Zeitschrift für hessische Geschichte und Literatur. Jg. VII. Kassel 1893. S. 71—72.*   [2919

Faust, A. B.: „The Hessians." *In: The German element in the United States. By A. B. Faust. Second edition. New York 1927 [= no. 42]. Vol. I. S. 349—356; Appendix S. 628—629.*   [2920

Field, Thomas W.: The battle of Long Island with connected preceding events and the subsequent American retreat. *Introductory narrative by Thomas W. Field with authentic documents. Brooklyn, N. Y.: Published by the Long Island Historical Society 1869. pp. IX, 549, ill., maps.* = Memoirs of the Long Island Historical Society. Vol. II.   [2921

Good, James I.: The Hessian soldiers of the Revolution. *In: The Pennsylvania-German. Vol. XII. Lititz, Pa. 1911. pp. 736—737.*   [2922

H. E.: Die Überfahrt des letzten hessischen Rekrutentransports nach Amerika 1782. *In: Mitteilungen an die Mitglieder des Vereins für hessische Geschichte und Landeskunde. Kassel 1909—1907. S. 147.*   [2923

[Harnier, Erasmus]: Die Überfahrt des letzten hessischen Rekrutentransportes nach Amerika 1782. *[Eine hessische Argonautenfahrt im Jahre 1782, verfaßt von E. Harnier.] Mitgetheilt von* A. Woringer. *In: Mitteilungen an die Mitglieder des Vereins für hessische Geschichte und Landeskunde. Jg. 1909—1910. Kassel 1910. S. 147—170.*   [2923a

Heidelbach, Paul: Das in London aufbewahrte Verzeichnis der Truppen von Hessen-Kassel. *In: Hessenland. Zeitschrift für hessische Geschichte und Literatur. Jg. XX. Kassel 1906. S. 118—122.*   [2924

Hertwig, J. G.: Die Hessischen Söldlinge. *In: Der Deutsche Pionier. Jg. VI. Cincinnati, O. 1874—1875. S. 346—351.* [2925

Johnson, Henry P.: The campaign of 1776 around New York and Brooklyn. *Including a new and circumstantial account of the battle of Long Island and the loss of New York with a review of events to the close of the war. Brooklyn, N. Y.: Published by the Long Island Historical Society 1878. pp. X, (1), 13—209, ill., maps.* = Memoirs of the Long Island Historical Society Vol. III.   [2926

[Lith, v. d.]: Feldzug der Hessen nach Amerika. *In: Ephemeriden über Aufklärung, Literatur und Kunst. Bändchen II. Marburg: in der jüngeren kriegerischen Buchhandlung 1785. S. 1—60.*   [2927

[Losch, Philipp]: Sklaverei und Soldatenhandel im Hessenlande. *In: Hessische Blätter. In Verbindung mit Freunden herausgegeben von Wilhelm Hopf. Jg. XXXVII, Nr. 3446. Melsungen 1908. S. (4).*   [2928

— Zur Geschichte des kurhessischen Staatsschatzes. *Nach unveröffentlichten Quellen. Kassel: Hess. Volksbund 1923. 15 S.*   [2928a

Lowell, Edward J.: The Hessians and the other German auxiliaries of Great Britain in the Revolutionary War. *New York, N. Y.: Harper & Brothers 1884. pp. VIII, (1), (1), 328, maps. [Bibliography. pp. 293—296.]*   [2929

[**Lowell, Edward J.**]: Die Hessen und die anderen deutschen Hilfstruppen im Kriege Groß-Britanniens gegen Amerika 1776—1783. *Von . . . Übersetzt mit Autorisation des Verfassers von O. C. Freiherrn von Verschuer. Zweite erweiterte Aufl. Braunschweig u. Leipzig: Richard Sattler 1902. XI, 250 S., Karten.* [2929a

Maurer, Fritz: Das angeblich in London aufgefundene Verzeichnis der hessischen Subsidientruppen. *Nachtrag zu dem in Nr. 4 dieses Blattes veröffentlichten Brief eines Hessen [= Nr. 2952]. In: Hessenland. Zeitschrift für hessische Geschichte und Literatur. Jg. XX. Kassel 1906. S. 65.* [2930

Mellik, . . .: *The Hessians in New Jersey; just a little in their favor. [See Cronau, R.: Drei Jahrhunderte deutschen Lebens in Amerika. 2. Aufl. 1924 [= Nr. 34]. S. 674.]* [2930a

Schwarzkopf, K.: Über den Anteil der Hessen an der Kapitulation von Yorktown 1781. *In: Mitteilungen an die Mitglieder des Vereins für hessische Geschichte und Landeskunde. Kassel 1882. S. 28—30.* 2931

Pfister, F.: Die Fahrt der ersten hessischen Heeresabteilung von Portsmouth nach Neu-York. Ein Beitrag zur Geschichte des Amerikanischen Krieges. *In: Zeitschrift des Vereins für hessische Geschichte und Landeskunde. Bd. II. Kassel 1840. S. 380—394.* [2932

— The voyage of the first Hessian army from Portsmouth to New York 1776. *New York City, N. Y.: Chas. Fred. Heartman 1915. pp. (1), 9—31. (Translation from the German of F. Pfister's historical sketch, published some 50 years ago in a German periodical.) = Heartman's Historical Series, no. 3.* [2932a

Pfister, H. v.: (Hessische Teilnehmer am amerikanischen Befreiungskriege). *In: Mitteilungen an die Mitglieder des Vereins für hessische Geschichte und Landeskunde. Nr. X. Kassel 1863. S. 11—12.* [2933

[—] Kanada als hessische Niederlassung. *In: Hessische Blätter. In Verbindung mit Freunden herausgegeben von Wilhelm Hopf. Bd. XI, Nr. 548. Melsungen 1879. S. 1.*

— Gedenktage aus dem Nordamerikanischen Kriege der Hessen-Casseler. *In: Allgemeine Militär-Zeitung. Jg. LXIV. Nr. 85 u. 86. Darmstadt 1889. S. 673—675; 684—686.* [2933b

Pfister, H. v.: [Über den Soldatenhandel H. v. Pfister wider den Casseler Geschichtsverein und dessen Antwort.] *In: Mitteilungen an die Mitglieder des Vereins für hessische Geschichte und Landeskunde. Jg. 1898. Kassel 1899. S. 24—31.* [2933c

— Noch einmal der sog. Soldatenhandel hessischer Fürsten. *In: Hessische Blätter. In Verbindung mit Freunden herausgegeben von Wilhelm Hopf. Melsungen 1899. Nr. 2557.* [2933d

[—] Friedrich II. und die neuere Geschichts-Schreibung. Ein Beitrag zur Widerlegung der Märchen über angeblichen Soldaten-Handel hessischer Fürsten. *Melsungen: Druck und Verlag von W. Hopf 1872. 53 S. Zweite mit einer Beleuchtung Seumens vermehrte Auflage. Melsungen 1879. 69 S. Gekürzte Übersetzung in: The Pennsylvania Magazine of History and Biography. Vol. XXIII. Philadelphia, Pa., July 1899. pp. 157—183.* [2933e

[**Preser, Carl**]: Der Kurfürst von Hessen, seine Dynastie und seine Gegner. *Vom Verfasser der „Göttlichen Mission Preußens". Heft 1. Wien 1869. 16 S.* [2934

— Der Soldatenhandel in Hessen. Versuch einer Abrechnung. *Marburg: N. G. Elwert'sche Verlagsbuchhandlung 1900. V—VII, 98 S. [Veränderte Neuausgabe des vorigen Buches.]* [2934a

— Über die angeblich nach Amerika verkauften Hessen. *In: Hessenland. Zeitschrift für hessische Geschichte und Literatur. Jg. II. Kassel 1888. S. 4—7; 24—27; 36—38; 50—52; 68—70. — Nochmals über die verkauften Hessen. In: Hessenland. Jg. III. Kassel 1889. S. 22—25.* [2934b

[—] Der angebliche Verkauf der Hessen nach Amerika. *(Auszug aus dem Aufsatz Presers im Hessenland, Kassel 1888 [= Nr. 2934b], unter Voranstellung von sieben Sätzen von H. v. Pfister. In: Allgemeine Militär-Zeitung. Jg. LXV, Nr 52—58. Darmstadt 1890. S. 410—412; 418—419; 426—428; 434—436; 442—444; 450—452; 458—460.* [2934c

— Und noch einmal: Die Hessen in Amerika! *[Besprechung und Abwehr des Buches von Edward J. Lowell in deutscher Übersetzung. Leipzig 1902 = Nr. 2929a] In: Hessenland. Zeitschrift für hessische Geschichte und Literatur. Jg. XVI. Kassel 1902. S. 32—34; 46—49.* [2934d

R., J.: Die hessischen Gefangenen im nordamerikanischen Freiheitskrieg. *[Übersetzung aus der New York Times vom 10. Nov. 1889.] In: Hessenland. Zeitschrift für hessische Geschichte und Literatur. Jg. V. Kassel 1891. S. 63—66.* [2935

R., Cl. D.: Deutsche Soldaten in Newport während der Jahre 1776—1779. Dessen Belagerung im Jahre 1778. *[Auszüge aus einem Vortrage von J. G. Rosengarten. Abgedruckt in: Rhode Island Historical Magazine. Vol. VII, No. 2.] In:Hessenland. Zeitschrift für hessische Geschichte und Literatur. Jg. III. Kassel 1889. S. 110—112; 145—147; 160—161.* [2936

P.[= Schenk zu Schweinsberg, Gustav Freiherr]: Geworbene Ausländer unter den Hessen in Amerika. *In: Allgemeine Militär-Zeitung. Jg. LXV. Nr. 22. Darmstadt 1890. S. 171—172.* [2937

Schenk zu Schweinsberg, Gustav Freiherr: Der angebliche Verkauf der Hessen nach Amerika. *In: Allgemeine Militär-Zeitung. Jg. LXV Nr. 66. Darmstadt 1890. S. 524.* [2937a

Schlieffen, Martin Ernst: Einige Betreffnisse und Erlebungen Martin Ernst von Schlieffen. *Berlin:G.Reimer 1830—1840. XII, 1278 S.*
[Die hessischen Hülfstruppen. S.184ff. Beilagen Nr. 137ff. S. 142ff. [2938

Sener, S. M.: The Lancaster barracks, where the British and Hessian prisoners were destained during the Revolution. *In: Notes and Queries. Edited by W. H. Egle. Fourth series, vol. II. 1894. Harrisburg, Pa. 1895. pp.280—283; 285—288; 291—295; 300—305; Separate print . . . Harrisburg, Pa.: Harrisburg Publishing Co. 1895. pp. 20.* [2938a

Shaaber, Andrew: The Hessian camp at Reading, Pa. 1781—1783. *Paper read before the Berks County Historical Society. Reprint from: The Reading Eagle. In: The Pennsylvania-German. Vol. XI. Lititz, Pa. 1910. pp. 477—487.* [2938 b

Slafter, Edmund F.: Landing of the Hessians, 1776. *A paper read at the meeting of the Massachusetts Historical Society, February 11, 1904. Boston, Mass. 1904. pp. 10.*
(Reprint from the Proceedings of the Massachusetts Historical Society.) [2939

Stern, Bernhard: Über die Schlacht bei Flatbusch 27. August 1776. *In: Mitteilungen an die Mitglieder des Vereins für hessische Geschichte und Landeskunde. Jg. 1907—1908. Kassel 1908. S. 37—40.* [2939a

Werthern, Frhr. von: Die hessischen Hülfstruppen im nordamerikanischen Unabhängigkeitskriege 1776—1783. *Vortrag gehalten am 23. November 1894 im Offiziercasino des Husaren-Regiments Hessen-Homburg. Cassel: Theodor Kay 1895. 47 S., Karte* [2940

Woringer, A.: Erinnerungen an die hessischen Truppen in Nordamerika. *In: Hessenland. Hessisches Heimatblatt. Zeitschrift für hessische Geschichte, Volks- und Heimatkunde, Literatur und Kunst. Jg. XXXIII. Kassel 1919. S. 54—57.* [2941

— Hessische Soldaten im nordamerikanischen Unabhängigkeitskrieg 1776—1783. *In: Nachrichten der Gesellschaft für Familienkunde in Kurhessen u. Waldeck. Jg. VIII. Kassel 1933. S. 25.* [2942

Etat der erforderlichen Zahlung für das Hochlöbl. Hessische Leib-Infanterie-Regiment in Amerika pro Febr. 1776. *In:August Ludwig Schlözers Briefwechsel meist historischen und politischen Inhalts. Theil VI. Heft XXXVI. Nr. 48. Göttingen 1780. S. 342—344.* [2943

Fürstl. Hessen-Casselsche Verordnung wegen des seit dem Marsch eines Corps Hessischer Truppen nach Amerika geschehenen Erlasses der halben Contribution 30. VII. 1776. *In: August Ludwig Schlözers Briefwechsel meist historischen und politischen Inhalts. Theil VIII. Heft XLVIII. Nr. 67. Göttingen 1781. S. 388—390.* [2944

Paulmann, . . .: Hessische Regimentstagebücher meist aus dem Amerikanischem Feldzug *[im der Landesbibliothek zu Kassel]. In: Nachrichten der Gesellschaft für Familienkunde in Kurhessen und Waldeck. Jg. III. Kassel 1928. S. 28—30.* [2945

August Ludwig Schlözers Briefwechsel meist historischen und politischen Inhalts. *Theil 1—10, Heft 1—60. (Nebst Registern über das ganze Werk). Göttingen: Verlag der Vandenhoekschen Buchhandlung [1776] 1777—1782.*

Theil II. Heft VIII. Nr. 20: New Yorks Island, im Gebiete Harlem 5 engl. Meilen von der Stadt Neujork und 100 Yards von Hornhuck am East River, den 18. Sept. 1776. *Von dem seel. Hrn. Lieut.* Hinrichs, *an den Herausgeber. S. 99—108.*

Theil III. Heft XIII. Nr. 5: Briefe aus N. Amerika. *(I).* Rhode Island, vom 24. Jun. 1777. *Von einem Hessischen . . . an seinen Bruder. S. 27—35; (II).* Aus dem Lager bei Duar House, den 31. Aug. 1777 *von einem Braunschweigischen . . . in der Bourgoynischen Armee. S. 35—42.*

Theil III. Heft XV. Nr. 21: Bei Philadelphia, on the Neck, 18. Jan. 1778; *von Hrn. Hauptman H. (Eingelaufen in Göttingen, 7. April). S. 149—153.*

Theil III. Heft XVII. Nr. 36: Vermischte Briefe. *I.* Philadelphia, 7. Mai 1778. *S. 259—267; II.* Auszug Schreibens eines deutschen Offiziers, datiert: dans les Baraques près de Boston, le 5 févr. 1778. *S. 268—269; IV.* Castle-Town in New Hampshire, 20. Jul. 1777. *S. 275—282.*

Theil IV. Heft XX. Nr. 22: On the neck bei Philadelphia, 2. June 1778. *Von Hrn. Hauptman H. S. 115—117.*

Theil IV. Heft XXI. Nr. 31. Newport auf Rhode-Island, 8. Sept. 1778. *S. 174.*

Theil IV. Heft XXIII. Nr. 49: Vertrauliche Briefe aus Kanada. St. Anne, 9. Marz—20. Apr. 1777. *Eingelaufen in Niedersachsen. 1. Aug. 1777. S. 288—323.*

Theil IV. Heft XXIV. Nr. 51: Vertrauliche Briefe aus Neu-England. Cambridge vom 15. Nov. 1777—10. Okt. 1778. *S. 341—587.*

Theil V. Heft XXV. Nr. 1: Savannah in Georgien, 16. Jan. 1779. *By D. S. H. .n, Auditeur. S. 8.*

Theil V. Heft XXV, Nr. 7: Von den Wilden auf Long Island bei Neu York in Amerika. *Aus einem Schreiben eines Waldeckschen Feld-Predigers, an einen Gelehrten in Arolsen, vom Junius 1777. S. 31—34.*

Theil V. Heft XXVII. Nr. 30: Liste der Generals Personen, die in der Armee der Rebellen dienen, vom Monat Mai 1778. *S. 195.*

Theil V. Heft XXIX. Nr. 38: Erster Feldzug der Braunschweiger in Kanada im J. 1776. *S. 267—279.*

Theil V. Heft XXX. Nr. 59: Staunton in Virginien, 1. Jun. 1779. *Eingelaufen in Braunschweig, den 10. Novemb. S. 413—420.*

Theil VI. Heft XXXVI. Nr. 48. Etat der erforderlichen Zahlung für das hochlöbl. Hessische Leib Infanterie-Regiment in Amerika, pro Febr. 1776. *S. 342—344.*

Theil VII. Heft XLI. Nr. 63: Copia eines Schreibens von dem General Major von Steuben, *an den Geheimen Rat. . . in:* Hechningen: im Lager zu Neu Windsor am

Nord Fluß, den 4. Jul. 1779. *S. 327—337.*

Theil VII. Heft XLII. Nr. 67: Brookland, bei Neu York 7. Sept. 1776. *Von einem Hessischen Feld-Prediger. S. 362—363.*

Theil IX. Heft LIV. Nr. 60: Neu York, 11. Sept. 1780 [von einem deutschen Officier]. *S. 383—385;* Ebendaher, 8. Okt. 1780. *S. 385;* Ebendaher, 19. Decemb. 1780. *S. 385—387.* [2945a

Letters of Brunswick and Hessian officers during the American Revolution. *Translated by* William L. Stone. *(Assisted by* August Hund]. *Albany, N. Y.: Joel Munsell's Sons 1891. pp. (1), X, 9—258, X, (1), ill.*

[English translation of no. 2945a.]
[2945 b

Letters from America 1776—1779. Being letters of Brunswick, Hessian and Waldeck officers with the British armies during the Revolution. *Translated by* Ray W. Pettengill. *Boston, Mass. and New York. N. Y.: Houghton Mifflin Co.; The Riverside Press Cambridge 1924. pp. (1), XXVI, 281.*

[English translation of no. 2945a]
[2945 c

Briefe als Anhang von: Der Soldatenhandel deutscher Fürsten nach America (1775 bis 1783). Von F. Kapp. Berlin 1864. = *Nr. 2945a].*

I Earl von Suffolk an Sir Joseph Yorke. *(St. James, Sept. 1, 1775.)*

II Sir Joseph Yorke an den Earl von Suffolk. *(Hague, Sept. 5, 1775.) S. 228—229.*

III Der Erbprinz von Hessen-Cassel an König Georg III. *(Hanau, le 19. Août 1775.) S. 230.*

IV Der Erbprinz von Hessen-Cassel an Sir Joseph Yorke. *(Hanau, le 20. Août 1775.) S. 230—231.*

V Der Fürst von Waldeck an den Earl von Suffolk. *(Arolsen, le 13. Novembre 1775.) S. 231—232.*

VI Earl von Suffolk an den Fürsten von Waldeck. *(St. James, le 24. Novembre 1775.) S. 232.*

VII Der Fürst von Waldeck an den Earl von Suffolk. *(Arolsen, le 30. Decembre 1775.) S. 232.*

VIII Georg III. an den Fürsten von Waldeck und den Prinzen von Hanau. *(St. James, January 2, 1776.) S. 233.*

IX Herzog von Braunschweig an König Georg III. *(Brunsvick, le 5. Decembre 1775.) S. 233—234.*

X Translation of a treaty between his Majesty and the reigning Duke of Bruns-

wick. *(Signed at Brunswick the 9th of January, 1776.) S. 234—238.*
XI Erbprinz Carl von Braunschweig an den General von Schlieffen. *(Brunswick, le 5. Decembre 1775.) S. 238.*
XII Translation of a treaty between his Majesty and the Landgrave of Hesse-Cassel. *(Signed Cassel the 15th of January 1776.) S. 238—243.*
XIII Der Erbprinz von Hessen-Cassel an den König Georg III. *(Hanau, le 17. Mars 1776.) S. 243—244.*
XIV Der Erbprinz von Hessen an den Earl von Suffolk. *(Hanau, 1. May 1776.) S. 244.*
XV Suffolk an den Erbprinzen von Hessen. *(St. James, May 14, 1776.) S. 244—245.*
XVI Der Erbprinz von Hessen-Hanau an den Earl von Suffolk. *(Hanau, 21. July 1776.) S. 245—246.*
XVIII A. Malsburg an den Earl von Suffolk. *(Hanau, 27. Novembre 1776.) S. 251.*
B. Der Erbprinz von Hanau an den Earl von Suffolk. *(Hanau, 4. Decembre 1776.) S. 251—252.*
XIX Sir Joseph Yorke an den Earl von Suffolk. *(Hague, April 1, 1777.) S. 252—256.*
XX Earl von Suffolk an Faucitt. *(St. James, 14. January 1777.) S. 256—257.*
XXIII Der Fürst von Anhalt-Zerbst an Sir Joseph Yorke. *(Le 29e Avril 1777.) S. 258—261.*
XXIV Oberst August Sigmund v. Koeseritz an — —. *(Zerbst, 20. Mai 1777.) S. 261—262.*
XXV Feronce an Faucitt. *(Brundwick, le 23. Decembre 1777.) S. 262.*
XXVI Elliott (englischer Gesandter in Berlin) an den Earl von Suffolk. *(Berlin, 8th November 1777.) S. 263.*
XXVII Sir Joseph Yorke an den Earl von Suffolk. *(Hague, Dec. 5th 1777.) S. 264—265.*
XXVIII Der Fürst von Anhalt-Zerbst an Sir Joseph Yorke. *(Dec. 10. 1777.) S. 265—266.* [2945 d

[Woringer, A.]: Auszüge aus Tagebüchern und Aufzeichnungen hessischer Offiziere und Regiments-Chroniken im amerikanischen Befreiungskrieg. *Von A. Woringer zur Verfügung gestellt und mit einer Vorbemerkung von Julius Goebel. In: Deutsch-Amerikanische Geschichtsblätter. Jahrbuch der Deutsch-Amerikanischen Gesellschaft von Illinois. Jg. 1920—1921. Vol. XX—XXI. Chicago, Ill. 1922. S. 251—279.* [2945 e

Schwarzkopf, K.: Valentin Osteroth und seine Erlebnisse im nordamerikanischen Freiheitskriege. *In: Mittheilungen an die*

Mitglieder des Vereins für hessische Geschichte und Landeskunde. Jg. 1876. I. Vierteljahrsheft. Kassel 1876. S. 2—3. [2946

[Bardeleben, Heinrich von]: Tagebuch des Hessischen Offiziers Heinrich von Bardeleben. *(29. Februar 1776, bis 22. Juni 1777). Mit einer Vorbemerkung des Herausgebers, J. G.[oebel]. In: Deutsch-Amerikanische Geschichtsblätter (German-American Historical Review). Jahrbuch der Deutsch-Amerikanischen Historischen Gesellschaft von Illinois. Jg. 1927—28. Bd. XXVII—XXVIII. Chicago, Ill. 1928. S. 7—119.* [2947

[Baurmeister]: Baurmeister's narrative of the capture of New York, September, 1776. *[Translated by A. A. Bierstadt.] From the original M. S. in the possession of George Bancroft. [Dated: „In Camp at Helgate," Sept. 24, 1776.] In: Magazine of American History. Vol. I. New York, N. Y. and Chicago, Ill. 1877. pp. 33—39.* [2947 a

[Cöster, G. C.]: Protocoll der Amtshandlungen, die, der Feldprediger G. C. Cöster bei den beiden löblichen Regimentern von Donop und von Loßberg und anderen verrichtet. *Angefangen am 14. März 1776. Mit einer Vorbemerkung von Julius Goebel. In: Deutsch-Amerikanische Geschichtsblätter. Jahrbuch der Deutsch-Amerikanischen Gesellschaft von Illinois. Jg. 1920—21. Vol. XX—XXI. Chicago, Ill. 1922. S. 280—304.* [2947 b

[Dörnberg, K. L. Frhr. von]: Tagebuchblätter eines hessischen Offiziers aus der Zeit des nordamerikanischen Unabhängigkeitskrieges. *[28. März 1779—10. Juni 1781] Herausgegeben von G. Marseille. 2 Teile. Pyritz: Druck der Backe'schen Buchdruckerei 1899/1900. 29 S.; 24 S., Karte. = Beilage zum Programm des Königlichen Bismarck-Gymnasiums zu Pyritz, Ostern 1899; . . . 1900.* [2948

[Dubuy, v.]: Beitrag zur Geschichte der hessischen Truppen in Amerika. Bericht des Majors v. Dubuy (aus dem Jahre 1780) *mitgetheilt von Hoffmeister. In: Mittheilungen an die Mitglieder des Vereins für hessische Geschichte und Landeskunde. Nr. XI. Kassel Okt. 1863. S. 8—10.* [2948 a

[Heinrichs, Johann]: The Hessians in Philadelphia. A German officer's impression on our city. *From the Correspon-*

dence of Professor Schlözer of Göttingen, vol. III. pp. 149ff. In: The Pennsylvania Magazine of History and Biography. Vol. I. Philadelphia, Pa. 1877. pp. 40—43. [Vgl. Nr. 4945a.]   [2949

[Heinrichs, Johann]: Extracts from the letter-book of Captain Johann Heinrichs of the Hessian Jäger Corps, 1778—1780. Translated by Julius F. Sachse. In: The Pennsylvania Magazine of History and Biography. Vol. XXII. Philadelphia, Pa. 1898. pp. 137—170.   [2949a

Heister, L. C. von: Auszüge aus dem Tagebuche eines vormaligen kurhessischen Offiziers über den Nordamerikanischen Freiheitskrieg 1776 und 1777. Mitgetheilt durch den Lieut. von Heister. I., im ersten Garde-Regiment zu Fuß. In: Zeitschrift für Kunst, Wissenschaft und Geschichte des Krieges. Heft 3. Berlin, Posen und Bromberg 1828. S. 223—270.   [2950

Heringen, v.: Einige Briefe aus dem amerikanischen Kriege. I. Schreiben eines Hessischen Officiers d. d. Long Island den 1. September 1776. (Vermuthlich von Oberst Heringen des Rgts. v. Schenk.) In: Preußisches Militair-Wochenblatt. Jg. XVIII. Berlin 1833. No. 863 und 864. S. 4854—4856; 4858—4859. II.[= Nr. 2975e].   [2950a

Henkelmann und Schirmer: Zwei Briefe hessischer Offiziere [Henkelmann und Schirmer, 1783 aus Halifax]. Von A. Woringer. In: Hessenland. Zeitschrift für hessische Geschichte und Literatur. Jg. XX. Kassel 1906. S. 339—342.   [2950b

[Koch, Berth]: Ein kurhessischer Infanterist im Siebenjährigen und amerikanischen Unabhängigkeitskrieg. In: Zeitschrift für Heereskunde. Berlin 1932. S. 337—456.   [2951

[Krafft, Charles Philip von]: Journal of Lieutnant John Charles Philip von Krafft, of the Regiment von Bose, 1776—1784. Translation in: Collections of the New York Historical Society for the year 1882. New York, N. Y. 1883. pp. 202, maps. Biographical sketch of Lieutnant von Krafft, with a prefatory note, by Thomas H. Edsall. pp. IX—XII.   [2951a

Schwarzkopf, K.: Aufzeichnungen des Feldpredigers Georg Köster über das Regiment von Donop und von Loßberg im amerikanischen Freiheitskriege. In:

Mitteilungen an die Mitglieder des Vereins für hessische Geschichte und Landeskunde. Jg. 1901. Kassel 1903. S24—25   [2951b

[Kümmel, H.]: Tagebuch des Pfarrers H. Kümmel, Feldprediger bei den hessischen Regimentern v. Huyne und v. Bünau 1776—1783. In: Hessische Blätter. In Verbindung mit Freunden herausgegeben von Wilhelm Hopf. Melsungen 1883. Nr. 946—948.   [2951c

[—] Aus dem Tagebuch eines hessischen Feldpredigers [H. Kümmel] im amerikanischen Kriege. In: Hessenland. Zeitschrift für hessische Geschichte und Literatur. Jg. VIII. Kassel 1894. S. 72—76; 87—91.   [2951d

Leiste, Christian: [See no. 3382.]

Maurer, Fritz: Brief eines Hessen [Reg. Feldscher Maurer] aus der Zeit des englisch-nordamerikanischen Krieges [datiert: Lowelly Sally, den 25. März 1776]. In: Hessenland. Zeitschrift für hessische Geschichte und Literatur. Jg. XX. Kassel 1906. S. 48—50.   [2952

[Münchhausen, Ernest von]: The battle of Germantown described by a Hessian officer. — Extracts from the journal and report of Captain Frederick Ernest von Münchhausen. Translated by Joseph G. Rosengarten. In: The Pennsylvania Magazine of History and Biography. Vol. XVI. Philadelphia, Pa. 1892. pp. 197—201, map.   [2952a

[Münscher, Joh.]: Noch einmal die „verkauften Hessen" in Amerika. [Brief von Joh. Münscher, Soldat aus Hitzerode, an seinen Vater datiert: Jamaica auf Long Island, 8. Dec. 1782.] In: Hessenland. Zeitschrift für hessische Geschichte und Literatur. Jg. XI. Kassel 1897. S. 161—162.   [2952b

[Reuber, Johannes]: Das Tagebuch des Grenadiers Reuber [im Batt. Rall]: 1. Theil, der Feldzug der Hessen in Nordamerika. Besprochen von F. W. Junghans. In: Mittheilungen des Hanauer Bezirksvereins für Geschichte und Landeskunde an seine Mitglieder pro 1885. Kassel 1885. S. LXXVIII—LXXX; . . . für 1892. Kassel 1893. S. 94.   [2953

[—] Der amerikanische Feldzug der Hessen nach dem Tagebuch des Grenadiers Johannes Reuber von Niedervellmar 1776—1783. Von F. W. Junghans. In: Hessenland. Zeitschrift für hessische Geschichte und Literatur. Jg. VIII. Kassel

1894. S. 155—157; 167—168; 183—186.
[2953a
[Wiederholdt,A]: Tagebuch des Capt. Wiederholdt. Vom 7. October 1776 bis 7. December 1780. *Transcribed by* **C. Große,**
and edited by **M. D. Learned.** *In: Ameri-*
cana Germanica. A quarterly. Vol. IV.
Philadelphia, Pa. 1901—1902. pp.
XVII, 19—93. [2954
[—] „Hauptmann Wiederhold's diary."
In: Annals of the Penn Square, Reading.
By J. Bennet Nolan. Philadelphia, Pa.
1933 [= no. 3640a]. pp. 17—30. [2954a
[H., v.]: Auszug eines Schreibens aus Ame-
rica an Sr. Excellenz den Herrn General-
lieutnant von . . . *[s. l., 1776.] S. 3—24.*
[Geschrieben Long Island, 1 ten Sept.
1776. 20 S. Anhang (1). Aus dem Reise-
journal des Hrn. Generaladjudanten von
D. an einen Freund in L. *S. 21—22;*
(2) Aus dem Schreiben eines Hessischen
Feldpredigers, aus Brookland bey Neu
Jork, vom 7ten Sept. *S. 23—24.]* [2955
[Schw., M. J. C.]: Schreiben eines hessischen
Feldpredigers, Brookland den 7. Sept.
1776. *[Gezeichnet M. J. C. Schw.] In:*
Chr. Schubarts Teutsche Chronik aufs
Jahre 1776. Jg. III. Stück 94. Ulm:
gedruckt bey Christian Ulrich Wagner
1776. S. 737—742. [2955a
Fortgesetztes Schreiben eines Hessischen
Officiers aus Amerika, welches die
weiter vorgefallenen Attaquen und ge-
machten Eroberungen enthält. *[s. l.]*
1776. 16 S. [2955b
„Journal" der hessischen Söldnertruppen
1778 *(im Besitz der Gräfin Schlieffen-*
Potsdam): „Vom 1 ten Julio bis den 31 ten
Dezembris 1778." Mit einer Vorbemer-
kung von Kurt Schomburg. Faksimile.
In: Deutschland und Amerika. Germany
and USA. The Steuben Memorial. Berlin
1932 [= Nr. 2888e]. S. 36—44. [2955c

Strieder, Fr. W.: Grundlage zu einer hessischen Gelehrten- und Schriftsteller-Ge-
schichte. *Bd. 1—18. Cassel 1781—Mar-*
burg 1819.
[Enthält zahlreiche Biographien von
Teilnehmern am Amerikanischen Feld-
zug u. a. B. Ewald (Bd. IV. S. 5);
v. d. Lith *(Bd. XVIII. S. 340);* Münchhausen *(Bd. XVIII. S. 387);* Ochs *(Bd.*
XVIII. S. 420); Seume *(Bd. XVIII.*
S. 399); Wiederhold *(Bd. XVII. S. 32).*
[2956
Büttner, Johann Carl: Büttner, der Amerikaner. *Eine Selbstbiographie Johann*

Carl Büttners, jetzigen Amts-Chirurgus
in Senftenberg und ehemaligen nordameri-
kanischen Kriegers. 2. Auflage . . .
Camenz: C. S. Krausche 1828. XIX,
137 S., ill. [2957
Rev. Samuel Dubendorff. *In: Notes and*
Queries. Edited by W. H. Egle. Third
series, vol. I. 1884—1887. Harrisburg,
Pa. 1887. p. 294. Reprint in: Third
series, vol. I. Harrisburg, Pa. 1895.
p. 531.
[Chaplain to one of the regiments of the
Hessian mercenaries, later removed to
Lykeus Valley, Dauphin Co. (in 1780).]
[2958
Landau, G.: Emmerich. *In: Historisches*
Jahrbuch Leipzig 1854. S. 148. [2959
Losch, Philipp: Eine althessische Familie in
Dänemark: (1) Joh. v. Ewald *[Capitän*
der hessischen Jäger in Amerika]. In:
Hessenland. Zeitschrift für hessische Ge-
schichte und Literatur. Jg. XX. Kassel
1906. S. 2—5. [2960
Lith, v. d.: Wilhelm Frhr. v. Knyphausen,
Hessen-Kasselischer General-Lieutnant
. . . In: Hessische Denkwürdigkeiten.
Herausgegeben von Karl Wilhelm Justi.
Theil III. Marburg 1802. S. 442—448;
siehe auch S. 498. [2961
Wilhelm, Baron Innhausen and Knyphausen. *In: The Pennsylvania Maga-*
zine of History and Biography. Vol. XVI.
Philadelphia, Pa. 1892. pp. 239—245,
ill. [2961a
Rogge-Ludwig, K.: Über Barth. Koch und
seine Erlebnisse im amerikanischen Freiheitskriege 1776—1782. *In: Mitthei-*
lungen an die Mitglieder des Vereins für
hessische Geschichte und Landeskunde.
Jg. 1876. T. 1. Vierteljahrsheft. Kassel
1876. S. 1—2. [2962
Hohenhausen, Leopold von: Biographie des
Generals von Ochs. *Ein politisch-mili-*
tärischer Beitrag zur Geschichte des nord-
amerikanischen und des französischen
Revolutionskrieges, sowie der Feldzüge in
Spanien, Rußland und Deutschland. (Aus
den Orginalpapieren des Generals und son-
stigen authentischen Mittheilungen.) He-
rausgegeben von . . . Cassel: Im Verlage
der Luckhardt'schen Hofbuchhandlung
und gedruckt bei J. H. Hampe 1827
V, (1), 344 S., ill. [2963
Massicotte, E. Z.: Le baron Schaffalisky
(a Hessian officer, who settled in Canada).
In: Bulletin des recherches historiques
Beauceville, Canada. Vol. 29 S. 134.
[2964

Woringer, August: Ein Kasselaner [W. E. Schoppach [im Stabe Washingtons. *In: Volk und Scholle. Heimatblätter für beide Hessen, Nassau und Frankfurt a. M. Jg. VI. Darmstadt 1928. S. 234—236.* [2965

Justi, K. W.: Johann Ludwig Friedrich von Stamford, Obervorsteher der hohen Samt-Hospitäler, Major . . . *In: Hessische Denkwürdigkeiten. Herausgegeben von Karl Wilhelm Justi. Vierter und letzter Theil. Zweite Abtheilung. 1805. S. 73—75.* [2966

Wangenheim, Otto Freiherr von: Biographical notes on Friedrich Adam Julius, Freiherrn von Wangenheim, *written by his grandson Otto, Freiherr von Wangenheim (Gotha). Translation by* **Charlotte Große.** = *J. G. Rosengarten communication. In: The Pennsylvania-German Society. Proceedings and Addresses at Philadelphia, Oct. 25, 1896. Vol. VII. Reading, Pa. 1897. pp. 24—30.* [2967

Stryker, William Scudder: The battle of Trenton and Princeton. *Boston, Mass. and New York, N. Y. Houghton, Mifflin Co. 1896. pp. 514.* [2968
Kriegsgerichtliches Erkenntniß über die Gefangennehmung der Hessen bei Trenton, den 26. Dezember 1776. *(Bisher ungedruckt.) Herausgegeben von* **Friedrich Kapp.** *In: Der Deutsche Pionier. Jg. XIV. Cincinnati, O. 1882—1883. Deutsch-amerikanische Dokumente. S. 401—405.* [2968a
[Kapp, Friedr.]: Report of the court-material for the trial of the Hessian officers captured by Washington at Trenton, December 26, 1776. *Translated from a German copy communicated by* **Frederick Kapp.** *Edited by* William S. Stryker. *In: The Pennsylvania Magazine of History and Biography. Vol. VII. Philadelphia, Pa, 1883. pp. 45—49.* [2968b
Franklin, Benjamin: Lettre du Landgrave de Hesse au commandant de ses troupes en Amérique *(à Cassel 1777) [s. l. 177. .) pp. 6.*
Translations and reprints:
Brief des Landgrafen von Hessen an den Commandanten seiner Truppen in Amerika. *[Deutsche Übersetzung der Original-Flugschrift von 1777.] In: Der Uriasbrief des Grafen von Schaumburg. Von* **Ph. Losch** *in: Hessische Chronik. Jg. II. Kassel 1913. S. 84—85.*

Lettre du comte de Chamb
urg, écrite de Rome au .baron de Hohendorff, commandant des troupes Hessois en Amérique. *In: L'Espion dévalisé. By* **Baudouin de Guémadeuc.** *Londres [Neuchatel] 1782. Chapter XVII. pp. 205 —209.*
Ein Brief des Grafen von Chamburg, von Rom aus an den Baron von Hohendorf, Kommandanten der Hessischen Truppen in Amerika, geschrieben. *In: Der geplünderte Spion. [Von* **Baudouin de Guémadeuc.]** *Aus dem Französischen übersetzt. London [Leipzig: Barth] 1783. S. 261ff.*
Wörtlich abgedruckt in: Der Uriasbrief des Grafen von Schaumburg. Von Ph. Losch in: Hessische Chronik. Jg. II. Kassel 1913. S. 86—87.
Brief des Grafen von Schaumburg, Prinzen von Hessen-Cassel, an den Commandeur seiner Truppen in Amerika, 8. Febr. 1777 *[nach dem Druck in „The Reveille", Nr. 31. Okt. 1845, St. Louis]. In: Der Uriasbrief des Grafen von Schaumberg. Von Ph. Losch in: Hessische Chronik. Jg. II. Kassel 1913. S. 38—39.*
Lettre du Landgrave de Hesse au commandant de ses troupes en Amérique. *(Aus Band Nr. 600 der Flugschriften in der Bibliothek der Historical Society of New York City.) Edited by* **Fr. Kapp.** *In: Der Soldatenhandel deutscher Fürsten nach Amerika (1775—1783). By Fr. Kapp. Berlin 1864 [= no.2901]. Appendix no. XXIX. pp. 267—268; German translation. pp. 196—197.*
Copie d'une lettre du comte de Schaumberg, écrite de Rome le 18 févr. 1777 au baron d'Hohendorf, commandant des troupes hessoises en Amérique, *beiliegend einen Brief aus Versailles vom 13. März 1777. In: Lescure, Correspondance secrète inédite sur Louis XVI. . . . de 1777— 1792 p. d'apres les ms. de la Bibl. Imp. de St.-Pétersbourg. Paris 1866. S. 3ff.*
What the Hessians of 1776 were thought by the father of their country. — Letter of the Prince of Hesse Cassel, dated Febr. 8, 1777 sent to Baron Hohendorff. *In: Littel's Living Age. Fifth series, vol. VIII. October numbers 1874. Boston, Mass. 1874. p. 64.*
Lettre du Landgrave de Hesse, au commandant de ses troupes en Amérique, 1777. *Edited by* J. G. Rosengarten. *In: Proceedings of the American Philosophi-*

*cal Society held at Philadelphia for pro-
moting useful knowledge. Vol. XXXIX.
Philadelphia, Pa. 1900. pp. 149—150.*
A remarkable letter. Edited by **Frank
R. Diffenderffer.** *In: Papers and Addresses of the Lancaster County Historical Society. Vol. VI. Lancaster, Pa.
1902. pp. 85—89.
In: Franklin, Benjamin. Works, including the private as well as the official
& scientific correspondence. Compiled and
edited by John Bigelow. Vol. VII. New
York 1905. S. 191.*   [2969
Schrader, Hermann: Der Bilderschmuck der
deutschen Sprache in Tausenden volks-
thümlicher Redensarten. Nach Ursprung und Bedeutung erklärt. 2. Aufl.
*Weimar: Emil Felber 1894. 543 S.
[Führt die Redensart „Ab nach Kassel"
auf den sog. „Soldatenhandel" der hessischen Fürsten zurück und bringt eine
Wiedergabe des Uriasbriefes vom 8. II.
1777. S. 357—358.]*   [2969a
Brunner, Hugo: Ein gefälschter Brief Landgraf Friedrichs II. und seine Quelle. *In:
Zeitschrift des Vereins für hessische Geschichte und Landeskunde. Neue Folge,
XXIV. Bd. (Der ganzen Folge XXXIV.
Bd.). Kassel 1899. S. 420—425.* [2969b
[Ditfurth, M. v.]: Bemerkungen über einige
besonders wichtige Gesichtspunkte für
die heeresgeschichtlichen Arbeiten in
den kleineren deutschen Contingenten.
*In:Neue Militär-Zeitung. Herausgegeben
von einer Gesellschaft deutscher Offiziere.
Jg. III. Darmstadt 1858. Nr. 13. S. 97
—99; Nr. 14. S. 106—108; Nr. 15.
S. 115—117.
[Bemerkungen über die Unechtheit des
Briefes des Landgrafen von Hessen, die
Löher [= Nr. 78] in seinem Buche ver-
öffentlichte.*   [2969c
Grotefend, Wilhelm: Ein gefälschter Brief.
*In: Hessenland. Zeitschrift für hessische
Geschichte und Literatur. Jg. IX. Kassel
1895. S. 70—71.*   [2969d
Landau, G.: Der angeblich von einem hessi-
schen Fürsten in bezug auf die 1776 bei
Trenton erfolgte Niederlage hessischer
Truppen geschriebene Brief. *In: Perio-
dische Blätter der Geschichts- und Alter-
thums-Vereine zu Kassel, Darmstadt,
Frankfurt a. M. und Wiesbaden. Nr. 3.
Okt. 1857. Kassel 1857. S. 39—40.* [2969e
L[andau], D[oktor]: Landgraf Friedrich II.
und die todten Hessen von Trenton. *In:
Die Grenzboten, Zeitschrift für Politik*

*und Literatur, Herausgegeben von Gustav
Freytag und Julian Schmidt. Jg. XVII.
Semester II. Bd. III. Leipzig 1858.
S. 92—101.*   [2969f
Losch, Philipp: Der Uriasbrief des Grafen
von Schaumburg. Zur Geschichte der
öffentlichen Meinung über den sog.
Soldatenhandel. *In: Hessische Chronik.
Monatsschrift für Familien- und Orts-
geschichte in Hessen und Hessen-Nassau.
Jg. II. Darmstadt 1913. S. 37—40; 83
—88; 99—105.*   [2969g
— Der Uriasbrief des Grafen von Schaum-
burg. Zur Geschichte der öffentlichen
Meinung über den sog. Soldatenhandel.
*[Erweiterter Neudruck von Nr. 2969g.]
In: Hessische Blätter. In Verbindung
mit Freunden herausgegeben von Wilhelm
Hopf. Nr. 4050—4054. Melsungen 1914.
S. 130—132; 138—139; 147—148; 154
—155; 162—164.*   [2969h
— Historische Wahrheit und journalisti-
scher Anstand. *[Entgegnung zu Aus-
führungen des Berliner „Vorwärts" über
den sog. Uriasbrief des Prinzen von
Hessen-Kassel vom 8. 2. 1777.]. In:
Hessenland. Illustrierte Monatsblätter für
Heimatforschung, Kunst und Literatur.
Jg. XXXVII. Kassel 1923. S. 219—
220.*   [2969i

Putnam, J.: Proclamation. Sintemal der
König von Großbrittanien hat Mittel
gefunden etc. *[Aufforderung an die
Deutschen zur Desertion.] Datiert: White
Plains Nov. 16, 1777. [Albany, N. Y. ?]
1777.
Abgedruckt in: Eelking. Deutsche Hilfs-
truppen. [= Nr. 2897]. Bd. I. S. 229ff.*
                                          [2970
Emmerich, A.: An die Deutschen in Ame-
rika. Germantown, Pa. 1777 *[Antwort
auf Putnams Proclamation]. Abgedruckt
in Eelking. Deutsche Hülfstruppen
[= Nr. 2897]. Bd. I. S. 229ff. In:
Deutsch-Amerikanisches Magazin Bd. I.
S. 399.*   [2970a
Mirabeau, Honore Gabriel: Avis aux Hessois
. . . . .1775. pp. 12.
Reprints:
Avis aux Hessois et autres peuples de
l'Allemagne, vendus par leurs Princes
à l'Angleterre, à Clèves: chez Bertol 1777.
pp. 16; In: L'Espion dévalisé. [By
Baudouin de Guémadeuc] Londres 1782.
Chapt. XVI. pp. 195—204;
In: Der geplünderte Spion. Von
[Baudouin de Guémadeuc]. Aus dem*

Französischen übersetzt. London (Leipzig: Barth) 1783.
In: Essai sur le déspotisme. By Gabriel Mirabeau. Troisième édition, corrigée de la main de l'auteur sur l'exemplaire de la second édition achété à sa vente. Précédé de la lettre de M. de S. M. aux Auteurs de la Gazette Littéraire, &c. suive de L'avis aux Hessois, &c. de la réponse aux conseils de la raison. Paris: Le Jay 1792. pp. 309—318.
,,Rath an die Hessen und die übrigen von ihren Fürsten an England verkauften Völker Deutschlands." Edited by Fr. Kapp. [German translation of: Avis aux Hessois . . . À Cleves chez Bertol 1777.] In: Der Soldatenhandel deutscher Fürsten nach Amerika (1775 bis 1783). By Fr. Kapp. Berlin 1864 [= no. 2901]. pp. 186—192.
Avis aux Hessois et autres peuples de l'Allemagne, vendus par leurs Princes à l'Angleterre, à Cleves: chez Bertol 1777. Edited by J. G. Rosengarten. In: Proceedings of the American Philosophical Society held at Philadelphia for promoting useful knowledge. Vol. XXXIX. Philadelphia, Pa. 1900. pp. 150—154.
Warning to the Hessians. — (Mirabeau avis aux Hessois). Edited by J. G. Rosengarten. In: German American Annals. New series, vol. XII. Philadelphia, Pa. 1914. pp. 228—232. [2970b
Aanspraak aande Hessische eu andere Volkeren van Duitschland, door hunne Vorsten verkogt aan Groot-Brittanie. Te Kleef, bij Bertol 1777. 16 S.
[Holländische Übersetzung von Nr. 2970c.] [2970c
Vriend-broederlijke Vermaning en Raadgeeving aan de Hessische en andere Duitsche Hulpbeuden, welke door hunne Vorsten aan het Engelsche Ministerie zijn verkogt. Gedruckt na de Copij. Te Cleef bij Berthol, en alomme te bekommen 1777. 16 S.
[Freiere Übertragung von Nr. 2970.] [2970d
Waarschouwing der Reede tegen het Geschrift getijtelt Vriendbroederlijke Vermaaning en Raadgeeving . . . Te Amsteldam: Bij F. H. Demter, Boekverkoper. [s. a.]. 16 S.
[Englische Gegenschrift gegen Nr.2970d ,,Vriend-broederlijke Vermaning . . ."] [2970e
Sr.idorf: Conseils de la raison. Amsterdam 1777. . . .

[Antwort auf (Reply to) Avis aux Hessois.] — Vgl. Nr. 2911, S. 30 (See no. 2911, p. 30). [2970f
Mirabeau, Honoré Gabriel: Response aux Conseils de la Raison. . . . . .
Reprints:
Essai sur le despotisme. Troisième édition, corrigée de la main de l'auteur sur l'exemplaire de la seconde édition acheté à sa vente. Précédé de la lettre de M. de S. M. aux Auteurs de la Gazette Littéraire, &c. suive de l'avis aux Hessois, &c. de la réponse aux conseils de la raison. Paris: Le Jay 1792. pp. 319—336 [2970g
[Schlieffen, Martin Ernst oder Luchet?]: Des Hessois en Amérique, de leur Prince et des déclamateurs [s. l.] 1782.
Abgedruckt in: Einige Betreffnisse und Erlebungen Martin Ernst von Schlieffen. Berlin: G. Reimer 1830. Beilagen zu dem zweiten Bande der Nachrichten von einigen Häusern des Geschlechts der von Schlieffen oder Schlieben vor Alters Schliwin oder Schliwingen No. 138. S. 142—146. [2970h
[Schlieffen, Martin Ernst]: Von den Hessen, ihren Fürsten und den Schreyern [Des Hessois en Amérique.] Aus dem Französischen. [s. l.] 1782. 22 S.
[Deutsche Übersetzung von Nr. 2970h.] [2970i
Wahrheit und Guter Rath an die Einwohner Deutschlands besonders in Hessen. Philadelphia, Pa.: Carl Cist 1783.
[Aufforderung zur Desertion.] [2970k
Warnung eines hessischen Feldwebels an seine redliche Landsleute gegen die ihnen unter der Masque der Wahrheit und Gutes Raths von einem Verräther seines Vatterlands gelegten Schlingen. New York, N. Y. 1783.
[Entgegnung auf Nr. 2970k.] [2970l
Pfister, H. v.: Über die Heeresverlassung hessischen Soldaten im Nordamerikanischen Unabhängigkeitskriege. In: Zeitschrift des Vereins für hessische Geschichte und Landeskunde. Jg. X. Kassel 1865. S. 361—373. [2970m
Russel, Ch. E.: ,,Things the Hessians learned." In: H. Salomon & the Revolution. By Ch. E. Russel. New York, N. Y. 1930. p. 60ff. [2970n
Fürer, J.: Ein zeitgenössisches Urtheil über den ,,Soldatenhandel" Landgraf Friedrich's II. und seine Würdigung. [Erklärung zweier desertierter hessischer Fähnriche des Regiments von Knyphausen: Führer und Kleinschmidt, 1782].

In: Hessenland. Zeitschrift für hessische Geschichte und Landeskunde. Jg. XIV. Kassel 1900. S. 5—8; 21—23; 35—37. [2970 o]

Seume, J. G.: Schreiben aus Amerika nach Deutschland. Halifax 1782. *In: Neue Literatur- und Völkerkunde. Herausgegeben von J. W. v. Archenholtz. Für das Jahr 1789. No. X. Leipzig Okt. 1789. Bd. II. S. 362—381.* [2971]
— Mein Leben. *Leipzig: Georg Joachim Göschen 1813. 285 S.* [2971 a]
[—] Mein Leben, von Johann Gottfried Seume. *Edited with an introduction and notes by* J. Henry Senger. *Boston, Mass.: Guin & Co.; The Athenaeum Press 1899. pp. VII. 136.* [2971 b]
Czernecki, J.: J. G. Seume. Jego zycie dziela i zaslugi. *Lwów 1889. [Enthält den Uriasbrief.]* [2971 c]
Eisentraut, G.: Johann Gottfried Seume's Rekrutenzeit 1781—1783. *In: Mitteilungen an die Mitglieder des Vereins für hessische Geschichte und Landeskunde. Jg. 1909—1910. Kassel 1910. S. 66—71. Vollständig abgedruckt in: Hessenland. Zeitschrift für hessische Geschichte und Literatur. Jg. XXIV. Kassel 1910. S. 57—59; 78—80; 89—91; 107—109; 122—124.* [2971 d]

Frederking, Hugo: An meine altpreußischen Landsleute und Freunde! Der Wahrheit die Ehre! Ein offener Brief zu den verleumderischen Behauptungen des Dichters J. G. Seume über den hessischen Landgrafen Friedrich II. *Bromberg: A. Dittmann 1889. 12 S.* [2971 e]
Planer, Oskar und Reißmann, Camillo: Johann Gottfried Seume. Geschichte seines Lebens und seiner Schriften. *Leipzig: G. J. Göschen 1898. VI (1) 724 S., ill.* [2971 f]
Pflug, Ferd.: „Seume unter den hessischen Werbern." *In: Geschichtsbilder. Erzählungen und Skizzen von Ferdinand Pflug. 2. Aufl. Glogau (um 1888) Bd. I. Glogau: Carl Flemming. S. 192—204, ill.* [2971 g]
Schoof, Wilhelm: Seumes Beziehungen zu Hessen. Eine literatur-historische Skizze. *In: Hessenland. Zeitschrift für hessische Geschichte und Literatur. Jg. XIII. Kassel 1899. S. 54—55.* [2971 h]
Ein Denkmal für eine Geschichtslüge. *[Eine Stellungnahme des Vorstandes des Vereins für hessische Geschichte und Landeskunde" zu Seumes Äußerungen über den Soldatenhandel.] In: Mitteilungen an die Mitglieder des Vereins für hessische Geschichte und Landeskunde. Jg. 1906/07. Kassel 1907. S. 129—138.* [2971 i]

Anhalt

[Sintenis, Friedrich Wilhelm]: Sintenis' Chronik der Stadt Zerbst 1758—1817. *Mitgeteilt von* Reinhold Specht. *In: Zerbster Jahrbuch. Jg. XV. Zerbst 1930.* S. 92ff. *[über den amerikanischen Subsidienvertrag und den Feldzug des Zerbster Regiments S. 115ff.].* [2972]

Ansbach-Bayreuth

Döhla, Johann Konrad]: Amerikanische Feldzüge, 1777—1783; Tagebuch von Johann Konrad Döhla. *Herausgegeben mit Anmerkungen versehen von* H. A. **Rattermann.** *In: Deutsch-Amerikanisches Magazin. Vierteljahrsschrift für Geschichte, Literatur, Wissenschaft, Kunst, Schule und Volksleben der Deutschen in Amerika. . . herausgegeben von H. A. Rattermann. Bd. I. Cincinnati, O. 1887. S. 57—86; 239—269; 373—402; 546—567.* [2973]

[Döhla, Johann Konrad]: Tagebuch eines Bayreuther Soldaten des Johann Conrad Döhla aus dem Nordamerikanischen Freiheitskrieg von 1777—1783. *Mit einem Vorwort von W. Frhr. v. Waldenfels. Bayreuth: Lorenz Ellwanger vorm. Th. Burger 1913. 411 S., ill., Karte.* = Sonderabdruck aus dem „Archiv für Geschichte und Altertumskunde von Oberfranken" 1912 und 1913. (Band XXV, Heft 2.) [2973 a]

[Döhla, Johann Konrad]: Amerikanische Feldzüge 1777—1783. Tagebuch von Johann Conrad Döhla. *In: Deutsch-Amerikanische Geschichtsblätter. Jahrbuch der Deutsch-Amerikanischen Historischen Gesellschaft von Illinois. Jg. 1917. Bd. XVII Chicago, Ill. 1917. S. 9—358.* [2973b

— Extracts from Döhla's diary, 1777—1783. *Paper. In: The Pennsylvania-German Society. Proceedings and Addresses at Philadelphia, Pa., Oct. 17, 1913. Vol. XXIV. Lancaster, Pa. 1916. pp. 29—33.* [2973c

[Popp, Stephan]: Popp's journal 1777—1783 *(Abstracts from a manuscript in the city library at Bayreuth, Germany, with the title:,,History of the North American War, especially of the part taken in it by the two regiments from Bayreuth and Anspach, described by one who served in the Bayreuth Regiment, named Stephen Popp, from 1777—1783. I was twenty-two years of age when we marched to America.")* Translated by **Joseph G. Rosengarten**. *In: The Pennsylvania Magazine of History and Biography. Vol. XXVI. Philadelphia, Pa. 1902. pp. 25—41; 245—254, maps.* [2973d

Schöepf, Johann David: *[Siehe Nr. (see nos.) 3354, 3355.]*
Meusel, J. G.: Schöpf, Johann David. *In: Lexikon der vom Jahr 1750—1800 verstorbenen Teutschen Schriftsteller. Bd. XII. Leipzig 1812. S. 364—371. [Bibliographie.]* [2973e
Ratzel, Friedrich: Schöpf, Johann David S., Naturforscher und Reisebeschreiber. *In: Allgemeine Deutsche Biographie. Bd. XXXII. Leipzig 1891. S. 350—352.* [2973f
Peters, Hermann: Johann David Schöpf. *Ein deutscher Naturforscher des vorigen Jahrhunderts in Nordamerika. In: Pharmaceutische Rundschau. Milwaukee, Wisc. 1895, July.* [2973g
Morrison, Alfred J.: Doctor Johann David Schoepf. *In: German American Annals. New series. Vol. VIII. Philadelphia, Pa. 1910. pp. 255—264.* [2973h
Genzmer, George Harvey: Schöpf, Johann David (1752—1800), physician, scientist, traveler. *In: Dictionary of American biography. Under the auspices of the American Council of Learned Societies. Vol. XVI. Edited by Dumas Malone. London-New York 1935. pp. 457—458. [Bibliography.]* [2974

Braunschweig

Zimmermann, Paul: Beiträge zum Verständnis des zwischen Braunschweig und England am 9. Jan. 1776 geschlossenen Subsidienvertrages. *In: Jahrbuch des Geschichtsvereins für das Herzogtum Braunschweig. Jg. XIII. Wolfenbüttel 1914. S. 160—176.* [2974a
Weidmann, Paul: Deutsches Archivmaterial zur Nordamerikanischen Geschichte. *In: Hamburg-Amerika-Post Bd. II. Hamburg 1930. S. 76—83. [Betrifft Braunschweiger Hilfstruppen — u. a. Abdruck des Diensteides zu Herzog Georg von England.]* [2974b
Verzeichniß der Offiziere der Braunschweig'schen Hülfstruppen, welche nach dem Frieden von Versailles 1783 in Amerika blieben oder wieder dahin zurückgekehrt sind. *(Nach in der M. v. Eelking's ,,Leben und Wirken des herzogl. Braunschw. General-Lieutnants Friedrich Adolph Riedesel", Bd. III. S. 391 ff., aufgeführten Namensliste aller braunschweig'schen Offiziere, die in Amerika*

dienten.) *In: Der Deutsche Pionier. Jg. XV. Cincinnati, O. 1883—1884. S. 285—287.* [2974c
Schrader W.: Jean Baptiste Feronce von Rothenkreutz. *In: Braunschweigische Heimat. Zeitschrift des Braunschweiger Landesvereins für Heimatschutz. Jg. XXII. Braunschweig 1931. S. 104—109, ill.* [2974d
August Ludwig Schlözers Briefwechsel meist historischen und politischen Inhalts. *Theil 1—10, Heft 1—60. (Nebst Registern über das ganze Werk.) Göttingen: Verlag der Vandenhoekschen Buchhandlung [1776] 1777—1782. [Vgl. Nr. 2945a]* [2974e
Stone, W. L.: Letters of Brunswick and Hessian officers during the American Revolution. *Translated by* **William L. Stone**. *(Assisted by* **August Hund**) *Albany, N. Y.: Joel Munsell's Sons 1891. [See no. 2945b]* [2974f
Pettengill: Letters from America 1776—1779. Being letters of Brunswick,

Hessian and Waldeck officers with the British armies during the Revolution. *Translated by* **Ray W. Pettengill.** *Boston, Mass. and New York, N. Y.: Houghton Mafflin Co.; The Riverside Press Cambridge 1924.*
[See no. 2945c]   [2974g
Droysen, Hans: Die Braunschweigischen Truppen im Nordamerikanischen Unabhängigkeitskriege. Aus den Briefen der Herzogin Philippine Charlotte von Braunschweig. *Mitgeteilt von H. Droysen. In: Jahrbuch des Geschichts-Vereins für das Herzogtum Braunschweig. Jg. XIII. Wolfenbüttel 1914. S. 145—159.*   [2974h
[Du Roy]: Vertrauliche Briefe aus Kanada und Neu-England vom J. 1777 und 1778. *Aus Herrn Prof. Schlözers Briefwechsel, Heft XXIII und XXIV. [= Nr. 2945a]. Göttingen: Verlag der Witwe Vandenhoek 1779. 84 S.*   [2974i
[—] Journal of Du Roi the Elder, lieutnant and adjutant, in the service of the Duke of Brunswick, 1776—1777. *[See: Schlözer's Vertrauliche Briefe aus Kanada und Neuengland vom Jahre 1777 und 1778 aus dem Briefwechsel, Heft XXIII und XXIV [no. 2945a].] Translated from the original German manuscript in the Library of Congress, Washington, D. C. by* **Charlotte S. J. Epping.** *In: German American Annals. New series, vol. VIII. Philadelphia, Pa. 1910. pp. 40—64; 77—128; 131—244. Also separate print: New York, N. Y.: D. Appleton & Co. 1911. pp. (1), 189, ill. = Americana Germanica. Monographs devoted to the comparative study of the literary, linguistic and other cultural relations of Germany and America. No. 15*   [2974k
Melsheimer, F. V.: Tagebuch von der Reise der Braunschweigischen Auxiliar Truppen von Wolfenbüttel nach Quebec, *entworfen von . . . Feldprediger bei dem Hochfürstl. Braunschweigischen Dragoner Regiment. Frankfurt und Leipzig 1776. S. 3—40; Erste Fortsetzung. Frankfurt und Leizpig 1776. S. 3—32.*   [2974l
[—] Tagebuch der Seereise von Stade nach Quebec in Amerika durch die zweyte Division Herzoglicher Braunschweigischer Hülfsvölker. *Von einem Officier unter des Herrn Obersten Specht Regimente. Frankfurth und Leipzig 1776. 48 S.*   [2974m

Prowell, George R.: Frederick Valentine Melsheimer, a pioneer entomologist, a noted clergyman and author. *Or paper read before the Historical Society of York County, April 8, 1897. In: Proceedings and Collections of the Historical Society of York County. Vol. I, no. 2. York, Pa. 1903. pp. 17—26.*   [2974n
— Frederick Valentine Melsheimer. *In: The Pennsylvania-German. Vol. IX. Cleona, Pa. 1908. pp. 213—217.*   [2974o
Genzmer, George Harvey: Melsheimer, Friederich Valentin (1749—1814) Lutheran clergyman, entomologist. *In: Dictionary of American biography. Under the auspices of the American Council of Learned Societies. Vol. XII. Edited by Dumas Malone. London-New York 1933. pp. 518—519.*   [2974p
[Papet, von . . .]: Rückblick auf die Jahre 1776 bis 1783, in denen ein Braunschweigisches Truppenkorps in Amerika diente. *[Auszug aus einem Tagebuch, das von dem 1776 mit ausmarschirten Lieutenant v. Papet geführt ist.] In: Braunschweigisches Magazin. Bd. XXXVIII. Braunschweig: Zu finden in Fürstl. Intelligenz-Comtoir 1825. 21stes Stück. Sp.. 329—360; 22tes Stück. Sp. 361—370.*   [2974q
[—] The Brunswick contingent in America 1776—1783. *Translation from: Braunschweigisches Magazin of May 21, 1825. In: The Pennsylvania Magazine of History and Biography. Vol. XV. Philadelphia, Pa. 1891. pp. 218—224.* [2974r
Remer, Julius August: Amerikanisches Archiv, *herausgegeben von . . . 3 Bde. Braunschweig: Verlag der Fürstl. Waisenhaus-Buchhandlung 1777/78. (12), 267 S., (2); (6), 294 S.; (14), 334 S.*   [2974s
Eelking, Max von: Leben und Wirken des Herzoglich Braunschweig'schen General-Lieutenants Friedrich Adolph Riedesel, Freiherrn zu Eisenach. *Nebst vielen Original-Correspondenzen und historischen Aktenstücken aus dem siebenjährigen Kriege, dem nordamerikanischen Freiheits-Kampfe und dem französischen Revolutions-Kriege. 3 Bde. Leipzig: Verlag von Otto Wigand 1856. XVI, 288 S., ill.; X, 450 S., Karte; IV, 400 S.*
[Vgl. Nr. 2974y]   [2974t
[Riedesel, Frederike Charlotte Louise (von Massow), Freifrau von]: Auszüge aus den Briefen und Papieren des Generals

Freyherrn von Riedesel und Seiner Gemalinn, geborenen von Massow. Ihre beyderseitige Reise nach America und ihren dortigen Aufenthalt betreffend. *Zusammengetragen und geordnet von ihrem Schwiegersohne* Heinrich dem XLIV. **Grafen Reuß.** *[Berlin]: Gedruckt als Manuscript für die Familie. [1800] 386 S.* [2974 u

[Riedesel, Frederike Charlotte Louise (von Massow), Freifrau von]: Die Berufs-Reise nach America. Briefe der Generalin von Riedesel auf dieser Reise und während ihres sechsjährigen Aufenthalts in America zur Zeit des dortigen Krieges in den Jahren 1776 bis 1783 nach Deutschland geschrieben. *Berlin: Haude und Spencer 1800. X, 352 S., zweite Auflage. Berlin: Haude und Spencer 1801. X, 352 S.* [2974 v

[—] Reize van noodzaaklijkheid en pligt na America; in eene reeks van oorspronglijke en echte Brieven door de echtgenoote van den Generaal Riedesel. *Naar het Hoogduitsch. Haarlem: A. Loosjes 1802. pp. VIII, 220.* [2974 w

[—] Letters and journals relating to the War of the American Revolution, and the capture of German troops at Saratoga. *By Mrs. General Riedesel. Translated from the original German by* **William L. Stone.** *Albany, N. Y.: Joel Munsell 1867. pp. 235, ill.* [2974 x

[Riedesel, Friedrich Adolph]: Memoirs and letters and journals, of Major General Riedesel during his residence in America. *Translated from the original German of* **Max von Eelking** *by* **William L. Stone.** *2 vols. Albany, N. Y.: J. Munsell 1868. pp. (1), VIII, 306, ill.; 248, ill.* *[Translation of vol. II and part of vol. III of the author: ,,Leben und Wirken des herzoglich braunschweigischen Generallieutnants Friedrich Adolph Riedesel. 1856. [= no. 2974.]* [2974 y

[Riedesel, Friedrich Adolph - Riedesel, Frederike Charlotte Louise (von Massow), Freifrau von]: Briefe und Berichte des Generals und der Generalin von Riedesel

während des nordamerikanischen Kriegs in den Jahren 1776—1783 geschrieben. *Freiburg i. B. und Tübingen: Akademische Verlagsbuchhdlg. von J. C. B. Mohr 1881. 305 S.* [2974 z

McLean, Mrs. Donald: The Baroness De Riedesel. *In: Proceedings of the New York State Historical Association. Fourth annual meeting . . . Vol. III. 1903. pp. 39—44.* [2975

Parker, Amelia Campbell: Baroness Riedesel and other women in Burgoyne's army. Heroines on the wrong side. *In: The Quarterly Journal of the New York State Historical Association. Vol. IX, no. 2. Geneva, N. Y. 1928. pp. 109—118.* [2975 a

Sinnickson, Lina: Fredericka Baroness Riedesel. *In: The Pennsylvania Magazine of History and Biography. Vol. XXX. Philadelphia, Pa. 1905. pp. 385—408, ill.* [2975 b

Schüler v. Senden, E.: Denkwürdigkeiten aus den hinterlassenen Papieren E. Schüler's von Senden, Königlich Preußischen Generals der Infanterie a. D. . . . *In: Zeitschrift für Kunst, Wissenschaft und Geschichte des Krieges. Heft 8 und 9. Berlin, Posen und Bromberg 1839. Abschnitt I.: ,,Der Feldzug in Amerika." In: Heft 8. S. 137—189; Abschnitt II: ,,Die Gefangennahme und Rückkehr nach Europa! In: Heft 9. S. 257—286.* [2975 c
Auszug einiger Briefe eines Braunschweigischen Officiers aus Amerika an einen Freund in Deutschland. *[Erster Brief: ,,Am Bord Jupiter den 19. August 1781."] In: Journal von und für Deutschland. Herausgegeben von Siegmund Freyherrn von Bibra. Jg. VI. Eilftes Stück 1789. S. 445—450.* [2975 d
Einige Briefe aus dem amerikanischen Kriege *(1) [= Nr. 2950 b];* (II) Brief eines braunschweigischen Offiziers aus Canada an einen Freund in Braunschweig. *In: Preußisches Militair-Wochenblatt. Jg. XVIII. Berlin 1833. No. 865. S. 4862—4864.* [2975 e

Hanau

Huffnagel, J. P.: Brief eines Hintersteinauers nach Amerika 1781 *[an den hanauischen Jäger Joh. Wilh. Huffnagel]. In: Unsere Heimat. Mitteilungen des*

Heimatbundes. Verein für Heimatschutz und Heimatpflege im Kreise Schlüchtern. Jg. XIX. Schlüchtern 1927. S. 138. [2975 f

274	Die deutschen Söldnertruppen

Pausch, George: Journal during Burgoyne's compaign. *Translated and annoted by* **William L. Stone.** *Albany, N. Y. . . . . 1886. pp. 185. = No. 14 of Munsell's Historical series, Albany 1887.* [2975g

Strecker, R.: H.-Hanauer Truppen a. d. Wetterau im amerikanischen Freiheitskriege. *In: Friedberger Geschichtsblätter. Jg. I. Friedberg i. Hessen 1919. S. 120 —127.* [2975h

Heiler, Carl: Von Hanau nach Quebec. *[Auszug aus dem „Journal vom 15. März 1776 an, da das hessen-hanauische Regiment nach Amerika marschiert ist".] In: Volk und Scholle. Heimatblätter für beide Hessen, Nassau u. Frankfurt a. M. Jg. IX. Darmstadt 1931. S. 292—295.* [2975i

Woringer, August: Beiträge zur Geschichte des Hanauer Militärs. *In: Hanauer Magazin. Monatsblätter für Heimatkunde. Herausgegeben von der Waisenhaus-Buchdruckerei (Hanauer Anzeiger) und dem Hanauer Geschichtsverein. Jg. IX. Hanau 1929. S. 65—72; 77—80; 92—93.* [2975k

— Die Zollentrichtung der hanauischen Truppen 1776. *In: Hanauer Magazin. Monatsblätter für Heimatkunde. Her-*

ausgegeben von der Waisenhaus-Buchdruckerei (Hanauer Anzeiger) und dem Hanauer Geschichtsverein. Jg. VII. Hanau 1928. S. 25—31. [2975l

[Vaupel, . . .]: Ein Brief des Feldwebels Vaupel aus der amerikanischen Gefangenschaft von 1782 *nach dem im Archiv des Hanauer Geschichtsvereins befindlichen Orginal veröffentlicht von Dr. Heiler. In: Hanauer Magazin. Monatsblätter für Heimatkunde. Herausgegeben von der Waisenhaus-Buchdruckerei (Hanauer Anzeiger) und dem Hanauer Geschichtsverein. Jg. X. Hanau 1931. S. 85—88.* [2975m

Losch, Philipp: Wilhelm von Hessen-Hanau und der Subsidienvertrag von 1776. *In: Hanauer Magazin. Monatsblätter für Heimathunde. Herausgegeben von der Waisenhaus-Buchdruckerei (Hanauer Anzeiger) und dem Hanauer Geschichtsverein. Jg. XI. Hanau 1932. S. 31—32.* [2975n

Frey, J.: Gelnhäuser als Angehörige von hessen-hanauischen Truppenteilen in der Zeit von 1777—1783. *In: Nachrichten der Gesellschaft für Familienkunde in Kurhessen und Waldeck. Jg. VI. Kassel 1931. S. 45—48.* [2975o

Waldeck

Curtze, L.: Geschichte und Beschreibung des Fürstenthums Waldeck. *Arolsen: Speyer'sche Buchhandlung 1850 XIII, (2), 664 S. [Der amerikanische Feldzug S. 564ff.]* [2976

Woringer, A.: Ein waldeckischer Indianerhäuptling. *[J. K. Brandenstein aus Königshagen, von seinen Landsleuten 1778 auf Florida entdeckt.] In: Nachrichten der Gesellschaft für Familienkunde in Kurhessen und Waldeck. Jg. VII. Kassel 1932. S. 125.* [2976a

[Waldeck, Philipp]: Waldeck's diary of the Revolution 1776—1780. *Edited by* **M.**

D. Learned *and* **Rudolph Cronau.** *In: German American Annals. New series, vol. I. Philadelphia, Pa. 1903. pp. 97—116; 178—186; 225—232; 275—283; 357—364; 420—428; 577—592; 734—745; Vol. II. 1904. pp. 59—64; 192—198; 252—257; 309—318; 367—378; 435—445. Also separate print: Philadelphia, Pa.: Americana Germanica Press 1907. pp. X, 146, ill. = Americana Germanica. Monographs devoted to the comperative study of the literary, linguistic and other cultural relations of Germany and America. Edited by M. D. Learned. No. 6.* [2976b

Zweibrücken

Cronau, Rudolf: „Die deutschen Truppen-
abteilungen im französischen Hilfsheer."
*In: Drei Jahrhunderte deutschen Lebens
in Amerika. Eine Geschichte der Deutschen in den Vereinigten Staaten. Berlin
1909 [= Nr. 34]. S. 242—245; 2. Aufl.
1924. S. 246—248.*   [2977

Faust, A. B.: „The Germans in the French
services." *In: The German element in the
United States. By A. B. Faust. Second
edition. New York 1927 [= no. 42].
Vol. I. S. 344—349.*   [2977a

Heigel, Karl Theodor v.: Die Beteiligung
des Hauses Zweibrücken am nordamerikanischen Befreiungskrieg. *München 1912. 20 S.
= Sitzungsberichte der Königlich Bay-
erischen Akademie der Wissenschaften.
Philosophisch-philologische und historische Klasse. Jg. 1912, 6. Abhdlg.* [2977b

[Zweibrücken, Graf Wilhelm von]: My Cam-
paigns in America. *A journal kept by
Count William de Deux-Ponts 1780—1781.
Translated from the French Manuskript.
With an introduction and notes by* **Sa-
muel Abbot Green.** *Boston, Mass.:
J. K. Wiggin and Wnr. Parsons Lunt
1868. pp. XVI (1) 176.*   [2977c

Vereinigungen

Societies

Kunze, Johann Christoph: Von den Absichten und dem bisherigen Fortgang der privilegirten Deutschen Gesellschaft zu Philadelphia in Pennsylvanien. *In einer vor der Gesellschaft gehaltenen Rede. Philadelphia, Pa.: Melchior Steiner 1782. 62 S.* [2978

Seidensticker, Oswald: Geschichte der Deutschen Gesellschaft von Pennsylvanien. Von der Zeit der Gründung bis zum Jahre 1876. Festgabe zum Jubeljahre der Republik. *Verfaßt auf Veranlassung der Deutschen Gesellschaft. Philadelphia, Pa.: Verlag von Jg. Kohler 1876. 336 S.* [2979

— and **Heinrici, Max:** Geschichte der Deutschen Gesellschaft von Pennsylvanien 1764—1917. *Philadelphia, Pa.: Graf & Breuninger 1917. (4), 633 S. Teil I.* Von der Gründung im Jahre 1764 bis zum Jubeljahre der Republik 1876. *By O. Seidensticker. (Neudruck) 7— 250 S.; Teil II.* Von 1876—1917. *By M. Heinrici. 251—633 S.* [2980

Hundertjährige Feier der Incorporation der Deutschen Gesellschaft von Pennsylvanien, gehalten am 11. Oct. 1881. *Philadelphia, Pa.: Globe Printing House 1882. 36 S.* [2981

Centennialfeier der Deutschen Gesellschaft von Pennsylvanien. *(Aus verschiedenen Wechselblättern zusammengestellt.) In: Der Deutsche Pionier. Jg. XIII.* Cincinnati, O. 1881—1882. 369—372 S. [2982

[Hennighausen, Louis P.]: Geschichte der Deutschen Gesellschaft von Maryland. *In: Deutsch-Amerikanische Geschichtsblätter. Jg. IX, Nr. 4. Chicago, Ill. 1909. S. 131—142; Jg. X. Nr. 1. S. 2—18.* [2983

Scholtz, Karl A. M.: German pilgrim fathers. *In: Society for the History of the Germans in Maryland dedicates this publication to the German Society of Maryland in commemoration of the celebration of this 150th anniversary. Baltimore, Md.: Schneidereith & Sons 1933, [pp. 24]. pp. 5—16.* [2984

U.[nger, P.]: Die Deutsche Gesellschaft von Maryland. *Eine Skizze. In: Der Deutsche Pionier. Jg. I.* Cincinnati, O. 1869 —1870. S. 370—374. [2985

Regeln für die Deutsche Gesellschaft in dem Staate von Neu York. Germantown, [Pa.]: Gedruckt bei Michael Billmeyer 1787. *Neudruck in: Heinrich Wansey's Tagebuch einer Reise durch die vereinigten Staaten von Nord-Amerika im Sommer des Jahres 1794. Aus dem Englischen. Mit Anmerkungen des Übersetzers, und einer Vorrede über Auswanderung und Länderkauf in Nord-Amerika von C. A. Böttinger. Berlin 1797 [= Nr. 3401]. Anhang. S. 221—232.* [2986

Niemeier, O.: Geschichte der Deutschen Gesellschaft von New York. Nach den Quellen bearbeitet von ... *In: Der Deutsche Pionier. Jg. II.* Cincinnati, O. 1870— 1871. S. 75—79; 212—216. [2987

Eickhoff, Anton: Die Deutsche Gesellschaft der Stadt New York. = Anhang zu: In der neuen Heimath. Geschichtliche Mittheilungen über die deutschen Einwanderer in allen Theilen der Union. *Herausgegeben von A. Eickhoff. New York, N. Y.: E. Steiger & Co. 1884. Anhang. 164 S.* [2988

Cronau, Rudolf: Denkschrift zum 150. Jahrestag der Deutschen Gesellschaft der Stadt New York 1784—1934. *New York, N. Y.: German Society of the City of New York. (Manufactured by Chas. H. Bohn & Co., Inc.) 1934. 97 S., ill. Mit englischer Übersetzung:* Historical sketch. German Society of the City of New York. 150th anniversary 1784 —1934. *pp. [55—]97.* [2988a

Der Freibrief, Beschlüsse und Nebengesetze der Deutschen Vereinigten Unterstützungs-Gesellschaft, zu Germantaun, Incorporirt den 6ten December 1813. — *The charter, resolutions and by-laws of the German United Assistance Society of Germantown. Incorporated, December 6, 1813. Skippacksville, Montgomery Co.: Charles A. Pulte 1836. 29 S.; pp. 29.* [2989

Worner, William Frederic: The German Society of Lancaster *for relief of distressed immigrants (1818—1833). In: Papers and Addresses of the Lancaster County Historical Society. Vol. XXXV. Lancaster, Pa. 1931. pp. 1—8.* [2990

Constitution und Nebengesetze der Chambersburger Deutschen Gesellschaft. Angenommen am 5ten September 1835. *Dr. J. Pulte. Chambersburg, Pa.: Victor Scriba 1835. 12 S.* [2991

Rattermann, H. A.: Ludwig Gall. *In: Der Deutsche Pionier. Jg. XIII. Cincinnati, O. 1881—1882. S. 42—56.*

Der Aufsatz enthält: Verfassung, Beamten- und Mitgliederliste der Gründung der deutschen Gesellschaft von Harrisburg, gegründet Aug., 1820. *S. 53—54.* [2992

— Ludwig Lambert Gall. *In: Notes and Queries. Edited by W. H. Egle. Second series. Harrisburg, Pa. 1883. pp. 32—36; 38—42.*

The article includes an English translation of the ,,Constitution" of the German Society of Harrisburg, Pa. (founded 7th Aug. 1820). pp. 39—42.

Reprint in: First and second series, vol. II. Harrisburg, Pa. 1895. pp. 107—113; 116—117, resp. 118—121. [2993

Der deutsche Pressverein von Pennsylvanien und das deutsche Element Amerika's. *In: Der Deutsche Pionier. Jg. VII. Cincinnati, O. 1875—1876. S. 418—419.* [2994

R.: Der deutsche Pressverein von Pennsylvanien. *In: Der Deutsche Pionier. Jg. VII. Cincinnati, O. 1875—1876. S. 463—466.* [2995

A German historical society. *(Suggested in): Notes and Queries. Edited by W. H. Egle. Third series, vol. II. 1887—1890. Harrisburg, Pa. 1891. p. 520.* [2996

,,The Pennsylvania German Society." *In: Notes and Queries. Edited by W. H. Egle. Third series, vol. II. 1887—1890. Harrisburg, Pa. 1891. pp. 540—541.* [2997

Diffenderffer, Frank R.: A Pennsylvania German society. *From the Lancaster*

,,New Era". *Reprint in: Notes and Queries. Edited by W. H. Egle. Third series, vol. II. 1887—1890. Harrisburg, Pa. 1891. pp. 524—525. Reprint in: Third series, vol. III. Harrisburg, Pa. 1896. pp. 547—548.* [2998

Richards, H. M. M.: The Pennsylvania-German Society. Its origin, its mission, its growth. *In: The Pennsylvania-German. Vol. VII. Lebanon, Pa. 1906. pp. 112—119, ill.* [2999

Buckenham, John Edgar Burnett: The Pennsylvania-German Society. *Constitutions and by-laws, founders, annual meetings, officers and members during the first twenty-five years of its existence. Narrative and critical history and church records published in the first twenty-five volumes of its proceedings. Compiled and edited by . . . and published by the Society, October 15, 1915. Lancaster, Pa. 1917. In: The Pennsylvania-German Society. Proceedings and Addresses . . . 1914. Vol. XXV. Lancaster, Pa. 1917. Separate pagination. pp. 49.*

. . . Published by the Society, November 2, 1916. In: . . . 1916. Vol. XXVII. Lancaster, Pa. 1920. Separate pagination. pp. 52. [3000

Strassburger, Ralph Beaver: Why you should be a member — How you can become a member of the Pennsylvania German Society. *A summary of the Society's proud history and its purposes. What the Pennsylvania Germans have done for America since 1683. A great historical institution. Norristown, Pa.: Norristown Press 1929. pp. 12.* [3001

Charter of the Pennsylvania-German Society. *Proceedings and Addresses . . . 1930. Vol. XLI. Norristown, Pa.: Norristown Herald. 1933. pp. 13—23.* [3001a

The Krefeld Society. *In: The Pennsylvania Magazine of History and Biography. Vol. XXXVIII. Philadelphia, Pa. 1914. p. 251.* [3002

The Society of the descendants of the Schwenkfeldian exiles. *Organized, Philadelphia, Febr. 8, 1921.*

[See nos. 1606—1627] [3003

Jacobson, H. A. History of the Moravian Historical Society, 1857—1907. *Read at annual vesper, Sept. 26, 1907. In: Transactions of the Moravian Historical Society. Vol. VIII. 1906—1908. Nazareth, Pa. 1909. pp. 29—36.* [3004

Anhang

Appendix

Bittinger, John W.: Address of welcome. ... *at York, Oct. 11, 1893. In: Vol. IV. 1894. pp. 8—11.* [3031

Zimmerman, Thomas. C.: Response to J. W. Bittinger' address. ... *at York, Oct. 11. 1893. In: Vol. IV. 1894. pp. 11—18.* [3032

Fisher, Henry L.: Annual address *of the president.* ... *at York, Oct. 11, 1893. In: Vol. IV. 1894. pp. 19—40.* [3033

Hark, J. Max: „Deutsch Amerika." *Toast at the annual banquet.* ... *at York, Oct. 11, 1893. In: Vol. IV. 1894. pp. 101—105.* [3034

Fisher, Henry L.: „The Pennsylvania-Germans and the Scotch-Irish." *Toast at the annual banquet.* ... *at York, Oct. 11, 1893. In: Vol. IV. 1894. pp. 105—106.* [3035

Zimmerman, Thomas C.: „Newspapers, the great moving force of the times." *Toast at the annual banquet.* ... *at York, Oct. 11, 1893. In: Vol. IV. 1894. pp. 107—114.* [3036

Trimmer, D. K.: „The Colonial." *Toast at the annual banquet.* ... *at York, Oct. 11, 1893. In: Vol. IV. 1894. pp. 114—119.* [3037

Ermentrout, James H.: Address of welcome. ... *at Reading, Oct. 3, 1894. In: Vol. V. 1895. pp. 6—10.* [3038

Schmauk, Theodore Emanuel: Response to J. N. Ermentrout's address. ... *at Reading, Oct. 3, 1894. In: Vol. V. 1895. pp. 11—13.* [3039

Heckman, George C.: „German colonization in America." *Annual address of the president.* ... *at Reading, Oct. 3, 1894. In: Vol. V. 1895. pp. 13—29.* [3040

Mosser, Henry: „The Schuylkill Valley." *Toast at the annual banquet.* ... *at Reading, Oct. 3, 1894. In: Vol. V. 1895. pp. 86—91.* [3041

Reinoehl, Adam C.: „Civil liberty and self-government." *Toast at the annual banquet.* ... *at Reading, Oct. 3, 1894. In: Vol. V. 1895. pp. 92—93.* [3042

Pennypacker, Samuel W.: „The Pennsylvania-German antiquarian." *Toast at the annual banquet.* ... *at Reading, Oct. 3, 1894. In: Vol. V. 1895. pp. 94—100.* [3043

Schaeffer, N. C.: „The progress of education." *Toast at the annual banquet.* ... *at Reading, Oct. 3, 1894. In: Vol. V. 1895. pp. 101—107, ill.* [3044

Montgomery, Morton L.: „The heritage of Conrad Weiser." *Toast at the annual banquet.* ... *at Reading, Oct. 3, 1894. In: Vol. V. 1895. pp. 108—113, ill.* [3045

Buehrle, Robert K.: „The influence of our race in literature." *Toast at the annual banquet.* ... *at Reading, Oct. 3, 1894. In: Vol. V. 1895. pp. 114—116.* [3046

Houck, Henry: „Our mothers and housewives." *Toast at the annual banquet.* ... *at Reading, Oct. 3, 1894. In: Vol. V. 1895. pp. 117—120.* [3047

Levering, J. Mortimer: Address of welcome. ... *at Bethlehem, Oct. 16, 1895. In: Vol. VI. Reading, Pa. 1896. pp. 6—7.* [3048

Pennypacker, Samuel W.: Extracts of the annual address *of the president.* ... *at Bethlehem, Oct. 16, 1895. In: Vol. VI. 1896. pp. 8—14, ill.* [3049

Richard, M. C.: „The Pennsylvania-German in the Lehigh Valley." *Toast at the annual banquet.* ... *at Bethlehem, Oct. 16, 1895. In: Vol. VI. 1896. pp. 76—82.* [3050

Grumbine, Lee L.: „The Pennsylvania-German in journalism and literature." *Toast at the annual banquet.* ... *at Bethlehem, Oct. 16, 1895. In: Vol. VI. 1896. pp. 82—98.* [3051

Kuhns, Oscar: „The Pennsylvania-German in education." *Toast at the annual banquet.* ... *at Bethlehem, Oct. 16, 1895. In: Vol. VI. 1896. pp. 98—103.* [3052

Schweinitz, Paul de: „The Pennsylvania-German in the church." *Toast at the annual banquet.* ... *at Bethlehem, Oct. 16, 1895. In: Vol. VI. 1896. pp. 103—111.* [3053

Schantz, F. J. F.: „The Pennsylvania-German Society." *Toast at the annual banquet.* ... *at Bethlehem, Oct. 16, 1895. In: Vol. VI. 1896. pp. 111—120.* [3054

Stille, Charles J.: Address of welcome. ... *at Philadelphia, Oct. 25, 1896. In: Vol. VII. 1897. pp. 9—11.* [3055

Pennypacker, Samuel W.: Response to J. Ch. Stille's address of welcome. ... *at Philadelphia, Oct. 25, 1896. In: Vol. VII. 1897. pp. 11—14.* [3056

Diffenderffer, Frank Ried: Annual address *of the president.* ... *at Philadelphia, Oct. 25, 1896. In: Vol. VII. 1897. pp. 14—18.* [3057

Martin, E. K.: Adress of welcome. ... *at Lancaster, Oct. 22, 1897. In: Vol. VIII. 1898. pp. 8—14.* [3058

Richards, Matthias H.: Response to E. K. Martin's address of welcome. ... *at Lancaster, Oct. 22, 1897. In: Vol. VIII. 1898. pp. 14—17.* [3059

Schmauk, Theodore Emanuel: Annual address *of the president.* ... *at Lancaster, Oct. 22, 1897. In: Vol. VIII. 1898. pp. 17—20.* [3060

Ettinger, George T.: Address of welcome. ... *at Allentown, Oct. 14, 1898. In: Vol. IX. 1899. pp. 8—9.* [3061

Schantz, F. J. F.: Response to G. T. Ettinger's address of welcome. ... *at Allentown, Oct. 14, 1898. In: Vol. IX. 1899. pp. 9—17.* [3062

Schaeffer, N. C.: Annual address *of the president.* ... *at Allentown, Oct. 14, 1898. In: Vol. IX. 1899. pp. 18—20.* [3063

Mentzer, J. F.: Address of welcome. ... *at Ephrata, Oct. 20, 1899. In: Vol. X. 1900. pp. 7—11.* [3064

Spangler, Henry T.: Response to J. F. Mentzer's address of welcome. ... *at Ephrata, Oct. 20, 1899. In: Vol. X. 1900. pp. 11—12.* [3065

Hertz, D. Rhine: Remarks by . . . . . . *at Ephrata, Oct. 20, 1899. In: Vol. X. 1900. pp. 13—16.* [3066

Schmauk, Theodore Emanuel: Annual address *of the president. . . . at Ephrata, Oct. 20, 1899. In: Vol. X. 1900. pp. 16—21.* [3067

Field, B. Rush: Address of welcome. . . . *at Easton, Oct. 26, 1900. In: Vol. XI. 1902. pp. 7—8.* [3068

Heckman, George C.: Response to B. R. Field's address of welcome. . . . *at Easton, Oct. 26, 1900. In: Vol. XI. 1902. pp. 8—12.* [3069

Schantz, F. J. F.: Annual address *of the president. . . . at Easton, Oct. 26, 1900. In: Vol. XI. 1902. pp. 13—19.* [3070

Gilbert, D. M.: Address of welcome. . . . *at Harrisburg, Oct. 25, 1901. In: Vol. XII. 1903. pp. 9—11.* [3071

Schantz, F. J. F.: Response to D. M. Gilbert's address of welcome. . . . *at Harrisburg, Oct. 25, 1901. In: Vol. XII. 1903. pp. 11—14.* [3072

Himes, Charles Francis: Annual address *of the president, containing an obituary enlogy of William Henry Egle. . . . at Harrisburg, Oct. 25, 1901. In: Vol. XII. 1903. pp. 15—31.* [3073

Fornance, Joseph: Address of welcome. . . . *at Norristown, Oct. 3, 1902. In: Vol. XIII. 1904. pp. 7—9.* [3074

Fry, Jacob: Response to J. Fornance's address of welcome. . . . *at Norristown, Oct. 3, 1902. In: Vol. XIII. 1904. pp. 9—12.* [3075

Dubbs, Joseph H.: Annual address *of the president. . . . at Norristown, Oct. 3, 1902. In: Vol. XIII. 1904. pp. 12—24.* [3076

Grumbine, Lee L.: Address of welcome. . . . *at Lebanon, Oct. 22, 1903. In: Vol. XIV. 1905. pp. 6—11.* [3077

Hess, Abraham: Greeting from the City of Lebanon. . . . *at Lebanon, Oct. 22, 1903. In: Vol. XIV. 1905. pp. 12—14.* [3078

Roller, John E.: Response. . . . *at Lebanon, Oct. 22, 1903. In: Vol. XIV. 1905. pp. 14—23.* [3079

Morris, Elliston P.: Address of welcome. . . . *at Germantown, Oct. 25, 1904. In: Vol. XV. 1906. pp. 6—9.* [3080

Evans, L. Kryder: Response to E. P. Morris' address of welcome. . . . *at Germantown, Oct. 25, 1904. In: Vol. XV. 1906. pp. 9—12,* [3081

Stahr, John S.: Annual address *of the president. . . . at Germantown, Oct. 25, 1904. In: Vol. XV. 1906. pp. 13—23.* [3082

Endlich, Gustav A.: Address of welcome. . . . *at Reading, Oct. 27, 1905. In: Vol. XVI. 1907. pp. 6—8.* [3083

Lemberger, Joseph L.: Response to G. A. Endlich's address of welcome. . . . *at Reading, Oct. 27, 1905. In: Vol. XVI. 1907. pp. 9—11.* [3084

Beaver, James Addams. Annual address *of the president. . . . at Reading, Oct. 27, 1905. In: Vol. XVI. 1907. pp. 11—19.* [3085

Haas, John A. W.: Address of welcome. . . . *at Allentown, Nov. 2, 1906. In: Vol. XVII. 1908. pp. 8—11.* [3086

Zimmerman, Thomas C.: Response to the addresses of welcome. . . . *at Allentown, Nov. 2, 1906. In: Vol. XVII. 1908. pp. 11—19.* [3087

Endlich, Gustav A.: Annual address *of the president. . . . at Allentown, Nov. 2, 1906. In: Vol. XVII. 1908. pp. 19—33.* [3088

Nead, Benjamin Matthias: Annual address *of the president. . . . at Philadelphia, Dec. 8, 1907. In: Vol. XVIII. 1909. pp. 6—14.* [3089

Stahr, John S.: Address of welcome. . . . *at Lancaster, Pa., Nov. 6, 1908. In: Vol. XIX. 1910. pp. 6—9.* [3090

Lamberton, James M.: Response to J. S. Stahr's address of welcome. . . . *at Lancaster, Pa., Nov. 6, 1908. In: Vol. XIX. 1910. p. 9.* [3091

Wanamaker, John: Annual address *of the president. (Spoken into the Edison phonograph). . . . at Lancaster, Pa., Nov. 6, 1908. In: Vol. XIX. 1910. pp. 10—16.* [3092

Zimmerman, Thomas C.: New President's address. . . . *at Lancaster, Pa., Nov. 6, 1908. In: Vol. XIX. 1910. pp. 18—23.* [3093

— Response to the addresses of welcome. . . . *at Bethlehem, Pa., Oct. 29, 1909. In: Vol. XX. 1911. pp. 6—9.* [3094

— Annual address *of the president. . . . at Bethlehem, Pa., Oct. 29, 1909. In: Vol. XX. 1911. pp. 9—29.* [3095

Roller, John E.: Annual address *of the president. . . . at York, Pa., Oct. 14, 1910. In: Vol. XXI 1912. pp. 6—23.* [3096

Schmauk, Th. E. - Sener, S. M. - Heilman, S. P. and others: Discussion called forth by the paper of Albert G. Rau. ,,The trades among the Pennsylvania-German." . . . *at York, Pa., Oct. 14, 1910. In: Vol. XXI. 1912. pp. 28—30.* [3097

— - Stapleton, A. - Croll, C. A.: Discussion called forth by the paper of Edwin M. Fogel. ,,Some Pennsylvania-German superstitions." . . . *at York, Pa., Oct. 14, 1910. In: Vol. XXI. 1912. pp. 31—33.* [3098

— ,,The twentieth anniversary of our society." Toast. . . . *at York, Pa., Oct. 14, 1910. In: Vol. XXI. 1912. pp. 37—42.* [3099

Hess, Abraham: ,,The meeting twenty years ago in Lancaster." Toast. . . . *at York, Pa., Oct. 14, 1910. In: Vol. XXI. 1912. pp. 42—44.* [3100

Bair, Robert C.: ,,The meeting in York." Toast. . . . *at York, Pa., Oct. 14, 1910. In: Vol. XXI. 1912. pp. 44—47.* [3101

Richards, H. M. M.: ,,The past membership of the society." Toast. . . . *at York, Pa., Oct. 14, 1910. In: Vol. XXI. 1912. pp. 47—50.* [3102

Glessner: ,,The new members." Toast. . . . *at York, Pa., Oct. 14, 1910. In: Vol. XXI. 1912. pp. 50—52.* [3103

Schaeffer, N. C.: „The work of the Society." Toast. . . . at York, Pa., Oct. 14, 1910. In: Vol. XXI. 1912. pp. 52—56. [3104

Evans, L. Kryder: „Pennsylvania German wives, new style and old style." Toast. . . . at York, Pa., Oct. 14, 1910. In: Vol. XXI. 1912. pp. 56—57. [3105

Jacobs, Henry E.: „The future." Toast. . . . at York, Pa., Oct. 14, 1910. In: Vol. XXI. 1912. pp. 57—59. [3106

— Annual address of the president. . . . at Harrisburg, Pa., Oct. 20, 1911. In: Vol. XXII. 1913. pp. 6—14. [3107

Baer, Geo. F.: „London and Philadelphia." Toast. . . . at Harrisburg, Pa., Oct. 20, 1911. In: Vol. XXII. 1913. pp. 18—21. [3108

Fackenthal, B. F.: Address of welcome. . . . at Riegelsville, Pa., Oct. 4, 1912. In: Vol. XXIII. 1915. pp. 7—15, ill. [3109

Richards, H. M. M.: Annual address of the president. „Shaping the destiny of the world." . . . at Riegelsville, Pa., Oct. 4, 1912. In: Vol. XXIII. 1915. pp. 16—32. [3110

Smith, Edgar Fahs: Address of welcome. . . . at Philadelphia, Pa., Oct. 17, 1913. In: Vol. XXIV. 1916. pp. 6—9. [3111

Fackenthal, B. F.: Annual address of the president. . . . at Philadelphia, Pa., Oct. 17, 1913. In: Vol. XXIV. 1916. pp. 9—17. [3112

Sachse, Julius F.: Address of president-elect. . . . at Philadelphia, Pa., Oct. 17, 1913. In: Vol. XXIV. 1916. pp. 40—42. [3113

— Annual address of the president. . . . at Lancaster, Pa., Nov. 13, 1914. In: Vol. XXV. 1917. pp. 15—26. [3114

Yerkes, Harman: Annual address of the president. . . . at Reading, Oct. 15, 1915. In: Vol. XXVI. 1918. pp. 6—15. [3114a

Ettinger, George T.: Annual address of the president. . . . at Norristown, Pa., Nov. 2, 1916. In: Vol. XXVII. 1920. pp. 8—24 [3115

Evans, L. Kryder: Annual address of the president. . . . at Philadelphia, Pa., Oct. 8, 1919. In: Vol. XXX. 1924. pp. 8—12. [3117

Schweinitz, Paul de: Annual address of the president, containing an answer to the question „Which is the first American Foreign Mission Board?" and a list of the first American foreign missionaries. . . . at Ephrata, Oct. 8, 1920. In: Vol. XXXI. 1925. pp. 7—20. [3118

Beck, Walter C.: Address of welcome. . . . at Selinsgrove, Pa., Oct. 10, 1924. In: Vol. XXXV. 1929. pp. 6—7. [3119

Richards, H. M. M.: Response to W. C. Beck's address of welcome. . . . at Selinsgrove, Pa., Oct. 10, 1924. In: Vol. XXXV. 1929. pp. 7—10. [3120

Shimer, Edgar Dubs: Annual address of the president. . . . at Selinsgrove, Pa., Oct. 10, 1924. In: Vol. XXXV. 1929. pp. 11—20. [3121

Wingard, Edgar R.: „Our community." [Selinsgrove, Snyder Co., Pa.] Toast. . . . at Selinsgrove, Pa., Oct. 10, 1924. In: Vol. XXXV. 1929. pp. 30—31. [3122

Aitkens, Charles T.: „Our Pennsylvania German heritage." Toast. . . . at Selinsgrove, Pa., Oct. 10, 1924. In: Vol. XXXV. 1929. pp. 31—35. [3123

Musser, Frank C.: Address of welcome. . . . at Lancaster, Oct. 9, 1925. In: Vol. XXXVI. 1929. p. 6. [3124

Richards, H. M. M.: Response to address of welcome. . . . at Lancaster, Oct. 9, 1925. In: Vol. XXXVI. 1929. pp. 6—9. [3125

Fretz, F. K.: Address of welcome. . . . at Easton, Oct. 12, 1928. In: Vol. XXXIX. 1930. pp. 6—8. [3126

Museen und Ausstellungen

Museums and Exhibitions

Barber, Edwin Atlee: Tulip ware of the Pennsylvania-German potters. *An historical sketch of the art of slip-decoration in the United States. Philadelphia, Pa.: Printed for the Museum Memorial Hall, Fairmont Park 1903. pp. 233, ill.* = *Art Handbook of the Pennsylvania Museum and School of Industrial Art.* [3127

Downs, Joseph: A Pennsylvania-German house. *In: The Pennsylvania Museum Bulletin. Vol. XXII, no. 108. December, 1926. Philadelphia, Pa. 1926. pp. 265 —275, ill.* [3128

— The house of the Miller at Millbach. The architecture, arts, and crafts of the Pennsylvania Germans. *[s. l.]: Published by the Pennsylvania Museum of Art, Philadelphia, Pa. 1929. pp. (31), ill.* [3129

Hensel, W. U.: Jacob Eichholtz, painter. *Some ,,loose leaves" from the ledger of an early Lancaster artist. An address delivered at the opening of an exposition of ,,The evolution of Portraiture in Lancaster County, Pa. under the auspices of the Lancaster Historical Society and the Iris Club, Woolworth Building, Lancaster, Pa., Nov. 22, 1912.* *(Revised Catalog of Eichholtz's Work). pp. 38, ill.* *Reprint in: The Penn Germania. Vol. II. = Old series, vol. XIV. 1913. pp. 81—96; 161—175.* [3130

Lambert: Pennsylvania at the Jamestown exposition, Hampton Roads, Va. 1907. *Philadelphia, Pa.: Published by the Pennsylvania Commission 1908. pp. V, (2), 360, ill.* [3131

Mercer, Henry C.: Tools of the nation maker. A description catalogue of objects in the Museum of the Historical Society of Bucks County, Pa. *Collected and arranged by . . . Doylestown, Pa.: Printed for the Society at the Office of the Bucks County Intelligencer 1897. pp. (2), 5—87. With Pennsylvania-German index. pp. 85—87.* = *Contributions to American History by the Bucks County Historical Society, no. 1.* [3132

Mercer, Henry C.: The decorated stove plates of the Pennsylvania Germans. *Doylestown, Pa.: McGinty's Job Press 1899. pp. 26, ill.* = *Contributed to American History by the Bucks County Historical Society, no. 6.* [3133

— The bible in iron or the pictured stoves and stove plates of the Pennsylvania Germans *with notes on colonial fire-backs in the United States, the ten-plate stove, Franklin's fireplace and the tile stoves of the Moravians in Pennsylvania and North Carolina, together with a list of colonial furnaces in the United States and Canada. Published for the Bucks County Historical Society. Doylestown, Pa.: McGinty 1914. pp. IV, 174, ill.* [3134

— The zithers of the Pennsylvania Germans. *Read January 20, 1923. In: A Collection of Papers read before the Bucks County Historical Society. Vol. V. Easton, Pa. 1926. pp. 482—497, ill.* [3135

Stoudt, John Baer: The liberty bells of Pennsylvania. *Presented to the Pennsylvania-German Society at the annual meeting in the Pennsylvania building at the Sesqui-Centennial on Friday, October 8, 1926. Norristown, Pa.: Norristown Press 1930. In: The Pennsylvania-German Society. Proceedings and Addresses . . . 1926. Vol. XXXVII. Norristown, Pa. 1930. Separate pagination. pp. XVI, 204, (1), ill.* [3136

The Perkiomen Valley museum. *In: The Perkiomen Region. Vol. VI, no. 2. 1928. pp. 54—57.* [3137

Pennsylvanien

Pennsylvania

Geschichte, allgemein

History, general

Pennsylvania, State of: [Colonial records.] *Philadelphia, Pa.: Printed by J. Severns & Co. 1851—53. 16 vols.:*
— Minutes of the Provincial Council of Pennsylvania, from the organization to the termination of the proprietary government. *March 10, 1683—September 27, 1775. Published by the state . . . Edited by* Samuel Hazard. *Philadelphia, Pa.: Printed by J. Severns & Co. 1851—52. Vols. 4—10 have imprint: Harrisburg, Pa.: Printed by T. Fenn & Co. 1851—52. 10 vols.*
= *[Colonial records] vols. 1—10. [Contents see appendix pp. 288—290.]* [3139
— Minutes of the Supreme Executive Council of Pennsylvania, from its organization to the termination of the Revolution. *[March 4, 1777—Dec. 20, 1790.] Published by the state . . . Harrisburg, Pa.: Printed by T. Fenn & Co. 1852—53. 6 vols.*
= *[Colonial records] vols. 11—16.*[3140
— Pennsylvania archives . . . *[First series], vols. 1—12; Second series, vols. 1—19; Third series, vols. 1—30; Fourth series, vols. 1—12; Fifth series, vols. 1—8; Sixth series, vols. 1—15; Seventh series, vols. 1—5. Philadelphia, Pa.: Printed by J. Severns & Co. 1852—56; Harrisburg, Pa. 1874ff., ill., maps and 2 atlases (27 fold maps; 5 fold fac-similes.). [Title varies]: [First series] ,,Pennsylvania archives selected and arranged from original documents in the office of the secretary of the commonwealth, conformably to acts of the General Assembly. Febr. 15, 1851, and March 1, 1852; second to third series (lithographed t—p.): ,,Pennsylvania archives. Second [—third] series. Published second series, vol. 13 ,,reprinted"; Second series, vol. 14 — third series, vol. 30, ,,printed" under direction of . . . [the] secretary of com-*monwealth . . ."; *Fourth [—fifth] series: ,,Pennsylvania archives. Fourth—fifth series . . . edited . . . under the direction of . . . [the] secretary of the commonwealth."* Editors: *[First series]* Samuel Hazard. *— Second series, vols. 1—14,* J. B. Linn *and* W. H. Egle. *— Second series, vols. 15—19, and third series, vols. 1—26,* W. H. Egle. *— Third series, vols. 27—30, and fourth series,* G. E. Reed. *— Fifth series, vols. 1—8,* T. L. Montgomery. *[Contents see Appendix pp. 290—294.* [3141

Pennsylvania, State of: General index to the Colonial records, in 16 volumes, and to the Pennsylvania archives. [First series] in 12 vols., *prepared and arranged by* Samuel Hazard, *under an act of the General Assembly of Pennsylvania. Philadelphia, Pa.: Printed by J. Severns & Co. 1860. pp. VI, 653.* [3142

Amor, William C.: Lives of the governors of Pennsylvania with the incidential history of the state, from 1609 to 1872. *Philadelphia, Pa.: James K. Simon 1872. pp. XIII, 17—528, ill.; second edition. 1609—1873. Norwich, Conn.: T. H. Davis & Co. 1874. pp. XIII, 14—557.* [3143

Barber, John Warner: The history of New England, New York, New Jersey, and Pennsylvania. *Embracing the following subjects, viz.: Discoveries and settlements — Indian history — Indian, French and Revolutionary wars — religious history — biographical sketches — anecdotes, traditions, remarkable and unaccountable occurrences — with a great variety of curious and interesting relics of antiquity. Third edition. Hartford, Conn.: H. S. Parsons & Co. 1846. pp. VIII, 9—624, ill.* [3144

Bready, Marcia B.: The colonists of William Penn. *In: Western Pennsylvania Historical Society. Vol. V. Pittsburgh, Pa. 1922. pp. 259—264.* [3145

Cornell, William Mason: The history of Pennsylvania. *From the earliest discovery to the present time including an account of the first settlements by the Dutch, Swedes and English, and of the colony of William Penn, his treaty and pacific measures with the Indians; and the gradual advancement of the state to its present aspect of opulence, culture, and refinement. Philadelphia, Pa.: John Sully & Co. 1876. pp. 575.* [3146

Davis, W. W .H.: Law governing the settlement of new countries. *In: A Collection of Papers read before the Bucks County Historical Society. Vol. III. Easton, Pa. 1909. pp. 341—344.* [3147

Day, Sherman: Historical collections of the State of Pennsylvania; *containing a copious selection of the most interesting facts, traditions, biographical sketches, anecdotes, etc., relating to its history and antiquities; both general and local, with topographical descriptions of every county and all the larger towns in the state. Philadelphia, Pa.: Published by George W. Gorton — New Haven Conn.: Durrie and Peck. 1843. pp. 708, ill.* [3148

Donehoo, George P.: Pennsylvania. A history. *Edited by . . . With an introduction by Thomas L. Montgomery. 7 vols. New York, N. Y. — Chicago, Ill.: Lewis Historical Publishing Co. 1926. Contents: Vol. I—IV History; Vol. V— VII Biography.* [3149

— Pennsylvania. A history. *Editor in chief . . . Biographical part. New edition. New York & Chicago: Lewis Historical Publishing Co. Inc. 1931. pp. 469, ill.* [3150

Ebeling, Christoph Daniel: Der Staat Pennsylvania. *2 Bde. Hamburg: Carl Ernst Bohn 1797, 1803. 914 S.; (2), 528, (15) S. = Erdbeschreibung und Geschichte von Amerika. Die vereinigten Staaten von Nordamerika. Bd. IV und VI.* [3151

Egle, William Henry: An illustrated history of the Commonwealth of Pennsylvania, civil, political, and military, from its earliest settlement, and to the present time, including historical descriptions of each county and industrial resources. *Harrisburg, Pa.: De Witt C. Goodrich & Co. 1876. pp. XII, 1186, ill.* [3152

Egle, William Henry: Bi-centennial edition. History of the Commonwealth of Pennsylvania, civil, political and military, from its earliest settlement to the present time, including historical descriptions of each county in the state, their towns, and industrial resources. *Third edition revised and corrected. Philadelphia, Pa.: E. M. Gardner 1883. pp. XII, 13—1204, ill., maps.* [3153

— Historical register: notes and queries, historical and genealogical, relating to interior Pennsylvania. *Vol. 1—2. (Published quarterly (irregular). Jan., 1883 —Dec., 1884. Harrisburg, Pa.: L. S. Hart 1883—1884. 2 vols. pp. 318; 318, map.* [3154

— Notes and queries, historical, biographical and genealogical: chiefly relating to interior Pennsylvania. *Edited by . . . First-second series. Third series. Vol. I —II. Harrisburg, Pa.: Telegraph Printing and Binding House 1881—1891. 4 vols.*
[First series issued in 5 parts, undated, with a general title-page bearing date 1881; second series in 8 parts, undated with a general title-page, bearing date 1883; Third series, vol. I in 8 parts. 1884— 1887 with a general title-page, dated 1887; third series, vol. 2 in 7 parts. 1887—1890, with a general title-page, dated 1891.
Titles varies: 1881: Notes and queries, historical and genealogical; 1884—1890. Notes and queries: historical, biographical and genealogical, chiefly relating to interior Pennsylvania. Caption and cover title: 1883—85: Notes and queries chiefly relating to the history of Dauphin Co.; 1886—90: Notes and queries, historical, biographical and genealogical. Title pages read: Notes and queries: historical, biographical and genealogical, chiefly relating to interior Pennsylvania. [3155

— Notes and queries, historical, biographical and genealogical, relating chiefly to interior Pennsylvania. *Edited by . . . First-second series, vol. 1—2, 1894—1895; Third series, vol. 1—3, 1895—96; Fourth series, vol. 1—2, 1893—1895; annual vols. 1896—1900. Harrisburg, Pa.: Harrisburg Publishing Co. 1894—1901. 12 vols. [First-Third series:] Reprint of articles which appeared originally in the Harrisburg Daily Telegraph 1878—1883; some of them having been issued also in pamphlet form.*

Notes and queries. Table of contents. *Published by* **M. W. McAlarney**. *Harrisburg, Pa. [s. d.] pp. 40.* [3156
Ferree, Barr: Pennsylvania: a primer. *New York, N. Y.: The Pennsylvania Society 1904. pp. 256.*
= *Supplemantary paper in: Year Book of the Pennsylvania Society. 1904. New York, N. Y. 1914.* [3157
Fisher, Sydney George: The making of Pennsylvania. *An analysis of the elements of the population and the formative influences that created one of the greatest of the American states. Philadelphia, Pa.: J. B. Lippincott Co. 1896. pp. VIII, 7—380, map. Second edition 1900.* [3158
— Pennsylvania, colony and commonwealth, *Philadelphia, Pa.: Henry T. Coates & Co. 1897. pp. XIII, 442, maps.* [3159
— The Quaker colonies. *A chronicle of the proprietors of the Delaware. New Haven, Conn.: Yale University Press 1921. pp. IX, 244, ill., map.*
= *Textbook edition: The Chronicles of America series. I. vol. 8.* [3160
Fiske, John: The Dutch and Quaker colonies in America. *2 vols. Boston, Mass. and New York, N. Y.: Houghton, Mifflin Co.; The Riverside Press, Cambridge 1899. pp. XVI, 294; XVI, 400.* [3161
Godcharles, Frederic A.: Daily stories of Pennsylvania. *Prepared for publication in the leading daily newspapers of the state. Milton, Pa. 1924. pp. XIII, 958, ill.* [3162
Gordon, Thomas F.: The history of Pennsylvania, from its discovery by Europeans to the Declaration of Independence in 1776. *Philadelphia, Pa.: Carey, Lea & Carey 1829. pp. VII, VIII, 628.* [3163
Hazard, Samuel: The register of Pennsylvania devoted to the preservation of facts and documents and every other kind of useful information respecting the State of Pennsylvania. *Edited by . . . Vol. I. (Issued in weekly series.) Philadelphia, Pa.: W. F. Geedes. 1828. semiannually ff. — Vol. XVI. 1835.* [3164
— Annals of Pennsylvania, from the discovery of the Delaware 1609—1682. *Philadelphia, Pa.: Hazard and Mitchell 1850. pp. VIII, 664.* [3165
Holcomb, William P.: Pennsylvania boroughs. *Baltimore, Md.: N. Murray, Publication agent, Johns Hopkins University 1886. pp. (1), 7—51.*

= *Johns Hopkins Unicersity Studies in Historical and Political Science. Fourth series, no. IV.*
[Borough of Germantown. pp. 23—33.] [3166
Hulbert, Archer Butler: Soil, its influence on the history of the United States. With special reference to migration and the scientific study of local history. *New Haven, Conn.: Yale University Press; London: Humphrey Milford, Oxford University Press 1930. pp. (5), 227, ill.*
,,Human seed on stony ground." = *Chapter XIII. pp. 120—126; ,,Penn's forest empire."* = *Chapter XIV. pp. 127 —136; ,,The Keystone state."* = *Chapter XVI. pp. 146—155.]* [3167
Jenkins, Howard M.: Pennsylvania, colonial and federal. A history: 1608—1903. *Editor . . . 3 vols. Philadelphia, Pa.: Pennsylvania Historical Publishing Association 1903. pp. XIV, 601; XII, 585; X, 608, ill.* [3168
Keith, Charles P.: Chronicles of Pennsylvania from the English Revolution to the peace of Aix-La-Chapelle 1688—1748. *2 vols. Philadelphia, Pa.: Patterson & White Co. 1917. Vol. I. pp. IX, 456; Vol. II. pp. (1), 457—481.*
The Germans = *Vol. II, Chapter XVII. pp. 511—551; Unitas Fratrum and attempted church unity* = *Chapter XXV. pp. 813—847.* [3169
Krahmer, Wolff: William Penn als Kolonisator von Pennsylvania insbesondere seine Politik gegenüber den Indianern. *Diss. Frankfurt a. M. 1928. Frankfurt a. M.: Graphische Anstalt Schirmer & Mahlau 1928. 96 S.* [3170
Kriebel, H. W.: Settlement of the counties of Pennsylvania. *In: The Pennsylvania-German. Vol. VIII. Lebanon, Pa. 1907. pp. 3—9. Note the adenda: ,,The first settlement in Berks County." Vol. VIII. 1907. p. 134.* [3171
Martin, Asa Earl and **Shenk, Hiram Herr:** Pennsylvania history told by contemporaries. *New York, N. Y.: The Macmillan Co. 1925. pp. XXI, 621.* [3172
McClure, A. K.: Old time notes of Pennsylvania. A connected and chronical record of the commercial, industrial and educational advancement of Pennsylvania, and the inner history of all political movements since the adoption of the Constitution of 1838. *2 vols. Philadelphia, Pa.: The John C. Winston Co.*

1905. pp. XXXIV, 17—599, ill.; pp. XXI, (7), 17—632, ill.   [3173

Pennypacker, Samuel Whitaker: Historical and biographical sketches. *Philadelphia, Pa.: Robert A. Tripple 1883. pp. 416. [See no. 356]*   [3174

— Pennsylvania in American history. *Philadelphia, Pa.: William J. Campbell 1910. pp. 494.*   [3175

— Pennsylvania, the Keystone. A short history. *Philadelphia, Pa.: Christopher Soyer Co. 1914. pp. 316.*   [3176

Proud, Robert: The history of Pennsylvania, in North America from the original institution and settlement of that province, under the first proprietor and governor William Penn in 1681, till after the year 1742, *with an introduction respecting the life of W. Penn . . . to which is added a brief description of the said province and the general state, in which it flourished, principally between the years 1760—1770. The whole including a variety of things, useful and interesting to be known, respecting that country in early time &c. Written principally between the years 1776—1780. 2 vols. Philadelphia, Pa.: Zachariah Poulson, jr. 1797—98. Vol. I. 1797. pp. 508, 1 portr.; Vol. II. 1798. pp. 373; Appendix pp. 146.*

[Germans, Vol. II. 1798. pp. 273—274; Part IV. Religious State of Pennsylvania. pp. 337—355; Of the Mennonites. pp. 341—345; Of the Dunkards, or Dumplers. pp. 345—348; Of the Swenckfelders. pp. 348—350; Of the Unitas Fratrum, or United Brethren, commonly called Moravians. pp. 351—355.]   [3177

Rhoads, Mrs. H. S.: The early settlers of Pennsylvania. *Paper read before the Lebanon Chapter, D. A. R. and later before the Lebanon County Historical Society, Nov. 30, 1928. In: Papers . . . of the Lebanon County Historical Society. Vol. IX, no. 10. Lebanon, Pa. 1928. pp. 311—324, ill.*   [3178

Schmieder, Oscar: ,,Die mittleren Staaten (das ehemalige Neu-Holland und Neu-Schweden). *In: Landeskunde Nordamerikas. Vereinigte Staaten und Canada. Von O. Schmieder. Leipzig u. Wien 1933 [= Nr. 20]. S. 78—95.*

[Die vorrevolutionäre deutsche Einwanderung. S. 82—83; Die Kolonisation Pennsylvaniens. S. 83—87.]   [3179

Sharpless, Isaac: Two centuries of Pennsylvania history. *Philadelphia, Pa.: J. B. Lippincott Co. 1900. pp. XIII. 9—385, ill. = Lippincott Educational Series.*   [3180

Shenk, Hiram H. and **Shenk, Esther:** Encyclopedia of Pennsylvania. *Editor: Hiram H. Shenk; associate editor: Esther Shenk. Harrisburg, Pa.: Publishers National Historical Association 1932. pp. VI, 593, ill.*   [3181

Shepherd, William Robert: History of proprietary government in Pennsylvania. *Thesis of Ph. D., University Faculty of Political Science, Columbia College, New York City, N.Y., New York 1896. pp. 168. = Studies in History, Economies and Public Law. Vol. 6.*   [3182

[Smith, Samuel]: History of the Province of Pennsylvania *by S. Smith. Edited by* **William M. Mervine.** *Published by the Colonial Society of Pennsylvania. Philadelphia, Pa.: J. B. Lippincott. 1913. pp. XIII, 231.*

,,An account of the Mennonites and Swenckfelders" *= Chapter XVI. pp. 168—179; ,,Of the Dunkards or Dumplers — and of the Moravians". = Chapter XVII. pp. 180—197.]*   [3183

Southwick, A. F.: Ethnic elements of colonial Pennsylvania and the population of today. *In: The Western Pennsylvania Historical Magazine. Vol. VI. Pittsburgh, Pa. 1923. pp. 234—249.*   [3184

Swank, James M.: Progressive Pennsylvania. A record of the remarkable industrial development of the Keystone State, with some account of its early and its later transportation systems, its early settlers, and its prominent men. *Philadelphia, Pa.: J. B. Lippincott Co. 1908. pp. VII, 360, ill.*   [3185

Walton, Joseph S. and **Brumbaugh, Martin G.:** Stories of Pennsylvania or school readings from Pennsylvania history. *New York, N. Y. — Cincinnati, O. — Chicago, Ill.: American Book Co. 1897. pp. 300, ill.*

[The Germans in Pennsylvania. pp. 45—73; The Moravians. pp. 75—82.]   [3186

Warwick, Charles F.: Warwick's keystone commonwealth. A review of the history of the great state of Pennsylvania, and a brief record of the growth of its chief city, Philadelphia. *Philadelphia, Pa. 1913. pp. 439.*   [3187

Watson, John F.: Annals of Philadelphia, *being a collection of memoirs, anecdotes and incidents of the city and its inhabi-*

tants from the days of the pilgrim founders intended to preserve the recollection of olden time, and to exhibit society in its changes of manners and customs, and the city in its local changes and improvements, to which is added an appendix containing olden time researches and reminiscences of New York City. Philadelphia, Pa.: E. L. Carvey & A. Hart; New York, N. Y.: *G. & C. & H. Carvill 1830. pp. XII, 740, 78, ill.*

Second edition: Annals of Philadelphia and Pennsylvania, in the olden time; *being a collection of memoirs, anecdotes, and incidents of the city and its inhabitants and of the earliest settlements of the inland part of Pennsylvania, from the days of the founders. Philadelphia, Pa.:* A. Hart, J. W. Moore, J. Pennington, U. Hunt and H. F. Anners 1850. *pp. XVI, 609, ill. pp. VII, 591, ill. Third edition: 2 vols. Philadelphia, Pa.: Whiting & Thomas 1856. pp. XVI, 609, ill.; 1857. pp. VII, 642, ill.*

Fourth edition: Enlarged with many revisions and additions by Willis P. Hazard. *3 vols. Philadelphia, Pa.:* J. M. Stoddart 1879. *pp. . . . ; . . . ; 524, ill. Fifth edition: 3 vols. Philadelphia, Pa.:* Edwin S. Stuart, 1898. *pp. XVI, 609, ill.; VII, 634, (6), ill.; 524, ill.* [3188

Watson, John F.: Historic tales of olden time, concerning the early settlement and progress of Philadelphia and Pennsylvania. *For the use of families and schools. Philadelphia, Pa.:* E. Littell & Thomas Holden *1833. pp. XII, 13—316, ill.*

[Settlement of Germantown, pp. 52—56; Frontier towns: Lancaster. pp. 64—68; Germans. pp. 224—227.] [3189

Pennsylvania Historical Commission: Marking the historic sites of early Pennsylvania. *Reports of the Pennsylvania Historical Commission. Harrisburg, Pa. . . . ill., maps.* [3190

Charter to William Penn and laws of the Province of Pennsylvania, passed between the years 1682—1700. *Preceded by Duke of York's laws in force from the year 1676 to the year 1682, with an appendix containing laws relating to the organization of the provincial courts and historical matter. Published under the direction of John Blair Linn. Compiled and edited by* George Stoughton, Benjamin M. Nead, Thomas McCamant. *Harrisburg, Pa.: Lane & Hart, State Printer 1879. pp. 614.* [3191

Constitutions of Pennsylvania. Constitution of the United States. *Analytically indexed and with index of legislation prohibeted in Pennsylvania. Prepared by* John H. Fertig, *and* Frank M. Hunter, *under the direction of* James N. Moore, *Director. Legislative Reference Bureau. Harrisburg, Pa.:* Wm. Stanley Ray, State Printer 1916. *pp. 301.* [3192

Pennypacker, Samuel Whitaker: Pennsylvania colonial cases: The administration of Law in Pennsylvania prior to A. D. 1700 as shown in the cases decided in the Court proceedings. *An address delivered before the Law Academy of Philadelphia, on the evening of October 21, 1891. Philadelphia, Pa.:* Rees Welsh & Co. *1892. pp. (1), 23—24; (2), 25—185.* [3193

Breisch, C. C., Frey, R. S. and Glidden, B. R.: The township law. *Harrisburg, Pa. 1922. pp. 593. = Bulletin no. 23. Commonwealth of Pennsylvania. Legislative Reference Bureau.* [3194

Fertig, John H. and Welsh, Elmer S.: The borough law. *Harrisburg, Pa. 1918. pp. 442. = Bulletin no. 19. Commonwealth of Pennsylvania. Legislative Reference Bureau.* [3195

Geseze der Republik Pennsylvanien in übersetzten Auszügen. *Enthaltend die brauchbaren öffentlichen Geseze bis zu dem Jahr 1805, einschließlich; so wie auch die Regierungs-Verfassungen der Vereinigten Staaten und von Pennsylvanien. Herausgegeben unter Authorität eines Gesezes der General Assembly — passiert im April, 1805. Reading, Pa.: Gedruckt und herausgegeben von Johann Ritter und Carl Keßler 1807. (7), XLIX, 766, (12) S.* [3196

Handbuch für Deutsche; enthaltend Formen zu Handschriften, welche den Bürgern der Vereinigten Staaten nützlich und dienlich seyn können *als: Bande, Noten, Reseten, Überschreibungen, Verträge, Vollmachten, Letzte Willen oder Testamente, Versteigerungs-Bedingungen, Ausweisungen über Verodnungen der Gesetze über obige und andere Gegenstände. Nebst allerley Formen in der englischen Sprache. Auch Interessen Tabellen und eine Tabelle zum Gebrauch für Sägemüller. Zweite und verbesserte Auflage. Reading, Pa.: Gedruckt und herausgegeben von Johann Ritter und Comp. 1828. VIII, 108 S.* [3197

Anhang

Appendix

[Colonial Records]: Minutes of the Provincial Council of Pennsylvania, from the organization to the termination of the proprietary government. *[March 10, 1683. — September 27, 1775.] Published by the state . . . Edited by* Samuel Hazard. *Philadelphia, Pa.: Printed by J. Severns & Co. 1851—52. Vols. 4—10 have imprint: Harrisburg: Printed by T. Fenn & Co. 1851—52.* 10 vols. = *[Colonial records], vol. 1—10.*

Table of contents relative to German immigration:

Colonial Records. Vol. II. 1852:
At a Council Phila. 5th 1 mo. 1700—01: A petition subscribed by ffr. Danl. Pastorius, by order & in behalf of the German Corporation. *pp. 13—14.*
At a Council 15th 3 mo., 1706: A petition of Joannes Koster, and about 150 other high and low Germans, to the Govr. and Council, praying to be naturalized. *pp. 241—242.*
At a Council, 1st March, 1708—9: Two several petitions, concerning the administration of the affairs of the Frankfort Comp. (petition for an ejectment of Jno Henry Sproegel and Daniel Falkner, presented by F. D. Pastorius & Johannes Jawert). *pp. 429—432.*
At a Council, 29th Sept., 1709: Bill for naturalizing the Germans . . . being intituled an Act for the better Enabling of Divers Inhabitants of the Province of Pennsylvania, To Hold and Enjoy Lands, Tenements, and Plantation in the same Province, by which are naturalized the persons following, vizt: ffrancis Daniel Pastorius . . . etc. *pp. 493—494.*
Colonial Records. Vol. III. 1852:
At a Council . . . Sept. 17, 1717: „Foreigners to be reported to Council, and take the Oath of Allegiance." — The Governor [William Keith] observ'd to the Board that great numbers off fforeigners from Germany . . . having lately been imported into this Province, daily dispersed themselves immediately after landing, without producing any Certificate . . . *p. 29.*
At a Council . . . Sept. 9, 1717: List of Palatines exhibited — 164 imported by Capt. Richmond, 91 by Capt. Towor, 108 by Capt. Eyers. *p. 29.*
At a Council, . . . Febr. 10th, 1724—25: Petition from divers Palatines, to be allowed to purchase lands, read . . . *p. 241.*

Message to the House from the Governor P. Gordon relative to the naturalization of Germans on the character of the said Germans, now inhabitants of the County of Lancaster. Jan. 16th, 1729—30. *p. 374.*
Petition of several Germans praying to be naturalized and message of Governor P. Gordon to the House, advicing to pass a bill for their naturalization. Jan. 9th, 1730—31. *pp. 392—393.*
Message to the House from Governor P. Gordon relative the naturalization „of several natives of Germany, now inhabitants of this Province." Jan. 16th, 1735. *pp. 587—588.*
„Paper being drawn up to be signed by those Palatines, who should come into this Province with an Intention to settle therein, pursuant to the order of this Board" . . . presented, read and approved at a Council, Philadelphia, Sept. 21st 1727. *p. 283.*
Signed lists, laid before the Board . . .
At a Council, Philadelphia, Sept. 21st 1727 . . . „of the names of 109 Palatines, who with their families making in all 400 persons, imported into this Province in the ship William and Sarah, William Hill, master from Rotterdam, but last from Dover. *pp. 283—284.*
. . . Sept. 27, 1727 . . . 53 Palatines, with their families . . . all about 200 persons, imported . . . the ship James Goodwill, David Crocket, mr., but last from Falmouth . . . *pp. 284—285.*
. . . Sept. 30th, 1727 . . . 70 Palatines . . . with their families . . . all about 300 persons, imported in the ship Malley, Jno Hodgeson, master, from Rotterdam, but last from Deal . . . *pp. 287—288.*
. . . Oct. 2d, 1727 . . . 53 Palatines . . . with their families . . . all about 140 persons, . . . imported in the ship Adventure, Jno Davies, master, from Rotterdam but last from Plymouth. *p 288.*
. . . Oct. 16th, 1727 . . . 46 Palatines . . . with their families . . . all about 200 persons, . . . imported in the ship Friendship of Pristol, John Davies, mr., from Rotterdam, but last from Cows . . . *p. 290.*
. . . Aug. 24th, 1728 . . . 80 Palatines, . . . with their families . . . all about 200 persons, imported in the ship Mortonhouse, John Coultas, master, from Rotterdem, but last from Deal . . . *pp. 327—328.*
. . . Sept. 4th, 1728 . . . 30 Palatines, . . . with their families . . . all about 100 persons, . . . imported in the ship Albany, Lazarus Oxman, master, from Rotterdam, but last from Portsmouth . . . *pp. 328—329.*

... Sept. 11th, 1728 ... 42 Palatines, ... with their families ... all about 90 persons, ... imported ... in the ship James Goodwill, David Crockat, master, from Rotterdam, but last from Deal ... *pp. 331—332*

At the courthouse of Philadelphia, Aug. 19th, 1729 ... 72 Palatines who ... with their families ... all about 180 persons ... imported ... in the ship Mortonhouse, James Coultas, master, from Rotterdam, but last from Deal ... *pp. 367—368.*

... Sept. 15th, 1729 ... 50 Palatines ... with their families ... all about 126 persons ..., imported ... in the ship Allen, James Craigie, master, from Rotterdam, but last from Cows ... *pp. 368—369.*

... Aug. 29th, 1730 ... 77 Palatines ... with their families ... all about 260 persons, ... imported ... in the ship Thistle of Glasgow, Colin Dunlap, mr., from Rotterdam, but last from Dover ... *pp. 384—385.*

... Sept. 5th, 1730 ... 46 Palatines ... with their families ... all about 130 persons, ... imported ... in the ship Alexr. & Aun, William Clymer, master, from Rotterdam, but last from Deal ... *p. 386.*

... Nov. 30th, 1730 ... 24 Palatines ... with their families ... all about 52 persons, ... imported ... in the ship Joyce, William Ford, master, from Boston ... *pp. 389—390.*

... Aug. 17th, 1731 ... 39 Palatines ... with their families ... in all 107 persons ... imported ... in the ship Samuel, Hugh Peircy, master, from Rotterdam ... *p. 410.*

... Sept. 11 th, 1731 ... 57 Palatines ... with their families ... in all 175 persons ... imported ... in the ship Pennsylvania Merchant, Jno Stedman, master, from Rotterdam, but last from Dover ... *pp. 413—414.*

... Sept. 21, 1731 ... 106 Palatines ... with their families ... in all 269 persons ... imported ... in the ship Britannia, of London, Michael Franklyn, mr., from Rotterdam, but last from Cowes. *pp. 414—415.*

... Oct. 14th, 1731 ... 33 Palatines ... with their families ... in all 78 persons ... imported in the Snow Louther, Joseph Fisher, master, from Rotterdam, but last from Dover. *pp. 415—416.*

... May 15th, 1732 ... 13 Palatines ... with their families ... in all — persons ... imported in the ship Norris, Thomas Lloyd, mr., from Boston ... *pp. 428—429.*

... Aug. 11th, 1732 ... 106 Palatines ... with their families ... in all about 279 persons ... imported in the ship Samuel, of London, Hugh Peircy, master, from Rotterdam, but last from Cowes ... *pp. 431—432.*

... Sept. 11th, 1732 ... 70 Palatines ... with their families ... in all 168 persons ... imported in the ship Pennsylvania. Merchant, John Stedman, master from Rotterdam, but last from Plymouth ... *pp. 452—453.*

... Sept. 19th, 1732 ... 112 Palatines ... with their families in all 330 persons ... imported in the ship Johnson of London, David Crockat, mr., from Rotterdam, but last from Deal ... *pp. 453—454.*

... Sept. 21st, 1732 ... 72 Palatines ... with their families ... in all 188 persons ... imported in the Pink Plaisance, John Paret, mr., from Rotterdam, but last from Cowes ... *pp. 454—455.*

... Sept. 23rd, 1732 ... 57 Palatines ... with their families ... in all 145 persons ... imported ... in the ship Adventure, Robert Curson, mr., from Rotterdam, but last from Cowes ... *pp. 455—456.*

... Sept. 25th, 1732 ... 115 Palatines ... with their families ... in all — persons ... imported in the ship Loyal Judith, of London, Robert Turpin, master, from Rotterdam, but last from Cowes ... *pp. 456—457.*

... Sept. 26th, 1732 ... 61 Palatines ... with their families ... in all 191 persons ... imported ... in the ship Mary, of London, John Gray, master, from Rotterdam, but last from Cowes ... *pp. 457—458.*

... Sept. 30th, 1732 ... 55 Palatines ... with their families ... in all 170 persons ... imported in the ship Dragon, Charles Hargrave, master, from Rotterdam, but last from Plymouth ... *pp. 458—459.*

... Oct. 11th, 1732 ... 42 Palatines ... with their families ... in all — persons ... imported ... in the ship Pleasant, James Morris, master, but last from Deal ... *pp. 465—466.*

... Oct. 17th, 1732 ... 61 Palatines ... with their families ... in all 169 persons ... imported in the Pink, John & William of Sunderland, Constable Tymperton, master, from Rotterdam, but last from Dover ... *pp. 466—467.*

... Aug. 17th, 1733 ... 90 Palatines ... with their families ... in all 291 persons, ... imported ... in the ship Samuel of London, Hugh Percy, master, from Rotterdam, but last from Deal ... *pp. 515—516.*

... Aug. 17th, 1733 ... 58 Palatines ... with their families ... in all 172 persons, ... imported in the ship Eliza, of London, Edward Lee, master, from Rotterdam, but last from Dover ... *pp. 516—517.*

... Aug. 28th, 1733 ... 84 Palatines ... with their families ... in all 226 persons ... imported ... in the ship Hope, of London, Daniel Reid, master, from Rotterdam, but last from Cowes ... *pp. 517—518.*

... Sept. 18 th, 1733 ... 67 Palatines, ... with their families ... in all 187 persons ... imported ... in the Briganteen Pennsylvania Merchant, of London, John Stedman, mr., from Rotterdam, but last from Plymouth ... *pp. 518—519.*

... Sept. 28th, 1733 ... 43 Palatines ... with their families, ... in all 137 persons ...

imported in the Briganteen Richard & Elizabeth, of Philadelphia, Christopher Clymer, master, from Rotterdam, but last from Plymouth . . . *p. 519.*

. . . Sept.29th, 1733 . . . 34 Palatines . . . with their families . . . in all 170 persons . . . imported . . . in the Pink Mary of Dublin, James Benn, master, from Rotterdam, but last from Plymouth . . . *pp. 519—520.*

. . . Oct. 12th, 1733 . . . 15 Palatines . . . with their families . . . in all 62 persons . . . imported in the ship Charming Betty, John Ball, master, from London . . . *p. 524.*

. . . Sept. 12th, 1734 . . . 89 Palatines . . . with their families . . . in all 261 persons . . . imported in the ship Saint Andrew, John Stedman, master, from Rotterdam, but last from Plymouth . . . *pp. 568—569.*

. . . Sept. 23rd, 1734 . . . 49 Palatines . . . with their families . . . in all 127 persons . . . imported . . . in the ship Hope, Daniel Reid, master, from Rotterdam, but last from Cowes . . . *p. 570.*

. . . May 29th, 1735 . . . 54 Palatines . . . with their families . . . in all 176 persons . . . imported . . . in the ship Mercury, of London, William Wilson, Master, from Rotterdam, but last from Cowes . . . *pp. 593—594.*

Colonial Records. Vol. IV. 1851:

. . . Sept. 1st 1736 . . . 151 Foreigners from the Palatinate & other places . . . with their families . . . in all 388 persons . . . imported here in the ship, of London, Ralph Harle, master, from Rotterdam, but last from Cowes . . . *pp. 58—60.*

. . . Sept. 16th, 1736 . . . 112 Foreigners from the Palatinate, and other places . . . with their families . . . in all 330 persones . . . imported . . . in the ship Princes Auguste, Samuel Merchant, master, from Rotterdam, but last from Cowes . . . *pp. 72—73.*

. . . Oct. 19th, 1736 . . . 37 Foreigners from the Palatinate, . . . with their families . . . in all 110 persons . . . imported . . . in the Brigantine John, of Perth Amboy, George Frazer, master, from Rotterdam, but last from Dover . . . *pp. 99—100.*

Germans proceed west of the Susquehanna; — discover their error and are willing to return. ,,The President [James Logan] acquainted the Board . . . that the Dutch people or Germans, who with others going over from this side of Susquehanna River to the west of it, had been prevailed on by some Agents from Maryland to acknowledge the authority of thet Province.'' . . . at a Council . . ., Aug. 24, 1736 . . . *pp. 56—58; — p. 64ff.; p. 71.*

At a Council, . . . May 12th, 1739: ,,A petition of sundry Germans and other Foreigners (now inhabitants of this Province) praying that they may be granted the Benefit of Natural born Subjects of Great Britain by an Act of Naturalization, was read''. *p. 331.*

At a Council, . . . May 14th, 1739: Message of the Governor Georg Thomas to the Assembly upon the above application. *p. 332.*

At a Council, . . . Jan. 26th, 1741—42: Message from the Governor George Thomas and answer to the Governor from the House, relative to a petition of ,,Several of the most substantial Germans now Inhabitants of this Province, . . . setting forth in Substance. That for want of a Convenient House for the reception of such of their Country men as, on their Arrival here laboured under Diseases . . . recommend to the Assembly the Erecting of a proper Building at the public Expence . . . *pp. 507—710 ff.*

,,Act for naturalizing such foreign Protestants, as are settled or shall settle in this Province, who not being of the people called Quakers, do conscientiously refuse taking any Oath, and the Amendment proposed to the same'' . . . read ,,in assembly, 11 mo., 13, 1742''. *pp. 628—629; p. 638.*

[3198

Pennsylvania Archives: Pennsylvania archives . . . *[1st series] vol. 1—12; 2d ser., vol. 1—19; 3d ser., vol. 1—30; 4th ser., vol. 1—12; 5th ser., vol. 1—18; 6th ser., vol. 1—15; 7th ser., vol. 1—5. Philadelphia 1852—56; Harrisburg, 1874. ill. maps and 2 atlases (27 fold maps; 5 fold fascim.)*

From the table of contents:

Pennsylvania Archives. Second series. Edited by **John B. Linn** and **Wm. H. Egle.**

Vol. I. Harrisburg 1896:

Minutes of the Board of War, from March 14, 1777, to August 7, 1777. *pp. 3—75.*

Minutes of the Nay Board, from Febr. 18, 1777, to Sept. 24, 1777. *pp. 77—241.*

List of officers and men of the Pennsylvania navy. 1775—1781. *pp. 243—382.*

Papers relating to the Pennsylvania navy. 1775—1781. *pp. 383—434.*

Papers relating to British prisoners in Pennsylvania. *pp. 435—498.*

Memorandum book of the Committee and Council of Safety. 1776—1777. *pp. 499—562.*

List of sick soldiers in Philadelphia, December, 1776. *pp. 563—579.*

Papers relating to the War of the Revolution, 1775—1777. *pp. 581—799.*

. . . *Vol. II. Harrisburg 1896:*

Names and persons for whom marriage licenses were issued in the Province of Pennsylvania, previous to 1790. *pp. 1—292.*

Persons naturalized in the Province of Pennsylvania 1740—1773. *pp. 293—415.*

Officers and soldiers in the service of the Province of Pennsylvania, 1744—1764. *pp. 417—528.*

Indian traders. 1743—48. *pp. 531—532.*

Indian traders licenses, dispended in the Secretary' Office. 1767—68. *pp. 533—538.*

Ships registers 1762—1776. *pp. 542—577.*

Papers relating to the Province of Pennsylvania, Prior to the Revolution. *pp. 579—637.*

Instructions to Conrad Weiser . . . 1749. *588—589.*

Address from the German Protestant . . . 1754. *pp. 590—591.*

. . . *Vol. III Harrisburg 1896:*

Names of persons who took the Oath of Allegiance to the State of Pennsylvania between the years 1776 and 1794. *pp. 1—86.*

Papers relating to the War of the Revolution, 1777. *pp. 87—136.*

Papers relating to the War of the Revolution, 1778. *pp. 137—226.*

Papers relating to the War of the Revolution, 1779. *pp. 227—298.*

Memorials against calling a convention, 1779. *pp. 299—332.*

Papers relating to the War of the Revolution, 1780. *pp. 333—390.*

Papers relating to the War of the Revolution, 1781. *pp. 391—470.*

Resolves of the Committee for the province with the instructions to their representatives in Assembly and an essay of the constitutional power of Great Britain. 1774. *pp. 471—546.*

Proceedings of the Convention for the Province of Pennsylvania, held at Philadelphia, from January 23, 1775, to January 28, 1775. *pp. 547—582.*

Officers of the State of Pennsylvania in the Revolution and under the Constitution of 1776. *pp. 583—698.*

. . . *Vol. IV. Harrisburg 1896:*

Papers relating to what is known as the Whisky Insurrection in western Pennsylvania 1794. *pp. 1—462.*

Papers relating to the defence of the frontiers 1790—1796. *pp. 525—652.*

. . . *Vol. V. Harrisburg 1896:*

Papers relating to the Colonies on the Delaware 1614—1682. *Harrisburg, Pa.: Clarence M. Busch 1895. pp. 1—912.*

. . . *Vol. VI. Harrisburg 1895:*

Papers relating to the French occupation in western Pennsylvania 1631—1764. *pp. 1—665.*

. . . *Vol. VII. Harrisburg 1895:*

Papers relating to provincial affairs: in Pennsylvania 1682—1750. *(maps) pp. 1—318.*

Papers relating to the boundary dispute between Pennsylvania and Maryland 1734—1760. *pp. 319—425.*

The narrative of Marie Le Roy and Barbara Leininger 1759. *pp. 427—438.*

Journal of Col. James Burd of the Provincial service, 1760. *pp. 439—444.*

Journal of Col. James Burd of the Augusta Regiment, 1760. *pp. 445—456.*

Journal kept at Fort Augusta, 1763. *pp. 457—484.*

Papers relating to the Dutch and Swedish settlements on the Delaware River. *pp. 485—873.*

. . . *Vol. VIII. Harrisburg 1878:*

Record of Pennsylvania Marriages, prior to 1810. Vol. I. Harrisburg 1880.

Marriage record of the Reformed Church. Falkner Swamp, Montgomery Co., Pa. 1748—1800. *pp. 599—617. [Reprint 1896. pp. 611—629.]*

Marriage record of the Lutheran Church, New Hanover, Montgomery County, Pa. 1745—1809. *pp. 619—647. [Reprint 1896. pp. 631—660.]*

Marriage record of the German Reformed Church, at Philadelphia, 1748—1802. *pp. 649—731. [Reprint 1896. pp. 661—746].*

. . . *Vol. IX. Harrisburg 1880:*

Record of Pennsylvania Marriages, prior 1810. Vol. II. Harrisburg 1880.

Marriage Register of the Moravian Church, Bethlehem, 1742—1800. *pp. 107—127. [Reprint 1895. pp. 107—128.]*

Marriage register of the Moravian Church, Nazareth 1742—1800. *pp. 129—134. [Reprint 1895. pp. 129—135.]*

Marriage register of the Moravian Church Lititz, 1743—1800. *pp. 135—146. [Reprint 1895. pp. 137—148.]*

Marriage register of the Moravian church, Philadelphia, 1743—1800. *pp. 147—151. [Reprint 1895. pp. 149—153.]*

Marriage register of the Moravian Church at Emaus 1758—1800. *pp. 153—154. [Reprint 1865. pp. 155—158.]*

Marriage record of St. Michael's and Zion Lutheran Church, Philadelphia, 1745—1800. *pp. 285—440. [Reprint 1895. pp. 291—457.]*

. . . *Vol. X. Harrisburg 1880:*

Pennsylvania in the War of the Revolution, Battalions and Line 1775—1783. *Vol. I. Harrisburg, Pa.: Lane & Hart 1880. (ill. map.) pp. I—IV; 1—782.*

. . . *Vol. XI. Harrisburg 1880:*

Pennsylvania in the War of the Revolution, Battallions and Line 1775—1783 *Vol. II. Harrisburg, Pa.: Lane & Hart 1880. pp. 1—805.*

(Continental Line. The German Regiment, July 12, 1776—January 1, 1781.) *(ill.) pp. 71—83.*

(The Corps of Count von Ottendorff. 1776—1780.) *pp. 85—95.*

. . . *Vol. XII. Harrisburg 1880:*

Muster rolls of the Pennsylvania volunteers in the war of 1812—1814, with con-

19*

temporary papers and documents. *Vol. I.*
Harrisburg: Lane & Hart 1880. (ill.) pp.
I—XXIV; 1—805.

... *Vol. XIII. Harrisburg 1880:*
Pennsylvania in the War of the Revolution, associated battalions and militia.
1775—1783. *Edited by* **William H. Egle.**
Vol. I. Harrisburg: E. K. Meyers 1890.
(ill.) pp. (1) 1—794.

... *Vol. XIV. Harrisburg 1888:*
Pennsylvania in the War of the Revolution, associated battalions and militia.
1775—1783. *Edited by* **William H. Egle.**
Vol. II. Harrisburg: E. K. Meyers 1888.
(ill., map.) pp. (2) 1—791.

... *Vol. XV. Harrisburg 1890:*
Journals and diaries of the War of the Revolution with lists of officers and soldiers. 1775—1783. *Edited by* **William H. Egle.** *Harrisburg: E. K. Meyers 1893. (ill., map.) pp. I—IV; 5—784.*

... *Vol. XVI. Harrisburg 1890:*
The Breviate in the Boundary dispute between Pennsylvania and Maryland. *Harrisburg: E. K. Meyers 1891. (maps) pp. III—XI; 1—790.*

... *Vol. XVII. Harrisburg 1890:*
Names of foreigners who took the Oath of Allegiance ... 1727—1775 ... with the foreign arrivals, 1786—1808. *Edited by* **William E. Egle.** *Harrisburg 1892. pp. 787.*

... *Vol. XVIII. Harrisburg 1890:*
Documents relating to the Connecticut settlement in the Wyoming valley. *Edited by* **William H. Egle.** *Harrisburg: E. K. Meyers 1893. (maps.) pp. III—IV; 1—792.*

... *Vol. XIX. Harrisburg 1890:*
Minutes of the Board of Property of the Province of Pennsylvania. *Vol. I. Edited by* **William H. Egle.** *Harrisburg: E. K. Meyers 1893. pp. 1—787.*

Pennsylvania Archives. Third series. Edited by **William H. Egle.**

... *Vol. I. Harrisburg 1894:*
Minutes of the Board of Property and other references to lands in Pennsylvania, including Proprietary (old) rights. *Harrisburg: Clarence M. Busch 1894. (map.) pp. 1—1807.*

... *Vol. II. Harrisburg 1894:*
Minutes of the Board of Property and other references to lands in Pennsylvania, including Proprietary (old) rights. *Harrisburg: Clarence M. Busch 1894. pp. 1—1802*

... *Vol. III. Harrisburg 1894:*
Old rights, Proprietary rights, Virginia entries and soldiers entitled to Donation Lands. With an explanation of Reed's map of Philadelphia. *Harrisburg: Clarence M. Busch 1896. (ill.) pp. (1) 1—771.*

... *Vol. IV. Harrisburg 1894:*
Draughts of the Proprietary Manors in the Province of Pennsylvania as preserved in the Land Department of the Commonwealth. *Harrisburg, Pa.: Clarence M. Busch 1895. (maps.) p. 5.*

... *Vol. V. Harrisburg 1896:*
State of the accounts of the County Lieutenants during the War of the Revolution, 1777—1789. *Vol. I. Harrisburg: Clarence M. Busch 1896. pp. (1) 1—791.*

... *Vol. VI. Harrisburg 1896:*
State of the accounts of the County Lieutenants during the War of the Revolution 1777—1789. *Vol. II. Harrisburg: Clarence M. Busch 1896. pp. I—IV; 1—788.*

... *Vol. VII. Harrisburg 1896:*
State of the accounts of the County Lieutenants during the War of the Revolution 1777—1789. *Vol. III. Harrisburg: Clarence M. Busch 1896. pp. I—IV 1—799.*

... *Vol. VIII. Harrisburg 1896:*
Commissions issued by the Province of Pennsylvania with official proclamations. *Vol. I. Harrisburg: Clarence M. Busch 1896. pp. (1) 1—793.*

... *Vol. IX. Harrisburg 1896:*
Commissions issued by the Province of Pennsylvania with official proclamations. *Vol. II. Harrisburg: Clarence M. Busch 1896. pp. 1—797.*

... *Vol. X. Harrisburg 1896:*
Commissions issued by the Province of Pennsylvania with official proclamations. *Vol. III. Harrisburg: Clarence M. Busch 1896. pp. (1) 1—820.*

... *Vol. XI. Harrisburg 1897:*
Provincial papers: Proprietary tax lists of the County of Chester for the years 1765, 1766, 1767, 1768, 1769, 1771. *Harrisburg, Pa.: Wm. Stanley Ray 1897. (map.) pp. (1) V—XIII; (1) 1—783.*

... *Vol. XII. Harrisburg 1897:*
Provincial papers: Proprietary and other tax lists of the County of Chester for the years 1774, 1779, 1780, 1781, 1785. *Harrisburg: Wm. Stanley Ray 1897. (map.) pp. III—XI; 1—823.*

... *Vol. XIII. Harrisburg 1897:*
Provincial papers: Proprietary and other tax lists of Bucks for the years 1779, 1781, 1782, 1783, 1784, 1785, 1786. *Harrisburg, Pa.: Wm. Stanley Ray 1897. pp. III—XIII; 1—820.*

... *Vol. XIV. Harrisburg 1897:*
Provincial papers: Proprietary, supply, and state tax lists of the City and County of Philadelphia for the years 1769, 1774 and 1779. *Harrisburg, Pa.: Wm. Stanley Ray 1897. pp. III—VIII; 1—838.*

... *Vol. XV. Harrisburg 1897:*
Provincial papers: Supply, and state tax lists of the City and County of Phila-

delphia for the years 1779, 1780 and 1781. *Harrisburg, Pa.: Wm. Stanley Ray 1897.* *pp. III—VI; 1—789.*

. . . *Vol. XVI. Harrisburg 1897:* Provincial papers: Supply, and state tax lists of the City and County of Philadelphia for the years 1781, 1782, 1783. *Harrisburg, Pa.: Wm. Stanley Ray 1898.* *pp. III—VI; 1—837.*

. . . *Vol. XVII. Harrisburg 1897:* Provincial papers: Proprietary and state tax lists of the County of Lancaster, for the years 1771, 1772, 1773, 1779 and 1782. *Harrisburg, Pa.: Wm. Stanley Ray 1898.* *pp. III—VIII; 1—896.*

. . . *Vol. XVIII. Harrisburg 1897:* Provincial papers: Proprietary and state tax lists of the County of Berks for the years 1767, 1768, 1779, 1780, 1781, 1784, 1785. *Harrisburg, Pa.: Wm. Stanley Ray 1898. pp. III—XI; 1—814.*

. . . *Vol. XIX. Harrisburg 1897:* Provincial papers: Proprietary, supply, and state tax lists of the Counties of Northampton and Northumberland, for the years 1772 to 1787. *Harrisburg, Pa.: Wm. Stanley Ray 1898. pp. III—XII; 1—805.*

. . . *Vol. XX. Harrisburg 1897:* Provincial papers: State and supply transcripts of the County of Cumberland for the years 1778, 1779, 1780, 1781, 1782 and 1785. *Harrisburg, Pa.: Wm. Stanley Ray 1898. pp. III—IX; 1—781.*

. . . *Vol. XXI. Harrisburg 1897:* Provincial papers: Returns of taxables of the County of York, for the years 1779, 1780, 1781, 1782 and 1783. *Harrisburg, Pa.: Wm. Stanley Ray 1898. pp. III— VIII; 1—820.*

. . . *Vol. XXII. Harrisburg 1897:* Provincial papers: Returns of taxables for the Counties of Bedford (1773 to 1784), Huntingdon (1788), Westmoreland (1783, 1786), Fayette (1785, 1786), Allegheny (1791), Washington (1786) and Census of Bedford (1784) and Westmoreland (1783). *Harrisburg, Pa.: 1898. pp. III—XI; 1—782.*

. . . *Vol. XXIII. Harrisburg 1897:* Muster rolls of the navy and line, militia and rangers 1775—1783, with a list of pensioners 1818—1832. *Harrisburg, Pa. 1898.*

. . . *Vol. XXIV. Harrisburg 1897 (1898):* Warrantees of land in the several counties of state of Pennsylvania 1730—1898. *Vol. I.*

. . . *Vol. XXV. Harrisburg 1897 (1898):* Warrantees of land in the several counties of state of Pennsylvania (1730—1898). *Vol. II.*

. . . *Vol. XXVI. Harrisburg 1897 (1898):* Warrantees of land in the several counties of state of Pennsylvania (1730—1898). *Vol. III.*

. . . *Vol. XXVII—XXX. Harrisburg, Pa. 1899:* General index to volumes XI—XXVI. *Edited by* Geo Edward Reed. A—Cost. = *Vol. XXVII;* Co—Jo. = *Vol. XXVIII;* K—Ref. = *Vol. XXIX;* Ref—Zy. = *Vol. XXX.*

Pennsylvania Archives. Fourth series. Papers of the Governors. *Edited by* George Edward Reed *12 vols. Harrisburg, Pa. (The State of Pa.) 1900—1902:*

. . . *Vol. I. Papers of the Governors 1681 —1747. pp. V—XII, 1—917:* The character of the province, the several frames of government, the laws agreed upon in England. *p. 1 ff.* The administration of William Markham 1681—1682 and 1691—1699. *p. 67 ff.* The administration of William Penn 1682—1684 and 1699—1701. *p. 97 ff.* The administration of John Blackwell 1688—1690. *p. 129 ff.* The administration of Benjamin Fletcher 1693—1695. *p. 151 ff.* The administration of Andrew Hamilton 1701—1703. *p. 179 ff.* The administration of John Evans 1704—1709. *p. 185 ff.* The administration of Charles Gookin 1709—1717. *p. 293 ff.* The administration of Sir William Keith 1717—1726. *p. 339 ff.* The administration of Patrick Gordon 1727—1736. *p. 421 ff.* The administration of James Logan 1736—1738. *p. 559 ff.* The administration of George Thomas 1738—1747. *p. 663 ff.*

. . . *Vol. II. Papers of the Governors 1747 —1759. pp. I—III, 1—1001:* The administration of Anthony Palmer 1747—1748. *p. 1 ff.* The administration of James Hamilton 1748—1754. *p. 87 ff.* The administration of Robert Hunter Morris 1754—1756. *p. 297 ff.* Papers of the Proprietors 1718—1776. *p. 647 ff.* The administration of William Denny 1756—1759. *p. 725 ff.*

. . . *Vol. III. Papers of Governors 1759 —1785. pp. I—III, 1—1076:* The 2nd and 3rd administration of John Hamilton 1759—1771. *p. 1 ff.* The 1st administration of John Penn 1763—1771. *p. 233 ff.* The 2nd administration of John Penn 1773—1776. *p. 437 ff.* The administration of Richard Penn 1771—1773. *p. 521 ff.* The Committee of Safety 1775—1776, and the Council of Safety 1776—1777. *p. 541 ff.* The constitution of 1776. *p. 625 ff.*

The administration of Thomas Wharton, Junr. 1777—1778. *p. 649 ff.*

The administration of George Bryan 1778. *p. 673 ff.*

The administration of Joseph Reed 1778—1781. *p. 705 ff.*

The administration of William Moore 1779—1782. *p. 825 ff.*

The administration of James Porter 1781—1782. *p. 855 ff.*

The administration of John Dickinson 1782—1785. *p. 861 ff.*

. . . *Vol. IV. Papers of Governors 1785—1817. pp. I—III, 1—985.*

The administration of Benjamin Franklin 1785—1788. *p. 1 ff.*

The acting presidential papers of Charles Biddle 1784—1787. *p. 31 ff.*

The acting presidential papers of Peter Mühlenberg 1787—1788. *p. 45 ff.*

The acting presidential papers of David Redick 1788. *p. 51 ff.*

The acting presidential papers of George Ross 1788—1790. *p. 55 ff.*

The acting presidential papers of Thomas Mifflin 1788—1790. *p. 61 ff.*

The constitution of 1790. *p. 113.*

The gubernatorial administration of Thomas Mifflin 1790—1799. *p. 137 ff.*

The administration of Thomas M'Kean 1799—1808. *p. 435 ff.*

The administration of Simon Snyder 1808—1817. *p. 655 ff.*

. . . *Vol. V. Papers of the Governors 1817—1832. pp. I—III, 1—1026, ill.:*

The administration of William Findlay 1817—1820. *p. 1 ff.*

The administration of Joseph Hiester 1820—1823. *p. 239 ff.*

The administration of Andrew Schulze 1823—1829. *p. 487 ff.*

The administration of George Wolf 1829—1835. (Period from 1829—1832.) *p. 856 ff.*

. . . *Vol. VI. Papers of the Governors 1832—1845. pp. I—III, 1—1101, ill.:*

Papers of the Governors. Wolf *(Continued)* Period from 1832—1835. *p. 1 ff.*

The administration of Joseph Ritner 1835—1839. *p. 247 ff.*

The constitution of 1838. *p. 497 ff.*

The administration of David Rittenhouse Porter 1839—1845. *p. 527 ff.*

. . . *Vol. VII. Papers of the Governors 1845—1858. pp. I—III, 1—979, ill.:*

The administration of Francis Raun Shunk 1845—1848. *p. 1 ff.*

The administration of William Freame Johnston 1848—1852. *p. 277 ff.*

The administration of William Bigler 1852—1855. *p. 507 ff.*

The administration of James Pollock 1855—1858. *p. 779 ff.*

. . . *Vol. VIII. Papers of the Governors 1858—1871. pp. V—VII, 1—1201, ill.:*

The administration of William Fisher Packer 1858—1861. *p. 1 ff.*

The administration of Andrew George Curtin 1861—1867. *p. 321 ff.*

The administration of John White Geary 1867—1873. *(Continued.) p. 767 ff.*

. . . *Vol. IX. Papers of the Governors 1871—1883. pp. V—VII, 1—959, ill.:*

The administration of John White Geary 1867—1873. *(Continued.) p. 1 ff.*

The administration of John Frederick Hartranft 1873—1879. *p. 203 ff.*

The administration of Henry Martyn Hoyt 1879—1883. *p. 709 ff.*

. . . *Vol. X. Papers of the Governors 1883—1891. pp. V—VII, 1—1122, ill.:*

The 1st administration of Robert Emory Pattison 1883—1887. *p. 1 ff.*

The administration of James Addams Beaver 1887—1891. *p. 525 ff.*

The 2nd administration of Robert Emory Pattison 1891—1895. *(Continued.) p. 957 ff.*

. . . *Vol. XI. Papers of the Governors 1891—1897. pp. V—VII, 1—808, ill.:*

The and administration of R. E. Pattison. *(Continued.) p. 1 ff.*

The administration of Daniel Hartman Hastings 1895—1899. *(Continued.) p. 495 ff.*

. . . *Vol. XII. Papers of the Governors 1897—1902. pp. V—VII, 1—963, ill.:*

The administration of D. H. Hastings. *(Concluded.) p. 1 ff.*

The administration of William Alexis Stone 1899—1903. *p. 371 ff.*

General index to the fourth series. *p. 641 ff.*

Pennsylvania Archives. Fifth series. Edited by **Thomas Lynch Montgomery.** *Harrisburg, Pa.: Harrisburg Publishing Co. 1906. 8 vols.*

Muster rolls of officers and soldiers of the French and Indian War and the War of the Revolution.

Pennsylvania Archives. Sixth series. Edited by **Thomas Lynch Montgomery.** *Vol. XV and XVI. Harrisburg, Pa. 1907.*

Index to Fifth series. A—Lear. = *Vol. XV.* Leard—Z. = *vol. XVI.*   [3199

Pionierwege und -landstraßen
Pioneer Roads and Highways

Hulbert, Archer Butler: Historic highways of America . . . Series of 16 vols. Cleveland, O.: The A. H. Clark Co. 1902—1905, ill., maps.

Vol. 1: Paths of the mound-building Indians and great game animals.

Vol. 2: Indian thoroughfares.

Vol. 3: Washington's road (Nemacolin's path) the first chapter of the old French War.

Vol. 4: Braddock's road and three relative papers.

Vol. 5: The old Glade (Forbes's road Pennsylvania state road).

Vol. 6: Boone's wilderniss road.

Vol. 7: Portage paths, the keys of the continent.

Vol. 8: Military roads of the Mississippi basin.

Vol. 9: Waterways of westward expansion.

Vol. 10: The Cumberland road.

Vol. 11 and 12: Pioneer roads and experiences of travelers.

Vol. 13 and 14: The great American canals: Vol. I. The Chesapeake and Ohio canal and the Pennsylvania canal; Vol. II. The Erie canal.

Vol. 15: The future of road making in America; a symposium.

Vol. 16: Index.   [3200

MacGill, Caroline E.   History of transportation in the United States before 1860. Prepared under the direction of Balthasar Henry Meyer by . . . and a staff of collaborators. Published by the Carnegie Institution of Washington. Washingtown, D. C.: Press of Gibson Brothers, Inc. 1917. pp. XI, 678, maps. = Carnegie Institutions of Washington. Publication no. 215c.

[Bibliography. pp. 609—649.]

Early trails, roads, and natural waterways. = Chapter I. pp. 3—64.

Tolls and transportation costs on early roads and canals. = Chapter II. pp. 65—93.

Traffic by rivers, trails, and roads in the trans-Appalachian region. = Chapter III. pp. 94—116.

Canals and waterways in Pennsylvania. = Chapter VII. pp. 207—248.

Railroads in the Middle Atlantic states. = Chapter XIV. pp. 382—413.
                                          [3201

Parkins, A. E.: The development of transportation in Pennsylvania. In: The Bulletin of the Geographical Society of Philadelphia. Vol. XIV, no. 3. Philadelphia, Pa., July, 1916. pp. 92—114; Vol. XV, no. 1. Jan., 1917. pp. 1—18, maps.   [3202

Plummer, Wilbur: Road policy of Pennsylvania. Thesis of Ph. D. University of Pennsylvania. Philadelphia, Pa. 1925. pp. 121, maps.

[Bibliography. pp. 112—121.]   [3203

Eshleman, H. Frank: The Great Conestoga road. In: Papers and Addresses of the Lancaster County Historical Society. Vol. XII. Lancaster, Pa. 1908. pp. 215—232, maps.   [3204

Gossler, Jacob L.: An old turnpike road with mere mention of some persons and places incident thereto. Printed for private distribution. New York, N. Y.: The Baker & Taylor Co. 1888. pp. 122.
                                          [3205

Hotchkin, Samuel Fitch: The York road, old and new. Philadelphia, Pa.: Binder & Kelly, 1892. pp. 516, ill.   [3206

Landis, Charles I.: History of the Philadelphia and Lancaster turnpike. The first long turnpike in the United States. In: The Pennsylvania Magazine of History and Biography. Vol. XLII. Philadelphia, Pa. 1918. pp. 1—28; 127—140; 235—258; 358—360; Vol, XLIII. 1919. pp. 84—90; 182—190. ill., maps.   [3207

— The first long turnpike in the United States. In: Papers and Addresses of the Lancaster County Historical Society. Vol. XX. Lancaster, Pa. 1918.

pp. 205—228; 235—258; 265—340, ill., maps. [3208

Klein, Theo B.: Roads and highways in eastern Pennsylvania and in Lebanon County. *In: Papers read before the Lebanon County Historical Society. Vol. II. Lebanon, Pa. 1901—1904. pp. 255—273.* [3209

Montgomery, Morton L.: Ancient milestones of Berks County highways. *A paper read Sept. 13, 1910. In: Transactions of the Historical Society of Berks County. Vol. III. Reading, Pa. 1923. pp. 50—68, ill.; pp. 155—164, ill.* [3210

Richards, Louis: Earliest county bridges in Berks County. *A paper read Dec. 9, 1913. In: Transactions of the Historical Society of Berks County. Vol. III. Reading, Pa. 1923. pp. 277—292.* [3211

Sachse, Julius Friedrich: The wayside inns on the Lancaster roadside between Philadelphia and Lancaster. *Lancaster, Pa.: The New Era Printing Co. 1912-14. = Part XXIV. „A narrative and critical history", prepared at the request of the Pennsylvania-German Society. In: The Pennsylvania-German Society. Proceedings and Addresses . . . 1910. Vol. XXI. Lancaster, Pa. 1912. Separate pagination. pp. 5—77, ill.; . . . 1911. Vol. XXII. Lancaster, Pa. 1913. Separate pagination. pp. 109, ill.* [3212

Searight, Thomas B.: The old pike. A history of the National road with

incidents, accidents and anecdotes thereon. *Uniontown, Pa.: Published by the author. Richmond, Ind.: M. Cullaton & Co. 1894. pp. 384, ill.* [3213

Travelling in 1784 and 1835. *In: Hazard's Register of Pennsylvania. Vol. 15. Philadelphia, Pa. 1835. p. 387.* [3214

Report on Pennsylvania. *From a M. S. volume, entitled „Haldimand Papers. Reports of the Indian Nations, &c." [The towns. — The German farmers.] In: The Perkiomen Region, Past and Present. Vol. II. Philadelphia, Pa. 1900. pp. 95—96.* [3215

Charles, Edwin: Canal lore. *Early conditions leading to the building of canals in Pennsylvania. In: The Pennsylvania-German. Vol. XII. Lititz, Pa. 1911. pp. 385—394, ill.* [3216

Fackenthal, B. F.: Improving navigation on the Delaware River with some account of its ferries, bridges, canals and floods. *Paper read at Point Pleasant, Bucks County, Pa., meeting, Sept. 10, 1927; revised April, 1932. In: A Collection of Papers read before the Bucks County Historical Society. Vol. VI. Allentown, Pa. 1932. pp. 103—230, ill.* [3217

Gausler, W. H.: Reminiscences of the Lehigh and Delaware canal from 1840 to 1856. *In: The Penn Germania. Vol. I. = Old series, Vol. XIII. Lititz, Pa. 1912. pp. 452—456.* [3218

Die Eingeborenen und der französisch-indianische Krieg[1])
The Aborigines, and the French and Indian War[2])

Beauchamp, Wm. M.: The life of Conrad Weiser as it relates to his services as official interpreter between New York and Pennsylvania and as envoy between Philadelphia and the Onondaga councils. *Compiled and edited by . . . Published by the Onandoga Historical Association at Syracuse, N. Y. 1925. Syracuse, N. Y.: The Syracuse Press 1925. pp. (2), 7—122, (3), ill.* [3219

Berlin, Alfred Franklin: A bit of Lehigh County Indian history. *In: The Pennsylvania-German. Vol. VII. Lebanon, Pa. 1906. pp. 227—231, ill.* [3220

— Lehigh County Indian history. *In: The Pennsylvania-German. Vol. XI. Lititz, Pa. 1910. pp. 288—290.* [3221

Brunner, D. B.: The Indians of Berks County, Pa. *being a summary of all the tangible records of the aborigines of Berks County, and containing cuts and descriptions of the varieties of relics found within the county. Written for the Society of Natural Sciences, Reading, Pa. Reading, Pa.: The Spirit of Berks Book Job and Printing Office 1881. pp. (1), 5—177, ill.; Second and revised edition. Reading, Pa.: Egle Book Print 1897. pp. (2), 5—257, ill.* [3222

Cronau, Rudolf: ,,Der Franzosenkrieg." *In: Drei Jahrhunderte deutschen Lebens in Amerika. Eine Geschichte der Deutschen in den Vereinigten Staaten. Von R. Cronau. Berlin 1909 [=Nr. 34]. S. 152—169, ill.; 2. Aufl. 1924. S. 151—168, ill.* [3222a

Donehoo, George P.: Christian Frederick Post's part in the capture of Fort Duquesne and in the conquest of the Ohio. *In: The Penn Germania. Vol. II. = Old series, vol. XIV. Cleona, Pa. 1913. p. 6.* [3223

— A short history of the Indian trails of Pennsylvania. *In: Proceedings and*

Collections of the Wyoming Historical and Genealogical Society. 1919. Vol. XVII. Wilkes-Barre, Pa. 1919. pp. 67—94. [3224

Donehoo, George P.: A history of the Indian villages and place names in Pennsylvania with numerous historical notes and references. *Harrisburg, Pa.: The Telegraph Press 1928. pp. XIV, 290.* [3225

Eshleman, H. Frank: Lancaster County Indians. *Annals of the Susquehannocks and other Indian tribes of the Susquehanna territory from about the year 1500 to 1763, the date of their extinction . . . Lancaster, Pa., [Lititz, Pa.]: Express Printing Co. 1909. pp. 415.* [3226

[Heckewelder, Johann]: Johann Heckewelder's Evangelischen Predigers zu Bethlehem Nachricht von der Geschichte den Sitten und Gebräuchen der Indianischen Völkerschaften, welche ehemals Pennsylvania und die benachbarten Staaten bewohnten. *Aus dem Englischen übersetzt und mit den Angaben anderer Schriftsteller über eben dieselben Gegenstände (Carver, Loskiel, Long, Volney) vermehrt von* Fr. Hesse. *Nebst einem die Glaubwürdigkeit und den anthropologischen Werth der Nachrichten Heckewelder's betreffenden Zusatze von* G. E. Schulze. *Göttingen: Vandenhoeck und Ruprecht 1821. XLVIII, 582, (2) S.* [3227

— History, manners and customs of the Indian nations who once inhabited Pennsylvania and the neighboring states. *By the Rev. John Heckewelder, of Bethlehem, Pa. New revised edition with an introduction and notes by* William C. Reichel. *Philadelphia, Pa.: Publication Fund of the Historical Society of Pennsylvania 1876. pp. XLVI, 47—465, ill. = Memoirs of the Historical Society of Pennsylvania. Vol. XII.* [3228

Rawle, William: A vindication of the Rev. Heckeweller's History of the Indian nations. *Read at a meeting of the council*

---

[1]) Siehe auch unter: Die Missionen der Brüdergemeinde = Nr. 1706—1795.
[2]) See also: Moravian Indian missions = nos. 1706—1795.

on the 15th day of February, 1826. *In: Memoirs of the Historical Society of Pennsylvania. Vol. I. = Part II. Philadelphia, Pa. 1826. pp. 258—275.* [3229

Heilman, S. P.: A final word as to Regina, the German captive. *In: Papers read before the Lebanon County Historical Society. Vol. III. Lebanon, Pa. 1905—1906. pp. 202—251.* [3229a

Heller, W. J.: The disappearance of the Lenni Lenape from the Delaware and their subsequent migrations. *In: The Penn Germania. Vol. I. = Old series, vol. XIII. Lititz, Pa. 1912. pp. 711—717.* [3230

Kern, D. N.: Indian relics of Lehigh County, Pa. *In: The Pennsylvania-German. Vol. XII. Lititz, Pa. 1911. pp. 169—170.* [3231

[Le Roy, Maria und Leininger, Barbara]: *Die Eerzehlungen von Maria le Roy und Barbara Leininger, welche vierthalb Jahr unter den Indianern gefangen gewesen, und am 6ten May in dieser Stadt glücklich angekommen. Aus ihrem eignen Mund niedergeschrieben und zum Druck befördert. Philadelphia, gedruckt und zu haben in der teutschen Buchdruckerey, das Stück vor 6 Pentz. MDCCLIX. 14 S.* [3231a

[— - —] The narrative of Marie Le Roy and Barbara Leininger, who spent three and one half years as prisoners among the Indians, and arrived safely in this city on the sixth of May. *Written and printed as dedicated by them. Philadelphia, Pa.: German Printing Office 1759. Translation from the German of the original narrative. In: Pennsylvania Archives. Second series. Edited by John B. Linn and Wm. H. Egle. Vol. VII. Harrisburg, Pa. 1895. pp. 427—438.* [3232

[— - —] The narrative of Marie Le Roy and Barbara Leininger, for three years captives among the Indians. *Translated by Edmund de Schweinitz. In: The Pennsylvania Magazine of History and Biography. Vol. XXIX. Philadelphia, Pa. 1905. pp. 407—420.* [3233

MacMinn, . . .: On the frontier with Colonel Antes or the struggle for supremacy of the red and white races in Pennsylvania. *Camden, N. J.: S. Chew & Sons 1900. pp. 513, ill.* [3234

Morrison, John: David Zeisberger and his Delaware Indians. *In: Ontario Historical Society. Papers and Records. Vol.*

XII. *Toronto, Ca. 1914. pp. 176—202.* [3235

[Mühlenberg, H. M.]: Pastor Mühlenberg über die Indianer. *(Abdruck aus den „Hallischen Nachrichten", S. 247.) In: Der Deutsche Pionier. Jg. V. 1873—74. Cincinnati, O. 1874. S. 248—249.* [3236

[Post, Frederick]: Journal of Frederick Post's journey from Philadelphia to Wyoming, June the 20th, 1758. *In: Colonial Records of Pennsylvania. Vol. VIII. 1852. pp. 142—145.* [3237

Richards, Henry Melchior Mühlenberg: The Pennsylvania-German in the French and Indian War. *A historical sketch. Lancaster, Pa.: New Era Printing Co. 1905. = Part XV. „A narrative and critical history", prepared at the request of the Pennsylvania-German Society. Proceedings and Addresses . . . 1904. Vol. XV. Lancaster, Pa. 1906. Separate pagination. pp. 559, ill., maps.* [3238

Richards, H. M. M. and Heilman, S. P.: Regina, the German captive Regina Hartman. *Part. I. The location. By H. M. M. Richards; Part. II. The story. By S. P. Heilman. In: Papers read before the Lebanon County Historical Society. Vol. II. 1901—1904. Lebanon, Pa. 1904. pp. 81—97.* *[See no. 3228a]* [3238a

Sipe, C. Hale: The Indian chiefs of Pennsylvania or a story of the part played by the American Indian in the history of Pennsylvania, *based primarily on the Pennsylvania Archives and Colonial Records, and built around the outstanding chiefs. With introduction by George P. Donehoo. Butler, Pa.: The Ziegler Printing Co. 1927. pp. (1), (5), 13—569.* [3239

— The Indian wars of Pennsylvania. *An account of the Indian events, in Pennsylvania, of the French and Indian War, Pontiac's War, Lord Dunmore's War, the Revolutionary War and the Indian uprising from 1789 to 1795. Tragedies of the Pennsylvania frontier, based primarily on the Pennsylvania Archives and Colonial Records. Harrisburg, Pa.: The Telegraph Press 1929. pp. (5), (5), 17—793, map.; Supplement to the first edition. Harrisburg, Pa. 1931. pp. (3), 7—115; Second edition, including supplement to first edition. Harrisburg, Pa.: The Telegraph Press 1931. pp. (5), (5), 17—908.* [3240

Spindler, Adaline Bream: Our aboriginal predecessors: *on the origin and relation of the various Indian tribes of North-America. In: Papers and Addresses of the Lancaster County Historical Society. Vol. XXI. Lancaster, Pa. 1917. pp. 85—92.* [3241

Walton, Joseph Solomon: Conrad Weiser and the Indian policy of colonial Pennsylvania. *Philadelphia, Pa.: G. W. Jacobs & Co. [1900.] pp. (5) 9—420, ill.* [3242

Weiser, Conrad]: Conrad Weiser's report of his journey to Shamokin, in obedience to the governor's letter of the 26th January last: — Jan. 31. 1742-3 — Febr. 9th. *In: Colonial Records of Pennsylvania. Vol. IV. 1851. pp. 640—646.* [3243

[—] Conrad Weiser's report of his journey to Onondago on the affairs of Virginia, in obedience to the orders of the governor in council, 13 June, 1743, *delivered to the governor the 1st September. In: Colonial Records of Pennsylvania. Vol. IV. 1851. pp. 660—669.* [3244

[—] Conrad Weiser — his report of his journey to Shamokin. Dated, „Shamokin, May 2d, 1744". *In: Colonial Records of Pennsylvania. Vol. IV. 1851. pp. 680—685.* [3245

[—] The journal of Conrad Weiser, Esqr., Indian interpreter to Ohio. — Aug. 11, 1748—Sept. 28, 1748. Dated „Pennsburg, Sept. 29th, 1748". *In: Colonial Records of Pennsylvania. Vol. V. 1851. pp. 348—358.* [3246

[—] A journal of the proceedings of Conrad Weiser in his journey to Onondago, with a message from the honorable Thomas Lee, Esquire, president of Virginia, to the Indians there. — Aug. 15, 1750 to Oct. 1, 1750 — Dated, „The 10th of October, 1750". *In: Colonial Records of Pennsylvania. Vol. V. 1851. pp. 470—480.* [3247

[—] Mr. Weiser's journal of his proceedings at Onondago. — 1751, June 27th to July 10th. *In: Colonial Records of Pennsylvania. Vol. V. 1851. pp. 541—543.* [3248

[—] Journal of Conrad Weiser to the Mohocks' Country. — July 24th, 1753 to Aug. 30th. — „Dated in Philadelphia the 2d September, 1753." *In: Colonial Records of Pennsylvania. Vol. V. 1851. pp. 642—647.* [3249

[Weiser, Conrad]: Letter from Mr. Weiser, relating to Teedyuscung and the Indians now at Easton. *See: Minutes of a council held at Philadelphia, 3rd November, 1756. In: Colonial Records of Pennsylvania. Vol. VII. 1851. pp. 308 —311.* [3250

[—] Mr. Weiser's report of his sentiments about certain Indian affairs (request of Teedyuscung . . .) Letter to the governor, dated, „September 19th, 1757". *Read at a council, Philadelphia, 19th Sept., 1757. In: Colonial Records of Pennsylvania. Vol. VII. 1851. pp. 735—736.* [3251

[—] „Memorandum of the News Will Sock, and a Cayuga Indian named Jorachgnison, both lately come from the Six Nation, taken the 6th of May, 1758", *written down by* Conrad Weiser *and at council, Philadelphia, 8th of May, 1758. In: Colonial Records of Pennsylvania. Vol. VIII. 1852. pp. 118—121.* [3252

[—] Notes of the Iroquois and Delaware Indians. *Communications from Conrad Weiser to Christopher Saur, which appeared in the years 1746—1749 in his newspaper printed at Germantown, entitled „The High German Pennsylvania Historical Writer, or A Collection of important Events from the Kingdom of Nature and the Church" and from his Saur's Almanacs. Compiled by Abraham H. Cassel. Translated by Helen Bell. In: The Philadelphia Magazine of History and Biography. Vol. I. Philadelphia, Pa. 1877. pp. 163—167; 319—323; Vol. II. 1878. pp. 407—410.* [3253

Weiser, R.: Regina, the German captive; or true piety among the lowly. *Philadelphia, Pa.: General Council Publication Board 1919. pp. 252, ill.* [3253a

[Zeisberger, David]: David Zeisberger's history of the northern American Indians. *Edited by* **Archer Butler Hulbert** and **William Nathaniel Schwarze.** *Columbus, O.: The F. J. Heer Printing Co. 1910. pp. II, 189. = Ohio Archaeological and Historical Quaterly. Vol. XIX. Jan. & April, 1910. No. 1—2.* [3254

Conditions of Pennsylvania during the year 1755. A translation of a French pamphlet found in the Ducal Library at Gotha, Germany. *[„État présent de la Pensilvanie où l'on trouve le détail de ce* qui s'y est passé depuis la défaite du Général Braddock jusqu'à la prise d'Oswego, avec une carte particulière de cette colonie. MDCCLVI."] Paper read by Julius F. Sachse at the 24th annual meeting at Lancaster, Pa., Nov. 13, 1914. Lancaster, Pa.: The New Era Printing Co. 1917. In: The Pennsylvania-German Society. Proceedings and Addresses . . . 1914. Vol. XXV. Lancaster, Pa. 1917. Separate pagination. pp. 38, ill., map. [3255

Report of the commission to locate the site of the frontier forts of Pennsylvania. Edited by William Henry Egle. State Librarian. 2 vols. Harrisburg, Pa.: Clarence M. Busch 1896. pp. V, 627, ill., maps; pp. 636, ill., maps.; Second edition. Edited by Thomas Lynch Montgomery. Harrisburg, Pa.: Wm. Stanley Ray 1916. pp. XVII, 627, ill., maps; 636, ill., maps.

(1) Richards, H. M. M.: The Indian forts of the Blue Mountains. Vol. I. pp. 1—347.

(2) Buckalew, John M.: The frontier forts within the North and West Branches of the Susquehanna River. Vol. I. pp. 349—418.

(3) Reynolds, Sheldon: The frontier within the Wyoming Valley region. Vol. I. pp. 419—466.

(4) Weiser, Jay Gilfillan: The frontier forts in the Cumberland and Juniata Valleys. Vol. I. pp. 467—627.

(5) Albert, George Dallas: The frontier forts of western Pennsylvania. Vol. II. pp. 1—636.

Montgomery, Th. L.: Prefatory note. Second edition. Vol. I. pp. VI—XVII. [3256

Fears of an Indian outbreak in 1757. [Appeal for contributions, published in Saur's Germantown newspapers, July, 1757.] In: The Perkiomen Region, Past and Present. Vol. I. Philadelphia, Pa. 1895. p. 157. [3257

Murder of ten Indians by Frederick Stump. In: The Penn Germania. Vol. II. = Old series, vol. XIV. Lititz, Pa. 1913. pp. 97—100. [3258

List of Pennsylvania settlers murdered, scalped and taken prisoners by Indians, 1755—1756. Copied from the Conrad Weiser papers in the manuscript department of the Historical Society of Pennsylvania — [settlers in what are now the Counties of Berks, Dauphin, Lancaster, Lebanon, Monroe and Northampton, and the Valley of the Lehigh]. In: The Pennsylvania Magazine of History and Biography. Vol. XXXII. Philadelphia, Pa. 1908. pp. 309—319. [3259

Indian invasion of Northampton County 1755—1756. (Notes on the Provincial troops quartered in Nazareth and vicinity.) In: The Pennsylvania Magazine of History and Biography. Vol. XXXVI. Philadelphia, Pa. 1912. p. 120. [3260

In the French and Indian War. (An original journal of Lieut. Andrew Engle, an officier of the frontiers during the French and Indian marauds from 1755 to 1764.) In: Notes and Queries. Edited by W. H. Egle. Annual vol. 1897. Harrisburg, Pa. 1898. p. 13. [3261

Six months on the frontier of Northampton County, Pa., during the Indian War, October, 1755— June, 1756. (Recorded by the chroniclers of Nazareth.) In: The Pennsylvania Magazine of History and Biography. Vol. XXXIX. Philadelphia, Pa. 1915. pp. 345—352. [3262

Some account of the capture, captivity and release from Indians, of a little girl, 1755. [Maria Christiana Schmidt, b. in Conewago, near York, Pa., Aug. 1, 1746.] In: The Pennsylvania Magazine of History and Biography. Vol. XLIII. Philadelphia, Pa. 1919. p. 284. [3263

Die Nachbarn der Deutschen in Pennsylvanien

The Neighbors of the Pennsylvania-Germans

Niederländer und Schweden

Dutch and Swedes

Acrelius, Israel: A history of New Sweden; or the settlements on the River Delaware. *By* Israel Acrelius. *Provost of the Swedish churches in America, and rector of the old Swedes Church, Wilmington, Del. [Stockholm: Harberg & Hasselberg 1759.] Translated from the Swedish with an introduction and notes by* William M. Reynolds. *Published under the joint auspices of the Historical Societies of Pennsylvania and Delaware. Philadelphia, Pa.: Publication Fund of the Historical Society of Pennsylvania. 1874. pp. VII—L; 17—458, ill., map. = Memoirs of the Historical Society of Pennsylvania. No. 11.* [3264

Arfwedson, Carolus David: A brief history of the colony of New Sweden *which, by the kind permission of the Faculty of Philosophy at Upsala, . . . the author publicy presented in the Gustivianeum, on the 19th day of November, 1825 . . . Upsala: Set up by the Typographers of the Royal Academy. Translation of the Swedish text by* K. W. Granlund: *of the Latin text by* Edward T. Horn. *Edited by* Julius F. Sachse. *Lancaster, Pa. 1909. In: The Pennsylvania German Society, Proceedings and Addresses . . . 1907. Vol. XVIII. Lancaster, Pa. 1909.*

Separate pagination. pp. 44, ill., map. [3265

Carson, Hampton L.: Dutch and Swedish settlements on the Delaware. *A paper read before the Historical Society of Pennsylvania, Nov. 9, 1908. In: The Pennsylvania Magazine of History and Biography. Vol. XXXIII. Philadelphia, Pa. 1909. pp. 1—21.* [3266

Hoffsten, E. G.: The Swedes in Philadelphia to-day. *In: German American Annals. Vol. I. Philadelphia, Pa. 1903—08. pp. 371—383, ill.* [3267

Schmauk, Theodore E.: The Lutheran Church and the Province of Pennsylvania in the seventeenth century. *In: The Lutheran Church Review. Vol. XV. Philadelphia, Pa. 1896. pp. 134—151.* [3268

Seidensticker, Oswald: Beziehungen der Deutschen zu den Schweden in Pennsylvanien. Kulturgeschichtlicher Beitrag. *In: Der Deutsche Pionier. Jg. VI. Cincinnati, O. 1874—1875. S. 400—405; 426—432.* [3269

Ward, Christopher: The Dutch and Swedes on the Delaware 1609—64. *Philadelphia, Pa.: University of Pennsylvania Press 1930. pp. XI, 393, ill.* [3270

Engländer

English

Dunaway, Wayland Fuller: The English settlers in colonial Pennsylvania. *In: The Pennsylvania Magazine of History and Biography. Vol. LII. Philadelphia, Pa. 1928. pp. 317—341.* [3271

Applegarth, Albert C.: Quakers in Pennsylvania. (Customes and laws.) *Baltimore, Md.: The Johns Hopkins Press 1892. pp. 5—84. = Johns Hopkins University Studies in Historical and Political Science. Tenth series, pp. VIII—IX; 385—464.* [3272

Bowden, James: The history of the Society of Friends in America. *2 vols.*

London: Charles Gilpin; printer: London: Richard Barrett 1850. pp. VIII, 426, maps; Vol. II. 1854. pp. 411, maps.
[3273

Jones, Rufus M., Sharpless, Isaac and Gummere, Amelia M.: The Quakers in the American colonies. London: Macmillan & Co., 1911. pp. XXXII, 603, 3 maps.
[3274

Pound, Arthur: The Penns of Pennsylvania and England. New York, N. Y.: The Macmillan Co. 1932. pp. XX, 349, ill., map.
[3275

Perry, William Stevens: Historical collections relating to the American colonial Church. Vol. II. Pennsylvania. Hartford, Conn.: The Church Press 1871. pp. III—XXI, 607.
[Protestant Episcopal Church in Pennsylvania.]
[3276

Egle, William H.: Documents relating to the Connecticut settlement in the Wyoming Valley. Edited by . . . Harrisburg, Pa.: E. K. Meyers 1893. pp. IV, 792, maps.
= Pennsylvania Archives. Second series, vol. XVIII.
[3277

Walliser
Welsh

Browning, Charles H.: Welsh settlement of Pennsylvania. Philadelphia, Pa.: William J. Campbell 1912. pp. 631, ill., maps.
[3278

Eshleman, H. Frank: Two centuries of Caernarvon history. In: Papers and Addresses of the Lancaster County Historical Society. Vol. XXVI. Lancaster, Pa. 1922. pp. 145—151.
[3279

Jenkins, Howard M.: Historical collections relating to Gwynedd. A township of Montgomery County, Pa., settled 1698, by Welsh immigrants. With some data

referring to the adjoining township of Montgomery, also a Welsh settlement. Philadelphia, Pa.: Ferris Bros. 1884. pp. (5), 396, (4), ill.
[3280

Lincoln, J. B.: The story of Caernarvon. In: Papers and Addresses of the Lancaster County Historical Society. Vol. XVIII. Lancaster, Pa. 1914. pp. 59—79.
[3281

Owen, B. F.: The Welsh of Cumru Township. In: Transactions of the Historical Society of Berks County. Vol. I, no. 7. Reading, Pa. 1904. pp. (6).
[3282

Irland-Schotten
„Scotch-Irish"

Armor, William C.: Scotch-Irish bibliography of Pennsylvania. In: Proceedings and Addresses of the Eighth Congress 1896. The Scotch-Irish Society of America. Vol. VIII. Nashville, Tenn. 1897. pp. 253—289.
[3283

Black, George Fraser: Scotland's mark on America. With a foreword by John Foord. New York, N. Y.: The Scottish Section of „America's Making". 1921. pp. 126.
[3284

Chambers, George: Tribute to the principles, virtues, habits and public usefulness of the Irish and Scotch early settlers of Pennsylvania. Second edition. Chambersburg, Pa.: M. A. Foltz. 1871. pp. 172.
[3285

Ford, Henry Jones: The Scotch-Irish in America. Princeton, N. Y.: Princeton University Press. 1915. pp. 607.

[„Pennsylvania. The Scotch-Irish centre" Chapter IX. pp. 260—290.]
[3286

Hanna, Charles A.: The Scotch-Irish or the Scot in North Britain, North Ireland and North America. 2 vols. New York, N. Y. and London: G. P. Putnam's Sons, The Knickerbocker Press 1902. pp. V—IX; 623, 2 maps; III—IV, 602, 1 map.
[Scotch-Irish Bibliography. In: Vol. II. pp. 531—551.]
[3287

Linehan, John C.: The Irish-Scots and the „Scotch-Irish." An historical and ethnological monograph, with some reference to Scotia major and Scotia minor. Concord, N. H.: The America-Irish Historical Society 1902. pp. 138.
[3288

MacLean, J. P.: An historical account of the settlement of Scotch Highlanders in

America prior to the peace of 1783 together with notices of Highland Regiments and biographical sketches. *Cleveland, O.: Helman-Taylor Co. 1900. pp. XVI, 17—459, ill.* [3289
Ross, Peter: The Scot in America. *New York, N.Y.: The Raeburn Book Co. 1896. pp. XI, 446.* [3290

Christian, Bolivar: The Scotch-Irish settlers in the Valley of Virginia. *Alumm address at Washington College, Lexington, Va. Richmond: Macfarlane & Fergusson 1860. pp. 38.* [3291
Hensel, W. U.: The Scotch-Irish: Their impress on Lancaster County, Pa. *In: Papers and Addresses of the Lancaster County Historical Society. Vol. IX. Lancaster, Pa. 1905. pp. 246—268.* [3292

McIlhaney, Asa K.: The Irish settlement in the Forks of the Delaware. *Reprint from: ,,The Presbyterian", July and August, 1847, submitted for publication by ... In: The Penn Germania. Vol. I. = Old series, vol. XIII. Lititz, Pa. 1912. pp. 632—640.* [3293
Meyer, T. P.: The Germans of Pennsylvania, their comming and conflicts with the Irish. *In: The Pennsylvania-German. Vol. XI. Lititz, Pa. 1910. pp. 38—47. Reviewed and corrected by* **Martin I. J. Gfiffen.** *ibid. pp. 124—126.* [3294
Stewart, John: Scotch-Irish occupancy and exodus. *Read March 30th, 1899. In: Kittochtinny Historical Society. Papers read before the Society from Febr. 1899 to Febr. 1901. Vol. II. Chambersburg, Pa. 1903. pp. 14—28.* [3295

Iren
Irish

Maginniss, Thomas Hobbs: The Irish contribution to America's independence. *Philadelphia, Pa.: Published by the Doire Publishing Co. Press of Wm. F. Fell Co. 1913. pp. 140.* [3296
McGee, Thomas D'Arcy: A history of the Irish settlers in North America from the earliest period to the census of 1850.

Boston, Mass.: Office of the ,,American Celt" 1851. pp. 180. [3297
Myers, Albert Cook: Immigration of the Irish Quakers into Pennsylvania 1682—1750, with their early history in Ireland. *Swarthmore, Pa.: The author; Lancaster, Pa.: Press of the New Era Printing Co. 1901. pp. V—XXII, 477, ill.* [3298

Hugenotten und sogenannte „Hugenotten"
Huguenots and so-called „Huguenots"

Bachert, A. C.: Huguenot absorption in America. *In: The Pennsylvania-German. Vol. XI. Lititz, Pa. 1910. pp. 21—28.* [3299
Baird, Charles W.: History of the Huguenot emigration to America. *2 vols. New York, N. Y.: Dodd, Mead & Co. 1885. pp. XIX; 21—354; XI, 13—448, ill.* [3300
Dunaway, Wayland Fuller: The French racial strain in colonial Pennsylvania. *In: The Pennsylvania Magazine of History and Biography. Vol. LIII. Philadelphia, Pa. 1929. pp. 322—342.* [3301
Landis, C. I.: Madame Mary Ferree and the Huguenots of Lancaster County, Pa. *In: Papers and Addresses of the Lancaster County Historical Society. Vol. XXI. Lancaster, Pa. 1917. pp. 101—124, maps.* [3302
Laux, James B.: The Huguenot element in Pennsylvania. *Address delivered before*

the Huguenot Society of America, in Assembly Hall, United Charities Building, New York City, April 30, 1896. pp. 21. [3303
Laux, James B.: Our [Laux family's] Huguenot ancestry: *the ancient home in France. In: The Pennsylvania-German. Vol. XII. Lititz, Pa. 1911. pp. 259—266.* [3304
Ranck, Henry H.: The Huguenots and American life. *In: The Reformed Church Review. Fifth series, vol. III. Lancaster, Pa. 1924. pp. 327—346.* [3305
Roberts, Charles Rhoads: The first Huguenot settlers in the Lehigh Valley. *Allentown, Pa. Nov. 21, 1918. pp. 23, ill.* [3306
Stapleton, A.: Memorials of the Huguenots in America, with special reference to their emigration to Pennsylvania. *Carlisle, Pa.: Huguenot Publishing Co. 1901. pp. IX, 164, ill.* [3307

Frühe Beschreibungen, Tagebücher und Briefe
Early Descriptions, Journals and Letters

Beschreibungen aus dem 17. Jahrhundert
Descriptions of the 17th century

Recueil de diverses pieces, concernant la Pensylvanie. *La Haye: A. Troyel 1684. pp. 118.*
  Contents: — [Penn, W.]: *Brief recit de la province de Pensylvanie, nouvellement accordé par le roy . . . au sieur Guillaume Penn . . .*
  Furly, [B.]: *Eclaircissemens de monsieur Furly, sur plusieurs articles, touchant l'etablissement de la Pensylvanie (dated: A Roterdam ce 6. mars, 1684).*
  Penn, [W.]: *Lettre de monsieur Penn... Contenant une description generale de la dite province [dated]: A Philadelphie ce 8. [i. e. 16]. Aoust 1683. Vn recit alregé de la situation, et grandeur de la ville de Philadelphia.*
  Paschall, T.: *Extrait d'une lettre escrite de Pensylvanie, par Thomas Paskel à J. J. [de] Chippenham en Angleterre en date du 10 fevrier 1683, nouveau style.*
  Deutsche Ausgabe: Beschreibung der in America new-erfunden Provinz Pensylvanien. Derer Inwohner Gesetz, Arth, Sitten und Gebrauch: auch samlicher reviren des Landes sonderlich der Haupt-stadt Philadelphia. *Hamburg 1684. 32 S.*
  English translation: Collections of various pieces concerning Pennsylvania, printed in 1684. *Translated by* Samuel W. Pennypacker. *In: The Pennsylvania Magazine of History and Biography. Vol. VI. Philadelphia, Pa. 1882. pp. 312—328.* [3308

Heuser, Emil: Pennsylvanien im 17. Jahrhundert und die ausgewanderten Pfältzer in England. *Mit drei Faksimile-Drucken. Neustadt a. d. Haardt: Ludwig Witter 1910. (1), 82 S., ill.*
  [Enthält Auszüge der frühen Landbeschreibungen unter Bezug auf die pfälzische Auswanderung.] [3309

Myers, Albert Cook: Narratives of early Pennsylvania, West New Jersey and Delaware, 1630—1707. *Edited by . . . New York, N. Y.: Charles Scribner's Sons 1912. pp. XIV, (1), 476, maps, ill. Original narratives of early American history. Reproduced under the auspices of the American Historical Association.*

  Contents:

  (1) From the „Korte Historiael ende Journaels Aenteyckeninge" by David Pietersz de Vries, *1630—1633, 1644 (1655).*
  (2) Relation of Captain Thomas Yong, *1634.*
  (3) From the „Account of the Swedish Churches in New Sweden", by Reverend Israel Acrelius, *1759.*
  (4) Affidavit of four men from the „Key of Calmar", 1638.
  (5) Report of Governor Johan Printz, *1644.*
  (6) Report of Governor Johan Printz, *1647.*
  (7) Report of Governor Johan Rising, *1654.*
  (8) Report of Governor Johan Rising, *1655.*
  (9) Relation of the Surrender of New Sweden, by Governor Johan Clason Rising, *1655.*
  (10) The Epistle of Penn, Lawrie *and* Lucas, *respecting West Jersey, 1676.*
  (11) The present state of the Colony of West Jersey, 1681.
  (12) Some account of the Province of Pennsylvania, by William Penn, *1681.*
  (13) Letter from William Penn *to the Committee of the Free Society of Traders, 1683.*
  (14) Letter of Thomas Paschall, *1683.*
  (15) A further account of the Province of Pennsylvania, by William Penn, *1685.*

(16) Letters of Doctor **Nicholas More,** *and others, 1686.*

(17) A short description of Pennsylvania, by **Richard Frame,** *1692.*

(18) An historical and geographical account of Pennsylvania and of West-New-Jersey, by **Gabriel Thomas,** *1698.*

(19) Circumstantial geographical description of Pennsylvania, by **Francis Daniel Pastorius,** *1700.*

(20) Letter of **John Jones,** *1725.*
[3310

Budd, Thomas: Good order established in Pennsylvania New Jersey in America, *being a true account of the country; with its produce and commodities there made. Philadelphia, Pa.: Wm. Bradford 1685. pp. 39, (1).* [3311

[Penn, William]: Some account of the Province of Pennsylvania in America; lately granted under the great seal of England to William Penn, etc. *Together with privileges and powers necessary to the well-governing thereof. Made public for the information of such as are or may be disposed to transport themselves or servants into those parts. London: Printed and sold by Benjamin Clark 1681. pp. 10.*

[German translation: Amsterdam 1681, see no. 215] [3312

— A brief account of the Province of Pennsylvania, lately granted by the king, under the great seal of England, to William Penn and his heirs and assigns. *Colophon: [London: Printed for Benjamin Clark 1681.] pp. 8, map.*

[Boston, 1924: American series; photostat reproductions by the Massachusetts Historical Society, no. 115.]

... London: Printed for Benjamin Clark 1682. pp. 14.

[German translation: Amsterdam 1682, see no. 216] [3313

— Letter from William Penn to the Committee of the Free Society of Traders. *London 1683.*

[German translation see no. 217] [3314

[—] Missive van William Penn, Eygenaar en Gouverneur van Pennsylvania, in America. *Geschreven aan de Commissarissen van de Vrye Societeyt der Handelaars, op de selve Provintie, binnen London resideerende ... Waar by noch gevoehgt is een Beschrijving ... de Hooft-Stadt Philadelphia ... Amsterdam: Jacob Claus 1684. pp. 23, map of Philadelphia.* [3315

Penn, William: Information and direction to such persons as are inclined to America, more especially those related to the Province of Pennsylvania. *[London 1684?] pp. 4. [An original copy in the Library of the Pennsylvania Historical Society, Philadelphia, Pa.]*

Boston, 1924; American series; photostat reproductions by the Massachusetts Historical Society, no. 122. [3316

[Webb, Robert]: Detailed information and account for those who are inclined to America and are interested in settling in the Province of Pennsylvania, with a preface. *Containing various noteworthy things concerning the present condition and the government of the province. Never before printed but now first published by Robert Webb, Amsterdam, By Jacob Claus. ... 1686. [Translation of Nader Informatie en Bericht voor die gene die genegen zijn, om zich na America te begeeven, en in de Provincie van Pensylvania geinteresseerd zijn, of zich daar zoeken neder te zetten. Met een Vorreden behelzende verscheydene aanmerkelijke zaken vanden tegenwoordige toestand, en Regeering dier Provincie; Nooit voor dezen in druk geweest: mar un eerst uitgegeven door Robert Webb, Amsterdam, by Jacob Claus ... 1686.]*
In: The Pennsylvania Magazine of History and Biography. Vol. XLIX. Philadelphia, Pa. 1925. pp. 115—140.
Introduction to the above: A rare Dutch document concerning the Province of Pennsylvania in the seventeenth century. *By* **Daniel Shumway.** *In: The Pennsylvania Magazine of History and Biography. Vol. XLIX. Philadelphia, Pa. 1925. pp. 99—114.* [3317

Thomas, Gabriel: An historical and geographical account of the Province and Country of Pennsylvania; and of West-New-Jersey in America. *The richness of the soil, the sweetness of the situation, the wholesomeness of the air, the navigable rivers, and others, the prodigious encrease of corn, the flourishing condition of the City of Philadelphia, with the stately buildings, and other improvements there. The strange creatures as birds, fishes, and fowls, with the several sort of minerals, purging waters, and stones, lately discovered. The natives, aborigines, their language, religion, laws, and customs; the first planters, the Dutch, Swedes, and English, with the number of its inhabi-*

20

tants, as also a touch upon George Keith's new religion, in his second change since he left the Quakers. London: Printed for and sold by A. Baldwin 1898. pp. (6), 55. An historical and geographical account of the Province and Country of Pennsylvania and of West-New-Jersey in America. *London: Printed and sold by A. Baldwin 1698. Separate title page and pagination. pp. (9), 34, map. Lithographed reprint: New York, N. Y.: For Henry Austin Brady 1848.*

Reprint: An account of Pennsylvania and West-New-Jersey *by* Gabriel Thomas. *Reprinted from the original edition of 1698. With an introduction by C y r u s T o w n-s e n d B r a d y. Cleveland, O.: The Burrows Brothers Co. 1903. pp. 83, map.*
[German translation: Frankfurt und Leipzig 1702, see no. 237] [3318

Pastorius, Franz Daniel: *Vgl.: Deutsche Flugblätter zur Auswanderung nach Amerika; see: German pamphlets which influenced the emigration to America.*

Beschreibungen aus dem 18. Jahrhundert
Descriptions of the 18th century

Mereness, Newton D.: Travels in the American colonies. *Edited under the auspices of the National Society of the Colonial Dames of America. New York, N. Y.: The Macmillan Co. 1916. pp. 693.* [3319
Achenwall, Gottfried: Einige Anmerkungen über Nordamerika, und über dasige Grosbritannische Colonien. *(Aus mündlichen Nachrichten des Hrn. Dr. Franklins.) In: Hannoverisches Magazin . . . Fünfter Jahrgang vom Jahr 1767. Hannover: H. E. C. Schlüter 1768. 17tes Stück, Spalte 257—272; 18tes Stück, Spalte 273—296; 31stes Stück, Spalte 481—496; 32stes Stück, Spalte 497—508.* [3320
— Herrn Hofrath Achenwalls in Göttingen Anmerkungen über Nordamerika und über dasige Grosbritannische Colonien, *aus mündlichen Nachrichten des Herrn Dr. Franklins. Frankfurt und Leipzig 1769. 94 S.*
[Neudruck aus Hannoverisches Magazin 1767, vgl. Nr. 3320] [3321
— Einige Anmerkungen über Nord-Amerika und über dasige Grossbritanische Colonien. *Aus mündlichen Nachrichten des Herrn Dr. Franklins, verfasst von . . . Nebst Herrn John Wesleys Schrift von den Streitigkeiten mit den Colonien in Amerika. Helmstedt: Johann Heinrich Kühlin 1777. 72 S.* [3322
[—] Achenwall's observations on North America, 1767. *(Translation of ,,Some Observations on North America and the British Colonies from verbal information of Dr. Franklin'' published by Professor*

Achenwall in the ,,Hanoverian Magazine'', in the volume beginning 1767. pp. 258 [= no. 3320].) Translated by J. G. Rosengarten. *In: The Pennsylvania Magazine of History and Biography. Vol. XXVII. Philadelphia, Pa. 1903. pp. 1 —19.*
Reprint in: The Pennsylvania-German Society. Proceedings and Addresses . . . Vol. XIII. Lancaster, Pa. 1904. pp. 69 —90. [3323
[Anburey, Thomas]: Travels through the interior parts of America; in a series of letters. *By an officer. Vol. II. London: William Lane 1789. pp. 558, ill.* [3324
[—] Anburey's Reisen im inneren Amerika. *Aus dem Englischen übersetzt von* Georg Forster. *In: Magazin von merkwürdigen neuen Reisebeschreibungen, aus fremden Sprachen übersetzt und mit erläuternden Anmerkungen begleitet. Bd. VI. Berlin: In der Vossischen Buchhandlung 1792. 1—372 S., ill.* [3325
[Beauchamp, . . .]: Journal of Beauchamp's journey from Mobile to the Choctaws, 1746. *In: Mereness: Travels in the American colonies. New York, N. Y. 1916 [= no. 3319]. pp. 259—297.* [3326
Burnaby, Andrew: Travels through the Middle settlements in North-America, in the years 1759—1760. With observations upon the state of the colonies. *London: T. Payne 1775. pp. VIII, 106.* [3327
Castiglioni, Luigi: Viaggio negli Stati Uniti dell' America Settentrionale fatto negli anni 1785, 1786, e 1787. *Con*

alcune osservazioni sui vegetabili piu utili di quel paese. 2 vols. Milano: Guiseppe Marelli 1790. pp. XII, 403; VI, 402. [3328

[Castiglioni, Luigi]: Luigi Castiglioni's . . . Reise durch die vereinigten Staaten von Nord-Amerika in den Jahren 1785, 1786 und 1787. *Nebst Bemerkungen über die nützlichsten Gewächse dieses Landes. Aus dem Italienischen von* **Magnus Petersen.** *Erster Theil. Memmingen: Andreas Seyler 1793. pp. (12), 495, ill.* [3329

[Cazenove, Theophile]: Cazenove Journal 1794. A record of the journey of Theophile Cazenove through New Jersey and Pennsylvania. *(Translated from the French.) Edited by* **Rayner Wickersham Kelsey.** *Haverford, Pa.: Published by the Pennsylvania History Press; Lancaster, Pa.: Press of the New Era Printing Co. 1922. pp. XVII, 103, ill., map.* = Haverford College Studies, no.13. [3330

[Chastellux, de]: Travels in North-America, in the years 1780, 1781, and 1782. *By the Marquis de Chastellux. Translated from the French by an English Gentleman who resided in America at that period. With notes by the translator. 2 vols. Dublin: Printed for Messrs. Colles, Moncrieffe, White, H. Whitestone, Bryne, Cash, Marchbank, Heery, and Moore, 1787. pp. XV, 462, map; XV, 430, ill., map.* [3331

[Crèvecœur, J. Hector St. John]: Letters from an American farmer; *describing certain provincial situations, manners, and customs, not generally known; and conveying some idea of the late and present interior circumstances of the British Colonies in North America. Written for the information of a friend in England. By J. Hector St. John, a farmer in Pennsylvania. London: Thomas Davies 1782. pp. (3), (3), (2), 318, map.* [3332

[—] Sittliche Schilderungen von Amerika, *in Briefen eines amerikanischen Guthsbesitzers an einen Freund in England. Von* J. Hector St. John. *Aus dem Englischen. Liegnitz und Leipzig: David Siegert 1784. 462 S., Karte.* [3333

[—] Lettres d'un cultivateur American, *écrites a W. S. Ecuyer, depuis l'année 1770, jusqu'à 1781. Traduites de l'Anglois. 2 vols. Paris: Cuchet 1784. pp. XXIV, IV, 422; IV, 400, (2).*

2 vols. Maestricht: J. E. Dufour & Phil. Roux 1785. pp. XXIV, 458; 432. [3334

[Crèvecœur, J. Hector St. John]: Letters from an American farmer. *By J. Hector St. John Crèvecœur. Reprint from the original edition. With a prefatory note by* **W. P. Trent** *and an introduction by* **Ludwig Lewisohn.** *New York, N. Y.: Fox Duffield & Co. 1904. pp. XXXVII, 355.* [3335

[—] Lettres d'un cultivateur Américan *addressées a Wm. S . . . on Esqr. depuis l'année 1770 jusqu'en 1786, par M. St. John de Crèvecœur, traduites de l'Anglois. 3 vols. Paris: Cuchet Libraire 1787. pp. XXXII, 478, ill.; 438, (6), maps; (2), 592, maps.* [Pensylvanie. (Philadelphie, 25 Sept., 1773.) In: Vol. II. pp. 228—248.] [3336

[—] Briefe eines Amerikanischen Landmanns an den Ritter W. S. in den Jahren 1770 bis 1781. *Aus dem Englischen ins Französische von . . . und jetzt aus dem Französischen übersetzt und mit einigen Anmerkungen begleitet von* **Johann August Ephraim Götze.** *3 Bände. Leipzig: Siegfried Lebrecht Crusins 1788—1789. VI, (2), 512 S.; VI, (2), 512 S.; (2), 668 S.* [Pennsylvania. In Bd. II. 1788. S. 247—270.] [3337

[Ellery, Wm.]: A visit to Bethlehem and Lititz in 1777, compiled from the Diary of the Hon. Wm. Ellery, *by* T. W. Higginson *for "Scribner's Magazine" Jan., 1880. In: Transactions of the Moravian Historical Society. Vol. II. Nazareth, Pa. 1886. pp. 125—128.* [3338

[Falckner, Daniel]: Daniel Falckner's Curieuse Nachricht from Pennsylvania . . . [siehe Nr. 234 u. 235]

[Fithian, Philip Vicars]: Fithian's journal. From Path Valley to Sunbury in 1775. *Annoted by* John Blair Linn. *In: Historical Register. Notes and Queries, historical and genealogical relating to interior Pennsylvania for the year 1883. Vol. I. Harrisburg, Pa. 1883. pp. 91—94; 177 —181; 285—288. Vol. II. for the year 1884. Harrisburg, Pa. 1884. pp. 13—18; 99—119; 194—201; 241—247.* [3340

[Franklin, Benjamin]: A true and impartial state of the Province of Pennsylvania. *Containing, an exact account of the nature of its government; the power of the proprietaries, and their governors, as well as those which they derive under the Royal*

grant, as those they have assumed in manifest violation thereof, their father's character, and the rights of the people: also the rights and privileges of the Assembly, and people which they claim under the said grant, charter, and laws of their country, confirmed by the royal approbation. With a true narrative of the dispute between the governors and assemblies, respecting the grants of supplies so often made by the latter, and rejected by the former. In which is demonstrated; by incontestable vouchers, that arbitrary proprietary instructions, have been the true and only cause of the refusal of such supplies, and the late defenceless state of the province. The whole being a full answer to the pamphlets intitled A brief state, and A brief view &c. of the conduct of Pennsylvania . . . Philadelphia, Pa.: Printed by W. Dunlap 1759. pp. (1), V, 173; 34.
[*Attributed to Benjamin Franklin.*]
[3341

G.: A historical review of North America: *containing a geographical, political and natural history of the British and other European settlements, the United and apocryphal states, and a general state of the laws. To which is added a description of the interior parts of North America, general face of the country, mountains, forests, rivers, and the most noted towns, cities, seats, and public buildings . . . In 2 vols. By a Gentleman immediately returned from a tour of that continent. Dublin: C. Brown 1789. pp. XXVIII, 268; IX, 377.*
[3342

Jardine, L. J.: A letter from Pennsylvania *[Burlington, Dec. 16, 1794.]* to a friend in England: containing valuable information with respect to America. *Bath, N. Y.: R. Cruttwell 1795. pp. (1), 31.*
[3343

[Kalm, Peter]: Des Herren Peter Kalm's Professors der Haushaltungskunst in Aobo, und Mitgliedes der königlichen schwedischen Akademie der Wissenschaften Beschreibung der Reise die er nach dem nördlichen America auf dem Befehl gedachter Akademie und öffentliche Kosten unternommen hat. *Eine Übersetzung. Unter dem Königlichen Pohlnischen und Churfürstlichen Sächsischen allergnädigsten Privilegis. 3 Bde. Göttingen: Verlag der Wittwe Abrams Vandenhoek 1754, 1757, 1764. (18), 568 S., ill.; 592 S., ill.; (4), 648 S., ill.*

= *Sammlung neuer und merkwürdiger Reisen zu Wasser und zu Lande. Theil IX—XI.*
[*Pennsylvania, Sept. — Nov., 1748. Vgl. Bd. II. S. 180—470.].*
[3344

Kalm, Peter: Travels into North America; *containing its natural history, and a circumstantial account of its plantations and agriculture in general, with the civil, ecclesiastical and commercial state of the country, the manners of the inhabitants, and several curious and important remarks on various subjects. By· Peter Kalm. Translated into English by* **John Reinhold Forster.** *3 vols. Vol. I. Warrington: William Eyers 1770. pp. XVI, 400, ill., map; Vol. II and Vol. III. London: Printed for the editor and sold by T. Lowndes 1771. pp. 352, ill.; VIII, (8), 318, (14), ill., map.*
[3345

[Marshe, Witham]: Marshe's ,,Journal of the Treaty with the Six Nations by the Commissioners of Maryland and other provinces at Lancaster, June, 1774. *In: Notes and Queries. Third series, vol. I. Harrisburg, Pa. 1895. pp. 264—305.*
[3346

Mittelberger, Gottlieb: Gottlieb Mittelbergers Reise nach Pennsylvanien im Jahre 1750 und Rückreise nach Teutschland im Jahre 1754. *Enthaltend nicht nur eine Beschreibung des Landes nach seinem gegenwärtigen Zustande, sondern auch eine ausführliche Nachricht von den unglückseligen und betrübten Umständen der meisten Teutschen, die in dieses Land gezogen sind, und dahin ziehen, Frankfurt und Leipzig 1756. (6), 120 S.* [3347

[—] Gottlieb Mittelberger's journey to Pennsylvania in the year 1750 and return to Germany in the year 1754, *containing not only a description of the country according to its present condition, but also a detailed account of the sad and unfortunate circumstances of most of the Germans that have emigrated, and are emigrating to that country. Translated from the German by* **Carl Theo Eben.** *Philadelphia, Pa.: Privately printed for Joseph Y. Jeanes. 1898. pp. 129, 1 fac-simile.* [3348

Learned, Marion Dexter: Gottlieb Mittelbergers Reise nach Pennsylvanien und ihre Bedeutung als Kulturbild. *In: Fifth Annual Report of the Society for the History of the Germans in Maryland. Baltimore, Md. 1891. pp. 23—33.*
[3349

Huch, C. F.: Mittelbergers Reise nach Pennsylvanien. *In: Mitteilungen des Deutschen Pionier-Vereins in Philadelphia, Heft 22. Philadelphia, Pa. 1911. S. 29—32.* [3350]

Oldmixon, M.: Groß-Britannisches America. *Nach seiner Erfindung, Bevölkerung und allerneuesten Zustand. Aus dem Englischen übersetzet durch* M. Vischer. *Hamburg: In Verlegung Zacharias Hertels 1710. (14), 879 S. [Geschichte von Pennsylvanien S. 209 —247.]* [3351]

Rousselot de Surgy, Jacques Philibert: Histoire naturelle et politique de la Pennsylvanie, et de l'etablissement des Quakers dans cette contrée. *Traduite de l'Allemand. P. M. D. S., censeur royal. Présédée d'une carte géographique. Paris: Ganeau 1768. pp. XX, 372, (4), map.*

[The compiler's chief sources were a German translation of P. Kalm's ,,Resa till Norra Amerika" and Gottlieb Mittelbergers' ,,Reise nach Pennsylvanien im Jahre 1750" (= no. 3344).] [3352]

Rush, Benjamin: An account of the progress of population, agriculture, manners, and government in Pensylvania. *In a letter from . . ., M. D., and professor of chemistry in the University of Pensylvania, to Thomas Percival, M.D.F.R.S. etc., etc. (Read December 6, 1786). In: Memoirs of the Literary and Philosophical Society of Manchester. Vol. III. Warrington 1790. pp. 183—199.*

Also appeared in: The Columbian Magazine or Monthly Miscellany . . . of the year 1787. Vol. I. Philadelphia, Pa. 1786/87. No.: November, 1786. pp. 117 —122. [3353]

Russel, William: Geschichte von Amerika von dessen Entdeckung an bis auf das Ende des vorigen Krieges. *Nebst einem Anhange, welcher eine Geschichte des Ursprunges und des Fortganges des gegenwärtigen unglücklichen Streites zwischen Groß-Brittannien und seinen Colonien enthält. Aus dem Englischen übersetzt. 4 Bde. Leipzig: im Schwickertschen Verlage 1779. XV, 782 S.; (11) 752 S.; (2) 660 S.; (3) 480, (32) S. Karten, ill. [Bd. III Geschichte u. Beschreibung der Colonien Neu York, Neu Jersey und Pennsylvanien S. 356ff. Virginien und Maryland S. 398ff. Carolina, Georgien . . . S. 419ff.]* [3353a]

Schöpf, Johann David: Reise durch einige der mittleren und südlichen vereinigten nordamerikanischen Staaten von Ost-Florida und den Bahama-Inseln unternommen in den Jahren 1783 und 1784. *2 Bde. Erlangen: Johann Jacob Palm 1788. (20), 644 S., Karte; (4), XXXII, 551 S.* [3354]

— Travels in the Confederation 1783— 1784. *From the German of* J.D. Schoepf *translated and edited by* Alfred J. Morrison. *2 vols. Philadelphia, Pa.: William Campbell 1911. pp. X, 426; (1), (1), 344.* [3355]

Beschreibungen aus der Zeit nach 1789

Descriptions of the Postrevolutionary Period

[Arfwedson, Carolus David]: A brief history of the Colony of New Sweden *which, by the kind permission of the Faculty of Philosophy at Upsala, . . .* Carolus David Arfwedson *of West Goth, the author publicly presented in the Gustivianeum, on the 19th day of November, 1825 . . . Upsala (Set up by the Typographers of the Royal Academy) Translation of the Swedish text by* K. W. Granlund; *of the Latin text by* Edward T. Horn; *edited by* Julius F. Sachse. *Lancaster, Pa.: New Era Printing Co. 1909.*

= Part XX. ,,A narrative and critical history", prepared by authority of the Pennsylvania-German Society. *Proceedings and Addresses . . . 1907. Vol.XVIII. Lancaster, Pa. 1909. Separate pagination pp. 44., ill., map.* [3356]

Ashe, Thomas: Travels in America performed in the year 1806 for the purpose of exploring the rivers Allegheny, Monongahela, Ohio, and Mississippi of their banks and vicinity. *London: Richard Phillips 1809. pp. 316 (4).* [3357]

Bernhard, Herzog zu Sachsen-Weimar-Eisenach: Reise Sr. Hoheit des Herzogs Bernhard zu Sachsen-Weimar-Eisenach durch Nord-Amerika in den Jahren 1825 und 1826. *Herausgegeben von*

Heinrich Luden. 2 Bde. Weimar:
Wilhelm Hoffmann; Jena: Druck von
Friedrich Mauke 1828. XXXI, 317 S.,
ill., Karten; IV, 323 S., ill., Karten.
[3358
Bernhard, Herzog zu Sachsen-Weimar-Eisenach: Travels through North America, during the years 1825 and 1826. *2 vols. Philadelphia, Pa.: Carey, Lea & Carey 1828. pp. IV, 9—212; 238.* [3359
Brauns, E.: Practische Belehrungen und Rathschläge für Reisende und Auswanderer nach Amerika. *Braunschweig: Herzogl. Waisenhaus Buchdruckerei 1829 IV, 5—492 S.*
[„Die Landwirtschaft der Deutschen in Nordamerika": S. 169—187; „Geschichte der Deutschen Einwanderung" S. 188—209; „Wird die deutsche Sprache in Amerika bestehen oder untergehen." S. 210—222.] [3360
Bremer, Friederike: Die Heimath in der neuen Welt. *Ein Tagebuch in Briefen, geschrieben auf zweijährigen Reisen in Nordamerika und auf Cuba. Stuttgart: Franck'sche Verlagshandlung. 1854, 3 Bde. Bd. I, 462 S.; Bd. II, 520 S.; Bd. III, 534 S.* [3360a
Bülow, D. von: Briefe eines Deutschen in America. *In: Minerva. Ein Journal historischen und politischen Inhalts herausgegeben von J. W. v. Archenholz. Zweiter Band für das Jahr 1796. Hamburg: B.G. Hoffmann 1796. Briefe 1—4. S. 73—103; Briefe 5—9. S. 486—517; Briefe 9—14. In: Bd. IV von 1796. S. 385—424; Brief 15. In: Bd. I von 1797. S. 105—113.* [3361
— Der Freistaat von Nordamerika in seinem neuesten Stand. *2 Bde. Berlin: Johann Friedrich Unger 1797. (4), 309; 285 S.* [3362
Büttner, J. G.: Briefe aus und über Nordamerika *oder Beiträge zu einer richtigen Kenntniß der Vereinigten Staaten und ihrer Bewohner, besonders der deutschen Bevölkerung, in kirchlicher, sittlicher, socialer und politischer Hinsicht, und zur Beantwortung der Frage über Auswanderung, nebst Nachrichten über Klima und Krankheiten in diesen Staaten. 2 Bde. Dresden und Leipzig: Arnoldische Buchhandlung 1845. VIII, 215; VI, 225 S.* [3363
— Die Vereinigten Staaten von Nord-Amerika. Mein Aufenthalt und meine Reisen in denselben vom Jahre 1834 bis 1841. *2 Bde. Hamburg und Leipzig:*

Verlag von Schuberth & Co. 1846. VI, (1), (1), 440; (1), 450 S. [3364
Cooper, Thomas: Some information respecting America. *Collected by . . . London: J. Johnson 1794. pp. IV, 240, map.* [3365
Dwight, Margaret van Horn: A journey to Ohio in 1810 as recorded in the journal of M. v. Horn Dwight. *Edited with an introduction by* **Max Farrand.** *New Haven, Conn.: Yale University Press 1920. pp. VI, 64.* [3366
Ebeling, Christoph Daniel: Erdbeschreibung und Geschichte von Amerika. *Die vereinigten Staaten von Nordamerika. 7 Bde. Hamburg: Carl Ernst Bohn; Bd. VII: Hoffman and Campe 1797—1816.*
[Der Staat Pennsylvania = Bd. IV und VI vgl. Nr. 3151] [3367
Eggerling, H. W. E.: Kurze Beschreibung der Vereinigten Staaten von Nord-Amerika, *nach ihren politischen, religiösen, bürgerlichen und gesellschaftlichen Verbindungen, nebst besonderer Berücksichtigung und Hinweisung dort zu gründender Niederlassungen Europäischer Einwanderer. Besonders diesem Letzteren gewiedmet. Wiesbaden: H. W. Rittersche Buchhandlung 1832. pp. XIV, 279; Zweite durchaus vermehrte und verbesserte Auflage. Mannheim: Tobias Löffler 1833. 344 S.* [3368
Fearon, Hy Bradshaw: Sketches of America. *A narrative of a journey of 5000 miles through the eastern and western states of America; contained in eight reports addressed to the 39 English families by whome the author was deputed in June, 1817, to ascertain whether any, and what part of the United States would be suitable for their residence. With remarks on Mr. Birbeck's „Notes" and „Letters". London: printed by Strahan and Spottiswoode for Longman, Hurst, Rees, Orme, and Brown. 1819. pp. XXV, 454.*
[Fifth report: Leave Philadelphia for the western country; Pennsylvania farms etc. pp. 181 ff.] [3369
Gall, Ludwig: Meine Auswanderung nach den Vereinigten-Staaten in Nord-Amerika, im Frühjahr 1819 und meine Rückkehr nach der Heimath im Winter 1820. *2 Bde. Trier: F. A. Gall 1822. Erster Theil, meine Beweggründe und mein Wirken zur Erleichterung der Auswanderung nach den Vereinigten-Staaten und mein Reisetagebuch enthaltend.*

VI, (2), 408, (2) S., ill., *Karten; Zweiter Theil,* meine Wahrnehmungen im Umgang mit den Amerikanern und mein Wirken zur Erleichterung der Ansiedlung in den Vereinigten-Staaten enthaltend. *(2), 428, (2) S., ill., Karten.* [3370

[Gilpin, Joshua]: Journey to Bethlehem, [Pa., in 1802]. *In: The Pennsylvania Magazine of History and Biography. Vol. XLVI. Philadelphia, Pa. 1922. pp. 15—38; 122—153, ill.* [3371

[—] Journal of a tour from Philadelphia thro the western counties of Pennsylvania in the months of September and October, 1809. *In: The Pennsylvania Magazine of History and Biography. Vol. L. Philadelphia, Pa. 1926. pp. 64—78; 163—178; 380—382; Vol. LI. 1927. pp. 172—190; 351—375, map; Vol. LII. 1928. pp. 29—58.* [3372

Harris, Thaddeus Mason: The journal of a tour into the territory Northwest of the Allegheny mountains, made in the spring of the year 1803. *Reprint from Boston edition, 1805 in: Early Western travels. 1748—1846. Edited by Reuben Gold Thwaites. Vol. III. Cleveland, O.: Arthur H. Clark Co. 1904. pp. 309— 382, 2 maps.* [3373

[Harris, William Tell]: Bemerkungen auf einer Reise durch die Vereinigten Staaten von Nord-Amerika, in den Jahren 1817, 1818 und 1819, von William Tell Harris, in einer Reihe von Briefen an Freunde in England. *Aus dem Englischen übersetzt von* C. Fl. Leidenfrost. *Weimar: im Verlag des G. H. S. pr. Landes-Industrie-Comptoirs 1822. VIII, 236 S. =Neue Bibliothek der wichtigsten Reisebeschreibungen zur Erweiterung der Erd- und Völkerkunde; . . . herausgegeben von F. J. Bertuch. Zweite Hälfte der ersten Centurie. Dreißigster Band, [1. Hälfte.]* [3374

[Hill, Thomas]: A journey on horseback from New Brunswick, New Jersey, to Lycoming County, Pa., in 1799. *In: The Pennsylvania Magazine of History and Biography. Vol. XIV. Philadelphia, Pa. 1890. pp. 189—198.* [3375

[Humboldt, Alexander v.]: Pennsylvanien in historischer, statistischer und naturhistorischer Hinsicht. *Ein interessantes Lesebuch für die Jugend. Hamburg und Altona: Gottfried Vollmer 1805 S. 236, ill.*

= *Alexander v. Humboldts Reisen um die Welt und durch das Innere von Südamerika. Interessantes Lesebuch für die Jugend. Vom Verfasser von Cooks Reisen um die Welt. [F. W. v. Schütz.] Bd. VI.* [3375a

Kelsey, Rayner Wickersham: At the forks of the Delaware 1794—1811. Chronicles of early travel to Easton and neighboring parts of Pennsylvania and New Jersey, including extracts from a hitherto untranslated and unpublished manuscript. *A paper read at Easton, Pa., Nov. 13, 1919 before the Northampton County Historical and Genealogical Society. Haverford, Pa.: The Pennsylvania History Press 1920. pp. VII, 18, ill.* [3376

Kohl, J. G.: Reisen in Canada und durch die Staaten von New York und Pennsylvanien. *Stuttgart und Augsburg: J. G. Cotta'scher Verlag 1856. IV, 576 S. [Zu den deutschen Grafschaften. = Kapitel XLVII, S. 528—547; Bethlehem. = Kapitel XLVIII, S. 547—558; Der Blaue Rücken. = Kapitel XLIX, S. 558 —569; Durch New Jersey. = Kapitel L. S. 570—576.]* [3378

— Travels in Canada and through the States of New York and Pennsylvania. *Translated by Mrs. Percy Sinnett. 2 vols. London: George Manwaring 1861. pp. X, 345; pp. IV, 357. [The German counties. = Chapter XVIII. pp. 283—304. Bethlehem. = Chapter XIX. pp. 305—318; The Blue Ridge. = Chapter XX. pp. 319— 334; Through New Jersey. = Chapter XXI. pp. 335—342.]* [3379

Lamprecht, Karl: „Americana." *Reiseeindrücke, Betrachtungen, geschichtliche Gesamtansicht. Freiburg im Breisgau: Verlag von Hermann Heyfelder 1906. (1), (1), 147 S.* [3380

La Rochefaucauld Liancourt, de (Fr. Alex Frederick): Reisen in den Jahren 1795, 1796 und 1797 durch alle am der See belegenen Staaten der Nordamerikanischen Republik; imgleichen durch Ober-Canada und das Land der Irokesen. Nebst zuverlässigen Nachrichten von Unter-Canada. *Aus der französischen Handschrift übersetzt. 3 Bde. Hamburg: Benjamin Gottlob Hoffmann 1799. XX, 629 S.; IV, 588 S.; VIII, 784 S.* [3381

Leiste, Christian: Beschreibung des Brittischen Amerika zur Ersparung der englischen Karten. *Wolfenbüttel: Gedruckt*

*mit Bindseilschen Schriften. 1778. 572,
(1) S., Karte.*   [3382
[Lincklaen, John]: Travels in the years 1791
and 1792 in Pennsylvania, New York
and Vermont. Journals of John Linck-
laen, agent of the Holland Land Company. *With a biographical sketch and
notes. New York, N. Y. and London:
G. P. Putnam's Sons; The Knickerbocker Press 1897. pp. XI, 162, ill.,
map.*   [3383
List, Friedrich: Friedrich List, Grundlinien
einer politischen Ökonomie und andere
Beiträge der amerikanischen Zeit 1825 —
1832. *Herausgegeben von William Notz.
Berlin: Verlag von Reimar Hobbing 1931.
XIV, 530 S., ill.*   [3384
Lutynes, Gotthilff Nicolas: Etwas über den
gegenwärtigen Zustand der Auswanderungen und Ansiedlungen im Staate
von Pennsylvanien in Nord-Amerika,
besonders in Ansehung der Deutschen.
Hamburg: Carl Ernst Bohn 1796. 23 S.
                                   [3385
— Über den gegenwärtigen Zustand der
Auswanderungen, und Ansiedlungen im
Staate von Pennsylvanien in Nord-
Amerika, besonders in Ansehung der
Deutschen. *In: Amerikanisches Maga-
zin oder authentische Beiträge zur Erd-
beschreibung, Staatskunde und Geschichte
von Amerika, besonders aber der ver-
einten Staaten. Herausgegeben von Hege-
wisch-Kiel und Ebeling-Hamburg. Erster
Band. Zweites Stück. Hamburg: Carl
Ernst Bohn 1796. S. 25—40.*   [3385a
Lyell, Charles: Travels in North America;
with geological observations on the
United States, Canada and Nova Sco-
tia. *2 vols. London: John Murray 1845.
pp. XIII, (1), 316; pp. . . .
[German patois in Pennsylvania. Vol.
I. p. 102.]*   [3386
**Maximilian, Alexander Phillipp, Prinz von
Wied [Neuwied]:** Reise in das innere
Nord-Amerika 1832—34. *2 Bde. Co-
blenz 1839—41. XVI, 653, (1) S. Karte;
XXII, (2), 687 S., ill.
Englische Ausgabe:* Travels in the inte-
rior of North America. *Translated from
the German by* H. Evans Lloyd. *London:
Ackermann and Co.; Cook and Co.,
Printers. 1843. pp. X, (1), 520, ill., map.
Reprint in: Early western travels 1748—
1846 . . . Edited with notes, introduc-
tions, index, etc. by* Reuben Gold Thwai-
tes. *Vol. XXII, 2 parts. Cleveland, O.:*

*The Arthus H. Clark Co. 1906. pp. 393;
395.
Französische Ausgabe: Paris 1840—1843.*
                                   [3387
Melish, John: Travels through the United
States of America in the years 1806 and
7, 1809, 10 and 11; including an account
betwixt America and Britain, and travels
through various parts of Britain, Ireland
and Canada. *2 vols. Philadelphia, Pa.:
Thom. Geo. Palmer 1812. pp. 444;
492. Second edition: With corrections and
improvements to 1815. 2 vols. Philadelphia, Pa.: Published by John Melish
1815. pp. 444; 492.*   [3388
[—] John Melish's Reisen durch die Vereinigten Staaten von America, in den
Jahren 1806, 1807, 1809, 1810, und
1811. *Aus dem Englischen, und mit Anmerkungen begleitet von* J. Ernst Ludwig
Brauns. *Weimar: Im Verlage des Gr.
H. S. pr. Landes-Industrie-Comptoirs
1819. pp. XVIII, 378, maps.
= Neue Bibliothek der wichtigsten Reisebeschreibungen zur Erweiterung der Erd-
und Völkerkunde; . . . herausgegeben von
F. J. Bertruch. Zweite Hälfte der ersten
Centurie, siebenzehnter Band.*   [3389
[Michaux, F. A.]: F. A. Michaux's Reise in
das Innere der Nordamerikanischen
Freistaaten, westwärts der Alleghany-
Gebirge. *Aus dem Französischen. Mit
einigen Zusätzen und Anmerkungen her-
ausgegeben von* T. F. Ehrmann. *Weimar:
Im Verlage des F. S. pr. Landes-Indu-
strie-Comptoirs 1805. XIV. 250 S.,
Karte.
= Bibliothek der neuesten und wichtigsten Reisebeschreibungen zur Erweiterung
der Erdkunde nach einem systematischen
Plane bearbeitet und in Verbindung mit
einigen anderen Gelehrten gesammelt und
herausgegeben von M. C. Sprengel, fortgesetzt von T. F. Ehrmann. Siebenzehnter
Band, 2. Hälfte.*   [3390
— Travels to the westward of the Allegany
Mountains, in the States of the Ohio,
Kentucky, and Tennessee, and return
to Charlestown, through the Upper Carolinas; *containing details on the present
state of agriculture and the naturel productions of these countries; as well as information relative to the commercial connections of these states with those situated
to the eastward of the mountains and with
Lower Louisiana. Undertaken in the
year X, 1802, under the auspices of his
Excellency M. Chaptol, minister of the*

interior. Translated from the original French by **B. Lambert.** *London: J. Mawman 1805. pp. XVI, 350, map.* [3391

Michaux, F. A.: Travels to the westward of the Alleghany Mountains in the States of the Ohio, Kentucky, and Tennessee, in the year 1802. *Containing accounts relative to the present state of agriculture, and the natural productions of those districts; together with particulars of the commercial relations which subsist between these states, and those to the eastward of the mountains, and of Lower Louisiana. Translated from the French. London: Printed for Richard Phillips . . . by Barnard & Sultzer 1805. pp. IV, 5—96, map.* [3392

[Mühlenberg, H.]: Dr. H. Mühlenbergs, Predigers in Lancaster, Bemerkungen auf einer Reise von Lancaster nach Philadelphia. *[Etliche Bemerkungen auf einer Reise von Lancaster nach Philadelphia und wieder zurück. Den 11. April 1796 trat ich eine Reise von Lancaster nach Philadelphia zu Pferde an...] In: Amerikanisches Magazin oder authentische Beiträge zur Erdbeschreibung, Staatskunde und Geschichte von Amerika, besonders aber der vereinten Staaten. Herausgegeben von Hegewisch und Ebeling. Erster Band. Drittes Stück. Hamburg: Carl Ernst Bohn 1796. S. 129—135.* [3392a

Myers, J. C.: Sketches on a tour through the northern and eastern states, the Canadas and Nova Scotia. *Harrisburg, Va.: J. H. Wartmann & Bro. 1849. pp. XVII, 475.* „State of Pennsylvania." = Chapters XLII and XLIII. pp. 435—460; „State of Maryland." = Chapter XLIV. pp. 461—475.] [3393

[Nicklin, P. H.]: A pleasant peregrination through the prettiest parts of Pennsylvania. *Performed by Peregrine Prolix. Philadelphia, Pa.: Grigg & Elliot. 1836. pp. XV, 17—148.* [3394

Rheinländer, Ein [*Pseudonym für* **Gottlieb, G. A.**]: Nachrichten und Erfahrungen über die vereinigten Staaten von Amerika, gesammelt auf einer Reise in den Jahren 1806 bis 1808 *von einem Rheinländer. Frankfurt a. M.: Friedrich Gerhard 1812. IV, 259 S., Karte.* [3395

Royall, Anne: Mrs. Royall's Pennsylvania, or travels continued in the United States. *2 vols. Washington, D. C.: Printed for the author. 1829. pp. 276.* [3396

[Stahlschmidt, Johann Christian]: Die Pilgerreise zu Wasser und zu Lande, oder Denkwürdigkeiten der göttlichen Gnadenführung und Fürsehung in dem Leben eines Christen, der solche, auch besonders in seinen Reisen durch alle vier Haupttheile der Erde reichlich an sich erfahren hat. Von ihm selbst beschrieben in Briefen an einen seiner Christlichen Mitbrüder in den Jahren 1797 und 1798. *Nürnberg: Im Verlag der Raw'schen Buchhandlung, und in Commission bei Wittib, Hutmacher zu Mühlheim bei Köln am Rhein 1799. XXXVI, 452 S.* [38. Brief: Verfassers Ankunft in Philadelphia.] [3397

Stuart, James: Three years in North America. *2 vols. Edinburgh: Robert Cadell 1833. pp. IX, 495; VI, 580. [See: Vol. II. pp. 522—523.]* [3398

Sutcliff, Robert: Travels in some parts of North America, in the years 1804, 1805, and 1806. *Second improved edition. York, Pa.: W. Alexander 1815. pp. XVI, 17—309, ill.* [3399

Wakefield, Proscilla: Excursions in North America described in letters from a gentleman and his young companion to their friends in England. *Second edition. London: Darton, Harvey, and Darton 1810. pp. X, 420, (2).* [3400

[Wansey, Heinrich]: Heinrich Wansey's Tagebuch einer Reise durch die vereinigten Staaten von Nord-Amerika im Sommer des Jahres 1794. *Aus dem Englischen. Mit Anmerkungen des Uebersetzers, und einer Vorrede über Auswanderung und Länderkauf in Nord-Amerika von* **C. A. Böttinger.** *Berlin: Vossische Buchhandlung 1797. XXXVI, 37—232 S., ill. Anhang.* Regeln für die Deutsche Gesellschaft in dem Staate von Neu-York. *Germantown, gedruckt bei Michael Billmeyer 1787 [Abdruck]. S. 221—232.* [3401

Weld, Isaac: Travels through the states of North America and the provinces of Upper and Lower Canada, during the years 1795, 1796 and 1797. *London: Printed for John Stockdale 1799. pp. XXIV, 464, ill., maps. Fourth edition. 2 vols. London: John Stockdale 1807. pp. XIX, (1), 427; VIII, 376, ill., maps.* [3402

— Reise durch die nordamerikanischen Freistaaten und durch Ober- und Unter-

Canada in den Jahren 1795, 1796 und 1797. *Aus dem Englischen frei übersetzt. Berlin: Haude und Spener 1800. (6), 410 S.*   [3403

[Weld, Isaac]: Isaac Weld's Reisen durch die Staaten von Nordamerika, und die Provinzen Ober- u. Unter-Canada, während den Jahren 1795, 1796 u. 1797. *Aus dem Englischen übersetzt. Berlin und Hamburg 1801. 475 S., ill., Karte. = Bibliothek der neuesten und interessantesten Reisebeschreibungen. Band IV.*   [3404

— Reisen durch die vereinigten Staaten von Nord-Amerika und durch die Provinzen Ober- und Unter Kanada in den Jahren 1795, 1796 und 1797. *Nach der letzten Ausgabe aus dem Englischen übersetzt mit Anmerkungen. 2 Bde. Zweite Auflage. Berlin: C. G. Flitt-*

nersche Buchhandlung 1820. (6), XIV, 395 S., ill.; .... S.   [3405

Pennsylvanien in historischer, statistischer und naturhistorischer Hinsicht. *Ein interessantes Lesebuch für die Jugend. Hamburg und Altona: Gottfried Vollmer [1805]. 236 S.*

= *Alexander von Humbolds Reisen um die Welt und durch das Innere von Südamerika. Interessantes Lesebuch für die Jugend vom Verfasser von Cooks Reisen um die Welt. Bd. VI. Hamburg und Altona: Gottfried Vollmer [1805].*   [3406

A diary of 1822. *On a journey made from Horsham, Montgomery County, Pa. to New Lisbon, in Northeastern Ohio and back. In: The Pennsylvania Magazine of History and Biography. Philadelphia, Pa. 1925. pp. 61—74.*   [3407

Reise- und Tagebücher[1])
Journals and Diaries[2])

Frank, John: John Frank of German Flatts, 1756—1840, his contemporaries and his account book, beginning with entries bearing the date of 1774. *By Robert Earl. In: Papers read before the Herkimer County Historical Society during the years 1899, 1900, 1901 to July 1, 1902. Vol. II. Herkimer and Ilion, N.Y. 1902. pp. 347—354.*   [3408

Fritsch, Catherine: Notes of a visit to Philadelphia, made by a Moravian sister in 1810. *Contributed and translated from the original Mss. in German by A. R. Beck. In: The Pennsylvania Magazine of History and Biography. Vol. XXXVI. pp. 346—361.*   [3409

[Guldin, Samuel]: Diary of Samuel Guldin, relating to his journey to Pennsylvania, June to September, 1710. *In: Journal of the Presbyterian Historical Society. Vol. XIV. Philadelphia, Pa. 1930. pp. 28—41, 64—73.*   [3410

Helffrich, John Henry: Diary of the Rev. John Henry Helffrich, September 6, 1771 —January 14, 1772. *Translated from the German by William J. Hinke. In: The Pennsylvania Magazine of History and*

Biography. *Vol. XXXVIII. Philadelphia, Pa. 1914. pp. 65—82.*   [3411

Herr, Benj.: Benj. Herr's journal 1830. *In: German American Annals. New series, vol. I. Philadelphia, Pa. 1903. pp. 8—31.*   [3412

Jungmann, Johann Georg: Ein Manuscript aus dem vorigen Jahrhundert. Lebenslauf des Johann Georg Jungmann in Bethlehem. *(Von ihm selbst eigenhändig niedergeschrieben.) In: Der Deutsche Pionier. Jg. I. Cincinnati, O. 1869—1870. S. 230—237.*   [3413

Krauss, John: Account book of John Krauss. For 1806. *In: The Perkiomen Region. Vol. VIII, no. 2. Pennsburg, Pa. 1930. pp. 43—55; . . . for 1807. In: Vol. IX, no. 1. 1931. pp. 3—12; No. 2. pp. 49—53; . . . for 1808. In: Vol. IX, no. 3. pp. 70—77.*   [3414

[Lischy, Jacob and Rausch, Christian Henry]: Diary of Lischy's and Rauch's journey among the Reformed congregations in Pennsylvania, in the month of February, 1745. *Translated and edited by W. J. Hinke. In: The Reformed Church Review. Fourth series, vol. IX. Philadelphia, Pa. 1905. pp. 74—90.*   [3415

Meurer, John Philip: From London to Philadelphia, 1742. *Compiled from the journal (in German) of John Philip*

---

[1]) Reisetagebücher von Mährischen Missionaren und Brüdern siehe Nr. 1752—1795.

[2]) Moravian itineraries see nos. 1752—1795.

Meurer. In: The Pennsylvania Magazine of History and Biography. Vol. XXXVII. Philadelphia, Pa. 1913. pp. 94—106. [3416

Miller, Aaron: Diary of Aaron Miller, written while in quest of Ohio wheat lands. *In: Ohio Archaeological and Historical Quarterly. Vol. XXXIII. Columbus, O. 1924. pp. 67—79.* [3417

Muhlenberg, F. A. C.: F. A. C. Muhlenberg's report of his first trip to Shamokin, sent to his father. *Translated from Hallesche Nachrichten, revised edition. Vol. II. p. 714—720. By J. W. Early. In: The Lutheran Church Review. Vol. XXV. Philadelphia, Pa. 1906. pp. 535—544.* [3418

Muhlenberg, F. A.: Diary of F. A. Muhlenberg. From the day of his ordination, October 25, 1770 until August, 1774. *Translated by J. W. Early. In: The Lutheran Church Review. Vol. XXIV. Philadelphia, Pa. 1905. pp. 127—137, 388—390, 562—571, 682—694; Vol. XXV. 1906. pp. 134—147, 345—356.* [3419

[Mühlenberg, Henry Melchior]: Journal of a voyage from Philadelphia to Ebenezer, in Georgia, &c., in the years 1774 and 1775, by Henry Melchior Mühlenberg, D. D. *Translated from an unpublished German manuscript by J. W. Richards. In: The Evangelical Review. Gettysburg, Pa. Vol. I. 1849—50. pp. 390—419, 534—560; Vol. II. 1850—51. pp. 15—134; Vol. III. 1851—52. pp. 115—129, 418—435, 583—590; Vol. IV. 1852—1853. pp. 172—203.* [3420

Naas, Johannes: Reisetagebuch des Johannes Naas aus Crefeld, von Rotterdam bis Germantown in Pennsylvanien. *[„Germantown, den 17ten October 1733."] Neudruck in: Der Deutsche Pionier. Jg. XII. Cincinnati, O. 1880—1881. Alte deutsch-amerikanische Dokumente. S. 340—350.* [3421

Ramsauer, John: A rare old diary [of John Ramsauer of Lincoln County, N. C.]. *In: The Penn Germania. Vol. II. = Old series, vol. XIV. Lititz, Pa. 1913. pp. 22—25.* [3422

[Schlatter, Michael]: Diary of the Rev. Michael Schlatter, June 1st to December 15th, 1746. *Edited by W. J. Hinke. In: Journal of the Presbyterian Historical Society. Vol. III. Philadelphia, Pa. 1906. pp. 105—121, 158—176.* [3423

Schultz, Christopher: Reise Beschreibung von Altenau bis Pennsylvanien. *(Account of the journey from Altoona to Philadelphia, 1734. Written by Christopher Schultz. [Free translation of the journey of the main body of Schwenkfelder immigrants, who arrived Sept. 22, 1734; it appears in print in German in the Appendix of the „Erläuterung", pp. 462—72].) In: The genealogical record of the Schwenkfelder families ... Edited by Samuel Kriebel Brecht. New York, N. Y. — Chicago, Ill. 1923. [= no. 1609]. pp. 45—50.* [3424

Schultz, David: David Shultze's journal. *In: The Perkiomen Region, Past and Present. Vol. II. Philadelphia, Pa. 1900. p. 165; David Shultze's coming to America: pp. 181—182, 187—189; Vol. III. 1901. Journal of 1752: p. 2, pp. 10—15; ... of 1757: pp. 81—82; 90—93, p. 98, pp. 106—110; ... of 1759: pp. 124—127, 140—144; ... of 1768: p. 146, pp. 155—159, p. 164, pp. 169—174.* [3425

— The David Schultz diary for 1769. *With notes of the editor, H. W. Kriebel. In: The Perkiomen Region. Vol. VI, no. 4. Pennsburg, Pa. 1928. pp. 109—113, 113—115; ... for 1774. In: Vol. VII, no. 1. 1929. pp. 8—15; ... for 1780. In: Vol. VII, no. 2. 1929. pp. 34—47; ... for 1782. In: Vol. VII, no. 3. 1929. pp. 66—73; ... for 1786. In: Vol. VII, no. 4. 1929. pp. 106—111; ... for 1790. In: Vol. VIII, no. 1. 1930. pp. 3—9.* [3426

Johnson, Elmer E. S.: David Schultz manuscripts in the Samuel W. Pennypacker collection at Pennsburg. *In: The Perkiomen Region. Vol. I, no. 1. Pennsburg, Pa. 1921. pp. 4—5.* [See no. 3425—3456] [3427

[Weiser, Conrad]: Copy of a family register, now in possession of Daniel Womelsdorf, of Womelsdorf, Berks County. *Translated from the German by Hiester H. Muhlenberg. In: Collections of the Historical Society of Pennsylvania. Vol. I. pp. 1—6.* [3429

— Conrad Weiser's Tagebuch. *Herausgegeben von I. D. Rupp. In: Der Deutsche Pionier. Jg. II. Cincinnati, O. 1870—1871. S. 182—186, 216—221.* [3430

— The journal of Conrad Weiser. *Translated from the German of the original. Edited by Benjamin Brink. In: Olde Vlster. An historical and genealogical*

*magazine. Vol. II. Kingston, N. Y.
1906. pp. 199—204, 229—235.* [3431
[Weiser, Conrad]: A Conrad Weiser diary.
*[Transcription and translation of a diary
by* Conrad Weiser, *owned by Howell
Souders, of Tamaqua, Pa., edited by*
George Gebert.*] In: The Penn Germania.
Vol. I. = Old series, vol. XIII. Lititz,
Pa. 1912. pp. 764—788.* [3432
Weiser, C. Z.: Authentic autobiography of
Conrad Weiser. *In: The life of (John)
Conrad Weiser, the German pioneer, and
patriot of two races. By C. Z. Weiser.
Second edition. Reading, Pa.: Daniel
Miller 1899 [= no. 7656]. pp. 118—127.*
[3432a
Diary of a voyage from Rotterdam to
Philadelphia in 1728. [„Auszug einiger

*Send-Schreiben in Pensylvanien, wo-
rinnen die gantze Reise, von Rotterdam
nach Pensylvanien, fleissig aufgezeichnet,
und dieses Landes Clima, dessen Bewohner Handlung, andere Gewerbe, Ordnung, etc. entdecket ist;... Dem Nächsten
zur nöthigen Nachricht durch den Druck
mitgetheilet.   Im Jahr Christi 1729.]
Translated by* Julius F. Sachse. *Lancaster, Pa.: New Era Printing Co. 1909.
= Part XIX. „A narrative and critical
history", prepared at the request of the
Pennsylvania-German Society. In: The
Pennsylvania-German Society. Proceedings and Addresses . . . 1907. Vol.
XVIII. Lancaster, Pa. 1909. Separate
pagination. pp. 25, ill.* [3433

Briefe[1])

Letters[2])

Blattenbach, Jacob and **Frey, Heinrich:**
Letters, translated from the German,
directed to Joseph Blattenbach, resp. to
Heinrich Frey, Pennsylvania emigrants
of 1680, by their fathers: — *Bruchsal,
Febr. 1, 1681 signed Jacob Blattenbach;
Heilbronn, Febr. 6, 1681 signed by Heinrich Frey. In: Historical Sketches. A
Collection of Papers prepared for the
Historical Society of Montgomery County,
Pa. Vol. IV. Norristown, Pa. 1910.
pp. 289—291.* [3434
[Pastorius, Franz Daniel: *Vgl. Nr. (see nos.)
219—221, 223—226, 228—232, 237.]*
Letters relating to the settlement of Germantown in Pennsylvania 1683-4, *from
the Könneken Manuscript in the Mini-
sterial-Archiv of Lübeck. Reproduces in
fac-simile under the direction of* J. F.
Sachse. *Lübeck and Philadelphia 1903.
pp. XII, 35, ill.*
   (Missive I) **[Pastorius, F. D.]:** Copy
of a letter sent from America by a son
to his parents. *pp. 2—6.*
   (Missive II) [—] Positive news from
America, about the Province of Pennsylvania, from a German who has
journeyed hither, de dato, Philadelphia,
March 7, 1684. *pp. 7—29.*
   (Missive VII) **Op Den Graeff,
Hermans:** Copy of a letter from German-

town, — i. e. the German city in Pennsylvania, — dated February 12, 1684.
(Evidently written by . . .) pp. 31—34.
   (Missive VIII) **Walle, van der:**
A fragment of an open letter by . . .
from Philadelphia *[mentioned in Pastorius missive. p. 13]. pp. 35.* [3435
Wertmuller, Joris: „Missive uyt German
Town in Pennsylvania." *In: Twee
missiven geschreven uyt Pensilvania
d'Eene door een Hollander, woonachtig
in Philadelphia, d'Ander door en Switzer
woonachting in German Town Dat is
Hoogduytse Stadt. Von den 16 en
26 Maert 1684. Nieuwe Stijl. Tot
Rotterdam, by Pieter van Alphen. Anno
1684. pp. (2).* [3436
[Pastorius, Franz Daniel]: Beschreibung
von Pennsylvanien, Epistola ad [Georgi-
um Leonhardium] Modelium, rectorem
scholae Windsheimensis. *Datiert: Germanopoli, 1.Dec. 1688. In: W.E. Tenzel's
Monatliche Unterredungen einiger guten
Freunde von allerhand Büchern und anderen annehmlichen Geschichten. Leipzig,
Aprilis 1691. S. 278—288.* [3437
[—] Auszug aus einem Briefe an seinen
Vater in Windsheim, datiert 20. Junii
1692. *In: W. E. Tentzel's Monatliche Unterredungen einiger guten Freunde. Leipzig, Februarius 1693. S.162—164.* 3437a
[—] Zwei unbekannte Briefe von Pastorius. *Reprints from Tentzel's „Monat-

---

[1]) Soweit sie als Einzeldruck erschienen.
[2]) As far as published as single publications.

lichen Unterredungen einiger guten Freunde von allerhand Buechern und anderen annehmlichen Geschichten". April 1691, resp. Februar 1693 [= no. 223]. Herausgegeben von Julius Goebel. In: German American Annals. New series, vol. II. Philadelphia, Pa. 1904. pp. 492—503. [3437b]
[Falckner, Daniel]: A contribution to Pennsylvania history. Missives to Rev. August Herman Francke from Daniel Falckner, New York, 1704. *(Reproduced in both the original and English translation.) Supplement with a genealogical chart of Daniel Falckner. Edited by Julius F. Sachse.* Lancaster, Pa.: New Era Printing Co. 1909. In: The Pennsylvania-German Society. Proceedings and Addresses . . . 1907. Vol. XVIII. Lancaster, Pa. 1909. Separate pagination. pp. 19, (2), ill. [3438]
[Furley, Benjamin]: A letter of Benjamin Furley. — Rott. 7 August, 1702, to Messre. Justus & Daniel Falckner. In: The Pennsylvania Magazine of History and Biography. Vol. X. Philadelphia, Pa. 1886. pp. 474—476. [3439]
[—] Letter of Benjamin Furley to John Henry Sprogell. — Rotterdam, 5th April, 1709. In: The Pennsylvania Magazine of History and Biography. Vol. XXVII. Philadelphia, Pa. 1903. pp. 376—377. [3440]
Briefe deutscher Auswanderer aus dem Jahre 1709. Herausgegeben von Julius Goebel. In: Deutsch-Amerikanische Geschichtsblätter. Jahrbuch der Deutsch-Amerikanischen Historischen Gesellschaft von Illinois. Jg. 1912. Vol. XII. Chicago, Ill. 1913. S. 124—189. [3441]
On the way to Pennsylvania 1710. *[Letter of 6 Bernese Mennonites from London to their Brethren in Amsterdam.]* In: The Mennonite Year Book and Almanac for 1911. Quakertown, Pa. 1911. p. 35. [3442]
[Pastorius, Franz Daniel]: Letter of Francis Daniel Pastorius to his son. — Germantown, the 27th of November 1714. In: The Pennsylvania Magazine of History and Biography. Vol. XVIII. Philadelphia, Pa. 1894. p. 121. [3443]
[Sauer, J. Christoph]: An early description of Pennsylvania. Letter of Christopher Sower, written in 1724, describing conditions in Philadelphia and vicinity, and the sea voyage from Europe. *(Translation of the German original.)*

Contributed by R. W. Kelsey. In: The Pennsylvania Magazine of History and Biography. Vol. XLV. Philadelphia, Pa. 1921. pp. 243—254. [3444]
Wistar, Caspar: Caspar Wistar's letter of December 4, 1732. — Continental emigrants warned against coming to Pennsylvania. — In: The Perkiomen Region, Past and Present. Vol. II. Philadelphia, Pa. 1900. pp. 119—120. [3445]
[Sauer, J. Christoph]: Wittgensteiner Auswanderungsbriefe aus alter Zeit. Herausgegeben von W. Lückert. In: Das schöne Wittgenstein. Seine Bewohner und Freunde in Gegenwart und Vergangenheit, mit den ,,Mitteilungen des Vereins für Geschichte und Heimatkunde Wittgensteins", Jg. 1927. Heft 1. Laasphe 1927. S. 31f.
[Der erste Brief stammt von dem Germantowner Buchdrucker J. Chr. Sauer und ist datiert: Germantown, den 18. Oktober 1738; der zweite Brief ist ohne Unterschrift, datiert Germantown 16. November 1738.] [3446]
[Sauer, J. Christoph]: Two Germantown letters of 1738. Translated with an introduction by Waldemar Westergood. In: The Pennsylvania Magazin of History and Biography. Vol. LVI. Philadelphia, Pa. 1932. pp. 9—14.
[Letter I signed: J. Christoph Sauer, Germantown, Pa. 18. October 1738; letter II dated: Germantown (Pa.) 16. November 1738; German originals = no. 3446] [3447]
[Seipt, David]: An immigrant's letter, 1734. *[Written by David Seipt, Germantown, Dec. 20, 1734.]* In: The Pennsylvania-German. Vol. IX. Cleona, Pa. 1908. pp. 367—370. [3448]
[Boehm, John Philip]: Life and letters of the Rev. John Philip Boehm, founder of the Reformed Church in Pennsylvania 1683—1749. Edited by William J. Hinke. Philadelphia, Pa.: Publication and Sunday School Board of the Reformed Church in the United States 1916. pp. XXVI, 501, ill., map. [3449]
Mühlenberg, Henry Melchior: Vgl. Hallische Nachrichten [= Nr. 1195—1198].
[Thomas, Geo.]: Letter of Governor George Thomas to Conrad Weiser. *(Dated ,,Philada, Febry. 26, 1741/2.)* In: The Pennsylvania Magazine of History and Biography. Vol. XXXVI. Philadelphia, Pa. 1912. p. 500.

[The governor's attitude to Count Zinzendorf and missionary intentions among the Indians.] [3450
[Weiser, Conrad]: Letter of Conrad Weiser to Richard Peters, secretary. *(Written at ,,Tulpehokin, February the 18, 1744—5. In: The Pennsylvania Magazine of History and Biography. Vol. XXXVII. Philadelphia, Pa. 1913. p. 382.* [3451
[Bechtel, John]: An interesting letter by John Bechtel. *(To Ludwig von Thurnstein in Marienborn, Germany, dated ,,Germantown, d. 6ten January, 1745".) [German original and English translation.] In: The Perkiomen Region, Past and Present. Vol. II. Philadelphia, Pa. 1900. pp. 64—66.* [3452
[Bechtel, John]: A letter of John Bechtel. Dated Germantown, 1745. *In: Germantown history. Papers read before the Site and Relic Society of Germantown. Vol. I. Germantown, Pa. 1915. pp. 23—24.* [3453
[Weiser, Conrad]: Letter of Conrad Weiser, 1747/8. *In: The Pennsylvania Magazine of History and Biography. Vol. XXIII. Philadelphia, Pa. 1899. p. 537.* [3454
Spangenberg, Augustus: A letter to Governor Morris from Mr. Spangenberg. Dated ,,B' th^m, Jun. 26, 1756". *In: Colonial Records of Pennsylvania. Vol. VII. 1851. pp. 173—174.* [3455
[Krause, . . .]: Brief eines Herrn Krause zu Glogau an Pastor H. M. Muhlenberg, vom 26. März, 1753. *Mitgetheilt von Dr. W. J. Mann. In: Der Deutsche Pionier. Jg. XV. Cincinnati, O. 1883—1884. S. 154—158.* [3456
[Weiser, Conrad]: In the French and Indian War. *(Letter, dated Heidelberg, Berks Co., Dec. 22, 1755 to Governor Morris, of Pa., written by Conrad Weiser.) In: Notes and Queries. Edited by W. H. Egle. Third series, vol. I. 1884—1887. Harrisburg, Pa. 1887. pp. 400—401. Reprint in: Third series, vol. II. Harrisburg, Pa. 1896. pp. 125—126.* [3457
[Spangenberg, Augustus]: Letter from Mr. Spangenberg, directed to the governor. Dated ,,Bethel, May 2nd, 1756". *In: Colonial Records of Pennsylvania. Vol. VII. 1851. pp. 118—119.* [3458
[Weiser, Conrad]: Letter from Colonel Weiser to Governor Denny. Dated, ,,Heidelberg, in the County of Berks,

October 19th, 1756". *In: Colonial Records of Pennsylvania. Vol. VII. 1851. pp. 302—303.* [3459
[Arndt, Jacob]: Northampton County, Pa., documents. (1). Letter of Capt. Jacob Arndt to Gov. Denny, 1757. *In: The Pennsylvania Magazine of History and Biography. Vol. XXXVIII. Philadelphia Pa. 1914. p. 381.* [3460
[—] A letter to Governor Denny from Major Arndt. *[Stating the distress caused by Indians on the frontiers in Tulpihocken.] Dated, ,,Fort Augusta, Septem. 20th, 1759." In: Colonial Records of Pennsylvania. Vol. VIII. 1852. p. 401.* [3461
A letter from Pennsylvania Mennonites to Holland in 1773. *Edited by* Harold S. Bender. *In: The Mennonite Quarterly Review. Vol. III. Goshen, Ind. 1929. pp. 225—234.* [3462
[Homrighausen, Sebastian and John]: Dual letter from Wittgenstein, May 31, 1773. Written by Sebastian and John Homrighausen to their brother-in-law, Rev. John Philip Leydich. *(Translated reprint.) In: Historical Notes, relating to the Pennsylvania Reformed Church. Vol. I. Philadelphia, Pa. 1900. pp. 117—120. Reprint in: The Perkiomen Region. Vol. II. Philadelphia, Pa. 1900. pp. 154—159.* [3463
[Dreisbach, Simon]: Colonial correspondence. *[Letter of Simon Dreisbach, member of the Indian Creek Church, Allen Township, Northampton County, Pa. to Rev. John Henry Helffrich, Jan., 1773]: edited and annotated by* John Baer Stoudt. *In: The Reformed Church Review. Fourth series, vol. XVIII. Philadelphia, Pa. 1914. pp. 206—218.* [3464
[Kunze, J. C.]: Von der bei den Deutschen in Philadelphia angelegten lateinischen Schule. Ein Schreiben des Herrn Pastor Kunze, vom 16. Mai 1773. *In: August Ludwig Schlözers Neuer Briefwechsel historischen und politischen Inhalts. Theil I. Heft IV. Nr. 39. Göttingen: Verlag der Vandenhoekschen Buchhandlung 1776. S. 206—217.* [3465
[Miller, Peter]: A genuine letter from a member of the Society called Dunkards to a Lady of the Penn family, with her answer. *(To the Honorable Lady J. P., Ephrata, 30th of June, 1774, signed P. M.; Answer dated, Sept. 29th, 1774.)*

In: The Columbian Magazine, or Monthly Miscellany. Vol. II. Philadelphia, Pa. 1788. (January, 1788). pp. 31—33. [3466

[Muhlenberg, H. M.]: Letter of Rev. H. M. Muhlenberg, 1774. (Translated.) In: The Pennsylvania Magazine of History and Biography. Vol. XXXV. Philadelphia, Pa. 1911. pp. 117—118. [3467

[Kunze, J. C. - Helmuth, J. H. C.]: Briefe von deutschen evangelischen Geistlichen in Pennsylvanien, an Hrn. Prof. Freylinghausen in Halle. (1) Philadelphia, den 18. Jul. 1775 von Hrn. Pastor Kunze; (II) Lancaster, den 25. Aug. 1775, von Hrn. Pastor Helmuth. In: August Ludwig Schlözers Neuer Briefwechsel historischen und politischen Inhalts. Theil I. Heft III. Nr. 29. Göttingen: Verlag der Vandenhoekschen Buchhandlung 1776. S. 152—153; 153—156. [3468

[Mühlenberg, Heinrich Melchior]: Zwei bisher ungedruckte Briefe des Patriarchen Heinrich Melchior Mühlenberg, sen. [(1) „Neuprovidence, in der Grafschaft Montgomery, den 6ten September 1785", addresses to Messrs. Eike und Westphal; (2) „Philadelphia, Freitags, den 10. Mertz 1775, to the Rev. Emanuel Schultze, Tulpehocken Pr. favor of Mr. Breitenbach.] In: Der Deutsche Pionier. Jg. XII. Cincinnati, O. 1880—1881. Alte deutsch-amerikanische Dokumente. S. 143—147; 184—185. [3469

[Müller, Peter]: Letter of Peter Miller. [Brother Jabez of the Ephrata community] to James Read, [Ephrata the 10th Oct. 1776]. In: The Pennsylvania Magazine of History and Biography. Vol. XXXVIII. Philadelphia, Pa. 1914. pp. 227—231. [3470
— A letter from Peter Müller to James Read, Esq. (Dated „Ephrata the 10th Oct. 1776). Contributed by Edward Biddle. In: The Pennsylvania Magazine of History and Biography. Vol. LII. Philadelphia, Pa. 1928. pp. 381—383. [Second print of letter, which was issued in vol. XXXVIII. pp. 227—231 the first time.] [3471

[Andre, John]: Major John Andre's German letter. [Lancaster, April 26, 1776.] By Charles I. Landis. Read June 5, 1914. In: Papers and Addresses of the Historical Society of Lancaster County. Vol. XVIII. Lancaster, Pa. 1914. pp. 127—155. [3472

Revolutionary letters. In: Trancactions of the Moravian Historical Society. Vol. I. Nazareth, Pa. 1858—1876. pp. 79—80; 136—138. [3473

K.: Drei Briefe aus Pennsylvanien — 1784. [(I) Nachricht von einer kleinen wiedertäuferischen Gemeine in Nordamerika. Ephrata in der Grafschaft Lancaster in Pennsylvanien, den 29. April 1784 [= Nr. 1148]; (II) Reading in der Grafschaft Berks in Pennsylvanien; (III) „Neue Universität in Nordamerika." Veröffentlicht in der „Berlinischen Monatsschrift", Mai und Juni 1785.] Abgedruckt in: Der Deutsche Pionier. Jg. XIII. Cincinnati, O. 1881—1882. S. 16—17. [3474

[Hillegas, Michael]: Selected letters of Michael Hillegas, treasurer of the United States. (1777—1780, from the letter-book of Michael Hillegas, now in the Manuscript Department of the Historical Society of Pennsylvania). In: The Pennsylvania Magazine of History and Biography. Vol. XXIX. Philadelphia, Pa. 1905. pp. 232—239. [3475

[Heckewelder, C. R. and Ettwein, J.]: Three letters written at Bethlehem, Pennsylvania, in 1778. [No. 1 and 2 written by Christ Ren s Heckewelder. No. 3 by Johannes Ettwein.] In: The Pennsylvania Magazine of History and Biography. Vol. XXXVI. Philadelphia, Pa. 1912. pp. 293—302. [3476

[Rittenhouse, David]: A letter from David Rittenhouse, Esq. to the Hon. Francis Hopkinson, respecting the generation of clouds in the atmosphere. Dated: Bethlehem, Sept. 9, 1786. Read before the Philosophical Society Febr. 16, 1787. In: The Columbian Magazine, or Monthly Miscellany . . . of the year 1787. Vol. I. (March, 1787). Philadelphia, Pa. 1787. pp. 301—303. [3477

Brief eines Deutschen aus Neu-Jersey. (Datiert: Paramos in Neu Jersey, den 24. Dec. 1789.) In: Amerikanisches Magazin oder authentische Beiträge zur Erdbeschreibung, Staatskunde und Geschichte von Amerika, besonders aber der vereinten Staaten. Herausgegeben von Hegewisch-Kiel und Ebeling-Hamburg. Erster Band. Drittes Stück. Hamburg: Carl Ernst Bohn 1796. S. 136—148. [3477a

[**Ettwein, John**]: Selections from the correspondence of Right Reverend John Ettwein, of Bethlehem, Pa. *[(1) Bishop Ettwein to Hon. Arthur Lee; (2) Henry Drinker to Bishop Ettwein, Philadelphia, 8th 8. mo., 1791; (3) Bishop Ettwein to President Ezra Stiles, June 24, 1793; (4) dito, 3 Aug., 1793; (5) Hon. A. J. Dallas to Bishop Ettwein, Philadelphia, 15 June, 1797.] In: The Pennsylvania Magazine of History and Biography. Vol. XXXIX. Philadelphia, Pa. 1915. pp. 219—220.* [3478

[**Rittenhouse, David**]: Letter of David Rittenhouse to Benjamin Franklin Baché — Jan. 10th, 1794. *In: The Pennsylvania Magazine of History and Biography. Vol. XXIII. Philadelphia, Pa. 1899. p. 116.* [3479

[**Bollman, . . .**]: Auszug eines Schreibens von Doctor Bollmann aus Philadelphia d. 20. Juni, 1796. *In: Berlinische Monatsschrift. Herausgegeben von Biester. Bd. XXVIII. Julius bis Dezember, 1796. Gedruckt zu Dessau; Berlin: Verlag der Haude- und Spenerschen Buchhandlung in Berlin. S. 446 —464.* [3480

[**Storch, . . .**]: Merkwürdige Verfälle. Auszüge aus Briefen usw. Aus einem am 25. Februar 1796 geschriebenen Briefe des Hrn. Storch, deutschen Predigers in Nord-Carolina, an Hrn. Generalsuperintendenten Velthusen in Stade. *In: Amerikanisches Magazin oder authentische Beiträge zur Erdbeschreibung, Staatskunde und Geschichte von Amerika, besonders aber der vereinten Staaten. Herausgegeben von Hegewisch-Kiel und Ebeling-Hamburg: Carl Ernst Bohn 1796. S. 176—179.* [3480 a

[**Bausman, Lorentz**]: A few Bausman letters *[written by L. Bausman, Reformed schoolmaster, 1793—1800]. Translated and edited by Lottie M. Bausman. In: The Pennsylvania-German. Vol. XI. Lititz, Pa. 1910. pp. 226—229.* [3481

[**Zeisberger, David**]: Brief von David Zeisberger an John Heckewelder. *[Goshen, den 4. Januar 1803.] In: Der Deutsche Pionier. Jg. XII. Cincinnati, O. 1880—1881. Alte deutsch-amerikanische Dokumente. S. 185.* [3482

[**Möllinger, Martin**]: The correspondence of Martin Mellinger with relatives in the Rheinish Paiatinate, 1807—1839. *Translated and edited by Harold Bender.*

In: The Mennonite Quarterly Review. Vol. V. Goshen, Ind. - Scottdale, Pa. 1931. pp. 42—64. [3483

Briefe an die Mennonisten Gemeine, in Ober Canada. *Mit einer Zugabe. Berlin, (Ober Canada): Heinrich Eby 1840. 47 S.*

(1) Brief an eine Anzahl zur Mennonisten Gemeine gehoerigen Familien, welche im Jahre 1800 von Pennsylvanien nach dem Niagara District in Ober Canada gezogen, *[datiert ,,Bedminster Taunship, Bucks Caunty, Pennsylvanien, den 4. September 1801", geschrieben von* **Jacob Gross**]. *S. 2—14;*

(2) Ein Brief aus Treußen an Benjamin Eby in der Provinz Ober Canada, *datiert ,,Herrnhagen, den 2ten July 1820", geschrieben von* **Isebrand Wiebe**. *S. 15 —23;*

(3) Ein Brief aus Brandenburg an Benjamin **Eby**, *datiert ,,Brenkenhofswalde bei Diesen an der Netz, in der Neumarkt Landschaft Brandenburg, den 16ten Januar, 1819", geschrieben von* **Wilhelm Lange**. *S. 24—29;*

(4) Auszug eines Briefes aus Baiern an Jacob Meyer, *(datiert ,,Herdhof bey Neuburg an der Donau, den 31sten May 1824", geschrieben von* **Daniel Mueller** *and* **Heinrich Mueller**]. *S. 30—32;*

(5) Ein Brief aus Daenemark an die Mennoniten in Canada, in America, *[datiert ,,Friedrichsstadt an der Eider, im Herzogthum Schleswig, Koenigreich Daenemark, den 29sten August, 1838", geschrieben von* **Carl Justus van der Smissen**]. *S. 33—42;*

(6) Zugabe: Eine Kurze und Aufrichtige Erklärung . . . *(= Petition of 1775 to Pennsylvania Colonial Assembly vs. Military burdens.) S. 43—47.* [3484

[**Smissen, Carl Justus van der**]: Zweyter Brief aus Daenemark an die Mennonisten Gemeine in Canada, *datiert von Friedrichstadt, Mai 19, 1840, geschrieben von . . . Berlin, Canada: Heinrich Eby 1841. 23 S.*

[Vgl. Nr. 3484, Nr. (5).] [3485

Sherrick, David: [Briefe zwischen Mennoniten in Canada und Baden, Germany.] *[s. l. 1863.] pp. 24.*

[Vgl.: ,,Two centuries of American Mennonite literature." A bibliography of Mennonitica Americana 1727—1928. By H. S. Bender. *Goshen, Ind. 1929 [no. = 909]. p. 29.]* [3486

[**Krehbiel, Jacob**]: A few words about the Mennonites in America in 1841: A contemporary document by Jacob Krehbiel. *Translated and edited by* **Harold S. Bender.** *In: The Mennonite Quarterly Review. Vol. VI. Goshen, Ind. — Scottdale, Pa. 1932. pp. 43—57; 110—121.* [3487

[Helffenstein, . . .]: Some Helffenstein letters. *Edited by . . . In: Papers and Addresses of the Lancaster County Historical Society. Vol. I. 1896—1897. Lancaster, Pa. 1897. pp. 218—225.* [3488

Marshall, Christopher: Letters of Christopher Marshall to Peter Miller, of Ephrata. *(Selected from the letter-book of the former in the Library of the Historical Society of Pennsylvania. In: The Pennsylvania Magazine of History and Biography. Vol. XXVIII. Philadelphia, Pa. 1904. pp. 71—77.* [3489

[**Muhlenberg, Peter**]: Letters o Generals Daniel Morgan and Peter Muhlenberg. *Contributed by* **George W. Schmucker.** *In: The Pennsylvania Magazine of History and Biography. Vol. XXI. Philadelphia, Pa. 1897. pp. 488—492.* [3490

[**Spangenberg, A. G.**]: A letter from Bishop Spangenberg to Rev. John Rogers of Philadelphia. *In: Transactions of the Moravian Historical Society. Vol. I. Nazareth, Pa. 1858—1876. pp. 139—141.* [3491

Letters of Mennonite clergymen. *Edited by* **F. R. D.[iffenderffer].** *In: Papers and Addresses of the Lancaster County Historical Society. Vol. VI. Lancaster, Pa. 1902. pp. 41—45.* [3492

Beschreibungen und Landeskunden jüngerer Zeit

General and Geographical Descriptions of more Recent Time

Archambault, A. Margaretta: A guide book of art, architecture, and historic interests in Pennsylvania. *Philadelphia, Pa.: The John Winston Co. 1924. pp. XIV, 509, ill.* [3493

Bowen, Eli: The pictorial sketch-book of Pennsylvania *or its scenery, internal improvements, resources and agriculture. Popularly described. Philadelphia, Pa.: Willis P. Hazard 1852. pp. (4), 9—268, (2).*
[Locomotive sketches with pen and pencil. From Philadelphia to Pittsburg. pp. 13—192, ill., map.; Second edition. Philadelphia, Pa.: William Bromwell 1853. pp. 7—309: 13—270, ill., map.] [3494

Bump, Charles Weathers: Down the historic Susquehanna. *A summer's jaunt from Otsego to the Chesapeake. Baltimore, Md.: Press of the Sun Printing Office 1899. pp. (2), 184.* [3495

Burrows, Thomas H.: State-book of Pennsylvania, *containing an account of the geography, history, government, resources, and noted citizens of the state; with a map of the state and each county. For the use of schools and families. Philadelphia, Pa.: Uriah Hunt & Son 1846. pp. 5—314, ill., maps.* [3496

Druckerman, Benjamin: An ecological survey of Pennsylvania with particular reference to its limestone soils. *In: The Bulletin of the Geographical Society of Philadelphia. Vol. XXIV. (No. 3.) Philadelphia, Pa. 1926. pp. 135—150.* [3497

Eaton, Rebecca: Geography of Pennsylvania for the use of schools and private families. *Second edition with corrections and additions. Philadelphia, Pa.: Edward C. Biddle 1837. pp. VIII, 5—282, ill.* [3498

Faris, John T.: Seeing Pennsylvania. *Philadelphia, Pa. & London: J. B. Lippincott Co. 1919. pp. 350, ill., map.* [3499
— Old trails and roads in Penn's land. *Philadelphia, Pa. & London: J. B.*
Lippincott Co. 1927. pp. 5—259, ill., map.* [3500

Gordon, Thomas F.: A gazetteer of the State of Pennsylvania. *First part, contains a general description of the state . . . Second part embraces ample descriptions of its counties, towns, cities, villages, mountains . . . alphabetically arranged. Philadelphia, Pa.: T. Belknap 1832. pp. (2), 9—63; 508, map.* [3501

James, Henry F.: The agricultural industry of southeastern Pennsylvania. *In: Bulletin of the Geographical Society of Philadelphia. Vol. XXVI. Philadelphia, Pa. 1928. pp. 29—59; 123—147; 208—229; 305—322; vol. XXVII. 1929. pp. 87—126; 167—197, maps.* [3502

Nutting, Wallace: Pennsylvania beautiful (Eastern). *Illustrated by the author with many examples of landscapes and old houses in all the counties herein described. Framingham, Mass.: Old America Co. 1924. pp. 302, ill.* [3503

Rath, G. vom: Pennsylvanien. Geschichtliche, naturwissenschaftliche und soziale Skizzen. *Nach einem Vortrage in Freundeskreisen. Heidelberg: Carl Winter's Universitätsbuchhandlung 1888. IV, 155 S.* [3504

Rolfe, Deette: Geological influences in the economic development of the Pennsylvania piedmont plateau. *In: The Bulletin of the Geographical Society of Philadelphia. Vol. XIII, no. 4. Philadelphia, Pa. 1915. pp. 133—154, ill., maps.* [3505

Rupp, Daniel: The geographical catechism of Pennsylvania, and the western states; *designed as a guide and pocket companion for travellers and emigrants, to Pennsylvania, Ohio, Indiana, Illinois, Michigan and Missouri; containing a geographical and early historical account of these several states, from their first settlement up to the present time. Harrisburg, Pa.: John Winebrenner 1836. pp. IV, 384.* [3506

Scott, Joseph: Geographical description of Pennsylvania: *also of the counties respectively, in the order in which they were established by the legislature. With an alphabetical list of the townships in each county, and their population in 1800. Philadelphia, Pa.: Robert Cochran 1806. pp. 147.* [3507

Smith, J. Russell: North America. *Its people and the resources, development, and prospects of the continent as an agricultural, industrial, and commercial area. London: G. Bell and Sons, Ltd. 1924. ppi VIII, 849, ill., maps. [The northern piedmont. = Chapter IX. pp. 183—195; The Appalachian Ridge and valley region. = Chapter X. pp. 196—212; The Appalachian plateau and the Carolina Mountains. = Chapter XI. pp. 213—230.]* [3508

Thralls, Zoe A.: The geography of Pennsylvania. *New York, N. Y.: The Macmillan Co. 1929. pp. 112, ill., maps.* [3509

Tower, Walter S.: A regional and economic geography of Pennsylvania. *In: The Bulletin of the Geographical Society of Philadelphia. Vol. IV. Philadelphia, Pa. 1906. pp. 57—76, map; pp. 113—136, map; pp. 193—217, map; pp. 271—281; vol. V. 1907. pp. 37—49; 93—107; 164—181.* [3510

Trego, Charles B.: A geography of Pennsylvania: *containing an account of the history, geographical features, soil, cli-*

mate, geology, botany, zoology, population, education, government, finances, productions, trade, railroads, canals &c. of the state; with a separate description of each county, and questions for the convenience of teachers. To which is appended, a travellers' guide, or table of distances on the principal rail road, canal and stage routes in the state. Philadelphia, Pa: Edward C. Biddle 1843. pp. 384, ill., map. [3511

Watts, Ralph L.: Rural Pennsylvania. *New York, N. Y.: The Macmillan Co. 1925. pp. XVII, 331. = Rural State and Province Series. Edited by L. H. Baily.* [3512

Wharton, Anne Hollingsworth: In old Pennsylvania towns. *Philadelphia, Pa. and London: J. B. Lippincott Co. 1920. pp. 5—352, ill.* [3513

Wyer, Samuel S.: The Smithonian Institution's study of natural resources applied on Pennsylvania's resources based on latest governmental data. *Columbus, O. 1922. pp. 150, ill., maps. Reprint. 1925. pp. 182, ill., maps.* [3514

The Pennsylvania manual. *Published by the Commonwealth of Pennsylvania. Compiled under the direction of Department of Property and Supplies, Bureau of Publications. Harrisburg, Pa. Biennial publication issued regularly since the first edition of 1924. Fifth edition, Harrisburg, Pa. 1931. pp. 1370, ill.* [3515

Ortsnamen

Place Names

Donehoo, George P.: The changing of historic place names. *With an introduction and glossary of some historic names changed or misspelled in Pennsylvania. Published under the auspices of the Pennsylvania Alpine Club, J. Herbert Walker, Secretary and Historian. Second edition, revised and enlarged.*

Altoona, Pa.: Tribune Press 1921. pp. 14. [3516

Espenshade, A. Howry: Pennsylvania place names. *Harrisburg, Pa.: The Evangelical Press 1925. pp. (1), 5—375, map. = The Pennsylvania State College Studies in History and Political Science, no. 1. College series, no. 1.* [3517

Heimatgeschichte

Local Historiography

Südost- und Zentral-Pennsylvanien

Southeastern and Central Pennsylvania

Adams County

Ault, John: A historical sketch of Christ's Church, in Union Township, Adams County, Pa. *Organized May 4, 1747. Published by the Congregation. Gettysburg, Pa.: H. J. Stahle, printer, ,,Compiler" office 1876. pp. 17.* [3518

Baker, Joseph Baer: History of the St. James Evangelical Lutheran Church of Gettysburg, Penna. 1775—1921. *Gettysburg, Pa.: Gettysburg Compiler Press 1921. pp. 318, ill.* [3519

Billheimer, Stanley: Christ Evangelical Lutheran Church of Lower Bermudian, Adams County, Pa. *In: The Pennsylvania-German. Vol. X. Lititz, Pa. 1909. pp. 456—459, ill.* [3520

Boyer, Cora: Mummasburg Mennonite Church, *[Franklin Township, Adams County, Pa.]. In: Christian Monitor. A monthly magazine for the home. Vol. XXIII, no. 8. Scottdale, Pa. 1931. p. 241.* [3521

Egle, William Henry: Provincial papers: Returns and taxables of the County of York for the years 1779, 1780, 1781, 1782 and 1783. *Edited by . . . Harrisburg, Pa.: Wm. Stanley Ray 1898. pp. VIII, 820.* = *Pennsylvania Archives. Third series, vol. XXI.* [3522

Foulk, Paul L. and **Eichelberger, Percy S.:** Adams County in the World War. April 6, 1917 to November 11, 1918. *Harrisburg, Pa.: The Evangelical Press 1921. pp. 298, ill.* [3523

Gobrecht, N. A.: Tombstone inscriptions of persons born prior to 1800 and past 16 years at death at Arendtsville, Adams County, Pa. *Transcribed by . . . In: The Pennsylvania-German. Vol. X. Lititz, Pa. 1909. Appendix. Genealogical record of pioneer Pennsylvania families. pp. 15—17.* [3524

Hay, Charles A.: Historical discourse. Christ Church, (Evangelical Lutheran) Gettysburg, Pa. *Read before the congregation, Feb. 18, 1877. Published by order of the Trustees and Church Council. Gettysburg, Pa.: Star and Sentinel 1878. pp. 31.* [3525

Lewars, Elsie Singmaster: Lutheran institutions in the battle of Gettysburg and its anniversary. *In: The Lutheran Quarterly. Vol. XLIII. Gettysburg, Pa. 1913. pp. 516—523.* [3526

McSherry, William: History of Saint Aloysius [Catholic] Church of Littlestown, Penn'a. *Gettysburg, Pa.: J. E. Wible 1893. pp. 127, ill.* [3527

Myers, Albert Cook: Some Adams County records. Inscriptions from Sunny Side cemetery, York Springs; Inscriptions in the Lutheran church graveyard at York Springs. *In: Notes and Queries. Edited by W. H. Egle. Annual vol. 1899. Harrisburg, Pa. 1900. pp. 210—212.* [3528

Reily, John T.: Conewago. *A collection of Catholic local history. Gathered from the fields of Catholic missionary labor within our reach. Martinsburg, W. Va.: Herold Print 1885. pp. IV, 5—220, (3), ill.* [3529

Rupp, I. Daniel: The history and topography of Dauphin, Cumberland, Franklin, Bedford, Adams and Perry Counties: *Containing a brief history of the first settlers, notices of the leading events, incidents and interesting facts, both general and local, in the history of the counties, general and statistical descriptions of all the principal boroughs, towns, villages, &c. with an appendix. Lancaster, Pa.:*

Gilbert Hills. 1846. pp. XII, 25—606, ill. [3530

Schuler, H. A.: The Hampton furnace. Reminiscences of an important industry and its old-time owner. *In: The Pennsylvania-German. Vol. VII. 1908. pp. 233—240, ill.* . [3531

Stump, Adam and **Anstadt, Henry:** History of the Evangelical Lutheran Synod of West Pennsylvania of the United Lutheran Church in America. 1825— 1925. *Edited by . . . Published by action of the Synod in the celebration of its Centennial. Chambersburg, Pa.: J. R. Kerr & Bro. 1925. pp. 696, ill.* *[Adams County Conference. pp. 193 —288.]* [3532

History of Cumberland and Adams Counties, Pa. *Containing history of the counties, their townships, towns, villages, schools, churches, industries, etc.; portraits of early settlers and prominent men; biographies; history of Pennsylvania, statistical and miscellaneous matter, etc., etc. 3 vols. Chicago, Ill.: Warner, Beers & Co. 1886. pp. X, 16—132; 588; 516, ill,\ maps.* [3533

Semi-Centennial anniversary of Christ Church and School. *Gettysburg, Pa. February 8—10, 1878. Gettysburg, Pa.: The ,,Star and Sentinel" Office 1878. pp. 40.* [3534

Bedford County

[Blackburn, E. Howard]: History of Bedford and Somerset Counties, Pa., with genealogical and personal history. *Bedford County, by E. Howard Blackburn; . . . Under the editorial supervision of William H. Koontz. 3 vols. New York, N. Y. — Chicago, Ill.: The Lewis Publishing Co. 1906. Vol. I. Bedford County. pp. X, 548, ill.; vol. II. Somerset County [See no. 5380]; vol. III. Bibliographical. pp. 553, ill.* [3535

[Byers, William L.]: A brief history of Bedford County. *Published by the Inquirer Printing Co. Bedford, Pa., March, 1924. pp. 49.* [3536

Carney, W. H. Bruce: History of the Alleghany Evangelical Lutheran Synod of Pennsylvania . . . *Published by the authority of Alleghany Synod in commemoration of its seventy-fifth anniversary, and in the Quadricentennial of the Reformation. 2 vols. Philadelphia, Pa.:* *Printed for the Synod by the Lutheran Publication Society 1918. pp. XII, 454; 455—871, ill., map.* *[,,Churches of Juniata Conference." = Chapter XI. pp. 252—357, ill.]* [3537

Egle, William Henry: Provincial papers. Returns of taxables for the Counties of Bedford (1773 to 1784), Huntingdon (1788), Westmoreland (1783, 1786), Fayette (1785, 1786), Allegheny (1791), Washington (1786) and Census of Bedford (1784) and Westmoreland (1783). *Edited by . . . Harrisburg, Pa. 1898. pp. XI, 782.* = *Pennsylvania Archives. Third series, vol XXII.* [3538

Jones, U. J.: History of the early settlement of the Juniata Valley: embracing an account of the early pioneers, and the trials and privations incident to the settlement of the valley. *Philadelphia, Pa.: Henry B. Ashmeed 1856. pp. 380. [,,The cove — early settlement by Dunkards . . ." = Chapter XVIII. pp. 207—217.]* [3539

L., W. F.: Burial records from the Reformed church graveyard at Bedford, Pa. *In: Notes and Queries. Edited by W. H. Egle. Annual vol. 1899. Harrisburg, Pa. 1900. pp. 118—121.* [3540

Replogle, Emma A. M.: Indian Eve and her descendants. *An indian story of Bedford County, Pa. Huntingdon, Pa.: J. L. Rupert 1911. pp. 128.* [3541

Rupp, I. Daniel: The history and topography of Dauphin, Cumberland, Franklin, Bedford, Adams and Perry Counties: *Containing a brief history of the first settlers, notices of the leading events, incidents and interesting facts, both general and statistical descriptions of all the principal boroughs, towns, villages, &c. with an appendix. Lancaster, Pa.: Gilbert Hill 1846. pp. XII, 25—606, ill.* [3542

Schell, William P.: The annals of Bedford County, Pa. *Consisting of condensed sketches of the most important events which occurred during the century from January, 1750—1850. Prepared for Old Home Week, August 4—10, 1907. Bedford, Pa.: Gazette Publishing Co., Print 1907. pp. 72; Appendix. pp. 15.* [3543

Welfley, W. H.: Bedford County marriages, 1791—1798. *In: The Pennsylvania-German. Vol. XII. Lititz, Pa. 1911. pp. 626—627.* [3544

History of Bedford, Somerset and Fulton
Counties, Pennsylvania. *With illu-
strations and biographical sketches of
some of its pioneers and prominent men.
Chicago, Ill.: Waterman, Watkins & Co.
1884. pp. IX, 15—672, ill.* [3545
Biographical review. Vol. XXXII. *Con-
taining life sketches of leading citizens of
Bedford and Somerset Counties, Pa.
Boston, Mass.: Biographical Review
Publishing Co. 1899. pp. (2), 9—345,
ill.* [3546
Bedford, Pa. S. *ttled in 1751. Fort erected
1758. Tout laid out 1766. Town
incorporated* 1 795. *Bedford, Pa. [. . .]:
Inquirer Printing Co. [1928] pp. 27.* [3547

Berks County

Balthasar, F. W.: The story of Berks
County, Pa. *Reading, Pa.: F. W.
Balthaser-Reading Eagle Press, 1925.
pp. XVIII, 373, ill.* [3548
Barnet, Edward: Some account of Reading,
in Pennsylvania 1817. *In: The Port
Folio. Vol. IV for 1817. Philadelphia,
Pa.: Harrison Hall; London: John
Souter 1817. pp. 370—372.* [3549
Bickel, P. J. and Stoudt, John Baer: Tomb-
stone inscriptions at Bern Church. *Tran-
scribed by . . . In: The Pennsylvania-
German. Vol. X. Lititz, Pa. 1909.
Appendix: Genealogical record of pioneer
Pennsylvania families. pp. 6—11.* [3550
Billett, Michael C.: History of party
politics in Berks County, Pa., 1854—
1860. *Thesis of M. A., University of
Pennsylvania, Philadelphia, Pa. 1931.
Typewritten pp. (2), 114, (15).* [3551
Body, Adam S.: The history of Shillington
1733—1928. *Dedicated to the 20 anni-
versary committee of the incorporation of
the Borough of Shillington, Reading, Pa.:
Reading Eagle Press 1928. pp. 36, ill.* [3552
Brane, C. I. B.: An historical souvenir of
several of the United Brethren churches
of Reading and vicinity. *Reading, Pa.:
Behney & Bright Book and Job Printing
1909. pp. VII, 9—72, ill.* [3553
Conner, Philip S. P.: The early registers of
the Catholic Church in Pennsylvania.
*Paper read May 5th 1887. In: Records
of the American Catholic Historical
Society of Philadelphia, Pa. Vol. II.
Philadelphia, Pa. 1889. pp. 22—28.* [3554

[Croll, P. C.]: Historical pilgrimages into
Pennsylvania-Germandom. Down the
Lebanon Valley. *In: The Pennsylvania-
German. Vol. II. Lebanon, Pa. 1901.
pp. 123—132, ill.; pp. 165—183, ill.
[See no. 295]* [3555
[—] Historical pilgrimages into Pennsylvania-Germandom. Over the Oley pike
to Boyertown and back. *In: The Pennsylvania-German. Vol. III. Lebanon,
Pa. 1902. pp. 113—132, ill.
[See no. 925]* [3556
—Annals of Womelsdorf, Pa. and community. 1723—1923. *History's yardstick
for two hundred years. [s. l. (Reading,
Pa.: Reading Eagle).] 1923. pp. 150, ill.* [3557
[—] The Tulpehocken Bi-Centennial com-
memorated in a four day celebration
at Womelsdorf, Pa., June 28th, 29th,
30th and July 1st, 1923. *Being a
series of historical sketches covering two
hundred years 1723—1923. Edited by the
chairman of the celebrating committee: . . .
Published by the Authority of the Executive Committee. [s. l. 1923.] pp. 212, ill.* [3558
— Conrad Weiser and his memorial park.
A little history in 3 parts. *Reading, Pa.:
Reading Eagle Press 1926. pp. 186, ill.* [3559
— Annals of the Oley Valley. Over two
hundred years of local history of an
American Canaan. *Reading, Pa.: Reading Eagle Press 1926. pp. 148, map.* [3560
Dampman, John B.: A short history of the
newspapers of Reading, Pa. *Compiled
by . . . Presented by* John D. Mishler
*to the Reading Press Club. Reading,
Pa.: Press of Pengelly & Bro. [s. d.]
pp. 55.* [3561
Deatrick, W. W.: The Keystone State
Normal School at Kutztown. *A paper
read June 8, 1909. In: Transactions of
the Historical Society of Berks County.
Vol. II. 1905—1909. Reading, Pa.
1910. pp. 378—385, ill.* [3562
[—] The Centennial history of Kutztown,
Pa. Celebrating the Centennial of the
incorporation of the borough 1815—
1915. *Compiled by the Historical Committee of the Kutztown Centennial Association,* W. W. Deatrick, *chairman.
Kutztown, Pa.: Press of the Kutztown
Publishing Co. 1915. pp. XII, (2),
247, ill.* [3563
De Long, Irwin Hoch: Pennsylvania grave-
stone inscriptions. Cemetery of Christ,

De Long's Reformed Church, Bowers, Berks County, Pa. *Contributed by . . . In: Publications of the Genealogical Society of Pennsylvania. Vol. IX, no. 1. Philadelphia, Pa. 1924. pp. 74—84. Reprint from: Publications of the Genealogical Society of Pennsylvania. Lancaster, Pa.: Wickersham Press 1925. pp. 14.* [3564

De Long, Irwin Hoch: *An early nineteenth century constitution of a union church. Lancaster, Pa. Privately printed 1931. pp. 27.* [3564a

— An early eighteenth century Reformed Church. *A contribution to church and family history. Lancaster, Pa. Privately printed 1934. IX, pp. 85, ill.* [3565

Dickert, Thomas W.: The history of St. Stephen's Reformed Church, Reading, Pa. 1884—1909. *Reading, Pa.: I. M. Beaver 1909. pp. XIII, 17—392, ill.* [3566

Early, John W.: Baptismal and other records of the „Little Tulpehocken Church". *In: Notes and Queries. Edited by W. H. Egle. Annual vol. 1899. Harrisburg, Pa. 1900. pp. 185—188; 190—194; 205—208; 212—215; 216—219.* [3567

— Historical sketch of the church on Oley Hills. *An address delivered Nov. 14, 1899. In: Transactions of the Historical Society of Berks County. Vol. I, no. 10. Reading, Pa. 1904. pp. (7).* [3568

— The oldest churches of Berks County. *A paper read March 12, 1901. In: Transactions of the Historical Society of Berks County. Vol. I, no. 19. Reading, Pa. 1904. pp. (11).* [3569

— A bit of early school history. *An address delivered Sept. 9, 1902. In: Transactions of the Historical Society of Berks County. Vol. I, no. 26. Reading, Pa. 1904. pp. (3).* [3570

— The church history of Berks County. *Paper read at the observance of the Sesqui-Centennial of the County of Berks, Pa., March 11, 1902. In: Transactions of the Historical Society of Berks County. Vol. I, no. 23. Reading, Pa. 1904. pp. 8—16.* [3571

— A journey over the route travelled by Rev. F. A. C. Muhlenberg in his trips to Shamokin, 1777. *In: The Pennsylvania-German. Vol. IX. Cleona, Pa. 1908. pp. 339—346. [Reading - Womelsdorf - Rehrersburg - Pinegrove - Tremont . . .]* [3572

— Indian massacres in Berks County and the story of Regina, the Indian captive. *A paper read June 12, 1906. In: Transactions of the Historical Society of Berks County. Vol. II. 1905—1909. Reading, Pa. 1910. pp. 107—140.* [3573

Early, John W.: Bern church records, 1739 —1835. Bern Township, Berks County, Pa. *In: Publications of the Genealogical Society of Pennsylvania. Vol. V, no. 1. Philadelphia, Pa. 1912. pp. 38—52.* [3574

— Höhn's church records, 1745—1805. St. John's Reformed, commonly called „Hain's Church", Heidelberg Township, Berks County, Pa. *In: Publications of the Genealogical Society of Pennsylvania. Vol. V, no. 1. Philadelphia, Pa. 1912. pp. 53—109.* [3575

— The northwest boundary of Berks County as originally constituted. *A paper read March 10, 1914. In: Transactions of the Historical Society of Berks County. Vol. II. Reading, Pa. 1910. pp. 302—315.* [3576

— Centennial of Friedens Evangelical Lutheran Church, Myerstown, Pa. *In: The Penn Germania. Vol. II. = Old series, vol. XIV. Lititz, Pa. 1913. pp. 32—36.* [3577

— Reading's German Reading Association. 1803—1840. *A paper read Dec. 12, 1911. In: Transactions of the Historical Society of Berks County. Vol. III. Reading, Pa. 1923. pp. 144—149.* [3578

— Our own pilgrim fathers. *Paper read March 14, 1916. In: Transactions of the Historical Society of Berks County. Vol. III. Reading, Pa. 1923. pp. 426—440.* [3579

— Lutheran ministers of Berks County. Sketches of the lives of those who have lived and labored in this county. *Reading, Pa.: Central Luther League of Reading and vicinity. [s. d.] pp. 111.* [3580

Egle, William Henry: Provincial papers: Proprietary and state tax lists of the County of Berks for the years 1767, 1768, 1779, 1780, 1781, 1784, 1785. *Edited by . . . Harrisburg, Pa.: Wm. Stanley Ray, 1898. pp. XI, 814. = Pennsylvania Archives. Third series, vol. XVIII.* [3581

Endlich, G. A.: Political and social history of the county. *Paper read at the observance of the Sesqui-Centennial of the County of Berks, Pa., March 11, 1902. In: Transactions of the Historical Society of Berks County. Vol. I, no. 23. Reading, Pa. 1904. pp. 21—27.* [3582

Ermentrout, John S.: 1776—1876. A Centennial memorial. Historical sketch of Kutztown, and Maxatawny, Berks County, Penn'a. *Prepared by . . . Kutztown, Pa.: Ulrick & Gehring's steam job print. 1876. pp. 58.* [3583

Fegley, H. Winslow: Old charcoal furnaces situated in eastern section of Berks County. *Paper read June 15, 1905. In: Transactions of the Historical Society of Berks County. Vol. II. 1905—1909. Reading, Pa. 1910. pp. 25—36, ill.* [3584

Fox, Cyrus: Reading and Berks County, Pa. A history. *Editor in Chief . . . 3 vols. New York, N. Y.: Lewis Historical Publishing Co., Inc. 1925. pp. (2), 427, ill.; pp. 429—580. Biographical: pp. 1a—6f.; 192, ill; 193—462, ill.* [3585

Fry, Jacob: The history of Trinity Lutheran, Church, Reading, Pa., 1751—1894. *Reading, Pa.: Published by the Congregation. — Press Eagle Job Office. 1894. pp. 300.* [3586

Furey, Francis T.: Father Schneider's Goshenhoppen registers 1741—1764. *Trancsribed for the Society, and translated and prepared for publication by Fr. T. Furey. In: Records of the American Catholic Historical Society of Philadelphia, Pa. Vol. II. Philadelphia, Pa. 1889. pp. 316—332.* [3587

Gehman, J. B.: History of Reading mission *[of the Mennonite Church.] In: Christian Monitor. A monthly magazine for the home. Vol. XIX, no. 8. Scottdale, Pa. 1927. pp. 238—239, ill.* [3588

Gerhart, Charles W.: „A century of Reading." *A paper compiled by* Chas. W. Gerhart *and read Jan. 8, 1901 by* Thomas Zimmerman. *In: Transactions of the Historical Society of Berks County. Vol. I., no. 18. Reading, Pa. 1904. pp. 24.* [3589

Gruber, Michael Alvin: Tombstone inscriptions of persons born to 1801, as found in the graveyard at the „Little Tulpehocken Church," located one and a half miles westward of Bernville, Berks County, Pa. *Collected and arranged by . . . In: The Pennsylvania-German. Vol. VII. Lebanon, Pa. 1906. pp. 80—81.* [3590

— The Lutheran congregation of Heidelberg *[Township, Berks County, Pa.] In: The Pennsylvania-German. Vol. IX. Cleona, Pa. 1908. pp. 175—180.* [3591

Gruber, Michael Alvin: Tombstone inscriptions, Bernville, Pa. *In: The Penn Germania. Vol. II. = Old series, vol. XIV. Lititz, Pa. 1913. pp. 45—50* [3592

— Tombstone inscriptions, St. Daniel's (Corner) Church, Berks County, Pa. *In: The National Genealogical Society Quarterly Vol. IX, no. 3. Washington, D. C. 1920. pp. 33—39, ill.* [3593

Hoch, D. K.: The Penn Street viaduct spanning the Schuylkill River at Reading, Pa. History of Penn Street bridges and of the movement that led to the erection of the present structure. *Compiled by county controller . . . as a supplement to his annual report. [Reading, Pa.] 1914. pp. 10, ill.* [3594

Horine, M. C.: The history of St. James Lutheran Church. Reading, Pa. 1850—1900. *Reading, Pa.: Published by the Congregation — Eagle Book and Job Press 1900. pp. 72, ill.* [3595

Jones, Alfred S.: Reading's inns of long ago. *An address delivered May 14, 1901. In: Transactions of the Historical Society of Berks County. Vol. I., no. 20. Reading, Pa. 1904, pp. (8).* [3596

— Old time school teachers. *An address delivered November 12, 1901. In: Transactions of the Historical Society of Berks County. Vol. I. no 21. Reading, Pa. 1904. pp. 12.* [3597

— Old time battalions in Berks County. *A paper read June 11, 1907. In: Transactions of the Historical Society of Berks County. Vol. II. 1905—1909. Reading, Pa. 1910. pp. 198—212.* [3598

Jones, Richmond L.: Early naturalizations in Berks County. *Paper read June 10, 1913. In: Transactions of the Historical Society of Berks County. Vol. III. Reading, Pa. 1923. pp. 238—243.* [3599

J.[ordan], J. W.: The Moravians. *(= a „Brief" of the Moravian land in Oley, Pa.) In: Notes and Queries. Edited by W. H. Egle. Annual vol. 1900. Harrisburg. Pa. 1901. p. 141, map.* [3600

Kehs, Irwin W.: The Catholic Church at Bally. *. Paper read Oct. 24, 1908. In: Historical Sketches. A Collection of Papers prepared for the Historical Society of Montgomery County, Pa. Vol. IV. Norristown, Pa. 1910. pp. 135—138, ill.* [3601

[Keim, De B. Randolph]: First annual report of the Board of Trade of Reading, Pa., for the year ending December 31, 1881, *embracing a description of the City* of Reading as a centre of manufacture and place of residence, and the reports of officers and standing committees, including various statistical tables, exhibiting the trade and commerce of the city. Reading, Pa.: Coleman Printing House 1882. pp. 162. [3602

Kershner, W. J.: Record of St. John's Reformed Church, Sinking Spring 1883—1913. [s. l , s. d.] pp. (2), 58. [3603

— Centennial anniversary, Sept. 15—16, 1894. History of St. John's Reformed Church, Sinking Spring, Pa. Reading, Pa.: Mohr Publishing Co. [1894] pp. 43, ill. [3604

—-Lerch, Adam G.: History of St. John's (Hain's) Reformed Church in Lower Heidelberg Township, Berks County, Penna. Reading, Pa.: I. M. Beaver 1916. pp. 494, ill. [3605

History of St. John's (Hain's) Reformed Church of Lower Heidelberg Township, Berks County, Pennsylvania, Bicentennial supplement 1935. Edited by Committee appointed by the consistory. 1935. pp. II, 333, ill. [3605a

[Kidd, H. S.]: Lutherans in Berks County. Two centuries of continuous organized church life. 1723—1923. Published by the Reading Conference of the Evangelical Lutheran Ministerium of Pennsylvania and adjacent states. Chairman of Committee: . . . Kutztown and Reading, Pa.: William S. Rhode Publishing Co. 1923. pp. 503, ill., maps. [3606

Kriebel, H. W.: A subscription-school in Hereford, 1814—1854. In: The Pennsylvania-German. Vol. VIII. Lebanon, Pa. 1907. pp. 527—530. [3607

Levan, F. K.: Maxatawny prior to 1800. In: The Pennsylvania-German Society. Proceedings and Addresses at York, Oct. 11, 1893. Vol. IV. Lancaster, Pa. 1894. pp. 73—90. [3608

[Lindemuth, C. I.]: The Tulpehocken settlement. [A map showing the pioneer homesteads 1723, drawn by C. L. Lindemuth.] In: The Pennsylvania-German. Vol. V. Lebanon, Pa. 1904. pp. 190—191, map. [3609

Mast, C. Z.: The Maiden Creek congregation [of the Amish.] In: Christian Monitor. A monthly magazine for the home. Vol. XV., no. 8. Scottdale, Pa. 1923. pp. 243—244, ill. [3610

Mengel, Levi W.: Former scientists and scientific societies of Reading. A paper read March 11, 1911. In: Transactions of the

Historical Society of Berks County. Vol. III. Reading, Pa. 1923. pp. 99—114, ill. [3611

Middleton, Thomas C.: Goshenhoppen registers. (Second series) 1765—1785. Translated and annotated by Thomas C. Middleton. In: Records of the American Catholic Historical Society of Philadelphia. Vol. III. Philadelphia, Pa. 1891. pp. 295—397. (Third series) 1787—1800. In: Vol. VIII. 1897. pp. 330—393; Baptisms (1801—1807); marriages (1801—1819); and deaths (1801—1818). (Fourth series). In: Vol. XI. 1900. pp. 43—60; 196—207; 303—307. [3612

Miller, Daniel: History of the Reformed Church in Reading, Pa. Introduction by B. Bausman. Reading, Pa.: Daniel Miller 1905. pp. VIII. 9—468, ill. [3613

— Early history of the Reformed Church in Reading, Pa. In: The Pennsylvania-German. Vol. VII. Lebanon, Pa. 1906. pp. 391—397, ill. [3614

— The early Moravians in Berks County. In: The Pennsylvania-German. Vol. X. Lititz, Pa. 1909. pp. 23—31; 67—73. [3615

— Early history of the Reformed Church in Reading, Pa. A paper read September 11, 1906. In: Transactions of the Historical Society of Berks County. Vol. II. 1905—1909. Reading, Pa. 1910. pp. 141—152, ill. [3616

— The early Moravian settlements in Berks County. A paper read September 8, 1908. In: Transactions of the Historical Society of Berks County. Vol. II. 1905—1909. Reading, Pa. 1910. pp. 309—334, ill. [3617

— The · Weisers and the Tulpenhocken settlement. In: The Penn Germania. Vol. I. = Old series, vol. XIII. Lititz, Pa. 1912. pp. 625—626. [3618

— The German newspapers of Berks County. A paper read March 8, 1910. In: Transactions of the Historical Society of Berks County. Vol. III. Reading, Pa. 1923. pp. 4—23. [3619

[Mohr, Howard C.]: Historical pilgrimages into Pennsylvania-Germandom. Down the Schuylkill Valley. In: The Pennsylvania-German. Vol. III. Lebanon, Pa. 1902. pp. 27—43, ill. [See no. 295] [3620

Montgomery, Morton L.: First families of Berks County. In: Historical Register. Notes and Queries, historical and genealo-

gical relating to interior Pennsylvania for the year 1883. Vol. I. Harrisburg, Pa. 1883. pp. 18—26. [3621

Montgomery, Morton L.: Political handbook of Berks County, Pa. *Reading, Pa.: Press of B. F. Owen 1883. pp. 104.* [3622

— Baptisms of Trinity Lutheran Church, Reading, Pa. *Communicated by . . . In: Historical Register: Notes and Queries, historical and genealogical relating to interior Pennsylvania for the year 1883. Vol. I. Harrisburg, Pa. 1883. pp. 104—108.* [3623

— Early furnaces and forges of Berks County, Pa. *In: The Pennsylvania Magazine of History and Biography. Vol. VIII. Philadelphia, Pa. 1884. pp. 56—81.* [3624

— History of Berks County in Pennsylvania. *Philadelphia, Pa.: Everts, Peck and Richards 1886. pp. X, 1204, ill., maps.* [3625

— School history of Berks County, in Pennsylvania. *Philadelphia, Pa.: J. B. Rodgers Printing Co. 1889. pp. 302, ill., map.* [3626

— History of Berks County, Pa., in the Revolution from 1774 to 1783. *Vol. arranged in two books. Book I. Revolution; Book II. Biographical sketches. Reading, Pa.: Chas. F. Haage 1894. pp. 295.* [3627

[—] 1748—1898. History of Reading, Pa. and the anniversary proceedings of the Sesqui-Centennial, June 5—12, 1898. *Compiled by* M. L. Montgomery *for the Executive Committee. Reading, Pa.: Times Book Print 1898. pp. 298, ill., maps.* [3628

— Berks County militia at the battles of Brandywine and Germantown in the Revolution. *Paper prepared for the Historical Society of Berks County, Pa. and read March 14, 1905. In: Transactions of the Historical Society of Berks County. Vol. II. 1905—1909. Reading, Pa. 1910. pp. 10—24.* [3629

— Statement of men supplied by the County of Berks in the Civil War. *Prepared by . . . In: Transactions of the Historical Society of Berks County. Vol. II. 1905—1909. Reading, Pa. 1910. pp. 1—5.* [3630

— Historical and biographical annals of Berks County, Pa., *embracing a concise history of the county and a genealogical and biographical record of representative*

families. Chicago, Ill.: J. H. Beers & Co. 1909. pp. XXXII, 784, ill., maps; pp. XX, 785—1723, ill. [3631

Mosser, H.: History of the First Reformed Church, Reading, Pa. 1755—1898. *Published by the consistory, Reading, Pa.: Daniel Miller 1898. pp. 71, ill.* [3632

[Muhlenberg, Hiester H.]: A forgotten retrospect. The reminiscences of Hiester H. Muhlenberg, 1846. *Forward by* J. Bennett Nolan. *Published by the Berks County Historical Society. Reading, Pa. 1926. pp. 21, ill., map.* [3633

Myers, William H.: Quarto-Centennial history of Grace Lutheran Church, Reading, Pa. 1878—1903. *Reading, Pa.: Press of Pengelly & Bro. 1903. pp. 152, ill.* [3634

Nolan, J. Bennett: The Reading militia in the Great War. *Published under the auspices of the Historical Society of Berks County. Reading, Pa.: F. A. Woerner. 1919. pp. 208.* [3635

— Early narratives of Berks County. *Published under the auspices of the Historical Society of Berks County. Reading, Pa.: Reading Eagle Press 1927. pp. 189, ill.* [3636

— Early maps of our town. Assembled and described. *Published and distributed by The Pennsylvania Trust Company. Reading, Pa.: Press of Edward Pengelly & Bro. 1928. pp. 31; maps. 11.* [3637

— The foundation of the Town of Reading in Pennsylvania. *Published under the auspices of School District of Reading, Pa. 1929. Reading, Pa.: Edward Pengelly & Bro. 1929. pp. 210, ill., maps.* [3638

— The first decade of printing in Reading, Pennsylvania. *Published and distributed by Reading National Bank and Trust Company. Reading, Pa.: Reading Eagle Press 1930. pp. 64, ill.* [3639

— George Washington and the Town of Reading in Pennsylvania. *Published under the auspices of the Chamber of Commerce of Reading, Pennsylvania. Reading, Pa.: Reading Eagle Press 1931. pp. 162, ill.* [3640

— Annals of the Penn Square, Reading. *Philadelphia, Pa.: University of Pennsylvania Press 1933. pp. (1) (1) 106, ill.* [3640a

Rapp, E. M.: The eight-cornered schoolbuilding at Sinking-Spring. *In: The Pennsylvania-German. Vol. VIII. Lebanon, Pa. 1907. pp. 517—523, ill.* [3641

Richards, H. M. Muhlenberg: Berks County in the French and Indian War. *A paper read March 10, 1908. In: Transactions of the Historical Society of Berks County. Vol. II. 1905—1909. Reading, Pa. 1910. pp. 275—293.* [3642

Richards, Louis: Washington's visits to Berks County and funeral ceremonies in Reading. *An address delivered December 12, 1899. In: Transactions of the Historical Society of Berks County. Vol. I., no. 11. Reading, Pa. 1904. pp. (4).* [3643

— War's alarms in Reading during the Confederate invasion of 1863, and the rally of Pennsylvania militia for home defence. *Paper read Sept. 12, 1905. In: Transactions of the Historical Society of Berks County. Vol. II. 1905—1909. Reading, Pa. 1910. pp. 37—63.* [3644

— Early Berks County tombstone inscriptions. *In: The Pennsylvania-German. Vol. XII. Lititz, Pa. 1911. pp. 48—52; 87—90; 163—165; 235—237; 362—365; 494—497.* [3645

— Earliest county bridges in Berks County. *A paper read Dec. 9, 1913. In: Transactions of the Historical Society of Berks County. Vol. III. Reading, Pa. 1923. pp. 277—292.* [3646

Rogers, Mrs. Harry: Items [names of late soldiers] taken from Administrations. *Vol. 4, Berks County, Pa. and . . . Vol. V. [1792—1800.] In: The Pennsylvania Magazine of History and Biography. Vol. XLVII. Philadelphia, Pa. 1923. pp. 178—183.* [3647

Rupp, I. Daniel: History of the Counties of Berks and Lebanon: *containing a brief account of the Indians, who inhabited this region of the country, and the numerous murders by them; notices of the first Swedish, Welsh, French, German, Irish and English settlers, giving the names of nearly five thousand of them, biographical sketches, topographical descriptions of every township, and of the principal towns and villages; the religious history with much useful statistical information; notices of the press and education. Lancaster, Pa.: G. Hills 1844. pp. VI, (3), 14—513, ill.* [3648

— Die erste deutsche Ansiedlung von Tulpehocken, Penn. *In: Der Deutsche Pionier. Jg. II. Cincinnati, O. 1870—1871. pp. 5—8.* [3649

Sallade, W. H.: The graveyards of Hereford Township, Berks County, Pa. *In: The Pennsylvania-German. Vol. X. Lititz, Pa. 1909. Appendix: Genealogical record of pioneer Pennsylvania families. pp. 25—29.* [3650

Schaeffer, Charles H.: The Berks County banking institutions. *A paper read January 14, 1902. In: Transactions of the Historical Society of Berks County. Vol. I., no. 22. Reading, Pa. 1904. pp. 8.* [3651

Schaeffer, N. C.: Education in Berks County before the Revolution. *Paper read at the observance of the Sesqui-Centennial of the County of Berks, Pa., March 11, 1902. In: Transactions of the Historical Society of Berks County. Vol. I., no. 23. Reading, Pa. 1904. pp. 17—20.* [3652

Schantz, F. J. F.: Historical discourse at the Sesqui-Centennial of Christ Evangelical Church on the Tulpehocken, near Stouchsburg, Berks County, Pa., on Sunday, Sept 3, 1893. *Published by request of Church Council. Lebanon, Pa.: Weigley & Co. 1894. pp. 27, ill.* [3653

[Schoepf, John D.]: Travels trough Berks County in 1783. *By Dr. John D. Schoepf, surgeon of the German auxiliary troops in the service of England, 1776—83. [Translation of a part of his work, published at Erlangen in 1788 (= no. 3354—3355).] In: The Pennsylvania Magazine of History and Biography. Vol. V. Philadelphia, Pa. 1881. pp. 74—81.* [3654

Scholl, William H.: Early dentistry and dental practitioners in Reading. *A paper read June 13, 1911. In: Transactions of the Historical Society of Berks County. Vol. III. Reading, Pa. 1923. pp. 115—123.* [3655

[Schultz, Christopher K.]: „Stohr Stophel's" day book. *[Christopher K. Schultz's day book opened for a store in Colebrook Township., Berks County, April, 1819.] In: The Perkiomen Region. Vol. V, no. 3. Pennsburg, Pa. 1927. pp. 57—59.* [3656

Schuyler, William Bishop: Memoirs of the Rev. Augustin Bally, S. J. *In: Records of the American Historical Society of Philadelphia. Vol. XX. Philadelphia, Pa. 1909. pp. 209—249.* [3657

Seidensticker, Oswald: Plaudereien aus Berks County in Pennsylvanien. *In: Der Deutsche Pionier. Jg. X. Cincinnati, O. 1879—1880. pp. 306—308.* [3658

Shaaber, Andrew: The Hessian camp at Reading, Pa. 1781—1783. *A paper read*

June 14, 1910. In: Transactions of the Historical Society of Berks County. Vol. III. Reading, Pa. 1923. pp. 24—49, ill., map. [3659

Stahle, William: The description of the Borough of Reading: *containing its population, institutions, trade, manufactures, &c, &c., with a notice of its first settlement, and many curious historical matters. Reading, Pa.: Published by the author 1841. pp. V, (2), 9—68.* [3660

Stähle, Maj. William: Die Beschreibung der Stadt Reading im Staat Pennsylvanien: *enthaltend ihre Bevölkerung, öffentlichen Lehr-Anstalten, Handel, Fabriken, Manufacturen u. s. w., u. s. w., mit Bemerkungen über ihr erstes Settlement und vielen seltenen historischen Materien. Verdeutscht von* **G. Hav. Wagner.** *Reading, Pa.: Johann Ritter & Co. 1841. pp. V, (1), 9—67.* [3661

Stapleton, A.: The „Oley" (Lutheran and Reformed) churches. *In: Notes and Queries. Edited by W. H. Egle. Annual vol. 1897. Harrisburg, Pa. 1898. pp. 161—162.* [3662

— The Amity (Lutheran) Church. *In: Notes and Queries. Edited by W. H. Egle. Annual vol. 1897. Harrisburg, Pa. 1898. pp. 207—209.* [3663

— Records of „Hill Church" in Berks County, Pa. *In: Notes and Queries. Edited by W. H. Egle. Annual vol. 1898. Harrisburg, Pa. 1899. pp. 169—171; 173—175; 178—180.* [3664

— Early records of the „Mertz" Church in Rockland township, Berks County. *In: Notes and Queries. Edited by W. H. Egle. Annual vol. 1900. Harrisburg, Pa. 1901. pp. 66—68; 70—74; 75—78; 81—84.* [3665

— Berks County Revolutionary soldiers. *In: Notes and Queries. Edited by W. H. Egle. Annual vol. 1900. Harrisburg, Pa. 1901. pp. 118—121.* [3666

— Records of the Reformed Church in Oley, Berks County, Pa. *In: Notes and Queries. Edited by W. H. Egle. Annual vol. 1900. Harrisburg, Pa. 1901. pp. 128—131.* [3667

— The Huguenot element in the settlement of Berks County. *A paper read September, 14, 1909. In: Transactions of the Historical Society of Berks County. Vol. II. 1905—1909. Reading, Pa. 1910. pp. 386—401, ill.* [3668

Steinmetz, Mary Owen: Union cemetery, Pleasantville, Berks County, Pa. *[Tombstones of persons born prior to 1800.] In: The National Genealogical Society Quarterly. Vol. XI, no. 1. Washington, D. C. 1922. pp. 7—8.* [3669

— Tombstone inscriptions from old Forest church and Lutheran church cemeteries, Geigertown, Berks County, Pa. *In: The National Genealogical Society Quarterly. Vol. XII, no. 2. Washington, D. C. 1923. pp. 17—20.* [3670

Stoudt, John Baer: Great religious revival which occured in the Oley Valley 175 years ago. *In: Transactions of the Historical Society of Berks County. Vol. III. Reading, Pa. 1923. pp. 255—270.* [3671

— Tombstone inscriptions at the De Long's Reformed Church, Bower's station, Berks County, Pa. *Transcribed by . . . In: The Pennsylvania-German. Vol. X. Lititz, Pa. 1909. Appendix: Genealogical record of pioneer Pennsylvania families. pp. 11—13.* [3672

— Marriage record of Zion Lutheran Church, Richmond Township, Berks County, Pa. 1744—1758. *[also called Moselem Lutheran Church.] In: The Pennsylvania-German: Vol. XI. Lititz, Pa. 1910. pp. 711—714.* [3673

— Baptisms of Indians in Oley prior to 1732. *A paper read Sept. 9, 1913. In: Transactions of the Historical Society of Berks County. Vol. III. Reading, Pa. 1923. pp. 244—254.* [3674

Strunck, Amos K.: Beamten von Berks Caunty, für jedes Jahr, von 1752 bis 1860. Gleichfalls, die Stimme der Caunty bey den Präsident- u. Gouvernörs Wahlen. *Reading, Pa.: Carl Kessler 1859. 124 S.* [3675

Wagner, A. E., Balthaser, F. W. and **Hoch, D. K.:** The story of Berks County (Pennsylvania). *Reading, Pa.: Eagle Book and Job Press 1913. pp. 253, ill.* [3676

Wollenweber, L. A. (Alter vom Berge): Aus Berks County's schwerer Zeit. *Eine geschichtliche Erzählung. Reading, Pa.: Druck von W. Rosenthal 1875. 40 S.* [3677

Zimmerman, Thomas C.: Conrad Weiser memorial tablet. *Dedicatory address delivered before the Berks County Teacher's Institute, October 30, 1907. In: Transactions of the Historical Society of Berks County. Vol. II. 1905—1909.*

Reading, Pa. 1910. pp. 224—242; — Dedicatory exercises upon the unveiling of the memorial tablet to Conrad Weiser. pp. 243—247.   [3678

Book of biographies. *This volume contains biographical sketches of leading citizens of Berks County, Pa. Buffalo, N. Y.: Biographical Publishing Co. 1898. pp. V, 11—739, (1).*   [3679

Observance of the Sesqui-Centennial of the County of Berks, Pa. *By the Historical Society of Berks County, Court House, March 11, 1902. pp. 39.* [3680

The first settlement in Berks County. *Extract from the Reformed Church Record, Jan. 24, 1907. In: The Pennsylvania-German. Vol. VIII. East Greenville, Pa. 1907. p. 134.*   [3681

Fear of „Papists" in Berks County, Pa., in 1755. *In: Records of the American Catholic Historical Society of Philadelphia. Vol. XXI. Philadelphia, Pa. 1910. pp. 168—169.*   [3682

Indian troubles in 1756. *In: The Perkiomen Region, Past and Present. Vol. I. Philadelphia, Pa. 1895. pp. 134—135.*   [3683

Early Berks County families. *In: Notes and Queries. Edited by W. H. Egle. Annual vol. 1900. Harrisburg, Pa. 1901. pp. 58—59.*   [3684

Early Berks County wills. *In: Notes and Queries. Edited by W. H. Egle. Annual Vol. 1900. Harrisburg, Pa. 1901. pp. 34—36.*   [3685

Reading. *Written for the Ladies' Garland. In: The Ladies' Garland. Philadelphia, Pa. 1839. Vol. II, no. 8. pp. 189—190, ill.*   [3686

Fair-day at Reading, Penna. — *In: The Pennsylvania Magazine of History and Biography. Vol. XXIII. Philadelphia, Pa. 1899. pp. 395—396.*   [3687

First annual report of the Board of Trade of Reading, Pa., for the year ending December 31, 1881, including a description of the city, *showing its advantages as a manufacturing centre, and attractions as a place of residence. Reading, Pa.: Coleman Printing House 1882. pp. 162.*   [3688

Industrial history of Berks County. *(Berks County industrially.) Published by* **Lew. C. Hulshizer.** *Reading, Pa.: Norton Printing House 1907. pp. 280, ill.*   [3689

Reading: its representative business men, and its points of interest. *New York,*

N. Y.: Mercantile Illustr. Co. 1893. pp. 134, ill.   [3690

Industrial Reading. A story of the city's progress and development. *Prepared by the Reading National Bank and Trust Company. Reading, Pa.: Albright & Stenton 1929. pp. 34, ill.*   [3691

Bernville: A historical sketch. *In: The Pennsylvania-German. Vol. VIII. East Greenville, Pa. 1907. pp. 480—486, ill.*   [3692

Roll of Captain Reiff's company in the Revolution, from East Oley, Berks County, Pa., May, 1777. *Contributed by* **A. Stapleton.** *In: The Pennsylvania Magazine of History and Biography. Vol. XXXIV. Philadelphia, Pa. 1910. pp. 491—492.*   [3693

1860. Zur Jubelfeier 1885. Geschichte und Entstehung der Deutschen evang.-Lutherischen St. Johannes-Gemeinde, sowie deren Kirche, Kapelle, Tag- und Sonntagsschule in Reading, Pa. *Reading, Pa.: Druck von Theodore Wischan 1885. pp. . . . .*   [3694

St. Peter Catholic Church, Reading, Pa. *Reading, Pa.: Pengelly & Bro. 1909. pp. 87, ill.*   [3695

The twin daughters of a union-church. *[The Alsace churches in the north of the City of Reading, Pa.] Reprint from „The Lutheran". In: The Pennsylvania-German. Vol. XII. Lititz, Pa. 1911. p. 564.*   [3696

Historical souvenir of the Hereford-Huff's Union Church in Hereford Township, Berks County, Pa. *Issued at the celebration of its Centennial, Oct. 31, 1915. Reading, Pa.: I. M. Beaver 1915. pp. 32, ill.*   [3697

Historical souvenir of Christ (Yocum's) Evangelical Lutheran and Reformed Church, Grill, Cumru Township, Berks County, Pa. *Issued at the first Centennial celebration 1924. Founded 1823, — organized 1854. Sept. 14—17, 1924.* **W. J. Kershner,** *Reformed Pastor —* **Harry E. Herman,** *Lutheran Pastor. [s. l. 1924.] pp. 19, ill.*   [3698

Graduate catalogue of the Reading high schools 1856 to 1899. *Published by the Alumni Association. Reading, Pa.: James E. Norton & Co. July 1, 1899. pp. 256, ill. Second edition. 1856 to 1905. Reading, Pa. 1905. pp. 328, ill.*   [3699

Historical pilgrimages into Pennsylvania-Germandom. A trip over the old Easton road. *In: The Pennsylvania-*

German. Vol. III. Lebanon, Pa. 1902. pp. 67—86, ill.
[See no. 295]   [3700
Pilgrimage of the Society to the old Moravian Church building in Oley Township, Sept. 8, 1908. *In: Transactions of the Historical Society of Berks County. Vol. II. Reading, Pa. 1910. pp. 306—308.*   [3701
Visit to historic places of Berks. Commemorate bravery of the early inhabitants of Tulpehocken region at the open-air meeting at Strausstown, June 19, 1915. *In: Transactions of the Historical Society of Berks County. Vol. III. Reading, Pa. 1923. pp. 373—380, ill.*   [3702
Pilgrimage of the Society to Kutztown, Pa., Sept. 29, 1916. *In: Transactions of the Historical Society of Berks County. Vol. III. Reading, Pa. 1923. pp. 454—459.*   [3703
Tenth pilgrimage. The Historical Society of Berks County, Friday, Oct. 2, 1914. *In: Transactions of the Historical Society of Berks County. Vol. III. Reading, Pa. 1923. pp. 327—332.*   [3704

Blair County

Africa, J. Simpson: History of Huntingdon and Blair Counties, Pa. *2 parts. Philadelphia, Pa.: Louis H. Everts. 1883. Blair County. pp. IV, 3—261, ill., map.*   [3705
Carney, W. H. Bruce: History of the Alleghany Evangelical Lutheran Synod of Pennsylvania. . . . *Published by the authority of Alleghany Synod in commemoration of its seventy-fifth anniversary, and of the Quadricentennial of the Reformation. 2 vols. Philadelphia, Pa.: Printed for the Synod by the Lutheran Publication Society 1918. pp. XII, 454; 455—871, ill., map. [„Churches of Northeast Conference." = Chapter XII. pp. 358—535.]* [3706
Davis, Tarring S. and Shenk, Lucile: A history of Blair County, Pennsylvania. *Under editorial supervision of* Tarring S. Davis. *Associate editor* Lucile Shenk. *2 vols. Harrisburg, Pa.: Publishers National Historical Association, Inc. 1931. pp. VIII, 322; Vol. II. Biographical. pp. VIII, 205, ill.* [3707
Dean, John: Blair County and its people. *Historical address. Delivered at Holli-*

daysburg, June 12, 1896. Reprint in: Twentieth century history of Altoona and Blair County, Pa. . . . By Jesse C. Sell. Chicago, Ill. 1911 [= no. 3709]. pp. 60—69.   [3708
[Ewing, Jas. H. and **Slep, Harry]:** History of the City of Altoona and Blair County including sketches of the shops of the Pennsylvania Railroad Co. *Edited by . . . Altoona, Pa.: Harry Sleps Mirror Printing House 1880. pp. 262, ill.*   [3709
Sell, Jesse C.: Twentieth century history of Altoona and Blair County, Pa. and representative citizens. *Chicago, Ill.: Published by the Richmond-Arnold Printing Co. 1911. pp. 972, ill.*   [3710
Semi-Centennial history of Blair County. 1896. *For visitors and citizens. Prepared especially for the first fifty years of the county's growth. Held June 11 and 12, 1896, at Hollidaysburg, Pa. A souvenir [s. l. 1896.] pp. 116, (1), ill., Appendix. How the Semi-Centennial was celebrated. pp. 16.*   [3711
Martinsburg Centennial souvenir. *A pictorial and descriptive booklet containing the history of Martinsburg and the borough council, schools and churches, and a list of patrons with their biographies, civic organizations and business cards and many other things of interest in the life of a growing community. 1832—1932. Published by the Centennial Souvenir Booklet Committee. Martinsburg, Pa., June 29—July 4, 1932. Martinsburg, Pa.: Morrisons Cove Herald. 1932. pp. 83, ill.*   [3712

Bucks County

Battle, J. H.: History of Bucks County, Pa.; *including an account of its original exploration; its relation to the settlements of New Jersey and Delaware; its erection into a separate county, also its subsequent growth and development, with sketches of its historic and interesting localities, and biographies of many of its representative citizens. Edited by . . . Philadelphia, Pa.; Chicago, Ill.: A. Warner & Co. 1887. pp. VIII, 9—1176, ill., map.*   [3713
Bell, Herbert C.: Durham Township, *[Bucks Co., Pa.] By* H. C. Bell, *assisted by* Charles Laubach *and* B. F. Fackenthal, jr. *Philadelphia, Pa.: A. Warner & Co. 1887. pp. 23.*   [3714

Buck, William J.: History of Bucks County, Pa. *By* W. J. Buck *with an appendix, containing* history of the early settlement of the Township of Wrightstown *by* **Charles W. Smith**. *Willow Grove, Pa. 1855. pp. 118; 24.* [3715

— Local sketches and legends pertaining to Bucks and Montgomery Counties, Pa. *[s. l.]: Printed for the author 1887. pp. VI, 9—340.* [3716

— The German population in Bucks County. *Read Oct. 11, 1882. In: A Collection of Papers read before the Bucks County Historical Society. Vol. I. Easton, Pa. 1908. pp. 57—65.* [3717

Buehrle, Robert K.: The Swamp of Tinicum and Nockamixon. *Read Jan. 18, 1910. In: A Collection of Papers read before the Bucks County Historical Society. Vol. IV. Easton, Pa. 1917. pp. 84—89.* [3718

Cabeen, Francis von A.: An old Dutch oven in New Britain. *Read Jan. 25, 1916. In: A Collection of Papers read before the Bucks County Historical Society. Vol. IV. Easton Pa. 1917. pp. 576—579.* [3719

Davis, William Watts Hart: The history of Bucks County, Pa., from the discovery of the Delaware to the present time. *Doylestown, Pa.: Democrat Book and Job Office Print. 1876. pp. XII, (4), 17—875; (3), 3—54, maps.* [3720

— Historical address *delivered by . . . at the Centennial celebration of Doylestown, Pa., March 1, 1878. [s. l. 1878.] pp. 26.* [3721

— History of Doylestown, old and new. From its settlement to the close of the nineteenth century, 1745—1900. *Doylestown, Pa.: Intelligencer Print. 1904. pp. 373; 11.* [3722

— History of Bucks County, Pa. from the discovery of the Delaware to the present time. *Second edition revised and enlarged with a genealogical and personal history of Bucks County. Prepared under the editorial supervision of* **Warren S. Ely** and **John W. Jordan**. *3 vols. New York, N. Y. Chicago, Ill.: The Lewis Publishing Co. 1905. pp. XIV, 482, ill., maps; pp. IX, 399. Appendix, pp. 98, ill., maps; pp. XIX, 732, ill.* [3723

— Plumstead Township. *[Bucks Co., Pa.] April 21, 1885. In: A Collection of Papers read before the Bucks County Historical Society. Vol. I. 1909. pp. 305—313.* [3724

Davis, William Watts Hart: Bedminster Township. *Read July 19, 1892. In: A Collection of Papers read before the Bucks County Historical Society. Vol. II. Easton, Pa. 1909. pp. 69—82.* [3725

— Settlement of Tinicum Township. *[Bucks Co., Pa.] Read Aug. 14, 1900. In: A Collection of Papers read before the Bucks County Historical Society. Vol. II. Easton, Pa. 1909. pp. 615—621.* [3726

— Law governing the settlement of new countries. *Read January 18, 1904. In: A Collection of Papers read before the Bucks County Historical Society. Vol. III. Easton, Pa. 1909. pp. 341—344.* [3727

Ely, Warren S.: The Tohickon settlers. *Read Oct. 6, 1903. In: A Collection of Papers read before the Bucks County Historical Society. Vol. III. Easton, Pa. 1909. pp. 296—306.* [3728

— A Lutheran mission in Northampton Township in 1748. *Read January 16, 1926. In: A Collection of Papers read before the Bucks County Historical Society. Vol. VI. Allentown, Pa. 1932. pp. 44—52.* [3729

Fackenthal, B. F.: Saint John Reformed Church of Riegelsville, Pa. showing the development and growth of the congregation from its organization in 1849 to January 1, 1911. *Its pastors and officers; the erection of buildings; its financial operations and constitution; founding of the Riegelsville Academy and Public Library; to which is added an alphabetical list of all its members, past and present. Also some accounts of the Riegelsville Union cemetery. Riegelsville, Pa.: Published for private circulation by B. F. Fackenthal, jr. Easton, Pa.: Eschenbach Printing Co. 1911. pp. 221.* [3730

Fisher, Allen S.: Lutheranism in Bucks county, 1734—1934. *With a restudy of the Indians of eastern United States to more definitely prove Lutheran missions among the Lenape of the Delaware valley, 1638—1740. Tinicum, Pa. 1935. pp. 208, ill.* [3730a

Grim, George M.: Historic sketch of Ottsville and vicinity. *Read Oct. 4, 1910. In: A Collection of Papers read before the Bucks County Historical Society. Vol. IV. Easton, Pa. 1917. pp. 103—107.* [3731

Gross, A. Haller: The old spring-houses of Bucks County. *Read Jan. 21, 1913. In: A Collection of Papers read before the Bucks County Historical Society. Vol. IV. Easton, Pa. 1917. pp. 396—397, ill.* [3732

Gross, H. W.: [Deep Run] Mennonite school and meeting house, with sketch of Mr. Moritz Loeb. *Read Oct. 24, 1914. In: A Collection of Papers read before the Bucks County Historical Society. Vol. IV. Easton, Pa. 1917. pp. 537—539.* [3733

Heller, William J.: Bucks County north of the Lehigh River. *Read Oct. 5, 1909. In: A Collection of Papers read before the Bucks County Historical Society. Vol. IV. Easton, Pa. 1917. pp. 42—50.* [3734

Hess, Asher L.: Picturesque and historic Durham Valley. *In: The Pennsylvania-German. Vol. IX. Cleona, Pa. 1908. pp. 195—204, ill.* [3735

Hindenach, C. E.: Education in Durham Township. *Read July 28, 1885. In: A Collection of Papers read before the Bucks County Historical Society. Vol. I. Easton, Pa. 1909. pp. 316—325, ill.* [3736

Hinke, William John: Church record of Neshaminy and Bensalem, Bucks County, 1710—1738. *Edited by . . . In: The Journal of the Presbyterian Historical Society. Vol. I. Philadelphia, Pa. 1901. pp. 111—134.* [3737

— A history of the Tohickon Union Church, Bedminster Township, Bucks County, Pa. With a copy of church records: Reformed congregation 1745—1869; Lutheran congregation 1749—1840. *Prepared and translated at the request of the Pennsylvania-German Society. Meadville, Pa.: The Tribune Publishing Co. 1925. In: The Pennsylvania-German Society. Proceedings and Addresses . . . 1920. Vol. XXXI. Meadville, Pa. 1925. Separate pagination. pp. XII, 483, ill.* [3738

— Early history of Keller's Lutheran Church, Bedminster Township, Bucks County. *Read May 2, 1931. In: A Collection of Papers read before the Bucks County Historical Society. Vol. VI. Allentown, Pa. 1932. pp. 363—378.* [3739

Jaekel, Frederic B.: Squirrel-tailed bake-oven in Bucks County. *Read Jan. 25, 1916. A Collection of Papers read before the Bucks County Historical Society.* *Vol. IV. Easton, Pa. 1917. pp. 579—586.* [3740

Jordan, John W.: Scraps of „Bucks" before 1750. *Read July 15, 1890. In: A Collection of Papers read before the Bucks County Historical Society. Vol. I. Easton, Pa. 1908. pp. 536—548.* [3741

Keichline, William H.: Early history of Bedminster Township, *[Bucks Co., Pa.] Recollections of* William H. Keichline. *Read by* Warren S. Ely, *June 12, 1920. In: A Collection of Papers read before the Bucks County Historical Society. Vol. V. Meadville, Pa. 1926. pp. 261—274.* [3742

Krauss, Fred. A.: Quakertown. *In: The Pennsylvania-German. Vol. XI. Lititz, Pa. 1910. pp. 718—723, ill.* [3743

Larison, George H.: The mode of life in our early settlements. *Read July 26, 1887. In: A Collection of Papers read before the Bucks County Historical Society. Vol. I. Easton, Pa. 1908. pp. 458—467.* [3744

Leatherman, J. Kirk: An old backeoven in Plumstead Township. *[Bucks Co., Pa.] Read Jan. 25, 1916. In: A Collection of Papers read before the Bucks County Historical Society. Vol. IV. Easton, Pa. 1917. pp. 572—574.* [3745

Lyman, Richard M.: Mennonites of German Friends, *[with reference to their settlement in Bucks County, Pa. Read July 18, 1882.] In: A Collection of Papers read before the Bucks County Historical Society. Vol. I. Easton, Pa. 1908. pp. 39—44.* [3746

Mercer, Henry C.: Notes on the Moravian pottery of Doylestown. *Read February 10, 1914. In: A Collection of Papers read before the Bucks County Historical Society. Vol. IV. Easton, Pa. 1917. pp. 482—487.* [3747

Mercer, William R.: Bucks County samplers. *Read June 18, 1921. In: A Collection of Papers read before the Bucks County Historical Society. Vol. V. Meadville, Pa. 1926. pp. 347—356, ill.* [3748

Michener, Henry C.: Complete report of the Bucks County Bi-Centennial celebration. Held at Doylestown, Pa. August 31, Sept. 1 and 2, 1882. *Reported by . . . [Doylestown, Pa.]: Published by Paschall Brothers, Bucks County Intelligencer [1882]. pp. 39.* [3749

Nickel, Warren: 1751—1901. 150th anniversary of St. Matthew's Evangelical Lutheran congregation at Keller's Church. *[Bedminister Township, Bucks*

County, Pa.] August 22, 1901. [s. l., 1901.] pp. (17). [3750
Rosenberger, S. M.: The German element in Bucks County. Read January 21, 1902. In: A Collection of Papers read before the Bucks County Historical Society. Vol. III. Easton, Pa. 1909. pp. 118—122. [3751
Ruth, John A.: St. Luke's Church, Nockamixon [Township, Bucks County, Pa.] In: The Pennsylvania-German. Vol. XII. Lititz, Pa. 1911. pp. 711—716. [3752
Scheerz, Greer: Tobacco and ist culture in Bucks County. Read Jan. 19, 1924. In: A Collection of Papers read before the Bucks County Historical Society. Vol. V. Meadville, Pa. 1926. pp. 612—620. Remarks by B. F. Fackenthal, jr. pp. 621—623, ill. [3753
Scheetz, Grier: Bucks County potters. Read May 23, 1911. In: A Collection of Papers read before the Bucks County Historical Society. Vol. IV. Easton, Pa. 1917. pp. 192—197. [3754
Souder, John J.: Early churches in the First Mennonite Conference. In: Christian Monitor. A monthly magazine for the home. Vol. XXV. Scottdale, Pa. 1933. pp. 46—47. [3755
Swain, Frank K.: Passing events. Two papers. In: A Collection of Papers read before the Bucks County Historical Society. Vol. V. Meadville, Pa. 1926. Paper no. 1. Read Jan. 15, 1921. pp. 324—339; Paper no. 2. Read Jan. 21, 1922. pp. 407—418. [3756
Wagner, Scott R.: Address of welcome, by . . . [to St. John Reformed Church of Riegelsville, Pa., Oct. 5, 1909.] In: A Collection of Papers read before the Bucks County Historical Society. Vol. IV. Easton, Pa. 1917. pp. 35—38, ill. [3757
Bedminster Township meeting [of the Bucks County Historical Society], Deep Run Mennonite meeting house, Oct. 24, 1914. In: A Collection of Papers read before the Bucks County Historical Society. Vol. IV. Easton, Pa. 1917. pp. 533—536, ill. [3758
The East Swamp cemetery. In: The Mennonite Year Book and Almanac for 1919. Quakertown, Pa. 1919. p. 34. [3759

Carbon County

Brenckman, Fred: History of Carbon County, Pa., also containing a separate account of the several boroughs and townships in the county. Harrisburg, Pa.: James J. Nungesser 1913. pp. 626, ill. [3760
Laclair, J. D.: Patriotism of Carbon County, Pa., and what her people contributed during the war for the preservation of the Union. Mauch Chunk, Pa. 1867. pp. 120. [3761
Rice, William H.: The Gnadenhütten massacres. A brief history of two historic tragedies. In: The Pennsylvania-German. Vol. VII. Lebanon, Pa. 1906. pp. 26—31, ill.; 71—79, ill. [3762
Rupp, I. Daniel: History of Northampton, Lehigh, Monroe, Carbon, and Schuylkill Counties: containing a brief history of the first settlers, topography of townships, notices of leading events, incidents, and interesting facts in the early history of these counties: with an appendix. Lancaster, Pa.: Published and sold by G. Hills; Harrisburg, Pa.: Hickok and Cantine 1845. pp. XIV, 568, ill. [3763
Portrait and biographical record of Lehigh, Northampton and Carbon Counties, Pa. Containing biographical sketches of prominent and representative citizens of the counties, together with biographies and portraits of all the presidents of the United States. Chicago., Ill.: Chapman Publishing Co. 1894. pp. (1), 19—999, ill. [3764

Centre County

Early, J. W.: „Emanuel's Church at the Loop." (formerly known as „Early's Church", Centre County, Pa.) In: Notes and Queries. Edited by W. H. Egle. Annual vol. 1898. Harrisburg, Pa. 1899. pp. 23—28. [3765
— Additional items concerning the „Loop" Church and the first settlers in that section. In: Notes and Queries. Edited by W. H. Egle. Annual vol. 1898. Harrisburg, Pa. 1899. pp. 31—33. [3766
— Record of baptisms. „Emanuel's Church at the Loop." In: Notes and Queries. Edited by W H. Egle. Annual vol. 1898. Harrisburg, Pa. 1899. pp. 108—110; 112—119; 121—215. [3767
Linn, John Blair: History of Centre and Clinton Counties, Pa. Philadelphia, Pa.: Louis H. Everts 1883. pp. X, 672, ill., maps. [3768
Maynard, D. S.: Industries and institutions of Centre County with historical sketches of principal villages &c; &c. Com-

piled by . . . Bellefonte, Pa.: Republican Job. Printing House 1877. pp. 340; Appendix: Soldiers of the late war furnished by Centre County. pp. 16. [3769

Rupp, I. Daniel: History and topography of Northumberland, Huntingdon, Mifflin, Centre, Union, Columbia, Juniata and Clinton Counties, Pa., *embracing local and general events, leading incidents, descriptions of the principal boroughs, towns, villages, etc. with a copious appendix: embellished by engravings. Compiled by authentic sources. Lancaster, Pa.: G. Hills 1847. pp. 562, (2), ill.* [3770

Stapleton, A.: Heckman's Church of Penn's Valley, Pa. *In: Notes and Queries. Edited by W. H. Egle. Annual vol. 1900. Harrisburg, Pa. 1901. pp. 195—196.* [3771

Commemorative biographical record of Central Pennsylvania, including the Counties of Centre, Clinton, Union and Snyder, *containing biographical sketches of prominent and representative citizens and of many of the early settled families. Chicago, Ill.: J. B. Beers, Publishers 1898. pp. (1), 1676, ill.* [3772

Chester County

Cope, Gilbert and **Ashmead, Henry Graham:** Historic homes and institutions and genealogical and personal memoirs of Chester and Delaware Counties, Pa. *Editors of genealogical departments: Chester County, by Gilbert Cope. Delaware County, by Henry Graham Ashmead. 2 vols. New York, N. Y. — Chicago, Ill.: The Lewis Publishing Co. 1904. pp. X, 600, ill.; VI, 598, ill.* [3773

Egle, William John: Provincial papers: Proprietary tax lists of the County of Chester for the years 1765, 1766, 1767, 1768, 1769, 1771. *Edited by . . . Harrisburg, Pa.: Wm. Stanley Ray, 1897. pp. XIII, 783, map.*
= *Pennsylvania Archives. Third series, vol. XI.* [3774

— Provincial papers: Proprietary and other tax lists of the County of Chester for the years 1774, 1779, 1780, 1781, 1785. *Edited by . . . Harrisburg, Pa.: Wm. Stanley Ray. 1897. pp. XII, 823, map.*
= *Pennsylvania Archives. Third series, vol. XII.* [3775

Fluck, J. Lewis: A history of the Reformed churches in Chester County. *Compiled by . . . Norristown, Pa.: Herold Printing and Binding Rooms 1892. pp. VII, (1), 13—139, (1), ill.* [3776

Futhey, J. Smith and **Cope, Gilbert:** History of Chester County, Pa., with genealogical and biographical sketches. *2 vols. Philadelphia, Pa.: Louis H. Everts 1881. pp. 342, ill., maps; pp. 343—782, XLIV.* [3777

[Grubb, N. B.]: The Phoenixville Mennonite Church *(with interments as far as they could be obtained.) In: The Mennonite Year Book and Almanac for 1923. Quakertown, Pa. 1923. pp. 22—24 ill.* [3778

— Beidler's or Chester Valley Mennonites. *In: The Mennonite Year Book and Almanac for 1923. Quakertown, Pa. 1923. pp. 24—25, ill.* [3779

Heathcote, Charles William: History of Chester County, Pa. *West Chester, Pa.: Horace F. Temple 1926. pp. VIII, 129, ill., maps.* [3780

Pennypacker, Samuel Whitaker: Annals of Phoenixville and its vicinity: from the settlement to the year 1871. *Giving the origin and growth of the borough, with information concerning the adjacent townships of Chester and Montgomery Counties and the Valley of the Schuylkill. Philadelphia, Pa.: Bavis & Pennypacker 1872. pp. 295, ill., map.* [3781

Pleasants, Henry: The history of the Old Eagle School, Tredyffrin, in Chester County, Pa. *With alphabetical lists of interments in the graveyard and of German settlers in Chester County, and a poems presenting the suggestive features of the place. Prepared at the request of the Trustees of the Old Eagle School. Philadelphia, Pa.: The John C. Winston Co. 1909. pp. (5), (1), (1), 180, ill.* [3782

[Sheeder, Frederick]: East Vincent Township, Chester County, Pa. *[written: ,,East Vincent, at Sheeders industry, February 18, 1846." Edited by* **Samuel W. Pennypacker.]** *In: The Pennsylvania Magazine of History and Biography. Vol. XXXIV. Philadelphia, Pa. 1910. pp. 74—98; 194—212; 361—380, ill.* [3783

Thomson, W. W.: Chester County and its people. *Edited by . . . Chicago, Ill. & New York, N. Y.: The Union History Co. 1898. pp. XXIV, 51—982, ill.* [3784

Urner, Isaac N.: A history of the Coventry Brethren Church in Chester County,

Pennsylvania. The second oldest Brethren Church in America. *Philadelphia, Pa.: J. B. Lippincott Co. 1898. pp. 51, ill.*

[See also: Genealogy of the Urner family . . . [= no. 7612].] [3785

Wanger, George F. P.: Vincent Mennonite Church burying ground near Spring City, Chester County, Pa., formerly known as „Rhoads' burying ground". *Copied by . . . In: The National Genealogical Society Quarterly. Vol. IX, no. 4. Washington, D. C. 1921. pp. 55—63.* [3786

— Tombstone inscriptions: Parkerford Baptist Church, Chester County, Pa. *In: National Genealogical Society Quarterly. Vol. XIV. Washington, D. C. 1925. pp. 39—43.* [3787

[Wiley, Samuel T.] and **Garner, Winfield Scott:** Biographical and portrait cyclopedia of Chester County, Pa., *comprising a historical sketch of the county by Samuel T. Wiley, together with more than five hundred biographical sketches of the prominent men and leading citizens of the county. Philadelphia, Pa. — Richmond, Ind. — Chicago, Ill.: Gresham Publishing Co. 1893. pp. XV, 17—879, ill.* [3788

Clinton County

Linn, John Blair: History of Center and Clinton Counties. Pa. *Philadelphia, Pa.: Louis H. Everts 1883. pp. X, 672, ill., maps.* [3789

Rupp, I. D.: History and topography of Northumberland, Huntingdon, Mifflin, Centre, Union, Columbia, Juniata and Clinton Counties, Pa., *embracing local and general events, leading incidents, descriptions of the principal boroughs, towns, villages, etc., etc. with a copious appendix: embellished by engravings. Compiled from authentic sources by . . . Lancaster, Pa.: G. Hills 1847. pp. 574, ill.* [3790

Commemorative biographical record of Central Pennsylvania, including the Counties of Centre, Clinton, Union and Snyder, *containing biographical sketches of prominent and representative citizens and of many of the early settled families. Chicago, Ill.: J. H. Beers, Publishers. 1898. pp. (1), 1676.* [3791

Columbia County

Battle, J. H.: History of Columbia and Montour Counties, Pa., *containing a history of each county; their townships, towns, villages, schools, churches, industries, etc.; portraits of representative men, biographies; history of Pennsylvania, statistical and miscellaneous matter, etc. Chicago, Ill.: A. Warner & Co. 1887. pp. IX, 15—542; 220, ill., map.* [3792

Dennis, W. V.: Organizations affecting farm youth in Locust ? ownship, Columbia County. *State C llege, Pa. 1931. pp. 43, ill.*

= *Bulletin no. 265 (June, 1931) of the Pennsylvania State College, School of Agriculture and Experiment Station, State College, Pa.* [3793

Freeze, John G.: A history of Columbia County, Pa. From the earliest times. *Bloomsburg, Pa.: Elwell & Bittenbender 1883. pp. (1), (3), 572, ill.* [3794

Henkel, D. M.: Golden souvenir programm in commemoration of the 50th anniversary of the building of St. Matthew's Evangelical Lutheran Church of Catawissa, Pa. *Including a history of a half century of the growth and development of the congregation . . . Sunday, Nov. 25th, 1900. Catawissa, Pa.: News Item Print 1900. pp. 22, ill.* [3795

Houtz, A.: A pastorate of thirty-five years. *[Orangeville charge, Columbia Co., Pa.] Reading, Pa.: Daniel Miller 1904. pp. 114, ill.* [3796

Historical and biographical annals of Columbia and Montour Counties, Pa., *containing a concise history of the two counties and a genealogical and biographical record of representative families. 2 vols. Chicago, Ill.: J. H. Beers & Co. 1915. pp. XXII, 671, ill.; XI, 673—1260, ill.* [3797

The one hundred twenty fifth anniversary celebration of Briar Creek Township's oldest church 1800 to 1925, Briar Brick Church of St. Peter's Union Church. *A brief history of the Lutheran and Reformed congregations for a century and a quarter. Berwick, Pa.: Learn 1925. pp. 35, ill.* [3798

Cumberland County

Albert, Chas. S. and **Stock, J. C.:** History of the first Evangelical Lutheran Church of Carlisle, Penn'a. *Also a Semi-Centennial history of the Sunday-school by*

22*

J. C. Stock. *Carlisle, Pa.: Herald Prin-
ting Co. 1876. pp. 28.*   [3799
Betz, I. H.: Historical pilgrimages into
Pennsylvania-Germandom and Scotch
Irishdom. From Winchester to Harris-
burg. *In: The Pennsylvania-German.
Vol. V. Lebanon, Pa. 1904. pp. 8—22;
61—72, ill.*   [3800
— Some Cumberland County physicians
of forty years ago. *(Delivered at the Ha-
milton Library, Nov. 1, 1907. pp. 15.*
                                       [3801
Brereton, T. J.: Scenes and incidents of the
Cumberland Valley. *In: Kittochtinny
Historical Society. Papers. Vol. III.
Chambersburg, Pa. 1904. pp. 39—51.*
                                       [3802
Burkhart, J. Paul: The Diller Mennonite
Church, Newville, Pa. *In: Christian
Monitor. A monthly magazine for the
home. Vol. XIX, no. 8. Scottdale, Pa.
1927. pp. 246—247.*   [3803
Egle, William Henry: Provincial papers:
State and supply transcripts of the
County of Cumberland, for the years
1778, 1779, 1780, 1782 and 1785. *Edited
by . . . Harrisburg, Pa.: Wm. Stanley
Ray 1898. pp. X, 781.
= Pennsylvania Archives. Third series,
vol. XX*   [3804
Fegley, H. N.: June, 1872—June, 1922. The
pastor's golden jubilee souvenir. St.
Mark's Evangelical Lutheran Church,
Mechanicsburg, Pa. Fiftieth anniver-
sary, June 2, 1922. *pp. 45, ill.*   [3805
Floyd, David Bittle: History of Zion's Lu-
theran congregation of Newville, Pa.
from 1795—1895. A centennial sermon.
*Published by and at the request of the
W. H. and F. M. Society of the Congre-
gation. Newville, Pa.: J. C. Fosnot 1895.
pp. 32, ill.*   [3806
Ganss, H. G.: History of St. Patrickts
[Catholic] Church, Carlisle, Pa. *Phila-
delphia, Pa.: D. J. Gallagher & Co. 1895.
pp. 215, ill.*   [3807
— History of St. Patrick's Church, Car-
lisle, Pa. *In: Records of the American
Catholic Historical Society. Vol. VI.
Philadelphia, Pa. 1895. pp. 266—422,
ill.*   [3808
Heathcote, C. W.: Lutheran Church in the
Cumberland Valley. *In: Kittochtinny
Historical Society. Papers. Vol. VII.
Chambersburg, Pa. 1912. pp. 106—121.*
                                       [3810
— The seventy fifth year. A history of the
Second Evangelical Lutheran Church

1836—1911, also a brief history of
General Synod Lutheranism in the
Cumberland Valley. *Chambersburg, Pa.:
Repository Press . . . pp. 41, ill.*   [3811
Hemminger, J. D.: Local history. Bridges
of Cumberland County, Pa. *Paper read
before the Hamilton Library Association,
Carlisle, Pa., Febr. 17, 1905. pp. 30.*
                                       [3812
Keller, J. H.: Feast of dedication of Mt.
Zion Evangelical Lutheran Church,
Shippensville, Pa., Dec. 5 to 13, 1913.
pp. 42, ill.   [3813
Klein, Theodore B. and Brown, Isaac B.:
Extracts from part one of the Annual
Report of the Department of Internal
Affairs for 1904: Early history and
growth of Carlisle *by* Theodore B.
Klein; Early footprints of development
and improvements in Northwestern
Pennsylvania *by* Isaac B. Brown.
*Harrisburg, Pa.: Wm. Stanley Ray 1905.
pp. 75, maps.*   [3814
Miller, J. R.: Local history reminiscences
of the Walnut Bottom road. *(Paper
read before the Historical Society of
Cumberland County, Pa., Nov. 25, 1904).
pp. 32.*   [3815
— Local history. Odds and ends of Cumberland County history. *(Paper read
before the Cumberland County Historical
Society, March 26, 1912.) pp. 27.*   [3816
Murray, Joseph A.: Local history. Louther
manor. *(Read before Historical Meeting
of the Hamilton Library Association,
Carlisle, Pa., and reprinted for the Historical Department.) pp. 11.*   [3817
Nevin, Alfred: Centennial biography. Men
and mark of Cumberland Valley, Pa.
1776—1876. *Philadelphia, Pa.: Fulton
Publishing Co. 1876. pp. VII, 5—452,
ill.*   [3818
Orr, John G.: Early highways. *No. 4.* Tou-
rists of a century ago. *In: Kittochtinny
Historical Society. Papers. Vol. VII.
Chambersburg, Pa. 1912. pp. 152—185.*
                                       [3819
Parkinson, Sarah Wodds: Memories of Carlisle's old graveyard . . . *Containing a list
of the inscriptions on all stones in the
enclosure in 1898 and describing a walk
through a part of the graveyard. Published
by Mary Kirtley Lamberton. Carlisle,
Pa.: The Sentinel [s. d.] (1929) pp. 258,
ill.*   [3820
Riley, Theodore M.: A garrison town in
Pennsylvania. *[Carlisle.]* Fifty years
ago. *In: The Pennsylvania-German.*

Vol. VII. Lebanon, Pa. 1906. pp. 55—63, ill. [3821

Rupp, I. Daniel: The history and topography of Dauphin, Cumberland, Franklin, Bedford, Adams and Perry Counties: *containing a brief history of the first settlers, notices of the leading events, incidents and interesting facts, both general and local, in the history of these counties, general and statistical descriptions of all the principal boroughs, towns, villages &c. with an appendix. Lancaster, Pa.: Gilbert Hills. 1846. pp. XII, 25—606, ill.* [3822

Schwarz, J. R. and Zeamer, J.: The Cumberland blue book. *A compendium of information of lower Cumberland County and an illustrated historical chapter. Directory . . . of Camp Hill and vicinity. J. R. Schwarz, publisher - J. Zeamer, historian. Harrisburg, Pa.: Mt. Pleasant Press 1908. pp. 100, ill.* [3823

Seilhammer, Geo. O.: The German settlement. *In: Kittochtinny Historical Society. Papers. Vol. V. Chambersburg, Pa. 1908. pp. 267—285.* [3824

Stewart, Harriet Wylie: History of the Cumberland Valley, Pa. *[s. l., s. d.] pp. 146, ill.* [3825

Stump, Adam and Anstadt, Henry: History of the Evangelical Lutheran Synod of West Pennsylvania of the United Lutheran Church in America 1825—1925. *Editet by . . . Published by action of the Synod in the celebration of the Centennial. Chambersburg, Pa.: J. R. Kerr & Bro. 1925. pp. 696, ill.*
[Cumberland Valley Conference pp. 289—440.] [3826

Swope, G. E.: Tombstone inscriptions in the neighborhood of Newville. *In: Notes and Queries. Edited by W. H. Egle. Annual vol. 1898. Harrisburg, Pa. 1899. pp. 206—207.* [3827

— Tombstone inscriptions, Ziegler's Church, Mifflin Township, Cumberland County, Pa. *In: Notes and Queries. Edited by W. H. Egle. Annual vol. 1897. Harrisburg, Pa. 1898. pp. 218—219.* [3828

Wing, Conway P.: 1731. History of Cumberland County, Pa. *Philadelphia, Pa.: James D. Scott 1879. pp. 272, V, ill.* [3829

History of Cumberland and Adams Counties, Pa. *Containing history of the counties, their townships, towns, villages, schools, churches, industries, etc., portraits of early settlers and prominent men;* biographies; history of Pennsylvania, statistical and miscellaneous matter, etc., etc. 3 vols. Chicago, Ill.: Warner, Beers & Co. 1886. pp. X, 16—132; 588; 516; ill., maps. [3830

1751. Cumberland County Sesqui-Centennial. Carlisle, Pa., Wednesday and Thursday, Oct. 23 and 24, 1901. *Mount Holly Springs, Pa.: Stationary and Printing Co. pp. 26, ill.* [3831

Carlisle, old and new. *By the Civic Club of Carlisle, Pa. Harrisburg, Pa.: J. Horace McFarland 1907. pp. VIII, 173, ill.* [3832

1765—1915. Memorial program of the 150th anniversary of the first Evangelical Lutheran Church of Carlisle, Pa. 1915. *pp. 82, ill.* [3833

Dauphin County

[Awl, F. A.]: An interesting register. „A list of freeholders of Dauphin County, A. D. 1794." *[A manuscript presented to the Dauphin County Historical Society by Col. F. Awl, in 1888.] In: Notes and Queries. Edited by W. H. Egle. Third series, vol. II. 1887—1890. Harrisburg, Pa. 1891. pp. 336—337; 339—340; 340—342; 349—350; 353—354; 357—358.* [3834

[Bergstresser, Fuller]: St. Peter's Lutheran Church, Middletown, Pa. 1767—1917. The book of memories. *Being the one hundred and fiftieth anniversary of the completion of Old St. Peter's Lutheran Church and the one hundred and fifty-third anniversary of the organization of the congregation. Committee in charge of the publication:* **D. P. Deatrick, D. W. C. Laverty, M. H. Gingerich, Fuller Bergstresser.** *[s. l., 1917.] pp. 153.* [3835

Boyer, W. W.: Old Market Street, old Market Square, *[Harrisburg, Pa.] Interesting recollection of an old citizen. In: Notes and Queries. Edited by W. H. Egle. Fourth series, vol. I. 1891—1893. Harrisburg, Pa. 1893. pp. 59—63.* [3836

Brehm, J. J.: Story of Messiah Lutheran Church, *[Harrisburg.] Harrisburg, Pa.: W. Elmer McCormick 1908. pp. 38, ill.* [3837

[Croll, P. C.]: Historical pilgrimages into Pennsylvania - Germandom. Historic Harrisburg. *In: The Pennsylvania-German. Vol. I., no. 4. Lebanon, Pa. 1900. pp. 35—43, ill.*
[See no. 295.] [3838

[Croll, P. C.]: Historical pilgrimages into Pennsylvania-Germandom. Over an old state road from the Susquehanna to the Swatara. *In: The Pennsylvania-German. Vol. II. Lebanon, Pa. 1901. pp. 73—85.*
[See no. 295.]   [3839
Donehoo, George P.: Harrisburg and Dauphin County. A sketch of the history for the past twenty-five years. 1900—1925. *Dayton, O.: The National Historical Association 1925. 2 vols. pp. (1), (5), 17—231, ill.; pp. 17—278, ill.* [3840
— Harrisburg, the city beautiful, romantic and historic. *Harrisburg, Pa.: The Telegraph Press 1927. pp. XVI, 265, ill.*
                              [3841
E., L. J.: Old church records (of Fetterhoff's Church, in Armstrong Valley). *In: Notes and Queries. Edited by W. H. Egle. Third series, vol. I. 1884—1887. Harrisburg, Pa. 1887. pp. 299—300. Reprint in: Third series, vol. I. Harrisburg, Pa. 1895. pp. 538—539.* [3842
Early, J. W.: A journey over the route travelled by Rev. F. A. C. Mühlenberg in his trips to Shamokin, 1777. *In: The Pennsylvania-German. Vol. IX. Cleona, Pa. 1908. pp. 339—346.*
[. . . . „Klinger's Church, ... „Weiser Lands" . . .]   [3843
Egle, William Henry: Contributions to the biographical history of Dauphin County. *In: Notes and Queries, Edited by W. H. Egle. First series, part I. Harrisburg, Pa. 1881. pp. 20—24; 24—29; 30—35; 55—59; 61—65; 66—69. Reprint in: First and second series, vol. I. Harrisburg, Pa. 1894. pp. 317—322; 323—329; 330—336; 358—363; 365—370; 372—377.*   [3844
— Hummelstown. *In: Notes and Queries. Edited by W. H. Egle. First series, part. II. Harrisburg, Pa. 1881. p. 80. Reprint in: First and second series, vol. I. Harrisburg, Pa. 1894. pp. 398—399.* [3845
— Heroes of the Revolution. Rolls of the companies of Captains Jacob Fridley and Richard Manning — the former raised in the neighborhood of Hummelstown, the latter in Upper Paxtang. *In: Notes and Queries. Edited by W. H. Egle. First series, part III. Harrisburg, Pa. 1881. p. 107. Reprint in: First and second series, vol. I. Harrisburg, Pa. 1894. pp. 424—425.* [3846
—] Dauphin County burials, *[„burial records in our possession prior to 1810".]*

In: Notes and Queries. Edited by W. H. Egle. First series, part V. Harrisburg, Pa. 1881. pp. 180—181; 189—190; 197—199; Second series, Harrisburg, Pa. 1883. pp. 44—45. Reprint in: First and second series, vol. II. Harrisburg, Pa. 1895. pp. 24—26; 35—37; 47—50; 123—126.   [3847
Egle, William Henry: Contributions to the biographical history of Dauphin County. *In: Notes and Queries. Edited by W. H. Egle. Second series. Harrisburg, Pa. 1883. pp. 108—113; 117—121; 124—127; 128—131; 280—284; 289—291; 294—297; Reprint in: First and second series, vol. II. Harrisburg, Pa. 1895. pp. 201—206; 211—215; 220—224; 225—230; 391—396; 399—403; 405—410.* [3848
— History of the Counties Dauphin and Lebanon in the Commonwealth of Pennsylvania: biographical and genealogical. *Philadelphia, Pa.: Everts & Peck 1883. pp. IX, 616; VI, 360, ill., maps.*   [3849
— 1785—1885. Centenary memorial of the erection of the County of Dauphin and the founding of the City of Harrisburg. *Harrisburg, Pa.: Telegraph Printing House 1886. pp. 397, ill.*   [3850
— Genealogical data. *In: Notes and Queries. Edited by W. H. Egle. Third series, vol. I. 1884—1887. Harrisburg, Pa. 1887. pp. 40—41; 52—53; 59—62; 83—84; 92—93; 103—104; 127—129; 140—142; 149—152; 171—172; 179—181. Reprint in: Third series, vol. I. Harrisburg, Pa. 1895. pp. 72—73; 87—91; 98—104; 133—137; 152—154; 175—179; 216—221; 239—243; 253—258; 342—346; 356—361.*   [3851
— Some genealogical notes. *[relating to Dauphin County, Pa.] In: Notes and Queries. Edited by W. H. Egle. Third series, vol. I. 1884—1887. Harrisburg, Pa. 1887. pp. 366—367; 369—370; 404; 408—409; 412; 415—416; 460—461; 462—463; 481—482; 488—489; 496—498; 523—524; 528—529; 549—550; 563—564. Reprint in: Third series, vol. II. Harrisburg, Pa. 1896. pp. 72—74; 77—80; 127—128; 133—134; 137—139; 142—145; 212—214; 215—217; 247—249; 257—260; 263—266; 276—278; 294—296; 321—324; 342—345.*
                              [3852
[—] Dauphin County marriages eighty years ago. *(Copied from „Oracle of Dauphin" and „Morgenrothe" and*

„Guardian".) In: Notes and Queries. Edited by W. H. Egle. First and second series, vol. I. Harrisburg, Pa. 1894. pp. 182—185; 193—196; 198—202. [3853

[Egle, William Henry]: Names of persons who took the Oath of Allegiance to the State of Pennsylvania in Paxtang Township, 1778—79. *In: Notes and Queries. Edited by W. H. Egle. First and second series, vol. I. Harrisburg, Pa. 1894. pp. 226—228; . . . in* Hanover Township, *1777—1779. pp. 231 —234; . . . in* Londonderry Township, *1777—1778. pp. 236—238.* [3854

[—] Transcript of inscriptions in Tox graveyard, Susquehanna Township. *In: Notes and Queries. Edited by W. H. Egle. Third series, vol. I. 1884—1887. Harrisburg, Pa. 1887. pp. 269—270. Reprint in: Third series, vol. I. Harrisburg, Pa. 1895. pp. 497—498.* [3855

[—] Millersburg. *In: Notes and Queries. Edited by W. H. Egle. First and second series, vol. I. Harrisburg, Pa. 1894. p. 262.* [3856

[—] Interesting notes from the records of the Land Department. *In: Notes and Queries. Edited by W. H. Egle. Third series, vol. II. 1887—1890. Harrisburg, Pa. 1891. pp. 176—177; 179—180; 185—186; 187—188.* [3857

[—] Contributions to the genealogy of Dauphin County. *In: Notes and Queries. Edited by W. H. Egle. Fourth series, vol. I. 1891—1893. Harrisburg, Pa. 1893. pp. 171—173; 180—181.* [3858

[—] Wiconisco in 1775. *(„Taxable of Wisconisky, Paxtang Township") Reprint in: Notes and Queries. Edited by W. H. Egle. First and second series, vol. I. Harrisburg, Pa. 1894. pp. 21—22.* [3859

[—] Londonderry in 1775. *In: Notes and Queries. Edited by W. H. Egle. First and second series, vol. I. Harrisburg, Pa. 1894. pp. 22—24.* [3860

[—] Ye ancient inhabitants. *[Lancaster County assessment lists of the region, now Dauphin County, prior to the formation of latter county in 1785, edited by . . .] In: Notes and Queries. Edited by W. H. Egle. First and second series, vol. I. Harrisburg, Pa. 1894.* East End of Hanover, 1769. *pp. 83—84;* North End of Paxtang, 1749. *pp. 95—96.* East End of Derry, 1751; East End of Hanover. *pp. 142—143.* West End of Hanover *pp. 143—144.* Paxtang, 1770.

pp. 179—181. Upper Paxtang, Wiconisco district, 1778. *pp. 271—272.* West End of Hanover; East End of Hanover, 1756. *pp. 350—352;* West End of Derry, 1755. *p. 400;* West End of Derry, 1757. *p. 401.* West Hanover, 1772. *pp. 404—405;* West side of Derry, 1758. *pp. 442—445; First and second series, vol. II. 1895.* Paxtang and Middletown *[s. d.] pp. 15—17;* Londonderry Township, 1778. *pp. 55—56;* Hanover, 1759. *pp. 209—210.* [3861

[Egle, William Henry]: [Dauphin County, Pa. assessment lists.] *In: Notes and Queries. Edited by W. H. Egle. Third series, vol. I. Harrisburg, Pa. 1895.* Londonderry, 1777. *pp. 466—467;* West End of Derry, 1751. *Third series, vol. II. 1896. pp. 17—18;* East End of Derry, 1751. *pp. 22—24;* West End of Derry, 1755. *pp. 31—32;* East End of Derry, 1755. *p. 38;* South End of East side of Derry, 1757. *p. 72;* West End of Derry, 1759. *p. 88.* [3862

[—] Upper Paxtang in the Revolution. *In: Notes and Queries. Edited by W. H. Egle. First and second series, vol. I. Harrisburg, Pa. 1894. pp. 177—179.* [3863

Ehrehart, C. J.: Emmaus orphan house. Middletown Bor., Dauphin Co. *In: The Evangelical Review. Vol. XII. Gettysburg, Pa. 1860—61. pp. 575—590.* [3864

Eshleman, E. M.: Tombstone-inscriptions in the old Hummelstown Lutheran churchyard. *In: The Pennsylvania-German. Vol. VIII. Lebanon, Pa. 1907. pp. 365—370, ill.* [3865

Geety, W. W.: An early settler in Clark's Valley. Ludwig Minsker. *In: Notes and Queries. Edited by W. H. Egle. First series, part III. Harrisburg, Pa. 1881. pp. 93—94; see also p. 111. Reprint in: First and second series, vol. I. Harrisburg, Pa. 1894. pp. 410—411; see also. p. 436.* [3866

Gilbert, D. M.: 1795—1895. Services commemorative of the one hundredth anniversary of Zion Evangelical Lutheran Church, Harrisburg, Pa., November 10 —11, 1895. *Edited by . . . Harrisburg, Pa.: Harrisburg Publishing Co 1896. pp. 148, ill.* [3867

Graydon, Alexander]: Dauphin County in 1789. *[Letter written in reply to several questions propounded by Jedediah Morse, the geographer.] In: Notes and Queries.*

Edited by W. H. Egle. Second series. Harrisburg, Pa. 1883. pp. 277—280. Reprint in: First and second series, vol. II. Harrisburg, Pa. 1895. pp. 385—390. [3868

H., A. B.: The origin of Dauphin County, names of places etc. In: Notes and Queries. Edited by W. H. Egle. First series, part V. Harrisburg, Pa. 1881. pp. 171—173; 176—179; 179—180. Reprint in: First and second series, vol. II. Harrisburg, Pa. 1895. pp. 13—15; 19—23. [3869

Hamilton, A. Boyd: Historical memoranda. Middletown-on-Swatara. [Harrisburg, Pa. 1878.] pp. 47. [3870

Hayden, Horace Edwin: Squire Weitzel's marriages, 1806 to 1830. In: Notes and Queries. Edited by W. H. Egle. Second series. Harrisburg, Pa. 1883. pp. 84—86. Reprint in: First and second series, vol. II. Harrisburg, Pa. 1895. pp. 176—178. [3871

Hutchinson, C. H.: The chronicles of Middletown, containing a compilation of facts, biographical sketches, reminiscences, anecdotes, etc., connected with the history of one of the oldest towns in Pennsylvania. [s. l.] 1906. pp. VII, 8—266, ill. [3872

Inglewood, Marian: Then and now in Harrisburg. Harrisburg, Pa. 1925. pp. 181, ill. [3873

Ivan: Historical localities [in Dauphin Co., Pa.] In: Notes and Queries. Edited by W. H. Egle. Fourth series, vol. I. 1891—1893. Harrisburg, Pa. 1893. pp. 34—37. [3874

Keefer, Horace Andrew: Early iron industries of Dauphin County. Harrisburg, Pa.: Telegraph Press 1927. pp. 35, ill. = Publications of the Dauphin County Historical Society. [3875

Kelker, Luther Reily: History of Dauphin County, Pa. With genealogical memoirs. 3 vols. New York, N. Y. and Chicago, Ill. The Lewis Publishing Co. 1907. pp. VIII. 488; 489—1136; 727, ill., maps. [3876

Lubold, D. G.: History of Berrysbury Seminary. Address delivered at a reunion of alumni and students held at Berrysburg, Pa. Thursday, Aug. 11, 1904. Elizabethville, Pa.: Elizabethville Echo 1904. pp. 28, ill. [3877

M., C. H. [H., H. B.]: Oak-Dale forge. In: Notes and Queries. Edited by W. H. Egle. First series, part II. Harrisburg,

Pa. 1881. pp. 71—72. Reprint in: First and second series, vol. I Harrisburg, Pa. 1894. pp. 378—379. [1894 signed: H. B. H.] [3878

Morgan, George H.: Annals comprising memoirs, incidents and statistics of Harrisburg from the period of its first settlement. For the past, the present, and the future. Harrisburg, Pa.: Geo. A. Brooks 1858. pp. II, 400. Revised and enlarged edition by L. Francis Morgan Black. 1906. pp. VII, 488, ill. [3879

— Centennial. The settlement, formation and progress of Dauphin County, Pa. from 1785 to 1876. Prepared under the directions of the commissioners of said county. Harrisburg, Pa.: Telegraph Steam Book and Job Printing House 1877. pp. 239. [3880

Mumma, David: Centennial memorial of the founding of Shoop's Church in Lower Paxton Township, Dauphin County, Pa. and addresses of Hon. David Mumma. Founded Nov. 9th, 1784. Commemoration Nov. 9th, 1884. Harrisburg, Pa.: Lane S. Hart 1884. pp. 15. [3881

P.[arthemore], E. W. S.: Some old family graveyards. In: Notes and Queries. Edited by W. H. Egle. Third series, vol. I. 1884—1887. Harrisburg, Pa. 1887. pp. 90—91; 148—149; 162—163. Reprint in: Third series, vol. I. Harrisburg, Pa. 1895. pp. 148—151; 251—253; 313—314. [3882

— Shoop's church records. Baptisms from 1783 to 1830. In · Notes and Queries. Edited by W. H. Egle. Third series, vol. I. 1884—1887. Harrisburg, Pa. 1887. pp. 104—108; 109—112; 114—117; 119—121; Reprint in: Notes and Queries. Third series, vol. I. Harrisburg, Pa. 1895. pp. 179—184; 186—191; 194—199; 202—207. [3883

— Tombstone records of St. Peter's church graveyard, Middletown. In: Notes and Queries. Edited by W. H. Egle. Third series, vol. I. 1884—1887. Harrisburg, Pa. 1887. pp. 130—132; 137—138. Reprint in: Third series, vol. I. Harrisburg, Pa. 1895. pp. 223—225; 233—235. [3884

— Old Shoop's Church (in Lower Paxtang Township, Dauphin Co.). In: Notes and Queries. Edited by W. H. Egle. Third series, vol. I. 1884—1887. Harrisburg, Pa. 1887. pp. 184—186. Reprint in: Third series, Vol. I. Harrisburg, Pa. 1895. pp. 368—371. [3885

P.[arthemore], E. W. S.: Tombstone insription in Shoop's Church burial ground. *In: Notes and Queries. Edited by W. H. Egle. Third series, vol. I. 1884—1887. Harrisburg, Pa. 1887. p. 186; pp. 189—191; 195—196. Reprint in: Third series, vol. I. Harrisburg, Pa. 1895. p. 371; pp. 377—379; 385—387.* [3886

— Tombstone records in cemetery at Union Deposit, Dauphin County. *In: Notes and Queries. Edited by W. H. Egle. Third series, vol. I. 1884—1887. Harrisburg, Pa. 1887. pp. 205—206. Reprint in: Third series, vol. I. Harrisburg, Pa. 1895. pp. 402—404.* [3887

— Tombstone records in German Reformed graveyard, corner High and Pine streets, Middletown. *In: Notes and Queries. Edited by W. H. Egle. Third series, vol. I. 1884—1887. Harrisburg, Pa. 1887. pp. 292—293. Reprint in: Third series, vol. I. Harrisburg, Pa. 1895. pp. 528—530.* [3888

— In Armstrong and Powell's Valley. *(Tombstone transcriptions.) In: Notes and Queries. Edited by W. H. Egle. Third series, vol. I. 1884—1887. Harrisburg, Pa. 1887. pp. 513—514; 519—520. Reprint in: Third series, vol. II. Harrisburg, Pa. 284—286; 288—290.* [3889

— Neidig's [U. B.] meeting house *(about 3 miles E. of Harrisburg, in the Village of Oberlin). In: Notes and Queries. Edited by W. H. Egle. Third series, vol. II. 1887—1890. Harrisburg, Pa. 1891. pp. 9—11. Reprint in: Third series, vol. II. Harrisburg, Pa. 1896. pp. 391—394.* [3890

— Tombstone records of Shell's Lutheran and Reformed Church *(in East Hanover Township, Dauphin County, Pa.). In: Notes and Queries. Edited by W. H. Egle. Third series, vol. II. 1887—1890. Harrisburg, Pa. 1891. pp. 138—141; Reprint in: Third series, vol. III. Harrisburg, Pa. 1896. pp. 67—72.* [3891

— Records of St. Peter's Lutheran Church, Middletown, Pa. *In: Notes and Queries. Edited by W. H. Egle. Third series, vol. II. 1887—1890. Harrisburg, Pa. 1891. pp. 473—476; 478—481; 483—485; 486—489; 493—496; 500—502; 505—508; 510—513; 516—518; 520—523; 525—527; 528—530; 531—534; 536—537; 546—547; 548—550; 550—552.* [3892

Parthemore, E. W. S.: Nintey-five years old. Memorandum of John Shoop, of Shoop's Church, the oldest native of Dauphin County. *In: Notes and Queries. Edited by W. H. Egle. Third series, vol. II. 1887—1890. Harrisburg, Pa. 1891. pp. 541—542.* [3893

— Records of the Hill Lutheran Church in Derry Township, Dauphin County, Pa. *Harrisburg, Pa.: Harrisburg, Pa.: Harrisburg Publishing Co. 1892. pp. 14, ill.* [3894

— Additional records of St. Peter's Church, Middletown. Burials 1818—1821. *In: Notes and Queries. Edited by W. H. Egle. Fourth series, vol. I. 1891—1893. Harrisburg, Pa. 1893. p. 9.* Baptisms 1814—1817. *pp. 10—11.* Baptisms II. Wenricks and Shoops. *pp. 15—18.* [3895

— „Hill" Lutheran Church. Derry Township, Dauphin County, Pa. Records of baptisms, etc. *In: Notes and Queries. Edited by W. H. Egle. Fourth series, vol. I. 1891—1893. Harrisburg, Pa. 1893. pp. 67—69, ill.; 79—80; 82—83; 84—85; 86—87; 91—92; 95—96.* Minutes of the church etc. *pp. 100—102; p. 106;* Inscriptions in the graveyard. *pp. 107—108.* [3896

— Tombstone inscriptions in St. John's Lutheran church graveyard, Wiconisco. *In: Notes and Queries. Edited by W. H. Egle. Fourth series, vol. II. 1894. Harrisburg, Pa. 1895. pp. 167—171.* [3897

— Hoffman's Reformed Church, Lykens Valley, Dauphin County, Pa. *(giving transcriptions of tombstones). In: Notes and Queries. Edited by W. H. Egle. Fourth series, vol. II. 1894. Harrisburg, Pa. 1895. pp. 227—232.* [3898

— The old grist mills of Dauphin County. *In: Notes and Queries. Edited by W. H. Egle. Fourth series, vol. II. Harrisburg, Pa. 1895. pp. 345—347.* [3899

— Long's Church, Powell's Valley, Dauphin County, Pa. *(including transcriptions of tombstones). In: Notes and Queries. Edited by W. H. Egle. Annual vol. 1896. Harrisburg, Pa. 1897. pp. 115—118.* [3900

— Scraps of Dauphin County history. *Harrisburg, Pa.: Harrisburg Publishing Co. 1896. pp. 16.* [3901

— Earliest Mennonite Church in Dauphin County. *In: Notes and Queries. Edited by W. H. Egle. Annual vol. 1896. Harrisburg, Pa. 1897. pp. 60—61.* [3902

R., H.: The Huguenots of Lykens Valley. *In: Notes and Queries. Edited by W. H. Egle. Third series, vol. II. 1887—1890. Harrisburg, Pa. 1891. p. 281. Reprint in: Third series, vol. III. Harrisburg, Pa. 1896. pp. 305—307.* [3903

R., W. F.: The first professional butcher of Paxtang Valley. (Daniel Martin, a Pennsylvania German.) *In: Notes and Queries. Edited by W. H. Egle. Third series, vol. I. 1884—1887. Harrisburg, Pa. 1887. pp. 223—225. Reprint in: Third series, vol. I. Harrisburg, Pa. 1895. pp. 426—428.* [3904

— The taverns of Paxtang Valley. *In: Notes and Queries, Edited by W. H. Egle. Third series, vol. I. 1884—1887. Harrisburg, Pa. 1887. pp. 240—243. Reprint in: Third series, vol. I. Harrisburg, Pa. 1895. pp. 446—451.* [3905

Rupp, I. Daniel: The history and topography of Dauphin, Cumberland, Franklin, Bedford, Adams and Perry Counties: *Containing a brief history of the first settlers, notices of the leading events, incidents and interesting facts, both general and local, in the history of these counties, general & statistical descriptions of all the principal boroughs, towns, villages, &c. with an appendix. Lancaster Pa.: Gilbert Hills 1846. pp. XII, 25—606, ill.* [3906

Schaeffer, C. W.: A discourse exhibiting the history of the Evangelical Lutheran Church in Harrisburg, Pa. *Harrisburg, Pa.: Geo. Bergner 1846. pp. 20.* [3907

Swartz, Joel: 1776—1876. A Centennial discourse on the history of Zion's Evangelical Lutheran Church, Harrisburg, Pa. *Delivered Nov. 5th. 1876. Harrisburg, Pa.: W. P. Swartz & Bro. 1877. pp. 25.* [3908

Commemorative biographical encyclopedia of Dauphin County, Pa., *containing sketches of prominent and representative citizens, and many of the early Scotch-Irish and German settlers. Edited under the assistence of* **William H. Egle.** *Chambersburg, Pa.: J. M. Runk & Co. 1896. pp. XIX, 1196, ill.* [3909

Families of the County of Dauphin in 1790. The first U. S. Census. *Harrisburg, Pa.: Harrisburg Publication Co. 1890. pp. 30. = Publications of the Dauphin County Historical Society.* [3910

Address delivered before the Dauphin County Historical Society in the State

Capital. Harrisburg, Pa., July 4, 1876. *[s. l. 1876.] pp. 85.* [3911

Souvenir book. Millersburg Centennial celebration. Sept. 1—4—5, 1907. *Published by the Committee on printing and advertising. Williamsport, Pa.: Grit Press 1907. pp. (78); advertisement pp. (34).* [3912

Noted inns prior to 1800. *In: Notes and Queries. Edited by W. H. Egle. Third series, vol. I. 1884—1887. Harrisburg, Pa. 1887. pp. 39—40. Reprint in: Third series, vol. I. Harrisburg, Pa. 1895. p. 71* [3913

The upper end. *Interesting reminiscences of early settlement. In: Notes and Queries. Edited by W. H. Egle. Third series, vol. I. 1884—1887. Harrisburg, Pa. 1887. pp. 251—253; 255—256. Reprint in: Third series, vol. I. Harrisburg, Pa. 1895. pp. 462—465; 468—470.* [3914

Some old marriages. *In: Notes and Queries. Edited by W. H. Egle. Third series, vol. I. 1884—1887. Harrisburg, Pa. 1887. pp. 279—280; 282—283; 290—291. Reprint in: Third series, vol. I. Harrisburg, Pa. 1895. pp. 510—511; 516—517; 524—526.* [3915

The mill-dam troubles of 1793 and 1794. *In: Notes and Queries. Edited by W. H. Egle. Third series, vol. I. 1884—1887. Harrisburg, Pa. 1887. pp. 320—322. Reprint in: Third series, vol. II. Harrisburg, Pa. 1896. pp. 9—11.* [3916

Early settlers of the „Upper End". *In: Notes and Queries. Edited by W. H. Egle. Third series, vol. I. 1884—1887. Harrisburg, Pa. 1887. pp. 511—512. Reprint in: Third series, vol. II. Harrisburg, Pa. 1896. pp. 282—284.* [3917

Ye olden times. The inns and taverns of Harrisburg. *In: Notes and Queries. Edited by W. H. Egle. Third series, vol. II. 1887—1890. Harrisburg, Pa. 1891. pp. 118—119; 121—123; 125—126; 131—133; 136—137. Reprint in: Third series, vol. III. Harrisburg, Pa. 1896. pp. 39—41; 44—46; 49—51; 59—63; 65—66.* [3918

The first census. The families in Dauphin County in 1790. *Reprint in: Notes and Queries. Edited by W. H. Egle. Third series, vol. II. 1887—1890. Harrisburg, Pa. 1891. pp. 431—433; 434—437; 437—440; 443—446; 447—448; 449—450; 451—455; 456—460; 461—464; 466—468; 469—472.* [3919

In Conewago Township, Dauphin County, Pa. *In: Notes and Queries. Edited by W. H. Egle. Fourth series, vol. I. 1891—1893. Harrisburg, Pa. 1893. p. 14.* [3920

The militia of 1812—1814. Roll of Capt. Shell's Company of the Second Battalion, 98th Regiment, First Brigade. *In: Notes and Queries. Edited by W. H. Egle. Third series, vol. I. 1884—1887. Harrisburg, Pa. 1887. pp. 340—341. Reprint in: Third series, vol. II. Harrisburg, Pa. 1895. pp. 43—44.* [3921

A militia roll of 1839. An enrollment of the militia comprised within the bounds of the Seventh Company of the First Battalion Ninety-eighth Regiment of Pennsylvania. *Reprint in: Notes and Queries. Edited by W. H Egle. Annual vol. 1900. Harrisburg, Pa. 1901. pp. 116—118.* [3922

Tombstone records in Lutheran churchyard, Hummelstown. *In: Notes and Queries. Edited by W. H. Egle. Third series, vol. I. 1884—1887. Harrisburg, Pa. 1887. pp. 6—8; 9—10; 12—14; 15—16. Reprint in: Third series, vol. I. Harrisburg, Pa. 1895. pp. 9—11; 13—15; 19—21; 24—25.* [3923

Dunkard meeting house in Derry. *In: Notes and Queries. Edited by W. H. Egle. Third series, vol. I. 1884—1887. Harrisburg, Pa. 1887. pp. 50—51. Reprint in: Third series, vol. I. Harrisburg, Pa. 1895. pp. 84—85.* [3924

St. Peter's Lutheran Church at Middletown. *In: Notes and Queries. Edited by W. H. Egle. Third series, vol. I. 1884—1887. Harrisburg, Pa. 1887. pp. 138—139. Reprint in: Third series, vol. I. Harrisburg, Pa. 1895. pp. 235—236.* [3925

Tombstone records in German Baptist church-yard, Lower Paxtang Township Dauphin County. *In: Notes and Queries. Edited by W. H. Egle. Third series, vol. I. 1884—1887. Harrisburg, Pa. 1887. pp. 291—292. Reprint in: Third series, vol. I. Harrisburg, Pa. 1895. pp. 528—530.* [3926

Tombstone inscriptions in the Fisher graveyard, Lower Swatara Township, Dauphin County. *In: Notes and Queries. Edited by W. H. Egle. Third series, vol. I. 1884—1887. Harrisburg, Pa. 1887. p. 306. Reprint in: Third series, vol. I. Harrisburg, Pa. 1895. p. 548.* [3927

Records *[tombstone transcriptions]* of Fetterhoff Church *(2 miles NE. of the Town of Halifax.) In: Notes and Queries. Edited by W. H. Egle. Third series, vol. I. 1884—1887. Harrisburg, Pa. 1887. pp. 323—325. Reprint in: Third series, vol. II. Harrisburg, Pa. 1896. pp. 14—16.* [3928

Register of marriages and baptisms kept by the Rev. Traugott Frederick Illing in connections with the churches of St. Peter's (Lutheran) Middletown, and Caernarvon (Episcopal) Lancaster County, Pa. *Harrisburg, Pa.: Harrisburg Publishing Co. 1891. pp. 43.* [3929

Wenrich, Church. Tombstone inscriptions in graveyard of Mount Zion Evangelical Lutheran and Reformed Church. *In: Notes and Queries. Edited by W. H. Egle. Third series, vol. II. 1887—1890. Harrisburg, Pa. 1891. p. 162. Reprint in: Third series, vol. III. Harrisburg, Pa. 1896. pp. 110—111.* [3930

Tombstone records in German Baptist church yard, Lower Paxtang Township. *In: Notes and Queries. Edited by W. H. Egle. Third series, vol. I. 1884—1887. Harrisburg, Pa. 1887. pp. 291—292. Reprint in: Third series, vol. I. Harrisburg, Pa 1895. pp. 526—527.* [3931

History of Zion's Evangelical Lutheran Church of Lykens. *In: Notes and Queries. Edited by W. H. Egle. Fourth series, vol. I. 1891—1893. Harrisburg, Pa. 1893. pp. 136—138* [3932

1793—1903. Historical souvenir and directory of the United Brethren Church, Highspire, Pa. *Highspire, Pa.: [Harrisburg, Pa.: The Evangelical Press.] 1903. pp. . . .* [3933

Dedication program. Zion Lutheran Church. Hummelstown, Pa. Containing a brief history of the congregation from 1753 A. D. — 1912. A. D. *March, 17—21, 1912. pp. 38, ill.* [3934

Franklin County

Betz, I. H.: Historical pilgrimages into Pennsylvania-Germandom and Scotch Irishdom. From Winchester to Harrisburg. *In: The Pennsylvania-German. Vol. V. Lebanon, Pa. 1904. pp. 8—22; 61—72, ill.* [See no. 295] [3935

Bonnell, W. Wilson: A history of the German Reformed Church, Chambersburg, Pa., *with an appendix, also a sermon on the convenant and ist blessings. Chambersburg, Pa.: Publication Office of the*

German Reformed Church 1844. pp. IV, 5—57, ill. [3936
Cooper, John M.: Facts suggested by paper read by M. A. Foltz at September meeting. *Read Nov. 3, 1898. In: The Kittochtinny Historical Society. Papers read before the Society during the year ending March 1, 1899. Vol. I. Chambersburg, Pa. 1900. pp. 84—89. [See no. 3946].* [3937
— The tradition concerning our limestone lands. *(Read Sept. 28, 1899.) In: Kittochtinny Historical Society. Papers read before the Society from Febr. 1899 to Febr. 1901. Vol. II. Chambersburg, Pa. 1903. pp. 74—92. [See: Orr, J. G., no. 3936].* [3938
Cort, Cyrus: Memorial of Enoch Brown and eleven scholars, who were massacred in Antrim Township, Franklin County, Pa., by the Indians, during the Pontiac War, July 26, 1764, *containing addresses of* George W. Ziegler, Cyrus Cort, Peter A. Witmer, F. A. Woods *and* Wm. H. Egle *and poem of* John M. Cooper, *at the dedication of the Enoch Brown Park and monuments, 3 miles north of Greencastle, Pa. Aug. 4, 1885, with Centennial sermons, appendix etc. Edited by . . ., in behalf of the Enoch Brown Monument Committee. Lancaster, Pa.: Steinman & Hensel 1886. pp. (1), 108, ill.* [3939
Cremer, C. W.: The Seventh Day Baptist of Snow Hill. *Read May 1, 1908. In: The Kittochtinny Historical Society, Papers read before the Society Febr., 1908 to Febr., 1910. Vol. VI. Chambersburg, Pa. 1910. pp. 10—30. Reprint in: The Pennsylvania-German. Vol. XII. Lititz, Pa. 1911. pp. 173—174.* [3940
— Historical incidents connected with Waynesboro and Franklin County. *Read by R. C. Gordon, April 29, 1920. In: The Kittochtinny Historical Society. Papers read before the Society, Febr., 1915 to April, 1922. Vol. IX. Chambersburg, Pa. 1923. pp. 346—370.* [3941
Davison, Watson R.: „Reminiscences of Greencastle." *Read Oct. 22, 1921. In: The Kittochtinny Historical Society. Papers read before the Society, Febr., 1915 to April, 1922. Vol. IX. Chambersburg, Pa. 1923. pp. 534—552.* [3942
Deatrich, Charles M.: Historical sketch of Saint Thomas, formerly Campbellstown. *Read at Oct. meeting, 1904. In: The Kittochtinny Historical Society. Papers read before the Society from March, 1903*

to Febr., 1905. Vol. IV. Chambersburg, Pa. 1906. pp. 244—285. [3943
Egle, William Henry: Provincial papers: State and supply transcripts of the County of Cumberland for the years 1778, 1779, 1780, 1782 and 1785. *Edited by . . . Harrisburg, Pa.: Wm. Stanley Ray 1898. pp. X, 781.*
= *Pennsylvania Archives. Third series, vol. XX.* [3944
Focht, D. H.: History of the Grindstone Hill Evangelical Lutheran Church: *a discourse portraying the history of the Grindstone Hill Evangelical Lutheran Church, in Franklin County, Pa. Delivered on Christmas, Monday, Dec. 25th, 1854. Gettysburg, Pa.: H. C. Neinstedt 1855. pp. 46.* [3945
Foltz, M. A.: The German influence in Pennsylvania: with special reference to Franklin County. *Read Sept. 22, 1898. In: The Kittochtinny Historical Society. Papers read before the Society during the year ending March 1, 1899. Vol. I. Chambersburg, Pa. 1900. pp. 62—83. [See no. 3937]* [3946
— The transitions of a century. *Read Dec. 27, 1900. In: The Kittochtinny Historical Society. Papers read before the Society from Febr. 1899 to Febr. 1901. Vol. II. Chambersburg, Pa. 1903. pp. 259—280.* [3947
[—] The Germans in Franklin County, Pa. Extracts of a paper of M. A. Foltz, on on „The German influence in Pennsylvania": *With special reference to Franklin County, read before The Kittochtinny Historical Society, Sept. 22, 1898. In: The Pennsylvania-German. Vol. IX. Cleona, Pa. 1908. pp. 307—312.* [3948
— A notable publication house in Chambersburg 1835—1864. *[M. Kieffer & Co.] (Read Jan. 31, 1907). In: The Kittochtinny Historical Society. Papers read before the Society from March, 1905 to Febr., 1908. Vol. V. Chambersburg, Pa. 1908. pp. 183—199.* [3949
—-**Harbaugh, Linn:** Historical sketch of Zion Reformed Church, Chambersburg, Pa. 1780—1911. *Chambersburg, Pa.: Public Opinion Print 1911. pp. 100, ill.* [3950
Garrard, Lewis H.: Chambersburg in the colony and the Revolution. A sketch. *Philadelphia, Pa.: J. B. Lippincott & Co. 1856. pp. V, 60.* [3951

Harbaugh, Linn: An early literary by-path along the Conococheque. *[Paper on the „Journal" of Rev. Michael Schlatterer 1747—1748.] Read Dec. 26, 1902. In: The Kittochtinny Historical Society. Papers read before the Society from March, 1901 to Febr., 1903. Vol. III. Chambersburg, Pa. 1904. pp. 197—208.* [3952

Heathcote, C. W.: Lutheran Church in the Cumberland Valley. *Read May 2, 1911. In: The Kittochtinny Historical Society. Papers read before the Society from Febr., 1910 to Febr., 1912. Vol. VII. Chambersburg, Pa. 1912. pp. 106—121.* [3953

— The German Lutherans of Chambersburg and vicinity. *In: The Penn Germania. New series, vol. III. = Old series, vol. XV. Cleona, Pa. 1914. pp. 61—64.* [3954

Hunsecker, Catherine: Civil War reminiscences. *In: Christian Monitor. A monthly magazine for the home. Vol. XVI, no. 1. Scottdale, Pa. 1924. pp. 406—407.* [3955

Horst, John L.: Historical sketch of the Mennonites of Franklin County, Pa. *In: Mennonite Year Book and Directory 1925. Scottdale, Pa. 1925. pp. 31—33.* [3956

Klinefelter, F.: Historical sketch of the Sunday school of Zion Evangelical Lutheran Church, Greencastle, Pa. *Presented at the 75th anniversary of the school, Oct. 4, 1885. Greencastle, Pa.: Press Printing House 1885. pp. 19, (2).* [3957

Leisenring, E. H.: Historical sketch. First Evangelical Lutheran Church, Chambersburg, Pa. Rose Day, June 4, 1899. *Chambersburg, Pa.: Public Opinion Print. pp. 10.* [3958

Maclay, J. P.: History of the early physicians of Chambersburg. *Read March 29, 1921. In: The Kittochtinny Historical Society. Papers read before the Society Febr., 1915 to April, 1922. Vol. IX. Chambersburg, Pa. 1923. pp. 477—491.* [3959

M'Cauley, I. H.: Historical sketch of Franklin County, Pa. *Prepared for the Centennial celebration held at Chambersburg, Pa., July 4, 1876. Chambersburg, Pa.: John M. Pomeroy, publisher. To which is added a valuable appendix by* **J. L. Suesserott, D. M. Kennedy** *and others. D. F. Pursel, publisher. Chambersburg, Pa.: Issued by D. F. Pursel*

1878. pp. 322, ill; Second enlarged edition. Harrisburg, Pa.: Patriot Publishing Co. 1878. pp. (1), 5—294. [3960

McIlvaine, J. S.: The banks of Chambersburg. *Read Dec. 5, 1902. In: The Kittochtinny Historical Society. Papers read before the Society from March, 1901 to Febr., 1903. Vol. III. Chambersburg, Pa. 1904. pp. 178—196.* [3961

Mason, Carol Y.: Land economy of Amberson valley. *Pa. In: Economic Geography. Vol. XII. Worcester, Mars 1936. pp. 265—272, ill.* [3961a

Martin, J. E.: Marion Mennonite Church, *[near Chambersburg, Franklin Co., Pa.] In: Christian Monitor. A monthly magazine for the home. Vol. XXIII, no. 9. Scottdale, Pa. 1931. pp. 272—233, ill.* [3962

Martin, S. A.: Colleges of the Cumberland Valley. *Read April 28, 1910. In: The Kittochtinny Historical Society. Papers read before the Society, Febr., 1910, to Febr., 1912. Vol. VII. Chambersburg, Pa. 1912. pp. 15—28.* [3963

Mullan, James M.: Fort Loudon. *Read at April meeting, May 5 th, 1904. In: The Kittochtinny Historical Society. Papers read before the Society from March, 1903 to Febr., 1905. Vol. IV. Chambersburg, Pa. 1906. pp. 230—243.* [3964

Nead, Benjamin Matthias: Waynesboro. The history of a settlement in the county formerly called Cumberland but later Franklin, in the Commonwealth of Pennsylvania, in its beginnings; through its growth into a village and borough, to its Centennial period and to the close of the present century: *including a relation of pertinent topics of general state and county history. Published under the auspices of the Waynesboro Centennial Association. Harrisburg, Pa.: Harrisburg Publishing Co. 1900. pp. 428, ill.* [3965

Orr, John G.: The traditions relating to the barrens of the limestone lands of the Cumberland Valley, with special reference to Franklin County *Read May 3, 1901. In: The Kittochtinny Historical Society. Papers read before the Society from March, 1901 to Febr., 1903. Vol. III. Chambersburg, Pa. 1904. pp. 18—31.* [3966

— „Fort Stauffer." *Read May 3. 1901. In: The Kittochtinny Historical Society. Papers read before the Society from March, 1901 to Febr., 1903. Vol. III.*

Chambersburg, Pa. 1904. pp. 31—34.
[3967
Orr, John G.: Early grist mills of Lurgan
Township. *Read Febr. 27, 1902. In: The
Kittochtinny Historical Society. Papers
read before the Society from March, 1901 to
Febr., 1903. Vol. III. Chambersburg,
Pa. 1904. pp. 75—128, ill.* [3968
— Early highways. *In: The Kittochtinny
Historical Society. Papers read before
the Society from March, 1905 to Febr.,
1908. Vol. V. Chambersburg, Pa. 1908.
pp. 9—23; 223—251; 1908—1910. Vol.
VI. Chambersburg, 1910. pp. 140—169.
1910—1912. Vol. VII. Chambersburg,
Pa. 1912. pp. 152—185, ill.* [3969
— Fords, ferries and bridges. *Read Febr.
24, 1921. In: The Kittochtinny Histo-
rical Society. Papers read before the So-
ciety, Febr., 1915 to April, 1922. Vol.
IX. Chambersburg, Pa. 1923. pp. 462
476.* [3970
— The pioneer church at Orrstown. *Read
Jan. 31, 1918. In: The Kittochtinny
Historical Society. Papers read before
the Society, Febr., 1915 to April, 1922.
Vol. IX. Chambersburg, Pa. 1923. pp.
127—137.* [3971
— The birth, growth and passing of the
country school. *Read Oct. 25, 1917. In:
The Kittochtinny Historical Society.
Papers read before the Society, Febr.,
1915 to April, 1922. Vol. IX. Chambers-
burg, Pa. 1923. pp. 106—117.* [3972
— Sketch of Salem Church, Plessant Hall,
Penna. *Read March 31, 1922. In: The
Kittochtinny Historical Society. Papers
read before the Society Febr., 1915 to
April, 1922. Vol. IX. Chambersburg,
Pa. 1923. pp. 618—632.* [3973
Rupp, I. Daniel: The history and topogra-
phy of Dauphin, Cumberland, Franklin,
Bedford, Adams and Perry Counties:
*Containing a brief history of the first
settlers, notices of the leading events, incidents and interesting facts, both general
and local, in the history of these counties,
general and statistical descriptions of all
the principal boroughs, towns, villages,
&c. with an appendix. Lancaster, Pa.:
Gilbert Hills 1846. pp. XII, 25—606, ill.*
[3974
Seibert, George: Die Zerstörung der Stadt
Chambersburg durch die Rebellen am
30. Juli 1864. *Nach persönlicher Er-
kundigung an Ort und Stelle, sowie nach
den veröffentlichten Berichten des Augen-
zeugen Dr. B. S. Schneck. Philadelphia,*

Pa.: J. Kohler 1865. 48 S., Karten.
[3975
Seibert, G. C.: The burning of Chambersburg, Pa. *In: The Pennsylvania-German. Vol. IX. 1908. pp. 291—302, ill.*
[3976
Seilhammer, Geo. O.: The German settlement. *Read Oct. 10, 1907. In: The
Kittochtinny Historical Society. Papers
read before the Society from March, 1905
to Febr., 1908. Vol. V. Chambersburg,
Pa. 1908. pp. 267—285.* [3977
Stump, Adam and **Anstadt, Henry:** History
of the Evangelical Lutheran Synod of
West Pennsylvania of the United Lu-
theran Church in America 1825—1925.
*Edited by . . . Published by action of the
Synod in the celebration of its Centennial.
Chambersburg, Pa.: J. R. Kerr & Bro.
1925. pp. 696, ill.*
*[Cumberland Valley Conference. pp.
289—440.]* [3978
Wiestling, Edward B.: Old iron works of the
Cumberland Valley. *Paper read before
the Kittochtinny Historical Society, May
25, 1922. Vol. X, no. 1. Chambersburg,
Pa. 1922. pp. 3—14.* [3979
Biographical annals of Franklin County,
Pa., *containing genealogical records of
representative families, including many
of the early settlers, and biographical
sketches of prominent citizens. Chicago,
Ill.: The Genealogical Publishing Co.
1905. pp. IX, 706, ill.* [3980
History of Franklin County, Pa., *containing
a history of the county, its townships,
towns, villages, schools, churches, industries, etc., portraits of early settlers and
prominent men; biographies; history of
Pennsylvania, statistical and miscellaneous matter, etc., etc. Chicago, Ill.:
Warner Beers & Co. 1887. pp. VII, 15
—968, ill., maps.* [3981
Old Mercersburg. *By the Womans Club of
Mercersburg, Pa. New York, N. Y.:
Published under the auspices of the Journal of the American History by Frank
Allaben Genealogical Co. 1912. pp. 215,
ill.* [3982

Fulton County

History of Bedford, Somerset and Fulton
Counties, Pa. *With illustrations and
biographical sketches of some of its pio-
neers and prominent men. Chicago, Ill.:
Waterman, Watkins & Co. 1884. pp.
IX, 15—672, ill.* 983

Huntingdon County

Africa, J. Simpson: History of Huntingdon and Blair Counties, Pa. *2 parts. Philadelphia, Pa.: Louis H. Everts 1883.* Huntingdon County. *pp. VI, 500, ill., map.* [3984

Carney, W. H. Bruce: History of the Alleghany Evangelical Lutheran Synod of Pennsylvania . . . *Published by the authority of Alleghany Synod in commemoration of its seventy-fifth anniversary and the Quadricentennial of the Reformation. 2 vols. Philadelphia, Pa.: Printed for the Synod by the Lutheran Publication Society 1918. pp. XII, 454, 455—871, ill., map.* [Churches of the Juniata Conference.= Chapter XI. *pp. 252—357, ill.]* [3985

Egle, William Henry: Provincial papers: Returns of taxables for the Counties of Bedford (1773 to 1784), Huntingdon (1788), Westmoreland (1783, 1786), Fayette (1785, 1786) Allegheny (1791), Washington (1786), and Census of Bedford (1784) and Westmoreland (1783). *Edited by . . . Harrisburg, Pa. 1898. pp. XI, 782.* = *Pennsylvania Archives. Third series, vol. XXII.* [3986

Guss, A. L.: Remember the days of old. An historical lecture delivered at the ,,Farewell Meeting" held in the old Lutheran Church in Huntingdon, Pa., on the evening of May 1st, 1876. *Published by request. Huntingdon, Pa.: The Globe Office 1876. pp. 55.* [3987

Jones, U. J.: History of the early settlement of the Juniata Valley: *embracing an account of the early pioneers, and the trials and privations incident to the settlement of the valley, predatory incursions, massacres, and abductions by the Indians during the French and Indian Wars, and the War of the Revolution, &c. Harrisburg, Pa.: Harrisburg Publishing Co. 1889. pp. 429, ill.* [3988

Jordan, John W.: A history of the Juniata Valley and ist people. *Under the editorial supervision of . . . 3 vols. New York, N. Y.: Lewis Historical Publishing Co. 1913. pp. (5), 496; 497—944; 945—1403, ill.* [Huntingdon County. *pp. 68—94.]* [3989

Lytle, Milton Scott: History of Huntingdon County in the State of Pennsylvania from the earliest times to the centennial

anniversary of American independence, July 4, 1876. *Lancaster, Pa.: William H. Roy 1876. pp. XIV, (2), 17—361, ill.* [3990

Rupp, I. Daniel: History and topography of Northumberland, Huntingdon, Mifflin, Centre, Union, Columbia, Juniata and Clinton Counties, Pa., *embracing local and general events, leading incidents, descriptions of the principal boroughs, towns, villages, etc., etc. with a copious appendix: embellished by engravings. Compiled from authentic sources. Lancaster, Pa.: G. Hills 1847. pp. 574, ill.* [3991

Historic Huntingdon 1767—1909. *Souvenir edition. Being a brief account of the history of Huntingdon from its earliest settlements to the present day, comprising many historical facts, now published for the first time, regarding its formation, divisions and government, together with its military, educational and industrial progress. Sept. 5—11, 1909. Published by the Historical Committee of the Old Home Week Association. Huntingdon, Pa.: Press of the Monitor Co. 1909. pp. 183, ill., map.* [3992

Historical sketch of the Huntingdon Reformed Church. *Beginning with the granting of a site by the founder of the town and continuing to the present time. Portraits of the pastors during the past forty years. Officers of the various organizations. List of members. Huntingdon, Pa.: J. C. Blair Co. 1906. pp. 5—32, ill.* [3993

Juniata County

Bressler, John F.: Mennonite churches of Snyder and Juniata Counties, Pa. *In: Christian Monitor. A monthly magazine for the home. Vol. XXIII, no. 7. Scottdale, Pa. 1931. pp. 208—209, ill.* [3994

Holman, W. H. J.: History of Messiah Evangelical Lutheran congregation of the Borough of Mifflintown, Juniata County, Pa. *Mifflintown, Pa. 1903. pp. 90. ill.* [3995

Jordan, John W.: A history of the Juniata Valley and its people. *Under the editorial supervision of . . . 3 vols. New York, N. Y.: Lewis Historical Publishing Co. 1913. pp. (5), 496; 497—944; 945—1403, ill.* [Juniata County. *pp. 142—180.]* [3996

Rupp, I. Daniel: History and topography of Northumberland, Huntingdon, Mifflin, Centre, Union, Columbia, Juniata and Clinton Counties, Pa., *embracing local and general events, leading incidents, descriptions of the principal boroughs, towns, villages, etc., etc. with a copious appendix: embellished by engravings. Compiled from authentic sources by . . . Lancaster, Pa.: G. Hills 1847. pp. 574, ill.* [3997

Commemorative biographical encyclopedia of the Juniata Valley, comprising the Counties of Huntingdon, Mifflin, Juniata and Perry, Pa. *Containing sketches of prominent and representative citizens and many of the early settlers. Chambersburg, Pa.: J. M. Runk & Co. 1897. pp. VII, 682, ill.; 683—1375, ill.* [3998

Lancaster County

Alspach, T. A.: Souvenir of the seventy-fifth anniversary of the founding of St. Paul's Reformed Church, Duke and Orange streets, Lancaster, Pa. 1850—1925. *Lancaster, Pa.: Lancaster Press Inc. 1925. pp. 46, ill.* [3999

Bausmann, Lottie M.: The liberality of Lancaster County, 1793—94. *In: Papers and Addresses of the Lancaster County Historical Society. Vol. XIX. Lancaster, Pa. 1915. pp. 315—325.* [4000

— Transportation troubles in Lancaster County during the Revolution. *In: Papers and Addresses of the Lancaster County Historical Society. Vol. XIX. Lancaster, Pa. 1915. pp. 333—345.* [4001

— A bibliography of Lancaster County, Pa. 1745—1912. *Publication of the Pennsylvania Federation of Historical Societies. Philadelphia, Pa.: Patterson & White Co. 1916. pp. IV, 460.* [4002

Beck, Abraham Reinke: The Moravian graveyards of Lititz, Pa. 1744—1905. *In: Transactions of the Moravian Historical Society. Vol. VII. Nazareth, Pa. 1906. pp. 217—321;* Index to the Moravian graveyards of Lititz, Pa. *pp. 323—336.* [4003

Beck, Herbert H.: Lititz as an early musical centre. *In: Papers and Addresses of the Lancaster County Historical Society. Vol. XIX. Lancaster, Pa. 1915. pp. 71—81.* [4004

Beck, Herbert H.: The military hospital at Lititz, 1777—1778. *In: Papers and Addresses of the Lancaster County Historical Society. Vol. XXIII. Lancaster, Pa. 1918. pp. 5—14.* [4005

— The story of Shultz's mill on Beaver Creek. *In: Papersand Addresses of the Lancaster County Historical Society. Vol. XXXI. Lancaster, Pa. 1927. pp. 97—100.* [4006

— Augustine Herrman, Lancaster County's first map maker. *In: Papers and Addresses of the Lancaster County Historical Society. Vol. XXXV. Lancaster Co., Pa. 1931. pp. 261—266, map. [See nos. 613—620]* [4007

Bomberger, Henry H.: Pioneers and transportation on Newport road. *In: Papers and Addresses of the Lancaster County Historical Society. Vol. XXXVI. Lancaster, Pa. 1932. pp. 101—110, ill.* [4008

[Bradford, Arthur B.]: First settlement of Columbia. *From M. S. S. documents of the Historical Society of Pennsylvania. In: Hazard's Register of Pennsylvania. Vol. IX. Philadelphia, Pa. 1832. pp. 113—115; 145—148.* [4009

Brickenstein, H. A.: Sketch of the early history of Lititz, 1742—75. *In: Transactions of the Moravian Historical Society. Vol. II. Nazareth, Pa. 1886. pp. 343—374.* [4010

Bruning, Mary J.: The Conestoga Collegiate Institute and ist founder. *In: Papers and Addresses of the Lancaster County Historical Society. Vol. XXXV. Lancaster, Pa. 1931. pp. 227—229, ill.* [4011

Burkholder, Joseph C.: Benedict Brechbuhl, Hans Burkholder and the Swiss Mennonite migration to Lancaster County, Penna. The Swiss emigration. *In: Papers and Addresses of the Lancaster County Historical Society. Vol. XXXI. Lancaster, Pa. 1927. pp. 57—62.* [4012

Byrne, Jacob Hill: Typical old Lancaster buildings and architecture. *In: Papers and Addresses of the Lancaster County Historical Society. Vol. XXVI. Lancaster, Pa. 1922. pp. 138—143.* [4013

— The old graveyard between Walnut, Chestnut, Lime, and Cherry streets, Lancaster City, Pa. *In: Papers and Addresses of the Lancaster County Historical Society. Vol. XXXIV. Lancaster, Pa. 1930. pp. 25—30.* [4014

Carmichael, H. I.: Re-opening of church and dedication of pipe organ, Custer memorial pews and memorial windows in the Immanuel U. E. Church, Adamstown, Pa., Sunday, March 20th, 1927. *[s. l. 1927.] pp. 28.* [4015

Christ, Henry S.: Souvenir of St. Joseph's Catholic Church. 1849—1924. *Lancaster, Pa.: The Manor Press 1924. pp. (16), ill.* [4016

Clare, Israel Smith: A brief history of Lancaster County, with special reference to the growth and development of its institutions, designed for the school and home. *Edited by* **A. Lyle**. *Lancaster, Pa.: Argus Publishing Co. 1892. pp. VII, 317, ill., 3 maps.* [4017

— Lancaster County history. *In: The Pennsylvania-German. Vol. X. Lititz, Pa. 1909. pp. 198—209.* [4018

Clark, Martha B.: Some early Lancaster notables — Valentine Krug; John Jacob Krug; Caspar Sniger, jr., John Dehuff. — *In: Papers and Addresses of the Lancaster County Historical Society. Vol. VIII. Lancaster, Pa. 1904. pp. 3— 13.* [4019

Conyngham, Redmond: Historical sketches *(relating to the history of Lancaster County) containing facts not generally known, compiled by* . . . *In: Notes and Queries. Edited by* **W. H. Egle**. *Fourth series, vol. II. 1894. Harrisburg, Pa. 1895. pp. 9—11; 20—22; 24—29; 30— 32; 34—37; 47—49; 54—56; 58—62; 64—67; 69—71; 74—78; 82—85; 91— 95; 109—113; 124—126; 133—135; 140—141.* [4020

Cramer, W. Stuart: History of the First Reformed Church, Lancaster, Pa. 1736 —1904. *Prepared by* . . . *Authorized by the Consistory. Vol. I. Lancaster, Pa.: Wickersham Printing Co. 1904. pp. XV, (1), 171, ill.* [4021

— In commemoration of the Sesqui-Centennial First Reformed Church, Lancaster, Penna, July 4th, 1926. *[s. l. 1926.] pp. 16.* [4022

[Croll, P. C. - Redsecker, J. H.]: Historical pilgrimages into Pennsylvania-Germandom. Through the state's garden county. *In: The Pennsylvania-German. Vol. I, no 2. Lebanon, Pa. 1900. pp. 22— 42, ill.*
[See no. 295] [4023

— Historical pilgrimages into Pennsylvania-Germandom. Up the historic Susquehanna. *In: The Pennsylvania-*

German. Vol. I, no. 3. Lebanon, Pa. 1900. pp. 21—39, ill.
[See no. 295] [4024

De Long, Irwin Hoch: Inscriptions of the tombstones in Carpenter's graveyard, Lancaster County, Pa. *[left of the road from Paradise to Strasburg.] In: National Genealogical Society Quarterly. Vol. XIV. Washington, D. C. 1925. pp. 33 —39.* [4025

Demuth, Henry C.: Demuth's 1770. The history of a Lancaster tradition. Being a brief history of the Demuth of a Lancaster tobacco shop, which was founded at Lancaster in the Province of Pennsylvania in the year of our Lord 1770. *[s. l.] 1925. pp. 16, ill.* [4026

[Diffenderffer, Frank Ried]: The three Earls. *An historical sketch and proceedings of the Centennial Jubilee, held at New Holland, Pa., July 4, 1876. New Holland, Pa.: Ranck & Sandoe 1876. pp. 115.*
[Historical sketch prepared by **Frank R. Diffenderffer**. *pp. 17—76; Appendix: pp. 77—95.]* [4027

— New Holland school house. *How (it) was built. In: Papers and Addresses of the Lancaster County Historical Society. Vol. II. Lancaster, Pa. 1898. pp. 181— 212.* [4028

— A new Ephrata imprint — Donegal Lancaster. *In: Papers and Addresses of the Lancaster County Historical Society. Vol. V. Lancaster, Pa. 1901. pp. 134—143.* [4029

— The Philadelphia and Lancaster turnpike; and biographical sketch of Col. Matthias Slough. *In: Papers and Addresses of the Lancaster County Historical Society. Vol. VI. Lancaster, Pa. 1902. pp. 116—149.* [4030

— Early Lancaster playbills and playhouses. *In: Papers and Addresses of the Lancaster County Historical Society. Vol. VII. Lancaster, Pa. 1903. pp. 24 —43; Notes on the same subject by* **S. M. Sener**. *pp. 43—45.* [4031

— Politics 75 years ago. Letters of Hon. Amos Ellmaker to Thaddeus Stevens. *In: Papers and Addresses of the Lancaster County Historical Society. Vol. VIII. Lancaster, Pa. 1904. pp. 36—47.* [4032

— The early settlement and population of Lancaster County and City. *In: Papers* and *Addresses of the Lancaster County Historical Society. Vol. IX. Lancaster, Pa. 1905. pp. 151—171.* [4033

Diffenderffer, Frank Ried: The story of a picture. *In: Papers and Addresses of the Lancaster County Historical Society. Vol. IX. Lancaster, Pa. 1905. pp. 182 —230, ill.* [4034

— Date stones, with examples. *In: Papers and Addresses of the Lancaster County Historical Society. Vol. IX. Lancaster, Pa. 1905. pp. 359—385.* [4035

— An early road petition. *In: Papers and Addresses of the Lancaster County Historical Society. Vol. X. Lancaster, Pa. 1906 pp. 145—156.* [4036

— The last one. *(Fulling mill.) In: Papers and Addresses of the Lancaster County*

— *Historical Society. Vol. X. Lancaster, Pa. 1906. pp. 295—303, ill.* [4037

— Historical sketch of the Lancaster County Agricultural and Horticultural Society from its organisation on September 3, 1866, until 1905. *Prepared for and read before the Society at the annual meeting on the last mentioned date. Lancaster, Pa.: The New Era Printing Co. 1911. pp. 22.* [4038

— A history of the Farmers Bank of Lancaster, the Farmers National Bank and the Farmers Trust Company of Lancaster. 1810—1910. *Lancaster, Pa.: Published by the Farmers Trust Company of Lancaster 1910. Lancaster, Pa.: Wickersham Printing Co. 1910. pp. 228.* [4039

— Some historical mistakes corrected *(concerning Reformed Church at Maytown). In: Papers and Addresses of the Lancaster County Historical Society. Vol. XXI. Lancaster, Pa. 1917. pp. 143— 144.* [4040

Dorley, Anthony F.: Historical sketch of St. Anthony's Church, Lancaster, Penna., 1870—1895. Together with a history of Sacred Heart Academy and St., Anthony's parochial school in commemoration of the silver jubilee year, 1895. *Lancaster, Pa.: Lancaster Lithographing Co. 1895. pp. 75, ill.* [4041

Drepperd, Carl W.: A glimpse of Lancaster in 1802. *Michaud's record. In: Papers and Addresses of the Lancaster County Historical Society. Vol. XXVI. Lancaster Pa. 1922. pp. 89—91.* [4042

— Lancaster City in 1843. *In: Papers and Addresses of the Lancaster County Hi-*

storical Society. Vol. XXVI. Lancaster, Pa. 1922. pp. 93—99, map. [4043

Dubbs, Joseph Henry: The names of the townships. *In: Papers and Addresses of the Lancaster county Historical Society. Vol. I. Lancaster, Pa. 1897. pp. 3—13.* [4044

— Earliest Reformed Church in Lancaster County. *In: Papers and Addresses of the Lancaster County Historical Society. Vol. V. Lancaster, Pa. 1901. pp. 3—16.* [4045

— Rustic art in Lancaster County. *In: Papers and Addresses of the Lancaster County Historical Society. Vol. VII. Lancaster, Pa. 1903. pp. 17—20.* [4046

— Lancaster book plates. *In: Papers and Addresses of the Lancaster County Historical Society. Vol. VIII. Lancaster, Pa. 1904. pp. 29—35.* [4047

E., S.: Marriage licenses at Lancaster 1791— 1799. *(Copied from a book in the Quarter Sessions office in Lancaster.) In: Notes and Queries. Edited by W. H. Egle. Third series, vol. I. 1884—1887. Harrisburg, Pa. 1887. pp. 531—534; 536—537; 542—544; 546—547; Reprint in: Third series, vol. II. Harrisburg, Pa. 1896. pp. 297—301; 304—306; 311—313; 316 —318.* [4048

Egle, William Henry: Provincial papers. Proprietary and state tax lists of the County of Lancaster, for the years 1771, 1772, 1773, 1779 and 1782. *Edited by ... Harrisburg, Pa. 1898. pp. VIII, 896. = Pennsylvania Archives. Third series, vol. XVII.* [4049

Ellis, Franklin and **Evans, Samuel:** History of Lancaster County, Pennsylvania, *with biographical sketches of many of its pioneers and prominent men. Philadelphia, Pa.: Everts & Peck 1883. pp. VIII, 1101, ill, map.* [4050

Erisman, George F. K.: Rope making in Lancaster, Pa. at the Martin rope walk. *In: Papers and Addresses of the Lancaster County Historical Society. Vol. XXXI. Lancaster, Pa. 1927. pp. 47— 52.* [4051

Eshleman H. Frank: The birth of Lancaster County. *In: Papers and Addresses of the Lancaster County Historical Society Vol. XII. Lancaster, Pa. 1908. pp. 5 —39.* [4052

— Early Lancaster taxables — 1754. *In: Papers and Addresses of the Lancaster County Historical Society. Vol. XIII. Lancaster, Pa. 1909. pp. 263—277.*

[„List of German taxables, property-holders etc., in Lancaster Borough, 1754." pp. 270—277.] [4053

Eshleman, H. Frank - Hostetter, A. K. - Steigerwalt, Chas.: Report of true character, time and place of the first regular settlement in Lancaster County. In: Papers and Addresses of the Lancaster County Historical Society. Vol. XIV. Lancaster, Pa. 1910. pp. 21—71, 3 maps. [4054

— Address delivered Sept. 8, 1910 at the Bi-Centennial celebration of Lancaster County's first settlement. In: Papers and Addresses of the Lancaster County Historical Society. Vol. XIV. Lancaster, Pa. 1910. Appendix. pp. 29. [4055

— The meaning of Lancaster County's two hundred years of history. 1710—1910. Papers delivered Sept. 8, 1910, at Willow Street, Lancaster County, Pa. on the occasion of observance of the 200th anniversary of the first settlement in Lancaster County, Pa. In: The Pennsylvania-German. Vol. XII. Lititz, Pa. 1911. pp. 1—14. [4056

— Early Columbia and vicinity. In: Papers and Addresses of the Lancaster County Historical Society. Vol. XVIII. Lancaster, Pa. 1914. pp. 29—41. [4057

— Map of old „Conestoga", earliest settlement on Conestoga River 1715 to 1729. (Circa). In: Papers and Addresses of the Lancaster County Historical Society. Vol. XIX. Lancaster, Pa. 1915. Between pp. 292 and 293; key to map of land-owners. p. 292. [4058

— Assessment lists and other documents of Lancaster County prior to the year 1729. In: Papers and Addresses of the Lancaster County Historical Society. Vol. XX. Lancaster, Pa. 1916. pp. 155—194. [4059

— Items in the Pennsylvania Gazette concerning Lancaster County. In: Papers and Addresses of the Lancaster County Historical Society.: 1734—1750. In: Vol. XXII. 1918. pp. 21—26; 1750—1760. In: Vol. XXIII. 1919. pp. 133—148; 1761—1770. In: Vol. XXIV. 1920. pp. 5—25; 1771—1775. In: Vol. XXV. 1921. pp. 41—51. 1776—1781. In: Vol. XXVI 1922. pp. 3—17. [4060

— The legislative career of Emanuel Carpenter. In: Papers and Addresses of the Lancaster County Historical Society. Vol. XXIV. Lancaster, Pa. 1920. pp. 153—168. [4061

Eshleman, H. Frank: Early Lancaster County history in the Provincial Records and Archives. 1727—1750. Compiled by . . . Read by Ben. B. Lippold. In: Papers and Addresses of the Lancaster County Historical Society. Vol. XXVI. Lancaster, Pa. 1922. pp. 19—35. [4062

— History of Lancaster County's highway system. (From 1714 to 1760.) In: Papers and Addresses of the Lancaster County Historical Society. Vol. XXVI. Lancaster, Pa. 1922. pp. 37—80, map. [4063

— Maps and pictures of old Lancaster. Report to the Society of an exhibition of pictures. By the committee on entertainment, H. Frank Eshleman, Pres . . . In: Papers and Addresses of the Lancaster County Historical Society. Vol. XXVI. Lancaster, Pa. 1922. pp. 127—132, maps. [4064

— A running story of Lancaster County from Hazard's Register (1613 to 1835). Compiled by . . . . In: Papers and Addresses of the Lancaster County Historical Society. Vol. XXVII. Lancaster, Pa. 1923. pp. 39—70. [4065

— Four great surveys in Lancaster County. [The John Estaugh and Co. tract 1716/17; Land on Pequea below Beaver Creek 1728; The Amos Strettle tract; Tract in west side of Little Conestoga 1734.] In: Papers and Addresses of the Lancaster County Historical Society. Vol. XXVIII. Lancaster, Pa. 1924. pp. 9—14, 4 maps. [4066

— Lancaster County history in the several series of the Pennsylvania Archives and other provincial and state source books. In: Papers and Addresses of the Lancaster County Historical Society. Vol. XXIX. Lancaster, Pa. 1925. pp. 23—32. [4067

— Lancaster County in province, state and nation. (A Bi-Centennial Review). In: Papers and Addresses of the Lancaster County Historical Society. Vol. XXXIII. Lancaster, Pa. 1929. pp. 21—43; 45—63. [4068

Evans, Samuel: Contributions to Lancaster County genealogy. In: Notes and Queries. Edited by W. H. Egle. Fourth series, vol. I. 1891—1893. Harrisburg, Pa. 1893. pp. 109—110; 112—113; p. 118; pp. 140—141; 144—145; 148—149; 151—152; 155—156; 158—160; 167—168.

23*

[Genealogical data relating mostly to English and Scotch-Irish families, but a few German ones.] [4069

Evans, Samuel: When was Strasburgh erected into a twonship. *In: Papers and Addresses of the Lancaster County Historical Society. Vol. I. 1896—1897. Lancaster, Pa. 1897. pp. 146—149.* [4070

[Falkenstein, G. N. and **Reber, D. C.]:** History of the Church of the Brethren of the Eastern District of Pennsylvania. *By the Committee appointed by District Conference. Lancaster, Pa.: Press of the New Era Printing Co. 1915. pp. XVII, 670, ill.* [4071

Flickinger, S. H.: Early settlers of Lancaster County, Pa. *(List of Lancaster County settlers who came between the years 1700 and 1718 and had purchased and held lands there before 1729). In: Genealogy. Journal of American ancestry. Vol. II. New York, N. Y. 1912. p. 220.* [4072

— Lancaster tombstone inscriptions. *(From the family graveyard on the Paul farm, along Indian Creek, West Cocalico Township, Lancaster Co., Pa.) In: Genealogy. Journal of American ancestry. Vol. II. New York, N. Y. 1912. p. 270.* [4073

— Marriage licenses in Lancaster, Pennsylvania, 1791—1799. *In: Genealogy. Journal of American ancestry. Vol. II. New York, N. Y. 1912. pp. 308—309; Vol. III. 1913. pp. 3—4; p. 21; 71; pp. 97—98. Vol. IV. pp. 13—14; 67—69.* [4074

Franklin, Walter M.: The people who made Lancaster County. *In: Papers and Addresses of the Lancaster County Historical Society. Vol. I. Lancaster, Pa. 1897. pp. 181—203.* [4075

— Historical points of interest along the Strasburg trolley road. *In: Papers and Addresses of the Lancaster County Historical Society. Vol. VII. Lancaster, Pa. 1903. pp. 3—14.* [4076

Fry, Harold Curtis: Union churches in Lancaster County, Pa. *Thesis of M. of Sacred Theology, Lutheran Theological Seminary, Gettysburg, Pa. 1930. Typewritten. pp. 278, (5).* [4077

Gerhard, D. W.: A history of the New Holland charge of the Reformed Church in Lancaster County, Pa. *New Holland, Pa.: Ranck & Sandoe 1877. pp. V, 7—140.* [4078

Goll, George Philip: Leaves from a century plant. The history of the St. John's

Evangelical Lutheran Church. Maytown, Lancaster County, Pa. 1765—1904. *Authorized by the Church Council. Lancaster, Pa.: Wickersham Printing Co. 1904. pp. XI, (4), 181, ill.* [4079

Gossler, Jacob L.: An old turnpike road with mere mention of some persons and places incident thereto. *Printed for private distribution. New York, N. Y.: The Baker & Taylor Co. 1888. pp. 122.* [4080

Gotwald, W. V.: History of St. John's Evangelical Lutheran Church, Lancaster, Pa., Sept. 22 d, 1867. *Lancaster, Pa.: Inquirer Book and Job Printing Office 1868. pp. 23.* [4081

[Groff, Michael W.]: Record of deaths kept by Michael Groff of West Earl Township, Lancaster County, Pa. *Published by his friends. Farmersville, Pa.: E. H. Burkholder 1884. pp. 29.* [4082

Hark, J. Max: An historical sketch of the old Moravian chapel, Lancaster, Pa. *Read at the reopening Sept. 30, 1890. pp. . . . .* [4083

Harris, Alex: A biographical history of Lancaster County: *being a history of early settlers and eminent men of the county; as also much other unpublished historical information, chiefly of a local character. Lancaster, Pa.: Elias Barr & Co. 1872. pp. V, 638.* [4084

Hart, Francis P.: Reminiscences of the Moravian Church, at Lititz, Penn'a., the Centennial exercises of August 13—14, 1887, and an appendix *containing notes, incidents, biographical sketches of all the ministers who served the church from the Count Zinzendorf down to the present. — Some of the old time customs, missionary work, etc. Lititz, Pa.: Record Steam Print 1887. pp. (1), 63.* [4085

Hassler, Jno. W.: Memorial volume of the Evangelical Lutheran Church, New Holland, Lancaster County, Pa. *An historical discourse delivered at the one hundred and fiftieth anniversary of the congregation. With additional historical particulars. From A. D. 1730 to 1880. New Holland, Pa.: Geo. H. Ranck 1880. pp. 64.* [4086

Hay, Ellis S.: One hundred and thirty and three years. Sketch of the Reformed Church of Maytown, Pa. *Marietta, Pa.: The Times Printing House 1898. pp. VI, 7—66, ill.* [4087

Hensel, Leander T.: The ark: a famous last century mansion. *In: Papers and Addresses of the Lancaster County Historical*

Society. Vol. II. Lancaster, Pa. 1898. pp. 146—156. [4088
Hensel, Leander T.: An old oil mill. *(Eden Township.) In: Papers and Addresses of the Lancaster County Historical Society. Vol. II. Lancaster, Pa. 1898. pp. 213—215.* [4089
[Hensel, W. U.]: Resources and industries of the City of Lancaster, Lancaster County, Pa., *with some account of its historical importance: its advantages of location: plan of city government: its churches and schools; literary and social life. Together with compendium and statistics illustrating the growth and extent of its commercial and manufacturing interests; its railroad connections and its public conveniences and also the organization of its Board of Trade and the preeminent inducements offered for the establishment here of new industrial enterprises. An abstract and brief chronicle of the time. Compiled and published for the Lancaster Board of Trade. Lancaster, Pa. 1887. pp. IX, 98. Part. II.* Some representative business interests of Lancaster, Pa. *1887. pp. V, 72.* [4090
— Lancaster in 1777—1780. *In: Papers and Addresses of the Lancaster County Historical Society. Vol. VIII. Lancaster, Pa. 1904. pp. 230—236.* [4091
— Tour through the northeastern section of Lancaster County. *In: Papers and Addresses of the Lancaster County Historical Society. Vol. VIII. Lancaster, Pa. 1904. pp. 256—266.* [4092
— „Trinity and the town." *An address delivered at the 150th anniversary celebration of the laying of the corner stone of Trinity Lutheran Church, Lancaster, Pa. [s. l. 1911.] pp. 12.* [4093
— A withered twig. Dark lantern glimpses into the operation of Know Nothingism in Lancaster sixty years ago. *In: Papers and Addresses of the Lancaster County Historical Society. Vol. XIX. Lancaster, Pa. 1915. pp. 174—181.* [4094
Herz, D. R.: History of Ephrata, Penna. *Giving a brief sketch of the settlement of the state and county, the Battle of Brandwine, the cloister and monument to be erected at Mount Zion and the Borough of Ephrata. Philadelphia, Pa.: H. Ferkler 1894. pp. 80, ill.*
= *Patriots Day, Ephrata, Penna., Sept. 11th, 1894.*
Second edition . . . Sept. 11th, 1895. pp. 32; 80, ill. [4095

Hildebrand, Jacob: Reminiscences of Strasburg. *In: Papers and Addresses of the Lancaster County Historical Society. Vol. I. Lancaster, Pa. 1897. pp. 97—108.* [4096
Hiller, Caspar: Conestoga, reminiscences of an old township. *In: Papers and Addresses of the Lancaster County Historical Society. Vol. I. Lancaster, Pa. 1897. pp. 24—26.* [4097
Hinke, William J.: History of Swamp and Muddy Creek congregations. *In: Rev. John Waldschmidt memorial 1724—1786. Monument erected under the auspices of the Swamp Reformed Church, unveiled and dedicated, Sunday, Oct. 17, 1915. Reading, Pa. 1915 [= no. 7627]. pp. 20—29.* [4098
— The Reformed Church in Lancaster County during the eighteenth century. *Read at Swamp Church, Sept. 29, 1929 and at a meeting of the Lancaster County Historical Society, Oct. 4, 1929. In: Papers and Addresses of the Lancaster County Historical Society. Vol. XXXIII. Lancaster, Pa. 1929. pp. 149—158.* [4099
— History of the Muddy Creek Reformed congregation. *Address delivered in the Muddy Creek Reformed Church, Oct. 2, 1932. In: Papers read before the Lancaster County Historical Society, Vol. XXXVI, No. 11, Lancaster, Pa. 1932. pp. 272—295, ill.* [4100
Hoffman, H. M.: John Vogan, founder of Voganville. *In: Papers and Addresses of the Lancaster County Historical Society. Vol. XXIV. Lancaster, Pa. 1920. pp. 211—213.* [4101
Hostetter, Albert K.: Early history of Penn Square. *In: Papers and Addresses of the Lancaster County Historical Society. Vol. XXVI. Lancaster, Pa. 1922. pp. 133—135.* [4102
— The Survivor's Club. *In: Papers and Addresses of the Lancaster County Historical Society. Vol. XXVII. Lancaster, Pa. 1923. pp. 133—142.* [4103
Houston, J. W.: Flax culture in Lancaster County. *In: Papers and Addresses of the Lancaster County Historical Society. Vol. IV. Lancaster, Pa. 1900. pp. 155—168.* [4104
Huber, Levi B.: Two hundred years of farming in Lancaster County. *In: Papers and Addresses of the Lancaster County Historical Society. Vol. XXXV. Lancaster Pa. 1931. pp. 97—110.* [4105
Hunter, J. V. R. - Steinmetz, Mary Owen: Muster rolls of soldiers from Lancaster

County in the war of 1812. *In: Papers and Addresses of the Lancaster County Historical Society. Vol. XXXVI. Lancaster, Pa. 1932. pp. 161—165.* [4106

I., W. E.: Tombstone records of Lutheran and Reformed graveyard, Elizabethville, Pa. *In: Notes and Queries. Edited by W. H. Egle. Annual vol. 1897. Harrisburg, Pa. 1898. pp. 167—169.* [4107

Jordan, John W.: Moravian Church at Lancaster. *[List of pastors] 1748—1870. In: Notes and Queries. Edited by W. H. Egle. Third series, vol. II. 1887—1890. Harrisburg, Pa. 1891. p. 349; Reprint in: Third series, vol. III. Harrisburg, Pa. 1896. pp. 417—418.* [4108

— The military hospital at Bethlehem and Lititz during the Revolution. *In: The Pennsylvania Magazine of History and Biography. Vol. XX. Philadelphia, Pa. 1896. pp. 137—157.* [4109

— Retrun of the sick at Lititz hospital, August 23, 1778. *In: The Pennsylvania Magazine of History and Biography. Vol. XXXVI. Philadelphia, Pa. 1912. pp. 379—381.* [4110

— Extracts from Moravian diaries at Bethlehem. *(Relating to early events in Lancaster, Pa.) In: Papers and Addresses of the Lancaster County Historical Society. Vol. XXVII. Lancaster, Pa. 1923. pp. 91—95;* Items from letters: *pp. 96—97.* [4111

[Kaufmann, A. K. and others]: 1812—1912. Souvenir book. Old Home Week and Hope Hose Company No. 1 Centennial. Manheim, Pa., June 30 to July 5, 1912. *Published by the Committee on Printing and Advertising [s. l., 1912.] pp. XVI, 180, ill.* [4112

Kemper E. Charles - Eshleman, H. Frank: Revolutionary pensioners living in Lancaster County, Pennsylvania, in 1840. *By E. Ch. Kemper. In: Papers and Addresses of the Lancaster County Historical Society. Vol. XXVII. Lancaster, Pa. 1923. p. 98;* Notes on the above pensioniers *by H. F. Eshleman. pp. 99—101.* [4113

Klein. H. M. J.: Lancaster's golden century 1821—1921. *A chronicle of men and women who planned and toiled to build a city strong and beautiful. Published by Hager and Co. to commemorate one hundred years of the house of Hager, April, 1921. Lancaster, Pa.: Wickersham Printing Co. 1921. pp. 130, ill.* [4114

Klein, Martin John and **Williams, E. Melvin:** Lancaster County, Pennsylvania, a history. *Editor-in-chief:* H. M. J. Klein; *staff historian* E. Melvin Williams. *4 vols. New York, N. Y. & Chicago, Ill.: Lewis Historical Publishing Co. 1924. pp. VII, 544; 545—1172;* Biographical vols. *3—4: pp. 224: 225—484, ill., maps.* [4115

Klein, Philip S.: Early Lancaster county politics. *In: Pennsylvania history. Official organ of the Pennsylvania Historical Association vol. III. Philadelphia, Pa. 1936. pp. 98—114.* [4115a

Knittle, John F.: Souvenir programm in commemoratum of the 150th anniversary of the founding of Zion Evangelical Church, Manheim, Pa. from Sunday, Sept. 19th, 1920 to Sunday, Sept. 26th, 1920. *[s. l., 1920.] pp. (14), ill.* [4116

Kocher, Alfred L.: The early architecture of Lancaster County. *In: Papers and Addresses of the Lancaster County Historical Society. Vol. XXIV. Lancaster, Pa. 1920. pp. 91—106, ill.* [4117

Kriebel, H. W.: Seeing Lancaster County from a trolley window. *In: The Pennsylvania-German. Vol. X. Lititz, Pa. 1909. pp. 372—382, map.; pp. 417—434; 473—483; 529—540; 611—617, ill. Issued also as separate print: Lititz, Pa.: The Express Printing Co. 1910. pp. 80, ill., map.* [4118

Landis, Charles I.: Major John Andre's German letter. *In: Papers and Addresses of the Lancaster County Historical Society. Vol. XVIII. Lancaster, Pa. 1914. pp. 127—155.* [4119

— Abraham Witmer's bridge. *In: Papers and Addresses of the Lancaster County Historical Society. Vol. XX. Lancaster, Pa. 1916. pp. 155—174, ill.* [4120

— A list of the original Lancaster subscribers to the capital stock of the Philadelphia and Lancaster turnpike. *In: Papers and Addresses of the Lancaster County Historical Society. Vol. XXII. Lancaster, Pa. 1918. pp. 93—100.* [4121

— City Hall and its hlstory. *In: Papers and Addresses of the Lancaster County Historical Society. Vol. XXII. Lancaster, Pa. 1918. pp. 107—122, ill.* [4122

— The beginnings of artificial roads in Pennsylvania. *In: Papers and Addresses of the Lancaster County Historical Socitey. Vol. XXIII.. Lancaster, Pa. 1919. pp. 99—107.* [4123

Landis, David Bachman: The musical and literary organizations and their leaders of Landisville and vicinity. *In: Papers and Addresses of the Lancaster County Historical Society. Vol. X. Lancaster, Pa. 1906. pp. 3—27.* [4124
— How the Landisville Church of God originated. *In: Papers and Addresses of the Lancaster County Historical Society. Vol. XXXIII. Lancaster, Pa. 1929. pp. 169—174.* [4125
Landis, D. H.: Historical sketch of Zion's Reformed Church and also historical items of general interest of Millersville and its environs. *Prepared by the request of the Executive Committee of Zion's Reformed anniversary (held, June 14, 16, and 18, 1922. Millersville, Pa.) Lancaster, Pa.: The Monor Press 1922. pp. 46, ill.* [4126
Landis, David M.: The awakening of the early progress of the Pequea, Conestoga and the other Susquehanna Valley settlement as shown by official letters, etc. of the time. *In: Papers and Addresses of the Lancaster County Historical Society. Vol. XXV. Lancaster, Pa. 1921. pp. 5—16.* [4127
Learned, Marion Dexter: An American ethnographical survey. *In: German American Annals. New series, vol. V. Philadelphia, Pa. 1907. pp. 30—53. Includes:* The preliminary report. „The Conestoga expedition, 1902." *pp. 37—49;* „List of surveys and chart made by the late Jacob Hildebrand, Esq., of Stosberg." *pp. 50—53, map. See no. 2176.* [4128
Lerbscher, August - Cavin, Albert: Items of interest from the Neue Unpartheyische Lancaster Zeitung, und Anzeigs-Nachrichten. *In: Papers and Adresses of the Lancaster County Historical Society. Vol. XXXIV. Lancaster, Pa. 1930. pp. 1—10; 97—107; Vol. XXXV. 1931. pp. 25—36.* [4129
Lesher, Pierce: Remarks on Andrew Ream, Revolutionary pensioner. *In: Papers and Addresses of the Lancaster County Historical Society. Vol. XXVII. Lancaster, Pa. 1923. p. 117.* [4130
— Notes on Reamstown, Lancaster County, Pa. *In: Papers and Addresses of the Lancaster County Historical Society. Vol. XXX. Lancaster, Pa. 1926. pp. 67—71.* [4131
Lippold, John W.: Old Trinity steeple. *In: Papers and Addresses of the Lancaster*

County Historical Society. Vol. XXXI. Lancaster, Pa. 1927. pp. 127—133. [4132
Lippold, John W.: Old Trinity graveyard. *In: Papers and Addresses of the Lancaster County Historical Society. Vol. XXXII. Lancaster, Pa. 1928. pp. 109—117.* [4133
Long, Henry G.: Some early printers. *In: Papers and Addresses of the Lancaster County Historical Society. Vol. III. Lancaster, Pa. 1899. pp. 203—212.* [4134
Lowe, W. J.: Donegal Reformed Church at Milton Grove; Maytown Reformed Church at Maytown. *In: Papers and Addresses of the Lancaster County Historical Society. Vol. XXII. Lancaster, Pa. 1918. pp. 35—50, ill.* [4135
Magee, D. F.: Grandfathers' clocks: *Their making and their makers in Lancaster County. In: Papers and Addresses of the Lancaster County Historical Society. Vol. XXI. Lancaster, Pa. 1917. pp. 63—77.* [4136
Martin, C. H.: Provincial, continental and federal revenues of Lancaster County, Pa. *In: Papers and Addresses of the Lancaster County Historical Society. Vol. XXV. Lancaster, Pa. 1921. pp. 27—38.* [4137
— Early federal revenues of Lancaster County, Pa. *In: Papers and Adresses of the Lancaster County Historical Society. Vol. XXVI. Lancaster, Pa. 1922. pp. 25—32.* [4138
— Federal revenus of Lancaster County, Pa. From about 1850 to date. *In: Papers and Addresses of the Lancaster County Historical Society. Vol. XXVI. Lancaster, Pa. 1923. pp. 107—116, ill.* [4139
Mayser, F. P.: Kurzgefaßte Geschichte der Deutschen Evangelisch - Lutherischen Zions-Gemeinde zu Lancaster, Pa. *Auf Beschluß des Kirchenraths als Beitrag zum 75 Jahresfest der Einweihung der ersten Kirche zusammengestellt. Lancaster, Pa.: Lancaster Printing and Publishing Co. 1903. 50 S., ill.* [4140
[—] 1827. The Centennial of the founding of Zion Lutheran congregation, Lancaster, Pa., May 1—8, 1927. *Containing the congregation's autobiography, cuts of its pastors and church. Crders of services for the celebration of its Centennial and a chronological table of its history. Lancaster, Pa.: Press of the Conestoga Publishing Co. 1927. pp. (16), ill.* [4141

McClure, David: Lancaster in 1772. *In: Papers and Addresses of the Lancaster County Historical Society. Vol. V. Lancaster, Pa. 1901. pp. 106—112.* [4142

Mombert, J. I.: An authentic history of Lancaster County in the State of Pennsylvania. *Lancaster, Pa.: J. E. Barr & Co. 1869. pp. VIII, 617; 175, ill., maps.* [4143

[Müller, Susanna]: An old German midwife's record. *(Kept by Susanna Müller, of Providence Township, Lancaster County, Pa. during the years 1791 —1815.) Edited by M. D. Learned and C. F. Brede. In: German American Annals. New series, vol. I. Philadelphia, Pa. 1903. pp. 73—96; 156—177, ill.* [4144

Nevin, Wilberforce: A comparison of Lancaster, England, and Lancaster, Pennsylvania. *Written in 1880 in Lancaster, England, for the Philadelphia Press of which he was the associate editor. Reprint made by Walter C. Hager. [s. l., s. d.] pp. 8.* [4145

[Parthemore, E. W. S.]: Register of marriage and baptisms kept by the Rev. Traugott Frederick Illing in connection with the churches of St. Peter's (Lutheran), Middletown and Caernarvon, (Episcopal), Lancaster County, Pa. *Harrisburg, Pa.: Harrisburg Publishing Co. 1891. pp. 43.* [4146

Phelps, E. J.: Souvenir of St. Joseph's Church, Lancaster, Pa. *Lancaster, Pa.: The New Era Printing Co. 1897. pp. 42, ill.* [4147

— Historical and illustrated sketch of Lancaster, Penna. *Published by . . . Lancaster, Pa.: The New Era Print. 1897. pp. 118, ill.* [4148

Rauck, Geo. H.: Historical sketch of Trinity Lutheran Sunday school, New Holland. *Read at jubilee-anniversary, June 7, 1903. New Holland, Pa.: The Clarion Printing Co. 1903. pp. 11.* [4149

Reuß, Francis X.: Catholic chronicles of Lancaster County, Pa.: *Some data relating to St. Peter's Church at Columbia, Pa., being a supplementary to and corrective of the sketch of that church published in vol. IV of these records in 1893. In: Records of the American Catholic Historical Society of Philadelphia. Vol. IX. Philadelphia, Pa. 1898. pp. 210—222.* [4150

— A contribution of the history of St. Peter's Church, Columbia, Lancaster Coun-

ty, Pa. *Part III. In: Records of the American Catholic Historical Society. of Philadelphia. Vol. XVI. Philadelphia, Pa. 1905. pp. 187—201.* [4151

Riddle, William: The early school systems of Lancaster City. *In: Papers and Addresses of the Lancaster County Historical Society. Vol. VIII. Lancaster, Pa. 1904. pp. 183—210.* [4152

— One hundred and fifty years of school history in Lancaster, Pa. *Lancaster, Pa. The New Era Printing Co. 1905. pp. XIX, 442, ill.* [4153

— Cherrished memoires of old Lancaster Town and Shire. *Lancaster, Pa.: Intelligencer Printing House 1910. pp. VII, 334, ill.* [4154

— The story of Lancaster: old and new. Being a narrative history of Lancaster, Pa. from 1730 to the Centennial year 1918. *Lancaster, Pa.: The New Era Printing Co. 1917. pp. XV, 292, ill.* [4155

Roddy, H. Justin: Physical and industrial geography of Lancaster County, Pa. *Lancaster, Pa.: The New Era Printing Co. 1916. pp. VI, 113, ill., maps.* [4156

Rupp, I. Daniel: History of Lancaster County. *To which is prefixed a brief sketch of the early history of Pennsylvania. Compiled from authentic sources. Lancaster, Penn.: Gilbert Hills 1844. pp. 524, ill.* [4157

Schaeffer, C. F. and Muhlenberg, F. A.: Memorial volume of the Evangelical Lutheran Church of the Holy Trinity, Lancaster, Pa. *Discourses delivered on the occasion of the Centenary Jubilee with additional historical particulars. From A. D. 1761—1861. Lancaster, Pa.: John Baer's Sons 1861. pp. VIII, 144, ill.* [4158

Schantz, F. J. F.: History of the Brickerville congregation in Lancaster County, Pa. *In: Papers and Addresses of the Lancaster County Historical Society. Vol. III. Lancaster, Pa. 1899. pp. 57—99.* [4159

Sener, Samuel M.: Historical sketch of the ancient parish of St. Mary's, Lancaster, Pa. *Reprinted from: U. S. Catholic Historical Magazine 1887. pp. 12.* [4160

— Additional historical notes in reference to St. Mary's at Lancaster. *[Separate print s. l., s. d.] pp. 5.* [4161

— Some Lancaster Catholics and other historical notes. *[Separate print s. l., s. d.] pp. 6.* [4162

Sener, Samuel M.: The Catholic Church at Lancaster, Penn'a. *Arranged from notes furnished by the author . . . and edited by Rev.* **Thomas C. Middletown.** *In: Records of the American Catholic Historical Society. Vol. V. Philadelphia, Pa. 1894. pp. 307—356.*
Separate issue. Philadelphia, Pa. 1894. pp. 52. [4163
— The Lancaster barracks, where the British and Hessian prisoners were destained during the Revolution. *In: Notes and Queries. Edited by W. H. Egle. Fourth series, vol. II. 1894. Harrisburg, Pa. 1895. pp. 280—283; 285—288; 291—295; 300—305; Separate print . . . Harrisburg, Pa.: Harrisburg Publishing Co. 1895. pp. 20.* [4164
— Old time heroes of the War of the Revolution and war of 1812—14. *Harrisburg, Pa.: Harrisburg Publishing Co. 1895. pp. 11.* [4165
— Historical memoranda. *[from old files, newspapers and court records, relating to Lancaster Co.] In: Notes and Queries. Etited by W. H. Egle. Fourth series, vol. II. 1894. Harrisburg, Pa. 1895. pp. 8—9; 23—24; 44—46; 53—54; 68—69; 188—189.* [4166
— An old time „Militia" company. *(Roll of the Marietta volunteer company of 1831). In: Notes and Queries. Edited by W. H. Egle. Fourth series, vol. II. Harrisburg, Pa. 1895. p. 87.* [4167
— Lafayette's visit to Lancaster. *In: Notes and Queries. Edited by W. H. Egle. Fourth series, vol. II. 1894. Harrisburg, Pa. 1895. pp. 209—212.* [4168
— Inscriptions in Lititz churchyard. *In: Notes and Queries. Edited by W. H. Egle. Annual vol. 1896. Harrisburg, Pa. 1897. pp. 87—88.* [4169
— Old Moravian families. *(Compiled mostly from the records of the Moravian Church, Lancaster). In: Notes and Queries. Edited by W. H. Egle. Annual vol. 1898. Harrisburg, Pa. 1899. pp. 45—47.* [4170
— Lancaster County divorces. 1788—1800. *In: Notes and Queries. Edited by W. H. Egle. Annual vol. 1899. Harrisburg, Pa. 1900. p. 101.* [4171
— Some Lancaster interments. *In: Notes and Queries. Edited by W. H. Egle. Annual vol. 1899. Harrisburg, Pa. 1900. 178—180.* [4172
— Millersville and other early towns established by lotteries. *In: Papers and Addresses of the Lancaster County Historical Society. Vol. IV. 1899—1900. Lancaster, Pa. 1900. pp. 23—30.* [4173
Sener, Samuel M.: Muster roll of the „Lancaster Phalanx". *In: Notes and Queries. Edited by W. H. Egle. Annual vol. 1900. Harrisburg, Pa. 1901. pp. 5—6.* [4174
— Early Lancaster baptisms. *(Baptisms at St. Mary's Roman Catholic Church, at Lancaster, Pa.) In: Notes and Queries. Edited by W. H. Egle. Annual vol. 1900. Harrisburg, Pa. 1901. pp. 124—126.* [4175
— Lancaster Reformed Church records. *(Records of the German Reformed Church, at Lancaster, Pa.) In: Notes and Queries. Edited by W. H. Egle. Annual vol. 1900. Harrisburg, Pa. 1901. pp. 158—159.* [4176
— Lancaster townstead, *In: Papers and Addresses of the Lancaster County Historical Society. Vol. V. Lancaster, Pa. 1901. pp. 121—133.* [4177
— Revolutionary days. *In: Papers and Addresses of the Lancaster County Historical Society. Vol. VI. Lancaster, Pa. 1902. pp. 10—32, ill.* [4178
Seyfert, A. G.: Samuel Bowman and the village he founded. *In: Papers and Addresses of the Lancaster County Historical Society. Vol. I. Lancaster, Pa. 1897. pp. 133—140.* [4179
— Bowmansville, *[Brecknock Township, Lancaster Co., Pa.] In: The Pennsylvania-German. Vol. XII. Lititz, Pa. 1911. pp. 351—353.* [4180
— Migration of Lancaster County Mennonites to Waterloo County, Ontario, Canada, from 1800 to 1825. *In: Papers and Addresses of the Lancaster County Historical Society. Vol. XXX. Lancaster, Pa. 1926. pp. 33—41, ill.* [4181
[—] Excerpts from the address of Hon. A. G. Seyfert, representing the Lancaster County Historical Society at the dedication of the Mennonite memorial, Waterloo County, Ontario, Canada, Aug. 28, 1926. *In: Papers and Addresses of the Lancaster County Historical Society. Vol. XXX. Lancaster, Pa. 1926. pp. 117—119.* [4182
— A page of Lancaster County history, during Civil War times. *[The Knights of the Golden Circle.] In: Papers and Addresses of the Lancaster County Historical Society. Vol. XXXI. Lancaster, Pa. 1927. pp. 111—117.* [4183

Seyfert, A. G.: Lancaster County's super-
intendents of public instruction. *In:
Papers and Addresses of the Lancaster
County Historical. Society. Vol. XXXII.
Lancaster, Pa. 1928. pp. 55—63, ill.*
[4184
— Members of Congress who represented
Lancaster County in the United States
Congress from 1789 to the present time.
*In: Papers and Addresses of the Lan-
caster County Historical Society. Vol.
XXXIV. Lancaster, Pa. 1930. pp. 49—
62, ill.* [4185
Sheedy, Morgan M.: Historical address delivered on the 169th anniversary of the
organization and the 57th anniversary of the consecration of St. Mary's
Church, Lancaster, Pa., Sunday, March
26, 1911. *In: Records of the American
Catholic Historical Society of Philadelphia. Vol. XXVI. Philadelphia, Pa.
1915. pp. 346—360.* [4186
Sheetz, Levi F.: Centennial souvenir historical and pictorial, Mount Joy and
history of Florin. *Containing a complete
directory and numerous illustrations . . .
All matter relating to fraternal organizations in charge of W. D. Chandler.
Mount Joy, Pa.: Published by the Centennial Publishing Co. 1912. pp. 160,
ill.* [4187
Shenk, H. H.: Lancaster County petitions
etc., to the Supreme Executive Council
1784—1790. *In: Papers and Addresses of the Lancaster County Historical
Society. Vol. XXV. Lancaster, Pa.
1921. pp. 67—86.* [4188
Sieger, P. George: Silver jubilee souvenir
Emmanuel Lutheran Church, Lancaster,
Pa. *Twenty-fifth anniversary, June,
1921. Lancaster, Pa.: The New Era
Printing Co. 1921. pp. 40, ill.* [4189
Steiner, Edward A.: From Ephrata to
Wisky Hill. *In: The Outlook. Vol. 88,
no. 14. New York, N. Y., April 4, 1908.
pp. 778—782.* [4190
Steinman, George: Lancaster Borough. *In:
Papers and Addresses of the Lancaster
County Historical Society. Vol. IV.
Lancaster, Pa. 1900. pp. 143—152.* [4191
Steinmetz, H. L.: Political divisions of Lan-
caster County. *In: Papers and Ad-
dresses of the Lancaster County Historical
Society. Vol. V. Lancaster, Pa. 1901.
pp. 36—51.* [4192
Steinmetz, Mary Owen: Revolutionary sol-
diers and patriots of Lancaster. *In:
Papers and Addresses of the Lancaster*

*County Historical Society. Vol. XXXV.
Lancaster, Pa. 1931. pp. 314—315.*
[See also: Worner, W. F. no. 4221]
[4193
Tobias, D. C.: A history of Bethany charge
of the Reformed Church in Lancaster
County, Pa. *Lititz, Pa.: Record Printing
Office 1881. pp. 43.* [4194
[Waldschmidt, John]: Baptismal and mar-
riage records, Rev. John Waldschmidt,
Cocalico, Moden Krick, Weisseichen
Land, and Seltenreich Gemeinde, Lan-
caster County, Pa. 1752—1786. *Translated by Luther R. Kelker. In: Pennsylvania Archives. Sixth series, vol. VI.
Harrisburg, Pa. 1907. pp. 153—264;
Communion services and communicants.
pp. 265—282.* [4195
Weaver, Martin G.: Fords and bridges,
across the Conestoga from Morgantown
to Hinkletown. *In: Papers and Addresses of the Lancaster County Historical
Society. Vol. XXIV. Lancaster, Pa.
1920. pp. 115—124.* [4196
— A history of New Holland, Pennsylvania, *covering its growth and activities
during two hundred years of existence,
1728—1928, as compiled by . . . New Holland, Pa.: The New Holland Clarion
1928. pp. 184, ill., map.* [4197
— Spring Grove, Weaverland and Blue
Ball. Settlement and development. *In:
Papers and Addresses of the Lancaster
County Historical Society. Vol. XXXV.
Lancaster, Pa. 1931. pp. 149—167.*
[4198
— Mennonites of Lancaster Conference,
*containing biographical sketches of Men-
nonite leaders, histories of congregations,
missions, and Sunday schools; record of
ordinations; and other interesting historical data. Scottdale, Pa.: Mennonite Publishing House 1931. pp. XVI, 496,
ill.* [4199
Whitteker, J. E.: 1730—1905. An outline
history of a church. A memorial of the
hundred and seventy-fifth anniversary
of Trinity Lutheran Church, Lancaster,
Pa. *Lancaster, Pa.: Wickersham Printing Co. 1905. pp. 44, ill.* [4200
[—] 1761—1911. One hundred and fiftieth
anniversary of laying of the corner stone
of the Evangelical Lutheran Church of
the Holy Trinity, Lancaster, Pa., May
18th, 1911. *[Lancaster, Pa.] 1911. pp.
15, ill.* [4201
Witmer, T. Richard: Lancaster County in
the eighteenth century. *Lancaster, Pa.:*

Inquirer Printing and Publishing Co. 1926. pp. 22, (1). [4202

Worner, William Frederic: Old St. James churchyard. *In: Papers and Addresses of the Lancaster County Historical Society. Vol. XX. Lancaster, Pa. 1916. pp. 99—125.* [4203

— St. Michael's Lutheran Church at Strasburg. *In: Papers and Addresses of the Lancaster County Historical Society. Vol. XXIV. Lancaster, Pa. 1920. pp. 177—186, ill.* [4204

— The Strasburg Scientific Society. *In: Papers and Addresses of the Lancaster County Historical Society. Vol. XXV. Lancaster, Pa. 1921. pp. 133—145, ill.* [4205

— Old Dutch burying ground, Strasburg Township, Lancaster County. *Contributed and copied by . . . In: Publications of the Genealogical Society of Pennsylvania. Vol. IX, no. 2. Philadelphia, Pa. 1925. p. 175.* [4206

— The graveyard adjoining the old Methodist Church on South Decatur street, Strasburg, Lancaster County. *Contributed and copied by . . . In: Publications of the Genealogical Society of Pennsylvania. Vol. IX, no. 2. Philadelphia, Pa. 1925. p. 176.* [4207

— Notes of local interest from Pennsylvania Packet and General Advertiser from Nov. 29 1777 to June 17, 1778. *Collected by . . . Supplementary to series of H. Frank Eshleman. In: Papers and Addresses of the Lancaster County Historical Society. Vol. XXX. Lancaster, Pa. 1926. pp. 125—132.* [4208

— Old Lancaster tales and traditions. *Lancaster, Pa.: Lancaster Press 1927. pp. X, 261, ill.* [4209

— New Holland Debating Society. *In: Papers and Addresses of the Lancaster County Historical Society. Vol. XXXII. Lancaster, Pa. 1928. p. 143.* [4210

— Mittelberger's notes on Lancaster. *In: Papers and Addresses of the Lancaster County Historical Society. Vol. XXXII. Lancaster, Pa. 1928. pp. 144—145.* [4211

— Strasburg academies. *In: Papers and Addresses of the Lancaster County Historical Society. Vol. XXXII. Lancaster, Pa. 1929. pp. 13—28, ill.* [4212

— Captain Wiederholdt in Lancaster. *In: Papers and Addresses of the Lancaster County Historical Society. Vol. XXXIII. Lancaster, Pa. 1929. pp. 65—68.*
[See no. 2954] [4213

Worner, William Frederic: Baron Riedesel in Lancaster. *In: Papers and Addresses of the Lancaster County Historical Society. Vol. XXXIII. Lancaster, Pa. 1929. pp. 69—73.*
[See no. 2974t.] [4214

— Petition for a school in Lancaster County in 1785. *In: Papers and Addresses of the Lancaster County Historical Society. Vol. XXXIII. Lancaster, Pa. 1929. pp. 73—76.* [4215

— William Priest in Lancaster. *In: Papers and Addresses of the Lancaster County Historical Society. Vol. XXXIII. Lancaster, Pa. 1929. pp. 77—78.* [4216

— The Sunday-school Society. *In: Papers and Addresses of the Lancaster County Historical Society. Vol. XXXIII. Lancaster, Pa. 1929. pp. 175—188.* [4217

— Alexander von Humboldt in Lancaster. *In: Papers and Adresses of the Lancaster County Historical Society. Vol. XXXIV. Lancaster, Pa. 1930. pp. 76—77.* [4218

— Governor Shulze in Lancaster. *In: Papers and Addresses of the Lancaster County Historical Society. Vol. XXXIV. Lancaster, Pa. 1930. pp. 107—109.* [4219

— Fairs for benefit of the Lutheran Sunday school. *In: Papers and Addresses of the Lancaster County Historical Society. Vol. XXXIV. Lancaster, Pa. 1930. p. 119.* [4220

— Revolutionary soldiers and patriots of Lancaster County, Pa. *In: Papers and Addresses of the Lancaster County Historical Society. Vol. XXXIV. Lancaster, Pa. 1930. pp. 146—167.*
[See also: Steinmetz, Mary Owen, no. 4193] [4221

— Opposition to cherry fairs in Strasburg. *In: Papers and Addresses of the Lancaster County Historical Society. Vol. XXXIV. Lancaster, Pa. 1930. pp. 188—189.* [4222

— Mechanics' Society of the City and County of Lancaster. *In: Papers and Addresses of the Lancaster County Historical Society. Vol. XXXIV. Lancaster, Pa. 1930. pp. 226—237.* [4223

— Prevention of horse-racing and gambling in 1812. *In: Papers and Addresess of the Lancaster County Historical Society. Vol. XXXIV. Lancaster, Pa. 1930. pp. 249—250.* [4224

— Agricultural societies in Lancaster County. *In: Papers and Addresses of the Lancaster County Historical Society.*

Vol. XXXIV. Lancaster, Pa. 1930. pp. 278—280. [4225

Worner, William Frederic: An early threshing machine in Lancaster. *In: Papers and Addresses of the Lancaster County Historical Society. Vol. XXXIV. Lancaster, Pa. 1930. p. 284.* [4226

— The German Society of Lancaster *[for relief of distressed immigrants (1818—1833)].* In: *Papers and Addresses of the Lancaster County Historical Society. Vol. XXXV. Lancaster, Pa. 1931. pp. 1—8.* [4227

— A religious riot in Lancaster *[at Zion German Lutheran Church in 1834.]* In: *Papers and Addresses of the Lancaster County Historical Society. Vol. XXXV. Lancaster, Pa. 1931. pp. 13—15.* [4228

— Associations for the detection of horse thieves. *In: Papers and Adresses of the Lancaster County Historical Society. Vol. XXXV. Lancaster, Pa. 1931. pp. 20—21.* [4229

— Public-house keepers in Lancaster County in 1772. *In: Papers and Addresses of the Lancaster County Historical Society. Vol. XXXV. Lancaster, Pa. 1931. pp. 21—22.* [4230

— Military activities in Lancaster during the war of 1812. *In: Papers and Addresses of the Lancaster County Historical Society. Vol. XXXV. Lancaster, Pa. 1931. pp. 205—227.* [4231

— The Conestoga Collegiate Institute. *In: Papers and Addresses of the Lancaster County Historical Society. Vol. XXXV. Lancaster, Pa. 1931. pp. 233—238, ill.* [4232

— Old-time customs in Lancaster. *In: Papers and Addresses of the Lancaster County Historical Society. Vol. XXXVI. Lancaster, Pa. 1932. pp. 121—136, ill.* [4233

Zell, Lydia D.: Epitaphs. *In: Papers and Addresses of the Lancaster County Historical Society. Vol. II. Lancaster, Pa. 1898. pp. 244—247.* [4234

Zook, John G.: Historical and pictorial Lititz. *Edited by . . . Lititz, Pa.: Express Printing Co. 1905. pp. 218, ill.* [4235

[—] Historic Lititz. *[Made up almost entirely of extracts from historical and pictoral Lititz, edited by G. Zook.]* In: *The Pennsylvania-German. Vol. X. Lititz, Pa. 1909. pp. 210—220, ill.* [4236

Portrait and biographical record of Lancaster County, Pa. *Containing biographical sketches of prominent and re-presentative citizens of the county together with biographies and portraits of all the presidents of the United States. Chicago, Ill.: Chapman Publishing Co. 1894. pp. 690, ill.* [4237

Biographical annals of Lancaster County. Pa., *containing biographical and genealogical sketches of prominent and representative citizens and many of the early settlers. Chicago, Ill.: J. H. Beers & Co. 1903. pp. XVIII, 1524, ill.* [4238

Report of committee appointed to conduct celebration of 200th anniversary of first permanent white settlement in Lancaster County. *In: Papers and Addresses of the Lancaster County Historical Society. Vol. XIV. Lancaster, Pa. 1910. pp. 197—243, ill.* [4239

Report on the Centennial observance of Lancaster City. *In: Papers and Addresses of the Lancaster County Historical Society. Vol. XXII. Lancaster, Pa. 1918. pp. 57—70, ill.* [4240

Chronology of first settlement of Lancaster County. *[Part of ,,Chronology" in official programm of exercises commemorating the Bi-Centennial of the first settlement of Lancaster County, Pa.]* In: *The Pennsylvania-German. Vol. XI. Lititz, Pa. 1910. pp. 585—589.* [4241

The Switzers land. *(A document in the office of the Secretary of Internal Affairs, endorsed ,,Return of 6500 acres, besides ye allowance of 6 p. cent to ye Switzers, 1710.")* In: Notes and Queries. Edited by W. H. Egle. Second series. Harrisburg, Pa. 1883. pp. 262—264. Reprint in: First and second series, vol. II. Harrisburg, Pa. 1895. pp. 360—362.* [4242

Conestoga assessment for 1718. *[Earliest assessment list yet found, containing the names of the first inhabitants of this locality, distinguished as ,,English" and ,,Dutch inhabitants".]* Contributed by **Gilbert Cope.** *In: Notes and Queries. Edited by W. H. Egle. Second series. Harrisburg, Pa. 1883. pp. 49—50. Reprint in: First and second series, vol. II. Harrisburg, Pa. 1895. pp. 131—132.* [4243

Tax return for substitutes. *(A copy of a return of John Ewing, Captain, for a township in Lancaster, whose location is uncertain.)* In: Notes and Queries. Edited by W. H. Egle. Fourth series. Vol. II. 1894. Harrisburg, Pa. 1895. pp. 43—44.* [4244

Heads of families, census 1790. Elizabeth, Lancaster County, Pa. *In: Genealogy. Journal of American ancestry. Vol. II. New York, N. Y. 1912. p. 314.* [4245

Heads of families, census 1790. Heidelberg, Lancaster, County, Pa. *In: Genealogy. Journal of American ancestry. Vol. II. New York, N. Y. 1912. p. 348.* [4246

Petition of some inhabitants of Lancaster County, Pa., December, 1777, praying that the whole strength of the state might be called into active service. *In: The Pennsylvania Magazine of History and Biography. Vol. XXIV. Philadelphia, Pa. 1900. pp. 246—247.* [4247

Wanted a guard. *[Copy of a petition of the burgesses and inhabitants of the Borough of Lancaster, about 1777.] In: Notes and Queries. Edited by W. H. Egle. Fourth series, vol. I. 1891—1893. Harrisburg, Pa. 1893. pp. 83—84.* [4248

Extracts from the Brethren's house and congregation diaries of the Moravian Church at Lititz, Pa., relating to the Revolutionary War. *Translated literally by* **Abraham Reincke Beck.** *In: The Penn Germania. Vol. I. = Old series, vol. XIII. Lititz, Pa. 1912. pp. 849—862.* [4249

Horse contract. N. 780. *[Copy of the rough draft of a certificate to be signed by inhabitants of Lancaster wgich accompanied Captain Mathias Slough's vouchers for the purchase of horses „bought by him for the French service", 20th September, 1780.] In: Notes and Queries Edited by W. H. Egle. Fourth series, vol. I. 1891—1893. Harrisburg, Pa. 1893. p. 81.* [4250

Revolutionary soldiers. — „Returns of the recruits enlisted by the Classes of Lancaster County agreeable to an Act of Assembly passed June 25, 1781." *In: The Pennsylvania Magazine of History and Biography. Vol. XIX. Philadelphia, Pa. 1895. pp. 125—127.* [4251

Captain Alexander Martin's Company. *(A copy of a muster roll of . . . of militia of Col. Peter Grubb's Battalion, of Lancaster County, on their march for the camp in ye Jerseys). In: Notes and Queries. Edited by W. H. Egle. Fourth series, vol. II. 1894. Harrisburg, Pa. 1895. p. 56.* [4252

Captain Nathaniel Page's Company. *(A copy of a muster roll of . . ., of Lancaster County, of Colonel Matthias Slough's Battalion, destined for the camp in the Jersey's Sept., 11, 1776.) Reprint in: Notes and Queries. Edited by W. H. Egle. Fourth series, vol. II. 1894. Harrisburg, Pa. 1895. pp. 55—56.* [4253

Captain Joseph Wright's Company. *(A copy of a muster roll of a detachment of . . . of the militia of Colonel Matthias Slough's Battalion, of Lancaster County, September 11, 1776, destined for the Jersey's). In: Notes and Queries. Edited by W. H. Egle. Fourth series, vol. II. 1894. Harrisburg, Pa. 1895. p. 56.* [4254

Captain Martin Weaver's Company, 1777—78. *(A copy of the muster roll . . . of Lancaster County, militia, now in the service of the U. S., commended by Colonel John Rogers.) In: Notes and Queries. Edited by W. H. Egle. Annual vol. 1898. Harrisburg, Pa. 1899. pp. 125—126.* [4255

Lancaster county militia, 1807. *In: The Pennsylvania Magazine of History and Biography. Vol. XXVIII. Philadelphia, Pa. 1904. p. 239.* [4256

Old time heroes. Revolutionary and war of 1812 pensioners in Lancaster County. *In: Notes and Queries. Edited by W. H. Egle. Fourth series, vol. II. pp. 262—269.* [4257

Mennonites of Donegal and Manor Townships address letter to Governor Mc Kean. *[March 11, 1800.] Edited by* **W. F. Worner.** *In: Papers and Addresses of the Lancaster County Historical Society. Vol. XXXIV. Lancaster, Pa. 1930. pp. 179—180.* [4258

Industries of Pennsylvania. Cities of Lancaster, Columbia and Mount Joy. *Historical and descriptive review — industries, institutions, manufacturing . . . Philadelphia, Pa.: Richard Edwards, editor and publisher 1880. pp. 164. ill.* [4259

Lancaster Intelligencer. Greater Lancaster edition. *Vol. LXIV, no. 46. Lancaster, Pa., Monday evening, October 24, 1927. pp. 120, ill.* [4260

Intelligencer Journal. Bi-Centennial edition. *Vol. LXV, no. 249. Lancaster, Pa., Saturday, June 22, 1929. pp. 180, ill.* [4261

A history of Strasburg, Lancaster County, Pa. *until the Sesqui-Centennial year. By the graduating class of 1926 of Strasburg High School. Strasburg, Pa.: News Print 1926. pp. 80, ill.* [4262

The town regulations of Lititz, Pa. 1759. *[Copy of the English version of the regu-*

lations adopted for the Moravian ,,settlement" at Lititz, Pa., in 1759.] In: The Penn Germania. Vol. I. = Old series, vol. XIII. Lititz, Pa. 1912. pp. 731— 736. [4263

Lititz, Lancaster County, Penna. (Items from the records of the Town of Lititz, 1774 and 1775). In: The Pennsylvania Magazina of History and Biography. Vol. XXXVI. 1912. p. 122. [4264

Pencillings about Ephrata. By a visitor. Philadelphia, Pa.: J. B. Chandler 1856. pp. 24; . . . 1860. pp. 40. [4265

Lancaster County, Pa. The garden spot of the United States. The picturesque and historical east end. Lancaster, Pa. 1908. pp. 28. [4266

Tavern keepers in 1783. (List of tavern-keepers in 1783 for Lancaster Co., embracing at that time those in what are now Dauphin and Lebanon Counties.) In: Notes and Queries. Edited by W. H. Egle. Annual vol. 1900. Harrisburg, Pa. 1901. pp. 167—168. [4267

A Lancaster, Pa., lottery. In: Genealogy. A monthly magazine of American ancestry. Vol. VI. New York, N. Y. 1916. p. 20. [4268

Birth and baptismal register of the First Reformed Church, Lancaster, Pa. In: The Pennsylvania-German Society. Proceedings and Addresses . . . 1893. Vol. IV. Lancaster, Pa. 1894. pp. 249—292; . . . 1894. Vol. V. Reading, Pa. 1895. pp. 203—266. [4269

Birth and baptismal register of Trinity Lutheran Church Lancaster, Pa. Prepared for publication by J. Max Hark, S. M. Sener and J. S. Stahr. In: The Pennsylvania-German Society. Proceedings and Addresses . . . 1892. Vol. III. Lancaster, Pa. 1893. pp. 191—292; . . . 1893. Vol. IV. Lancaster, Pa. 1894. pp. 189— 248; . . . 1894. Vol. V. Reading, Pa. 1895. pp. 173—200; . . . 1895. Vol. VI. Reading, Pa. 1896. pp. 251—283, ill. [4270

25 jubilee of St. Stephen's Lutheran Church, corner Duke and Church Str., and the 20th anniversary of Rev. E. Meister, as pastor of the congregation. Fest-Programm für die Festzeit vom 15. bis zum 18. Juli. Lancaster, Pa. 1900. pp. 48, ill. [4271

Fourtieth anniversary souvenir. Christ Evangelical Lutheran Church 1867, Michaelmas 1907, September 29th. Lancaster, Pa.: Rider Printer 1907. pp. 93, ill. [4272

The watchman. Christ Lutheran Church' Lancaster, Penna. Fiftieth anniversary souvenir 1867—1917. [s. l. 1917.] pp. 11. [4273

Two hundredth anniversary Emanuel Evangelical Lutheran Church, Brickerville, Pa. 1730—1930. History and program. [s. l. 1930.] pp. (15). [4274

A brief history of the United Brethren [Moravian] congregation at Lititz, Pa., from 1742 to 1757. Lancaster, Pa.: Printed by John Baer & Sons 1857. pp. 23. [4275

Marriage register of the Moravian Church, Lititz. 1743—1800. In: Record of Pennsylvania marriages, prior to 1810. Vol. II. Harrisburg, Pa. 1880. = Pennsylvania Archives. Second series, vol. IX. Edited by John B. Linn and Wm. H. Egle. Harrisburg, Pa. 1880. pp. 135— —146.

Reprint: Harrisburg, Pa. 1895. pp. 137 —148. [4276

An ancient burying ground. (Some records of the old Moravian cemetery at Milton Grove, in Lancaster, Co.) In: Notes and Queries. Edited by W. H. Egle. Annual vol. 1897. Harrisburg, Pa. 1898. pp. 46—47. [4277

Baptismal records from St. Mary's Church, Lancaster, Pa., Jan. 25, 1787— Sept. 20, 1795. In: Records of the American Catholic Historical Society of Philadelphia. Vol. XXV. 1914. pp. 35—51; 259—276; 342—351; Marriage records. pp. 351—355. [4278

Burials in Penryn cemetery, Penryn, Pa. List compiled, May 30, 1928. Ephrata, Pa.: ,,Review"-Print 1928. pp. 20. [4279

Lancaster Orphan's Court records. (1762— 1769.) In: Notes and Queries. Edited by W. H. Egle. Annual vol. 1900. Harrisburg, Pa. 1901. pp. 194—195. [4280

Lancaster firemen in 1766. [List of members of the Friendship, Union, and Sun Fire Companies of Lancaster.] In: The Pennsylvania Magazine of History and Biography. Vol. III. Philadelphia, Pa. 1879. p. 469. [4281

Thirty- five years of ,,The Clio". A historical review of the Cliosophic Society of Lancaster, Pennsylvania. Organized, Nov. 19, 1879. Compiled and published by order of the Society, for its members. A. D. 1914. Lancaster, Pa. 1914. pp. 142. [4282

Lancaster, Penn., burial records. (Tombstone inscriptions.) Old cemetery, Ephrata — Lutheran cemetery, Ephrata. — Adamstown cemetery — Muddycreek cemetery, Reamstown. *In: Genealogy. Journal of American ancestry. Vol. IV. New York, N. Y. 1914. p. 87.* [4283

Lebanon County

Albright, S. C.: Graves that tell a tale. Notes from the records of the Moravian cemetery at Hebron, near Lebanon, Pa. *In: Papers read before the Lebanon County Historical Society. Vol. VIII, no. 2. Lebanon, Pa. 1920—1928. pp. 41—86.* [4284

Bassler, J. H.: The Myerstown academy. *In: Papers read before the Lebanon County Historical Society. Vol. III. Lebanon, Pa. 1905—1906. pp. 358—399, ill.* [4285

— The color episode of the 149th regiment, Pennsylvania volunteers in the first day's fight at Gettysburg, July 1, 1863. *In: Papers read before the Lebanon County Historical Society. Vol. IV. Lebanon, Pa. 1906—1909. pp. 80—110.* [4286

Berger, A. C. and orthes: Agricultural production and marketing in Lebanon County, Pa. *A report of the results of a survey of agricultural conditions in Lebanon County, Pa., for the purpose of furnishing an economic basis for a production and marketing program. By . . . and* **P. R. Taylor, B. H. Critchfield** *and* **R. S. Kiefer.** *State College, Pa. 1925. pp. 47, ill., maps. = Pennsylvania State College, School of Agriculture and Experiment Station. Bulletin no. 198.* [4287

Bierman, Benjamin: A visit to Annville sixty years ago. *In: Papers read before the Lebanon County Historical Society. Vol. I. Lebanon, Pa. 1898—1901. pp. 135—147.* [4288

Bierman, E. Benjamin: Lebanon County in our state legislature. *In: Papers read before the Lebanon County Historical Society. Vol. II. Lebanon, Pa. 1901—1904. pp. 353—396.* [4289

— The first twenty-five years of Lebanon Valley College. *In: Papers read before the Lebanon County Historical Society. Vol. III. Lebanon, Pa. 1905—1906. pp. 114—136, ill.* [4290

Boger, Cyrus: The Humberger School Association and its school. *In: Papers read before the Lebanon County Historical*

Society. Vol. V. Lebanon, Pa. 1909—1912. pp. 336—362. [4291

Bowman, C. A.: Beginning of the Evangelical Church in Lebanon County. *In: Papers read before the Lebanon County Historical Society. Vol. VIII. Lebanon, Pa. 1920—1924. pp. 133—144.* [4292

Bowman, Charles M.: Lebanon County. — A story of its newspapers. *In: Papers read before the Lebanon County Historical Society. Vol. I. Lebanon, Pa. 1898—1901. pp. 393—403.* [4293

Boyer, Alfred W.: Company B, 103rd ammunition train in the World War. *Paper read before the Lebanon County Historical Society. Vol. VIII. Lebanon, Pa. 1920—1924. pp. 388—460, ill.* [4294

Brane, C. I. B.: The United Brethren Church in Lebanon County. *In: Papers read before the Lebanon County Historical Society. Vol. II. Lebanon, Pa. 1901—1904. pp. 205—252, ill.* [4295

Brendle, Abram S.: The early history of Schaefferstown, Pa. *In: Papers read before the Lebanon County Historical Society. Vol. I Lebanon, Pa. 1898—1901. pp. 9—16.* [4296

— A brief history of Schaefferstown, *(written by A. S. Brendle.) York, Pa.: Dispatch Publishing Co. pp. V, 6—233, ill. 3 plans.* [4297

— A historical sketch of Schaefferstown. *The Pennsylvania-German. Vol. VIII. Lebanon, Pa. 1907. pp 68—72; 112—116; 173—177, ill.* [4298

Breslin, William M.: A history of Lebanon County up to 1876. *In: Papers read before the Lebanon County Historical Society. Vol. VI. Lebanon, Pa. 1912—1916. pp. 121—140.* [4299

Brownmiller, E. S.: 1727. 1744. 1837. 1887. Memorial discourse. A brief history of the first Tulpehocken Lutheran congregation, now known as Zion's (Reeds') Lutheran Church. *Delivered at the Semi-Centennial of the erection of the present church edifice, Nov. 26, 1887. [s. l. 1887.] pp. 7.* [4300

Butz, C. A.: History of St. Paul, commonly called Klopp Reformed Church, Hamlin, Pa. *Annville, Pa.: Journal Publishing Co. 1908. pp. 62, ill.* [4301

Christ, Adam: St. Mary's Catholic Church, Lebanon, Pa. *In: Papers read before the Lebanon County Historical Society. Vol. II. Lebanon, Pa. 1901—1904. pp. 346—350.* [4302

[**Croll, P. C.**]: Art work of Lebanon County. *Published in 9 parts. Chicago, Ill.: The W. H. Parish Publishing Co. 1895. pls. 51. pp. 14.* Historical and descriptive sketch of Lebanon County, Pa. *By* P. C. Croll. [4303
— Ancient and historic landmarks in the Lebanon Valley. *Philadelphia, Pa.: Lutheran Publishing Society. 1895. pp. XII, 13—334, ill.* [4304
— Distinguished visitors of Lebanon County. *In: Papers read before the Lebanon County Historical Society. Vol. I. Lebanon, Pa. 1898—1901. pp. 85—120.* [4305
[—] Historical pilgrimages into Pennsylvania-Germandom. Down the Lebanon Valley. *In: The Pennsylvania-German. Vol. II. Lebanon, Pa. 1901. pp. 123—132, ill.; 165—183, ill.* *[See: no. 295]* [4306
— Lebanon and its environs; a brief historical sketch. *In: The Pennsylvania-German Society. Proceedings and Addresses at Lebanon, October 22, 1903. Vol. XVI, Lancaster, Pa. 1905. pp. 38—51.* [4307
— Quaint and historic markers and inscriptions of Lebanon County. *In: Papers read before the Lebanon County Historical Society. Vol. III. Lebanon, Pa. 1905—1906. pp. 323—355, ill.* [4308
— Lebanon County imprints and bibliography. *In: Papers read before the Lebanon County Historical Society. Vol. IV. Lebanon, Pa. 1906—1909. pp. 153—199.* [4309
Daugherty, Carroll Roop: Lebanon, Pennsylvania, as an industrial center. *Thesis, University of Pennsylvania; Philadelphia, Pa. 1924. Typewritten pp. . . .* [4310
Early, Martin H.: A history and directory of Palmyra, Pa., also of Campbelltown, Bindnagles and Gravel Hill churches, *containing a brief history of the first settlers, notices of the leading events, incidents and interesting facts, also unpublished information, chiefly of a local character. Compiled by . . . [s. l. 1898.] pp. 80, ill.* [4311
Early, J. W.: Baptismal record of the Evangelical Lutheran congregation, at Campbellstown, Lebanon County. *In: Notes and Queries. Edited by W. H. Egle. Annual vol. 1898. Harrisburg, Pa. 1899. pp. 132—135; 137—140;* Mar-

riages by Rev. J. G. Lochmann. *ibid. p. 147;* Record of burials. *ibid. pp. 147—151.* [4312
Early, J. W.: Records of „The Hill Church". *In: Notes and Queries. Edited by W. H. Egle. Annual vol. 1898. Harrisburg, Pa. 1899. pp. 231—237; 240—247; 248—250; 256—259; 261—263; 266—269; 270—274; 276—279; 279—283; 285—287; 289—291; 296—300; 301—308.* [4313
— Campbellstown Evangelical Lutheran church. *In: Notes and Queries. Edited by W. H. Egle. Annual vol. 1899. Harrisburg, Pa. 1900. pp. 227—228.* [4314
— The Bindnagel Church. *In: Papers read before the Lebanon County Historical Society. Vol. I. Lebanon, Pa. 1898—1901. pp. 57—70.* [4315
— Palmyra, its history and its surroundings *In: Papers read before the Lebanon County Historical Society. Vol. IV. Lebanon, Pa. 1906—1909. pp. 253—291.* [4316
— A few historical facts of interest. Rev. John Casper Stoever's original Tulpehocken Church; the Northkill Church, or church in Bern Township; the Oley Hill Church; the two Stoewers. *In: The Lutheran Church Review. Vol. XXVII. Philadelphia, Pa. 1908. pp. 660—664.* [4317
— The Palmyra Academy. *In: Papers read before the Lebanon County Historical Society. Vol. V. Lebanon, Pa. 1909—1912. pp. 3—20, ill.* [4318
— Centennial of Friedens Evangelical Lutheran Church, Myerstown, Pa. *In: The Penn Germania. Vol. II. = Old series, vol. XIV. Cleona, Pa. 1913. pp. 32—36.* [4319
Egle, William Henry: History of the Counties of Dauphin and Lebanon in the Commonwealth of Pennsylvania: biographical and genealogical. *Philadelphia, Pa.: Everts & Peck 1883. pp. IX, 616, VI, 360, ill., maps.* [4320
— Hill Church. *In: Notes and Queries. Edited by W. H. Egle. Third series, vol. I. 1884—1887. Harrisburg, Pa. 1887. p. 50; Reprint in: Third series, vol. I. Harrisburg, Pa. 1895. p. 84.* [4321
— Provincial papers: Proprietary and state tax lists of the County of Lancaster, for the years 1771, 1772, 1773, 1779 and 1782. *Edited by . . . Harrisburg, Pa. 1898. pp. VIII, 896.* *= Pennsylvania Archives. Third series, vol. XVII.* [4322

Egle, William Henry: Lebanon County in history, biography and genealogy. *In: Papers read before the Lebanon County Historical Society. Vol. I. Lebanon, Pa. 1898—1901. pp. 2—8.* [4323

Fisher, I. Calvin: A history of St. Mark's Reformed Church· and Sunday school, Lebanon, Pa. *Compiled and edited by . . . Lebanon, Pa.: Weigley & Co. 1895. pp. 74, ill.* [4324

Fox, Clarence R.: An old colonial homestead. (The Henry S. Heilman house and treasures.) *Read before the Lebanon Chapter, D. A. R. and later before the Lebanon Historical Society. Nov. 30, 1928. In: Papers read before the Lebanon County Historical Society. Vol. IX. Lebanon, Pa. 1925—1928. pp. 327—336, ill.* [4325

Francis, J. G.: The Church of the Brethren (Dunkers) in Lebanon County. *In: Papers read before the Lebanon County Historical Society, Sept. 15, 1916. Vol. VIII. Lebanon, Pa. 1920—1924. pp. 87—129, ill.* [4326

Freeman, William C.: Our county. *Address. In: Papers read before the Lebanon County Historical Society. Vol. V. Lebanon, Pa. 1909—1912. pp. 28—34.* [4327

Gobin, J. P. S.: Lebanon in the wars of the nation. *In: Papers read before the Lebanon County Historial Society. Vol. I. Lebanon, Pa. 1898—1901. pp. 177—181* [4328

Grittinger, Henry C.: The iron industries of Lebanon County. *In: Papers read before the Lebanon County Historical Society. Vol. III. Lebanon, Pa. 1905—1906. pp. 3—30.* [4329

Grumbine, Lee L.: The origin and significance of our township names. *In: Papers read before the Lebanon County Historical Society. Vol. I. Lebanon, Pa. 1898—1901. pp. 121—133.* [4330

— The women of Lebanon. *In: Papers read before the Lebanon County Historical Society. Vol. I. Lebanon, Pa. 1898 —1901. pp. 191—196.* [4331

Grumbine, E.: Two dead and lost churches of the Swatara. *In: Papers read before the Lebanon County Historical Society. Vol. I. Lebanon, Pa. 1898—1901. pp. 291—304.* [4332

— An early educational project of Lebanon Town. *In: Papers read before the Lebanon County Historical Society. Vol. III. Lebanon, Pa. 1905—1906. pp. 145 —154.* [4333

Grumbine, E.: Folk-lore of Lebanon County. *Papers read before the Lebanon County Historical Society. Vol. III. Lebanon, Pa. 1905—1906. pp. 254—294.* [4334

— Stories of old Stumpstown. *Extracts from the author's paper read before and printed by the Lebanon County Historical Society, 1909—1910. In: The Pennsylvania-German. Vol. XII. Lititz, Pa. 1911. pp. 212—218.* [4335

— Stories of old Stumpstown. A history of interesting events, traditions and anecdotes of early Fredericksburg. *In: Papers read before the Lebanon County Historical Society. Vol. V. Lebanon, Pa. 1909—1912. pp. 153—276, ill.* [4336

— The history of Greenville (Bethel Township). *In: Papers read before the Lebanon County Historical Society. Vol. VII. Lebanon, Pa. 1916—1919. pp. 257—262.* [4337

— An old time religious meeting (Bethel Township, June 1854.) *In: Papers read before the Lebanon County Historical Society. Vol. XVII. Lebanon, Pa. 1916— 1919. pp. 266—270.* [4338

— An old tragedy of Jackson Township Lebanon County, Pa. *Posthumus paper by Ezra Grumbine. Foreword by Charles D. Weirick. In: Papers read before the Lebanon County Historical Society. Jan. 25, 1925. Vol. IX. Lebanon, Pa. 1925—1928. pp. (1), 39—51.* [4339

Guilford, Wm. M.: Lebanon in the councils of the nation. *In: Papers read before the Lebanon County Historical Society. Vol. I. Lebanon, Pa. 1898—1901. pp. 187— 191.* [4340

— Notes an medical history of Lebanon County. *In: Papers read before the Lebanon County Historical Society. Vol. IV. Lebanon, Pa. 1906—1909. pp. 204 —219, ill.* [4341

Hark, Max: Moravian influence in the settlement and early development of Lebanon County. *In: Papers read before the Lebanon County Historical Society. Vol. VI. Lebanon, Pa. 1912—1916. pp. 191—204.* [4342

Heilman, Henry S.: The mills of the Quittapahilla. *In: Papers read before the Lebanon County Historical Society. Vol. II. Lebanon, Pa. 1901—1904. pp. 295—314.* [4343

Heilman, S. P.: The first trial, conviction and execution for murder in Lebanon County. *In: Papers read before the Lebanon County Historical Society. Vol.*

II. *Lebanon, Pa. 1901—1904. pp. 155—178.* [4344

Heilman, S. P. and **Musser, Daniel:** The fire companies of Lebanon. *In: Papers read before the Lebanon County Historical Society. Vol. III. Lebanon, Pa. 1905—1906. pp. 405—446, ill.* [4345

— A story of beginnings and first things in Lebanon County. *In: Papers read before the Lebanon County Historical Society. Vol. VI. Lebanon, Pa. 1912—1916. pp. 27—45.* [4346

Heilman, U. Henry: Descriptive and historical memorials of Heilman Dale. *In: Papers read before the Lebanon County Historical Society. Vol. IV. Lebanon, Pa. 1906—1909. pp. 407—459, ill., map.* [4347

[—] Heilman Dale. *Quoted from a paper by* U. H. Heilman. *,,Descriptive and historical memorials of Heilman-dale'', read before the Lebanon County Historical Society, April, 1909. In: The Pennsylvania-German. Vol. XI. Lititz, Pa. 1910. pp. 110—111.* [4348

— The old Hill Church and a court trial. *In: Papers read before the Lebanon County Historical Society. Vol. IX. Lebanon, Pa. 1925—1928. pp. 107—120, ill.* [4349

Hiester, J. E.: Twenty-fifth anniversary of Palatinate college. *In: Papers read before the Lebanon County Historical Society. Vol. III. Lebanon, Pa. 1905—1906. pp. 137—142.* [4350

Hinke, William J.: The Reformed Church within the bounds of Lebanon Classis during the eighteenth century. *Address delivered before Lebanon Classis at its one hundreth annual session, June 1, 1920. In: The Reformed Church Review. Fourth series, vol. XXV. Philadelphia, Pa. 1921. pp. 46—64.* [4351

— and **Happel, Wm. D.:** First (Tabor) Reformed Church. History of pastors and congregation, 1760—1935. *Published by the Consistory of the church as part of the celebration of the 175th anniversary of the founding of the congregation. October 27th to November 3rd, 1935. [s. l. 1935.] pp. 127, ill.* [4351a

Jordan, John W.: Note on the Moravian Church in Lebanon County. *In: The Pennsylvania Magazine of History and Biography. Vol. IX. Philadelphia, Pa. 1885. pp. 113—114.* [4352

— Marriage records, Moravian congregation, at Lebanon, Pa. 1751—1811. *In: Notes and Queries. Edited by W. H.*

Egle. *Third series, vol. I. 1884—1887. Harrisburg, Pa. 1887. pp. 570—571. Reprint in: Notes and Queries, third series, vol. II. Harrisburg, Pa. 1896. pp. 354—355.* [4353

Klein, Theo B.: Roads and highways in eastern Pennsylvania and in Lebanon County. *In: Papers read before the Lebanon County Historical Society. Vol. II. Lebanon, Pa. 1901—1904. pp. 255—273.* [4354

Klopp, D. Earnest: A history of Tabor, First Reformed Church, Lebanon, Pa. *Commemorative of the 100th anniversary of the laying of the corner stone, June 26th, 1792. Lebanon, Pa.: M. H. Berger. Philadelphia, Pa. 1892. pp. 70, ill.* [4355

Krall, John, M.: Colonial events: Eastern Pennsylvania and Schaefferstown. *In: Papers read before the Lebanon County Historical Society. Vol. II. Lebanon, Pa. 1901—1904. pp. 104—109.* [4356

— Millbach history and lore. *In: Papers read before the Lebanon County Historical Society. Vol. VI. Lebanon, Pa. 1912—1916. pp. 265—282, ill.* [4357

Learned, Marion Dexter: The Pennsylvania German and his English and Scotch-Irish neighbors. *In: Papers read before the Lebanon County Historical Society. Vol. II. Lebanon, Pa. 1901—1904. pp. 317—329.* [4358

Lemberger, Joseph L.: The Lebanon Academy. The pioneer classical school of Lebanon, Pa. *In: Papers read before the Lebanon County Historical Society. Vol. IV. Lebanon, Pa. 1906—1909. pp. 225—251, ill.* [4359

Mays, George: ,,Battalion'' or Training Day at Schaefferstown in the olden time. *In: Papers read before the Lebanon County Historical Society. Vol. I. Lebanon, Pa. 1898—1901. pp. 149—168.* [4360

— The Palatine and Scotch-Irish settlers of Lebanon County, Pa. *In: Papers read before the Lebanon County Historical Society. Vol. I. Lebanon, Pa. 1898—1901. pp. 305—326.* [4361

— The Jewish colony at Tower Hill — Schaefferstown, Lebanon County, Pa. *Philadelphia, Pa.; Lebanon, Pa.: Press of Report Publishing Co. 1905. pp. 20.* [4362

Mays, Thomas J.: Early Lebanon County recollections. *In: Papers read before the Lebanon County Historical Society. Vol. III. Lebanon, Pa. 1905—1906. pp. 309—312.* [4363

McCurdy, E. E.: The western border of Lebanon County. *In: Papers read before the Lebanon County Historical Society. Vol. III. Lebanon, Pa. 1905—1906. pp. 67—76.* [4364

Miller, Daniel: The Moravian Church in Bethel *[Township, Lebanon County, Pa.] In: The Pennsylvania-German. Vol. XI. Lititz, Pa. 1910. pp. 28—32.* [4365

— The German newspapers of Lebanon County. *In: Papers read before the Lebanon County Historical Society. Vol. V. Lebanon, Pa. 1909—1912. pp. 131—150.* [4366

[Parthemore, E. W. S.]: Records of the Bindnagle Church. *In: Notes and Queries. Edited by W. H. Egle. Third series, vol. I. 1884—1887. Harrisburg, Pa. 1887. pp. 435—438; 440—442; 447—448; 457—458; 458—459; 464—465; 471—472; 476—477; 479—481; 518—519; 534—536; 540—542; see also pp. 486—487. Reprint in: Third series, vol. II. Harrisburg, Pa. 1896. pp. 173—176; 181—184; 192—194; 206—208; 208—211; 219—221; 230—233; 237—239; 243—246; 290—291; 302—304; 308—310; see also pp. 254—255.* [4367

— Londonderry's oversees in the long ago. *In: Notes and Queries. Edited by W. H. Egle. Fourth series, vol. I. 1891—93. Harrisburg, Pa. 1893. pp. 221—222; 235—236.* [4368

— A trip into the „Swatara" region of Lebanon County, Pa. *Read at the monthly meeting of the Dauphin County Historical Society, Dec. 13, 1894. Harrisburg, Pa.: Harrisburg Publishing Co. 1895. pp. 13.* [4369

— In the Swatara region. A two days' trip through the valley. *In: Notes and Queries. Edited by W. H. Egle. Fourth series, vol. II. 1894. Harrisburg, Pa. 1895. pp. 200—203; 206—208; 216—218.* [4370

— A trip no. 2. into the „Swatara" region or among the „Bethel Moravian" settlement of Bethel Township, Lebanon County, Pa. *Read at the 28 anniversary of the Dauphin County Historical Society, May 13, 1897. Harrisburg, Pa.: Harrisburg Publishing Co. 1897. pp. 13.* [4371

— The Moravian settlement in Bethel Township, Lebanon County. *In: Notes and Queries Edited by W. H. Egle. Annual vol. 1897. Harrisburg, Pa. 1898. pp. 70—77.* [4372

Parthemore, E.W.S.: Tombstone inscriptions, Bellview, Lebanon County, U. B. church graveyard. *In: Notes and Queries. Edited by W. H. Egle. Annual vol. 1898. Harrisburg, Pa. 1899. pp. 43—45.* [4373

Ranck, Henry H.: The history of St. John's Reformed Church, 1858—1901. *Lebanon, Pa.: Lebanon Daily Times Print 1901. pp. 246, (4), ill.* [4374

Redsecker, J. H.: The Hebron diary during the Revolutionary period. *In: Papers read before the Lebanon County Historical Society. Vol. I. Lebanon, Pa. 1898—1901. pp. 8—16.* [4375

— Some doctore of the olden time. *In: Papers read before the Lebanon County Historical Society. Vol. I. Lebanon, Pa. 1898—1901. pp. 329—356.* [4376

— The Women's Aid Society of Lebanon during the War of Rebellion. *In: Papers read before the Lebanon County Historical Society. Vol. III. Lebanon, Pa. 1905—1906. pp. 157—167.* [4377

Richards, H. M. M.: Lebanon County in the French and Indian War. *In: Papers read before the Lebanon County Historical Society. Vol. II. Lebanon, Pa. 1901—1904. pp. 57—77.* [4378

— Lebanon County's emergency volunteers at Gettysburg. *In: Papers read before the Lebanon County Historical Society. Vol. III. Lebanon, Pa. 1905—1906. pp. 170—199.* [4379

— Lebanon County's part in the Revolutionary War. *In: Papers read before the Lebanon County Historical Society. Vol. IV. Lebanon, Pa. 1906—1909. pp. 382—404.* [4380

— Lebanon County in the foreign wars of the United States. 1898—1901. *In: Papers read before the Lebanon County Historical Society. Vol. V. Lebanon, Pa. 1909—1912. pp. 366—391.* [4381

— American Iron and Steel Manufacturing Company, Lebanon's great iron works. *In: Papers read before the Lebanon County Historical Society. Vol. VI. Lebanon, Pa. 1912—1916. pp. 442—467, ill.* [4382

— Company D., 109th Machine Gun Battalion of the World War. *In: Papers read before the Lebanon County Historical Society, Oct. 19, 1923. Vol. VIII. Lebanon, Pa. 1920—1924. pp. 335—387.* [4383

— Our educational system in its early growth. *Paper read Sept. 26, 1930. In:*

24*

Papers read before the Lebanon County Historical Society. Vol. X, no. 2. Lebanon, Pa. 1932 pp. 65—98, ill. [4384

Rockey, John L.: The eastern border of Lebanon County. *In: Papers read before the Lebanon County Historical Society. Vol. III. Lebanon, Pa. 1905—1906. pp. 53—66.* [4385

Roop, H. U.: The educational work of Lebanon County. *(Brief abstract.) In: Papers read before the Lebanon County Historical Society. Vol. II. Lebanon, Pa. 1901—1904. pp. 330—336.* [4386

Rupp, I. Daniel: History of the Counties of Berks and Lebanon: *containing a brief account of the Indians, who inhabited this region of the country, and the numerous murders by them; notices of the first Swedish, Welsh, French, German, Irish and English settlers, giving the names of nearly five thousand of them, biographical sketches, topographical descriptions of every township, and of the principal towns and villages; the religious history with much useful statistical information; notices of the press and education. Lancaster, Pa.: C. Hills. 1844. pp. VI, (3), 14—513, ill.* [4387

— Die erste deutsche Ansiedlung von Tulpehocken, Penn. *In: Der Deutsche Pionier. Jg. II. Cincinnati, O. 1870—1871. S. 5—8.* [4388

Ruth, John and **Schmauk, Theodore E.:** The early churches of Lebanon County. *An address delivered at the 3d annual banquet of the Lebanon County Historical Society, Dec. 21, 1900. Reported by John Ruth and subsequently revised by Th. E. Schmauk. In: Papers read before the Lebanon County Historical Society. Vol. I. Lebanon, Pa. 1898—1901. pp. 358—384, ill.* [4389

Sachse, Julius Friedrich: A photographic ramble in the Millbach Valley *(Lebanon Co., Penna.) Reprint from: The American Journal of Photography, Sept., 1896. Philadelphia, Pa.: Press of Alfred J. Ferris 1896. pp. 15, ill.* [4390

Schantz, F. J. F.: Myerstown — its men and events of the past. *In: Papers read before the Lebanon County Historical Society. Vol. IV. Lebanon, Pa. 1906—1909. pp. 5—19.* [4391

Schmauk, Theodore E.: Old Salem in Lebanon, a history of the congregation and town. *Lebanon, Pa.: Press of Report Publishing Co. 1898. pp. XI, 208, ill.* [4392

[Schmauk, Theodore E.]: The history of Eighth street, Lebanon, Penn'a. *By Th. E. Schmauk. Paper read before the Lebanon County Historical Society, Oct. 21, 1898. Edited by P. C. Croll, and again presented before the Society, April 28, 1922. In: Papers read before the Lebanon County Historical Society. Vol. VIII. Lebanon, Pa. 1920—1924. pp. 211—250, ill., map.* [4393

Seltzer, A. Frank: Steitztown. *In: Papers read before the Lebanon County Historical Society. Vol. III. Lebanon, Pa. 1905—1906. pp. 79—83.* [4394

Shenk, Hiram H.: The Anville Academy. *In: Papers read before the Lebanon County Historical Society. Vol. II. Lebanon, Pa. 1901—1904. pp. 399—433.* [4395

— The Know-nothing party in Lebanon County. *In: Papers read before the Lebanon County Historical Society. Vol. IV. Lebanon, Pa. 1906—1909. pp. 54—78.* [4396

— Some hitherto unpublished documents pertaining to Lebanon County's part in the War of the Revolution. *In: Papers read before the Lebanon County Historical Society. Vol. VII. Lebanon, Pa. 1916—1919. pp. 39—63.* [4397

— The Myerstown riot of 1793. *In: Papers read before the Lebanon County Historical Society. Vol. VII. Lebanon, Pa. 1916—1919. pp. 430—444.* [4398

— A history of the Lebanon Valley in Pennsylvania. *2 vols. Published by The National Historical Association, Inc. Harrisburg, Pa.: Telegraph Press 1930. pp. (3), 17—372. ill.; Personal sketches: pp. (3), 17—255, ill.* [4399

Shuey, D. B.: Walmer's Church and the old school house. *In: The Pennsylvania-German. Vol. VIII. Lebanon, Pa. 1907. pp. 334—336.* [4400

Stein, Thomas S.: Annville's oldest burial-place and its memories. *In: Papers read before the Lebanon County Historical Society. Vol. VI. Lebanon, Pa. 1912—1916. pp. 345—413, ill., [Part II. Inscriptions. pp. 357—411.]* [4401

— Centennial history of Lebanon Classis of the Reformed Church in the United States. *Together with brief sketches of various churches, congregations and prominent workers in the kingdom. 1820—1920. Compiled by . . . Lebanon, Pa.: Sowers Printing Co. 1920. pp. XIV, 473, ill., map.* [4402

Stein, Thomas S.: Annville Township. An election district. *In: Papers read before the Lebanon County Historical Society. Vol. VIII. Lebanon, Pa. 1920 —1924. pp. 147—157.* [4403
— Granny Forney's cake and beer chop. *In: Papers read before the Lebanon County Historical Society, Jan. 14, 1927. Vol. IX. Lebanon, Pa. 1925—1928. pp. 241 —259, ill.* [4404
Strouss, B. Morris: The founding of Fredericksburg. *In: Papers read before the Lebanon County Historical Society. Vol. VI. Lebanon, Pa. 1912—1916. pp. 97 —113, map.* [4405
Wagner, Henr.: Kurzgefaßte hundertjährige Geschichte der Berg Kirche in Libanon County, Pa. *Herausgegeben von F. W. Kremer, Chambersburg, 1855. 8 S.* [4406
Warner, Joseph H.: Annville: township and town. *In: Papers read before the Lebanon County Historical Society. Vol. V. Lebanon, Pa. 1909—1912. pp. 69— 127, ill.* [4407
Wheeler, George: Richard Penn's manor of Andolhea. *In: The Pennsylvania Magazin of History and Biography. Vol. LVIII. Philadelphia, Pa. 1934. pp. 193—212, map.* [4408
Woelfly, Simon J.: Swatara Collegiate Institute, Jonestown, Lebanon County, Pa. *In: Papers read before the Lebanon County Historical Society. Vol. IV. Lebanon, Pa. 1906—1909. pp. 23—51, ill.* [4409
Young, Hiram: A brief history of Schaefferstown. *[s. l. ca. 1900]. pp. 234.* [4410
Yundt, Thomas M.: A history of Bethany Orphans' Home of the Reformed Church in the United States. Located at Womelsdorf, Pa. *Revised and enlarged by Wilson F. Moore. Philadelphia, Pa.: Publication Board of the Reformed Church in the United States. pp. 165.* [4411
Zerbe, Charles, M.: Lebanon County: — A brief of its celebrated law cases. *In: Papers read before the Lebanon County Historical Society. Vol. I. Lebanon, Pa. 1898—1901. pp. 385—392.* [4412
— Annals of Schaefferstown with some reference to the early Jewish community. *In: Papers read before the Lebanon County Historical Society. Vol. IV. Lebanon, Pa. 1906—1909. pp. 294—316.* [4413
Zimmerman, Thomas C.: Lebanon: A bit of retrospect, reminiscence and sentiment. *In: Papers read before the Lebanon County Historical Society. Vol. I.*

Lebanon, Pa. 1898—1901. pp. 73—80. Reprint in: Olla Podrida, consisting of addresses . . . Reading, Pa. 1908 [= no. 413]. pp. 139—167. [4414
Biographical annals of Lebanon County, Pa. *containing sketches of prominent and representative citizens and many of the early settled families. Chicago, Ill.: J. H. Beers & Co. 1904. pp. XII, 772, ill.* [4415
Revolutionary pensioners, living in Lebanon County, in 1800. *In: Notes and Queries. Edited by W. H. Egle. Third series, vol. I. 1884—1887. Harrisburg, Pa. 1887. pp. 344—345. Reprint in: Third series, vol. II. Harrisburg, Pa. 1896. p. 49.* [4416
Some old marriages. *(Copied from the old Moravian Church records near Lebanon, 1751—1811.) In: Notes and Queries. Edited by W. H. Egle. Fourth series, vol. I. 1891—1893. Harrisburg, Pa. 1893. pp. 18—19.* [4417
Marriage record of Hebron Church. *In: Notes and Queries. Edited by W. H. Egle. First series, vol. IV. Harrisburg, Pa. 1881. pp. 137—139. Reprint in: First and second series, vol. I. Harrisburg, Pa. 1894. pp. 461—464.* [4418
The Hebron diary. Extracts from the diary of the Moravian Church at Hebron, now Lebanon, Pa. 1775—1783. *Translated by Jacob H. Redsecker. In: Notes and Queries. Fourth series, vol. II. 1894. Harrisburg, Pa. 1895. pp. 332—338; 341—345; 347—351; 353—356; 356— 365.* [4419
Extracts from the records of the Moravian congregation at Hebron, Pa., 1775— 1781. — *Extracts from the German, of remnants of the diary of the pastor, Rev. P. C. Bader, translated. In: The Pennsylvania Magazine of History and Biography. Vol. XVIII. Philadelphia, Pa. 1894. pp. 449—462.* [4420
Souvenir. [Unveiling of the Stoever monument.] *Annville, Pa.: Press of the Annville Journal. 1895. pp. (17).* [4421
Some old tax lists. (Tax for the King's use, Heidelberg, 1758; Lebanon tax, 1751.) *Reprint in: Notes and Queries. Edited by W. H. Egle. Annual vol. 1898. Harrisburg, Pa. 1899. pp. 18—21.* [4422
Baptismal records of the First Reformed Church at Lebanon, Pa., from 1769 to 1780. *In: Notes and Queries. Edited by W. H. Egle. Annual vol. 1900. Harrisburg, Pa. 1901. pp. 88—91.* [4423

Lehigh County

Abel, Allen E.: The Emaus Moravian congregation. *(Translated and compiled from original sources.) In: Proceedings and Papers read before the Lehigh County Historical Society. Vol. II. Allentown, Pa. 1910. pp. 47—53.* [4424

Bailey, Harry D.: Several hours with the pioneers. *In: Annual Proceedings of the Lehigh County Historical Society. Allentown, Pa. 1924. pp. 83—87, ill.* [4425

Balliet, L. B.: A Lehigh County English school seventy years ago. *In: The Pennsylvania-German. Vol. VIII. Lebanon, Pa. 1907. pp. 523—527, ill.* [4426

Bartholomew, Allen R.: Brief history. Salem Reformed Church, Allentown, Pa. 1875—1900. *Published by the consistory. Allentown, Pa.: John H. Ritter 1901. pp. 166, ill.* [4427

Ben [Pseudonym für Benjamin F. Trexler]: Skizzen aus dem Lecha-Thale. Eine Sammlung von Nachrichten über die ersten Ansiedlungen der Weißen in dieser Gegend. *Allentown, Pa.: Drukkerei des ,,Friedens-Bote" — Trexler & Härtzell 1880—1886. 260 S.* [4428

Bossard, James Herbert: The churches of Allentown. A study in statistics. *Thesis of Ph. D. University of Pennsylvania, Philadelphia, Pa., Allentown, Pa.: Jacks 1918. pp. 116.* [4429

Brunner, Edmund de S.: Cooperation in Coopersburg. *New York, N. Y.: Missionary Education Movement of the United States and Canada 1916. pp. XVI, 95, ill. = Library of Christian Progress.* [4430

Cooper, C. J.: History of Jerusalem Church, Eastern Salisbury. *Read at the Sesqui-Centennial July 25, 1909. In: Proceedings and Papers read before the Lehigh County Historical Society. Vol. II. Allentown, Pa. 1910. pp. 69—99, ill; Also separately printed pp. 35, ill.* [4431

— History of Jerusalem Church, Eastern Salisbury. *In: Proceedings and Papers read before the Lehigh County Historical Society. Vol. II. Allentown, Pa. 1910. pp. 69—99, ill.* [4432

Croll, P. C.: Historical pilgrimages into Pennsylvania-Germandom. Fishing along two Lehigh County streams. *In: The Pennsylvania-German. Vol. VI. Lebanon, Pa. 1905. pp. 310—327, ill. [See no. 295]* [4433

— Historical pilgrimages into Pennsylvania-Germandom. Down the Little Lehigh from source to mouth. *In: The Pennsylvania-German. Vol. VI. Lebanon, Pa. 1905. pp. 366—378, ill. [See no. 295]* [4434

Darms, J. M. G.: The New Salem, Allentown, Pa. *Allentown, Pa.: Berkemeyer, Keck & Co. 1915. pp. 63, ill.* [4435

De Long, S.: Slatington, Pa. *In: The Pennsylvania-German. Vol. XI. Lititz, Pa. 1910. pp. 589—593, ill.* [4436

Egle, William Henry: Provincial papers: Proprietary, supply, and state tax lists of the counties of Northampton and Northumberland, for the years 1772 to 1787. *Edited by . . . Harrisburg, Pa.: Wm. Stanley, Ray 1898. pp. XII, 805. = Pennsylvania Archives. Third series, vol. XIX.* [4437

Fogel, E. M.: Fogelsville. *In: Annual Proceedings of the Lehigh County Historical Society, Allentown, Pa. 1930. pp. 9—12.* [4438

[Fretz, Franklin Kline]: Historical sketch of St. John's Lutheran Church. 1740—1915, Easton, Pa. *Easton, Pa.: Free Press Publishing Co. 1915. pp. 64, ill.* [4439

Gardner, G. F.: Geschichte der Ev. Luth. St. Peters-Gemeinde zu Allentown, Pa. 1867—1892. *Allentown, Pa.:Trexler und Hartzell, ,,Welt-Bote" Druckerei 1892. 12 S.* [4440

[Geissinger, D. H. - Kolb, Reuben]: 1832—1882. Jubilate Deo. memorial volume, St. John's Lutheran Church, Easton, Pa. *Containing an account of the jubilee services, the historical sermon, the charters of the Church and the Benevolent Society, and a list of the officers of the church and the officers, teachers, and pupils of the Sunday school. Published by authority of the Church Council. pp. 84, ill.* [4441

Greiss, George A.: 1762—1912. 150th anniversary November 10—17, 1912. St. Paul's Evangelical Lutheran Church, S 8th Street, Allentown, Pa. *[s. l., s. d.] pp. 33, ill.* [4442

Hartman, William L.: The mayors of Allentown. *In: Proceedings and Papers read before the Lehigh County Historical Society. Vol. I. Allentown, Pa. 1908. pp. 205—225, ill.* [4443

— The mayors of a typical Pennsylvania German city (Allentown, Pa.). *In: The Pennsylvania-German. Vol. IX. Cleona, Pa. 1908. pp. 147—152, ill.* [4444

Hauser, James J.: A history of Lehigh County, Pennsylvania. *From the earliest settlement to the present time including much valuable information for the use of schools, families, libraries. Emaus, Pa.: Times Publishing Co. 1901. pp. 94, ill. Second edition: Allentown, Pa.: Jacks 1902. pp. 128.* [4445
— Northampton Town and Allentown. A historical sketch. *In: The Pennsylvania-German. Vol. VII. Lebanon, Pa. 1906. pp. 102—111; 208—211; 244—252, ill.* [4446
— History of Salomons' Reformed Church, Macungie. *In: Proceedings and Papers read before the Lehigh County Historical Society. Vol. II. Allentown, Pa. 1910. pp. 100—105.* [4447
Hecker, L. P., Schaadt, Jas. L. and Hottenstein, Marcus S.: History petition for character, constitution, bylaws, and list of members of the Lehigh County Agricultural Society, organized at Egypt, Pa., Jan. 24, 1852. *Allentown, Pa.: Press of Berkemeyer, Keck & Co. 1902. pp. 54, ill.* [4448
Helffrich, Wm. A.: Geschichte verschiedener Gemeinden in Lecha und Berks Counties, wie auch Nachricht über die sie bedienenden Prediger, vornehmlich über die Familie Helffrich, deren Ursprung und Ausbreitung in Europa, nach authentischen Quellen, und deren Immigration und Verbreitung in Amerika, nebst einem Rückblick in das kirchliche Leben Ostpennsylvaniens. *Allentown, Pa.: Trexler & Hartzell 1891. 104 S.* [4449
Henninger, Milton C.: History of the Bar Association of Lehigh County. *In: Proceedings. Lehigh County Historical Society. Annual publication for the year 1923. Allentown, Pa. 1923. pp. 14—46.* [4450
Henry, M. S.: History of the Lehigh Valley, *containing a copious selection of the most interesting facts, traditions, biographical sketches, anecdotes, etc. relating to its history of all its internal improvements, progress of the coal and iron trade, manufactures, etc. Easton, Pa.: Published by Bixler & Corwin 1860. pp. XII, 436, ill.* [4451
Jordan, John W., Green, Edgar Moore and Ettinger, George T.: Historic homes and institutions and genealogical and personal memoirs of the Lehigh Valley, Pa. *Under the editional editorship . . . 2 vols.*

New York, N. Y. — Chicago, Ill. The Lewis Publishing Co. 1905. pp. VII, 516, ill. V, 528, ill. [4452
K.[eller, E.]: In memoriam. Names and age of ministers of the gospel of the different denominations buried in the Protestant public cemetries at Allentown, Pa. *Collected in 1909 and alphabetically arranged by . . . In: The Pennsylvania-German. Vol. X. Lititz, Pa. 1909. pp. 626—627.* [4453
Kistler, J. G.: Lynn's honor roll. *In: The Pennsylvania-German. Vol. X. Lititz, Pa. 1909. pp. 594—597.* [4454
Kloß, H.: „Allentown." *In: Handwörterbuch des Grenz- und Auslanddeutschtums. Bd. I. Breslau 1933 [= Nr. 93]. S. 89.* [4454a
Krick, Thomas H.: History of Mickley's Church. *In: Proceedings and Papers read before the Lehigh County Historical Society. Vol. II. Allentown, Pa. 1910. pp. 26—36, ill.* [4455
— History of Trinity Reformed Church, Coplay, Lehigh County, Pa. With records of baptisms, confirmations, marriages, burials, and present membership. *Prepared and arranged by . . . Allentown, Pa.: H. Ray Haas & Co. 1922. pp. 128.* [4456
Lambert, James F. and Reinhard, Henry J.: A history of Catasauqua in Lehigh County, Pa. *Allentown, Pa.: The Searle & Dressler Co., Inc. 1914. pp. XVI, 408, ill.* [4457
Laux, James B.: Fusion of races in Lehigh County. *In: Proceedings and Papers read before the Lehigh County Historical Society. Allentown, Pa. 1922. pp. 3—11.* [4458
Mathews, Alfred and Hungerford, Austin N.: Histories of the Counties of Lehigh and Carbon in the Commonwealth of Pennsylvania. *Philadelphia, Pa.: Everts & Richards 1884. pp. XI, 802, ill., map.* [4459
[Meckstroth, W. L. - Bond, Wm. F.:] Joint anniversary of the Reformed and Lutheran congregations. *November, 1923, Longswamp Union Church. Edited by . . . [s. l.] 1923. pp. 29, ill.* [4460
Mickley, Minnie F.: Old Egypt church yard. Tombstone inscriptions in old Egypt church yard, Egypt, Lehigh County, Pa. *In: Notes and Queries. Edited by W. H. Egle. Annual volume 1898. Harrisburg, Pa. 1899. pp. 74—76; 81—85; 86—89; 93—96.* [4461

Mickley, Minnie F.: Founders and organizers of Mickley's Church, Whitehall Township. *In: Proceedings and Papers read before the Lehigh County Historical Society. Vol. II. Allentown, Pa. 1910. pp. 38—42.* [4462

Miller, C. C.: Golden anniversary 1873—1923. St. John's Evangelical Lutheran Church, Coplay, Pa. *[s. l.; s. d.] pp. 72.* [4463

Mohr, Ella J.: The Lehigh County fair. *In: The Pennsylvania-German. Vol. XI. Lititz, Pa. 1910. pp. 547—549, ill.* [4464

Morrison, T. Maxwell: Coopersburg survey. Being a study of the community around Coopersburg, Lehigh County, Pa. *Taken under the auspices of the Coopersburg Neighborhood Association and the Moravian Country Church Commission. Edmund de S. Brunner, Secretary. Easton, Pa.: Moravian Country Church Commission 1914. pp. 34, ill.* [4465

Neimeyer, Tilghman: A partial burial record of the Western Salisbury Lutheran and Reformed cemeteries. *In: The Pennsylvania-German. Vol. X. Lititz, Pa. 1909. Appendix: Genealogical record of pioneer Pennsylvania families. pp. 17—24.* [4466

Roberts, Charles R.: Records of Egypt Reformed Church, Lehigh County, Pa. 1734—1834. *Translated by . . . with notes. 1905. Harrisburg, Pa.: Harrisburg Publishing Co. 1906. In: Pennsylvania Archives. Sixth series, vol. VI. Harrisburg, Pa. 1907. pp. 151.* [4467

— Sketches of some settlers in Lehigh County prior to 1750. *In: Proceedings of the Lehigh County Historical Society. Vol. I, no. 2. 1906. pp. (7). Reprint in: Proceedings and Papers read before the Lehigh County Historical Society. Vol. I. Allentown, Pa. 1908. pp. 50—61.* [4468

— Historic buildings of the Lehigh Valley. *In: The Pennsylvania-German. Vol. VII. Lebanon, Pa. 1906. pp. 313—314; 428—429; ill. Vol. VIII. 1907. pp. 72—73; 169—170; 598—599, ill.* [4469

—-Schindel, J. D.: History of Egypt Church. *Read before the Lehigh County Historical Society. Allentown, Pa. (1908). pp. 72, ill.* [4470

— History of the Reformed congregation of Egypt Church. *In: Proceedings and Papers read before the Lehigh County Historical Society. Vol. I. Allentown, Pa. 1908. pp. 71—100, ill.* [4471

Roberts, Charles R.: Revolutionary patriots of Allentown and vicinity. *In: Proceedings and Papers read before the Lehigh County Historical Society. Vol. I. Allentown, Pa. 1908. pp. 197—204.* [4472

— Tombstone inscriptions of Lower Milford Township, Lehigh County, Pa. *Transcribed by . . . In: The Pennsylvania-German. Vol. X. Lititz, Pa. 1909. Appendix: Genealogical record of pioneer Pennsylvania families. pp. 13—15.* [4473

— A glimpse at Allentown, Pa. *In: The Pennsylvania-German. Vol. XI. Lititz, Pa. 1910. pp. 291—298, ill.* [4474

— Lehigh County, Pa. *Reprint from: "Chronicle and News." Allentown, Pa. Anniversary and industrial number, Aug. 3, 1912. In: The Penn Germania. Vol. I. = Old series, vol. XIII. Lititz, Pa. 1912. pp. 742—747.* [4475

— Allentown, Pa., in the Revolution. *Paper read before the Lehigh County Historical Society. In: The Penn Germania. Vol. I. = Old series, vol. XIII. Lititz, Pa. 1912. pp. 158—160.* [4476

—, Stoudt, John Baer, Krick, Thomas H. and Dietrich, William J.: History of Lehigh County, Pa. and a genealogical and biographical record of its families. *3 vols. Allentown, Pa.: Lehigh Valley Publishing Co. 1914. pp. XI, 1101, ill. maps. Genealogical and biographical: pp. 774, 744 a—744 d, XI, ill. pp. 775—1466, XI, ill.* [4477

[—] 1770—1918. *History of Trout Hall, home of the Lehigh County Historical Society. Issued by the Lehigh County Historical Society. [s. l.] 1918. pp. 18, ill.* [4478

— Men of Lehigh County in the various wars. *In: Proceedings and Papers read before the Lehigh County Historical Society, Allentown, Pa. 1922. pp. 12—28.* [4479

— Fragments of early history. *In: Annual Proceedings of the Lehigh County Historical Society. Allentown, Pa. 1924. pp. 88—91.* [4480

— The Jennings or Geisinger farm and its owners. *In: Annual Proceedings of the Lehigh County Historical Society. Allentown, Pa. 1930. pp. 5—8.* [4481

— Early settlers in the vicinity of Friedensville. *In: Annual Proceedings of the Lehigh County Historical Society. Allentown, Pa. 1930. pp. 27—30.* [4482

Roberts, Charles Rhoades: Lecha Kaunti un Ellentaun. *In: Hamburg-Amerika-Post. Bd. II, H. 9. Hamburg 1930. S. 292—294.* [4482a]

Rupp, I. Daniel: History of Northampton, Lehigh, Monroe, Carbon and Schuylkill Counties: *containing a brief history of the first settlers, topography of townships notices of leading events, incidents, and interesting facts in the early history of the counties: with an appendix. Lancaster, Pa.: Published and sold by G. Hills; Harrisburg, Pa.: Hickok and Cantine 1845. pp. XIV, 568, ill.* [4483]

Schantz, F. J. F.: Historical discourse at the Sesqui-Centennial of Jordan Evangelical Lutheran congregation of South Whitehall Township, Lehigh County, Pa. *Sunday, June 10th, 1894. Published by request. Allentown, Pa.: Haines & Worman 1894. pp. 40, ill.* [4484]

— Das 155ste Jahresfest der Jerusalem Kirche in Salzburg Township, Lecha County, Pennsylvanien am Sonntag, den 13ten September 1896. *Predigt. Auf Verlangen der Kirchengemeinde gedruckt. [s. l.; s. d.] 11 S.* [4485]

— Allentown and its vicinity about sixty years ago. *In: Proceedings and Papers read before the Lehigh County Historical Society. Vol. I. Allentown, Pa. 1908. pp. 154—183, ill.* [4486]

Schindel, J. D.: History of the Lutheran congregation of Egypt Church. *In: Proceedings and Papers read before the Lehigh County Historical Society. Vol. I. Allentown, Pa. 1908. pp. 102—121, ill.* [4487]

— The Egypt Church. *In: Proceedings and Papers read before the Lehigh County Historical Society. Vol. I. Allentown, Pa. 1908. pp. 123—140.* [4488]

Schmucker, B. M.: Historical discourse. At the twenty-fifth anniversary of the consecration of St. John's Church, Allentown, Pa. *Allentown, Pa.: Brobst, Diehl & Co. 1880. pp. 20.* [4489]

Schuler, H. A.: The Hampton furnace, reminiscences of an important industry and its old-time owners. *In: The Pennsylvania-German. Vol. VII. Lebanon, Pa. 1906. pp. 233—240, ill. Reprint: In: Proceedings and Papers read before the Lehigh County Historical Society. Vol. I. Allentown, Pa. 1908. pp. 141—152, ill.* [4490]

Seiberling, F. C.: Lynn Township and its professional men. *In: The Pennsylvania-German. Vol. IX. Cleona, Pa. 1908. pp. 158—165, ill.* [4492]

Shuman, J. C.: History of St. Henry's Church [Lehigh Co., Pa.]. *In: The Pennsylvania-German. Vol. XI. Lititz, Pa. 1910. pp. 343—345.* [4491]

Singmaster, J. A.: The 150th anniversary of St. Paul's Evangelical Lutheran Church, Allentown, Pa. *In: The Lutheran Quarterly. Vol. XLIII. Gettysburg, Pa. 1913. pp. 1—13.* [4493]

Stoudt, John Baer: History of Jerusalem Lutheran and Reformed Church of Western Salisbury, Lehigh County, Pa. With complete records of all members of both congregations, baptisms, confirmations, marriages and burials. *Prepared and arranged by Tilghman Neimeyer, John B. Stoudt, Myron O. Rath, Jacob J. Reinhard, Marcus J. Kemmerer, Committee. Edited by . . . Allentown, Pa.: H. Ray Haas & Co. 1911. pp. 283, ill.* [4494]

— Rev. Michael Schlatter in the Lehigh Valley June 24—July 2, 1747. *In: The Reformed Church Review. Fourth series, vol. XX. Philadelphia, Pa. 1916. pp. 83—97.* [4495]

Trexler, B. F.: Some changes in the Lehigh Valley in my life. *In: The Pennsylvania-German. Vol. XI. Lititz, Pa. 1910. pp. 299—300.* [4496]

Weiser, Charles W.: Sketches of men once living in Lehigh County who were considered eccentric men. *In: Annual Proceedings of the Lehigh County Historical Society. Allentown, Pa. 1924. pp. 100—106.* [4497]

— The early hotels of Allentown. *In: Annual Proceedings of the Lehigh County Historical Society. Allentown, Pa. 1924. pp. 92—99.* [4498]

Wuchter, A. C.: Jacob's Church, Jacksonville, Lehigh County, Pa. *In: The Pennsylvania-German. Vol. X. Lititz, Pa. 1909. pp. 162—165, ill.* [4499]

Commonwealth of Pennsylvania. Manufacturing and mercantile resources of the Lehigh Valley, including historical sketches of the prominent towns. A descriptive industrial and statistical review. Progress enterprise, development. *Philadelphia, Pa.: Industrial Publishing Co. 1881. pp. 205, ill.* [4500]

Portrait and biographical record of Lehigh, Northampton and Carbon Counties, Pa. *Containing biographical sketches of prominent and representative citizens of the counties, together with biographies and portraits of all presidents of the United States. Chicago, Ill.: Chapman Publishing Co. 1894. pp. (1), 19—999.* [4501

Marriage register of the Moravian Church at Emaus. 1758—1800. *In: Record of Pennsylvania marriages, prior to 1810. Vol. II. Harrisburg, Pa. 1880. = Pennsylvania Archives. Second series, vol. IX. Edited by John B. Linn and Wm. H. Egle. Harrisburg, Pa. 1880. pp. 153—154.
Reprint Harrisburg, Pa. 1895. pp. 155—158.* [4503

Records of St. Paul's Evangelical Lutheran congregation *[familiarly known as the „Blue Church", within the present limits of Upper Saucon Township]* Lehigh County, Pa. 1750—1764. *Contributed by* Clarence E. Beckel. *In: The Pennsylvania Magazine of History and Biography. Vol. XXXV. Philadelphia, Pa. 1911. pp. 188—198.* [4504

Ein 170 Jahre alter deutscher Wohnsitz in Amerika. *[Bogert Platz in Salzburg Township, nahe Allentown, Pa.] Reprint from: Allentown Republikaner. In: Der Deutsche Pionier. Jg. VIII, Cincinnati, O. 1876. S. 59.* [4505

Saint Luke's Evangelical Lutheran Church, Easton, Pa. *[s. l. 1891.] pp. 56, ill.* [4506

A golden sheaf of history. Fiftieth anniversary. Historical shetch. St. Paul's Evangelical Lutheran congregation, Catasauqua, Pa. 1852—1902. *[s. l. 1902.] pp. 72, ill.* [4507

From Mountainville to Macungie. *In: The Pennsylvania-German. Vol. XI. Lititz, Pa. 1910. pp. 333—339, ill.* [4508

Ziegler's Church, Pa. *Reprint from: Reformed Church Record. In: The Pennsylvania-German. Vol. XII. Lititz, Pa. 1911. p. 234.* [4509

1762. 150th anniversary of the founding of the City of Allentown, Pennsylvania. 1912. *Issued by the Lehigh County Historical Society. Allentown, Pa.: Berkemeyer, Keck & Co. 1912. pp. (2), ill.* [4510

An act of assembly (passed April 1st, 1778 and a petition of the Mennonites in

Saucon, then Northampton, now Lehigh County). *In: The Mennonite Year Book and Almanac for 1915. Quakertown, Pa. 1915. pp. 36—38.* [4511

Interments at the Saucon Mennonite Church, Saucon Lehigh County, Pa. *In: The Mennonite Year Book and Almanac for 1915. Quakertown, Pa. 1915. pp. 38—47.* [4512

Seventy-fifth anniversary history of St. John's Evangelical Lutheran Church, Allentown, Pa. 1855—1930. *[s. l. 1930.] pp. 39, ill.* [4513

Characters who lived in Allentown during the '70s and '80s of last century. *In: Annual Proceedings of the Lehigh County Historical Society. Allentown, Pa. 1930. pp. 51—53.* [4514

Allentown had a branch of Young Men's Christian Association that ceased to exist before the Civil War. *In: Annual Proceedings of the Lehigh County Historical Society. Allentown, Pa. 1930. pp. 56—57.* [4515

Three hundred visit the Mechling farms. Two hundreth anniversary of arrival of progenitor is observed. *Morning Call, June 16, 1929. In: Annual Proceedings of the Lehigh County Historical Society. Allentown, Pa. 1930. pp. 61—64, ill.* [4516

The story of a patent. *[Extract from the Patent issued by the Commonwealth of Pennsylvania, June 3, 1791 to Adam Sherer, for a certain tract of land in Upper Milford Township, Lehigh County, Pa.] In: The Perkiomen Region. Vol. IX, no. 2. Pennsburg. Pa. 1931 p. 64* [4517

Luzerne County

Bradsby, H. C.: History of Luzerne County, Pa. with biographical selections. *Chicago, Ill.: S. B. Nelson & Co. 1893. pp. IX, 17—1509, ill., map.* [4518

Kulp, Geo. B.: Families of the Wyoming Valley. Biographical, genealogical and historical sketches of the Bench and Bar of Luzerne, County, Pa. *3 vols. Wilkes-Barre, Pa.: E. B. Yordy 1885—1890. pp. VIII, 504, (3); VII, 505—1038, (7); IX, 1039—1423.* [4519

Nagel, Peter Conrad: Geschichte der St. Nickolaus Kirche und Schule in Wilkes-Barre, Pa., nebst einem Bericht über die

Schwestern der Christlichen Liebe in den Vereinigten Staaten. *Wilkes-Barre, Pa.: Druck des „Leucht-Thurms". 1895. 92 S., ill.* [4520

Pearce, Stewart: Annals of Luzerne County, Pa., a record of interesting events, traditions, and anecdotes. From the first settlement in Wyoming Valley to 1860. *Philadelphia, Pa.: J. B. Lippincott & Co. 1860. pp. XII, 13—554, ill., map. Second edition . . . to 1866. Philadelphia, Pa. 1866. pp.XII,13—564,ill.,map.* [4521

Plumb, Henry Blackman: History of Hanover Township including Sugar Notch, Ashley, and Nanticoke Boroughs, and also a history of Wyoming Valley in Luzerne County, Pa. *Wilkes-Barre, Pa.: Robert Baur 1885. pp. 499, map.* [4522

Stofflett, Sefellen E.: Reformed church history of Hazleton and vicinity. *Hazleton, Pa., July, 1924. pp. 106, ill.* [4523

[Wagner, John]: 1874—1899. Silver jubilee souvenir of Trinity Evangelical Lutheran Church, Hazleton, Pa. Celebration, June 27 to July 2, 1899. *Hazleton, Pa.: Published by the order of the Church Council 1899. pp. 90, ill.* [4524

History of Luzerne County. Pa. with illustrations and biographical sketches of some of its prominent men and pioneers. *New York, N. Y.: W. W. Munsell & Co. 1880. pp. 452, ill.* [4525

Lycoming County

[Anspach, J. M.]: 1871—1896. Silver jubilee souvenir of Saint Paul's Lutheran congregation. Williamsport, Pa. Celebration, June 13—15, 1896. *Williamsport, Pa.: The Sun Printing and Binding Co. 1897. pp. 54, ill.* [4526

Frederick, T. J.: Historical sketch of the Lutheran Church in Nippenose Valley, Lycoming County, Pa., *prepared by . . . and delivered in both churches the first and second Sunday of January, 1887.* Also a brief history of the settlement of Nippenose Valley *written by Col. Jacob Sallade (originally published in the Sun & Banner. Williamsport, Pa.: Scholl Brothers, Power Printing House 1887. pp. 50.* [4527

Meginness, J. F.: Otzinachson: A history of the West Branch Valley of the Susquehanna: *its first settlement, privations endured by the early pioneers, Indian wars, predatory incursions, abductions and massacres together with an account of the*

fair play system and the scenes of the Big Runaway; copies of curious old documents, biographical sketches of the leading settlers, together with anecdotes, statistics, and much valuable matter entirely new. Revised edition. Vol. I. Williamsport, Pa.: Gazette and Bulletin House 1889. pp. 702, V, maps.
[First edition 1856.] [4528

Meginness, J. F.: Biographical annals of deceased residents of the West Branch Valley of the Susquehanna, from the earliest times to the present. *Williamsport, Pa.: Gazette and Bulletin Printing House 1889. pp. 272.* [4529

— History of Lycoming County, Pa. *Including its aboriginal history; the colonial and revolutionary periods; early settlement and subsequent growth; organization and civil administration; the legal and medical professions; internal improvements; past and present history of Williamsport; manufacturing and lumber interests; religious, educational, and social development; geology and agriculture; military record; sketches of boroughs, townships and villages; portraits and biographies of pioneers and representative citizens, etc., etc. Edited by . . . Chicago, Ill.: Brown, Runk & Co. Publishers; Press of John Morris Co., Chicago 1892. pp. XV, 17—1268, ill., maps.* [4530

[—] List of books and pamphlets printed and written in Lycoming County, Pa. *By John of Lancaster. [Pseudonym]. In: Notes and Queries. Edited by W. H. Egle. Annual vol. 1897. Harrisburg, Pa. 1898. pp. 29—33.* [4531

Leisenring, Edwin H.: 1852—1882. Celebration of the thirtieth anniversary of the formation of the Evangelical Lutheran Church, Muncy, Lycoming County, Pa., on Sunday, Nov. 5, 1882. *pp. 9.* [4532

Steck, J. M.: 1791—1891. Historical addresses on the Centennial of Immanuel's Lutheran Church of Muncy Valley, Pa. *Delivered July 23, 1891, at the Muncy Front Ponds. Published by request. Williamsport, Pa.: Keystone Lithograph Co. 1891. pp. 36, ill.* [4533

— „A backward look," or reminiscences of the Lutheran Church in Lycoming County. *An address delivered at the dedicatory services of Messiah's Lutheran Church, South Williamsport, Pa., June 16, 1890. Rewritten and enlarged. pp. 55.* [4534

[Tome, Philip]: Pioneer life: or, thirty years a hunter. Being scenes and adventures in the life of Philip Tome, fifteen years interpreter for Cornplater and Gov. Blacksnake, chiefs on the Alleghany River. *[Reprint of a scarce edition of 1854.] With a preface by* Henry W. Shoemaker, *and an appendix by* A. Monroe Aurand, jr. *Harrisburg, Pa.: Privately printed by The Aurand Press 1928. pp. IX, 173, ill.* [4535

Mifflin County

Cochran, Joseph: History of Mifflin County, its physical peculiarities, soil, climate, &c, including an early sketch of the State of Pennsylvania. *Vol. I. Harrisburg, Pa.: Patriot Publishing Co. 1879. pp. 422, ill.* [4536

James, Henry F.: The Kishacoquillas Valley. A study in human geography. *In: The Bulletin of the Geographical Society of Philadelphia, Pa. Vol. XXVIII, (no. 4.) Philadelphia, Pa. 1930. pp. 223—239, ill.* [4537

Jordan, John W.: A history of the Juniata Valley and its people. *Under the editorial supervision of ... 3 vols. New York, N. Y. Lewis Historical Publishing Co, 1913. pp. (5), 496; 497—944; 945—1403, ill. [Mifflin County. pp. 68—141.]* [4538

Peachey, Samuel W.: Amish in Kishacoquillas Valley, Mifflin County, Pa. *Scottdale, Pa.: Mennonite Publishing House 1930. pp. 48.* [4539

Rupp, I. Daniel: History and topography of Northumberland, Huntingdon, Mifflin, Centre, Union, Columbia, Juniata and Clinton Counties, Pa., *embracing local and general events, leading incidents, descriptions of the principal boroughs, towns, villages, etc., etc. with a copious appendix: embellished by engravings. Compiled from authentic sources. Lancaster, Pa.: G. Hills 1847. pp. 562, (2), ill.* [4540

History of that part of the Susquehanna and Juniata Valleys embraced in the Counties of Mifflin, Juniata, Perry, Union, and Synder in the Commonwealth of Pennsylvania. *2 vols. Philadelphia, Pa.: Everts, Peck & Richards 1886. pp. 894, ill., maps; VI, 895—1602, ill., map.* [4541

Monroe County

Burrell, . . .: Reminiscences of George La Bar, the centenarian of Monroe County,

Pa., who is still living in his 107th year! and incidents in the early settlement of the Pennsylvania side of the River Valley from Easton to Bushkill. *Philadelphia, Pa.: Claxton, Remsen & Haffelfinger. 1870. pp. VIII, 9—111, ill.* [4542

[Hughes, Geo. C.]: The bells ringing the message of progress in Monroe County, Pa., and tributary country where industry and recreation meet. *Edited by . . . East Stroudsburg, Pa.: The Hughes Press 1915. pp. 136, ill.* [4543

Jordan, John W., Green, Edgar Moore and Ettinger, George T.: Historic homes and institutions and genealogical and personal memoirs of the Lehigh Valley, Pa. *Under the editorial editorship . . . 2 vols. New York, N. Y. — Chicago, Ill.: The Lewis Publishing Co. 1905. pp. VII, 516, ill.; V, 528, ill.* [4544

Keller, Robert Brown: History of Monroe County, Pa. *Stroudsburg, Pa.: The Monroe Publishing Co. 1927. pp. 500, ill.* [4545

Mathews, Alfred: History of Wayne, Pike and Monroe Counties, Pa. *Philadelphia, Pa.: R. T. Peck & Co. 1886. pp. X, 1283, ill., map. [Monroe County: pp. 982—1278.]* [4546

Rupp, I. Daniel: History of Northampton, Lehigh, Monroe, Carbon and Schuylkill Counties: *containing a brief history of the first settlers, topography of townships, notices of leading events, incidents, and interesting facts in the early history of these counties: with an appendix. Lancaster, Pa.: Published and sold by G. Hills; Harrisburg, Pa. Hickok and Cantine 1845. pp. XIV, 568, ill.* [4547

Tyson, Carroll B.: The Poconos. *Illustrated with photographs of the region and map. Philadelphia, Pa.: Innes & Sons 1929. pp. (5), 193, ill.* [4548

[Wuchter, A. C.]: The 100th anniversary 1806 Salem Church, Gilbert, Pa., Nov. 10th and 11th, 1906. History and biography. *Stroudsburg, Pa.: Times Print 1906. pp. 36, ill.* [4549

— Salem Church, Monroe County, Pa. *In: The Pennsylvania-German. Vol. X. Lititz, Pa. 1909. pp. 15—23.* [4550

Hark, J. Max: Meniológoméka. Annals of a Moravian Indian village an hundred and thirty years ago. *In: Transactions of the Moravian Historcial Society. Vol. II. Nazareth, Pa. 1886. pp. 129—144.* [4551

Hillmann, Ralf Ridgway: Old Dansbury and the Moravian mission. *Buffalo, N. Y.:*

*Kenworthy Printing Co. 1934. pp. 1—
100, ill., maps.* [4552
Leibert, Eugene: Wechquetank. *A paper
read before the Moravian Historical Society. Sept. 13, 1900. In: Transactions
of the Moravian Historical Society. Vol.
VII. Nazareth, Pa. 1906. pp. 57—82.*
[4553
Dedication of the monument at Wechquetank. *In: Transactions of the Moravian
Historical Society. Vol. VIII. Nazareth, Pa. 1900. pp. 3—5, ill.* [4554
Dedication of the monument at Meniológoméka, October 22, 1901. *In: Transactions of the Moravian Historical Society. Vol. VII. Nazareth, Pa. 1906.
pp. 17—27.* [4555
Monroe County reverie. *Reprint from:
Monroe County Record, Oct., 1912. In:
The Penn-Germania. Vol. II. = Old
series, vol. XIV. Cleona, Pa. 1913. pp.
20—21.*
*[Relative to Dottersville, Polks Town-
ship.]* [4556

Montgomery County

Anderson, M. M.: A glimpse of the Perkiomen Valley. *In: The Pennsylvania-
German. Vol. IX. Cleona, Pa. 1908.
pp. 508—510, ill.* [4557
Auge, M.: Lives of the eminent dead and
biographical notices of prominent living
citizens of Montgomery County, Pa.
*Norristown, Pa.: Published by the au-
thor 1879. pp. VIII, 9—568.* [4558
— Clock and watchmakers of Montgomery
County. *In: Historical Sketches. A Col-
lection of Papers prepared for the Historical Society of Montgomery County, Pa.
Vol. I. Norristown, Pa. 1895. pp. 187—
196.* [4559
Barker, Charles R.: Persons naturalized in
Montgomery County 1750—56, and 1760
—62. *In: The Perkiomen Region. Vol.
IX, no. 3. Pennsburg, Pa. 1931. pp. 66
—69.* [4560
Bean, Theordore W.: History of Montgomery
County. *Philadelphia, Pa.: Everts &
Peck 1884. pp. X, 1197. LXXXVIII,
ill. maps.* [4561
Bechtel, J. B.: The Mennonite home for the
aged. Located at Frederick, Montgo-
mery County, Pa. *In: Mennonite Year
Book and Almanac for 1922. Quaker-
town, Pa. 1922. pp. 43—45, ill.* [4562
Bechtel, Jesse F.: Boyertown Mennonite
Church burying ground. Boyertown,

Berks County, Pa. *Copied by . . ., Nov.
17 and 19, 1928. In: The Perkiomen
Region. Vol. VII, no. 2. Pennsburg,
Pa. 1929. pp. 47—54; Vol. VIII, no. 1.
1930. p. 15.* [4563
Beck, Clara A.: A „wheat market" of colonial days. *In: The Pennsylvania-German. Vol. XII. Lititz, Pa. 1911. pp.
177—179, ill.* [4564
— St. John's Lutheran Church, Centre
Square, Pa. *In: Historical Sketches. A
Collection of Papers prepared for the Historical Society of Montgomery County,
Pa. Vol. V. Norristown, Pa. 1925. pp,
52—72, ill. Appenda. In: Vol. VI. 1929.
pp. 400—401.* [4565
— Men, women and events in the early hi-
story of Whitpain Township. *In: Historical Sketches. A Collection of Papers
prepared for the Historical Society of
Montgomery, County, Pa. Vol. V. Norristown, Pa. 1925. pp. 202—209, ill.*
[4566
— Revolutionary heroes buried in St.
John's cemetery. *[At Centre Square,
Pa.] In: Historical Sketches. A Collec-
tion of Papers prepared for the Historical
Society of Montgomery County, Pa. Vol.
VI. Norristown, Pa. 1929. pp. 39—46.*
[4567
Becker, J. L.: Christ Lutheran congregation.
*[Mainland, Towamencin Twp., Mont-
gomery County, Pa.] Read Sept. 16,
1899. In: Historical Sketches. A Collec-
tion of Papers prepared for the Historical
Society of Montgomery County, Pa. Vol.
III. Norristown, Pa. 1905. pp. 85—93.*
[4568
Boggs, Edward F.: Colonial architecture in
Montgomery County. *In: Historical
Sketches. A Collection of Papers pre-
pared for the Historical Society of Mont-
gomery County, Pa. Vol. V. Norristown, Pa. 1925. pp. 23—34, ill.* [4569
Boorse, John C.: Some unwritten history of
Towamensing. *Read Sept. 16, 1899. In:
Historical Sketches. A Collection of Papers prepared for the Historical Society of
Montgomery County, Pa. Vol. III. Norristown, Pa. 1905. pp. 57—66.* [4570
— The Towamensing Mennonite meeting
house. *In: Historical Sketches. A Collection of Papers prepared for the Historical Society of Montgomery County, Pa.
Vol. III. Norristown, Pa. 1905. pp.
390—391.* [4571
Brecht, Samuel K.: The Hosensack academy. *In: The Pennsylvania-German.*

Vol. XI. Lititz, Pa. 1910. pp. 664—669.
[4572

Brendle, D. D.: A description of the Skippack Creek and Valley. *In: The Perkiomen Region. Vol. I, no. 3. Pennsburg, Pa. 1922. pp. 42—48.* [4573
— History of Wentz's Reformed Church. *In: Historical Sketches. A Collection of Papers prepared for the Historical Society of Montgomery County, Pa. Vol. V. Norristown, Pa. 1925. pp. 36—51, ill.* [4574

Brendle, Thomas R.: Falckner Swamp, 1725—1925. *In: The Reformed Church Rewiew. Fifth series, vol. IV. Lancaster, Pa. 1925. pp. 326—340.* [4575
— The Skippack Reformed Church. *In: The Reformed Church Review. Fifth series, vol. IV. Lancaster, Pa. 1925. pp. 367—382.* [4576

Buck, William J.: History of Montgomery County within the Schuylkill Valley, *containing sketches of all the townships, boroughs and villages, in said limits, from the earliest period to the present time; with an account of the Indians, the Swedes, and other early settlers, and the local events of the Revolution; besides notices of the progress in population, improvements, and manufactures; prepared chiefly from original materials. Norristown, Pa.: E. L. Acker 1859. pp. V. 7—124, III.* [4577
— Taxables of New Hanover Township for 1779. *In: The Perkiomen Region. Past and Present. Vol. I. Philadelphia, Pa. 1895. pp. 185—189.* [4578
— Assessment of Frederick Township for 1776. *Communicated by . . . In: The Perkiomen Region, Past and Present. Vol. I. Philadelphia, Pa. 1895. pp. 69—71.* [4579
— Assessment of Providence Township for 1776. *Communicated by . . . In: The Perkiomen Region, Past and Present. Vol. II. Philadelphia, Pa. 1900. pp. 47—52.* [4580

Cassel, Abraham H.: Franconia and Lower Salford stories. *Read Oct. 28, 1896. In: Historical Sketches. A Collection of Papers prepared for the Historical Society of Montgomery County, Pa. Vol. II. Norristown, Pa. 1900. pp. 154—161, ill.* [4581
[—] Old Goshenhoppen Church, Montgomery County, Pa. *In: The National Genealogical Society Quarterly. Vol. XVI., no. 1. Washington, D. C. 1828. pp. 12—13.* [4582

Clemmer, Abram - Clemmer, A. G.: Record of tombstone inscriptions Franconia Mennonite cemetery. *Compiled by . . . Aug. 1929. In: The Perkiomen Region. Vol. VIII, no. 3—4. 1930. pp. 87—141.* [4583

[**Croll, Michael**]: The docket of Michael Croll, *[of Upper Salford Township],* Justice of Peace. *[1787—1795.] In: The Perkiomen Region, Past and Present. Vol. I. Philadelphia, Pa. 1895. pp. 39—46.* [4584

Dannehower, William F.: The Green Lane Forge. *In: The Perkiomen Region. Vol. III, no. 2. Pennsburg. Pa. 1924. pp. 22—29.* [4585
— „The thousand acres." *[Tract of land situated partly in Upper Salford (now Salford) Township, Montgomery County, and partly in Rockhill Township, Bucks County, Pa.] In: The Perkiomen Region. Vol. III, no. 2. Pennsburg, Pa. 1924. pp. 30—38.* [4586
— The Sumney Town Academy. *In: The Perkiomen Region. Vol. III, no. 4. Pennsburg, Pa. 1925. pp. 60—90. ill.* [4587

Davis, L. H.: 1776—1876. The Centennial celebration at Pottstown, Pa., July 4, 1876 and historical. sketch, *written by L. H. Davis, at the request of the Centennial Committee. Pottstown, Pa. 1876. pp. 80.* [4588

De Long, Calvin M.: The early churches of the Goshenhoppen region. *Read October, 1908. In: Historical Sketches. A Collection of Papers prepared for the Historical Society of Montgomery County, Pa. Vol. IV. Norristown, Pa. 1910. pp. 84—97, ill.* [4589
— The early churches of the Goshenhoppen region. *Read Oct., 1908. In: The Pennsylvania German. Vol. X. Lititz, Pa. 1909. pp. 541—551, ill.* [4590
[—] Photographic history of New Goshenhoppen Reformed Church, East Greenville, Pa. *Published in connection with the celebration of the 200th anniversary of the founding of the church, Oct. 9, 1927. Pennsburg, Pa.: Town and County Prompt Print 1927. pp. 18.* [4591
— An interesting old legal document *[concerning the engagement of Nicholas Weinel, recently arrived from Germany, as schoolmaster in the congregation of the New Goshenhoppen Reformed Church 1802.] In: The Perkiomen Region. Vol. V, no. 1. Pennsburg, Pa. 1927. pp. 16—17.* [4592

[De Long, Calvin M.]: The New Goshenhoppen Reformed Church. Bicentennial and interesting historical side-lights. *By the pastor. In: The Perkiomen Region. Vol. VI, no. 2. Pennsburg, Pa. 1928. pp. 34—49, ill.* [4593

Detwiler, Jones: First troop of Montgomery County cavalry. *Read Febr. 22, 1899. In: Historical Sketches. A Collection of Papers prepared for the Historical Society of Montgomery County, Pa. Vol. II. Norristown, Pa. 1900. pp. 313—328.* [4594

— The lost *[Reformed]* Church at Whitemarsh. *Read Sept. 18, 1895. In: Historical Sketches. A Collection of Papers prepared for the Historical Society of Montgomery County, Pa. Vol. II. Norristown, Pa. 1900. pp. 177—183.* [4595

Develin, Dora Harvey: Historic Lower Merion and Blockley; also the erection or establishment of Montgomery County, Pa. *Bala Lower Merion Philadelphia, Pa.: George H. Buchanan Co. 1922. pp. (4). 5—→131, ill., maps.* [4596

Dotterer, Henry S.: Marriages in Goshenhoppen, 1731—1790. *Communicated ... In: Historical Register: Notes and Queries, historical and genealogical relating to interior Pennsylvania for the year 1884. Vol. II. Harrisburg, Pa. 1884. pp. 137 —144; 179—189.* [4597

— The Perkiomen Region, Past and Present. *Monthly magazine. Vol. I. Sept., 1894 to Aug., 1895. Philadelphia, Pa.: Perkiomen Publishing Co. 1895. pp. 201. Vol. II. April 1899 to March 1900. Philadelphia, Pa. 1900. pp. 201. Vol. III. May 1900 to April 1901. Philadelphia, Pa. 1901. pp. 195. [Discontinued.]* [4598

— A Red Letter Day at St. James's [Episcopel] Perkiomen. *In: The Perkiomen Region. Past and Present. Vol. I. Philadelphia, Pa. 1895. pp. 33—35.* [4599

— The first quarter century of Falkner Swamp Reformed Church. *Read at Falkner Swamp Reformed Church, October 31, 1897. In: Historical Notes, relating to the Pennsylvania Reformed Church. Philadelphia, Pa. 1900. Vol. I. pp. 86— 89; 106—109; see also pp. 139—141.* [4600

— Whitemarch Reformed congregation in the Holland archives. *Read Sept. 23, 1897. In: Historical Sketches. A Collection of Papers prepared for the Historical Society of Montgomery County, Pa.*

Vol. II. Norristown, Pa. 1900. pp. 184 —195. [4601

[Dotterer, Henry S.]: Falkner Swamp. The Markley school house. *Reprint from: The Weekly Item, Schwenksville, Pa. April 30, 1880. In: The Perkiomen Region. Vol. III., no. 3. Pennsburg, Pa. 1925. pp. 48—52.* [4602

Egle, William Henry: Provincial papers: Proprietary, supply, and state tax lists of the City and County of Philadelphia for the years 1769, 1774 and 1779. *Edited by . . . Harrisburg, Pa.: Wm. Stanley Ray 1897. pp. VIII, 838. = Pennsylvania Archives. Third series, vol. XIV.* [4603

— Procincial papers: Supply, and state tax lists of the City and County of Philadelphia for the years 1779, 1780 and 1781. *Edited by . . . Harrisburg, Pa.: Wm. Stanley Ray 1897. pp. VI, 789. = Pennsylvania Archives. Third series, vol. XV.* [4604

— Provincial papers: Supply, and state tax lists of the City and County of Philadelphia for the years 1781, 1782, 1783. *Edited by . . . Harrisburg, Pa.: Wm. Stanley Ray 1898. pp. VI, 837. = Pennsylvania Archives. Third series, vol. XVI.* [4605

Evans, L. Kryder: Historical sketch of Pottstown. *Read Oct. 10, 1905. In: Historical Sketches. A Collection of Papers prepared for the Historical Society of Montgomery County, Pa. Vol. III. Norristown, Pa. 1905. pp. 345—366.* [4606

Fegely, W. O.: Augustus Lutheran Church, Trappe, Penna. 1743. *Philadelphia, Pa.: E. A. Wright Co. 1931. pp. (32), ill.* [4607

Fisher, Daniel: Norristown as it was in 1814 and 1815. *In: Historical Sketches. A Collection of Papers prepared for the Historical Society of Montgomery County, Pa. Vol. V. Norristown, Pa. 1925. pp. 115—142, ill.* [4608

Fisher, John S.: Address by Governor Fisher at the Bicentennial exercises of the New Goshenhoppen Reformed Church, East Greenville, Pa. *In: The Perkiomen Region. Vol. VI, no. 2. Pennsburg, Pa. 1928. pp. 46—48.* [4609

Fry, J.: Governor Shunk's visits to the Trappe. *In: The Perkiomen Region, Past and Present. Vol. II. Philadelphia, Pa. 1900. p. 153.* [4610

— Reminiscences of Trappe. *In: Historical Sketches. A Collection of Papers pre-*

pared for the Historical Society of Montgomery County, Pa. Vol. V. Norristown, Pa. 1925. pp. 159—161, ill. Reprint in: The Perkiomen Region. Vol. IX, no. 1. Pennsburg, Pa. 1931. p. 29. [4611

[Geissenhaimer, F. W.]: Title of the New Goshenhoppen Church property. [Paper of F. W. Geissenhaimer, translated by H. W. Kriebel.] In: The Perkiomen Region. Vol. VI, no. 1. 1928. p. 21. [4612

Geist, George W.: The story of the first Pennsylvania copper mine. Reprinted from: „The Mineral Collector." Vol. XIV, no. 6. Aug. 1907. In: The Perkiomen Region. Vol. II, no. 1. 1923. pp. 3—7. [4613

[Gordon, Thomas F.]: The Perkiomen region, as described in Thomas F. Gordon's Gazetteer of Pennsylvania, 1832. In: The Perkiomen Region, Past and Present. Vol. I. Philadelphia, Pa. 1895. pp. 11—16. [4614

Gottshall, W. S.: The Mennonite Church and congregation of Schwenksville, Pa. In: The Mennonite Year Book and Almanac for 1896. Quakertown, Pa. 1896. p. 33, ill. [4615

Gotwals, W. C.: Tombstone inscriptions on the Evansburg Mennonite graveyard, taken on January 7, 1908. In: The Perkiomen Region. Vol. I., no. 4. Pennsburg, Pa. 1922. p. 74. [4616

[Grob, Samuel]: Mennonite home anniversary. Circular: The merry youngster of 1920 who attended Frederick Institute, Pennsylvania, as students, at any time between the date of its establishment in 1857 and that of his close as an educational institution, about 1870, are hereby invited and requested to attend the anniversary of the Mennonite Old Folks' Home on the same hallowed, historic spot, Saturday, September, 18th, 1920. Signed by . . . Reprint in the Perkiomen Region. Vol. VII, no. 3. Pennsburg, Pa. 1929. pp. 57—59. [4617

[Grubb, N. Bertolet]: Falkner Swamp. The Markley school house. Reprint from: Schwenksville Item, April 30, 1880. In: The Pennsylvania-German. Vol. XI. Lititz, Pa. 1910. pp. 689—692. [4618

— Traditions and some reminiscences. In memory of my ancestors, and boyhood days. Issued on the occasion of a joint pilgrimage of the Montgomery and Berks County Historical Societies thru histo-

rical Frederick . . . Sept. 24th, 1910. pp. (8). [4619

Grubb, N. Bertolet: Traditions and reminiscences of Frederick [Township, Montgomery County, Pa.] In: Historical Sketches. A Collection of Papers prepared for the Historical Society of Montgomery County, Pa. Vol. IV. Norristown, Pa. 1910. pp. 281—291, ill. [4620

— A Towamencin tax list, Jan. 21, 1733. Copied by . . . In: The Pennsylvania-German. Vol. XII. Lititz, Pa. 1911. p. 117. [4621

— Herstine's meeting house [and] burials at Herstine's. In: Mennonite Year Book and Almanac for 1922. Quakertown, Pa. 1922. pp. 41—42, ill. [4622

Harley, J. A.: A history and geography of Montgomery County, Pa., together with county and township government. Designed for the use of schools and the general reader. 1883. pp. VII, 9—108, map. Rev. edition. Philadelphia, Pa. 1891. pp. VIII, 9—114, map. [4623

Hauck, J. K.: Recollections of Swamp Door. In: Historical Sketches. A Collection of Papers prepared for the Historical Society of Montgomery County, Pa. Vol. V. Norristown, Pa. 1925. pp. 164—166. [4624

Hauck, I. M.: „Kuttlefleck Hall" [Frederick Sunday school.] In: The Perkiomen Region. Vol. III, no. 3. Pennsburg, Pa. 1925. pp. 46—48. [4625

Hay, E. G.: History of the English Lutheran Church of Pottsville, Pa. from its origin, May 16th, 1847 to Sept. 1st, 1888. Pottsville, Pa.: Robt. D. Colborn 1888. pp. VIII, 9—167, ill. [4626

Heckler, James Y.: History of Lower Salford Township, in sketches, concerning with a history of Harleysville. Harleysville, Pa.: Weekly News Office 1888. pp. (7), 456, 10, ill. [4627

Heebner, Joseph R.: Worcester or Methacton Mennonite meeting house and burying ground. In: The Perkiomen Region. Vol. I, no. 5. Pennsburg, Pa. 1922. pp. 84—89. [4628

Hendricks, J. H.: An historical address at the twenty-sixth anniversary of the pastorate of Rev. J. H. Hendricks, A. M., of the Trinity Christian churches at Collegeville and Skippackville, Pa. Containing an account of the origin, past history, present status and outlook for the future, of said churches, with some statistics of pastoral work done, by the pastor.

Skippack, Pa.: A. E. Dambly's Estate. 1888. pp. 20. [4629

Hengey, R. G.: Indian Creek Reformed Church and Furman's graveyard. *Compiled by . . . In: The Perkiomen Region. Vol. V., no. 3. Pennsburg, Pa. 1927. pp. 55—56.* [4630

Heysham, Theodore: Norristown. 1812— 1912. A brief history of the Borough of Norristown, *memorializing its one hundreth anniversary, together with maps showing the complete evolution of the borough and views of the town in the dress of its first Centennial, groups of citizens, distinguished guests, and scenes from the first historical pageant. Norristown, Pa.: Herald. 1913. pp. 71, ill.* [4631

Hinke, Wm. J.: The cornerstone of the old Goshenhoppen Church. *In: The Perkiomen Region, Past and Present. Vol. III. Philadelphia, Pa. 1901. pp. 168— 169.* [4632

— Record of the Goshenhoppen Reformed Church, 1731—1761. *Edited by . . . In: The Perkiomen Region, Past and Present. Vol. III. Philadelphia, Pa. 1901. pp. 76—80; 94—96; 110—112; 121— 123; 137—140; 150—155; 175—176; 185—188.* [4633

— The early history of Wentz's Reformed Church, Montgomery County, Pa. *In: Journal of the Presbyterian Historical Society. Vol. III. Philadelphia, Pa. 1906. pp. 332—346.* [4634

— A history of the Goshenhoppen Reformed Church, Montgomery County, Pa. (1727—1819.) *Lancaster, Pa.: The New Era Printing Co. 1920. = Part. XXIX. „A narrative and critical history", prepared at the request of the Pennsylvania-German Society. In: The Pennsylvania-German Society. Proceedings and Addresses . . . 1916. Vol. XXVII. Lancaster, Pa. 1920. Separate pagination. pp. XVII, 5—271, ill.;* Church records of the Goshenhoppen Reformed charge 1731—1833. *In: . . . 1917. Vol. XXVIII. Langaster, Pa. 1922. Separate pagination. pp. 272—490.* [4635 The stone church at New Goshenhoppen. Built in 1769. *In: The Perkiomen Region. Vol. I., no. 5. Pennsburg, Pa. 1922. pp. 83—84.* [4636

— A hundred years of history in the old Goshenhoppen Reformed Church, 1730 —1830. *In: The Perkiomen Region. Vol. IV, no. 1. Pennsberg, Pa. 1926. pp. 1 —18.* [4637

Hobson, F. G., Buck, William J. and **Dotterer, Henry S.:** The Centennial celebration of Montgomery County at Norristown, Pa., Sept. 9, 10, 11, 12, 1884. *An official record of its proceedings. Edited by . . . Norristown, Pa.: Published by the Centennial Association of Montgomery County. 1884. pp. XI, 467.* [4638

Holstein, William H.: The Second Troop, Montgomery County, Pa. *In: Historical Sketches. A Collection of Papers prepared for the Historical Society of Montgomery County, Pa. Vol. I. Norristown, Pa. 1895. pp. 184—186.* [4639

Hoover, Hiram, C.: History of the First Troop of Cavalry of Montgomery County, Pa. *In: Historical Sketches. A Collection of Papers prepared for the Historical Society of Montgomery County, Pa. Vol. I. Norristown, Pa. 1895. pp. 176—183.* [4640

Huber, S. M. K.: Christ Reformed congregation, Mainland, Towamencin Twp., Montgomery County, Pa. *Read Sept. 16, 1899. In: Historical Sketches. A Collection of Papers prepared for the Historical Society of Montgomery County, Pa. Vol. III. Norristown, Pa. 1905. pp. 81—84.* [4641

Hunsicker, Clifton S.: Montgomery County, Pa. A history. *By . . . with the co-operation of the Historical Society of Montgomery County, Pa. 3 vols. New York, N. Y. — Chicago, Ill.: Lewis Historical Publishing Co. 1923. pp. (2), 416, ill., 340, ill.; 341—717, ill.* [4642

Jellett, Edwin C.: Herstein meeting. *Limerick Twp., Montgomery County, Pa.: upon Sumneytown road, 2 miles eastward from Colebrook, or Swamp pike. Read April 30, 1910. In: Historical Sketches. A Collection of Papers prepared for the Historical Society of Montgomery County, Pa. Vol. IV. Norristown, Pa. 1910. pp. 225—234, ill.;* **Wanger, George F. P.:** Herstein meeting — Addenda to *Vol. IV. In: Vol. V. 1925. pp. 393— 396.* [4643

Jenkins, Howard M.: Historical collections relating to Gwynedd. *A township of Montgomery County, Pa., settled 1698, by Welsh immigrants. With some data referring to the adjoining township of Montgomery, also a Welch settlement. Philadelphia, Pa.: Ferris Bros. 1884. pp. (5), 396, (4), ill.* [4644

[Johnson, A. D.]: Death records. *[Lansdale and vicinity, 1861 to 1927.] In: The*

Perkiowen Region. Vol. VI, no. 2. 1928 pp. 58—64; No. 3. 1928. pp. 90—96; No. 4. Pennsburg, Pa. 1928. pp. 98— 103.   [4645

Jordan, John W.: Aid for sufferers from Indian incursion. *[Donations from Skippack, Franconia Twp., and Perkiomen Twp., Montgomery County, Pa.] In: The Perkiomen Region, Past and Present. Vol. III. Philadelphia, Pa. 1901. p. 134.*   [4646

— Moravian notes. *Communicated by . . . In: The Perkiomen Region, Past and Present. Vol. II. Philadelphia, Pa. 1900. pp. 89—90.*   [4647

— Henry Antes' Moravian school in 1745. *Read at Camp Pottsgrove, Sept. 25, 1910. In: Historical Sketches. A Collection of Papers prepared for the Historical Society of Montgomery County, Pa. Vol. IV. Norristown, Pa. 1910. pp. 171— 172.*   [4648

Kistler, William U.: Early organ builders in northern Montgomery County. *Read October 24, 1908. In: Historical Sketches. A Collection of Papers prepared for the Historical Society of Montgomery County, Pa. Vol. IV. Norristown, Pa. 1910. pp. 112—117.*   [4649

Kline, J. J.: The Lutheran Church in New Hanover (Falckner Swamp), Montgomery County, Pa. *Lancaster, Pa.: New Era Printing Co. 1911. = Part. XXII. „A narrative and critical history", prepared at the request of the Pennsylvania-German Society. In: The Pennsylvania-German Society. Proceedings and Addresses . . . 1909. Vol. XX. Lancaster, Pa. 1911. Separate pagination. pp. VI, 444, ill. [Includes list of baptisms from 1740 to 1825. pp. 198—343; list of the catechumens and adult baptisms, who were confirmed from 1743 to 1825. pp. 345—391; record of marriages pp. 392—417; list of deaths pp. 418—444.]*   [4650

Kratz, Henry W.: Washington at Pennybecker's mills. *Read Sept. 16, 1896. In: Historical Sketches. A Collection of Papers prepared for the Historical Society of Montgomery County, Pa. Vol. II. Norristown, Pa. 1900.   pp. 162—176, ill.*   [4651

Krauss, H H.: Historical development of St. Paul's Lutheran Church, Red. Hill, Pa. *In: The Perkiomen Region. Vol. VII, no. 3. Pennsburg, Pa. 1929. pp. 88—90.*   [4652

[Krauss, John]: Account book of John Krauss. For 1806. *In: The Perkiomen Region. Vol. VIII, no. 2. Pennsburg, Pa. 1930. pp. 43—55;*
. . . for 1807. *In: Vol. IX, no. 1. 1931. pp. 3—12; No. 2. pp. 49—53.*
. . . for 1808. *In: Vol. IX, no. 3. pp. 70 —77. [See no. 6871.]*   [4653

Kretschmann, Ernest T.: 1743—1893. The old Trappe Church. *A memorial of the Sesqui-Centennial services of Augustus Evangelical Lutheran Church, Montgomery County Pa. Philadelphia, Pa.: Publish ed by the congregation. 1893. pp. 182, ill.*   [4654

Kriebel, Howard Wiegner: A brief history of Montgomery County, Pa. *with an accompanying map. Prepared under the supervision of the School Directors' Association for the use of Schools. Norristown, Pa.: The School Directors' Association 1923. pp. 216, ill., maps.*   [4655

— Perkiomen land grants or patents. *In: The Perkiomen Region. Vol. V, no. 1. Pennsburg, Pa. 1925. pp. 5—11.* [4656

[—] From Brandywine through the Perkiomen Valley to Valley Forge, Sept. and Oct. 1777. *= The Perkiomen Region. Vol. V, no. 4. pp. 62—108, ill.*   [4657

— The good old times. *In: The Perkiomen Region. Vol. VI, no. 3. Pennsburg, Pa. 1928. pp. 77—84.*   [4658

— Perkiomen Valley water power. *(Lists of mills along the Perkiomen Creek and its tributaries.) In: The Perkiomen Region. Vol. VI, no. 1. Pennsburg, Pa. 1929. pp. 10—13.*   [4659

— Account books *(partial list of . . . in custody of the Schwenkfelder Historical Society.) In: The Perkiomen Region. Vol. VII, no. 1. Pennsburg, Pa. 1929. pp. 21—22.*   [4660

— Perkiomen Valley water power. *(A list compiled from the records of Montgomery County, Pa. showing the mills with names of owners in various townships of the Perkiomen region at various periods.) In: The Perkiomen Region. Vol. VIII, no. 1. Pennsburg, Pa. 1930. pp. 10—13.*   [4661

— Prices in other days. *(Gleaned from account books in the Schwenkfelder Historical Library.) In: The Perkiomen Region. Vol. VIII, no. 1. Pennsburg, Pa. 1930. pp. 26—29.*   [4662

Longaker, A. B.: Men of Montgomery County in state and national legislation.

In: reponse to a toast, 1882. In: Historical Sketches. A Collection of Papers prepared for the Historical Society of Montgomery County, Pa. Vol. I. Norristown, Pa. 1895. pp. 146—148. [4663

Mann, Charles S.: Fort Washington's historic environment. *Read Sept. 23, 1897. In: Historical Sketches. A Collection of Papers prepared for the Historical Society of Montgomery County, Pa. Vol. II. Norristown, Pa. 1900. pp. 201—213.* [4664

Mathews, Edward: Towamencin Township. *Read Sept. 16, 1899. In: Historical Sketches. A Collection of Papers prepared for the Historical Society of Montgomery County, Pa. Vol. III. Norristown, Pa. 1905. pp. 67—75, ill.* [4665
— Hatfield Township. *Read Oct. 8, 1901. In: Historical Sketches. A Collection of Papers prepared for the Historical Society of Montgomery County, Pa. Vol. III. Norristown, Pa. 1905. pp. 156—160.* [4666
— The Peter Wentz house, General Washington's headquarters in Worcester. *In: Historical Sketches. A Collection of Papers prepared for the Historical Society of Montgomery, County, Pa. Vol. IV. Norristown, Pa. 1910. pp. 313—319, ill.* [4667

McDermott, William: Banks and banking. *In: Historical Sketches. A Collection of Papers prepared for the Historical Society of Montgomery County, Pa. Vol. I. Norristown, Pa. 1895. pp. 94—121.* [4668

Messinger, S. L.: History of St. Luke's Reformed Church, Trappe, Pa. *In: The Pennsylvania-German. Vol. IX. Cleona, Pa. 1908. pp. 255—261, ill.* [4669

Nyce, George S.: Old epitaphs. Leidig's burying ground. *[Located in the southwestern part of Frederick Township, east of Swamp Creek.] Copied by . . . In: The Perkiomen Region, Past and Present. Vol. I. Philadelphia, Pa. 1895. pp. 8—9; p. 29; pp. 54—57.* [4670
— Epitaphs in Falkner Swamp Reformed churchyard. *Copied by . . . In: The Perkiomen Region, Past and Present. Vol. I. Philadelphia, Pa. 1895. pp. 90—91; p. 110; pp. 115—117; 132—134; 136—137; p. 152; pp. 165—167.* [4671

Parsons, Luther C.: The early history of the Evangelical Lutheran congregation of St. Paul's Church, Ardmore, Pa. *In:*

Historical Sketches. A Collection of Papers prepared for the Historical Society of Montgomery County, Pa. Vol. IV. Norristown, Pa. 1910. pp. 320—332. [4672

Pennypacker, Samuel Whitacker: Bebber's Township *[since 1725: Skippack and Perkiomen Township, Montgomery County, Pa.]* and the Dutch patroons of Pennsylvania. *In: The Pennsylvania Magazine of History and Biography. Vol. XXXI. Philadelphia, Pa. 1907. pp. 1—18.* [4673
[—] The outing at Camp, Pottsgrove and address of S. W. Pennypacker. *In: Historical Sketches. A Collection of Papers prepared for the Historical Society of Montgomery County, Pa. Vol. IV. Norristown, Pa. 1910. pp. 265—273, ill.* [4674
— Historical address [,,Centennial of the founding of Norristown"], May 10th 1912. *In: Historical Sketches. A Collection of Papers prepared for the Historical Society of Montgomery County, Pa. Vol. V. Norristown, Pa. 1925. pp. 82—91.* [4675
— Pennypacker's mill, [Schwenksville, Pa.]. *In: Historical Sketches. A Collection of Papers prepared for the Historical Society of Montgomery County, Pa. Vol. VI. Norristown, Pa. 1929. pp. 53—55, ill.* [4676

Proctor, Joseph: [Emmanuel] Leidy's Church. *Read Oct. 8, 1901. In: Historical Sketches. A Collection of Papers prepared for the Historical Society of Montgomery County, Pa. Vol. III. Norristown, Pa. 1905. pp. 167—170, ill.* [4677

Reed, W. H.: Commissioners of Montgomery County 1784—1790. *(Addenda to the list found in Bean's History of Montgomery County, Pa. 1884. p. 322.) In: The Perkiomen Region, Past and Present. Vol. II. Philadelphia, Pa. 1900. p. 179.* [4678
— The Henry Rittenhouse farm. *Read Jan., 29, 1898. In: Historical Sketches. A Collection of Papers prepared for the Historical Society of Montgomery County, Pa. Vol. II. Norristown, Pa. 1900. pp. 306—312.* [4679
— Indian Creek Reformed Church in Franconia township. *In: Lieut. Col. Jacob Reed. Proceedings at the dedication of the monument . . ., Norristown, Pa. 1905. pp. 151—183.* [4679a

25*

Reed, W. H.: Properties exempted from taxation in 1815. *In: Historical Sketches. A Collection od Papers prepared for the Historical Society of Montgomery County, Pa. Vol. IV. Norristown, Pa. 1910. pp. 139—145.* [4680
— A Whitpain school in 1808. *Read April 30, 1910. In: Historical Sketches. A Collection of Papers prepared for the Historical Society of Montgomery County, Pa. Vol. IV. Norristown, Pa. 1910. pp. 165—170.* [4681

Richard, Marion Gilbert: A history of the Upper Dublin Evangelical Lutheran Church, Montgomery County, Pa. *An address delivered at the Sesqui-Centennial anniversary exercises, Nov. 1, 1903. Philadelphia, Pa.: Printed for the congregation by the Lutheran Publication Society. 1903. pp. 27, ill.* [4682

Richards, H. Branson: The corner-stone laying and the consecration of the second Trappe Church. *In: The Lutheran Church Review. Vol. XXVIII. Philadelphia, Pa. 1909. pp. 395—403.* [4683

Richards, J. W.: Centenary jubilee of the Evangelical Lutheran Church of Augustus, Trappe, May 2, A. D. 1843. *Sermon. Pottstown, Pa.: J. C. Slemmer pp. 43.* [4684

Roberts, Ellwood: Biographical annals of Montgomery County, Pa., *containing genealogical records of representative families, including many of the early settlers and biographical sketches of prominent citizens. 2 vols. New York, N. Y. — Chicago, Ill.: T. S. Benham & Co. and The Lewis Publishing Co. 1904. pp. IX, 544, ill.; V, 542, ill.* [4685

Roth, Geo W.: History of the Falkner Swamp Reformed Church, New Hanover, Montgomery County, Pa. *[s. l.] 1904. pp. 73.* [4686

Roush, J. L.: Sumneytown and vicinity. A brief historical sketch. *In: The Pennsylvania-German. Vol. IX. Cleona, Pa. 1908. pp. 51—58, ill.; 359—361.* [4687

Ruoff, Henry Wilson: Biographical and portrait cyclopedia of Montgomery County, Pennsylvania, *containing biographical sketches of prominent and representative citizens of the county, together with an introductory historical sketch. Edited by . . . Philadelphia, Pa.: Biographical Publishing Co. 1895. pp. 652, ill.* [4688

Saylor, Wilmer and **Hoffman, Clinton:** History of Pennsburg in Montgomery

County. *In: The Perkiomen Region. Vol. IX., no. 2. Pennsburg, Pa. 1931. pp. 59—62.* [4689

[Scheffley, A. W.]: A census of Keelor's Reformed congregation. *(From congregational records 1863. Reprint in: The Perkiomen Region. Vol. 3, no. 1. Pennsburg, Pa. 1924. pp. 2—6.* [4690

Schmidt, N. F.: The Schwenksville cemetery. *In: The Perkiomen Region. Vol. I, no. 1. Pennsburg, Pa. 1921. pp. 5—6.* [4691
— The old Perkiomen copper mine. *In: The Perkiomen Region. Vol. I, no. 2. Pennsyburg, Pa. 1922. pp. 30—32; no. 6. 1922. pp. 101—103.* [4692

Schmucker, B. M.: The Lutheran Church in Pottstown. *An historical dicourse delivered Sept. 24, 1882, at the Decennial commemoration of the consecration of Emmanuel Lutheran Church. Pottstown, Pa. 1882. pp. 48.* [4693

Schrack, David: Norriton Tonwship. *In: Historical Sketches. A Collection of Papers prepared for the Historical Society of Montgomery County, Pa. Vol. I. Norristown, Pa. 1895. pp. 122—133.* [4694

Schuler, H. A.: The Perkiomen region and its people. A descriptive and historic survey. *In: The Pennsylvania-German. Vol. VII. Lebanon, Pa. 1906. pp. 7—16, ill.* [4695

Schuyler, William Bishop: Historical sketch of St. Aloysius' [Catholic] parish, Pottstown, Pa. *Written for the 50th anniversary of the dedication of the Old Church. Norristown, Pa.: Times Printing House 1906. pp. 64, ill.* [4696

Sheeleigh, Mathias: Sketch of Montgomery County, Pa. *In: Historical Sketches. A Collection of Papers prepared for the Historical Society of Montgomery County, Pa. Vol. I. Norristown, Pa. 1895. pp. 232—239.* [4697

Shelly, A. S.: In the manor of Douglas. *In: The Perkiomen Region, Past and Present. Vol. I. Philadelphia, Pa. 1895. pp. 94—95.* [4698

[Schultz, David]: David Shultze's journal. *In: The Perkiomen Region, Past and Present. Vol. II. Philadelphia, Pa. 1900. p. 165;* David Shultze's comming to America; *pp. 181—182; 187—189; Vol. III. 1901: Journal of 1752. pp. 1—2; 10—15; . . . of 1757. pp. 81—82; 90—93; p. 98; pp. 106—110; . . . of 1759. pp. 124—127; 140—144; . . . of 1768. p. 146; pp. 155—159; p. 164; pp. 169—174.* [4699

[Schultz, David]: The David Schultz diary for 1769. *With notes of the editor,* **H. W. Kriebel.** *In: The Perkiomen Region. Vol. VI, no. 4. Pennsburg, Pa. 1928. pp. 109 —113; 113—115; . . .* for 1774. *In: Vol. VII, no. 1. 1929. pp. 8—15; . . .* for 1780. *In: Vol. VII, no. 2. 1929. pp. 34—47; . . .* for 1782. *In: Vol. VII, no. 3. 1929. pp. 66—73; . . .* for 1786. *In: Vol. VII, no. 4. 1929. pp. 106—111; . . .* for 1790. *In: Vol. VIII, no. 1. 1930. pp. 3—9.* [4700

Smyth, S. Gordon: The Plymouth road-tax list of 1854. *In: Historical Sketches. A Collection of Papers prepared for the Historical Society of Montgomery County, Pa. Vol. V. Norristown, Pa. 1925. pp. 276—292, ill.* [4701

Souder, John D.: History of Franconia township. *Harleysville, Pa.: Benjamin L. Gehman 1886. pp. V, 102.* [4702

— Private burying grounds of Franconia Township. *Read Oct. 8, 1901. In: Historical Sketches. A Collection of Papers prepared for the Historical Society of Montgomery County, Pa. Vol. III. Norristown, Pa. 1905. pp. 161—166.* [4703

— Early churches in the First Mennonite Conference District. *In: Christian Monitor. A monthly magazine for the home. Vol. XXV. Scottdale, Pa. 1933. pp. 46—47.* [4704

Stapleton, A.: Records of the New Hanover Lutheran Church, Falkner Swamp, Montgomery County Penna. 1703— 1800. *In: Notes and Queries. Edited by W. H. Egle. Annual volume 1898. Harrisburg. Pa. 1899. pp. 183—185; 188— 190; 192—195; 207—211.* [4705

Strassburger, Ralph Beaver: Our judiciary Norristown, March 1, 1929. Montgomery County's judiciary. *Historical series, reprinted from the Times Herold, Norristown, Pa. Norristown, Pa. 1929. pp. VII. 11—106.* [4706

Stump, A. M.: Program and historical sketch of St. Paul's Evangelical Lutheran Church. *[Red Hill, Pa., Upper Hanover Township, Montgomery County.] 180th anniversary 1739—1919. June 22, 1919. pp. 5, ill.* [4707

Swartley, Samuel R.: The Franconia Mennonite congregation. *In: The Perkiomen Region. Vol. VIII, no. 3—4 Pennsburg, Pa. 1930. pp. 69—73.* [4708

Swenk, Thomas: The Trappe seventy-five years ago. *Recollectians. of . . .,* octo-

genarian. *In: The Perkiomen Region, Past and Present. Vol. II. Philadelphia, Pa. 1900. p. 13, pp; 24—26; p. 38; pp. 57—58; 76—77; p. 99; pp. 109 —110; 126—129.* [4709

Swenk, Thomas: Word picture of the school in the Trappe, when honest Jacob Fry, jr., then a young man, was our teacher. *In: The Perkiomen Region, Past and Present. Vol. II. Philadelphia, Pa. 1900. pp. 139—142.* [4710

Tallis, John R.: Privats graveyards of our region. *In: The Perkiomen Region. Vol. I, no. 1. Pennsburg, Pa. 1921. pp. 2—3.* [4711

— The Zieber-Schwenk graveyard. *In: The Perkiomen Region. Vol. I, no. 2. Pennsburg, Pa. 1922. pp. 21—33.* [4712

— Leydich burying ground. *In: The Perkiomen Region. Vol. II, no. 2. Pennsburg, Pa. 1923. pp. 25—31.* [4713

— List of soldier graves, in the Perkiomen Valley, that are decorated by the Roy Leidy Legion Post, of Schwenksville. *Contributed by . . . In: The Perkiomen Region. Vol. III, no. 1. Pennsburg, Pa. 1924. pp. 6—8.* [4714

— The old Salford store ledger M. *In: The Perkiomen Region. Vol. II, no. 2. Pennsburg, Pa. pp. 31—36.* [4715

Titus, T. T.: A historical sketch of St. Paul's Evangelical Lutheran Church, Lower Merion, Montgomery County, Pa. *A discourse delivered in the church on March 4, 1860. Philadelphia, Pa.: Lutheran Publication House. 1860. pp. 19.* [4716

Vanderslice, J. M.: A land of prosperous farmers. *[Montgomery County.] Reprint from: The County Gentleman. In: The Pennsylvania-German. Vol. VIII. Lebanon, Pa. 1907. p. 493.* [4717

Wanger, George F. P.: Pottstown's efforts to become a county seat. *Read Oct. 10, 1905. In: Historical Sketches. A Collection of Papers prepared for the Historical Society of Montgomery County, Pa. Vol. III. Norristown, Pa. 1905. pp. 367— 378. maps.* [4718

— The day-book of John Potts, founder of Pottsgrove, now Pottstown, Pa. *In: The Pennsylvania-German. Vol. VIII. East Greenville, Pa. 1907. pp. 126—129.* [4719

— Herstein's meeting. *From Historical Society of Montgomery County, Pa., Sketches. Vol. V. 1915. pp. 393—394. In: The Perkiomen Region. Vol. XI,*

no. 1. Pennsburg, Pa. 1931. pp. 30—31.
[4720

Wanger, George F. P.: Tombstones, Price burial ground, Lower Salford Township, Montgomery County, Pa. *In: The National Genealogical Society Quarterly. Vol. VIII, no. 4. Washington, P. C. 1920. pp. 62—64. Vol. IX, no. 1. 1920. pp. 14—15.* [4721

Wanger, Irving P.: The forming of Montgomery County. *Read Oct. 7, 1907. In: Historical Sketches. A Collection of Papers prepared for the Historical Society of Montgomery County, Pa. Vol. IV. Norristown, iPa. 1910. pp. 45—61.*
[4722

Warner, Robley A.: 1765—1915. Historical sketch of the Evangelical Lutheran congregation of Saint Paul's Church, Ardmore, Lower Merion Township, Pa. *Philadelphia, Pa.: John C. Clark Co. Second edition 1915. pp. 53, ill.* [4723

[Wehler, E. Chas.]: 1740—1890. Proceedings of the Sesqui-Centennial of Boehm's Reformed Church founded 1740 — Sesqui-Centennial celebrated Sept. 11, 1890. *Edited by . . . Norristown, Pa.: Herold Printing 1891. pp. 156, ill.* [4724

Weiser, C. Z.: A monograph of the New Goshenhoppen and Great Swamp Reformed charge. 1731—1881. *Reading, Pa.: Daniel Miller 1882. pp. 166.* [4725

[—] Educational history of Upper Hanover. *(From: Perkiomen Valley Press, June 30, 1877.) Reprint in: The Perkiomen Region. Vol. III, no. 3. Pennsburg, Pa. 1925. pp. 43—46.* [4726

Wenger, John C.: The alms book of the Skippack Mennonite Church 1738—1936. *In: The Mennonite Quaterly Review. Vol. X. Goshen, Ind.-Scottdale, Pa. 1936. pp. 138—148.* [4726a

Wiley, Samuel T.: Biographical and portrait of Montgomery County, Pa., *containing biographical sketches of prominent and representative citizens of the county, together with an introductory historical sketch. Philadelphia, Pa.: Biographical Publishing Co. 1895. pp. 652, ill.* [4727

Williams, Thomas: Some old-time Montgomery County schools and school houses. *Read Oct. 6, 1900. In: Historical Sketches. A Collection of Papers prepared for the Historical Society of Montgomery County, Pa. Vol. III. Norristown, Pa. 1905. pp. 94—113.* [4728

[Yeakel, Reuben]: History of the Evangelical Association. *(Extracts of the History of the Evangelical Association, edited by Reuben Yeakel in 1894, relating to the religious life of the upper end of the Perkiomen Valley a century ago.) In: The Perkiomen Region. Vol. VII, no. 3. Pennsburg, Pa. 1929. pp. 80—87.*
[4729

Yeakle, William A.: Whitemarsh. *In: Historical Sketches. A Collection of Papers prepared for the Historical Society of Montgomery County, Pa. Vol. I. Norristown, Pa. 1895. pp. 16—89.* [4730

Marriage record of the Reformed Church, Falkner Swamp, Montgomery County, Pa. 1748—1800. *In: Record of Pennsylvania marriages, prior to 1810. Vol. I. Harrisburg, Pa. 1880. = Pennsylvania Archives. Second series, vol. VIII. Edited by John B. Linn and Wm. H. Egle. Harrisburg, Pa. 1878. pp. 599—617.*
Reprint Harrisburg, Pa. 1896. pp. 611—629. [4731

Marriage record of the Lutheran Church, New Hanover, Montgomery County, Pa. 1745—1809. *In: Record of Pennsylvania marriages, prior to 1810. Vol. I. Harrisburg, Pa. 1880. = Pennsylvania Archives. Second series, vol. VIII. Edited by John B. Linn and Wm. H. Egle. Harrisburg, Pa. 1878. pp. 619—647.*
Reprint Harrisburg, Pa. 1896. pp. 631—660. [4732

Kirchen — Matricul: der Evangelisch Lutherischen Gemeinde in Neu Providenz, Pennsylvania. (Augustus Ev. Luth. congregation, Trappe, Pa.) *Translated, collected and arranged by* Julius Friedrich Sachse. *In: The Pennsylvania-German Society. Proceedings and Addresses at Bethlehem, Oct. 16, 1895. Vol. VI. Reading, Pa. 1896. pp. 159—248; . . . 1896. Vol. VII. Reading, Pa. 1897. pp. 476—533.*
[Birth and baptisms. (1729—1799.) Vol. VI. pp. 177—283; Record of marriages (1730—1774.) Vol. VII. pp. 477—509; Confirmations (1745—1778) pp. 509—523; Burials (1745—1777) pp. 524—530.] [4733

The Evangelical Lutheran Church of the Trinity, Norristown, Pa. A souvenir history of its reconstruction, Sept. 15, 1895. *Norristown, Pa.: The Herold. 1896. pp. 68, ill.* [4734

The Mennonite home of the Eastern District Conference. *In: Mennonite Year Book and Almanac for 1897. Quakertown, Pa. 1897. pp. 23—24, ill.* [4735
Whitefield at Skippack and Falkner Swamp. *In: Historical Notes, relating to Pennsylvania Reformed Church. Vol. I. Philadelphia, Pa. 1900. pp. 83—85.* [4736
Tombstone inscription from the Lower Skippack Mennonite cemetery. *In: Mennonite Year Book and Almanac for 1912. Quakertown, Pa. 1912. pp. 28—29.* [4737
Interments in the Gottschall Mennonite cemetery, Schwenksville, Pa. *In: Mennonite Year Book and Almanac for 1921. Quakertown, Pa. 1921. pp. 35—38.* [4738

„The Perkiomen Region, Past and Present." Philadelphia, Pa. 1895 ff. *Items without naming the authors:*
Early patents to Montgomery countians. (1794—1836.) *In: Vol. I. 1895. p. 31.* [4739
Marriages by John Wentz, justice of the peace, of Whitpain Township. (1803—1806). *In: Vol. I. 1895. p. 72.* [4740
Old Trappe Church in 1760. *[= List of subscribers to the support of Rev. Henry Melchior Muhlenberg, pastor of New Providence Lutheran congregation, in the year 1760.] In: Vol. I. 1895. pp. 95—96.* [4741
The patent to the Frankfort Company. *[Dated 25th of October, 1701, concerning the land variously named in early deeds: the German Tract, The Manatawny Tract, The Frankfort Company's land and The Great Tract of twenty-two thousand three hundred and seventy-seven acres and today comprising part of the land upon which Pottsgrove Township, all of New Hanover Township and part of Upper Hanover Township.] In: Vol. I. 1895. pp. 98—101.* [4742
Ejectment of the Frankfort Company. *In: Vol. I. 1895. pp. 121—123.* [4743
Petition for a road in Salford Township. 1737, December. *In: Vol. I. 1895. p. 137.* [4744
Payments for land by original purchasers in the Perkiomen country. Extracts from the journal kept in the Land Office of the proprietaries. *In: Vol. I. 1895. pp. 27—28; p. 48; p. 53; pp. 73—74; 86—87; 104—105; 118—119; 140—141; p. 151; Vol. II. 1900. p. 23; p. 63; p.*

100; p. 114; Vol. III. 1901. p. 15; p. 31; p. 47; p. 64; p. 80. [4745
Primitive settlers of Falkner Swamp. *In: Vol. II. 1900.* Elias Affee. *p. 35;* Daniel Schoener. *p. 35;* Kilian Keely. *p. 105;* John George Wanner. *p. 138;* Johannes Dunkell. *p. 138;* Frederick Antes. *pp. 160—161; 177—178.* [4746
Petition for a road to Manatawny. *(Endorsed „March, 1709".) In · Vol. II. 1900. p. 135.* [4747
An interesting land deal in Frederick Township. *(A copy of the deed for 200 acres purchased by Andrew Frey, August 5, 1718 and the transfer by him of the tract, May 1, 1728, to Ludwig Engelhart, Henry Stetler, George Kraus, and Christopher Sheagle.) In: Vol. III. 1901. pp. 37—38.* [4748
New Goshenhoppen in 1759. *In: Vol. III. 1901. p. 130.* [4749
Washington at the home of Col. Frederick Antes. *In: Vol. III. 1901. pp. 178—180.* [4750
Our Revolutionary sires. *In: Vol. I. 1895 p. 30; p. 47; p. 64; p. 72; p. 85; p.106; p. 135; p. 156; p. 167; Vol. II. 1900. p. 7; p. 18; p. 70; p. 86; p. 112; p. 119; p 138; p. 149; p. 169; pp. 185—186; Vol. III. 1901. p. 21; p. 35; p. 52; p. 66; p. 83; p. 97; p. 122; p. 159; p. 174; p. 180.* [4751

„The Perkiomen Region" Pennsburg, Pa. 1921 ff. *Items without naming the authors:*
The Young's Hollow Farms. *In: Vol. I, no. 1. 1921. pp. 9—11.* [4752
Translation of the Records of the Lutheran congregation at old Goshenhoppen. *In: Vol. I, no. 1. 1921. pp. 11—19. No. 3. 1922. pp. 54—60; no. 4. 1922. pp. 75—80; no. 5. 1922. pp. 95—100; no. 6. 1922. pp. 116—120; Vol. II, no. 1. 1923. pp. 14—20; no. 2 1923. pp. 36—40; no. 3. 1923. pp. 53—60; no. 4. 1923. pp. 75—80; Vol. III, no. 1. 1924. pp. 17—20; no. 2 1924. pp. 38—40. no. 3. 1925. p. 60.* [4753
Collecten Buch vor die Reformirte Gemeind an der Schippach in Worcester Township, Philadelphia County, in der Provintz Pennsylvanien, 1763. *In: Vol. I, no. 2. 1922. pp. 35—40.* [4754
Our last redemptioner. *[1818. Conrad Daur, late of Wurttemberg. Taken from the docket of Philip Reed, Esq. of Marlborough. p. 180.] In: Vol. I, no. 3. 1922. p. 52.* [4755

„Memorandum what money Christian Sheid 'recd. from the sundry persons for the use of the ministers place *[made for the Lutheran congregation at Old Goshenhoppen some time between 1770—1790.] Contributed by* E. B. Brenner. *In: Vol. I, no. 3. 1922. p. 53.* [4756

List of subscribers to Sumneytown Academy. *In: Vol. I, no. 3. 1922. p. 53.* [4757

A list of deaths. *(1847—1849. — On a loose leaf of a book found in „Squire" Philip Reeds' ledger of Marlborough Township.) Contributed by* W. H. Reed. *In: Vol. I, no. 4. 1922. p. 66.* [4758

The Marlborough Tonwship book. *In: Vol. I, no. 4. 1922. pp. 67—74.* [4759

Tax list of Upper Hanover township for the year 1785. *Transcribed by* Raymond Kline. *In: Vol. I, no. 6. 1922. pp. 103—104.* [4760

Nicolaus Korndoerffer. *[And a translation of his account book, containing lists of his pupils.] In: Vol. I, no. 6. pp. 104—108;* The remaining entries in the account book of Nicolaus Korndoerffer. *In: Vol. II, no. 1. 1923. pp. 11—13.* [4761

Tax duplicate for Frederick Township, 1816. *In: Vol. II. no. 3. 1923. pp. 43—46.* [4762

Removing a landmark. The old hotel at Sumneytown an historic hostlerie. — A murder that stopped the construction of a railroad. *Reprint from: Perkiomen Press," Tuesday, April 22, 1884. In: Vol. II, no. 3. 1923. pp. 48—50.* [4763

Old mills in the vicinity of Sumneytown, 1865 *(Edwin Benner's record). In: Vol. II, no. 3. 1923. p. 51.* Persons killed in mills, 1790—1867. *(Edwin Benner's Record.) p. 52.* [4764

Corner stone laying of Keelor's (Reformed and Lutheran Union Church.) *Reprint from the „Bauern Freund", Oct. 2, 1833. In: Vol. II, no. 3. 1923. p. 52.* [4765

Marlborough Township. *(Deed of erection of the . . . March 3, 1742.) In: Vol. II, no. 3. 1923. p. 53.* [4766

Two petitions for bridges over the Branch Creek. *In: Vol. II, no. 4. 1923. p. 62.* [4767

Book of education. *Lists of children between the age of five and twelve years whose parents are unable to pay for their schooling, in Montgomery County 1821—23. In: Vol. II, no. 4. 1923. pp. 62—63.* [4768

History of Keelor's [Reformed and Lutheran Union Church]. *In: Vol. II. no. 4. 1923. pp. 65—68.* [4769

The Sumneytown bridge, 1787—1923. *In: Vol. II, no. 4. 1923. pp. 68—70.* [4770

Assessment for Marlborough 1785. *In: Vol. II, no. 4. 1923. pp. 70—74.* [4771

Assessment for Marlborough 1795. *In: Vol. III, no. 3. 1925. pp. 57—60.* [4772

A Salford road petition. *[1755.] Reprint in: Vol. V, no. 1. 1927. p. 17.* [4773

Early family names [of the Perkiomen region, occuring in the list of taxables for the year 1734]. *In: Vol. V, no. 1. 1927. p. 18.* [4774

MacCall Manor [of Douglas Township, Montgomery County, Pa.]. *In: Vol. V, no. 2. 1927. pp. 29—35.* [4775

Marriage records. *(From the Bauern Freund, German weekly, published in Sumneytown by Enos Brenner, during the first four years, from the first issue August 6, 1828, to July 8, 1832.) In: Vol. V, no. 3. 1927. pp. 42—54.* [4776

„The German tract." *[Known variously as the Frankfort, the Manatawny, the German, the Sproegell tract, or even as Falkner Swamp in Philadelphia County, but what is now Montgomery County, Pa.] In: Vol. VI, no. 1. 1928. pp. 2—21.* [4777

Early residents of New Hanover Township. *[Collected from land conveyances.] In: Vol. VI, no. 1. 1928. pp. 21—29.* [4779

The Manor of Gilberts [of Upper Providence Township, Montgomery County, Pa.]. *In: Vol. VI, no. 3. 1928. pp. 66—76, map.* [4780

The Perkiomen railroad. *Reprint from the „Reading Eagle". In: Vol. VI, no. 4. 1928. pp. 114—116.* [4781

An old school circular, *(of the Mennonite Seminary Wadsworth, Medina County, Ohio.) Reprint in: Vol. VI, no. 4. 1928. pp. 124—128.* [4782

A supervisor's accounts (of George Schultz, April 16, 1830 to Febr. 22, 1831). *In: Vol. VII, no. 1 1929. pp. 16—18.* [4783

The Valentine Geiger plantation (of New Hanover Township). *In: Vol. VII, no. 2. 1929. pp. 59—61.* [4784

Constitution of the Washington Hall Debating Society of the Trappe. *In: Vol. VII, no. 2. 1929. pp. 61—64.* [4785

The Falkner Swamp church property. *In: Vol. VII, no. 3. 1929. pp. 73—74.* [4786

Building a school house. *(Reproduction of a paper in the Schwenkfelder Historical Library, giving the expenses for erecting the school house on the land of Jacob M. Oberholtzer, Douglass, in 1846.) In: Vol. VII, no. 4. 1929. pp. 116—117.* [4787

A school experiment. *Report, concerning the erection of a schoolhouse in the Lower end of Upper Milford Township, Lehigh County. 1842 to 1854. In: Vol. VII, no. 4. 1929. pp. 118—121.* [4788

The Skippack Society for the Detection of Horse Thieves. *(Introductory page of a minute book, contributed to the Schwenkfelder Historical Library by Jesse S. Kriebel estate). In: Vol. VIII, no. 1. 1930. pp. 13—15.* [4789

Supervisor's account, Worcester Township, 1837. *(Made by George Schultz as supervisor of East Worcester Road District). Reprint in: Vol. VIII, no. 1. 1930. pp. 16—26.* [4790

Practical benevolence. *(Two sets of papers in the Schwenkfelder Historical Library, illustrating the method of helping one's neighbors in case of misfortune before the days of universal insurance.) In: Vol. VIII, no. 2. 1930. pp. 55—57.* [4791

A Kriebel family record. *(Accounts of George Kriebel with two of his sons, Andrew K. and Abraham K., 1855 to 1859.) In: Vol. VIII, no. 2. 1930. pp. 60—61.* [4792

Music in the Upper End [of Montgomery County, Pa.]. *Reprint rom ,,Norristown Times Herold", Jan. 10, 1930. In: Vol. VIII, no. 2. 1930. pp. 61—62.* [4793

Franconia Township [Montgomery County, Pa.], historical data. *In: Vol. VIII, no. 3—4. 1930. pp. 66—141.* [4794

Residents of Franconia Township 1850. *Copied from the original records in Washington, D. C. In: Vol. VIII, no. 3—4, 1930. pp. 81—86.* [4795

A Krausdale choral union. *In: Vol. IX, no. 1. 1931. pp. 13—14.* [4796

Lea K. Heist, seamstress and milliner. *In: Vol. IX, no. 1. 1931. pp. 25—26* [4797

A collection list. *(Being a list of contributions for the pastor's salary of Rev. Daniel Weiser of the Great Swamp Reformed Church in the year 1835.) Translated in: Vol. IX, no. 1. 1931. pp. 27—28.* [4798

List of taxables in Upper Hanover Township. *In: Vol. IX, no. 2. 1931. pp. 55—59.* [4799

The Macungie road. *In: Vol. IX, no. 2. 1931. p. 64.* [4800

Montour County

Battle, J. H.: History of Columbia and Montour Counties, Pa., *containing a history of each county; their townships, towns, villages, schools, churches, industries, etc.,* portraits of representative men; biographies, history of Pennsylvania, statistical and miscellaneous matter, etc. *Chicago, Ill.: A. Warner & Co. 1887. pp. IX, 15—542; 220, ill., map.* [4801

Brower, D. H. B.: *Danville, Montour County, Pa. A collection of historical and biographical sketches. Harrisburg, Pa.: Lane S. Hart. 1881. pp. 288.* [4802

Historical and biographical annals of Columbia and Montour Counties, Pa., *containing a concise history of the two counties and a genealogical and biographical record of representative families. 2 vols. Chicago, Ill.: J. H. Beers & Co. 1915. pp. XXII, 671, ill.; XI, 673—1260, ill.* [4803

Northampton County

Atchley, Kathryn and Atchley, William: Inscriptions alphabetically arranged of the tombstones in the old cemetery at Stone Church, Penna. *Transcribed by . . . Published by Rev. W. E. Wenner. [s. l. s. d.] pp. 14.* [4803a

Beitel, Calvin G.: The Penn titles to Northampton County lands. *[s. l.] 1900. pp. 34, 2 maps.* [4804

Brickenstein, H. A.: Peter Boehler's oak-tree. *Read March 9th, 1857. In: Transactions of the Moravian Historical Society. Vol. I. Nazareth, Pa. 1858—1876. pp. 14—17.* [4805

Brong, W. H.: History of the Plainfield Church. *[Plainfield Township, Northampton Co., Pa.] In: The Pennsylvania-German. Vol. X. Lititz, Pa. 1909. pp. 305—317; 362—371, ill.* [4806

Condit, Uzal W.: The history of Easton, Penna. from the earliest time to the present. 1739—1885. *Easton, Pa.: George W. West. pp. 501, ill.* [4807

Croll, P. C.: Historical pilgrimages into Pennsylvania-Germandom. A detour on the Forks of the Delaware. *In: The Pennsylvania-German. Vol. V. Lebanon, Pa. 1904. pp. 121—143, ill. [See no. 295]* [4808

[Dreisbach, Simon]: Colonial correspondence. *[Letter of Simon Dreisbach, member of the Indian Creek Church, Allen Township, Northampton Co., Pa. to Rev. John Henry Helffrich, Jan. 1773.] Edited and annoted by* John Baer Stoudt. *In: The Reformed Church Review. Fourth series, vol. XVIII. Philadelphia, Pa, 1914. pp. 206—218.* [4809

Egle, William Henry and Jordan J. W.: The Barony of Nazareth. *In: Notes and Queries. Edited by W. H. Egle. Fourth series, vol. I. 1891—1893. Harrisburg, Pa. 1893. p. 153; pp. 157—158.* [4810
— Provincial papers: Proprietary and state tax lists of the Counties of Northampton and Northumberland, for the years 1772—1787. *Edited by . . . Harrisburg, Pa.: Wm. Stanley Ray. 1898. pp. XII, 805. = Pennsylvania Archives. Third series, vol. XIX.* [4811
Eyerman, John: The old grave-yards of Northampton and adjacent counties in the State of Pennsylvania. *Vol. I. Easton, Pa.: Private Press at Oakhurst. House 1899. pp. 149. Vol. II, no. 1—2 1901. pp. 34. No. 3. 1901. pp. 35—58.* [4812
— A genealogical index of the wills of Northampton County, Pa., 1752—1802. *Compiled by . . . (Typewritten. First edition. 1 copy 1897; Second edition. 5 copies 1917; Third edition. 3 copies 1925.) Greenwich, Conn. 1925. Typenwritten. pp. 111. [One copy at the library of Congress, Washington, D. C.]* [4813
Fretz, Franklin K.: Historical sketch of St. John's Lutheran Church. 1740—1915. *Easton, Pa.: Free Press Publishing Co. 1915. pp. 64.* [4814
Geisinger, D. H. and Kolb, Reuben: 1832—1882. Memorial volume. St. John's Lutheran Church, Easton, Pa. *Containing an account of the jubilee services, the historical sermon, the charters of the church and benevolent society, . . . Edited by . . . Published by authority of the Church-Council. [s. l., s. d.] pp. 85, ill.* [4815
[Hamm, George B.]: Shepherds at the end of the wildernis 1734—1926. *[Brief biographical sketches of the ministers, who served the Christ Reformed congregation of Lower Saucon Church.] [s. l. 1926.] pp. 32.* [4816
Heller, W. J.: The rise and decline of the First Lutheran congregation at the Forks of the Delaware. *Read before the Northampton County Historical and Genealogical Society. In: The Pennsylvania-German. Vol. XI. Lititz, Pa. 1910. pp. 138—147.* [4817
— Easton from a trolley window. *In: The Pennsylvania-German. Vol. XII. Lititz, Pa. 1911. pp. 421—436, ill., maps; pp. 449—466; 545—557; 642—654.* [4818

Heller, W. J.: Historic Easton from the window of a trolley-car. *Easton, Pa. 1911. pp. 181, ill. = Reprint of a series of articles published in The Pennsylvania-German Magazine during the year 1911, to which is added the story of the Treaty of Easton and other of items local interest.* [4819
— History of Northampton County, Pa. and the grand valley of the Lehigh. *Under supervision and revision of William J. Heller, assisted by an advisory board of editiors. 3 vols. Boston, Mass., New York, N. Y., Chicago, Ill.: The American Historical Society. 1920. pp. (3), 429, ill., map; 431—536; 296, ill.; 297—655, ill.* [4820
Henry, James: Christian's Spring, *[a settlement of single Brethren situated at the distance of 2 miles from Nazareth]. In: Transactions of the Moravian Historical Society. Vol. I. Nazareth, Pa. 1858—1876. pp. 64—77.* [4821
— Nazareth and the Revolution. *An address. In: Transactions of the Moravian Historical Society. Vol. II. Nazareth, Pa. 1886. pp. 37—42.* [4822
— Events at Nazareth in the year 1800. *In: Transactions of the Moravian Historical Society. Vol. IV. Nazareth, Pa. 1895. pp. 26—28.* [4823
— The Nazareth cemetries. *In: Transactions of the Moravian Historical Society. Vol. IV. Nazareth, Pa. 1895. pp. 29—32.* [4824
Hinke, William J.: Early history of the Lower Saucon Reformed Church 1734—1832. *Address delivered at the Lower Saucon Reformed Church, near Hellertown, Pa., Oct. 17, 1926. In: Journal of the Presbyterian Historical Society. Vol. XII. Philadelphia, Pa. 1926. pp. 464—479.* [4825
Horn, A. P.: Proceedings of the re-union of Apple's Church and of the Boehm family. *Celebrated at Apple's or New Jerusalem Reformed and Lutheran Church, Leithsville, Northampton, County, Pa. September 14, 1895. Hellertown, Pa.: H. D. Laubach 1902. pp. 154, ill.* [4826
Jacobson, Henry A.: Revolutionary notes concerning Nazareth, Friedensthal and Christian's Spring. *Compiled by . . . In: Transactions of the Moravian Historical Society. Vol. II. Nazareth, Pa. 1886. pp. 43—48.* [4827
— The Moravian Sister's House at Nazareth, Pennsylvania. *Notes compiled by . . . In: Transactions of the Moravian Historical Society. Vol. XI, part 1. Bethlehem, Pa. 1931. pp. 64—67.* [4828

Jordan, John W.: The Friedensthal printing office. *In: The Pennsylvania Magazine of History and Biography. Vol. VIII. Philadelphia, Pa. 1884. p. 108.* [4829

Jordan, John W.: Inscriptions on the gravestones in the Moravian cemetery at Nazareth, Pa. *In: Notes and Queries. Edited by W. H. Egle. Fourth series, vol. I. 1891—1893. Harrisburg, Pa. 1893. pp. 169—171; 173—176.* [4830

—, Green, Edgar Moore and Ettinger, George T.: Historic homes and institutions and genealogical and personal memoirs of the Lehigh Valley, Pa. *Under the editorial editorship . . . 2 vols. New York, N. Y. — Chicago, Ill. : The Lewis Publishing Co. 1905. pp. VII, 516, ill.; V, 528, ill.* [4831

Kelsey, Raymer Wickersham: At the Forks of the Delaware 1794—1811. Chronicles of early travel to Easton and neighboring parts of Pennsylvania and New Jersey, *including extracts from a hitherto untranslated and unpublished manuscript. A paper read at Easton. Pa., Nov. 13, 1919, before the Northampton County Historical and Genealogical Society. Haverford, Pa.: The Pennsylvania History Press 1920. pp. VII, 18, ill.* [4832

Kieffer, Henry Martyn: Sketch of the First Reformed Church of Easton, Pa. *In: The Pennsylvania-German Society. Proceedings and Addresses at Easton, Oct. 26, 1900. Vol. XI. Lancaster, Pa. 1902. pp. 23—27.* [4833

[—]: Some of the first settlers of „The Forks of the Delaware" and their descendants. *Being a translation from the German of the Record books of The First Reformed Church of Easton, Pa. from 1760—1852. Translated and published by . . . Together with an historical introduction. In commemoration and fifty-seventh anniversary of the founding of the Commonwealth 1745—1902. Easton, Pa., Lancaster, Pa.: Press of the New Era Printing Co. 1902. pp. VII, 404, ill.* [4834

Kluge, Edw. T.: The Moravian graveyards at Nazareth, Pa. 1744—1904. *In: Transactions of the Moravian Historical Society. Vol. VII. Nazareth, Pa. 1906. pp. 85—191;* Index to the Moravian cemeteries of Nazareth. *pp. 197—207.* [4835

Kohl, J. G.: *[Vgl. Nr. (see nos.) 3378—3379]*

Laubach, John R.: The old octagonal schoolhouse on the Bath road. *In: The Pennsylvania-German. Vol. VIII. Lebanon, Pa. 1907. pp. 515—517, ill.* [4837

Levering, J. M.: Some notes on the family of William Parsons, the founder of Easton and their relation to the Moravian Church, with some connected matter. *In: Transactions of the Moravian Historical Society. Vol. VII. Nazareth, Pa. 1906. pp. 41—55.* [4838

McCann, John E.: History of Catholicity in Northampton County, Pa. from the earliest times to the present. A. D. 1737 —1920. *In: Records of the American Catholic Historical Society of Philadelphia. Vol. XXXI. Philadelphia, Pa. 1920. pp. 339—348; Vol. XXXII. 1921. pp. 61—92.* [4839

McIlhaney, Asa K.: An historic pilgrimage along mountain by-ways. *In: The Pennsylvania-German. Vol. IX. Cleona, Pa. 1908. pp. 316—321; Vol. XI. Lititz, Pa. 1910. pp. 94—102; 489—494; Vol. XII. 1911. pp. 227—234; 414—420; 472—478, ill.* [4840

— An old graveyard with a history. *(Union cemetery, Bath, Pa.) In: The Pennsylvania-German. Vol. XI. Lititz, Pa. 1910. pp. 715—717, ill.* [4841

Oerter, A, L.: The Whitefield house on the Ephrata property at Nazareth, Pa. 1740 —1914. *Bethlehem, Pa.: Times Publishing Co. 1914. pp. 39, ill.* [4842

Rau, Albert G.: Historical sketch of the Whitefield house. *Read at annual Vesper, held September 26, 1907. In: Transactions of the Moravian Historical Society. Vol. VIII, Nazareth, Pa. 1909. pp. 37—42.* [4843

Rau, Robert: Sketch of the Moravian congregation at Gnadenhütten on the Mahoning. *In: Transactions of the Moravian Historical Society. Vol. II. Nazareth, Pa. 1886. pp. 399—414.* [4844

[Reichel, Gotthold Benjamin]: A journey to Bethlehem and Nazareth, in September and October, 1815, described by Gotthold Benjamin Reichel. *Translated from the original German M. S. by Helen Bell. In: Transactions of the Moravian Historical Society. Vol. IV. Nazareth, Pa. 1895. pp. 127—161.* [4845

[Reichel, William Cornelius]: A red rose from the olden time; or a ramble through the annals of the Rose Jnn, on the Barony of Nazareth, in the days of the province: *based on ,,The old Inns at Nazareth".* A *paper read at the Centenary of the ,,Nazareth Inn",* June *9th, 1871.* Philadelphia, Pa.: King & Baird *1872. pp. 50.* [4846

[Reichel, William Cornelius]: A red rose from the olden time: or, a ramble through the annals of the Rose Inn and the Barony of Nazareth, in the days of the province, 1752—1772. Edited by John W. Jordan, 1883. *In: Transactions of the Moravian Historical Society. Vol. II. Nazareth, Pa. 1886. pp. 271—302;* The old inn at Nazareth *1771. pp. 303—308;*Appendix. *[Containing matter supplementary to the preceding history]* by John W. Jordan. *pp. 309—322.* [4847

[—] Friedensthal and its stockaded mill. A Moravian chronicle, 1749—1767. By *... and contributed by* John W. Jordan. *In: Transactions of the Moravian Historical Society. Vol. II. Nazareth, Pa. 1877—1886. pp. 1—36.* [4848

Reid, Grace Stuart: The Barony of the Rose. A historical monograph. *New York, N. Y.: The Grafton Press 1904. pp. 58, ill.* [4849

Reitz,J. J.: History of Emmanuel's Church, Petersville *[Northampton Co.], Pa. In: The Penn Germania. Vol. I.* = *Old series, vol. XIII. Lititz, Pa. 1912. pp. 433—443; 551—561, ill.* [4850

Rupp, I. Daniel: History of Northampton, Lehigh, Monroe, Carbon, and Schuylkill Counties: *containing a brief history of the first settlers, topography of townships, notices of leading events, incidents, and interesting facts in the early history of these counties: with an appendix. Lancaster, Pa.: Published and sold by G. Hills; Harrisburg, Pa.: Hickok and Cantine 1845. pp. XIV, 568, ill.* [4851

Souder, John D.: Early churches in the First Mennonite Conference District. *In: Christian Monitor. A monthly magazine for the home. Vol. XXV, no. 2. Scottdale, Pa. 1933. pp. 46—47. [Mennonite settlement in Northampton County. p. 47.]* [4852

Stoudt, John Baer, Borger, Preston D., Smith, James W. and Werner, Herbert T.: A history of Grace Reformed Church Northampton, Pa. *Together with an account of the Dry Run and Stemton union Sunday schools, a complete record of baptisms, confirmations, marriages, deaths, the officers and members of the*

congregation and Sunday school. In commemoration of the fifteenth anniversary of the laying of the cornerstone, Oct. 18, 1897—Oct. 20, 1912. Northampton, Pa.: Clement News Print. Arranged and prepared by . . . 1912. pp. 66, ill. [4853

Stoudt, John Baer: The life and times of Col. John Siegfried. *Prepared at the request of the Col. John Siegfried Memorial Committee and issued in connection with the unveiling of the monument on the old Mennonite cemetery on West Twenty First street, memorial day, May 30, 1914. Northampton, Pa.: The Cement News Print 1914. pp. 62, (4).* [4854

W.[eaver] E. A.: Northampton in the Revolution. Newspaper notes and sketches. *In: Notes and Queries. Edited by W. H. Egle, Fourth series, vol. I. 1891—1893. Harrisburg, Pa. 1893. pp. 207—208; 210—211; 259—260; 262—263; 265—266.* [4855

— Centennial of journalism in Northampton County. *In: The Pennsyvania Magazine of History and Biography. Vol. XVIII. Philadelphia, Pa. 1894. pp. 121—122.* [4856

— Local historical and biographical notes collected *by . . . from files of newspapers published in Easton, Pa.; Germantown, Pa. 1906. pp. 315, (4).* [4857

1752. History of Northampton County, Pennsylvania; *with illustrations descriptive of its scenery. A new illustred historical, descriptive & biographical souvenir. Public buildings, fine blocks, and important manufactories. Philadelphia, Pa., Reading, Pa.: Peter Fritts, 1877. pp. 293, ill., maps.* [4858

Portrait and biographical record of Lehigh, Northampton and Carbon Counties, Pa. *Containing biographical sketches of prominent and representative citizens of the counties, together with biographies and portraits of all the presidents of the United States. Chicago, Ill.: Chapman Publishing Co. 1894. pp. (1), 19—999, ill.* [4859

Early Northampton County wills. *In: Notes and Queries. Edited by W. H. Egle. Annual vol. 1900. Harrisburg, Pa. 1901. pp. 52—53.* [4860

Some of the expenses in the founding of Easton, Pa. *In: The Pennsylvania Magazine of History and Biography. Vol. XXXVIII, Philadelphia, Pa. 1914. pp. 110—114.* [4861

The „Drylands" of Northampton County. *In: The Pennsylvania Magazine of History and Biography. Vol. XXI. Philadelphia, Pa. 1897. pp 502—503.* [4862
Petition against erecting a court-house and jail at Easton, Pa., 1765. *(From the original in the Historical Society of Pennsylvania.) In: The Pennsylvania Magazine of History and Biography. Vol. XXIII. Philadelphia, Pa. 1899. pp. 386—389.* [4863
From Nazareth to the Delaware Water Gap in 1748. *(Entries taken from the note-book of three Moravian clergymen.) In: The Pennsylvania Magazine of History and Biography. Vol. XXVII. Philadelphia, Pa. 1903. pp. 375—376.* [4864
Gnadenhuetten on the Mahoning. Historical and commemorative. 1746—1755. *The memorial office in honor of the missionary martyrs who fell at Gnadenhuetten on the Mahoning, Nov. 24th, 1755, celebrated in Trinity Evangelical Lutheran Church, Nov. 24, 1905. In: Transactions of the Moravian Historical Society. Vol. VII. Nazareth, Pa. 1906. pp. 349—386.* [4865
Some Revolution worthies. *[Brief sketch of the Revolutionary services of Northampton County patriots.] In: Notes and Queries. Edited by W. H. Egle. Fourth series, vol. I. 1891—1893. Harrisburg, Pa. 1893.* Frederick Nagel: *p. 161;* John L. Geiger: *p. 161;* John Ohl: *p. 162;* Simon Keller: *p. 162;* George and John Sauer: *pp. 162—163;* Aaron Depul: *p. 165;* Jacob Rieper: *p. 165;* Daniel Labar: *p. 165;* George P. Kesler: *p. 165.* Additional: *pp. 182—183.* [4866
Sketches of several Northampton County, Pa. slaves. *In: The Pennsylvania Magazine of History and Biography. Vol. XXII. Philadelphia, Pa. 1898. pp. 503—504.* [4867
Marking the cattle in 1755. *(Ear-marks filed by the Moravian at the commissioner's office of Northampton.) In: Notes and Queries. Edited by W. H. Egle. Third series, vol. II. 1887—1890. Harrisburg, Pa. 1891. p. 486. Reprint in: Third series, vol. III. Harrisburg, Pa. 1896. p. 519.* [4868
Shows forbidden. *Reprint of an advertisement which appeared June 18, 1829, in the „Friedens-Bothe" of Allentown, Pa., „Borough of Northampton of 1829." In: The Perkiomen Region. Vol. VIII,*

no. 2. Pennsburg, Pa. 1930. p. 62. [4869
Marriage register of the Moravian Church, Nazareth. 1742—1800. *In: Record of Pennsylvania marriages, prior to 1810. Vol. II. Harrisburg, Pa. 1880. = Pennsylvania Archives. Second series, vol. IX. Edited by John B. Linn and Wm. H. Egle. Harrisburg, Pa. 1880. pp. 129—134. Reprint Harrisburg, Pa. 1895. pp. 129—135.* [4870
Zum hundertjährigen Fest der Christus-Kirche zu Schönersville, Pa. *Eine kurze Geschichte dieser zwei vereinigten Gemeinden. Verzeichnis der Gräber auf dem alten Kirchhof. Verzeichnis der Gräber auf dem Kirchhof der Christus Kirche zu Schönersville, Pa. [s. l. 1880.] (6) S.* [4871
1780—1910. History of Christ Lutheran and Reformed Church, Shoenersville, Pa., *with a complete record of all members of both congregations and Sunday-school. Record of persons buried on old and new cemeteries. Bethlehem, Printing Co. 1910. pp. 73, ill.* [4872
Church records of the Williams Township. *[Evangelical Lutheran]* congregation, *[Northampton Co., Pa.] Lancaster, Pa.: New Era Printing Co. 1909. In: The Pennsylvania-German Society. Proceedings and Addresses . . . 1907. Vol. XVIII. Lancaster, Pa. 1909. Separate pagination pp. 102.* [4873
Mennonite burial records. Inscription from the settlement churchyard at Siegfried, Northampton County, Pa. *In: Genealogy. A monthly magazine of American ancestry. Vol. VI. New York, N.Y. 1916. pp. 182—184; Vol. VII. 1917. pp. 8—9* [4874
History of St. Thomas' Evangelical Lutheran and Reformed Church, Altonah, Pa. and record of burials 1848—1923 *by the pastors. Bethlehem, Pa.: Bethlehem Printing Co. 1923. pp. 47, ill.* [4875

Bethlehem — Stadt
City of Bethlehem

Beck, James M.: Bethlehem and its military hospital. *An address delivered at the unveiling of a tablet erected by the Pennsylvania Society of Sons of the Revolution, June 19, 1897, in memory of the soldiers of the Continental Army, who suffered and died at the Military Hospital at Bethlehem*

Pa. [s. l.]: Printed by the Society 1897.
pp. 17, ill. [4876
[Berg, J. F.]: Bethlehem, Pa. *In: The*
Evangelical Quarterly devoted to Chri-
stian Literature and Theology. Edited
by J. F. Berg. Vol. II. Philadelphia,
Pa. 1861. pp. 326—337. [4877
Cornelius, Emily F.: With the Moravians at
Easter. *In: The Mennonite Year Book*
and Almanac for 1919. Quakertown, Pa.
1919. pp. 24—25. [4878
Croll, P. C.: Historical pilgrimages into
Pennsylvania-Germandom. Moravian
headquarters, old Bethlehem. *In: The*
Pennsylvania-German. Vol. V. Le-
banon, Pa. 1904. pp. 166—181, ill. Ap-
pendix p. 182.
[See no. 295] [4879
— Historical pilgrimages into Pennsylvania-Germandom. A stroll' through
modern Bethlehem. *In: The Pennsyl-*
vania-German. Vol. VI. Lebanon, Pa.
1905. pp. 210—229, ill.
[See no. 295] [4880
Erbe, Hellmuth: Bethlehem, Pa. Eine
kommunistische Herrnhuter Kolonie
des 18. Jahrhunderts. *Stuttgart: Aus-*
land und Heimat Verlags-Aktiengesell-
schaft 1929. 191 S., ill., Karten.
= *Schriften des Deutschen Ausland-In-*
stituts Stuttgart. A: Kulturhistorische
Reihe. Bd. XXIV. [4881
Erbe, H. W. and **Kegel, F.:** „Bethlehem."
In: Handwörterbuch des Grenz- und Aus-
landdeutschtums Bd. I. Breslau 1933
[= Nr. 93]. S. 422—425. [4881a
Gilpin, Joshua: Journey to Bethlehem, *[Pa.*
in 1802]. In: The Pennsylvania Maga-
zine of History and Biography. Vol.
XLVI. Philadelphia, Pa. 1922. pp.
15—38; 122—153. [4882
H., H.: Brother Stolz's beat. *In: The Cen-*
tury. Illustrated Monthly Magazine. Vol.
XXIII. = New series, vol. I. New York,
N.Y. 1881—1882. pp. 499—512, ill. [4883
Jordan, John W.: Bethlehem water works.
In: The Pennsylvania Magazine of Hi-
story and Biography. Vol. VIII. Phila-
delphia, Pa. 1884. pp. 118—119. [4884
— Bethlehem during the Revolution. Ex-
tracts from the diaries in the Moravian
archives at Bethlehem, Pa. *In: The*
Pennsylvania-Magazine of History and
Biography. Vol. XII. Philadelphia,
Pa. 1888. pp. 385—406, ill.; Vol. XIII.
Philadelphia, Pa. 1889. pp. 71—89. [4885
- An historical sketch of the Widows'
House at Bethlehem, Pa. 1768—1892.

In: Transactions of the Moravian Hi-
storical Society. Vol. IV. Nazareth, Pa.
1895. pp. 101—124, ill. [4886
Jordan, John W.: The military hospitals at
Bethlehem and Lititz during the Revo-
lution. *In: The Pennsylvania Magazine*
of History and Biography. Vol. XX.
Philadelphia, Pa. 1896. pp. 137—157.
[4887
— The Bethlehem ferry, 1743—1794. *In:*
The Pennsylvania Magazine of History
and Biography. Vol. XXI. Philadel-
phia, Pa. 1897. pp. 104—111. [4888
King, Wilbur L.: An abondoned cemetery.
[Methodist Episcopal church graveyard,
Centre Str., Bethlehem, Pa.] In: The
Pennsylvania-German. Vol. XI. Lititz,
Pa. 1910. pp. 351—353. [4889
Laux, James B.: Brother Albrecht's secret
chamber. *A legend of the ancient Mora-*
vian Sun Inn of Bethlehem, Pa. Lititz,
Pa.: Express Printing Co. 1914. pp. 62.
[4890
Leibert, Augustus H.: Historical and stati-
stical matter relating to the Widows'
Society of Bethlehem. *Collected and*
compiled from the minutes of the Society
by . . . In: Transactions of the Moravian
Historical Society. Vol. X. Nazareth,
Pa. 1917. pp. 37—104. [4891
— A chronicle of the first century of Bethlehem 1741—1841. *[Bethlehem, Pa.]*
1921. pp. (8), ill. [4892
Levering, Joseph Mortimer: A history of
Bethlehem, Pa. *1741—1892, with some*
accounts of its founders and their early
activity in America. Issued as a me-
morial volume by the Sesqui-Centennial
Committee of the Moravian congregation
of Bethlehem. Bethlehem, Pa.: Times
Publishing Co. 1903. pp. XIV, (1),
809, ill., maps. [4893
Martin, John Hill: Historical sketch of
Bethlehem in Pennsylvania with some
account of the Moravian Church. *Phila-*
delphia, Pa.: Printed for Orrin Rogers by
John L. Pile. 1872. pp. III, 5—191,
ill.; Second edition. Philadelphia, Pa.:
John L. Pile 1873. pp. III, 5—191, ill.
[4894
Meyers, Elizabeth Lehman: A century of
Moravian sisters. A record of Christian
community life. *New York, N. Y.: Fle-*
ming H. Revell Co. 1918. pp. 7—243, ill.
[4895
— The Moravian Revolutionary Church at
Bethlehem, commonly called „The old
chaple". *Read before the Pennsylvania*

German Society at Bethlehem, Oct. 5, 1923. In: The Pennsylvania German Society. Proceedings and Addresses. Vol. XXXIV. 1929. pp. 55—66, ill.   [4896

Mortimer, C. B.: Bethlehem and Bethlehem school. *New York, N. Y.: Stanford & Delisser 1858. pp. 208.*   [4897

Oerter, Albert L.: Tile stoves of the Moravians at Bethlehem, Pa. *In: A Collection of Papers read before the Bucks County Historical Society. Vol. IV. Easton, Pa. 1917. pp. 479—481.*   [4898

Ogden, John C.: An excursion into Bethlehem and Nazareth, in Pennsylvania, in the year 1799; *with a succint history of the Society of the United Brethren, commonly called Moravians. Philadelphia, Pa.: Charles Gist 1800. pp. 167; Second edition. Philadelphia, Pa.: Charles Gist. pp. 167.*   [4899

Rau, Albert G.: The Bethlehems. *In: The Pennsylvania-German. Vol. XI. Lititz, Pa. 1910. pp. 552—558, ill.*   [4900

Rau, Robert: The physicians of early Bethlehem. *(A paper communicated at the annual meeting of the Moravian Historical Society, Sept,. 1891.) In: Transactions of the Moravian Historical Society. Vol. XI. Part 1. Bethlehem, Pa. Pa. 1931. pp. 56—61.*   [4901

— The first apothecary in Bethlehem. *(Paper written in 1891). In: Transactions of the Moravian Historical Society. Vol. XI. Part 1. Bethlehem, Pa. 1931. pp. 62—63.*   [4902

Reichel, William Cornelius: The Crown Inn, near Bethlehem, Pa. 1745. *A history, touching the events that occured at that notable hostelry, during the reigns of the second and third Georges, and rehearsing the transmission of ,,The Simpson Tract,'' in Lower Saucon Township, Bucks Co., in unbroken chain of title, from William Penn ... to Jasper Payne, of Bethlehem for the sole use and behoof of his Moravian Brethren, between 1681 and 1746: being a partial unfolding of the particular annals of early Moravian settlement, and other settlement, in the Province of Pennsylvania. Philadelphia, Pa.: King and Baird 1872. pp. 7—162, ill., map.*   [4903

[—] The old Sun Inn at Bethlehem, Pa. 1758, now the Sun Hotel. *An authentic history. Second edition. Doylestown, Pa.: W. W. H. Davis 1876. pp. 48, ill.*   [4904

[—] The old Moravian Sun Inn. *In: The Pennsylvania-German Society. Procee-*

dings and Addresses at Bethlehem, Oct. 16, 1895. Vol. VI. Reading, Pa. 1896. pp. 43—75, ill.   [4905

Ruth, John A.: The Town of Bethlehem. *In: A Collection of Papers read before the Bucks County Historical Society. Vol. III. Easton, Pa. 1909. pp. 24—31.*   [4906

Schultze, Augustus: A brief history of the Widows' Society of Bethlehem, *compiled from the minutes of the Society. In: Transactions of the Moravian Historical Society. Vol. II. Nazareth, Pa. 1886. pp. 51—124.*   [4907

— The old Moravian cemetery of Bethlehem, Pa. 1742—1897. *In: Transactions of the Moravian Historical Society. Vol. V. Nazareth, Pa. 1899. pp. 99—267;* Index to the old Moravian cemetery, Bethlehem, Pa. *pp. 271—294.*   [4908

— Guide to the old Moravian cemetery of Bethlehem, Pa. 1742—1910. *Lancaster, Pa.: [The New Era Printing Co.] 1912. In: The Pennsylvania-German Society. Proceedings and Addresses ... 1910. Vol. XXI. Lancaster, Pa. 1912. Separate pagination pp. IV, 218.*   [4909

Schweinitz, Edmund De: The chapel and its contiguous buildings on Church Street at Bethlehem. *In: Transactions of the Moravian Historical Society. Vol. I. Nazareth, Pa. 1858—1876. pp. 125—135.*   [4910

Stewart, Harriet Washburn: Christmas eve at Bethlehem. *In: The Pennsylvania-German. Vol. XII. Lititz, Pa. 1911. pp. 708—710.*   [4911

Walters, Raymond: Bethlehem long ago and to-day. *Bethlehem, Pa.: Carey Printing Co. 1923. pp. 152. (7), ill.*   [4912

Proposition to make Bethlehem, Penna., the seat of government in 1780. *Correspondence between Lewis Weiss, of Philadelphia, and the Rev. John Ettwein, of Bethlehem, 1780. Contributed by* John W. Jordan. *In: The Pennsylvania Magazine of History and Biography. Vol. II. Philadelphia, Pa. 1878. pp. 153—156.*   [4913

Extracts from the diary of the Bethlehem congregation 1756. *Reprint from ,,The Moravian'' July 6 and 13, 1910. In: The Penn Germania. Vol. II. = Old series, vol. XIV. Lititz, Pa. 1913. pp. 187—193.*   [4914

Trades represented in Bethlehem, 1756. *In: The Pennsylvania Magazine of Hi-*

story and Biography. Vol. XXXIX.
Philadelphia, Pa. 1915. pp. 244—245.
[4915
Excerpts from the waste books of the Sun
Inn, at Bethlehem, Pa. 1760—1799. In:
The Pennsylvania Magazine of History
and Biography. Vol. XXXIX. Phila-
delphia, Pa. 1915. pp. 469—475. [4916
Washington's army stores at Bethlehem,
Pa. from September 17 to December
24, 1777. In: The Pennsylvania Maga-
zine of History and Biography. Vol. XL.
Philadelphia, Pa. 1916. p. 362. [4917
The old Moravian Sun Inn, Bethlehem, Pa.
An authentic history. Philadelphia, Pa.:
J. B. Lippincott Co. 1893. pp. 40, ill.
[4918
Marriage register of the Moravian Church,
Bethlehem, 1742—1800. In: Record of
Pennsylvania marriages, prior to 1810.
Vol. II. Harrisburg, Pa. 1880. =
Pennsylvania Archives. Second series,
vol. IX. Edited by John B. Linn and
Wm. H. Egle. Harrisburg, Pa. 1880.
pp. 107—127.
Reprint Harrisburg. Pa. 1895. pp. 107
—128. [4919
The handbook of the Moravian congregation
of Bethlehem, Pa. incorporated as „The
congregation of United Brethren of the
Borough of Bethlehem and its vicinity.
Bethlehem, Pa.: Published by order of
Church-Council, Nov. 13, 1890. 1891.
pp. XIV, 130.
Silver anniversary 1887—1912. Holy Tri-
nity Evangelical Lutheran Church,
Bethlehem, Pa. Rev. Luther D. Lazarus,
Pastor. Published under the auspices of
the Luther League. May, 1912. [s. l.
1912.] pp. 54, ill. [4921

Northumberland County

Bell, Herbert C.: History of Northumberland
County, Pa., including its aboriginal history; the colonial and revolutionary periods; early settlement and subsequent
growth; political organization; agricultural mining, and manufacturing interests; internal improvements; religious,
educational, social, and military history;
sketches of its boroughs, villages and townships; portraits and biographies of pioneers and representative citizens, etc., etc.
Edited by . . . Chicago, Ill.: Brown,
Runk & Co. 1891. pp. XI, 17—1256,
ill., map. [4922

Egle, William Henry: Provincial papers:
Proprietary and state tax lists of the
Counties of Northampton and Northum-
berland, for the years 1772 to 1787. Edited by . . . Harrisburg, Pa.: Wm. Stan-
ley Ray. 1898. pp. XII, 805.
= Pennsylvania Archives. Third series,
vol. XIX. [4923
Gotwald, W. H.: History of the Evangelical
Lutheran Church at Milton, Pa. Pub-
lished by the congregation. Philadelphia,
Pa.: Lutheran Publication Society. 1882.
pp. 32. [4924
[Meginness, John F.]: Tombstone inscrip-
tions at Milton. By John of Lancaster
[Pseudonym]. In: Notes and Queries.
Edited by W. H. Egle. Fourth series,
vol. I. 1891—1893. Harrisburg, Pa.
1893. pp. 181—182. [4925
[—] First enumeration of taxable in-
habitants of Muncy Township in 1796.
By John of Lancaster [Pseudonym].
Contributed by . . . In: Notes and Queries.
Edited by W. H. Egle. Fourth series, vol.
I. 1891—1893. Harrisburg, Pa. 1893.
pp. 202—204. [4926
[—] Annals of Montoursville, Pa. from the
earliest times to the present. Montours-
ville, Pa.: Globe Press 1898. pp. 122,
maps. [4927
Musser, F. B.: St. Jacob's (or Reed's)
Church [Ralpho Township, Northumberland County, Pa.]. In: The Penn Germania. Vol. I. = Old series, vol. XIII.
Lititz, Pa. 1912. pp. 889—894. [4928
Reimensnyder, J. M.: The 29th anniversary
of the pastor of Trinity Lutheran
Church, Milton, Pa., and the history of
Trinity Lutheran Church from 1796 to
1916 with important memorandum and
sermon. Souvenir edition. Milton, Pa.
1916. pp. 10, ill. [4929
Rupp, I. Daniel: History and topography
of Northumberland, Huntingdon, Mifflin, Centre, Union, Columbia, Juniata
and Clinton Counties, Pa., embracing
local and general events, leading incidents,
descriptions of the principal boroughs,
towns, villages, etc., etc. with a copious
appendix: embellished by engravings.
Compiled from authentic sources by . . .
Lancaster, Pa.: G. Hills 1847. pp. 574,
ill. [4930
Steck, J. M. and Ritter, William McK.: 1795
—1895. Historical addresses on the
Centennial of Follmer Lutheran Church,
Turbot Township, Northumberland
County, Pa. Delivered Aug. 29, 1895, in

Sypher's Grove. History of the church by J. M. *Steck;* History of the Sunday-school *by William Mck. Pitter.* York, Pa.: *P. Anstadt & Sons 1896. pp. 63.* [4931

Weber, J. H.: 1791—1891. History of Zion's Evangelical Lutheran Church with a synopsis of the Centennial services of the church, and of the Semi-Centennial of the Sunday-school, Sunbury, Pa. *Introduction by J. J. Reimensnyder. Published for the congregation. Philadelphia, Pa.: Lutheran Publication House Print. 1891. pp. 109.* [4932

Genealogical and biographical annals of Northumberland County, Pa., *containing a genealogical record of representative families, including many of the early settlers, and biographical sketches of prominent citizens, prepared from data obtained from original sources of information. Chicago, Ill.: J. L. Floyd & Co. 1911. pp. XII, 988, ill.* [4933

Jacob Conrad takes up lots in Sunbury, Pa., 1772. *(Note of Jno Lukens.) Reprint in: The Pennsylvania Magazine of History and Biography. Vol. XXXVIII. Philadelphia, Pa. 1914. p. 121.* [4934

Perry County

Focht, D. H.: Churches between the mountains. A history of the Lutheran congregations in Perry County, Pa. *Baltimore, Md.: T. Newton Kurtz 1862. pp. XII, 13—370, ill.* [4935

Groh, M. H.: A brief historical sketch of the Landisburg charge, Reformed Church in United States. *Landisburg, Pa.: Job Print [1888.] pp. (1), 426.* [4936

Hain, H. H.: History of Perry County, Pa., *including descriptions of Indian and pioneer life from the time of earliest settlement. Sketches of its noted men and women and many professional men. Harrisburg, Pa.: Hain-Moore Co. 1922. 1088, ill., map.* [4937

Jordan, John W.: A history of the Juniata Valley and its people. *Under the editorial supervision of . . . 3 vols. New York, N. Y.: Lewis Historical Publishing Co. 1913. pp. (5), 496; 497—944; 945—1403, ill. [Perry County. pp. 181—226.]* [4938

Rothrock, Lewis Frederick: Forty-five years of agriculture in Perry County, [Pa.] *Thesis of M. Sc. University of Wisconsin,*

Madison, Wis. Typewritten. pp. 70, (2), map. [4939

Rupp, I. Daniel: The history and topography of Dauphin, Cumberland, Franklin, Bedford, Adams, and Perry Counties: *Containing a brief history of the first settlers, notices of the leading events, incidents and interesting facts, both general and local in the history of these counties, general and statistical descriptions of all the principal boroughs, towns, villages, &c. with an appendix. Lancaster, Pa.: Gilbert Hills 1846. pp. XII, 25—606, ill.* [4940

[Scott, W. D. E.]: Souvenir of the Centennial anniversary of the Evangelical Lutheran Church in Loysville, Perry County, Pa., *containing a brief sketch of the congregation and pastors who, during a century have ministered in her pulpit, together with the names of contributors to the monument erected at the grave of Rev. John William Heim. Loysville, Pa.: Orphan Home Print 1894. pp. (42), ill.* [4941

— 1883—1903. Twentieth anniversary, Loysville charge Evangelical Lutheran Charge, Loysville, Pa. *Loysville, Pa.: Orphan Home Print 1903. pp. 20, ill.* [4942

Wright, Silas: History of Perry County in Pennsylvania, from the earliest settlement to the present time. *Lancaster, Pa.: Wylie & Griest 1873. pp. VII, 9—290, ill., 2 maps.* [4943

History of that part of the Susquehanna and Juniata Valleys embraced in the Counties of Mifflin, Juniata, Perry, Union and Snyder in the Commonwealth of Pennsylvania. *2 vols. Philadelphia, Pa.: Everts, Peck & Richards 1886. pp. 894, ill. maps; pp. VI, 895—1602, ill., map.* [4944

Philadelphia County

Brumbaugh, Gajus Marcus: Early landowners, citizens, etc., of Philadelphia, Pa. 1683, 1692, 1698, census of 1720—1730. *In: The National Genealogical Society Quarterly. Vol. XIV, no. 4. Washington, D. C. 1925. pp. 49—58.* [4945

Egle, William Henry: Provincial papers: Proprietary, supply, and state tax lists of the City and County of Philadelphia for the years 1769, 1774 and 1779. *Edited by . . . Harrisburg, Pa.: Wm. Stanley Ray 1897. pp. VIII, 838.*

= *Pennsylvania Archives Third series,
vol. XIV.* [4946

Egle, William Henry: Provincial papers:
Supply, and state tax lists of the City and
County of Philadelphia for the years 1779,
1780 and 1781. *Edited by ... Harrisburg,
Pa.: Wm. Stanley Ray 1897. pp. VI, 789.
= Pennsylvania Archives. Third series,
vol. XV.* [4947

— Provincial papers: Supply, and state
tax lists of the City and County of Philadelphia for the years 1781, 1782 and
1783. *Edited by . . . Harrisburg, Pa.:
Wm. Stanley Ray. 1898. pp. VI, 837.
= Pennsylvania Archives. Third series,
vol. XIV.* [4948

Mervine, Wm. M.: Abstracts of wills of
Philadelphia County. *Contributed by
. . . Recorded in Administration Book
B. In: Publications of the Genealogical
Society of Pennsylvania. Vol. III. Philadelphia, Pa. 1906—1908. pp. 170—
171; . . .* Administration Book C. *ibid.
pp. 172—183; . . .* Administration Book
E. *ibid. pp. 183—189; . . .* Administration Book F. *ibid. Vol. IV. Philadelphia, Pa. 1912—14. pp. 174—195; . . .*
Administration Book G. 1754—1812.
ibid. pp. 195—217; . . . Administration
Book H. 1765—1799. *ibid. pp. 217—
219; . . .* Administration Book K. 1799
1812. *ibid. pp. 220—238; . . .* Administration Book L. 1812—1817. *ibid.
pp. 238—240; 271—276; . . .* Administration Book M. 1817—1824. *ibid. pp.
276—289; . . .* Administration Book N.
1824—1831. *ibid. pp. 289—302; . . .*
Administration Book O. 1832—1838.
ibid. pp. 302—321; . . . Administration
Book P. 1838—1849. *ibid. pp. 321—
322.* [4949

Rawle, William Brooke: The first tax list
for Philadelphia County. A. D. 1693.
*Introductory note by . . . In: The Penn-
sylvania Magazine of History and Biography. Vol. VIII. Philadelphia, Pa.
1884. pp. 82—105.* [4950

Landholders of Philadelphia County, 1734.
*(A list of names of the Inhabitants of the
County of Philadelphia, with the quan-
tity of land they respectively hold therin
according to the uncertaine Returns of
Constables.) In: Publications of the Genealogical Society of Pennsylvania. Vol.
I. Philadelphia, Pa. 1895/98. pp. 166—
184.* [4951

Some Philadelphia County farmers send
relief to the poor of Boston, 1775. *In:*

*The Pennsylvania Magazine of History
and Biography, Vol. XXVIII. Philadelphia, Pa. 1904. pp. 242—243.* [4952

Assessment of damages done by the British troops during the occupation of
Philadelphia, 1777—1778. *(Copied
from the original in the library of the Historical Society of Pennsylvania.) In:
The Pennsylvania Magazine of History
and Biography. Vol. XXV. Philadelphia, Pa. 1901. pp. 323—335; 544—559.* [4953

Philadelphia — Stadt
City of Philadelphia

Eberlin, Harold Donaldson and **Lippincott,
Horace Mather:** The colonial homes of
Philadelphia and its neighborhood.
*Philadelphia, Pa. and London: J. B.
Lippincott Co. 1912. pp. 366, ill.* [4954

Faris, John T.: Old churches and meeting
houses in and around Philadelphia. *Philadelphia, Pa. and London: J. B.
Lippincott Co. 1926. pp. XVI, 261, ill.
[Content see no. 865]* [4955

Jackson, Joseph: Encyclopedia of Philadelphia. *Vol. I. Harrisburg, Pa.: The National Historical Association 1931. pp.
V, 310, ill.; (will be continued ff.)* [4956

Mease, James: The picture of Philadelphia,
*giving an account of its origin, increase
and improvements in arts, sciences, manufactures, commerce and revenue. With a
compendious view of its societies, literary,
benevolent, patriotic and religious, its po-
lice — the public buildings — the prison
and penetentiary system — institutions,
monied and civil — museum. Philadelphia, Pa.: B. & T. Kite 1811. pp. XII,
376, ill. Second edition. 2 vols. Philadelphia, Pa.: Robert Desilver 1831. pp.
XII, 358, ill.; VI, 128, ill.* [4957

Oberholtzer, Ellis Paxson: Philadelphia. A
history of the city and its people. *4 vols.
Philadelphia, Pa.; Chicago, Ill.; St.
Louis, Mo.: The S. J. Clarke Publishing
Co. . . . pp. 452, ill., maps; 464, ill.,
maps; Vol. III and IV: Biographical.
pp. 627, ill.; pp. 531.* [4958

Ritter, Abraham: Philadelphia and her merchants, as constituted fifty & seventy
years ago, *illustrated by diagrams of the
river front, and portraits of some of its
prominent occupants together with sketches of character, and incidents and anecdotes of the day. Philadelphia, Pa.: Published by the author. 1860. pp. 223, ill.* [4959

Scharf, J. Thomas and Westcott, Thompson: History of Philadelphia 1609—1884. *3 vols. Philadelphia, Pa.: L. H. Everts & Co. 1884. pp. X, 852, (4), ill., maps; pp. VI, 853—1702, ill.; pp. VI, 1703— 2399, ill., maps.* [4960

Shoemaker, John v.: Founder's week memorial volume. *Containing an account of two hundred and twenty-fifth anniversary of the founding of the City of Philadelphia, and histories of its principal scientific institutions, medical colleges, hospitals, etc. Philadelphia, Pa.: Published by the City of Philadelphia in commemoration of the 225th anniversary of its founding 1909. pp. XVI, 912, ill.* [4961

Watson, John F.: Annals of Philadelphia, *being a collection of memoirs, |anecdotes and incidents of the city and its inhabitants from the days of the pilgrim founders intended to preserve the recollection of olden time, and to exhibit society in its changes of manners and customes, and the city in its local changes and improvements, to which is added an appendix containing olden time researches and reminiscences of New York City. Philadelphia, Pa.: E. L. Carvey & A. Hart; New York, N. Y.: G. & C. H. Carvill 1830. pp. XII, 740, 78, ill. Second edition: Annals of Philadelphia and Pennsylvania, in the olden time; being a collection of memoirs, anecdotes, and incidents of the city and its inhabitants and of the earliest settlements of the inland part of Pennsylvania, from the days of the founders. Philadelphia, Pa.: A. Hart, J. W. Moore, J. Pennington, U. Hunt and H. F. Anners 1850. pp. XVI, 609, ill.; pp. VII, 591, ill. Third edition: 2 vols. Philadelphia, Pa.: Whiting & Thomas 1856. pp. XVI, 609, ill.; 1857. pp. VII, 542, ill. Fourth edition: Enlarged with many revisions and additions by* Willis P. Hazard. *3 vols. Philadelphia, Pa.: J. M. Stoddart 1879. pp. . . .; Fifth edition: 3 vols. Philadelphia, Pa.: Pa.: Edwin S. Stuart, 1898. pp. XVI, 609, ill.; VII, 634, (6), ill.; 524, ill.* [4962

Helmuth, J. Heinrich C.: Bericht von dem sogenannten gelben Fieber in Philadelphia für den nachdenkenden Christen. *Philadelphia, Pa.: Steiner & Kämmerer 1793. 104 S.* Todten Liste von den Monaten August, September und October in Philadelphia, 1793. *10 S.* [4963

Deutsche in Philadelphia

Germans in Philadelphia

A.: The German Society's library. *In: Hazard's Register of Pennsylvania. Vol. VII. Philadelphia, Pa. 1831. p. 267.* [4964

Baum, Maria L.: Historical sketch of St. Matthew's Lutheran Church of Philadelphia. *Prepared by . . . [s. l., s. d.] pp. 8.* [4965

Berg, Joseph F.: The ancient land-mark being the substance of a discourse preached Sept. 29, 1839, on the Centenary anniversary of the organization of the Reformed Church on Race street, Philadelphia. *Philadelphia, Pa.: D. Weidner 1840. pp. 47.* [4966

Binder, Clarence K.: A contribution to the history of the Lutheran Sunday school in Philadelphia. *In: The Lutheran Church Review. Vol. XV. Philadelphia, Pa. 1896. pp. 420—432.* [4967

Bomberger, J. H. A.: Five years' ministry in the German Reformed Church, in Race street, below Fourth, Philadelphia. *An anniversary sermon, preached, January 8, 1860, and an ecclesiastical appendix. Philadelphia, Pa.: Lindsay & Blackiston 1860. pp. 72.* [4968

Bosse, Georg von: Philadelphia und sein Deutschtum. *Ein Gedenkblatt im Ausstellungsjahr 1926. Dargeboten von . . . Philadelphia, Pa.: Graf & Breuninger 1926. 44 S., ill.* [4969

Carson, James: Trial of Frederick Eberle and others, at a nisi prius court, held at Philadelphia, July, 1816 *before the Honorable Jasper Yeates, Justice. For illegally conspiring together by all means lawful and unlawful, ,,with their bodies and lives" to prevent the introduction of the English language into the service of St. Michael's and Zion's Churches, belonging to the German Lutheran congregation, in the City of Philadelphia. Taken in short hand. Philadelphia, Pa.: Published for the reporter 1817. pp. 240.* [4970

Dotterer, Henry S.: Philadelphia Reformed church burial ground. *(Inscriptions in the stones marking the graves in the lot of the First German Reformed Church of Philadelphia, in West Laurel Hill Cemetery, copied by* H. S. Dotterer, *Dec. 3, 1889.) In: Historical Notes, relating to the Pennsylvania Reformed Church. Vol. I. Philadelphia, Pa. 1900. pp. 28—31.* [4971

26*

Dotterer, Henry S.: The Philadelphia Reformed congregation in 1734. *Read at the commemoration by Philadelphia Classis of the 150th anniversary of the organization of the Reformed Church in the United States, Sept. 29, 1897. In: Historical Notes, relating to the Pennsylvania Reformed Church. Vol. I. Philadelphia, Pa. 1900. pp. 65—66.* [4972

Evers, Fritz Otto: Fest-Buechlein zum 175jährigen Jubiläum der Zions-Gemeinde, Philadelphia. 1742—1917. *Philadelphia, Pa.: Craig, Finley & Co. 1917. (20) S., ill.* [4973

Gillingham, Harrold E.: Some early Philadelphia instrument makers. *In: The Pennsylvania Magazine of History and Biography. Vol. LI. Philadelphia, Pa. 1927. pp. 289—308.* [4974

Griffin, Martin I. J.: The Church of the Holy Trinity, Philadelphia. Its first pastor, Rev. John Baptist Charles Helbron. The first opposition to ecclesiastical authority. *In: Report of the American Catholic Historical Society of Philadelphia. Vol. XXI. Philadelphia, Pa. 1910. pp. 1—45, ill.* [4975

— The Rev. Peter Helbron, second pastor of Holy Trinity Church, Philadelphia. Usurpation of pastoral rights by Rev. John N. Goetz and Rev. William Elling. Opposition of the trustees to Bishop Carroll. *In: Records of the American Catholic Historical Society of Philadelphia. Vol. XXIII, Philadelphia, Pa. 1912. pp. 1—21.* [4976

— The Reverend John Nepomucene Goetz, third pastor, and the Reverend William Elling, assistant of Holy Trinity Church, Philadelphia. *In: Records of the American Catholic Historical Society of Philadelphia. Vol. XXIII. Philadelphia, Pa. 1912. pp. 94—124.* [4977

[—] The Church of the Holy Trinity, Philadelphia. *In: Records of the American Catholic Historical Society of Philadelphia. Vol. XXIII, Philadelphia, Pa. 1912. pp. 249—261.* [4978

Hertkorn, Francis John: 1789—1914. A retrospect of Holy Trinity parish as a souvenir of the 125th anniversary of the foundation of the church. *Philadelphia, Pa.: Press of F. McManus, jr. & Co. 1914. pp. 135, ill.* [4979

Hinke, William J.: The early history of the first Reformed Church of Philadelphia, Pa. 1727—1734. *In: Journal of the Presbyterian Historical Society. Vol. II.*

Philadelphia, Pa. 1904. pp. 292—309. [4980

Horne, David van: A history of the Reformed Church in Philadelphia. *Published by request. Philadelphia, Pa.: Reformed Church Publication Board. 1876, pp. VI, 7—104, ill.* [4981

Huch, C. F.: Die deutsche Einwanderungsgesellschaft von Philadelphia. *In: Mitteilungen des Deutschen Pionier-Vereins von Philadelphia. Heft 7. 1908. [Philadelphia, Pa. 1908.] S. 27—30.* [4982

— Deutsche Zeitungen in Philadelphia während der ersten Hälfte des neunzehnten Jahrhunderts. *In: Deutsch-Amerikanische Geschichtsblätter. Jg. IX, Nr. 1. Chicago, Ill. 1909. S. 23—27.* [4983

— Die Deutschen in Philadelphia ums Jahr 1847. *In: Mitteilungen des Deutschen Pionier-Vereins von Philadelphia. Heft 17. 1910. [Philadelphia, Pa. 1910.] S. 13—21.*
Adruck in: Deutsch-Amerikanische Geschichtsblätter. Jg. 1910. Bd. X, Nr. 4. Chicago, Ill. 1910. S. 233—240. [4984

— Die deutsche Sprache in den deutschen Kirchen. *In: Mitteilungen des Deutschen Pionier-Vereins von Philadelphia. Heft 20. 1911. [Philadelphia, Pa. 1911.] S. 23—26.*
Abdruck in: Deutsche Erde. Zeitschrift für Deutschkunde. Herausgegeben von Paul Langhaus. Jg. XI. Gotha 1912. 57—58. [4985

Jacobs, Henry E.: Gloria Dei Church, Philadelphia 1700—1925. *Commemorative discourse preached at the 225th anniversary of its dedication. June 14, 1925. In: The Lutheran Church Review. Vol. XLIV. Philadelphia, Pa. 1925. pp. 185—194.* [4986

Jordan John W.: Colonial families of Philadelphia. *2 vols. New York, N. Y. — Chicago, Ill. The Lewis Publishing Co. 1911. pp. (1), 924, ill.; 925—1759, ill. Under others the following families of Germanic origin:* Wistar-Wister family. *pp. 257—275;* Pennypacker family. *pp. 480—493;* Tyson family. *pp. 689—733;* Lukens family. *pp. 744—751;* Pepper family. *pp. 1088—1097;* Updegrave family. *pp. 1190—1204;* Lukens family. *pp. 1470—1473;* Conard or Conrad family. *pp. 1474—1479;* Tunis family. *pp. 1556—1567;* Wagner family. *pp. 1572—1581;* W. Hinckle Smith family. *pp. 1643—1656.* Baker family. *pp.*

1657—1663; Stull family. *pp. 1678—1682;* Suter family. *pp. 1709—1711;* Diehl family. *pp. 1723—1737.* [4987

Jordan, William H.: Reminiscences of the old First Moravian Church of Philadelphia 1742—1901. *A paper read before the Moravian Historical Society and the First Moravian Church. Philadelphia, Pa. 1901. pp. 19, ill.* [4988

Kirlin, Joseph L. J.: Catholicity in Philadelphia. From the earliest missionaries down to the present time. *Philadelphia, Pa.: John Jos. McVey 1909. pp. XV, 546.* [4989

McCallen, William J.: Temporary schism over the election of father William Elling, to the pastorate of Holy Trinity Church, Philadelphia 1797—1806. *In: Records of the American Catholic Historical Society of Philadelphia. Vol. XXIV. Philadelphia, Pa. 1913. pp. 193—216.* [4990

[Mühlenberg, Henry Melchior]: Mühlenbergs short sketch of the Lutheran congregation in Philadelphia 1795. *Reprints from Philadelphia Gazette 1795. Edited by J. F. Sachse. In: The Lutheran Church Review. Vol. XXI. Philadelphia, Pa. 1902. pp. 81—87.* [4993

Murphy, Thomas: One hundred years of the Presbyterian church of Frankford. *Philadelphia, Published by the church. 1872, pp. 167. [A German Ref. church, from 1769—1802].* [4993a

Pennypacker, Samuel Whitaker: The Pennsylvania Dutchman in Philadelphia. *Address at the annual meeting of the Pennsylvania-German Society in 1896, held in Philadelphia, Pa. Philadelphia, Pa. 1907. pp. 12.* [4994

Pfatteicher, E. P.: The Lutheran problems in Philadelphia. *In: The Lutheran Church Review. Vol. XXXVIII. Philadelphia, Pa. 1919. pp. 44—47.* [4995

[Reuß, Francis X.]: Baptismal registers of Holy Trinity Church of Philadelphia A. D. 1790—1795. Priests named therein — John Baptist Charles Helbron, Peter Helbron, Laurence Peter Phelan and William Elling. *From the originals by Fr. X. Reuss. Edited with notes by Thomas Cooke Middleton. In: Records od the American Catholic Historical Society of Philadelphia. Vol. XXI. Philadelphia, Pa. 1910. pp. 65—76; 145—154; vol. XXII. 1911. pp. 20; 65—83.* [4996

[—] Marriage registers of the Holy Trinity Church of Philadelphia, Pa. A. D. 1791

—1799. Priests named therein — John Charles Helbron, Peter Helbron and Laurence Peter Phelan. *From the originals by Francis X. Reuss. Edited with notes by Thomas Cooke Middleton. In: Records of the American Catholic Historical Society of Philadelphia. Vol. XXIV. Philadelphia, Pa. 1913. pp. 140—161.* [4997

Ritter, Abraham: History of the Moravian Church in Philadelphia, from its foundation in 1742 to the present time. *Comprising notices, defensive of its founder and patron, Count Nicholas Ludwig von Zinzendorf. Together with an appendix. Philadelphia, Pa.: Hayes and Zell 1857. pp. XX, 17—281, ill.* [4998

Sachse, Julius F.: The religious and social conditions of Philadelphia during the first decade of the federal constitution, 1790—1800. *In: The Lutheran Church Rewiew. Vol. XX. Philadelphia, Pa. 1901. pp. 491—517, ill.* [4999

Seidensticker, Oswald: Die Deutschen von Philadelphia im Jahr 1776. *In: Der Deutsche Pionier. Jg. VIII. Cincinnati, O. 1876—1877. S. 190—195; 245—250; 284—287; 343—348. Abdruck in: Mitteilungen des Deutschen Pionier-Vereins von Philadelphia. Heft 10, 1909. [Philadelphia, Pa. 1909.] S. 1—20.* [5000

Sibole, Edward E.: Centennial. A brief narrative of events in the first hundred years of the Evangelical Lutheran congregation of Saint John's Church, Philadelphia 1806—1906. *[Philadelphia, Pa. 1906.] pp. (1), 7—136, ill.* [5001

Wischan, F.: Kurze Geschichte der deutschen evangel. luther. Gemeinden in und um Philadelphia und der lutherischen Synoden Amerikas. *(1892). = Teil II in: Die lutherische Kirche in Amerika. Leipzig: Theodor Rother 1893 [= Nr. 226]. S. 79—240, ill.* [5002

[Hiltzheimer, Jacob]: Extracts from the diary of Jacob Hiltzheimer, of Philadelphia, 1768—1798. *In: The Pennsylvania Magazine of History and Biography. Vol. XVI. Philadelphia, Pa. 1892. pp. 93—102; 160—177; 412—422. [At the age of nineteen, left his native City of Manheim, on the Rhine, and emigrated to Philadelphia, 1748.]* [5003

[—] Extracts from the diary of Jacob Hiltzheimer of Philadelphia. 1765—1798. *Edited by his great-grandson, J. Cox Parsons. Philadelphia, Pa.:*

Press of Wm. F. Fell & Co. 1893. pp. VIII, 9—270. [5004

[Hiltzheimer, Jacob]: Jacob Hiltzheimer's diary. *In: Historical Notes, relating to the Pennsylvania Reformed Church. Vol. I. Philadelphia, Pa. 1900. pp. 21—22; 37—38;* Record of a methodical church officer of the past century. *pp. 111—112;* Philadelphia Reformed church records. *pp. 123—125.* [5005

[Wister, Sally]: Journal of Miß Sally Wister. *In: The Pennsylvania Magazine of History and Biography. Vol. IX. Philadelphia, Pa. 1885. pp. 318—333; 463—478; Vol. X. 1886. pp. 51—60.* [5006

[Wollenweber, L. A.]: Aus den Aufzeichnungen von L. A. Wollenweber über seine Erlebnisse in Amerika, namentlich in Philadelphia. *Herausgegeben von C. F. Huch. In: Mittheilungen des Deutschen Pionier-Vereins von Philadelphia. Heft . . , 19 . . Philadelphia, Pa. 19 . . . . S.*
Abdruck in: Deutsch-Amerikanische Geschichtsblätter. Jg. 1910. Bd. X, Nr. 1. Chicago, Ill. 1910. S. 45—60, Nr. 2. S. 67—105; Nr. 3. S. 130—147. [5007
— Zwei treue Kameraden. Die beiden ersten deutschen Ansiedler in Pennsylvanien. *[Heinrich Frey u. Joseph Plattenbach.] Historische Erzählung aus der ersten Epoche der deutschen Einwanderer in Pennsylvanien, im Jahre 1680. Philadelphia, Pa.: Verlag von Jg. Kohler, Nr. 911 Arch Straße. 1880. 72 S., ill.* [5007a

[Tyson, J. R.]: Sketch of the Wistar Party of Philadelphia. *Being a reprint of the edition of 1846 with a continuation to the present time. (Printed for the members only.) Philadelphia, Pa. 1898. pp. 3—17, 19, 21, 23, ill.* [5008

Carson, Hampton L.: The Centenary of the Wistar Party. An historical address. *Delivered by appointment in the Hall of the Historical Society of Pennsylvania, May 4th, 1918. With the roll of members 1818—1918. Philadelphia, Pa.: Printed for the Wistar Association 1918. [Lancaster, Pa.: Press of the New Era Printing Co.] pp. 36.* [5009

„A list of those persons that refuse to go to Camp, 'till they are compelled," *is addressed to Colonel Timothy Matlack, 1776. In: The Pennsylvania Magazine of History and Biography. Vol. XXIV.* *Philadelphia, Pa. 1900. pp. 380—381.* [5010
Where Count Zinzendorf resided in Philadelphia. *In: The Pennsylvania Magazine of History and Biography. Vol. XXXIX. Philadelphia, Pa. 1915. pp. 494—495.* [5011
German Lutheran congregation of Philadelphia. *In: Hazard's Register of Pennsylvania. Vol. IV. Philadelphia, Pa. 1829. pp. 369—373.* [5012
Zum Andenken an die hundertjährige Jubelfeier in der deutschen evangl. luther. Sct. Michaelis Kirche in Philadelphia, am 14. Junius, 1843. *Dem Druck übergeben, auf Verlangen des Kirchenrathes. Philadelphia, Pa.: Conrad Zentler 1843. 104 S.* [5013
The records of St. Michaelis and Zion congregation of Philadelphia. *[Birth and baptisms of the Evangelical Lutheran congregation in Philadelphia, 1745—1762.] Copied, collated, arranged and edited by* Julius F. Sachse. *In: The Pennsylvania-German Society. Proceedings and Addresses . . . 1896. Vol. VII. Reading, Pa. 1897. pp. 535—576; . . . 1897. Vol. VIII. Lancaster, Pa. 1898. pp. 199—222; . . . 1898. Vol. IX. Lancaster, Pa. 1899. pp. 449—468.* [5014
Marriage record of St. Michael's and Zion [Lutheran] Church, Philadelphia. 1745 —1800. *In: Record of Pennsylvania Marriages, prior to 1810. Vol. II. Harrisburg, Pa. 1880. = Pennsylvania Archives. Second series, vol. IX. Edited by John B. Linn and Wm. H. Egle. Harrisburg, Pa. 1880. pp. 285—440.*
Reprint Harrisburg, Pa. 1895. pp. 291—457. [5015
Record of marriages in the St. Michaelis and Zion Evangelical Lutheran congregation in Philadelphia. Commenced Anno 1745. *In: The Pennsylvania German Society. Proceedings and Addresses . . . 1903. Vol. XIV. Lancaster, Pa. 1905. Separate pagination pp. 140, ill.* [5016
An historical sketch of the Sunday school of the Evangelical Lutheran Church of St. John, Philadelphia. *Published by the Missionary, Tract and Book Society of St. John's Church. Philadelphia, Pa.: Sherman & Co. 1871. pp. 70.* [5017
Fünfunddreißig Jahre der Evangelisch Lutherischen St. Jacobus Gemeinde, Ecke der Dritten Str. und Columbia Ave. in Philadelphia. Pa. *Zu haben beim Kirchenrat der Gemeinde. 1890. 80 S.* [5018

Marriage record of the German Reformed Church at Philadelphia, 1748—1802. *In: Record of Pennsylvania marriages, prior to 1810. Vol. I. Harrisburg, Pa. 1880. = Pennsylvania Archives. Second series, vol. VIII. Edited by John B. Linn and Wm. H. Egle. Harrisburg, Pa. 1896. pp. 649—731. Reprint Harrisburg, Pa. 1896. pp. 661— 746.* [5019

The Reformed Church of Frankford. Its transition from the German Reformed to the Presbyterian denomination. *In. Historical Notes, relating to the Pennsylvania Reformed Church. Vol. I. Philadelphia, Pa. 1900. pp. 27—28.* [5020

Marriage register of the Moravian Church, Philadelphia, 1743—1800. *In: Record of Pennsylvania marriages, Prior to 1810. Vol. II. Harrisburg, Pa. 1880. = Pennsylvania Archives. Second series, vol. IX. Edited by John B. Linn and Wm. H. Egle. Harrisburg, Pa. 1880. pp. 147—151. Reprint Harrisburg, Pa. 1895. pp. 149— 153.* [5021

Register of members and their children belonging to the Moravian congregation in Philadelphia in 1766. *In: Notes and Queries. Edited by W. H. Egle. Annual vol. 1896. Harrisburg, Pa. 1897. pp. 212—215.* [5022

Register of members and their children, Moravian congregation, Philadelphia, 1757. *In: The Pennsylvania Magazine of History and Biography. Vol. XXXV. Philadelphia, Pa. 1911. pp. 254—256.* [5023

Historical sketch of the First Schwenkfeldian Church in Philadelphia. *In: Mennonite Year Book and Almanac for 1900. Quakertown, Pa. 1900. pp. 34— 35.* [5024

Fiftieth anniversary of the First Mennonite Church of Philadelphia 1865—1915. *. . . Philadelphia, Pa., Sept. 26th, Oct. 3rd, 1915. Philadelphia, Pa.: The Harrison Press. pp. 54, ill.* [5025

First Mennonite congregation of Philadelphia. Historical sketches of Mennonite congregations. *In: Mennonite Year Book and Almanac for 1928. Quakertown, Pa. 1898. pp. 29—30, ill.* [5026

Holy Trinity baptismal records — Register number two, 1796—1802. Edited by F. E. Tourscher. *In: Records of the American Catholic Historical Society of Philadelphia. Vol. XXXIV, 1923. pp. 151*

—194. Vol. XXXV. 1924. pp. 159—177. Vol. XXXVIII. pp. 168—192. Vol. XXXIX, pp. 54—62. [5027

[Frank, Henry]: Das heutige Philadelphia. *Ein illustrirter Führer durch alle oeffentliche Gebäude, Institute, Eisenbahnen, sowie Plätze von Interesse.* Nebst einer vollständigen Liste aller bedeutenden deutschen Gesellschaften und Vereine, *und einer Karte von Philadelphia. Philadelphia, Pa.: Herausgegeben von Henry Frank 1885. 96 S. ill.* [5028

Deutsche Institute in Philadelphia. *(Kirchen; Wohltätige Gesellschaften; Bildungsvereine; Gesangvereine; Volksfestvereine; Turn- und Schützenvereine; Deutsche Zeitungen in Philadelphia.) In: German Day 1892 [=Nr. 391]. S. 34—44* [5029

Germantown, the 22d Ward of the City of Philadelphia

Albert, Luther E.: A sermon commemorative of the fiftieth anniversary of Trinity Lutheran Church, Germantown, April 18th, 1886. *[s. l.] pp. 16, ill.* [5030

[Bechtel, John]: A letter of John Bechtel. Dated Germantown, 1745. *In: Germantown history. Papers read before the Site and Relic Society of Germantown. Vol. I. Germantown, Pa. 1915. pp. 23—24.* [5031

Bender, Harold S.: The foundation of the Mennonite Church in America at Germantown, 1683—1708. *In: Mennonite Quarterly Review. Vol. VII. Goshen, Ind.-Scottdale, Pa. 1933. pp. 227—250.* [5032

Bennett, R. P. D.: The religious history and the significance of the founding of Germantown. A sermon preached in Summit Presbyterian Church, Oct. 4, 1908. *[s. l. 1908.] pp. . . . .* [5033

Blicknell, Joseph D.: The Wissahickon in history, song and story. *Written for the City History Society of Philadelphia and read at the meeting of Oct. 10, 1906. Philadelphia, Pa.: Printed for the Society, 1908. In: Publication of the City of Philadelphia. Vol. I, no. 1. pp. 1—24.* [5034

Campbell, Jane: A newcomer in Germantown. *Address delivered Oct. 25, 1913. In: Germantown history, consisting of papers read before the Site and Relic So-*

ciety of Germantown. Vol. II, no. 1. Germantown, Pa. 1916. pp. 25—38. [5035

Clayton, Beatrice: Francis Daniel Pastorius. *From a sketch written for the Philadelphia „Public Ledger". In: The Mennonite Yearbook and Almanac for 1902. Quakertown, Pa. 1902. pp. 42—44, ill.* [5036

Conrad, Henry C.: Address of Hon. Henry C. Conrad, associate Judge Superior Court of Delaware, at the dedication of the Pastorius Memorial at Germantown, Pa., November 10, 1920. *In: The Mennonite Year Book and Almanac for 1922. Quakertown, Pa. 1922. pp. 45—46.* [5037

Cronau, Rudolf: „Die Mennoniten und die Gründung Germantowns." *In: Drei Jahrhunderte deutschen Lebens in Amerika. Eine Geschichte der Deutschen in den Vereinigten Staaten. Von R. Cronau. Berlin 1909 [= Nr. 34]. S. 49—69, ill.; 2. Aufl. 1924. S. 49—69, ill.* [5037a

Croon, Helmuth: Zur Geschichte der Krefelder Auswanderung von 1683. *In: Die Heimat. Mitteilungen der Vereine für Heimatkunde in Krefeld und Uerdingen. Herausgegeben im Auftrage der Vereine von K. Rembert. Jg. V. Heft 1. Crefeld: Druck von Th. Gippers 1926. S. 36—39.* [5038

De Yoe, Luther: History of Trinity Lutheran Church. Germantown Avenue & Queen Lane. Germantown, Philadelphia. 1836 to 1925. *[s. l. 1925.] pp. 52. ill.* [5039

Dotterer, Henry S.: The church at Market Square. *Read at a meeting in the chapel of Market Square Presbyterian Church, Germantown, Philadelphia, Nov. 17, 1898. In: The Perkiomen Region, Past and Present. Vol. II. Philadelphia, Pa. 1900. pp. 9—12; 30—32; 39—46; 59—62; 74—76. In: Historical Notes relating to the Pennsylvania Reformed Church. Vol. I. Philadelphia, Pa. 1900. pp. 13—16; 23—26; 39—42; 55—58; 69—74. [Also separately issued. Philadelphia, Pa.: Perkiomen Publishing Co. 1899. pp. 22.]* [5040

Dripps, J. Frederick: History of the First Presbyterian Church in Germantown. The Centennial services. The present church organizations. Germantown, Oct., 1909. *Philadelphia, Pa.: Press of Allen, Lane & Scott 1909. pp. II, 3—302, ill.* [5041

Eiselmeier, J.: Franz Daniel Pastorius, der Gründer von Germantown. *In: Die*

neue Zeit (The new Era). Wochenschrift für Politik, Kultur und Literatur. Bd. XIV. Nr. 50. New Ulm, 14. Mai 1932. S. 3—6. [5042

Erkelenz, Anton: 250 Jahre deutsche Kolonisation in USA. Zum 6. Oktober 1683. *In: Die Hilfe. Zeitschrift für Politik, Wirtschaft und geistige Bewegung. Jg. XXXIX, Nr. 20. Berlin 1933. S. 515—516.* [5042a

Faris, John T.: Old churches and meetinghouses in and around Philadelphia. *Philadelphia, Pa. and London: J. B. Lippincott Co. 1926. pp. XVI, 261, ill. [Three old churches in Germantown. pp. 35—38; Intimate glimpses of Germantown meeting. pp. 178—184; In Germantown and Frankford. pp. 193—196.]* [5043

Faust, A. B.: „The first permanent German settlement, at Germantown, 1689." *In: The German element in the United States. By A. B. Faust. Second edition. New York. N. Y. 1927. Vol, I. = Chapter II. pp. 30—52.* [5044

— Francis Daniel Pastorius and the 250th anniversary of the founding of Germantown. *Philadelphia, Pa. Carl Schurz Memorial Foundation, Inc. 1934. pp. 22.* [5045

Gillingham, Harrold E.: Benjamin Lehman, a Germantown cabinetmaker. *In: The Pennsylvania Magazine of History and Biography. Vol. LIV. Philadelphia, Pa. 1930. pp. 289—306, ill.* [5046

Götz, Karl: Große Deutschamerikaner. Franz Daniel Pastorius. *In: Deutsche Arbeit. Führerzeitschrift des Vereins für das Deutschtum im Ausland. Jg. XXIX. Dresden 1929—1930. S. 260—266.* [5046a

Grubb, N. B.: The Dirk Keyser house. *In: The Mennonite Year Book and Almanac for 1902. Quakertown, Pa. 1902. p. 104, ill.* [5047

— 1683—1708—1770. The Mennonite Church of Germantown. *Philadelphia, Pa. 1906. pp. 11, ill.* [5048

Harshberger, John W.: Some old gardens of Pennsylvania. *In: The Pennsylvania Magazine of History and Biography. Vol. XLVIII. 1924. pp. 289—300. [Rosicrucum garden on the Wissahickon. pp. 289—290.]* [5049

Haverstick, Horace: The Billmeyer house. *Read February 7, 1902. In: Germantown history, consisting of papers read before the Site and Relic Society of Germantown. Vol. I. Germantown, Pa. 1915. pp. 25—30.* [5050

[Hemsath, W. Karl]: 1728—1928. Programme, Bi-Centennial celebration of St. Michael's Lutheran Church of Germantown. *With historical notes. [s. l. 1928.] pp. 32, ill.* [5051

Hennighausen, Louis P.: The first German settlement in North America. *In: Fourth Annual Report of the Society for the History of the Germans in Maryland, Baltimore, Md. 1890. pp. 25—31.* [5052

Hinke, William J.: The early history of the German Reformed Church at Germantown. *Address delivered before the City History Club of Philadelphia, May 7, 1903. In: Dr. Naaman Keyser & others, History of Old Germantown, Germantown, Philadelphia, 1907. [=no. 5070]. Vol. I, pp. 381—402.* [5052a

[Hocker, Edward W.]: A century of the National Bank of Germantown. *Philadelphia, Pennsylvania 1814—1914. Dedicated to the former presidents and cashiers by the directors. Philadelphia, Pa.: Innes & Sons 1914. pp. 66.* [5053

— Germantown 1683—1933. *The record that a Pennsylvania community has achieved in the course of 250 years. Being a history of the people of Germantown, Mount Airy and Chestnut Hill. Germantown Pa., published by the author; Philadelphia Pa., printed by Camp News Company, 1933. pp. 331.* [5054

Holcomb, William P.: Pennsylvania boroughs. *Baltimore, Md. 1886. pp. 51. = Johns Hopkins University Studies of History and Political Science. Fourth series, no. IV. 1886. [Germantown, its origin and form of government. Vol. IV. pp. 151—170.]* [5055

Hotchkin, S. F.: Ancient and modern Germantown, Mount Airy and Chestnut Hill. *Philadelphia, Pa.: P. W. Ziegler & Co. 1889. pp. 538, (10).* [5056

Hull, William I.: William Penn and the Dutch Quaker migration to Pennsylvania. *Swarthmore, Pa.: Swarthmore College 1935. pp. XIII, 445, ill. = Swarthmore College Monographs on Quaker History. No. 2.* [5056a

Jackson, Joseph: A history of the Germantown Academy. *Published upon the one hundred and fiftieth anniversary of the school's founding, 1910. Philadelphia, Pa.: Press of S. H. Burbank & Co. 1910. pp. XVI, 321.* [5057

Jellett, Edwin C.: German-Towne. Its founders and their progenitors and what we owe them. *Germantown, Pa.: Press of ,,Independent-Gazette". 1903. pp. 25, ill.* [5058

Jellett, Ewin C.: Germantown, old and new. Its rare and notable plants. *Germantown, Pa.: Independent-Gazette, 1904. pp. 104, ill.; Second edition 1904/05. pp. 114.* [5059

— Germantwon gardens and gardeners. *Germantown, Philadelphia, Pa.: Horace F. McCann 1914. pp. 96, ill.* [5060

— Grumblethorpe. *In: Germantown history, consisting of papers read before the Site and Relic Society of Germantown. Vol. I. Germantown, Pa. 1915. pp. 99—121, ill.* [5061

— Gardens and gardeners of Germantown: *Address delivered Jan. 19, 1912. In: Germantown history, consisting of papers read before the Site and Relic Society of Germantown. Vol. I. Germantown, Pa. 1915. pp. 251—343, ill.* [5062

— Historical outing to Germantown. *In: Historical sketches. A Collection of Papers prepared for the Historical Society of Montgomery County, Pa. Vol. VI. Norristown, Pa. 1929. pp. 76—79, ill.* [5063

Jenkins, Charles F.: The guide book to historic Germantown. *Prepared for the Site and Relic Society. Germantown, Pa.: Innes & Sons, Philadelphia, Pa. 1902. pp. 167, ill., map; Second edition. 1904. pp. . . . ill., map.; Third edition. 1915. pp. 161, ill., map.; Fourth edition 1926. pp. 161, ill., map.* [5064

— Washington visits Germantown. *Germantown, Pa.: Germantown Historical Society. Philadelphia, Pa. 1932. pp. (1), 6—91, ill.* [5065

Johnson, Sarah Wheeler: Noted women of Germantown. *In: Germantown history, consisting of papers read before the Site and Relic Society of Germantown. Vol. II, no. 2. Germantown, Pa. 1916. pp. 41—53.* [5066

Jones, Horatio Gates: Historical sketch of the Rittenhouse paper-mill; the first erected in America. A. D. 1690. *Paper read before the Historical Society of Pennsylvania, May 11, 1863. In: The Pennsylvania Magazine of History and Biography. Vol. XX. Philadelphia, Pa. 1896. pp. 315—333, ill.* [5067

Kapp, Friedrich: Die deutschen Pilgerväter. *In: Deutsche Rundschau. Herausgegeben von Julius Rodenberg. Vol. XXXVIII. Berlin 1884. pp. 130—138.* [5068

Keyser, Naaman Henry: Old historic Germantown. *An address with illustrations presented at the fourteenth annual meeting. Lancaster, Pa.: The New Era Printing Co. 1906. In: The Pennsylvania-German Society. Proceedings and Addresses at Germantown, Oct. 25, 1904. Vol. XV. Lancaster, Pa. 1906. Separate pagination. pp. 78, ill.* [5069

—-**Kain, C.** Henry - **Garber, John** Palmer - **McCann, Horace F.:** History of old Germantown. *With a description of its settlement and some account of its important persons, buildings and places connected with its development. Germantown, Philadelphia, Pa.: Horace F. McCann 1907. pp. 453, XXI, ill., map.* [5070

— Early transportation to Germantown. *Read April 18, 1902. In: Germantown history, consisting of papers read before the Site and Relic Society of Germantown. Vol. I. Germantown, Pa. 1915. pp. 39—55, ill.* [5071

Keyser, Peter D.: A history of the Upper Germantown burying-ground, Germantown Avenue (Main Street) above Washington Lane. *In: The Pennsylvania Magazine of History and Biography. Vol. VIII. Philadelphia, Pa. 1884. pp. 414—426.* [5072

— Inscriptions in the Upper Germantown burying-ground. *In: Pennsylvania Magazine of History and Biography. Vol. IX. Philadelphia, Pa. 1885. pp. 82—88.* [5073

Keyser, Romaine: The Concord school house. *Read March 29, 1903. In: Germantown history, consisting of papers read before the Site and Relic Society of Germantown. Vol. I. Germantown, Pa. 1915. pp. 56—72.* [5074

Kretschmann: Historical sketch of the Evangelical Lutheran Christ Church of Chestnut Hill, prepared for the 25th anniversary of the consecration of the church, June 22, 1896. *Philadelphia, Pa.: Craig Finley & Co. 1896. pp. 46.* [5075

Kriebel, H. W.: Old Germantown. *Extracts from various publications. In: The Pennsylvania-German. Vol. IX. Cleona, Pa. 1908. pp. 443—450, ill.* [5076

Learned, Marion Dexter: Francius Daniel Pastorius. The founder of Germantown. *In: German American Annals. New series, vol. V. Philadelphia, Pa. 1907. pp. 131—171; 195—234; 259—*

293; 323—356; vol. VI. 1908. pp. 3—31; 65—101; 121—156; 187—237, ill., maps. [5077

Learned, Marion Dexter: The life of Francis Daniel Pastorius, the founder of Germantown. *With an appreciation of Pastorius by Samuel Whitaker Pennypacker. Philadelphia, Pa.: William J. Campbell 1908. pp. X, 324, ill., maps.* [5078

[—] Das Leben von Franz Daniel Pastorius. *Nach: ,,Leben von F. D. Pastorius" von M. D. Learned [= Nr. 5078]. In: Deutsch-Amerikanische Geschichtsblätter. Jg. IX. Chicago, Ill. 1909. Nr. 1. S. 2—5; Nr. 2. S. 47—50.* [5079

Lichtenstein, Gaston: Germantown, Pa. *In: When Tarboro was once incorporated, also Reverend James Moir, Edgecombe changes her county seat, and Germantown, Pennsylvania. Reprinted from the Tarborough Southerner, Tarboro, N. C. Richmond, Va.: Capital Printing Co. 1910. pp. 24—27.* [5080

Macfarlane, John J.: History of early Chestnut Hill. *Read at a meeting of the City History Society of Philadelphia. Nov. 11, 1914. Enlarged and revised for publication. Philadelphia, Pa.: Published by the Society 1927. pp. 168, ill., maps.* [5081

Meynen, Emil: Germantown. *In: Deutsche Arbeit, Zeitschrift des Volksbundes für das Deutschtum im Ausland. Jg. XXXIV. Berlin 1934. S. 176—183, ill.* [5082

— Germantown, Pennsylvanien 1683—1933. *In: Die Heimat, Zeitschrift für niederrheinische Heimatpflege, herausgegeben von K. Rembert. Jg. XIII. Krefeld 1934. S. 105—112, ill.; Neudruck Berlin, Hiehold & Co., 1935. 15 S., ill.* [5083

Morris, Elliston P.: Memoirs of old Germantown, particularly of Market Square. *Read April 18, 1902. In: Germantown history, consisting of papers read before the Site and Relic Society of Germantown. Vol. I. Germantown, Pa. 1915. pp. 8—12.* [5084

Müller, Bernhard: ,,Frankfurter Landkompagnie, Pastorius und Germantown." *In: Frankfurt/Amerika. I. Alte und neue Beziehungen von Bernhard Müller; II. Frankfurt im Sezessionskriege von Ludwig Heilbrunn. Frankfurt am Main: Herausgegeben vom Wirtschaftsamt der Stadt Frankfurt am Main, Abteilung für*

Werbe- und Ausstellungswesen, anläßlich der Ausstellung Frankfurt-America. 1926. S. 14—32. [5085

Pancoast, Mary E.: A short history of St. Michael's Church, Germantown, *1902. pp. 44, ill.* [5086

[Pastorius, Franz Daniel]: *Siehe auch Nr. (see nos.) 219—221, 223—226, 228—232, 237, 3310, 3435.*

Pennypacker, Samuel Whitacker: The settlement of Germantown and the causes which led to it. *Paper read before the Historical Society, Oct. 20, 1879. In: The Pennsylvania Magazine of History and Biography. Vol. IV. Philadelphia, Pa. 1880. pp. 1—41. Reprinted in: S. W. Pennypacker: Historical and biographical sketches. Philadelphia, Pa. 1883 [= no. 356]. pp. 9—58.* [5088

— An address at the Bi-Centennial celebration of the settlement of Germantown, and the beginning of German emigration to America, *in the Philadelphia Academie of Music, on the evening of October 6th, 1883. Philadelphia, Pa.: Pennypacker & Rogers 1883. pp. 10.* [5089

— The settlement of Germantown, Pa., and the beginning of German immigration to North America. *Lancaster, Pa. 1899. = Part IV. ,,A narrative and critical history", prepared at the request of the Pennsylvania-German Society. In: The Pennsylvania-German Society. Proceedings and Addresses . . . 1898. Vol. IX. Lancaster, Pa. 1899. pp. 51—345, ill., map.* [5090

— Early German settlers. *Reprint from Germantown Independent Gazette. No. 14, 1902. In: The Pennsylvania School Journal. Vol. LI. Lancaster, Pa. 1902. pp. 295—297.* [5091

Powers, Fred Perry: Tales of old taverns. *Address delivered March 17, 1911. In: Germantown history, consisting of papers read before the Site and Relic Society of Germantown. Vol. I. Germantown, Pa. 1915. pp. 195—231, ill.* [5092

Pullinger, Herbert: Old Germantown. *Introduction by Charles F. Jenkins. Philadelphia, Pa.: David McKay Co. 1926. pp. 57, ill.* [5093

Rattermann, H. A.: Eine Ehrenrettung des Franz Daniel Pastorius. *In: Deutsch-Amerikanische Geschichtsblätter. Jg. XI. Chicago, Ill. 1911. S. 212—222.* [5093a

[Rattermann, H. A.]: A vindication of Francis Daniel Pastorius. *Free translation of an article by . . ., published in the: ,,Deutsch-Amerikanische Geschichtsblätter," Oct. 1911. In: The Penn Germania. Vol. I. = Old series, vol. XIII. Lititz, Pa. 1912. pp. 17—24.* [5093b

— Pastorius und die Gründung von Germantown, Pa. Replik an Herrn Wilhelm Kaufmann *[Vgl. Nr. 214s]. In: Deutsch-Amerikanische Geschichtsblätter. Jahrbuch der Deutsch-Amerikanischen Historischen Gesellschaft von Illinois Jg. 1912. Vol. XII. Chicago, Ill. 1912. S. 559—567.* [5093c

Rembert, Karl: Die ersten deutschen Einwanderer in Amerika. *In: Die Heimat. Mitteilungen des Vereins für Heimatkunde in Krefeld. Jg. IV, Heft 2. Krefeld 1925. S. 131—135, ill.* [5094

Rohrbach, Paul: ,,Pastorius und die Gründung von Germantown." *In: Das Deutschtum über See. Von P. Rohrbach. Karlsruhe 1931 [= Nr. 97a]. S. 15—19.* [5094a

Sachse, Julius Friedrich: Quaint old Germantown in Pennsylvania. *Paper read at the annual meeting. Illustrated with 60 copies of the original sketches of John Richard. Lancaster, Pa.: The New Era Printing Co. 1915. In: The Pennsylvania-German Society. Proceedings and Addresses at Riegelsville, Pa., Oct. 4, 1912. Vol. XXIII. Lancaster, Pa. 1915. Separate pagination. pp. 7; 60 plates.* [5095

Seidensticker, Oswald: Franz Daniel Pastorius (1651—1719) und die Gründung von Germantown (1684). *In: Der Deutsche Pionier. Jg. II. Cincinnati, O. 1870—1871. S. 136—143; 169—178; 206—211; 241—248; 275—279; 300—307; 334—340; 379—383; Jg. III. 1871—1872. S. 8—12; 56—58; 78—83.* [5096

— Die erste Deutsche Einwanderung in Amerika und die Gründung von Germantown im Jahre 1683. *Festschrift zum deutsch-amerikanischen Pionier-Jubiläum am 6. Okt. 1883. Philadelphia, Pa.: Globe Printing House 1883. 94 S.* [5097

Shoemaker, Thomas H.: A list of the inhabitants of Germantown and Chestnut Hill in 1809. *In: The Pennsylvania Magazine of History and Biography. Vol. XV. Philadelphia, Pa. 1891. pp. 449—480; Vol. XVI. 1892. pp. 42—63.* [5098

Shoemaker, Thomas H.: The middle ward fire company, of Germantown. *In: The Pennsylvania Magazine of History and Biography. Vol. XVIII. Philadelphia, Pa. 1894. pp. 429—448, ill.*   [5099

[Sower, Charles G., Falkenstein, Georg N. and Brumbaugh, Martin G.]: Bishop Christopher Sower of Germantown. Memorial services, presentation of tablet. Church of the Brethren. Germantown, January 1, 1899. *[s. l.] (Privately printed.) pp. 31, ill.*   [5100

Spencer, David: Historic Germantown. *Germantown, Philadelphia, Pa.: Horace F. McCann 1908. pp. 193, ill.*   [5101

Swigart, Milton C.: Souvenir. Bi-Centennial of the Germantown Church of the Brethren 6613 Germantown Ave., Philadelphia, Sunday, Oct. 11th, 1908. *Germantown, Pa.: The Germantown News 1908. pp. 14.*   [5102

— 200th anniversary of the first baptism and love feast held in the old mother church, Germantown, Philadelphia, Pa., Dec. 23rd and Christmas Day, Dec. 25, 1923. *Edited by . . . Rockton, Pa.: Keystone Printing Office 1924. pp. 28, ill.*   [5103

Thomas, Robert: A century of Methodism in Germantown. *Germantown, Pa.: Press of Germantown Independent. 1895. pp. 70, (6).*   [5104

Travis, William: History of the Germantown Academy. Compiled from the minutes of the trustes. From 1760 to 1877. *Edited by Horace Wemyss Smith. Philadelphia, Pa.: Ferguson Bros. & Co. 1882. pp. 64.*   [5105

Turner, Beatrice Pastorius: William Penn and Pastorius. *An address delivered before the Pennsylvania Society of the Colonial Dames of America, Jan. 28, 1932. In: The Pennsylvania Magazin of History and Biography, Vol. LVII. Philadelphia, Pa. 1933. pp. 66—90.*   [5106

Ward, Townsend: The Germantown road and its associations. *In: The Pennsylvania Magazine of History and Biography. Vol. V. Philadelphia, Pa. 1881. pp. 1—18; 121—140; 241—258; 365—392; Vol. VI. 1882. pp. 1—20; 129—155; 257—283; 377—401, ill.*   [5107

Watson, John F.: Notes of the early history of Germantown. *In: Hazard's Register of Pennsylvania. Vol. I. Philadelphia, Pa. 1828. pp. 279—284; 289—293.* [A correction to above article. *p. 335.]*   [5108

Weygandt, Cornelius: The Wissahickon hills. Memoirs of leisure hours out of doors in an old countryside. *Philadelphia, Pa.: University of Pennsylvania Press 1930. pp. XIII, 366, ill.*   [5109

Whayman, Horace W.: Some early German settlers in Germantown, Pa. and their descendants in the old territory. *In the ,,Old Northwest" Genealogical Quarterly 1904. Vol. VII. Columbus, O. 1904. pp. 123—128; 183—186.* *[See: Ohio.]*   [5110

Willits, I. Pearson: The early physicians of Germantown. *In: Germantown history, consisting of papers read before the Site and Relic Society of Germantown. Vol. I. Germantown, Pa. 1915. pp. 135—150.*   [5111

Zell, Hannah Ann: Recollections of the School House Lane meeting. *Read April 18th, 1902. In: Germantown history, consisting of papers read before the Site and Relic Society of Germantown. Vol. I. Germantown, Pa. 1915. pp. 13—15.*   [5112

Ziegenfuß, S. A.: A brief and succinct history of Saint Michael's Evangelical Lutheran Church of Germantown, Pa., 1730—1905. One hundred and seventy-fifth anniversary, Nov. 12—14, 1905. *Philadelphia, Pa.: General Council Publication House 1905. pp. 42, (2), ill.*   [5113

Articles of an agreement between the members of the Frankfort Company, 1686. *In: The Pennsylvania Magazine of History and Biography. Vol. XV. Philadelphia, Pa. 1891. pp. 205—211.*   [5114

Letters relating to the settlement of Germantown in Pennsylvania, 1683—84, from the Könneken Manuscript in the Ministerial Archiv of Lübeck. *Reproduced in fac-simile under the direction of J. F. Sachse. Lubeck and Philadelphia 1903. pp. XII, 35, ill.*

(Missive I.) **[Pastorius, F. D.]:** Copy of a letter sent from America by a son to his parents. *pp. 2—6.*

(Missive II.) **[Pastorius, F. D.]:** Positive news from America, about the Province of Pennsylvania, *from a German who has journeyed hither, de date, Philadelphia, March 7, 1684. pp. 7—29.*

(Missive VII.) **Op den Graeff, Hermans:** Copy of a letter from Germantown, — i. e. the German city in Pennsylvania, — *dated February 12, 1684. (Evidently written by . . .) pp. 31—34.*

(Missive VIII.) **Walle, van der:** A fragment of an open letter *by . . . from Philadelphia (mentioned in Pastorius missive p. 13). p. 35.* [5115
An interesting document on the early history of Germantown. *[Reply of the ministers and elders of the Mennonite Church in Altona, Germany to an appeal to send a delegate to Germantown, Pa., to ordain a bishop in the regular way. (Letter to Claes Beerends, op Pennsylvanien Ao 1702: Martio).] Edited by* **Harold S. Bender.** *In: The Mennonite Quarterly Review. Vol. V. Goshen, Ind.-Scottdale, Pa. 1931. pp. 284—285.* [5116
Old Germantown. *In: Lippincott's Magazine of Popular Literature and Science. Old series, vol. XXXIII. = New series, vol. VII. Philadelphia, Pa. 1884. pp. 113—128, ill.;* New Germantown and Chestnut Hill. *pp. 321—335.* [5117
German Lutheran congregation of Germantown. *In: Hazard's Register of Pennsylvania. Vol. V. Philadelphia, Pa. 1830. pp. 193—196.* [5118
Cost of a Mennonite church. [Mennonite meeting house in Germantown, 1770.] *From the church records. In: The Mennonite Year Book and Almanac for 1900. Quakertown, Pa. p. 14, ill.* [5119
A bit of Germantown school history, 1763. *In: The Pennsylvania Magazine of History and Biography. Vol. XXXIII. Philadelphia, Pa. 1909. pp. 374—375.* [5120
Accounts concerning the building of the Stone meeting house at Germantown, A. D. 1705. *In: The Pennsylvania Magazine of History and Biography. Vol. XXXIII. Philadelphia, Pa. 1909. pp. pp. 375—377.* [5121
Early Mennonite homestead in Germantown, *[home built by Rev. Jacob Gottschalk]. In: The Mennonite Year Book and Almanac for 1910. Quakertown, Pa. 1910. pp. 29—30, ill.* [5122
How the Franconia Conference supplied ministers for the Germantown Church in 1796. *In: The Mennonite Year Book and Almanac for 1911. Quakertown, Pa. 1911. 22—24.* [5123
Burials at Germantown Mennonite Church. *In: The Mennonite Year Book and Almanac for 1913. Quakertown, Pa. 1913. pp. 30—32.* [5124
Der Freibrief, Beschlüsse und Nebengesetze der Deutschen Vereinigten Unterstützungs-Gesellschaft, zu Germantown,

Incorporirt den 6ten December 1813. — The charter, resolutions and by-laws of the German United Assistance Society of Germantown. Incorporated, December 6, 1813. *Skippacksville, Montgomery Co.: Charles A. Pulte 1836. 29 S.; pp. 29.* [5125
Names of stockholders in the Germantown and Philadelphia Turnpike Company, about 1800. *In: The Pennsylvania Magazine of History and Biography. Vol. XXIII. Philadelphia, Pa. 1899. pp. 537—539.* [5126
Centennial anniversary of the foundation of Germantown Academy 1860. *Germantown, Pa.: Printed for the Academy, 1860. [C. Sherman & Son, Printers] pp. 59.* [5127
Germantown. Past and present. Oct. 5th to 10th, 1896. *Business men's parade souvenir. Compliments of the Germantown Independent Gazette. Germantown, Pa. 1896. pp. (72), ill.* [5128
A sketch of The Saving Fund Society of Germantown and vicinity. Founded 1854. *Published on the fiftieth anniversary of its founding. Germantown, Philadelphia, Pa. 1904.: Innes & Sons. pp. 39.* [5129
Germanopolis. 225th anniversary of the settlement of Germantown by Francis Daniel Pastorius. The first permanent German settlement in America. Official historical souvenir book of Germantown. 1883—1908. *Germantown, Pa.: Independent-Gazette. Publishing House of Horace F. McCann. pp. (90), ill.* [5130
Ein Denkmal zur Erinnerung an die ersten deutschen Einwanderer in Amerika und die Gründung von Germantown. *In: Deutsch-Amerikanische Geschichtsblätter. Jg. VIII. Chicago, Ill. 1908. S. 43—44.* [5131
Monument at Germantown. *Hearing before the committee on the Library of the house of Representatives on H. R. 9137. 61st Congress, second session. Washington, D. C.: Government Printing Office 1910. pp. 23.* [5132
Zur Feier der Übernahme des Pastorius Denkmals im Krefelder Heimatmuseum, 27. Mai 1931. *In: Die Heimat. Mitteilungen der Vereine für Heimatkunde in Krefeld-Ürdingen am Rhein. Jg. X, Heft 2. Krefeld, 15. Juli 1931. S. 73—88.* [5133
1683—1933. 250th Anniversary of the Settlement of Germantown. *Under the aus-*

pices of the Germantown Historical Society Germantown, Philadelphia Pa. Friday, October 20. Annual meeting of the Pennsylvania German Society. Saturday, October 21. Germantown's community celebration. Sunday, October 22. Religious observances. (The historical text by **Edward W. Hocker.)** *Germantown, Pa. Fleu & Fetterolf Inc. 1933. pp. 68, ill.*   [5134

Schuylkill County

Barr, J. W.: Biographical notes of Pine Grove, 1841—1916. *Pine Grove, Pa.: Anderson & Reber 1916. pp. 109.*
                                                    [5135
Chambers, George: Historical sketch of Pottsville, Schuylkill County, Pa. *Read at Union Hall, Pottsville, July 4th 1876. Pottsville, Pa.: Standard Publishing Co. 1876. pp. 19.*   [5136
Channell, G. W.: Port Carbon and her people. *Paper, Febr. 18, 1912. In: Publications of the Historical Society of Schuylkill County. Vol. IV. Pottsville, Pa. 1912. pp. 156—167.*   [5137
DeLong, Irwin Hoch: Some tombstone inscriptions from the cemetery in Friedensburg, Pa. *In: The National Genealogical Society Quarterly. Vol. XVI, no. 3. Washington, D. C. 1928. pp. 38—40.*
                                                    [5138
Derr, Chas. F.: The Derr foundry. *Paper, May 28, 1913. In: Publications of the Historical Society of Schuylkill County. Vol. IV. Pottsville, Pa. 1912. pp. 213—232.*   [5139
[Early, J. W. - Lubold, D. G.]: Wills of early settlers of Schuylkill County. *The wills were nearly all written in German, and are recorded at Reading. These abstracts were made by . . . In: Publications of the Historical Society of Schuylkill County. Vol. I. Pottsville, Pa. 1907. pp. 228—235.*   [5140
Eastmann, Elisabeth: Early days in Pottsville. *Paper, Dec. 27, 1911. In: Publications of the Historical Society of Schuylkill County. Vol. IV. Pottsville, Pa. 1912. pp. 185—192.*   [5141
Edwards, Richard: Industries of Pennsylvania, Reading, Pottsville, Ashland, Shenandoah, Minersville, Birdsboro, Schuylkill Haven, Mahanoy City. *Philadelphia, Pa.: Richard Edwards, Editor and publisher 1881. pp. (1), 33—64, ill.; pp. (2), 159—242.*   [5142

Elliot, Ella Zerbey: Old Schuylkill tales. A history of interesting events, traditions and anecdotes of the early settlers of Schuylkill County, Pa. *Pottsville, Pa.: Published by the author; Philadelphia, Pa.: George F. Lasher 1906. pp. 344, ill.*   [5143
— Blue book of Schuylkill County. *Who was who, and why in interior eastern Pennsylvania, in colonial days — The Huguenots and Palatines — Their service in Queen Ann's, French and Indian, and Revolutionary wars — History of the Zerbey, Schwalm, Miller, Merkle, Minnich, Staudt and many, other representative families. Pottsville, Pa.: „Republican", Joseph H. Zerbey. 1916. pp. VI, 7—456, ill., maps.*   [5144
Emhardt, Chas. E., Bushar, John F. and **Palmer Frank C.:** 1846—1899. History of the Good Intent Fire Co., No. 1. Pottsville, Pa. Organized Oct. 5, 1846. Incorporated Febr. 2, 1860. *(Advertising compiled by Eugene Peltier.) Pottsville, Pa.: Daily Republican Book Rooms 1899. pp. 96, ill.*   [5145
Gebert, George: Souvenir program and historical sketch of Zion's English Evangelical Lutheran Church, Tamaqua, Pa., on its 30th anniversary, June 24, 26, 27, 1906. *[s. l. 1906.] pp. 23, ill.*   [5146
Graeff, Charles: Reminiscences of Tamaqua's early days. *Reprinted from: Correspondence to the „Tamaqua Courier" of Dec. 31, 1903. In: Publications of the Historical Society of Schuylkill County. Vol. I. Pottsville, Pa. 1907. pp. 334—342.*   [5147
— Mrs. Susan Moyer tells of life in a bygone age. *Reprinted from: Correspondence in the Tamaqua Courier, March 28, 1904. In: Publications of the Historical Society of Schuylkill County. Vol. I. Pottsville, Pa. 1907. p. 435.*   [5148
Hanse, Louisa S.: The Orwigsburg Academy and the Arcadian Institute. *Paper, June 24, 1908. In: Publications of the Historical Society of Schuylkill County. Vol. II. Pottsville, Pa. 1910. pp. 345—354.*   [5149
Hay E. G.: History of the English Lutheran Church of Pottsville, Pa., from ist origin, May 16th, 1847, to September 1st, 1888. *Pottsville, Pa.: Robt. D. Colborn 1888. pp. (2), VIII, 9—167.*   [5150
Henning, D. C.: Old Home Week. Official program and historical sketches of Pottsville, Schuylkill County, Pa., Sept.

2—8, 1906. *Published by the Executive Committee, Pottsville, Pa.: Pottsville Daily Republican, Miner's Journal, Evening Chronicle 1906. pp. XVI, 51, ill. map. = Early annals of Pottsville by D. C. Henning. pp. (1) 5—50.* [5151

Henning, D. C.: The German peddler's grave. *[¹/₂ mile N. of Mahonoy City.] Paper, March 29, 1905. In: Publications of the Historical Society of Schuylkill County. Vol. I. Pottsville, Pa. 1907. pp. 183—192.* [5152

— The unique settlement house on the Indian frontier of the Blue Mountains. *Paper, Oct. 24, 1906. In: Publications of the Historical Society of Schuylkill County. Vol. I. Reading, Pa. 1907. pp. 413—423.* [5153

— Old Academy-scholars' names. *Paper, January 30, 1907. In: Publications of the Historical Society of Schuylkill County. Vol. II. Reading, Pa. 1910. pp. 1 —3.* [5154

— Early annals of Pottsville. *Published under the auspices of the Executive Committee of Pottsville's Old Home Week, Sept. 2—8, 1906. In: Publications of the Historical Society of Schuylkill County. Vol. II. Reading, Pa. 1910. pp. 104— 150, map.* [5155

— Sesqui-Centennial of the Red Church. *Address, Oct. 8, 1905. In: Publications of the Historical Society of Schuylkill County. Vol. II. Pottsville, Pa. 1910. pp. 445—459.* [5156

— Tales of the Blue Mountains. *Pottsville, Pa. 1911. pp. 237. With a biographical sketch of the author. pp. 3—5. = Publications of the Historical Society of Schuylkill County. Vol. III.* [5157

— The German settler and farmer of the days along the Blue Mountains. *In: Publications of the Historical Society of Schuylkill County. Vol. III. Pottsville, Pa. 1911. pp. 19—35.* [5158

— Tales of the Blue Mountains. *In: Publications of the Historical Society of Schuylkill County. Vol. IV. Pottsville, Pa. 1912. pp. 121—133.* [5159

Hoch, John: Reminiscences of Pinegrove, Pa. *Paper, Dec. 30, 1903. In: Publications of the Historical Society of Schuylkill County. Vol. I. Pottsville, Pa. 1907. pp. 61—65.* [5160

[Hubler, Guy G.]: History of St. Paul's Lutheran Church, Gordon, Pa., 35th anniversary 1876—1911. *Special anniversary services and home-coming week,*

Sept. 3rd to 8th, 1911. [s. l. 1911.] pp. 34, ill. [5161

Karsch, Carl Gustav: 1841—1916. 75th anniversary of Zion's Evangelical Lutheran Church, 4th and Lewis Streets, Minersville, Pa. and a brief survey of the history of the congregations. June 25, 26, 27, 28, 29, 1916. *Pottsville, Pa.: Chronicle Print 1916. pp. (25), ill.* [5162

Lubold, Daniel G.: Pioneer Lutheran ministers of Schuylkill County. *Paper, Nov. 30, 1905. In: Publications of the Historical Society of Schuylkill County. Vol. I. Pottsville, Pa. 1907. pp. 311—323.* [5163

— Jacob's Church; its history and records. *Paper, May 30, 1904. In: Publications of the Historical Society of Schuylkill County. Vol. I. Pottsville, Pa. 1907. pp. 247—276.* [5164

[— and Shenk, Fred.]: East Brunswick Township schools from 1766—1927, Schuyklill County, Pa. (History of the schools of East Brunswick Township. *By D. G. Lubold;* Consolidated school building of East Brunswick Township. *y F. Shenk.) Pottsville, Pa.: Book Rooms „Republican" — „Morning Paper" Pottsville, Pa. 1927. pp. 39, ill.* [5165

Lyon, T. H. B.: History of Mahanoy City and the building of Mahanoy tunnel. *Paper, May 31, 1905. In: Publications of the Historical Society of Schuylkill County. Vol. I. Pottsville, Pa. 1907. pp. 216—227.* [5166

McCool, Sarah A.: Schuylkill County. Historic gleamings. *A chronicle of the principal events in the history, and a record of the part taken by individuals and families, in the settlement and development of the county, from its first organization to the present time. Chapter I—XCII. In: Shenandoah Weekly Herald. Vol. V. Shenandoah, Pa. 1874, no. 6. Febr. 7, 1874 — Vol. VI, no. 48. Nov. 27, 1875.* [5167

Miesse, Charles: Points on coal and the coal business, *containing an explanation of how coal was formed, coal veins, how they were deposited. A description of the coal flora, vegetation, coal discovery, introduction, history, mining preparation and marketing, shipping, statistics, data, gases and fires in mines, biographical sketches and record of coal operators, etc., etc. History of the Anthracite coalregion and its surrounders, with miscellany.*

*Myerstown, Pa.: Feese & Uhrich 1887.
pp. XVII, 464.*   [5168
Miller, Jonathan W.: History of Frackville,
Schuylkill County, Pa. *Pottsville, Pa.:
Miners' Journal 1904. pp. V, 90, ill.*
                                    [5169
Newell, W. H.: Early days of Schuylkill
County. *Paper, June 3, 1904. In: Pub-
lications of the Historical Society of
Schuylkill County. Vol. I. Pottsville,
Pa. 1907. pp. 43—51.*   [5170
— An old town of Schuylkill County.
*[Schuylkill Haven.] Paper, Febr. 22,
1905. In: Publications of the Historical
Society of Schuylkill County. Vol. I.
Pottsville, Pa. 1907. pp. 288—295.* [5171
— Schuylkill County in the Mexican War.
*Paper, June 27, 1906. In: Publications
of the Historical Society of Schuylkill
County. Vol. I. Pottsville, Pa. 1907. pp.
324—333.*   [5172
— Leno, a legend of Pinedale. *Paper, Oct.
24, 1906. In: Publications of the Histo-
rical Society of Schuylkill County. Vol. I.
Pottsville, Pa. 1907. pp. 424—434.*
                                    [5173
— Legends and traditions of Schuylkill
County. *Paper, Jan. 31, 1912. In:
Publications of the Historical Society of
Schuylkill County. Vol. IV. Pottsville,
Pa. pp. 193—197.*   [5174
Paxson, Isaac: Reminiscences of Schuylkill
Haven in the Civil War. *Paper, Nov.
24th, 1909. In: Publications of the Hi-
storical Society of Schuylkill County.
Vol. II. Pottsville, Pa. 1910. pp. 418—
444.*   [5175
— Recollections of my early farm life in
Schuylkill County. *Paper, April 24,
1907. In: Publications of the Historical
Society of Schuylkill County. Vol. II.
Pottsville, Pa. 1910. pp. 17—34.* [5176
— Reminiscences of Schuylkill Haven.
*Paper, April 26, 1911. In: Publications
of the Historical Society of Schuylkill
County. Vol. IV. Pottsville, Pa. 1912.
pp. 71—92.*   [5177
Richards, Louis: The German peddler's
grave: a mountain tragedy of 1797.
*Read Dec. 14, 1909. In: Transactions of
the Historical Society of Berks County.
Vol. II. 1905—1909. Reading, Pa.
1910. pp. 402—411.*   [5178
Rupp, I. Daniel: History of Northampton,
Lehigh, Monroe, Carbon and Schuylkill
Counties: *containing a brief history of the
first settlers, topography of townships,
notices of leading events, incidents, and*

*interesting facts in the early history of
these counties: with an appendix. Lancaster, Pa.: Published and sold by G.
Hills; Harrisburg, Pa.: Hickok and Cantine 1845. pp. XIV, 568, ill.*   [5179
Russel, James Y.: Historical notes of the
early days of Pottsville, *written by Captain . . . in 1888. Edited by* **Wm. G.
Wells.** *In: Publications of the Historical
Society of Schuylkill County. Vol. II.
Pottsville, Pa. 1910. pp. 151—158.* [5180
Schalk, Adolph W. and **Henning, D. C.:** History of Schuylkill County, Pa. *Including a genealogical and biographical
record of many families and persons in
the county. Edited by . . . 2 vols. State
Historical Association . . . 1907. pp. (3),
17—330, ill.; 17—554, ill.*   [5181
Seltzer, Livingston: History of McKeans-
burg, Schuylkill County's oldest town.
*Paper, March 29, 1905. In: Publi-
cations of the Historical Society of Schuylkill County. Vol. I. Pottsville, Pa.
1907. pp. 177—182.*   [5182
Spayd, H. H.: The early settlement of
Minersville and history of its schools.
*Paper, April 27, 1904. In: Publications
of the Historical Society of Schuylkill
County. Vol. I. Pottsville, Pa. 1907.
pp. 67—78.*   [5183
Stapleton, A.: Murder of the Neiman family
in 1780. *In: Notes and Queries Edited
by W. H. Egle. Annual vol. 1897. Harrisburg, Pa. 1898. pp. 145—146.* [5184
Steinhagen, Henry John: 1842—1917. A
retrospect of St. John the Baptist's parish of Pottsville, Pa., as a souvenir of
the 75th anniversary of the foundation
of the church. *Nov. 10th, 1917. pp. 70,
ill.*   [5185
Stichter, George B.: Early school days in
Lower Schuylkill County. *Paper, February 26, 1903. In: Publications of the
Historical Society of Schuylkill County.
Vol. II. Pottsville, Pa. 1910. pp. 177—
185, ill.*   [5186
Wallace, Francis B.: Memorial of the patriotism of Schuylkill County, in the
American slaveholder's rebellion. *Compiled by . . . Pottsville, Pa.: Benjamin
Bannan 1865. pp. XII, 13—548, IX,
map.*   [5187
Weller, H. A.: Friedens Church at the Little
Schuylkill. A history of the congregation
and community. *Published by the congregation in commemoration of the Centenary of the dedication of the first church
edifice of the congregation. Pottsville,*

Pa.: *Daily Republican Book Rooms 1898. pp. VI, 86, ill.* [5188

Weller, H. A.: Zion, the „Old Red Church" in West Brunswick Township, Schuylkill County Pa. *In: The Pennsylvania-German. Vol. VII. Lebanon, Pa. 1906. pp. 22—26, ill.* [5189

— Introduction to the history of the Red Church *[— Zion's of West Brunswick Township.] A letter written by . . . and read, Dec. 30, 1903. In: Publications of the Historical Society of Schuylkill County. Vol. I. Pottsville, Pa. 1907. pp. 281 —287.* [5190

— A documentary history of the old Red (Zion) Church in West Brunswick Township, Schuylkill County, Pa. *Translated from the documentary records of said church and compiled for the Historical Society of Schuylkill County. In: Publications of the Historical Society of Schuylkill County. Vol. II. Pottsville, Pa. 1910. pp. 187—269, ill.* [5191

Wells, W. G.: The history of the public schools of Pottsville. *Paper, March 25, 1908. In: Publications of the Historical Society of Schuylkill County. Vol. II. Pottsville, Pa. 1910. pp. 278—294.* [5192

Wiley, Samuel T. and Ruoff, Henry W.: Biographical and portrait cyclopedia of Schuylkill County, Pa., *comprising a historical sketch of the county. By Samuel T. Wiley. Together with about five hundred and fitfy biographical sketches of the prominent men and leading citizens of the county. Carefully revised and edited by Henry W. Ruoff. Philadelphia, Pa.: Rush, West and Co. 1893. pp. (1), 7—752, ill.* [5193

History of Schuylkill County, Pa. *with illustrations and biographical sketches of some of its prominent men and pioneers. New York, N.Y.: W.W. Munsell & Co. 1881. pp. 5—390; R 1—R60, ill., map.* [5194

History of the County of Schuylkill. *In honor of the county's Centenary. July 2 to 8, 1911. Pottsville, Pa.: Dives, Pomeroy & Stewart [1911.] (1), 7—104, ill.* [5195

Schuylkill County, Pa. *Genealogy-family history-biography containing historical sketches of old families and representative and prominent citizens past and present. 2 vols. Chicago, Ill.: J. H. Beers & Co. 1916. pp. XVI, 608, ill.; pp. XIV, 609—1219, ill.* [5196

Our home week. Official programm and historical sketches of Pottsville. Schuylkill County, Pa. *Published by the Executive Committee. Pottsville, Pa.: Pottsville Daily Republican, Miners Journal, Evening Chronicle 1906. pp. XVI—51, ill., map.*
Including: **Henning, D. C.:** Early annals of Pottsville. *pp. 5—51.* [5197

Industrial review. Orwigsburg — Schuylkill Haven, etc. *Pottsville, Pa.: Daily Republican Book Rooms 1898. pp. (62), ill.* [5198

Centennial anniversary, Orwigsburg Pa. 1813—1913. *History of Orwigsburg and illustrations of residences and business houses. Published by the Civic Association. Pottsville, Pa.: Seiders 1913. pp. (24); 44 illustration plates). Advertisments.* [5199

Schuyklill Haven. 1750. Historical data 1925. The 175th anniversary September 3d to 6th, 1925. *Published by authority of the Civic Club of Schuylkill Haven, Pa. Schuylkill Haven, Pa.: Copyright 1925 by G. I. Bensinger 1925. pp. 200, ill.* [5200

First purchasers of lots in Orwigsburg Pa. *From a small pass-book found among the papers of Christopher Lesher, Esq. deceased. In: Publications of the Historical Society of Schuylkill County. Vol. I. Pottsville, Pa. 1907. pp. 53—60.* [5201

Account of sales at the public vendues of John Bonawitz's Pinegrove Township., Oct., 1828. *In: Publications of the Historical Society of Schuylkill County. Vol. II. Pottsville, Pa. 1910. pp. 168—176.* [5202

A letter of the American Revolution. *In: Publications of the Historical Society of Schuylkill County. Vol. I. Pottsville, Pa. 1907. pp. 462—466.* [5203

Muster Roll of Co. B. 1st Regt. Pa. Vols. War with Mexico. Dec. 5, 1846. *From a copy in possession of Col. Daniel Nagle, Pottsville, Pa. In: Publications of the Historical Society of Schuylkill County. Vol. I. Pottsville, Pa. 1907. pp. 484—487.* [5204

Snyder County

Aurand, A. M., Klose, W. J. and Keller, J. F.: History of Beaver Springs, Penn'a, and Centennial souvenir book. *Published in commemoration of the celebration of the one hundredth anniversary of*

the founding of the town. 1806—1906.
(A. M. A u r a n d, *editor;* W. J. Klose
and J. F. Keller, *historians) Beaver
Springs, Pa.: Aurand Printing and
Publishing House 1906. pp. (136), ill.*
                                    [5205
Boyer, D. S. and Wampole, J. F.: History
of the Freeburg Lutheran charge, em-
bracing St. Peter's at Freeburg, Salem
or Row's at Salem, St. John's or
Schnee's at Fremont, Bottschaft's or
Grubb's, St. Peter's or Sieber's at
Globe Mills, St. Paul's, or Artley's.
From 1775 to 1891. *Prepared by . . .
Freeburg, Pa.: E. S. Mills, Commercial
Printing House, Millerstown, Pa. 1891.*
, *pp. 87, ill.*   [5206
Bressler, John F.: Mennonite churches of
Snyder and Juniata Counties, Pa. *In:
Christian Monitor. A monthly magazine
for the home. Vol. XXIII, no. 7. Scott-
dale, Pa. 1931. pp. 208—209, ill.*
                                    [5207
Genszler, G. W.: A short history of Selins-
grove. *In: The Pennsylvania-German.
Vol. VIII. Lebanon, Pa. 1907. pp. 204
—209; 252—258, ill.*   [5208
Grift, A. K.: The Hassinger Church, *[Sny-
der Co.], Pa. In: The Pennsylvania-
German. Vol. IX. Cleona, Pa. 1908.
pp. 415—420, ill.*   [5209
Schnure, William Marion: Selinsgrove,
Pennsylvania chronology. *Vol. I:* 1700
—1850. *Middleburg, Pa.: Middleburg
Post 1918. pp. 150, ill.; Vol. II:* 1851—
1920. *Selinsgrove, Pa.: Reprinted from
,,The Selinsgrove Times". 1929. pp. 215,
ill.*   [5210
Shuman, J. C.: History of St. Henry's
Church, *[near Troxelville, Snyder Co.,
Pa.] In: The Pennsylvania-German.
Vol. XI. Lititz, Pa. 1910. pp. 343—345.*
                                    [5211
Stapleton, A.: Early Snyder County families. *In: Notes and Queries. Edited
by W. H. Egle. Annual vol. 1899. Harris-
burg, Pa. 1900. pp. 165—167.*   [5212
Wagenseller, Geo. W.: Snyder County mar-
riages 1835—1899. Miscellaneous marriages 1868—98. Rev. Caspar's marriage
record, 1839—82. Rev. Shindel's marriage record, 1835—88. Rev. C. G. Er-
leumger's marriage record 1840—75.
*With an index of surnames. Compiled by
. . . Middleburgh, Pa.: Wagenseller Publishing Co. 1899. pp. 266.*   [5213
— Tombstone inscriptions of Snyder
County. *All the epitaphs taken from the*

*markers in every burying ground of Sny-
der County. A complete record from the
time of the settlement of this territory by
the pioneers before the Revolutionary War
down to the year 1904. Compiled by . . .
Middleburgh, Pa.: Wagenseller Publishing Co. 1904. pp. 279.*   [5214
Wagenseller, Geo. W.: Snyder County annals. *Vol. I. A collection of all kinds
of historical items affecting Snyder
County from the settlement of the first
pioneers in this section, to the names
of the soldiers in the World War, 1917
—1919. [Compiled by* G. W. W a g e n-
seller; *assisted by* Clara R. Winey.]
*Middleburgh, Pa.: The Middleburgh
Post 1919. pp. (2), 364, ill.*   [5215
**Wagenseller, John F. and Drumheller, Leon
S.:** History and souvenir of St. Paul's
Reformed Church, Selinsgrove, Pa. Re-
dedication number. 1856—1915. *February 7, 1915. Edited by . . . [Selins-
grove 1915.] pp. 48. (including advertisements), ill.*   [5216
Yutzy, Jacob: The golden jubilee memorial
anniversary of the Evangelical Lutheran
Church, Selin's Grove, Pa. *Published
by J. A. Lumbard. [s. l.; s. d.] pp. 117,
ill.*   [5217
Commemorative biographical record of
Central Pennsylvania, including the
Counties of Centre, Clinton, Union and
Snyder, *containing biographical sketches of prominent and representative citizens and of many of the early settled fa-
milies. Chicago, Ill.: J. H. Beers, Pub-
lishers. 1898. pp. (1), 1676, ill.* [5218
The Snyder County Historical Society Bul-
letin. Proceedings and addresses. *Vol.
I., no. 1—10. Middleburgh, Pa.: Reprin-
ted from The Middleburgh Post 1913—
1921. pp. 228, ill.*   [5219
Souvenir book of Selinsgrove, Pa. *By the
Book Committee 160th anniversary of the
Penn's Creek Massacre. Selinsgrove, Pa.,
Oct. 14—15—16, 1915. pp. 104, ill.* [5220

Union County

Beaver, P. H.: German supplanters. *In: The
Pennsylvania-German. Vol. IX. Cleona,
Pa. 1908. pp. 461—463.*
[Buffalo Valley, Union County.]
                                    [5221
Chamberlain, E. A.: A history of St. Peter's
Lutheran-Presbyterian Church, New
Columbia. *(Address delivered at New Co-*

lumbia in St. Peter's Church at the Harvest Home Service, Sept. 26, 1914.) [s. l. 1914.] pp. 16., ill.   [5222

Gramley, A. D.: Memorial booklet commemorating the unveiling of the marker on the site of the first Evangelical Church. Program of exercises held August second, 1927, at three P. M., under the auspices of the Historical Society of the Evangelical Church by which the marker was erected. Editor: ... [Cleveland, O.]: Published by order of the Historical Society of the Evangelical Church 1927. pp. 46, ill.   [5223

Linn, John Blair: Annals of Buffalo Valley, Pennsylvania. 1755—1855. [Collated by . . .] Harrisburg, Pa.: Lane & Hart 1877. pp. 621, ill., map.   [5224

Owens, J. G.: Folk-lore from Buffalo Valley, Central-Pennsylvania. In: The Journal of American Folk-Lore. Vol. IV (No. XIII). Boston-New York 1891. pp. 115—128.   [5225

Rupp, I. Daniel: History and topography of Northumberland, Huntingdon, Mifflin, Centre, Union, Collmbia, Juniata, and Clinton Counties, Pa., embracing local and general events, leading incidents, descriptions of the principal boroughs, towns, villages, etc. etc. with a copious appendix: embellished by engravings. Compiled from authentic sources by . . . Lancaster, Pa.: G. Hills 1847. pp. 574, ill.   [5226

Stapleton, A.: Burials at New Berlin, Pa. In: Notes and Queries. Edited by W. H. Egle. Annual vol. 1898. Harrisburg, Pa. 1899. pp. 66—68.
[Union County, Penns Creek Valley.]   [5227

Umble, John: The Amish Mennonites of Union County, Pa. In: The Mennonite Quarterly Review. Vol. VII. Goshen, Ind. — Scottdale, Pa. 1933. pp. 71—96; 162—190.   [5228

Commemorative biographical record of Central Pennsylvania, including the Counties of Centre, Clinton, Union, and Snyder, containing biographical sketches of prominent and representative citizens and of many of the early settled families. Chicago, Ill..: J. B. Beers, Publishers 1898. pp. (1), 1676, ill.   [5229

The early dead at Mifflinburg. In: Notes and Queries. Edited by W. H. Egle. Annual vol. 1899. Harrisburg, Pa. 1900. pp. 88—91.   [5230

Wyoming County

[Chapman, . . .]: Count Zinzendorf. Reprint from „Chapman's Wyoming" in: Hazard's Register of Pa. Vol. VI. Philadelphia, Pa. 1830. p. 123.   [5231

Johnson, Frederick C.: Count Zinzendorf and the Moravian and Indian occupancy of the Wyoming Valley 1742—1763. In: Proceedings and Collections of the Wyoming Historical and Genealogical Society for the years 1902—1903. Vol. VIII. Wilkes-Barre, Pa. 1904. pp. 119—180, ill.   [5232

Reichel, W. C.: Wyalusing, and the Moravian mission at Friedenshuetten. In: Transactions of the Moravian Historical Society. Vol. I. 1858—1876. Nazareth, Pa. 1876. pp. 179—224.   [5233

Tombstone records. St. John's cemetery, Butler Township. [Wyoming Co.] In: Proceedings and Collections of the Wyoming Historical and Genealogical Society. For the years 1923—1924. Vol. XIX. Wilkes-Barre, Pa. 1926. pp. 236—252.   [5234

York County

Albright, S. C.: The story of the Moravian congregation at York, Pa. York, Pa.: The Maple Press Co. 1927. pp. XIX, 224, ill.   [5235

Betz, I. H.: A pioneer church of the United Brethren in Christ in the upper end of York County. A history of Salem or „Stone Church" from its beginning 1844 to 1908. Read at the dedication. [s. l., s. d.] pp. 3—16.   [5236

— Historical pilgrimages into Pennsylvania Germandom. A town and county of the olden time. Historic York, Pa. In: The Pennsylvania-German. Vol. IV. Lebanon, Pa. 1903. pp. 215—228; 265—286.
[See no. 295]   [5237

Bowersox, George Edward: History of Christ Evangelical Lutheran congregation of Shrewsbury, York County, Pa. Prepared for the occasion of its Centenary celebration, November 19 to 26, 1922. [s. l. 1922.] pp. 56.   [5238

Carter, W. C. and Glossbrenner, A. J.: History of York County, from its erection to the present time. York, Pa.: A. J. Glossbrenner 1834. pp. 183; 30, ill. [5239

[— - —] History of York County from its erection to the present time [1729—1834]. New edition; with additions edi-

27*

ted by A. Monroe Aurand, Jr. Harrisburg, Pa.: Privately printed: The Aurand Press 1930. pp. XVI, 221.   [5240

Edwards, Richard: Industries of Pennsylvania. York County. York, Hannover, Glen Rock, Wrightsville &c. Philadelphia, Pa.: Richard Edwards; Editor and publisher 1881. pp. (3), (2), 99—156.   [5241

Egle, William Henry: Provincial papers: Returns and taxables of the County of York for the years 1779, 1780, 1781, 1782 and 1783. Edited by . . . Harrisburg, Pa.: Wm. Stanley Ray 1898. pp. VIII, 820.
= Pennsylvania Archives. Third series, vol. XXI.   [5242

Ehehalt, C. M.: The Borough of Red Lion, York County, Pa. Pictorial souvenir. Golden jubilee, 1880—1930. June seventh to fourteenth inclusive. Fifty years of progress. Edited by . . . York, Pa.: The York Printing Co. 1930. pp. 204, ill.   [5243

[Ehehalt, „Rudi" C. M.]: Official souvenir year book 1927. Dedicated to no less noble and honorable a class of people than the thousands of cigar merchants and friends of tobacco of the U.S.A. for their information and guidance in the great battle of cigars. By The York County Cigar Manufactures Association. Headquarters: Red Lion, Pa. York, Pa.: Trimmer Printing Co. 1927. pp. 120.
[Contents see no. 2670]   [5244

Eslinger, A. N.: Local history of Dillsbury, Pa. With notes and comments, from the earliest known settlement to the present. 1902. Dillsbury, Pa.: Dillsbury Bulletin Print 1902. pp. 34, ill.   [5245

Evans, . .: Troubles of early settlers in York County. In: Notes and Queries. Edited by W. H. Egle. Third series, vol. I. 1884—1887. Harrisburg, Pa. 1887. pp. 416—418; 422—424; Reprint in: Third series, vol. II. Harrisburg, Pa. 1896: pp. 145—148; 155—158.   [5246

Foin, J. C.: Historical sketch of St. Joseph's [Catholic] Church, Hannover, Pa. 1877—1902. In remembrance of the 25th anniversary of the church. Sept. 16th, 1902. Hanover, Pa.: Press of the Anthony-Hostetter Co. 1902. pp. 32, ill.   [5247

Garrett, Walter E.: History of the Kreutz Creek charge of the Reformed Church. Published by the joint consistory of the Kreutz Creek charge. Philadelphia, Pa.:

Publication and Sunday School Board of the Reformed Church. 1924. pp. IX, (1), 250, ill.   [5248

[Gibson, John]: The historical sketch and account of the Centennial celebration at York, Pa., July 4, 1876. Containing an accurate account of the proceedings from the time of the passage of the resolution by the Town Council to celebrate the Nation's birth and the appointment of a committee to carry out the spirit of the resolution, up to close of the celebration . . . the elaborate and venerable historical sketch, prepared by John Gibson. pp. 17—134. York, Pa.: Democratic Press Print. 1876. pp. 155, ill.   [5249

— History of York County, Pa., from the earliest period to the present time, divided into general, special, township and borough histories, with a biographical department appended. Chicago, Ill.: F. A. Battey Publishing Co. 1886. pp. IX, 772, 207, ill., maps.   [5250

Gobrecht, N. A. - Gobrecht, John C.: Old Pennsylvania-German graveyard records. Old Reformed graveyard, Hanover, Pa. In: The Pennsylvania-German. Vol. V. Lebanon, Pa. 1904. pp. 184—188.   [5251

Gotwald, L. A.: Our history and our success. A sermon delivered in St. Paul's Evangelical Lutheran Church of York, Pa., Oct. 29th, 1876. Published by the congregation. York, Pa.: Miram Young 1876. pp. 27.   [5252

Hall, Clifford J. and Lehn, John P.: York County and the World War, being a war history of York and York County and a record of the services rendered to their country by the people of this community. Compiled, edited and published by . . . York, Pa. 1920. pp. 424, ill.   [5253

Hawkins, Charles A. and Landis, Houston E.: Some facts concerning York and York County, 1749—1899. A Sesqui-Centennial memento. By A. Ch. Hawkins and H. E. Landis. Prepared by direction of M. B. Gibson, H. E. Niles and Geo. S. Billmeyer, committee. York, Pa.: Press of York Daily. 1901. pp. 144, ill.   [5254

Hay, Ellis S.: One hundred and forty-four years. A sketch of Emmanuel Reformed Church, Hanover, Pa. 1765—1909. Hanover, Pa.: Anthony Printing Co. pp. 73, ill.   [5255

Herring, S. Edward: Centennial historical sketch of the Lutheran Church in America, together with a history, and the names of the present members and patrons of the Lutheran Church in Wrightsville, Pa. *Delivered July 9th, 1876. Wrightsville, Pa.: Wrightsville Star 1876. pp. 17.* [5256

Jordan, John C.: York in its relation to the Revolution. Lecture delivered before the York County Historical Society, May 21, 1903. *In: Proceedings and Collections of the Historical Society of York County. Vol. I, no. 3. York, Pa. 1903. pp. 27—50.* [5257

— York, Penna, in the Revolution. *In: The Pennsylvania Magazine of History and Biography. Vol. XXXII. Philadelphia, Pa. 1908. pp. 487—497.* [5258

Jordan, John W.: Contributions to Pennsylvania-German genealogy. *[York County.] In: Notes and Queries. Edited by W. H. Egle. Fourth series, vol. I. 1891—1893. Harrisburg, Pa. 1893. pp. 238—240.* [5259

— Records of the Moravian Church at York. *In: Notes and Queries. Edited by W. H. Egle. Fourth series, vol. II. 1894. Harrisburg, Pa. 1895. pp. 245—247; 250—251.* [5260

— Register of interments in the Moravian cemetery, York, Penna, 1752—1792. *In: Notes and Queries. Edited by W. H. Egle. Fourth series, vol. II. 1894. Harrisburg, Pa. 1895. pp. 254—255.* [5261

— Fragments of history and biography relating to the Moravians in York County. 1744—1782. *Compiled by . . . pp. 35.* [5262

[Koller, J. C.]: 1743—1893. Memorial volume of the Sesqui-Centennial services in St. Matthew's Lutheran Church, Hanover, Pa., Nov. 19th to 26th, 1893. *Published by the Committee. York, Pa.: York Daily Print 1893. pp. 122, ill.* [5263

Murphy, R. E.: The economic geography of York, Pennsylvanien. *State College, Pa. 1935. = Pennsylvania State College, Mineral Industries Exper. Station Bull. 17.* [5263 a

— Johnstown and York: a comparative study of two industrial cities. *In: Annals of the Association of American Geographers. Vol. XXV. Lancaster, Pa. 1935. pp. 175—196.* [5263 b

[Neisser, George]: Incidents in the history of York, Pa. 1778. *(Extracted from the diary of Rev. George Neisser, Moravian*

minister.) *In: The Pennsylvania Magazine of History and Biography. Vol. XVI. Philadelphia, Pa. 1892. pp. 433—438.* [5264

[Neisser, George]: Items of history of York, Pa., during the Revolution. *(Selected from the diaries of the Moravian congregation at York, Rev. George Neisser, pastor.) In: The Pennsylvania Magazine of History and Biography. Vol. XLIV. Philadelphia, Pa. 1920. pp. 309—324.* [5265

P.[arthemore, E. W. S.]: Contributions in York County genealogy. *In: Notes and Queries. Edited by W. H. Egle. Fourth series, vol. I. 1891—1893. Harrisburg, Pa. 1893. pp. 164—165.* [5266

Prowell, George R.: The City of York, past and present. *York, Pa.: Gazette Print 1904. pp. 48, ill.* [5267

— A brief history of York County. *Published by request for the use of teachers and others, desiring to obtain the leading facts relating to local history. York, Pa. 1906. pp. 67, ill.* [5268

— History of York County, Pa. 2 vols. *Chicago, Ill.: J. H. Beers & Co. 1907. pp. VI, (1), 1118, ill., map; pp. 1058, ill.* [5269

Reily, John T.: Conewago. A collection of Catholic local history. *Gathered from the fields of Catholic missionary labor within our reach. Martinsburg, W. Va.: Herold Print. 1885. pp. IV, 220, (3), ill.* [5270

Schmucker, Beale M.: The Lutheran Church in York, Pa. *In: The Quarterly Review of the Evangelical Lutheran Church. New series, vol. XVIII. Gettysburg, Pa. 1888. pp. 473—529.* [5271

Spangler, F. L.: The inundation of York, Penn'a. A graphic description of the great flood with an account of the violent rain storm of June 25, 1884. *York, Pa.: York Daily Printing House. 1884. pp. 103, ill.* [5272

Stapleton, A.: Some York County colonial burial places. *In: Notes and Queries. Edited by W. H. Egle. Annual vol. 1899. Harrisburg, Pa. 1900. pp. 138—140.* [5273

— Burial records from Mennonite graveyard, Hanover, Pa. *In: Notes and Queries. Edited by W. H. Egle. Annual vol. 1899. Harrisburg, Pa. 1900. pp. 204—205.* [5274

Stoner, Bertha: Traditions of Kreutz Creek Valley. *Essay read at the commencement of the York Collegiate Institute, June 11, 1910. In: The Pennsylvania-German.*

Vol. XI. Lititz, Pa. 1910. pp. 424—426.
[5275
Stump, Adam and **Anstadt, Henry:** History of the Evangelical Lutheran Synod of West Pennsylvania of the United Lutheran Church in America. 1825—1925. *Edited by* ... *Published by action of the Synod in the celebration of the Centennial. Chambersburg, Pa.: J. R. Kerr & Bro. 1925. pp. 696, ill.*
[York County Conference. pp. 441— 688.]   [5276
Trump, Sarah: 1760—1910. One hundred and fiftieth anniversary of Immanuel Lutheran Church, Manchester, Md. *A historical sketch prepared for the Women's Home and Foreign Missionary Society. [s. l. 1910.] pp. 23.*   [5277
W., M. A.: History of St. Mary's [Catholic] parish. York, Pennsylvania 1852—1927. *On the occasion of the Diamond jubilee by M. A. W. York, Pa.: The York Printing Co. 1927. pp. 39, ill.*
[5278
Wentz, Abdel Ross: The beginnings of the German element in York County, Pa. *Lancaster, Pa.: The New Era Printing Co. 1916. = Part XXVI. ,,A narrative and critical history," prepared by authority of the Pennsylvania-German Society. In: The Pennsylvania-German Society. Proceedings and Addresses ... 1913. Vol. XXIV. Lancaster, Pa. 1916. Separate pagination pp. 7—217, ill.*   [5279
Germans proceed west of the Susquehanna; — discover their error and are willing to return. *,,The President [James Logan] acquainted the Board . . . that the Dutch people or Germans, who with others going over from this side of Susquehanna River to the West of it, had been prevailed on by some agents from Maryland to acknowledge the authority of that Province: . . . at a Council at Philadelphia, Aug. 24, 1736 . . . see: Colonial Records of Pennsylvania. Vol. IV. 1851. pp. 56—58; p. 64ff.; p. 71.*   [5280
York, Pa., family names in 1800. *[List of family names compiled from an original copy of the York borough county tax duplicate for the year 1807—08.] Reprint from the ,,York Gazette," May 27, 1911. In: The Pennsylvania-German. Vol. XII. Lititz, Pa. 1911. pp. 443—444.*
[5281
York's Centenary memorial comprising detailed description of the Centennial celebration, in the City of York, Sep-

tember 23d and 24th, 1887. *York, Pa.: Hiram Young 1887. pp. 226, ill.*
[5282
Souvenir sketch book of York City and vicinity. *Prepared expressly for the benefit of Christian delegates to the convention of '94. York, Pa.: York Daily Printing House 1894. pp. VII, 88, ill.*
[5283
Picturesque and industrial York, Penna. Knights Templar edition. *Issued in commemoration of the fifty-first annual conclave of the Grand Commandery, Knights Templar of the State of Pennsylvania, May, 1904.* [**Charles M. Mc Elhinay, Bruce Irvin Susong, Alfred Collins,** *publishers.] [s. l. 1904.] (71) f.*   [5284
Memorial souvenir, commemorating the 150th anniversary of York as the capital of the United States of America. *York, Pa. Oct. 13—15, 1927. York, Pa. [1927.] pp. 64, ill.*   [5285
York, Pennsylvania. Its progress and development. *Prepared by York Trust Company, 21 East Market Street. York, Pa. 1930. pp. 31, ill.*   [5286
Wrightsville's book of facts. *A souvenir inspired by the sixtieth anniversary of an event of the Civil War, which occurred at Wrightsville, York County, Pa., known as ,,Farthest East reached by the Confederate Army". June the 28th, 1863— 1923. Including a classified professional and business directory. Prepared by the Historical Committee. York, Pa.: H. O. Birnstock, Trimmer Printing Co. 1923. pp. 96.*   [5287
Tobacco. *Weekly trade review. Established 1886. Published by the Tobacco Trade Journal Company. [Pennsylvania number.] Issued annually in May. East Stroudsburg, Pa.*
Schettel, James W.: York and Adams Counties prove right to title ,,Home of 5c Cigar". *In: Vol. LXXXIV, no. 5. 1927. pp. 20—24, 49—50, ill.*
— York County cigar production sets a fast pace for the entire country. *In: Vol. XXXVI, no. 6. 1928. pp. 19—21; 32—34.*
— York County maintains its famed position in the cigar industry. *In: Vol. XC, no. 6. 1930. pp. 15—21, ill.*
Red Lion, the cigar city, celebrating golden jubilee of progress. *In: Vol. XC, no. 6. 1930. p. 22, pp. 31—35, ill.*
Laughton, Herbert J.: How cigar industry has made history in the Borough of

Dallastown. *In: Vol. XC, no. 6. 1930. p. 37, pp. 39—40, ill.*
Cigar industry foundation of the Borough of East Prospect, Pa. *In: Vol. XCII, no. 6. 1931. pp. 33—35, 38—40, ill.* [5288
Memorial of the fiftieth year 1836—1886. Published by St. Paul's English Evangelical Lutheran Church, York, Pa., June 1886. *Philadelphia, Pa.: Lutheran Publication House Print. 1886. pp. 95, ill.* [5289
1743—1893. Memorial volume of the Sesqui-Centennial Services of St. Matthew's Evangelical Lutheran Church, Hanover, Penn'a, Nov. 19th, to 26th, 1893. *Published by the Committee, York, Pa.: York Daily Print. pp. 122, ill. Including* Koller, J. C.: Historical discourse. pp. 7—46. [5290
Church register of the United Reformed and Lutheran Church, called Blimyers, in Hopewell Township, York County, Pa.

Commenced March 19, 1767, by Rev. Geo Bager, *(Lutheran) and* William Otterbein *(Reformed). Transcribed and translated. In: The Pennsylvania-German Society. Proceedings and Addresses . . . 1897. Vol. VIII. Lancaster, Pa. 1898. pp. 155—196.* [5291
Records of the Moravian Church, York, Pennsylvania: Soul-register of the members of the congregation and society and their children in Yorktown in the year 1780. *In: Publications of the Genealogical Society of Pennsylvania. Vol. IV, no. 3. Philadelphia, Pa. 1911. pp. 324—369.* [5292
Tenth anniversary of the dedication of the chapel. St. Matthew's Lutheran Church, York, Pa., April 15th —22d, 1917. *York, Pa.: The York Printing Co. 1917. pp. 16, ill.* [5293
Fragments of history and biography to the Moravians in York County 1744—1782. *[s. l., s. d.] pp. 35.* [5294

West- und Nordwest-Pennsylvanien
Western and Northwestern Pennsylvania

Allgemeines
General

Blough, Jerome E.: History of the Church of the Brethren of the Western District of Pennsylvania. *Elgin, Ill.: Brethren Publishing House 1916. pp. 600, ill.* [5295
Burgess, Ellis Beaver: History of the Pittsburgh Synod of the General Synod of the Evangelical Lutheran Church 1748—1845—1904. *Together with a brief sketch of each congregation of the Synod. Published by the authority of the Synod. Philadelphia, Pa.: Lutheran Publication Society. 1904. pp. 488, ill.* [5296
— Memorial history of the Pittsburgh Synod of the Evangelical Lutheran Church 1748—1845—1924. *Together with a sketch of each of the 317 congregations found in the fellowship of the Synod in the year of the merger. Greenville, Pa.: Published for the Synod by the Beaver Co. 1925. pp. 814, ill.* [5297
Chapman, Thomas J.: The Valley of Conemaugh. *Altoona, Pa.: McCrum & Dern 1865. pp. 202.*

[Description of Cambria County and parts of Somerset, Indiana, and Westmoreland Counties.] [5298
Egle, William Henry: Provincial papers. Returns of taxables for the Counties of Bedford (1773—1784), Huntingdon (1788), Westmoreland (1783, 1786), Fayette (1785, 1786), Allegheny (1791), Washington (1786) and Census of Bedford (1784) and Westmoreland (1783). *Edited by . . . Harrisburg, Pa. 1898. pp. XI, 782. = Pennsylvania Archives. Third series, vol. XXII.* [5299
Fullerton, James N.: Squatters and titles to land in early western Pennsylvania, or an introduction to early western Pennsylvania land titles. *In: Western Pennsylvania Historical Magazine. Vol. VI. Pittsburgh, Pa. 1923. pp.165—176.* [5300
Lady, David B.: The history of the Pittsburgh Synod of the Reformed Church in the United States, *prepared in commemoration of its fiftieth anniversary. Assisted by (others) . . . Greensburg, Pa.: Chas. M. Henry Printing Co. 1920. pp. (10), 569, ill.* [5301

Oberly, Frank C.: Lutheran pioneer missionaries of western Pennsylvania. *A sketch of their field and their work. In: The Lutheran Church Review. Vol. XXVII. Philadelphia, Pa. 1908. pp. 259—270; 456—468.* [5302]

[Rupp, I. Daniel]: Early history of western Pennsylvania, and of the west, and of western expeditions and campaigns, from MDCCLIV to MDCCCXXXIII. *By a gentleman of the Bar. With an appendix containing, besides copious extracts from important Indian treaties, minutes of conferences, journals, etc., a topographical description of the Counties of Allegheny, Westmoreland, Washington, Somerset, Greene, Fayette, Beaver, Butler, Armstrong, etc. Pittsburg, Pa.: Daniel W. Kauffman—Harrisburg, Pa.: William O. Hickok 1846. pp. VI, VI, 17—352. Appendix. pp. 752, map.* [5303]

Scheffer, J. A.: Some Pennsylvania-German settlers in the western part of the state. *In: The Pennsylvania-German. Vol. X. Lititz, Pa. 1909. pp. 169—170.* [5304]

Ulery, William F.: History of the Southern Conference of the Pittsburgh Synod of the Evangelical Lutheran Church. *By . . . Edited and published by* **W. F. Ulery** *and* **A. L. Youndt,** *Committee of Conference. Greensbury, Pa.: Church Register Co. 1902. pp. XV, (1), 416, map; Second enlarged edition 1903. pp. XV, 431, ill., map.* [5305]

Allegheny County

Burgess, Ellis Beaver: History of the Pittsburgh Synod of the Evangelical Lutheran Church 1748—1845—1904. *Together with a brief sketch of each congregation of the synod. Edited by the same author. Philadelphia, Pa.: Printed for the Synod by the Lutheran Publication Society. 1904. pp. 488, ill.* [*"The churches of Allegheny County." = Chapter VIII. pp. 176—249, ill.]* [5306]
— Memorial history of the Pittsburgh Synod of the Evangelical Lutheran Church 1748—1845—1924. *Together with a sketch of each of the 317 congregations found in the fellowship of the Synod in the year of the merger. Greenville, Pa.: Published for the Synod by the Beaver Printing Co. 1925. pp. 814, ill.* [*"Churches of the Allegheny County." = Chapter IX. pp. 223—331, ill.]* [5307]

Donehoo, George P.: Christian Frederick Post's part in the capture of Fort Duquesne and in the conquest of the Ohio. *In: The Penn Germania. Vol. II. = Old series, vol. XIV. Lititz, Pa. 1913. pp. 1—6.* [5308]

Egle, William Henry: Provincial papers: Returns of taxables for the Counties of Bedford (1773—1784), Huntingdon (1788), Westmoreland (1783, 1786), Fayette (1785, 1786), Allegheny (1791), Washington (1786) and Census of Bedford (1784) and Westmoreland (1783). *Edited by . . . Harrisburg, Pa. 1898. pp. XI, 782.*
= Pennsylvania Archives. Third series, vol. XXII. [5309]

Jordan, John W.: Genealogical and personal history of the Allegheny Valley, Pa. *Under the editorial supervision of . . . 3 vols. New York, N. Y.: Lewis Historical Publishing Co. 1913. pp. VIII, 416; 417—752; 753—1162, ill.* [5310]

Lady, David B. (and **Wiant, H. H.**): The history of the Pittsburgh Synod of the Reformed Church in the United States. *Prepared in commemoration of its fiftieth anniversary by . . . Greensburg, Pa.: Chas. M. Henry Printing Co. 1920. pp. (10), 569, ill.*
[*"Allegheny Classis." By H. H. Wiant. = Chapter XXVII. pp. 498—546, ill.]* [5311]

History of Allegheny County, Pa. *including its early settlement and progress to the present time; a description of its historic and interesting localities; its cities, towns and villages; religious, educational, social and military history; mining manufacturing and commercial interests; improvements, resources, statistics etc., also portraits of some of its prominent men, and biographies of many of its representative citizens. In 2 parts. Chicago, Ill.: A. Warner & Co. 1889. pp. VIII, 9—758; 5—790, ill., map.* [5312]

Memoirs of Allegheny County, Pa. *Personal and genealogical with portraits. 2 vols. Madison, Wisc.: Northwestern Historical Association 1904. pp. 560, ill.; 530 ill.* [5313]

Armstrong County

Burgess, Ellis Beaver: History of the Pittsburgh Synod of the Evangelical Lutheran Church 1748—1845—1904. *Together with a brief sketch of each congregation of the Synod. Edited by the same* author. *Philadelphia, Pa.: Printed for the Synod by the Lutheran Publication Society. 1904. pp. 488, ill.* [*„The churches of Armstrong County."* = *Chapter X. pp. 294—363, ill.]* [5314

— Memorial history of the Pittsburgh Synod of the Evangelical Lutheran Church 1748—1845—1924. *Together with a sketch of each of the 317 congregations found in the fellowship of the Synod in the year of the merger. Greenville, Pa.: Published for the Synod by the Beaver Printing Co. 1925. pp. 814, ill.* [*„Churches of Armstrong County."* = *Chapter X. pp. 331—399, ill.]* [5315

Earhart, D.: History of the Evangelical Lutheran Church at Leechburg, Pa. *In: The Lutheran Church Review. Vol. XIX. Philadelphia, Pa. 1900. pp. 422—433.* [5316

Hammond, Olive L.: Social life and customs in early Armstrong County, Pa. *Thesis of M. A., University of Pittsburgh. Pittsburgh, Pa. 1930. Typewritten pp. (4), 80.* [5317

[Wiley, Samuel T.]: Biographical and historical cyclopedia of Indiana and Armstrong Counties, Pa. *Philadelphia, Pa.: John M. Gresham & Co. 1891. pp. 636, ill.* [5318

Armstrong County, Pa. Her people, past and present, *embracing a history of the county and a genealogical and biographical record of representative families. 2 vols. Chicago, Ill.: J. H. Beers & Co. 1914. pp. XXIV, 496; X, 497—995, ill.* [5319

Beaver County

Bausman, Joseph H.: History of Beaver County, Pa. and its Centennial celebration. *2 vols. New York, N. Y.: The Knickerbocker Press 1904. pp. XXXIII, 612; 613—1315, ill. maps.* [5320

Jordan, John W.: Genealogical and personal history of Beaver County, Pa. *Under the editorial supervision of . . . 2 vols. New York, N. Y.: Lewis Historical Publishing Co. 1914. pp. 546; 547—1125, ill.* [5321

History of Beaver County, Pa.: *including the early settlement; ist erection into a separate county; its subsequent growth and development; sketches of its boroughs; villages and townships; portraits of some of its prominent men; biographies of many of its representative citizens; statis-*

tics, etc. Philadelphia, Pa. and Chicago, Ill.: A. Warner & Co. 1888. pp. VII, 11—908, ill., map. [5322

Bradford County

Reichel, W. C.: Wyalusing and the Moravian mission at Friedenshuetten. *In: Transactions of the Moravian Historical Society. Vol. I. Nazareth, Pa. 1858—1876. pp. 179—224.* [5323

Butler County

Bagger, Henry Horneman: An historical sketch of the first English Evangelical Lutheran Church of Butler County, Pa. *1843—1923. Butler, Pa.: Miller Printing Co. 1923. pp. 30, ill.* [5324

Brown, Robert C.: History of Butler County, Pa., *embracing its physical features; aborigines and explorers; public lands and surveys; pioneers; early settlement and subsequent growth; organization and civil administration sketches and boroughs, townships and villages Chicago, Ill.: R. C. Brown & Co. 1895. pp. XVI, 17 —1360. ill., map.* [5325

McKee, James A.: 20th century history of Butler and Butler Counties, Pa. and representative citizens. *Edited and compiled by . . . Chicago, Ill.: Richmond — Arnold Publishing Co. 1909. pp. 1487, ill.* [5326

Sipe, C. Hale: History of Butler County, Pa. *2 vols. Topeka, Kans. — Indianapolis, Ind.: Historical Publishing Co. 1927. pp. (20), 65—696, ill.; pp. (8), 737—1343, ill.* [5327

1796—1883. History of Butler County, Pa. *With illustrations and biographical sketches of some of its prominent men and pioneers. Chicago, Ill.: Waterman, Watkins & Co. 1883. pp. VIII, 9—454.* [5328

Cambria County

Carney, W. H. Bruce: History of the Alleghany Evangelical Lutheran Synod of Pennsylvania . . . *Published by the authority of Alleghany Synod in commemoration of its seventy-fifth anniversary and of the Quadricentennial of the Reformation. 2 vols. Philadelphia, Pa.: Printed for the Synod by the Lutheran Publication Society. 1918. pp. XII, 454; 455—871, ill., map.* [5329

Chapman, Thomas J.: The Valley of the Conemaugh. *Altoona, Pa.: McCrum & Dern 1865. pp. 202.* [5330

McLaurin, J. J.: The story of Johnstown: its early settlement, rise and progress, industrial growth, and appalling flood on May 31st, 1889. *Prefatory note by John R. Paxton. Harrisburg, Pa.: James M. Place 1890. pp. 380, ill.* [5331

Meise, John: Schantz and Johnstown. *A souvenir for the dedication of the Joseph Schantz monument in connection with the fourteenth convention of the German-American Alliance of Pennsylvania. Johnstown, Pa.: Published by the Schantz Memorial Committee. 1913. pp. 176. ill. (English and German.)* [5332

Murphy, R. E.: The geography of Johnston, Pennsylvania. *State College, Pa. 1934. = Pennsylvania State College, Mineral Industries Exper. Station Bull 13. [See also no. 5263b.]* [5332a

Storey, Henry Wilson: History of Cambria County, Pa. with genealogical memoirs. *3 vols New York, N. Y. — Chicago, Ill.: The Lewis Publishing Co. 1907. pp. VII, 590, III, ill.; pp. 575, VI, (1), ill.; pp. 679, VII, ill.* [5333

Swank, James M.: Cambria County pioneers. *A collection of brief biographical and other sketches relating to the early history of Cambria County. Pa. Philadelphia, Pa.: Allen, Lane & Scott 1910. pp. 138.* [5334

Who founded Johnstown, Pa. *In: Notes and Queries. Edited by W. H. Egle. Annual vol. 1897. Harrisburg, Pa. 1898. pp. 230—231.* [5335

Clearfield County

Aldrich, Lewis Cass: History of Clearfield County, Pennsylvania *with illustrations and biographical sketches of some of its prominent men and pioneers. Edited by . . . Syracuse, N. Y.: D. Mason & Co. 1887. pp. 3—731.* [5336

Irwin, K. E.: Souvenir history. Trinity Lutheran Church. Du Bois, Pa. *Tenth anniversary June 4, 1916. Du Bois, Pa.: The Du Bois Daily Express Print. pp. 63, ill.* [5337

Snyder, John Franklin: 1804—1904. Clearfield County's Centennial celebration at Clearfield, Pa., July 26, 27, 28 and 29. *Clearfield, Pa.: Raftsman's Journal 1904. pp. (88), ill.* [5338

Swoope, Roland D.: Twentieth century history of Clearfield County, Pa. and representative citizens. *Chicago, Ill.: Published by Richmond — Arnold Publishing Co. 1911. pp. 981, ill.* [5339

Wall, Thomas Lincoln: Clearfield County, Pa., present and past. *Library edition. Clearfield, Pa.: Published by the author 1925. pp. X, 296, ill.* [5340

Commemorative biographical record of Central Pennsylvania, including the Counties of Centre, Clearfield, Jefferson and Clarion, *containing biographical sketches of prominent and representative citizens, and of many of the early settled families. Chicago, Ill.: J. H. Beers & Co. 1898. pp. (1), 1676, ill.* [5341

Clarion County

Burgess, Ellis Beaver: History of the Pittsburgh Synod of the Evangelical Lutheran Church 1748—1845—1904. *Together with a brief sketch of each congregation of the Synod. Edited by the same author. Philadelphia, Pa.: Printed for the Synod by the Lutheran Publication Society. 1904. pp. 488, ill. [„The churches of Clarion County." = Chapter XI. pp. 364—395, ill.]* [5342

— Memorial history of the Pittsburgh Synod of the Evangelical Lutheran Church 1748—1845—1924. *Together with a sketch of each of the 317 congregations found in the fellowship of the Synod in the year of the merger. Greenville, Pa.: Published for the Synod by the Beaver Printing Co. 1925. pp. 814, ill. [„Churches of Clarion County." = Chapter XIII. pp. 453—483.]* [5343

Davis, A. J.: History of Clarion County, Pa. *with illustrations and biographical sketches of some of its prominent men and pioneers. Edited by . . . Syracuse, N. Y.: D. Mason & Co. 1887. pp. 664, LXXII, ill.* [5344

Lady, David B. (and **Darbaker, H. D.**): The history of the Pittsburgh Synod of the Reformed Church in the United States. *Prepared in commemoration of its fiftieth anniversary by . . . Greensburg, Pa.: Chas. M. Henry Printing Co. 1920. pp. (10), 569, ill. [„Clarion Classis." By H. D. Darbaker. = Chapter XXIV. pp. 359—415, ill.]* [5345

Commemorative biographical record of Central Pennsylvania, including the

Counties of Centre, Clearfield, Jefferson and Clarion, *containing biographical sketches of prominent and representative citizens, and of many of the early settled families. Chicago, Ill.: J. H. Beers & Co. 1898. pp. (1), 1676, ill.* [5346

Crawford County

Bates, Samuel P.: Our county and its people. *A historical and memorial record of Crawford County, Pa. [Boston]: W. A. Ferguson & Co. 1899. pp. XV. 972, ill., maps.* [5347

History of Crawford County, Pa., *containing a history of the county; its townships, towns, villages, schools, churches, industries, etc.; portraits of early settlers and prominent men; biographies; history of Pennsylvania; statistical and miscellaneous matter, etc., etc. Chicago, Ill.: Warner, Beers & Co. 1885. pp. XI, 15—1186, ill., map.* [5348

Elk County

History of the Counties of McKean, Elk, Cameron and Potter, Pa., *with biographical selections including their early settlement and development; a description of the historic and interesting localities; sketches of their cities, towns and villages; portraits of prominent men; biographies of representative citizens; outline history of Pennsylvania; statistics. Chicago, Ill.: J. H. Beers & Co. 1890. pp. XIII, 17—1261, maps. ill.* [5349

Erie County

Russell, . . .: Dauphin County settlers on lake Erie. *In: Notes and Queries. Edited by W. H. Egle. Third series, vol. II. 1887—1890. Harrisburg, Pa. 1891. pp. 2—4. Reprint in: Third series, vol. II. Harrisburg, Pa. 1896. pp. 386—387.* [5350

Fayette County

Bell, Edmund Hayes: Echoes of early Brownsville. *In: Western Pennsylvania Historical Magazine. Vol. VII. Pittsburgh, Pa. 1924. pp. 10—23.* [5351

[Bowman, James Lowry]: Some historical notes of South-West Pennsylvania. *Edited by Edmund Hayes Bell. In:*

Western Pennsylvania Historical Magazine. Vol. X. Pittsburgh, Pa. 1927. pp. 48—57; 117—125; 187—190. [5352

Egle, William Henry: Provincial papers: Returns of taxables for the Counties of Bedford (1773 to 1784), Huntingdon (1788), Westmoreland (1783, 1786), Fayette (1785, 1786), Allegheny (1791), Washington (1786) and Census of Bedford (1784) and Westmoreland (1783). *Edited by . . . Harrisburg, Pa. 1898. pp. XI, 782.*
= *Pennsylvania Archives. Third series, vol. XXII.* [5353

Ellis, Franklin: History of Fayette County, Pa. with biographical sketches of many of its pioneers and prominent men. *Edited by . . . Philadelphia, Pa.: L. H. Everts & Co. 1882. pp. 841, ill., map.* [5354

Gresham, John M. and Wiley, Samuel T.: Biographical and portrait cyclopedia of Fayette County, Pa. *Editorialy managed by John M. Gresham, assisted in the compilation by Samuel T. Wiley. Chicago, Ill.: John M. Gresham & Co. 1889. pp. VIII, 9—602, ill.* [5355

Hadden, James: A history of Uniontown, the county seat of Fayette County, Pa. *Akron, O.: New Werner Co. 1913. pp. VIII, 824, ill., map.* [5356

Hart, J. Percy and Bright, W. H.: Hart's history and directory of the three towns, Brownsville, Bridgeport, West Brownsville. Also abridged history of Fayette County & Western Pennsylvania. *Edited and compiled by J. Percy Hart, assisted by W. H. Bright. Cadwallader, Pa.: J. Percy Hart 1904. pp. 368, ill., maps. pp. 369—686 Advertisements.* [5357

[Jordan, John W.-Hadden, James]: Genealogical and personal history of Fayette and Greene Counties, Pa. *Under the editorial supervision of . . . 3 vols. New York, N. Y.: Lewis Historical Publishing Co. 1912. pp. (4), 306; 307—614; 615—922, (14), ill.* [5358

Metzler, A. J.: Masontown, Pa., Mennonite Church. *In: Christian Monitor. A monthly magazine for the home. Vol. XXIV, no. 5. Scottdale, Pa. 1932. pp. 145—146, ill.* [5359

Indiana County

Burgess, Ellis Beaver: History of the Pittsburgh Synod of the Evangelical Lutheran Church 1748—1845—1904. *Together*

with a brief sketch of each congregation of the Synod. Edited by the same author. Philadelphia, Pa.: Printed for the Synod by the Lutheran Publication Society. 1904. pp. 488, ill.
[,,The churches of Indiana County." = Chapter IX. pp. 250—293, ill.] [5360

Burgess, Ellis Beaver: Memorial history of the Pittsburgh Synod of the Evangelical Lutheran Church 1748—1845 —1924. *Together with a sketch of each of the 317 congregations found in the fellowship of the Synod in the year of the merger. Greenville, Pa.: Published for the Synod by the Beaver Printing Co. 1925. pp. 814, ill.*
[,,Churches of Indiana County." = Chapter XVI. pp. 531—563, ill.]
[5361

Wiley, Samuel T.: Biographical and historical cyclopedia of Indiana and Armstrong Counties, Pa. *Philadelphia, Pa.: John M. Gresham & Co. 1891. pp. 636, ill.* [5362

Welch, Charles Howard: History of Mount Union, Shirleysburg and Shirley Township. *Mount Union, Pa.: The Mount Union Times Office 1909—10. pp. (29), 752, ill.* [5363

Jefferson County

McKnight, W. J.: 1755—1844. A pioneer history of Jefferson County, Pennsylvania and my first recollections of Brookville, Pennsylvania, 1840—1843, when my feet were bare and my cheeks were brown. *Philadelphia, Pa.: J. B. Lippincott Co. 1898. pp. 670, ill.*
[Lutheran Church. pp. 265—266; Intentured apprentices, white slavery, and redemptioners. pp. 284—296.] [5364

Scott, Kate M.: History of Jefferson County, Pennsylvania. *With illustrations and biographical sketches of some of its prominent men and pioneers. Syracuse, N. Y.: D. Mason & Co. 1888. pp. 753, ill.*
[5365

Commemorative biographical record of Central Pennsylvania, including the Counties of Centre, Clearfield, Jefferson and Clarion, *containing biographical sketches of prominent and representative citizens and of many of the early settled families. Chicago, Ill.: J. H. Beers & Co. 1898. pp. (1), 1676, ill.* [5366

Lawrence County

Moravian mission. *A historical spot in Lawrence County. The old settlement — East and West Moravian — The town and its business men, with old residents. In: Notes and Queries. Edited by W. H. Egle. Third series, vol. I. 1884—1887. Harrisburg, Pa. 1887. pp. 558—559.*
[5367

Mercer County

[Durant, S. W.]: 1796. History of Mercer County, Pa. *Philadelphia, Pa.: L. H. Everts & Co. 1877. pp. 156, ill., map.*
[5368

White, J. G.: A twentieth century history of Mercer County, Pa. *A narrative account of its historical progress, its people, and its principal interests, prepared under the general editorial supervision of J. G. White. 2 vols. Chicago, Ill.: The Lewis Publishing Co. 1909. pp. XX, 560, ill.; pp. 561—1111, ill.* [5369

History of Mercer County, Pa. Its past and present. *Including its aboriginal history; its early settlement and development; a description of its historic and interesting localities; sketches of its boroughs, townships and villages; neighborhood and family histories; potraits and biographies of pioneers and representative citizens; statistics, etc. also a condensed history of Pennsylvania. Chicago, Ill.: Brown, Runk & Co. 1888. pp. VIII, 15—1210, ill., map.*   [5370

Somerset County

Bittinger, Elmer E.: Mennonite Church at Springs, Pa. *In: Christian Monitor. A monthly magazine for the home. Vol. XXIV, no. 5. Scottdale, Pa. 1932. pp. 208—209, ill.*   [5371

Blough, Jerome E.: History of the Church of the Brethren of the Western District of Pennsylvania. *Elgin, Ill.: Published by the Brethren Publishing House 1916. pp. (1), 7—600, ill.*   [5372

Carney, W. H. Bruce: History of the Allegany Evangelical Lutheran Synod of Pennsylvania . . . *Published by the authority of Alleghany Synod in commemoration of its seventy-fifth anniversary, and of the Quadricentennial of the Reformation. 2 vols. Philadelphia, Pa.: Printed for the Synod by the Lutheran Publi-*

*cation Society. 1918. pp. XII, 454, 455
—871, ill., map.*
[„Churches of the Somerset Conference."
= Chapter XIII. pp. 536—781, ill.]
[5373
Egle, William Henry: Provincial papers:
Returns of taxables for the Counties of
Bedford (1773 to 1784), Huntingdon
(1788), Westmoreland (1783, 1786),
Fayette (1785, 1786), Alleghany (1791),
Washington (1786) and Census of Bedford (1784) and Westmoreland (1783).
*Edited by . . . Harrisburg, Pa. 1898. pp.
XI, 782.
= Pennsylvania Archives. Third series,
vol. XXII.*   [5374
Lady, David B. (and Truxal, A. E.): The history of the Pittsburgh Synod of the Reformed Church in the United States.
*Prepared in commemoration of its fiftieth
anniversary by . . . Greensburg, Pa.:
Chas. M. Henry Printing Co. 1920. pp.
(10), 569, ill.*
[„Somerset Classis." By A. E. Truxal.
= Chapter XXVI. pp. 446—497, ill.]
[5375
[Rupp, I. Daniel]: Early history of Western
Pennsylvania, *and of the West and of
western expeditions and campaigns, from
MDCCLIV to MDCCCXXXIII. By a
gentleman of the Bar. With an appendix
containing, besides copious extracts from
important Indian treaties, minutes of
conferences, journals, etc., a topographical description of the Counties of Allegheny,Westmoreland,Washington, Somerset, Greene, Fayette, Beaver, Butler,
Armstrong, etc. Pittsburg, Pa.: Daniel
W. Kaufman — Harrisburg, Pa.: William O. Hickok 1846. pp. VI, VI, 17—
352. Appendix pp. 752.*   [5376
Saylor, E. C.: Births and baptisms of Somerset County, Pa. *2 vols. Berlin, Pa. 1929
[Typewritten.]
Vol. I:* Reformed and Lutheran Church
records of Berlin, Sommerset County,
Pa. *Translated from the German script.
pp. 180; Vol. II.* Church book and baptismal register. Belonging to the Evangelical Lutheran congregation of Berlin,
Bedford County, Pa., *containing the
births of children and the time of their
baptism, from the year 1788, and the
following years, entered and registered as
follows. pp. 178.*   [5377
Shetler, Sanford G.: Stahl Mennonite
Church, Johnstown, Pa. *In: Christian
Monitor. A monthly magazine for the*

*home, Vol. XXIV, no. 3. Scottdale, Pa.
1932. pp 82—84, ill.*   [5378
Shoup, J. B.: Parish record. A brief account, historical and statistical of the
several congregations, comprising the
Hooversville pastorate, of the Allegheny
Evangelical Lutheran Synod. *Philadelphia, Pa.: Lutheran Publication Society. 1880. pp. 24.*   [5379
Welfley, William H.: History of Bedford
and Somerset Counties, Pa., with genealogical and personal history....; Somerset County, by William H. Welfley.
Under the editorial supervision of **William H. Koontz.** *3 vols. New York, N.
Y.) Chicago, Ill.: The Lewis Publishing
Co. 1906. Vol. I.* Bedford County. *[See
No. 3535]; Vol. II.* Somerset County. *pp.
XI, 695, ill.; Vol. III.* Bibliographical
pp. 553, ill.   [5380
— Berlin and Brothers Valley. *In: The
Pennsylvania German. Vol. X. Lititz,
Pa. 1909. pp. 506—509; 552—557.* [5381
— Early printing in Somerset, Pa. *In:
The Pennsylvania German. Vol. XI.
Lititz, Pa. 1910. pp. 148—149.* [5382
**Wilson, L. Newin, Compton, D. and Hay,
Ed. R.:** A history of the Wilhelms and
the Wilhelm charge. *By the Historical
Committee . . . Meyersdale, Pa.: The
Wilhelm Press 1919. pp. 9—204, ill.
[Meyersdale, Pa., St. Paul's Church,
Somerset County, Pa.]*   [5383
History of Bedford, Somerset and Fulton
Counties, Pa. *With illustrations and biographical sketches of some of its pioneers
and prominent men. Chicago, Ill.: Waterman, Watkins & Co. 1884. pp. IX, 15—
672, ill.*   [5384

Washington County

Crumrine, Boyd: History of Washington
County, Pa., with biographical sketches of many prominent men. *Edited by
. . . Philadelphia. Pa.: L. H. Everts &
Co. 1882. pp. 1002, ill., map.*   [5385
Egle, William Henry: Provincial papers:
Returns of taxables for the Counties of
Bedford (1773 to 1784), Huntingdon
(1788), Westmoreland (1783, 1786), Fayette (1785, 1786), Allegheny (1791),
Washington (1786) and Census of Bedford (1784) and Westmoreland (1783).
*Edited by . . . Harrisburg, Pa. 1898. pp.
XI, 782.
= Pennsylvania Archives. Third series,
vol. XXII.*   [5386

Wood, Mary Ellison: Abstracts of wills of Washington County, registered at Little Washington, Pa. *In: Publications of the Genealogical Society of Pennsylvania. Vol. VI, no. 2. Philadelphia, Pa. 1916. pp. 135—180.* [5387

Westmoreland County

Albert, George Dallas: History of the County of Westmoreland, Pa., *with biographical sketches of many of its pioneers and prominent men. Edited by . . . Philadelphia, Pa.: L. H. Everts & Co. 1882. pp. 727, ill.* [5388
Boucher, John N.: History of Westmoreland County, Pa. *3 vols. New York, N. Y.: Chicago, Ill.: The Lewis Publishing Co. 1906. pp. VII, 678, ill., map. pp. XI, 649, ill.; pp. IX, 659, ill.* [5389
Burgess, Ellis Beaver: History of the Pittsburgh Synod of the Evangelical Lutheran Church 1748—1845—1904. *Together with a brief sketch of each congregation of the synod. Edited by the same author. Philadelphia, Pa.: Printed for the Synod by the Lutheran Publication Society. 1904. pp. 488, ill.*
[„The churches of Westmoreland County." = Chapter VII. pp. 136—175, ill.] [5390
— Memorial history of the Pittsburgh Synod of the Evangelical Lutheran Church 1748—1845—1924. *Together with a sketch of the 317 congregations found in the fellowship of the Synod in the year of the merger. Greenville, Pa.: Published for the Synod by the Beaver Printing Co. 1925. pp. 814, ill.*
[„Churches of Westmoreland County." = Chapter XX. pp. 627—725, ill.] [5391
Cort, Cyrus: Historical sermon. In the First Reformed Church of Greensburg, Pa., Oct. 13, 1907, during the sessions of the Pittsburg Synod to commemorate the services of the pioneer pastor of the Reformed Church in western Pennsylvania on the 125th anniversary. *[1907.] pp. 48, ill.* [5392
Egle, William Henry: Provincial papers: Returns of taxables for the Counties of Bedford (1773 to 1784), Huntingdon (1788), Westmoreland (1783, 1786), Fayette (1785, 1786), Allegheny (1791), Washington (1786), and Census of Bedford (1784) and Westmoreland (1783). *Edi-*

ted by . . . *Harrisburg, Pa. 1898. pp. XI, 782.*
= *Pennsylvania Archives. Third series, vol. XXII.* [5393
Hassler, Edgar W.: Old Westmoreland: A history of western Pennsylvania during the Revolution. *Pittsburgh, Pa.: J. R. Weldin & Co. 1900. pp. 4, VI, 5—200.* [5394
Huber, Vincent: Sportman's Hall. *In: Records of the American Catholic Historical Society. Vol. III. Philadelphia, Pa. 1888—1891. pp. 142—173, ill.* [5395
Kellogg, Joseph M.: Westmoreland County, Pa., petitions; Revolutionary. *In: The National Genealogical Society Quarterly. Vol. XVI, no. 3. Washington, D. C. 1928. pp. 60—63.* [5396
Lady, David B. (and **Bright, E. D.**): The history of the Pittsburgh Synod of the Reformed Church in the United States. *Prepared in commemoration of its fiftieth anniversary by . . . Greensburg, Pa.: Chas. M. Henry Printing Co. 1920. pp. (10), 569, ill.*
[Westmoreland Classis." By E. D. Bright. = Chapter XXIII. pp. 269—358, ill.] [5397
Ressler, Rhoda M.: Mennonite Church at Scottdale, Pa. *In: Christian Monitor. A monthly magazine for the home. Vol. XXIII., no. 4. Scottdale, Pa. 1931. pp. 112—113, ill.* [5398
[Rupp, I. Daniel]: Early history of western Pennsylvania, and of the west, and of western expeditions and campaigns, from MDCCLIV to MDCCCXXXIII. *By a gentleman of the Bar. With an appendix containing, besides copious extracts from important Indian treaties, minutes of conferences, journals, etc., a topographical description of the Counties of Allegheny, Westmoreland, Washington, Somerset, Greene, Fayette, Beaver, Butler, Armstrong, etc. Pittsburg, Pa.: Daniel W. Kauffman; Harrisburg, Pa.: William O. Hickok 1846. pp. VI, VI, 17—352; Appendix pp. 752, map.* [5399
Wood, Mary Ellison: Abstracts of wills of Westmoreland County, registered at Greensburg, Pa. *Abstracted and contributed by . . . In: Publications of the Genealogical Society of Pennsylvania. Vol. V, no. 3. Philadelphia. Pa. 1914. pp. 326—350; Vol. VI, no. 1. 1915. pp. 31—63.* [5400
Zundel, William Arter: Fort Allen in Westmoreland County, Pa. *In: The Penn-*

sylvania-German Society. Proceedings and Addresses. Vol. XXXIII. . . . 1923. Part II. pp. 21—38. [5401

Zundel, William Arter: History of olp Zion Evangelical Lutheran Church in Hempfield Township, Westmoreland County, Pa. near Harold's. *Published by the Church Council Waverly, Ia.: Wartburg Press 1922. pp. XI, 266, ill.* [5402

A history of the Reformed Church within the bounds of the Westmoreland classis. *Edited by a Committee of Classis. Philadelphia, Pa.: Reformed Church Publication Board 1877. pp. 232.* [5403

Address and sermons delivered at the one hundredth anniversary of the laying of the corner-stone of the Denmark-Manor Church 1811—1911. *Reading, Pa.: I. M. Beaver 1911. pp. 97, ill.* [5404

Tombstone inscriptions. Old Union graveyard, German Reformed and Lutheran, Greensburg, Westmoreland County, Pa. *(Only old stones copied). In: Publications of the Genealogical Society of Pennsylvania. Vol. VI, no. 1. Philadelphia, Pa. 1915. pp. 26—29.* [5405

Centennial. Brush Creek Church. Hempfield Township, Westmoreland County, Pa. August 17, 1816—August 17, 1916. *[s. l. 1916.] pp. 55, ill.* [5406

Father Peter Helbron's, Greensburg, Pa. Register. First series, 1799 to 1802. *Copied from the original book by Rev. Father* **John,** *O. S. B. Translated by* **Lawrence F. Flick.** *In: Records of the American Catholic Historical Society of Philadelphia. Vol. XXVI. Philadelphia, Pa. 1915. pp. 250—263; Vol. XXVII. 1916. pp. 65—73; 161—173; 346—355; Vol. XXVIII 1917. pp. 85—90; 135—149; 266—276; 297—309.* [5407

Maryland

Allgemeines
General

[Andrews, Matthew Page]: Tercentenary history of Maryland. *4 vols. Chicago, Ill. — Baltimore, Md.: The S. J. Clarke Publishing Co. 1925. Vol. I. by M. P. Andrews. pp. 953, ill., map. Vol. II and III. issued anonymously. pp. 1041, ill.; pp. 1041, ill.; Vol. IV. compiled principally by* **Henry Fletcher Powell.** *pp. 919, ill.* [5408

Brumbaugh, Gajus Marcus and **Hodges, Margaret Roberts:** Revolutionary records of Maryland. *Part I. Washington, D. C.: Rufus H. Darby 1924. pp. VIII, 56.* [5409

— Maryland, records, colonial, revolutionary, county and church from the original sources. *Vol. I. Baltimore, Md.: Williams & Wilkins Co. 1915. pp. IX, 513, ill., map.; Vol. II. Lancaster, Pa.: Lancaster Press, Inc. 1928. pp. XVI, 688, ill.* [5410

Clark, Wm. Bullock: The geography of Maryland. *Baltimore, Md.: Johns Hopkins Press 1918. pp. (6), 41—167, (4), ill.* [5411

Edwards, Richard: Statistical gazetteer of the State of Maryland and the District of Columbia, *giving a full and comprehensive review of the history, progress, present condition, commercial, railroad, manufacturing and industrial resources of every city and town in the state and district. Baltimore, Md.: J. S. Waters; Washington, D. C.: Wm. M. Morrison & Co. 1856. pp. (19), 84—328.* [5412

Fisher, R. S.: Gazetteer of the State of Maryland *compiled from the returns of the seventh census of the United States, and other official documents. New York, N. Y.: J. H. Colton; Baltimore, Md.: James S. Waters 1852. pp. IV, 5—122, map.* [5413

Gould, Clarence Pembroke: The land system in Maryland, 1720—1765. *Baltimore, Md. 1913. pp. (1), (1), 9—100. = Johns Hopkins University Studies of History and Political Science. Series XXXI, no. 1. 1913.* [5414

Kennedy, Joseph, C. G.: Historical account of Maryland. *Washington, D. C.: Gideon & Co. 1852. pp. 40. [Out of the author's ,,History and statistics of Maryland."]* [5415

McSherry, James: History of Maryland; from its first settlement in 1634, to the year 1848. *Baltimore, Md.: John Murphy 1849. pp. XII, 13—405, ill.; edited 1852: For the use of schools. Baltimore, Md.: John Murphy & Co. 1852. pp. XII, 13—418; Edited and continued by* **Bartlett B. James.** *Baltimore, Md.: The*

Baltimore Book Co. 1904. pp. 437, ill.
                                        [5416
Mereness, Newton D.: Maryland as a pro-
prietary province. *New York, N. Y.:
The Macmillan Co. 1901. pp. XX, 530.*
                                        [5417
Scharf, J. Thomas: History of Maryland
from the earliest period to the present
day. *3 vols. Baltimore, Md.: John B.
Piet 1879. pp. XVI, 556, ill., map; pp.
XIV, 635, ill., maps; pp. XIII, (1), 782,
XXXVIII, ill.*   [5418
— History of western Maryland being a
history of Frederick, Montgomery, Carroll, Washington, Alleghany, and Garrett
Counties from the earliest period to the
present day; *including biographical
sketches of their representative men. 2
vols. Philadelphia, Pa.: Louis H. Evers
1882. pp. 788, ill., maps; pp. IV, 789—
1560, ill.*   [5419
— The natural and industrial resources
and advantages of Maryland, *being a
complete description of all the counties of
the state and the city of Baltimore . . .
Annapolis, Md.: C. H. Baughman & Co.
1892. pp. 240.*   [5420
Steiner, Bernard Christian: Description of
Maryland. *Baltimore, Md.: The Johns
Hopkins Press 1904. pp. 94.
= Johns Hopkins University Studies in
History and Political Science. Series
XXII, no. 11—12.
[A bibliography 1526—1903.]*   [5421
Williams, T. J. C.: The State of Maryland.
A description of its lands, products and
industries. *Compiled by . . . for the
Board of Public Works. Baltimore, Md.:
The Sun Job Printing Office 1906. pp.
168, ill.; Edition, 1908. pp. 194, ill.,
map.*   [5422
History and statistics of Maryland, accor-
ding to the returns of the 7th census of
the United States, 1850. *Washington,
D. C.: Gideon & Co. 1852. pp. III, 104.*
                                        [5423
Maryland, its resources, industries and in-
stitutions. *Prepared for the World's Fair
Managers of Maryland by members of
Johns Hopkins University and others.
Baltimore, Md.: The Sun Job Printing
Office, 1893. pp. VI, 504, (1), ill., maps.*
                                        [5424
The State of Maryland and its advantages
for immigrants especially farmers, ma-
nufactures, and capitalists. *Pub-
lished by the State Bureau of Immigra-
tion, Baltimore, Md. U. S. A. 1909. Bal-*

*timore, Md.: The Sun Job Printing Of-
fice 1909. pp. 55; Deutsche Ausgabe:*
Der Staat Maryland und die Vorteile,
die er Einwanderern, special Landwirten
und Industriellen, und Kapitalisten bie-
tet. *Herausgegeben von der Staats-Ein-
wanderungsbehörde in Baltimore, Md.
U. S. A. Baltimore, Md.: Schneidereith
& Söhnen 1909. 80 S. ill.*   [5425

Deutschpennsylvanier und Deutsche
Pennsylvania-Germans and Germans

Faust, Albert B.: ,,The early Germans . . .
of Maryland." *In: The German element
in the United States. By A. B. Faust.
Second edition New York, 1927 [= no.
42].Vol. I. = Chapter VI. pt. 2. pp. 161
—176.*   [5426
— Undercurrents of German influence in
Maryland. *Address delivered at the 25
anniversary of the founding of the So-
ciety for the History of the Germans in
Maryland, Febr. 21, 1911. In: Annual
Report of the Society for the History of
the Germans in Maryland. Baltimore,
Md. 1929. pp. 5—13.*   [5427
Henninghausen, Louis P.: The redemptioners
and the German Society of Maryland.
An historical sketch. *In: Second Annual
Report of the Society for the History of
the Germans in Maryland. Baltimore,
Md. 1888. pp. 33—54.*   [5428
— Die Revolte der Deutschen gegen die
Regierung von Maryland. *In: Third
Annual Report of the Society for the Hi-
story of the Germans in Maryland. Balti-
more, Md. 1889. S. 45—59.*   [5429
— Auszüge aus den Archiven des Staates
Maryland. *In: Fourth Annual Report
of the Society for the History of the Ger-
mans in Maryland. Baltimore, Md. 1890.
S. 11—14.*   [5430
— Early German settlement in western
Maryland. *In: Sixth Annual Report of
the Society for the History of the Germans
in Maryland. Baltimore, Md. 1892. pp.
pp. 13—25.*   [5431
— History of the German Society of Maryland. *Compiled by . . . Read at the meetings of the Society for the History of the
Germans in Maryland. 1909. Baltimore,
Md.: W. E. C. Harrison & Sons 1909.
203, ill.*   [5432
— Geschichte der Deutschen Gesellschaft
von Maryland. *Extracts out of the author's book: ,,History of the German Society of Maryland." Baltimore, Md.*

1909 [= Nr. 5432]. In: Deutsch-Amerikanische Geschichtsblätter. Jg. IX. Chicago, Ill. 1909. S. 131—142; Jg. X. 1910 S. 2—18. [5433

Henninghausen, Louis P.: Die Deutschen in Maryland. *Skizze. In: Das Buch der Deutschen in Amerika. Philadelphia, Pa. 1909 [= Nr. 59]. S. 179—186.* [5434

Hoffmann, J. Leonard: Twenty-fifth anniversary of the Society for the History of the Germans in Maryland. *In: Mitteilungen des Deutschen Pionier-Vereins in Philadelphia. Heft 20. Philadelphia, Pa. 1911. pp. 17—19.* [5435

Hofmann, Julius: The Germans of Maryland during the colonial period. *Published for the Star Spangled Banner Centennial. September, 1914. Baltimore, Md.: Schneidereith & Sons 1914. pp. E. (12); G. (12).* [5436

Mayer, F. B.: Memoranda in reference to early German emigration to Maryland. *In: Fifth Annual Report of the Society for the History of the Germans in Maryland. Baltimore, Md. 1891. pp. 15—19.* [5437

[Morris, Jno. G.]: An incident in the history of the Germans in Maryland. *Translated from: ,,Der Deutsche Pionier.'' Vol. IX, (1877). p. 157. In: Fourth Annual Report of the Society for the History of the Germans in Maryland. Baltimore, Md. 1890. pp. 35—36.* [5438

Nead, Daniel Wunderlich: The Pennsylvania-German in the settlement of Maryland. *Lancaster, Pa.: The New Era Printing Co. 1914. = Part XXV. ,,A narrative and critical history,'' prepared at the request of the Pennsylvania-German Society. In: The Pennsylvania-German Society. Proceedings and Addresses ... 1911. Vol. XXII. Lancaster, Pa. 1913. Separate pagination. pp. 304, ill., maps.* [5439

Raddatz, C. F.: German-American families in Maryland. *In: Sixth Annual Report of the Society for the History of the Germans in Maryland. Baltimore, Md. 1892. pp. 43—50.* [5440

Schultz, Edward T.: First settlement of Germans in Maryland. *A paper read .. before the Frederick County Historical Society, Jan. 17th, 1896 and before the Society of the History of the Germans in Maryland, March, 17th, 1896. (Published by request.) Frederick, Md.: David H. Smith 1896. pp. 60, ill., map.* [5441

U.[nger P.]: Die Deutsche Gesellschaft in Maryland. Eine Skizze. *In: Der Deutsche Pionier. Jg. I. Cincinnati, O. 1869—1870. S. 370—374.* [5442

Weishaar, J. A.: The German element in Maryland. *In: Fifteenth Annual Report of the Society for the History of the Germans in Maryland. Baltimore, Md. 1901. pp. 13—34.* [5443

Wentz, Abdel Ross: History of the Evangelical Lutheran Synod of Maryland of the United Lutheran Church in America 1820—1920, *together with a brief sketch of each congregation of the Synod and biographies of the living sons of the Synod in the ministry. Edited by the same author. Harrisburg, Pa.: Printed for the Synod by the Evangelical Press 1920. pp. 641, ill.* [5444

Der Fortschritt des Deutschtums in Maryland. Biographische Notizen abgedruckt aus: Deutsche Correspondent, Baltimore. *In: Der Deutscher Pionier. Jg. XIII. Cincinnati, O. 1881—1882. S. 400—402.* [5445

Maryländer Deutsche im Revolutionskriege. *Abdruck aus: ,,Baltimore Correspondent.'' In: Der Deutsche Pionier. Jg. XVII. Cincinnati, O. 1885—1886. S. 322—325.* [5446

Baltimore — Stadt

City of Baltimore

Albert, C. S.: The first twenty-five years of the history of St. Mark's English Lutheran Church, Baltimore. *Baltimore, Md.: Lantz & Arnold 1885. pp. 43.* [5447

Deutsche Literarische Bureau, Das: Baltimore. Seine Vergangenheit und Gegenwart, mit besonderer Berücksichtigung des deutschen Elements. *Herausgegeben von dem Literarischen Bureau. Baltimore, Md.: C. C. Bartgis & Bro. 1887. 343 S., ill.* [5448

Evers, Fritz: Zion in Baltimore. (1755—1930). *Schlichte Gedenkblätter, der Gemeinde dargeboten zur Jubelfeier ihres 175jährigen Bestehens am 19. Oktober 1930. Baltimore, Md.: Schneidereith 1930. 47 S., ill.* [5449

Frey, Jacob: Reminiscences of Baltimore. *Edition de luxe. Baltimore, Md.: Maryland Book Concern 1893. pp. (2), 468, ill.* [5450

Hall, Clayton Colman: Baltimore, its history and its people. *By various contributors; Clayton Colman Hall, ge-*

*neral editor. 3 vols. New York, N. Y. —
Chicago, Ill.: Lewis Historical Publishing Co. 1912. Vol. I. History. pp.
(2), 9—721, ill. map; Vol. II and III. Biography. pp. 488, ill.; 489—936, ill.* [5451
Heiner, Elias: Centenary sermon delivered
in the Second Street Church on Sabbath
morning, Dec. 8th, 1850, on the occa-
sion of the Centenary celebration of the
First Reformed congregation of Balti-
more. *Second edition. Baltimore, Md.:
Sherwood & Co. 1850. pp. IV, 5—52.
ill.* [5452
— Reminiscences of a quarter of a century.
*A sermon delivered in the First German
Reformed Church, Second Street, Balti-
more, Jan. 13, 1861. Published by the
Consistory Baltimore, Md.: John D.
Toy 1861. pp. 23.* [5453
Heldt, A.: „Baltimore." *In: Handwörter-
buch des Grenz- und Auslanddeutschtums.
Bd. I. Breslau 1933 [= Nr. 93]. S. 205
—207.* [5453a
Hennighausen, L. P.: The German Day in
Baltimore, October 6th, 1890. *In: Fifth
Annual Report of the society for the Hi-
story of the Germans in Maryland. Balti-
more, Md. 1891. pp. 43—72.* [5454
— Reminiscences of the political life of the
German-Americans in Baltimore during
1850—1860. *In: Seventh Annual Re-
port of the Society for the History of the
Germans in Maryland. Baltimore, Md.
1893. pp. 53—59; Eleventh and Twelfth
Annual Report . . . Baltimore, Md. 1898.
pp. 3—18.* [5455
— The Germans in the defence of Balti-
more in the war of 1812 to 1814. *In:
Sixteenth Annual Report of the Society
for the History of the Germans in Mary-
land. 1907. pp. 57—60.* [5456
— Die Deutschen bei der Vertheidigung
Baltimore's im Kriege von 1812—1814.
*From: Sixteenth Annual Report of the So-
ciety for the History of the Germans in
Maryland. In: Deutsch-Amerikanische
Geschichtsblätter. Jg. VIII. Nr. 2. Chi-
cago, Ill. 1908. S. 75—77.* [5457
Hines, Charles: The beginnings of English
Lutheranism in Baltimore. *In: The
Lutheran Quarterly. Vol. LVI. Gettys-
burg, Pa. 1926. pp. 287—303.* [5458
Hofmann, Julius: A history of Zion Church
in the City of Baltimore, 1755—1897.
*Published in commemoration of its Ses-
qui-Centennial, Oct. 15, 1905. Baltimore, Md. C. W. Schneidereith & Sons
1905. pp. 81, ill.* [5459

Keidel, George C.: The earliest German newspapers of Baltimore. An essay. *I. The
eighteenth century. Washington, D. C.:
Privately printed 1927. pp. 12, fac-
simile.* [5460
Leyh, E. F.: Baltimore Deutsch-Amerikaner
in Handel und Industrie. *In: Sixth
Annual Report of the Society fot the Hi-
story of the Germans in Maryland. Bal-
timore, Md. 1892. S. 77—85.* [5461
McCreary, George W.: The first book in
Baltimore-Town. Nicholas Hasselbach,
printer. *The book reprinted with a sketch
of Hasselbach's life and work. Baltimore,
Md.: Press of Kohn & Pollock 1903. pp.
XIII, 48, ill.* [5462
Morris, J. G.: The German in Baltimore.
*In: Eighth-Tenth Annual Report of the
Society for the History of the Germans in
Maryland. Baltimore, Md. 1896. pp. 11
—19.* [5463
Newcomer, Harry D.: Twenty-fifth anni-
versary. Grace English Lutheran
Church, Broadway and Gough St., Bal-
timore, Md., Sept. 25th to Oct. 2nd
1910. *[s. l., 1910.] pp. 31, ill.* [5464
Raine, Friedrich: Die deutschen Pioniere
Baltimore's. *Festrede gehalten von Oberst
Friedrich Raine, beim 150jährigen Jubiläum der Stadt Baltimore am 11. Okt.
1880. In: Der Deutsche Pionier. Jg.
XII. Cincinnati, O. 1880—1881. S. 321
—328.* [5465
Scharf, J. Thomas: The chronicles of Baltimore; *being a complete history of „Baltimore Town" and Baltimore City from
the earliest period to the present time. Baltimore, Md.: Turnbull Brothers 1874.
pp. VIII, 756.* [5466
— History of Baltimore City and County
from the earliest period to the present
day: *including biographical sketches of
their representative men. Philadelphia,
Pa.: Louis H. Everts 1881. pp. X, 13—
947, ill., map.* [5467
Scheib, H.: The Zion Church of the City of
Baltimore. *In: Second Annual Report
of the Society for the History of the Germans in Maryland. Baltimore, Md.
1888. pp. 57—73, maps.* [5468
Scholtz, Karl A. M.: The Germans as an
integral part of the community. *In:
Deutsche Feier des zweihundert jährigen
Bestehens der Stadt Baltimore. Sonntag,
15. September 1929 in der Zions Kirche.
[Published by the Society for the History
of the Germans in Maryland.] Baltimore,
Md. [s. d.] pp. (7).* [5469

Unger, P.: Das Deutschtum Baltimore's. *In: Der Deutsche Pionier. Jg. II. Cincinnati, O. 1870—1871. S. 202—205; Jg. III. 1871—1872. S. 106—109.* [5470

Genealogy and biography of leading families of the City of Baltimore and Baltimore County, Md., *containing portraits of many well known citizens of the past and present. New York, N. Y. — Chicago, Ill.: Chapman Publishing Co. 1897. pp. (1), (11), (1), 27—1061, ill.* [5471

Register of the first English Lutheran Church, Baltimore, from February, 1827 to March, 1859. *Baltimore, Md.: Frederick A. Hanzsche 1859. pp. 61.* [5472

The German Reformed congregation in Baltimore Town. *In: [Annual Report of the] Society for the History of the Germans in Maryland. Baltimore, Md. 1929. pp. 29—31.* [5473

Ludwig Stassfort's letter to his father. *Baltimore, den 4ten May '40. In: [Annual Report of the] Society for the History of the Germans in Maryland. Baltimore, Md. 1929. pp. 15—21. (English and German.)* [5474

Baltimore County

Jones, Charles Stork: History of St. Paul's Evangelical Lutheran Church in Baltimore County, Md. *Hampstead, Md.: W. B. Wooden & Co. 1902. pp. 62, ill.* [5475

Keidel, George C.: Semi-Centennial Salem Lutheran Church. *In: The Argus. Vol. XVIII, no. 2. Sept. 30, 1899. Catonsville, Md. 1899. pp. 3, col. 2—4.* [5476

— The Catonsville Lutheran Church. A sketch of its origin. *Washington, D. C.: Privately printed; Lancaster, Pa.: The New Era Printing Co. 1919. pp. 12.* [5477

— Catonsville pioneers of the Lutheran faith. *In: The National Genealogical Society Quarterly. Vol. IX, no. 2. Washington, D. C. 1920. pp. 20—22.* [5478

Prechtel, George: Saint Paul's Lutheran Church of Arcadia, Baltimore County. *In: [Annual Report of the] Society for the History of the Germans in Maryland. Baltimore, Md. 1929. pp. 23—26;* names of members of St. Paul's Church. *pp. 27—28.* [5479

Carroll County

Everhart, O. T.: A history of the Everhart and Shower families, from 1744 to 1883. *Embracing six generations. Also a sketch of Manchester, Md. Hanover,* York Co., Pa.: O. T. Everhart 1833. pp. VI, 7—142. [5480

Hafer, L. B.: A brief history of Trinity Lutheran Church Taneytown, Md. *Taneytown, Md.: The Carroll Record Print 1911. pp. 58, ill.* [5481

Miller, P. H.: History of Grace Evangelical Lutheran Church, Carroll Street, of the City of Westminster, Md. from 1868 to 1894 with some account of earlier efforts to establish a Lutheran congregation in Westminster, *with an appendix containing short sketches of the different Lutheran congregations and charges in Carroll County, Md. Westminster, Md.: Published by Lawyer, Edwin J. [Lancaster, Pa.]: The New Era Print 1894. pp. 283.* [5482

Tawney, G. A.: The founder of Taneytown. *In: The Maryland Historical Magazine. Vol. XI. Baltimore, Md. 1916. pp. 74—75.* [5483

Montgomery County

Brumbaugh, G. M.: Unpublished Revolutionary records of Maryland. List of patriots who took the oath of fidelity and support to the government. *Edited by . . . [,, A list of Persons in Montgomery County who have taken the following Oath before the different magistrates as mentioned below; and returned by them to Montgomery Court."] In: The National Genealogical Society Quarterly. Vol. VI, no. 1. Washington, D. C. 1917. pp. 1—21.* [5484

Frederick County

Betz, I. H.: Historical pilgrimages into Pennsylvania Germandom. From York, Pa., to Harper's Ferry, W. Va. *In: The Pennsylvania-German. Vol. IV. Lebanon, Pa. 1903. pp. 355—374. [See no. 295]* [5485

Brumbaugh, Gajus Marcus: Census of 1776, Frederick County, Md. *In: Maryland records, colonial, revolutionary, county and church from original sources. Vol. 1. Baltimore, Md. 1915. pp. 177—257, ill.* [5486

— Earliest records of All Saints' parish, Frederick, Md., 1727—1781. *In: Maryland records, colonial, revolutionary, county and church from original sources. Vol. 1. Baltimore, Md. 1915. pp. 258—262.* [5487

— Unpublished Revolutionary records of Maryland. List of citizens who took the

28*

oath of fidelity and support to the government, March, 1778. *Edited by . . .
[,,A list of Persons in Frederick County
who have taken the following Oath before
the different Magistrates as mentioned
below; and returned then to Frederick
Court."] In: The National Genealogical
Society Quarterly. Vol. VI, no. 2. Washington, D. C. 1917. pp. 33—34.*   [5488
Brumbaugh, Gajus Marcus: ,,State of his
Lordship's manor of Monococy, 1767."
*In: Maryland records, colonial, revo-
lutionary, county and church from original
sources. Vol. II. Baltimore, Md. 1928.
pp. 51—56; ,,. . . Monocosy in Frederick.
County, April, 1768." pp. 56—60.*   [5489
Cary, John D.: Frederick, Maryland-De-
scription . . . *taken from: ,,The Key"
published there by John D. Cary and
printed by Matthias Bartgis in 1798.
In: The Pennsylvania Magazine of
History and Biography. Vol. XXIII.
Philadelphia, Pa. 1899. p. 116.*   [5490
Diehl, George: History of the Lutheran
Church of Frederick, Md. *In: The Evan-
gelical Review. Gettysburg, Pa. 1855—56.
pp. 459—476.*   [5491
— History of the Lutheran Church of
Frederick, Md. *A discource delivered in
the Old Lutheran Church of Frederick,
Md., Dec. 2, 1855, being the last Sabbath
service in the Old Church. Gettysburg,
Pa.: H. C. Neinstedt 1856. pp. 23.* [5492
— Jubilee of the Sunday school of the
Evangelical Lutheran Church of Frede-
rick, Md., September 25th, 1870. Hi-
storical discourse. *By G. Diehl, and ad-
dresses. Baltimore, Md.: F. A. Hanzsche's
Steam Press 1870. pp. 36.*   [5493
Eschbach, E.: Historic sketsch of the Evan-
gelical Reformed Church of Frederick,
Md. *Frederick, Md.: Great Southern Ptg.
& Mfg. Co. 1894. pp. 67.*   [5494
— The Centenary of the town steeple of
Frederick, Maryland. A historical ser-
mon. *In: Journal of the Presbyterian Hi-
storical Society. Vol. IV. Philadelphia,
Pa. 1908. pp. 315—327, ill.*   [5495
Garrott, Nellie Carter: Official poll of pre-
sidential election in Frederick County,
Md., Nov. 9 to 12, 1796; 1917 voters.
*In: Maryland records, colonial, revo-
lutionary, county and church from origi-
nal sources by G. M. Brumbaugh. Vol. I.
Baltimore, Md. 1915. pp. 271—295.*
                                     [5496
Gentzler, J. Winfield: The Middletown
Lutheran Church trouble or the Midd-

letown trouble in the Lutheran Church.
[s. l., s. d.] pp. 23.   [5497
Gruber, Michael Alvin: Tombstone inscriptions, Frederick, Md. — Inscriptions
from tombstones in the burial grounds
connected with the Lutheran and Reformed denominations at Frederick,
Md. *In: The National Genealogical Society Quarterly. Vol. VIII, no. 1. 2. Washington, D. C. 1919. pp. 19—27.*   [5498
Helfenstein, Ernest: Tombstone inscriptions
from the original church yard of All
Saints' parish, Frederick, Md. *(Complete). In: Maryland records, colonial,
revolutionary, county and church from
original sources, by G. M. Brumbaugh.
Vol. I. Baltimore, Md. 1915. pp. 263
—270.*   [5499
Helman, James A.: History of Emmits-
burg, Md. *with a prelude of historical
fact of Frederick County, and a romance
entitled disappointed, or the recluse of
Huckle's field. Frederick, Md.: Citizens
Press 1906. pp. 124.*   [5500
McCardell, Abby Gertrude: Frederick Coun-
ty marriages: Evangelical Reformed
Church, Frederick, Md. *In: Maryland
records, colonial, revolutionary, county
and church from original sources, by
Gajus Marcus Brumbaugh. Vol. II. Bal-
timore, Md. 1928. pp. 498—513.* [5501
Oerter, A. L.: The history of Graceham,
Frederick County, Md. *Bethlehem, Pa.:
Times Publishing Co. 1913. pp. 189, ill.
= Part of Vol. IX. Transactions of the
Moravian Historical Society.*   [5502
— Graceham, Frederick County, Md. An
historical sketch. *In: Transactions of
the Moravian Historical Society. Vol.
IX. 1909—1912. Nazareth, Pa. 1913.
pp. 119—305, ill.*   [5503
Schmucker, B. M.: History of the Lutheran
congregation at Frederick, Md. *In:
The Quarterly Review of the Evangelical
Church. New series, vol. XIII. Gettys-
burg, Pa. 1883. pp. 516—540.*   [5504
Shafer, Sary Andrew: Frederick Town.
,,The garden spot of Maryland." *In:
American historic towns. Historic towns
of the Southern States. Edited by Lyman
P. Powell. New York-London: G. P.
Putnam's Sons. The Knickerbocker Press
1904. pp. 75—99.*   [5505
Sioussat, St. George Leakin: Economics and
politics in Maryland, 1720—1750, and
the public services of Daniel Dulany
the elder. *Baltimore, Md.: The Johns
Hopkins Press 1903. pp. 84.*

= *Johns Hopkins University Studies in Historical and Political Science. Series XXI, nos. 6—7.*
[„Dulany and emigrations". = *Chapter V. pp. 76—84.]* [5506

Williams, T. J. C. and **McKinsey, Folger:** History of Frederick County, Md. from the earliest settlements to the beginning of the war between the states *by T. J. C. Williams,* continued from the beginning of the year 1861 down to the present time *by Folger McKinsey. To this is added a biographical record of representative families prepared from data obtained from original sources of information. 2 vols. Frederick, Md. L. R. Titsworth & Co.; Hagerstown, Md.: The Mail Publishing Co. 1910. pp. (6), 685, ill.; (2), 693—1635, ill.* [5507

Frederick County substitutes: *A list of the substitutes procured by the following persons and passed by the Lieutenant Frederick County as part of the quota of said county agreeable to the late act of Assembly. In: The Maryland Historical Magazine. Vol. VI. Baltimore, Md. 1911. pp. 256—261.* [5508

The Brengle home guard. *Reprint from: „The Maryland Historical Magazine", June 1912. In: The Penn Germania. Vol. I.* = *Old series, vol. XIII. Lititz, Pa. 1912. pp. 725—727.* [5509

Journal of the Committee of Observation of the Middle District of Frederick County, Md. *In: The Maryland Historical Magazine. Vol. X. Baltimore, Md. 1915. pp. 301—321; Vol. XI. 1916. pp. 50—66; 157—175; 237—260; 304 —321; Vol. XII. 1917. pp. 10—21.* [5510

The Centennial celebration in Frederick County, Md., on June 28th, 1876. *Centennial Central Committee. Frederick, Md.: Baughman Brothers. 1879. pp. 64.* [5511

Addresses and abstracts of sermons delivered at the first re-union of Lutheran clergymen, born in the Middletown Valley, Frederick County, Md., held in the Lutheran Church at Middletown, July 26th and 27th, 1882. *Boonsboro, Md.: R. N. Monroe, Times Office 1882. pp. 34.* [5512

Sesqui-Centennial services of the Evangelical Reformed Church, Frederick, Maryland, May 9, 14, and 16, 1897. Rev. E. R. Eschbach, D. D., pastor. *Frederick, Md. 1897. pp. 91* [5513

German Reformed Church of Frederick. *In: Maryland Historical Magazine. Vol. X. Baltimore, Md. 1915. pp. 59—60.* [5514

Washington County

Bell, Herbert C.: History of Leitersbury District, Washington County, Md.; *including its original land tenure; first settlement; material development; religious education, political and general history; biographical sketches, etc. Leitersburg, Md.: Published by the author. 1898. pp. 337, ill., map.* [5515

Betz, I. H.: Historical pilgrimages into Pennsylvania-Germandom and Scotch Irishdom. From Winchester to Harrisburg. *In: The Pennsylvania-German. Vol. V. Lebanon, Pa. 1904. pp. 8—22; 61—72, ill.* *[See no. 295]* [5516

Gruber, Michael: Tombstone inscriptions, Hagerstown, Md. *(302 names).* — Inscriptions from the tombstones in the burial grounds connected with the Lutheran and Reformed denominations and the cemetery at Hagerstown, Md. *In: The National Genealogical Society Quarterly. Vol. VIII, no. 1 and 2. Washington, D. C. 1919. pp. 1—16.* [5517

Hartmann, J. Stewart: The history of Christ Reformed Church Cavetown, Md. *1827—1927. A century. Hagerstown, Md.: Maryland Printery 1927. pp. (4), 91, ill.* [5518

Hesse, Ferdinand: History of the Smithsbury charge composed of Trinity Smithsburg, Md., Mt. Moriah, Foxville Md., St. Paul's Greensburg, Md. *Hagerstown, Md.: Press of Hagerstown Bookbinding and Printing Co. 1912. pp. 125, ill.* [5519

Sollers, Basil: Der Gründer von Hagerstown. *[Jonathan Hager.] Nach einem Bericht im „Deutschen Correspondent." In: Der Deutsche Pionier. Jg. XVII. Cincinnati, O. 1885—1886. S. 305—307.* [5520

— Jonathan Hager, the founder of Hagerstown. *In: Second Annual Report of the Society for the History of the Germans in Maryland. Baltimore, Md. 1888. pp. 17—30.* [5521

Stapleton, A.: Pennsylvania-German graveyards in the south. *In: Notes and Queries. Edited by W. H. Egle. Annual vol. 1899. Harrisburg, Pa. 1900. pp. 128—129.* [5522

Wenner, Jessie Shafer: A historical sketch and directory of Trinity Lutheran Church, Hagerstown, Md. *Hagerstown, Md.: Hagerstown News Print 1891. pp. 15.* [5523

Williams, Thomas J. C.: A history of Washington County, Md., from the earliest settlements to the present time, including a history of Hagerstown. *To this is added a biographical record of representative families prepared from data obtained from original sources of information. 2 vols. Chambersburg, Pa. John M. Runk & L. R. Titsworth, Hagerstown, Md.: Mail Publishing Co. 1906. pp. 602; 611—1347, ill.* [5524

Extracts from the minutes of the proceedings of the Committee of Observation for the Elizabethtown (now Hagerstown) District during the years 1775, '76 and '77. *Baltimore, Md. 1862. pp. 20* [5525

Proceedings of the Committee of Observation for Elizabeth Town District. *[Washington County Md.] In: The Maryland Historical Magazine. Vol. XII. Baltimore, Md. 1917. pp. 142—163; 261—275; 324—347; Vol. XIII. 1918. pp. 28—53; 227—248.* [5526

Objectors to the movement for national independence in 1776, *[in Hartford Co., Md.]. In: The Mennonite Year Book*

Washington County marriages 1777—1804. *In: Maryland records, colonial, revolutionary, county and church from original sources by Gajus Marcus Brumbaugh. Vol. II. Baltimore, Md. 1928. pp. 522 —534.* [5528

Allegany County

Lowdermilk, Will. H.: History of Cumberland, (Md.) from the time of the Indian town, Caiuctucuc, in 1728, up to the present day, *embracing an account of Washington's first campaign and battle of Fort Necessity, together with a history of Braddock's expedition &c. Washington, D. C.: James Anglim 1878. pp. 496, LVIII, ill., maps.* [5529

Thomas James W. and **Williams T. J. C.:** History of Allegany County, Md., *including its aboriginal history; the colonial and revolutionary period; its settlement by the white race and subsequent growth; a description of its valuable mining, industrial and agricultural interests; master spirits; character sketches of founders, military and professional men, etc. 2 vols. . . . : L. R. Titsworth & Co. 1923. pp. VII, 696, ill.; 699—1290, ill.* [5530 *and Almanac for 1919. Quakertown, Pa. 1919. pp. 234.* [5527

Washington, D. C.

Bender, Gustav: Die ersten Deutschen im District Columbia. *In: Das Buch der Deutschen in Amerika. Philadelphia, Pa. 1909 [= Nr. 59]. S. 187—189.* [5531

Domer S. and **Alden, L. D.:** 1843—1893. History of St. Paul's English Lutheran Church, *and of the work of the church and Sunday school for the Semi-Centennial year, including additional reports to June 30, 1893, with a synopsis of the Semi-Centennial services of the church and Sunday-school, April 6 and 17, 1893. Compiled and edited by . . . Published by the congregation. Washington, D. C.: McGill & Wallace Press 1893. pp. 271.* [5532

Waring, Luther Hess: History of the Evangelical Lutheran Church of Georgetown,

D. C., Wisconsin Ave. & Volta Place, N. W. Washinton, District of Columbia 1769—1909. *Prepared for the 140th anniversary. October 31, 1909. Washington, D. C.: Press of Byron & Adams 1909. pp. 28, ill.* [5533

1849 Ebenezer 1889. Forty years pastorate. Anniversary celebration Luther Place Memorial Church. Nov. 24 — Dec. 1, 1889. *Published by the vestry. Washington, D. C.: E. Beresford 1889. pp. 30, ill.* [5534

Historical sketch of Luther Place Memorial Church, 1873—1923, golden jubilee, April 8th to 15th, 1923. *Compiled by the Historical Committee of the Golden Jubilee Committee. Published by the Congregation. [s. l.] 1923. pp. 32. ill.* 5535

Die Ausbreitung der Deutschpennsylvanier nach dem Süden

The Pennsylvania-German Expansion to the South

Virginia und Westvirginien

Virginia and West Virginia

Geschichte von Virginia und Westvirginien, allgemein

History of Virginia and Westvirginia, general

Amber, Charles Henry: Sectionalism in Virginia from 1776 to 1861. *Chicago, Ill.: The University of Chicago Press 1910. pp. IX, 366, maps.* [5536

Atkinson, Geo. W. and Gibbens, Alvaro F.: Prominent men of West Virginia. *Biographical sketches of representative men in every honorable vocation, including politics, the law, theology, medicine, education, finance, journalism, trade, commerce and agriculture . . . Wheeling, W. Va.: W. L. Gallin 1890. pp. XIV, 7—1022, ill.* [5537

Bruce, Alexander Philip: Virginia, rebirth of the old Dominion. *5 vols. Chicago, Ill. and New York, N. Y.: The Lewis Publishing Co. 1929. pp. LIII, 524, ill.; pp. 7—534, ill.; vol. III—V. Virginia biography by special staff writers. pp. 532, ill.; pp. 513, ill.; pp. 498, ill. [„Westward movements-German and] Scotch-Irish." In: Vol. I. Chapter II. pp. 324ff.]* [5538

Kemper, Chas. E.: The early westward movement of Virginia, 1722—1734. *As shown by the proceedings of the colonial council. Edited and annotated by . . . In: The Virginia Magazine of History and Biography. Vol. XII. Richmond, Va. 1904—1905. pp. 337—352; Vol. XIII. 1905—1906. pp. 1—16; 113—138; 281 —297; 351—374.* [5539

Koontz, Louis K.: The Virginia frontiers, 1754—1763. *Baltimore, Md.: The Johns Hopkins Press. 1925. pp. IX, 11—186. = Johns Hopkins University Studies in Historical and Political Science. Series XLIII, no. 2.* [5540

Martin, Joseph: A new and comprehensive gazetteer of Virginia and the District of Columbia: . . . *to which is added a history of Virginia from its first settlement to the year 1754 . . . Charlottesville, Va.: Published by Joseph Martin; Moseley & Tompkins Printers. 1835. pp. 636, map.* [5541

Tyler, Lyon Gardiner: Encyclopedia of Virginia biography. *Under the editorial supervision of . . . 5 vols. New York, N.Y.: Lewis Historical Publishing Co. 1915. pp. 387, ill.; pp. 376, ill.; pp. 389, ill.; pp. 560. ill.; pp. (1), 561—1144, ill.* [5542

Bruce, Philip Alexander and Tyler, Lyon Gardiner: History of Virginia. *6 vols. Chicago, Ill. and New York, N. Y.: The American Historical Society 1924. Vol. I.: Colonial period 1607—1763, by Philip Alexander Bruce. pp. LXXI, 424, ill., maps; Vol. II: The federal period, 1763—1861, by Lyon Gardiner Tyler. pp. (1), 7—542, ill.; Vol. III. Virginia since 1861. pp. (1), 7—421; Vol. IV—VI. Virginia biography, by special staff of writers. pp. 580, ill.; pp. 568, ill.; pp. 649, ill.* [5543

Key to inscriptions on Virginia highway markers. *Published by the State Commission on Conservation and Development. Richmond, Va.: Division of Purchase and Printing 1930. pp. 125, map.* [5544

The Virginia highway historical markers. *The tourist guide book of Virginia featuring the inscriptions on the official markers along the historic and romantic highways of the mother state. First issue — May, 1930. Strasburg, Va.: Shenandoah Publishing House, Inc. 1930. pp. 224. ill.* [5545

Virginia. *Published by the Department of Agriculture and Immigration of the State*

*of Virginia. Compiled under the direction
of George W. Koiner, Commissioner.
Richmond, Va.: Davis Bottom, Superintendent of Public Printing 1926. pp.
240, ill.* [5546
Virginia farm statistics. 1923. *Compiled
jointly by the United States Department
of Agriculture, Bureau of Agricultural
Economics and Virginia Department of
Agriculture Division of Agricultural
Statistics. Richmond, Va.: Davis Bottom,
Superintendent Public Printing 1924.
pp. 108, ill., maps. Annually ff.* [5547

Shenandoah Tal, allgemein
Shenandoah Valley, general

Chalkley, Lyman: Before the dates of the
wilderness road. *The settlement of
southwestern Virginia. In: The Virginia
Magazine of History and Biography.
Vol. XXX. Richmond, Va. 1922. pp.
183—202.* [5548
Gordon, Armistead C.: In the picturesque
Shenandoah Valley. *With an intro-
duction by Philip Alexander Bruce.
Richmond, Va.: Garrett & Massie, Inc.
1930. pp. XIX, 201, ill.* [5549
Gray, R. L.: The wonderful Shenandoah
Valley. *[Staunton, Va. 1932.] pp. 307,
ill.* [5550
Hays, Kizzie: Glimpses of pioneer life in the
Shenandoah Valley. *In: The Penn Ger-
mania. Vol. I. = Old series, vol. XIII.
Lititz, Pa. 1912. pp. 695—696.* [5551
Kercheval, Samuel: A history of the Valley
of Virginia. *Winchester, Va.: Samuel
H. Davis 1833. pp. XLVI, 47—486.
Second edition. Revised and extended.
Woodstock, Va.: John Gatewood 1850.
pp. XXVIII, 29—347; Third edition.
Revised and extended. Woodstock, Va.:
W. N. Grabill 1902. pp. XXX, 31—403.* [5552
Kemper, Charles E.: Valley of Virginia
notes. *Contributed by . . . In: The Virginia Magazine of History and Bio-
graphy. Vol. XXX. Richmond, Va.
1922. pp. 398—402; Vol. XXXI. 1923.
pp. 245—252.* [5553
— The settlement on the valley. *In: The
Virginia Magazine of History and Biography. Vol. XXX. Richmond, Va. 1922.
pp. 168—182.* [5554
Lewis, Thomas: The Fairfax line. *With
notes and index by John W. Wayland.
New Market, Va.: The Henkel Press
1925. pp. 100, ill.* [5555

Wayland, John W.: A bird's-eye view of the
Shenandoah Valley. *Staunton, Va.:
The McClure Co. 1924. pp. 16, map.* [5556

Deutschpennsylvanier und Deutsche
Pennsylvania Germans and Germans

Bell, Sadie: The church, the state, and the
education in Virginia. *Thesis of Ph. D.
University of Pennsylvania. Philadel-
phia, Pa. 1930. pp. VII—XII, 796.
[The German Protestants. pp. 51—55;
Educational activities and tendencies of
minor Evangelical groups. pp. 572—579.]* [5557
Bente, C. W.: Die deutschen in West-
Virginien. *In: Das Buch der Deutschen
in Amerika. Philadelphia, Pa. 1909
[= Nr. 59]. pp. 190—194.* [5558
Cassell, C. W., Finck, W. J. and **Henkel,
Elon O.:** History of the Lutheran
Church in Virginia and East Tennessee.
*Edited by . . . Published by authority of
the Lutheran Synod of Virginia. Stras-
burg, Va.: Shenandoah House, Inc. 1930.
pp. XVII, 401, ill.* [5559
Ehrenfeld, Charles L.: An historic bible.
*(George Miller's family bible.) In: Notes
and Queries. Edited by W. H. Egle.
First series, part IV. Harrisburg, Pa.
1881. pp. 130—131; Reprint in: First
and second series, vol. I. Harrisburg, Pa.
1894. pp. 452—453.* [5560
Faust, A. B.: „The Germans in Virginia."
*In: The German element in the United
States. By A. B. Faust. Second edition
New York, N. Y. 1927 [= no. 42]. Vol.
I. = Chapter VII. pp. 177—211.* [5561
Finck, William J.: Virginia Lutheranism.
*The factors entering into the making of
the history of the Lutheran Church in
Virginia and East Tennessee. Historical
address delivered at the Centennial celebration of the Evangelical Lutheran Synod
of Virginia, Woodstock, Va., July 24,
1929. In: The Lutheran Church Quarterly
Vol. III. Gettysburg, Pa. 1930. pp. 373
—387.* [5562
Funkhouser, A. P.: The United Brethren
in Christ Virginia Conference. *By A. P.
Funkhouser. Compiled by O. T. Morton. Dayton, Va.: Ruebush-Kieffer Co.
1921. pp. 315.* [5563
Garrison, J. S.: Historical sketch of the
Virginia Classis of the Reformed Church,
1825—1925. *[Harrisburg, Va. 1925.]
pp. 28.* [5564

Gilbert, D. M.: 1776—1876. The Lutheran Church in Virginia. *A historical discourse delivered before the Evangelical Lutheran Synod of Virginia, at its fortyseventh convention, held in Strasburg, Shenandoah County, Va., Aug. 3rd—8th, 1876. Published at the request of the Synod. New Market, Va.: Henkel & Co. 1876. pp. 43; Appendix pp. 16.* [5565
— 1829—1879. The Synod of Virginia, its history and work. *Delivered at Woodstock, Va., Thursday, Aug. 28th, 1879. New Market, Va.: Henkel & Co. 1879. pp. 20.* [5566
— A chapter of colonial Luthero-Episcopal church history. *(An address delivered at the laying of the corner stone of Emanuel Evangelical Lutheran Church, Woodstock, Va., Friday, Aug. 8, 1884.) In: The Quarterly Review of the Evangelical Lutheran Church. New series, vol. XIV. Gettysburg, Pa. 1884. pp. 479—500; Separate reprint: Gettysburg, Pa.: J. E. Wible 1884. pp. 24.* [5567
Hartman, Peter S.: Civil War reminiscenses *In: The Mennonite Quarterly Review. Vol. III. Goshen, Ind. 1929. pp. 203—219.* [5568
Hays, Heber M.: On the German dialect spoken in the Valley of Virginia. *In: Dialect notes. Publication of the American Dialect Society. Vol. III, part IV. New Haven, Conn.: Published by the Society; printed by the Tuttle, Morehouse & Taylor Co. 1908. pp. 263—278. Reprint in: The Pennsylvania-German. Vol. X. Lititz, Pa. 1909. pp. 510—520.* [5569
Heatwole, L. J.: The organization and growth of the Mennonite Church in Virginia. *In: The Mennonite Year Book and Directory. 1905. Scottdale, Pa. 1905. p. 12; p. 15; p. 16.* [5570
— Early settlement of Mennonites in Virginia. *In: The Mennonite Year Book and Directory 1920. Scottdale, Pa. 1920. pp. 6—8.* [5571
Kaufmann, Wm.: Auf alten deutschen Spuren. In Virginia. *In: Deutsch-Amerikanische Geschichtsblätter. Jg. VIII, Nr. 1. Chicago, Ill. 1908. S. 9—15.* [5572
Schuricht, Hermann: Der Anteil der Deutschen an der Kolonisierung Virginiens. *Vortrag gehalten vor dem geselligwissenschaftlichen Verein in New York. In: „Freidenker", vom 3., 10., 17., 24., und*

31. Januar 1897. Abdruck ohne die Anmerkungen des Originals in: Mitteilungen des Deutschen Pionier-Vereins von Philadelphia. Heft 26. [Philadelphia, Pa. 1912.] S. 19—34. Abdruck in: Deutsche Erde. Zeitschrift für Deutschkunde. Herausgegeben von Paul Langhans. Jg. XII. Gotha 1913. S. 141—150. [5573
Schuricht, Hermann: History of the German element in Virginia. *Contributed by the author as a corresponding member of, and published by the Society for the History of the Germans in Maryland. 2 vols. Baltimore, Md.: Theo Kroh & Sons. 1898/1900. pp. 160, VIII; 239, V. Issued as appendices to the Annual Report of the Society for the History of the Germans in Maryland. Vol. I. in eleventh and twelfth Reports for 97—1898; vol. II. in thirteenth and fourteenth Reports for 1899—1900.* [5574
— Anglicized and corrupted German names in Virginia. *Compiled by . . . In: The Pennsylvania-German. Vol. XII. Lititz, Pa. 1911. pp. 305—306.* [5575
Stöver, Johann Caspar: Kurtze Nachricht von einer Evangelisch-Lutherischen Deutschen Gemeinde in dem Americanischen Virginien, und zwar an den eußersten Grentzen des Ammts Spotsilvanien wohnend, *aufgesetzet von Johann Caspar Stöver, ersterern Prediger dieser Gemeinde. Hannover, gedruckt bey L. C. Holwein. 1737. 4 S.* [5575a
Strickler, Ann V.: Colony west of the Blue Ridge proposed by Jacob Stauber and others, 1731, etc. *Some additional documents. Contributed and edited by . . . In: The Virginia Magazine of History and Biography. Vol. XXXV. Richmond, Va. 1927. pp. 175—190; Vol. XXXVI. 1928. pp. 54—70.* [5576
Wayland, John Walter: The Germans in the Valley. *In: The Virginia Magazine of History and Biography. Vol. IX. Richmond, Va. 1901—1902. pp. 337—352; Vol. X. 1902—1903. pp. 33—48; 113—130.* [5577
— The Germans in Virginia. An appeal. *In: The Virginia Magazine of History and Biography. Vol. X. Richmond, Va. 1902—1903. pp. 210—211.* [5578
— The German element of the Shenandoah Valley of Virginia. *Charlottesville, Va: The Michie Co. 1907. pp. XI, 272.* [5579

Wayland, John Walter: Index to: The German element of the Shenandoah Valley of Virginia. *[= no. 5578]* *Charlottesville, Va. 1908. pp. 273—312.* [5580
— The Pennsylvania-German in the Valley of Virginia. *In: The Pennsylvania-German. Vol. X. Lititz, Pa. 1909. pp. 1—5.* [5581
Zigler, D. H.: History of the Brethren in Virginia. *Elgin, Ill.: Brethren Publishing House 1908. pp. XVI, 278, ill., map. Second edition. Elgin, Ill. 1914. pp. XVI, 17—340, ill., map.* [5582
Experience of Mennonite settlers in Virginia. *In: The Mennonite Year Book and Almanac for 1911. Quakertown, Pa. 1911. p. 18.* [5583
Moravian diaries of travels through Virginia. *Edited by* William J. Hinke *and* Charles E. Kemper. *In: The Virginia Magazine of History and Biography. Vol. XI. 1903—1904. pp. 113—131; 225—242; 370—393; Vol. XII. 1904—1905. pp. 55—82; 134—153; 271—281. [See: Schnell, L.; Gottschalk; Spangenberg; Grube, B. [= nos. 1756 —1758, 1759, 1780—1782, 1785].]* [5584

Loudoun County, Va.

Goodhart, Briscoe: The Pennsylvania Germans in Loudoun County, Virginia. *In: The Pennsylvania-German. Vol. IX. Cleona, Pa. 1908. pp. 125—133, ill.* [5585
— The German settlement. Early history of this interesting section of Loudoun County. *[Va.] Written for the Telephone [Hamilton]. Clippings, Va.: Loudoun Telephone, Jan. 26 and Febr. 2, 1900 [mounted and bound in bookform]. [At Library of Congress, Washington, D. C.]* [5586

Berkeley and Jefferson Counties, W. Va.

Aler, Vernon F.: Aler's history of Martinsburg and Berkeley County, W. Va. *From the origin of the Indians, embracing their settlement of the Valley; also including the wars between the settlers and their mode and manner of living. Besides a variety of valuable information consisting of the past and present history of the county including a complete sketch of the late wars, strikes early residents, origanizations, etc., accompanied by personal sketches and interesting facts of the present day. Hagerstown, Md.: The Mail Publishing Co. 1888. pp. 438.* [5587

Cartmell, Thomas Kemp: Shenandoah Valley, pioneers and their descendants. A history of Frederick County, Va. *From its formation in 1738 to 1908. Compiled mainly from original records of old Frederick County, now Hampshire, Berkeley, Shenandoah, Jefferson, Hardy, Clarke, Warren, Morgan and Frederick. Winchester, Va. Eddy Press 1909. pp. VII, 587, ill.* [5588

Culler, M. L.: A Centennial discourse or historical sketch of the Lutheran congregation of Martinsburg, W. Va., from 1775—1876. *Delivered in the Lutheran Church, June 18th, 1876. Published by and at request of the congregation. Martinsburg, W. Va.: Independent Printing Co. 1876. pp. 20.* [5589

Dandrige, Danske: Historic Shepherdstown. *Charlottesville, Va.: The Michie Co. 1910. pp. VI, 362, map.* [5590

Evans, Willis F.: History of Berkeley County, W. Va. *[Wheeling]: Willis F. Evans 1928. pp. 347.* [5591

Norris, J. E.: History of the Lower Shenandoah Valley counties of Frederick, Berkeley, Jefferson and Clarke, *their early settlement and progress to the present time; genealogical features; a description of their history and interesting localities; cities, towns and villages; portraits of some of the prominent men, and biographies of many of the representative citizens. Edited by . . . Chicago, Ill.: A. Warner & Co. 1890. pp. VIII, 9—812, ill.* [5592

Augusta County, Va.

Catlett, Clay and **Fishburne, Elliott G.:** An economic and social survey of Augusta County. *A laboratory study in the School of Rural Social Economics of the University of Virginia. Charlottesville, Va.: University of Virginia 1928. pp. X, 168, ill. = University of Virginia Record Extension Series. Vol. XII, no. 7. Jan., 1928.* [5593.

Heatwole, L. J.: Early settlers in Virginia. *In: Christian Monitor. A monthly magazine for the home. Vol. XIV, no. 3. Scottdale, Pa. 1922. pp. 466—467.* [5594
— Old settler stories of Virginia. *In: Christian Monitor. A monthly magazine*

*for the home. Vol. XIV, no. 7. Scott-
dale, Pa. 1922. pp. 592—593.* [5595
Kemper, Charles E.: Historical notes from
the records of Augusta County, Va.
*Part I. In: Papers and Addresses of the
Lancaster County Historical Society.
Vol. XXV. Lancaster, Pa. 1921. pp.
89—92. Part II. by Charles E.
Kemper; read by* Charles I. Landis. *In:
Vol. XXV. pp. 147—155.* [5596
Peyton, J. Lewis: History of Augusta
County, Va. *Staunton, Va.: Samuel M.
Yost & Son 1882. pp. VII, 387, (7).*
[5597
Waddell, Jos. A.: Annals of Augusta County, Virginia, *with reminiscences illustrative of the vicissitudes of its pioneer settlers; biographical sketches of citizens lo-
cally prominent, and those who have
found families in the southern and we-
stern states; a diary of the war, 1861—65
and a chapter on reconstruction. Rich-
mond, Va.: Wm. Ellis Jones 1886. pp.
VII, 374, map.*
Annals of Augusta County, Va. Supplement. *Richmond, Va.: J. W. Randolph & English 1888. pp. (2), 381—
460.
Second edition, revised and enlarged:*
Annals of Augusta County Va. from
1726—1871. *Staunton, Va.: C. Russell
Caldwell 1902. pp. X, 545, map.* [5598
Waddell's history of Augusta County, Va.
An additional chapter.
*[Account of manners and customs.] In:
The Virginia Magazine of History and
Biography. Vol. VII. Richmond, Va.
1899/1900. pp. 106—112.* [5599
Waddell, Joseph A.: Indian wars in Augusta
County, Va. — *with: A register of the
persons who have been either killed,
wounded, or taken prisoners by the enemy,
in Augusta County, as also such as have
made their escape. In: The Virginia Ma-
gazine of History and Biography. Vol.
II. Richmond, Va. 1895. pp. 399—404.*
[5600

Frederick County, Va.

Cartmell, Thomas Kemp: Shenandoah Valley, pioneers and their descendants. A
history of Frederick County, Va. From
its formation in 1738 to 1908. *Compiled
mainly from original records of old Frederick County, now Hampshire, Berkeley, Shenandoah, Jefferson, Hardy, Clarke, Warren, Morgan and Frederick. Win-*

*chester, Va. Eddy Press 1909. pp. VII,
587, ill.* [5601
Chalkley, Lyman: Wills in Frederick County, Va. prior to 1805. *Contributed by . . .
In: The Virginia Magazine of History
and Biography. Vol. XVIII. Richmond, Va. 1910. pp. 204—212.* [5602
Greene, Katherine Glass: Winchester, Virginia and its beginnings 1743—1814
*from its founding by Colonel James Wood
to the close of the life of his son, Brigardier-
General and Governor, James Wood, with
the publication for the first time of
valuable manuscripts, relics of their long
tenure of public offices. Strasburg, Va.:
Shenandoah Publishing House. 1926.
pp. 441, ill.* [5603
Gruber, M. A.: Early German settlement of
Winchester, Va. *In: The Pennsylvania-
German. Vol. V. Lebanon, Pa. 1904.
pp. 93—94.* [5604
Morton, Frederic: The story of Winchester
in Virginia, the oldest town in the
Shenandoah Valley. *Strasburg, Va.:
Shenandoah Publishing House 1925.
pp. 336, ill.* [5605
Norris, J. E.: History of the Lower Shenandoah Valley Counties of Frederick,
Berkeley, Jefferson and Clarke, *their
early settlement and progress to the present time; genealogical features; a description of their historic and interesting
localities; cities, towns, villages; portraits of some of the prominent men and
biographies of many of the representative
citizens. Edited by . . . Chicago, Ill.:
A. Warner & Co. 1890. pp. VIII, 9—
812, ill.* [5606
Pickeral, J. Julian and Fogg, Gordon: An economic and social survey of Frederick
County. *A laboratory study in the
School of Rural Social Economics of the
University of Virginia. Charlottesville,
Va.: University of Virginia 1930. pp.
142, ill. map.
=University of Virginia Record Extension Series. Vol. XV, no. 2. August,
1930.* [5607

Page County, Va.

Kemper, Charles E.: Adam Muller (Miller),
first white settler in the Valley of Virginia. *In: The Virginia Magazine of
History and Biography. Vol. X. Richmond, Va. 1902—1903. pp. 84—86* [5608
Strickler, Harry M.: Massanutten settled
by the Pennsylvania pilgrim 1726. The

first white settlement in the Shenan-
doah Valley. *Strasburg, Va.: Shenan-
doah Publishing House 1924. pp. 184,
ill., map.*   [5609
Milbourne, Virginia S.: „History of Page
County, Va." *[In the making].* [5610
Naturalization paper of Adam Miller *[„the
first white settler in the Valley on the
Shenandoah"]. Contributed by* **Lizzie B.
Miller** *in: William Mary College and
Quarterly, vol. IX, no. 2. Williamsburg,
Va., October, 1900.
Reprint in: The Pennsylvania-German.
Vol. ¹IX. Cleona, Pa. 1908. p. 421.*
[5611

Rockingham County, Va.

Braun, Johannes: Circular Schreiben an die
Deutschen Einwohner von Rockingham
und Augusta, und den benachbarten
Counties. *Harrisonburg, Va.: Laurentz
Wartmann 1818. 419 S.*
[Vgl. Nr. 2757]   [5612
Heatwole, Jacob E.: A historical sketch of
the Bank Church, Rockingham County,
Va. *In: The Mennonite Year Book and
Directory 1907. Scottdale, Pa. 1907. p.
28, p. 30.*   [5613
Heatwole, L. J.: A congregation of Menno-
nites *[Weaver's congregation near Har-
risonburg, Rockingham County, Va.]*
that has existed for one hundred years.
*In: The Mennonite Year Book and Direc-
tory. 1927. Scottdale, Pa. 1927. pp. 29—
30.*   [5614
Hinke, William J.- Kemper, Charles E.: Record of the Peaked Mountain Church,
Rockingham County, Va. *In: William
and Mary College Quarterly. Vol. XIII.
Williamsburg, Va. 1905. pp. 247—256;
Vol. XIV. 1905/06. pp. 9—18, 186—
193.*   [5615
Humbert, Reuben L.: Harrisonburg, Va.
Industrial survey. An economic and
social appraisal . . . *compiled by . . .
under the supervision and direction of the
Industry and Trade Extension Committee
of the Chamber of Commerce. Harrisonburg, Va.: P. & L. Press. First edition, April 23, 1926. pp. 31, ill.; Second
edition, 1926; Third edition, 1928.* [5616
Stirewalt, J. P.: A brief history of Rader's
Lutheran Church near Timberville, Va.
*(Rockingham Co.) from May 20, 1765 to
April 11, 1921. New Market, Va.: Henkel & Co's. Lutheran Publication Establishment 1922. pp. 81, ill.*   [5617

Strickler, Harry M.: Old tenth legion marriages. Marriages in Rockingham County, Virgina, from 1778 to 1816. *Taken
from the marriage bonds. Compiled by
. . . Dayton, Va.: Joseph K. Ruebush Co.
1828. pp. (1), 5—128.*   [5618
— Tenth legion tithables. *(Rockingham
Division.)* Rockingham County, Virginia tithables for 1792. *A list of all the
white males above 16 years of age in the
county and all the slaves above 12 in the
county in 1792. Compiled by . . . Luray,
Va.: Published by the author. 1930 pp.
(1), 5—77, map.*   [5619
Wayland, John W.: A history of Rockingham County, Va. *Dayton, Va.: Ruebush — Elkins Co. 1912. pp. (5), VIII,
9—467, (6).*
[Bibliography. pp. 462—467.] [5620
[—] The Germans in Rockingham County,
Va. *(Extracts from: „History of Rockingham County, Va.) By J. W. Wayland.
In: The Penn Germania. New series,
vol. III. = Old series, vol. XV. Cleona,
Pa. 1914. pp. 162—172.*   [5621
— Virginia Valley records. *Genealogical
and historical materials of Rockingham
County, Va. and related regions. Strasburg, Va.: Shenandoah Publishing House
Inc. 1930. pp. (2), 7—491, map.* [5622
Weaver, H. D.: Weavers Mennonite Church,
near Harrisonburg, Va. *In: Christian
Monitor. A monthly magazine for the
home. Vol. XXIV, no. 10. Scottdale, Pa.
1932. pp. 302—303, ill.*   [5623

Rockbridge County, Va.

Morton, Oren F.: A history of Rockbridge
County, Va. *Staunton, Va.: The Mc-
Clure Co., Inc. 1920. pp. (6), 574, ill.*
[5624

Shenandoah County, Va.

Duttera, W. B. and others: Historical souvenir. 200th anniversary Reformed
Church in the United States, and 100th
anniversary Virginia Classis. *With report Mill Creek charge in the shadow of the
Shenandoah National Park, Mt. Jackson,
Va., Shenandoah County, region of the
famous caverns. Mt. Jackson. Va.: Published by W. B. Duttera 1925, pp. 52.* [5625
Wayland, John W.: A history of Shenandoah County, Va. *Strasburg, Va.:
Shenandoah Publishing House 1927. pp.
874, ill., maps.*
[Bibliography. pp. 773—776.] [5626

Grafschaften des Westens und Südwestens:
Western and southwestern counties:

Bath County, Va.

Morton, Oren F.: Annals of Bath County, Va. *Staunton, Va.: The McClure Co., Inc. 1917. pp. VI, 208, map.* [5627

Highland County, W. Va.

Morton, Oren F.: A history of Highland County, Va. *Monterey, Va.: Published by the author; Roanoke, Va.: Stone Printing and Manufacturing Co. 1911. pp. 419, ill., maps.* [5628
— A handbook of Highland County and supplement to Pendleton and Highland history. *Monterey, Va.: The Highland Recorder 1922. pp. (2), 109, ill.* [5629

Pendleton County, W. Va.

Morton, Oren F.: A history of Pendleton County, W. Va. *Franklin, W. Va.: Published by the author; Dayton, Va.: Ruebush — Elkins Co. 1910. pp. VII, 493.* [5630

Botetourt County, Va.

Painter, F. V. N.: The Lutheran Church in Botetourt County, Va. *Together with a brief note of the Lutheran Church in general. Published by the council. Salem, Va.: Conservative Book and Job Print 1877. pp. 56.* [5631

Floyd County, Va.

Humbert, R. L.: Industrial survey, Floyd County, Virginia. *By . . ., in collaboration with others. Blacksburg, Va.: Engineering Extension Division, Virginia Polytechnic Institute. May, 1930. pp. 55, ill., map.* [5632

Montgomery County, Va.

Humbert, R. L.: Industrial survey, Montgomery County and City of Radford, Virginia. *By . . ., in collaboration with others . . . Blacksburg, Va.: Engineering Extension Division, Virginia Polytechnic Institute. April, 1929. pp. 91, ill., map.* [5633

Pulaski County, Va.

Heavener, U. S. A.: German New River settlement — Virginia. *[s. l. 1929.] pp. 75, ill.* [5634

Humbert, R. L.: Industrial survey, Pulaski County, Virginia. *By . . ., in collaboration with others . . . Blacksburg, Va.: Engineering Extension Division, Virginia, Polytechnic Institute. October, 1929. pp. 74, ill., map.* [5635
Johnston, David E.: A history of Middle New River settlements and contiguous territory. *Huntington, W. Va.: Standard Printing and Publishing Co. 1906. pp. (3), 7—500, XXXI.* [5636

Roanoke County, Va.

Humbert, R. L.: Industrial survey, Roanoke County, Virginia. *By . . ., in collaboration with others . . . Blacksburg, Va.: Engineering Extension Division, Virginia, Polytechnic Institute. October, 1929. pp. 70, ill., map.* [5637
Jack, George S. and **Jacobs, E. B.:** History of Roanoke County. *By George S. Jack.* — History of Roanoke City and history of the Norfolk & Western Railway Company. *By E. B. Jacobs. Roanoke. Va.: Stone 1912. pp. 255, ill.* [5638
McGauley, William: History of Roanoke County, Salem, Roanoke City, Va. and representative citizens. *Edited and compiled by . . . 1734—1900. Chicago, Ill.: Published by Biographical Publishing Co. 1902. pp. 560, ill., map.* [5639
Vernon, J. J. and **Richards, H. I.:** The agricultural situation in Roanoke and its trade territory, *with special reference to the adjustment of agricultural production and distribution in Roanoke's trade territory to meet home market demands. Blacksburg, Va. 1925. pp. 70, ill., maps. = Bulletin 240 (March 1925) of the Virginia Polytechnic Institute, Virginia Agricultural Experiment Station, Blacksburg, Va.* [5640

Tazwell County Va.

Harman, John Newton: Annals of Tazwell County, Va. from 1800 to 1922, (1924). *2 vols. Richmond, Va.: W. C. Hill Printing Co. 1922, 1924. Vol. I. in 2 parts: Part I. containing records of courts etc., from 1800 to 1852; Part II: containing a republication of Bickley's history of the ,,Settlement and Indian wars of Tazwell County" published 1852. Rich-*

mond, Va. 1922. pp. 467; Vol. II. 1853
—1924. Richmond, Va. 1925. pp. 653.
[5641

Pendleton, Wm. C.: History of Tazwell
County and Southwest Virginia 1748—
1920. Richmond, Va.: W. C. Hill
Printing Co. 1920. pp. XVI, 3—700,
ill.   [5642

Wythe County, Va.

Humbert, R. L.: Industrial survey, Wythe
County, Virginia. By . . ., in collaboration with others . . . Blacksburg, Va.:
Engineering Extension Division, Virginia Polytechnic Institute. August,
1929; Reprint 1930. pp. 72, ill., map.
[5643

Nordkarolina

North Carolina

Geschichte von Nordkarolina, allgemein

History of North Carolina, general

North Carolina, State of: The colonial records of North Carolina. Published under supervision of the Trustees of the Public Libraries, by order of the General
Assembly. Collected and edited by William L. Saunders. Vol. I: 1662—1712;
Vol. II: 1713—1790; [Vols. III—X;
XI—XXVI; XXVII—XXX.] Ra-
leigh, U. C.: P. M. Hale, Printer of the
State [differently: Winston, Goldsboro,
Charlotte — Raleigh: E. M. Uzell & Co]
1886 [—1914]. Since vol. XI.: The
state records (1776—1790). Collected
and edited by Walter Clark; Vol. XXVII
—XXX. Index to the colonial and state
records of North Carolina, covering vol.
I—XXV. Compiled and edited by Ste-
phen B. Weeks.   [5644
Arthur, John Preston: Western North Ca-
rolina. A history (from 1730 to 1913).
Published by the Edward Buncombe
Chapter of the Daughters of the American
Revolution of Asheville, N. C. Raleigh,
N. C.: Edwards & Broughton Printing
Co. 1914. pp. 5—710, ill.   [5645
Ashe, Samuel A.: Biographical history of
North Carolina. From colonial times
to the present. Editor-in-chief . . . 8 vols.
Greensboro, N. C.: Charles L. Van Nop-
pen 1905—1917.   [5646
Clemens, William Montgomery: North and
South Carolina marriage records from
the earliest colonial days to the Civil
War. Compiled and edited by . . . New
York, N. Y.: E. P. Dutton & Co. 1927.
pp. X, 295.   [5647
Connor, R. D. W., Boyd, William K. and
Hamilton J. G. de Roulhac: History of
North Carolina. 6 vols. Chicago, Ill.
and New York, N. Y.: The Lewis Pub-

lishing Co. 1919. Vol. I.: The colonial
and revolutionary periods 1584—1783.
By R. D. W. Connor. pp. IX, 519,
ill.; Vol. II.: The federal period 1783—
1860. By William K. Boyd. pp.
VIII, 407, ill.; Vol. III. North Caro-
lina since 1860. By J. G. de Roulhac
Hamilton. pp. VIII, 434, ill.; Vol.
IV—VI: North Carolina biography by
special staff of writers. pp. 400, ill.;
405, ill.   [5648
Connor, R. D. W.: Race elements in the
white population of North Carolina.
Raleigh, N. C.: Edwards & Broughton
Printing Co. 1920. pp. 115.
= North Carolina State Normal & In-
dustrial College. Historical Publications.
No. 1.   [5649
— North Carolina. Rebuilding an ancient
commonwealth. 1584—1925. Issued in
4 vols. Chicago, Ill. and New York,
N. Y.: The American Historical Society,
Inc. 1928—1929. pp. LXI, 613, ill.;
pp. 7—698, ill.; vol. III and IV: Bio-
graphies. pp. 559, ill.; pp. 635, ill.
[5650
Franklin, W. Neil: Agriculture in colonial
North-Carolina. In: North Carolina
Historical Review. Issued quarterly. Vol.
III, no. 4. Raleigh, N. C. 1926. pp.
538—574.   [5651
Grimes, J. Bryan: Abstract of North Carolina wills compiled from original and recorded wills in the office of the secretary
of state. Published under the authority
of the Trustees of the Public Libraries.
Raleigh, N. C.: E. M. Uzell & Co. 1910.
pp. VII, 670.   [5652
Hobbs, Samuel Huntington: North Caro-
lina, economic and social. Chapel Hill,
N. C.: The University of North Carolina
Press 1930. pp. XVIII. 403.   [5653

Pittnam, Thomas M.: Industrial life in colonial Carolina. *In: The North Carolina Booklet. Vol. VII, no. 1. 1907. Raleigh. N. C. 1907. pp. 50—58.* [5654

Wheeler, John H.: Historical sketches of North Carolina, from 1548 to 1851. *Compiled from original records, official documents, and traditional statements. With biographical sketches of her distinguished statesmen, jurists, lawyers, soldiers, divines, etc. 2 vols. Philadelphia, Pa.: Lippincott, Grambo and Co. 1851. pp. XXII, 23—138; 480; ... A reprint of the original edition as written in 1851 by Col. John H. Wheeler with a foreward by Magnolia McKay Shuford. New York, N. Y.: Frederick H. Hitchcock 1925. pp. 19; XII, 23—138; 480.* [5655

— Reminiscences and memoirs of North Carolina and eminent North Carolinians. *Columbus, O.: Columbus Printing Works 1884. pp. 478.* [5656

Western North Carolina. Historical and biographical. *Charlotte, N. C.: A. D. Smith & Co.; Raleigh, N. C.: Edwards & Broughton, Printers 1890. pp. 465, ill.* [5657

Clark, Walter: Indian Massacre and Tuscarora War 1711—'13. *Raleigh N. C.. Capital Printing Co. 1902. pp. 16. = North Carolina Booklet. Vol. II, no. 4.* [5658

Rand, James Hall: The Indians of North Carolina and their relations with the settlers. *Chapel Hill, N. C.: Published by the University; Durham, N. C.: The Seeman Printery 1913. pp. 41. = The University of North Carolina: The James Sprunt Historical Publications. Published under the direction of the North Carolina Historical Society. Vol. XII, no. 2.* [5659

[Kocherthal, Joshua]: Ausführlich- und umständlicher Bericht von der berühmten Landschaft Carolina in dem Engelländischen America gelegen. *An Tag gegeben von ... Vierter Druck. Mit Anhängen zweyer Engelischen Authoren gethanen Beschreibung, und eines auff der Reyse dahin begriffenen Hochteutschen auss London. Benachrichtigung; Nebst einer Land-Carte von Carolina vermehrt. Frankfurt am Mayn: Georg Heinrich Oehrling 1709. 80 S.* [5660

Lawson, John: The history of Carolina, *containing the exact description and natural history of that country; together with the present state thereof, and a journal of a thousand miles, travel'd thro' several nations of Indians giving a particular account of their customs, manners, etc. London: Printed for T. Warner 1718. pp. (4), 258, ill.* [5661

[Lawson, John]: Allerneueste Beschreibung der Provintz Carolina in West Indien. *Samt einem Reise-Journal von mehr als Tausend Meilen unter allerhand Indianischen Reisen. Auch einer accuraten Land-Carte und andere Kupfer Stichen. Aus dem Englischen übersetzt durch* **M. Visher.** *Hamburg: Gedruckt und verlegt durch seel. Thomas von Wierings Erben ... Anno 1712. (7), 365, (3), S., ill., Karte.* [5662

Ochs, Joh. Rudolff: Amerikanischer Wegweiser oder kurtze und eigentliche Beschreibung der englischen Provintzen in Nord-Amerika, sonderlich aber der Landschafft Carolina, *mit großem Fleiß zusammen getragen und an den Tag gegeben durch ... neben einer neuen und correcten Land-Karten von Nord- und Süd Carolina. Bern ... 1711. ...* [5663

Deutschpennsylvanier

Pennsylvania Germans

Allen, Oliver H.: The German Palatines in North Carolina. *In: The North Carolina Booklet. Vol. IV, no. 12. 1905. Raleigh, N. C. 1905. pp. 9—27.* [5664

Bassett, John Spencer: Anti-Slavery leaders of North Carolina. *Baltimore, Md.: The Johns Hopkins Press 1898. pp. 74. = John Hopkins University Studies in Historical and Political Science. Series XVI, no. 6. [Includes sketches of Hinton Rowan Helper. pp. 11—29; of Benjanim Sherwood Hedrick. pp. 29—47.]* [5665

Bender, H. S.: Mennonites in North Carolina. *In: The Mennonite Quarterly Review. Vol. I. no. 3. Goshen, Ind., July, 1927. pp. 69—71.* [5666

Bernheim, G. D.: History of the German settlements and of the Lutheran Church in North and South Carolina from the earliest period of the colonization of the Dutch, German and Swiss settlers to the close of the first half of the present century. *Philadelphia, Pa.: The Lutheran Book Store 1872. pp. XVI, 25 —557.* [5667

[**Bernheim, G. D.**]: Early Lutheran settlements in North Carolina. *Condensed from Rev.G.D. Bernheim's History of the Lutheran churches in the Carolinas. In: The colonial records of North Carolina, published under the supervision of the Trustees of the Public Libraries, by order of the General Assembly. Collected and edited by William L. Saunders. Vol. VIII. 1769 to 1771. Raleigh, N. C. 1890 [= no. 5644]. pp. 758—796.* [5668

— The first twenty years of the history of St. Paul's Evangelical Lutheran Church, Wilmington, N. C. *Wilmington, N. C.: S. G. Hall 1879. pp 71.* [5669

— - **Cox, George H.**: The history of the Evangelical Lutheran Synod and Ministerium of North Carolina *in commemoration of the completion of the first century of its existence. Philadelphia, Pa.: Published for the Synod by the Lutheran Publication Society 1902. pp. VIII, 9 —189, ill.* [5670

Boyd, William K. and **Krummel, Charles A.**: German tracts concerning the Lutheran Church in North Carolina during the eighteenth century. *In: The North Carolina Historical Review. Vol. VII. Raleigh, N. C. 1930. pp. 79—147; 225 —282.* [5671

Bruncken, Ernest: Das deutsche Element in Nord Carolina. *In: Deutsch-Amerikanische Geschichtsblätter. Jg. V. Heft 4. Chicago, Ill. 1905. S. 71.* [5672

Ch[eshire], J. B.: *I.* White Haven parish; *II.* Robert Johnston Miller; *III.* Fraternal relations: The Diocesan Convention and the Lutheran Synod. *[s. l.] 1885. pp. 39.* [5673

[**Clapp, Jacob C.** and **Leonard, J. C.**]: Historic sketch of the Reformed Church in North Carolina. *By a board of editors under the Classis of North Carolina. Edited by . . . With an introduction by the late* **Geo. Wm. Welker**. *Philadelphia, Pa.: Publication Board of the Reformed Church in the United States 1908. pp. 327, ill.* [5674

Connor, R. D. W.: Program of exercises for North Carolina Day. (The settlements of the Germans) Friday, December 18, 1908. *Compiled by . . . Raleigh, N. C.: Issued from the Office of the State Superintendent of Public Instruction 1908. pp. 95.* [5675

— „The Germans in North Carolina." *In: Race elements in the white population of North Carolina. Raleigh, N. C. 1920*

[= no. 5649]. Chapter V. pp. 91—111. [5676

Cox, Geo. H.: The beginnings of the Lutheran Church in North Carolina. *Delivered at the 120th annual convention of the United Evangelical Lutheran Synod of North Carolina. [s. l.]: Published by the Synod. pp. 12.* [5677

Gehrke, William H.: The beginnings of the Pennsylvania-German element in Rowan and Cabarrus counties, North Carolina. *In: The Pennsylvania Magazine of History and Biography. Vol. LVIII. Philadelphia, Pa. 1934. pp. 342 —369.* [5678

— The transition from the German to the English language in North Carolina. *In: The North Carolina Historical Review. Vol. XII. Boston, Mass. 1935. pp. 1—19.* [5679

Leonard, J. C.: The Germans in North Carolina. *Address. Reprint from the Dispatch of Lexington, N. C. In: The Pennsylvania-German. Vol. X. Lititz, Pa. 1909. pp. 266—272.* [5680

[—] Deutsche Familien Namen in Nord Carolina, u. A. *[entnommen einem im „The Pennsylvania-German", Juni 1909 veröffentlichten Artikel von C. J. Leonard). Jn: Deutsch-Amerikanische Geschichtsblätter. Jg. IX, Nr. 3. Chicago, Ill. 1909. S. 98—100.* [5681

Lohr, L. L.: The Germans in North Carolina west of the Catawba. *In: The Pennsylvania-German. Vol. XII. Lititz, Pa. 1911. pp. 206—211.* [5682

Mannhardt, Emil: Die deutsche Einwanderung in Nord-Carolina und ihre Nachkommen. *In: Deutsch-Amerikanische Geschichtsblätter. Jg. V, Heft 1. Chicago, Ill. 1905. S. 2—17.* [5683

Nash, Francis: The history of Orange County. *Part I. In: The North Carolina Booklet. Vol. X, no. 2. Raleigh, N. C. 1910. pp. 55—113.* [5684

[**Shober, Gottlieb**]: A comprehensive account of the rise and progress of the blessed Reformation of the Christian Church. *By Doctor Luther: Began on the thirty-first of October, A. D. 1517. Interspersed with views of his character and doctrine extracted from his books; And how the church, established by him, arrived and progressed in North America — as also the constitution and rules of that church, in North Carolina and adjoining states, as existing in October, 1817. Printed for the German* and *English Synod of North Carolina and adjoining states. Baltimore, Md.: Schaeffer & Maund 1818. pp. XII, 213.* [5685

Snyder, W. A. and Schultz, G. J.: An historical sketch of St. Paul's Evangelical Lutheran congregation, Wilmington, N. C. *By W. A. Snyder, assisted by G. J. Schultz. Published by the fiftieth anniversary committee [1908.] pp. 49.* [5686

[Storch, . . .]: Merkwürdige Vorfälle. Auszüge aus Briefen usw. Aus einem am 25. Februar 1796 geschriebenen Briefe des Hrn. Storch, deutschen Predigers in Nord-Carolina, an Hrn. Generalsuperintendenten Velthusen in Stade. *In: Amerikanisches Magazin oder authentische Beiträge zur Erdbeschreibung, Staatskunde und Geschichte von Amerika, besonders aber der vereinten Staaten. Herausgegeben von Hegewisch-Kiel und Ebeling-Kiel. Hamburg: Carl Ernst Bohn 1796. S. 176—179.* [5686a

Velthusen, Johann Caspar: Rede und Gebet bey Einsegnung Herrn Carl August Gottlieb Storch zum evangelischen Gehülfsprediger für Nordcarolina. *Leipzig: S. L. Crusius 1788. 24 S.* [5687

— Nachricht von der evangelischen Kirchenverfassung in Nordcarolina. *Helmstadt 1786. . . S.* [5688

— Nordcarolinische Kirchennachrichten, *herausgegeben von . . . Erstes Heft Leipzig: Siegried Lebrecht Crusius 1790. 44 S.; Zweytes und letztes Heft. (Hierzu zugleich die Anzeige des Rechnungsabschlusses) Stade: gedruckt bey Heinrich Andreas Friederich 1792, 664 S.* [5689

[—] Briefe aus Nord Carolina. *Abdruck von: „Nordcarolinische Kirchennachrichten, herausgegeben von Johann Caspar Velthusen, Herzgl. Mecklenb. Oberkirchenrath und öffentl. Lehrer der Theol. zu Rostock. Erstes Heft." Leipzig 1790. In: Der Deutsche Pionier. Jg. XIII. Cincinnati, O. 1881—1882. S. 311—317; 352—359.* [5690

Wagener, I. A.: Die Deutschen in Nord Carolina. *In: Der Deutsche Pionier. Jg. III. Cincinnati, O. 1872—1873. S. 42—45; 91—95.* [5691

Welker, G. William: „Early German Reformed settlements in North Carolina." *In: The Colonial records of North Carolina, published under the supervision of the Trustees of the Public Libraries, by order of the General Assembly. Collected and edited by* **William L. Saunders.** *Vol. VIII. 1769—1771. Raleigh, N. C.: Josephius Daniels 1890 [= no. 5644]. pp. 727—757.* [5692

[Welker, G. William]: A historical sketch of the Classis of North Carolina *by the late G. W. Welker with notes and introduction by* **Joseph L. Murphy.** *Hickory, N. C.: A. L. Crouse 1895. pp. 35.* [5693

Whitsett, William Thornton: Landmarks and pioneers. *[Extracts from an address delivered at St. Paul's Lutheran Church, near Burlington, N. C., at the historical celebration, Sunday, August 16, 1925.] Whitsett, N. C.: Publishers „Saber and Song" 1925. pp. 8.* = *Whitsett Historical Monographs. No. 1.* [5694

— Founders of church and state. *(Extracts from the historical address delivered before the Eastern Conference of the United Lutheran Synod of North Carolina, Sept., 2, 1925, at Melanchthon Church, Liberty, N. C.) Whitsett, N. C.: Publishers „Saber and Song" 1926. pp. 14.* = *Whitsett Historical Monographs. No. 3.* [5695

Alamance County, N. C.

Whitsett, William Thornton: A brief history of Alamance County, N. C. with sketches of the Whitsell family and the Huffman family. *Burlington, N. C.: A. D. Pate & Co., Printers 1926. pp. 32, ill.* = *Whitsett Historical Monographs. No. 4.* [5696

Cabarrus County, N. C.

Barringer, Rufus: Early German settlers in eastern Cabarrus County. *An address of . . . delivered at the Lutheran commemoration in Concord, N. C., November 10, 1883. In: Wheeler, John H.: Reminiscences and Memoirs of North Carolina and eminent North Carolinians. Columbus, O.: Columbus Printing Works 1884. pp. XXXIX—XLVIII; also in: The University Monthly [N. C. University Magazine]. Vol. IV. 1884. pp. 275—289.* [5697

Gehrke, William H.: The beginnings of the Pennsylvania-German element in Rowan and Cabarrus counties, North Carolina. *In: The Pennsylvania Magazine of History and Biography. Vol. LVIII. Philadelphia, Pa. 1934. pp. 342—369.* [5698

Steffey, Sidney: A brief history of St. John's Evangelical Lutheran Church of Cabarrus County, N. C. from its earliest settlement to the present time. *Concord, N. C.: The Times Steam Book and Job Presses 1899. pp. 69.* [5699

Catawba County, N. C.

Allen, Frank Field: Catawba County, N. C. *Some of its economic conditions and problems. Thesis of M. A., University of North Carolina. Chapel Hill, N. C. 1917. Typewritten. pp. (2), 69.* [5700
Hahn, Geo. W.: The Catawba soldier of the Civil War. *A sketch of every soldier from Catawba County, N. C., with the photograph, biographical sketch, and reminiscence of many of them, together with a sketch of Catawba County from 1860 to 1911 — a complete history of these valiant men, in war and peace. Edited and compiled . . . Hickory, N. C.: Clay Printing Co. 1911. pp. 385, ill.* [5701
Johnson, J. M. and **Strait, E. D.:** Farm management in Catawba County, N. C. *Washington, D. C., July, 1922. pp. 23. = United States Department of Agriculture Bulletin. No. 1070.* [5702
Murphy, J. L.: Henry Weidner, his life and character. A memorial-service held at J. W. Robinson's May 30, 1894. *Dedicated to the descendants of Henry Weidner. Hickory, N. C.: Published by Hickory Printing Co., Publishers of Press and Corolinian. 1895. pp. 22.* [5703
Shuford, Richard Harvey: Co-operative institutions among the farmers of Catawba County. *In: The University of North Carolina Record. Durham, N. C.: The Seeman Printery 1914. pp. 3—15; also separate. = Extension series, no. 8.* [5704
Smith, Carroll O.: St. John's Church in Catawba Co., N. C. *One hundred and twenty-five years old. In: Theological monthly. Published by the Evangelical Lutheran Synod of Missouri, Ohio, and other states. Vol. V. St. Louis, Mo.: Concordia Publishing House 1925. pp. 105—110; 136—141; 168—173.* [5705
Whitener, Russel W.: The growth and development of education in Catawba County. *Thesis o M. A., University of North Carolina, Department of Education. Chapel Hill, N. C. 1924. Typewritten. pp. 65, map.* [5706

Yoder, G. M.: First permanent settlement in Catawba County, N. C. *In: The Pennsylvania-German. Vol. XI. Lititz, Pa. 1910. p. 752.* [5707
Survey of Hickory, N. C. *Source book of facts and figures, with supplement covering Catawba County. Prepared by* **Walter J. Matherly, Claudius T. Murchison, Edgar T. Thompson, P. W. Wagner, J. J. Rhyne** and **C. E. Moore** *and published by the Hickory Chamber of Commerce. July 1, 1925. pp. 37, ill. New edition. Sept. 1, 1927. pp. 43, ill.* [5708

Davidson County, N. C.

Leonard, Jacob Calvin: Centennial history of Davidson County, North Carolina. *Raleigh, N. C.: Edwards & Broughton Co. 1927. pp. IX—XVI, 523, ill.* [5709
Sink, M. Jewell: Davidson County: Economic and social. *A laboratory study in the Department of Rural Social-Economics, University of North Carolina. Chapel Hill, N. C., May, 1925. pp. 86 (advertisements) — 99. = Vol. II. County series, no. 3.* [5710

Guilford County, N. C.

Riser, Y. von A.: A sermon and two addresses. *Delivered on Memorial Day, May 5, 1918. Friedens Lutheran Church in Guilford County, North Carolina near Gibsonville. Columbia, S. C.: Lutheran Board of Publication 1918. pp. 36.* [5711
Stockard, Sallie W.: The history of Guilford County, N. C. *Knoxville, Tenn.: Gaut-Ogden Co. 1902. pp. 197, ill.* [5712
Whitsett, William Thornton: History of Brick [Reformed] Church [Guilford Co., N. C.] and the Clapp family. *Greensboro, N. C.: Harrison Printing Co. 1925. pp. 28, ill. = Whitsett Historical Monographs. no. 2.* [5713

Lincoln County, N. C.

Bynum, Curtis: Marriage bonds of Tryon and Lincoln Counties, North Carolina. *Abstracted and indexed. [s. l.] 1929. pp. 184.* [5714
Hoke, W. J.: What Lincoln County did in the late war. *In: Our Living and our Dead; devoted to North Carolina — her past, her present and her future. Official*

organ N. C. branch Southevan Historical Society. Vol. I. Raleigh, N. C.: S. D. Pool, Editor 1874—1875. pp. 429—434. [5715

Nixon, Alfred: History of Daniel's Evangelical Lutheran and Reformed churches, Lincoln Co., N. C. *Hickory, N. C.: A. L. Crouse & Son 1898. pp. 44, ill.* [5716

[—] Roster of the ex-confederate soldiers living in Lincoln County *with the address of A. Nixon delivered before the United Daughters of the Confederacy and Confederate Veterans in Court House, Lincolnton, N. C., on Memorial Day, May 10th, 1907. Lincolnton, N. C.: The Lincoln County News Print 1907. pp. 19.* [5717

— The history of Lincoln County. *In: The North Carolina Booklet. Vol. IX, no. 3. Raleigh, N. C. 1910. pp. 111—178.* [5718

Nixon, Joseph R.: Exercises of Lee and Jackson Day. Lincolnton, N. C., January 23, 1915. *Published by . . . [s. l., s. d.] pp. 15.* [5719

— The German settlers in Lincoln County and western North Carolina. *In: The James Sprunt Historical Publications. Published under the direction of the North Carolina Historical Society. Vol. XI, no. 2. Chapel Hill, N. C.: Published by the University of North Carolina 1912. pp. 25—62.* [5720

[Ramsauer, John]: A rare old diary *[of John Ramsauer of Lincoln Co., N. C.] In: The Penn Germania. Vol. II. = Old series, vol. XIV. Lititz, Pa. 1913. pp. 22—25.* [5721

Randolph County, N. C.

Burgess, Fred: Randolph County: economic and social. *A laboratory study at the University of North Carolina, Department of Rural Social Economics. May, 1924. pp. (1), (1), 9—89, ill.* [5722

Rowan County, N. C.

Bean, Eugene H.: Rowan County (N. C.) records. *Early settlers. Contributed by . . . In: The National Genealogical Society Quarterly. Vol. III, no. 3. Washington, D. C. 1914. pp. 14—22.* [5723

Cox, Geo. H.: History of the Organ Church, Rowan County, N. C., with an account of the Centennial celebration of the first edifice, May 6, 1894. *Newberry,*

S. C.: Aull & Houseal 1894. pp. 46, ill. [5724

Curry, Cora C.: Heidelberg Evangelical Lutheran Church records. (Old Dutch meeting House), Rowan County (now Davie), N. C. *In: National Genealogical Society Quarterly. Vol. XIX. Washington, D. C. 1931. pp. 4—10.* [5725

Gehrke, William H.: The Beginnings of the Pennsylvania-German element in Rowan and Cabarrus counties, North Carolina. *In: The Pennsylvania Magazine of History and Biography Vol. LVIII. Philadelphia, Pa. 1934. pp. 342—369.* [5726

McCubbins: Rowan County wills. *Compiled by . . . In: The North Carolina Booklet. Vol. X. Raleigh, N. C. 1910/11. pp. 223 —225; Vol. XI. 1911—12. pp. 59—69; 117—130; 187—190. [Mostly non-German.]* [5727

Pickens, Wiley M.: The development of education in Rowan County. *Thesis of M. A., University of North Carolina, Department of Education. Chapel Hill, N. C. 1924. Typewritten. pp. (1), 117.* [5728

Rumple, Jethro: A history of Rowan County, North Carolina. *Containing sketches of prominent families and distinguished men, with an appendix. Salisbury, N. C.: J. J. Bruner 1881. pp. VIII, 508, X.*

Republished by the Elizabeth Maxwell Steele Chapter Daughters of the American Revolution, Salisbury, N. C., Charlotte, N. C.: Observer Printing Hause 1916. pp. 618;

Reprint: Raleigh, N. C.: Edwards & Broughton Co. 1929. pp. 428. [5729

A misstatement in the „Episcopal Journal" of Bishop Ravenscroft corrected. *(Signed by)* John Beard, George Vogler, Elders; James Brown, Robert Mull, Deacons. *[Concerning the German Lutheran congregation in the Town of Salisbury, N. C.] Salisbury, N. C.: Philo White 1827. pp. 7.* [5730

Grafschaft Forsyth — Herrnhuter in Nordkarolina

Forsyth County, N. C. — Moravians in North Carolina.

Blackwelder, Ruth: The attitude of the North Carolina Moravians toward the American Revolution. *Thesis of M. A.,*

29*

University of North Carolina, Department of History. Chapel Hill, N. C. 1930. Typewritten. pp. (1), 60. [5731
Blackwelder, Ruth: The attitude of the North Carolina Moravians toward the American Revolution. In: The North Carolina Historical Review. Vol. IX. Raleigh, N. C. 1932. pp. 1—21. [5732
Clewell, John Henry: History of Wachovia in North Carolina. The Unitas Fratrum or Moravian Church in North Carolina during a century and a half. 1752—1902. From the original German and English manuscripts and records in the Wachovia Archives, Salem, North Carolina. New York, N. Y.: Doubleday, Page & Co. 1902. pp. XIV, 365, ill., maps. [5733
— Moravian settlement in North Carolina. Raleigh, N. C.: Capital Printing Co. 1902. pp. 21.
= North Carolina Booklet. Vol. II, no. 4. [5734
— The Moravian Eastern Salem, North Carolina. [Winston Salem.] pp. 16. [5735
Crews, Hall: Old Salem, now a part of Winston-Salem, N. C. Photographs by Kenneth Clark. Measured drawings from the George F. Lindsay collection. In: The monograph series recording the architecture of the American Colonies and the early Republic. Vol. XV, no. 2. Edited and Published by Russel F. Whitehead. New York City, N. Y.: Russel F. Whitehead 1929. pp. 31—44, plate XVI—XXX. [5736
Fries, Adelaide L.: Records of the Moravians in North Carolina. Edited by . . . 4 vols. Raleigh, N. C.: Edwards & Broughton Printing Co. 1922, 1925, 1926. Vol. I: 1752 —1771. pp. 511, ill., maps; Vol. II: 1752 —1775. pp. VIII, 515—973, ill.; Vol. III. 1776—1779. pp. (1), (1), 977—1490, ill.; Vol. IV: 1780—1783. pp. (1), 1494 —1962, ill.
= Publications of the North Carolina Historical Commission. [5737
— Forsyth County. Salem, N. C. 1898. Winston, N. C.: Stewart's Printing House 1898. pp. (1), 132, ill. [5738
— Historical sketch of Salem Female Academy. Salem, N. C.: Christ & Keehlin 1902. pp. 32.
Reprint in: North-Carolina University Magazine. Vol. XIII. Raleigh, N. C. 1893—4. pp. 16—24, ill. [5739
— Der North Carolina land und colonie etablissement. In: The North Carolina

Booklet. Vol. IX, no. 4. Raleigh, N. C. 1910. pp. 199—214, map. [5740
Fries, Adelaide L.: The Pflegerin. In: The North Carolina Booklet. Vol. XIII no. 4. Raleigh, N. C. 1914. pp. 222—233. [5741
— An early Fourth of July celebration. In: The Journal of American History. Vol. IX. New York, N. Y. 1915. pp. 467—474. [5742
— The town builders. Winston-Salem, N. C., December, 1915. Raleigh, N. C.: Edwards & Broughton 1915. pp. 17. [5743
— Moravian tile stoves of Salem, N. C. In: A Collection of Papers read before the Bucks County Historical Society. Vol. IV. Easton, Pa. 1917. pp. 477—479. [5744
— and **Pfohl, J. Kenneth:** The Moravian Church yesterday and today. Raleigh, N. C.: Edwards & Broughton Co. 1926. pp. XI, 153, ill. [5745
— The Moravian contribution to colonial North Carolina. In: The North Carolina Historical Review. Vol. VII. Raleigh, N. C. 1930. pp. 1—14. [5746
— A history of Hope congregation in North Carolina. In: The Indiana Magazine of History. Vol. XXVI, no. 4. Bloomington, Ind. 1930. pp. 279—287. [5747
[Hinshaw, Ida Clifton]: Cornwallis and the Moravians. (Extract from an article „Cornwallis in North America" in: The Journal of American History. Second quarter, 1912.) In: The Penn Germania. Vol. II. = Old series, vol. XIV. Lititz, Pa. 1913. pp. 135—136. [5748
Holder, Edward M.: Community life in Wachovia 1752—1780. Thesis of M. A., University of North Carolina, Department of History. Chapel Hill, N. C. 1929. Typewritten. pp. 142.
[Bibliography pp. 139—142.] [5749
Holdich, L. A.: A visit to the Moravians. In: The Ladies' Repository: A monthly periodical, devoted to literature and religion. Vol. XX. Nov., 1860. Cincinnati, O., etc. . . . 1860. pp. 664—667. [5750
Kirkland, Winifried: The Easter people. In: The Ladie's Home Journal. Philadelphia, Pa.: The Curtis Publishing Co. April, 1922. pp. 12—13; p. 156, ill. [5751
— The Easter people. A pen-picture of the Moravian celebration of the resurrection. New York, N. Y.: Fleming H. Revell Co. 1923. pp. 61, ill. [5752

Kirkland, Winifried: A Christmas city of the old South. *In: The North American Review. Vol. CCXVIII. New York, N.Y. 1923. pp. 790—804.* [5753
— Where the star still shines. *New York, N. Y.: Fleming H. Revell Co. 1924. pp. 64, ill.* [5754
Oldham, Edward A.: The Moravian Easter. *In: The American Magazine, April, 1888... pp 654—656.* [5755
Patterson, Mrs. Lindsay: „Dear Salem" of North Carolina. *In: „House Beautiful." Boston, Mass., April, 1918. pp. 291 —293, ill.* [5756
Reichel, Levin T.: The Moravians in North Carolina. *An authentic history. Salem, N. C.: O. A. Keehln; Philadelphia, Pa.: J. B. Lippincott and Co. 1857. pp. IV, 13—206.* [5757
[—] „Succinct history of the settlement of the Unitas Fratrum of the United Brethren, in North Carolina." *(Believed to have been written by Bishop Reichel). In: The history of North Carolina, from the earliest period. By Martin, Francois — Xavier. Vol. I. New Orleans, La: A. T. Penniman & Co. 1829. Appendix. pp. XXIV—LXI; reprinted in: The colonial records of North Carolina. Vol. V. Raleigh, N. C. 1887 [= no. 5644]. pp. 1144—1163.* [5758
Robbins, D. P.: Descriptive sketch of Winston-Salem, its advantages and surroundings, Kernersville, etc. *compiled under the auspices of the Chamber of Commerce from a matter of fact standpoint. Winston, N. C.: Sentinel Job Print 1888. pp. 96.* [5759
Rondthaler, Edward: The memorabilia of fifty years 1877 to 1927. *Raleigh, N. C.: Edwards & Broughton Co. 1928. pp. XI, 520, ill.;* Appendix to the memorabilia of fifty years, containing memorabilia of 1928, 1929, 1930. Memoir of Bishop Edward Rondthaler who fell asleep January 31, 1931. By J. Kenneth Pfohl. The distinguished community service award. *Raleigh, N. C.:*

Edwards & Broughton Co. 1931. pp. VIII, 58, ill. [5760
Schwarze, Edmund: Missions of the Moravians in North Carolina among southern Indian tribes. *In: Proceedings of the 22nd annual session of the State Literary and Historical Association of Carolina. Raleigh, Dec. 7—8, 1922. Raleigh, N. C.: Bynum Printing Co. 1923. pp. 53—69.* [5761
— History of the Moravian missions among southern Indian tribes of the United States. *Bethlehem, Pa.: Times Publishing Co. 1923. pp. XVII, 331, ill. = Transactions of the Moravian Historical Society. Special series. Vol. I.* [5762
Siewers, Charles N.: Forsyth County: economic and social. *A laboratory study at the University of North Carolina, Department of Rural Social Economics. May, 1924. pp. (1), 7—92, (advertisement) —110, ill.* [5763
Swink, D. M.: The early settlement of the Moravians in North Carolina. *In: The North Carolina University Magazine. Vol. XVII, no. 4. Chapel Hill, N. C. 1900. pp. 187—192.* [5764
Thomas, N. A.: The Salem Tavern. *Reprint from the Winston-Salem „Journal". [Winston-Salem, N. C., s. d.] pp. 24, ill.* [5765
Thrasher, Max Bennett: The southern old Salem. *In: New England Magazine. New series, vol. XX. Boston, Mass., 1899. pp. 190—200, ill.* [5766
Winkler, A. V.: Souvenir of the twin cities of North Carolina, Winston-Salem, Forsyth County. Descriptive and historical. *Salem, N. C.: Blum's Steam Power Press Print 1890. pp. 5—77, (advertisements) — 92, ill.* [5767
Guide book of N. W. North Carolina *containing historical sketches of the Moravians in North Carolina, a description of the country and its industrial pursuits. Salem, N. C.: L. V. & E. T. Blum, Printers 1878. pp. 109.* [5768

Der deutschpennsylvanische Anteil an der Erschließung des Westens

The Pennsylvania-German Part in the Winning of the West

Allgemeines
General

Bender, D. H.: Mennonites west of the Mississippi. *In: The Mennonite Year Book and Directory 1921. Scottdale, Pa. 1921. pp. 16—18.* [5769

Bolliger, Theodore P.: The westward expansion of the Reformed Church. *Prepared for the Historical Society of the Reformed Church in the United States in part at the annual meeting of the Society, Lancaster, Penn., on May 12, 1926. Typewritten. pp. 48. [Archives of the Hist. Soc. of the Reformed Church in the U. S., Lancaster, Pa.]* [5770

Croll, P. C.: Early Lutheran annals in the „Far West". *Reprint from: The Lutheran Observer, Dec. 13 and 17, 1912 and Jan. 3, 1913. In: The Penn Germania. Vol. II. = Old series, vol. XIV. Cleona, Pa. 1913. pp. 181—186.* [5771

Henninghausen, L. P.: Early western settlement. *In: Fifth Annual Report of the Society for the History of the Germans in Maryland. Baltimore, Md. 1891. pp. 37—40.* [5772

Johnson, Roy H.: The Lutheran Church and the western frontier; 1789 to 1830. *In: The Lutheran Church Quarterly. Vol. III. Gettysburg, Pa. 1930. pp. 225—248.* [5773

Kephart, Horace: Pennsylvania's part in the winning of the West. *An address delivered before the Pennsylvania Society of St. Louis, Dec. 12, 1901. St. Louis, Mo.: Published by the Bureau of Publicity of the Louisiana Purchase Exposition 1902. pp. 19.* [5774

[—] Pennsylvania's part in the winning of the West. *Extracts of an address delivered before the Pennsylvania Society of St. Louis, Mo., December 12, 1901. In: The Pennsylvania-German. Vol. IX. Cleona, Pa. 1908. pp. 205—212.* [5775

Mannhardt, Emil: Die sogenannten Scotch-Irish. *In: Deutsch-Amerikanische Geschichtsblätter. Jg. IV. Chicago, Ill. 1904. Heft 1. S. 1—6.* [5776

Schade, A. E.: Denkschrift über Henry L. Yesler. Gebürtig aus Leitersburg, Md. (1811). Gründer der Stadt Seattle, Washington. *In: Seventh Annual Report of the Society for the History of the Germans in Maryland. Baltimore, Md. 1893. S. 29—35.* [5777

Stapleton, A.: Early Pennsylvania-German emigration north and west. *In: Notes and Queries. Edited by W. H. Egle. Annual vol. 1899. Harrisburg, Pa. 1900. p. 93.* [5778

Yeakel, Frederic D.: The Pennsylvania-German in the Far-West. *In: The Pennsylvania-German. Vol. VIII. Lebanon, Pa. 1907. pp. 53—55.* [5779

Western pioneers. *In: Christian Monitor. A monthly magazine for the home. Vol. XIV, no. 5. Scottdale, Pa. 1922. pp. 528—529.* [5780

A summer's outing. *[List of 200 families (many of whom came originally from eastern Pennsylvania) visited by Jonas Y. Schultz of the Upper Perkiomen Valley on a trip to Canada, Michigan, Illinois and Ohio in the summer of 1867.] In: The Perkiomen Region. Vol. VII. no. 1. Pennsburg, Pa. 1929. pp. 18—20.* [5781

G., K.: Der erste Flachbootschiffer des Mississippi. *In: Der Deutsche Pionier. Jg. I. Cincinnati, O. 1869—1870. S. 335—336.* [5782

R.[attermann, H. A.]: Deutsche, die Pioniere der Flußschiffahrt im Westen der Vereinigten Staaten. *In: Der Deutsche Pionier. Jg. XIII. Cincinnati, O. 1881—1882. S. 69—70.* [5783

The first flat boat on the Mississippi. *Reprint from the „Cincinnati Mirror" in: Hazard's Register of Pennsylvania. Vol. XIII. Philadelphia, Pa. 1834. p. 295.* [5784

Tennesee — Kentucky

Faust, A. B.: ,,The winning of the West: *I.* The German settlers in Kentucky and Tennessee." *In: The German element in the United States. By A. B. Faust. Vol. I. Second edition. New York 1927 [= no. 42]. = Chapter XII. pp. 357— 390.* [5785

Harbaugh, D.: A history of the Evangelical Lutheran congregation of Hopeful Church, Boone County Ky. *A discourse delivered at its 48th anniversary, Jan. 6, 1854, pp. . . .* [5786

Lentz, H. Max: A history of the Lutheran churches in Boone County, Ky. together with sketches of the pastors who have served them. *York, Pa.: P. Anstadt & Sons 1902. pp. VIII. 9—130, ill.* [5787

Rattermann, H. A.: Eine alte deutsche Gemeinde in Kentucky. *Vortrag gehalten vor dem deutschen Pionier-Verein von Covington, Ky. In: Der Deutsche Pionier. Jg. X. Cincinati, O. 1880—1881. S. 65—73; 93—99; 136—143.* [5788

— Die deutschen Pioniere von Kenton County, Kentucky. *Vortrag gehalten vor dem deutschen Pionier-Verein von Covington, Kentucky, am 6. Sept. 1877. In: Der Deutsche Pionier. Jg. IX. Cincinnati, O. 1877—1878. S. 258—264; 309—315; 352—357.* [5789

— Die ersten deutschen Pioniere von Campbell County, Kentucky. *Vortrag gehalten vor dem Verein der deutschen Pioniere von Newport, Ky., am 4. Juli 1877. In: Der Deutsche Pionier. Jg. IX. Cincinnati, O. 1877—1878. S. 184—194.* [5790

[Rattermann, H. A.]: Die deutschen Pioniere von Lexington, Kentucky, nebst Notizen über die ersten deutschen Ansiedler der Blaugras-Region in jenem Staate. *In: Der Deutsche Pionier. Jg. X. Cincinnati, O. 1878—1879. S. 273—278; 368—373; Jg. XI. 1879—1880. S. 65—72; 181 —184; 425—431; Jg. XII. 1880—1881. S. 298—305; 444—450.* [5791

Stein, Louis E.: Das Deutschtum in Kentucky. *Aus: ,,Westl. Post", 7.Okt. 1904. In: Deutsch-Amerikanische Geschichtsblätter. Jg. VIII, Nr. 1. Chicago, Ill. 1908. S. 16—21.* [5792

Cassell, C. W., Finck, W. J. and **Henkel, Elon O.:** History of the Lutheran Church in Virginia and East Tennessee. *Edited by . . . Published by the authority of the Lutheran Synod of Virginia. Strasburg, Va.: Shenandoah Publishing House. Inc. 1930. pp. XVII, (1), 401, ill.* [5793

Taylor, Oliver: Historic Sullivan. A history of Sullivan County, Tennessee with brief biographies of the makers of history. *Bristol, Tenn.: The King Printing Co. 1909. pp. XIII, 330, ill.* [5794

New York

Behe, Stacy D.: The Pennsylvania-Germans in western New York. *In: The Pennsylvania-German. Vol. VIII. Lebanon, Pa. 1907. pp. 12—13.* [5795

Laux, James B.: Emigration from Pennsylvania to Seneca County, N. Y. *In: The Pennsylvania-German. Vol. X. Lititz, Pa. 1909. pp. 107—109.* [5796

Sexton, John L.: Pennsylvanians in the ,,Genesee country". *In: Historical Register: Notes and Queries, historical and genealogical relating to interior Pennsylvania for the year 1883. Vol. I. Harrisburg, Pa. 1883. pp. 86—90; 188—193.* [5797

Stapleton, A.: The Pennsylvania-German in the Seneca country, State of New York. *In: Notes and Queries. Edited by W. H Egle. Annual vol. 1897. Harrisburg, Pa. 1898. p. 1.* [5798

Swope, G. E.: Pennsylvania German Lutheran at Dansville, N. Y. *In: Notes and Queries. Edited by W. H. Egle. Annual vol. 1898. Harrisburg, Pa. 1899. pp. 140—141.* [5799

W.[illers], Diedrich: Pennsylvania immigration into New York. *In: Notes and Queries. Edited by W. H. Egle. First series, part I. Harrisburg, Pa. 1881. pp. 16—17. Reprint in: First and second series, vol. I. Harrisburg, Pa. 1894. p. 312.* [5800

— Early Pennsylvania German settlers in western New York. *In: Notes and Queries. Edited by W. H. Egle. Annual vol. 1898. Harrisburg, Pa. 1899. pp. 90 —93; 99—102; 110—112; 120—121.* [5801

Deutsche Loyalisten in Kanada

German Loyalists in Canada

Canniff, W.: History of the settlement of Upper Canada, with special reference to the Bay Quinté. *Toronto, Ont. Dudley & Burns 1869. pp. 671.* [5802

Carnochan, Janet: Early churches in the Niagara Peninsula, Stamford and Chippewa with marriage records . . . *In: Ontario Historical Society. Papers and Records. Vol. VIII. Toronto, Ont. 1907. pp. 149—225.* [5803

— Inscriptions and graves in the Niagara Peninsula. *In: Niagara Historical Society. Vol. III, No. 19. Niagara, Ont. 1910. pp. 126.* [5804

— Names only but much more. *In: Niagara Historical Society. Vol. IV, No. 27. Niagara, Ont. 1910. pp. 126.* [5805

Casselman, Alexander C.: The German U. E. Loyalists of the County of Dundas, Ontario. *In: The United Empire Loyalists' Association of Ontario. Vol. III. Toronto, Ont. 1900. pp. 53—76.* [5806

Croil, James: Dundas. *Montreal, Que.: B. Dawson & Son 1861. pp. 352.* [5807

Cruikshank, Ernest: The story of Butler's Rangers and the settlement of Niagara. *Welland, Ont.: Lundy's Lane Historical Society. 1893. pp. 114.* [5808

— The Loyalists of New York. *In: The United Empire Loyalists' Association of Ontario. Vol. I. Toronto, Ont. 1898. pp. 49—62.* [5809

— Ten years of the Colony of Niagara 1780—1790. *In. Niagara Historical Society. Vol. II, No. 17. Niagara, Ont. 1908. pp. 50.* [5810

— Notes on the history of the District of Niagara 1791—93. *In: Niagara Historical Society. Vol. IV, No. 26. Niagara, Ont. 1913. pp. 51.* [5811

Cumberland, R. W.: The U. E. Loyalist settlements, between Kingston and Adolphustown. *In: Bulletin of the Departments of History and Political and Economic Science in Queen's University, Kingston, Ont., Canada. No. 45. May 1923. pp. 24.* [5812

Herrington, Walter: Pioneer life on the Bay of Quinté. *In: Lennox and Addington Historical Society. Papers and Records. Vol. VI. Nappanee, Ont. 1915. pp. 7—34.* [5813

Lehmann, Heinz: Zur Geschichte des Deutschtums in Kanada. *Band I:* Das Deutschtum in Ostkanada. *Stuttgart 1931 [= Nr. 757]. (2), 125 S. [Besonders Kapitel III: Das Deutschtum in der Provinz Quebec. S. 40—67; Kapitel IV: Das Deutschtum in der Ontario. S. 48ff.]* [5814

Noyes, Ino P.: The Canadian Loyalists and early settlers in the District of Bedford. *St. Johns, Que. The News Typ 1900. pp. 20.* [5815

— The Missisquoi Germans or Dutch. *In: Reports of the Missisquoi County Historical Society. No. 2. St. Johns, Que. 1907. pp. 31—35.* [5816

— Canadian Loyalists and early settlers in the District of Bedford. *In: Reports of the Missisquoi County Historical Society. No. 3. St. Johns, Que. 1908. pp. 90—107.* [5817

Pierce, Lorne A.: The German Loyalist in Upper Canada. *In: The Canadian Magazine. Vol. LV. Toronto, Ont. Aug., 1920. pp. 290—296.* [5818

Sabine, Lorenzo: The American Loyalists, or biographical notes of adherents to the British Crown in the War of Revoluntion. *Boston, Mass.: C. C. Little & J. Brown 1847. pp. 733.* [5819

Siebert, W. H.: The American Loyalists in the eastern seigniories and townships of the Province of Quebec. *In: Proceedings and Transactions of the Royal Society of Canada. Third series, vol. VII. Ottawa, Toronto, London 1913. Section 2. pp. 3—41.* [5820

Stein, Paul: A story of the rear of Addington County. *In: Lennox and Addington Historical Society. Papers and Records. Vol. II. Nappanee, Ont. 1910. pp. 14—21.* [5821

Tasker, L. H.: The U. E. Loyalist settlement at Long Point, Lake Erie. *In: Ontario Historical Society. Papers and Records. Vol. II. Toronto, Ont. 1900. pp. 9—128.* [5822

Tucker, W. Bowman: The Camden Colony of the seed of the righteous. A story of the United Empire Loyalists. *With genealogical tables. Montreal, Can.:*

John Lovell & Son., Limited 1908. pp.
(1), XVI, 216, (9), ill. [5823
Tucker, W. Bowman: The romance of the
Palatine Millers. A tale of Palatine
Irish-Americans and United Empire
Loyalists. Second edition of „The
Camden Colony" revised and enlarged.
Montreal, Que.: Published by the author;
Southam Press Montreal Limited 1929.
pp. (1), (1), XXXIV, 369, ill. [5824
United Empire Loyalist Centennial Com-
mittee: The centennial of the settlement
of Upper Canada by the United Empire

Loyalists 1784—1884. The celebrations
at Adolphustown, Toronto and Niagara.
With an appendix containing a copy of
the U. E. list, preserved in the Crown
Lands Department at Toronto. Toronto,
Ont.: Rose Publishing Comp. 1885.
pp. 334. [5825
A Lutheran church record. [Ebenezer
Church, Fredericksburg Township, Lennox and Addington Districts, Ont.]
1793—1832. In: Ontario Historical Society. Papers and Addresses. Vol. VI.
Toronto, Ont. 1905. pp. 136—167. [5826

Mennoniten-Siedlungen in Ontario, Kanada

Mennonite Settlements in Ontario, Canada

Allen, A. S.: Reminiscences of early Waterloo. In: Thirteenth Annual Report of
the Waterloo Historical Society. Kitchener, Ont. 1925. pp. 139—143. [5827
Bender, Harold S.: New source material for
the history of the Mennonites in Ontario. In: The Mennonite Quarterly Review. Vol. III. Goshen, Ind. 1929. pp.
42—53.
Contains: (I) A list of claims by residents of (present) Waterloo County,
mostly Mennonites, for losses suffered
when employed in military transport,
in October 1813. pp. 42—46;
(II) Outline of several journeys from
eastern Pennsylvania to Waterloo
Township and return in 1817, 1819, and
1845 by Joseph Bowman. pp. 46—48;
(III) Statistics regarding Mennonite
ministers and population in Ontario
about 1825. pp. 49—53;
(IV) A form for the Oath of Allegiance.
p. 53. [5828
Breithaupt, W. H.: Early history of the
County of Waterloo. In: First Annual
Report of the Waterloo Historical So-
ciety. Berlin, Ont. 1913. pp. 8—9.
[5829
— Some German settlers of Waterloo
County. In: First Annual Report of the
Waterloo Historical Society. Berlin,
Ont. 1913. pp. 11—15. [5830
— Waterloo County history. In: Ontario
Historical Society. Papers and Records.
Vol. XVII. Toronto, Ont. 1919. pp.
43—47. [5831
— Waterloo County newspaper. In: Ninth
Annual Report of the Waterloo Historical

Society, Kitchener, Ont. 1921. pp. 152—
159. [5832
Breithaupt, W. H.: The settlement of Waterloo County. In: Ontario Historical Society. Papers and Records. Vol. XXII.
Toronto, Ont. 1925. pp. 14—17, ill. [5833
— First settlements of Pennsylvania-Men-
nonites in Upper Canada. In: Ontario
Historical Society. Papers and Re-
cords. Vol. XXIII. Toronto, Ont. 1926.
pp. 8—14. [5834
— First settlements of Pensylvania-Men-
nonites in Upper Canada. In: Chri-
stian Monitor. A monthly magazine for
the home. Vol. XIX. Scottdale, Pa. 1927.
No. 6. pp. 180—183, ill. [5835
— Waterloo County millers. In: Sixteenth
Annual Report of the Waterloo Historical
Society. Waterloo, Ont. 1928. pp. 78—
80. [5836
Burkholder, L. J.: The early Mennonite
Settlements in Ontario. In: The Men-
nonite Quarterly Review. Vol. VIII.
Goshen, Ind. — Scottdale, Pa. 1934.
pp. 103—122. [5837
Casselman, A. C.: „The settlement of the
Mennonites and Tunkers." In: Canada
and its provinces . . . Vol. XVII. Sec-
tion IX. The Province of Ontario 1914
[see no. 753]. pp. 47—49. [5838
Cruikshank, E. A.: The reserve of the Six
Nations on the Grand River and the
Mennonite purchase of Block no. 2. In:
Fifteenth Annual Report of the Waterloo
Historical Society. Waterloo, Ont. 1927.
pp. 303—350.
[Map showing the Six Nations Reserve
see Seventh Annual Report 1919.] [5839

Dunham, B. Mabel: The trail of the Conestoga. *With foreward by the Rt. Hon. W. L. Mackenzie King. Toronto, Ont.: The Macmillan Co. of Canada 1924. pp. (2), 342.* [5840

— Toward Sodom. *Toronto, Can.: The Macmillan Co. of Canada 1927. pp. VII, 336.* [5841

Eby, A.: Die Ansiedlung und Begründung der Mennoniten Gemeinschaft in Canada. *Milford Square, Pa.: J. G. Stauffer 1872. III, 5—31 S. Abdruck aus: Der Mennonitische Friedensbote. Herausgegeben von der östlichen Mennoniten District Conferenz. Jg. XVI. Milford Square, Pa. Nr. 2ff.* [5842

Eby, Ezra E.: A biographical history of Waterloo Township and other townships of the county, *being a history of the early settlers and their descendants, mostly all of Pennsylvania Dutch origin, and also much other unpublished historical information chiefly of a local character. Berlin, Ont., Canada. 2 vols. 1895/1896. pp. III, (1), 887; 712.* [5843

Gingerich, Mary Etta: Hagey Mennonite Church, Preston, Ont. *In: Christian Monitor. A monthly magazine for the home. Vol. XXIV, no. 2. Scottdale, Pa. 1932. pp. 48—50, ill.* [5844

[Klotz, Otto]: Sketch of the history of the village Preston. *Reprint from Preston Progress 1886. In: Fifth Annual Report of the Waterloo Historical Society. Kitchener, Ont. 1917. pp. 24—40, ill.* [5845

— Preston. Reminiscences. *In: Ninth Annual Report of the Waterloo Historical Society. Kitchener, Ont. 1921. pp. 171—182.* [5846

Lehmann, Heinz: ,,Das Deutschtum in der Provinz Ontario." *In: Zur Geschichte des Deutschtums in Kanada. Band I. Das Deutschtum in Ostkanada. Von H. Lehman. Stuttgart 1931 [= Nr. 757]. = Kapitel IV. S. 48—114.* [5847

— Das evangelische Deutschtum in Kanada. *In: Auslanddeutschtum und evangelische Kirche. Jahrbuch 1935. München 1935. S. 218—252. [Die Mennoniten in Ontario. S. 14—20.]* [5847a

Munro, Ross: The Snider flour mills, Waterloo. *Reprint from ,,Saturday Night", Sept. 10, 1927. In: Fifteenth Annual Report of the Waterloo Historical Society.*

Waterloo, Ont. 1927. pp. 383—384, ill. [5848

Nicolay, C. L.: Berlin, a German settlement in Waterloo County, Ontario, Canada. *Read in the Germanic Association, University of Pennsylvania, Jan. 14, 1807. In: German American Annals. New series vol. V. Philadelphia, Pa. 1907. pp. 105—121.* [5849

Panabaker, D. N.: The Town of Hespeler. *A sketch of the early years of its development, including some general references to the settlers associated with its early industries. In: Tenth Annual Report of the Waterloo Historical Society. Kitchener, Ont. 1922. pp. 213—224, ill.* [5850

— Address of the president, Waterloo County Pioneers' Memorial Association, turning — the — sod exercises, June 24, 1924. *In: Ontario Historical Society. Papers and Records. Vol. XXII. Toronto, Ont. 1925. pp. 182—185.* *[See no. 5868]* [5851

Pearce, Thomas: School history, Waterloo County and Berlin. *In: Second Annual Report of the Waterloo Historical Society, Berlin, Ont. 1914. pp. 33—48, ill.* [5852

Ruccius und **Lehmann, H.:** ,,Berlin" *(Kitchener), Grafschaft Waterloo, Ontario. In: Handwörterbuch des Grenz- und Auslanddeutschtums. Bd. I. Breslau 1933 [= Nr. 93]. S. 389—390.* [5852a

Seyfert, A. G.: Migration of Lancaster County Mennonites to Waterloo County, Ontario, Canada, from 1800 to 1825. *In: Papers and Addresses of the Lancaster County Historical Society. Vol. XXX. Lancaster, Pa. 1926. pp. 33—41, ill.* [5853

— Excerpts from the address of Hon. A. G. Seyfert, representing the Lancaster County Historical Society at the dedication of the Mennonite memorial, Waterloo County, Ontario, Canada, Aug. 28, 1926. *In: Papers and Addresses of the Lancaster County Historical Society. Vol. XXX. Lancaster, Pa. 1926. pp. 117—119.* *[See no. 5868]* [5854

Sherk, A. B.: The Pennsylvania Germans of Waterloo County, Ontario, Canada. *In: Ontario Historical Society. Papers and Records. Vol. VII. Toronto, Ont. 1906. pp. 98—109.*

Reprint in: The Pennsylvania-German. Vol. XII. Lititz, Pa. 1911. pp. 280—287. [5855

Sherk, A. B.: The Pennsylvania-Germans in Canada. *In: The Pennsylvania-German. Vol. VIII. Lebanon, Pa. 1907. pp. 101—104., map.* [5856

— Recollections of early Waterloo. *In: Third Annual Report of the Waterloo Historical Society. Berlin, Ont 1914. pp. 13—19.* [5857

[Sherk, Michael Gonder]: Pen pictures of early pioneer life in Upper Canada, *by a „Canuck" of the fifth generation. Toronto, Ont.: William Briggs 1905. pp. XIV, 15—280, ill.* [5858

— An old family account book. *In: Ontario Historical Society. Papers and Records. Vol. VII. Toronto, Ont. 1906. pp. 120—139.* [5859

Smith, Clyde: The Amishman. *Toronto, Ont. William Briggs 1912. pp. 132.* [5860

Smith, Geo.: The Amishman. *In: Ontario Historical Society. Papers and Records. Vol. XVII. Toronto, Ont. 1919. pp. 40—42.* [5861

Snyder, E. W. B.: Waterloo County forests and primitive economics. *In: Sixth Annual Report of the Waterloo Historical Society. Kitchener, Ont. 1918. pp. 14—36.* [5862

Wambold, I. A.: Early Mennonite settlers in Canada. *In: The Mennonite Year Book and Directory 1920. Scottdale, Pa. 1920. pp. 8—10.* [5864

Wells, Clayton W.: A historical sketch of the Town of Waterloo, Ontario. *In: Sixteenth Annual Report of the Waterloo Historical Society. Waterloo, Ont. 1928. pp. 22—67, ill., map.* [5865

Transcript of original deed for the German Company Tract, Waterloo Township. *In: Seventh Annual Report of the Waterloo Historical Society. Kitchener, Ont. 1919. pp. 87—90.* [5866

Briefe an die Mennonisten Gemeine, in Ober Canada. *Mit einer Zugabe. Berlin (Ober Canada): Heinrich Eby 1840. 47 S.*
[Inhaltsangabe siehe Nr. 3484] [5866a

Zweyter Brief aus Daenemark an die Mennonisten Gemeine in Canada, datiert von Friedrichstadt, Mai 19, 1840, *geschrieben von Carl Justus van der Smissen. Berlin, Canada: Heinrich Eby 1841. 23 S.*
[Vgl. Nr. 3485] [5866b

More source material for Ontario Mennonite history. *In: The Mennonite Quarterly Review. Vol. V. Scottdale, Pa. —Goshen, Ind. 1931. pp. 221—224.*
Contains: *(I) Memorandum of assessment for Willoughby Township, [Lincoln County, Ont.] 1839, Papers of Michael Gonder;*
(II) Affidavit of Mennonist for militia exemption. p. 222.
(III) An early Ontario Mennonite conference of 1836. (A translation of the German reports in the local Berlin, Ontario [now Kitchener] Weekly Newspaper.) pp. 222—224. [5867

The Waterloo County pioneers' memorial tower. *In: Fourteenth Annual Report of the Waterloo Historical Society. Kitchener, Ont. 1926. pp. 185, ill.*
Appendix: Organization of the Waterloo County Pioneers' Memorial Association. *pp. 202—203, ill.*
Addresses delivered at the dedication of the memorial tower, Aug. 28, 1926. *pp. 204—249;*
By **A. G. Seyfert.** *pp. 204—211;*
By **D. N. Panabaker:** A tribute to the pioneers. *pp. 212—216;*
By **John S. Martin:** Characteristics of the Pennsylvania German in Canada. *pp. 217—219;*
By **W. H. Breithaupt.** *pp. 220—225;*
By **E. A. Cruikshank.** *p. 226;*
By **James H. Coyne.** *p. 227;*
By **S. F. Coffman:** The adventure of faith. *pp. 228—233;*
By **J. P. Jaffray:** Blazing the trail in New Dumfries. *pp. 234—236;*
By **M. G. Sherk:** The Pennsylvania-German in history. *pp. 237—246;*
By **C. F. Derstine:** Significance of the memorial tower. *pp. 247—249.* [5868

Berlin. Celebration of Cityhood 1912. *Issued by authority of the City of Berlin, Ontario. Issued in commemoration of its celebration of Cityhood, July 17, 1912. Published by the German Printing & Publishing Co. Berlin, Ont., Can. 1912. 120 leaves.* [5869

Preston mill historical tablet. *In: Sixteenth Annual Report of the Waterloo Historical Society. Waterloo, Ont. 1928. p. 77, ill.* [5870

Johnston, William: History of the County of Perth from 1825 to 1902. *Stratford, Ont.: W. M. O'Beirne 1903. pp. VIII, 11—565, ill.* [5872

Ohio

Allgemeines

General

Bolliger, Theodore P.: History of the First Reformed Church, Canton, O. *Cleveland, O.: Central Publishing House [1929.] pp. XIII, 208, ill.* [5873

Bradford, J. E.: ,,The German churches." *Part of a paper: The Centennial churches of the Miami Valley. In: Ohio Archaeological and Historical Quarterly. Vol. XXV. Columbus, O. 1916. pp. 251—252.* [5874

Buehring,. . .: The beginnings of Lutheranism in Ohio. *Thesis of M. A., Faculty of the Graduate School of Arts and Literature. University of Chicago, Ill., July, 1923. Typewirtten. pp. 119 (5).* [5875

Cosler, Elsie Jane: Historical reminiscences of Hawker Reformed Church. *Compiled by . . . Dayton, O. 1923. pp. 39, ill.* [5876

Detweiler, Dorothy: North Salem Church, Huntsville, Ohio. *In: Christian Monitor. A monthly magazine for the home. Vol. XXIII. No. 10. Scottdale, Pa. 1931. p. 305.* [5877

Ernsberger, C. S.: A history of the Wittenberg Synod of the General Synod of the Evangelical Lutheran Church 1847—1916. *Together with a brief sketch of each congregation of the Synod. Edited by the same author. Published by the authority of the Synod. Columbus, O.: Lutheran Book Concern. 1917. pp. 582, ill.* [5878

Faust, A. B.: ,,The winning of the West. II. The settlement of the Ohio Valley." *In: The German element in the United States. By A. B. Faust. Vol. I. Second edition. New York 1927 [= no. 42]. = Chapter XIII. pp. 391—431.* [5879

Garland, D. Frank: An historical sketch of the First Evangelical Lutheran Church of Dayton, Ohio, U. S. A. *Dayton, O.: United Brethren Publishing House. 1907. pp. 37, ill.* [5880

Garst, Jesse O.: History of the Church of the Brethren of the Southern District of Ohio *by the Historical Committee . . . Editional supervision by . . . Dayton, O.: The Otterbein Press 1921. pp. 605, ill.* [5881

Gerig, Kathryn: Oak Grove Amish Mennonite congregation, Wayne County, Ohio. *In: Christian Monitor. A monthly magazine for the home. Vol. XXIII, no. 6.*

Scottdale, Pa. 1931. pp. 176—177, ill. [5882

Giorg, Kara [Pseudonym für **Brühl, Georg**]: Das erste im Staate Ohio geborene weiße Kind. *[Johann Louis Roth, geb. 4. Juli 1773.] In: Der Deutsche Pionier. Jg. II. Cincinnati, O. 1870—1871. S. 296—297.* [5883

Hanna, Charles A.: Ohio Valley genealogies. Relating chiefly to families in Harrison, Belmont and Jefferson Counties, O. and Washington, Westmoreland and Fayette Counties, Pa. *New York: Privately printed 1900. pp. 128.* [5884

[Henkel, Paul]: Rev. Paul Henkel's journal. His missionary journey to the State of Ohio in 1806. *Translated from the German by* **F. E. Cooper**, *edited by* **Clement L. Martzolff**. *In Ohio Archaeological and Historical Publications. Vol. XXIII. Columbus 1914. pp. 162—218.* [5885

Hentz, J. P.: History of the Evangelical Lutheran congregation in Germantown, O. and biographies of its pastors and founders. *Dayton, O.: Christian Publishing House Print. 1882. pp. VII, 9—102.* [5886

— Twin Valley, its settlement and subsequent history 1798—1882. *Dayton, O.: Christian Publishing House 1883. pp. XI, 13—288.* [5887

— Germantown, Ohio. *In: The Pennsylvania-German. Vol. XII. Lititz, Pa. 1911. pp. 655—664.* [5888

Hirschy, N. C.: Extracts of a historical sketch of the Mennonite Church at Wadsworth, O. *In: The Mennonite Year Book and Almanac for 1904. Quakertown, Pa. 1904. pp. 32—36, ill.* [5889

Hostetler, Carl: Kolb's Church. Walnut Creek Township, Holmes County, Ohio. *In: Christian Monitor. A monthly magazine for the home. Vol. XXIII. No. 3. Scottdale, Pa. 1931. pp. 80—81, ill.* [5890

Hostetler, Ellis: Martin's Church, near Orrville, Ohio. *In: Christian Monitor. A monthly magazine for the home. Vol. XXIV. No. 12. Scottdale, Pa. 1932. pp. 367—368.* [5891

John of Lancaster [Pseudonym of **Meginness, John F.**]: Drifted west. Early Pennsylvania settlers in Tuscarawas County, Ohio. *In: Notes and Queries. Edited by W. H. Egle. Fourth series, vol. I. 1891*

The Winning of the West

461

—*1893. Harrisburg, Pa. 1893. pp. 374 —377.* [5892

Klauprecht, Emil: Deutsche Chronik in der Geschichte des Ohio Thales und seiner Hauptstadt Cincinnati in's Besondere, *umfassend eine ausführliche Darstellung der Abentheuer, Ansiedlungen und des allgemeinen Wirkens der Deutschen im Flußgebiete von der Entdeckung des Mississippi-Thales an bis auf unsere Tage. Zusammengestellt nach authentischen Quellen. Cincinnati, O.: Druck und Verlag von G. Hof & M. A. Jacobi 1864. 198 S.* [5893

Martzolff, Clement L.: Zane's trace. *In: Ohio Archaeological and Historical Quarterly. Vol. XIII. Columbus, O. 1904. pp. 297—331, ill.* [5894

— Lutheranism in Perry County, Ohio. *In: Ohio Archaeological and Historical Quarterly. Vol. XXVIII. Columbus, O. 1919. pp. 375—395.* [5895

Mechling, G. W.: History of the Evangelical Lutheran District Synod of Ohio, covering fifty-three years 1857—1910. *Dayton, O.: Press of the Giele & Pelaun Co. 1911. pp. 208.* [5896

Metzler, Mildred: Midway Church, Columbiana County, Ohio. *In: Christian Monitor. A monthly magazine for the home. Vol. XXIII. No. 12. Scottdale, Pa. 1931. pp. 368—369, ill.* [5897

[Miller, Aaron]: Diary of Aaron Miller, written while in quest of Ohio wheat lands. *In: Ohio Archaeological and Historical Quarterly. Vol. XXXIII. Columbus, O. 1924. pp. 67—79.* [5898

Miller, S. H.: The Amish in Holmes County, O. *In: The Mennonite Year-book and Directory 1908. Scottdale, Pa. 1908. pp. 31—32, ill.* [5899

Neuhauser, J. H.: An historical sketch of the 55th anniversary of the First English Evangelical Lutheran Church, Shelby, O. 1859—1914. *pp. 52, ill.* [",,Most of the original members migrated from the State of Pennsylvania, largely from Perry County, Pa."] [5900

Povemire, H. M.: Baptism by Rev. Jacob Leist recorded in Israel's Lutheran and Reformed Church records at Amanda, Fairfield County, O. *In: National Genealogical Society Quarterly. Vol. XVIII. Washington, D. C. 1930. pp. 83—84.* [5901

Prince, B. F.: Beginnings of Lutheranism in Ohio. *In: The Lutheran Quarterly.*

Vol. XLIII. Gettysburg, Pa. 1913. pp. 116—130. [5902

Prince, B. F.: Beginnings of Lutheranism in Ohio. *In: Ohio Archaeological and Historical Quarterly. Vol. XXIII. Columbus, O. 1914. pp. 268—283.* [5903

R.[attermann, H. A.]: ,,Germany," die erste deutsche Niederlassung im Miamithale. *In: Der Deutsche Pionier. Jg. X. Cincinnati, O. 1878—1879. S. 346—361, Karte.* [5904

[—] Der erste Versuch einer Ansiedlung im Miamithale. *In: Der Deutsche Pionier Jg. X. Cincinnati, O. 1878—1879. S. 380—381.* [5905

— ,,Die Deutschen in Ohio und Indiana.' *In: In der neuen Heimath. Geschichtliche Mittheilungen über die deutschen Einwanderer in allen Theilen der Union. Herausgegeben von A. Eickhoff. New York, N. Y. 1884 [= Nr. 39]. = Abschnitt VIII, S. 229—314.* [5906

— Die deutschen Pioniere von Lucas County, Ohio mit besonderer Berücksichtigung des Deutschtums der Stadt Toledo. *In: Der Deutsche Pionier. Jg. XV. Cincinnati, O. 1883—1884. S. 30—37; 117—123; 245—250; 287—297; 312—318; 450—453; Jg. XVI. 1884—1885. S. 143—149; 282—285; 475—478.* [5907

— [Die Deutschen in Ohio.] *Festred gehalten bei Gelegenheit des ,,Deutschen Tages" in Greenville, O. 2. Okt. 1895. In: H. A. Rattermann. Gesammelte ausgewählte Werke. Bd. XVI. Cincinnati, O.: Selbstverlag des Verfassers, 1912 = Abhandlungen, Vorträge und Reden. Bilder aus Deutsch-Amerikanischer Geschichte. Vermischte Schriften. Erster Theil. S. 397—409.* [5907a

Rohrbach, Paul: ,,Die Deutschen im Ohio Gebiet." *In: Das Deutschtum über See. Von P. Rohrbach. Karlsruhe 1931 [= Nr. 97a]. S. 66—71.* [5907b

S., D. F.: From the Sprague farm cemetery, near Minerva, Stark County, Ohio. *In: Genealogy, Journal of American ancestry. Vol. I. New York, N. Y. 1912. p. 197.* [5908

Sheatsley, C. .V: History of the Evangelical Lutheran Joint Synod of Ohio and other states from the earliest beginnings to 1919. *Century Memorial Edition. Columbus, O.: Lutheran Book Concern. 1919. pp. 312, ill.* [5909

Smith, Arthur Harms: A history of the East Ohio Synod of the General Synod of the Evangelical Lutheran Church 1836

—1920. *Together with a brief sketch of each congregation of the Synod. Prepared and edited by . . . Published by the authority of the Synod. Columbus, O.: Lutheran Book Concern. 1924. pp. 250, ill.* [5910

Spielmann, C.: Abriß der Geschichte der evangelisch-lutherischen Synode von Ohio u. a. Staaten, in einfacher Darstellung, von ihren ersten Anfängen bis zum Jahre 1846. *Nebst einem Anhang. Columbus, O.: Ohio Syndical-Druckerei 1880. 197 S.* [5911

Suntheimer, Ralph: Berlin Church, Holmes County, Ohio. *In: Christian Monitor. A monthly magazine for the home. Vol. XXIII. No. 5. Scottdale, Pa. 1931. p. 145.* [5912

Thomas, William Hannibal: Memoirs of Otterbein half a century ago. *In: The United Brethren Review. Vol. XVI. Dayton, O. 1905. pp. 201—207.* [5913

Trepte, Helmut: Deutschtum in Ohio bis zum Jahre 1820. *Diss. phil., Universität Leipzig. In: Deutsch-Amerikanische Geschichtsblätter. German American Historical Review. Jahrbuch der Deutsch-Amerikanischen Gesellschaft von Illinois. Jg. 1932. Vol. XXXII. Chicago, Ill. 1932. S. 153—408, ill., Karte. [Bibliographie. S. 396—408.]* [5914

[Treyer, David A.]: Ein unparteiischer Bericht von den Hauptumstaenden, welche sich ereigneten in den sogenannten Alt-Amischen Gemeinden in Ohio, vom Jahr 1850 bis ungefaehr 1861, wodurch eine vollkommene Spaltung entstand. *Abgeschrieben den 11. August 1898. 16 S.* [5915

Umble, John: Early Sunday schools at West Liberty, Ohio. *In: The Mennonite Quarterly Review. Vol. IV. Goshen, Ind.-Scottdale, Pa. 1930. pp. 6 —50.* [5916

— Early Mennonite Sunday schools of northwestern Ohio. *In: The Mennnonite Quarterly Review. Vol. V. Goshen, Ind.-Scottdale, Pa. 1931. pp. 100—111; 179 —197; 260—271.* [5917

— The Fairfield County, Ohio, background of the Allen County, Ohio, Mennonite settlement, 1799—1860. *In: The Mennonite Quarterly Review. Vol. VI. Goshen, Ind.-Scottdale, Pa. 1932. pp. 5—29.* [5918

— The Allen County, Mennonite settlement. *In: The Mennonite Quarterly Review. Vol. VI. Goshen, Ind.-Scottdale, Pa. 1932. pp. 81—109.* [5919

Whayman, Horace W.: Some early German settlers in Germantown, Pa., and their descendants in the old territory. *In: The ,,Old Northwest'' Genealogical Quarterly 1904. Vol. VII. Columbus, O. 1904. pp. 123—128; 183—186.* [5920

Die deutschen Pioniere des Scioto-Thales. *In: Der Deutsche Pionier. Jg. VII. Cincinnati, O. 1875—1876. S. 140—145; 187—190; 223—229; 283—285; 375 —379; 405—409; 455—458.* [5921

Relic department of the Centennial. German Department. (List of articles.) *In: Ohio Archaeological and Historical Quarterly. Marietta Centennial Number. Vol. II. Columbus, O. 1888—1889. pp. 248— 249.* [5922

1845—1895. First Lutheran Church, Springfield, Ohio. *Springfield, O.: The New Era Co. 1895. pp. 70.*
Including: Prince, B. T.: History of the First Lutheran Church, Springfield, Ohio. *pp. 10—37.* [5923

Inscription from German cemetery three miles east of Alum Creek on Broad Street, Columbus, O., and Sixty Rods South of Street. *In: The ,,Old Northwest'' Genealogical Quarterly. Vol. IX. Columbus, O. 1906. pp. 187—188.* [5924

Souvenir booklet. Centennial. One hundred years of Reformed church history in Ohio and adjacent states. *Programm Merger Meeting Ohio and Central Synods. Ohio and Central Synodical Womens Missionary Societies. The Centennial and Merger Meetings were held 1923, in First and Trinity Reformed Churches, Canton O. [s. l.] 1923. pp. 133, ill.* [5925

David Ziegler, the first mayor of Cincinnati, Ohio. *See: nos 7749—7753.*

Chaddock, Robert E.: Ohio before 1850. A study of the early influence of Pennsylvania and southern populations in Ohio. *Thesis of Ph. D. Columbia University, New York City, N. Y. 1908. New York, N. Y.: Columbia University Longmans, Green & Co., agents 1908. pp. 155, map.* [5927

Grafschaftsgeschichte
County Histories
Ashland County

Knapp: History of Ashland County, Ohio. *. . . 1863. pp. . . . .* [5928

[—] Pioneers of Ashland County, Ohio. *[List of the original settlers of Ashland*

County, Ohio, showing from what states and counties they came.] Gleaned from Knapp's History of Ashland County, Ohio 1863. In: The Pennsylvania-German. Vol. XII. Lititz, Pa. 1911. pp. 166—168. [5929

Auglaize County

Williamson, C. W.: History of western Ohio and Auglaize County with illustrations and biographical sketches of pioneers and prominent public men. *Columbus, O.: Press of W. M. Linn & Sons 1905. pp. III, 860, ill.* [5930

Clark County

Prince, Benjamin F.: A standard history of Springfield and Clark County, Ohio. *An authentic narrative of the past, with particular attention to the modern era in the commercial, industrial, civic and social development. Prepared under the editorial supervision of* **Benjamin F. Prince.** *Assisted by a board of advisory editors. Chicago, Ill. and New York, N. Y.: The American Historical Society 1922. 2 vols. pp. XXIV, 562, ill.; Vol. II. Biographical. pp. 433, ill.* [5931

Fairfield County

Graham, A. A.: History of Fairfield and Perry counties, Ohio. *Their past and present, containing a comprehensive history of Ohio; a complete history of Fairfield and Perry counties; their townships, cities, villages, towns, schools, churches, societies, industries, statistics etc.; a history of their soldiers in the late war; portraits of early settlers and prominent men; miscellaneous matter; maps of the counties; biographies and histories of pioneer families, etc., etc. Chicago, Ill.: W. H. Beers & Co. 1883. pp. (5), 19—596, ill., maps.* [5932

Miller, Charles C.: History of Fairfield County, Ohio and representative citizens. *Edited and compiled by . . . Chicago, Ill.: Published by Richmond-Arnold Publishing Co. 1912. pp. XVII, 19—820, ill.* [5933

Scott, Hervey: A complete history of Fairfield County, Ohio. 1795—1876. *Columbus, O.: Siebert & Lilley 1877. pp. VI, (3), 304.* [5934

Umble, John: The Fairfield county, Ohio, background of the Allen county, Ohio, Mennonite settlement, 1799—1860. *In:*

Mennonite Quarterly Review. Vol. VI. Goshen, Ind.-Scottdale, Pa. 1932. pp. 5—29. [5935

Wiseman, C. M. L.: Centennial history of Lancaster, Ohio and Lancaster people. 1898. The one hundredth anniversary of the settlement of the spot where Lancaster stands. *Lancaster, O.: C. M. L. Wiseman 1898. pp. 5—397; 401—407.* [5936

— Pioneer period and pioneer people of Fairfield County, Ohio. *Columbus, O.: F. J. Heer 1901. pp. 430.* [5937

Holmes County vgl. (see): Wayne County
Jefferson County

Doyle, Joseph B.: 20th century history of Steubenville and Jefferson County, Ohio and representative citizens. *Chicago, Ill.: Richmond-Arnold Publishing Co. 1910. pp. (1), 11—1197, ill.* [5938

Mahoning County

Sanderson, Thos. W.: 20th century history of Youngstown and Mahoning County, Ohio and representative citizens. *Chicago, Ill.: Biographical Publishing Co. 1907. pp. (3), 11—1030, ill.* [5939

Montgomery County

The history of Montgomery County, Ohio, *containing a history of the county; its townships, cities, towns, schools, churches, etc.; general and local statistics; portraits of early settlers and prominent men; history of the Northwest Territory; History of Ohio; . . . Chicago, Ill.: W. H. Beers & Co. 1882. pp. VIII, 19—460, ill., map.* [5940

Conover, Frank: Centennial portrait and biographical record of the City of Dayton and Montgomery County, Ohio, *containing biographical sketches of prominent and representative citizens, together with the biographies and portraits of the governors of Ohio. [s. l.]: A. W. Bowen & Co.; Logansport, Ind.: Press of Wilson, Humphreys & Co. 1897. pp. 1310, ill.* [5941

Drury, A. W.: History of the City of Dayton and Montgomery County, O. 2 vols. *Chicago, Ill. — Dayton, O.: The S. J. Clark Publishing Co. 1909. pp. 941, ill.; Vol. II. Biographical. pp. 1081, ill.* [5942

Perry County vgl. (see): **Fairfield County**

Pickaway County

Cleaf, Aaron R. van: History of Pickaway County, Ohio and representative citizens. *Edited and compiled by . . . Chicago, Ill.: Biographical Publishing Co. 1906. pp. 882, ill.* [5943

Richland County vgl. auch (see also): **Ross County**

Baughman, A. J.: History of Richland County, Ohio from 1808 to 1908. Also biographical sketches of prominent citizens of the county. *2 vols. Chicago, Ill.: The S. J. Clarke Publishing Co. 1908. pp. 7—590, ill.; 595—1175, V, ill.* [5944

Graham, A. A.: History of Richland County, Ohio *(including the original boundaries) its past and present, containing a condensed comprehensive history of Ohio, including an outline history of the Northwest, a complete history of Richland County; its townships, cities, towns and villages, schools, churches, societies, industries, statistics. . . . Compiled by . . . Mansfield, O.: A. A. Graham & Co. 1880. pp. (5), 11—941, ill., map.* [5945

Ross County

1796. History of Ross and Highland Counties, Ohio, with illustrations and biographical sketches. *Cleveland, O.: W. W. Williams 1880. pp. (3), 9—532, ill., maps.* [5946

Evans, Lyle S.: A standard history of Ross County, Ohio. *An authentic narrative of the past, with particular attention to the modern era in the commercial, industrial, civic and social development. Under the editorial supervision. . . . 2 vols. Chicago, Ill. and New York, N. Y.: The Lewis Publishing Co. 1917. pp. XXIX, 484, ill.; 487—934, ill.* [5947

Seneca County

Baughman, A. J.: History of Seneca County Ohio. *A narrative account of its historical progress, its people and its principal interests. 2 vols. Chicago, Ill. — New York, N. Y.: The Lewis Publishing Co. 1911. pp. XXXII, 488, ill.; 493 —969, ill.* [5948

Lang, W.: History of Seneca County from the close of the Revolutionary War to

July, *1880; embracing many personal sketches of pioneers, anecdotes, and faithful descriptions of events pertaining to the organization of the county and its progress. Springfield, O.: Transcript Printing Co. 1880. pp. 691, (1), XII, ill.* [5949

Stark County

Räber, Johann: Rückerinnerungen an die frühe Geschichte von Stark County, [Ohio] und seine ältesten größeren Städte. *In: Der Deutsche Pionier. Jg. III. Cincinnati, O. 1871—1872. S. 18 —21; 51—54; 86—90; 155—157; 189 —191; 218—221; 247—250; 285—287; 347—350; 374—378.* [5950

Tuscarawas County

The history of Tuscarawas County, Ohio, *containing a history of the county; its townships, towns, churches, schools etc., general and local statistics; military record; portraits of early settlers and prominent men; history of the northwest territory; history of Ohio; miscellaneous matters etc., etc. Chicago, Ill.: Warner, Beers & Co. 1884. pp. VIII, 19—882, ill., map.* [5951

Wayne County

Douglas, Ben: History of Wayne County, Ohio, from the days of the pioneers and first settlers to the present time. *Indianapolis, Ind.: Robert Douglas 1878. pp. 868, ill.* [5952

Commemorative biographical record of the counties of Wayne and Holmes, Ohio, *containing biographical sketches of prominent and representative citizens, and many of the early settled families. Chicago, Ill.: J. H. Beers & Co. 1889. pp. (1), 11—836, ill.* [5953

History of Wayne County, Ohio. *2 vols. Indianopolis, Ind.: B. F. Bowen & Co. 1910. pp. (15), (6), 17—896; (13), (6), 913—1494; appendix pp. 1—14.* [5954

Memoirs of the Miami Valley. *Edited by* John C. Hover, Joseph D. Barnes, Walter D. Jones, Charlotte Reeve Conover, Williard J. Wright, Clayton A. Leiter, John Ewing Bradford, W. C. Culkins. *3 vols. Chicago, Ill.: Robert O. Law Co. 1919. pp. XXVII, 17—636, map. pp. XXXI, 17—644. Vol. III. Biographical. pp. 5—794, ill.* [5955

Ohio-Missionen der Brüdergemeinde[1])

Ohio Moravian Missions[2])

Bickenderfer, Jesse: Establishment of the Moravian congregations in Ohio. *In: Transactions of the Moravian Historical Society. Vol. I. 1858—1876. Nazareth, Pa. 1876. pp. 154—176.* [5956

Faris, John T.: „Gnadenhütten, Ohio where the Moravians built a town that passed away. *New York, N. Y. and London: Harper & Brothers 1924. pp. 99—102.* [5957

Farrar, William M.: The Moravian massacre. *In: Ohio Archaeological and Historical Quarterly. Vol. III. Columbus, O. 1890. pp. 271—297.* [5958

Forrest, Earle R.: History of Washington County, Pa. *Vol. I. Chicago, Ill.: The S. J. Clarke Publishing Co. 1926. Chapter XXII: 1754—1780. Founding of the Ohio missions. The story of the Moravians; Chapter XXIII: The storm gathers; Chapter XXIV: Events that led up to the massacre at Gnadenhutten; Chapter XXV: The massacre at Gnadenhutten; Chapter XXVI. Later history of Gnadenhutten. pp. 121—146, ill.* [5959

Giorg, Kara [Pseudonym für Brühl, Georg]: Die ersten Niederlassungen in Ohio. *[Die mährischen Brüder.] In: Der Deutsche Pionier. Jg. I. Cicinnati, O. 1869—1870. S. 65—75; 102—108; 133—138.* [5960

Hildreth, Samuel: Contributions to the early history of the Northwest, including the Moravian missions in Ohio. *Cincinnati, O.: 1864. pp. . .* [5961

Howells, W. D.: Gnadenhütten. *In: The Atlantic Monthly. A magazine of literature, science, art, and politics. Vol. XXIII. Boston, Mass.: Fields, Osgood & Co. 1869. pp. 95—115.* [5962

Huebner, Francis, C.: The Moravian missions in Ohio. *Washington, D. C.: Simms & Lewis. 1898. pp. 128, ill.* [5963

Hulbert, Archer Butler: The Moravian records. „A rough catalogue of the manuscripts preserved in the archives of the Moravian Church and Malin Library." *In: Ohio Archaeological and Historical*

Quarterly. Vol. XVIII. Columbus, O. 1909. pp. 199—226, ill. [5964

John of Lancaster [Pseudonym of Meginness, John F.]: „Schönbrunn." Zeisberger's beautiful spring. *In: Notes and Queries. Edited by W. H. Egle. Fourth series, vol. I. 1891—1893. Harrisburg, Pa. 1893. pp. 359—360.* [5965

Oerter, M. F.: A brief historical sketch of the Moravian congregation at Sharon, Tuscarawas County, Ohio. Written for the Centennial of the congregation. *Canal Dover, O.: Seibert Printing Co. 1915. pp. 36, ill.* [5966

Randell, E. O.: Heckewelder's narrative. *In: Ohio Archaeological Historical Quarterly. Vol. XVIII. Columbus, O. 1909. pp. 258—261.* [5967

Weinland, Joseph E.: The romantic story of Schoenbrunn, the first town of Ohio. *A brief account of the founding of the town, its destruction, and the finding of the lost town site after 146 years. Also a short description of the rebuilding of the town, and the founding of Schoenbrunn Memorial Park as a memorial to our pioneers. Dover, O.: Seibert Printing Co. 1928. pp. 56, ill.* [5968

[Zeisberger, David]: The Moravian records. Volume two. The diaries of Zeisberger relating to the first mission in the Ohio basin. *Edited by Archer Butler Hulbert and William Nathaniel Schwarze. In: Ohio Archaeological and Historical Quarterly. Vol. XXI. Columbus, O. 1912. pp. 125.* [5969

Die deutschen Siedlungen im Scioto-Thale. *From: Portsmouth, O., Correspondent. — Louis F. Korth, Herausgeber. In: Deutsch-Amerikanische Geschichtsblätter. Jg. VIII, Nr. 1. Chicago, Ill. 1908. S. 7—9.* 5970

The Gnadenhuetten Centennial. Sept. 29, 1798. *In: Ohio Archaeological and Historical Publications. Vol. VII. Columbus, O. 1899. pp. 297—313.* [5971

A true history of the massacre of ninety-six Christian Indians, at Gnadenhuetten. Ohio. March 8th, 1782. *Published by the Gnadenhuetten Monument Society. Org. Oct. 7th, 1843. New Philadelphia, O.: Ohio Democrat Office 1847. pp. 12. New print 1870. pp. 12.* [5972

---

[1]) Siehe auch Nr. 1706—1795.
[2]) See also nos. 1706—1795.

Indiana

Betz, I. H.: The Studebacker brothers. The wagon builders of South Bend, Indiana. *In: The Pennsylvania-German. Vol. XI. Lititz, Pa. 1910. pp. 194—204, ill.* [5973

Borntreger, Hans E.: Eine Geschichte der ersten Ansiedlung der Amischen Mennoniten und die Gründung ihrer ersten Gemeinde im Staate Indiana, nebst einer kurzen Erklärung über die Spaltung die in dieser Gemeinde geschehen ist. *Elkhart, Ind.: Mennonite Publishing Co. 1907. 24 S.* [5974

Christophel, Allen B.: Yellow Creek congregation, near Goshen, Ind. *In: Christian Monitor. A monthly magazine for the home. Vol. XXIV, no. 5. Scottdale, Pa. 1932. pp. 237—238, ill.* [5975

Dunn, Jacob P.: The Moravian mission near Anderson. *In: Indiana Magazine of History. Vol. IX. Bloomington, Ind. 1913. pp. 73—83.* [5976

Fritsch, W. A.: Die frühesten deutschen Ansiedler in Indiana bis zum Jahre 1850. *In: Deutsch-Amerikanische Geschichtsblätter. Jg. VIII, Nr. 1. Chicago, Ill. 1908. S. 2—7.* [5977

Funk, John F.: An address by John F. Funk on the occasion of the ninety-second anniversary of his birth at the Mennonite Church, Elkhart, Ind., April 6, 1927. *[s. l.] pp. 14.* [5978

Kolb, A. B.: Pennsylvania-German settlers in Indiana. *In: The Pennsylvania-German. Vol. VIII. Lebanon, Pa. 1907. pp. 51—53.* [5979

Rarick, Ralph G.: History of the Mississinewa Church of the Brethren, Delaware County, Indiana. *Prepared and published by . . . Elgin, Ill.: Brethren Publishing House 1917. pp. 222, ill., map.* [5980

Schrock, Delton S.: A brief history of Clinton Frame Church. *Scottdale, Pa.: Mennonite Publishing House 1927. pp. 11.* [5981

Shuey, D. B.: A Pennsylvania German settlement in Indiana [Mulberry, Ind.]. *In: The Pennsylvania-German. Vol. IX. Cleona, Pa. 1908. pp. 487—490, ill.* [5982

Troyer, Glen L. and others: Mennonite church history of Howard and Miami counties, Indiana. *By the Y. P. C. A. Historical Committee: Glen L. Troyer, John W. Horner, Sadie Miller Mishler, Kathryn King, Melvin Myers. Scottdale, Pa.: Mennonite Publishing House 1916. pp. 189, ill.* [5983

Taylor, R. S.: Restoring a worn-out farm. *Reprint from: Tennessee Sun. In: The Pennsylvania-German. Vol. XI. Lititz, Pa. 1910. p. 638.* [5984

Tedrow, William L.: Our church. A history of the Synod of Northern Indiana of the Evangelical Lutheran Church. *Ann Arbor, Mich.: The Inland Press 1894. pp. VI, 295.* [5985

[Tschetter, Paul]: The diary of Paul Tschetter. *[Description of a journey to America 1873 with Lorentz Tschetter, both of Hutterthal, South Russia.] Translated and edited by* I. M. Hofer. A brief biography of Paul Tschetter, 1842——1919. *By his son* W. Tschetter. *In: The Mennonite Quarterly Review. Vol. V. Goshen, Ind.-Scottdale, Pa. 1931. pp. 112—127; 198—219, map. [Relative to Amish and Mennonites of Elkhart Co., Indiana.]* [5986

Winger, Otho: History of the Church of the Brethren in Indiana. *Elgin, Ill.: Brethren Publishing House 1917. pp. 479, ill.* [5987

Yoder, Reuben: A Report. A history of the Amish in Elkhart County and reports of Amish Conferences, 1862, 1864, 1865 and 1868. [5988

History of Elkhart County, Ind., *together with sketches of its cities, villages and townships, educational, religious, civil, military, and political history. History of Indiana, embracing accounts of the pre-historic races, aborigines, French, English and American conquests, and a general review of its civil, political and military history. Chicago, Ill.: Chas. C. Chapman & Co. 1881. pp. 1181, ill.* [5989

Pictorial and biographical memoirs of Elkhart and St. Joseph Counties, Indiana, *together with biographies of many prominent men of Northern Indiana and of the whole state, both living and dead. Chicago, Ill.: Goodspeed Brothers 1893. pp. XII, 777.* [5990

Weaver, Abraham E.: A standard history of Elkhart County, Indiana. *An authentic narrative of the past, with par-*

ticular attention to the modern era in the commercial, industrial, educational, civic and social development. Under the editorial supervision of . . . 2 vols. Chicago, Ill. and New York, N. Y.: The American Historical Society. 1916. pp. XXVIII, 403, ill., map. pp. 407—944, ill. [5991

History of Northeast Indiana, La Grange, Steuben, Noble and DeKalb Counties. *Under the editorial supervision of* Ira Ford, Orville Stevens, William H. McEwen, William H. McIntosh. *2 vols. Chicago, and New York: The Lewis Publishing Co. pp. XXXIV, 612, ill.; 463, ill.* [5992

Illinois

Croll, P. C.: Early Lutheran annals in the „Far West". *Reprint from: „The Lutheran Observer, Dec. 13 and 27, 1912 and Jan. 3, 1913. In: The Penn Germania. Vol. II. = Old series, vol. XIV. Lititz, Pa. 1913. pp. 181—186.* [5993
Harkey, S. W.: The early history of Lutheranism in Illinois. *In: The Evangelical Review. Vol. XVII. Gettysburg, Pa. 1866. pp. 526—546.* [5994
Haupert, Albert P.: The Moravian settlement in Illinois. *An address delivered before the Illinois State Historical Society, in the Senate Chamber of the State Capital at Springfield, Ill., May 5, 1922, and printed in the Proceedings of said society. Bethlehem, Pa.: Bethlehem Printing Co. 1922. pp. 16.* [5995
[Hoffmann, E. B.]: Deutsche Ansiedlungen in St. Clair County, Ill. *Abdruck aus: St. Louis „Anzeiger des Westen". In: Der Deutsche Pionier. Jg. XIII. Cincinnati, O. 1881—1882. S. 107—110.* [5996
Mannhardt, Emil: Die Deutschen in McLean County und Bloomington. *In: Deutsch-Amerikanische Geschichtsblätter, Vierteljahrsschrift herausgegeben von der Deutsch-Amerikanischen Historischen Gesellschaft von Illinois. Chicago, Ill. Jg. IV. 1904. S. 6—25. [Besonders S. 20—21.]* [5997
— The Pennsylvania-German in Illinois. *In: The Pennsylvania-German. Vol. VIII. Lebanon, Pa. 1907. pp. 13—15.* [5998
Shambaugh, Adam: Early days on the Wabash. *. . . 1890. pp. . . .*

[Gives an account of the United Brethren families settling in that part of the country; note Drury, 1924. p. 386.] [5999
Sifferd, C. W.: The Lutheran Church in southern Illinois. *In: The Lutheran Quarterly. Vol. XLI. Gettysburg, Pa. 1911. pp. 412—423.* [6000
Weber, Harry F.: Centennial history of the Mennonites of Illinois 1829—1929. *Published by the Mennonite Historical Society, Goshen College, Goshen, Ind. Scottdale, Pa.: Press of the Mennonite Publishing House. 1931. pp. VII—XVI, 680, ill., maps. = Studies in Anabaptist and Mennonite History. . . . Published by the Mennonite Historical Society, Goshen College, Goshen, Ind. No. 3.* [6001
Deutsche Namen in St. Clair County, Illinois, vor dem Jahre 1800. *In: Der Deutsche Pionier. Jg. XIII. Cincinnati, O. 1881—1882. S. 20—21.* [6002
History of the Waddams Grove Church. *A history of the Waddams Grove congregation of the Church of the Brethren, in Stephenson and Jo Daviess Counties, Illinois, and adjoining counties of Wisconsin. Including an account of the annual meeting of 1856, Enoch Eby's Mission to Denmark, in 1877, and the minutes of the first three district meetings of northern Illinois, held at Waddams Grove, in 1862, 1871 and 1882. Elgin, Ill. : Brethren Publishing House 1910. pp. 123, ill.* [6003

Iowa

Bender, Ruth: A study of the Pennsylvania-German dialect as spoken in Johnson County, Iowa. *Thesis of M. A., State University of Iowa, Iowa City, Ia. 1929. (Typewritten) pp. 72.* [6004

[Blough, Albert P.]: South Waterloo Church of the Brethren, Waterloo, Iowa. *Historical sketch and dedicatory program. 1913. pp. (7), ill.* [6005

30*

Fouse, D. S.: Pennsylvania-German colonies in Iowa. *In: The Pennsylvania-German. Vol. VIII. Lebanon, Pa. 1907. pp. 147—151, ill.* [6006

Gingerich, Melvin: The Amish Mennonites in Iowa. *Thesis of M. A., State University of Iowa, Iowa City, Ia. Department of History. Iowa City, Ia. 1930. [Typewritten] pp. 151.*
[Bibliography pp. 127—134.] [6007

Guengerich, J. D.: Early frontier life in Iowa. *(Extracts from an address at a family reunion.) In: Christian Monitor. A monthly magazine for the home. Vol. XIV, no. 6. Scottdale, Pa. 1922. pp. 561—562.* [6008

Guengerich, S. D.: A brief history of the Amish settlement in Johnson County, Iowa. *In: The Mennonite Quarterly Review. Vol. III. Goshen, Ind. 1929. pp. 243—248.* [6009

Haughtelin, J. D.: History of Coon River congregation. A history of Coon River congregation of the Church of the Brethren, in the Middle District of Iowa, to March 1, 1913. *Compiled and written by . . . Elgin, Ill.: Brethren Publishing House. 1913. pp. 105, ill.* [6010

Kephart, Cyrus J.: Historical souvenir of the Church of the United Brethren in Christ at Lisbon, Iowa 1836—1904. *Lisbon, Ia.: Lisbon Herold 1904. pp. 44.* [6011

Kirkpatrick, Ellis Lore: A study of the social life of the Brethren, as depicted by the English River congregation near South English, Keokuk County, Iowa. *Thesis of M. S., University of Kansas. Lawrence, Kan. 1920. Tpyewritten pp. (7), 128.* [6012

— The English River congregation of the Church of the Brethren. *Iowa City, Ia.: Published by the State Historical Society of Iowa; Athens Press 1930. pp. 107. = Iowa Monograph Series: No. 2. Edited by Benj. F. Shambaugh.* [6013

Mohler, John E.: The Dunkers in Iowa. *In: The Annals of Iowa. A historical quarterly. Vol. VII. Third series. Des Moines, Ia.: Published by the Historical Department of Iowa, Jan., 1906. pp. 270—282, ill.* [6014

Rodabaugh, Willis P. and **Brower, A. H.:** A history of the Church of the Brethren in southern Iowa. *Compiled by . . . Elgin, Ill.: Brethren Publishing House 1924. pp. 323, ill.* [6015

Snyder, J. S., Haughtelin, J. D. and **Miller, S. B.:]** Compiled minutes of the German Baptist Brethren Church (called Dunkers) of the Middle District of Iowa. Published by authority of the District Meeting of Middle District of Iowa, held at Garrison, Iowa, Sept. 26, 1906. *Committee on publication: J. S. Snyder, J. D. Haughtelin, — S. B. Miller, Elgin, Ill.: Brethren Publishing House 1907. pp. 88.* [6016

Swartzendruber, J. F.: Mother's story. *In: Christian Monitor. A monthly magazine for the home. Vol. XIV, no. 8. Scottdale, Pa. 1922. pp. 624—625.* [6017

Tungeln, H. von: A rural survey of Orange Township, Blackhawk County, Iowa. *Ames, Iowa 1918, pp. 397—450, ill., map.*
= Agricultural Experiment Station, Iowa State College of Agriculture and Mechanic Arts. (Rural Sociology Section.) Bulletin no. 184. [6018

Wick, Barthinius L.: The Amish Mennonites A sketch of their origin, and of their settlement in Iowa, with their creed in an appendix. *Iowa City, Ia: Published by the State Historical Society 1894. pp. 60.* [6019

—————

Brewer, Luther A. and **Wick, Barthinius L.:** History of Linn County Iowa from its earliest settlement to the present time. *Cedar Rapids, Ia.: The Torch Press 1911. pp. XV, 496.*
[Lisbon and the United Brethren Church. pp. 291—297.] [6020

Hartman, John C.: History of Black Hawk County, Iowa and its people. *2 vols. Chicago, Ill.: The S. J. Clarke Publishing Co. 1915. pp. 432; 497.*
[Orange Township. pp. 83—84; 332—333.] [6021

Metre, Isaiah Van: History of Black Hawk County, Iowa and representative citizens. *Chicago, Ill.: Biographical Publishing Co. 1904. pp. 801.*
[German Baptist Brethren. pp. 282—284.] [6022

History of Johnson County, Iowa, *containing a history of the county, and its townships, cities and villages from 1836 to 1882 . . . Iowa City, Ia. 1883. pp. 966.* [6023

Michigan

Russel, John Andrew: The Germanic influence in the making of Michigan. *Detroit, Mich.: University of Detroit 1927. pp. 415.*
[*Bibliography: 367—374.*]   [6024

Shrock, Delton: History of Pleasant View Church, near Chief, Michigan. *In: Christian Monitor. A monthly magazine for the home. Vol. XX, no. 9. Scottdale, Pa. 1928. pp. 277—278.*   [6025

Wisconsin

Lacher, J. H. A.: The German element in Wisconsin. *Published for the Benefit of the Salomon Brothers Memorial Fund by Muehlenberg Unit.,36. Milwaukee, Steuben Society of America 1926. pp. 60.* [6026

Levi, Kate Asaphine Everest: Geographical origin of German immigration to Wiscon-

sin. *Madison, Mich.: State Historica Society of Wisconsin 1898. pp. (2) 341—398. Folded map.*
Reprinted from State Historical Society of Wisconsin. Collections, vol. XIV.
[6027

Kansas

Craik, E.: History of the German Baptist Brethren in Kansas. *McPherson Published by the author; Press of Daily Republican 1922. pp. 397.*   [6028

Ruppenthal, J. C.: Pennsylvania Germans in Central Kansas. *In: The Penn Germania. New series, vol. III, no. 1. = Old series, vol. XV. Cleona, Pa. 1914. pp. 33—38.*   [6029

Troyer, Ida: History of the West Liberty Mennonite Church located in McPher-

son County, Kansas. *In: Christian Monitor. A monthly magazine for the home. Vol. XXI, no. 10. Scottdale, Pa. 1929. pp. 306—308.*   [6030

River Brethren in Kansas. How the colony that went out from Lancaster County about 30 years ago has prospered. *Reprint from Kansas Star. In: The Pennsylvania-German. Vol. X. Lititz, Pa. 1909. p. 347.*   [6031

Nebraska

Long, Francis A.: The Pennsylvania-German in the Elkhorn Valley. *In: The*

Pennsylvania German. Vol. VIII. Lebanon, Pa. 1907. pp. 55—57.   [6032

Minnesota

Haupt, A. J. D.: The Pennsylvania-German in Minnesota. *In: The Pennsylvania-*

German. Vol. IX. Cleona, Pa. 1908. pp. 277—279.   [6033

North Dakota

Martin, Ruby: Fairview Mennonite Church near Surrey, North Dakota. *In: Christian Monitor. A monthly magazine for*

the home. Vol. XXIV, no. 4. Scottdale, Pa. 1932. pp. 113—114, ill.   [6034

Biographisches und genealogisches Schrifttum

Biographical and Genealogical Papers

Allgemeines

General

[U. S.] Library of Congress: American and English genealogies in the Library of Congress. *Compiled under the direction of the chief of the catalogue division. Second edition. 2 vols. Washington, D. C. 1919. Vol. I. A to Lesa; Vol. II. Lesh to Z. pp. IV, 688; 689—332.* [6035

The American genealogist, being a catalogue of family histories. *A bibliography of American genealogy or a list of the title pages of the books and pamphlets on family history, published in America, from 1771 to date. Fourth edition. Prepared by the publishers. Former editions were edited by William H. Whitmore in 1862, 1868 and 1875. Albany, N. Y.: Joel Munsell's Sons, publishers 1897. pp. 328.* [6036

List of titles of genealogical articles in American periodicals and kindred works. *Giving the name, residence and earliest date of the first settler of each family, and adding deficiencies in brackets. Designed as a companion volume to our „American Genealogist", Albany, N. Y.: Joel Munsell's Sons, Publishers 1899. pp. 165.* [6037

Index to American genealogies and to genealogical material contained in all works such as town histories, county histories, local histories, historical society publications, biographies, historical periodicals, and kindred works. *Alphabetically arranged. Enabling the reader to ascertain whether the genealogy of any family, or any part of it, is printed, either by itself or embodied in other works. Fifth edition. Revised, improved and enlarged, containing nearly 50000 references. First and second editions were edited by* **Daniel S. Durrie.** *Albany, N. Y.: Joel Munsell's Sons, publisher 1900. pp. 352.*

Supplement 1900 to 1908 to the Index of Genealogies. *Published in 1900. Albany, N. Y.: Joel Munsell's Sons, publishers 1908. pp. 107.* [6038

Library Catalogue of the Institute of American generalogy. *Chicago, Ill. 1934. 80 S.* 6038a

Helbig, Richard E.: German - American genealogies, chiefly Pennsylvanian, found in the New York Public Library. *In: The Pennsylvania-German. Vol. VII. Lebanon, Pa. 1906. pp. 303—307.* [6039

Ruederer, H.: Deutsche Familienforschung in den Vereinigten Staaten von Amerika. *In: Archiv für Sippenforschung und alle verwandten Gebiete. Jg. V. Görlitz, O.-L. 1928. S. 284—285.* [6039a

Staudt, Richard Wilh.: Genealogie in Amerika. *Sonderheft der Vierteljahrsschrift für Wappen-, Siegel- und Familienkunde. Herausgegeben vom Verein „Herold" in Berlin. Jg. LIV, Heft 4. Berlin 1928. 24 S.* [6039b

Virkus, Frederick Adams: The abridged compendium of American genealogy; first families of America; a genealogical encyclopedia of the United States, *edited by . . . under direction of* **Albert Nelson Marquis** *. . . Vol. 1—(4). Chicago, Ill.: A. N. Marquis & Co. 1925—(30), ill.* [6040

The national cyclopedia of American biography being the history of the United States as illustrated in the lives of the founders, builders, and defenders of the republic, and the men and women who are doing the work and moulding the thought of the present time. *Edited by distinguished biographers, selected from each state, revised and approved by the most eminent historians, scholars, and statesmen of the day. Vol. I—XXI, A—C, and Index and Conspectus. New York, N. Y.: James T. White & Co. 1898—1906.* [6041

Dictionary of American biography. *Under the auspices of the American Council of Learned Societies. Edited by* Allen Johnson *[since vol. IV:* Allen Johnson *and* Dumas Malone; *since vol. IX:* Dumas Malone]. *New York, N. Y.: Charles Scribner's Sons. Vol. I. 1928. ff. [Contents: see Appendix S. 583—591.]* [6042

National Society of the Daughters of American Revolution: Lineage book — National Society of the Daughters of the American Revolution. *Vol. I. 1890—1891. ff. — (Vol. CXXV. 1916).* [6043

American ancestry: giving the name and descent in the male line, of Americans whose ancestors settled in the United States previous to the Declaration of Independence. *A. D. 1776. 12 vols. Albany, N. Y.: J. Munsell's Sons 1887—1899. [Contents: — Vol. I.* The City of Albany, State of New York, 1887, *edited by* Thomas P. Hughes. *— Vol. II. (Local series)* Columbia County, State of New York, 1887, *edited by* Th. P. Hughes. *— Vol. III—XII.* Embracing lineages from the whole of the United States, *1888 —1898. Edited by* Frank Munsell.] [6044

Pennsylvanien, allgemein

Pennsylvania, general

Egle, William Henry: Pennsylvania genealogies; Scotch-Irish and German. *Harrisburg, Pa.: Lane & Hart 1886. pp. VIII,, 720; Second edition. Harrisburg, Pa. 1896. pp. 798.* [6045

[Jordan, John Woolf]: Colonial and Revolutionary families of Pennsylvania; genealogical and personal memoirs. *Editor . . . 3 vols. New York, N. Y.: The Lewis Publishing Co. 1911. pp. . . . [Paged continiously.]* [6046

[—] Encyclopedia of Pennsylvania biography. *By John W. Jordan. 1—(20) vols. New York, N. Y.: The Lewis Historical Publishing Co. 1914—(1932). [Vols. 1—7 paged continiously; vol. 11 not numbered. Vols. 1—13 edited by* John W. Jordan; *vols. 14—16 edited by* Thomas Lynch Montgomery; *vol. 17 edited by* Ernest Spofford; *vols. 18—(20) by* Frederic A. Godcharles.] [6047

— Genealogical and personal history of western Pennsylvania. *Editor-in-chief . . . 3 vols. New York, N. Y.: Lewis Historical Publishing Co. 1915. pp. (3), 528; 529—1088; 1089—1789, ill.* [6048

Seilhammer, G. O.: Genealogical notes. *Arranged in alphabetical orders. 8 vols. Typewritten. [At the State Library of Pa., Harrisburg.]* [6049

The biographical encyclopedia of Pennsylvania of the nineteenth century. *Philadelphia, Pa.: Galaxy Publishing Co. 1874. pp. 672, ill.* [6050

A biographical album of prominent Pennsylvanians. *Three series. Philadelphia, Pa.: The American Biographical Publishing Co. 1888—1889—1890. First series:* Statesmen, military, officers, journalists, educators and prominent persons recently deceased. *pp. 446, ill.; Second series:* State officials, judges, lawyers, physicians, artists, etc. *pp. 364, ill.; Third series:* Financiers, railroad officials, merchants, manufacturers, inventors, publishers, and other practical men of affairs. *pp. 380, ill.* [6051

Encyclopaedia of contemporary biography of Pennsylvania. *3 vols. New York, N. Y.: Atlantic Publishing and Engraving Co. 1890, 1898. pp. 317; IV, 5—284; 318, ill.* [6052

Deutschpennsylvanien

Pennsylvania-German

Crone, Frank L.: Some Pennsylvania Dutch genealogies. *In: The Indiana Magazine of History. Vol. XV. Indianopolis, Ind. 1919. pp. 48—52.*

[Crone; Switzer, Weaver; Steel families.] [6053

De Long, Irwin Hoch: Genealogical gleanings from different sources; (Pa.) *In:*

The National Genealogical Society Quarterly. Vol. XII, no. 2. Washington, D. C. 1923. pp. 20—21. [6054

Ely, Warren S. (Mrs.): Family bibles in the Library of the Bucks County Historical Society. *Inscriptions copied by . . . In: A Collection of Papers read before the Bucks County Historical Society. Vol. VI. Allentown, Pa. 1932. pp. 425—466.*
[Among others the following German family bibles: Jacob Angene, John Georg Emig, Hardman, Oberholtzer, Summers A. Smith, Stover.] [6055

Jordan, John W.: Contributions to Pennsylvania-German genealogy. *In: Notes and Queries Edited by W. H. Egle. Fourth series, vol. I. 1891—1893. Harrisburg, Pa. 1893. pp. 26—27; 32—34; 192—193.* [6056

— Contributions to Pennsylvania-German genealogy. [York County.] *In: Notes and Queries. Edited by W. H. Egle. Fourth series, vol. I. 1891—1893. Harrisburg, Pa. 1893. pp. 238—240.* [6057

Kriebel, Howard Wiegner: Family bibles. *(Partial list of . . .: [Gilbert, Funk-Oberholtzer, Stichter, Gottwalls, Rothrock, John Hersh, Schneider, Rummel, Hartranft, Schwartz, Freiderich, Neuman, Gottschalk, Alderfer, Wyker, Krebil, Markley] . . . in custody of the Schwenkfelder Historical Society and the genealogical data recorded in them.) In: The Perkiomen Region. Vol. VII, no. 1. Pennsburg, Pa. 1929. pp. 24—26; No. 2. pp. 54—57; No. 3. pp. 90—94; No. 4. pp. 122—128.* [6058

Brief notices of colonial families. *In: The Perkiomen Region, Past and Present. Vol. I. Philadelphia, Pa. 1895.* John Steger. *pp. 46—47;* Ulrich Hartman. *p. 47;* Hieronimus Dotterer. *pp. 57—58;* John Jacob Schrack. *pp. 58—59;* Henry Bitting. *pp. 59—60;* Philip Reinhart Erhard. *pp. 101—102;* Jacob Markley. *p. 102;* Frederick Reimer. *pp. 102—103;* Georg Schwenk. *p. 117;* John Campell. *p. 138;* Benedict Mintz. *p. 138;* Peter Conrad. *p. 157. Vol. III. 1901.* The Stapleton and Specht families. *pp. 19—21;* Michael Schwenck. *pp. 35—37;* John Zieber, of Ferderick Twp. *pp. 67—68;* John Krey. *p. 82.* Justus Wright. *pp. 127—128;* Jacob Rothrock. *p. 147;* John Joseph Bull. *p. 147.* [6059

Where they came from. *In: The Perkiomen Region, Past and Present. Vol. I. Philadelphia, Pa. 1895:* Evert In de Haven. *p. 6;* Frederick Pennebecker. *p. 6;* Joseph Wiand. *p. 31;* Simon Keppler. *p. 31;* Jacob Markley. *p. 62; Vol. II. 1900.* Johann Adam Rau. *p. 8;* Hans Ulrich Ammann. *p. 8;* Johann George Gaukler. *p. 8;* Frantz Thomas Hartman. *p. 21;* Johannes Rheiner. *p. 137;* Rudolf Egg. *p. 137;* John Scheidel. *p. 149;* John Cress. *p. 149;* George and Jacob Graemeling. *p. 169;* Michael Bauer. *p. 194;* Andrew Weiler. *p. 194. Vol. III. 1901.* Johannes Bastian Seibert. *p. 50;* Philip and Frederick Drescher. *p.37;* Adam Gebhard, George Horn, George Reh, Nicolaus Peter. *p. 82.* [6060

Genealogical records of pioneer Pennsylvania families. *In: The Pennsylvania-German. Vol. X. Lititz, Pa. 1909. Appendix pp. 32.*
(I) Introduction. *pp. 1—4.*
(II) A letter of Louis Richards. *p. 5.*
(III) Tombstone inscriptions at Bern Church. *Transcribed by* P. J. Bickel and John Baer Stoudt. *pp. 6—11.*
(IV) Tombstone inscriptions at the De Long's Reformed Church, Bowers Station, Berks County, Pa. *Transcribed by* J. Baer Stoudt. *pp. 11—13.*
(V) Tombstone inscriptions of Lower Milford Township, Lehigh County, Pa. *Transcribed by* Charles R. Roberts. *pp. 13—15.*
(VI) Tombstone inscriptions of persons born prior to 1800 and past 16 years at death at Arendtsville, Adams County, Pa. *Transcribed by* N. A. Gobrecht. *pp. 15—17.*
(VII) A partial burial record of the Western Salisbury Lutheran and Reformed cemeteries, *By* Tilghman Neimeyer. *pp. 17—24.*
(VIII) The graveyards of Hereford Township, Berks County, Pa. *By* W. H. Sallade. *pp. 25—29.*
(IX) Death notices in ,,Die Biene" 1846—1848, *published in Bethlehem, Pa. pp. 29—31.* [6061

A noteworthy list of subscribers *[1420 names of subscribers, found in the Baer folio bible of 1819, Lancaster, Pa.] Reprint in: The Pennsylvania-German. Vol. XI. Lititz, Pa. 1910. pp. 409—415.* [6062

Nead, Daniel Wunderlich: Index to proper names mentioned in the Proceedings and Addresses of the Pennsylvania-

German Society. *Prepared by . . . Lancaster, Pa.: New Era Printing Co. 1898. In: The Pennsylvania-German Society. Proceedings and Addresses . . . 1897. Vol. VIII. Lancaster, Pa. 1898. Separate pagination.* pp. 100. [6063

The Penn Germania Genealogical Club. *In: The Penn Germania. Vol. I. = Old series, vol. XIII. Lititz, Pa. 1912.* pp. 276—279; 375—378; 466—469; 562—566; 650—654; 779—783; 895—901. *Vol. II. — Old series, vol. XIV. 1913.* pp. 62—65; 144—149; 225—229.
[6064

The Pennsylvania German Society: List of the Pennsylvania-German Society. Biographical sketches. *In: The Pennsylvania-German Society. Proceedings and Addresses 1892. Vol. III. 1893.* pp. 149—188; . . . 1893. Vol. IV. 1894. pp. 157—187; . . . 1894. Vol. V. 1895. pp. 153—170; . . . 1895. Vol. VI. 1896. pp. 141—157; . . . 1896. Vol. VII. 1897. pp. 441—475. [6065

— Obituaries. In memoriam. *In: The Pennsylvania-German Society. Proceedings and Addresses. Vol. II, 1892ff. [See Appendix S. 581—583.]* [6066

Pennsylvanische Heiratslisten

Pennsylvania Marriage Licenses

Names and persons for whom marriage licenses were issued in the Province of Pennsylvania, previous to 1790. *In: The Pennsylvania Archives. Second series. Edited by John B. Linn and Wm. H. Egle. Vol. II. Harrisburg, Pa. 1896.* pp. 292. [6067

Pennsylvania marriage licenses, issued by Governor James Hamilton, 1748—1752. *[List from an account book in the Manuscript Department of the Historical Society of Pennsylvania, — „The Honourable James Hamilton Esq., his account current with Richard Peters" — a list of marriage licenses not included in those printed in the Pennsylvania Archives, Second series, vol. II.] In: The Pennsylvania Magazine of History and Biography. Vol. XXXII. Philadelphia, Pa. 1908.* pp. 71—78; 233—236; 345—350; 471—486. [6068

Pennsylvania marriage licenses, 1762—1768. *In: The Pennsylvania Magazine of History and Biography. Vol. XL. Philadelphia, Pa. 1916.* pp. 104—107; 208—221; 319—334; 436—457; *Vol. XLI. 1917.* pp. 224—246; 334—358; 489—501.
[6069

Kirchenbücher[1])

Church-Records[2])

Bucher, John Conrad: Record of marriages performed by Rev. *John Conrad Bucher.* 1763—1769. *(Copy of the original records), contributed by* Luther R. Kelker. *In: The Pennsylvania Magazine of History and Biography. Vol. XXV. Philadelphia, Pa. 1901.* pp. 375—381. [6070

[Helffrich, Johannes Heinrich]: Register of marriages and burials between the years 1790 and 1810. *By the Rev. Johannes Heinrich Helffrich. Con-*

tributed by **Clarence E. Beckel.** *In: Publications of the Genealogical Society of Pennsylvania. Vol. V, no. 1. Philadelphia, Pa. 1912.* pp. 6—23. [6071

[Henkel, Paul]: Marriages performed by Rev. *Paul Henkel* in Rockingham, Shenandoah, Augusta and Botetourt Counties, Va. and other localities. *Most are clearly indicated as shown „Paul Hinckle — his book." Copied by* **Cora C. Curry.** *In: The National Genealogical Society Quarterly. Vol. XII, no. 2. Washington, D. C. 1923.* pp. 30—31.
[6072

[Van Hoff, A. H.]: A baptismal register. 1816—1844. (Supposed to be that of

---

[1]) Soweit nicht regional eingeordnet.
[2]) Most of the church records will be found arranged regionally.

Rev. *Van Hoff*.) *In: Notes and Queries.*
Edited by W. H. Egle. Third series,
vol. II. 1887—1890. Harrisburg, Pa.
1891. pp. 385—386; p. 382; Marriage
register: *pp. 388—389; 392—393; 395*
—396; Reprint in: Third series, vol. III.
Harrisburg, Pa. 1896. pp. 451—453;
456—457; resp. pp. 457—459; 460—462;
462—465.   [6073
[Stoever, John Casper]: Rev. *John Casper*
Stoever's record of baptism and marriages from 1730 to 1779. *Edited by*
F. G. F. Schantz. *In: Notes and Queries.*
Edited by W. H. Egle. Annual vol. 1896.
Harrisburg, Pa. 1897. pp. 2—7; 10—14;
16—19; 22—25; 27—31; 33—37; 39—43;
45—48; 51—54; 55—59; 61—65; 68—72;
74—76; 80—86; 88—94; 96—101; 104
—108; 111—114.   [6074
[—] Records of Rev. *John Casper*
Stoever. Baptismal and marriage 1730
—1779. [Translated from the German
and edited by] F. J. F. Sch[antz]. *Har-*
risburg, Pa.: Harrisburg Publishing Co.
1896. pp. 77.   [6075
[Wack, George]: Marriages by Rev. *George*
Wack. [„*Record of marriages solem-*
nized by me, Georg Wack, minister of

the Gospel in Montgomery County."]
Communicated by **W. H. Reed.** *In:*
Historical Notes, relating to the Pennsyl-
vania Reformed Church. Vol. I. Phila-
delphia, Pa. 1900. pp. 10—12; 31—32;
53—54; 90—91; 104—106; 125—128;
142—144; 159—160; p. 170.   [6076
[Wack, George]: Marriages by Rev. *George*
Wack. Contributed by **W. H. Reed.** *In:*
The Perkiomen Region, Past and Present.
Vol. II. Philadelphia, Pa. 1900. p. 1;
pp. 27—29; 66—67; 83—88; 115—116;
130—132; 147—148; p. 164; p. 180;
pp. 195—196; Vol. III. 1901. p. 16;
p. 32; p. 48.   [6077
Collections of the Genealocigal Society of
Pennsylvania. *In: Publications of the*
Genealogical Society of Pennsylvania.
Vol. VI, no. 3. Philadelphia, Pa. 1917.
pp. 309—318. Church records — Lutheran. *p. 312;* Moravian. *p. 313;* — Reformed. *p. 313.*   [6078
Hinke, Wm. J.: Oldest Reformed church
records in Pennsylvania. *In: The Na-*
tional Genealogical Society Quarterly.
Vol. VI, no. 3. Washington, D. C. 1917.
p. 57.   [6079

Familientage

Family Reunions

Pennsylvania-German family-reunions *[in*
1907.] In: The Pennsylvania-German.
Vol. VIII. Lebanon, Pa. 1907. p. 454;
Additional family-reunions. *p. 510.* [6080
Family reunions in *[1909.] In: The Penn-*
sylvania-German. Vol. X. Lititz, Pa.
1909. pp. 467—469.   [6081
Family reunions. *[List of Pennsylvania-*
German family reunions and their smee-
tings.] In: The Pennsylvania-German

Vol. XI. Lititz, Pa. 1910. pp. 579
—585.   [6082
Family reunions; List of, held in 1911. *In:*
The Pennsylvania-German. Vol. XII.
Lititz, Pa. 1911. pp. 613—615.   [6083
Family reunions. *[Stray notes respecting*
some of the reunions of 1912.] In: The
Penn Germania. Vol. I. = Old series,
vol. XIII. Lititz, Pa. 1912. pp. 875
—883.   [6084

Deutsche Vor- und Familiennamen

German Names

American Council of Learned Societies:
Report of committee on linguistic and
national stocks in the population of the
United States. *In: Annual Report of the*
American Hisorical Association for the
year 1931. Vol. I. — Proceedings.

Washington, D. C.: United States Go-
vernment Printing Office 1932. pp. 103
—452.
[Contents see no. 855a.]   [6085
Bachert, A. E.: Corrupted patronymics.
A bane in genealogical research. „*Bacher*

(boshair); Baucher (bö-sha); Bochart (bo-shär); Boucher (bö-sha), etc., etc." In: *The Pennsylvania-German. Vol. XII. Lititz, Pa. 1911. pp. 604—607.* [6085a

Große, Friedrich: Des deutschen Volkes verlorene Söhne als Angelsachsen. *In: Deutsche Erde. Zeitschrift für Deutschkunde. Herausgegeben von Paul Langhans. Jg. X. Gotha 1911. S. 140—141.* [6086

Heiderich, Wilhelm: Veränderung deutscher Familiennamen in den Vereinigten Staaten. *In: Volk und Rasse. Illustrierte Monatsschrift für deutsches Volkstum. Jg. VIII. München 1933. S. 46—48.* [6086a

Kapp, Friedrich: „Einige deutsche, amerikanisierte Namen in New York." *In: Die Deutschen im Staate New York bis zum Anfang des neunzehnten Jahrhunderts. Von Friedrich Kapp. Leipzig 1868 [= Nr. 440]. Anhang. Nr. 8. S. XXVII—XXVIII.* [6087

Kehr, Cyrus: Identification of nationality. *In; The Pennsylvania-German. Vol. XI. Lititz, Pa. 1910. pp. 742—744.* [6088

Kekule von Stradowitz, Stephan: Deutsche Familiennamen unter fremden Völkern. *In: Mitteilungen der Akademie zur wissenschaftlichen Erforschung und zur Pflege des Deutschtums. Deutsche Akademie. Jg. 1928. München 1928. S. 901—915.* [6089

Kuhns, Oscar: Pennsylvania-German surnames. *In: The Pennsylvania-German Society. Proceedings and Addresses at Reading, Oct. 3, 1894. Vol. V. Reading: Pa. 1895. pp. 121—131.* [6900

— Origin of Pennsylvanian surnames. *In: Lippincott's monthly magazine. Vol. LIX. Jan. to June, 1897. Philadephlia, Pa. 1897. pp. 395—399.* [6091

— Studies in Pennsylvania German family names. *In: Americana Germanica. A quarterly. Vol. IV. Philadelphia, Pa. 1901—1902. pp. 299—341.*

[includes an alphabetical list of current Pennsylvania German names with both their German and the Anglicize forms. pp. 303—341.] [6092

Rupp, I. Daniel: General remarks on the origin of surnames; interpretation of baptismal names, which occur in the Collection of Thirty Thousand Names of German, Swiss and other Immigrants; to which are added other baptismal names, both of males and females. *Collected and arranged by . . . Harrisburg, Pa.: Theo. F. Scheffer 1856. pp. 37.* [6093

[Schoedler, D. E.]: Origin of names. *In' The Historical Journal. Vol. II. Williamsport, Pa. 1894. pp. 384—390.* [6094

Schuricht, Hermann: Anglicized and corrupted German names in Virginia. *Compiled by . . . In: The Pennsylvania-German. Vol. XII. Lititz, Pa. 1911. pp. 305—306.* [6095

Familiengeschichten und Biographien

Family Histories and Biographies

A

[Houtz, Mrs. S. J. (Kline)]: Family memorial of John Phillip **Achenbach** and descendants in the United States. *Topeka, Kan.: The Mail Printing House. pp. 39.*

[who came to America from Wiehenstein, Westphalia about 1754.] [6096

Delk, Edwin Heyl: The life and works of Rev. Charles S. **Albert,** D. D. *Edited by . . . Philadelphia, Pa.: The Lutheran Publication Society 1915. pp. IV, 5—443, ill.*

[b. at Hanover, Pa., Aug. 17, 1847, son of Rev. John Jacob Albert and Julia Diehl.] [6097

The **Albrights.** Records of the Albright family from Schaefferstown, Penn. *In: Genealogy. A journal of American ancestry. Vol. XI, no. 4. Pompton Lakes, N. J. 1923. p. 57.* [6098

Memoir of Cathrine E. **Alleman,** wife of Rev. M. J. Alleman, of Aaronsburg, Pa. *By one who knew and loved her. Baltimore, Md.: T. Newton Kurtz 1855. pp. XI, 131.*

[Daughter of William and Susan Shellman, b. in Fredericktown, Md. Sept. 16, 1823.] [6099

An early German family. **Alleman.** *In: Notes and Queries. Edited by W. H. Egle. Fourth series, vol. I. 1891—1893. Harrisburg, Pa. 1893. p. 65.* [6100

Ashe, S. A.: John Wesley **Alspaugh** *(Banker). In: Biographical history of North Carolina. Edited by S. A. Ashe. Vol. VIII. Greensboro, N. C. 1917. pp. 1—5, ill.*

[b. in Forsyth Co., N. C., July 22, 1831; descendant of Henry Alspaugh, who came to N. C. from Germany about the time of the Revolutionary War, and settled among the Moravians.] [6101

The family of **Alter.** *In: Notes and Queries. Edited by W. H. Egle. Third series, vol. I. 1884—1887. Harrisburg, Pa. 1887. pp. 286—288. Reprint in: Third series, vol. I. Harrisburg, Pa. 1895. pp. 521—524.*

[Jacob Alter, a native of Switzerland, came to America about 1765, and located in Lancaster Co., Pa.] [6102

Laux, James B.: The **Alter** family. *In: The Pennsylvania-German. Vol. XI. Lititz, Pa. 1910. pp. 147—148.*

[Descendants of Johan Jacob Alter, who landed at Philadelphia, Pa., Sept., 1753 and m. about 1768 to Margaretha Landis of Lancaster Co., Pa.] [6103

— Dr. David **Alter.** Scientist: discoverer of the spectrum analysis and inventor of the first electric telegraph and electric motor. *In: The Pennsylvania-German. Vol. XI. Lititz, Pa. 1910. pp. 130—138.*

[b. in Allegheny Township, Westmoreland Co., Pa., Dec. 3, 1807, descendant of Johan Jacob Alter, who emigrated to Pa., 1753.] [6104

Means, Della: Dr. David **Alter,** a local scientist. *In: Western Pennsylvania Historical Magazine. Vol. I. Pittsburgh, Pa. 1918. pp. 224—238, ill.* [6105

„Anna Reinwald **Anders** and her descendants." *In: The genealogical record of the Schwenkfelder families. Edited by S. K. Brecht. New York, N. Y. — Chicago, Ill. 1923. pp. 1279—1309.* [6106

„George **Anders** and his descendants." *In: The genealogical record of the Schwenkfelder families. Edited by S. K. Brecht, New York, N. Y. — Chicago, Ill. 1923. p. 414.* [6107

Lessig, Othniel B.: The **Antes** family. *Address delivered at the joint meeting of the Historical Societies of Montgomery and Berks Counties, Sept. 24, 1910. In: Historical Sketches. A Collection of Papers prepared for the Historical Society of Montgomery County, Pa. Vol. IV. Norristown, Pa. 1910. pp. 274—280.*

[Descendants of Philip Frederick Antes and his wife Anna Catherine who emigrated from Freinsheim, Palatinate to America between 1716—1723.] [6108

Descendants of Anna Margaretha **Antes**. *In: The Perkiomen Region, Past and Present. Vol. III. Philadelphia, Pa. 1901. pp. 6—9; 25—27.* [6109

Heinrich **Antes**. *Reprint from „Weltbote", Allentown. In: Der Deutsche Pionier. Jg. XIV. Cincinnati, O. 1882—1883. pp. 70—71.* [6110

McMim, Edwin: A German hero of the colonial times of Pennsylvania; or the life and times of Henry **Antes**. *Morristown, N. J.: William J. Lowell 1886. pp. (1), 4—305, ill.*
[„The descendants of Henry Antes." Chapter XXII. pp. 284—305.] [6111

[Egle, William Henry]: Henry **Antes**. *In: Notes and Queries. Edited by W. H. Egle. Third series, vol. I. 1884—1887. Harrisburg, Pa. 1887. pp. 17—18. Reprint in: Third series, vol. I. Harrisburg, Pa. 1895. p. 28.* [6112

Antes, Henry: Family record of Henry **Antes**, of Frederick Township. *In: The Perkiomen Region, Past and Present. Vol. I. Philadelphia, Pa. 1895. pp. 51—52.* [6113

Dotterer, Henry S.: Henry **Antes**. *Paper read at Fagleysville, Pa., March 19, 1898. In: The Perkiomen Region, Past and Present. Vol. II. Philadelphia, Pa. 1900. pp. 106—108; 123—125; 145—147.* [6114

[Meginness, John F.]: The **Antes** family. *History of the progenitor and his children in America. By John of Lancaster. In: Notes and Queries. Edited by W. H. Egle. Annual vol. 1898. Harrisburg, Pa. 1899. pp. 222—227.* [6115

Jordan, John W.: Visit to the homestead of Henry **Antes**. *In: The Pennsylvania-German. Vol. XI. Lititz, Pa. 1910. pp. 686—689.* [6116

Meginness, John F.: Henry **Antes**. *In: Notes and Queries. Edited by W. H. Egle. Annual vol. 1899. Harrisburg, Pa. 1900. p. 76.*
[Son of Joseph Antes and a great-grandson of Col. John Henry Antes.] [6117

Dotterer, Henry S.: John **Antes**. *traveller, missionary and author. In: The Perkiomen Region, Past and Present. Vol. I. Philadelphia, Pa. 1895. pp. 92—94; p. 111; pp. 120—121; 142—144; 158—160; 168—171; 181—182.* [6118

McMinn, Joseph H.: Souvenir. Fourth annual reunion of the descendants and friends of Lieut. Col. John Henry **Antes**. *Sept. 4, 1911. [s. l., s. d.] pp. (7)* [6119

M.[eginness], John F.: Philip **Antes** of the west branch. *In: Notes and Queries. Edited by W. H. Egle. Annual vol. 1899. Harrisburg, Pa. 1900. pp. 1—2.* [6120

Arndt, John Stover: The story of the **Arndts**. The life, antecedents and descendants of Bernhard **Arndt**, who emigrated to Pennsylvania in the year 1731. *Philadelphia, Pa.: The Christopher Sower Co. 1922. pp. 427, ill.* [6121

[—] Captain John **Arndt**. An interesting autobiography of a Revolutionary patriot. *(Copied from the Arndt family bible, by Susan Arndt Fried.) In: Notes and Queries. Edited by W. H. Egle. Annual vol. 1897. Harrisburg, Pa. 1898. pp. 170—174.* [6122

Aurand, Frederick: History of the American branch of the **Aurand** family from 1725 to 1900. *Beaver Springs, Pa.: A. M. Aurand 1900. pp. 4—23, ill.*
[Descendants of Henry Aurand and Anna Christina (b. Hoff), who lived at or in Straas Ebersbach, Germany and whose son John emigrated to Pa., 1753.] [6123

B.

Bachman bible records. *From a bible printed in Zurich, by Christoffe Froschower, and completed the 26th of March, 1536. In the possession of Mr. J. Kennedy Stout, Washington, D. C. Contributed by John Baer Stoudt. In: Publications of the Genealogical Society of Pennsylvania. Vol. V, no. 3. Philadelphia, Pa. 1914. pp. 269—270.* [6124

Bachman, De Forest L.: Bachman. *After 25 years of peaceful repose this memorial to my father Colonel Amos W. **Bachman** is dedicated to my beloved mother. Oct. 28, 1913. [s. l., s. d.] pp. 10 f., ill.* [6125

[Haskell, John Bachman]: John **Bachman** D. D. LL. D. Ph. D. The pastor of St. John's Lutheran Church, Charleston. *[Collected by J. Bachman Haskell, edited by C. L. Bachman.] Charleston, S. C.: Walker, Evans & Gogswell 1888. pp. XI, 5—436, ill.*
[Whose „paternal ancestor, was a native of the Canton of Berne, Switzerland." After visiting England, he came to America as private secretary to William Penn. Finally he settled near Easton, Pa.] [6126

Minnich, Michael Reed: The Rev. Dr. John **Bachman**, Audubon's colaborer. *Paper read before the Historical Society of*

*Montgomery County, Oct. 7, 1903. In:
Historical Sketches. A Collection of Papers prepared for the Historical Society
of Montgomery County, Pa. Vol. III.
Norristown, Pa. 1905. pp. 226—232, ill.
[Whose paternal ancestor came from
Canton of Berne, and maternal progenitors from the Kingdom of Würtemberg,
Germany.]*   [6127
Baker family. *In: Colonial families of Philadelphia. Edited by John W. Jordan.
New York, N. Y.-Chicago, Ill.: The Lewis
Publishing Co. 1911. Vol. II. pp. 1657
—1663.
[August Becker, of the Village of
Bonnheim, Duchy of Hesse-Darmstadt,
b. in 1621, d. Febr. 25, 1676; Johann
Hilarius Becker, b. Febr. 25, 1705,
emigrated to Pa. between 1753 and 1756.]*
     [6128
Baer, Samuel A.: The **Baer** family. *In:
The Pennsylvania-German. Vol. VII.
Lebanon, Pa. 1906. pp. 333—337, ill.*
     [6129
Bare, Daniel M. and **Bare, Robert Bruce:**
Genealogy of Johannes **Baer**, 1749
—1910. *Compiled by . . . Harrisburg,
Pa.: Central Printing and Publishing
House 1910. pp. (1), (1), 7—288, ill.,
map.
[Descendants of Johannes and Anna
Maria Baer.]*   [6130
G., E. B.: A **Baer** line. *In: Genealogy. Journal of American ancestry. Vol. II. New
York, N. Y. 1912. p. 333.
[Descendants of George Baer, b. in
1715 in Bavaria, Germany.]*   [6131
Betz, I. H.: Rachel **Bahn**, the York County
poetess. *In: The Pennsylvania-German.
Vol. VII. Lebanon, Pa. 1906. pp. 99
—102, ill.*   [6132
E.[gle], W. H.: The **Balsbaugh** family. *In:
Notes and Queries. Edited by W. H.
Egle. Second series. Harrisburg, Pa.
1883. pp. 269—270. Reprint in: First
and second series, vol. II. Harrisburg,
Pa. 1895. pp. 373—375.
[George Balsbach, a native of Fahrenbach, in the Pfaltz, Germany, b. 1706,
came to America prior to 1750, and was
one of the earliest of the German settlers
on Spring Creek, Derry Township,
Dauphin Co.]*   [6133
Hensel, L. W.: The Martin **Barr** family.
*In: Papers and Addresses of the Lancaster County Historical Society. Vol.
II. 1897—8. Lancaster, Pa. 1898. pp.
216—217.*   [6134

Wilson, Woodrow: Daniel Moreau **Barringer**
jr. *(Geologist). In: Biographical history
of North Carolina. Edited by S. A. Ashe.
Vol. I. Greensboro, N. C. 1905. pp. 145
—147, ill.
[Son of Daniel Moreau Barringer and
Elizabeth (Wethered) Barringer; b. in
Raleigh, N. C., May 25, 1860.]*   [6135
Means, Paul B.: Paul Brandon **Barringer**
*(College president). In: Biographical
history of North Carolina. Edited by
S. A. Ashe. Vol. I. Greensboro, N. C.
1905. pp. 135—144, ill.
[son of General Rufus Barringer and
Eugenia Morrison; b. in Concord, N. C.
Febr. 13, 1857.]*   [6136
— John Alston **Barringer** *(Lawyer). In:
Biographical history of North Carolina.
Edited by S. A. Ashe. Vol. I. Greensboro,
N. C. 1905. pp. 130—134, ill.
[Eldest son of Rev. William Barringer
and Lavinia Margaret Alston; b. Aug. 30,
1851.]*   [6137
Barringer, Paul B. and **Barringer, D. M.:**
Victor Clay **Barringer** *(Judge). In:
Biographical history of North Carolina.
Edited by S. A. Ashe. Vol. I. Greensboro, N. C. 1905. pp. 125—129, ill.
[Youngest son of General Paul Barringer and Elizabeth Brandon; b. at
Poplar Grove, Cabarrus Co., N. C.
March 29, 1827.]*   [6138
Cansler, E. T.: Rufus **Barringer** *(Confederate general). In: Biographical history of North Carolina. Edited by S. A.
Ashe. Vol. I. Greensboro, N. C. 1905.
pp. 116—124, ill.
[Son of General Paul Barringer, b.
Dec. 2, 1821, at Poplar Grove, Cabarrus
Co., N. C.]*   [6139
Crawford, Leonidas W.: William **Barringer**
*(Clergyman). In: Biographical history
of North Carolina. Edited by S. A. Ashe.
Vol. I. Greensboro, N. C. 1905. pp. 110
—115, ill.
[Fourth son of General Paul Barringer
of Cabarrus Co., N. C., b. on Dutch
Buffalo Creek, Febr. 18, 1816.]*   [6140
Barringer, D. M.: Daniel Moreau **Barringer**
*(Minister to Spain). In: Biographical
history of North Carolina. Edited by
S. A. Ashe. Vol. I. Greensboro, N. C.
1905. pp. 100—109, ill.
[Eldest son of General Paul Barringer
of Cabarrus; b. near Concord, July 30,
1806.]*   [6141
— and **Barringer, Paul B.:** General Paul
Barringer *(General in the war of 1812).*

In: Biographical history of North Carolina. Edited by S. A. Ashe. Vol. I. Greensboro, N. C. 1905. pp. 95—99, ill.
[Eldest son of Captain John Paul Barringer and Catherine (Blackwelder); b. Sept. 26, 1778.] [6142

Barringer, D. M. and **Barringer, Paul B.:** John Paul **Barringer** *(Revolutionary patriot). In: Biographical history of North Carolina. Edited by S. A. Ashe. Vol. I. Greensboro, N. C. 1905. pp. 89—94.*
[b. in the Duchy of Würtemberg, Germany, June 4, 1721, sailed from Rotterdam to America, landing at Philadelphia, Pa., Sept. 30, 1743, became the founder of the North Carolina family.] [6143

Foin, Julius C.: Rev. Louis **Barth,** a pioneer missionary in Pennsylvania and an administrator of the Diocese Philadelphia. *Paper read May 5, 1887. In: Records of the American Catholic Historical Society of Philadelphia. Vol. II. Philadelphia, Pa. 1889. pp. 29—37.*
[b. at Münster, Alsace.] [6144

Bartholomew, Allen R.: First Bartholomew reuion, August 30, 1919. *Address. [s. l.] 1919. pp. 12.* [6145

Stapleton, A.: The **Bashore** family of Pennsylvania. *In: Notes and Queries. Edited by W. H. Egle. Annual vol. 1897. Harrisburg, Pa. 1898. pp. 180—181.*
[The emigrants of this name were „Brethren" or „Dunkards."] [6146

[Weiser, Clement Z.]: Henry B. **Bassler** funeral discourser. *By . . . Contributed by J. L. Roush. In: The Perkiomen Region. Vol. III, no. 1. Pennsburg, Pa. 1924. pp. 8—13.*
[Pastor of the Reformed Church, b. near Zionsville, Lehigh Co., Pa. 1804; d. Febr. 17, 1883.] [6147

H. S. P.: In memoriam: Capt. John Henry **Bassler.** *In: Papers and Addresses of the Lebanon County Historical Society. Vol. VII. 1916—1919. Lebanon, Pa. 1919. pp. 17—19, ill.*
[Son of Henry and Barbara (Unger) Bassler.] [6148

Memorial of the Rev. H. Louis **Baugher,** D. D., Aug. 6, 1840 — Febr. 2, 1899. *Published by his friends. Philadelphia, Pa.: Lutheran Publication Society Print 1900. pp. 55, ill.*
[b. Aug., 1840.] [6149

Adamson, Lorena Blanche: Bible record of Christian and Elizabeth **Baughman.** *In: The National Genealogical Society Quarterly. Vol. XVII, no. 4. Washington, D. C. 1929. p. 72.* [6150

The **Baums** of Derry. *In: Notes and Queries. Edited by W. H. Egle. Third series, vol. I. 1884—1887. Harrisburg, Pa. 1887. pp. 329—330. Reprint in: Third series, vol. II. Harrisburg, Pa. 1896. pp. 24—26.*
[Adam Baum, a native of the Palatinate, emigrated to America about 1760.] [6151

Keyser, L. S. and **Larimer, L. H.:** Professor David H. **Bauslin,** D. D. L. L. D. — A biographical sketch. *By L. S. Keyser. The eternal values of the life of Professor David H. Bauslin. Funeral sermon preached by L. H. Larimer. In: The Lutheran Quarterly. Vol. LII. Gettysburg, Pa. 1922. pp. 271—280; 281—288.*
[b. at Winchester, Va. 1853.] [6152

Ranck, Henry Haverstick: The life of Reverend Benjamin **Bausman,** D. D. LL. D. *Philadelphia, Pa.: The Publication. and Sunday School Board of the Reformed Church in the United States. 1912. pp. (1), 7—8; (2), 13—439, ill.*
[Descendant of Bausman family at Freilaubersheim, Palatinate and son of Johannes Bausman, landed in Philadelphia, Pa. 1802.] [6153

Lambright, Harvey: Family record of Samuel J. **Beachy** and his descendants. *Millersburg, Ind.: R. F. D. I. 1918. pp. 28.*
[b. in Somerset Co., Pa. 1825.] [6154

[Egle, W. H.]: Henry **Beader.** *In: Notes and Queries. Edited by W. H. Egle. Third series, vol. I. 1884—1887. Harrisburg, Pa. 1887. p. 18. Reprint in: Third series, vol. I. Harrisburg, Pa. 1895. p. 28.* [6155

Bear, Walter Scott: A genealogy of the **Bear** family and biographical record of the descendants of Jacob Bear [Bär]. *1747—1906. Harrisburg, Pa.: Central Printing and Publishing House 1906. pp. 216, ill.* [6156

Burr, Frank A.: Life and achievements of James Addams **Beaver.** Early life, military services and public career. *Philadelphia, Pa. Ferguson Bros. & Co. 1882. pp. 224.* [6157

Dandridge, Danske: George Michael **Bedinger:** a Kentucky pioneer. *Charlottsville, Va.: The Michie Co. 1909. pp. IV, 232, ill.*
[Descendants of Adam Büdinger, who emigrated from Alsace to America 1737,

and son of Henry Bedinger and his wife Magdalena von Schlegel, in what is now York Co., Pa.] [6158

Jordan, John W.: John Bechtel: His contributions to literature, and his descendants. *In: The Pennsylvania Magazine of History and Biography. Vol. XIX. Philadelphia, Pa. 1895. pp. 137 —151.*

[b. Oct. 3, 1690, at Weinheim in the Palatinate, emigrated to Pa. in 1726, and settled in Germantown.] [6159

Eby, Simion P.: John Beck: The eminent teacher. *In: Papers and Addresses of the Lancaster County Historical Society. Vol. II. 1897—98. Lancaster, Pa. 1898. pp. 111—139.* [6160

Becker, Leah B.: A biographical history of the Becker family and their early settlement in America, *and other unpublished information belonging thereto. Lititz, Pa.: Express Printing Office 1901. pp. 129, ill.*

[Valentine Becker and his 3 brothers, namely: George, Conrad and Michael, emigrated to America, 1737.] [6161

Flickinger, S. H.: A Pennsylvania family graveyard. *[Inscriptions from the tombstones in the Becker family graveyard on the Martin Becker farm in Clay Township, Lancaster, County.] In: Genealogy. Journal of American ancestry. Vol. I. New York, N. Y. 1912. p. 179.* [6162

Custer, Milo: Beeler biography and genealogy. *Compiled and printed by . . . Bloomington, Ill. 1918. pp. 20, ill.*

[Descendants of Samuel Beeler, son of Samuel Beeler (?) of German descent.] [6163

„Abraham Beer (Beyer) and his descendants." *In: The genealogical record of the Schwenkfelder families. Edited by S. K. Brecht. New York, N. Y. — Chicago, Ill., 1923. pp. 1313—1431.* [6164

Wenger, Joseph H.: History of the descendants of Abraham Beery, born in 1718, emigrated from Switzerland to Pennsylvania in 1736, *and a complete genealogical family register with biographies of many of his descendants, from the earliest available records to the present time, giving dates in three centuries. South English, Ia.: Published by the author 1905. pp. 328.* [6165

— History of the descendants of Nicholas Beery. Born in 1707. Emigrated from

Switzerland to Pennsylvania in 1727. *And a complete genealogical family register with biographies of many of his descendants, from the earliest available records to the present time. Dates in three centuries. By . . . South English, Ia. [s. l.] Febr. 22, 1911. pp. 496, ill.* [6166

Fretz, A. J.: A genealogical record of the descendants of Jacob Beidler of Lower Milford Township, Bucks Co., Pa. *Together with historical and biographical sketches. With an introduction by H. B. Garner. [s. l.] 1903. pp. XVI, 549, ill., map.*

[b. in Germany about 1708 or 1709, emigrated to America in the early part of the 18th century.] [6167

Mast, C. Z.: The Beiler family. *In: Christian Monitor a monthly magazine for the home. Vol. XV, no. 3. Scottdale, Pa. 1923. pp. 83—85, ill.*

[whose ancestor emigrated from Switzerland and landed at Philadelphia, 1737.] [6168

Ashe, S. A.: Alfred H. Belo, *(Editor). In: Biographical history of North Carolina. Edited by S. A. Ashe. Vol. V. Greensboro, N. C. 1906. pp. 8—13, ill.*

[b. in Salem, N. C. May, 1839, of Moravian stock and son of Frederick Edward Boehlo (Belo).] [6169

John Benner, tanner, early settler and prosperous tradesman in New Hanover Township. *In: The Perkiomen Region, Past and Present. Vol. II. Philadelphia, Pa. 1900. pp. 78—82.*

[Johannes Böhner (Behner, Bener, Beaner, Beener, Benner), who settled as early as 1731 at Falkner Swamp.] [6170

Bergey, D. H.: The Bergey family. *In: The Pennsylvania-German. Vol. VII. Lebanon, Pa. 1906. pp. 331—332.* [6171

— The progenitors of the Bergey family in America. *Published for the Bergey family Association. [s. l.] 1907. pp. 18.*

[John Ulrich Berge came from Germany about the year 1717, and settled in Lower Salford Township, now Montgomery Co.] [6172

— Genealogy of the Bergey family. A record of the descendants of John Ulrich Bergey and his wife Mary. *New York, N. Y.: Frederick H. Hitchcock 1925. pp. XIV, 1150, ill.*

[who purchased a tract of about 250 acres of land in Lower Salford Twp.,

Montgomery Co., Pa. 1726, and ti is believed that he came from Switzerland.] [6173

Bertolet, Daniel H.: A genealogical history of the Bertolet family, the descendants of Jean Bertolet. *Compiled by . . . Published by the Bertolet Family Association (Incorp.) 1914. Harrisburg, Pa.: Press of the United Evangelical Publishing House 1914. pp. 260, ill.*

[Jean Bertolet of Huguenot ancestry, b. at Chateau d'Oex in Switzerland, in the District of Bern, lived in Minnfeldten (Minfeld), Germany, came to America in the fall of the year 1726 and settled at Oley, Berks Co., Pa.] [6174

Johannes Bertolet. *In: The Perkiomen Region, Past and Present. Vol. II. Philadelphia, Pa. 1900. p. 122.*

[Great-grandson of Jean (John) Bertolet, who settled in Oley, Pa., as early as 1726.] [6175

Samuel Bertolet, of Frederick Township. *In: The Perkiomen Region, Past and Present. Vol. II. Philadelphia, Pa. 1900. pp. 96—97.*

[The first of the name to settle in Falkner Swamp was Samuel Bertolet, son of Abraham Bertolet of Oley, and a grandson of Jean Bertolet, the Huguenot immigrant who came in 1726.] [6176

Bethel family burials. — Inscriptions from Mt. Bethel cemetery, Columbia, Pa. *In: Genealogy. Journal of American ancestry. Vol. IV. New York, N. Y. 1914. p. 60.* [6177

A Revolutionary widow. [Elizabeth **Betz.**] *In: Notes and Queries. Edited by W. H. Egle. Fourth series, vol. I. 1891—1893. Harrisburg, Pa. 1893. p. 30.* [6178

Dr. Israel H. **Betz.** By a friend. *In: The Pennsylvania-German. Vol. XI. Lititz, Pa. 1910. pp. 578—579, ill.*

[b. in Lancaster, Pa. 1841.] [6179

Brown, Harry W.: The second **Betzner** reunion. *In: Eighth Annual Report of the Waterloo Historical Society. Kitchener, Ont. 1920. pp. 133—139.* [6180

P.[arthemore], E. W. S.: The family of **Beyerly.** *In: Notes and Queries. Edited by W. H. Egle. Third series, vol. II. 1887—1890. Harrisburg, Pa. 1891. pp. 503—505. Reprint in: Third series, vol. III. Harrisburg, Pa. 1896. pp. 532—536.*

[Genealogy record of Caspar Beyerly, b. Aug. 24, 1727; d. Nov. 7, 1794.] [6181

Bibighaus, Samuel H.: Descendants of John **Bibighaus,** of Bedminster, Bucks County, Pa. *[s. l.] 1888. pp. 44.*

[Descendants of Martin Bibighaus of Ahlretshausen, a village in Sayn, Witgenstein Co., Germany, who emigrated to America, 1770.] [6182

Grumbine, E.: Hon. Jacob L. **Bicksler.** *In: Papers read before the Lebanon County Historical Society. Vol. V. Lebanon, Pa. 1909—1912. pp. 265—268.*

[b. Jan. 31, 1814, son of Daniel Stettler Bicksler, and descendant of Peter Bicksler, who emigrated to Pa., 1727.] [6183

Steinmetz, Mary Owen: Bieber-Lescher burial ground in Oley Township, Berks County, Pa. (and) Bieber-family record. *In: The National Genealogical Society Quarterly. Vol. XI, no. 1. Washington, D. C. 1922. pp. 8.* [6184

Stapleton, A.: Binder and **Sensendorfer** families. *In: Notes and Queries. Edited by W. H. Egle. Annual vol. 1898. Harrisburg, Pa. 1899. pp. 217—220.* [6185

Pine, John B.: Abraham **Bininger.** *In: The New York Genealogical and Biographical Record. Vol. XXXIII. New York, N. Y. 1902. pp. 135—137.*

[b. Jan. 18, 1720 in Bulock (or Baden-Bulach) in Canton Zurich, Switzerland; came over with his father, Christian, and mother to America, in 1734, went to Purysburg, S. C.; became acquainted with the Moravians and joined them at Bethlehem, 1742.] [6186

Abraham M. **Bininger.** *In: Hunt's Merchants' Magazine Year Book 1871. New York, N. Y. 1871. pp. 450—451.*

[Descendant of Abraham Bininger, German immigrant of the middle of the 17th century; nephew of Abraham Bininger, the founder of the groceryhouse Bininger & Co.]. [6187

Draper, Armos G.: Isaac W. **Bininger,** Revolutionary pensioner. *In: The National Genealogical Society Quarterly. Vol. XV, no. 3. Washington, D. C. 1927. p. 45.*

[Son of Abraham Bininger, who was b. in Bulach, Canton Zurich, Switzerland, Jan. 18, 1720 and landed in Georgia, North America, April 22, 1734.] [6188

York County, Pa., genealogical notes, 1780, *(relating to* Peter **Binkele,** *b. March 2, 1704 in Switzerland, and his issue.)* *In: The Pennsylvania Magazine of History and Biography. Vol. XXXI. Philadelphia, Pa. 1907. p. 243.* [6189

Peachey, Samuel M.: A memorial history of Peter **Bitsche,** and a complete family register of his lineal descendants and those related to him by intermarriage from the year 1767 to 1892. *Chronologically arranged. With an appendix of those not received in time for their proper place. Lancaster, Pa.: John Baer's Sons 1892. pp. 205.*   [6190

The family of **Bittinger**. *In: Notes and Queries. Edited by W. H. Egle. Second series. Harrisburg, Pa. 1883. p. 214; pp. 247—248. Reprint in: First and second series, vol. II. Harrisburg, Pa. 1895. p. 309; pp. 337—339.*   [6191

Bittinger, Lucy Forney: Bittinger and **Bedinger** families. Descendants of Adam Büdinger. *[s. l.; s. d.] (1904). pp. 63. [Descendants of Adam Büdinger (b. 1698, d. about 1768), native of the Village of „Dorschel in the principality of Lichtzstine", near Strasburg; emigrated in 1737.]*   [6192

— Memorials of the Reverend Baugher **Bittinger, D. D.** *By his daughter . . . Woodsville, N. H.: Press of F. W. Bittinger 1891. pp. 230, ill. [Third son of Joseph and Lydia (Bair) Bittinger; b. March 30, 1823, in Berwick Twp., Adam Co., Pa.]*   [6193

Diehl, G.: Rev. David F. **Bittle**. *In: The Quarterly Review of the Evangelical Lutheran Church. New series, vol. VII. Gettysburg, Pa. 1877. pp. 541—570. [b. near Myersville, Frederick Co., Md. 1811, the son of Thomas and Mary Beale Bittle.]*   [6194

Bittner, Jacob Webster: Genealogical record and history of the **Bittner-Werley** families. Descendants of Michael Bittner; Sebastian Werley 1753—1930. *Kutztown, Pa. 1930. pp. XXV, 239, ill. [Michael Büttner; Sebastian Werlein.]*   [6195

Mast, C. Z.: The **Blank** family. *In: Christian Monitor. A monthly magazine for the home. Vol. XV, no. 6. Scottdale, Pa. 1924. pp. 595—597, ill. [whose pioneer ancester landed in Philadelphia, 1752.]*   [6196

Blauch, D. D.: History of the **Blauch** family. *In: The Pennsylvania-German. Vol. X. Lititz, Pa. 1909. pp. 500—505, ill.*   [6197

The **Blickensderfer** family. *In: The Pennsylvania-German. Vol. IX. Cleona, Pa. 1908. pp. 322—323. [Descendants of „Anabaptist" Blickensderfer (or Pleickensdoerfer) of the Kohlhoff, Palatinate, Germany, whose five*

sons, Christian, John, Jacob, Ulrich and Jost, emigrated to America. 1748 —1753.]   [6198

Blickensderfer, Jacob: History of the **Blickensderfer** family in America. *[s. l.; s. d.] (Lebanon, Pa. 1899). pp. 56. [Descendants of Christian Blickensderfer, b. March 6, 1724 at the Kohlhof, in the Palatinate who m. Jan. 7, 1748 Catherine Shürger, both Mennonites; emigrated to America 1753.]*   [6199

Egle, William Henry: Boas family. *In: Pennsylvania genealogies. Harrisburg, Pa. 1896 [= no. 6045]. pp. 98—106. [Descendants of Frederick Boas, b. in 1739 in the Canton of Zürich, Switzerland.]*   [6200

Horn, A. P.: Proceedings of the re-union of Apple's Church and of the **Boehm** family. *Celebrated at Apple's or New Jerusalem Reformed and Lutheran Church, Leithsville, Northampton County, Pa. Sept. 14, 1895. Edited by . . . Hellertown, Pa.: H. D. Laubach 1902. pp. (2), (1), 9—154, ill.*   [6201

Wakeley, J. B.: The Patriarch of one hundred years; being reminiscences, historical and biographical, of Rev. Henry **Boehm**. *With several additional chapters, containing an account of the exercises on his one hundredth birthday; his sermon before the Newark Conference and the addresses then delivered; his Centennial sermons in Trinity Church, Jersey City, and in Johnstreet Church, New York, and the addresses made on those occasions. Phonographically reported. New York, N. Y.: Nelson & Phillips 1875. pp. 587, ill.*   [6202

R.[attermann, H. A.]: Ein deutsch-amerikanischer Patriarch. *[Heinrich* **Böhm]** *In: Der Deutsche Pionier. Jg. VIII. Cincinnati, O. 1876—1877. S. 25—35, ill.*

Unter dem Titel „Ein Patriarch von hundert Jahren. Heinrich Böhm, der Begründer des deutschen Methodismus" abgedruckt in: H. A. Rattermann. Gesammelte Werke. Bd. X. Cincinnati, O.: Selbstverlag des Verfassers 1911. S. 226 —238. [Enkel von Jacob Böhm, Auswanderer aus der deutschen Schweiz, geb. 8. Juni 1775.]   [6203

John Philip **Böhm.** *Original papers in the records of the (Collegiate) Reformed Protestant Dutch Church of the City of New York, translated by* **T. W. Chambers.**

In: The Mercersburg Review. Vol. XXIII. Philadelphia, Pa. 1876. pp. 528—557. [6204

Dotterer, Henry S.: Rev. John Philip **Boehm.** *Prepared for the Sesqui-Centennial anniversary of Boehm's Reformed Church, in Whitpain Township, Montgomery County, Pa., held September 11, 1890. Philadelphia, Pa. 1890. pp. 27.* [6205

— Reverend John Philip **Boehm,** pioneer Reformed preacher in Pennsylvania. *Sketch read at the Sesqui-Centennial anniversary of Boehm's Church in Whitpain, Montgomery County, Pa., Sept. 11, 1890. In: The Pennsylvania-German. Vol. VIII. Lebanon, Pa. 1907. pp. 243—248, ill.* [6206

— An interesting confirmation *[concerning genealogical data of John Philip Boehm, the founder of the German Reformed Church in Pennsylvania, and his son Anton Wilhelm Boehm.] In: The Perkiomen Region, Past and Present. Vol. II. Philadelphia, Pa. 1900. p. 19.* [6207

Hinke, William J.: Life and Letters of the Rev. John Philip Boehm, Founder of the Reformed Church in Pennsylvania, 1683—1749. *Philadelphia, Publication and S. S. Board of the Reformed Church in the U. S., 1916. pp. XXVI, 501, ill.* [6207a

[Stein, Thos. S. - Lantz, C. R. - Grittinger, H. C.]: Prof. Cyrus **Boger,** A. M. *In: Papers read before the Lebanon County Historical Society. Vol. VI. Lebanon, Pa. 1912—1916. pp. 147—149, ill. [Descendant of Mathias Boger, an immigrant from the Palatinate.]* [6208

Ein 170 Jahre alter deutscher Wohnsitz in Amerika. *[The farm-homestead of the* **Bogert** *family, Salzburg Township, Lehigh County, Pa.] Reprint from „Allentown Republikaner." In: Der Deutsche Pionier. Jg. VIII. Cincinnati, O. 1876—1877. p. 59.* [6209

The first printed genealogy. *[Family record of the* **Bollinger** *family, printed at Ephrata in 1763.] In: Notes and Queries. Edited by W. H. Egle. Third series, vol. II. 1887—1890. Harrisburg, Pa. 1891. p. 228. Reprint in: Third series, vol. III. Harrisburg, Pa. 1896. pp. 229—230.* [6210

Egle, William Henry: Bomberger family. *In: Egle's „Pennsylvania genealogies." Harrisburg, Pa. 1896 [= no. 6045]. pp. 107—112.*

[Descendants of Christian Bamberger, who emigrated from Eschelbrun, Baden, Germany to Pennsylvania 1722.] [6211

An unique old-time release. *[Eschelbronn, May 22, 1722. — Translation from the German of a release given to Christian* **Bomberger,** *the first Bomberger settler of Lancaster County, who located NW. of Lititz, Pa. 1726.] In: The Pennsylvania-German. Vol. XII. Lititz, Pa. 1911. pp. 607.* [6212

Bomberger, Christian Martin Hess.: Christian **Bomberger,** pioneer. *Compiled from an address delivered by the writer at the first annual reunion of the Bomberger family, Lititz, Springs Grounds, Aug. 29, 1922. Jeanette. Pa.: Press of Jeanette Publishing Co. 1923. pp. 22, ill.* [6213

Jacob Cauffman **Bomberger.** *In: Notes and Queries. Edited by W. H. Egle. Annual vol. 1897. Harrisburg, Pa. 1898. pp. 99—101.*

[b. Dec. 17, 1817, at Mifflintown, Pa., d. Harrisburg 18, 1897. He was 5th in descent from Christian Bomberger who emigrated from Eshelbrun, Baden, Germany to America.] [6214

Borneman, J. H.: The history of the **Borneman** family in America, since the first settlers, 1721 to 1878. *Published by J. H. Borneman. Boyertown, Pa. 1881. pp. (1), 5—114.*

[of Swiss ancestry; descendants of Daniel Borneman.] [6215

Borntreger, John E.: Descendants of Martin **Borntreger,** the emigrant of 1767. *Scottdale, Pa.: Mennonite Publishing House 1923. pp. 291.* [6216

Kenkel, F. P.: Christian **Börstler.** Autobiographische Aufzeichnungen eines deutschen Pioniers in Maryland. *Mitgetheilt von . . . In: Deutsch-Amerikanische Geschichtsblätter. Jg. I. Chicago, Ill. 1901. Heft 1. S. 17—22.* [6217

Wieand, J. B.: The **Bortz** family. *In: The Pennsylvania-German. Vol. VII. Lebanon, Pa. 1906. pp. 279—280, ill.* [6218

Burkhardt, Franklin A.: The **Boucher** family (Bowsher, Bauscher, Bausher, Bousher) Comprising a genealogy of branches of **Strawn, Harpster, Tedrow, Cryder, Reichelderfer, Critchfield, Stahl, Straw, Brant** and other families. Descendants of Daniel Boucher of Albany Township, Berks County, Pa. Notes of other Boucher families. Henry Boucher descendants *(Indiana, Pa.)* A brief history of the Ohio reunions of kindred families. *New York, N. Y.: Press of Francis E. Burkhardt 1917. pp. 402.* [6219

Jenkins, John S.: „William C. Bouck (1786 —1859) governor of New York." *In: Lives of the governors of the State of New York. Auburn, N. Y. Derby, Miller & Co. 1851. pp. 689—721.*

[his great-grandfather having been one of the first of a company of German Palatines, to settle in the Schoharie Valley beyond Heldersberg.] [6219a

[Bowman, S. L.]: The Bowman family. A historical and memorial volume from the earliest traditions to the present time 1886. *Harrisburg, Pa.: Publishing Department M. E. Book Rooms 1886. pp. XV, 258, ill.* [6220

Brief sketch of a Lykens Valley octogenarian. *[John J. Bowman.] In: Notes and Queries. Edited by W. H. Egle. Fourth series, vol. I. 1891—1893. Harrisburg, Pa. 1893. pp. 223—224.*

[b. in the City of Lancaster, Pa. Febr. 12, 1807.] [6221

S., R. S.: Bowman family burials. *(Tombstone inscriptions from the Lutheran cemetery, in Mapleton, Stark County, O.) In: Genealogy. Journal of American ancestry. Vol. II. New York, N. Y. 1912. p. 342.* [6222

Bowman, H. M.: The Mennonite settlements in Pennsylvania and Waterloo with special reference to the Bowman family. *In: Tenth Annual Report of the Waterloo Historical Society. Kitchener, Ont. 1922. pp. 225—247, ill.*

[Descendants of Weyndel Bowman, a Switzer.] [6223

Bowman, Alfred S.: The Jesse Bowman, sr. lineage. *By his grandson . . . Scotia, Schenectady County, N. Y. 1931. pp. (I), 98, ill.*

[Christopher Bauman was b. near Ems, Germany in 1733, and was of Swiss-German descent; he emigrated about 1753 to Bucks Co., Pa.] [6224

[Egle, W. H.]: John F. Bowman. *In: Notes and Queries. Edited by W. H. Egle. First and second series, vol. I. Harrisburg, Pa. 1894. pp. 204—205.*

[b. in Lancaster County, May 10, 1771.] [6225

Bowser, Addison Bartholomew: The Bowser family history. *Authorized and published by the Bowser Reunion which meets annually at Kittanming, Arm-*

strong County, Pa., on the last Tuesday of August. *Chicago, Ill.: Excelsior Printing Co. 1922. pp. 310, ill.* [6226

Gruber, Michael Alvin: Boyer, Bayer, Beyer, Beier, Baier, — Pennsylvania records. *In: The National Genealogical Society Quarterly. Vol. X, no. 2. Washington, D. C. 1921. pp. 81—84.* [6227

Boyer, Charles Clinton: American Boyers. *Kutztown, Pa.: Press of the Kutztown Publishing Co. 1915. pp. X, 11—531.* Appenda to American Boyers 1916. *pp. 61; Addenda 1918. pp. 18, ill.* [6228

[L., D. G.]: Account of sales at the public vendues of Henry Boyer's personal property, held in Tulpehocken, April 13 and 14, 1757. *In: Publications of the Historical Society of Schuylkill County. Vol. II. Pottsville, Pa. 1910. pp. 159—167.* [6229

[B., J.]: An old family register. — Family register of Jacob Bozart *(Bostart). In: Notes and Queries. Edited by W. H. Egle. Third series, vol. II. 1887—1890. Harrisburg, Pa. 1891. pp. 60—62.* Reprint in: *Third series, vol. II. Harrisburg, Pa. 1896. pp. 445—448.*

[m. to Ester Mollinger 1721.] [6230

Dotterer, Henry S.: Philip Brandt, of New Hanover. *In: The Perkiomen Region, Past and Present. Vol. I. Philadelphia, Pa. 1895. pp. 37—38.*

[In 1734 he was the owner of 100 acres of land in Hanover Township; he was the „first fellow traveller" of Rev, Henry Melchior Muhlenberg, when latter arrived. Nov. 25, 1742 and was going to meet the people of the congregation of New Providence and New Hanover.] [6231

Branner, John Casper: Caspar Branner of Virginia and his descendants. *Privately printed, Stanford University, California, 1913. San Francisco, Ca.: Taylor, Nash & Taylor 1913. pp. VII, 469, ill., map.*

[Descendants of Caspar Branner, b. about 1729; d. about 1792; m. Catherine . . . b. about 1730; d. about 1800, both of German origin; they settled in the Shenandoah Valley before 1760.] [6232

S.[ener], S. M.: The Breneman family. *In: Notes and Queries. Edited by W. H. Egle. Fourth series, vol. II. 1894. Harrisburg, Pa. 1895. pp. 171—173.* [6233

— A Breneman bible. *In: Notes and Queries. Edited by W. H. Egle. Annual vol. 1896. Harrisburg, Pa. 1897. p. 33.* [6234

Gerberich, Albert H.: Brenneman bible records. *In: National Genealogical Society Quarterly. Vol. XVIII. Washington, D. C. 1930. p. 82.* [6235]

Brendlinger, Ellsworth: Genealogy and biography of the Brentlinger family. 1927. *Dayton, O.: Press of The Groneweg Printing Co. 1927. pp. 5—165, ill.*

[Descendants of Conrad Brendlinger, b. 1728; George Brentlinger, b. in 1765, in Frederick Co., Md.; seems to have been the first to cross the border line of Ohio]. [6236]

The Bretz family. *In: Notes and Queries. Edited by W. H. Egle. Third series, vol. I. 1884—1887. Harrisburg, Pa. 1887. p. 20. Reprint in: Third series, vol. I. Harrisburg, Pa. 1895. pp. 35—36.*

[John Bretz, b. Dec. 15, 1771; d. April 1845, early settler in Upper Paxtang, Dauphin Co.] [6237]

Parthemore, E. W. S.: Genealogy of the Ludwig Bretz family 1750—1890. *Harrisburg, Pa.: Harrisburg Publishing Co. 1890. pp. 5—142.*

[who belonged to the German race and settled as early as 1760 in what is now Lancaster Co.] [6238]

The Bretz and Boyer family. *In: Notes and Queries. Edited by W. H. Egle. Third series, vol. I. 1884—1887. Harrisburg, Pa. 1887. p. 113. Reprint in: Third series, vol. I. Harrisburg, Pa. 1895. pp. 192—193.* [6239]

Kriebel, H. W.: Elias Brey, the gunmaker. *In: The Perkiomen Region. Vol. VII, no. 3. Pennsburg, Pa. 1929. pp. 76—80.*

[Son of John Adam and Elizabeth Brey; b. Nov. 2, 1817, in Montgomery Co., Pa.] [6240]

Parthemore, E. W. S.: The first member of the Bricker family in America. *In: Papers and Addresses of the Lancaster County Historical Society. Vol. III. Lancaster, Pa. 1899. pp. 20—21.*

[Peter Bricker, who emigrated from Germany and landed at Philadelphia, 1732.] [6241]

Green, A. G.: Historical sketch of the Bright family. *A paper read before the Historical Society of Berks County, Pa., Nov. 13, 1900. In: Transactions of the Historical Society of Berks County. Vol. I. no. 15. Reading, Pa. 1904. pp. 27, (3), ill.*

[Michael Brecht, the first emigrant to America, came from Schriessheim, a market town in the Palatinate; b. 1706; came to Germantown, Pa. 1726.] [6242]

Brinker — Capt. Abraham Brinker. *In: Genealogy. Journal of American ancestry. Vol. III. New York, N. Y. 1913. p. 52.* [6243]

De Long, Irwin Hoch: Descendants of Otto Henrich Wilhelm Brinkman. *Lancaster, Pa.: Privately printed; Lancaster Press, Inc. 1925. pp. VI, 47, ill.*

[emigrated from Kirchlengern, Westphalia, Germany, to the United States of America some time between 1829—1837.] [6244]

Brinser, H. S.: Bishop Brinser and the Brinser meeting house. *In: The Pennsylvania-German. Vol. II. Lebanon, Pa. 1901. pp. 23—31, ill.*

[Rev. Mathias Brinser, founder and first bishop of the United Zion's Children; b. May 10, 1795; d. July 27, 1889; his grandfather, Christian Brinser came from Baden, Germany.] [6245]

S.[eidensticker], Oswald: Biographische Notizen über Pastor S. K. Brobst aus Allentown, Pa. *In: Der Deutsche Pionier. Jg. IX. Cincinnati, O. 1877—1878. S. 60—62.*

[geb. in Berks Co., Pa. 16. Nov. 1822.] [6246]

Rattermann, H. A.: Pastor Samuel Kistler Brobst. Ein Vorkämpfer deutschen Wesens in Amerika. *Aus dem „Deutschen Pionier". Jg. IX abgedruckt in: H. A. Rattermann. Gesammelte Werke. Bd. X. Cincinnati, O.: Selbstverlag des Verfassers 1911. S. 203—210.* [6246a]

[Schuler, H. A.]: Reverend Samuel K. Brobst, Sunday-school founder, minister and editor. *In: The Pennsylvania-German. Vol. Lebanon, Pa. 1907. pp. 360 —364, ill.* [6247]

Diehl, T. H.: Reminiscences of Rev. S. K. Brobst and his times. *In: The Lutheran Church Review. Vol. XXIX. Philadelphia, Pa. 1910. 326—342; 478—499; 835—854.* [6248]

Brosius, Lewis W.: Genealogy of Henry and Mary Brosius and their descendants with other historical matters connected therewith, also some short accounts of other families bearing the Borsius name. *Compiled by . . . [s. l.] 1928. pp. (8), 472, ill.* [6249]

Brown, Richard L.: A history of the Michael Brown family of Rowan County, North Carolina. *Tracing its line of posterity from the original Michael Brown to the present generation and giving something of the times one hundred and fifty years*

ago, together with many historic facts of local and national interest. *Published under the auspices of the Michael Brown Family Association. 1921. pp. 190, ill.*
[6250

Brubacher, Benjamin: Brubacher family history. *In: Eleventh Annual Report of the Waterloo Historical Society. Kitchener, Ont. 1923. pp. 38—45.* [6251

Brubacher, Jacob N.: The Brubacher genealogy in America. *Elkhart, Ind.: Mennonite Publishing Co. 1884. pp. (1), 5—243.*

[Descendants of John, who came from Switzerland about 1710 and settled in Lancaster County, Pa.] [6252

Brubaker, Henry S.: The Brubaker genealogy. *Mount Joy, Pa.: The Mount Joy Bulletin 1912. pp. 344.*

[Descendants of John or Hans Brucker from Switzerland; emigrated about 1710.]
[6253

Abstracts of records from the bible of the Bruner family, of Germantown. *In: The Pennsylvania Magazine of History and Biography. Vol. XXI. Philadelphia. Pa. 1897. pp. 415—416.*

[Frederick Bruner, b. in Canton Basel, Switzerland, Sept., 1744.] [6254

Sener, S. M.: Evans-Bruner. *In: Notes and Queries. Edited by W. H. Egle. Annual vol. 1899. Harrisburg, Pa. 1900. p. 113.*
[6255

Bruner. *In: Notes and Queries. Edited by W. H. Egle. Annual vol. 1899. Harrisburg, Pa. 1900. p. 156.*

[Ulrich Brunner came to America in 1744, and settled in Morgantown, Berks Co., Pa.] [6256

Mengel, Levi W.: In memoriam. David B. Brunner. *Paper read before the Society, Jan. 12, 1904. In: Transactions of the Historical Society of Berks County. Vol. I. Reading, Pa. 1904. pp. (3), ill.*

[b. March 7, 1835; great-great-grandson of Peter Brunner, a Palatine emigrant of about 1736.] [6257

Brumbaugh, Gajus Marcus: Genealogy of the Brumbach families including those using the following variations of the original name, **Brumbaugh, Brumbach, Brumback, Brombaugh, Brownback,** and many other connected families. *New York, N. Y.: Frederick H. Hitchcock 1913. pp. XXV. pp. 850, ill., map.*
[6258

Brownback, Garret E. and Brownback, Oscar B.: The Gerhard Brumbach fa-

mily. *In: The Pennsylvania-German. Vol. XI. Lititz, Pa. 1910. pp. 163—172, ill.* [6259

Porter, Thos. Conrad: The Bucher album. *In: The Pennsylvania-German Society. Proceedings and Addresses at Reading, Oct. 3, 1894. Vol. V. Reading, Pa. 1895. pp. 133—140.* [6260

Egle, William Henry: Bucher family. *In: Egle's ,,Pennsylvania genealogies". Harrisburg, Pa. 1896 [= no. 6045]. pp. 120—142.*

[Descendants of Claus Bucher, b. in Neukirch, in the Canton of Schaffhausen, Switzerland in 1524.] [6261

Ayres, George Bucher: Reverend Captain John Conrad Bucher. *In: Notes and Queries. Edited by W. H. Egle. Second series. Harrisburg, Pa. 1883. pp. 298—300. Reprint in: First and second series, vol. II. Harrisburg, Pa. 1895. pp. 411—416.*

[b. at Harrisburg, Pa., Dec. 28, 1792.]
[6262

Dubbs, J. H.: Rev. John Conrad Bucher, *In: Notes and Queries. Edited by W. H. Egle. Third series, vol. I. 1884—1887. Harrisburg, Pa. 1887. pp. 228—230. Reprint in: Third series, vol. I. Harrisburg, Pa. 1895. pp. 432—434.* [6263

Stapleton, A.: Famous Pennsylvania-Germans. Rev. John Conrad Bucher, scholar, soldier and pioneer preacher. *In: The Pennsylvania-German. Vol. IV. Lebanon, Pa. 1903. pp. 291—308, ill.*
[6264

Ayres, George Bucher: John Jacob Bucher. *In: Notes and Queries. Edited by W. H. Egle. First series, part I. Harrisburg, Pa. 1881. pp. 17—19. Reprint in: First and second series, vol. I. Harrisburg, Pa. 1894. pp. 313—315.* [6265

Meyer, Henry: The Buchtel family. *In: The Pennsylvania-German. Vol. VIII. Lebanon, Pa. 1907. pp. 588—594, ill.*

[John Buchtel, the ancester, emigrated from Württemberg in 1753.] [6266

Yeakel, Frederic D.: Hon. Henry A. Buchtel, D. D., LL. D., governor of Colorado. *In: The Pennsylvania-German. Vol. VIII. Lebanon, Pa. 1907. pp. 268—269, ill.*

[b. near Akron, O., Sept. 30, 1847, his great-grandfather Peter Buchtel came from Switzerland to Pa. about 1750.]
[6267

Dandridge, Danske Dedinger: The Büddinger family in America. *In: The Penn-*

sylvania-German. Vol. XI. Lititz, Pa. 1910. p. 763. [6268
Buhrer, James D.: The ancestry and history of the Buhrer families. *Washington, D. C. [s. l., s. d.] (1916). pp. 51, ill.*
[of Swiss origin, from the villages in the Hegan.] [6269
Burgner, Jacob: History and genealogy of the Burgner family, in the United States of America as descendant from Peter Burgner, a Swiss emigrant of 1734. *First edition. Oberlin, O.: The Oberlin News Press 1890. pp. (1), VI, 172, ill.* [6270
Mast, C. Z.: The Burkholder family. *In: Christian Monitor. A monthly magazine for the home. Vol. XVIII. Scottdale, Pa. 1926. No. 10. pp. 309—310; No. 11. pp. 338—339; No. 12. pp. 370— 371; Vol. XIX, 1927. No. 1. pp. 19— 20; No. 2. pp. 51—52; Vol. XX, 1928. No. 3. p. 86, ill.*
[who traced back into the regions of Emmenthal, Canton Berne, Switzerland and whose first pioneer ancestor settled in Lancaster Co., Pa. as early as 1734.] [6271
[Burkholder, J. C.]: Report of the (first Burkholder family reunion.) Rhoads Park, Franklin County, Pa. *September 3, 1926. pp. 23.* The Burkholder family reunion. *Part II. Harrisburg, Pa., July 10, 1927. pp. 16. Part III. Harrisburg, Pa., March 1, 1928. pp. 69. Part IV. Harrisburg, Pa., April 1, 1929. pp. 37. Part V. Harrisburg, Pa., April 1, 1930. pp. 28. Part VI. Harrisburg, Pa., April 1, 1931. pp. 34, ill. Part VII. Harrisburg, Pa., April 1, 1932. pp. 105, ill.*
[is traced to the Canton Berne, Switzerland, the Emmenthal Valley and the Villages of Langnau and Ruderswyl.] [6272
Lacher, J. H. A.: Lincolns' stepmother of German stock. *[Sarah Bush Lincoln.] In: Unrolling the scroll. Published by the National Society. Vol. I. Chicago, Ill. 1928 [=no. 29]. pp. 85—87, ill.* [6273
Wyand, E. Clayton: A brief history of the Andrew Putnam **(Buttnam,** Putnam), Christian Wyandt **(Weyandt,** Weygandt, Voint, Wyand) and Adam Snyder families **(Schneider)** of Washington County, Md. *Hagerstown, Md.: Hagerstown Bookbinding and Printing Co. 1909. pp. (1), (4), 11—103, ill.* [6274
Martin, C. H.: Life of Andrew Byerly. *In: Papers and Addresses of the Lancaster*

County Historical Society. Vol. XXXIII. Lancaster, Pa. 1929. pp. 3—8.
[Emigrated 1738, and settled in Lancaster Co., Pa.] [7275
Egle, William Henry: Byers of Derry. *In: Egle's ,,Pennsylvania genealogies." Harrisburg, Pa. 1896 [= no. 6045]. pp. 765 —767.*
[Descendants of John Byers, a native of Germany who came to America prior to 1740.] [6276

C.

The **Capp** family in Pennsylvania. *In: Notes and Queries. Edited by W. H. Egle. Annual vol. 1896. Harrisburg, Pa. 1897. pp. 155—158.*
[Andreas Kapp, one of the Palatine settlers, at Livinstone Manor, N. Y. in 1710, who removed to Pa.] [6277
Walker, Edwin Sawyer: Genealogical notes of the **Carpenter** *[Zimmerman]* family including the autobiography and personal reminiscences of Dr. Seymour D. Carpenter, Lieutnant Colonel, in the war for the Union. *With genealogical and biographical index. Springfield, Ill.: Illinois State Journal Co. 1907. pp. XV, 11—242, ill.* [6278
Casanova, A. Y.: A **Carpenter** family of Lancaster. *In: The Pennsylvania-German. Vol. XI. Lititz, Pa. 1910. pp. 65 —76.*
[Descendants of Heinrich Zimmerman, b. at Wattenwil, Canton Berne, Switzerland Sept. 7, 1673, emigrated to America, arrived at Germantown, Pa. 1698.] [6279
Cassel, Daniel Kolb: A genealogical history of the **Cassel** family in America being the descendants of Julius Kassel or Yelles Cassel, of Kriesheim, Baden. Germany. *Containing biographical sketches of prominent descendants. Norristown, Pa.: Morgan R. Wills 1896. pp. 463, (2), ill.* [6280
Hocker, Edward W.: Abraham Harley **Cassel.** A biographical sketch. *In: The Pennsylvania-German. Vol. IX. Cleona, Pa. 1908. pp. 304—307.*
[b. in Towamencin Township, Montgomery Co., Pa. Sept. 21, 1820.] [6281
— Abraham Harley **Cassel.** *Read April 25, 1908. In: Historical Sketches. A Collection of Papers prepared for the Historical Society of Montgomery County, Pa. Vol. IV. Norristown, Pa. 1910. pp. 78—83.* [6282

Pennypacker, Samuel Whitaker: Abraham Harley **Cassel.** *An appreciation. In: The Pennsylvania-German. Vol. IX. Cleona, Pa. 1908. pp. 303—304, ill.* [6283

Smith, Charles D.: Rev. Leonard **Cassel.** *A memoir. Baltimore, Md.: Baltimore Methodist Print 1896. pp. 24.* [6284

P.[arthemore, E. W. S.]: A Dauphin County Centenarian. Miß Margaret or „Peggy" **Cassel.** *Paper read before the Dauphin County Historical Society, Nov. 11, 1895. In: Notes and Queries. Edited by W. H. Egle. Annual vol. 1896. Harrisburg, Pa. 1897. pp. 14—16.* [6285

Cauffman. *In: Rodenbough, Theo Francis: Autumn leaves . . New York, N. Y.: Clark & Zugalla 1892. pp. 13—24, ill.*
[Descendants of Joseph Kauffman of Alsace, Germany, who arrived at Philadelphia, Pa. 1749.] [6286

Willox, Joseph: Historical sketches of some of the pioneer Catholics of Philadelphia and vicinity: Joseph **Cauffmann.** *In: Records of the American Catholic Historical Society of Philadelphia. Vol. XV. Philadelphia, Pa. 1904. pp. 422—427;* Some notes: *In: Vol. XXI. Philadelphia, Pa. pp. 83—84.* See also Dr. Joseph Cauffman applying to Benjamin Franklin for service during the Revolutionary War. *In: Vol. XXI. 1910. pp. 77—82.*
[Founder of the family in this country; b. in Strasburg, Germany in 1720.] [6287

Christlieb, Benj. F.: The **Christlieb** family. *[s. l.] 1895. pp. 52.*
[Descendants of Frederick Charles Christlieb of Durkheim, Rheinish Bavaria, who emigrated to America in 1765.] [6288

Whitsett, William Thornton: History of Brick [Reformed] Church [Guilford County, N. C.] and the **Clapp** family. *Greesboro, N. C.: Harrison Printing Co. 1925. pp. 28, ill.*
= *Whitsett Historical Monographs, no. 2.* [6289

Class bible record. *Taken from a bible in the possession of Mrs. John Jacob Mohr, of Philadelphia. Translated from the German by* Samuel W. Pennypacker. *In: Publications of the Genealogical Society of Pennsylvania. Vol. IV, no. 1. Philadelphia, Pa. 1909. p. 22.* [6290

Clemmer, Abram: The **Clemmer** family of Montgomery County. *In: The Perkiomen Region. Vol. XIII. No. 3—4. Pennsburg, Pa. 1930. pp. 74—80.*

[Henrich Clemmer (Klemmer) arrived at Philadelphia Sept. 5, 1730 and settled in Franconia Township, Montgomery Co., Pa. as early as 1738.] [6291

Singmaster, J. A.: Dr. Jacob A. **Clutz,** D. D. LL. D. *In: The Lutheran Quarterly. Vol. LV. Gettysburg, Pa. 1925. pp. 389—391;* A tribute to Dr. Clutz. *By Archbishop Söderblom, Upsala. Translated from the Swedish Församlings-blaret by* Saby. *pp. 392—395.*
[b. and raised on a farm in Adams Co., Pa.] [6292

Steiner, M. S.: John S.[amuel] **Coffman,** Mennonite evangelist. His life and labors. *Spring Grove, Pa.: Mennonite Book and Tract Society 1903. pp. 139, ill.*
[Descendant of Isaac Coffman, who settled in Greenbeer Co., W. Va.] [6293

Haywood, Marshall De Lancey: Richard **Cogdell** (Revolutionary patriot). *In: Biographical history of North Carolina. Edited by S. A Ashe. Vol. II. Greensboro, N. C. 1905. pp. 64—66.*
[of Swiss origin, descended from one of the members of Baron de Graffenried's colony at New Bern, N. C.; b. July 8, 1724.] [6294

Cressman, Clayton W.: Notes on the **Cressman** family. *In: The Perkiomen Region. Vol. VI, no. 1. Pennsburg, Pa. 1928. p. 29.*
[Descendants of Nicholas Cressman, a native of Switzerland, he came — it is thought — to Limerick Twp., Montgomery Co. in 1727.] [6295

Croll, P. C.: The golden-wedding ring. A souvenir of the fiftieth anniversary of the marriage of John and Catherine **Croll** to the celebrated October 29, 1887. *2 parts: I.* Brief history of the Croll family; *II.* Biographical sketch of John Croll and his family. *Lancaster, Pa.: The Era Printing House 1887. pp. 106.* [6296

The **Croll** family. *In: Notes and Queries. Edited by W. H. Egle. Third series, vol. II. 1887—1900. Harrisburg, Pa. 1891. pp. 312—313. Reprint in: Third series, vol. III. Harrisburg, Pa. 1896. pp. 361—362.*
[Descendants of John Croll; b. Aug. 16, 1797; d. Nov. 14, 1825.] [6297

Croll, P. C.: The **Croll** family in America. *In: The Pennsylvania-German. Vol. II. Lebanon, Pa. 1901. pp. 32—42, ill;* The Croll family again. *Vol. V. 1904. pp. 31—42.* [6298

Croll, P. C.: 1880—1930. Croll-Greiss. *Fifty years. Golden Wedding Souvenir. [s. l.] 1930. pp. 89, ill.* [6299]

McCaskey, J. P.: Rev. John S. Crumbaugh. First Sunday school, superintendent and first pastor of St. John's Evangelical Lutheran Church, with some early childhood memoirs of this remarkable man, *written for his infant son. Printed for the Semi-Centennial of St. John's Lutheran Church, Lancaster, Pa. Sunday, May 17, 1903. pp. 16.* [6300]

Whittaker, Frederick: A complete life of General Geo. A. Custer. *New York, N. Y.: Sheldon & Co. 1876. pp. 257, ill.* [6300a]

Custer, G. A.: My life on the plains. *New York, N.Y. 1881. pp. . . .* [6300b]

Custer, Elisabeth Bacon: The boy general, story of the life of Maj. Gen. George A. Custer, as told in Teuting on the plains. *Edited by M. E. Burt. New York, N. Y.: Charles Scribners & Sons 1901. pp. . . .* [6300c]

Dellenbaugh, Frederick Samuel: George Armstrong Custer *(True stories of great Americans) New York, N. Y.: The Macmillan Co. 1917. pp. XV, 188.* [6300d]

Ronsheim, Milton: The life of General Custer. *In: Ohio Archaeological and Historical Quarterly. Vol. XXXIX. Columbus, O. 1930. pp. 667—670.*
[Said to be of Hessian ancestry.] 6301

D.

K.[eim], De B. R.: The De Benneville family. *In: Notes and Queries. Edited by W. H. Egle. Annual vol. 1898. Harrisburg, Pa. 1899. pp. 181—183.* [6302]

Hostetler, Ella M. (Doggett): Michael DeBolt and his descendants. *By one of them. Shelton, Nebraska: Clipper Press 1926. pp. 19, ill.*
[French Huguenot; emigrated 1739.] [6303]

Deckard, Percy Edward: Genealogy of the Deckard family showing also those descended from Decker, Deckert, Decher, Dechert, Decherd, etc. *Compiled by . . . Pittsburgh, Pa.: Pittsburgh Printing Co. 1932. pp. (1), 11—893, ill.* [6304]

Deibert, Daniel: Life and experience of Daniel Deibert, from his youth to his old age. *Schuylkill Haven, Pa. 1884. pp. 15.*
[Descendant of William Deibert, b. in Wittenburg, Germany.] [6305]

Hager, Walter C.: Jacob William Deichler. Artist and shoemaker. *In: Papers and Addresses of the Lancaster County Historical Society. Vol. XXIX. Lancaster, Pa. 1925. pp. 15—18, ill.* [6306]

The Deininger family. *In: Notes and Queries. Edited by W. H. Egle. Third series, vol. II. 1887—1890. Harrisburg, Pa. 1891. pp. 328—329; 329—330. Reprint in: Third series, vol. III. Harrisburg, Pa. 1896. pp. 381—383; 383—386.*
[John Adam Deininger, b. April 23, 1722 at Aicholz, near Halle, Germany, landed at Philadelphia, Pa. 1732.] [6307]

Memorial of the Rev. C. J. Deininger, pastor during nearly forty years of Lutheran churches in York County, Pa. *Published by his family. York, Pa.: Gazette Printing House 1885. pp. . . .*
[b. Aug. 30, 1822, at the ,,Loop'' in Centre County, son of Rev. A. G. Deininger.] [6308]

George Delker, a private soldier of the Revolution, from Philadelphia County, killed at the battle of Germantown, Oct. 4, 1777. *In: The Pennsylvania-Magazine of History and Biography. Vol. XXXI. Philadelphia, Pa. 1907. p. 510.* [6309]

Croll, P. C.: The Delong family in America. *In: The Pennsylvania-German. Vol. IV. Lebanon, Pa. 1903. pp. 375—383, ill.;* Additional Delong Genealogical data. *Vol. V. 1904 pp. 22—23.* [6310]

De Long, Irwin Hoch: Early occurrences of the family name De Long in Europe and America. *In: The Reformed Church Review. Fifth series, vol. III. Lancaster, Pa. 1924. pp. 267—280, ill.* [6311]

— The lineage of Malcolm Metzger Parker from Johannes DeLong. 1724 Pyeter Delangh — 1926 Malcolm Metzger Parker. *In commemoration of the 21st birth-day anniversary of their son Malcolm and as a special contribution to the celebration of the Sesqui-Centennial of the Declaration of Independence, Philadelphia, Pa. 1926, this publication is issued by Mr. and Mrs. Harry W. Parker, Pittsburgh, Pa. Lancaster, Pa.: The Art Printing Co. 1926. pp. VIII, 62, ill.* [6312]

— Pioneer Palatine pilgrims. *Also: A. Children of Peter De Long and his wife Elisabeth; B. The family bible of Rebecca Amanda Geist, a born De Long; C. The family bible of Dewald De Long; D. Benneville B. De Long and his children; E. De*

Long burials, Bowers, Pa.; F. Family bible now in possession of Mrs. Benneville Miller, Rockland Township, Berks County, Pa.; G. Additional European De Longs; H. Smith burials in Fairview cemetery, Allentown, Pa.; I. Records of early Hochs in Pennsylvania; J. Baptismal and marriage certificates of Joseph De Long; K. The alleged French or Huguenot origin of the De Longs. Lancaster, Pa.: Press of the Art Printing Co. *1928. pp. 36.* [6313

DeLong, Irwin Hoch: My ancestors. Lancaster, Pa. *1930. pp. XI, 108, ill., chart.* [6314

Demuth, Henry C.: Demuth's 1770. The history of a Lancaster tradition. *Being a brief history of the Demuth Tobacco Shop, which was founded at Lancaster in the Province of Pennsylvania in the year of our Lord 1770. [s. l.] 1925. pp. 16, ill.* [6315

Miller, Daniel: Life and labors of Rev. Levi K. **Derr,** D. D. *Reading, Pa.: Daniel Miller 1907. pp. 83, ill.*
[Son of Daniel Derr and his wife Susanna, Pa. — Germans.] [6316

Montgomery, Morton L.: Deturk family. *In: Historical Register: Notes and Queries, historical and genealogical relating to interior Pennsylvania for the year 1884. Vol. II. Harrisburg, Pa. 1884. pp. 92—98.*
[Isaac Deturk, or le Turck, as it is first written in legal documents, emigrated to this country about 1709, and tradition says, from Alsace, having landed with his sister Esther at New York, and settled at Esopus. On June 11, 1712, the commissioners of land of the Prov. of Pa. issued a warrant to him for 300 acres of land, to be laid out at a place called „Oley". In this he is described as „late of Frankendal" in Germany.] [6317

Steinmetz, C. M.: Inscriptions private burying ground on the farm of Seth L. De Turck, Oley, Berks County, Pa. *In: The National Genealogical Society Quarterly. Vol. XV., no. 2. Washington, D. C. 1927. p. 30.* [6318

D. B. Detweiler. *In: Seventh Annual Report of the Waterloo Historical Society. Kitchener, Ont. 1919. pp. 93—101.*
[b. April 10, 1860 near Roseville, North Dumfries Township, Ontario; grandson of Rev. Jacob Detweiler, coming from Bucks Co., Pa. to Ontario, 1822.] [6319

Death of Hon. Jones **Detweiler.** *In: The Perkiomen Region, Past and Present. Vol. III. Philadelphia, Pa. 1901. pp. 129—130.*
[b. in Upper Dublin Township, Montgomery Co., Pa. Nov. 11, 1828.] [6320

Diehl family. *In: Colonial families of Philadelphia. Edited by John W. Jordan. New York, N. Y. — Chigaco, Ill.: The Lewis Publishing Co. 1911. Vol. II. pp. 1723—1737, ill.*
[Nicholas Diehl was b. in Frankfort-the-Main, Germany, in Frankfort-on-the Main, Germany, in or about 1741. He arrived in Philadelphia, Pa. 1761, and purchased a good tract land on Tinicum Island, then in Ridley Township, Chester Co., Pa.] [6321

Diehl, E. H.: Diehl families of America. History, genealogy, reminiscences, &c. *[Ipava, Ill.] 1915. pp. (2), 9—229, ill.*
[Samuel Diehl, progenitor of one of the prominent branches was b. 1740 and resided in Loudon Co., Va.] [6322

— Long ago. Poetry, local public schools, reminiscences, genealogy. *Ipava, Ill. 1924. pp. (1), 5—239, (8), ill.* [6323

— Addenda to Diehl genealogy of 1915. *Berlin, Pa.: The Berlin Press 1930. pp. (2), 5—227, ill.* [6324

An account of the family reunion of the descendants of Samuel **Diehl** of Friend's Cove, Bedford County, Pa., held September 19, 1890, with a genealogical table of his descendants. *Bedford, Pa.: The Inquirer Steam Co. 1891. pp. 60.* [6325

Third reunion of the **Dietrich** family association. Souvenir programm. Sept. 1, 1906. Kutztown Park, Kutztown, Berks County, Pa. *Kutztown, Pa.: J. B. Esser 1906. pp. 20, ill.* [6326

Deatrick, W. W.: The Dietrichs in Europe and America. *Historical address delivered at the Dietrich family-reunion at Kutztown, Pa., Sept. 1, 1906. In: The Pennsylvania-German. Vol. VIII. Lebanon, Pa. 1907. pp. 428—434.* [6327

Dietterich, H. A.: A wonder of grace, thirty-three years in the ministry, being a short sketch of the life and labors of Rev. H. A. Dietterich. *Written by himself. York, Pa.: P. Anstadt & Sons 1892. pp. 415, ill.*
[b. in Columbia Co., Pa., April 21, 1838, son of Henry Dietterich.] [6328

Diffenbaugh, Milton Hess: Dieffenbach-Diffenbaugh . . . *Compiled by . . . Lan-*

caster, Pa. 1930. Genealogical tab., ill. (Blueprint, at Library of Congress, Washington, D. C.)

[Family tree of descendants of Adam Dieffenbaugh and Fraena (Franconia) Bare.] [6329

Family records. The **Diffenderfers** and **Frieses**. Unsere Quellen sind von Zeit zu Zeit eingetragene Familien-Ereignisse, wie sie sich auf den inneren Seiten der Deckel einer Schweizer Bibel (Basel 1729) vorfanden, und andere geschriebene Notizen aus alten Büchern im Besitze der Baltimorer Diffenderfer. In: Fifth Annual Report of the Society for the History of the Germans in Maryland. Baltimore, Md. 1891. pp. 91—95. [6330

Diffenderffer, Frank Ried: Some of the descendants of Sohn Michael **Dübendorf** 1695—1778 more especially those directly descended through his grandson David Diffenderffer 1752—1846. By his great-great-grandson. Lancaster, Pa.: Press of the New Era Printing Co. 1910. pp. 28, ill., map. [6331

Kopenhaver, W. M.: Rev. John Caspar **Dill**. In: The Pennsylvania-German. Vol. XI. Lititz, Pa. 1910. pp. 431—432. [Native of Wertheim, Franconia, Germany; came to America 1790.] [6332

Dillenback family genealogy. Notes in: The New York Genealogical and Biographical Record. Vol. XXIX. New York, N. Y. 1898. p. 115. [Martin Dillenback, b. in the Palatinate, landed in New York 1710.] [6333

Ringwalt, J. L.: The **Diller** family. [Philadelphia, Pa. 1877.] pp. 56. [Descendants of Caspar Diller, b. in Alsace, about 1670 or 1675 and d. at Loch Platz, Lancaster Co., Pa. 1770 or 1775.] [6334

Diller, J. S.: The **Dillers**. In: The Pennsylvania-German. Vol. XI. Lititz, Pa. 1910. pp. 216—219, map. [6335

— The Francis **Diller** family. In: The Pennsylvania-German. Vol. XI. Lititz, Pa. 1910. pp. 282—287, ill. [Francis Diller, of Biglen, Bernese Oberland, Switzerland, emigrated 1754 and purchased a farm, on a branch of Muddy Creek in Cocalico, now Brecknock Twp.,Lancaster Co., Pa.1760.] [6336

Ringwalt, Roland: The **Diller** family. Address delivered at Diller reunion, New Holland, Pa., June 17, 1910. In: The Pennsylvania-German. Vol. XI. Lititz, Pa. 1910. pp. 529—533. [6337

Diller, C. H.: Maryland **Dillers**. Abstract of a paper read at the first Diller reunion, New Holland, Pa., June, 1910. In: The Pennsylvania-German. Vol. XI. Lititz, Pa. 1910. pp. 534—535. [Descendants of Martin Diller, who removed from Musselman's farm near New Holland, Lancaster Co., Pa. to Johnsville, Frederick Co., Md. 1828.] [6338

Mountz, S. M.: Some **Diller** baptismal records. Abstract of a paper read at the 1st Diller reunion, New Holland, Pa., June, 1910. In: The Pennsylvania-German. Vol. XI. Lititz, Pa. 1910. pp. 535—536. [6339

Dings, Myron: The **Dings** family in America. Genealogy, memoirs and comments. Chicago, Ill. 1927. pp. 182, ill. [of Palatine ancestry.] [6340

Stetzel, Henry: A brief biography of Moses **Dissinger**, preacher of the Evangelical Association. Schaefferstown, Lebanon County, Pa.: Published by Isaac Iba [s. d.] (1905?) pp. 8. [6341

[Yost, Wm.]: Moses **Dissinger**-reminiscences. Introduction by S. P. Spreng. Reprint from: The Evangelical Messenger. April/May, 1911. In: The Penn Germania. Vol. I. = Old series, vol. XIII. Lititz, Pa. 1912. pp. 178—184, ill. [6342

Shenk, H. H.: A Lebanon County old time backwoods preacher. [Rev. Moses **Dissinger**.] In: Papers read before the Lebanon County Historical Society. Vol. VI. Lebanon, Pa. 1912—1916. pp. 416—439, ill. [6343

Page, Jane M.: William Urich **Ditzler**. Quaker by convincement. In: Quaker Biographies. A series of sketches, chiefly biographical, concerning members of the Society of Friends, from the 17th century to more recent times. Vol. V. Philadelphia, Pa.: Friend's Book Store. 1916. pp. 229—246. [b. in Lebanon, Pa., in 1821 of German parentage.] [6344

Pennypacker, Samuel Whitaker: Christopher **Dock**, the pious schoolmaster on the Skippack and his works. In: Historical and biographical sketches. Philadelphia, Pa. 1883 [= no. 356]. pp. 91—153. [6345

Brumbaugh, Martin G.: The life and works of Christopher **Dock**, America's pioneer writer on education, with a translation of his works into the English lan-

guage. With an introduction by Samuel
W. Pennypacker. Philadelphia, Pa.
& London: J. B. Lippincott Co. 1908.
pp. 272, ill. [6346
Will of Christopher **Dock**. [Febr. 1, 1762.]
Copied by Helen G. Breuninger. In:
The Perkiomen Region. Vol. II, no. 2.
Pennsburg, Pa. 1923. pp. 23—25. [6347
Hinke, William J.: Life and work of the
Rev. Peter Henry **Dorsius**. Read Jan.
19, 1918. In: A Collection of Papers
read before the Bucks County Historical
Society. Vol. V. Meadville, Pa. 1926.
pp. 44—67. [6348
Bergstresser, P.: A biography of Rev.
Thomas William Luther **Dosh**, D. D.
In: The Quarterly Review of the Lutheran
Church. Vol. XXI. Gettysburg, Pa.
1891. pp. 357—373.
[b. Nov. 21, 1830 at Strasburg, Va.,
descendant of Alsacian emigrants.] [6349
Dotterer, Henry S.: The **Dotterer** family.
Philadelphia, Pa. 1903. pp. (2), (2),
9—164, ill.
[Descendants of George Philip Dotterer,
who is b. in Europe; d. in Frederick
Twp., Philadelphia (now Montgomery)
Co., Pa., Nov. 5, 1741.] [6350
Dotterer family bible record. — Matthias
Dotter. In: National Genealogical So-
ciety Quarterly. Vol. XIV. Wash-
ington, D. C. 1925. p. 47. [6351
Hinke, William J.: Henry Sassaman **Dot-
terer**. 1841—1903. In: Journal of the
Presbyterian Historical Society. Vol. II.
Philadelphia, Pa. 1904. pp. 243—250,
ill.; Reprint in: Historical Sketches. A
Collection of Papers . . . Historical Society of Montgomery County, Pa. Vol.
III. Norristown, Pa. 1905. pp. 1—8.
[Descendant of George Philip „Dod-
derer" who came from Germany to Pa.
before the year 1722.] [6352
Betz, I. H.: Daniel **Drowbaugh**, the mechanic and inventor. In: The Pennsylvania-German. Vol. XI. Lititz, Pa.
1910. pp. 450—459.
[b. at Eberly's Mills, Cumberland Co ,
Pa. 1827, of Pennsylvania-German parents.] [6353
Dreisbach, Laura M.: History and genealogy of the **Dreisbach** family. [Vol. I.]
Allentown, Pa.: Press of Berkmeyer,
Keck & Co. 1924. pp. (1), 3—47, ill.;
Supplement to vol. I. Allentown, Pa.
1927. pp. (1), 3—26, ill.
[Simon Dreisbach, sr., the progenitor
of the Dreisbach family in America, was

b. in Witgenstein, Germany, Aug. 7, 1698;
d. March 31, 1785, buried at Kreidersville,
Northampton Co., Pa.] [6354
„George **Drescher** (Dresher) and his descen-
dants". In: The genealogical record of
the Schwenkfelder families. Edited by
S. K. Brecht. New York, N. Y. — Chicago, Ill. 1923. pp. 917—926. [6355
Dubbs, J. H.: The **Dubbs** family of Lower
Milford, Lehigh County, Pa. In: The
Pennsylvania-German. Vol. X. Lititz,
Pa. 1909. pp. 605—610, ill.
[Descendants of Jacob Dubs, b. Aug.
31, 1710, in the hamlet of Aesch, parish
of Birmensdorf, Canton of Zürich,
Switzerland, emigrated to America and
arrived at Philadelphia, Pa. Sept. 30,
1732.] [6356
— Jacob Dubs, of Milford. In: Pennsyl-
vania Magazine of History and Bio-
graphy, Vol. XVIII. Philadelphia, Pa.
1894. pp. 367—376. [6356a
Richards, George Warren: Joseph Henry
Dubbs. In: German American Annals.
New series, vol. VIII. Philadelphia,
Pa. 1910. pp. 94—96.
[b. in North Whitehall Twp., Lehigh
Co., Pa. Oct. 5, 1838; son of the Rev.
Joseph S. Dubbs, D. D., and his wife
Eleanor.] [6357
Stahr, J. S.: The Rev. Joseph Henry **Dubbs**,
D. D. L. L. D. An appreciation. In: The
Pennsylvania-German. Vol. XI. Lititz,
Pa. 1910. pp. 420—422. [6358
Rev. Samuel **Dubendorff**. In: Notes and
Queries. Edited by W. H. Egle. Third
series, vol. I. 1884—1887. Harrisburg,
Pa. 1887. p. 294. Peprint in: Third
series, vol. I. Harrisburg, Pa. 1895.
p. 531.
[A native of Germany; came to America
at the outset of the Revolution as chap-
lain to one of the regiments of the Hessian
mercenaries, later removed to Lykens
Valley, Dauphin Co. (in 1780).] [6359

E.

Egle, William Henry: Eagley family. In:
Egle's „Pennsylvania genealogies". Harrisburg, Pa. 1899 [=no. 6045]. pp. 767
—768. [6360
Parthemore, E. W. S.: The **Early** family.
Address prepared for the ninetieth anniversary of John Early. In: Notes and
Queries. Edited by W. H. Egle. Annual
vol. 1897. Harrisburg, Pa. 1898. pp.
48—51. [6361

Early, J. W.: The descendants of Christian Early. *In: The Pennsylvania-German. Vol. XI. Lititz, Pa. 1910. pp. 33—37.* [6362

— John Early (Johannes Oehrle) and his descendants. *In: The Pennsylvania-German. Vol. X. Lititz, Pa. 1909. pp. 74—76; 126—128.*
[Emigrated from Jesingen, Ober-amt Kirchlein, Germany, in 1750.] [6363

— John Early (Johannes Oehrle) and his descendants — by his second wife, Christina Regina Sichele. *In: The Pennsylvania-German. Vol. XI. Lititz, Pa. 1910. pp. 205—211.* [6364

— John Early (Johannes Oehrle) and his descendants. John William, Thomas and the daughters. *In: The Pennsylvania-German. Vol. XI. Lititz, Pa. 1910. pp. 398—403.* [6365

[Eberle, William H.]: A branch of the Eberle family. *By W. H. Eberle in his 84th year (1885) transcribed by his grandson W. H. Eberle. In: Papers and Addresses of the Lancaster County Historical Society. Vol. IV. Lancaster, Pa. 1900. pp. 75—85.* [6366

Wanger, George F. P.: Eberly (Daniel) bible record. *In: The National Genealogical Society Quarterly. Vol. XII, no. 2. Washington, D. C. 1923. p. 28.* [6367

E.[gle], J. H.: The Ebersole family. *In: Notes and Queries. Edited by W. H. Egle. Third series, vol. I. 1884—1887. Harrisburg, Pa. 1887. pp. 36—37. Reprint in: Third series, vol. I. Harrisburg, Pa. 1895. pp. 65—66.*
[Abraham Ebersole, a settler in now Swatara Twp., Dauphin Co., Pa.] [6368

Eby, Ezra E.: A biographical history of the Eby family, *being a history of their movements in Europe during the Reformation and their settlement in America; as also much other unpublished historical information belonging to the family. Berlin, Ont., Can.: Hett & Eby 1889. pp. 142.* [6369

Flickinger, S. H.: From a Pennsylvania family graveyard. *[Tombstone inscriptions from the Eby family graveyard, 1 mile west of the Town of Stevens, Lancaster County, Pa., on the Mentzer farm, formerly the farm of John Herman]. In: Genealogy. Journal of American ancestry. Vol. II. New York, N. Y. 1912. pp. 211—212.* [6370

Eby, Jacob: A brief record of the Ebys from their arrival in America to my grand-parents, Peter and Margaret, Hess Eby, their descendants, my uncles, aunts and cousins, their births, deaths and ages together with their companions as well as I was able to learn. *Lancaster, Pa. 1923. pp. 50.* [6371

Eby, Allan A.: The Eby family as related to the Brubachers. *In: Eleventh Annual Report of the Waterloo Historical Society. Kitchener, Ont. 1923. pp. 46—49.* [6372

Aby, Franklin Stanton: The Ebi family, the Ebie family of Stark County, Ohio, progeny of Theodorus Eby, the Swiss Mennonite pioneer of Lancaster County, Pa. United States of America. *Chicago, Ill.: Privately printed 1923. pp. 19.*
= *The Eby family bulletin, no. 1.* [6373

— The Swiss Eby family. Pioneer millwrights and millers of Lancaster County, Pa., United States of America. *Chicago, Ill.: Privately printed 1924. pp. 55.*
= *The Eby family bulletin, no. 2.* [6374

— Colonial documentary history of Theodorus Eby. (His relatives and descendants) the Swiss Mennonite pioneer of Lancaster County, Pa. United States of America. *Chicago, Ill.: Privately printed 1924. pp. 89, maps.*
= *The Eby family bulletin, no. 3.* [6375

Aby, Malvina (Stanton) and Aby, Franklin Stanton: The Aby family of Peoria County, Ill., and the Eaby family of Lancaster County, Pa., progeny of Theodorus Eby (1663—1732) the Swiss Mennonite pioneer of Lancaster County, Pa., United States of America. *Including Gideon Cole (1751—1826); Clark Stanton (1776—1850); Timothy Barnes (1780—1873). Chicago, Ill.: Privately printed 1924. pp. 101, maps.*
= *The Eby family bulletin, no. 4.* [6376

Aby, Franklin Stanton: Nicholaus Ebi-Eby (1825—1898) of Sheboygan County, Wis., United States of America, great-great-grand nephew of Theodorus Eby, the Swiss Mennonite pioneer of Lancaster County, Pa., United States of America. *Chicago, Ill.: Privately printed 1925. pp. . . .*
= *The Eby family bulletin, no. 5.* [6377

— The Eby group of American family names comprising the Eby — the Aby — the Eaby — the Ebi — the Ebie — the Ebey family and others. *Chicago, Ill.: Privately printed 1925. pp. . . .*
= *The Eby family bulletin, no. 6.* [6378

Sherk, A. B.: Ezra E. **Eby,** the historian and his work. *In: The Pennsylvania-German. Vol. IX. Lititz, Pa. 1908. pp. 273—277.*
[b. near the Town of Berlin, Ontario, Aug. 9, 1850, grandson of Rev. Ben Eby, the first bishop of the Mennonite Church at that place.]   [6379

Ehle, Boyd: Dominie John Jacob Ehle and his descendants. *Published by Enterprize and News, St. Johnsville, N. Y. 1930. pp. 51, ill.*
(Johann Jakob Oehl, born at Hachenburg. Nassau, 1689; came to N. Y. 1722; labored among Palatines; d. 1780.)
          [6379a

Aby, Franklin Stanton: The Eber group of family names, European and American, ancient and modern. *A contribution to comparative philology. Chicago, Ill.: Privately printed 1926. pp. . . .*
= The Eby family bulletin, no. 7. [6380

Eberhart, Ulrich: History of the Eberharts in Germany and the United States from A. D. 1265 to A. D. 1890 — 625 years. *Chicago, Ill.: Donohue & Henneberry 1891. pp. IV, (2), 5—263.* [6381

Zimmerman, T. C.: In memoriam George Brown **Eckert.** *Historical sketch delivered before the Historical Society of Berks County, Pa., Oct. 10, 1899. In: Transactions of the Historical Society of Berks County. Vol. I. Reading, Pa. 1904. pp. (2), ill.*
[b. in Reading, Sept. 13, 1840.] [6382

Hassler, J. W.: Memorials of deceased ministers. III. Lewis G. **Eggers.** *In: The Lutheran Church Review. Vol. II. Philadelphia, Pa. 1883. pp. 340—344.*
[b. in Seesen, Hanover, Germany, 1805, came to America with his parents about 1820.] [6383

Egle, William Henry: Genealogical record of the families of Beatty, **Egle,** Müller, Murray, Orth and Thomas. *Harrisburg, Pa.: Lane & Hart 1886. pp. (1), 126.*
[Marcus Egle, the first of the name in Pa. was b. about the year 1690 in the Canton of Zürich, Switzerland, not far from the City of Berne, from whence he and his family emigrated to America, in 1743 (prior to 1740).] [6384

— The family of **Egle.** *In: Egle's „Pennsylvania genealogies". Harrisburg, Pa. 1896 [= no. 6045]. pp. 159—186.*
          [6385

Dr. William Henry **Egle.** *Death of the editor of „Notes and Queries". With sermon of the Rev. E. F. Smith. In: Notes and*

Queries. Edited by W. H. Egle. Annual vol. 1900. Harrisburg, Pa. 1901. pp. 227—237. [6386

Death of William Henry **Egle,** M. D., ex-state librarian. *In: The Pennsylvania Magazine of History and Biography. Vol. XXV. Philadelphia, Pa. 1901. pp. 133—134.* [6387

William Henry **Egle,** A. M., M. D. *In: The „Old Northwest" Genealogical Quarterly. Vol. IV. Columbus, O. 1901. pp. 77—79, ill. Reprint from the National Cyclopedia of American Biography. Vol. VIII. p. 198, with addition of a few later facts.* [6388

Eichelberger, A. W.: Historical sketch of Philip Frederick **Eichelberger,** who came from Ittlingen, Germany in 1728, and his descendants with a family register. *Hanover, Pa.: Hanover Herold Print 1901. pp. . . .* [6389

Hensel, W. U.: Jacob **Eichholtz,** painter. *Some „Loose Leaves" from the ledger of an early Lancaster artist. An address at the opening of an exposition of „The evolution of portraiture in Lancaster County, Pa." under the auspices of the Lancaster County Historical Society and the Iris Club. Woolworth Building, Lancaster, Pa., Nov. 22, 1912. In: The Penn Germania. Vol. II. = Old series, vol. XIV. Cleona, Pa. 1913. pp. 81—89; 161—173. Reprint from the catalogue.* [6390

The **Eisenberg-Jones** family record. Eisenberg branch. A record of Lawrence Eisenberg and his descendants. *By the Historical Committee. Philadelphia, Pa. 1923. pp. 120, ill.* [6391

Pell, George P.: Adolphus Hill **Eller** (Lawyer). *In: Biographical history of North Carolina. Edited by S. A. Ashe. Vol. VIII. Greensboro, N. C. 1917. pp. 154—161. ill.*
[of German, Scotch and English ancestry, b. at New Hope, Wilkes County, April 9, 1861; his paternal ancestor came over from Germany along with the Palatine emigration 1730—40 and settled in Pa. His sons, including George Eller, removed to N. C. 1753.] [6392

Ellis, Nathaniel Missimer: Nathaniel Missimer **Ellis.** A brief autobiography, dedicated to his friend J. O K. Robarts. *In: Historical Sketches. A Collection of Papers prepared for the Historical Society of Montgomery County, Pa. Vol. III. Norristown, Pa. 1905. pp. 392—395, ill.*

[„my father of English, my mother of German descent."] [6393
Hensel, W. U.: Notes on Amos and Elias Ellmaker. In: Papers and Addresses of the Lancaster County Historical Society. Vol. XII. Lancaster, Pa. 1908. pp. 175—183. [6394
Ellmaker, J. Watson: The Ellmaker family. In: The Pennsylvania-German. Vol. X. Lititz, Pa. 1909. pp. 341—347, ill.
[Descendants of John Leonard Ellmaker, b. Jan. 3, 1697 at Gaulhof, Nuremberg, Germany, son of Elias and Mary Magdalena (Bremer) Oelmacher; he landed at Philadelphia, Pa., Aug. 1, 1726.] [6395
Schnerer, Frank E.: The Elser homestead and family history. In: Papers and Addresses of the Lancaster County Historical Society. Vol. XVI. Lancaster, Pa. 1912. pp. 51—59.
[Peter Elser, the first ancestor, was the son of Hans Adam and Mary Margaretha Elser, daughter of Frederick and Mary Babara Hager, and a native of Russheim, Germany; he arrived at Philadelphia, Sept. 28, 1749.] [6396
— The Elser homestead and family history. In: The Penn Germania. Vol. I. = Old series, vol. XIII. Lititz, Pa. 1912. pp. 737—741. [6397
Frederick, Virginia Shannon: Emmert — Zug (Zuck) notes. In: The National Genealogical Society Quarterly. Vol. XII, no. 1. Washington, D. C. 1923. p. 11. [6398
The Enders family. In: Notes and Queries. Edited by W. H. Egle. Third series, vol. I. 1884—1887. Harrisburg, Pa. 1887. pp. 129—130. Reprint in: Third series, vol. I. Harrisburg, Pa. 1895. pp. 221—222. [6399
E., L. J.: Enders family. In: Notes and Queries. Edited by W. H. Egle. Third series, vol. I. 1884—1887. Harrisburg, Pa. 1887. p. 197. Reprint in: Third series, vol. I. Harrisburg, Pa. 1895. pp. 388—389. [6400
The Enders family. In: Notes and Queries. Edited by W. H. Egle. Third series, vol. I. 1884–1887. Harrisburg, Pa. 1887. pp. 449—451. Reprint in: Third series, vol. II. Harrisburg, Pa. 1896. pp. 195—198.
[Philip Christian Enders, b. July 22, 1740, in Braunsigweiler, District of Zugenheim, Nassau, Germany; d. Febr. 26, 1809, in Halifax Township, Dauphin County, Pa.] [6401

Barnes, Vivian Englar: Genealogy of the Englar family, the descendants of Philip Englar 1736—1817, traced down for five generations from 1736. Taneytown, Md.: The Carroll Record Print 1929. pp. 5—79.
[Descendants of Philip Englar, (b. Dec. 30, 1730, d. April 15, 1817) supposed to be b. in Appenzell, near Saint Gallen, Switzerland; landed in Philadelphia, Pa. 1748.] [6402
Engle, Morris M.: History of the Engle family in America 1754—1927. The Engle history and family records of Dauphin and Lancaster Counties. The numerous lineal descendants of Ulrich Engel. Short sketches of Engle families not related. A sketch of the arrival and record of the origin of the Brethren in Christ Church of which a large number of these descendants are members. Compiled, arranged, indexed and published. Mt. Joy, Pa.: The Bulletin Press 1927. pp. 161 ,ill.
[Ulrich Engel of the Canton of Basel, Switzerland, landed at Philadelphia, Pa. Oct. 1, 1754.] [6403
The Enterline family. In: Notes and Queries. Edited by W. H. Egle. Third series, vol. I. 1884—1887. Harrisburg, Pa. 1887. pp. 135—137. Reprint in: Third series, vol. I. Harrisburg, Pa. 1895. pp. 229—233.
[Rev. John Michael Enterline, the ancestor, was a native of Bavaria, Germany, b. 1726; emigrated to America in 1768.] [6404
Zimmerman, T. C.: In memoriam. Hon. Daniel Ermentrout. Historical sketch delivered before the Historical Society of Berks County, Pa., Nov. 14, 1899. In: Transactions of the Historical Society of Berks County. Vol. I. Reading, Pa. 1904. pp. (6), ill.
[b. in Reading, Jan. 24, 1837, great-great-grandson of John Ermentrout, of the emigrant from the Palatinate of 1739.] [6405
Memorial address on the life and character of Daniel Ermentrout (Late a representative from Pa.) Delivered of Representatives in the House of Representatives and Senate. 56th Congress, 1. Session. Washington, D. C.: Government Printing Office. 1900. pp. 67, ill. [6406
Wagner, Jacob Alvin: Genealogical annals of Gauger — Eschbach families. Com-

piled by . . . Des Moines, Ia. 1912. pp.
132, ill.
   [Eschbach: descendants of John Eschbach, b. in the Palatinate, Germany, Dec.,
1747, arrived at Philadelphia, Pa., Nov.,
1750.]   [6407
S.[ener], S. M.: Eshleman. In: Notes and
Queries. Edited by W. H. Egle. Annual
vol. 1900. Harrisburg, Pa. 1901. p. 218.
   [Descendants of Jacob Eshleman, who
came to America, landing at Philadel-
phia, Pa., Aug. 19, 1729 and settled on
the Conestoga, Lancaster Co., Pa.]
                                         [6408
Mast, C. Z.: The Eshleman family. In:
Christian Monitor. A monthly magazine
for the home. Vol. XVI, no. 2. Scottdale,
Pa. 1924. pp. 436—437.   [6409
Demuth, C. B.: Aaron Eshleman, artist. In:
Papers and Addresses of the Lancaster
County Historical Society. Vol. XVI.
Lancaster, Pa. 1912. pp. 247—250.
                                         [6410
Esler — Diefendorff records. In: The Penn-
sylvania Magazine of History and Bio-
graphy. Vol. XVII. Philadelphia, Pa.
1893. p. 375.
   [Henry Esler, b. in Zurich, Switzer-
land, emigrated to Pa. 1758; d. 1770.]
                                         [6411
The Esling genealogy. In: Records of the
American Catholic Historical Society of
Philadelphia. Vol. II. Philadelphia,
Pa. 1889. pp. 333—366.
   [Descendants of John George Esling,
a native of the Palatinate, b. c. 1692 and
arrived at Philadelphia, Nov. 25, 1740.]
                                         [6412
Everhart, O. T.: A history of the Everhart
and Shower families, from 1744—1883.
Embracing six generations. Also a sketch
of Manchester, Md. Hanover, York
County, Pa.: O. T. Everhart 1833. pp.
VI, 7—142.   [6413
Miller, Allie Everhart: Everhart — Miller
and allied families. Compiled by . . .,
West Point, Miss. 1923—1931. [s. l.]
1931. pp. 181, X, ill.
   [„Everharts in Germany from 1265."
pp. 11—16; „Everharts in America
1771—1930." pp. 17—35.]   [6414
Eyerman, John: Genealogical studies. The
ancestry of Marguerite and John Eyerman. Easton, Pa.: Published for the
author by the Eshenbach Printing Co.
1902. pp. . . .
   [of Prenschdorf, near Worth, Alsace.]
                                         [6415

F.

Memorial of Benjamin Franklin **Fackenthal.** Born, Nov. 28, 1825 — died, Jan.
14, 1892. [New York, N. Y.] University
Printing Office Columbia University.
1917. pp. 65, ill.   [6416
Mrs. B. F. **Fackenthal,** jr. née Sarah Jane
Riegel, daughter of John Leidy and
Elisabeth (Shimer) Riegel. Buried in
the Riegelsville Union Cemetery, May
19, 1925. pp. 25, ill.   [6417
Fahnestock, A. K. & W. F.: Family memo-
rial of the **Fahnestocks,** in the United
States. The following records have been
gathered by . . . Harrisburg, Pa.: S. W.
Fleming 1879. pp. (1), 5—69, ill.
   [Descendants of Diedrich Fahnestock
from Halten, Westphalia, Germany. Left
for America in 1726. b. Febr. 2, 1696, d.
Oct. 10, 1775; buried at Ephrata, Lancaster County, Pa.]   [6418
Sachse, Julius Friedrich: Justus Falckner.
Mystic and scholar. Devout pietist in
Germany, hermit on the Wissahicken,
missionary on the Hudson. A Bi-Cen-
tennial memorial of the first regular or-
dination of an Orthodox pastor in Ame-
rica, done November 24, 1703, at Gloria
Dei, the Swedish Lutheran Church at
Wicaco, Philadelphia. Compiled from
original documents, letters and records
at home and abroad. Philadelphia, Pa.
Printed for the author; Lancaster, Pa.:
The New Era Printing Co. 1903. pp.
141, ill.   [6419
Rev. Ferdinand **Farmer** S. J. A priest of
Pennsylvania 1752—1786. In: The
American Catholic Historical Researches.
Vol. VII. Philadelphia, Pa. 1890. pp.
120—128.   [6420
Quirk, John F.: Father Ferdinand **Farmer,**
S. J. An apostolic missionary in three
states. [s. l; s. d.] pp. 14.   [6421
The **Faust** family record. In: The Per-
kiomen Region, Past and Present. Vol. I.
Philadelphia, Pa. 1895. pp. 195—196.
   [Peter Faust, son of Henry Faust of
Brünbach, Germany and Eva Elizabeth
Kämerin of Maubächel, Germany, came
to Pa. about 1750 and settled in Frederick
Township, Montgomery Co., Pa.]   [6422
Faust, Harry E.: First Fausts in Pennsyl-
vania. Lewisburg, Pa.: Press of the
University Print Shop. 1930. pp. 4.
                                         [6423
Bausman, Lottie M.: The old **Feeman**
homestead in the Lebanon Valley. In:

*The Pennsylvania-German. Vol. XI.
Lititz, Pa. 1910. pp. 680—684, ill.*
[*Valentin Vehman (Vihman, Feeman) of Heidelberg Twp., Lancaster Co.,
Pa., the ancestor, who applied and got
warrant of 250 acres, Oct. 29, 1737.*]
[6424

Koetteritz, John B.: The **Feeter** family. *In:
Papers read before the Herkimer Historical Society during the years 1896,
1897 and 1898. Vol. I. Herkimer and
Ilion 1899. pp. 50—56.*
[*Descendants of Lucas Feeter (Vetter)
of Schoenaich, Germany, the emigrant
of 1754, who settled to the north of Stone
Arabia.*]
[6425

The **Felder** family of South Carolina.
[s. l.; s. d.] pp. 12.
[*The progenitor, Hans Heinrich Felder
is said to have come from Zurich, Switzerland; settled with his wife Ursula and son
John Henry in Orangeburgh Township
in 1735.*]
[6426

Fenstermacher. *In: The Pennsylvania Magazine of History and Biography. Vol.
XXXV. Philadelphia, Pa. 1911. p. 254.*
[*Christian Fenstermacher, b. April 14,
1697, in Meysenheim, Zweibrücken,
emigrated to Pa. in 1741.*]
[6427

Fertig family notes. *In: Genealogy. A journal of American ancestry. Vol. V. 1915.
New York, N. Y. 1915. pp. 84.*
[6428

E.[gle], William Henry: The **Fetterhoff**
family. *In: Notes and Queries. Edited
by W. H. Egle. Third series, vol. I.
1884—1887. Harrisburg, Pa. 1887. pp.
306—307. Reprint in: Third series, vol.
I. Harrisburg, Pa. 1895. pp. 548—549.*
[*Frederick Fetterhoff, b. Aug. 6, 1765
probably in the Palatinate, Germany,
settled first in now Lancaster Co., Pa.*]
[6429

[Fetterhoff, John]: The life of Rev. John
Fetterhoff, one of the early fathers of
the United Brethren in Christ. *Written
by himself. Containing a summarized
memorandum of his religious life and
labors, privations and providences from
his early youth up to superannuated aged-
ness. With an introduction by W. O.
Tobey. Chambersburg, Pa.: United
Brethren in Christ Print 1883. pp. 284,
ill.*
[6430

Dietrich, W. J.: The **Fetterolf** family. *Paper
read before the Lehigh County Historical
Society. In: The Penn Germania. Vol.
I. = Old series, vol. XIII. Lititz, Pa.
1912. pp. 204—207.*

[*Peter Fetterolf, a native of Wachbach,
Germany, emigrated to Pa. and arrived
at Philadelphia, Aug. 20, 1730; settled
in Hereford Twp., Berks Co., Pa.*]
[6431

Fretz, A. J.: Prof. Adam H. **Fetterolf**, Ph.
D., L. L. D., president of Girard College.
*In: The Pennsylvania-German. Vol.
VIII. Lebonon, Pa. 1907. pp. 177—178,
ill.*
[*b. at Perkiomen, Montgomery Co.,
Pa. Nov. 24, 1841; descendant of Peter
Fetterolf, the emigrant.*]
[6432

Nixon, A.: The **Finger** family of Lincoln
County, N. C. with brief sketch of Saint
Matthews Church. *Lincolntown, N. C.:
Press of the Lincoln Journal 1903, pp.
26.*
[*Descendants of Peter Finger, a Penn-
sylvania Dutchman, who settled on
Leeper' Creek, Ironton Twp. Lincoln
Co. about 1778.*]
[6433

Koetteritz, John B.: Andrew **Finck**, major
in the Revolutionary War. *In: Papers
read before the Herkimer County Historical Society, during the year 1897.
Vol. I. Herkimer and Ilion, N. Y. 1898.
pp. 59—72.*
[*b. Febr. 1, 1751, grandson of Andrew
Fink, Palatine emigrant, who settled in
Stone Arabia as early as 1722.*]
[6434

Obituary. Henry **Fink.** *In: Notes and Queries.
Edited by W. H. Egle. Annual vol. 1898.
Harrisburg, Pa. 1899. p. 15.*
[6435

Kemper, Willis Miller: Genealogy of the
Fishback family in America, the descendants of John Fishback, the emigrant, with an historical sketch of his
family and of the colony at Germanna
and Germantown, Virginia 1714—1915.
*New York, N. Y.: Thomas Madison
Taylor 1914. pp. V, 359, ill., map.* [6436

Fishback, Reuben Dewitt: Genealogy of the
Fishback family, the descendants of Harman Fishback, the emigrant [1713—
1714] with additional data. *New York,
N. Y.: Published by Thomas Madison
Taylor 1926. pp. XIV, 60.*
[*b. at Truppach, near Siegen in Westphalia, Germany, arrived in Va., April,
1714.*]
[6437

Crone, Frank L.: **Fishels** buried at the Roth
Church, near Spring Grove and La
Botte, York County, Pa. *In: The
Pennsylvania Magazine of History and
Biography. Vol. XLIV. Philadelphia,
Pa. 1920. pp. 287—288.*
[6438

Obituary. Emory A. **Fisher.** *In: Notes and
Queries. Edited by W. H. Egle. Annual*

*vol. 1900. Harrisburg, Pa. 1901. pp.
109—110.* [6439
Harbaugh, Henry: Youth in earnest; as
illustrated in the life of Theodore David
Fisher, A. M. *Philadelphia, Pa.: S. R.
Fisher & Co. 1867. pp. 238.* [6440
The founder of Middletown. *(Copy of the
will of George F i s h e r.) In: Notes and
Queries. Edited by W. H. Egle. Third
series, vol. I. 1884—1887. Harrisburg,
Pa. 1887. pp. 11—12. Reprint in: Third
series, vol. I. Harrisburg, Pa. 1895. pp.
18—19.* [6441
Honeyman, A. van Doren: Hendrick **Fisher**
— the real German-American. *In:
Somerset County Historical Quarterly.
Vol. VIII. Somerville N. J. 1919. pp.
1—17, ill.*
[*b. about 1697, in the Palatinate as is
believed; came with his father to New
Jersey, 1703.]* [6442
Hendrick **Fisher's** children. *In: Somerset
Historical Quarterly. Vol. VIII. Somerville, N. J. 1919. pp. 154—160.* [6443
Betz, I. H.: The career of Henry Lee **Fisher.**
*In: The Pennsylvania-German. Vol. XI.
Lititz, Pa. 1910. pp. 2—9, ill.*
[*b. near Quincy, Franklin Co., Pa. in
1822; a grandson of Frederick Fisher,
who was b. in Germany in 1746 and came
to Philadelphia in 1764.]* [6444
Dotterer, Henry S.: Herman **Fisher,** of
Upper Hanover. *In: The Perkiomen
Region, Past and Present. Vol. I. Philadelphia, Pa. 1895. pp. 22—26.*
[*son of Jacob and Sophia Elizabeth
Fisher, who came from Freinsheim, Palatinate. They emigrated about 1726.]*
[6445
— Jacob **Fisher,** of New Goshenhoppen.
*In: The Perkiomen Region, Past and
Present. Vol. I. Philadelphia, Pa. 1895.
pp. 6—7.*
[*came from Freinsheim, Palatinate.]*
[6446
Strassburger, Ralph Beaver: Jacob **Fisher,**
the immigrant, an early settler in the
Perkiomen Valley. *Edited by . . . Norristown Pa.: Norristown Press 1927. pp.
39, ill.* [6447
[Fisher, John S.]: Address by Governor
Fisher *at the Bicentennial exercises of
the New Goshenhoppen Reformed Church,
East Greenville, Pa. In: The Perkiomen
Region. Vol. VI, no. 2. Pennsburg, Pa.
1928. pp. 46—48.* [6448
Fisher, Clarence Woodward: Genealogy
of Joseph **Fisher** and his descendants,

and of the allied families of **Farley,
Farlee, Fetterman, Pitner, Reeder** and
Shipman. *Compiled by . . . Troy, N. Y.:
E. H. Lisk 1890. pp. 243.*
*[who, b. in April 1734, in Saxony,
emigrated to New Jersey about 1747, and
after the close of the Revolutionary War
removed to Northumberland Co., Pa.]* [6449
Larison, C. W.: A sketch of the **Fisher** fa-
mily of old Amwell Township in Hunter-
don County, New Jersey. *Ringos, N.
J.: Published by the Fonic Publishing
House 1890. pp. IV, 5—148, CIL—
CLIX.*
*[Descendants of Peter Fisher, the Ger-
man.]* [6450
Harbaugh, H.: The bright light in the clouds.
A sermon delivered in St. John's Church,
Lebanon, Pa., Oct. 11, 1863 in com-
memoration of Theodore **D. Fisher,**
A. B. *Lebanon, Pa.: Worth & Reinoehl
1863. pp. 26.* [6451
Owen, Thomas McAdory: The **Fisher** fa-
mily. *In: The Gulf States Historical
Magazine. Vol. I. Montgomery, Ale.
1902. pp. 134—138.*
*[concerning the Fisher family of Ger-
man origin, in Rowan Co., N. C.]* [6452
P.[arthemore], E. W. S.: The **Fisler** family.
*In: Notes and Queries. Edited by W. H.
Egle. Annual vol. 1896. Harrisburg,
Pa. 1897. p. 119.*
*[John Ulrich Fisler, b. in Schwatz,
Wurtemberg, Germany in 1757, came to
America when quite a youth.]* [6453
Fitler, William Wonderly: Genealogy of
the **Fitler** and allied families, being the
ancestry of Edwin Henry Fitler of
Philadelphia and his wife Josephine
R. Baker. *By their son. Philadelphia,
Pa.: Printed for private circulation 1922.
pp. (1), (1), (1), 9—172, ill.*
*[Johan Georg Fiedler came from Ger-
many and arrived at Philadelphia, Pa.
1750.]* [6454
Fleisher family. *In: Notes and Queries.
Edited by W. H. Egle. Annual vol. 1896.
Harrisburg, Pa. 1897. pp. 127—128.*
*[Jacob Fleisher came from Germany,
and landed in Philadelphia, Pa. 1732.]*
[6455
Flick, Alexander C.: Captain Gerlach Paul
Flick, Pennsylvania pioneer. *In: The
Pennsylvania Magazine of History and
Biography. Vol. LIII. Philadelphia,
Pa. 1929. pp. 230—268.*
*[b. at Emmerichenhain, near Wies-
baden, Germany (?), on March 7, 1728;*

came to Pa., landing at Philadelphia, Pa., Sept. 23, 1751.] [6456
Flickinger, Robert Elliott: The Flickinger families in the United States. Records and tributes from materials gathered by . . . Des Moines, Ia.: Success Composition and Printing Co. 1926. pp. (2), 132, ill. [6457
— The Flickinger family history, including the Flickinger families in the United States of America. Andreas, Joseph, Johannes, Peter, Ulrick Flickinger, colonists; and a dozen later arrivals. Records and tributes from materials gathered . . . Des Moines, Ia.: Success Composition and Printing Co. 1927. pp. XII, 808, ill. [6458
F.[lickinger], S.H.: Pennsylvania Flickingers. In: Genealogy. Journal of American ancestry. Vol. II. New York, N. Y. 1912. p. 236. [6459
— Illinois Flickinger. In: Genealogy. Journal of American ancestry. Vol. I. ·New York, N. Y. 1912. p. 188. [6460
F.[lickinger], J. H.: New York Flickingers. In: Genealogy. Journal of American ancestry. Vol. I. New York, N. Y. 1912. p. 119. [6461
F., A. S.: An Arnold-Flickinger branch. In: Genealogy. Journal of American ancestry. New York, N. Y. 1912. p. 132. [6462
F., I. N.: The Eli Flickinger family. In: Genealogy. Journal of American ancestry. Vol. I. New York, N. Y. 1912. p. 109. [6463
C., W. M.: Flickinger family notes. In: Genealogy. Journal of American ancestry. Vol. III. New York, N. Y. 1913. p. 114. [6464
Flickinger deaths, in Northampton County, Pa., now Lehigh County, Pa. In: Genealogy. Journal of American ancestry. Vol. IV. New York, N. Y. 1914. p. 27. [6465
[Flickinger, D. K.]: Fifty-five years of active ministerial life by Bishop D. K. Flickinger D. D. for forty years a laborer in the mission work of West Africa, as missionary, missionary secretary, and later missionary bishop. With a preface by G. M. Mathes. Dayton, O.: United Brethren Publication House 1907. pp. 261, ill. [6466
[Focht, Benjamin K.]: In memorian: Dr. Martin Luther Focht. Lewisburg, Pa.: Saturday News Publishing Co. 1928. pp. (10), ill. [6467

The Follmer family. In: The Historical Journal. Vol. II. Williamsport, Pa. 1894. pp. 383—384.
[One of the largest in West Branch Valley, descendants of Jacob Follmer (Vollmer), who emigrated from Germany and settled near Reading, Pa., in 1737.] [6468
Follmer, Charles Carroll: History of the Follmer family. Compiled and edited by . . . Grand Rapids, Mich. 1899. pp. 104.
[Descendants of Jacob Follmer of Rosswog Voigeramt, Wurtemberg, Germany, who came to America in 1738.] [6469
Obituary. Andrew Foltz. In: Notes and Queries. Edited by W. H. Egle. Annual vol. 1898. Harrisburg, Pa. 1899. p. 15. [6470
Bittinger, Lucie Forney: The Forney family of Hanover, Pa. 1690—1893. Published for members of the families. Pittsburgh, Pa.: Press of Shaw Brothers 1893. pp. (1), (1), 59.
[Descendants of Johann Adam Forney of Wachenheim in the Haardt in the Palatinate.] [6471
F.[olker], H. O.: Sketches of the Forney family. Philadelphia, Pa.: Harper & Brothers 1911. pp. (4), 129. [6472
Forney, Charles William: Forney's five family records of genealogy of Benners, Clappers, Ettlemans, Forneys and Studys, with historical sketches. (For private circulation.) Boone, Ia.: Printed for the author by the Standard Printing Co. 1931. pp. V—XVII, 367, ill. [6473
Forney, John K.: Sketches and genealogy of the Forney family from Lancaster County, Pa. (In Part.) Abiline, Kan.: Printed for the author by the Reflector Printing Co. 1926. pp. 115, ill.
[Descendants of Peter Forney and his wife Anne, daughter of John Smith.] [6474
Obituary. John C. Forney. In: Notes and Queries. Edited by W. H. Egle. Fourth series, vol. II. Harrisburg, Pa. 1896. pp. 135—137. [6475
Haywood, Marshall De Lancey: Peter Forney. (Revolutionary patriot.) In: Biographical history of North Carolina. Edited by S. A. Ashe. Vol. V. Greensboro, N. C. 1906. pp. 98—106.
[b. in Lincoln Co. in April, 1756, son of General Jacob Forney, emigrant from Alsace, and Maria (Bergner) Forney, native of Berne, Switzerland.] [6476

32*

Obituary: Wien **Forney**. *In: Notes and Queries. Edited by W. H. Egle. Annual vol. 1898. Harrisburg, Pa. 1899. pp. 15—17.*   [6477

Buck, William J.: An early teacher of languages and music in Norristown. *[Charles* **Fortman**]. *In: Historical Sketches. A Collection of Papers prepared for the Historical Society of Montgomery County, Pa. Vol. I. Norristown, Pa. 1895. pp. 309—312, ill. [German by birth.]*   [6478

Brumbaugh, Gajus Marcus and **Fouse, John Garner**: Genealogy of the descendants of Theobald **Fouse** (Fauss), *including many other connected families. Baltimore, Md.: Waverly Press Williams & Wilkins Co. 1914. pp. XIII, 289, ill. [who was b. in ,,1725" (?), and lived in Rheinville, Rheinfelz, Bavaria, later moved to Zweibrücken, where he died 1765 and whose son Nicholas Fouse, b. 1748 at Zweibrücken landed in Baltimore, Md. 1784.]*   [6479

Heverly, C. F.: The **Fox** family. *Published by the Bradford County Historical Society, 1908. In: The Pennsylvania-German. Vol. XI. Lititz, Pa. 1910. pp. 212—215.*   [6480

Fox, Julius B.: Biography of Rev. Alfred J. **Fox**, M. D., Evangelical Lutheran minister of the Tennessee Synod, and physician. *By his son. With an introduction by his son A. Fox. Published for the author. Philadelphia, Pa.: Lutheran Publication Society. 1885. pp. XIII. 15—150, ill.*   [6481

[Frelinghuysen, T. J.]: Sermons. *Translated from the Dutch and prefaced by the author's life by* **Wm. Demarest** . . . *1856. pp. . . .*   [6481a

Hageman, F. J.: The life, character and services of Frederick T. Frelinghuysen, LL. D. *In: Proceedings of the New Jersey Historical Society. Second series, Vol. IX. Newark, N. J. 1887. pp. . . .*   [6481b

Parker, Cortlandt: A sketch of the life and public services of Theodore Frelinghuysen *1844. pp. . . .*   [6481c

Chambers, Talbot W.: Memoir of the life and character of the late Hon. Theodore Frelinghuysen. . . . *1863. pp. 22—27.*   [6481d

Hart, Charles Henry: The **Franks** family. *In: The Pennsylvania Magazine of History and Biography. Vol. XXXIV. Philadelphia, Pa. 1910. pp. 253—255.*

[Jacob Franks, the American emigrant of the family came to this country 1705 or 1711; his father was Aaron Franks or Naphtali Franks, of Germany.]   [6482

Freed, Jacob A.: Partial history of the **Freed** family and conecting families. *Souderton, Pa.: W. F. Goettler & Son 1923. pp. 113. [Descendants of Johannes Fried, who settled in what is now Skippack Twp., Montgomery Co., Pa. as early as 1724.]*   [6483

An unique will. *[Will of John* **Freed** *(Johannes Friet) living in the Township Scippack, Montgomery County, Pa., written by Christopher Dock in 1744.] In: The Perkiomen Region. Vol. IX, no. 2. Pennsburg, Pa. 1931. pp. 54—55.*   [6484

Fretz, A. J.: A brief history of John and Christian **Fretz**, and a complete genealogical family register with biographies of their descendants from the earliest available records to the present time. *With an introduction by J. Freeman Hendricks. Elkhart, Ind.: Mennonite Publishing Co. 1890. pp. 607, ill.*   [6485

— A brief history of John and Christian **Fretz**, and a complete genealogical family register to the fourth generation with accounts and addresses delivered ad the Fretz family reunions held at Bedminster, Pa. 1888, 1893, 1898 and 1903. *With an introduction by J. F. Hendricks. Milton, N. J.: Press of the Evergreen News 1904. pp. 125, ill.*   [6486

— The **Fretz** family. *In: The Pennsylvania-German. Vol. IX. Cleona, Pa. 1908. pp. 68—71, ill. [The earliest pioneers of that name are believed to have been John and Christian Fretz, who in company with a third brother Mark who died during the voyage, left their homes near the City of Manheim, in the Grandduchy of Baden, Germany, and arrived at Philadelphia, Pa. prior to 1727.]*   [6487

Fretz, John Stover (Mrs.): The ancestry of John Stover **Fretz**. *Paper read at Doylestown meeting, May, 2, 1931. In: A Collection of Papers read before the Bucks County Historical Society. Vol. VI. Allentown, Pa. 1932. pp. 379—385, ill. [Descendant of John Fretz [Fritsch], a German, who landed with 2 brothers in Philadelphia in 1725.]*   [6488

Reminiscences from early Mennonite families as recorded in **Fretz** family history. *In: The Mennonite Year Book and Almanac for 1914. Quakertown, Pa. 1914. pp. 33—34.* [6489

Frey, Samuel Clarence: Ancestry and postery (in part) of Gottfried **Frey.** 1605—1913. *York, Pa.: Dispatch-Daily Print 1914. pp. 388, ill., 2 maps.*
[b. in Weiler, what is Baden to-day, Aug. 4, 1721.] [6490

Henry Clay **Frick.** *In: The Western Pennsylvania Historical Magazine. Vol. III. Pittsburgh, Pa. 1920. pp. 1—2, ill.* [6491

Harvey, George: Henry Clay Frick, the man. *New York, N. Y. Charles Scribers & Sons 1928. pp. 382, ill.* [6491 a

Blair, W. A.: Francis **Fries.** *(Pioneer manufacturer of N. C.) In: Biographical history of North Carolina. Edited by A. S. Ashe. Vol. III. Greensboro, N. C. 1905. pp. 129—134, ill.*
[Descendant of Sigismund Eberhard von Fries, colonel in the emperor's army and commandant of the City Hoechst-am-Main, Germany; grandson of Peter Konrad Fries, son of John Christian William, the emigrant, and Elizabeth Nissen; b. in Salem, N. C. Oct. 17, 1812.] [6492

Manly, Clement: Francis Henry **Fries.** *(Manufacturer). In: Biographical history of North Carolina. Edited by S. A. Ashe. Vol. III. Greensboro, N. C. 1905. pp. 141—151, ill.*
[son of Francis Fries and Lizetta Vogler; b. in Salem, N. C., Febr. 1, 1855.] [6493

Stephenson, Gilbert Thomas: The life story of a trust man being that of Francis Henry **Fries,** president of The Wachovia Bank and Trust Company, Winston-Salem, N. C., since February 16, 1893. *New York, N. Y.: F. S. Crofts & Co. 1930. pp. 7—11, (1), (1), 17—267, ill.* [6494

Blair, W. A.: Henry Elias **Fries** *(Manufacturer). In: Biographical history of North Carolina. Edited by S. A. Ashe. Vol. III. Greensboro, N. C. 1905. pp. 152—156, ill.*
[son of Francis Fries and Lizetta Vogler; b. in Salem, N. C., Sept. 22, 1857.] [6495

Rondthaler, Edward: Henry William **Fries** *(Manufacturer). In: Biographical history of North Carolina. Edited by S. A. Ashe. Vol. III. Greensboro, N. C. 1905. pp. 135—137, ill.*

[son of John Christian William Fries and Elizabeth Nissen; b. in Salem, March 5, 1825.] [6496

Blair, W. A.: John William **Fries** *(Manufacturer). In: Biographical history of North Carolina. Edited by S. A. Ashe. Vol. III. Greensboro, N. C. 1905. pp. 138—140, ill.*
[son of Francis Fries and Lizetta Vogler, b. in Salem, N. C. Nov. 7, 1846.] [6497

The family **Fritchey.** *In: Notes and Queries. Edited by W. H. Egle. Third series, vol. I. 1884—1887. Harrisburg, Pa. 1887. pp. 301—302. Reprint in: Third series, vol. I. Harrisburg, Pa. 1895. pp. 540—542.*
[Descendants of Joseph Fritchey, native of Huffingen, Grand Dukedom of Baden, Germany, whose son, John Baptist Fritchey emigrated to America in 1823 and located at Harrisburg, Pa.] [6498

[Fritchey, John Godfrey]: A family record. *(Translation of original family record of John Godfrey Fritchey, contributed by John Q. A. Fritschey.) In: Notes and Queries. Edited by W. H. Egle. Fourth series, vol. I. 1891—1893. Harrisburg, Pa. 1893. p. 334.*
[John Godfrey Fritchey, b. in the Town of Schoenlinder, Leitmeritsche Creyse, 6 mi. from Dresden, Sept. 20, 1755 and came to America 1784.] [6499

Croll, P. C.: Famous Pennsylvania Germans. Barbara **Fritchie.** *In: The Pennsylvania-German. Vol. IV. Lebanon, Pa. 1903. pp. 339—347, ill.* [6500

Apple, J. H.: Barbara **Frietchie** at home. *In: The Pennsylvania-German. Vol. VII. Lebanon, Pa. 1906. pp. 366—370, ill.* [6501

Boston, Transcripts: Whittier's belief in Barbara **Frietchie.** *In: The Magazine of History, with notes and queries. Vol. XVI. Jan.-June, 1913. New York City, N. Y. 1913. pp. 120—121.* [6502

Landis, John H.: A Lancaster girl in history (Barbara **Frietchie**). *In: Papers and Addresses of the Lancaster County Historical Society. Vol. XXIII. Lancaster, Pa. 1919. pp. 85—93, ill.* [6503

The autobiography of John **Fritz.** *New York, N. Y.: John Wiley & Sons; London: Chapman & Hall 1912. pp. XV, 325, ill.*
[b. in Chester Co., Pa. 1822.] [6504

Martin, Thomas Commerford: John **Fritz,** iron master. *Reprint from „Century*

*Magazine." In: The Penn Germania.
Vol. II. = Old series, vol. XIV. Lititz,
Pa. 1913. pp. 202—208.*   [6505
Swank, James M.: John Fritz, the farmer's
boy. *In: The Penn Germania. Vol. II.
= Old series, vol. XIV. Lititz, Pa. 1913.
pp. 208—210.*   [6506
John Fritz. His support of higher education.
An appreciation. *In: The Penn Ger-
mania. Vol. II = Old series, vol. XIV.
Lititz, Pa. 1913. pp. 210—212.*   [6507
Fackenthal, B. F.: John Fritz, the iron
master. *Read before the Pennsylvania-
German Society at Bethlehem, Oct. 5,
1923. In: The Pennsylvania German
Society. Proceedings and Addresses.
Vol. XXXIV. . . . 1929. pp. 97—112,
ill.*   [6508
George Nelson **Fry**, president of the Board
of Control passes away. *In: Notes and
Queries. Edited by W. H. Egle. Fourth
series, vol. I. 1891—1893. Harrisburg,
Pa. 1893. pp. 45—46.*
[b. in Berks Co., Pa. June 9, 1829.]
                                   [6509
Fretz, A. J.: A brief history of Bishop
Henry **Funck** and other **Funk** pioneers
and a complete genealogical family
register, with biographies of their descendants from the earliest available
records to the present time. *Elkhart,
Ind.: Mennonite Publishing Co. 1899.
874, ill.*   [6510
Washburn, Mabel Thacher Rosemary: The
Funk family, one of the pioneer Mennonite families from Switzerland which
settled on large tracts of land in Lan-
caster County, Pa., in 1710. *In: The
Journal of American Genealogy. Vol.
I. Greenfield, Ind. 1921. pp. 213—228;
333—342; Vol. II. 1922. pp. 45—60;
169—184.*   [6511
Rev. Isaac K. **Funk**, D. D. LL. D. *In:
The Pennsylvania-German. Vol. VIII.
Lebanon, Pa. 1907. pp. 28—29, ill.
[b. at Clifton, O., Sept. 10, 1839, son
of John Funk and Martha Kauffman.]*
                                   [6512
Isaac Kaufmann **Funk**. *In: The Literary
Digest. Vol. XLIV, no. 15. New York,
N. Y., April 13, 1912. p. 735, ill.*
                                   [6513
A brief historical sketch of the life of John
F. **Funk** and his brother Abraham K.
Funk while engaged in the publishing
business as the Mennonite Publishing
Company, from 1864 to 1925. *Elkhart,
Ind.: James A. Bell Co. pp. 15.*   [6514

Loucks, Aaron: John F. **Funk**, pioneer publisher of Mennonite literature. *In:
Christian Monitor. A monthly magazine
for the home. Vol. XXII, no. 3. Scottdale, Pa. 1930. pp. 82—83, ill.
Reprint in: The Perkiomen Region. Vol.
IX, no. 2. Pennsburg, Pa. 1931. pp.
37—39.
[b. in Bucks Co., Pa., April 6, 1835.]*
                                   [6515
Kolb, Aaron C.: John Fretz **Funk**, 1835
—1930: an appreciation. *A conden-
sation of a biographical address delivered
at the Memorial Service for John Fretz
Funk, 1835—1930, held in Assem bly
Hall at Goshen College, Goshen, Indiana,
April 10th, 1932. In: The Mennonite
Quarterly Review. July, 1932. Vol. VI.
Goshen, Ind. — Scottdale, Pa. 1932. pp.
144—155; 250—263.*   [6516
Wayland, John W.: Joseph **Funk**. Father
of song in northern Virginia. *In: The
Pennsylvania-German. Vol. XII. Lititz,
Pa. 1911. pp. 580—594, ill.
Reprint: Dayton, Va.: The Ruebush-
Kieffer Co. pp. (12), ill.
[b. March 9, 1777, in Berks Co., Pa.,
son of Henry Funk and Barbara Sho-
walter.]*   [6517
Alderfer, David: Life and works of Joseph
Funk and his descendants. *In: Christian
Monitor. A monthly magazine for the
home. Vol. XXII. Scottdale, Pa. 1930.
No. 5. pp. 149—150; p. 159; No. 6. p.
181; p. 187, ill.*   [6518

G.

Allaben, Frank: History of the **Gable** family. *Compiled by . . . for Percival K.
Gable. Norristown, Pa. 1903. pp. (5), (2)
chart.
[Descendants of Johan Philip Gabel,
a son of Johan Jacob and Maria Margaret Gabel, who were residents of Ra-
bach, in Zweibruecken, the Pfalz, Germany. b. in 1698, m. in 1735 and came
to America 1739.]*   [6519
The **Garber** family. *In: Notes and Queries.
Edited by W. H. Egle. Annual vol. 1899.
Harrisburg, Pa. 1900. pp. 44—45.
[Descendants of Benedict Garber, b.
Oct. 18, 1732; d. June 12, 1817. He came
to America from Alsace, Germany, in
1741, when a lad, with his parents, and
died on shipboard.]*   [6520
Keidel, George C.: Dr. Abram P. **Garber:**
A biographical sketch. *In: Papers and*

Addresses of the Lancaster County Historical Society. Vol. XVIII. Lancaster, Pa. 1914. pp. 199—219.
[Bibliography pp. 214—219.] [6521
Garr, John Wesley and **Garr, John Calhoun:** Genealogy of the descendants of John **Gar**, or more particulary of his son, Andreas Gaar, who emigrated from Bavaria to America in 1732. *With portraits, coat-of-arms, biographies, wills, history, etc. Commenced in 1844 by John Wesley Garr and completed in 1894 by his son, John Calhoun Garr. Cincinnati, O.: Published by the author. Press of Raisbeck & Co. 1894. pp. XIII, (3), 608. ill.*
[In order to escape persecution . . . Andreas Gaar, at the head of 300 Palatines, left Illenschwang in 1732 for America, and settled in what is now Madison County, Va., where they were members of the first German Lutheran Church in-America.] [6522
De Long, Irwin H.: In memoriam. Rev. Frederick Augustus **Gast**, A. B. A. M. D. D. LL. D. *In: The Reformed Church Review. Fourth series, vol. XXI. Philadelphia, Pa. 1917. pp. 269—275.* [6523
Wagner, Jacob Alvin: Genealogical annals of **Gauger-Eschbach** families. *Compiled by . . . Des Moines, Ia. 1912. pp. 132, ill.*
[Gauger: descendants of Johann Conrad Gauger, who arrived at Philadelphia, Pa., Sept., 1736.] [6524
Stroh, Jacob: Frederick **Gaukel.** *In: Sixteenth Annual Report of the Waterloo Historical Society. Waterloo, Ont. 1928. pp. 86—87.*
[b. in Wurtemberg, Germany, in 1785.] [6525
In memoriam. Frederick **Gebhart.** Born May 7, 1798 — Died, Oct. 3, 1878. *Dayton, O.: United Brethren Publishing House 1879. pp. 46.*
[b. at Somerset, Pa.] [6526
Memorial of Mrs. Catherine W. **Gebhart.** *(Wife of Frederick Gebhart) who died February 28, 1877. Dayton, O.: United Brethren Publishing Hause 1877.*
[b. in Somerset Co., Pa., Oct. 12, 1801.] [6527
Gayman, A. James: The **Gehman** family. *In: The Pennsylvania-German. Vol. VII. Lebanon, Pa. 1906. pp. 301—302.* [6528
Mast, C. Z.: The **Gehman** family. *In: Christian Monitor. A monthly magazine for the home. Vol. XIX. Scottdale, Pa.*

1927. No. 10. p. 308; No. 11. pp. 341—342; No. 12. p. 374.
[whose ancestors were natives of Switzerland and arrived at Philadelphia 1732.] [6529
Valentine **Geiger,** New Hanover Township's first settler. *In: The Perkiomen Region, Past and Present. Vol. I. Philadelphia, Pa. 1895. pp. 66—68.*
[b. in Germany in 1685, accompanied his father-in-law to Pa. in 1717.] [6530
Bair, Samuel F.: Sketch of children of Valentin **Geiger.** Pioneer of the Geiger family in America. *By grandson of Sarah Geiger, a great-greatgrand-daughter of the pioneer. Pottstown, Pa. 1922. pp. (14).* [6531
Funk, John F.: Biographical sketch of Pre. John **Geil**, pastor of the Mennonite Church at Line Lexington, Bucks Co., Pa. *Elkhart, Ind.: Mennonite Publishing Co. 1897. pp. 45.* [6532
Wenger, Joseph H.: History of the descendants of J. Conrad **Geil** and his son Jacob Geil, emigrated from Württemberg, Germany, to America in 1754 and a complete genealogical family register and biographies of many of their descendants from the earliest available records to the present time. *Dates in three centuries. Elgin, Ill. 1914. pp. (1), (2), 7—275.* [6533
[Waage, O. F.]: Frederick William **Geissenhainer,** D. D. *In: The Perkiomen Region. Vol. V, no. 2. Pennsburg, Pa. 1927. pp 22—28.*
[son of Henry Athanasius and Sophia Henrietta Geissenhainer and b. at Muehlheim on the Ruhr, Dukedom of Bergen, now Prussia, June 26, 1771; arrived in Philadelphia, Pa. in 1793.] [6534
Schmucker, Beale M.: Memorials of deceased ministers, II. Augustus Theodorius **Geissenhainer.** *In: The Lutheran Church Review. Vol. II. Philadelphia, Pa. 1883. pp. 332—339.*
[son of Rev. Henry Anastasius Geissenhainer and Anna Maria Schaerer, of Whitpain Twp., Montgomery Co., Pa.] [6535
Gerberich, A. H. and **Gerberich, Albert H.:** History of the **Gerberich** family in America (1613—1925). *[s. l.] 1925. pp. 288. ill.* [6536
Gerhard genealogical notes. *In: The Pennsylvania Magazine of History and Biography. Vol. XXIV. Philadelphia, Pa. 1900. pp. 117—118.*

[Frederick Gerhard, b. March 26, 1714 at Langenselbold, Hesse Darmstadt, m. Jan. 23, 1737 to Elizabeth Fisher, sailed for Philadelphia, Pa. 1739.] [6537

Dickert, Thomas W.: Life of the Rev. Calvin S. **Gerhard,** D. D. *Edited by . . . Philadelphia, Pa.: Sunday School Board of the Reformed Church in the United States 1904. pp. VII, 11—256.* [6538

Kremer, Ellis N.: Rev. Emanuel Vogel **Gerhart,** D. D. LL. D. *In: The Reformed Church Review. Fourth series, vol. VIII. Philadelphia, Pa. 1904. pp. 565—575.* [6539

Herman, Theodore F.: The theology of the Rev. Prof. Emanuel Vogel **Gerhart.** *In: Addresses of the life and the theology of the Rev. H. Harbaugh and the Rev. E. VogelGerhart (1917). pp. 9—45.* [6540

— The theology of Prof. Emanuel V. **Gerhart.** *In: The Reformed Church Review. Fourth series, vol. XXII. 1918. pp. 211—238.* [6541

Good, James I.: Rev. E. V. **Gerhart,** D. D. as professor of theology at Tiffin, O. *Address delivered at Central Theological Seminary of the Reformed Church, May 6, 1920. . . . pp. 20.* [6542

Gernerd, Jeremiah M. M.: Heinrich **Gernhardt** and his descendants. *Historical facts and musings. — Cogitations on interesting genealogical problems — Records of the births, marriages and deaths of all branches of the family — Brief sketches of many of the members — And some interesting reminiscences of the Great Civil War. Williamsport, Pa.: Press of the Gazette and Bulletin 1904. pp. 315, ill.* [6543

Gesner, Anthon Temple: The **Gesner** family of New York and Nova Scotia. *Together with some notes concerning the families of* Bogardus, Brower, Ferdon and Pineo. *In commemnoration of the 202nd anniversary of the settlement of John Henry Gesner in America. 1710 1912. Middletown, Conn.: Pelton & King 1912. pp. (3), 7—30, ill.*

[Johann Hendrick Gesner, 1681—1745, ancestor of the Hudson River and Nova Scotia Gesners, left the Palatinate of the Rhine, and arrived in New York, June, 1710.] [6544

Gift, Aaron Kern: History of the **Gift,** Kern and Royer families. *Compiled by . . . Beaver Springs, Pa.: Herold Printing and Publishing Co. 1908. pp. VI, 7— 177, ill.* [6545

Glatfelter, Noah Miller: Record of Caspar **Glattfelder** of Glattfelden, Canton Zurich, Switzerland, immigrant, 1743, and his descendants, in part, comprising 861 families. *St. Louis, Mo.: Nixon-Jones Printing Co. 1901. pp. (2), 124, ill.* [6546

— Supplement to the Caspar **Glattfelder** Record embracing the addition of 545 families. *St. Louis, Mo.: Nixon-Jones Printing Co. 1910. pp. 36.* [6547

Glatfelter, S. F.: The **Glattfelder** family. *In: The Pennsylvania-German. Vol. IX. Cleona, Pa. 1908. pp. 396—398, ill.* [6548

[**Glattfelder, Casper**]: Will and inventory of Casper **Glattfelder.** *[1775.] In: The Pennsylvania-German. Vol. IX. Cleona, Pa. 1908. pp. 493—495.* [6549

[Glatfelter, Granville and Glatfelter, Noah]: **Glatfelters** in the war. *In: The Pennsylvania-German. Vol. IX. Cleona, Pa. 1908. p. 525.* [6550

Parr, Amos A.: Philip H. **Glatfelter.** *July 1890, to July 1905. In: The Pennsylvania-German. Vol. IX. Cleona, Pa. 1908. pp. 399—402.* [6551

[**Gleim, Harrison**]: German family of **Gleim.** *In: Notes and Queries. Edited by W. H. Egle. Annual vol. 1900. Harrisburg, Pa. 1901. pp. 156—158.* [6552

H., S. P.: In memoriam: Andrew B. **Gloninger,** M. D. *In: Papers read before the Lebanon County Historical Society. Vol. VII. Lebanon, Pa. 1916—1919. pp. 345—348, ill.*

[son of Dr. Cyrus D. and Julia A. (Beaumint) Gloninger and descendant of Philip Gloninger, the immigrant ancestor from Germany of the Gloninger family in Pa.] [6553

[**Drury, A. W.**]: Family of **Glossbrenner.** *In: Notes and Queries. Edited by W. H. Egle. Third series, vol. II. 1887—1890. Harrisburg, Pa. 1891. p. 209. Reprint in: Third series, vol. III. Harrisburg, Pa. 1896. pp. 192—193.* [6554

— The life of Bishop J. J. **Glossbrenner,** D. D. of the United Brethren in Christ. *With an appendix containing a number of his sermons and sketches. With an introduction by* James W. Hott. *Dayton, O.: Published for John Dodds by United Brethren Publishing House. 1889. pp. XV, 17—391, ill.* [6555

Gnagey, Elias: A complete history of Christian **Gnaegi** and a complete family register of his lineal descendants, and those related to him by intermarriage,

from the year 1774 to 1897, *containing some records of families not received in time to have them chronologically arranged in their proper places. Elkhart, Ind.: Mennonite Publishing Co. 1897. pp. 198.*
[who came from Switzerland to America between 1750 and 1760.] [6556

Darrach, Charles Gobrecht: Christian Gobrecht, artist and inventor. *In: The Pennsylvania Magazine of History and Biography. Vol. XXX. Philadelphia, Pa. 1906. pp. 355—358.*
[son of John Christopher Gobrecht, b. in Angerstein, Germany. Oct. 11, 1733, emigrated to Philadelphia, Pa. in 1755.]
[6557

Godshalk, Abraham: A family record and other matters which, it is hoped, will be good for the souls of men and women. *The family record back to the first emigrant who came to this country and settled at Germantown, then Philadelphia County, Pa. From the many of the descendants emigrated to Bucks County, of whome the author is a descendant. Harrisbourg, Pa.: The United Evangelical Press 1912. pp. (1), 7—304, ill.*
[Rev. Jacob Godshalk was b. in the Village of Goch, District of Cleves, Germany, about the year 1670 he came to Pa. and located in Germantown about 1699. He became a minister of the Mennonite Church there in 1708.] [6558

Hay, Charles A.: Memoirs of Rev. Jacob Goering, Rev. George **Lochman,** D. D., and Rev. Benjamin **Kurtz,** D. D., LL. D. *Philadelphia, Pa.: Lutheran Publication Society 1887. pp. 211, ill.*
[6559

Sherk, A. B.: Some incidents in the history of the **Gonder** family. *In: The Pennsylvania-German. Vol. XII. Lititz, Pa. 1911. pp. 302—304.*
[Michael Gonder (German: Gander), a Lancaster County man, was one of the Loyalists who went to Canada in the year 1789.] [6560

Good, James I.: The „**Good**" family. *In: The PennGermania. Vol. I. = Old series, vol. XIII. Lititz, Pa. 1912. pp. 457—459.*
[tracing back their ancestry to the region of Zweibrücken, Palatinate, Germany.] [6561

Latsha, Christiana Boyer: The Adam **Good** family history. *Lyndhurst, B. J.: Sentinel Print 1914. pp. (1), (1), (1), 9—150, ill.*

[A Good, (Guth) who was of German descent and settled in Penn Twp., Union Co., Pa., as early as 1813.] [6562

Richards, George Warren: In memoriam. James I. **Good,** D. D. LL. D. 1850—1924. *In: The Reformed Church Review. Fifth series, vol. III. Lancaster, Pa. 1924. pp. 113—118.* [6564

Omwake, George L.: James I. **Good.** *In: The Reformed Church Review. Fifth series, vol. III. Lancaster, Pa. 1924. pp. 118—121.* [6565

Hinke, William John: Rev. Prof. James I. **Good,** D. D. LL. D. *In: Journal of the Presbyterian Historical Society. Vol. XII. Philadelphia, Pa. (1924). pp. 65—81, ill.* [6566

— The contribution of Dr. James I. **Good** to Reformed Church history. *In: The Reformed Church Review. Fifth series, vol. III. Philadelphia, Pa. 1924. pp. 152—167.* [6567

Richards, George Warren: The Reverend James I. **Good,** D. D. LL. D., as a church historian. *In: Papers of the American Society of Church History. Second series. vol. VIII. New York, N. Y. and London: G. P. Putnam's Sons. The Knickerbocker Press 1928. pp. 199—209.*
[Descendant of Jacob Guth, who came from Zweibrücken and landed in Philadelphia, Pa., Sept. 9, 1765.] [6568

Zerbe, Alvin Sylvester: The life and labors of the Rev. Jeremiah Haak **Good.** D. D. Professor of dogmatic and practical theology in the Heidelberg Theological Seminary. (1868—1888). *Tiffin, O.: Commercial Printing Co. 1925. pp. 72.*
[b. in the Town of Rehrersburg, Berks Co., Pa., Nov. 22, 1822; son of Philip Augustus and Elizabeth (Haak) Good; descendant of Jacob Guth of Zweibrücken.] [6569

Grubb, N. B.: A genealogical history of the **Gottshall** family. Descendants of Rev. Jacob Gottshall with the complete record of the descendants of William Ziegler Gottshall. *Compiled by . . . Published by the Gottshall Family Association. [s. l.] 1924. pp. (1), 5—112, ill.*
[J. Gottshall, b. about 1670 came from Goch, District of Cleves, Germany to America, and settled in Germantown, in 1702.]
[6570

Allebach, H. G.: The **Gottschall** family. *In: The Pennsylvania-German. Vol. VII. Lebanon, Pa. 1906. pp. 281—283, ill.*
[6571

Fifth annual reunion of the **Gottschalk** family. *September 4th, 1909. Sanatoga Park, Pa. [s. l.; s. d.] pp. 16;* The **Gottschall** family *by* **H. G. Allebach.** *pp. 6—9.* [6572

Singmaster, J. A.: Frederick Gebhardt **Gotwald,** D. D. *In: The Lutheran Quarterly. Vol. LVI. Gettysburg, Pa. 1926. pp. 9—11, ill.*

[b. at Aaronsburg, Pa., 1869, on his father's side of German and on his mother's side of New England ancestry.] [6573

Constitution of the Hans **Graf** family association. *Organized at Lancaster, Pa., Aug. 22nd, 1866. Lancaster, Pa.: S. A. Wylie 1866. pp. 10.* [6574

Grove, Oliver P.: History of the **Graff** — **Groff** — **Grove** family. A. D. 1681 to A. D. 1900. *[s. l.; s. d.] pp. 20.* [6575

Graff, Paul: History of the **Graff** family of Westmoterand County. *Philadelphia, Pa. 1891. pp. 103, ill.*

[Descendants of Jacob Graff, who lived at Grafenauer Hof Castle, near Mannheim, Germany, and whose eldest son, Jacob, b. about 1726, came to America and settled near Lancaster, Pa.] [6576

Sandt, George W.: Lutheran leaders as I knew them. Rev. Emmanuel **Greenwald** D. D. Leader as Evangelical pastor. *In. The Lutheran Church Review. Vol. XXXVII. Philadelphia, Pa. 1918. pp. 445—449.* [6577

Haupt, C. Elvin: Samuel **Greenwald,** pastor and doctor of divinity. *Footprints of his life, together with his earliest extant and latest discourses. Lancaster, Pa.: G. L. Fon Dersmith 1889. pp. 181, ill.*

[b. Jan. 13, 1811, son of Christian G. and great-grandson of ,,Johnnes Gruenwald" of Zurich, Switzerland.] [6578

Egle, William Henry: Greenawalt of Lebanon. *In: Egle's ,,Pennsylvania genealogies". Harrisburg, Pa. 1896. [= no. 6045.] pp. 303—314.*

[Descendants of Philip Lorentz Greenawalt, b. June 10, 1725 in Hasslock, in Boehl, Germany.] [6579

Obituary. Jacob **Greenawalt.** *In: Notes and Queries. Edited by W. H. Egle. Annual vol. 1898. Harrisburg, Pa. 1899. p. 41.* [6580

Major Theodore D. **Greenawalt.** *In: Notes and Queries. Edited by W. H. Egle. Annual vol. 1897. Harrisburg, Pa. 1898. pp. 33—34.*

[b. in Harrisburg, Dec. 11, 1820, d. April 10, 1897. His great-grandfather,

Philip Lorentz Greenawalt, came to America in 1749, and settled at Ephrata, Lancaster Co., Pa.] [6581

Crater, Lewis: History of the **Greter, Grater** or **Crater** family. *Reading, Pa.: B. F. Owen & Co. pp. IV, 27, ill.*

[From 4 main roots, viz: Moritz Creeter, who arrived at Phila., Pa., Aug., 1729; Jacob Greeter, who arrived at Phila., Pa., Aug. 17, 1733; John Crater apparently a bro. of Moritz Creeter; and Michael Kreter.] [6582

Beck, Herbert H.: Peter Lehn **Grosh** (1798 —1859), an early Lancaster artist. *In: Papers and Addresses of the Lancaster County Historical Society. Vol. XVI. Lancaster, Pa. 1912. pp. 285—291.* [6583

Egle, William Henry: Gross family. *In: Egle's Pennsylvania genealogies. Harrisburg, Pa. 1896 [=no. 6045]. pp. 771—773.*

[Descendants of Jacob Gross, from Mayence on the Rhine, emigrated to America in 1759.] [6584

The **Gross** family. *Inscriptions from the Lutheran cemetery, Ephrata, Penn. In: Genealogy. Journal of American ancestry. Vol. III. New York, N. Y. 1913. p. 90.* [6585

Obituary. Daniel W. **Gross.** *In: Notes and Queries. Edited by W. H. Egle. Annual vol. 1896. Harrisburg, Pa. 1897. pp. 79—80.*

[b. in Middle Paxtang Twp., Dauphin Co., Pa. March 11, 1810, son of Abraham Gross and Anne Maria Wiestling.] [6586

Keen, WilliamW.: Addres son the unveilnig of the bronze statue of the late Professor Samuel David **Gross,** in Washington, D. C. *In: The American Journal of the Medical Sciences. Edited by Edward P. Davis. New series, vol. CXIII. Philadelphia and New York 1897. pp. 669—677.*

[b. near Easton, Pa. July 8, 1805.] [6586a

Croll, P. C.: Famous Pennsylvania-Germans. Prof. Samuel D. **Gross,** M. D., LL. D., D. C. L. *In: The Pennsylvania-German. Vol. VI. Lebanon, Pa. 1905. pp. 345—355, ill.*

[b. in Forks Twp., Northampton Co., Pa., July 8, 1805, son of Philip Gross.] [6587

Klotz, A. L.: Samuel David **Gross,** M. D., LL. D., D. C. L. late professor of surgery in Jefferson Medical College,

Philadelphia. *In: The Pennsylvania German Society. Proceedings and Addresses . . . Easton, Pa., Oct. 12, 1928. Vol. XXXIX. Norristown, Pa. 1930. Separate pagination. pp. 5—20, ill.* [6588

Maxwell, E. C.: Hon. Peter Stenger Grosscup. Judge of the United States Court of Appeals in Chicago. *In: The Pennsylvania-German. Vol. VIII. Lebanon, Pa. 1907. pp. 74—76, ill.*
[b. Febr. 15, 1852 at Ashland, O., son of Benjamin and Susannah (Bowermaster) Grosscup.] [6589

Fourth annual reunion. Grubb family. *Parkerford, Pa., October 24, 1908. pp. (24), ill.*
[Abraham Grubb (Grob) 5—19—1726, 7—27—1808, son of Henry Grubb who cam from Switzerland in 1717.] [6590

Wanger, G. F. P.: The Grubb family. *In: The Pennsylvania-German. Vol. VII. Lebanon, Pa. 1906. pp. 283—286, ill.* [6591

Jordan, John W.: Biographical sketch of Rev. Bernhard Adam Grube. *In: The Pennsylvania Magazine of History and Biography. Vol. XXV. Philadelphia, Pa. 1901. pp. 14—19, ill.*
[b. June 1, 1715 at Walschleben, a village near Erfurt, in Thuringia, Germany, entered the ministry of the Moravian Church in 1740, was dispatched to Pa. in 1748.] [6592

Strickland, W. P.: The life of Jacob Gruber. *New York, N. Y.: Published by Carlton & Porter 1860. pp. 384, ill.*
[b. Febr. 3, 1778, Bucks Co., Pa., son of John and Platina Gruber, both of German descent.] [6593

Kriebel, H. W.: Reverend Jacob Gruber, Methodist preacher. *In: The Pennsylvania-German. Vol. VIII. Lebanon, Pa. 1907. pp. 154—160, ill.* [6594

Genealogical notes. Gunkel (Kunkel). *In: Notes and Queries. Edited by W. H. Egle. Annual vol. 1896. Harrisburg, Pa. 1897. p. 32.*
[J. Michael Gunkel (Kunkel) came to America in 1749, landing at Philadelphia.] [6595

H.

Kocher, O. E.: The Haas family. *In: The Pennsylvania-German. Vol. VII. Lebanon, Pa. 1906. pp. 350—352.* [6596

Hayden, Horace Edwin: Michael Haas, of Strasburg Township, Lancaster County, Pa. *In: Notes and Queries. Edited by W. H. Egle. Third series, vol. II. 1887—*

1890. Harrisburg, Pa. 1891. p. 525. Reprint in: Third series, vol. III. Harrisburg, Pa. 1896. pp. 548—549.
[Hanse, or Hanze] b. on sea civ. 1753.] [6597

Hess, Abram: The life and services of General John Philip de Haas 1735—1786. *In: Papers read before the Lebanon County Historical Society. Vol. VII. Lebanon, Pa. 1916—1919. pp. 69—124, ill.*
[Descendant of the German family de Haas, of Baron Charles de Haas of Brandenburgh, Prussia.] [6598

Russel, Geo B.: Historical memoir of the late Rev. Nicholas P. Hacke, of Greensburg, Pa. *In: The Mercersburg Review. Vol. XXV. Philadelphia, Pa. 1878. pp. 579—599.*
[b. in Baltimore, Md., the son of Nicholas Hacke, a native of Bremen, who came to America 1792—93.] [6599

Heffner, Geo H.: Family records of the descendants of Henry Haeffner 1754—1886. *(Total number of souls in the six to seven generations probably about 1200 2000.)* Also the older generations of Johann Georg Haeffner (Rockland Stem), 1733—, Yost Heinrich Georg (Herborn, Nassau, Germany, born 1707), Georg Spohn, father of Conrad, (born 1755), Adam Dietrich, (born 1740), etc. *With biographical and historical notes. Kutztown, Pa.: Journal Steam Job Print 1866. pp. 56, ill.* [6600

Nixon, A.: A brief historical sketch of the Hager family of Lincoln County, N. C. *1902. pp. 15.*
[Descendants of William Hager [Heeker] who settled on the west bank of the Catawba about 1750.] [6601

Sollers, Basil: Der Gründer von Hagerstown Jonathan [Hager]. Nach einem Bericht im „Deutschen Correspondent." *In: Der Deutsche Pionier. Jg. XVII. Cincinnati, O. 1885—1886. S. 305—307.* [6602

— Jonathan Hager, the founder of Hagerstown. *In: Second Annual Report of the Society for the History of the Germans in Maryland. Baltimore, Md. 1888. pp. 17—30.* [6603

Hager & Bro. Lancaster, Pa. 80th anniversary 1827—1907. *Lancaster, Pa. Press of Wickersham Co. 1907. pp. 16, ill.*
[Christoph Hager, founder of the Hager business, is a son of Christoph H. who emigrated from Worms, Germany in 1766.] [6604

Hagner, Alexander B.: A personal narrative of the acquaintance of my father and myself with each of the presidents of the United States. *Washington, D. C.: Privately printed 1915. pp. 54.*
[The ancestor John Valentin Hagner, born near Heilbronn in Württemberg emigrated to Philadelphia, Pa. 1755.] [6604a

Richards, O. A.: Kaspar **Haidel** and his primitive tannery. With a brief account of the Schuylkill Indians. *In: The Pennsylvania-German. Vol. XI. Lititz, Pa. 1910. pp. 404—408.* [6605

Brinton, D. G.: Memoir of S. S. **Haldeman**, A. M. Ph. D., etc. *Read before the American Philosophical Society held at Philadelphia for promoting useful knowledge. Vol. XIX. March, 1880 to Dec., 1881. Philadelphia, Pa. 1882. pp. 279—285.*
[b. Aug. 12, 1812, at Locust Grove, 20 mi. below Harrisburg, of German origin; family came from Thun, in German Switzerland.] [6606

Haldeman, Horace L.: A memoir of Prof. Samuel Steman **Haldeman**, LL. D. *By his nephew . . . With an appendix by Francis X. Reuss. In: Records of the American Catholic Historical Society. Vol. IX. Philadelphia, Pa. 1898. pp. 257—292.* [6607

Croll, P. C.: Famous Pennsylvania-Germans. Prof. Samuel S. **Haldeman**, LL. D. *In: The Pennsylvania-German. Vol. VI. Lebanon, Pa. 1905. pp. 291—303, ill.* [6608

The **Haller** family. Inscriptions from the Zion Lutheran cemetery, York, Pa. *In: Journal of American ancestry. Vol. III. New York, N. Y. 1913. p. 104.* [6609

The **Handwerk** family. *In: The Pennsylvania-German. Vol. XII. Lititz, Pa. 1911. pp. 749—750.* [6610

Eaton, O. B.: Pleasant Henderson **Hanes** *(Manufacturer). In: Biographical history of North Carolina. Edited by S. A. Ashe. Vol. II. Greensboro, N. C. 1905. pp. 139—145.*
[b. at Fulton, Davie Co., N. C., Oct. 16, 1845; descendant of Marcus Höhns [Heintz] who emigrated from Kusel, Dutchy of Zweibruecken, Germany, landing at Philadelphia, Sept. 9, 1738, and lived a while in York Co., Pa., and settled on South Fork of Muddy Creek, neer Salem, N. C.] [6611

Blair, William A.: John Wesley **Hanes** *(Manufacturer). In: Biographical hi-*story *of North Carolina. Edited by S. A. Ashe. Vol. II. Greensboro, N. C. 1905. pp. 146—151, ill.*
[b. at Fulton, Davie Co., N. C., Febr. 3, 1850; son of Alexander Martin Hanes and Jane March Hanes.] [6612

Harbaugh, H.: Annals of the **Harbaugh** family in America from, 1736—1856. *Chambersburg, Pa.: M. Kieffer & Co. 1856. pp. 148.*
[Descendants of Yost Harbaugh, who came from Switzerland about 1736 and settled at Philadelphia, Pa.] [6613

Apple, T. G.: The late editor *[Rev. Henry Harbaugh, D. D.] In: The Mercersburg Review. Vol. XV. Philadelphia, Pa. 1868. pp. 165—179.* [6614

Harbaugh, Linn: Life of Henry Harbaugh, D. D. *With an introduction and eulogy. Philadelphia, Pa.: Reformed Church Publication Board 1900. pp. 302; Bibliography p. IV.* [6615

Croll, P. C.: Famous Pennsylvania-Germans. Rev. Henry **Harbaugh**, D. D. *In: The Pennsylvania-German. Vol. V. Lebanon, Pa. 1904. pp. 51—57, ill.* [6616

Dubbs, Jos. H.: The blessed memory of Henry Harbaugh. *(A response to a sentiment offered at the banquet of the Pennsylvania-German. Society, Lancaster, Nov. 6, 1908.) In: The Pennsylvania-German Vol. X. Lititz, Pa. 1909. pp. 12—14.* [6617

Rattermann, H. A.: Hendrich Harbaugh. Geschichtsschreiber und Dichter in Pennsylvanisch-Deutscher Mundart. *In: H. A. Rattermann. Gesammelte Werke. Bd. X. Cincinnati, O.: Selbstverlag des Verfassers 1911. S. 247—264.* [6617a

Kieffer, J. Spangler: Recollections of Dr. Harbaugh. *In: The Reformed Church Review. Fourth series, vol. XXI. Philadelphia, Pa. 1917. pp. 427—446.* [6618

Richards, George: The theology of the Rev. Prof. Henry Harbaugh, D. D. *In: Addresses of the life and the theology of the Rev. H. Harbaugh and the Rev. E. Vogel Gerhart (1917). pp. 49—82.* [6619

— The theology of Professor Henry **Harbaugh**. *Address delivered Oct., 1917 at Hagerstown, Md., during the annual session of Potomac Synod, at a service commemorating the one hundreth anniversary of the birth of H. Harbaugh. In: The Reformed Church Review. Fourth series, vol. XXII. 1918. pp. 185—210.* [6620

Harman, John Newton: Harman genealogy *(Southern branch)* with biographical sketches 1700—1924. *Richmond, Va.: W. C. Hill Printing Co. 1925. pp. 7 —376, ill.* [6621

Harnly, Henry H.: A history of the Harnly family, containing biographical sketches of the Harnly, Hoerner, Eby, Hershey, Sneider and related families. *Auburn, Ill. 1903. pp. 64.*

[whose ancestor Ulrich Harnly, leaving German Schweiz, reached America Sept. 26, 1737.] [6622

Harshberger, John William: The life and work of John W. Harshberger, Ph. D., *an autobiography with bibliography. Philadelphia, Pa.: Privately printed. The author. 1928. pp. 40.*

[The paternal ancestor came from near Coblenz, Rhineland, Germany, about 1735.] [6622a

Hartman, W. L.: The Hartman family. *In: The Pennsylvania-German. Vol. VII. Lebanon, Pa. 1906. pp. 344—350, ill.; Vol. VIII. 1907. pp. 160—169; 259 —267, ill.* [6623

Mast, C. Z.: The Hartman family. *In: Christian Monitor. A monthly magazine for the home. Vol. XVI. no. 4. Scottdale, Pa. 1924. pp. 499—501, ill.* [6624

Richards, H. M. M. - Heilman, S. P.: Regina, the German captive Regina Hartman. Part I. The location. *By H. M. M. Richards; Part. II. The story. By S. P. Heilman. In: Papers read before the Lebanon County Historical Society. Vol. II. 1901—1904. Lebanon, Pa. 1904. pp. 81—97.* [6625

Heilman, S. P.: A final word as to Regina, the German capitve. *In: Papers read before the Lebanon County Historical Society. Vol. III. Lebanon, Pa. 1905 —1906. pp. 202—251.* [6626

Weiser, R.: Regina, the German captive; or true piety among the lowly. *Philadelphia, Pa.: General Council Publication Board 1919. pp. 252, ill.* [6627

D., F. R.: Extract from an old will. *(Henry Hartman, Lampeter Township.) In: Papers and Addresses of the Lancaster County Historical Society. Vol. X. Lancaster, Pa. 1906. pp. 120—122.* [6628

The republican candidate for the governorship of Pennsylvania in 1875. *[John Frederick Hartranft.] Harrisburg, Pa.: Singerly Printing and Publishing House 1875. pp. 64.* [6629

De Peyster, John Watts: John Frederic Hartranft, governor of Pennsylvania. *[s. l., 1877?] Printed on one side of leaf only. pp. 20.* [6630

Ashman, William N.: An Address on the life and services of John F. Hartranft. *Published by the Committee on political education. Philadelphia, Pa.: The Pennsylvania Club 1890. pp. 44.* = *Pennsylvania Club Lectures, course of 1889—90.* [6631

Pratt, W. S. and Jacobus, M. W.: Memorial addresses upon the late Chester David Hartranft . . . *1915. pp. . . .* [6631a

[Schuler, H. A.]: General John Frederic Hartranft, Union leader and governor of Pennsylvania. *In: The Pennsylvania-German. Vol. VIII. Lebanon, Pa. 1907. pp. 475—477.* [6632

Tobias Hartranft and his descendants. *In: The Genealogical Record of the Schwenkfelder families. Edited by S. K. Brecht. New York, N. Y.-Chicago, Ill. 1923. pp. 683—854.* [6633

Hartzell. *[Note on a prospectus of a historical and genealogical record of the Hartzell family.] In: The Pennsylvania Magazine of History and Biography. Vol. X. Philadelphia, Pa. 1886. p. 122.* [6634

Cressman, Jesse S.: A short sketch of the life of the late Henry E. Hartzell. *In: The Perkiomen Region. Vol. III, no. 3. Pennsburg, Pa. 1925. pp. 52—56.*

[b. April 15, 1840 in Frederick Township, Montgomery Co., Pa.] [6635

Hartzell, J. Culver: In memory of George Henry Hartzell. *In: The Perkiomen Region. Vol. IX, no. 1. Pennsburg, Pa. 1931. pp. 19—21.*

[who arrived at Philadelphia, Sept. 21, 1732 and settled in Rockhill Twp., Bucks Co., Pa.] [6636

Lancaster County, Pa. inscriptions, from the Hauck family graveyard, on Norman Wenger's farm (formerly Rev. Israel Wenger's) in Meadow Valley, Ephrata Township, Lancaster County, Pa. *In: Genealogy Journal of American ancestry. Vol. IV. New York, N. Y. 1914. p. 59.* [6637

Fastnacht, A. G.: Rev. Daniel Jacob Hauer, D. D. *In: The Pennsylvania-German. Vol. XII. Lititz, Pa. 1911. pp. 717—721.* [6638

Haupt, William Henry: The Haupt family in America. The descendants of (1) Sebastian Haupt, arrived 1738, Philadelphia; (2) Joh. Nicholas Haupt, arrived

1740; (3) Johannes Haupt, Esq., arrived 1750 and 1754. Together with data of others, arriving before 1770 and late arrivals. *[1924.] Typewritten copy at the Library of Congress, Washington, D. C. pp. 68, ill.*   [6639

[Haupt, Herman]: Reminiscences of General Herman Haupt. *Director, chief engineer and general superintendent of the Pennsylvania railroad, contractor and chief engineer for the Hoosac Tunnel, chief of the Bureau of United States military railroads in the Civil War, chief engineer of the tidewater pipeline, general manager of the Richmond & Danville and Northern Pacific Railroads, President American Air Power Company etc. etc. giving hitherto unpublished official orders, personal narratives of important military operations, and interviews with president Lincoln, secretary Stanton, generalin chief Halleck, and with generals McDowell, Mc Clellan, Meade, Hancock, Burnside, and others in command of the armies in the field and his impressions of these men. [Written by himself.] With notes and a personal sketch by* **Frank Abial Flower.** *Milwaukee, Wis.-Wright & Joys Co. 1901. pp. XL, 43—331.*
        [6639a

Hauser, James J.: Six great-grandparents living, *[of the children of Mr. and Mrs. Victor H. Hauser, of Kutztown]. In: The Pennsylvania-German. Vol. VIII. Lebanon, Pa. 1907. pp. 370—371.* [6640

[Mayer, Brantz]: Notes on Hausil family. *(Extracts from a letter of Brantz Mayer to Rev. Dr. George Diehl, of Frederick, Oct. 17, 1877.) In: The Maryland Historical Magazine. Vol. X. Baltimore, Md. 1915. pp. 57—58.*
        [who m. at Rotterdam, Holl., Sybilla Magaretha Mayer (b. at Ulm, Wurttemberg, 1733).]   [6641

Nixon, A.: The Hauss family of Lincoln County, N. C. *Lincolntown, N. C.: The Lincoln Journal 1905. pp. 10.*
        [Descendants of Jacob Hauss, who arrived in Philadelphia, Pa., Sept. 1765, and settled on Leonards Fork, Lincoln Co., N. C. about 1770.]   [6642

Heatwole, D. A.: A history of the Heatwole family, from the landing of the ancestor of the race up to the present time. *Dale Enterprise: Office of the „Watchful Pilgrim" 1882. pp. 24.*
        [Mathias Heitwohl, a German emigrant, the ancestor of the Heatwoles in Rocking-

ham Co., Va., arrived at Philadelphia, Pa. Sept., 1748.]   [6643

Hecker, Edward J.: The Hecker family. Jacob Hecker - Mary Ann Nagel, married in Lehigh County, Pa., 1830, located in Ohio, 1845. *Indianopolis, Ind. 1930. pp. (15).*   [6644

Zimmerman, Thos. C.: In memoriam. Rev. George C. **Heckman,** D. D. *Historical sketch delivered before the Historical Society of Berks County, Pa., April 8, 1902. In: Transactions of the Historical Society of Berks County. Vol. I. Reading, Pa. 1904. pp. (2), ill.*
        [b. in Easton, Jan. 26, 1825.]   [6645

George **Heebner,** Schwenkfelder settler in Falkner Swamp. *In: The Perkiomen Region, Past and Present. Vol. III. Philadelphia, Pa. 1901. pp. 44—46.*
        [Georg Hübner, one of a colony of 184 persons of the Society of the Schwenkfelders came to Philadelphia, Sept. 12, 1734.]   [6646

J., H.: Genealogical register of the male and female descendants of Hans **Hege;** and also of the male and female descendants of Henry **Lesher,** and the relationship existing between the said two families. *Chambersburg, Pa.: M. Kieffer & Co. 1859. pp. IV, 5—46.*
        [landed at Philadelphia, Pa., Sept., 1727.]   [6647

Heilman, S. P.: The name Heilman in European, American and Lebanon history. *Paper read before the Lebanon County Historical Society, Nov. 2, 1917. In: Papers read before the Lebanon County Historical Society. Vol. VII. Lebanon, Pa. 1916—1919. pp. 221—252, ill.*   [6648

Richards, H. M. M.: Samuel Philip **Heilman,** M. D. *In: The Yearbook of the Pennsylvania Federation of Historical Society, 1920. Harrisburg, Pa. 1921. pp. 148 —150.*   [6649

Roberts, C. R.: Heimbach family. *Prepared by . . . for J. A. Heimbach, Allentown, Pa. In: The Pennsylvania-German. Vol. XI. Lititz, Pa. 1910. pp. 559—560.* [6650

Heinecke, Samuel: Genealogy from Adam to Christ; with the genealogy of Adam **Heinecke** and Henry **Vandersaal,** from 1747 to 1868. *To which is added a brief account of the author's travels as an evangelist, with some interesting incidents appertaining thereto with ten sermons composed by himself. Philadelphia, Pa.: Collins 1869. pp. (1), 5—231; Second*

edition: . . ., from 1747 to 1881. To
which is added a brief account of the
author's travels in about 16 years as an
evangelist and 12 sermons composed by
himself. Lancaster, Pa.: John A. Hiestand 1881. pp. (1), 5—302.   [6651
Wolff, Bernard C.: A discourse in commemoration of the Rev. Elias Heiner, D. D.
delivered in the German Reformed Church,
Second Str., Baltimore, Nov. 15, 1863.
pp. 74, ill.   [6652
Proctor, John Glagett: Johannes Heintz
and his descendants. Greenville, Pa.
1918. pp. 102, (8), IX.
[Descendants of Johannes Heintz,
immigrated from Dillenburg, Germany
in 1751.]   [6653
Hostetter, A. K.: Major Samuel Peter
Heintzelman. In: Papers and Addresses
of the Lancaster County Historical Society. Vol. XVII. Lancaster, Pa. 1913.
pp. 57—78, ill.   [6654
An autobiography. Rev. J. Albert Helffenstein. In: The Reformed Quarterly Review. Vol. XXVII. = New series, vol.
II. Philadelphia, Pa. 1880. pp. 50—73.
[b. in Germantown, Pa., 1788, son
of J. Albert C. Helffenstein, a native of
Germany.]   [6655
Helffrich, Wm. A.: Nachrichten über die
Familie Helffrich. In: Wm. A. Helffrich,
Geschichte verschiedener Gemeinden in
Lecha und Berks Counties . . . Allentown,
1891 [= Nr. 4449]. S. 71—104. [6655a
Helffrich, Wm. A.: Lebensbild aus dem
Pennsylvanisch-Deutschen   Prediger-
stand: oder Wahrheit in Licht und
Schatten. Allentown, Pa.: Heraus-
gegeben von N. W. A. und W. U. Helff-
rich 1906. (2), 549 S., ill.   [6656
Heller, W. J.: Genealogy of Christopher
Heller and his six sons. Paper read at
the 5th reunion of the Heller family as-
sociation at Island Park, Easton, Pa.,
August 29, 1908. In: The Pennsyl.
vania-German. Vol. XI. Lititz, Pa. 1910.
pp. 275—281.   [6657
Weeks, Stephen B.: Hinton Rowan Helper
(Author). In: Biographical history of
North Carolina. Edited by S. A. Ashe.
Vol. VIII. Greensboro, N. C. 1917. pp.
204—214.
[b. in Davie Co., N. C., Dec. 27, 1829.
His paternal grandfather (Helfer) came
to N. C. in 1752 from the vicinity of
Heidelberg, Germany.]   [6658
Stapleton, A. - [Henkel, Elon O.]: The
Henkel memorial 1717—1910. [On in-

side title-page. The Henkel memorial.
Historical, genealogical, biographical.
A serial publication devoted to collecting
and preserving the history of the Rev.
Anthony Jacob Henkel (known in history as Rev. Gerhart Henkel) an exiled
Lutheran clergyman who came from
Germany to Pennsylvania in 1717. One
of the founders of his church in America,
and father of a great and honorable
posterity, also to collect and preserve the
history of his worthy descendants of
whatsoever name or creed. Organ of The
Henkel Memorial Association. A. Stapleton, editor and publisher. York, Pa.
1910.] 2 series. New Market, Va.:
Henkel & Co. 1910. First series, 4 numbers. pp. 170; second series, 3 numbers.
pp. 171—280, ill. Second series, no. 3
edited by Elon O. Henkel.   [6659
Henkel, Elon O.: The Henkel family records.
A periodical publication devoted to collecting and preserving the history of
the Henkel family in Europe and America. 1635—1717. Edited by . . . No.
1—13. New Market, Va.: The Henkel
Press 1926—1935. No 1—6. 1926—
1931. pp. 262, ill.   [6660
— The Henkel family news letter. A se-
miannual supplement to the the Henkel
family records. Edited by . . . Published by authorithy of the Henkel Family
Association. No. 1—(3). New Market,
Va.: Henkel Press 1928—(1930). pp.
52.   [6661
Cury, Cora C.: Geiger-Hinkle note. By . . .,
historian of the Henkel Family Association. In: The Perkiomen Region.
Vol. VII, no. 3. Pennsburg, Pa. 1929.
p. 75.   [6662
Stapleton, A.: Famous Pennsylvania-Germans. Rev. Gerhart Henkel and his descendants. In: The Pennsylvania-German.
Vol. IV. Lebanon, Pa. 1903. pp. 243
—253, ill.   [6663
Finck, W. J.: Paul Henkel, the Lutheran
pioneer. In: The Lutheran Quarterly.
Vol. LVI. Gettysburg, Pa. 1926. pp. 307
—334.
[b. in Rowan Co., N. C., to which his
grandfather John Justus, and his father
Jacob, had migrated a few years before,
with the stream of settlers from Pennsylvania and Maryland to the Piedmont of
the Carolinas.]   [6664
Stapleton, A.: An important historical
error corrected. [Concerning Henkel
family history.] In: The Pennsylvania-

*German. Vol. VII. Lebanon, Pa. 1906.
pp. 397—400, ill.* [6665
Emig, Lelia Dromgold: Records of the annual **Hench** and **Dromgold** reunion
held in Perry County, Pa., from 1897
to 1912. The records contain the genealogies of Nicholas **Ickes,** Johannes
Hench, Zachariah **Rice,** John **Hartman,**
Thomas **Dromgold** and kindred families
who were among the early settlers of
Chester County, and served in the Revolution. *Harrisburg, Pa.: The United
Evangelical Press 1913. pp. 191, ill.*
[6666
Learned, Marion Dexter: Professor George
Allison **Hench.** In memoriam. *In: Americana Germanica. Vol. III. 1899. pp.
219—225.* [6667
Henry of Spring Creek *(about one mile north
of the Town of Palmyra, Lebanon Coun-
ty, Pa.). In: Notes and Queries. Edited
by W. H. Egle. Fourth series, vol. I.
1891—1893. Harrisburg, Pa. 1893. pp.
2—3.*
*[George Heinrich, b. April 22, 1722
in the Pfalz, Germany, emigrated with
his wife Elizabeth Balsbaugh and her
brother about the year 1752.]* [6668
Ferree, Barr: William Uhler **Hensel.** An
*appreciation . . . Pennsylvania Society
prepared for the annual meeting April
20, 1915. pp. 8.* [6669
Henshie, Lura Maye: A history and genealogy of the **Henshie** family in America
and their descendants. *Springfield, Ill.:
Springfield Job Printing 1928. pp. (3),
48, ill.*
*[Descendants of Hans Jacob Handschin
of Rickenbach, Canton St. Gallen,
Switzerland.]* [6670
Herbruck, Emil P.: Early years and late
reflections. *Cleveland O.: Central Printing House 1923. pp. XI, 257.*
*[Son of Peter Herbruck, who came
from a Reformed family in the Palatinate.]*
[6671
Cowen, Phoebe Strong: The **Herkimers** and
Schuylers. An historical sketch of the
two families with genealogies of the
descendants of George Herkimer, the
Palatinate, who settled in the Mohawk
Valley, N. Y., in 1721. *Albany, N. Y.:
Joel Munsell's Sons Publishers 1903.
pp. 147, ill.* [6672
Riehm, Friedrich: Die pfälzische Abstam-
mung des amerikanischen Generals
Herchheimer. *In: Pfälzisches Museum.
Jg. XLIII. — Pfälzische Heimatkunde.*

*Jg. XXII. Kaiserslautern 1926. S. 206
—209, ill.*
*[Getauft 20. Juni 1700, Sohn von
Georg und Magdalena Hörchemer aus
Sandhausen bei Heidelberg, Deutsches
Reich.]* [6673
Bagg, Mathew D.: The **Herkimer** papers.
Descriptive list of papers of George
Herkimer, Esq., the brother of General
Herkimer, received from H. G. Babcock.
*In: Transactions of the Oneida Hi-
storical Society at Utica, with the annual
addresses and reports for 1881. Utica,
N. Y. 1881. pp. 100—106, ill.* [6674
Earl, Robert: John Jost **Herkimer.** *In:
Papers read before the Herkimer County
Historical Society, during the year 1898.
Vol. I. Herkimer and Ilion 1899. pp.
5—8.* [6675
Lyttle, Eugene W.: Nicholas **Herkimer.** *In:
Proceedings of the New York State Historical Association. Fifth annual mee-
ting. Vol. IV. Albana, N. Y. 1904. pp.
19—29.* [6676
Greene, Nelson: The home and name of
General **Herkimer.** With notes and
comments on the Americanism of Herkimer and his troops, the Americanism
of the Revolutionary Mohawk Valley
and the present American ideal. *In:
Proceedings of the New York State Historical Association. The sixteenth meeting. Vol. XIV. Albany, N. Y. 1915.
pp. 365—402.* [6677
Hadcock, De Witt C.: Last hours of General
Herkimer. An intensly interesting article from the pen of . . . over 90 years
of age. *In: Papers read before the Herkimer County Historical Society, covering the period from May 1914 to November 1922. Vol. V. [s. l., 1922.] pp.
199—200.* [6678
Shaeffer, Nicholas: Rev. Lebrecht Frederick **Herman.** *In: The Pennsylvania-
German. Vol. X. Lititz, Pa. 1909. pp.
122—126.* [6679
Flickinger, S. H.: A **Herman** bible record.
*In: Genealogy. Journal of American
ancestry. Vol. I. New York, N. Y. 1912.
pp. 186.*
*[Descendants of George Herman, b.
Jan. 13, 1784; d. Oct. 6, 1863; and Eve
(Landis) Herman b. March 7, 1789, d.
Oct. 19, 1863.]* [6680
Funk, John F.: A biographical sketch of
Bish. Christian **Herr.** *Also a collection
of hymns written by him in the German
language. Compiled by* J. F. Funk.

Elkhart, Ind.: Mennonite Publishing Co. 1887. pp. 50. [6681

The Memorial Journal. *Official organ of the Hans* Herr *Memorial Association. Vol. I, no. 1. Lancaster, Pa., Nov., 1895. pp. 4. — (Nov. 9. July, 1896).* [6682

Herr, Theodore W.: Lineage and family record of descendants of Reverend Hans Herr from his birth A. D. 1639 made from the perfected genealogical records of the pioneer settlers of Lancaster County, Pa. from A. D. 1709 to A. D. 1729, and of all the lineal descendants of such pioneer settlers to the present time. *Adapted also for the use of any person. Compiled, arranged and published by . . . Lancaster, Pa.: New Era Printing 1901. 1 table, (3)f., ill.* [6683

— Genealogical record of Reverend Hans Herr and his direct lineal descendants from his birth A. D. 1639 to the present time, containing the names etc. of 13223 persons. *Compiled and arranged by . . . Lancaster, Pa.: Examiner Printing House 1908. pp. XII, (1), 785, ill.* [6684

Hans Herr and his descendants. *(View and extracts of Theodore W. Herr's „Genealogical record of Rev. Hans Herr and his direct lineal descendants . . . 1908.) In: The Pennsylvania-German. Vol. X. Lititz, Pa. 1909. pp. 116—118.* [6685

Martin, C. H.: The emigration of Hans Herr. *In: Papers and Addresses of the Lancaster County Historical Society. Vol. XXIX. Lancaster, Pa. 1925. pp. 77—82.* [6686

Obituary. Andrew Jackson Herr. *From Daily Telegraph, Saturday, March 17, 1894. Reprint in: Notes and Queries. Edited by W. H. Egle. Fourth series, Vol. II. 1894. Harrisburg, Pa. 1895. pp. 16—18.* [6687

The Hershey family. *In: Notes and Queries. Edited by W. H. Egle. Third series, vol. I. 1884—1887. Harrisburg, Pa. 1887. p. 327. Reprint in: Third series, vol. II. Harrisburg, Pa. 1896. pp. 18—20.*

[Andrew Hershey, b. 1721 in Switzerland; removed early in life with his parents to the Palatinate and sailed with his brother for America in 1719, where he settled in Lancaster Co., Pa.] [6688

Hershey Freindschaft. Seventh annual reunion of the Hershey family to celebrate the 203d anniversary of their arrival in America. Rocky Springs Park, Lancaster County, Pa., Sept. 7th, 1912. *Marietta, O. Washington L. Hershey, historian 1912. pp. 34.* [6689

Hershey, Scott Funk: History and records, of the **Hershey** family from the year 1600. *New Castle, Pa.: The Petite Book Co. 1913. pp. (1), 5—108, ill.*

[Christian Hershey, a bishop in the Mennonite Church; his 3 children, Benjamin, Andrew and Anna, located in Lancaster Co., Pa. in 1709. Another Hershey came to Lancaster Co. in 1711. In 1719 two brothers, Andrew Hershey and Benjamin Hershey, both ministers of the Mennonite Church arrived with their father, Hans Hersche. In 1739, a third brother, Christian Hershey, also a minister arrived. . . . So far known the Hersheys in this country are descended from the two families — the 1709 and the 1719 group.] [6690

Sener, S. M.: The Hershey family. *In: Notes and Queries. Edited by W. H. Egle. Annual vol. 1896. Harrisburg, Pa. 1897. pp. 206—207.*

[Andrew Hershey was b. in Switzerland in 1702, from whence his father removed to the Palatinate, at the Court of Friedensheim, in 1719, and he, with his father and brothers came to America and settled in Lancaster Co., Pa.] [6691

Schaff, I. James: Rev. John Hershey. *Reprinted from „The Religious Telescope." In: The Pennsylvania-German. Vol. XI. Lititz, Pa. 1910. pp. 617—620.* [6692

Hershey, Henry: Hershey family history. *Compiled by . . . Scottdale, Pa.: Mennonite Publishing House 1929. pp. 291.* [6693

Hertzler, John: A brief biographic memorial of Jacob **Hertzler** and a complete genealogical family register of his lineal descendants and those related by intermarriage, from 1730 to 1883, chronologically arranged. *Together with the necessary historical and other notes, also an appendix of the Christian Zug family. Elkhart, Ind.: Mennonite Publishing Co. 1885. pp. 370.*

[Jac. Hertzler b. 1703 of Swiss parents, landed in Philadelphia, Pa., Sept. 9th, 1749.] [6695

Hess, John H.: A family record of the **Hess** family from the first emigrant to this country down to the present time as far as could be obtained. *Mistakes excepted. Lititz, Pa.: Sunbeam 1880. pp. (2), 68.*

[Samuel Hess, came to this country in 1712.] [6696
Hess, John H.: A genealogy of the **Hess** family from the first emigrant to this country down to the present time as far as could be ascertained. *Lititz, Pa.: Express Print 1896. pp. (2), 248, (12).* *[Descendants of Samuel Hess, who settled at Pequea, Lancaster Co., Pa. in the year 1712.]* [6697
Hess, Asher S.: The Nicholas Hess family. *Paper prepared by Asher S. Hess and read by Jeremiah S. Hess at the 3rd annual reunion of the Hess family at Rittersville, Pa., Aug. 21, 1909. In: The Pennsylvania-German. Vol. X. Lititz, Pa. 1909. pp. 569—571.*
[Nicholas Hess, a native of Zweibruecken, in the Palatinate, Germany, landed in America about 1741; he settled in Springtown Township, Bucks Co., Pa.] [6698
Babcock, Wm. Emerson: Hess Higbee genealogy. *Compiled by . . . 1903—1909.* *[Mishawaka, Ind.] [s. l.] 1909. pp. (1), 5—175, ill.*
[William Hess, b. about 1750 and Mary Waltour Hess, residents of Westmoreland Co., Pa. and of German descent, were of the second generation of American birth.] [6699
Hess, Asher L.: Genealogical record of the descendants of Nicholas Hess, pioneer immigrant, together with historical and biographical sketches. *Compiled by . . . Allentown, Pa.: H. Ray Haas & Co. 1912. pp. (2), 5—332.*
[was a native of Zweibruecken, Germany, and emigrated to America about 1741.] [6700
Hester, Martin M.: History and genealogy of the descendants of John Lawrence **Hester** and Godfrey Stough. *1752—1905. Compiled by . . . [s. l.] 1905. pp. IX, 323; Addenda pp. 43; 30.*
[Descendants of John Lawrence Hoerster, b. in the Kingdom of Hanover, Germany, about 1738, emigrated to America 1771.] [6701
„Balthasar **Heydrick** and his descendants." *In: The genealogical record of the Schwenkfelder families. Edited by S. K. Brecht. New York, N. Y.-Chicago, Ill. 1923. pp. 859—883.* [6702
„Caspar **Heydrick**." *In: The genealogical record of the Schwenkfelder families. Edited by S. K. Brecht. New York, N. Y.-Chicago, Ill. 1923. p. 860.* [6703

„George **Heydrick**." *In: The genealogical record of the Schwenkfelder families. Edited by S. K. Brecht. New York, N. Y.-Chicago, Ill. 1923. p. 908.* [6704
„Abraham **Heydrick**." *In: The genealogical record of the Schwenkfelder families. Edited by S. K. Brecht. New York, N. Y.-Chicago, Ill. 1923. pp. 1312—1313.* [6705
Smyth, S. Gordon: Hans Joest **Heydt**. The story of a Perkiomen pioneer. *Paper read before the Historical Society of Montgomery County, February 22, 1909. In: Historical Sketches. A Collection of Papers prepared for the Historical Society of Montgomery County, Pa. Vol. IV. Norristown, Pa. 1910. pp. 118—133.*
[from Alsace, Germany.] [6706
— Hans Joest **Heydt**, the story of a Perkiomen pioneer. *In: The Pennsylvania-German. Vol. X. Lititz, Pa. 1909. pp. 330—338.* [6707
[Heyl, Christian]: Biographische Skizze eines alten Pioniers. *[Christian Heyl.] In: Der Deutsche Pionier. Jg. II. Cincinnati, O. 1870—1871. S. 130—136.*
[Einer der Gründer von Columbus, O., geb. 1788 in Zeidlops, Amt Brückenau, Deutsches Reich; er wanderte 1799 mit seinem Vater nach Amerika aus.] [6708
The family **Hiester** in Pennsylvania. *In: Der Deutsche Pionier. Jg. I. Cincinnati, O. 1869—1870. pp. 303—306.* [6709
Hill, V. E. C.: A genealogy of the **Hiester** family. *Printed for private distribution. Lebanon, Pa.: Report Publishing Co. 1903. pp. 65.* [6710
Richards, Henry Melchior Muhlenberg: The **Hiester** family. *Prepared by the authority of the Pennsylvania-German Society. In: The Pennsylvania-German Society. Proceedings and Addresses . . . 1905. Vol. XVI. Lancaster, Pa. 1907. Separate pagination: Pennsylvania-German genealogies. pp. 42.*
[Descendants of Johannes Hiester and wife Catherine of the Town of Elsoff, in the Grafschaft of Wittgenstein, Province of Westphalia, Germany, and offspring especially of three sons: John, who reached America in 1732 and settled at Goshenhoppen, Montgomery Co, Pa.; Joseph and Daniel, who took the oath of alliance at Philadelphia 1737.] [6711
Hiester, Isaac: The Hiester homestead in Germany. *A paper read March 12, 1907. In: Transactions of the Historical Society of Berks County. Vol. II. 1905—1909*

Reading, Pa. 1910. pp. 180—188, ill; Reprint in: The Pennsylvania-German. Vol. IX. Cleona, Pa. 1908. pp. 496—499.
[the Village of Elsoff in the Grafschaft of Wittgenstein, in the Province Westphalia, Germany.]   [6712

Obituary. Augustus O. **Hiester.** In: Notes and Queries. Edited by W. H. Egle. Fourth series, vol. II. Harrisburg, Pa. 1895. pp. 289—291.   [6713

Dotterer, Henry S.: Daniel **Hiester,** of Upper Salford. In: The Perkiomen Region, Past and Present. Vol. I. Philadelphia, Pa. 1895. pp. 18—20.
[Daniel Hüster (sick) and Joseph Hüster signed the declaration Sept. 26, 1737, having arrived at Philadelphia, in the ship St. Andrew.]   [6714

— The grave of Daniel **Hiester** the immigrant. In: The Perkiomen Region, Past and Present. Vol. III. Philadelphia, Pa. 1901. p. 103.   [6715

Egle, William Henry: Prominent Pennsylvanians: Gen. Gabriel **Hiester.** In: Historical Register: Notes and Queries, historical and genealogical relating to interior Pennsylvania for the year 1883. Vol. I. Harrisburg, Pa. 1883. p. 156.   [6716

Dotterer, Henry S.: General Daniel **Hiester.** In: The Perkiomen Region, Past and Present. Vol. I. Philadelphia, Pa. 1895. pp. 78—79; 82—84; 106—109; 124—126; 148—150; 163—165.   [6717

B.: Biography of Gov. **Hiester.** Reprint from the United States Gazette in: Hazard's Register of Pennsylvania. Vol. X. Philadelphia, Pa. 1832. pp. 23—24. [6718

Vaux, Richard: Sketch of the life of Joseph **Hiester,** governor of Pennsylvania. Read before the Historical Society of Pennsylvania on the presentation of his portrait to that institution, June 13th, 1887. Philadelphia, Pa.: Allen, Lane & Scott [1887]. pp. 23.   [6719

Richards, Henry Melchior Muhlenberg: Governor Joseph **Hiester.** A historical sketch. Lancaster, Pa. 1907. = Part XVII. ,,A narrative and critical history," prepared at the request of the Pennsylvania-German Society. In: The Pennsylvania-German Society. Proceedings and Addresses . . . 1905. Vol. XVI. Lancaster, Pa. 1907. Separate pagination pp. 51.
[b. in Bern Township, Berks Co., Pa.; Nov. 18, 1752; son of John Hiester,

migrant of 1732, and Mary Barbara Epler.]   [6720

[Stein, Thos. S. - Lantz, C. R. and Grittinger, H. C.]: Rev. J. E. Hiester, D. D. In: Papers read before the Lebanon County Historical Society. Vol. V. 1909—1912. pp. 400—403, ill.   [6721

Pedigree. Margaretta Pepper van **Reed,** of San Jose, Cal. In: The Perkiomen Region, Past and Present. Vol. III. Philadelphia, Pa. 1901. pp. 103—104.
[Descendant of Johannes Hiester and wife Catherine, resided at Elsoff, Wittgenstein, Germany.]   [6722

Steinmetz, C. M.: Inscriptions. High private burying ground, Poplarneck, Berks County. In: The National Genealogical Society Quarterly. Vol. XV, no. 3. Washington, D. C. 1927. pp. 35—36.   [6723

Minnich, Michael Reed: John Frederick **Hillegas,** 1685—1765. In: The Pennsylvania Magazine of History and Biography. Vol. XVIII. Philadelphia, Pa. 1894. pp. 85—89.   [6724

— The graves of John Frederick and Elizabeth Barbara **Hillegas.** In: The Perkiomen Region, Past and Present. Vol. I. Philadelphia, Pa. 1895. pp. 50—51. [6725

Egle, William Henry: Michael **Hillegas.** First treasurer of the United States. In: The Pennsylvania Magazine of History and Biography. Vol. XI. Philadelphia, Pa. 1887. pp. 406—409, ill.   [6726

Whitney, Emma St. Clair: Michael **Hillegas** and his descendants. By his great-granddaughter. Edition private. Pottsville, Pa.: Press of M. E. Miller 1891. pp. 118, ill.   [6727

Minnich, Michael Reed: Famous Pennsylvania Germans. Michael **Hillegas.** In: The Pennsylvania-German. Vol. II. Lebanon, Pa. 1901. pp. 147—155, ill.   [6728

— Some data of the Hillegas family. In: American Historical Register. Vol. I. Philadelphia, Pa. & Boston, Mass. Sept. 1894. pp. 23f.   [6728 a

— Memoir of the first treasurer of the United States [Michael Hillegas] with chronical data. Philadelphia, Pa.: Michael Reed Minnich 1906. pp. . . .   [6728 b

Huch, C. F.: Michael **Hillegas,** der erste Schatzmeister der Vereinigten Staaten. In: Mitteilungen des Deutschen Pionier-Vereins von Philadelphia. Heft III. Philadelphia, Pa. 1907. S. 2—11.

*Reprint in: Deutsch-Amerikanische Ge-
schichtsblätter. Jg. VII, Nr. 2. Chicago,
Ill. 1907. S. 97—104.* [6729
Biography of Michael Hillegas. First
treasurer of the United States. *Pub-
lished by Michael Hillegas Unit, no. 55.
S. S. A. New York, N. Y. 1924.* [6729a
An old-time will. Will of Father-in-law of
Michael Hillegas. 1732—1733. *Reprint
in: The Perkiomen Region. Vol. VIII,
no. 1. Pennsburg, Pa. 1930. p. 9.* [6730
Hensel, W. U.: An old time worthy. (Jacob
Hiltzheimer.) *In: Papers and Addresses
of the Lancaster County Historical So-
ciety. Vol. XI. 1906—1907. Lancaster,
Pa. 1907. pp. 328—354.* [6731
Hinkle family, inscriptions from the Mt.
Bethel cemetery, Columbia, Pa. *In:
Genealogy. Journal of American ancestry. Vol. IV. New York, Pa. 1914.
p. 69.* [6732
Inscriptions. Hoch private burying ground
near Pleasantville, Berks Co., Pa. on
farm of Gideon Hoch. *In: The National
Genealogical Society Quarterly. Vol. XV,
no. 2. Washington, D. C. 1927. pp. 30—
31.* [6733
S[ch]latter, Michael: Schwanen Gesang
oder letzte Arbeit des Weiland Ehr-
würdigen und Hochgelehrten Herrn
Johann Jacob Hochreutner. *Bestimmten
Prediger der ehrsamen Reformierten Gemeinde zu Lancaster, welcher auf eine
außerordentliche Weise nach Gottes all-
weiser Zulassung durch einen Büchsen-
Schuß aus dem Zeitlichen in das ewige
Leben den 14. Oktober 1748 im 27ten
Jahr seines Alters hingerückt wurde.
Zum Trost der getrübten Gemeinde in
Lancaster zu dem Druck befördert und mit
einer Zeitschrift versehen von Michael
Slatter, V. D. M. zu St. Gallen in der
Schweitz, gegenwärtig Reform. Prediger
in Philadelphia und Germantown in
Pennsylvanien. Philadelphia, Pa.: Johann Böhm 1748. 15 S.* [6734
Hochstetler, Harvey: Descendants of Jacob
Hochstetler, the immigrant of 1736. *Hi-
storical introduction by William F.
Hochstetler. An appendix of some fa-
milies closely connected by marriage and
some of similar names. Elgin, Ill.: Brethren Publishing House. 1912. pp. 1191,
ill.* [6735
P.[arthemore, E. W. S.]: Jacob Reider Hof-
fer. *In: Notes and Queries. Edited by
W. H. Egle. Fourth series, vol. I. 1891—
1893. Harrisburg, Pa. 1893. p. 158.*

*[b. in Conewago Twp., Dauphin Co.,
Pa., d. April 15, 1892.]* [6736
Hoffman, Laban Miles: Our kin being a hi-
story of the Hoffman, Rhyne, Costner,
Rudisill, Best, Hovis, Hoyle, Wilis,
Shetley, Jenkins, Holland, Hambright,
Gaston, Withers, Cansler, Clemmer and
Lineberger families. *Published by
Daniel E. Rhyne, Laban L. Jenkins and
L. M. Hoffman. Charlotte, N. C.: Press
of Queen City Printing Co. 1915. pp.
585, ill.* [6737
[Egle, William Henry]: Hoffman family, of
Lykens Valley. *In: Notes and Queries.
Edited by W. H. Egle. First and second
series, vol. I. Harrisburg, Pa. 1894. pp.
211—215.*
*[Descendants of John Peter Hoffman,
a native of Germany, b. in 1709, who lan-
ded at Philadelphia, Pa. in 1739.]* [6738
„Ursula Hoffman and her descendants.“
*In: The genealogical record of the
Schwenkfelder families. Edited by S. K.
Brecht. New York, N. Y. — Chicago, Ill.
1923. pp. 1179—1184.* [6739
Berlin, Alfred Franklin: Walter Jacob
Hoffman. *In: Proceedings and Papers
read before the Lehigh County Historical
Society. Allentown, Pa. 1921. pp. 30—
36.*
*[b. in Weidasville, Lowhill Twp.,
Lehigh Co., 1846.]* [6740
— Walter Jacob Hoffman, M. D., *physi-
cian, explorer and scientist. In: The
Pennsylvania-German. Vol. VIII. Le-
banon, Pa. 1907. pp. 583—585, ill.*
[6741
Hoffmeister-Weitzel. *In: Notes and Queries.
Edited by W. H. Egle. Annual vol. 1897.
Harrisburg, Pa. 1898. p. 165.*
*[Gottlieb Hoffmeister b. in Germany, d.
in Tennessee. m. June 12, 1781 in
Greenbrier Co. Va. Sarah Landerback,
b. in Va., d. in Tenn.]* [6742
Ashe, S. A.: Robert Frederick Hoke *(Con-
federate General). In: Biographical hi-
story of North Corolina. Edited by S. A.
Ashe. Vol. I. Greensboro, N. C. 1905.
pp. 309—321, ill.*
*[native of Lincolntown, N. C., b.
May 27, 1837; descendants of William
Hoke, a Lutheran minister of Alsace or
Lorraine and settler of York Co., Pa.]*
[6743
Welles, Edward: Sketch of Col. Matthias
Hollenback. *In: The Pennsylvania-
German. Vol. X. Lititz, Pa. 1909. pp.
53—57; 97—103, ill.*

[b. 1752 in Lebanon Twp., Lancaster (now Lebanon) Co., second in descent from Georg Hollenbach, who came from the Rhine provinces about 1717.] [6744

Welles, Edward: Falkner-Swamp. Early wills and inventories of the **Hollenbach** family. *In: The Pennsylvania-German. Vol. XII. Lititz, Pa. 1911. pp. 677—683.* [6745

Mast, C. Z.: The **Hooley** family. *In: Christian Monitor. A monthly magazine for the home. Vol. XIV, no. 11. Scottdale, Pa. 1922. pp. 721—722.*
[whose ancestors supposed to have come from Berne Canton.] [6746

H., S. P.: In memoriam. Georg Henry **Horst.** *In: Papers read before the Lebanon County Historical Society. Vol. VI. Lebanon, Pa. 1912—1916. pp. 315—317, ill.*
[Son of Henry and Sarah (Landis) Horst at Annville.] [6747

Ayres, George B.: The **Horter** family. *In: Notes and Queries. Edited by W. H. Egle. First series, part II. Harrisburg, Pa. 1881. pp. 2—3. Reprint in: First and second series, vol. I. Harrisburg, Pa. 1894. pp. 347—349.*
[believed to have emigrated from the City of Speyer, Germany.] [6748

Hostetler, C. K.: The **Hostetler** Indian story. *In: Christian Monitor. A monthly magazine for the home. Vol. XIV. Scottdale, Pa. 1922. No. 2. pp. 433—435.* [6749

Hostetter wills. *From original records. In: Genealogy. A monthly magazine of American ancestry. Vol. VII. Hackensack, N. J. 1917. pp. 81—82.* [6750

Drury, Marion R.: The life and career of James William **Hott** [Heiss] D. D., LL. D. Late bishop of the United Brethren in Christ. *With an introduction by* Lewis Bookwalter. *Dayton, O.: United Brethren Publishing House 1902. pp. XIX, 21—214, ill.* [6751

Huddle, W. D. - Huddle, Lulu May: History of the descendants of John **Hottel** (Immigrant from Switzerland to America) and an authentic genealogical family register of ten generations from the first of the name in America, 1732 to the present time, 1929, *with numerous brief biographical sketches, collected and compiled from many indisputable sources: Court and church records, old and late family records and tombstones of the many states in the Union. Strasburg, Va.: Shenandoah Publishing House, Inc. 1930. pp. XVI, 1183. ill.* [6752

Hottenstein. *In: Notes and Queries. Edited by W. H. Egle. Annual vol. 1899. Harrisburg, Pa. 1900. p. 219.*
[Jacob Hottenstein was b. Febr. 15, 1697, in Eslingen, Germany.] [6753

H., S. P.: In memoriam: Alfred Rhodes **Houck.** *In: Papers read before the Lebanon County Historical Society. Vol. VI. Lebanon, Pa. 1912—1916. pp. 325—327, ill.*
[Son of Henry and Susan Margaret (Bucher) Houck.] [6754

In memoriam. Henry **Houck.** Pennsylvania's beloved educator 1836—1917. *Biographical sketch. Loving tributes by educational co-workers: Governor* Martin G. Brumbaugh, O. T. Corson, Nathan C. Schaeffer. *Delivered at meeting of the State Teachers' Association at Johnstown, Pa., Dec. 28, 1917. Published under the direction of the Department of Public Instruction of the State of Pennsylvania. 1917. pp. 5—38.*
[b. at Palmyra, Lebanon Co., Pa., March 6, 1836, son of Samuel Houck and Rosanna Joutz.] [6755

H., S. P.: In memoriam: Henry **Houck,** Litt. D. *In: Papers read before the Lebanon County Historical Society. Vol. VII. 1916—1919. Lebanon, Pa. pp. 179—182, ill.*
[Son of Samuel Houck and Rosanna Joutz.] [6756

Houser, W. W. and others: Genealogy of the **Houser,** Rhorer, Dillman, Hoover families. *Compiled by . . . Blomington, Ill.: Pantagraph and Stationery Co. 1910. pp. 239, ill.*
[Descendants of Abraham Houser, b. near the Town of Wondenberg, Germany 1740.] [6757

[Egle, William Henry]: Daniel **Houser.** — *Biographical note. In: Notes and Queries. Edited by W. H. Egle. Third series, vol. I. 1884—1887. Harrisburg, Pa. 1887. p. 213. Reprint in: Third series, vol. I. Harrisburg, Pa. 1895. p. 413.* [6758

Diffenderffer, F. R.: Notes on Colonel **Houssacker.** *In: Papers and Addresses of the Lancaster County Historical Society Vol. X. Lancaster, Pa. 1906. pp. 304—309.* [6759

Randolph, Howard S. F.: The **Howser** [Hauser] family. *In: The New York Genealogical and Biographical Record. Vol. LX. New York, N. Y. 1929. pp. 79—91; 172—184.*
[Jacob Hauser or Howser, progenitor of the branch of the Howser family here

*traced, b. in the ,,Tudlinger District" of
Wurttemberg, Germany about 1721; m.
at the Lutheran Church, New York City,
March 1, 1752, to Elizabeth Bender (Binder), daughter of Christoph Bender, of
Wurttemberg.]*   [6760
Denig, John: Autobiography of the Rev.
Samuel **Huber,** elder in the Church of
the United Brethren in Christ; *containing sketches of his life and religious
experience, illustrated with deeply interesting and affecting facts and incidents,
showing forth the work of God in the conversion of souls &c., &c. Edited by . . .
Chambersberg, Pa.: M. Kiefer & Co.
1858. pp. VIII, 9—254.*   [6761
Egle, William Henry: Hoover: — Jacob
Hoover. *In: Notes and Queries. Edited
by W.H.Egle. Third series, vol. I. 1884
—1887. Harrisburg, Pa. 1887. p. 152.
Reprint in: Third series, vol. I. Harris-
burg, Pa. 1895. pp. 258—259.*   [6762
Hon. Hiram Conrad **Hoover.** 1822—1911.
*In: Historical Sketches. A Collection of
Papers prepared for the Historical Society
of Montgomery County, Pa. Vol. IV.
Norristown, Pa. 1910. pp. 1—4.
[Descendant of Jacob Huber, who emi-
grated from the Palatinate in 1751.]* [6763
Huber family graveyard, *(at Swatara sta-
tion, in Derry Township, Dauphin Co.).
In: Notes and Queries. Edited by W. H.
Egle. Third series, vol. I. 1884—1887.
Harrisburg, Pa. 1887. p. 65. Reprint
in: Third series, vol. I. Harrisburg, Pa.
1895. pp. 108—109.*   [6764
Clarke, Grace Julian: Andrew **Hoover** comes
to Indiana. *In: The Indian Magazine
of History. Vol. XXIV. Indianopolis,
Ind. 1928. pp. 223—241.*   [6765
Hoover, Harry M.: The **Huber-Hoover** fa-
mily history. *A biographical and genea-
logical history of the descendants of Hans
Huber from the time of his arrival in
Pennsylvania down to the 11th generation.
Scottdale, Pa.: Mennonite Publishing
House 1928. pp. 335, ill.*   [6766
The **Hoover** ancestry. *In: Genealogy. A
journal of American ancestry. Vol. X,
no. 7. Pompton Lakes, N. J. 1922. pp.
72—73.*   [6767
B.[rumbaugh], G.M.: Huber-Hoover records.
*In: The National Genealogical Society
Quarterly. Vol. XV, no. 1. Washington,
D. C. 1927. pp. 2—4.*   [6768
Kephart, Calvin: Hoover American ancestry.
*In: The National Genealogical Quarterly.
Vol. XVII, no. 1. Washington, D. C.*

*1929. pp. 6—8; no. 2. pp. 19—24; no. 4.
pp. 53—56.*   [6769
Staudt, Richard W.: Origin of the **Hoover**
families. *The story of a research in the
Palatinate. In: The National Genealogical Society Quarterly. Vol. XVII,
no. 1. Washington, D. C. 1929. pp. 1—6.*
                                        [6770
Macco, H. F.: Die angebliche Abstammung
des amerikanischen Präsidenten **Hoover**
aus Baden-Baden. *In: Der deutsche
Herold. Zeitschrift für Wappen-, Siegel-
und Familienkunde. Herausgegeben vom
Verein Herold in Berlin. Bd. LX. Berlin 1929. S. 55—56.*   [6771
— Die deutsche Abstammung des Präsi-
denten der Vereinigten Staaten Herbert
Hoover. *In: Der deutsche Herold. Zeit-
schrift für Wappen-, Siegel- und Fami-
lienkunde. Herausgegeben vom Verein
Herold in Berlin. Bd. LXI. Berlin
1930. S. 12—15; 27—30, ill.*   [6772
— Wahrheit und Dichtung in der Hoover-
forschung. *In: Der deutsche Herold.
Zeitschrift für Wappen-, Siegel- und
Familienkunde. Bd. LXI. Berlin 1930.
S. 43—44.*   [6773
— Tracing the genealogy of President
Herbert **Hoover.** *In: Passing through
Germany. Seventh edition 1930. Berlin:
Terramare Office 1930. pp. 60—67, ill.
[Descendants of Andreas Huber, b. in
Ellerstadt, Rheinpfalz, Jan. 29, 1723 and
emigrated to Pennsylvania 1740.]*   [6774
Staudt, R. W.: *The Huber-Hoover family
of Aesch, Switzerland and Trippstadt,
Palatinate, with some accent on migration
to Pennsylvania. Philadelphia, Pa. 1935.
21 S.*   [6774a
The **Hubleys** of Lancaster County. *In: Hi-
storical Register: Notes and Queries, hi-
storical and genealogical relating to
interior Pennsylvania for the year 1883.
Vol. I. Harrisburg, Pa. 1883. pp. 75—
76.*   [6775
P., A. C.: The **Hubley's** of Lancaster. *In:
Notes and Queries. Edited by W. H.
Egle. Annual vol. 1898. Harrisburg,
Pa. 1899. 1—3.*   [6776
[Meginness, John F.]: The **Hubley** family.
*Origin of the surname — Early strugg-
les — Captain Bernard* **Hubley.** *By
John of Lancaster. In: Notes and Queries.
[of Huguenot ancestry. Bernard, the
paternal ancestor of the Hubley family
in America fled to Switzerland and later
to Germany, from where he emigrated to*

Pennsylvania, landing at Philadelphia, 1732.] [6777

[Meginness, John F.]: Captain Bernard Hubley. By John of Lancaster. In: Notes and Queries. Edited by W. H. Egle. Annual vol. 1897. Harrisburg, Pa. 1898. pp. 13—14. [6778

Melchior Hübner (Heebner) and his descendants. In: The genealogical record of the Schwenkfelder families. Edited by S. K. Brecht. New York, N. Y.-Chicago, Ill. 1923. pp. 219—225. [6779

David Hübner (Heebner) and his descendants. In: The genealogical record of the Schwenkfelder families. Edited by S. K. Brecht. New York, N. Y.-Chicago, Ill. 1923. pp. 269—342. [6780

Hans Hübner (John Heebner) and his descendants. In: The genealogical record of the Schwenkfelder families. Edited by S. K. Brecht. New York, N. Y.-Chicago, Ill. 1923. pp. 1002—1149. [6781

Christopher Hübner (Heebner) and his descendants. In: The genealogical record of the Schwenkfelder families. Edited by S. K. Brecht. New York, N. Y.-Chicago, Ill. 1923. pp. 1557—1561. [6782

Hoffert, Franklin Pierce: The Huffard family history. 1729—1909. Compiled and published by . . . Indianopolis, Ind. 1909. pp. 265, (2), ill.
[Descendants of Christian Hoffart, who came from Schwartzenau, Germany to America and located at Germantown, Pa. 1729.] [6783

Henry, James: Memoir of Christian Gottlieb Hüffel, Episcopus Fratrum. In: Transactions of the Moravian Historical Society. Vol. IV. Nazareth, Pa. 1895. pp. 33—38. [6784

Huffmaster, James F.: Huffmaster - Hoffmeister family records. Galveston, Texas: Oscar Springer 1922. pp. (44)f., ill.
[Descendants of Gottlieb Hoffmeister, b. about 1757 in the vicinity of Frankfurt a. M., arrived in America about 1776 and settled in Shenandoah Co., Va.] [6785

Hummel, Levi: Notes on the Hummel family. In: The Penn Germania. Vol. II. = Old series, vol. XIV. Lititz, Pa. 1913. pp. 147—149. [6786

David Hummel. — Biographical note. In: Notes and Queries. Edited by W. H. Egle.

Third series, vol. I. 1884—1887. Harrisburg, Pa. 1887. p. 213.
Reprint in: Third series, vol. I. Harrisburg, Pa. 1895. p. 413. [6787

Major Frederick Hummel. In: Notes and Queries. Edited by W. H. Egle. Third series, vol. I. 1884—1887. Harrisburg, Pa. 1887. p. 63. Reprint in: Third series, vol. I. Harrisburg, Pa. 1895. p. 106.
[b. in Derry Twp., now Dauphin Co., Pa. Oct., 4, 1758; son of the first settler of that name.[[6788

Humrickhouse. — In: Notes and Queries. Edited by W. H. Egle. Annual vol. 1898. Harrisburg, Pa. 1899. p. 79.
[Peter Humrickhouse, b. in York Co., Pa., Oct. 10, 1753; m. Mary Post, the only daughter of Rev. Christian Frederick Post.] [6789

Humrichhouse, Harry H.: Rev. Christian Post and Peter Humrickhouse and some of the latter's family. [s. l.] 1913. pp. (1), 7—51. [6790

Hunsberger, Byron K.: The Hunsbergers. Compiled by . . . Part I. Switzerland. 1925. pp. 32; Part. II. The descendants of 31 Christian Hunsberger. Published by the Huntsberger-Hunsberger Family Association. 1926. pp. 115. [6791

Hunsicker. — Records on the fly-leaves of a copy of Saur's Bible. In: The Pennsylvania Magazine of History and Biography. Vol. XVI. Philadelphia, Pa. 1892. pp. 247—248. [6792

Hunsicker, Henry A.: A genealogical history of the Hunsicker family. By Henry A. Hunsicker, assisted by Horace M. Hunsicker. Printed for private circulation. Philadelphia, Pa.: J. B. Lippincott Co. 1911. pp. 358, ill.
[confined „to the compilation of the names belonging to the fifth branch of Henry Hunsicker (second generation), youngest son of the progenitor Valentine Hunsicker (first generation); Valentine Hunsicker, b. in the Canton Zurich, Switzerland, 1700, came with his maternal grandfather, Valentine Klemmer to America in 1717. d. March 30, 1771."] [6793

P.[arthemore], E. W. S.: A York County private graveyard. (Hursh's graveyard, near Oak Grove Schoolhouse, in York County hills, S. of Harrisburg.) In: Notes and Queries. Edited by W. H. Egle. Annual vol. 1896. Harrisburg, Pa. 1897. pp. 119—120. [6794

520   Familiengeschichte und Biographien

I.

Betz, I. H.: An interview with Lawrence
J. Ibach, the amateur astronomer. *In:*
The Pennsylvania-German. Vol. XII.
Lititz, Pa. 1911. pp. 202—205.   [6795
Rattermann, H. A.: Lorenz Ibach. Der
Hufschmied und Astronom. *In: H. A.*
Rattermann. Gesammelte Werke. Bd. X.
Cincinnati, O.: Selbstverlag des Verfassers
1911. S. 225—226.   [6795a
Famous Pennsylvania-Germans. General
John D. Imboden. *A relic of the late war*
and prominent citizen of Virginia. In:
The Pennsylvania-German. Vol. V.
Lebanon, Pa. 1904. pp. 3—7, ill.
  [b. Febr. 16, 1823, 6 miles S. E. of
Staunton, son of George and Isabella Im-
boden of Washinton Co., Va.]. · [6796

J.

H., A. R.: Das Leben und Wirken von
Vater Josua **Jäger** [Yeager], Evangelisch
Lutherischem Prediger; wie auch ein
Verzeichnis seiner Amtsgeschäfte. *Al-*
lentown, Pa.: Published at the Office
of the National Educator. 1889. 229 S.,
ill. Deutsch und Englisch.
  [Sohn des Rev. Johann Conrad Yeager
von York Co., Pa.; geb. 23. Sept. 1802.]
     [6797
Balthsar **Jäckel** (Balzer Yeakel) and his
descendants. *In: The genealogical re-*
cord of the Schwenkfelder families. Edited
by S. K. Brecht. New York, N. Y.-Chi-
cago, Ill. 1923. p. 344.   [6798
David **Jäckel** (Yeakel) and his descendants. *In: The genealogical record of*
the Schwenkfelder families. Edited by
S. K. Brecht. New York, N. Y.-Chicago,
Ill. 1923. pp. 465—564.   [6799
Matthias **Jäckel** (Yeakel) and his descendants. *In: The genealogical record of*
the Schwenkfelder families. Edited by
S. K. Brecht. New York, N. Y.-Chicago,
Ill. 1923. p. 886.   [6800
Regina (Hübner) **Jäckel** (Yeakel) and her
descendants. *In: The genealogical re-*
cord of the Schwenkfelder families. Edi-
ted by S. K. Brecht. New York, N. Y.-
Chicago, Ill. 1923. pp. 1257—1278.
     [6801
Abraham **Jäckel** (Yeakel) and his descen-
dants. *In: The genealogical record of*
the Schwenkfelder families. Edited by
S. K. Brecht. New York, N. Y.-Chicago,
Ill. 1923. pp. 1571—1577.   [6802

Genealogy of **Jacobs** family. *In: Papers and*
Addresses of the Lancaster County Hi-
storical Society. Vol. XII. Lancaster,
Pa. 1908. pp. 52—53.   [6803
In memoriam. Henry Eyster **Jacobs.** *In:*
Church History. Published by the Ame-
rican Society of Church History. Vol. I,
no. 3. Chicago, Ill. — Scottdale, Pa. 1932.
p. 163.   [6804
Henry Sylvester **Jacoby.** *In: The Pennsyl-*
vania-German. Vol. IX. Cleona, Pa.
1908. pp. 222—223, ill.
  [b. April 8, 1857 in Springtown Town-
ship, Bucks Co., Pa., son of Peter L. and
Barbara Jacoby, both of German descent.]
     [6805
Lorentz **Jacoby**, powder-maker. *In: The*
Perkiomen Region, Past and Present.
Vol. I. Philadelphia, Pa. 1985. pp.
109—110.
  [a native of Germany, who established
his business at Sumneytown, Montgomery
Co., Pa. in 1780.]   [6806
Jacoby, Henry Sylvester: The **Jacoby** family genealogy. A record of the descendants of the pioneer Peter Jacoby
of Bucks Co., Pa. *Lancaster, pa.: For*
the Committee on Publication by Lan-
caster Press. 1930. pp. XIII, 667. [6807
Clark, Olynthus: Joseph **Joder,** schoolmaster, farmer and poet. 1797—1887.
In: Transactions of the Illinois State
Historical Society for the year 1929.
Springfield, Ill. 1929. = Publication no.
36 of the Illinois State Historical Library.
pp. 135—165.   [6808
Caspar **John.** *In: The genealogical re-*
cord of the Schwenkfelder families. Edited
by S. K. Brecht. New York, N. Y.-Chi-
cago, Ill. 1923. p. 1002.   [6809
[Cassel, Abraham]: **Johnson** genealogy (Pa.)
and reminiscences. *In: The National*
Genealogical Society Quarterly. Vol. XVI.
no. 1. Washington, D. C. 1928. pp. 14—15.
  [Mathias Jantz, or Johnson emigrated
to America about 1730, or perhaps earlier,
and settled on a farm in Franconia Twp.
Montgomery County, Pa.]   [6810
Addresses and proceedings of the Historical Society of Pennsylvania, on the
death of John **Jordan,** jr., a vice-president of the society, *held April 28,*
1890. Philadelphia, Pa.: J. B. Lippin-
cott Co. 1890. pp. V—XL.
  [b. in Philadelphia, May 18, 1808,
son of John and Elizabeth (Henry) Jor-
dan; of German ancestry on his paternal
side.]   [6811

[Jungmann, Johann George]: Ein Manuscript aus dem vorigen Jahrhundert. Lebenslauf des Johann George Jungmann in Bethlehem. *(Von ihm selbst eigenhändig niedergeschrieben.) In: Der Deutsche Pionier. Jg. I. Cincinnati, O. 1869—1870. S. 230—237.*
[geb. in Hockenheim, Pfalz, Deutsches Reich, 19. April, 1720.] [6812

K.

Keagy, Franklin: A history of the Kägy relationship in Amerika, from 1715 to 1900. *Harrisburg, Pa.: Harrisburg Publishing Co. 1899. pp. 675, ill.* [6813
Wayland, John W.: One of the John Brown's men. *[John Henry Kagi.] In: The Pennsylvania-German. Vol. X. Lititz, Pa. 1909. pp. 484—494, ill.*
[b. at Bristolville, Trumbull Co., O., March 15, 1835, son of Abraham Nelf Kagey of Shenandoah Co., Va. and Anna Fansler, both of Pennsylvania-German descent.] [6814
Hartzler, R. Z.: Kaltglesser - Hartzler. *In: Notes and Queries. Edited by W. H. Egle. Annual vol. 1899. Harrisburg, Pa. 1900. p. 102.*
[Jacob Kalckglaesser emigrated from the Palatinate, Germany to Pa. in 1729.] [6815
Hillpot, Joseph: Kamerer. *(A record from the old family bible in possession of Joseph Kamerer, of Sugar Valley, Lycoming Co., Pa.) Translated by . . . In: Notes and Queries. Edited by W. H. Egle. Second series. Harrisburg, Pa. 1883. p. 284. Reprint in: First and second series, vol. II. Harrisburg, Pa. 1895. pp. 397 —398.*
[Christian Kamerer, b. Sept. 9. 1734; d. Sept. 26, 1804.] [6816
Hostetler, Pius: Life, preaching, labors of John D. Kauffman. *A short sketch of the life, preaching and labors of John D. Kauffman. Shelbyville, Ill.: Published by Pius Hostetler 1915. pp. 36.* [6817
Keck, John Melvin: The Keck family, with special reference to the descendants of Michael Keck who came to Ohio in 1806. *Compiled and edited by . . . pp. 71. Addenda pp. (4).* [6818
Goodwin, John S.: The Keeley family. *In: Notes and Queries. Edited by W. H. Egle. Annual vol. 1897. Harrisburg, Pa. 1898. pp. 181—184; 191—194.*

[Valtin Kuhle, Jonas Kohleer and Michael Kohler were among the „Foreigners" imported in the ship Mortonhouse, Aug. 24, 1728.] [6819
H., S. P.: In memoriam: Isaac Kegerreis. *In: Papers read before the Lebanon County Historical Society. Vol. VII. Lebanon, Pa. 1916—1919. pp. 337—338, ill.*
[son of Christian and Catherine (Kurtz) Kegerreis.] [6820
Keim, De B. Randolph: The Keim and allied families in America and Europe. 1698—1898. *A Bi-Centennial commemoration. A monthly serial of history, biography, genealogy and folklore, illustrating the causes, circumstances and consequences of the German, French and Swiss emigrations to America during the 17th, 18th and 19th centuries. Editor . . . Vol. I., no. 1—12. Published by the editor for subscribers only. Harrisburg, Pa.: Publishing Co. 1899. pp. 382; Vol. II, nos. 1—23. Harrisburg, Pa. 1899 —1900. pp. 385—736.* [6821
— The Keim lineage. *In: Notes and Queries. Edited by W. H. Egle. Annual vol. 1898. Harrisburg, Pa. 1899. pp. 212—213.*
[Johannes Keim, m. 1706; he settled on the Manatawny Creek, Oley Twp., Berks Co.] [6822
Keim, Henry May: Account of the Keim family. *Reading, Pa.: Printed privately 1874. pp. 26.*
[Descendants of John Keim, who settled about 1704 in Oley Twp., Berks Co., Pa.] [6823
Steinmetz, C. M.: Inscriptions Keim private burying ground, Berks County, Pa. *Copied by . . . In: The National Genealogical Society Quarterly. Vol. XV, no. 3. Washington, D. C. 1927. pp. 33—34;* Inscriptions. Second Keim private burying ground, Berks County, Pa. *p. 34.* [6824
K.[eim], De B. Randolph: Gen. George M. Keim. *In: Notes and Queries. Edited by W. H. Egle. Annual vol. 1898. Harrisburg, Pa. 1899. pp. 143—145.*
[b. in Reading, March 23d, 1805.] [6825
Hiester, Isaac: In memoriam. Henry May Keim. *Paper submittet to the society, April 11, 1899. In: Transactions of the Historical Society of Berks County. Vol. I. Reading, Pa. 1904. pp. (2), ill.*
[b. in Reading, Aug. 16, 1842.] [6826

A historical sketch of Michael **Keinadt** and Margaret Diller, his wife. The history and genealogy of their numerous posterity in the American States, up to the year 1893. *Prepared by a Committee appointed for that purpose by the ,,Michael Koiner Memorial Association.'' organized March 28th, 1892, at Staunton, Va.: Stoneburner & Prufer 1893. pp. . . .*

[b. Jan. 29, 1720 at Winterlingen, Wurttemburg, Germany, son of Conrad Keinadt; settled in Lancaster Co., Pa. and m. at New Holland Margaret Diller, daugther of Caspar Diller, Febr. 21. 1749.]   [6827

„Klam, Alma": Michael Keinadt and some of his descendants. *In: The .Pennsylvania-German. Vol. X. Lititz, Pa. 1909. pp. 618—622.*   [6828

,,Old Michael" *[John Michael **Keinzle**.]* Interesting reminiscence of the old sexton and high constable who rang the curfew bell and terrorized Wilkes Barre boys half a century ago. *Reprint from Wilkes-Barre Telephone. In: The Historical Record. A quaterly publication devoted principally to the early history of Wyoming Valley . . . Vol. I. Wilkes Barre, Pa. 1897. pp. 173—174.*

[came from Switzerland about the year 1802, and was elected high constable of Wilkes-Barre in 1806 and held the office until his death in 1846.]   [6829

Kelker, Rudolph F. Keller: Genealogisches Verzeichnis der Familie **Kölliker** von Herrliberg, Bezirk Meilen, Kanton Zürich, in der Schweiz, *abgefaßt im Sommer 1849 durch* **John Jacob Hess,** *Ev. Reform. Pfarrer daselbst [Translation of the above].* Genealogical record of the family of **Koelliker** of Herrliburg, District Meilen, Canton Zürich, Switzerland, *completed in the summer of 1849 by* **John Jacob Hess.** *To the above now, (1883),* added a record of the family of **Kelker,** since their arrival in this country, in 1743, *compiled from authentic sources, for the use of the members of the family. Harrisburg, Pa.: Lane & Hart 1883. pp. 132, (2).*   [6830

Keller, David Henry: The **Kellers** of Hamilton Township. *A study in democracy. Alexandria, La.: The Wall Printing Co. 1922. pp. VII, 134, ill., maps.*

[Descendants of Christopher Keller, who emigrated from Germany and settled in Hamilton in 1749.]   [6831

Mathews, Edward: Keller family history. *In: A Collection of Papers read before the Bucks County Historical Society. Vol. III. Easton, Pa. 1909. pp. 307 —316.*

[Descendants of Henry or Heinrich Keller, who arrived in Philadelphia 1738.]   [6832

Shumaker, E. S., Keller, Amos and **Jones, Zarel (Lulie):** Descendants of Henry **Keller** of York €ounty, Pa. and Fairfield County, Ohio. *Indianopolis, Ind.: Published by E. S. Shumaker 1924. pp. 594, ill.*

[b. May 13, 1755 on the family homestead east of York, Pa.]   [6833

Stapleton, A.: Some **Keller** family history. *In: Notes and Queries. Edited by W. E. Egle. Annual vol. 1897. Harrisburg, Pa. 1898. pp. 125—126.*

[Descendants of Jacob Keller of Nitsche, on the Rhine, in Hesse Darmstadt, whose son Christopher Keller came to America 1764.]   [6834

Diehl, M.: Biography of Rev. Ezra **Keller,** D. D., founder and first president of Wittenberg College. *With an introduction by S. Sprecher. Springfield, O.: Ruralist Publishing Co. 1859. pp. XXVI, 27—382, ill.*

[b. near Middletown, Frederick Co., Md., May 12, 1812, grandson of Jacob Keller, the German immigrant.]   [6835

Keller, Eli: History of the **Keller** family. *Tiffin, O.: Press of Will. H. Good 1905. pp. 192, ill.*

[Descendants of Joseph Keller, b. March 15, 1719, in Schwarzenacker, near the City of Zweibrücken, emigrated to Pa., landing at Philadelphia, Oct. 31, 1737.]   [6836

Egle, William Henry: Keller of Lancaster.'' *In: Egle's ,,Pennsylvania genealogies.'' Harrisburg, Pa. 1896. pp. 341—349.*

[Descendant of Johann Peter Keller, a native of Germany, emigrated to America prior to 1760.]   [6837

Keller family burials. *In: Genealogy. Journal of American ancestry. Vol. IV. New York, N. Y. 1914. p. 4.*   [6838

[Backenstove, William A.]: Two centuries of **Kemmerer** family history. 1730 —1929. *Compiled by the Kemmerer Family Association. Incorporated in 1902. Allentown, Pa.: Searle & Bachman Co. 1929. pp. 152, ill.*   [6839

Kemper, Willis Miller and **Wright, Harry Linn:** Genealogy of the **Kemper** family in the United States. *Descendants of John Kemper of Virginia with a short historical sketch of his family and of the German Reformed colony at Germanna and Germantown, Va. Chicago, Ill.: Geo. K. Hazlitt & Co. 1899. pp. 248, XIX.* [6840

The **Kemps** of Maryland. *In: Genealogy. Journal of American ancestry. Vol. III. New York, N. Y. 1913. p. 33.* [6841

Egle, William Henry: Kendig of Swatara. *In: Egle's „Pennsylvania genealogies." Harrisburg, Pa. 1896 [= no. 6045]. pp. 350—356.*
[Descendants of Martin Kendig, one of the earliest Swiss settlers of Lancaster Co., Pa.] [6842

John, Lewis Franklin: The life of Ezekiel Boring **Kephart**, statesman, educator, preacher and for 25 years bishop of the Church of the United Brethren in Christ. *Dayton, O.: Press of the United Brethren Publishing House 1907. pp. 417, ill.* [6843

Kephart, C. J. and Funk, W. R.: Life of Isaiah L. Kephart. . . . *1909. pp. . . .* [6843a

Kephart, Calvin Ira: John Kephart [1751—1822], minister of the Doylestown Mennonite congregation 1806—1822. A brief biography. *In: The Mennonite Quarterly Review. Vol. II. Goshen, Ind. 1928. pp. 119—122.* [6844

Mickley, Minnie F.: Our ancestors. The **Kern** family of America. *In: The National Geneological Society Quarterly. Vol. I., no. 1. Washington, D. C. 1912. pp. (4—6).*
[The first member of the Kern family of Whitehall Township, Northampton Co., now Lehigh Co., Pa. arrived in Philadelphia, Pa., in 1727, bearing the name Nicholas Kern (supposed to have come from Holland?).] [6845

Kephart, I. L.: Biography of Rev. Jacob Smith **Kessler**, of the Church of the United Brethren in Christ. *Compiled from his autobiography. With a sermon by the compiler. Published by the Publishing Committee of the East Pennsylvania Conference, of the Church of the United Brethren in Christ. Dayton, O.: W. J. Shuey 1867. pp. 246.* [6846

Hunt, John E.: The **Kester** ancestry and William Kester and family. *In: The Pound and Kester families containing an account of the ancestry of John Pound (born in 1735) and William Kester*

(born in 1733) and a genealogical record of all their descendants and other family historical matter. First edition. Chicago, Ill.: Regan Printing House 1904. pp. 303—583.
[Paul Küster and his wife Gertrude, and three sons, Arnold, Johannes and Hermans Küster, immigrated to America probably about 1685. They came from Crefeld, Germany.] [6847

John **Keylor**, of Colerain. *In: Notes and Queries. Edited by W. H. Egle. Annual vol. 1897. Harrisburg, Pa. 1898. p. 96.*
[Son of Jacob Keylor [Keuhler] of Raumland, on the Rhine, Germany, who emigrated to America in 1795.] [6848

Keyser, Charles S.: The **Keyser** family, descendants of Dirck Keyser of Amsterdam. *Compiled by . . . Philadelphia, Pa.: Press of Wm. Fell & Co. 1889. pp. 161, ill. = The Bi-Centennial reunion of the Keyser family in the old Mennonite meeting-house, Germantown, Pa., Oct. 10, 1888.* [6849

Keyser, Naaman H.: Charles Shearer **Keyser**. *A Penn-German whose influence for good still survives one of the founders of Fairmount Park, Philadelphia. In: The Pennsylvania-German. Vol. X. Lititz, Pa. 1909. pp. 77—78, ill* [6850

Kilmer, C. H.: History of the **Kilmer** family in America. *Compiled and edited by . . . Elmira, N. Y.: Advertiser Association 1897. pp. 214, ill.*
[Descendants of Philip Kelmer (Külmer) who came from Hesse-Cassel Germany to America and was among the Palatinates at the „Camp" what is now Germantown, N. Y.] [6851

[Stein, T. S., Lantz, C. R. and Grittinger, H. C.]: Hon. John H. **Kinports**. *In: Papers read before the Lebanon County Historical Society. Vol. VI. Lebanon, Pa. 1912—1916. pp. 249—252, ill.* [6852

Kistler, Charles E.: Hanjoerg **Kistler** and his descendants. *In: The Pennsylvania-German. Vol. VII. Lebanon, Pa. 1906. pp. 124—131, ill.*
[Johannes Kistler, a native of the Palatinate, Germany, came to Pennsylvania in 1737.] [6853

Kistler, John: Hanjoerg **Kistler** and his descendants. *In: The Pennsylvania-German. Vol. IX. Cleona, Pa. 1908. pp. 173—175.* [6854

Kitzmiller. *In: Notes and Queries. Edited by W. H. Egle. Annual vol. 1900. Harrisburg, Pa. 1901. pp. 198—199.*

[Descendants of Johannes Kitzmiller of Bethel Twp., Lancaster Co., Pa., d. prior to 1747.]   [6855

Kleppinger, Stanley J.: Kleppinger-Clippinger family history. *Bethlehem, Pa.: Bethlehem Printing Co. 1928. pp. (3), 7—209, ill.*

[Descendants of Johan Georg Kleppinger, b. Jan. 25, 1707, in the Palatinate, Germany, arrived at Philadelphia, Pa. 1737.]   [6856

Funk, Benjamin: Life and labors of Elder John Kline, the martyr missionary. *Collated from his diary. Elgin, Ill.: Brethren Publishing House 1900. pp. VIII, 9—480, ill.*   [6857

Martindale, Thos.: Mahlon N. Kline. *A brief record of a noted man. In: The Pennsylvania-German. Vol. XI. Lititz, Pa. 1910. pp. 220—222.*

[b. Febr. 6, 1846, near Hamburg, Berks Co., Pa.]   [6858

Kling, Margaret E.: Genealogical history of John Ludwig Kling and his descendants 1755—1924. *[s. l.] 1924. pp. 145.*

[Descendant of Henreck Kling, came from Hanover; landed at Philadelphia 1755 and made the journey on foot to the Palatine settlement of Stone Arabia, N. Y., 1757.]   [6859

Klinger. *In: Notes and Queries. Edited by W. H. Egle. Annual vol. 1899. Harrisburg. Pa. 1900. p. 53.*

[John Philip Klinger was b. July 11, 1723, in Poffenbeerfurt, Odenwald, Germany. He came to America and settled near Reading. Later on, he removed to Lykens Twp., Dauphin Co., near Klinger's Church, where he d. Sept. 30, 1811.]   [6860

Häberle, D.: Oberst Johannes Jakob Klock aus Sobernheim. *(Führer der Pfälzer im Mohawktal im Unabhängigkeitskrieg.) In: Pfälzisches Museum. Jg. XLI — Pfälzische Heimatkunde. Jg. XX. Kaiserslautern 1924. S. 124—125.*   [6861

Knauss, J. O.: The Knauss family. *In: The Pennsylvania-German. Vol. VII. Lebanon, Pa. 1906. pp. 287—292, ill.*   [6862

— and **Knauss, Tilghman John:** History and genealogy of the Knauss family in America, tracing back the records to Ludwig Knauss to the year 1723. *Compiled and arranged by . . . Emaus, Pa.: Published by the Knauss Family Association, Inc. 1915. pp. 242, ill.*   [6863

Magee, Anna J.: Memorials of the Kneass family of Philadelphia. *Contributed by*

. . . In: Publications of the Genealogical Society of Pennsylvania. Vol. VII, no. 2. Philadelphia, Pa. 1919. pp. 107—126.

[Johan Christian Kneass [Kniess, Kneass, Niess] was the first of his name in Pennsylvania, doubtless a native of the Palatinate, arrived at Philadelphia, 1753.]   [6864

Cassel, Daniel Kolb: A genealogical history of the Kolb, Kulp or Culp family and its branches in America with biographical sketches of their descendants from the earliest time, including Dielman Kolb in Germany. *Norristown, Pa.: Morgan R. Wills 1895. pp. 584, ill.*   [6865

Souder, John D.: The life and times of Dielman Kolb 1691—1756. *In: The Mennonite Quarterly Review. Vol. III. Goshen, Ind. 1929. pp. 33—41.*   [6866

— Dielman Kolb, 1691—1756, minister at Skippack and Salford, 1717—1756. *Reprint from the „Gospel Herald", Febr. 7, 1929 in: The Perkiomen Region. Vol. VII, no. 4. 1929. pp. 112—114.*

[Son of Dielman Kolb, sr., of Wolfsheim in the Palatinate, Germany.]   [6867

Stapleton, A.: The Krape family. *In: Notes and Queries. Edited by W. H. Egle. Annual vol. 1897. Harrisburg, Pa. 1898. p. 175.*

[John Henry Krape arrived at Philadelphia, Pa., from the fatherland, on the St. Michael, Sept. 8, 1753.]   [6868

Fretz, A. J.: A brief history of John Valentine Kratz and a complete genealogical family register with biographies of his descendants from the earliest available records to the present time. *With an introduction of R. W. Kratz of Pomona, Kan. Elkhart, Ind.: Mennonite Publishing Co. 1892. pp. X, 11—128.*

[Descendants of John Philip Kratz, Germany, whose youngest son John Valentine Kratz, b. in 1707, in the Palatinate emigrated to Pa. in 1727.]   [6869

The Krause family. *Sketch prepared from notes furnished by members of the family. In: The Pennsylvania-German. Vol. VII. Lebanon, Pa. 1906. pp. 298—301.*   [6870

Kriebel, H. W.: The successor to David Schultze. John Krauss, Esq., the surveyor, scrivener, conveyancer, organbuilder, machinist and mathematician. *In: The Perkiomen Region. Vol. VIII, no. 1. Pennsburg, Pa. 1930. pp. 29—31.*

[b. March 1, 1770 in Lower Milford, Lehigh Co., Pa., son of Balthasar Kraus, descendant of Ann Kraus who emigrated in 1733, with the original group of Schwenkfeldians.] [6871
Anna **Kraus** and her descendants. *In: The genealogical record of the Schwenkfelder families. Edited by S. K. Brecht. New York, N. Y. — Chicago, Ill. 1923. pp. 145—217.* [6872
Waage, Oswin F.: Rev. Elmer Frederick **Krauss,** D. D. *In: The Pennsylvania-German. Vol. IX. Cleona, Pa. 1908. pp. 156—158.*
[b. in Krausdale, Lehigh Co., Pa. Sept. 7, 1862, son of Isaac Y. Kraus and Theodora R. Waage.] [6873
Maria (Beyer) **Krauss** and her descendants. *In: The genealogical record of the Schwenkfelder families. Edited by S. K. Brecht. New York, N. Y. — Chicago, Ill. 1923. pp. 1563—1570.* [6874
Krauss, Fred A.: Samuel **Krauss,** clockmaker, of Sumneytown. *In: The Perkiomen Region, Past and Present. Vol. III. Philadelphia, Pa. 1901. pp. 53—56.*
[b. Aug. 5, 1807, at Krausdale Montgomery Co., Pa., descendant of the Krauss and Schultz families, who came to Pennsylvania in 1733 and 1734.] [6875
Schaeffer, C. W.: In memoriam. Charles Porterfield **Krauth,** D. D., LL. D. *In: The Lutheran Church Review. Vol. II. Philadelphia, Pa. 1883. pp. 143—153.*
[Descendant of Charles J. Krauth, who came to America before the end of the 18th century and resided in Montgomery Co., Pa.] [6876
Schmucker, Beale M.: Memorials of deceased ministers. I. Charles Porterfield **Krauth.** *In: The Lutheran Church Review. Vol. II. Philadelphia, Pa. 1883. pp. 254—279.* [6877
Spaeth, Adolph: A chapter of biography. Charles Porterfield **Krauth** and the Synod of Maryland, 1842—1845. *In: The Lutheran Church Review. Vol. X. Philadelphia, Pa. 1891. pp. 22—43;* Rev. Charles Porterfield Krauth. Childhood — College and seminary life, 1823 to 1841. *(A second chapter of biography.) In: The Lutheran Church Review. Vol. XII. Philadelphia, Pa. 1893. pp. 241—255;* Charles Porterfield Krauth and the General Synod up to the year 1859. *(Another chapter of biography and church history.) In: Vol. XIII. Philadelphia, Pa. 1894. pp. 5—50; 89—119.* [6878

Spaeth, Adolph: Charles Porterfield **Krauth,** D. D., LL. D. Norton professor of systematic theology and church polity in the Lutheran Theological Seminary in Philadelphia; professor of intellectual and moral philosophy, and vice-provost of the University of Pennsylvania. *2 vols. New York, N. Y.: The Christian Literature Co. 1898. pp. XIII, 425; XI, 443.* [6879
— Rev., Charles Porterfield **Krauth,** D. D., LL. D. *(From Herzog-Hauck Encyclopedia. Translated by E. Pfatteicher.) In: The Lutheran Church Review. Vol. XXII. Philadelphia, Pa. 1903. pp. 231—238.* [6880
Schmauk, Theodore E.: Dr. Charles Porterfield **Krauth** as a philosopher. *In: The Lutheran Church Review. Vol. XXIX. Philadelphia, Pa. 1910. pp. 420—439.* [6881
P.[arthemore], E. W. S.: Kreider family data, *In: Notes and Queries. Edited by W. H. Egle. Annual vol. 1900. Harrisburg, Pa. 1901. pp. 53—57.*
[Jacob Kreider, a Mennonite, came to America with his family prior to the year 1717, and settled on the Conestoga, Chester Co.] [6882
H., S. P.: In memoriam: Joseph H. **Kreider.** *In: Papers read before the Lebanon County Historical Society. Vol. VII. Lebanon, Pa. 1916—1919. pp. 459—461, ill.*
[son of David and Sarah (Henry) Kreider and great-grandson of Kreider, who came to America (Lebanon Co., Pa.) from Switzerland.] [6883
Frank zu Döfering, Karl Friedrich von and **Roberts, Charles Rhoads:** Kress family history. *Compiled written and published by Karl Friedrich von Frank zu Döfering. The genealogical material, concerning the American line of the Kress family was contributed by Charles Rhoads Roberts. Vienna, Austria: Carl Gerold's Son 1930. pp. IV, 770, ill.*
[Johannes Kress, Henry Kress, Caspar Kress and Carl Kress, four brothers of Steinau on the Road Hesse-Nassau, Germany emigrated by via of Philadelphia Oct. 4, 1752.] [6884
Christopher **Kribel** (Kriebel) and his descendants. *In: The genealogical record of the Schwenkfelder families. Edited by S. K. Brecht. New York, N. Y. — Chicago, Ill. 1923. pp. 227—267.* [6885
Melchior **Kribel** (Kriebel) and his descendants. *In: The genealogical record of the Schwenkfelder families. Edited by*

S. K. Brecht. New York, N. Y. — Chicago, Ill. 1923. pp. 347—411. [6886

Grumbine, E.: A bit of genealogy. The Grumbine family. In: Papers read before the Lebanon County Historical Society. Vol. V. Lebanon, Pa. 1909—1912. pp. 273—276, ill. [6887

Krumbine, Clinton B.: Genealogy of the Krumbein, Grumbine or Crumbine family with a history of Leonard Krumbein, the ancestor of nearly all who bear the name of Krumbein, Grumbine or Crumbine in America. Lebanon, Pa.: Clinton B. Krumbine 1918. pp. 265.
[who emigrated to Pa., 1754.] [6888

Barker, Charles R.: The Kuglers of Providence. In: The Perkiomen Region. Vol. VIII, no. 2. Pennsburg, Pa. 1930. pp. 34—52.
[Descendants of John Michael Kugler, who settled in what is now Montgomery Co., Pa. as early as 1742.] [6889

Kuhns, Oscar: A one-sided autobiography, containing the story of my intellectual life. New York, N. Y.: Eaton & Mains; Cincinnati, O.: Jennings & Graham 1913. pp. 236.
[b. in Columbia, Lancaster Co.] [6890

Ruppenthal, J. C.: Captain Henry Kuhn, a noted Penna. German. In: The Pennsylvania-German. Vol. XII. Lititz, Pa. 1911. pp. 377—378.
[b. Febr. 2, 1830 in Franklin Co., Pa., only son of Emanuel Kuhn.] [6891

Johnson, R. Windber: The ancestry of Rosalie Morris Johnson, daughter of Georg Calvert Morris and Elizabeth Kuhn, his wife. Compiled by . . . 2 vols. Philadelphia, Pa.: Ferris and Leach 1905; 1908. pp. (1), (1), (2), 294, ill.; (1), (1), 87.
[Kuhn: Vol. I. pp. 116—133. John Christopher Kuhn, son of George Martin and Barbara Kuhn, b. at Fürfeld, a village on the Neckar, Wurttemberg, Dec. 16, 1684; baptized Dec. 19, 1684. d. in Maiden-Creek Twp., Berks Co., Pa. 1754.] [6892

Conrad, Henry C.: 1683—1891. Thones Kunders and his children. Also a list of the descendants for six generations, of his youngest son Henry Cunders, „of Whitpain". Wilmington, Del.: Press of W. Costa 1891. pp. 105; 23. [6893

Conard or Conrad family. In: Colonial families of Philadelphia. Edited by John W. Jordan. New York, N. Y. — Chicago, Ill.: The Lewis Publishing Co. 1911. Vol. II. pp. 1474—1479.

[Thones Kunders, ancestor of the Pennsylvania families who now spell the name Conrad, Conard, and Connard, b. at Crefeld on the Rhine, 1648 was one of the company of Germans who took passage in the „Concord" which sailed from London, July 24, 1683; d. at Germantown, 1729.] [6894

Grubb, N. B.: Will of Dennis Kunders. In: The Mennonite Year Book and Almanac for 1908. Quakertown, Pa. 1908. p. 29. [6895

Egle, William Henry: Family of Kunkel. In: Egle's „Pennsylvania Genealogies". Harrisburg, Pa. 1896 [= no. 6045]. pp. 357—366.
[Descendants of Christian Kunkel, son of John Christian Kunkel, b. July 10, 1757, in the Palatinate, Germany.] [6896

Kuhns, Oscar: Notes on the Kuntz (Kuhns) and Brown families. In: The Pennsylvania-German. Vol. X. Lititz, Pa. 1909. pp. 278—282.
[The Kuhns family being traced back to the Town of Waldmohr, in the Province of Zweibrucken, where on Nov. 15, 1708 Johann Frantz Cuntz m. Anna Elizabeth Kirsch.] [6897

George Michael Kuntz. In: The Perkiomen Region. Vol. II. no. 4. Pennsburg, Pa. 1923. pp. 63—64.
[b. in Germany, arrived in America Sept. 24, 1727.] [6898

Oakley, Henrietta M.: Famous Pennsylvania Germans. Rev. John C. Kunze, D. D. In: The Pennsylvania-German. Vol. III. Lebanon, Pa. 1902. pp. 99—108, ill.
[b. Aug. 5, 1744 at Artem, near Mansfield, Germany, arrived at New York, Sept. 23, 1770.] [6899

[Egle, W. H.]: The Kurtz family. In Notes and Queries. Edited by W. H. Egle. Third series, vol. II. 1887—1890. Harrisburg, Pa. 1891. p. 476. Reprint in: Third series, vol. III. Harrisburg, Pa. 1896. pp. 513—514.
[Issue of Benjamin Kurtz, sr. and his wife Elizabeth Gardner Rankin, of York Co., Pa.] [6900

Mast, C. Z.: The Kurtz family. In: Christian Monitor. A monthly magazine for the home. Vol. XV, no. 9. Scottdale, Pa. 1923. pp. 273—275. [6901

Hutter, E. W.: Eulogy on the life and character of Rev. Benjamin Kurtz, D. D., LL. D. Delivered before the professors and students of the Missionary Institute, *and a large concourse of citizens and visitors, at Selinsgrove, Pa. Monday, May 28th, 1866. Philadelphia, Pa.: H. G. Leisenring Steam Printing House 1866. pp. 80.*

[b. in Harrisburg, 1795, son of Daniel and Elizabeth Kurtz.] [6902]

Cruikshank, Margaret A.: Life of Johann Nicolaus **Kurtz** *(missionary, clergyman, president of the Lutheran Ministerium). With notes of his brother* **Johann Wilhelm Kurtz,** *Lutheran clergyman. Edited by* **Benjamin Kurtz Miller.** *[Umschlag: Johann Nicolaus Kurtz.] Life and genealogy. [s. l.; s. d.] pp. 106, (5), ill.*

[son of Johann Georg Kurtz, b. in Lützellinden, Kreis Wetzlar, Germany who came to America via Philadelphia 1745.] [6903]

L.

Michael Anthony and Anne Shields-Lambing. *Their ancestors and their descendants. By a member of the family. Pittsburgh, Pa.: printed for the family by Fahey & Co. 1896. pp. 42, ill.*

[M. A. Lambing, b. Oct. 10, 1806, descendant of Christopher Michael Lambing who immigrated to America about 1740.] [6904]

Lambing, A. A.: Rev. Andrew Arnold **Lambing.** *In: Brief sketch of St. James Roman Catholic Church, Wilkinsburg, Pa. [s. l. 1912?] pp. 37—39.*

[Descendants of Christopher and Anne Mary (Wanner) Lambing, who emigrated from a place a few miles S. of Strasburg, in Alsace.] [6905]

Death of Right Reverend Monsignor Andrew Arnold Lambing, LL. D. *In: The Western Pennsylvania Historical Magazine. Vol. II. Pittsburgh, Pa. 1919. pp. 36—37, ill.*

[Descendant of Christian Lambing, who emigrated from Germany and settled in Bucks Co., Pa.] [6906]

Landis, D. B.: The **Landis** family of Lancaster County, *a comprehensive history of the Landis folk from the martyrs era to the arrival of the first Swiss settlers giving their numerous lineal descendants: also, an account record of members in the rebellion with a sketch of the start and subsequent growth of Landisville and Landis Valley, and a complete directory of living Landis adults etc., etc. Lancaster, Pa.: Press of the Weekly Inquirer 1888. pp. 90, ill.* [6907]

Genealogical data. Landis family. *In: Notes and Queries. Edited by W. H. Egle. Fourth series, vol. I. 1891—1893. Harrisburg, Pa. 1893. p. 14.*

[Rev. Benjamin Landis, Mennonite preacher, accompanied by his only son Benjamin, came to America from Switzerland in 1718.] [6908]

E.[gle], William Henry: **Landis** family. *In: Notes and Queries. Edited by W. H. Egle. Third series, vol. I. 1884—1887. Harrisburg, Pa. 1887. p. 11. Reprint in: Third series, vol. I. Harrisburg, Pa. 1895. pp. 16—17.* [6909]

Landis family reunions. *Reports of the:*

First reunion, Perkasie Park, Perkasie, Pa. Aug. 19, 1911. pp. 27.

Second reunion, Lititz, Springs Park, Lancaster Co., Pa. Aug. 3, 1912. pp. 35.

Third reunion, Ursinius College, Collegeville, Pa. Aug. 18, 1913. pp. 24.

Fourth reunion, Perkasie Park, Perkasie, Pa. Aug. 8, 1914. pp. 24.

Fifth reunion, Conestoga Park. Aug. 21, 1915. pp. 20.

Sixth reunion, Salem Reformed Church Allentown, Pa. Aug. 19, 1916. pp. 6.

Bicentennial of first Landis settlement in Lancaster County and seventh reunion, Lititz Springs Park, Aug. 4, 1917. pp. 32, ill., maps.

Eighth reunion, Perkasie Park, Perkasie, Pa. Aug. 23, 1919. pp. 20.

Nineth reunion, Fairmount Park, Philadelphia, Pa. Sept. 10, 1921. pp. 19.

Tenth reunion, M. E. camp grounds, Landisville, Pa. Aug. 25, 1923. pp. 15.

Eleventh reunion, Perkasie Park, Perkasie, Pa. Sept. 5, 1925. pp. 23.

Twelfth reunion. M. E. camp grounds, Landisville, Pa. Aug. 27, 1927. pp. 16.

Thirteenth reunion, Perkasie Park, Perkasie, Pa. Sept. 1, 1928. pp. 20.

Fourteenth reunion, M. E. camp grounds Landisville, Pa. Aug. 10, 1929. Lancaster, Pa.: D. B. Landis 1929. pp. 15, ill. [6910]

K., F.: John **Landis.** *In: Notes and Queries. Edited by W. H. Egle. Second series. Harrisburg, Pa. 1883. p. 336. Reprint in: First and second series, vol. II. Harrisburg, Pa. 1895. pp. 463—464.* [6911]

Ayres, George B.: John **Landis.** *In: Notes and Queries. Edited by W. H. Egle. Second series. Harrisburg, Pa. 1883. pp. 337—339. Reprint in: First and second series, vol. II. Harrisburg, Pa. 1895. pp. 464—466.* [6912]

528 Familiengeschichte und Biographien

B.: John **Landis.** *In: Notes and Queries. Edited by W. H. Egle. Second series. Harrisburg, Pa. 1883. pp. 340—341. Reprint in: First and second series, vol. II. Harrisburg, Pa. 1895. pp. 469—470.* [6913

Sener, S. M.: John **Landis** — Andrew D. Smolnikar. Two eccentric men of bygone days. *In: Notes and Queries. Edited by W. H. Egle. Annual vol. 1899. Harrisburg, Pa. 1900. pp. 122—123.* [6914

Robinson, Mary N.: John **Landis,** painter. *In: Papers and Addresses of the Lancaster County Historical Society. Vol. XVI. Lancaster, Pa. 1912. pp. 179—185.* [6915

Souder, John D.: John H. **Landis.** *Reprint from the Souderton Independent, March 1, 1929 in: The Perkiomen Region. Vol. VII, no. 4. Pennsburg, Pa. 1929. pp. 115—116.*
[d. aged 81 years and buried in Salford Mennonite burial grounds, Montgomery Co., Pa.] [6916

[Landes, Elisabetha]: Letter from the unwritten history of the **Landis** family. *Translated from the German by N. B. Grubb. In: The Mennonite Year Book and Almanac for 1914. Quakertown, Pa. 1914. pp. 36—37.* [6917

P.[arthemore], E. W. S.: The **Lantz** family. *In: Notes and Queries. Edited by W. H. Egle. Third series, vol. II. 1887—1890. Harrisburg, Pa. 1891. pp. 366—368. Reprint in: Third series, vol. III. Harrisburg, Pa. 1896. pp. 434—439.*
[Philip Lantz, b. in 1725, in Switzerland, emigrated to America, landing at Baltimore, Md. and settled in Lampeter Twp., Lancaster Co., Pa.] [6918

Lantz, Jacob W.: The **Lantz** family record. Being a brief account of the Lantz family in the United States of America. *[s. l.] 1931. pp. VII, 265, ill.*
[of German stock, they came from the City of Speyer, on the Rhine, Germany.] [6919

The Larue family. *In: Notes and Queries. Edited by W. H. Egle. Third series, vol. II. 1887—1890. Harrisburg, Pa. 1891. pp. 175—176. Reprint in: Third series, vol. III. Harrisburg, Pa. 1896. pp. 123—125.*
[Johan George Larue, a native of Switzerland, emigrated to America about 1740.] [6920

Lasher genealogy. *3 parts. New York, N. Y.: C. S. Williams. 1904. pp. (1), 5—270, ill., map.*

[Descendants of Sebastian Lasher, m. Elizabeth —, who was at West Camp, N. Y., in 1710.] [6921

R.[attermann, H. A.]: Friedrich **Lauer,** der Altmeister der Bierbrauer in den Vereinigten Staaten. *In: Der Deutsche Pionier. Jg. XVI. Cincinnati, O. 1884. S. 172—179.* [6922

1710—1910. Two hundredth anniversary celebration. The **Laux** — **Loux** — **Lauck** — **Laucks** — **Loucks** family association. *Brookside Park, York, Pa., June 18, 1910. York, Pa.: The York Printing Co. 1910. pp. 48, ill.* [6923

1710—1913. Two hundred and third anniversary of the founding of the family in America: **Laux, Loux, Lauck, Laucks, Loucks.** *Brookside Park, York, Pa., Sat., July 5, 1913. . . . [1913] pp. 24, ill.* [6924

The **Laux, Loux, Lauck, Laucks, Loucks** family. *In: The Pennsylvania-German. Vol. XII. Lititz, Pa. 1911. pp. 258—279, ill. [A symposium of addresses and papers.] . . .* First family association meeting. *pp. 258—259;*
James B. **Laux:** Our Huguenot ancestry: The ancient home in France. *pp. 259—266;*
Edwin A. **Loucks:** Landing in the New World — From exile in Germany to Shoharie. *pp. 267—271;*
Michael **Loucks:** From Shoharie to Tulpehocken, Pa. *pp. 272—275;*
David M. **Loucks:** The Louck's from Berks Co. to York Co., Pa. *pp. 276—277.* [6925

Laux, James B.: The **Laux** family of Bucks County, Pa. *In: A Collection of Papers read before the Bucks County Historical Society. Vol. V. Meadville, Pa. 1926. pp. 550—567, ill.* [6926

[Stoudt, John Baer]: Dedication of the memorial tablet to Frederick **Leaser.** Nov. 29, 1928. *[Frederick Leaser and the handling of the Liberty Bell. Address by J. B. Stoudt.] Published for the Leaser Family Association. Norristown, Pa.: Norristown Press 1928. pp. 32, ill.*
[Leaser (Liesser) family is of Swiss origin.] [6927

H., S. P.: In memoriam: Ambrose E. **Lehman** C. E. *In: Papers read before the Lebanon County Historical Society. Vol. VII. Lebanon, Pa. 1916—1919. pp. 185—188, ill.*
[son of Benjamin Bringhurst and Susanna (Mustin) Lehman and descen-

dant of Christian Lehman who d. as a Notary Public in Germantown 1774.] [6928
Lehman family. *In: Notes and Queries. Edited by W. H. Egle. Third series, vol. I. 1884—1887. Harrisburg, Pa. 1887. pp. 404—406. Reprint in: Third series, vol. II. 1896. pp. 128—131.*
[Martin Lehman, b. in Germany, Jan. 1, 1744, who came with his parents to America in 1746.] [6929
William Lehman. *[Inscriptions on the front of the monument of . . ., a representative of the City of Philadelphia in the General Assembly of the State, on the N. W. side of the Zion Lutheran Church, 4th Str. (Harrisburg).] In: Notes and Queries. Edited by W. H. Egle. First and second series, vol. II. Harrisburg, Pa. 1895. p. 271.* [6930
Ruschenberger, W. S. W.: A sketch of the life of Joseph Leidy, M. D., LL. D. *(Read before the American Philosophical Society, April 1, 1892.) In: Proceedings of the American Philosophical Society, April 1, 1892. In: Proceedings of the American Philosophical Society, held at Philadelphia, for promoting useful knowledge. Vol. XXX. Philadelphia, Pa. 1892. pp. 135—166.*
[Carl Leidy, the forefather of the American-born Leidys, came to America from Rheinisch Germany about 1724.] [6931
Croll, P. C.: Famous Pennsylvania-Germans. Joseph Leidy. *In: The Pennsylvania-German. Vol. VI. Lebanon, Pa. 1905. pp. 196—201, ill.* [6932
The Leinbach family. *Reprint from: Reading Eagle. In: The Penn Germania. Vol. I. = Old series, vol. XIII. Lititz, Pa. 1912. pp. 831—838.*
[Johannes Leinbach, the first of the name to settle in Pennsylvania, was b. in Langen-Selbold, Wetterau, Germany, March 9, 1674; he located in Oley Twp., Berks Co., Sept. 11, 1723.] [6933
Leipham reunion; family of Peter and Catharine Leipham. *In: Procceedings and Collections of the Wyoming Historical and Genealogical Society for the years 1925 and 1926. Vol. XX. Wilkes-Barre, Pa. 1929. pp. 48.* [6934
Rattermann, H. A.: Edmund Daniel Leisenring. Deutsch-amerikanischer Journalist. *Aus dem „Deutschen Pionier". Jg. XIV. Abgedruckt in: H. A. Rattermann: Gesammelte Werke. Bd. X. Cincinnati, O.:*

Selbstverlag des Verfassers 1911. S. 197—202. [6934a
S.[ener], S. M.: A hero of the Revolution. George Leonard. *In: Notes and Queries. Edited by W. H. Egle. Fourth series, vol. II. 1894. Harrisburg, Pa. 1895. pp. 37 —38.*
[b. in Lancaster, Sept. 13, 1755, son of Philip Leonard and a grandson of John George Leonard (Lennhart) who came from Germany and landed at Philadelphia, 1736.] [6935
Leonard, J. C.: Valentin Leonhardt, the Revolutionary War patriot of North Carolina. *In: The Pennsylvania-German. Vol. XI. Lititz, Pa. 1910. pp. 10—20, ill.*
[b. in Katzenbach, Kuhr Pfaltz, Germany, Oct. 13, 1718, reached Philadelphia, Pa. Oct. 25, 1746.] [6936
Jones, Horatio Gates: The Levering family; *or a genealogical account of Wigard Levering and Gerhard Levering, two of the pioneer settlers of Roxborough Township, Philadelphia County, Pa., and their descendants; and an appendix containing brief sketches of Roxborough and Manayunk. Philadelphia, Pa.: King & Baird 1858. pp. X, 193, ill.* [6937
Proceedings of the Levering family reunion, held at Levering, Knox County, Ohio. August 6, 1891. *Containing the movement, the proceedings of the organization, the addresses delivered. Published by order of the Association. Columbus, O.: J. L. Trauger 1892. pp. (1), 120.* [6938
Levering, John: Levering family, history and genealogy. *Published by the Levering Historical Association. Indianapolis, Ind.: Wm. B. Burford 1897. pp. 975, ill.* [6939
Family history of Rev. John Philip Leydich. *In: Historical Notes, relating to the Pennsylvania Reformed Church. Vol. I. Philadelphia, Pa. 1900. pp. 59—60.* [6940
Libhart, Antonio Canova: John Jay Libhart, artist. *In: Papers and Addresses of the Lebanon County Historical Society. Vol. XVI. Lancaster, Pa. 1912. pp. 241—246.* [6941
[Lichtenwalner, Charles]: Lichtenwalner family history. *Compiled and published by the Committee on Publication appointed by the Executive Committee of the Pennsylvania Branch of the Lichtenwalner family. Allentown, Pa.: Press*

of S. J. Brobst & Co. 1900. pp. 198.
[Descendants of Johannes Lichten-
wallner and his wife Barbara, who ar-
rived in Philadelphia Aug. 17, 1733.]
                                            [6942
Johannes Lick. *In: The Perkiomen Region.*
Vol. I, no. 3. Pennsburg, Pa. 1922. p. 52.
[Father of James Lick, founder of the
Lick Observatory.]   [6943
Croll, P. C.: Famous Pennsylvania-Ger-
mans. James Lick. *In: The Pennsyl-*
vania-German. Vol. V. Lebanon, Pa.
1904. pp. 149—159, ill.
   [b. Aug. 25, 1796 at Fredericksburg,
   Lebanon Co., Pa., son of Pennsylvania-
   German parents.]   [6944
Wyneken, Friedrich A.: James Lick und
sein Teleskop. Lebensskizze eines
Deutsch-Pennsylvaniers. *In: Deutsche*
Erde. Zeitschrift für Deutschkunde. Her-
ausgegeben von Paul Langhaus. Jg. XIII.
Gotha 1914—15. S. 25—27.   [6945
Light, Moses: The Light genealogy in America. *By . . ., of Manheim, Lancaster*
County, Pa. [s.l.] (Published for the
author.) 1896. pp. (1), 5—38.
   [The first John Light and two of his
   brothers, natives of Palatinate, Germany,
   left for America about 1719, one stopping
   in England and one in Baltimore, Md.
   John Light, above mentioned, settled in
   Lebanon Twp., Lancaster Co., Pa., now
   Lebanon Co., Pa. and secured a tract
   of land now a part of the City of Lebanon,
   patent dated April 2, 1742.]   [6946
Linabarger, Paul Myron and Linneberger,
Walter Franklin: A family of five re-
publics. A sketch of the origin of the
Leyenberger - Lineberger - Linabarger -
Lionberger families. *Published at the*
expense of the authors as a contribution
to the Monument Fund of the ,,Family
of five republics." Hammond, Ind.: W.
B. Conkey 1925. pp. 43.
   [Descendants of John Leyenberger,
   Lewis Leyenberger and Peter Leyen-
   berger from Wittelsheim, near Mulhouse,
   Alsace, who landed at Philadelphia on
   Aug. 26, 1735.]   [6947
Harbaugh, H.: Rev. Jacob Lischy. *In: The*
Mercersburg Quarterly Review. Vol.
VIII. Chambersburg, Pa. 1856. pp.
524—548.   [6948
Livergood family. Inscriptions from the
Mt. Bethel cemetery, Columbia, Penn.
In: Genealogy. Journal of American
ancestry. Vol. III. New York, N. Y.
1913. p. 81.   [6949

Stapleton, A.: Two Pennsylvania-German
families. The Lobach and Pott families,
of Berks County, and the establishment
of industries at Lobachville. *With hi-*
storical memoranda. In: Notes and Que-
ries. Edited by W. H. Egle. Annual vol.
1900. Harrisburg, Pa. 1901. pp. 187
—189.   [6950
Gilbert, D. M.: Rev. George Lochman, D.
D. *Paper read before the Historical So-*
ciety of Dauphin County. In: Notes and
Queries. Edited by W. H. Egle. Annual
vol. 1900. Harrisburg, Pa. 1901. pp. 22
—27; 29—33.
   [b. Philadelphia, Pa. 1773.]   [6951
Hagenbuch, Elizabeth A. - Lehr, Edward
Chester: Johann Heinrich Loehr and
his descendants. *[s. l.] pp. 16.*
   [b. Sept. 24, 1753 in Wallahalben,
   Prussian Saxony, and came to America
   1774.]   [6952
Lesh, (Loesch) William W.: A collection
of over 600 names. Descendants of Bal-
thasar and Susanna Phillipina Loesch,
Palatines from Gernsheim, near Worms,
Germany. *With historical notes. Wash-*
ington, D. C.: National Capital Press
1914. pp. 47; (1), ill. Supplemental list.
Descendants of Balthasar and Susanna
Phillipina Loesch of Gernsheim, near
Worms, Germany, who emigrated to
America in 1710. *Washington, D. C.*
1916. pp. 21.   [6953
Long, William Gabriel: History of the
Long family of Pennsylvania. *Publis-*
hed by the Long Family Organization of
Pennsylvania. Huntingdon, W. Va.:
Huntingdon Publishing Co. 1930. pp.
VII, 365, ill.
   [Descendants of Christian Lang, the
   emigrant ancestor, of the Palatinate,
   Germany, landed at Philadelphia, Pa.
   in 1683—84.]   [6954
The Long family. Inscriptions from the Lan-
caster cemetery, Lancaster, Pa. *In:*
Genealogy. Journal of American an-
cestry. Vol. IV. New York, N. Y. 1914.
p. 6.   [6955
Long. *In: Notes and Queries. Edited by W.*
H. Egle. Annual vol. 1900. Harrisburg,
Pa. 1901. p. 173.   [6956
Ashe, S. A.: Benjamin Franklin Long *(Jud-*
ge). In: Biographical history of North Ca-
rolina. Edited by S. A. Ashe. Vol. VIII.
Greensboro, N. C. 1917. pp. 306—313, ill.
   [b. near Graham, N. C., March 19,
   1852; son of Jacob Long and Jane Stuart
   Stockard.]   [6957

The will of Catharine H. **Long** of Lancaster City, Pennsylvania. *Died June 18, 1900. Together with an inventory of her personal property; a schedule of her real estate; and extracts from the will of her father, the late Hon. Henry G. Long, dec'd relating to the ,,Henry G. Long Asylum." A. D. 1900. pp. 21.* [6958

Joyner, J. Y.: Daniel Albright **Long** *(Educator). In: Biographical history of North Carolina. Edited by S. A. Ashe. Vol. VIII. Greensboro, N. C. 1917. pp. 296 —299.*
[b. on father's farm in Almanace Co., N. C., May 22, 1844; son of Jacob Long and Jane Stuart Stockard.] [6959

George Washington **Long** *(Physician). In: Biographical history of North Carolina. Edited by S. A. Ashe. Vol. VIII. Greensboro, N. C. 1917. pp. 304—305.*
[b. near Graham, N. C., July 15, 1848; son of Jacob Long and Jane Stuart Stockard.] [6960

Staley, W. W. - Newman, J. U.: Jacob **Long** *(Agriculturist). In: Biographical history of North Carolina. Edited by S. A. Ashe. Vol. VIII. Greensboro, N. C. 1917. pp. 286—291, ill.*
[b. near Graham, N. C., March 28, 1807; his paternal grandfather Conrad Long, in German spelled Lange, came from Germany to Pa. before the Revolution.] [6961

Ashe, S. A.: Jacob Alson **Long** *(Lawyer). In: Biographical history of North Carolina. Edited by S. A. Ashe. Vol. VIII. Greensboro, N. C. 1917. pp. 300—303, ill.*
[b. near Graham, N. C., April 6, 1846; son of Jacob Long and Jane Stuart Stockard.] [6962

Yeakel, R.[euben]: Bishop Joseph **Long,** the peerless preacher of the Evangelical Association. *Cleveland, O.: Thomas & Mattill 1897. pp. XII, 261, ill.* [6963

Staley, W. W.: William Samuel **Long** *(Educator). In: Biographical history of North Carolina. Edited by S. A. Ashe. Vol. VIII. Greensboro, N. C. 1917. pp. 292—295, ill.*
[b. near Graham, Almanace Co., Oct. 22, 1839, son of Jacob and Jane Stuart Stockard.] [6964

History of the **Longacre - Longaker - Longenecker** family. *Published for the Committee. Philadelphia, Pa.: Lutheran Publication Society. [s. d.] pp. VIII, 9—310.*

[Descendants of Ulrich and Daniel Longenecker, brothers, who emigrated to Pa. between 1722—1733.] [6965

Early Pennsylvania **Longacre** marriages. *In: Genealogy. A Journal of American ancestry. Vol. V. 1915. New York, N. Y. 1915. p. 74.*
[Longenecker]. [6966

Lower, Joseph Leaney: Some account of the **Lower** family in America, principally of the descendants of Adam Lower, who settled in Williamsburg, Pa., in 1779. *Compiled by . . . Cincinnati, O.: Monfort & Co. [s. d.] pp. 144.*
[b. in Württemberg, 1755.] [6967

Loy, M.: Story of my life. *By Prof. M. Loy, D. D. Third edition. Columbus, O.: Lutheran Book Concern 1905. pp. 440, ill.*
[son of an immigrant from Germany, who came to America in 1817; b. March 17, 1828 on the Blue Mountain in Cumberland Co., Pa.] [6968

Daniels, Annie M.: Lucken - Luken-family records. *In: The Pennsylvania Magazine of History and Biography. Vol. XXIII. Philadelphia, Pa. 1899. pp. 270—290.* [6969

Cooper, Theodore: Lucken genealogy. *In: The Pennsylvania Magazine of History and Biography. Vol. XXIII. Philadelphia, Pa. 1899. p. 408.* [6970

Some items from the account of the executors of John **Lukens,** deceased (1769 —1778). *In: The Pennsylvania Magazine of History and Biography. Vol. XXIV. Philadelphia, Pa. 1900. pp. 122—123.* [6971

Lukens family. *In: Colonial families of Philadelphia. Edited by John W. Jordan. New York, N. Y.-Chicago, Ill.: The Lewis Publishing Co. 1911. Vol. I. pp. 744—751, ill. Vol. II. pp. 1470 —1473.*
[Jan Lucken, ancestor of the Luckens family of America, b. in Crefeld, Germany; he arrived at Chester, on the Delaware Oct. 6, 1683, being one of the 13 original families of Germantown, Pa.] [6972

[Luckenbach, Abraham]: Biography of Brother Abraham **Luckenbach.** *Written by himself and left for his dear children. Translated from the German by H. E. Stocker. In: Transactions of the Moravian Historical Society. Vol. X. Nazareth, Pa. 1917. pp. 361—408.*

34*

[b. May 5, 1777 in Upper Saucon, Lehigh Co., of German parents.]   [6973
Hull, William: Rev. William H. **Luckenbach,** D. D. *In: The Lutheran Quarterly. Vol. XXVIII. Gettysburg, Pa. 1898. pp. 396—397.*
[b. at Doylestown 1828, the son of George B. Luckenbach and Julia A. Bisel; on the fathers side descendant of Germans who immigrated to America 1741 and settled at Bethlehem in Pa.]   [6974
Rush, Benjamin: An account oh the life and character of Christopher **Ludwick,** late citizen of Philadelphia, and Baker-General of the army of the United States during the Revolutionary War. *Philadelphia, Pa. 1801. pp. . . . .*
[b. on the 17th of October 1720, at Gießen in Hesse Darmstadt, in the Circle of the Upper Rhine in Germany.]   [6975
— An account of the life and character of Christopher **Ludwick,** late citizen of Philadelphia, and Baker-General of the army of the United States during the Revolutionary War. *First published in the year 1801. Revised and republished by direction of The Philadelphia Society for the Establishment and Support of Charity Schools. To which is added, an account of the origin, progress and present condition of that institution. Philadelphia, Pa.: Printed for the Society by Garden and Thompson 1831. pp. 61.*   [6976
[—] Life and Character of Christopher **Ludwick,** late citizen of Philadelphia, and Baker-General of the army of the United States during the Revolutionary War. *First published in the year 1801. Reprint in: Hazard's Register of Pennsylvania. Vol. IX. Philadelphia, Pa. 1832. pp. 161—164.*   [6977
R.[attermann, H. A.]: Christopher **Ludwig,** der Armeebäcker Washington's. *In: Der Deutsche Pionier. Jg. VIII. Cincinnati, O. 1876—1877. S. 18—25; Nachtrag zur Biographie Christopher Ludwigs. S. 73—74.*   [6978
Christopher **Ludwig,** Baker-General in the army of the United States during the Revolutionary War. *In: The Pennsylvania Magazine of History and Biography. Vol. XVI. Philadelphia, Pa. 1892. pp. 343—348.*   [6979
Huch, C. F.: Christoph **Ludwig,** der Bäcker-General. *In: Mitteilungen des Deutschen Pionier-Vereins von Philadelphia. Heft 7. Philadelphia, Pa. 1908. S. 19.*   [6980

Finck, William J.: Christopher **Ludwig.** *In: The Lutheran Church Review. Vol. XLVI. Mt. Airy, Philadelphia, Pa. 1927. pp. 361—372.*   [6981
Ludwig, M. R.: Ludwig genealogy. Sketch of Joseph Ludwig, who was born in Germany in 1699, and his wife and family, who settled at „Broad Bay" Waldoboro, Me. 1753. *Augusta, Me.: Kennebec Journal 1866. pp. 223.*   [6982
H., S. P.: Samuel R. **Ludwig.** *In: Papers read before the Lebanon County Historical Society. Vol. VII. Lebanon, Pa. 1916—1919. pp. 329—330, ill.*
[son of John and Mary (Long) Ludwig.]   [6983
Schick, Rudolph M.: De Benneville Keim **Ludwig,** Ph. D. 1839—1915. *In: Journal of the Presbyterian Historical Society. Vol. VIII. Philadelphia, Pa. 1916. pp. 193—198, ill.*   [6984
[Egle, William Henry]: Dr. John **Luther,** the second burgess of the Borough of Harrisburg. *In: Notes and Queries. Edited by W. H. Egle. First and second series, vol. I. Harrisburg, Pa. 1894. pp. 269—271.*   [6985
Hassler, John W.: A funeral sermon: preached sermon of Dr. John W. **Luther.** *Lancaster, Pa.: Pearsol & Geist 1870. pp. 15.*   [6986
Anderson, Rasmus: Descendants of Martin **Luther.** *Reprint from: The Lutheran, Nov. 28, 1907. In: The Pennsylvania-German. Vol. IX. Cleona, Pa. 1908. p. 84.*   [6987
Lybarger, Donald F. and Lybarger, Jesse J.: A brief history of the **Lybarger** family compiled by . . . *[Gettysburg-Reading, Pa.] 1915. pp. 8.*
[Descendants of Johann Adam Leberger who landed at Philadelphia Sept. 19, 1732.]   [6988
Lybarger, Donald: History of the **Lybarger** family. *Cleveland, O. 1921. pp. 5—100.*   [6989

M.

Brumbaugh, M. G.: Alexander **Mack.** *Address delivered at the unveiling of the Alexander Mack memorial tablet, Germantown Church, Pa., April 9, 1911. In: The Penn Germania. Vol. I. = Old series, vol. XIII. Lititz, Pa. 1912. pp. 254—259.*
[b. 1679 in the Village of Schriesheim, not far from Frankfort in the Upper Palatinate, Germany, became one of the

founders of the Church of Schwarzenau, reached Philadelphia, Sept. 29, 1729.]
[6990

[Dotterer, Henry Sassaman]: Descendants of Jacob **Markley** of Skippack, Montgomery County, Pa. *Published by the Markley Freundschaft. 1884. pp. (1), 5—36.*
[b. probably in Europe and settled in Skippack as early as 1725.]   [6991

Johnson, Alonzo Markley: Genealogy of John and Mary **Markley.** Compiled by . . . *La Junta, Colo.: Daily Democrat Print 1924. pp. 37.*
[John Markley, m. to Mary Springer, in 1793; moved to Hamilton Co., O. and bought land what was known as Five Mill Creek, they were known as Pa. Dutch.]   [6992

Stein, Thos. S.: The **Marshalls** of Berks and Lebanon Counties, Pa. *A historic-biographical sketch portraying the careers of a family of physicians. Anville, Pa.: Hiester Printing and Publishing Co. 1915. pp. 67, ill.*   [6993

Fries, Adelaide L.: Frederick William von **Marshall** *(Moravian colonist). In: Biographical history of North Carolina. Edited by S. A. Ashe. Vol. II. Greensboro, N. C. 1905. pp. 237—239.*
[b. in Stolpen, Saxony, Febr. 5, 1721, where his father Baron George Rudolph von Marshall of Herrn Grosserstaedt was commandant; in 1750 he m. Hedwig Elizabeth von Schweinitz, and in 1761 came to Pa. on important official matters connected with the Moravian congregation at Bethlehem.]   [6994

Dotterer, Henry S.: Frederick **Marsteller.** *In: Historical Register: Notes and Queries, historical and genealogical relating to interior Pennsylvania for the year 1883. Vol. I. Harrisburg, Pa. 1883. pp. 27—33.*
[b. in the Duchy of Hesse Darmstadt, Jan. 11., 1702; came with his family to this country, arriving at Philadelphia in 1729.]   [6995

Martins of Pennsylvania. Inscriptions from Mt. Zion cemetery, near Ephrata, Pa. *In: Genealogy. Journal of American ancestry. Vol. III. New York, N. Y. 1913. p. 112.*   [6996

[Meginness, John F.]: The **Masser** family. *By John of Lancaster. In: Notes and Queries. Edited by W. H. Egle. Annual vol. 1897. Harrisburg, Pa. 1898. pp. 190—191.*

[Descendants of Matthias and Barbara Masser, natives of Wurttemberg, Germany, and Switzerland respectively, whose son Henry Masser was b. in Oley Twp., Berks Co., Febr. 11, 1775.]   [6997

Mast, C. Z.: A brief history of Bishop Jacob **Mast** and other Mast pioneers and a complete genealogical family register and those related by intermarriage. *Scottdale, Pa.: Mennonite Publishing House Press 1911. pp. (5), 10—822, ill.*
[b. in 1738 in Switzerland of Swiss parents; emigrated to America an orphan boy in company with his four sisters and younger brother John in care of his uncle Johannes Mast; reached Philadelphia, Pa., Nov. 3, 1750.]   [6998

— The **Mast** family. *In: Christian Monitor. A monthly magazine for the home. Vol. XIV, no. 10. Scottdale, Pa. 1922. pp. 688—691, ill.*
[whose ancestors, the brothers Jacob and John Mast of Swiss parents and Amish faith, landed in Philadelphia, 1750.]   [6999

Fragments of family history. The **Maurers** of Goshenhoppen. *In: The Perkiomen Region, Past and Present. Vol. II. Philadelphia, Pa. 1900. p. 68.*   [7000

The **Maus** family, of Montour. *In: Notes and Queries. Edited by W. H. Egle. Annual vol. 1897. Harrisburg, Pa. 1898. pp. 132—133.*
[Philip Maus, a native of Prussia, b. in 1731, came with his parents to Philadelphia, Pa. when he was about 10 years of age.]   [7001

Mayer, Brantz: Memoir and genealogy of the Maryland and Pennsylvania family of **Mayer** which originated in the Free Imperial City of Ulm, Würtemberg: 1495—1878. *Baltimore, Md.: Privately printed for the family by William K. Boyle & Son. 1878. pp. 5—179, ill.*   [7002

Steiner, Bernard C.: Brantz **Mayer.** *In: The Maryland Historical Magazine. Vol. V. Baltimore, Md. 1910. pp. 1—22.*
[son of Christian Mayer and his wife Anne Katharine Baum, who emigrated from Ulm, Germany to Baltimore, Md.]   [7003

Keim, De B. R.: The **Mayer** family. *In: Notes and Queries. Edited by W. H. Egle. Annual vol. 1898. Harrisburg, Pa. 1899. pp. 129—130.*

[Christopher Bartholomew Mayer, founder in America of the Pennsylvania branch of the family of Ulmer-Mayers, b. at Carlesruhe, Germany, Nov., 1702.] [7004
Mayer, Harriet Hyatt: The Mayer family. *[Annisquam, Mass.]* 1911. pp. 8.
[The Pa. branch descended from Christopher Bartholomew Mayer of Ulm, b. Nov., 1702, and who came to Maryland 1752.] [7005
H.[einer], E.[lias]: Life of the Rev. Dr. Lewis Mayer. *In: The Mercersburg Review. Vol. III. Mercersburg, Pa. 1851. pp. 275—285.*
[b. at Lancaster, Pa., 1783, the son of George L. Mayer.] [7006
Stoever, M. L.: Memorial of Rev. Philip F. Mayer, D. D., late pastor of St. John's Lutheran Church, Philadelphia. *Philadelphia, Pa.: Smith, English & Co. 1859. pp. 70.*
[b. April, 1, 1781, in the City of New York, son of George Frederick Mayer, who immigrated from Swabia, Germany, and of Marie Magdalene Kamerdiener.] [7007
H., S. P.: In memoriam: Thomas J. **Mays**, A. M. M. D. *In: Papers read before the Lebanon County Historical Society. Vol. VII. Lebanon, Pa. 1916—1919. pp. 321—323, ill.*
[son of Georg W. and Sarah (Spayd) Mays.] [7008
Melcher **Meishter** (Melchior Meschter) and his descendants. *In: The genealogical record of the Schwenkfelder families. Edited by S. K. Brecht. New York, N. Y. — Chicago, Ill. 1923. pp. 927—937.* [7009
Gregorius **Meishter** (Meschter) and his descendants. *In: The genealogical record of the Schwenkfelder families. Edited by S. K. Brecht. New York, N. Y. — Chicago, Ill. 1923. pp. 565—628.* [7010
Mellick, Andrew D.: The story of an old farm or life in New Jersey in the eighteenth century. *With a genealogical appendix. Somerville, N. J.: The Unionist Gazette 1889. pp. XXIV, (2), 743, ill.*
[Moelich — Malick — Melick — Mellick genealogy. pp. 627—713.
Descendants of the German emigrants Moelich, who all came from Bendorf on the Rhine.] [7011
Honeyman, A. van Doren: The author of „The story of an old farm." *[Andrew D.*

Mellick.] *In: Somerset County Historical Quarterly. Vol. I. Somerville, N. J. 1912. pp. 23—34.*
[of Palatinate descendants; the original name: Moelich; on his mother's side descendant of Edward Fuller, one of the „Mayflower" emigrants.] [7012
Prowell, George R.: Frederick Valentine **Melsheimer**, a pioneer entomologist, a noted clergyman and author. *A paper read before the Historical Society of York County, April 8, 1897. In: Proceedings and Collections of the Historical Society of York County. Vol. I, no. 2. York, Pa. 1903. pp. 17—26.*
[b. at Regenborn in the Dukedom of Brunswick, Germany, Sept. 25, 1749; appointed chaplain of the Brunswick Dragoons, auxiliary troops 1776 and came with them to Quebeck.] [7013
— Frederick Valentine **Melsheimer**. *In: The Pennsylvania-German. Vol. IX. Cleona, Pa. 1908. pp. 213—217.* [7014
John Christopher **Meng**. *In: The Pennsylvania Magazine of History and Biography. Vol. XXII. Philadelphia, Pa. 1898. p. 376.*
[b. Sept. 22, 1697, in Mannheim, Germany, settled in Germantown, Pa., and Aug. 24, 1728 took the oath of allegiance.] [7015
George **Mentzel**. *In: The genealogical record of the Schwenkfelder families. Edited by S. K. Brecht. New York, N. Y. — Chicago, Ill. 1923. p. 662.* [7016
Melchior **Mentzel**. *In: The genealogical record of the Schwenkfelder families. Edited by S. K. Brecht. New York, N. Y. — Chicago, Ill. 1923. p. 662.* [7017
S.[ener], M. S.: Some **Mentzer** data. *In: Notes and Queries. Edited by W. H. Egle. Annual vol. 1899. Harrisburg, Pa. 1900. p. 33.*
[which family located in Lancaster Co., 1751. An emigration paper, granted on April 13, 1751, to Johan Maintzern, of Jagsfeld, Baden, Oberamt Jorlagh allows, said John Mentzer, his wife and four children to emigrate to Pa.] [7018
Mering, Warren: The „Merring" family. *Sussex, N. J.: Wantage Recorder Press 1929. pp. 50.*
[Descendants of the three brothers, Francis, Nicholas and George Mearing, iron refiners by trade, who came to New Jersey, Pa., arriving at Port Philadelphia, Pa. 1750.] [7019

De Long, Irwin Hoch: The Joel Mertz family bible. *In: The National Genealogical Society Quarterly. Vol. XVI, no. 3. Washington, D. C. 1928. pp. 37—38.*
[Descendants of Joel Mertz and Lovina Hoch, m. Oct. 25, 1863.] [7020
,,Eva Yeakel **Meschter** and her descendants." *In: The genealogical record of the Schwenkfelder families. Edited by S. K. Brecht. New York, N. Y. — Chicago, Ill. 1923. p. 1313.* [7021
Saur bible, first edition. It contains the record of Leonard **Metz**'s family. *In: The Perkiomen Region, Past and Present. Vol. I. Philadelphia, Pa. 1895. p. 35.*
[1763, June 21, Leonard Metz and Maria Histand were married.] [7022
Metzler, C. E.: The Bishop **Metzler** bible. *In: The Pennsylvania-German. Vol. XI. Lititz, Pa. 1910. pp. 611—613, ill.*
[Valentine Metzler, a bishop in the Mennonite Church b. in Europe, Febr. 14, 1726; came to America in 1738.] [7023
Hartman, John M.: A daughter of Germantown [Magaret **Metzler**]. *Read before the Site and Relict Society, Oct. 25, 1902. In: Germantown history. Vol. I. Germantown, Pa. 1915. pp. 31—36.* [7024
Meyer family. *In: Notes and Queries. Edited by W. H. Egle. Third series, vol. I. 1884 —1887, Harrisburg, Pa. 1887. p. 299.* [7025
Dr. John Adolph **Meyer.** *In: The Pennsylvania Magazine of History and Biography. Vol. XXIV. Philadelphia, Pa. 1900. pp. 245—246.*
[b. March 15, 1714, in Saxony, Germany, came to Pa. in 1742.] [7026
Meyers, Theodore B.: Lineage of the Christian **Meyer** family. *Compiled by . . . In: Olde Vlster. An historical and genealogical magazine. Vol. II. Kingston, N. Y. 1906. pp. 50—57; 177—183; 219—222; 313—318; 370—375; Vol. IV. Kingston, N. Y. 1908. pp. 53—56; 311 —314; Vol. V. Kingston, N. Y. 1909. pp. 378—382; Vol. VI. Kingston, N. Y. 1910. pp. 21—26; 218—222; 247—254; 281—286; 313—319; 343—349; 378— 383; Vol. VII. Kingston, N. Y. 1911. pp. 58—63; Vol. X. Kingston, N. Y. 1914. pp. 243—247.*
[Christian Meyer and wife came to America with the Palatine emigration in 1710, arriving in New York with Governor Hunter, June 24, 1710.] [7027

Fretz, A. J.: A genealogical record of the descendants of Christian and Hans **Meyer** and other pioneers, *together with historical and biographical sketches, illustrated with 87 portraits and other illustrations. Harleysville, Pa.: News Printing House 1896. pp. XV, (1), 17—739, ill.*
[settled in Montgomery Co., Pa., about 1720.] [7028
— Genealogy of the **Moyer** family. *Netcong, N. J.: Union Times Print 1909. pp. 144, (1), ill.*
[Christian Meyer, the progenitor of a family numerously represented in Montgomery, Bucks and adjacent counties, Pa. settled in Lower Salford Twp., Montgomery Co., Pa. sometime prior to 1719.] [7029
Meyer, Henry: Genealogy of the **Meyer** family. *Cleveland, O.: Lauer & Mattili 1890. pp. (1), (2), 9—131.*
[Henry (?) Meyer, came from the Palatinate, Prussia and settled among the early settlers on Mill Creek (Mühlbach), Lancaster Co., Pa.] [7030
Fretz, Allan M.: The Meyer or **Moyer** family. *In: The Pennsylvania-German. Vol. VII. Lebanon, Pa. 1906. pp. 275—279, ill.* [7031
Autobiography of William **Michael.** *Part I. — A trip southward. By George Erisman. In: Papers and Addresses of the Lancaster County Historical Society. Vol. XXV. Lancaster, Pa. 1921. pp. 62—64; Part II. A trip westward — Whiskey rebellion. By H. Frank Eshleman. pp. 99—107.*
[b. in Lancaster, State of Pennsylvania, April 1768.] [7033
Mickley, Minnie: The genealogy of the **Mickley** family of America. *Together with a brief genealogical record of the Michelet family of Metz, and some interesting and valuable correspondence, biographical sketches, obituaries and historical memorabilia. Newark, N. J.: Advertising Printing Office. 1893. pp. 182.* [7034
David **Mickley.** *In: Proceedings. Lehigh County Historical Society, Pa. Annual Publication for the year 1923. Allentown, Pa. 1923. pp. 64—65, ill.* [7035
Stapleton, A.: The **Miller** family, of York County. *In: Notes and Queries. Edited by W. H. Egle. Annual vol. 1897. Harrisburg, Pa. 1898. p. 132.*
[Descendants of Michael Miller, of Wurttemberg, Germany whose son Andrew

came with another brother to Pa. prior to 1755.] [7036

P.: Miller. *In: Notes and Queries. Edited by W. H. Egle. Annual vol. 1899. Harrisburg, Pa. 1900. p. 20.*

[children of John and Elizabeth Miller of Lebanon Co., Pa.] [7037

Miller, Frank Burton: The **Miller** family. *An address delivered before the Miller family reunion association at North Waldoboro, Maine, September 7, 1904. Rockland, Me.: The Calson Press Print 1909. pp. (2), 9—47.*

[Frank Miller, the ancestor came with Waldo's German emigrants to Maine, in 1753.] [7038

The **Miller** family magazine. *Genealogical, historical and biographical. Edited by William Montgomery Clemens. Published quarterly. New York City, N. Y. Vol. I. January, 1916. No. 1. ff. — Vol. II. April, 1917. No. 2. (Whole No. 6.) pp. 64; 65—96.* [7039

Mast, C. Z.: The **Miller** family. *In: Christian Monitor. A monthly magazine for the home. Vol. XVII. Scottdale, Pa. 1925. No. 7. pp. 213—214; no. 8. pp. 243—244; no. 9. pp. 278—279; p. 286, ill.* [7040

Lancaster County, Penn., **Miller** wills. *From original records. In: Genealogy. A monthly magazine of American ancestry. Vol. VII. New York, N. Y. 1917. pp. 153—155.* [7041

York County, Penn., **Miller** wills. *From original records. In: Genealogy. A monthly magazine of American ancestry. Vol. VIII, no. 2. New York, N. Y. 1918. pp. 13—15; no. 3. pp. 17—20.* [7042

A family of preachers. *(Rev. Adam Miller, sen. a native of Pennsylvania, and his six sons.) In: Notes and Queries. Edited by W. H. Egle. Fourth series, vol. I. 1891—1893. Harrisburg, Pa. 1893. p. 1.* [7043

Naturalization paper of Adam **Miller**. *[„the first white settler in the Valley on the Shenandoah".] Contributed by Lizzie B. Miller in: William and Mary College Quarterly, Vol. IX, no. 2. October, 1900. Reprint in: The Pennsylvania-German. Vol. IX. East Greenville, Pa. 1908. p. 421.* [7044

In memoriam. Daniel **Miller**. *In: Transactions of the Historical Society of Berks County. Vol. III. Reading, Pa. 1923. pp. 460—461, ill.* [7045

Bates, Bess Royer: Life of D. L. **Miller**. *Anniversary edition. Elgin, Ill.: Breth-*

ren Publishing House. 1924. pp. 340, ill. [7046

Miller, John Peery: The genealogy of the descendants of Frederick and Mary Elizabeth Peery **Miller**. *Compiled by . . . Xenia, O.: Smith Advertising Co. 1913. pp. 7—103, ill., map.*

[Frederick Miller, b. Dec., 1760 in Pa., d. Dec. 2, 1822, at his home, Bethel Twp., Clark Co., O.; m. Mary Elizabeth Peery, b. Dec., 1769, Cumberland Co., Pa., d. Sept. 24, 1844; both of German descendance.] [7047

Miller, Adam B.: History of George **Miller**, sr. and Catharina, his wife, and their descendants. *Dayton, O.: Groneweg Printing Co. 1926. pp. (4), 11—172, (5), ill.*

[George Miller, sr. b. about 1788, a native of Pa. of German descendance, member and a minister of the German Baptist Brethren Church.] [7048

Landis, James D.: A Revolutionary patriot and his worthy grandson. *[Johannes Mueller (John Miller); Emanuel Schaeffer.] In: Papers and Addresses of the Lancaster County Historical Society. Vol. XIX. Lancaster, Pa. 1915. pp. 189—199.* [7049

D.: Doctor John **Miller**, of Frederick Township. *(Montgomery Co., Pa.) Farmer, practioner of medicine, and officer in the church. Reprint from the Schwenksville Item, Friday, Sept. 23, 1881, in: The Perkiomen Region. Vol. IX, no. 1. Pennsburg, Pa. 1931. pp. 15—18.*

[of German or Swiss nativity, bought lands of Frederick Twp., Montgomery Co., Pa., Aug. 10, 1732.] [7050

Stein, Thos. S.: Biographical sketch of Rev. John Peter **Miller**. *Paper read before the Lebanon County Historical Society, Jan. 14, 1927. Vol. IX, no. 1. Lebanon, Pa. 1924—1929. pp. 261—267, ill.* [7051

Dapp, Charles Frederick: Johann Heinrich **Miller**. *In: German American Annals. New series, vol. XIV. Philadelphia, Pa. 1916. pp. 118—136.*

[German printer in the office of Benjamin Franklin, subsequently the proprietor and publisher of the „Staatsbote", b. at Rheden in the principality of Waldeck on the Upper Rhine, March 12, 1702.] [7052

H., S. P.: In memoriam: John Henry **Miller**. *In: Papers read before the Lebanon County Historical Society. Vol. VII. Lebanon, Pa. 1916—1919. pp. 455—457 ill.*

[son of Henry and Sabina (Tittle) Miller and great-grandson of John Miller, the first of the family in Pa., who came from the Palatinate, Germany 1729 and settled in what is now Lebanon Co.] [7053

Fox, Cyrus T.: In memoriam John R. **Miller.** A paper read Dec. 8, 1914. In: Transactions of the Historical Society of Berks County. Vol. III. Reading, Pa. 1923. pp. 233—340, ill. [7054

Steinmetz, Hiram Erb: Peter **Miller** — Michael Witman. In: Papers and Addresses of the Lancaster County Historical Society. Vol. VI, Lancaster, Pa. 1902. pp. 46—49. [7055

Winger, Otho: The life of Elder R. H. **Miller.** Elgin, Ill.: Brethren Publishing House 1910. pp. 269. [7056

Strong, Henry: Justice Samuel Freeman **Miller.** In: Annals of Jowa. Des Moines, Ja. 1894, Jan. [7056a

Gregory, C. N.: Samuel Freeman **Miller.** Jowa City, Ja.: State Historical Society of Jowa, 1908. = Jowa biographical series. [7056b

Stern, Horace: Samuel Freeman Miller, 1816—1890. In: Great American lawyers: history of the legal profession in America. By W. Draper Lewis. Vol. VI. Philadelphia, Pa.: John C. Winston & Co. 1909. pp. . . . [7056c

Miller, Allen H.: Yost D. **Miller** family record. Pekin, Ill.: Free Press 1927. pp. 46.

[who of Amish parents was b. in Somerset Co., Pa. 1814.] [7057

Washburn, Mabel Thacher Rosemary: Millspauch. In: The Journal of American Genealogy. Vol. III. Albany, N. Y. 1928. pp. 189—211.

[Mathias Millspauch (Miltzbagh, Milspaugh, Melsboch, Millspach, Miltzpatch, Melspaugh, Milspagh etc.), a early settler among the Palatines of what is now Orange County, and his descendanss.] [7058

Mishler, John Diefenbach: Mishler's memoirs. Many mistakes merely mentioned. 1847 — April 28 — 1907. Reading, Pa.: Press of Pengelly & Bro. 1907. pp. 191. [7059

Mishler, John Milton: History of **Mishler** families and their descendants. July, first, 1921. Reading, Pa.: Press of Edw. Pengelly & Bro. 1921. pp. 30, ill. [7060

Burkholder, Albert N.: Sketch of John D. **Missimer.** Read June 12, 1906. In: Transactions of the Historical Society of

Berks County. Vol. II. Reading, Pa. 1910. pp. 103—106, ill.

[b. 1847 at Dengler's (now Mount Penn).] [7061

Wilson, Benjamin Franklin: Genealogy of the **Mittong** family and connection. [s. l.] 1926. pp. (2), 7—187, ill.

[The Mittong families who hold their reunions annually at Beegum Grove, 2 miles west of Mannington, Marion Co., W. Va. are of German ancestry. The reunions are held in memory of Jacob M. Mittong, b. Sept. 1, 1821, d. Oct. 27, 1897.] [7062

Dunning, Cora Garber: Genealogy of the Ludwig **Mohler** family in America, covering a period from April 4, 1696, to June 15, 1921. [Ludwig Mohler and his descendants in the line of his sons Henry, of Lancaster, Pa., Jacob of Cocalico Twp., Lancaster Co., Pa. to the year 1795; of Jacob's grandson John Mohler, of Weyer's Cave, Augusta Co., Va., treating particularly of the line through Magdalena Mohler, who became the wife of Martin, son of Levi Garber, bishop of Middle River Dunker Church of Augusta Co., Va.] Lincoln, Nebr.: Published by the editor under the auspices of the Nebraska State Historical Society 1921. pp. (6), 9—63, ill.

[Ludwig Mohler, from Switzerland, arrived Aug. 29, 1730 in America; b. April 4, 1696, d. Jan. 6, 1754; buried near Ephrata, Pa.] [7063

Mohr, Richard G.: The **Mohr** family. In: The Pennsylvania-German. Vol. IX. Cleona, Pa. 1908. pp. 352—353. [7064

Moore, J. H.: The boy and the man. The story of a greatly handicapped boy working his way up to active manhood. Elgin, Ill.: Brethren Publishing House 1923. pp. 190, ill. [7065

Croll, P. C.: Rev. John G. **Morris,** D. D. LL. D. In: The Pennsylvania-German. Vol. VIII. Lebanon, Pa. 1907. pp. 59—62, ill.

[b. Nov. 14, 1803, in York, Pa., son of Dr. John Morris [Moritz] of the Village of Rinteln, in the Duchy of Brunswick, Germany, who came to America 1776.] [7066

Morris, John G.: Life reminiscences of an old Lutheran minister. Philadelphia, Pa.: Lutheran Publication Society 1896. pp. VI, 7—396, ill. [7067

Bachman, J. Fred: Charles **Moser.** A Pennsylvania German boy. Reading, Pa.:

I. M. Beaver 1916. pp (4), 9—348, ill.
[*Written in the way of a story.*] [7068
M., J. S.: The Moul family. *In: Genealogy. Journal of American ancestry. Vol. I. New York, N. Y. 1912. p. 103.* [7069
C., W. M.: Moul family notes. *In: Genealogy. Journal of American ancestry. Vol. III. New York, N. Y. 1813. p. 104.* [7070
Copy of the last will and testament of Abraham **Moyer,** dec. (1789). *In: The Perkiomen Region. Vol. IX, no. 1. Pennsburg, Pa., 1931. pp. 22—24.* [7071
Heebner, H. K.: Prof. James A. **Moyer,** A. M., engineer, scientist and author. *In: The Pennsylvania-German. Vol. VIII. Lebanon, Pa. 1907. pp. 125—126, ill.*
[*b. in Worcester, Pa. Sept. 13, 1874, son of Isaac Kulp and Jane Grater Moyer, of Norristown, Pa.*] [7072
Richards, H. M. M.: Descendants of Henry Melchior **Mühlenberg.** *Prepared by authority of the Pennsylvania-German Society. In: The Pennsylvania-German Society. Proceedings and Addresses . . . 1899. Vol. X. Lancaster, Pa. 1900. Separate pagination: Pennsylvania-German genealogies pp. 3—89.* [7073
Swank, James M.: ,,The Mühlenberg family of Pennsylvania.'' *In: Progressive Pennsylvania. A record of the remarkable industrial development of the keystone state . . . By James M. Swank. Philadelphia, Pa. 1908 [= no. 3185]. = Chapter XXVIII. pp. 289—297. Reprint in: The Pennsylvania-German. Vol. XI. Lititz, Pa. 1910. pp. 103—108.* [7074
[Oakley, Henriette Meir and Schwab, John Christopher]: Muhlenberg album. *[New Haven: Tuttle Morehouse & Taylor Press] 1910. pp. 6, pl. 30.* [7075
Richards, Henry Melchior Muhlenberg: The Muhlenberg family of Pennsylvania. *In: The National Genealogical Society Quarterly. Vol. II. no. 4. Washington, D. C. 1914. pp. 41—42; vol. III. 1914/15, no. 1. p. 10; no. 2. p. 6; no. 3. pp. 6—7; no. 4. pp. 9—11; vol. IV. 1915, no. 1. pp. 32—34.* [7076
[Mühlenberg, Heinrich Melchior]: Heinrich Melchior **Mühlenberg,** Patriarch der Lutherischen Kirche Nordamerika's. *Selbstbiographie, 1711—1743. Aus dem Missionsarchive der Franckischen Stiftungen zu Halle. Mit Zusätzen und Er-*

läuterungen von W. Germann. Allentown, Pa.: Brobst, Diehl & Co.; Halle a. d. S.: Waisenhausbuchhandlung 1881. X, (2), 256 S. [7077
Helmuth, Just Heinrich Christian: Denkmal der Liebe und Achtung welches Seiner Hoch,würden dem Herrn D. Heinrich Melchior **Mühlenberg,** verdienstvollsten Senior des Evangelisch Lutherischen Ministeriums in Nord-America, und treueifrigsten ersten Lehrers an der St. Michaels- und Zions-Gemeinde in Philadelphia ist gesetzet worden. *Samt desselben Lebenslaufe. Philadelphia, Pa.: Melchior Steiner 1788. 60 S., ill.* [7078
Muhlenberg, F. A.: Memoir of Henry Melchior **Mühlenberg,** D. D. *In: The Evangelical Review. Vol. III. Gettysburg, Pa. 1851—52. pp. 151—197.* [7079
Stoever, M. L.: Memoir of the life and times of Henry Melchior **Muhlenberg,** D. D. Patriarch of the Evangelical Lutheran Church in America. *For the Board of Publication. Philadelphia, Pa.: Lindsay & Blakiston 1856. pp. XII, 13—120.* [7080
Mann, W. J.: Vergangene Tage. Aus den Zeiten des Patriarchen Dr. H. M. **Mühlenberg.** *Vortrag gehalten bei der Reformationsfeier des Theol. Luth. Seminars, am 31. Oct. 1879, in der Evang. Luth. Zions-Kirche. Reading, Pa.: Pilger Buchhandlung; Allentown, Pa.: Brobst, Diehl & Co. 1879. 23 S.* [7081
Stricker, Wilhelm: Mühlenberg, Heinrich Melchior. *In: Allgemeine deutsche Biographie. Bd. XXII. Leipzig 1885. S. 460—461.* [7081a
Mann, W. J.: Life and times of Henry Melchior **Mühlenberg.** *Philadelphia, Pa.: G. W. Frederick 1887. pp. XVI, 547; Second edition. Philadelphia, Pa.: General Council Publication Board 1911. pp. XVI, 547, ill.* [7082
In memoriam. Henry Melchior **Mühlenberg** *1711, 1742, 1787. Commemorative excercises held by the Susquehanna Synod of the Evangelical Lutheran Church, at Selinsgrove, Pa., Oct 18 and 19, 1887. Published for the Synod's Committee. Philadelphia, Pa.: Lutheran Publication Society 1888. pp. 61.*
    Ochsenford, S. E.: Lutheranism in America prior to the coming of Mühlenberg. *pp. 3—20;*
    Focht, John B.: Pietism and Halle. *pp. 21—27;*

Wolf, E. J.: Heinrich Melchior Mühlenberg. *pp. 28—41;* [7082]
Morris, J. G.: Brief synopsis of the remarks on the Muhlenberg family. *pp. 42—50;*
Cressman, Mark S.: Lutheranism in America since the death of Mühlenberg. *pp. 51—61.* [7083]
Wolf, E. J.: Henry Melchior **Mühlenberg**. *A memorial address. In: The Quarterly Review of the Evangelical Lutheran Church. New series, vol. XVIII. Gettysburg, Pa. 1888. pp. 254—269.* [7084]
Newton, William Wilberforce: American religious leaders. Dr. [Henry Melchior] **Muhlenberg**. *Boston, Mass. and New York, N. Y.: Houghton, Mifflin & Co. 1890. pp. 272.*
[Reviewed by Henry E. Jacobs under: ,,A common-place Lutheran." In: The Lutheran Church Review. Vol. IX. Philadelphia, Pa. 1890. pp. 117—129.] [7085]
Mann, W. J.: Heinrich Melchior Mühlenbergs Leben und Wirken. *Zum 150. Jahrestag von Mühlenbergs Ankunft in der Neuen Welt. Philadelphia, Pa.: A Hellwege, Roxborough 1891. 77 S., ill. [Neudruck siehe Nr. 1226]* [7086]
Frick, William K.: Henry Melchior **Muhlenberg**, ,,patriarch of the Lutheran Church in America." *First and second edition. Philadelphia, Pa.: Lutheran Publication Society 1902. pp. IV, 5—200, ill.* [7087]
[Croll, P. C.]: Famous Pennsylvania Germans: Henry Melchior Muhlenberg. *In: The Pennsylvania-German. Vol. I, no. 3. Lebanon, Pa. 1900. pp. 3—11, ill.* [7088]
Schuchard, C. B.: A critical estimate of Henry Melchior **Muehlenberg** in the development of the American Lutheran Church. *Paper read before the Brooklyn Lutheran Pastoral Association. In: The Lutheran Church Review. Vol. XLVI. Mt. Airy, Philadelphia, Pa. 1927. pp. 373—390.* [7089]
Heyer, W. C.: Anna Weiser Muhlenberg. *(Mrs. Patriarch H. M M.) A morning star in the destiny of a continent. Shamokin, Pa.: The Leader Publishing Co. 1916. pp. (2), 5—38.* [7090]
[Seabury, Samuel]: Tribute to the memory of Frederick Augustus **Muhlenberg**, M. D. *Boston, Mass.: Marden & Kimball [1837] pp. (1), 5—27.* [7091]
Seidensticker, Oswald: Frederick Augustus Conrad **Muhlenberg**, speaker of the House of Representatives, in the first

congress, 1789. *In: The Pennsylvania Magazine of History and Biography. Vol. XIII. Philadelphia, Pa. 1889. pp. 184—206.* [7092]
Richards, Henry Melchior Muhlenberg: Famous Pennsylvania-Germans: Frederick Augustus Conrad **Muhlenberg**. *In: The Pennsylvania-German. Vol. III. Lebanon, Pa. 1902. pp. 51—60, ill.* [7093]
Seidensticker, Oswald: Friedrich August Conrad **Mühlenberg**. *Abdruck aus ,,Belletristisches Journal", 2. Mai 1889 in: Mitteilungen des Deutschen Pionier-Vereins von Philadelphia. Heft 8. Philadelphia, Pa. 1908. S. 1—14. Neudruck in: Deutsch-Amerikanische Geschichtsblätter. Jg. IX. Chicago, Ill. 1909. S. 12—22.* [7094]
Early, J. W.: Rev. F. A. C. **Muhlenbergs**' trips to Shamokin. *In: The Pennsylvania-German. Vol. XII. Lititz, Pa. 1911. pp. 542—544.* [7095]
Maisch, J. M.: Gotthilf Heinrich Ernst **Mühlenberg** als Botaniker. *Vortrag gehalten vor dem Pionierverein zu Philadelphia am 6. Mai 1886. Veröffentlicht in: Dr. Fr. Hoffmann's ,,Pharmaceutische Rundschau" Juni 1886. (Separat-Abdruck derselben) New York, N. Y.: Gustav Lauter 1886. 39 S., ill.* [7096]
Richards, Henry Melchior Muhlenberg: Famous Pennsylvania-Germans. Gotthilf Henry Ernst **Muhlenberg**, D. D. *In: The Pennsylvania-German. Vol. III. Lebanon, Pa. 1902. pp. 147—155, ill.* [7097]
Schiedt, R. C.: Gotthilf Heinrich Ernst **Mühlenberg**. The first president of Franklin College. *In: The Reformed Church Review. Fourth servies, vol. XVI. Philadelphia, Pa. 1912. pp. 504—516. Reprint in: The Lutheran Quarterly. Vol. XLIII. Gettysburg, Pa. 1913. pp. 59—69.* [7098]
Beck, Herbert H.: Henry E. **Muhlenberg**, botanist. *In: Papers and Addresses of the Lancaster County Historical Society. Vol. XXXII. Lancaster, Pa. 1928. pp. 99—107.* [7099]
Giorg, Kara [Pseudonym von Brühl, Georg]: Heinrich August **Mühlenberg**. *In: Der Deutsche Pionier. Jg. II. Cincinnati, O. 1870—1871. S. 194—197.* [7100]
Muhlenberg, Henry A.: The life of Major-General Peter **Muhlenberg** of the Revolutionary army. *Philadelphia, Pa.: Carey and Hart 1849. pp. XII, 13—456, ill.* [7101]

Ermentrout, Daniel: Remarks of Hon. Daniel Ermentrout, senator from Berks County, on the bill making appropriations for statues of Muhlenberg and Fulton. *The Pennsylvania Statuary Commission. Harrisburg, Pa.: Lane & Hart 1879. pp. 32.*   [7102

Stricker, Wilhelm: Mühlenberg, Peter M. *In: Allgemeine deutsche Biographie. Bd. XXII. Leipzig 1885. S. 461—463.*   [7102a

Germann, W.: Jugendleben des Generals Peter Mühlenberg. *In: Deutsch-Amerikanisches Magazin. Vierteljahrsschrift für Geschichte, Literatur, Wissenschaft, Kunst, Schule und Volksleben der Deutschen in Amerika. . . . herausgegeben von H. A. Rattermann. Bd. I. Cincinnati, O. 1887. S. 43—57; 186—201; 334—344.*   [7103

Wright, Marcus J.: A sketch of the life of General Peter Gabriel Muhlenberg. *Read before the District of Columbia Society of the Sons of the American Revolution, Jan. 16, 1901. In: Publications of the Southern History Association. Vol. V, no. 3. Washington, D. C. 1901. pp. 181—187.*   [7104

Famous Pennsylvania-Germans. Gen. John Peter G. Muhlenberg. *In: The Pennsylvania-German. Vol. III. Lebanon, Pa. 1902. pp. 3—21, ill.*   [7105

A statue of General Peter Muhlenberg. *[Sculptor: J. Otto Schweizer.] Reprint from „The Lutheran." In: The Pennsylvania-German. Vol. XI. Lititz, Pa. 1910. pp. 677—680.*   [7106

Staake, William H.: Address at the unveiling of the monument of General Peter Muhlenberg on German Day, October 6, 1910 at the City Hall, Philadelphia. *[Published by] The German Society of Pennsylvania. [Philadelphia, Pa. 1910.] pp. 18.*   [7107

Huch, C. F.: General Peter Mühlenberg. *In: Mitteilungen des Deutschen Pionier-Vereins von Philadelphia. Heft 2. Philadelphia, Pa. 1906. pp. 2—26.*   [7108

— Peter Mühlenbergs Jugendjahre. *In: Mitteilungen des Deutschen Pionier-Vereins in Philadelphia. Heft 18. Philadelphia, Pa. 1910. S. 34—36 Neudruck in: Deutsch-Amerikanische Geschichtsblätter. Jg. XI. Heft 2. Chicago, Ill. 1911. S. 79—80.*   [7109

Germann, William: The crisis in the early life of General Peter Mühlenberg. *In: The Pennsylvania Magazine of History and biography. Vol. XXXVII. Philadelphia, Pa. 1913. pp. 298—329; 450—470.*   [7110

Kuhlman, Arthur H.: Pulpit and battlefield. A story of Peter Muhlenberg and the American Revolution. *Columbus, O.: The Book Concern [s. d.] pp. 128.*   [7111

Ayres, Anne: The life and work of William August Muhlenberg. Doctor in divinity. *New York, N. Y.: Harper & Brothers. 1881. pp. XIV, 524, ill.* Fifth edition. *New York, N. Y.: Thomas Whittaker 1894. pp. XIV, 524, ill.*   [7112

Newton, William Wilberforce: Dr. William August Muhlenberg. *Boston, Mass. and New York, N. Y.: Houghton, Mifflin & Co. 1890. pp. X, (1), 272.* = *American religious leaders.*   [7113

Croll, P. C.: Famous Pennsylvania-Germans. William A. Muhlenberg. *In: The Pennsylvania-German. Vol. VI. Lebanon, Pa. 1905. pp. 243—249, ill.*   [7114

Halsted, N. O.: Dr. Muhlenberg and Saint Johnland. *In: The Pennsylvania-German. Vol. VI. Lebanon, Pa. 1905. pp. 251—262, ill.*   [7115

Newton, William Wilberforce: William Augustus Muhlenberg. A great Pennsylvania-German leader of religious thought and educator. *In: The Pennsylvania-German. Vol. XII. Lititz, Pa. 1911. pp. 293—296. ill,*   [7116

Ancestry of Rev. Dr. W. A. Muhlenberg. *In: The Pennsylvania-German. Vol. XII. Lititz, Pa. 1911. pp. 297—298.*   [7117

Egle, William Henry: Genealogical record of the families of Beatty, Egle, Müller, Murray, Orth and Thomas. *Harrisburg, Pa.: Lane & Hart 1886. pp. (1), 126.* [Müller and Lobinger *pp. 49—58; John Müller, son of Rudolph Müller, b. about 1715, in the Palatinate, Germany, emigrated with his family to America in 1752.]*   [7118

— Müller [Miller] and Lobinger. *In: Egle's, „Pennsylvania genealogies" Harrisburg. Pa. 1896 [= no. 6045]. pp. 495—504.* [Descendants of John George Müller, son of Rudolph Müller, b. in the Canton of Zürich, Switzerland, Sept. 21, 1715, emigrated to America in 1752.]   [7119

[—] Rev. Charles Edward Muench. *In: Notes and Queries. Edited by W. H. Egle. First and second series, vol. I. Harrisburg, Pa. 1894. pp. 205—206.* [a native of Mettenheim, Wartenburg, in the Palatinate of Chur Pfaltz on the Rhine, Germany, Jan. 7, 1769.]   [7120

[**Kriebel, H. W.**]: A Musser family record. *[Transcriptions data from two historic books belonging to the family of Henry S. Musser, of Marietta, Pa.] In: The Pennsylvania-German. Vol. X. Lititz, Pa. 1909. pp. 393—395.* [7121

In memoriam: Daniel Musser. *In: Papers read before the Lebanon County Historical Society. Vol. VII. Lebanon, Pa. 1916 —1919. pp. 33—35, ill. [son of John and Rebecca (Boltz) Musser.]* [7122

Hays, H. M.: Genealogy of the John Myers family. *In: The Pennsylvania-German. Vol. XI. Lititz, Pa. 1910. pp. 235—237. [John Myers came from Germany in the middle of the 18th century and settled in Pennsylvania.]* [7123

The Myers family. Inscriptions from the Mt. Bethel cemetery, Columbia, Pa. *In: Genealogy. Journal of American ancestry. Vol. III. New York, N. Y. 1913. p. 45.* [7124

N.

Correll, Ernst: The value of family history for Mennonite history, illustrated from Nafziger family history material of the eighteenth century. *In: The Mennonite Quarterly Review. Vol. II. Goshen, Ind. 1928. pp. 66—79; 151—154; 198—204.* [7125

Neff, Elizabeth Clifford: A chronicle together with a little romance regarding Rudolf and Jacob Näf of Frankford, Pa., and their descendants, including an account of the Neffs in Switzerland and America. *Cincinnati, O.: Press of Robt. Clarke & Co. 1886. pp. 352, ill.* [7126

— Addenda. Näf - Neff history. *Regarding the origin and meaning of the name of Neff. Together with the Revolutionary records of Captain Rudolph Neff. Ensign Aaron Scout, Major Thomas Smith, jr. Cleveland, O.: Plain Dealer Publishing Co. 1899. pp. 35.* [7127

Sener, S. M.: The Neffs of Lancaster. *In: Notes and Queries. Edited by W. H. Egle. Annual vol. 1896. Harrisburg, Pa. 1887. pp. 8—10.* [7128

Neff, Elmer Ellsworth: A memorial of the Neff family, with special reference to Francis Neff and some of his descendants. *Altoona, Pa.: Mirror Printing Co. 1931. pp. XIV, 132, ill. [Francis Neiff, Heinrich Neiff and Johann Heinrich Neiff, were banished from Switzerland on account of their re-*

ligious opinions (Mennonites) and were among the earliest settlers of Lancaster Co., Pa., about the year 1717.] [7129

Neff, Florence: The biography of Elder M. Neff and his writings. *Elgin, Ill.: Brethren Publishing House 1913. pp. 304, ill.* [7130

Two Revolutionary heroes. Colonel George Nagel; Captain Peter Nagel. *In: Notes and Queries. Edited by W. H. Egle. Fourth series. Vol. II. 1894. Harrisburg, Pa. 1895. pp. 46—47. [Sons of Joachim Nagel, b. in Isenberg, 3 miles from the City of Coblenz, in what is now Rhenish Province of Prussia about 1740, respectively Oct. 31, 1750.]* [7131

Fretz, A. J.: A genealogical record of the descendants of William Nash of Bucks County, Pa., *together with historical and biographical sketches. . . . Butler, N. J.: Pequannock Valley Argus 1903. pp. 89, 6, ill. [b. 1760, emigrated to America, settled in Bedminster Twp., Bucks Co., Pa. It is uncertain whether he was native of England or if he was a German.]* [7132

Neidig family. *In: Notes and Queries. Edited by W. H. Egle. Third series, vol. I. 1884 —1887. Harrisburg, Pa. 1887. pp. 276 —277. Reprint in: Third series, vol. I. Harrisburg, Pa. 1895. pp. 507—508.* [7133

Neighbour, L. B.: Descendants of Leonard Neighbour, immigrant to America, 1738. *Dixon, Ill.: Star Job Rooms 1906. pp. VIII, 48, ill., map. [Leonard Nachbar, founder of the traced Neighbour family, b. in Germany, May, 1698; arrived at Philadelphia, Pa., Sept. 11, 1738; d. at German Valley, N. J. Aug. 26, 1766.]* [7134

Melchior **Neuman** and his descendants. *In: The genealogical record of the Schwenkfelder families. Edited by S. K. Brecht. New York, N. Y.-Chicago, Ill. 1923. pp. 661—682.* [7135

Fretz, A. J.: A genealogical record of the descendants of Andrew **Newbaker** of Hardwick Township, Warren County, N. J., *together with historical and biographical sketches. Netnong, N. J.: Union Times Print 1908. pp. IV, 5—40, (1), ill. [b. in Germany or Holland in 1759 and emigrated to America prior to about 1790.]* [7136

Hildt, John: The life and journal of the Rev. 'd Christian **Newcomer**, late bishop of the United Brethren in Christ. *Hager-Town: F. G. W. Kapp 1834. pp. 330. = [Newcomers Memoirs or Journal.]* [7137

Roberts, Charles R.: History of the Newhard family of Pennsylvania. *Allentown, Pa. 1915. pp. 17.*

[emigrated from the neighborhood of Oberbach, Palatinate, Germany: (Georg Frederick, Michael and Georg Neuhard) and arrived at Philadelphia, 1737.] [7138

Keller, Eli: Rev. 'd. Peter Frederick Niemeyer. *In: The Pennsylvania-German. Vol. X. Lititz, Pa. 1909. pp. 165—166.*

[b. Aug. 24, 1733 in the City of Wismar, Sweden; emigrated to America 1753.] [7139

Reist, J. Clarence: The Nissley's. *Part II. Containing:* A genealogy of a branch of the Nissley family. *Compiled by . . . , April 1917;* Prospectus for forming a permanent Nissley organization *by* John E. Nissley. An incomplete history of five generations of Nissley's in America, *by J. Clarence Reist. Mount Joy, Pa. 1918. pp. 23, table.*

[Descendants of Jacob Nissley, who emigrated in 1717, and his brother John, who settled near Elizabethtown, Pa. — 1744.] [7140

Fries, Adelaide: The lure of historical research [a picture of Anna Nitschmann, „the Handmaid of the Lord"]. *In: The North Carolina Historical Review. Vol. I. Raleigh, N. C. 1924. pp. 121—137.* [7141

The Nyces of Frederick. *In: The Perkiomen Region, Past and Present. Vol. I. Philadelphia, Pa. 1895. pp. 189—194.*

[Hans Neues (De Nyce, Newes, Nice, Neiss, Nyce) was a resident of the Northern Liberties of Philadelphia; Oct. 20, 1720, he purchased land in Frederick Twp., Montg. Co., Pa.] [7142

Rev. Benjamin Markley Nyce. *In: The Perkiomen Region, Past and Present. Vol. I. Philadelphia, Pa. 1895. pp. 79—80.*

[Pastor of the First Presbyterian Church of Warsaw, Ind., descant of 2 old families of the Perkiomen Valley.] [7143

O.

Rev. John H. Oberholtzer. *Sketch of the founder of the New Mennonites. From: The Reading Eagle, Nov. 2, 1891. In:*

The Perkiomen Region. Vol. IX, no. 2. Pennsburg, Pa. 1931. pp. 39—40.

[b. in Hereford Twp., Montg. Co., Pa. in 1809.] [7144

[Schuler, H. A.]: Rev. John H. Oberholtzer, teacher, locksmith, preacher and publisher. *(Compiled from material, furnished by N. B. Grubb, and by H. P. Krehbiel's „History of the General Conference of the Mennonites of North America". St. Louis, Mo. 1898 [= no. 1055].) In: The Mennonite Yearbook and Almanace for 1908. Quakertown, Pa. 1908. pp. 34—38, ill.*

Reprint in: The Pennsylvania-German. Vol. VIII. Lebanon, Pa. 1907. pp. 420—423, ill. [7145

Loomis, Elisha S.: Some account of Jacob Oberholtzer who settled, about 1719, in Franconia Township, Montgomery County, Pa., and some of his descendants in America. *Cleveland, O.: The Mohler Printing Co., Berea, O. pp. (1), (1), (1), 15—412, (1), (1), ill.*

[b. a. 1686 in Switzerland, or possibly in the Palatinate, Germany.] [7146

Fretz, A. J.: A genealogical record of the descendants of Martin Oberholtzer, together with historical and biographical sketches and illustrated. . . . *Milton, N. J.: Press of the Evergreen News 1903. pp. 254.*

[b. in 1709, in Germany „30 miles from Frankfort-on-the-Main", and settled probably somewhere in Bedminster Twp., Bucks Co., Pa.; d. April 5, 1744.] [7147

Early, J. W.: Oehrlin - Oehrle - Early. *In: Notes and Queries. Edited by W. H. Egle. Annual vol. 1899. Harrisburg, Pa. 1900. pp. 21—22.*

[Descendants of Thomas Oehrlin, school teacher and town clerk of Jesingen, Wurttemberg, Germany, whose son John arrived at Philadelphia, 1752.] [7148

Oehrle (Early) genealogy. *In: Notes and Queries. Edited by W. H. Egle. Annual vol. 1899. Harrisburg, Pa. 1900. pp. 95—97.* [7149

Ohls, Henry Garnsey: Ohl family of Pennsylvania. *In: Notes and Queries. Edited by W. H. Egle. Annual vol. 1900. Harrisburg, Pa. 1901. pp. 113—115.* [7150

Longman, Rufus A.: The genealogy of the Oldfather family. *Compiled by . . . Cincinnati, O.: R. A. Longman 1911. pp. . . .*

[Descendants of Friedrich Altvater, who left Berlin, Germany about 1796 and settled near Berlin, Pa.] [7151

[Omwake, George Leslie]: The Omwakes of Indian Spring farm. *Pictorial, descriptive, biographical. Cincinnati, O. 1926. pp. (1), 7—96, ill.*

[Descendants of Leonhart Amweg and his son, Michael, who emigrated to America, landing at Philadelphia, Pa., Sept. 15, 1729; latter settled „near Cocalico Creek," Lancaster Co., Pa.] [7152

Pennypacker, Samuel W.: Abraham and Dirck Op den Graeff. *Reprint from: Penn Monthly, Sept., 1875. In: Historical and biographical sketches. Philadelphia, Pa. 1883 [= no. 356]. pp. 203 —221.* [7153

Updegrave family. *In: Colonial families of Philadelphia. Edited by John W. Jordan. New York, N. Y.-Chicago, Ill.: The Lewis Publishing Co. 1911. Vol. II. 1199—1204.*

[Herman Op den Graeff, b. in the Village of Aldekerk, or Aldekerry, on Lower Rhine, November 26, 1585. On Aug. 16, 1605 he m. Grietje Pletjes, and removed to Crefeld. He was a delegate from the Crefeld District to the Council of Dordrecht in 1632 when was formulated the first Mennonite confession of faith; d. at Crefeld, Dec. 27, 1642. Isaac Op De Grave, only son, b. at Crefeld, Germany, Febr. 28, 1616, father of 18 children, of whome 4, Herman, Dirck, Abraham, and Margaret were among the first colony of Germans and Palatinates, arrived in Pa., Oct., 1683.] [7154

[Op den Graeff, John William]: The Op den Graeff family. *In: The Mennonite. Year Book and Almanac for 1916. Quakertown, Pa. 1916. pp. 19—22.* [7155

Custer, Milo: Orendorff genealogy. *Bloomington, Ill. 1919. pp. (12), ill.*

[Christopher Orendorf, of German descent, was b. in Maryland about the year 1770, m. Elizabeth Phillips, 1791, and d. in Logan Co., Ill.] [7156

Larimer, L. H.: Samuel Alfred Ort. *A memoir. In: The Lutheran Quarterly. Vol. XLI. Gettysburg, Pa. 1911. pp. 245—248.*

[b. at Lewistown, Pa. 1843.] [7157

Egle, William Henry: Genealogical record of the families of Beatty, Egle, Müller, Murray, Orth and Thomas. *Harrisburg, Pa.: Lane & Hart 1886. pp. (1), 126.*

[Orth of Lebanon. pp. 85—104; Balzer or Balthasar Orth, b. May 5, 1703; emigrated from the Palatinate, Germany, to Lebanon Twp., Lancaster Co., Pa. about 1730.] [7158

Egle, William Henry: Orth family. *In: Notes and Queries. Edited by W. H. Egle. First series, part II. Harrisburg, Pa. 1881. pp. 74 —75. Reprint in: First and second series, vol. I. Harrisburg, Pa. 1894. pp. 383—384.*

[First of the family who emigrated from the Palatinate to Lancaster, now Lebanon Co., Pa. about 1725.] [7159

— Orth of Lebanon. *In: Egle's „Pennsylvania genealogies." Harrisburg, Pa. 1896. pp. 556—578.*

[Descendants of Balzer or Balthasar Orth, the Palatine emigrant.] [7160

Godlove S. Orth. *In: The Pennsylvania German. Vol. IX. Cleona, Pa. 1908. pp. 435—442, ill.*

[Descendant of Balzar or Balthasar Orth, the Palatine emigrant. [7161

[Egle, William Henry]: Rosina Kucher Orth. *In: Notes and Queries. Edited by W. H. Egle. Fourth series, vol. I. 1891— 1893. Harrisburg, Pa. 1893. pp. 388— 389.*

[b. in Lebanon Twp., Lancaster Co., Pa., March 19, 1741, second daughter of Peter and Barbara Kucher, who emigrated from the Palatinate, Germany, about the year 1737.] [7162

Wagenseller, Geo. W.: The descendants of Gottfried Orwig, 1719—1898. *Edited and compiled by . . . (Taken from: „The history of the Wagenseller family in America.") Middleburgh, Pa.: Wagenseller Publishing Co. 1898. pp. 181—208.*

[Gottfried Orwig, founder of the name in America, b., it is supposed, in Brunswick, Germany, Aug. 24, 1719, and arrived at Philadelphia, Pa., Oct. 2, 1741.] [7163

Freas, W. S.: Rev. Jonathan Oswald, D. D. — A memoir. *In: The Quarterly Review of the Evangelical Lutheran Church. Vol. XXII. Gettysburg, Pa. 1892. pp. 341— 353.*

[b. 7 miles from Hagerstown, 1806, the son of John and Eve Oswald, of German stock.] [7164

Lechner, C. S.: Genealogie Otterbein. *S. C. van Doesburgh 1927. pp. IX, 131, ill.* [7165

Cuno, Fr. W.: Johann Daniel Otterbein, weiland Inspector in Berleburg. *Nach seinem Leben und Wirken. In: Reformiertes Wochenblatt. Jg. XIX. Elberfeld 1874. S. 201—207; 209—216; 217— 221; 233—240; 241—244.* [7166

Batdorf, Grant D.: Rev. Philip William Otterbein. *Address delivered in the First*

Reformed Church of Lancaster, Pa. at
an unveiling of a tablet dedicated to the
memory of pastors of that church prior to
1850. In: The Reformed Church Review. Fourth series, vol. XX. Philadelphia, Pa. 1916. pp. 303—314.   [7167
Drury, A. W.: The life of Rev. Philip William Otterbein; founder of the Church
of the United Brethren in Christ. With
an introduction by Biship J. Weaver.
Dayton, O.: United Brethren Publishing
House. 1913. pp. XVIII, 17—384, ill.
                                    [7168
Hinke, Wm. J.: Philip William Otterbein
and the Reformed Church. In: Presbyterian and Reformed Review, Vol. XII,
1901. pp. 437—452.   [7168a
Overmyer, Barnhart B. - Overmyer, John C.:
Overmyer, history and genealogy from
1680—1905. Fremont, O.: Chas. S.
Beelman 1905. pp. (6), 927, 39, ill.,
map.
    [Descendants of John George Ober-
    mayer, a German emigrant who came
    to America from Baden, Germany, in
    1751.]   [7169

P.

Brownback, G. E.: Heivert Papen and the
Papen house of Germantown, Pa. In:
The Penn Germania. Vol. I. = Old
series, vol. XIII. Lititz, Pa. 1912. pp.
78—80, ill.
    [came in 1685 from Mulheim in the
    Palatinate.]   [7170
Parthemore, E. W. S.: Genealogy of the
Parthemore family. 1744—1885. Harrisburg, Pa.: Lane & Hart 1885. pp. VIII,
242.
    [John Frederick Parthemore, son of
    John Henry Parthemore, emigrated to
    America in 1744, landing at Philadel-
    phia Oct. 20; he resided prior to his emi-
    gration, at Sprendlingen, Rhein-Hessen,
    Grand-Duchy of Hesse-Darmstadt.] [7171
Sandt, George W.: Lutheran leaders as I
knew them. Rev. William A. Passavant,
D. D. Leader as philanthropist and
missionary apostle. In: The Lutheran
Church Review. Vol. XXXVII. Philadelphia, Pa. 1918. pp. 441—444. [7172
Seidensticker, Oswald: Franz Daniel Pastorius (1651—1719) und die Gründung
von Germantown (1684). In: Der Deutsche Pionier. Jg. II. Cincinnati, O.
1870—1871. S. 136—143; 169—178;
206—211; 241—248; 275—279; 300—

307; 334—340; 379—383; Jg. III. 1871
—72. S. 8—12; 56—58; 78—83.
    [geb. in Sommerhausen, Franken,
    Deutsches Reich, 26. Sept., 1651.] [7173
Pastorius. In: Notes and Queries. Edited by
W. H. Egle. Annual vol. 1899. Harrisburg, Pa. 1900. p. 156.
    [children of Christian Pastorius, of
    Warburg, Germany.]   [7174
Clayton, Beatrice: Francis Daniel Pastorius
(from a sketch written for the Philadelphia „Public Ledger.") In: The Mennonite Yearbook and Almanac for 1902.
Quakertown, Pa. 1902. pp. 42—44, ill.
                                    [7175
Learned, Marion Dexter: Francius Daniel
Pastorius. The founder of Germantown.
In: German American Annals. New
series, vol. V. Philadelphia, Pa. 1907.
pp. 131—171; 195—234; 259—293;
323—356; Vol. VI. 1908. pp. 3—31; 65—
101; 121—156; 187—237; ill., maps.
                                    [7176
— The life of Francis Daniel Pastorius, the
founder of Germantown. With an
appreciation of Pastorius by Samuel
Whitaker Pennypacker. Philadelphia,
Pa.: William J. Campbell 1908. pp. X,
324, ill., maps.   [7177
Das Leben von Franz Daniel Pastorius.
Nach: „Leben von F. D. Pastorius" von
M. D. Learned [= Nr. 7176—7177].
In: Deutsch-Amerikanische Geschichts-
blätter. Jg. IX. Chicago, Ill. 1909.
Nr. 1. S. 2—5; Nr. 2. S. 47—50. [7178
Götz, Karl: Große Deutschamerikaner.
Franz Daniel Pastorius. In: Deutsche
Arbeit. Führerzeitschrift des Vereins für
das Deutschtum im Ausland. Jg. XXIX.
Dresden 1929—1930. S. 260—266.
                                    [7178a
Turner, Beatrice Pastorius: William Penn
and Pastorius. An address delivered be-
fore the Pennsylvania Society of the Co-
lonial Dames of America, Jan. 28, 1932.
In: The Pennsylvania Magazine of History and Biography. Vol. LVII Philadelphia, Pa. 1933. pp. 66—90.   [7179
Taylor, Herman: The descendants of Henry
and Susannah Paul. Huntingdon, Ind.
1917. pp. (2), 68.
    [Descendants of Henry Paul, who or
    his ancestors came from Germany and
    spent the latter part of his life on a farm
    north of Martinsburg, Blair Co., Pa.]
                                    [7180
Pennypacker, Samuel Whitaker: The Pennypacker reunion, Oct. 4, 1877. Philadel-

phia, Pa.: Bavis and Pennypacker 1878.
pp. IV, 51. [7181
Die **Pennypackerische** Familie in Pennsylvanien. *Aus dem Englischen übersetzt. In: Herold der Wahrheit. Eine religiöse Monatsschrift. Jg. XV. No. 4. Elkhart, Ind. 1878. S. 56—59.* [7182
Pennypacker, Samuel Whitaker: Hendrick **Pannebecker**, surveyor of lands for the Penns. 1674—1754, Flomborn, Germantown and Skippack. *Privately printed. Philadelphia, Pa.: Edward Stern & Co. 1894. pp. 9—164, ill.* [7183
Pennypacker family. *In: Colonial families of Philadelphia. Edited by John W. Jordan. New York, N. Y. — Chicago, Ill.: The Lewis Publishing Co. 1911. Vol. I. pp. 480—493, ill.*

[Hendrick Pannebecker, a Dutch patroon, ancestor of American family, now generally bearing the name Pennypacker, b. in the rural Village of Flomborn, on the Rhine, not far from the City of Worms, March 21, 1674. He was, however, of Dutch lineage, his immediate ancestors having removed from Holland to the locality of his birth. He settled at Germantown as early as 1699, when he m. Eve Umstat who came with her parents Hans Peter and Barbara Umstat from Crefeld, 1685.] [7184
Pennypacker, Samuel Whitaker: The autobiography of a Pennsylvanian. *Philadelphia, Pa.: The John C. Winston Co. 1918. pp. 564, ill.* [7185
Hon. Samuel Whitaker **Pennypacker**, LL. D. *In: The Pennsylvania Magazine of History and Biography. Vol. XL. Philadelphia, Pa. 1916. p. 493.* [7186
Tower, Charlemagne: In memoriam. Hon. Samuel Whitaker **Pennypacker**. *(Minute presented by . . . at a stated meeting of the Council of the Historical Society of Pennsylvania, Oct. 23, 1916.) In: The Pennsylvania Magazine of History and Biography. Vol. XL. Philadelphia, Pa. 1916. pp. 494—495.* [7187
Carson, Hampton L.: The life and services of Samuel Whitaker **Pennypacker**. *In: The Pennsylvania Magazine of History and Biography. Vol. XLI. Philadelphia, Pa. 1917. pp. 1—125.*

[Bibliography pp. 119—125.] [7188
Montgomery, Thomas Lynch: A literary governor. (Samuel Whitaker **Pennypacker**.) *Read Nov. 10, 1916. In: Papers read before the Lebanon County Historical Society. Vol. VII. Lebanon, Pa. 1916—1919. pp. 147—154, ill.* [7189

Pepper family. *In: Colonial families of Philadelphia. Edited by John W. Jordan. New York, N. Y. — Chicago, Ill.: The Lewis Publishing Co. 1911. Vol. II. 1088—1097.*
[Johann Heinrich Pfeffer, b. near Strasburg, Elsass, Jan. 5, 1739, embarked from Rotterdam with 91 other Germans and Palatines for Philadelphia, Pa. Soon after his arrival he located at Schaefferstown, Lebanon Co., Pa.] [7190
William **Pepper**, M. D., LL. D., born, August 21, 1843. Died July 29, 1898. *[Memorial address held in the Chapel of the University of Pennsylvania Nov. 29, 1898.] In: Proceedings of the American Philosophical Society held at Philadelphia for promoting useful knowledge. Memorial volume I. Philadelphia, Pa. 1900. pp. 133—188, portrait.* [7191
Thorpe, Francis Newton: William **Pepper**, M. D., LL. D. (1843—1898). Provost of the University of Pennsylvania. *Philadelphia, Pa. & London: J. B. Lippincott Co. 1904. pp. 555, ill.* [7192
Croll, P. C.: William **Pepper**, M. D., LL. D. A biographical sketch. *In: The Pennsylvania-German. Vol. VII. Lebanon, Pa. 1906. pp. 51—55, ill.* [7193
Pershing, Edgar Jamison: The **Pershing** family in America. *A collection of historical and genealogical data, family portraits, traditions, legends, and military records. Philadelphia, Pa.: George S. Ferguson Co. 1924. pp. XI, 13—434.*
[The Pershing family in America traces back to six immigrants, but only five of them left descendants, and all came to America from Alsace or the Rhine Valley, as included in the Palatine. The first of the emigrants was Frederick Pershing (Friederich Pfoershing) landing at Philadelphia, Pa., Oct. 2, 1749.] [7194
Swank, James M.: Hon. Cyrus L. **Pershing**. 1825—1903. *[s. l.] 1904. pp. 9.*
[Descendant of Frederick Pershing (Friederich Pfoershing).] [7195
Tomlinson, Evert T.: The story of General **Pershing**. *New York-London: D. Appleton and Co. 1919. pp. XIII, 260, ill.* [7196
O'Laughlin, John Callan: Pershing. *Farmer, teacher, moralist, governor, statesman, diplomat, leader, business man, civilian, American. New York-London: G. P. Putnam's Sons, The Knickerbocker Press 1928. pp. V, 185, ill.* [7197

Staudt, Richard Wilh.: [Zur Herkunft der Familie Pershing.] *In: Genealogie in Amerika. Von R. W. Staudt. Vierteljahrsschrift für Wappen-, Siegel- und Familienkunde. Jg. LIV, Heft 4. Berlin 1928. S. 19f.*
[aus Flehingen bzw. Gaisenhausen, Baden, Deutsches Reich.]   [7197a

Mohr, P. P.: The Peter family. *In: The Pennsylvania-German. Vol. VII. Lebanon, Pa. 1906. pp. 352—354, ill.*
[Descendants of Caspar Peter, immigrant from Switzerland, who settled S. E. of Slatington as early as 1742.]   [7198

Peter, W. K.: History of the Peter family which originally settled in Heidelberg Township, Northampton, now Lehigh County, Pa. *Compiled by . . . Allentown, Pa.: Call Publishing Co. 1908. pp. 54, (1).*   [7199

Dotterer, Henry S.: Captain Jacob Peterman. *(His service in the Revolutionary War; his ancestry and his family.) In: The Perkiomen Region, Past and Present. Vol. III. Philadelphia, Pa. 1901. pp. 117—121; 135—137; p. 160; 167—168.*
[son of Christian Ludwick Piederman (Biedermann), a native of Anhalt and settler of Bristol Twp., Philadelphia Co. Pa.]   [7200

Stapleton. A.: Gustav Sigismund Peters, pioneer stereotyper and color-printer. *In: The Pennsylvania-German. Vol. VII. Lebanon, Pa. 1906. pp. 177—178, ill.*
[b. 1793 near the City of Dresden, Germany; d. March 26, 1847 in Harrisburg.]   [7201

Pfautz, John Eby: A family record of John Michael Pfautz, a native of Switzerland, Europe, who emigrated from the Palatinate to America, about the year 1707, and his posterity down to the year 1880. *Compiled by . . . Printed for the compiler and the Pfautz relationship. Lancaster, Pa.: John Baer's Sons 1881. pp. IV, 5—70.*   [7202

Sellers, Edwin Jaquett: Genealogy of Dr. Francis Joseph Pfeiffer of Philadelphia, Pa. and his descendants 1734—1899. *Philadelphia, Pa.: J. B. Lippincott Co. 1899. pp. 67, ill.*   [7203

Phifer, Charles H.: Genealogy and history of the Phifer family. *Edited by George E. Wilson. Charlotte, N. C.: Presbyterian Standard Publishing Co. 1910. pp. (1), 5—54.*

[Descendants of Martin Phifer, b. in Switzerland, Oct. 18, 1720; emigrated to Pa. 1737/38.]   [7204

Mecklenburgh: Memoir of Col. John Phifer, one of the signers of the Mecklenburgh Declaration of Independence. *In: The North Carolina University Magazine. Vol. V. Raleigh, N. C. 1856. pp. 418—420.*
[of Pennsylvania German lineage, son of Martin Phifer (Pfeifer), emigrant from Switzerland.]   [7205

Wing, C. P.: Molly Pitcher. *In: The Pennsylvania Magazine of History and Biography. Vol. III. Philadelphia, Pa. 1879. pp. 109—110.*
[before marriage: Mary Ludwig; she herself came probably from Germany.]   [7206

[Croll, P. C.]: Famous Pennsylvania-Germans. Molly Pitcher. *In: The Pennsylvania-German. Vol. II. Lebanon, Pa. 1901. pp. 99—108, ill.*   [7207

Murray, J. A.: Molly Pitcher (Molly McCauley). *In: Contributions of the local history of Carlisle, Pa. Reprinted under the auspices of the Hamilton Library Association, Historical Department. Carlisle, Pa. 1902. pp. 11.*   [7208

A short history of Molly Pitcher. The *heroine of the battle of Monmouth. Together with an account of the ceremonies incident to the unveiling of the cannon planted over her grave in the old graveyard in Carlisle, Pennsylvania, by The Patriotic Order of Sons of America, on June 28, 1905. Printed for the District of Cumberland County, P. O. S. of A. of Pa., 1905. Carlisle, Pa.: The Cornman Printing Co. pp. 58, ill.*   [7209

Mast, C. Z.: The Plank family. *In: Christian Monitor. A monthly magazine for the home. Vol. XV. no. 10. Scottdale. 1923. pp. 307—309, ill.*   [7210

Montgomery, Morton L.: Sketch of Dr. D. Heber Plank. *Read March 13, 1906. In: Transactions of the Historical Society of Berks County. Vol. II. Reading, Pa. 1910. pp. 101—102, ill.*
[b. in Caenarvon Twp., Berks Co., Nov. 12, 1842, son of David Plank and Rebecca, grandson of Peter Plank, bishop in the Mennonite Church and greatgrandson of Dr. Jacob de Plank, who emigrated from France in 1710, and settled in Oley Twp., Berks Co., about 1720.]   [7211

Fragments genealogiae. The German Poes. *In: The Kittochtinny Magazine. A ten-*

*tative record of local history and genea-
logy west of the Susquehanna. Vol. I,
no. 2. Chambersburg, Pa. 1905. pp.
192—205.* [7212
Dubbs, Joseph H.: Obituary eulogy of the
Rev. Thomas Conrad **Porter**, D. D.,
LL. D. *In: The Pennsylvania-German
Society. Proceedings and Addresses at
Harrisburg, Oct. 25, 1901. Vol. XII.
Lancaster, Pa. 1903. pp. 32—42.* [7213
Lubold, D. G.: The **Pott** family. *Paper,
June 3, 1904. In: Publications of the
Historical Society of Schuylkill County.
Vol. I. Pottsville, Pa. 1907. pp. 31—42.*
[7214
[Wanger, G. F. P.]: The Jacob **Price** family.
*In: The Pennsylvania-German. Vol.
XII. Lititz, Pa. 1911. p. 378.* [7215
— A genealogy of the descendants of Rev.
Jacob **Price**. Evangelist-pioneer. *Com-
piled for the Price Family Association.
Harrisburg, Pa.: The Evangelical Press
1926. pp. (2), VII—X, 832, ill.*
*[Descendants of Rev. Jacob Price
(John Jacob Preisz). b. in Witzenstein,
Prussia, toward the close of the 17th cen-
tury.]* [7216

Q.

Quinter, Mary N.: Life and sermons of
Elder James **Quinter**, late editor of
Gospel Messenger, president of Bre-
thren's Normal School, and author of
,,Trine Immersion". *By his daughter.
Mt. Morris, Ill.: Brethren Publishing
Co. 1891. pp. 426, ill.; Second edition.
Elgin, Ill.: Brethren Publishing House
1909. pp. VI, 7—426, ill.* [7217

R.

Raudenbusch. An old [Palatinate] passport *[of Ulrich Raudenbusch and Anna
Catharina Ehrlich, his wife, 1738]. In:
Notes and Queries. Edited by W. H.
Egle. Second series. Harrisburg, Pa.
1883. p. 239. Reprint in: First and
second series, vol. II. Harrisburg, Pa.
1895. p. 327.* [7218
Gotwald, Luther A.: Memorabilia concerning
the Rev. Lucas **Rauss**, one of the early
ministers of the Evangelical Lutheran
Church in America: including an account
of his ancestors and descendants. *York,
Pa.: O. Stuck. 1878. pp. 68.*
*[b. in Kronstadt, Transylvania, Oct. 17,
1723, son of Lucas and Justina Rauss,
who came to America 1749.]* [7219

Ream, S.: A genealogical history of the
Ream family in Fairfield County, Ohio.
*Cleveland, O.: Central Publishing House
1908. pp. 41.*
*[Descendants of Abraham Ream, who
was born in Reamstown, Pa. in 1746.]*
[7220
Lesher, Pierce: Remarks on Andrew **Ream**,
Revolutionary pensioner. *In: Papers
and Addresses of the Lancaster County
Historical Society. Vol. XXVII. Lan-
caster, Pa. 1923. p. 117.* [7221
Reber, Moris B.: Genealogy of the **Reber**
family descended from Johan Bernhard
Reber 1738. *Compiled by . . . Published
for the family. Reading, Pa. 1901. pp. 50.*
*[Descendants of Johan Bernhard Reber
from Langenselbold, Kreis Hanau, Reg.
Bez. Kassel, Prussia, who came to Ame-
rica, arriving at Philadelphia, Pa. 1738.]*
[7222
Reed, Willoughby H.: History and genea-
logy of the **Reed** family. *Johann Philib
Ried (Rieth, Riedt, Ritt, Rüdt, etc.) in
Europe and America, an early settler of
Salford Township (New Goshenhoppen
Region), Philadelphia County, Pa. Including Reeds other than our family of
this locality, an addenda. Norristown,
Pa.: Norristown Press 1929. pp. XVIII,
529, ill., maps.*
*[They left their home in Mannheim,
Baden, Germany (Palatinate) in 1727,
and arrived at Philadelphia, Oct. 16,
1727.]* [7223
— Lieut. Col. Jacob **Reed**. *Proceedings at
the dedication of the monument, erected to
his memory in Franconia Township, Pa.
under the auspices of the Historical Society of Montgomery County, Pa., Oct. 8,
1901. Norristown, Pa.: Press of The
New Era Printing Co. — Lancaster, Pa.
1905. pp. XVI, 198, ill.* [7224
— Michael H. **Reed**, postmaster of Skippack 80 years ago — an old time hatter.
*In: Historical Sketches. A Collection of
Papers prepared for the Historical Society of Montgomery County, Pa. Vol. V.
Norristown, Pa. 1925. pp. 264—275.*
[Descendant of Lieut. Col. Jacob Reed.]
[7225
P.[arthemore], E. W. S.: Notes on the
Reehm family. *In: Notes and Queries.
Edited by W. H. Egle. Third series, vol.
II. 1887—1890. Harrisburg, Pa. 1891.
pp. 248—250. Reprint in: Third series,
vol. III. Harrisburg, Pa. 1896. pp. 266
—268.* [7226

35*

Reehm. — *In: Notes and Queries. Edited by W. H. Egle. Third series, vol. I. 1884 —1887. Harrisburg, Pa. 1887. p. 3. Reprint in: Third series, vol. I. Harrisburg, Pa. 1895. p. 5.*
[Abraham Reehm, sen., d. in Oct., 1777, Lancaster Co.]   [7227
Sener, S. M.: The **Reesor** family. *In: Notes and Queries. Edited by W. H. Egle. Annual vol. 1898. Harrisburg, Pa. 1899. p. 140.*
[The Reesor family fled from Switzerland to Rhine Bairen, Germany. Peter Reesor, a Mennonite clergyman, arrived with his family in Lancaster Co., Pa. in 1739.]   [7228
Burkholder, L. J.: The **Reesor** reunion of 1928 and family chart. *Compiled by . . . Markham, Wash.: Economist and Sun 1928. pp. 16., ill.*   [7229
Jordan, John W.: Memorial notice of the Rev., William C. **Reichel**. *Paper read before the Historical Society of Pennsylvania, Nov. 13, 1876. In: The Pennsylvania Magazine of History and Biography. Vol. I. Philadelphia, Pa. 1877. pp. 104—107, ill.*
[b. at Salem, in Forsyth Co., N. C., May 9, 1824.]   [7230
Reichner, L. Irving: **Reichner** and Aiken genealogies. *Compiled and edited by . . . [s. l.; s. d.] pp. (3), (3), 3—226; Addenda and errata, Dec. 1, 1926. pp. 3.*
[Descendants of Georg Reichner (Richner, Riegner) b. Nov. 2, 1724; arrived at Philadelphia, Pa. 1751; d. near Trappe, Pa., April 2, 1777.]   [7231
Brinton, Edward Penrose: Col. Adam **Reigart**, 1739—1813. *In: Papers and Addresses of the Lancaster County Historical Society. Vol. XXX. Lancaster, Pa. 1926. pp. 75—79, ill.*   [7232
Ashe, S. A.: Robert Smith **Reinhardt**. *(Manufacturer.) In: Biographical history of North Carolina. Edited by S. A. Ashe. Vol. V. Greensboro, N. C. 1906. pp. 335 —338, ill.*
[b. at Rehobeth Furnace, Lincoln Co., N. C., Jan. 1858, descent from German pioneers of ,,Pennsylvania Dutch" stock, son of Franklin M. Reinhardt and Sarah Smith.]   [7233
Reinhold, D. G.: The **Reinhold** family. *In: The Pennsylvania-German. Vol. VII. Lebanon, Pa. 1906. pp. 295—298, ill.*   [7234
Reinhold, bible. *Contributed by Eli S. Reinhold. In: Publications of the Genealogical Society of Pennsylvania. Vol. VI, no. 1. Philadelphia, Pa. 1915. pp. 18—23.*   [7235
Christopher **Reinwald** and his descendants. *In: The genealogical record of the Schwenkfelder families. Edited by S. K. Brecht. New York, N. Y. — Chicago, Ill. 1923. pp. 629—660.*   [7236
George **Reinwalt** [Rinewald] and his descendants. *In: The genealogical record of the Schwenkfelder families. Edited by S. K. Brecht. New York, N. Y. — Chicago, Ill. 1923. pp. 414— 415.*   [7237
Reist, Henry G.: Peter Reist of Lancaster County, Pennsylvania and some of his descendants. *Schenectady, New York, 1933. pp. 118.*   [7237a
Reitz, J. J.: Family history and record book of the descendants of Johan Friedrich **Reitz**, the pioneer who landed at Philadelphia, Pa., September 7, 1748. *Allentown, Pa.: Searle & Bachman Co. 1930. pp. 289, ill.*
[emigrated from Flörsbach at that time in the principality of Hanau, but now (1930) in the District of Gelnhausen, Reg. Bez. Kassel, Prussia, Germany.]   [7238
Scheffer, J. A.: The Reverend Stephen Albion **Repass**, D. D. *A descendant of the Pennsylvania-German settlers in Virginia. In: The Pennsylvania-German. Vol. X. Lititz, Pa. 1909. pp. 282—286, ill.*
[b. Nov. 25, 1838.]   [7239
The **Rhoads** family. *Inscriptions from the Lutheran Reformed Church, Reamstown, Pa. In: Genealogy. Journal of American ancestry. Vol. III. New York, N Y. 1913. p. 44.*   [7240
Roberts, Charles **Rhoads**: Hon. Peter **Rhoads**. *By his great-great-grandson. In: Proceedings and Papers read before the Lehigh County Historical Society, Allentown, Pa. 1922. pp. 41—43.*
[b. in Whitehall Twp., 1737, the son of Daniel Roth, a native of Switzerland.]   [7241
Shull, David Franklin and Shull, Laura H. S.: Descendants of Christian **Riblet** and his son Bartholomew **Riblet** and genealogical family history, collected and compiled 1925. *Philadelphia, Pa.: 206S 41st Str. 1925. pp. 37.*
[(Huguenot) came from Germany, arriving in Philadelphia, Aug., 1733, and settled in Northampton Co., Pa.]   [7242

Hartman, J. M.: Genealogical notes of the family of Zachariah Rice. *In: The Pennsylvania Magazine of History and Biography. Vol. XXIV. Philadelphia, Pa. 1900. pp. 524—525.*

[Zachariah Rice or Reiss was b. in Germany, 1731, and arrived at Philadelphia, Pa., Sept. 16, 1751.]   [7243

Berry, Charles J.: The Richard genealogy, being a record of Charles and Jacob Richard and all their known descendants. *Published by the author. Minneapolis, Minn. 1926. Mimiographed. pp. IV, 176.*

[who came to America about the time 1740—1750.]   [7244

Hefelbower, S. G.: James William Richard, D. D., LL. D. Born Febr. 14, 1843. Died March 7, 1909. *In: The Lutheran Quarterly. Vol. XXXIX. Gettysburg, Pa. 1909. pp. 451—464.*

[whose ancestors on both sides, were mostly Germans, who had settled in the Shenandoah Valley in the 18th century.]   [7245

Richards, H. M. M.: The Richards (Reichert) family. *In: The Perkiomen Region, Past and Present. Vol. I. Philadelphia, Pa. 1895. pp. 174—175.*

[John Frederick Reichert, the founder of the family in America; b. in Augsburg about 1690; emigrated with his wife, Anna Maria, about 1718.]   [7246

— Early days of Prof. Matthias Henry Richards, D. D. By his son. *In: The Lutheran Church Review. Vol. XVIII. Philadelphia, Pa. 1899. pp. 347—359.*   [7247

Panabaker, D. N.: John G. Richter, F. A. S. *In: Sixteenth Annual Report of the Waterloo Historical Society. Waterloo, Ont. 1928. pp. 92—93.*   [7248

[Egle, William Henry]: Rickert: — (Hartman Rickert). *In: Notes and Queries. Edited by W. H. Egle. Third series, vol. I. 1884—1887. Harrisburg, Pa. 1887. p. 152; Reprint in: Third series, vol. I. Harrisburg, Pa. 1895. p. 259.*   [7249

H., S. P.: In memoriam: Samuel Riegel. *In: Papers read before the Lebanon County Historical Society. Vol. VI. Lebanon, Pa. 1912—1916. pp. 321—323, ill.*

[son of Abraham and Mary (McConnell) Riegel, descendants of Adam Raiguel, who landed in America Aug. 13, 1750.]   [7250

Gruber, M. A.: Rieth [Reed] genealogy. *(Gathered from Rev. John Caspar Stoe-*

ver's Record of baptism and marriages. [1730—1779], published in Egle's Notes and Queries. Annual vol. 1896; gathered from the tombstone inscriptions at Reed's Church, near Stouchsburg, Berks County, Pa.) In: The Pennsylvania-German. Vol. V. Lebanon, Pa. 1904. pp. 90—92.   [7251

Leonhardt Rieth, a noted Pennsylvania-German pioneer. *In: The Pennsylvania-German. Vol. IV. Lebanon, Pa. 1903. pp. 253—257, ill.*

[Palatine settler of the Schoharie, N. Y., who emigrated to Pa., Tulpehocken Valley 1723.]   [7252

Hennighausen, L. P.: Der Bildhauer William Henry Rinehart. *In: Sixteenth Annual Report of the Society for the History of the Germans in Maryland. Baltimore, Md. 1907. pp. 69—72.*

[(Reinhardt) b. 1826, Caroll Co. Md.]   [7253

Rusk, William Sener: Notes on the life of William Henry Rinehart, sculptor. *(With a tentative list of his works.) In: The Maryland Historical Magazine. Vol. XIX. Baltimore, Md. 1924. pp. 309—338; Rinehart's works. Vol. XX. 1925. pp. 380—383.*   [7254

R.[atterman, H. A.]: Johann Georg Ripper, *[der Begründer und Herausgeber der „Pennsylvanische Staatszeitung"]. In: Der Deutsche Pionier. Jg. XII. Cincinnati, O. 1880—1881. pp. 277—279.* [7255

The late John G. Riper. *Translated from the „Deutsche Pionier". In: Notes and Queries. Edited by W. H. Egle. First series, part IV. Harrisburg, Pa. 1881. pp. 152—153. Reprint in: First and second series, vol. I. Harrisburg, Pa. 1894. pp. 481—482.*

[founder and editor of „Pennsylvanische Staats-Zeitung". d. at Harrisburg, Pa., July 23, 1880. (?).]   [7256

Biddle, Edward W.: Governor Joseph Ritner. Historical address. *Read before the Hamilton Library Association, Carlisle, Pa., on Friday evening, Oct. 17, 1919. [s. l.; s. d.] (1919). pp. 10, ill.*   [7257

Rush, Benjamin: An eulogium intended to perpetuate the memory of David Rittenhouse, late president of the American Philosophical Society, *delivered before the Society in the First Presbyterian Church in High-street, Philadelphia, on the 17th Dec., 1796. Agreeably to appointment. Philadelphia, Pa.: J. Ormrod 1796. pp. (2), 5—46.*   [7258

[**Ebeling, C. D.**]: Kürzere Lebensbeschreibungen: David Rittenhouse. *In: Amerikanisches Magazin oder authentische Beiträge zur Erdbeschreibung, Staatskunde und Geschichte von Amerika, besonders aber der vereinten Staaten. Herausgegeben von Hegewisch-Kiel und Ebeling-Hamburg. Erster Band. Drittes Stück. Hamburg: Carl Ernst Bohn 1796. S. 165— 167; Zusätze zu David Rittenhousens Leben. In: Erster Band. Viertes Stück. Hamburg 1797. S. 13—16.* [7258a

Barton, William: Memoirs of the life of David **Rittenhouse**, LL. D. F. R. S.*late president of the American Philosophical Society, &c. interspersed with various notices of many distinguished men: with an appendix, containing sundry philosophical and other papers, most of which have not hitherto been published. Philadelphia, Pa.: Edward Parker 1813. pp. LXXVIII, 79—614, ill.* [7259

David **Rittenhouse**. *Reprint from The Encyclopaedia Americana. Vol. XI. in: Hazard's Register of Pennsylvania. Vol. X. Philadelphia, Pa. 1832. pp. 254— 255.* [7260

Pennypacker, Samuel Whitaker: David **Rittenhouse**. *In: Harper's New Monthly Magazine. Vol. LXIV. Dec., 1881 to May, 1882. New York, N. Y. 1882. pp. 838—849, ill.* [7261
[See no. 356]

Jones, Horatio Gates: Account of Andrew Bradford and Claus **Rittenhouse**. *In: The Pennsylvania Magazine of History and Biography. Vol. XII. Philadelphia, Pa. 1888. pp. 370—372.* [7262

Account of David **Rittenhouse** for surveying, 1774—1775. *In: The Pennsylvania Magazine of History and Biography. Vol. XV. Philadelphia, Pa. 1891. p. 246.* [7263

Holstein, Anna M.: Swedish Holsteins in America from 1644 to 1892. Comprising . . . the families of De Haven, **Rittenhouse**, Clay, Blackiston, Atlee, Coates and other descendants of Matthias Holstein of Wicago, Philadelphia, are included. *Norristown, Pa.: M. R. Wills 1892. pp. 5—305, (1), ill.* [7264

Cassel, Daniel K.: A geneo-biographical history of the **Rittenhouse** family and all its branches in America, *with sketches of their descendants from the earliest available records to the present time, including the birth of Wilhelm in 1644. With an introduction by* Alvah Rittenhouse. *Vol. I. Published by the Rittenhouse Memorial Association. Philadelphia, Pa. 1893. pp. XLIX, 272, ill.* [7265

Cassel, Daniel K.: History of the **Rittenhouse** family. *Part I. Germanotwn, Philadelphia, Pa. 1894. pp. 76, ill.* [7266

— History of the **Rittenhouse** family. *Germantown, Pa. 1894—95. pp. 128. [The first 76 pages were printed in 1894 as part I and the remainder in 1895 as part II; the whole is a continuation of the 1893 volume.]* [7267

— The family record of David **Rittenhouse**, including his sisters Esther, Anne and Eleanor. *Norristown, Pa.: Herald Printing and Binding Rooms. 1896. pp (1), 5—42, ill.* [7268

— The family record of David **Rittenhouse**, including his sisters, Anne, Esther and Eleanor. Also, Benjamin Rittenhouse and Margaret Rittenhouse Morgan. *Norristown, Pa.: Herald Printing And Binding Rooms. 1897. pp. 5—139, ill.* [7269

[**Croll, P. C.**]: Famous Pennsylvania-Germans. David **Rittenhouse**. *In: The Pennsylvania-German. Vol. II, no. 1. Lebanon, Pa. 1901. pp. 3—10, ill.* [7270

Fernow, B.: **Rittenhouse** note. *In: The Pennsylvania Magazine of History and Biography. Vol. XXIX. Philadelphia, Pa. 1905. pp. 503—504.* [7271

Rittenhouse's survey of the River Delaware, 1774. *(Note regarding . . .) In: The Pennsylvania Magazine of History and Biography. Vol. XXXVIII. Philadelphia, Pa. 1914. p. 241.* [7272

Babb, Maurice Jefferis: David **Rittenhouse**, biographical sketch. *In: University of Pennsylvania lectures. No. 4. Part II. April, 1915. pp. 595—608.* [7273

— David **Rittenhouse**. *In: The Pennsylvania Magazine of History and Biography. Vol. LVI. Philadelphia, Pa. 1932. pp. 193—224, ill.* [7274

Ritter, H. S.: The **Ritter** family. *In: The Pennsylvania-German. Vol. VII. Lebanon, Pa. 1906. pp. 292—295. ill.* [7275

— **Ritterana**. *Compiled by . . . Reading, Pa.: Weiler's Printing 1916. pp. 54. [Elios Ritter. temp. 1650. Emigrated to Maryland from Büdingen, Hessen-Darmstadt, Germany and temp. 1682 migrated from Maryland to Pa.]* [7276

Rockefeller, Henry Oscar (and others): The transactions of the **Rockefeller** Family Association for the five years, 1905—

1909 with genealogy. *Editor: ... [Associate editors:* Benjamin F. Rockefeller *and* Claudius Rockefeller.] *Vol. I. New York, N. Y.: The Knickerbocker Press 1910. pp. (2), V—XV, 383, ill.; ...* for the five years, 1910—1914, ... *Vol. II. New York, N. Y.: J. J. Little & Ives Co. 1915. pp. (2), 5—338, ill.; ...* for the eleven years, 1915—1925, ... *Vol. III. New York, N. Y.: J. J. Little & Ives Co. 1926. pp. IX, 294, ill.* [7277

Rockefeller, Henry O.: [Key to family tree of John Peter **Rockefeller** and his descendants.] *Brooklyn, N. Y. 1914. p. 1 and table.*
[who emigrated from Altwied, Germany and settled in Amwell, N. J. from 1743—1787.] [7278

— Key to the family tree of Diell **Rockefeller** and his descendants, who were born Rockefellers. *Brooklyn, N. Y. 1912. p. 1 and table.*
[who emigrated from Rengsdorf, Germany and settled in Germantown, N. Y. 1733—1769.] [7279

Rodenbough. *In: Rodenbough, Theo Francis: Autumn leaves . . . New York, N. Y.: Clark & Zugalla 1892. pp. 146—171.*
[Descendants of Heinrich Rodenbach, a native of the Palatinate, who arrived at Philadelphia, Pa. 1738.] [7280

Rohler records *(from a scrap book ,,commenced about the year 1832 by Mrs. Susan Henning, Suspension Bridge"). In: The Pennsylvania Magazine of History and Biography. Vol. XXXIV. Philadelphia. Pa. 1910. pp. 484—486.*
[,,John Rohrer; b. March, 1696, in Alsace; Maria Souder, his wife, b. February 24, 1716 in Mannheim, Germany.] [7281

Schweinitz, E. A. de: A sermon in memory of the Rev. Edward **Rondthaler,** professor in the theological seminary of the Moravian Church, and late pastor of the Moravian congregation in Philadelphia. *Philadelphia, Pa.: Published by the Board of Elders 1855. pp. 16.* [7282

Blair, William A.: Edward **Rondthaler** *(Moravian bishop). In: Biographical History of North Carolina. Edited by S. A. Ashe. Vol. VI. Greensboro, N. C. 1907. pp. 416—419, ill.*
[b. July 24, 1842, grandson of Emanuel Rondthaler.] [7283

P.: The **Roop** family. *In: Notes and Queries. Edited by W. H. Egle. Third series,*

vol. I. 1884—1887. Harrisburg, Pa. 1887. pp. 280—281. Reprint in: Third series, vol. I. Harrisburg, Pa. 1895. pp. 512—513.
[Descendants of Jacob Roop, of Cocalico Twp., Lancaster Co., Pa.; d. prior to 1777.] [7284

Mathes, Edward: The **Rosenberger** family of Montgomery County. *Historical and genealogical sketches. Harleysville, Pa.: Isaiah R. Haldeman 1892. pp. (5), 60.* [7285

Fretz, A. J.: A genealogical record of the descendants of Henry **Rosenberger** of Franconia, Montgomery Co., Pa. *together with historical and biographical sketches. With an introduction by Seward M. Rosenberger. [Milton, N. J.] 1906. pp. 337, ill.* [7286

Rosenberger, Jesse Leonard: The Pennsylvania-Germans. A sketch of their history and life of the Mennonites and of the side lights from the **Rosenberger** family. *Chicago, Ill.: The University of Chicago Press 1923. pp. X, 173, ill.* [7287

— Through three centuries. Clover and **Rosenberger** lives and times, 1620—1922 *Chicago, Ill.: The University of Chicago Press 1922. pp. VII—XII, 407, ill.*
[J. L. R. descendant of Henry Rosenberger, a Mennonite of Germany, who settled in Indian Creek Valley, Franconia Twp., Montgomery Co., Pa. since 1729.] [7288

Brower, Wm.: Johannes **Roth** (Rhodes) or gleamings from the life of a pioneer settler on the Schuylkill. *In: The Pennsylvania-German. Vol. X. Lititz, Pa. 1909. pp. 119—122.*
[Johannes Roth of Heppenheim, and his wife Barbara Müller of Wachtenheim on the Haardt, Germany, came to Pennsylvania in 1719.] [7289

Roth, David Luther: Johann **Roth:** Missionary. *Published for the author for private distribution. Greenville, Pa.: The Beaver Printing Co. 1922. pp. 240.*
[b. Febr. 3, 1726 in Saarmund.] [7290

Croll, P. C.: Famous Pennsylvania-Germans. Peter F. **Rothermel.** *In: The Pennsylvania-German. Vol. V. Lebanon. Pa. 1904. pp. 99—108, ill.*
[b. in the Village of Nescopeck, Luzerne Co., Pa., July 8, 1812, of German ancestry.] [7291

Rothermel, Abraham H.: The pioneer **Rothermel** family of Berks County, Pa., and their ancestral home of Walbach, Wurtemberg. *Paper read before the Berks County Historical Society, Dec. 12, 1911. In: The Penn Germany. Vol. I. = Old series, vol. XIII. Lititz, Pa. 1912. pp. 94—101, ill.* [7292

Rothermel, Abraham H.: The pioneer Rothermel family of Berks County. *Read Dec. 12, 1911. In: Transactions of the Historical Society of Berks County. Vol. III. Reading, Pa. 1923. pp. 134—143, ill.* [7293

Steinmetz, C. M.: Inscriptions. De Turk Rothermel private burying ground near Fleetwood, Berks County, Pa. *In: The National Genealogical Society Quarterly. Vol. XV, no. 2. Washington, D. C. 1927. pp. 31—32.* [7294

Rothrock. *In: The Pennsylvania Magazine of History and Biography. Vol. XXI. Philadelphia, Pa. 1897. pp. 498—499.*
[Philip Rothrock, b. Aug. 14, 1714, at Beiselheim, Palatinate, came to Pa. in 1733 and settled on the Skippack, Philadelphia Co., and later removed to York Co., Pa.] [7295

Exercises in appreciation of Dr. Joseph Trimble **Rothrock.** at West Chester, March 19, 1914. *Bulletin of the Chester County Historical Society. West Chester, Pa.: F. S. Hickman 1914. pp. 31, ill.* [7296

Dr. Joseph Trimble **Rothrock.** *In: The Pennsylvania Magazine of History and Biography. Vol. XLVII. Philadelphia, Pa. 1923. pp. 143—145.* [7297

Illick, Joseph S.: Joseph Trimble Rothrock, father of Pennsylvania forestry. *Read before the Pennsylvania-German Society at Bethlehem, Oct. 5, 1923. In: The Pennsylvania German Society. Proceedings and Addresses. Vol. XXXIV. 1929. pp. 94, ill.* [7298

Roush, Lester Le Roy: The Roush family in America. *In: Ohio Archaeological and Historical Quarterly. Vol. XXXVI. Columbus, O. 1927. pp. 116—144, ill.* [7299

— History of the **Roush** family in America from its founding by John Adam Rausch in 1736 to the present time. *By ... sixth generation from its founder ... Strasburg. Va.: Shenandoah Publishing House, Inc. 1928. pp. XXVI, 747, ill.* [7300

Genealogical data. **Royer** family. *In: Notes and Queries. Edited by W. H. Egle. Fourth series, vol. I. 1891—1893. Harrisburg, Pa. 1893. p. 14.*
[Sebastian Royer emigrated to America from the Palatinate.] [7301

The **Royer** family. *In: The Perkiomen Region, Past and Present. Vol. I. Philadelphia, Pa. 1895. pp. 153—156.*
[John Michael Reyer (Reier, Reiher, Royer), the founder of the family in Pa. was b. in Schwabbach, Württemberg, in the year 1686; he came from Rohrbach, Württemberg to America and signed the desclaration in Philadelphia, Pa., Sept. 25, 1732.] [7302

Francis, J. G.: Genealogical records of the Royer family in America or more especially those of Sebastian Royer's family, based on original records of Michael Zug. *Lebanon, Pa.: J. G. Francis 1928. pp. (2), XLV, (2), 654, ill.*
[Sebastian Royer (Reier or Ryer) with his four sons, emigrated from the Palatinate, Germany in the year 1718.] [7303

Johann Caspar **Rubel,** der erste deutsche Geistliche auf Long-Island. *In: Der Deutsche Pionier. Jg. III. Cincinnati, O. 1871—1872. pp. 250—253.*
[b. in Hessen-Kassel, came to Philadelphia, Pa. 1751.] [7304

Whitley, Edythe Johns, née Rucker: History of the Rucker family and their descendants. *Sketches of Carter Barton, Early, Johns, Lee, Martin, Pendleton, Reade, Seldon, Taliaferro, Witt and Wyatt families. Nashville, Tenn.: Hermitage Printing Co. 1927. pp. IX, 308.*
[Descendants of Peter Rucker, an emigrant of German nationality to Virginia in 1704.] [7305

Croll, P. C.: Prof. Charles **Rudy,** Ph. D. Remarkable career of a Pennsylvania-German in Paris. *In: The Pennsylvania-German. Vol. IV. Lebanon, Pa. 1903. pp. 195—205, ill. Appendix. pp. 205—207.*
[b. 1837 in Washington Twp., Lehigh Co., Pa., son of Durs Rudy, a Swiss emigrant, who landed at Philadelphia, in 1803.] [7306

Roberts, Charles Rhoads: Sketch of a Lehigh County boy who became a famous teacher — Charles **Rudy.** *In: Annual Proceedings of the Lehigh County Historical Society. Allentown, Pa. 1924. pp. 77—82, ill.* [7307

Roof, F. H.: Johannes **Rueff,** a pioneer of Oneida County, N. Y. *Read before the Society, Sept. 23, 1879. In: Transactions of the Oneida Historical Society, at Utica, with the annual addresses and*

reports for *1881. Utica, N. Y. 1881.
pp. 96—99.*
[*b. in the City of Durlach, Suabia,
Germany, Jan. 9, 1730, landed at Phila-
delphia, Pa. 1759.*]   [7308
Fox, E. L.: William Henry **Ruffner** and the
vise of the public free school system of
Virginia. *In: The John P. Branch
Historical Papers of Randolph-Macon
College. Richmond, Va. 1910, June.*
                                        [7308a
Pearson, C. C.: William Henry **Ruffner:**
Reconstruction statesman of Virginia.
*In: South Atlantic Quaterly. Vol. XX.
Durham, N. C. 1921. pp. 25—32; 137
—151.*   [7308b
Rembaugh, A. C.: Historical sketch of the
Rumbaugh family 1753 to 1888. [*s. l.;
s. d.] pp. 104.*
[*of Pfoutz's Valley, Perry Co., Pa.*]
                                        [7309
Runkel family graveyard. [*In West Hano-
ver Twp., Dauphin Co., on the farm owned
many years by the Runkel family.*] *In:
Notes and Queries. Edited by W. H.
Egle. Annual vol. 1899. Harrisburg, Pa.
1900. p. 51.*   [7310
Fisher, Ben. van D.: The **Runkle** family,
being an account of the Runkels in
Europe, and their descendants in America. *New York, N. Y.: T. A. Wrigth
1899. pp. 5—366, ill.*
[*Descendants of Adam Runkle who
settled about 1755 in Lebanon Twp.,
Hunterdon Co., N. J.*]   [7311
Rupp, I. Daniel: A brief biographic memorial
of Joh. Jonas **Rupp** and complete genealogical family register of his lineal
descendants from 1756 to 1875. *With
an appendix. W.-Philadelphia, Pa.:
L. W. Robinson 1875. pp. XI, (2), 13—
292, ill.*
[*b. at Reihen, near Sinsheim, Germany;
emigrated to Pa. 1751.*]   [7312
— En kurze G'schicht von mei'm Groß-
vater Johann Jonas **Rupp.** *In: Der
Deutsche Pionier. Jg. II. Cincinnati,
O. 1870—1871. S. 235—240.*   [7313
[**Ringwalt, Jessie E.**]: Der Historiograph
Pennsylvanien's — I. D. **Rupp.** *(Frei
nach dem Englischen der Frau Jessie
E. Ringwalt.) In: Der Deutsche Pionier.
Jg. VI. Cincinnati, O. 1874—1875. S.
351—356.*
[*geb. 10. Juli 1803 in East Pennsboro
(jetzt Hampden Twp., Cumberland Co.,
Pa.), Enkel von Jonas Rupp, dem Ein-
wanderer.*]   [7314

R.[attermann, H. A.]: Professor Israel Daniel **Rupp.** *In: Der Deutsche Pionier.
Jg. X. Cincinnati, O. 1878—1879. S.
200—205.*
    *Abdruck in: H. A. Rattermann. Ge-
sammelte Werke. Bd. X. Cincinnati, O.:
Selbstverlag des Verfassers 1911. S. 189
—196.*   [7315
Seidensticker, Oswald: Memoir of Israel
Daniel **Rupp,** the historian. *Paper read
before the Historical Society of Pa., Ja-
nuary 13, 1879. In: The Pennsylvania
Magazine of History and Biography. Vol.
XIV. Philadelphia, Pa. 1890. pp. 403
—413.*   [7316
Croll, P. C.: Prof. Israel Daniel **Rupp.** *A
biographical sketch. In: The Pennsyl-
vania-German. Vol. VII. Lebanon, Pa.
1906. pp. 3—7, ill.*   [7317
Richards, George W.: Rev. William **Rupp,**
D. D. *In: The Reformed Church Review.
Fourth series, vol. VIII. Philadelphia,
Pa. 1904. pp. 541—562.*   [7318
The life and work of Rev. Francis Jacob
Ruth, a pioneer of Lutheranism, in
North-Western Ohio. *Plymouth, O.:
Advertiser Steam Printing House 1888.
pp. 183, ill.*
    [*whose grandfather came „from Swit-
zerland" and resided near Reamstown,
in Lancaster Co., Pa.*]   [7319
William Penn **Ryman.** *Biographical sketch.
In: Proceedings and Collections of the
Wyoming Historical and Genealogical
Society. 1900. Vol. VI. Wilkes-Barre,
Pa. 1901. pp. 139—141.*   [7320

S.

Sahler, Louis Hasbrouck: The genealogy of
the **Sahlers,** of the United States of Ame-
rica, and of their kinsmen, the **Gross**
family. *Utica, N. Y.: L. C. Childs &
Son pp. 38, ill.*
[*Descendants of Abraham Sahler, who
settled at Perkiomen, Pa.*]   [7321
Sandt, George W.: The Adam **Sand** family.
Brief sketch of history of the first two
generations, together with the Adam
Sand and the Philip Corell Wills. [*s. l.;
s. d.] pp. 16, ill.*   [7322
[—] The **Sandt** family history. *Vol. II.
The third generation. 1928. pp. 24, ill.*
                                        [7323
Steinmetz, Mary Owen: Letter (relative to
the **Sassamanhausen** family). *In: The
Perkiomen Region. Vol. II, no. 3.
Pennsburg, Pa. 1923. pp. 42—43.*

[settled in Berks Co., Yost Heinrich Sassamanhausen becoming naturalized somewhere between January 9, 1729 to 1730.] [7324
Seidensticker, Oswald: Die beiden Christoph **Sauer** in Germantown. *In: Der Deutsche Pionier. Jg. XII. Cincinnati, O. 1880—1881. S. 10—15; 47—51; 89— 92; 178—182; 305—310; 350—357; 389—393; 437—444; Jg. XIII. 1881— 1882. S. 63—67; 114—118; 138—142.* [7325
Sower, Charles G.: Descendants of Christopher **Sower** of Germantown. *In: The Pennsylvania Magazine of History and Biography. Vol. VI. Philadelphia, Pa. 1882. pp. 127—128.* [7326
— Genealogical chart of the descendants of Christopher **Sower**, printer of Germantown, Philadelphia, Pa. *Philadelphia, Pa.: C. G. Sower 1887.* [7327
Christopher Saur, jr. loyalist. Extracts taken from Davis's ,,Memoir of Aaron Burr". *In: The Pennsylvania Magazine of History and Biography. Vol. XIII. Philadelphia, Pa. 1889. p. 125.* [7328
Meschter, Charles K.: Christopher **Sower**. An account of what happened to him during the American Revolution. *In: The Perkiomen Region, Past and Present. Vol. I. Philadelphia, Pa. 1895. pp. 182—184.* [7329
Sower, Charles G., Falkenstein, George N. and **Brumbaugh, Martin G.:** Bishop Christopher **Sower** of Germantown memorial services presentation of tablet. Church of the Brethren, Germantown, January 1, 1899. *[s. l.]: Privately printed 1899. pp. 31, ill.* [7330
Brumbaugh, Martin Grove: Famous Pennsylvania-Germans. Christopher **Sower**, jr. *In: The Pennsylvania-German. Vol. II. Lebanon, Pa. 1901. pp. 51—65, ill.* [7331
— The two Christopher **Sauers** in Germantown. *[s. l.; s. d.] Typewritten pp. 16. [Library of the University of Pennsylvania, Philadelphia, Pa.]* [7332
Anders, Daniel M.: The last years of Christopher **Sower**. *In: Historical Sketches. A Collection of Papers prepared for the Historical Society of Montgomery Co., Pa. Vol. V. Norristown, Pa. 1925. p. 162,ill.* [7333
Knauss, James O.: Christopher **Saur** the third. *In: Proceedings of the American Antiquarian Society at the Semi-annual*

meeting held in Boston. *April 15, 1931. New series, vol. XLI, part I. Worcester, Mass. 1931. pp. 235—253.* [7333a
Auge, M.: David **Sower**. The **Sower** family. *From: ,,Lives of eminent men of Montgomery County." By M. Auge. Norristown, Pa. 1879 [= no. 4558]. pp. 14.* [7334
Sayler, James Lanning: A history of the **Sayler** family being a collection of genealogical notes relative to Daniel Sayler of Frederick County, Md., who came to America about 1725—1730 and his descendants. *Albany, N. Y.: Joel Munsell's Sons 1898. pp. 164, ill. [b. in Switzerland, Jan. 15, 1708.]* [7335
Mason, Louis B.: The **Saylor** family. A genealogical sketch of the ancestry of Eliza Saylor Musselman. *New York, N. Y. 1919. [Manuskript at Lancaster County Historical Society.]* [7336
Shaeffer family. Inscriptions from Mt. Zion cemetery, Ephrata, Pa. *In: Genealogy. Journal of American ancestry. Vol. IV. New York, N.Y. 1914. p. 70.* [7337
A memorial sketch of Charles Ashmead **Schaeffer**. Born Aug. 14, 1843 — Died Sept. 23, 1898. President of the State University of Iowa 1887—1898. *Reprint from the Iowa Historical Record, April, 1899. Iowa City, Ia. 1899. pp. 16, ill. [His great-grandfather, David Frederick Schaeffer came from Frankfort, Germany, in 1776.]* [7338
Späth, A., Krauth, C. P., Mann, W. J. and **Schmucker, B. M.:** Memorial of Charles Fred. **Schaeffer**, D. D., late chairman of the Faculty and St. John's professor of systematic and pastoral theology in the Evangelical Lutheran Theological Seminary at Philadelphia. *Philadelphia, Pa., Published by the Alumni Association 1880. pp. ... [b. in Germantown, Pa., Sept. 3, 1807, son of Frederick David Schaeffer, pastor of St. Michaels Church.]* [7339
Jacobs, Henry E.: In memoriam. Charles William **Schaeffer**. Born at Hagerstown, Md., May 5, 1813. Entered into death Germantown, Philadelphia, March 15, 1896. *In: The Lutheran Church Review. Vol. XV. Philadelphia, Pa. 1896. p. 369.* [7340
Schaeffer, D. Nicholas: George **Schaeffer**, the pioneer. *In: The Pennsylvania-Ger-*

*man. Vol. VII. Lebanon, Pa. 1906. pp.
387—391, ill.*
  [arrived at Philadelphia, Aug., 1750.]
                                        [7341
Shimmell, L. S.: Our superintendent of pub-
lic instruction. [Nathan C. **Schaeffer.**]
*In: The Pennsylvania-German. Vol.
VIII. Lebanon, Pa. 1907. p. 318, ill.*
                                        [7342
Brown, J. A.: Rev. Salomon **Schaeffer.** *In:
The Lutheran Quarterly. Vol. XXIX.
Gettysburg, Pa. 1899. pp. 277—283.*
  *[a native of Loudoun Co., Va., whose
parents emigrated to America from Ger-
many.]*   [7343
P.[arthemore], E. W. S.: The family of
Schaffner. *In: Notes and Queries. Edi-
ted by W. H. Egle. Third series, vol. I.
1884—1887. Harrisburg, Pa. 1887. pp.
271—272. Reprint in: Third series, vol.
I. Harrisburg, Pa. 1895. pp. 500—502.*
  *[Henry Schaffner came to America in
the middle of the 18th century from Bos-
sell, Germany.]*   [7344
Robinson, Mary L.: Notes on the **Shaffner**
family. *In: Papers and Addresses of the
Lancaster County Historical Society. Vol.
XXI. Lancaster, Pa. 1917. pp. 5—7.*
                                        [7345
Tobias **Schall,** of Oley, and some of his
descendants. *In: The Perkiomen Region, Past and Present. Vol. I. Philadelphia, Pa. 1895. pp. 127—128.*
  *[came with his wife Magdalene and
his son George from Middle Shefflentz,
Palatinate to America in 1748.]*   [7346
Mast, C. Z.: The **Schantz** (or Johns) family.
*In: Christian Monitor. A monthly maga-
zine for the home. Vol. XV, no. 5. Scottdale, Pa. 1923. pp. 147—149.*
  *[whose ancestor Joseph Schantz was the
founder of Johnstown.]*   [7347
Bowman, H. M.: Jacob Y. **Shantz.** Pioneer
of Russian Mennonite immigration to
Manitoba. *In: Twelfth Annual Report
of the Waterloo Historical Society. Kit-
chener, Ont. 1924. pp. 85—100, ill.*
                                        [7348
Sharp family burials. *Inscriptions from the
burial ground of the Lutheran Reformed
Church, Reamstown, Pa. In: Genealogy.
Journal of American ancestry. Vol. III.
New York, N. Y. 1913. p. 113.*   [7349
Mumaw, Catharine: Shaum family history.
*A short sketch of the ancestry of grand-
father (John) Shaum and the record of
his lineage. Wooster, O.: Published by
Cath. Mumaw 1915. pp. 61.*   [7350

Cory, H. T.: Johan Adam **Schaus** (Shouse)
of Easton, Pa. and some of his descendants. *Typewritten copy 1931. pp. 11.*
  *[came to Philadelphia, Pa., Sept. 1,
1736.]*
  *[At Library of Congress, Washington,
D. C.]*   [7351
Kephart, C. I.: The **Scheib** (Sheip) family.
*In: The Perkiomen Region. Vol. II,
no. 1. Pennsburg, Pa. 1923. pp. 7—9.*
                                        [7352
Johnston, Laura Willhide: Descendants of
my great-grandparents. Being a record
of the descendants of my great-grandfather Peter **Scheibly** *(Family no. 1.);*
my great-grand-father **Wertz** *(Family
no. 818);* my grand-father Conrad **Willhide** *(Family No. 871);* my great-grandfather John Georg **Seiss,** jr. *(Family
no. 904.) . . . By . . . Assisted by* Frank
A. Johnston. *[s. l.] 1924. pp. 7—474,
ill.*   [7353
Christian **Scheid.** *In: The Perkiomen Region. Vol. II, no. 1. Pennsburg, Pa.
1923. p. 10.*   [7354
Brendle, Thos, R.,' Summers, G. Byron and
Kline, Raymond: Concerning Matthias
Scheiffley. *In: The Perkiomen Region.
Vol. I, no. 5. Pennsburg, Pa. 1922. pp.
93—95.*
  *[of Old Goshenhoppen, Montgomery
Co., Pa., son of Johann Caspar Scheiffele
and wife Anna, Lutherans from the District of Ulm, Germany.]*   [7355
Demissen, Christian: Schell, or researches
after the descendants of John Christian
Schell and John **Schell.** *Compiled by . . .
Detroit, Mich.: John F. Eby & Co. 1896.
pp. 94.*
  *[Hannes Krist or John Christian
Schell and Hannes or John Schell, two
brothers of the City of Baden-Baden, in
the Grand-Duchy of Baden, Germany,
emigrated to America and settled on German Flatts, N. Y. about the early of the
fiftees of the 18th century.]*   [7356
Schell, William P.: The ancestry of Ellen
Schell Garber. *Madison, Ind.: The Cou-
rier Co. [1898.] pp. 25.*
  *[Michael Schell, sr., the first Ameri-
can ancestor, emigrated from the Palatinate, b. in 1675 there; he landed at Philadelphia in 1732 and settled near
Goshenhoppen in Philadelphia Co., Pa.]*
                                        [7357
Minnich, Michael Reed: The **Schell** family.
*In: The Pennsylvania-German, Vol. II.
Lebanon, Pa. 1901. pp. 133—139.* [7358

Dotterer, Henry S.: Aaron F. **Shelly, M. D.**
*In: The Perkiomen Region, Past and
Present. Vol. I. Philadelphia, Pa. 1895.
pp. 20—21.*
   *[b. in the Great Swamp, Milford Twp.,
Bucks Co., Febr. 10, 1823, son of Francis
and Catharine (Funk) Shelly.]*   [7359
Musical triumphs of a young American in
Paris. Professor Albert **Shelley.** Albertus Shelley in Dresden. Albertus Shelley's gold medal. *In: The Perkiomen
Region, Past and Present. Vol. I. Philadelphia, Pa. 1895. p. 68; p. 110;
p. 128; p. 129.*   [7360

H., S. P.: In memoriam: Christian **Shenk.**
*In: Papers and Addresses of the Lebanon
County Historical Society. Vol. VII.
Lebanon, Pa. 1916—1919. pp. 21—23,
ill.*
   *[son of Jacob and Magdalena (Miller)
Shenk, descendant of . . . Schenk, a Ger-
man by birth, who settled in Heidelberg
Twp., Lebanon Co., Pa.]*   [7361

Shepherd, James E.: An address of the life
and character of the late judge David
Schenck. *Delivered at Guilford Battle
Ground on the occasion of the unveiling
of a monument to his memory — July 4,
1904. Greensboro, N. C.: Published by
the Guilford Battle Ground Co. 1904.
pp. 18.*
   *[b. in Lincolnton, N. C., March 24,
1835, of Swiss ancestry.]*   [7362

F.[lickinger], S. H.: Graves of the **Scherb**
family. *(From the family grave yard on
the Paul farm, along Indian Creek, Lancaster Co., Pa.) In: Genealogy. Journal
of American ancestry. Vol. II. New
York, N. Y. 1912. p. 287.*   [7363
Documents relating to early German settlers in America. The **Scherer** family.
   *[(1) a letter of health and passport; (2) a
certificate of church membership; (3) a
letter from the father in Germany to his son
in America; (4) a certificate of baptism;
(5) a love letter in rhymne. [1753—1767.]
Transcription, German and Dutch; translation, English. In: German American
Annals. New series, vol. IV. Philadelphia, Pa. 1906. pp. 252—263, fac-
similes.*   [7364

Sherk, Michael G.: A memoir of Rev. A. B.
Sherk. *By his son. In: Fourth Annual
Report of the Waterloo Historical Society. Kitchener, Ont. 1916. pp. 35—36,
ill.*   [7365

Greenwood, Isaac J.: Jacob and Hannah
(Lawrence) **Schieffelin** of New York.

*Reprint from New England Historical
and Genealogical Register for October,
1897. Boston, Mass.: David Clapp &
Son 1897. pp. 3—7.*
   *[The Schieffelin family traces their
decent from the German family of Scheuffelin; grandson of Jacob Schieffelin of
Weilham an-der-Teck, in the Duchy
of Wurttemberg, son of Jacob Scheuffelin,
m. at Philadelphia, Sept. 16, 1756 to Regina Ritzhauer.]*   [7366

Shimer, Allen R.: History and genealogy of
the **Shimer** family in America. *5 vols.
1908—1931. Vol. I. Allentown, Pa.:
Press of Berkemeyer, Keck & Co. 1908.
pp. (2), 7—147, ill.; vol. II. Allentown,
Pa. 1914. pp. (1), (1), 149—235, ill.;
vol. III. Allentown, Pa. 1921. pp. (3),
245—351, ill.; vol. IV. Allentown, Pa.
1927. pp. (1), (1), 361—440, ill.; vol.
V. Philadelphia, Pa.: Press of Kensington Local 1931. pp. (1), (1), 449—536,
ill.*
   *[one of the ancestors of the Shimer fa-
mily in America was Jacob Scheimer, in
Germantown, Pa. as early as 1722. It is
said that he came from Gersheim, Rheinpfalz, Bayern, Germany.]*   [7367

Abbott, Louisa J. - Abbott, Charles L.: The
Shinkle genealogy, comprising the descendants of Philipp Carl **Schenkel,**
1717—1897. *Cincinnati, O.: Press of
Curtis & Jennings 1897. pp. 5—348, ill.*
                                          [7368

Craig, Wm.: **Schindel** reminiscences. *[Rev.
Jeremiah Schindel, Lutheran minister in
Lehigh County, Pa.] In: The Pennsylvania-German. Vol. XI. Lititz, Pa.
1910. pp. 111—112.*   [7369

Roberts, J. O. K.: Mrs. Sallie **Shirey,** the
incomparable. *In: The Pennsylvania-
German. Vol. VIII. EastGreenville, Pa.
1907. pp. 378—379, ill.*
   *[b. 1812 in the Township of Amity,
Berks Co., Pa. of Pennsylvania-German
parents.]*   [7370
— A Pennsylvania German woman. *[Wi-
dow Sallie Shirey, Amity Township,
Berks Co.] In: Historical Sketches. A
Collection of Papers prepared for the Historical Society of Montgomery County,
Pa. Vol. VI. Norristown, Pa. 1929. pp.
243—245.*   [7371

H., S. P.: In memoriam: Howard C. **Shirk,**
Esq. *In: Papers read before the Lebanon
County Historical Society. Vol. VII.
Lebanon, Pa. 1916—1919. pp. 175
—176, ill.*

[son of Samuel Shirk and descendant of . . . Shirk, who emigrated from the Palatinate, Germany to Schoharie, New York and thence into Pennsylvania during Gov. Keith's colonial administration.]

Seyfert, A. G.: Joseph Shirk *[Scherck]*, astronomer, mathematician and inventor. *In: Papers and Addresses of the Lancaster County Historical Society. Vol. XXIX. Lancaster, Pa. 1925. pp. 87—91, ill.* [7373

Harbaugh, H.: The life of Rev. Michael Schlatter; *with a full account of his travels and labors among the Germans in Pennsylvania, New Jersey, Maryland and Virginia; including his services as chaplin in the French and Indian War and in the War of the Revolution, 1716— 1790. Philadelphia, Pa.: Lindsay & Blackiston 1857. pp. XXXI, 27—375, ill.* [7374

Gerhart, E. V.: The life and labors of Michael Schlatter. *[Review of: The life and labors of Rev. Michael Schlatter . . . 1716— 1790. By H. Harbaugh. Philadelphia, Pa. 1857 [= no. 7374].] In: The Mercersburg Quarterly Review. Vol. IX. Chambersburg, Pa. 1857. pp. 466—485.* [7375

Hinke, Wm. J.: Famous Pennsylvania-Germans. Michael Schlatter, the organizer of the Reformed Church in the United States. *In: The Pennsylvania-German. Vol. I., no. 4. Lebanon, Pa. 1900. pp. 3—21, ill.* [7376

Michael Schlatter memorial addresses at the Sesqui-Centennial services held in Hagerstown, Md., by the Synod of the Potomac, October 20. A. D., 1897, in honor of the pioneer organizer of Reformed churches in America. *Prepared for the occasion by* Cyrus Cort, John E. Roller *and* E. R. Eschbach, *and published by request of Synod, January, 1900. Reading, Pa.: Daniel Miller Printer 1900. pp. 61.* [7377

Evans, Samuel: Slaymaker of Lancaster. *In: Notes and Queries. Edited by W. H. Egle. Fourth series, vol. I. 1891—1893. Harrisburg, Pa. 1893. pp. 193—194; corrections. p. 211.*

[Mathias Slaymaker, the first of the name who emigrated to America, came from Strasburg, Germany about the year 1716.] [7378

Slaymaker, Henry Cochran: History of the descendants of Mathias Slaymaker, who emigrated from Germany and settled in the eastern part of Lancaster County, Pa. about 1710. *Compiled by . . . Lancaster, Pa. 1909. pp. (1), (1), 5—344.*

[Mathias Slaymaker or, as it is in the German, Schleiermacher, was b. and bred in Hesse Castle, in Germany.] [7379

Ellis, J. Howard: The Slingluff family. *In: The Pennsylvania-German. Vol. VII. Lebanon Pa. 1906. pp. 341—344, ill.*

[Heinrich Schlengeluff, a native of Waldeck, Germany emigrated to England and afterwards to America; arrived at Philadelphia, Pa., Aug. 19, 1729.] [7380

Diffenderffer, F. R.: Biographical sketch of Col. Matthias Slough. *In: Papers and Addresses of the Lancaster County Historical Society. Vol. VI. Lancaster, Pa. 1901—1902. pp. 139—149.* [7381

Jordan, John W.: Schlosser, George Ernst. *In: Notes and Queries. Edited by W. H. Egle. Third series, vol. II. 1887—1890. Harrisburg, Pa. 1891. pp. 205—206. Reprint in: Third series, vol. III. Harrisburg, Pa. 1896. pp. 188—189.*

[George Ernst⋅ Schlosser, b. Oct. 27, 1714, at St. Arnaud, Nassau—Saarbrück, came to Pennsylvania in 1751.] [7382

W., H. C.: Small family of York. *In: Notes and Queries. Edited by W. H. Egle. Third series, vol. II. 1887—1890. Harrisburg, Pa. 1891. p. 127. Reprint in: Third series, vol. III. Harrisburg, Pa. 1896. p. 52.*

[Lorenz Schmahl arrived at Philadelphia, Pa. from the Palatinate in Sept., 1742.] [7383

Small, Samuel: Genealogical records of George Small, Philip Albright, Johann Daniel Dünckel, William Geddes Latimer, Thomas Bartow, John Reid, Daniel Benezet, Jean Crommelin, Joel Richardson. *Compiled by . . . Revised and edited by* Anne H. Cresson. *Philadelphia, Pa.: Printed for private circulation. by J. B. Lippincott Co. 1905. pp. (3), 361, ill.* [7384

[Small, P. A. & S.]: Remiscences of one hundred years. 1809—1909. *York, Pa.: York Printing Co. 1909. pp. (18), ill.* [7385

Theodore Emanuel Schmauk. *In: The Lutheran Church Review. Vol. XXXIX. Philadelphia, Pa. 1920:*

Sandt, G. W.: A biographical sketch. *pp. 195—212;*

Jacobs, H. E.: Dr. Schmauk and the seminary. *pp. 213—219.*

Weller, H. A.: Dr. Schmauk as member of the Evangelical Lutheran Ministerium of Pennsylvania and president of the General Council. *pp. 220—225;*

Knubel, F. H.: Dr. Schmauk and the United Lutheran Church. *pp. 226—231;*

Haas, John A. W.: Dr. Schmauk as philosopher. *pp. 232—235.*

Selections from Dr. Schmauk's writings. *pp. 239—383.*

[See also no. 7387] [7386

Sandt, George W.: Theodore Emanuel Schmauk, D. D., LL. D. *A biographical sketch with liberal quotations from his letters and other writings. Philadelphia, Pa.: United Lutheran Publication House 1921. pp. XIV, 291, ill.*

[Descendant of Benjamin Friedrich Schmauk, who emigrated to Pa. 1819, from Wurttemberg.] [7387

Smouse, J. Warren: The history of the Smouse family of America. *Martinsburg, Pa.: Herald Print 1908. pp. 5—112, ill.*

[John Smouse (Schmaus,) son of Henry, b. April 5, 1721, set sail at Bremen to America, landing at Baltimore, Md., Sept. 19, 1738 and settled in Loudoun Co., Va., later removed to Bedford Co., Pa.] [7388

Rudisill, Abraham: Minutes of the Centennial celebration, held by the descendants of the Elder Mathias Smyser, May 3rd, 1845, on the farm of Samuel Smyser, in West Manchester Township, York, County, Pa. *[Written, printed and published by] . . . Carlisle, Pa.: Abraham Rudisill 1852. pp. 34.* [7389

The Smysers of York County. *In: Historical Register: Notes and Queries, historical and genealogical, relating to interior Pennsylvania for the year 1883. Vol. I. Harrisburg, Pa. 1883. pp. 154—155.* [7390

Xanders, Amanda Lydia Laucks: History of the Smyser family in America. September, 1731—September, 1931. *York, Pa.: The York Printing Co. 1931. pp. (3), 7—260, ill.*

[Mathias Schmeisser, b. Febr. 17, 1715 in the Village of Rugelbach, 6 miles W. of Dinkelsbühl, Germany, came to America, landing in Philadelphia, Pa., Sept. 21, 1731; he and his family settled in the neighborhood of Kreutz Creek, York Co., Pa.] [7391

In remembrance of Edward G. Smyser, June 15, 1820—Sept. 22, 1887. *Philadelphia, Pa.: Lutheran Publication Society. 1887. pp. 43, ill.* [7392

W. Hinckle Smith family. *In: Colonial families of Philadelphia. Edited by John W. Jordan. New York, N. Y. — Chicago, Ill.: The Lewis Publishing Co. 1911. Vol. II. pp. 1643—1656, ill.*

[Johann Frederick Schmidt, pioneer ancestor, b. at Frohse, near Ashersleben, principality · of Halberstadt, Germany, Jan. 9, 1746, sailed for Pa., Jan., 1769, became appointed pastor of the German Lutheran Church of Germantown, Philadelphia.] [7393

Nolan, J. Bennett: Johann Friederich Schmidt. Written for the exercises attendant upon the 175th anniversary of the foundation of the City of Reading. *Prepared for Publication by Mary Davis Stevens. Reading. Pa.: Reading Eagle Press 1923. pp. 24.* [7394

— The Smith family of Pennsylvania, Johann Friedrich Schmidt. 1746—1812. *By . . . of the sixth generation. Published by the family. Reading. Pa.: Reading Eagle Press 1932. pp. 203, ill.* [7395

Dr. I. S. Schminky. *In: Notes and Queries. Edited by W. H. Egle. Annual vol. 1900. Harrisburg, Pa. 1901. pp. 46—47.*

[b. in Upper Mahantongo Twp., Northumberland Co., son of John and Mary (Flower) Schminky. His grandfather emigrated from Germany and settled in Lancaster Co.] [7396

Mast, C. Z.: The Schmucker family. *In: Christian Monitor. A monthly magazine for the home. Vol. XV, no. 6. Scottdale, Pa. 1923. pp. 180—181; p. 188, ill.*

[whose pioneer ancestor Christian Schmucker landed at Philadelphia, May 8, 1752.] [7397

Wagner, Charles A.: Prof. Samuel C. Schmucker, A. M. Ph. D., teacher and writer. *In: The Pennsylvania-German. Vol. VIII. Lebanon, Pa. 1907. pp. 220—221, ill.*

[b. Dec. 18, 1860 in Allentown, son of Beale Melanchton and Christiana Maria (Pretz) Schmucker.] [7398

Diehl, S. S.: Dr. S. S. Schmucker. *In: The Quarterly Review of the Evangelical Lutheran Church. New series, vol. IV. Gettysburg, Pa. 1874. pp. 1—51.*

[b. at Hagerstown, Febr. 28, 1799, son of John George Schmucker.] [7399

Anstadt, Pa.: Life and times of Rev. S. S. Schmucker, D. D., first professor of theology in the Lutheran Theological Seminary at Gettysburg, Pa. *York, Pa.: P. Anstadt & Sons 1896. pp. VIII, 9—392, ill.* [7400

Spaeth, Adolph: The Schmuckers: Samuel S. and Beale. *(Translated from the: Realencyklopädie für Protestantische Theologie und Kirche. Third edition, by J. W. Early.) In: The Lutheran Church Review. Vol. XXV. Philadelphia, Pa. 1906. pp. 466—475.* [7401

Genealogical register of the male and female descendants of John Jacob **Schnebele**, now **Snively**; and also of the male and female descendants of Samuel **Bachtel** and the relationship existing between the said two families. *Chambersburg, Pa.: M. Kieffer & Co. 1858. pp. 31.*

[J. J. Schnebele, emigrated from Switzerland and arrived in Lancaster Co. between 1707—1718. This is the first Mennonite family history published in America.] [7402

Snively, William Andrew: Genealogical memoranda. Snively, A. D. 1659 — A. D. 1882. *Compiled and arranged by . . . [Brooklyn, N. Y.]: Printed for private circulation. [1883.] pp. 77.*

[Descendants of Johann Jacob Schnebele, b. in Switzerland in 1659, came to Lancaster Co., Pa. in 1714.] [7403

P.[arthemore], E. W. S.: Family of Snively. *In: Notes and Queries. Edited by W. H. Egle. Third series, vol. II. 1887—1890. Harrisburg, Pa. 1891. pp. 222—223. Reprint in: Third series, vol. III. Harrisburg, Pa. 1896. pp. 218—220.*

[John Jacob Schnebele, b. 1659 in Switzerland landed at Philadelphia, Pa. 1727.] [7404

— **Snaveley** family. *In: Notes and Queries. Edited by W. H. Egle. Third series, vol. II. 1887—1890. Harrisburg, Pa. 1891. p. 545. Reprint in: Third series, vol. III. Harrisburg, Pa. 1896. pp. 558—559.*

[History of John Ulrich Schnebli, who settled in what is now Lebanon Co., Pa. after 1755.] [7405

H., S. P.: In memoriam: Henry C. **Snavely**. *In: Papers read before the Lebanon County Historical Society. Vol. VI. Lebanon, Pa. 1912—1916. pp. 333—335, ill.*

[son of Joseph and Elisabeth (Brandt) Snavely; descendant of Caspar Schnebeli, who emigrated from Switzerland 1735 and settled in eastern Pennsylvania.] [7406

The **Schneiders** of Falkner Swamp. *In: The. Perkiomen Region, Past and Present. Vol. II. Philadelphia, Pa. 1900. pp. 142—144; 161—163; 172—176; 190—192; vol. III. 1901. pp. 28—30; 39—40.*

[Johannes Schneider, the founder, who settled near the Falkner Swamp churches, Montgomery Co., as early as 1718.] [7407

The **Schneider** family. Reunion, June 19th, 1915. *pp. 24, ill.*

[Descendants of Jacob Schneider and his wife, Magdalena, who emigrated 1729.] [7408

Allaben, Frank: Schneider family of Columbia County, New York. *A partial account of the German Palatinate stocks which settled in the Valley of Hudson in 1710. In: The Journal of American Genealogy. Vol. I. Greenfield, Ind. 1921. pp. 315—322.* [7409

Benjamin **Schneider**, missionary. *His ancestry, his early life and his conversion. In: Historical Notes, relating to the Pennsylvania Reformed Church. Vol. I. Philadelphia, Pa. 1900. pp. 81—82.* [7410

Good, James I.: Life of Benjamin Schneider, D. D. *A missionary of the Reformed Church in the United States through the American Board, at Broosa and Aintab, Turkey, 1834—1877. Board of Foreign Missions Reformed Church in the United States. Fifteenth and Race streets. Philadelphia, Pa. 1908. pp. 76.* [7410a

Houpt, C. Elvin: Memorials of deceased ministers. *IV.* Benaiah Christian **Snyder**. *In: The Lutheran Church Review. Vol. II. Philadelphia, Pa., 1883. pp. 345—349.*

[son of Conrad Snyder and Sarah Benner of Northampton Co., Pa.] [7411

Beaver, Frederick Philip: Data of the George **Snyder** family. *Collected by . . . [s. l.] Aug. 1, 1914. pp. 5—21, ill.*

[Descendants of Johannes Schneider, who came from the Canton of Berne, Switzerland, as near as can be ascertained, between 1730 to 1740.] [7412

Gov. Simon **Snyder**. *In: Notes and Queries. Edited by W. H. Egle. Third series, vol. I. 1884—1887. Harrisburg, Pa. 1887. p. 296. Reprint in: Third series, vol. I. Harrisburg, Pa. 1895. p. 534.*

[son of Anthony Snyder, who was b. in Plaemig, near Kretznach, in the Pala-

tinate, *Germany in Nov. 1725 and emigrated to America in 1744].*   [7413

Snider, W. W.: The **Snider** pioneer memorial. *In: Tenth Annual Report of the Waterloo Historical Society. Kitchener, Ont. 1922. pp. 248—250.*

[in memory of Christian Schneider and his family, one of the early settlers near, where is now the Village of Doon.]   [7414

Elias Weber Bingeman **Snider.** *In: Ninth Annual Report of the Waterloo Historical Society. Kitchener, Ont. 1921. pp. 183—188, ill.*

[b. in the Town of Waterloo, June 19, 1842, son of Rev. Elias Snider and Hannah Bingeman; descendant of Johannes Schneider who emigrated from Switzerland to Pennsylvania 1736.]   [7415

John Bricker **Snider.** *In: Fifth Annual Report of the Waterloo Historical Society. Kitchner, Ont. 1917. p. 58, ill.*

[b. in Waterloo, Aug. 22, 1840, son of Jacob C. Snider of Franklin Co., Pa.]   [7416

Shock, H. Harvey: Matthias **Schoch.** *Paper read at the Matthias Schoch marker in the Middle Creek Valley, Snyder Co., Pa. In: The Pennsylvania-German Society. Proceedings and Addresses at Selinsgrove, Pa., Oct. 10, 1924. Vol. XXXV. Norristown, Pa. 1929. pp. 24—29.*   [7417

Schofer, H. M.: History of the descendants of John George and Regina Dorothea **Schofer.** *[s. l.] 1897. pp. 110.*

[Descendants of John George Schofer. who emigrated from Loechgau, Bessigheim, Germany to Oley Twp., Berks Co., Pa. 1832.]   [7418

Wilder, Eloise (Walker): A memorial of the one hundreth anniversary of the marriage of Philip **Schoff** and Elizabeth Ramsay, April 10, 1794. *By their granddaughter . . .Greenfield, Ind.: Wm. Mitchell Printing Co. 1922. pp. 311, ill.*   [7419

Shoffner, C. L.: The history of one branch of the **Shoffner** family or John **Shofner** and his descendants, *including also records of the Shoffner reunions. Nashville, Tenn.: McQuiddy Printing Co. 1905. pp. 7—131, ill.*

[Michael Shoffner, the pioneer, was b. in Germany in 1721, near Frankfort-on-the-Main; and soon after landing at Philadelphia, about 1760, removed to Orange Co., N. C. where he d. in 1800.]   [7420

Scholl, John William: Scholl, Sholl, Shull genealogy. The colonial branches. *New York, N. Y.: The Grafton Press 1930. pp. XXXI, 879, ill.*   [7421

Fretz, C. D.: The Frederick **Scholl** family. *In: The Pennsylvania-German. Vol. XI. Lititz, Pa. 1910. pp. 376—379.*

[F. Scholl of the Palatinate, landed at Philadelphia, Sept., 1728 and first settled in Milford Twp., Bucks Co., Pa.]   [7422

Scholl, A. G.: Descendants of John Peter **Scholl** and his wife Anna Susanna Dorothea Scholl, and genealogical family history with short sketch of Philip Scholl and descendants. *Mifflintown, Pa.: The Juniata Herald Publishing Co. 1903. pp. 87, ill.*

[b. April 7, 1738, in the region of the Black Forest, Germany.]   [7423

Scholl, John William and **Shull, Horatio Gates:** The **Scholl** of Salford and Franconia. *In: The Perkiomen Region. Vol. I, no. 5. Pennsburg, Pa. 1922. pp. 89—93; no. 6. 1922. pp. 110—114.*   [7424

George **Scholtze** [Schultz or Shultz] and his descendants. *In: The genealogical record of the Schwenkfelder families. Edited by S. K. Brecht. New York, N. Y. — Chicago, Ill. 1923. pp. 87—143.*   [7425

Gregorius **Scholtze** (Schultz) and his descendants. *In: The genealogical record of the Schwenkfelder families. Edited by S. K. Brecht. New York, N. Y. — Chicago, Ill. 1923. pp. 908—915.*   [7426

George **Scholtze** (Schultz) and his descendants. *In: The genealogical record of the Schwenkfelder families. Edited by S. K. Brecht. New York, N. Y. — Chicago, Ill. 1923. pp. 939—961.*   [7427

Melchior **Scholtze** (Schultz). *In: The genealogical record of the Schwenkfelder families. Edited by S. K. Brecht. New York, N. Y. — Chicago, Ill. 1923. p. 964.*   [7428

Christoph **Scholtze** (Schultz) and his descendants. *In: The genealogical record of the Schwenkfelder families. Edited by S. K. Brecht. New York, N. Y. — Chicago, Ill. 1923. pp. 963—999.*   [7429

Susanna (Dietrich) **Scholtze** (Schultz) and her descendants. *In: The genealogical record of the Schwenkfelder families. Edited by S. K. Brecht. New York, N. Y. — Chicago, Ill. 1923. pp. 1185—1223.*   [7430

W., C. Z.: Anna Rosina **Schultzin.** *[Wife of David Schultz, the surveyor of Upper Hanover Township, Montgomery Co.,*

Pa.] In: The Perkiomen Region, Past and Present. Vol. I. Philadelphia, Pa. 1895. p. 80. [7431

Kriebel, H. W.: David Schultz: An old time „Bush Lawyer". *Paper read before the Montgomery County Historical Society, at the meeting at Perkiomen Seminary, Pennsburg, Oct. 24, 1908. In: The Pennsylvania-German. Vol. IX. Cleona, Pa. 1908. pp. 499—505.* [7432

— David Schultz. An old time „Bush Lawyer". *Read Oct. 24, 1908. In: Historical Sketches. A Collection of Papers prepared for the Historical Society of Montgomery County, Pa. Vol. IV. Norristown, Pa. 1910. pp. 98—111.*

[b. in Harpersdorf, Silesia, the son of George Schultz and Anna Huebner.] [7433

Christoph **Schultz.** *In: The Pennsylvania-German. Vol. XI. Lititz, Pa. 1910. pp. 649—658.*

[son of Melchior and Susanna Schultz, b. in Nieder-Harpersdorf, Silesia, Germany, March 26, 1718; d. near Clayton, Berks Co., Pa., May 9, 1789.] [7434

Magdalena **Shultze.** *In: The Perkiomen Region, Past and Present. Vol. III. Philadelphia, Pa. 1901. pp. 163—164.*

[daughter of David Shultze; b. Nov. 5 (6), 1759.] [7435

Obituary. Dr. Jacob **Shope.** *In: Notes and Queries. Edited by W. H. Egle. Annual vol. 1898. Harrisburg, Pa. 1899. pp. 293—294.* [7436

B., A. H.: Personal recollections of Dr. David **Shope.** *In: Notes and Queries. Edited by W. H. Egle. Third series, vol. I. 1884—1887. Harrisburg, Pa. 1887. p. 365. Reprint in: Third series, vol. II. Harrisburg, Pa. 1896. p. 71.* [7437

Genealogical notes. **Schott.** *In: Notes and Queries. Edited by W. H. Egle. Fourth series, vol. I. 1891—1893. Harrisburg, Pa. 1893. pp. 25—26.*

[Frederick Schott of Derry Twp., Dauphin Co., son of Frederick, sen. went 1812 to Seneca Co., N. Y.] [7438

Mathews, W. B.: Sketch of the life and services of the Hon. George L. Shoup. 1900. [7438a

Shouse, Thomas R.: The Shouse family. *Prepared by Thomas R. Shouse. Liberty, Mo. 1928. pp. (62).*

[Two Shouse brothers came to America from Germany and settled in Pennsylvania. One of them, Herny Shouse, mooved to Woodford Co., Ky. about 1750.] [7439

Everhart, O. T.: A history of the **Everhart** and **Shower** families, from 1744 to 1883. *Embracing six generations. Also a sketch of Manchester, Md. Hanover, York Co., Pa.: Oa.: O. T. Everhart 1833. pp. VI, 7—142.* [7440

Yoder, Silvanus: A brief history of biographical sketches together with a complete genealogy of the descendants of Peter **Schrock.** *Scottdale, Pa.: Mennonite Publishing House 1923. pp. 101, ill.*

[b. in Switzerland, about 1745.] [7441

Shriver, Samuel S.: History of the **Shriver** family and their connections. 1684—1888. *Published for the members of the family. Baltimore, Md.: Press of Guggenheimer, Weil & Co. 1888. pp. 160, ill.*

[Descendants of Andrew Schreiber, b. in Alsenborn, Oberamt Lautern, Germany, Sept. 6, 1712, and came to America in 1721.] [7442

[Shriver, Pearl J.]: History of the **Shriver** family. *[s. l., 1926.] pp. (46), (4), ill.*

[Descendants of Lewis Shriver (originally spelled Schreiber), b. in Beirach, Germany, in 1750 and on arriving in America (in Baltimore about 1790), settled in Greenmount, Cumberland Twp., Adams Co., Pa.] [7443

J.[ordan], J. W.: The **Schropp** family of Northampton County. *In: Notes and Queries. Edited by W. H. Egle. Third series, vol. II. 1887—1890. Harrisburg, Pa. 1891. pp. 189—190; Reprint in: Third series, vol. III. Harrisburg, Pa. 1896. pp. 158—160.*

[Descendants of John Conrad Schropp, of Germany, whose son, Matthew, b. March 21, 1722 at Kauffernen, Swabia, came to Pa, with the second Moravian colony in 1743.] [7444

Shryock, Joseph Grundy.: Shryock genealogy. *Descendants of the emigrant ancestor John Schryock, born in Germany in 1705, emigrated to America in 1733. Philadelphia, Pa. 1930. Blue print. pp. 15. Genealogical chart.*

[At Library of Congress, Washington, D. C.] [7445

Christopher **Schubert** and his descendants. *In: The genealogical record of the Schwenkfelder families. Edited by S. K. Brecht. New York, N. Y. — Chicago, Ill. 1923. p. 345.* [7446

David **Schubert** (Shoebert) and his descendants. *In: The genealogical record of the Schwenkfelder families. Edited by*

S. K. Brecht. New York, N. Y. — Chicago, Ill. 1923. pp. 1151—1174. [7447
Shuey, D. B.: History of the Shuey family
in America, from 1732—1876. Lan-
caster, Pa.: Published by the members
of the family 1876. pp. VIII, 9—279;
Second edition. Galion, O.: Published
for the members of the Shuey family.
    [Daniel Shuey came with Palatines to
    Pennsylvania in 1732.]   [7448
H., S. P.: In memoriam: Edward Shuey.
In: Papers read before the Lebanon
County Historical Society. Vol. VII.
Lebanon, Pa. 1916—1919. pp. 447—
449, ill.
    [son of Amos and Maria (Boeshore)
    Shuey.]   [7449
Shuford, Julius H.: A historical sketch of
the Shuford family. Hickory, N. C.:
A. L. Crouse & Son 1902. pp. 156,
ill.
    [Descendants of John Shuford, of Ger-
    man origin who came from Pennsylvania
    and was found in North Carolina as
    early as 1766.]   [7450
Ashe, S. A.: Abel Alexander Shuford (Ban-
ker). In: Biographical history of North
Carolina. Edited by S. A. Ashe . . . Vol.
VIII. Greensboro, N. C. 1917. pp. 462
—466, ill.
    [b. on his father's farm in Catawba Co.,
    N. C., Nov. 13, 1841; descendant of John
    Shuford, who came from Pa. to what is
    now Lincoln Co., before the Revolutionary
    War.]   [7451
Monteath, Arch. D.: George Archibald Shu-
ford. (Judge). In: Biographical history
of North Carolina. Edited by S. A. Ashe.
Vol. VIII. Greensboro, N. C. 1917. pp.
467—474, ill.
    [b. on his father's farm in Buncombe
    Co., N. C., Aug. 1, 1855, of German an-
    cestry, descendant of George Shuford,
    who removed from Pennsylvania to North
    Carolina on the Catawba River, acquiring
    land as early as 1755.]   [7452
Rosenberger, Elizabeth D.: Gabriel Schuler.
A vigorous pioneer. In: The Pennsyl-
vania-German. Vol. XII. Lititz, Pa.
1911. pp. 240—242.   [7453
Gabriel Shuler's will. [Febr. 15, 1776.]
Translated by Helen G. Brenninger. In:
The Perkiomen Region. Vol. II, no. 3.
Pennsburg, Pa. 1923. pp. 46—48.
                                        [7454
Kriebel, H. W.: Henry A. Schuler. In: The
Pennsylvania-German. Vol. IX. Cleona,
Pa. 1908. pp. 99—105, ill.

    [b. July 12, 1850, in Upper Milford
    Township, Lehigh Co., Pa., son of
    Thomas and Elizabeth (née Kemmerer)
    Schuler.]   [7455
Avellanus, Arcadius: To the memory of
Henry A. Schuler. In: The Pennsylvania-German. Vol. X. Lititz, Pa. 1909.
pp. 114—115.   [7456
Meginness, John F.: Governor John Andrew Shulze. In: The Historical Journal. Vol. I. Williamsport, Pa. 1888. pp.
105—109, ill.   [7457
Richards, H. M. M.: Lebanon County's
distinguished Governor John Andrew
Melchior Shulze. Read February 24,
1922. In: Papers read before the Lebanon County Historical Society. Vol.
VIII. 1921—1924. pp. 181—207, ill.
                                        [7458
Shoemaker, Edward: Some account of the
life and family of George Shoemaker,
for half a century, flour inspector of
Georgetown, D. C. Privately printed.
West Washington, D. C.: L. E. Mankin
[1882] pp. 18.
    [Descendant of Jonathan Shoemaker,
    a native of Pa., having been b. March 20,
    1756, at Cheltenham, near Philadelphia,
    Pa.]   [7459
Keith, Charles P.: „Benjamin Shoemaker".
In: The provincial councillors of Pennsylvania who held office between 1733 and
1776, and those earlier councillors who
where some time chief magistrates of the
province, and their descendants. By . . .
Philadelphia, Pa.: The W. S. Sharp
Printing Co., Trenton, N. J. 1883. pp.
242—264.
    [b. at Germantown, Aug. 3, 1704.] [7460
Shoemaker, Thomas H.: Shoemaker and
Schumacher family. In: The Pennsylvania Magazine of History and Biography. Vol. XVI. Philadelphia, Pa. 1892.
pp. 254—256.   [7461
— The Shoemaker family. Philadelphia,
Pa.: J. B. Lippincott 1893. pp. (1),
5—112.
    [Descendants of the three brothers Ja-
    cob Peter and Georg Schumacher from
    Kriegsheim, Palatinate, who came to Pa.
    between 1683—1686.]   [7462
— The Shoemaker family. Philadelphia,
Pa.: J. B. Lippincott 1893. pp. (1),
(5), 7—112, ill.
    [Jacob, Peter and Sarah, widow of Ge-
    orge, emigrated from Kriegsheim, Pala-
    tinate, to Pa. respectivily 1683, 1685, and
    1688.]   [7463

Shoemaker, Benjamin H.: Geneaolgy of the Shoemaker family of Cheltenham, Pennsylvania. *Compiled by . . . Printed for private circulation. Philadelphia, Pa.: J. B. Lippincott. 1903. pp. (VII), (IX), 524, ill.*
[Descendants of George and Sarah Shoemaker, m. in Heidelberg, Germany in 1662. Sarah, widow of George, emigrated with her children and arrived at Philadelphia, Pa. 1. mo. 20, 1686.] [7464

Mohr, Charles Shoemaker: The Shoemaker family of Shoemakersville, Pa. *In: The Pennsylvania-German. Vol. IX. Cleona, Pa. 1908. pp. 559—563, ill.* [7465

The Shoemaker family of Shoemakersville, Pennsylvania 1682—1909. *Reading, Pa.: Luther & Mohr 1909 pp. 42, ill.*
[Descendants of Carl (Charles, sr.) Shoemaker, who was a grandson of Jacob Schumacher (now Shoemaker) who emigrated to Pa. from Cresheim (Kriegsheim), Germany, Aug. 16, 1682.] [7466

Shoemaker family. *In: Colonial families of Philadelphia. Edited by John W. Jordan. New York, N. Y. — Chicago, Ill.: The Lewis Publishing Co. 1911. Vol. I. pp. 435—450.*
[of German origin, the name being anglicised from Schumacher; descendants of Georg and Sarah Shoemaker of Kriegsheim, Upper Palatinate. He sailed for Philadelphia, but died on the passage, his family arriving at Philadelphia, March 20, 1685—86.] [7467

Blair, Williams T.: The Michael Shoemaker book (Schumacher). *Printed for J. I. Shoemaker, Wyoming, Pa. Scranton, Pa.: International Textbook Press 1924. pp. XII, 995, ill.*
[Michael Schumacher was b. in the Dukedom of Zweibrucken, Germany, about 1715; arrived at Philadelphia, Pa. Aug. 30, 1737.] [7468

Gwinn, Sherman: Edward E. Shumaker. *His questions were hind-side-'fore but he got his answers straight. Out of the mountains came Edward E. Shumaker, bringing his Pennsylvania-Dutch dialect, and his incurable habit of asking questions — Men laughed at his curiously twisted sentences, but respected his determination to learn, a determination which, two years ago, saved an industry. In: The American Magazine for Sept., 1927. Vol. CIV. Springfield, O. 1927. p. 18; p. 144; p. 145; p. 147; p. 148; p. 149, ill.*
[b. in Somerset Co., Pa. 1882.] [7469

Marriage certificate, George and Sarah (Wall) Shoemaker, 1694. *In: The Pennsylvania Magazine of History and Biography. Vol. XVI. Philadelphia, Pa. 1892. pp. 461—462.* [7470

Obituary. George J. Shoemaker. *In: Notes and Queries. Edited by W. H. Egle. Annual vol. 1898. Harrisburg, Pa. 1899. p. 293.* [7471

Shuman, William C.: The George Shuman family. Genealogy and history. *From the time of arrival in America, in 1760, to the year 1913. Evanston, Ill.: Published by W. C. Shuman. — Press: Chicago, Ill.: Kenfield — Leach Co. pp. 341. ill.* [7472

Schumm, Wm. J. and others: History of the John George Schumm family. *1928. [s. l.] 1928. pp. 52, ill.*
[emigrated to America in 1833.] [7473

De Witt, W. R.: A discourse on the life and character of Francis R. Shunk. *Harrisburg, Pa. 1848. pp. 30.* [7474

P.[arthemore], E. W. S.: The family of Shuster. *In: Notes and Queries. Edited by W. H. Egle. Third series, vol. I. 1884 —1887. Harrisburg, Pa. 1887. pp. 314 —315; 315—316. Reprint in: Third series, vol. II. Harrisburg, Pa. 1896. pp. 1—5.*
[Lawrence Shuster, b. in Germany, April 19, 1749, came over to America with his mother, sister and 2 brothers in 1767.] [7475

Swarr, Jacob Mellinger: A biographical history of the Swarr [Schwahr] family of Lancaster County, Pa. *Lancaster, Pa.: L. B. Herr Print 1909. pp. 32, ill.* [7476

Swander, John I.: History of the Swander family. *(Published by Thomas S. Falkner and Pittinger Harry D. Committee) Tiffin, O.: Press of E. R. Good & Bro. [1899.] pp. 143, ill.* [7477

[—] Autobiography of Dr. I. Swander supplemented with selections of his written sermons preached during his early ministry . . . *With a foreward by John C. Bowman. Philadelphia, Pa.: Publication Board of the Reformed Church in the United States 1911. pp. 272.*
[Descendant of Frederick Schwander, who left the Canton of Berne, Switzerland and landed at Philadelphia in 1732.] [7478

[Shuman, J. C.]: Schwartz descendants. *In: The Pennsylvania-German. Vol. IX. Cleona, Pa. 1908. p. 143.* [7479

36*

Stapleton, A.: A neglected grave. *(Inscription of the tombstones of Albrecht Schweinforth, and his two sons, settlers of the Middcreek Valley, in (now) Snyder Co.) In: Notes and Queries. Edited by W. H. Egle. Annual vol. 1896. Harrisburg, Pa. 1897. p. 170.*
[A. Schweinforth emigrated to Pa. 1754.]   [7480
In memoriam. Edmund Alexander de Schweinitz, S. T. D., episcus fratrum. *Born March 20, 1825. Entered into rest December 18, 1887. Bethlehem, Pa.: The Comenius Press 1887. pp. 27.*
[son of Lewis David de Schweinitz.]
[7481
Pfohl, J. K. - Rondthaler, Edward: In memoriam. Elenor de Schweinitz Siewers. *Born, December 23rd, 1853. Entered into rest May 17th, 1927. [Winston-Salem, N. C. 1927.] pp. 11.*
[b. Salem, Dec. 23, 1853, daughter of Emil A. and Sr. Sophia Herman de Schweinitz.]   [7482
Ruffin, Sterling: Emil Alexander de Schweinitz *(Physician, chemist and educator). In: Biographical history of North Carolina. Edited by S. A. Ashe. Vol. III. Greensboro, N. C. 1905. pp. 394—400, ill.*
[of German ancestry, descendants of Hans Christian Alexander von Schweinitz, who came to Bethlehem, Pa. in 1770, son of Lewis David von Schweinitz; b. in Salem, N. C., Jan. 18, 1864.]   [7483
Johnson, Walter R.: Lewis David von Schweinitz, P. D. A memoir of the late Lewis David von Schweinitz, P. D., with a sketch of his scientific labours. *Read before The Academy of Natural Sciences of Philadelphia, May 12th, 1835. In: Hazard's Register of Pennsylvania. Vol. XV. Philadelphia, Pa. 1835. pp. 369—376.*   [7484
— A sketch of the life and scientific work of Lewis David von Schweinitz. *In: Journal of the Elisha Mitchell Scientific Society, 1885—1886. Third year. Raleigh, N. C.: Edwards, Broughton & Co. 1886. pp. 9—25.*   [7485
The Schwenk family. *In: The Perkiomen Region, Past and Present. Vol. III. Philadelphia, Pa. 1901. pp. 51—52.*
[7486
Genealogy of the Schwenk family. *Compiled by Enos S. Schwenk and his son John K. Schwenk. 1916. Revised and enlarged by Ralph Beaver Strassburger.*

Norristown, Pa.: The Norristown Press 1929. pp. (1), 5—282, (1).   [7487
Flores, P. W.: Martin Schwenk. *In: The Perkiomen Region, Past and Present. Vol. III. Philadelphia, Pa. 1901. pp. 188—191.*
[Martin Schwenk, a German, m. Anna Maria Dillinger, March 6, 1750, recorded in the church book of the Lutheran congregation of Milford Twp., Bucks Co., (now Lehigh Co.), Pa.] [7488
Genealogical notes. Schweyer (Schwoyer) — Nicholas Schweyer, sr. of Maxatawney Township, Berks Co. died in Sept., 1802. *In: Notes and Queries. Edited by W. H. Egle. Fourth series, vol. II. 1894. Harrisburg, Pa. 1895. p. 43.*   [7489
Swiger, Ira L.: A genealogical and biographical history of the Swiger family in the United States of America. *Fairmont, W. Va.: Press of Fairmont Printing & Publishing Co. 1916. pp. (4), 9—361, XVI, ill.*
[Descendants of John William and Mary Swiger, the emigrants to Virginia, 1755, later removed to Fayette Co., Pa.]
[7490
Swope, Gilbert Ernest: History of the Swope family and their connections 1678—1896. *Compiled and edited by . . . Lancaster, Pa.: T. B. & H. B. Cochran 1896. pp. (1), (1), 9—390, ill.*
[Descendants of Yost (Joseph) Swope, (Schwab, Swab,) founder of this branch of the Swope family in America, was b. Febr. 22, 1678, in the Town of Sinsheim, in the Duchy of Baden, Germany.] [7491
Obituary. Eli Swab. *In: Notes and Queries. Edited by W. H. Egle. Annual vol. 1898. Harrisburg, Pa. 1899. p. 255.*   [7492
Gilbert E. Swope, of Newville. *In: Notes and Queries. Edited by W. H. Egle. Annual vol. 1899. Harrisburg, Pa. 1900. p. 95.*   [7493
Walker, J. Herbert: John P. Swoope, trapper and hunter. *An appreciation of a great Huntingdon County woodsman. (Pennsylvania Alpine Club Bulletin No. 2.) In: Second Annual Publication of the Pennsylvania Alpine Club. 1918. Altoona, Pa. 1919. pp. 63—73.* [7494
Stapleton, A.: Seebolt family, of Union County, [Pa.]. *In: Notes and Queries. Edited by W. H. Egle. Annual vol. 1898. Harrisburg, Pa. 1899. p. 43.*
[Lenhart Zebolt emigrated from Wurttemberg, Germany, landing at Philadelphia, 1750.]   [7495

The **Sehner** family. *In: Records of the American Catholic Historical Society. Vol. II. Philadelphia, Pa. 1889. pp. 367—368.* [7496

An old Lancaster County family. — The family of Mrs. Ann Maria Sehner. *In: Notes and Queries. Edited by W. H. Egle. Third series, vol. II. 1887—1890. Harrisburg, Pa. 1891. pp. 64—65.* [7497

Sener, Samuel Miller: The Sehner ancestry. *Compiled from authentic records and illustrated with Wappen, or coat of arms, and Stammhaus in Schwaigern, Württemberg. 1500 to 1896. Dedicated to John Fick Sehner. Lancaster, Pa. 1896. pp. 16, ill.* [7498

Roush, J. L.: Rev. Samuel Seibert. Keelor's 1843—1852. *In: The Perkiomen Region. Vol. II, no. 3. Pennsburg, Pa. 1923. p. 48.* [7499

Laux, James B.: Seiler family data. *Contributed by . . . In: The Pennsylvania-German. Vol. XII. Lititz, Pa. 1911. p. 378.* [7500

David **Seibt** (Seipt) and his descendants. *In: The genealogical record of the Schwenkfelder families. Edited by S. K. Brecht. New York, N.Y. — Chicago, Ill. 1923. pp. 885—906.* [7501

Biographical sketch of Rev. Joseph Augustus **Seiss**, D. D., LL. D., L. H. D., president of the Pennsylvania-German Society, 1902—1903. *In: The Pennsylvania-German Society. Proceedings and Addresses at Harrisburg, Pa., Oct. 25, 1901. Vol. XII. Lancaster, Pa. 1903. pp. 52—56.* [7502

Sandt, George W.: Lutheran leaders as I knew them. Rev. Joseph A. **Seiss,** D. D. LL. D. The leader as preacher, seer and administrator. *In: The Lutheran Church Review. Vol. XXXVII. Philadelphia, Pa. 1918. pp. 88—93.* [7503

S.[ellers]. July 1886. *[s. l.]:* Siddall Brothers Printers 1886. *pp. 101, (every other side blank).*
[Philip Henry Sellers (Söller) was b. in Vinom (Weinheim,) near the City of Mannheim, in Germany; emigrated to Pa. in 1737 and settled on the North Branch of the Perkiomen.] [7504

Sellers, Edwin Jaquett: Partial genealogy of the **Sellers** and Wampole families of Pennsylvania. *Philadelphia, Pa.: Printed for private circulation by J. B. Lippincott Co. 1903. pp. 5—139.* [7505

Sellers, Edwin Jaquett: Sellers family of Pennsylvania and allied families. *Philadelphia, Pa.: Press of Allen, Lane & Scott 1925. pp. (1), 58.*
[Philip Heinrich Söller, of Weinheim, Palatinate, emigrated to Pa., 1728.] [7506

H., S. P.: In memoriam: Colonel A. Frank **Seltzer.** *In: Papers read before the Lebanon County Historical Society. Vol. VII. Lebanon, Pa. 1916—1919. pp. 191—193.*
[son of John Clark and Elisabeth (Faber) Seltzer and descendant of Mathias Seltzer, who emigrated from Seltzer Springs in the Duchy of Nassau, Germany about 1730.] [7507

A baptismal certificate. *[of Michael* **Senger,** *son of Michael Senger and Johanna (Schaefferin) Senger, 1788.] Translated from the German by* Gajus M. Brumbaugh. *In: The National Genealogical Society Quarterly. Vol. II, no. 1. Washington, D. C. 1913. p. 8.* [7508

Neitz, S.: Das Leben und Wirken des seeligen Johannes **Seybert,** ersten Bishofs der Evangelischen Gemeinschaft. *Verfasst von . . . Cleveland, O.: C. Hammer für die Evangelische Gemeinschaft 1862. 471 S.*
[geb. 1791 in Lancaster Co., Pa., Sohn von Heinrich Seybert, der als einer der Hessischen Söldner nach Amerika kam.] [7509

Stapleton, A.: Incidents from the life of Bishop John **Seybert.** *From Stapleton's „Flashlights on Evangelical History" [= no. 1880]. In: The Pennsylvania-German. Vol. X. Lititz, Pa. 1909. pp. 167—169.* [7510

Hall, William: The late Gustavus **Seyffarth,** Ph. D., D. D. *In: The Quarterly Review of the Evangelical Lutheran Church. New series, vol. XVII. Gettysburg, Pa. 1887. pp. 427—435.* [7511

Seyfert, A. G.: The hired boy. *In: The Pennsylvania-German. Vol. XI. Lititz, Pa. 1910. pp. 223—225;* — How I became schoolmaster in Brenock [Lancaster Co., Pa.] *In: Vol. X. 1909. pp. 567—569.* [7512

Stoudt, John Baer: The life and times of Col. John **Siegfried.** *Prepared at the request of Col. John Siegfried Memorial Committee and issued in connection with the unveiling of the monument on the old Mennonite cemetery on West Twenty First street, memorial day, May 30, 1914.*

Northampton, Pa.: The Cement News Print 1914. pp. 62, (4). [7513

Sigler — Bell. In: Notes and Queries. Edited by W. H. Egle. Annual vol. 1900. Harrisburg, Pa.1901.pp.173—174. [7514

Wentz, Abdel Ross - Alleman, Herbert C.: John Alden Singmaster, D. D., LL. D. By Abdel Ross Wentz; John Alden Singmaster, D. D., LL. D. An appreciation. By Herbert C. Alleman. In: The Lutheran Quarterly. Vol. LVI. Gettysburg, Pa. 1926. pp. 1—4; 5—8, ill.
[b. in Macungie, Pa. 1852, the son of James Singmaster and his wife Sarah Ann Mattern.] [7515

Smith, Allen J.: Edgar Fahs Smith, vice-provost, University of Pennsylvania. Reprint from: Old Penn Weekly Review. In: The Pennsylvania-German. Vol. IX. Cleona, Pa. 1908. pp. 346—348, ill.
[b. in York, Pa. 1854, son of Gibson Smith and Susann E. (Fahs) Smith.] [7516

Nixon, A.: In memoriam John Barnett Smith. November 26, 1827 — February 2, 1906. Lincolnton, N. C.: Press of the Lincoln Journal 1906. pp. 12, ill.
[son of David and Elizabeth (Arndt) Smith, both of Pennsylvania lineage.] [7517

Foltz, Henry Wesley: Descendants of Adam Spach. Compiled by Henry Wesley Foltz. Autobiography and memoirs of Adam Spach and his wife. Translated from the German records and prepared for this volume by Adelaide L. Fries. Published by Wachovia Historical Society, Winston-Salem, N. C., Raleigh, N. C.: Edwards & Broughton Printing Co. 1924. pp. XXVI, 170, 170a, ill.
[b. Jan. 20, 1720 in Pfaffenhofen, Alsace, Germany, d. Aug. 23, 1801 at Friedberg, N. C., m. Dec. 17, 1752 in Frederickstown, Md. to Maria Elizabeth Henter, b. April 1, 1731 in Wurttemberg, Germany, d. Oct. 26, 1799, in Friedberg, N. C.] [7518

Secrest, Abraham Thompson: Spaid genealogy from the first of the name in this country to the present time with a number of allied families and many historical facts. Columbus, O.: Privately printed for the compiler by Nitschke Bros. 1922. pp. (2), 395, ill.
[Descendants of Georg Nicholas Spaht from Cassel, a Hessian soldier, and settled at first in Hampshire Co., Va.] [7519

Risler, Jeremias: Leben August Gottlieb Spangenbergs, Bischofs der evangelischen Brüderkirche. Barby: Leipzig: in Commission bey Paul Gotthelf Kummer 1794. (18), 516 S. [7520

Ledderhose, K. F.: Das Leben Aug. Gottl. Spangenbergs, Bischofs der Brüdergemeine. Heidelberg: Universitätsbuchhandlung von Karl Winter 1846. (2), 131 S. [7521

Ledderhose, Charles T.: The life of Augustus Gottlieb Spangenberg, bishop of the Unity of the Brethren. From the German. London: William Mallalieu & Co. 1855. pp. (1), (1), 118, ill. [7522

Jordan, John W.: Bishop Augustus Gottlieb Spangenberg. In: The Pennsylvania Magazine of History and Biography. Vol. VIII. Philadelphia, Pa. 1884. pp. 233—240, ill. [7523

Reichel, Gerhard: August Gottlieb Spangenberg, Bischof der Brüderkirche. Tübingen: J. C. B. Mohr [Paul Siebeck] 1906. V—XVI, 291 S. [7524

Genealogy of Christian E. Spangler of Philadelphia, Pa. from 1737 to 1883. One hundred and fifty-one years. Seven generations [s. l.] pp. 13.
[Descendants of Michael Spangler, who emigrated from Heidelberg, Germany and arrived at Philadelphia, Pa., 1737.] [7525

Spangler, Edward W.: The annals of the families of Caspar, Henry, Baltzer, and George Spengler, who settled in York County respectively in 1729, 1732, 1732 and 1751: with biographical and historical sketches and memorabilia of contemporaneous local events. York, Pa.: The York Daily Publishing Co. 1896. pp. XII, 605, ill. [7526

Jacobs, H. E.: George Frederick Spieker. Born Nov. 17th, 1844. Died Sept. 7th, 1913. In: The Lutheran Church Review. Vol. XXXII. Philadelphia, Pa. 1913. pp. 564—571. [7527

Stapleton, A.: Notes on the Spyker family. In: Notes and Queries. Edited by W. H. Egle. Annual vol. 1897. Harrisburg, Pa. 1898. pp. 184—185.
[John, sr., John, jr., and Peter Spyker arrived at Philadelphia, 1737, and settled at the Tulpehocken, Berks Co., Pa.] [7528

Col. Henry Spyker of Berks County. In: Notes and Queries. Edited by W. H. Egle. Annual vol. 1897. Harrisburg, Pa. 1898. p. 19. [7529

Bell, P. G.: A portraiture of the life of Samuel Sprecher, D. D., LL. D. *Pastor, president of Wittenberg College and Seminary, and author. Philadelphia, Pa.: Published for the author by the Lutheran Publication Society, 1907. pp. VIII, 9 —146, ill.*
[*b. Dec. 28, 1810, son of Samuel Sprecher, who came to America from Germany and settled in Washington Co., Md. between Williamsport and Hagerstown.*]
[7530
Springer, M. C.: A genealogical table and history of the Springer family, in Europe and North America, for 8 centuries, from the earliest German princes; origin of the name, etc. *Philadelphia, Pa.: Press of Dickson & Gillin 1881. pp. 144, ill.* [7531
Stager, H. J.: „Freundschaft." Facts, incidents and tradition relating to the Stager-Rudy families and lineage, beginning with the year 1717. *Philadelphia, Pa. April 1912. Ashbury Park, N. J.: Kinmonth Press 1912. pp. 141, ill.* [7532
Hagy, Henry B.: In memoriam. Daniel W. Sheman. *Paper read before the society, March 8, 1904. In: Transactions of the Historical Society of Berks County. Vol. I. Reading, Pa. 1904. pp. (2).*
[*b. in Middletown, Aug. 26, 1837.*] [7533
Staudt, Richard W. and Stoudt, John Baer: The Staudt — Stoudt — Stout — family of Pennsylvania and their ancestors in the Palatinate. *A preliminary study. [s. l. (1925).] pp. 149.* [7534
The Stauffer family. *In: Notes and Queries. Edited by W. H. Egle. Fourth series, vol. I. 1891—1893. Harrisburg, Pa. 1893. pp. 403—404.* [7535
Bower, Henry S.: A genealogical record of the descendants of Daniel Stauffer and Hans Bauer and other pioneers *[Bechtel family; Johannes Moyer's family; Francis Buchwalter family; descendants of Samuel Bauer] together with historical and biographical sketches, and a short history of the Mennonites. With a history of the house of Hohenstaufen by* Fred Raumer. *Harleysville, Pa.: News Printing House 1897. pp. (1), 5—203, ill.* [7536
Stauffer, Henry: Stauffer. *Historical address delivered by . . . at the first Stauffer reunion which was held near Middlebranch, Stark Co., Ohio, Sept. 3, 1898. Akron, O. 1898. pp. 40.* [7537

Fretz, A. J.: A genealogical record of the descendants of Henry Stauffer and other Stauffer pioneers *together with historical and biographical sketches and illustrated with portraits and other illustrations. Harleysville, Pa.: The Harleysville News 1899. pp. 371, ill.* [7538
Snively, Kate S.: Genealogical memoranda. Stouffer. A. D. 1630 — A. D. 1903. *Compiled and arranged by . . . Greencastle, Pa. [1903]. pp. 104, ill.*
[*Daniel Stauffer b. in Thun, Switzerland, about A. D. 1630; Hans, his son, b. in Alsheim, near Mayence.*] [7539
Records of the proceedings of the John Stauffer Memorial Association, Ringtown, Pa. *Ringtown, Pa. 1911. pp. (2), 5—114, ill.*
[*John (Hans) Stauffer, b. in 1655, at Altzheim or Weisenau, Switzerland; m. Kinget Heistant, 1685; came to America, 1710.*] [7540
Veach, R. S.: The Veach and Stover families. *Strasburg, Va.: Shenandoah Publishing House 1913. pp. 170.* [7541
Stauffer, Ezra N.: Stauffer genealogy of America. And history of the descendants of Jacob Stauffer from the earliest available records to the present time. *Goshen, Ind. 1917. pp. 180.* [7542
Jordan, John W.: Biographical sketch of David McNelly Knox Stauffer. *In: The Pennsylvania Magazine of History and Biography. Vol. XXXVII. Philadelphia, Pa. 1913. pp. 202—206.*
[*civil engineer, author and antiquarian, son of Jacob Stauffer of Swiss, and Ann McNeely. of Scotch ancestry; b. in Mt. Joy, Pa. 1845; d. 1913.*] [7543
Steiner memoir. *Sketch of the Steiner family. 1311—1878. Cincinnati, O.: Press of Robert Clarke & Co. 1880. pp. 21.*
[*Rev. John Conrad, b. at Winterthur, in Switzerland, came to America 1749, d. July 6, 1762.*] [7544
Steiner, Lewis H. - Steiner, Bernard C.: The genealogy of the Steiner family, especially of the descendants of Jacob Steiner. *Baltimore, Md.: Press of the Friedenwald Co. 1896. pp. 103.* [7545
Stemen, C. B.: History of the Stemen family together with full particulars of the reunion held at Enslen's Grove, Allen County, Ohio, May 28th, 1881. *Fort Wayne, Ind.: Gazette Co. 1881. pp. 45, (3).*
[*Descendants of Christian Stehman who probably was b. near Red Stone, Pa., moved to Fairfield Co., O. 1803.*] [7546

Stichter, Joseph L.- Stichter, Joseph: Genea-
logy of the Stichter family 1819 to 1902.
*Compiled in Europe by J. L. Stichter
of Reading, Pa. and in America by
J. Stichter of Pottsville, Pa. Pottsville,
Pa.: Daily Republican Book Rooms
1902. pp. 41, ill.*   [7547
Dubbs, Jos. Henry: Baron Stiegel. *In: The
Pennsylvania Magazine of History and
Biography. Vol. I. Philadelphia, Pa.
1877. pp. 67—72.*   [7548
[—] Baron Heinrich Wilhelm Stiegel.
*(Übersetzt ins Deutsche aus: ,,The Penn-
sylvania Magazine of History and Bio-
graphy" Vol. I. [= Nr. 7548].) In: Der
Deutsche Pionier. Jg. XII. Cincinnati,
O. 1880—1881. S. 82—87.*   [7549
Siegling, J. H.: Baron Henry William
Stiegel. *In: Papers and Addresses of the
Lancaster County Historical Society.
Vol. I. Lancaster, Pa. 1896. pp. 44—65,
ill.*   [7550
Stine, M. H.: Baron Stiegel. *Philadelphia,
Pa.: Lutheran Publication Society. 1903.
pp. VI, 7—331.*   [7551
Grittinger, Henry C.: Henry William Stiegel.
*In: Papers read before the Lebanon Coun-
ty Historical Society. Vol. II. 1901—
1904. Lebanon, Pa. 1904. pp. 31—33.*
                                       [7552
Brown, Frank B.- Brendle, A. S.: The life of
Baron Henry W. Stiegel, iron and glass
manufacturer, pioneer, philanthropist,
preacher, teacher, etc., etc. *Schaefferstown, Lebanon County, Pa.: Published
by Isaac Iba. [s. d.] 8 S., ill.*   [7553
Huch, C. F.: Baron Heinrich Wilhelm Stiegel. *In: Mitteilungen des Deutschen
Pionier-Vereins von Philadelphia. Heft 5.
Philadelphia, Pa. 1907. S. 1—16.* [7554
[—] Henry William Stiegel. *Translated
and adapted from the German sketch ha-
ving appeared in the ,,Mitteilungen" of
the Deutsche Pioneer Verein, Philadel-
phia. In: The Pennsylvania-German.
Vol. IX. Cleona, Pa. 1908. pp. 71—76,
ill.*   [7555
Brendle, A. S.: Henry William Stiegel. *In:
Papers read before the Lebanon County
Historical Society. Vol. VI. Lebanon,
Pa. 1912—1916. pp. 59—76, ill.* [7556
Hensel, W. U.: Stiegel's life and legend. *In:
Papers and Addresses of the Lancaster
County Historical Society. Vol. XVIII.
Lancaster, Pa. 1914. pp. 227—235.* [7557
Baron Stiegel's prayer, written on the fly-
leaf of his hymn book during imprison-
ment. *In: The Pennsylvania-German.*

Vol. I., no. 3. Lebanon, Pa. 1900. p. 40.
                                       [7558
Genealogical notes, Stine. — Abraham
Stine of Bethel Township, Dauphin, now
Lebanon County died in May 1807. *In:
Notes and Queries. Edited by W. H.
Egle. Fourth series, vol. II. 1894. Harris-
burg, Pa. 1895. p. 43.*   [7559
Coover, George D.: Daniel Stine. *In: Papers
read before the Lebanon County Historical
Society. Vol. VI. Lebanon, Pa. 1912—
1916. pp. 151—154.*   [7560
Noppen, Leonard Charles von: Henry Jerome
Stockard *(Poet and educator.) In: Bio-
graphical history of North Carolina. Edi-
ted by S. A. Ashe. Vol. V. Greensboro,
N. C. 1906. pp. 383—394, ill.*

*[b. in Chatham Co., N. C., Sept. 15,
1858, son of James Gibbs Stockard and
Mary (Johnson) Stockard.]*   [7561
Staver, Addie Johnston - King, Nora Bar-
tholomew. A genealogical and biogra-
phical sketch of a branch of a family tree.
The Stoever family. *[s. l.] 1931. pp. 4
—55, ill.*   [7562
Early, John W.: The two Stoevers. John
Caspar Stoever of Virginia and John
Caspar Stoever of Pennsylvania. *In:
The Pennsylvania-German. Vol. XI.
Lititz, Pa. 1910. pp. 267—275*   [7563
Davis, Harry A.: Stoll bible records, South
Carolina. Furnished with annotations.
*In: The National Genealogical Society
Quarterly. Vol. XVII, no. 1. Washing-
ton, D. C. 1929. pp. 13—14.*

*[David Stoll is a grandson a Jacob Stoll
and Catharine, his wife, who came to
Purÿsburg, S. C. 1732, with a colony of
Huguenots under Col. John Pury.]* [7564
Stoltzfus, John, Sr. (?): Eine Familien Ge-
schichte . . . *Gap., Pa.: Office des
,,Waffenlosen Waechters", Samuel Ernst.
1876.*

*[Angeführt von H. S. Bender: Two cen-
turies of American Mennonite literature.
1929 (= Nr. 909). S. 42.]*   [7565
— A family history or memories of the
past with a glance into the future and
legacy of a minister. *(Translated from
the original German by H. S. B.) [s. l.]
1927. pp. 21.*   [7566
Mast, C. Z.: The Stoltzfus family. *In: Christian Monitor. A monthly magazine for
the home. Vol. XV, no. 2. Scottdale, Pa.
1923. pp. 50—53, ill.*

*[who emigrated from Zweibrücken,
Pfaltz and landed in Philadelphia on
Oct. 18, 1766.]*   [7567

Morris, John G.: The **Stork** family in the Lutheran Church or biographical sketches of Rev. Charles Augustus Gottlieb **Stork**, Rev. Theophilus **Stork**, D. D., and Rev. Charles A. **Stork**, D. D. *Philadelphia, Pa.: Lutheran Publication Society 1886. pp. 263.*
[Ch. Aug. Gottlieb Stork arrived in Baltimore, Md., June 27, 1788, and became pastor of 3 congregations, Salisbury, Organ, and Pine Church, N. C.] [7568
A memorial of Rev. T. **Stork**, D. D. who died March 28, 1874 in the sixtieth year of his age. *Prepared by his family. [s. l.; s. d.] pp. 31.* [7569

Dubbs, Joseph H.: William **Stoy.** *In: Papers and Addresses of the Lancaster County Historical Society. Vol. VI. 1901 —1902. Lancaster, Pa. 1902. pp. 92—98.* [7570
Andrew **Straub,** a German millwright, was the first settler on the site of Milton in 1762. *In: The Historical Journal. Vol. I. Williamsport, Pa. 1888. p. 168.* [7571

Dotterer, Henry S.: The Bucks County **Strassburgers.** *In: The Perkiomen Region, Past and Present. Vol. II. Philadelphia, Pa. 1900. pp. 90—94.*
[John Andrew Strassburger, b. Jan. 19, 1716, son of Johann Ulrich Strassburger of Ober-Diebach, came to America Oct., 1769 and located in Hill Twp., Bucks Co., Pa.] [7572

Strassburger, Ralph Beaver: The **Strassburger** family and allied families [sc. Yeager, Schneider, Stout, Hartzell, Kern, Schwenk, Bauer, Landis, Markley, Dotterer, Shoemaker, Kolb, Ziegler, Clemens and Lederach] of Pennsylvania. *Being the ancestry of Jacob Andrew Strassburger, Esquire of Montgomery County, Pa. By his son R. B. Strassburger. Gwynedd Valley, Pa.: Printed for private circulation 1922. pp. 520, ill.* [7573

Leitich, Ann Tizia: Ein Epos des Deutschtums in Amerika. *In: Der Auslanddeutsche. Halbmonatsschrift für Auslanddeutschtum und Auslandkunde. Mitteilungen des Deutschen Ausland-Institutes, Stuttgart. Jg. XIII, Nr. 10. Stuttgart 1930. S. 328—330.*
[Besprechung von Nr. 7573.] [7574

Dotterer, Henry S.: Rev. John Andrew **Strassburger.** *In: Historical Notes, relating to the Pennsylvania Reformed Church. Vol. I. Philadelphia, Pa. 1900. pp. 92—95.* [7575

Stricker, John (Jr.): General John **Stricker.** *In: Maryland Historical Magazine. Vol. IX. Baltimore, Md. 1914. pp. 209—218.*
[b. at Frederick Town, Md., descended from Swiss ancestors.] [7576

Strickler, Harry M.: Forerunners. A history or genealogy of the **Strickler** families, their kith and kin including **Kauffmans, Stovers, Burners, Ruffners, Beavers, Shavers, Brumbachs, Zirkles, Blossers, Groves, Brubakers, Neffs, Rothgebs** and many other early families of Shenandoah, Rockingham, Augusta, Frederick and Page Counties of the Shenandoah Valley. *From about 1700 to the present time, 1924. Harrisonburg, Virginia: Published by H. M. Strickler; Dayton, Va.: The Ruebush-Kieffer Co. 1925. pp. XV, 425, ill.* [7577

P.[arthemore], E. W. S.: **Stroh's** (Straw) graveyard (in Fishing Creek Valley, Dauphin Co., Pa.). *In: Notes and Queries. Edited by W. H. Egle. Annual vol. 1896. Harrisburg, Pa. 1897. pp. 170—171.* [7578

Eshleman, H. Frank: Outline of John **Strohm's** career in congress. *In: Papers and Addresses of the Lancaster County Historical Society. Vol. XXIII. Lancaster, Pa. 1919. pp. 60—62.*
[b. Oct. 16, 1793 in Little Britain Twp., Lancaster Co., Pa.] [7579

Martin, Christian Hess: Hon. John **Strohm.** *In: Papers and Addresses of the Lancaster County Historical Society. Vol. XXXIV. Lancaster, Pa. 1930. pp. 221—226.*
[b. Oct. 16, 1793 in Little Britain Twp., Lancaster Co., Pa.] [7580

Betz, I. H.: The **Studebaker** brothers. The wagon builders of South Bend, Indiana. *In: The Pennsylvania-German. Vol. XI. Lititz, Pa. 1910. pp. 194—204, ill.* [7581

Erskine, Albert Russel: History of the **Studebaker** Corporation. *Chicago, Ill.: The Studebaker Corporation. Printed by R. R. Donnelly & Sons Co. 1924. pp. IX—XXVII, 229, ill.* [7582

Stull family. *In: Colonial families of Philadelphia. Edited by John W. Jordan. New York, N. Y. — Chicago, Ill.: The Lewis Publishing Co. 1911. Vol. II. pp. 1678—1682.*
[John Adam Stoll, b. in Germany 1749, emigrated to America, arriving in Philadelphia, Pa. Dec. 24, 1772.] [7583

Steinmetz, C. M.: Stump private burying ground inscriptions; near Bernville [Berks Co., Pa.]. In: The National Genealogical Society Quarterly. Vol. XV, no. 2. Washington, D. C. 1927. p. 32.
[7584
[Stump, Christopher]: Last will of Christopher Stump. [Copy of the German original, Febr. 28, 1769.] In: The Pennsylvania-German. Vol. IV. Lebanon, Pa. 1903. pp. 229—233.   [7585
Grumbine, Ezra: Frederick Stump, the founder of Fredericksburg, Pa. In: Papers read before the Lebanon County Historical Society. Vol. VI. Lebanon, Pa. 1909—1912. pp. 205—221, ill., map.
    [b. in Heidelberg Twonship, Lancaster Co., now Lebanon Co., Pa., descendant of Christopher Stump (Stumb).]   [7586
Stutesman family. In: The Pennsylvania-German. Vol. IX. Cleona, Pa. 1908. pp. 525—526.
    [John Jacob Stutesman, presumely b. in Durkheim, on the Rhine, Germany, took the oath of allegiance to England at Philadelphia, Pa., Oct. 2, 1727.]   [7587
Adam Geiselhardt Summer; William Summer. In: History of the State Agricultural Society of South Carolina from 1839 . . . Published under the State Agricultural and Mechanical Society of South Carolina. Columbia, S. C.: The R. L. Bryan Co. 1916. pp. 233—235; 236—239.   [7588
Summers, G. Byron: 1752—1923. A history of George Summers of Douglas and Lower Dublin Townships, Montgomery County, Pa. [s. l.] 1923. pp. 34.
    [b. in Germany, about 1690, arrived in America 1752.]   [7589
— Isaac Sumney. In: The Perkiomen Region. Vol. I, no. 2. Pennsburg, Pa. 1922. 27—30.
    [of Huguenot ancestry, b. about 1724, founder of Sumneytown.]   [7590
[Hyde, Edmund M.]: In memoriam: The Reverend Henry William Super, D. D., LL. D. Second president of Ursinus College. Collegeville, Pa.: Thompson Brothers 1898. pp. 123.
    [son of John Super, native of Wurttemberg, Germany.]   [7591
Roberts, J. O. K.: A Suplee line of descent. In: The Pennsylvania-German. Vol. XII. Lititz, Pa. 1911. pp. 111—113.
    [Andreas Souplis, b. in France 1634, a Huguenot, emigrated to Germany, m. Gertrude Stiessinger, and came to America, landing at Philadelphia, Pa. early in 1684.]   [7592
Suter family. In: Colonial families of Philadelphia by John W. Jordan. New York, N. Y. — Chicago, Ill.: The Lewis Publishing Co. 1911. Vol. II. pp. 1709—1711.
    [Peter Suter, of German parentage, b. in Hagerstown, Md., July 17, 1806, d. in Cumberland, Md., June 8, 1897.]   [7593
Heatwole, L. J.: A sketch of the life and work of Emanual Suter. In: The Mennonite Year Book and Directory. 1906. Scottdale, Pa. 1906. pp. 31—32.   [7594

T.

Beck, A. R.: David Tannenberg. In: The Pennsylvania-German. Vol. X. Lititz, Pa. 1909. pp. 339—341.
    [b. March 21, 1728 in Berthelsdorf, Upper Lusatia, Germany; he came to Bethlehem, Pa. in 1749.]   [7595
Beck, Paul E.: David Tannenberger, organ builder. In: Papers and Addresses of the Lancaster County Historical Society. Vol. XXX. Lancaster, Pa. 1926. pp. 3—11.
        [7596
[Stein, Thos. S.]: Report of the Biographical Committee, embracing a sketch of Rev. John Conrad Tempelman. In: Papers read before the Lebanon County Historical Society. Vol. VIII. Lebanon, Pa. 1921—1924. pp. 161—177, ill.   [7597
Egle, William Henry: Genealogical record of the families of Beatty, Egle, Müller, Murray, Orth, and Thomas. Harrisburg, Pa.: Lane & Hart 1886. pp. 126.
    [Thomas of Heidelberg. pp. 107—126; Theodorus Thomas, a native of Switzerland, and a refugee from the Palatinate, Germany emigrated to America, 1736.]   [7598
— Thomas of Heidelberg. In: Egle's ,,Pennsylvania genealogies". Harrisburg, Pa. 1896 [no. 6045]. pp. 674—693.
    [Descendants of Theodorus Thomas, the emigrant of 1736.]   [7599
[Tome, Philip]: Pioneer life: or, thirty years a hunter. Being scenes and adventures in the life of Philip Tome, fifteen years interpreter for Cornplanter and Gov. Blacksnake, chiefs on the Alleghany River. [Reprint of a scarce edition of 1854.] With a preface by Henry W. Shoemaker, and an appendix by A. Monroe Aurand, jr. Harrisburg, Pa.:

Privately printed by The Aurand Press 1928. pp. IX, 173, ill. [7600

Betz, I. H.: Life and death of Samuel Too-mey. *In: The Pennsylvania-German. Vol. XI. Lititz, Pa. 1910. pp. 158—162.*
[b. in 1830 near Dover, York Co., Pa.] [7601

Memorial of Rev. David Loy **Tressler,** Ph. D., late president of Carthago College, who died Friday morning, February 20, 1880. *Philadelphia, Pa.: Lutheran Publication Society 1880. pp. 104.*
[son of Col. John Tressler; b. in the Village of Loysville, Pa., Febr. 15, 1839.] [7602

Reno, Claude Trexler: Minutes and proceedings of the first reunion of the **Trexler** family. Wednesday 28th, 1907. *Kutztown Park, Kutztown, Pa. Allentown, Pa. 1908. pp. 33.*
[Peter Trexler came to America sometime prior to 1720 and settled in Oley Twp., Berks Co., Pa.] [7603

Tyson family. *In: Colonial families of Philadelphia. Edited by John W. Jordan. New York, N. Y. — Chicago, Ill.: The Lewis Publishing Co. 1911. Vol. I. pp. 395—399.*
[Cornelius Tyson, b. in Crefeld in 1652, resided in Germantown as early as 1703.] [7604

Tyson family. *In: Colonial families of Philadelphia. Edited by John W. Jordan. New York, N. Y. — Chicago, Ill.: The Lewis Publishing Co. 1911. Vol. I. pp. 689—733, ill.*
[Reymier Teisen (Tyson) named in Penn's charter of Aug. 12, 1689 as one of the original incorporators of the Borough of Germantown; b. in Germany in or about the year 1659.] [7605
Fragments of a family history. *[Peter Tyson of Towamencin Township.] In: The Perkiomen Region, Past and Present. Vol. II. Philadelphia, Pa. 1900. p. 22.* [7606

U.

Uhler, George H.: Genealogy of the **Uhler** family from the year 1735 to the younger generation. *(Anastasius, b. in Germany about 1710. Christopher, b. 1741; Martin, b. 1745; Michael, b. 1746.) Lebanon, Pa. The Report Publishing Co. 1901. pp. (1), 35, ill.* [7607
Morris, John G.: Reminiscences of Rev. John Uhlhorn. *(Read before the German Historical Society of Maryland.) In: The*

Quarterly Review, of the Evangelical Lutheran Church. Vol. XXI. Gettysburg, Pa. 1891. pp. 197—205.
[b. in Bremen in 1793, came to Baltimore in 1822.] [7608

[Egle, William Henry]: The **Umholtz** family. *In: Notes and Queries. Edited by W. H. Egle. First and second series, vol. I. Harrisburg, Pa. 1894. pp. 209—210.* [7609

Sener, S. M.: The **Umholtz** family. *In: Notes and Queries. Edited by W. H. Egle. Annual vol. 1900. Harrisburg, Pa. 1901. p. 171.*
[Descendants of Michael Umholtz, b. Aug. 31, 1776, removed to Perry Co.] [7610

Butler, Russell Harris: Ungerfehr, Uncapher, Unkefer. Genealogica et biographica or genealogical notes concerning Martin **Ungerfehr** and his descendants, separated into two distinct branches, the larger branch being known by the name Uncapher while the smaller one is designated by the name Unkefer. *[s. l., 1925.] pp. 453, ill.*
[emigrated from near Dresden, Saxony, Germany and settled in Heidelberg Twp., York Co., Pa. in 1735.] [7611
Urner, Isaac N.: Genealogy of the **Urner** family and sketch of the Coventry Brethren Church in Chester County, Pennsylvania. *Philadelphia, Pa.: J. B. Lippincott Co., 1893. pp. 175, ill.* [7612

V.

Garland, D. F.: Milton **Valentine.** *In: The Lutheran Quarterly. Vol. XXXVII. Gettysburg, Pa. 1907. pp. 1—17, ill.*
[b. 1825 near Uniontown, Caroll Co., Md., the son of Jacob and Rebecca Valentine.] [7613
Vogt, Mary M.: Vogt and allied families. *Genealogical and biographical. Prepared and privately printed for . . . New York, N. Y.: The American Historical Society, Inc. 1925. pp. 57, ill.*
[Descendants of Johann Friedrich Helferich Vogt, parson at Madelungen and later at Grossenlupnitz.] [7614
Koetteritz, John B.: The history of William Feeter, a soldier in the War of American Independence, and of his father Lucas Vetter, the ancestor of the **Feeter** — **Feder** — **Feader** — **Fader** families in the United States and Canada, with genealogy of the family, *compiled at the request*

of James D. Feeter by John B. Koetteritz.
Little Falls, N. Y.: Press of Stebbins &
Burney 1901. pp. (3), 7—125, ill.
    [Lucas Vetter, d. 1483 near Derdingen,
in the present Kingdom of Wurttemberg,
Germany; Lucas Vetter b. 1696, m. in
1722 to Katharine Lenninger, moved to
Schoenaich, Wurttemberg; his eldest son,
Lucas Vetter, was the emigrant 1754. He
settled to north of Stone Arabia, Mohawk
Valley, N. Y.]   [7615
Honeyman, A. van Doren: Notes on the
Vosseler family. In: Somerset County
Historical Quarterly. Vol. III. Somer-
ville, N. J. 1914. pp. 26—31; 112—117;
206—211; 292—295; vol. IV. 1915.
pp. 123—125.
    [Descendants of Jacob Vosseler [Fus-
ler] who came as a Palatine, from Ger-
many to the Schoharie prior to 1750 and
located later near, where the Church of
Raritan in the Hills was situated, near
Pluckenim, N. J.]   [7616
Vosseler burying ground inscriptions, located west of South Branch [Somerset Co.,
N. J.]. In: Somerset County Historical
Quarterly. Vol. III. Somerville, N. J.
1914. pp. 303—304.   [7617

W.

Waage, O. F.: Rev. Frederick Waage. In:
The Penn Germania. Vol. I. = Old series
vol. XIII. Lititz, Pa. 1912. pp. 612—
616, ill.
    [b. Aug. 15, 1797 in Itzehoe, town in
the Dukedom of Holstein.]   [7618
Wagenseller, Geo. W.: The history of the
Wagenseller family in America with
kindred branches. Edited and compiled
by . . . Middleburgh, Pa.: Wagenseller
Publishing Co. 1898. pp. (3), (2), 9—
225, ill.   [7619
Wagenseller. In: Notes and Queries. Edited
by W. H. Egle. Annual vol. 1897. Harrisburg, Pa. 1898. pp. 214—215.
    [John Wagenseller, b. in Germany
1737.]   [7620
Anna Wagner (Wagener) and her descendants. In: The genealogical record of the
Schwenkfelder families. Edited by S. K.
Brecht. New York, N. Y. — Chicago,
Ill. 1923. pp. 1501—1556.   [7621
Anna Yeakel Wagner and her descendants. In: The genealogical record of
the Schwenkfelder families. Edited by
S. K. Brecht. New York, N. Y. — Chicago, Ill.: 1923. pp. 1433—1500.   [7622

Kitner, Nannie (Wagner): History of the
Wagner family. [s. l.]: Carroll Chronicle
Print [1917] pp. (10), ill.
    [John Wagner, b. in Germany came to
America and settled in eastern Pa., he
enlisted in the Revolutionary army.]
                                      [7623
The Wagners. In: The Perkiomen Region.
Vol. II. no. 4. Pennsburg, Pa, 1923. pp.
74—75.
    [of the upper end of Montgomery Co.,
Pa. — descendants of Jonas Bocher
Wagner and Esther, b. Schneider.]   [7624
Wagner family. In: Colonial families of
Philadelphia. Edited by John W. Jordan.
New York, N. Y. — Chicago, Ill.: The
Lewis Publishing Co. 1911. Vol. II.
pp. 1572—1581.
    [The Wagner family of Philadelphia
was founded in America 1743, by Rev.
Tobias Wagner, pastor of the Lutheran
Church at Horkheim, near Heilbronn,
Kingdom of Wurttemberg, who came as a
missionary to Reading, Pa. 1743.] [7625
Wagner, E. R.: Isaac Wagner family tree.
With comments of . . . San Francisco, Cal.
Harr Wagner Publishing Co. 1928. pp.
56, ill.
    [Descendants of Tobias Wagner, mini-
ster in Heilbronn, who came to America
1742.]   [7626
Hinke, Wm. J.: Rev. John Waldschmidt
memorial 1724—1786. Monument erected under the auspices of the Swamp
Reformed Church, unveiled and dedicated,
Sunday, Oct. 17, 1915. [Added to this:]
History of Swamp and Muddy Creek
congregations. By Wm. J. Hinke. Reading, Pa.: Reformed Church Record.
1915. pp. 29, ill.   [7627
Hinke, Wm. J.: In memory of the Rev.
John Waldschmidt. Address delivered
in Swamp Church, Lancaster County,
Oct. 17, 1915, at the dedication of a memorial monument of Rev. John Waldschmidt. In: The Reformed Church Review. Fourth series, vol. XX. Philadelphia, Pa. 1916. pp. 22—44.   [7628
Fackenthal, B. F.: Biographical notice of
Joseph B. Walter, M. D. In: A Collection of Papers read before the Bucks
County Historical Society. Vol. V.
Meadville, Pa. 1926. pp. 84—87, ill.
    [descendants of Michael Walter, whose
ancestors were residents of Alsace, Germany.]   [7629
[Waltz, Levi]: Waltz family history and
genealogical record, in family classifica-

tion, comprising upward of 3000 names, of lineal descendants of Frederick Reinhart Waltz. *Dayton, O.: Reformed Publishing Co. 1884. pp. XVI, 17—128.*

[banished from his native land, the Switzerland, in 1731, emigrated to America 1744 and settled in eastern Pa.] [7630

Richman, Carl L.: The Waltz family. *Compiled by . . . Tipton, Ind. 1926. Typewritten copy.*

[Descendants of Frederick Reinhart Waltz, banished from Switzerland in 1731.]

[At Library of Congress, Washington, D. C.] [7631

Croll, P. C.: John **Wanamaker**, merchant and philanthropist. *In: The Pennsylvania-German. Vol. IX. Cleona, Pa. 1908. pp. 16—21, ill.*

[b. in Philadelphia, Pa., July 11, 1838, descendant of early German settlers of Hunterdon County, N. J., of the name Wanamacher.] [7632

Gibbons, Herbert Adams: John **Wanamaker**. *2 vols. New York, N. Y. & London: Harper & Brothers. 1926. pp. XVI, 398; 497.* [7633

Apple, Joseph H.: The business biography of John **Wanamaker**, founder and builder. *America's merchant pioneer 1861 to 1922. With glimpses of Rodman Wanamaker and Thomas B. Wanamaker. New York, N. Y.: The Macmillan Co. 1930. pp. XXVI, (1), 471.* [7634

Diffenderffer, F. R.: Jacob Eshleman **Warfel**, painter. *In: Papers and Addresses of the Lancaster County Historical Society. Vol. XVI. Lancaster, Pa. 1912. pp. 251—252.* [7635

Andreas **Warner**. *In: The genealogical record of the Schwenkfelder families. Edited by S. K. Brecht. New York, N. Y. — Chicago, Ill.: 1923. p. 1002.* [7636

The **Weand** family. *In: The Perkiomen Region, Past and Present. Vol. I. Philadelphia, Pa. 1895. pp. 130—132.*

[Wigandt family of Freinsheim, Palatinate, from where various members of the family emigrated to America in the beginning of the 18th century.] [7637

L., M. W.: The **Weber** family, (of Lancaster County, Pa.). *In: Notes and Queries. Edited by W. H. Egle. Annual vol. 1896. Harrisburg, Pa.1897. pp.108—109.* [7638

S.[ener], M. S.: Some **Weaver** data. *In: Notes and Queries. Edited by W. H. Egle. Annual vol. 1899. Harrisburg, Pa. 1900. p. 15.*

[About 1715 or 1717 Jacob Weber, John Weber and Henry Weber settled in what is known as „Weber Thal" in Earl Twp., Lancaster Co., Pa.] [7639

Clemens, William Montgomery: Early marriage records of the **Weaver** family in the United States. *Official and authoritative records of Weaver marriages in the original states and colonies from 1628 to 1865. Edited by . . . New York, N. Y.: William M. Clemens 1916. pp. (1), 5—32.*

= The Clemens American Marriage Records. Vol. I. [7640

Stauffer, Ezra N. and others: **Weber** or **Weaver** family history. *Nappanee, Ind.: E. V. Publishing 1926. pp. 68.* [7641

Fouse, D. S.: Rev. John William **Weber**, pioneer Reformed preacher of Western Pennsylvania. *In: The Pennsylvania-German. Vol. VII. Lebanon, Pa. 1906. pp. 219—223.* [7642

Tompson, H. A.: Biography of Jonathan **Weaver**, a bishop in the Church of the United Brethren in Christ for 35 years. *With an introduction by Bishop N. Castle. Dayton, O.: United Brethren Publishing House 1901. pp. XVII, 19—477, ill.* [7643

Record of the deaths kept by Mary **Weaver** of West Earl Township, Lancaster County, Pa. *Published by her friends. Farmerville, Pa.: E. H. Burkholder 1900. pp. 39.*

[beginning with the great-great-grandfather of John B. Weaver, preacher of Elkhart Co., Ind.] [7644

Weidel, Jacob: Jacob **Weidel**. *Biographical sketch. In: Papers read before the Lebanon County Historical Society. Vol. II. Lebanon, Pa. 1901—1904. pp. 337—341.* [7645

Early, J. W.: In memoriam. William Murray **Weidman**. *In: Transactions of the Historical Society of Berks County. Vol. I. Reading, Pa. 1904. pp. (4), ill.*

[b. at Lebanon, May 8, 1836.] [7646

Steinmetz, C. M.: Inscriptions in the **Weidner** private burying ground near the Hoch cemetery, Berks County. *Copied by . . . In: The National Genealogical Society Quarterly. Vol. XV, no. 3. Washington, D. C. 1927. p. 33; Inscriptions Weidner burying ground. p. 34.* [7647

Murphy, J. L.: Henry **Weidner**, his life and character. *A memorial — service held at J. W. Robinson's, May 30, 1894. Dedi-*

cated to the descendants of Henry Weidner. Hickory, N. C.: Published by Hickory Printing Co., Publishers of Press and Carolinian 1895. pp. 22. [7648

K.: Rev. Revere Franklin **Weidner,** D. D., LL. D. *In: The Pennsylvania-German. Vol. IX. Cleona, Pa. 1908. pp. 153—156, ill.*

[b. in Center Valley, Lehigh County, Pa., Nov. 22, 1851, son of William P. and Eliza A. (Blank) Weidner.] [7649

Gerberding, G. H.: R. F. **Weidner,** D. D., LL. D. *A character sketch, an appreciation, a tribute. Waverly, Ia.: Wartburg Press 1916. pp. 136, (3), ill.* [7650

Weikert, Edward L.: History of the **Weikert** family from 1735—1930. *Work started in November, 1922 and completed in March, 1930. Harrisburg, Pa.: The Telegraph Press 1930. pp. (3), (3), 9—357, ill.*

[Descendants of John Andrew Weikert, b. 1735 in the Palatinate, Germany, emigrated to Pa. 1753.] [7651

The **Weirman** family. *(Inquiries by Albert Cook Myers and the answers to them by a member of the family. In: Notes and Queries. Edited by W. H. Egle. Annual vol. 1896. Harrisburg, Pa. 1897. pp. 139—141.* [7652

Romiger, Charles H. and **Bornman, Charles J.:** Noah **Weis,** wood carver. *An unappreciated genius. In: The Pennsylvania-German. Vol. XI. Lititz, Pa. 1910. pp. 673—676, ill.*

[b. about 1842, on the old Weis homestead, near Hosensack, Lehigh Co., Pa., of Pennsylvania-German parents.] [7653

W., F. N.: Adam **Weise.** *In: Notes and Queries. Edited by W. H. Egle. First and second series, vol. I. Harrisburg, Pa. 1894. pp. 288—291.*

[b. in New Goshenhoppen, Philadelphia, County, Pa., Dec. 23, 1751.] [7654

[Weiser, Conrad]: Copy of a family register . . . *[see nos. 3429—3432].*

Weiser, Clement Zwingli: The life of (John) Conrad **Weiser,** the German pioneer, patriot and patron of two races. *Reading, Pa.: Daniel Miller 1876. pp. 7, (4), 449; Second edition 1899. pp. 140, ill.* [7656

Diffenderffer, Frank R.: Conrad **Weiser.** *A neglected chapter of colonial history. In: The Mercersburg Review. Vol. XXIV. Philadelphia, Pa. 1877. pp. 293—314.* [7657

Montgomery, Morton L.: Lecture on the lief and times of Conrad **Weiser,** the first representative man of Berks County. *Reading, Pa.: Chas. F. Haage [1893.] pp. (2), 5—37, (1).* [7658

[Croll, P. C.]: Famous Pennsylvania Germans: Conrad **Weiser.** *In: The Pennsylvania-German. Vol. I, no. 1. Lebanon, Pa. 1900. pp. 3—17, ill.* [7659

Walton, Joseph Solomon: Conrad **Weiser** and the Indian policy of colonial Pennsylvania. *Philadelphia, Pa.: G. W. Jacobs & Co. [1900]. pp. (5), 9—420, ill.* [7660

The **Weiser** house. *With sketches by Hermann Faber. In: Mitteilungen des Deutschen Pionier-Vereins von Philadelphia. Heft 6. Philadelphia, Pa. 1907. S. 1—4.* [7661

Huch, C. F.: Conrad **Weiser.** *In: Mitteilungen des Deutschen Pionier-Vereins von Philadelphia. Heft 6. Philadelphia, Pa. 1907. S. 4—7.* [7662

Miller, Daniel: Conrad **Weiser** as a monk. *Read March 12, 1912. In: Transactions of the Historical Society of Berks County. Vol. III. Reading, Pa. 1923. pp. 169—181.* [7663

Richards, Henry Melchior Muhlenberg: The **Weiser** family. *Prepared by authority of the Pennsylvania-German Society. In: The Pennsylvania-German Society. Proceedings and Addresses . . . 1921. Vol. XXXII. Lancaster, Pa. 1924. Separate pagination: Pennsylvania-German genealogies. pp. 5—115, ill.* [7664

Beauchamp, Wm. M.: The life of Conrad **Weiser** as it relates to his services as official interpreter between New York and Pennsylvania and as envoy between Philadelphia and the Onandaga Councils. *Compiled and edited by . . . Published by the Onandaga Historical Association at Syracuse, N. Y. 1925. Syracuse, N. Y.: The Syracuse Press 1925. pp. (2), 7—122, (3), ill.* [7665

Richards, H. M. M.: Conrad **Weiser,** an early Lutheran patriot. *In: Papers read before the Lebanon County Historical Society. Vol. IX. Lebanon, Pa. 1925—1928. No. 5. pp. 165—185, ill.* [7666

Nolan, J. Bennett: Conrad **Weiser,** the interpreter. *Address before the annual meeting of the Society of Colonial Wars in the Commonwealth of Pa., March 13, 1930 at the Philadelphia Club, Philadelphia. = Historical Publications of the Society of Colonial Wars in the Common-*

*wealth of Pennsylvania. Vol. IV, no. 2.
Aug., 1930. pp. 3—8.*   [7667
Goebel, Julius: Conrad Weiser. *In: Deutsch-
Amerikanische Geschichtsblätter. German-
American Historical Review. Jahrbuch
der Deutsch-Amerikanischen Historischen
Gesellschaft von Illinois. Jg. 1930. Vol.
XXX. Chicago, Ill. 1930. S. 166—181.*
[7667a
Rev. Dr. Clement Z. **Weiser's** lineage. *In:
Historical Notes, relating to the Pennsyl-
vania Reformed Church. Vol. I. Phila-
delphia, Pa. 1900. p. 83.*   [7668
Conrad **Weiser.** His fear of Catholics —
His daughter's conversion — Her des-
cendants. *In: Records of the American
Catholic Historical Society of Philadel-
phia. Vol. XXI. Philadelphia, Pa.
1910. pp. 155—158.*   [7669
Murdock, William G.: Margaret **Weiser,**
daughter of Conrad Weiser. *In: The
Pennsylvania-German. Vol. XI. Lititz,
Pa. 1910. pp. 560—561.*   [7670
K.[riebel], W. H.: A brief sketch of Rev.
Georg Weiss, the first minister of the
Schwenkfelders in America. *In: The
Mennonite Year Book and Almanac for
1900. Quakertown, Pa. 1900. pp. 37—
40.*   [7671
„Georg **Weiss** and his descendants." *In:
The genealogical record of the Schwenk-
felder families. Edited by S. K. Brecht.
New York, N. Y. — Chicago, Ill. 1923.
pp. 855—857.*   [7672
Jordan, John W.: Lewis **Weiss.** *In: Notes
and Queries. Edited by W. H. Egle.
Third series, vol. II. 1887—1890. Harrisburg, Pa. 1891. pp. 358—360; 363—
365.*
*[Wilhelm Ludwig Weiss (his bap-
tismal name) b. Dec. 28, 1717 in Berlin,
Prussia, emigrated to America, landing
in Philadelphia, Dec., 1755.]*   [7673
— Lewis **Weiss,** of Philadelphia, conveyancer, lawyer, and judge. *In: The Pennsylvania Magazine of History and Biography. Vol. XV. Philadelphia, Pa.
1891. pp. 361—365.*   [7674
Hayden, Horace Edwin: A genealogical
sketch of the descendants of Johan Paul
Weitzel of Lancaster County, Pa., 1742.
*Reprint from: Harrisburg Telegram.
1881. pp. 9.*
[who emigrated to America 1742.] [7675
— **Weitzel** family of Pennsylvania. *In:
Notes and Queries. Edited by W. H.
Egle. Second series. Harrisburg, Pa.
1883. pp. 158—162; 164—168.*

*[Johann Paul Weitzel, and his wife
Charlotte emigrated to America 1742, and
settled in Lancaster Co., Pa.]*   [7676
Hayden, Horace Edwin: The **Weitzel** me-
morial. *Historical and genealogical record
of the descendants of Paul Weitzel of
Lancaster, Pa. 1740. Including brief
sketches of the families of Allen, Byers,
Bailey, Crawford, Davis, Hayden,
M'Cormick, Stone, White and others.
Wilkes-Barre, Pa.: E. B. Yordy 1883.
pp. (1), 5—81.*   [7677
Wenger, Jonas G., Wenger, Martin D. and
Wenger, Joseph H.: History of the descendants of Christian **Wenger** who emigrated from Europe to Lancaster County,
Pa. *in 1727, and a complete genealogical
family register with biographies of his
descendants from the earliest available
records to the present time. Elkhart, Ind.:
Mennonite Publishing Co. 1903, pp. 259.*
[7678
The **Wenrich** family bulletin. *Official organ
of the Wenrich Family Association. No. 1.
August, 1924. pp. 23. Annually ff. —
(No. 9.) 1932. pp. 32; 48; 64; 62; 56;
64; 61; all ill.*   [7679
Brendle, D. D.: Peter **Wentz.** *In: The Perkiomen Region. Vol. I, no. 3. Penns-
burg, Pa. 1922. pp. 49—52.*
*[who paid quit-rent for tracts of land
in Towamencin Twp., Montgomery Co.,
Pa. in 1717; d. 1749.]*   [7680
H., S. P.: In memoriam: David T. **Werner,**
Ph. D. *In: Papers read before the Lebanon County Historical Society. Vol. VII.
Lebanon, Pa. 1916—1919. pp. 341—
342, ill.*
*[son of David and Sarah (Groh) Wer-
ner, of South Lebanon Twp.]*   [7681
Snyder, William J.: Stenographic report of
proceedings had at the second reunion
of the **Wertz** family, held at Harrisburg,
Pa., October 25, 26, 27, 1912. *[Chicago,
Ill.] pp. 102, ill.*   [7682
Westhafer, Francis M.: The **Westhafer**
genealogy. *[s. l.] 1912. pp. (1), 7—62,
ill.*
*[Valentine Westhaeffer, b. in Hohen
Sachen Village, near Heidelberg, the Palatinate, now part of Germany, Jan. 1,
1703, came to America 1732 and settled
among the Moravians in Lancaster Co.
Pa.]*   [7683
P.[arthemore], E. W. S.: The **Wetzel** family
(of Pennsylvania and West Virginia).
*In: Notes and Queries. Edited by W. H.
Egle. Third series, vol. II. 1887—1890.*

Harrisburg, Pa. 1891. pp. 14—15. Reprint in: Third series, vol. II. Harrisburg, Pa. 1896. pp. 403—404.
[Martin and Jacob Wetzel came from Switzerland to Pa. about 1747.] [7684

Weygant, C. H.: Descendants of Rev. George Herman **Weygandt** of the Rhine, Palatinate. *In: The family record devoted for 1897 to the Sackett, the Weygant, and the Mapes families, and to ancestors of their intersecting lines. Published monthly by C. H. Weygant. Newburgh, N. Y. 1897. pp. 6—9; 19—22; 30—32; 43—45; 55—58; 66—70; 82—92; 102—113; 128—130; 141—146.* [7685

— History of the Palatine family of **Weygandt — Weigand — Weygant — Wygant — Weyant — Weiant** in America. *Newburgh, N. Y.: Journal Printing House and Book-Bindery 1899. Part II. Historical and Biographical. pp. 65—102.*
[Part I is not printed yet.] [7686

Reed, Luther D.: A benefactor of the church. B. Frank **Weyman**. *Born, March 26, 1842; died June 12, 1919. Address delivered at the funeral service in the First Church, Pittsburgh, Pa. In: The Lutheran Church Review. Vol. XXXVIII. Philadelphia, Pa. 1919. pp. 291—298.* [7687

Whitmer, T. Carl: Life of Rev. Carl Whitmer. *A lover of man. Philadelphia, Pa.: Publication and Sunday School Board of the Reformed Church in the United States. 1923. pp. . . . .*
[descendant of Peter and Mary Whitmer, Mennonites near Greencastle, Pa.] [7688

John Lehman **Wideman**. *In: Fifth Annual Report of the Waterloo Historical Society. Kitchener, Ont. 1917. p. 61, ill.*
[b. in the Township of Markham, York Co., Ontario, Dec. 27, 1833, son of Andrew Wideman, b. in Pa. 1805.] [7689

Kriebel, H. W.: Christopher **Wiegner**, the Towamencin diarist. *Paper read before the Historical Society of Montgomery County, May 25, 1904. In: Historical Sketches. A Collection of Papers prepared for the Historical Scoiety of Montgomery County, Pa. Vol. III. Norristown, Pa. 1905. pp. 271—289.*
[b. in Harpersdorf, Silesia, about 1712.] [7690

— Christopher **Wiegner**, the Towamencin diarist. *Paper read before the Montgomery County Historical Society, May*

25, 1904. In: The Pennsylvania-German. Vol. VII. Lebanon, Pa. 1906. pp. 400 —405, ill.; Vol. VIII. 1907. pp. 23—27. [7691

Hans **Wiegner** and his descendants. *In: The genealogical record of the Schwenkfelder families. Edited by S. K. Brecht. New York, N. Y. — Chicago, Ill. 1923. p. 415.* [7692

George **Wiegner** and his descendants. *In: The genealogical record of the Schwenkfelder families. Edited by S. K. Brecht. New York, N. Y. — Chicago, Ill. 1923. pp. 417—464.* [7693

Susanna Heydrick **Wiegner** and her descendants. *In: The genealogical record of the Schwenkfelder families. Edited by S. K. Brecht. New York, N. Y. — Chicago, Ill. 1923. pp. 1175—1178.* [7694

Susanna Seibt **Wiegner** and her descendants. *In: The genealogical record of the Schwenkfelder families. Edited by S. K. Brecht. New York, N. Y. — Chicago, Ill. 1923. pp. 1225—1255.* [7695

Myers, Albert C.: **Wierman** family, of Adams County. *In: Notes and Queries. Edited by W. H. Egle. Annual vol. 1898. Harrisburg, Pa. 1899. pp. 22—23.* [7696

Egle, William Henry: **Wiestling** family. *In: Egle's ,,Pennsylvania genealogies.'' Harrisburg, Pa. 1896. pp. 719—732.*
[Descendants of Samuel Christopher Wiestling, b. June 4, 1760 at Oschatz, in the District of Meissen, Germany.] [7697

Wilson, L. Nevin - Compton, D. - Hay, Ed. R.: A history of the **Wilhelms** and the Wilhelm charge *[St. Paul's Church, Meyersdale, Somerset Co.,Pa.] Meyersdale, Pa.: The Wilhelm Press 1919. pp. 9—204, ill.* [7698

Miller, J. E.: With John Henry **Williams**, our secretary. *Elgin, Ill.: General Mission Board, Church of the Brethren 1921. pp. 143, ill.* [7699

P.[arthemore], E. W. S.: **Winagle** family record. *In: Notes and Queries. Edited by W. H. Egle. Third series, vol. I. 1884 —1887. Harrisburg, Pa. 1887. pp. 68—69. Reprint in: Third series, vol. I. Harrisburg, Pa. 1895. pp. 112—114.*
[Mathias Windnagle, b. 1716; m. Maria Catharine (Ritter); d. 1786.] [7700

Genealogical data. **Windnagle**. *In: Notes and Queries. Edited by W. H. Egle. Fourth series, vol. I. 1891—1893. Harrisburg, Pa. 1893. p. 26.*

[John Mathias Windnagle, b. May 14, 1716 of Evangelical Lutheran parents in Switzerland, came to America, landing at Philadelphia, Pa., Sept. 21, 1742.] [7701

Kauffman, Daniel: The Wing family. *In: Christian Monitor. A monthly magazine for the home. Vol. XIV, no. 9. Scottdale, Pa. 1922. p. 655.* [7702

[Egle, William Henry]: Obituary. Mrs. Mary H. Winnebrenner. *In: Notes and Queries. Edited by W. H. Egle. Third series, vol. II. 1887—1890. Harrisburg, Pa. 1891. pp. 186—187.* [7703

P.[arthemore], E. W. S.: Wirt family of Lykens Valley. *In: Notes and Queries. Edited by W. H. Egle. Fourth series, vol. I. 1891—1893. Harrisburg, Pa. 1893. pp. 242—244; 246—247.*

[Descendants of John Jacob Wertz (Wert) who emigrated from Germany in the ship Mascliffe-Galley, George Durell commander, from Rotterdam.] [7704

Fretz, A. J.: A brief history of Jacob Wismer and a complete genealogical family register *with biographies of his descendants from the earliest available records to the present time. With an introduction by Eli Wismer. Elkhart, Ind.: Mennonite Publishing Co. 1893. pp. X, (1), 372, ill.*

[b. in Germany about 1684 and d. in Bedminster Twp., Bucks Co., Pa. 1787.] [7705

Wisner, G. Franklin: The Wisners in America and their kindred. *A genealogical and biographical history. Baltimore, Md. 1918. pp. 270, (1), XVIII; genealogical charts.*

[Johannes Weesner, of Switzerland, progenitor of most of the Wisner in America, came to America about 1714 as a lieutenant in the 10000 troops of Queen Anne's Swiss contingent, and settled upon Long Island.] [7706

Wissler, Henry: The Wissler family record. *Being a brief account of Andrew Wissler's branch of the Wissler family in the United States of America and Canada. Toronto, Can.: The Bryant Press 1904. pp. 95, ill.* [7707

Davids, Richard Wistar: The Wistar family. *A genealogy of the descendants of Caspar Wistar, emigrant in 1717. Compiled by . . . Philadelphia. Pa. 1896. pp. 3—52—62. First to third supplement to the Wistar family. pp. (3), (2), (4).*

[b. in the village of Hilspach, some 6 miles from Heidelberg, in the then Electorate of the Rhenish Palatinate.] [7708

Observation on the European derivation of the American family of **Wistars** and **Wisters.** *[s. l.; s. d. (1898.)] pp. 3—14, ill.; chart showing lineal succession of eldest sons of the male line of the American branch, issuing from Johannes Casper Wister.* [7709

Wistar — Wister family. *In: Colonial families of Philadelphia. Edited by John W. Jordan. New York, N.Y. — Chicago, Ill.: The Lewis Publishing Co. 1911. Vol. I. pp. 257—263.*

[Hans Caspar Wüster, ancestor of the Wistar and Wister families, „Jäger" or forester to the Prince Palatine, resided in the rural Village of Hilspach, 6 miles from Heidelberg, in the then Electorate of the Rehnish Palatinate; d. at Hilspach, Jan. 13, 1726; Caspar Wüster, b. at Hilspach, Febr., 1696, sailed for Philadelphia, Pa. where he arrived Sept. 16, 1717.] [7710

The **Wister** family. *In: Colonial families of Philadelphia. Edited by John W. Jordan. New York, N.Y. — Chicago, Ill.: The Lewis Publishing Co. 1911. Vol. I. pp. 264—275, ill.*

[John Wüster, second son of Hans Caspar and Anna Catharina Wüster, b. in Hillspach, Renish Palatinate, Nov. 8, 1708, emigrated to Pa., arrived in Sept., 1727.] [7711

Ruschenberger, W. S. W.: A sketch of the life of Caspar Wister, M. D. *Reprinted from the: Transactions of the College of Physicians of Philadelphia, November 5, 1890. Philadelphia, Pa.: Wm. J. Dornan 1891. pp. 3—34, ill.* [7712

W.[ister], C.[harles] J. jr.: The labour of a long life: a memoir of Charles J. **Wister.** *Part I and II. Germantown, Pa.: Collins Printing House 1866; 1886. pp. 9—200, ill., pp. 204, ill.; Poscriptum pp. 12. Added: Obituary notice of Caspar Wister, M. D. By Craig Biddle. Read before the American Philosophical Society, Oct. 4, 1889. pp. 19; Some incidents in the life of Dr. Caspar Wister, not introduced in the Memoir of Dr. W. S. W. Ruschenberger. pp. 30.*

[great-grandson of Hans Caspar and Anna Catharina Wister, of Hillspach, near Heidelberg, Chur Palatinate, Germany.] [7713

Wister, Jones: Jones **Wister's** reminiscences. *Philadelphia, Pa.: J. B. Lippincott Co. 1920. pp. XIII, 459, ill.* [7714

Hocker, Edward W.: Sally Wister. *In: Historical Sketches. A Collection of Papers prepared for the Historical Society of Montgomery County, Pa. Vol. VI. Norristown, Pa. 1929. pp. 182—184, ill.* [7715

Comfort, Mary Lawton: Thomas **Wistar**. 1798—1876. *In: Quaker biographies. Series II. Brief biographical sketches concerning certain members of the religious Society of Friends. Vol. II. Philadelphia, Pa.: Friends' Book Store. pp. 29—69, ill.*

[grandson of Caspar Wüster, who emigrated from Germany to Pennsylvania 1717.] [7716

Witwer, George and **Witwer, Ananias Cline**: Witwer genealogy of America. *Compiled by . . . South Bend, Ind.: L. P. Hardy Co. 1909. pp. (5), 9—256.*

[Michael Witwer, the ancestor, settled in what is now Earl Twp., Lancaster Co., Pa. in the year 1727.] [7717

Nicholas **Wohlfart**. *In: The Perkiomen Region. Vol. I, no. 6. Pennsburg, Pa. 1922. pp. 108—110.* [7718

A family baptismal record *[of the family of Michael* **Wolfarth**, *d. July, 1806, and Elizabeth Lutz]. In: Notes and Queries. Edited by W. H. Egle. First and second series, vol. II. Harrisburg, Pa. 1895. pp. 358—359.* [7719

Stapleton, A.: The **Wolf** family, of Bethel Township, Berks County. *In: Notes and Queries. Edited by W. H. Egle. Annual vol. 1897. Harrisburg, Pa. 1898. p. 189.*

[Michael Wolf, the emigrant, came to Pennsylvania in 1754.] [7720

Steele, Henry J.: The life and public services of Governor George **Wolf**. *In: The Pennsylvania-German Society. Proceedings and Addresses . . . Easton, October 12, 1928. Vol. XXXIX. Norristown, Pa. 1930. Separate pagination pp. 25, ill.*

[son of George Wolf who emigrated from the Lower Alsace to America and arrived at Philadelphia, Pa., Oct. 4, 1751.] [7721

Beck, Clara A.: Kith an kin of George **Wolf**, governor of Pennsylvania. 1829—1835. *Easton, Pa.: John S. Correll Co. 1930. pp. V, 66, ill.* [7722

Wolf, John M.: Threescore years of public-school work. *In: The Pennsylvania-German. Vol. IX. Cleona, Pa. 1908. pp. 6—11, ill.*

[John M. Wolf, b. in Hamilton Township, Adams Co., Pa., June 27, 1832.] [7723

[Fahnestock, Geo. Wolff]: A Centennial memorial of Christian and Anna Maria **Wolff**, March 25, 1863: with brief records of their children and relatives. *Philadelphia, Pa. 1863. pp. (1), VII—VIII, 9—113.*

[Georg Michael Wolff, a citizen of Churpfaltz, removed from Nieder Hochstadt, Germany, with his wife, and two sons John Barnardt and Conrad to Pennsylvania, 1739.] [7724

Sener, S. M.: The **Wolff** family. *In: Notes and Queries. Edited by W. H. Egle. Fourth series, vol. II. Harrisburg, Pa. 1895. pp. 14—16.*

[John George Wolff, b. Aug. 10, 1676 in Oberhochstadt, Palatinate, m. 1695, removed to Pennsylvania in 1739.] [7725

Wolff, Frederick Lawrence: A genealogy of the descendants of John N. **Wolff** (1729 —1771), veteran (1746) of the Third Inter Colonial War, a resident of Lancaster Co., Pa. and particularly of the descendants of his son John Wolff (1764—1831) veteran of the War of the Revolution, a resident of Lancaster, Pa. and Byron, Ohio. *A Bicentennial memorial of John Nicholas Wolff, (born [in Germany] 1729) and Anna Maria Bower Wolff, his wife. Omaha, Neb. 1929. Typewritten pp. 65.*

[at Library of Congress, Washington, D. C.] [7726

Cornman, Charles Albert and **Nead, Daniel Wunderlich**: Genealogical record of the **Wunderlich** family in America. *Seventeen branches. Compiled by Charles Albert Cornman, assisted by Daniel Wunderlich Nead. Carlisle, Pa.: Cornman Printing Co. 1911. pp. X, 211, XVIII, ill.*

[John and Daniel Wunderlich, sons of Johannes Wunderlich and Anna Maria Densler, of Ludwigsburg, Wurttemberg, emigrated to America, the former arriving at Philadelphia, Pa. on Oct. 16, 1751, and the latter on Sept. 26, 1753.] [7727

[Wurtz, Charles Pemberton]: A genealogical record of the **Wurts** family, the descendants of Reverend Johannes Conrad **Wirz**, who came to America from Zurich, Switzerland, in 1734, also a record of the ancestry of the Reverend Johannes Wirz, from the thirteenth century. *[s. l.] 1889. pp. 91, ill., charts.* [7728

Y.

Yeager, James Martin: A brief history of the Yeager, Buffington, Creighton, Jacobs, Lemon, Hoffman and Woodside families and their collateral kindred of Pennsylvania. *Compiled by . . . [s. l.] 1912. pp. 6—277, (1), ill.* [7729

Memorial to the Yerkes family. *In: Genealogical and biographical memorials of the Reading, Howell, Yerkes, Watts, Lathan and Elkins families. By* Josiah Granville Leach. *Printed for private circulation. Philadelphia, Pa.: J. B. Lippincott 1898. pp. 189—202, ill.*

[Anthony Yerkes, the founder of the Yerkes family in the United States, emigrated from Germany and settled in Germantown, Pa. about 1700.] [7730

Leach, Josiah Granville: Chronicle of the Yerkes family, with notes on the Leech and Rutter families. *Printed for private circulation. Philadelphia, Pa.: J. B. Lippincott 1904. pp. XII, 262.* [7731

Stapleton, A.: Some Yoder family history. *In: Notes and Queries. Edited by W. H. Egle. Annual vol. 1897. Harrisburg, Pa. 1898. pp. 152—153.*

[The first of this name in Pa.'s Provincial history was Yost Yoder, who located on the Manatawny Creek, near where Pleasantville is now situated, Oley Twp., Berks Co., Pa.] [7732

Yoder, G. M.: Long lived Yoders. *[Descendants of Conrad Yoder, one of the pioneers of South Fork Valley, N. C.] In: The Pennsylvania-German. Vol. XII. Lititz, Pa. 1911. p. 377.* [7733

Mast, C. Z.: The Yoder family. *In: Christian Monitor. A monthly magazine for the home. Vol. XV, no. 1. Scottdale, Pa. 1923. pp. 18—21.* [7734

M.[eginness], J. F.: Moses Yoder. *In: Notes and Queries. Edited by W. H. Egle. Annual vol. 1899. Harrisburg, Pa. 1900. pp. 121—122.*

[Descendants of Samuel Yoder, of Oley Twp., Berks Co., Pa.] [7735

Weaver, Ethan Allen: Descendants of Northampton County families. The Yohe — Stecher — Weygandt reunion held in Washington County, this state. *[sg. Germantown, Pa., Oct. 12, 1907.] pp. 5.* [7736

Yost, J. Irwin: The Yost family. *In: The Pennsylvania-German. Vol. VII. Lebanon, Pa. 1906. pp. 337—341, ill.* [7737

James **Young.** *In: Notes and Queries. Edited by W. H. Egle. Fourth series, vol. II. Harrisburg, Pa. 1895. pp. 278—200.*

[James Young, son of Peter and Sophia Young, b. at Swatara Hill, 2 mi. E. of Middletown, July 25, 1820. His father emigrated from Berks Co., Pa.] [7738

[Hollinshead, Benjamin M.]: Mountain Mary. (Die Berg Maria.) *Contributed by Mr.* Converse Cleaves, *of Philadelphia. In: The Pennsylvania-German. Vol. III. Lebanon, Pa.. 1902. pp. 133—142.*

[Mary Young, of Oley; she, her mother and sister, emigrated. from Germany, about the year 1765.] [7739

Miller, Daniel: Maria **Young,** the mountain recluse of Oley. *Read Dec. 10, 1912. In: Transactions of the Historical Society of Berks County. Vol. III. Reading, Pa. 1923. pp. 209—220.* [7740

Captain Peter **Young.** — *Biographical note. In: Notes and Queries. Edited by W. H. Egle. Third series, vol. I. 1884—1887. Harrisburg, Pa. 1887. pp. 108—109. Reprint in: Third series, vol. I. Harrisburg, Pa. 1895. pp. 185—186.*

[eldest son of Valentine and Margaret Young, Exeter Twp., Berks Co., b. about 1740.] [7741

Z.

Zahniser, Kate M. - Zahniser, Charles Reed: The Zahnisers. A history of the family in America. *Mercer, Pa.: Kate M. Zahniser, publisher; Pittsburg, Pa.: Spahr & Ritscher, printers. 1906. pp. (2), 7—218, ill.*

[Descendants of Valentine Zahneisen of Moersheim, Germany, who d. on the ship, having embarked to Pa. in the fall of 1753, leaving his widow Juliana and a small boy, Matthias.] [7742

Zartman, Rufus Calvin: The Zartman family. *Philadelphia, Pa.: Lyon & Armor 1909. pp. IX—XVI, 431, ill.*

[Alexander and Ann Catharina Zartman, the progenitors, came from Germany in the summer of A. D. 1728.] [7743

John **Zeamer** and his descendants. *Reprint from: ,,Biographical Annals of Cumberland County, Pa." Chicago, Ill.: J. H. Beers & Co. 1905. pp. 21, ill.* [7744

Gross, Luelja Zearing: The Zearings. A pioneer Illinois family, with an account of the life of James Roberts Zearing, M. D. *Reprinted from: The Transactions*

37*

of the Illinois State Historical Society for
1921. Springfield, Ill.: Phillips Bros.
Print 1921. pp. 76, ill.
[Two brothers, John Zearing, 1792—
1846, of Harrisburg, Pa. and Martin
Zearing, 1794—1855, of Mechanicsburg,
Pa., sons of Henry Zearing, made their
first tour in the West, 1834.]   [7745

H., S. P.: In memoriam; Benjamin Franklin Zerbe, M. B. In: Papers read before
the Lebanon County Historical Society.
Vol. VI. Lebanon, Pa. 1912—1916. pp.
329⌐330.
    [son of Dr. Jonathan and Martha A.
(Meyer) Zerbe; descendant of the Zerbe
family whose progenitor came from one
of the French Cantons of Switzerland and
settled in Berks Co., 1723, and on the
maternal side of the Schaeffer family,
whose ancestor, Alexander Schaeffer,
founded Schaefferstown (then known as
Heidelberg) 1743.]   [7746

Elliot, Ella Zerbey: Blue book of Schuylkill
County. Who was who and why in
interior eastern Pennsylvania, in colonial days — The Huguenots and Palatines — Their service in Queens Ann's,
French and Indian wars — History of
the Zerbey, Schwalm, Miller, Merkle,
Minnich, Staudt, and many other representative families. Pottsville, Pa.:
,,Republican", Joseph H. Zerbey. 1916.
pp. VI, 7—456, ill., maps.
[Reviewed by E. Müller under the title
,,Familienkunde in Amerika". In:
Familiengeschichtliche Blätter. Monatsschrift für die gesamte deutsche wissenschaftliche Genealogie. Jg. XX. Leipzig
1922. Sp. 45—46.]   [7746a

F.[lickinger], S. H.: Zern family burials.
(From the family grave yard on the Paul
farm, along Indian Creek, West Cocalico
Township, Lancaster Co., Pa.) In: Ge-
nealogy. Journal of American ancestry.
Vol. II. New York, N. Y. 1912. p. 279.
                                        [7747

Ziegler, Elder Jesse: The Ziegler family record. A complete record of the Ziegler
family from our ancestor, Philip Ziegler,
born in Bern, Switzerland, in 1734, down
to the seventh and eight generations; including also those who are directly descendant from the family as far as data
could be obtained. By . . ., assisted by
Daniel P. Ziegler. Royersford, Pa.: Published by Jesse Ziegler 1906. pp. 118.
                                        [7748

Der erste Mayor Cincinnatis ein Deutscher.
[David Ziegler.]   In: Der Deutsche
Pionier. Jg. I. Cincinnati, O. 1869—
1870. S. 11—15.
[geb. in Heidelberg, Deutsches Reich,
1748, kam nach Amerika 1775, um in die
Armee der Freiheitskämpfer einzutreten.]
                                        [7749

R.[attermann, H. A.]: David Ziegler, Cin-
cinnati's erster Bürgermeister. In: Der
Deutsche Pionier._Jg. X. Cincinnati, O.
1878—1879. S. 3—12.   [7750
— Captain David Ziegler. An officier of the
Pennsylvania line of the Revolution, and
the first chief magistrate of Cincinnati,
O. Read before the ,,Literary Club of
Cincinnati", Ohio, June 8, 1883. In:
Historical Register: Notes and Queries,
historical and genealogical relating to
interior Pennsylvania for the year 1883.
Vol. I. Harrisburg, Pa. 1883. pp. 269—
284.   [7751
Major David Ziegler. A brave and distin-
guished Revolutionary hero. In: Notes
and Queries. Edited by W. H. Egle.
Annual vol. 1897. Harrisburg, Pa. 1898.
pp. 1—2.   [7752
Katzenberger, Geo. A.: Major David Zieg-
ler. [Biography of the first Mayor of
Cincinnati.] In: Ohio Archaeological and
Historical Quarterly. Vol. XXI. Co-
lumbus, O. 1912. pp. 127—174, ill.; also
separately issued: Columbus, O.: The
F. J. Heer Printing Co. 1912. pp. 50.
                                        [7753
Father and son. The life story of Henry
Ziegler, D. D. 1816—1898 and of John
A. M. Ziegler, Ph. D., D. D. 1855. To-
gether with a concise outline of American
Lutheran history by the son. With an
introduction by Frank P. Manhart.
Published for the author. Philadelphia,
Pa.: The United Lutheran Press 1930.
pp. 285, ill.
[Henry Ziegler was b. in Center Co.,
Pa., near the Old Fort, on the 19th of
Aug., 1816, son of Jacob Ziegler, native
of Baltimore Co., Md.]   [7754
Zimmermann. — In: Notes and Queries.
Edited by W. H. Egle. Third series,
vol. I. 1884—1887. Harrisburg, Pa.
1887. pp. 264. Reprint in: Third series,
vol. I. Harrisburg, Pa. 1895. pp. 483—
484.
[Frederick Zimmermann, d. 1793 on
his farm located on the Colebrook road,
2 1/2 miles from the Town of Lebanon,
Pa.]   [7755

Hostetter, Albert K.: The ancestors of the Zimmerman-Carpenter families of Lancaster County. *In: Papers and Addresses of the Lancaster County Historical Society. Vol. XXIV. Lancaster, Pa. 1920. pp. 138—143.* [7756

Obituary. Conrad O. Zimmerman. *In: Notes and Queries. Edited by W. H. Egle. Fourth series, vol. II. Harrisburg, Pa. 1895. pp. 226—227.* [7757

Zimmerman, L. M.: Reminiscences after thirty years in the ministry. *Baltimore, Md.: Myer and Thalheimer 1917. pp. 220, ill.*

[b. Aug. 29, 1860, son of Henry Zimmerman, farmer near Manchester, Caroll Co., Md.] [7758

Nead, Benjamin M. and Fegley, H. Winslow: Colonel Thomas Cadwallader Zimmerman. A minute upon his death. *In: The Pennsylvania-German Society. Proceedings and Addresses at Lancaster, Pa., Nov. 13, 1914. Vol. XXV. Lancaster, Pa. 1917. pp. 11—15.* [7759

Richards, Louis: In memoriam Thomas C. Zimmerman. *Read March 9, 1915. In: Transactions of the Historical Society of Berks County. Vol. III. Reading, Pa. 1923. pp. 358—360, ill.* [7760

Reigner, Louis: Celia [Zorndorf] of Bernville. *In: The Pennsylvania-German. Vol. XII. Lititz, Pa. 1911. pp. 175—176.*

[b. Nov. 6, 1756.] [7761

Mast, C. Z.: The Zug (Zook) family. *In: Christian Monitor. A monthly magazine for the home. Vol. XIV, no. 12. Scottdale, Pa. 1922. pp. 752—754.*

[Christian, Moritz and Johannes Zug of the Canton of Berne, Switzerland arrived in Philadelphia, Pa. 1742.] [7761a

Andrew Zumault of Shenandoah County Va., Henry Zumault and heirs of District of Upper Louisiana. *Advertised in The Missouri Gazette and Public Advertiser, April 12, 1820. Copied by Miss Emma Curry. In: The National Genealogical Society Quarterly. Vol. XI, no. 2. Washington, D. C. 1922. pp. 27—28.* [7761b

Anhang

Appendix

The Pennsylvania-German Society: Obituaries. In memoriam. *In: The Pennsylvania-German Society. Proceedings and Addresses.*

Vol. II. 1892:
Reist, Levi Sheaffer. *p. 131.*
Reinhold, Henry Sherk. *p. 132.*

Vol. III. 1893:
Zahm, Samuel Hensel. *p. 143.*
Lehman, Samuel Kaufman. *p. 144.*
Muma, David. *p. 145.*
Dreher, Samuel S. *p. 146.*

Vol. IV. 1894:
Slaymaker, Samuel Cochran. *p. 152.*
Seidensticker, Oswald. *p. 153.*

Vol. V. 1895:
Coxe, Eckley B. *pp. 142—143.*
Glatz, A. Hiestand. *p. 144.*
Mühlenberg, Francis. *p. 145.*
Hecht, Charles Edward Ziegler. *pp. 146—147.*
Levan, Franklin Klein. *pp. 148—149.*
Young, James. *pp. 150—151.*

Vol. VI. 1896:
Funk, Josiah. *pp. 122—123.*
Fisher, Charles Gutzlaff. *pp. 124—125.*
Weidman, Grant. *pp. 126—127.*
Wilhelm, J. Schall. *pp. 128—129.*

Vol. VII. 1897:
Klotz, Robert. *pp. 416—417.*
Shindel, Jacob Andrew. *pp. 418—420.*
Levan, Lewis Sebastian. *pp. 421—422.*
Richards, George Henry. *p. 423.*
Zieber, Eugene. *pp. 424—425.*

Vol. VIII. 1898:
Weiser, Clement Zwingli. *pp. 151—152.*
Borhek, Ashton Christian. *pp. 153—154.*

Vol. IX. 1899:
Richards, Mathias Henry. *pp. 29—37.*
Heinitsh, Charles Augustus. *pp. 38—39.*
Landis, Henry. *pp. 40—41.*
Kauffman, Andrew J. *pp. 42—44.*
Latimer, James W. *pp. 45—46.*

Vol. X. 1900:
Trexler, Horatio. *pp. 29—30.*
Stille, Charles Janeway. *pp. 31—32.*
Ermentrout, Daniel. *pp. 33—35.*
Sheeleigh, Mathias. *pp. 36—37.*
Schwartz, James Ernst. *pp. 38—40.*

Vol. XI. 1902:
Egle, William Henry. *pp. 31—36.*
Hanold, Hiester Muhlenberg. *pp. 36—37.*
Heiges, George W. *pp. 37—39.*
Porter, Thomas Conrad. *pp. 39—42.*
Reinoehl, Adam Cyrus. *pp. 42—43.*
Sütter, Daniel. *pp. 43—45.*
Shea, Christian Bernard. *pp. 45—48.*
Eberly, Adam John. *pp. 49—50.*

Vol. XII. 1903:
Albright, Edwin. *pp. 59—61.*
Rutter, Amos. *pp. 61—63.*
Meily, John. *pp. 64—65.*
Maurer, Daniel C. *pp. 65—66.*
Heckman, George C. *pp. 67—69.*
Boyd, Peter Keller. *pp. 69—71.*
Dotterer, Henry Sassaman. *pp. 71—72.*

Vol. XIII. 1904:
Yohe, Samuel Straub. *pp. 31—32.*
Beidelman, William. *pp. 33—34.*

Landes, Gared Clemens. *pp. 31—32.*
Atlee, John. *pp. 33—34.*
Gorgas, William Luther. *pp. 35—38.*
Bobb, Henry. *pp. 39—41.*
Herbst, George Edwin Maurer. *pp. 42—44.*
Stonecipher, John Franklin. *pp. 45—46.*
Renninger, Josiah Stauffer. *pp. 47—49.*
Schaeffer, Nathan Christ. *pp. 50—56.*
Opp, Charles Henry. *pp. 57—59.*
Graff, William Knapp. *p. 60.*
Miller, John Henry. *pp. 61—65.*
Shimer, Joseph Rodenberg. *pp. 66—67.*
Borhek, Morris Augustus. *pp. 68—69.*

Vol. XXXI. 1925:
Seibert, William Adam. *pp. 29—30.*
Wieand, Charles Samuel. *pp. 31—32.*
McClintock, Andrew Hamilton. *pp. 33—36.*
Shindel, William Lincoln. *pp. 37—39.*
Sachse, Julius Friedrich. *pp. 40—46.*
Keller, Eli. *pp. 47—50.*
Horn, Frank Melchior. *pp. 51—56.*
Fry, Jacob. *pp. 57—60.*
Bricker, Luther Jackson. *p. 61.*
Schmauk, Theodore Emanuel. *pp. 62—66.*
Edelman, William. *pp. 67—68.*
Steinman, George. *pp. 69—70.*
Heller, William Jacob. *pp. 71—73.*
Rath, Myron Oscar. *pp. 74—75.*
Heilman, Samuel Philips. *pp. 76—79.*

Vol. XXXII. 1924:
Grittinger, Henry Clay. *pp. 15—16.*
Haldeman, Horace Leander. *pp. 17—19.*
Schadt, Thomas A. J. *pp. 20—21.*
Rosengarten, Joseph George. *pp. 22—23.*
Bruner, Alfred Cookman. *p. 24.*
Hiester, Isaac. *pp. 25—27.*
Weidman, Grant. *pp. 28—29.*
Summers, William. *pp. 30—31.*
Wonsetler, Franklin B. *pp. 32—33.*
Diffenderffer, Frank Ried. *pp. 34—45, ill.* [7762

Dictionary of American biography. *Under the auspices of the American Council of Learned Societies. Edited by* Allen Johnson; *since vol. IV:* Allen Johnson and Dumas Malone; *since vol. IX:* Dumas Malone. *New York, N. Y.: Charles Scribner's Sons. Vol. I 1928ff. [with bibliographies].*

Vol. I. 1928:
Adams, Joseph Alexander (1803—1880), wood engraver, inventor. *By* Ralph C. Smith. *p. 93.*
Albright, Jakob (1759—1808), religious leader. *By* Theodore D. Bacon. *pp. 136—137.*
Alter, David (1807—1881), physician, physicist. *By* Dinsmore Alter. *p. 230.*
Ammen, Daniel (1819—1898), noval officer and writer. *By* Allan Westcott. *pp. 258—259.*

Ammen, Jakob (1807—1894), Union soldier. *By* Thomas Marshall Spaulding. *p. 259.*
Antes, Henry (1701—1755), religious leader. *By* Edmund Kimball Alden. *p. 312.*
Appenzeller, Henry Gerhard (1858—1902), Methodist missionary to Korea. *By* Horace Newton Allen. *pp. 323—324.*
Apple, Thomas Gilmore (1829—1898), theologian educator. *By* George Fulmer Mull. *pp. 324—325.*
Bachman, John (1790—1874), naturalist, Lutheran clergyman. *By* Donald C. Peattie. *pp. 466—467.*
Baer, George Frederick (1842—1914), lawyer, railroad president. *By* W. J. Ghent. *pp. 489—490.*
Ballinger, Richard Achilles (1858—1922), lawyer, secretary of the interior. *By* Frederic Logan Paxson.

Vol. II. 1929:
Baugher, Henry Louis (1804—1868), Lutheran clergyman. *By* George Harvey Genzmer. *pp. 58—59.*
Bausman, Benjamin (1824—1909), clergyman of the German Reformed church. *By* George Fulmer Mull. *p. 60.*
Beaver, James Addams (1837—1914), governor of Pennsylvania. *By* Conrad H. Lanza. *pp. 112—113.*
Bedinger, Georg Michael (1756—1843), soldier, pioneer, congressman. *By* Ellis Merton Coulter. *p. 124.*
Beissel, Johann Conrad (1690—1768), founder of the Solitary Brethren of the Community of Seventh Day Baptists at Ephrata. *By* Paul S. Leinbach. *pp. 142—143.*
Benner, Philip (1762—1832), merchant and ironmaster. *By* Harold Underwood Faulkner. *pp. 189—190.*
Berger, Daniel (1832—1920), United Brethren clergyman. *By* Augustus Waldo Drury. *p. 214.*
Bigler, John (1805—1871), governor of California. *By* Robert Glass Cleland. *pp. 263—264.*
Bigler, William (1814—1880), governor of Pennsylvania. *By* Robert Glass Cleland. *p. 264.*
Boehler, Peter (1712—1775), bishop of the Unitas Fratrum. *By* Dora Mae Clark. *pp. 402—403.*
Boehm, Henry (1775—1875), Methodist itenerant preacher. *By* Ezra Squier Tipple. *pp. 403—404.*
Boehm, John Philip (1683—1749), German Reformed clergyman. *By* George Harvey Genzmer. *pp. 404—405.*
Boehm, Martin (1725—1812), Mennonite bishop, United Brethren bishop. *By* Dora Mae Clark. *pp. 405—406.*
Boltzius, Johann Martin (1703—1765), Lutheran clergyman. *By* George Harvey Genzmer. *pp. 425—426.*

Gerhard, William Wood (1809—1872), Philadelphia physician. *By* John F. Fulton. *pp. 218—219.*

Gerhart, Emanuel Vogel (1817—1904), German Reformed theologian, college president. *By* George Harvey Genzmer. *p. 219.*

Geyer, Henry Sheffie (1790—1859), lawyer, United States senator. *By* H. Edward Nettles. *p; 231.*

Gobrecht, Christian (1785—1844), engraver and die-sinker. By Joseph Jackson. *pp. 336—337.*

Goetschius, John Henry (1718—1774), Reformed Dutch clergyman. *By* George Harvey Genzmer. *pp. 357—358.*

Good, James Isaac (1850—1924), German Reformed clergyman. *By* George Harvey Genzmer. *pp. 375—376.*

Good, Jeremiah Haak (1822—1888), German Reformed clergyman. *By* George Harvey Genzmer. *pp. 376—377.*

Graff, Frederic (1817—1890), civil engineer. *By* Frank A. Taylor. *pp. 466—467.*

Graff, Frederick (1774—1847), engineer. *By* Ray Palmer Baker. *pp. 467—468.*

Grim, David (1737—1826), tavernkeeper, merchant, antiquarian. *By* A. Everett Peterson. *p. 629.*

Vol. VIII. 1932:

Gros, John Daniel (1738—1812), German Reformed clergyman, educator. *By* George Harvey Genzmer. *pp. 15—16.*

Gross, Samuel David (1805—1884), pioneer, surgeon, teacher, and author. *By* J. Chalmers Da Costa. *pp. 18—20.*

Gross, Samuel Weissel (1837—1889), surgeon and author. *By* J. Chalmers Da Costa. *pp. 20—21.*

Grosscup [Grosskopf] Peter Stenger (1852 —1921), jurist. *By* John T. Vance. *pp. 21—22.*

Grube, Bernhard Adam (1715—1808), Moravian missionary. *By* George Harvey Genzmer. *pp. 31—32.*

Hager, John Sharpenstein (1818—1890), lawyer, judge, United States senator. *By* Edgar E. Robinson. *pp. 82—83.*

Hagner, Peter (1772—1850), third auditor of the Treasury. *By* Frank Monaghan. *pp. 84—85.*

Haldeman, Samuel Steman (1812—1880), scientist, philologist. *By* George C. Harvey. *p. 94—95.*

Harbaugh, Henry (1817—1867), German Reformed clergyman, author. *By* George Harvey Genzmer. *pp. 237—238.*

Harshberger, John William (1869—1929), botanist, naturalist, teacher. *By* Horace B. Baker. *pp. 354—355.*

Hartranft, Chester David (1839—1914), clergyman of the Reformed Dutch Church. *By* Harris Elwood Staar. *pp. 367—368.*

Hartranft, John Frederick (1830—1889), soldier, politician. *By* Witt Bowden. *p. 368.*

Hartwig, Johann Christoph (1714—1796), Lutheran clergyman. *By* George Harvey Genzmer. *p. 370.*

Hartzell, Joseph Crane (1842—1928), missionary bishop of the Methodist Episcopal Church. *By* James R. Joy. *pp. 370—371.*

Haupt, Herman (1817—1905), civil engineer, author, inventor. *By* John H. Frederick. *pp. 400—401.*

Hauser, Samuel Thomas (1833—1914), pioneer miner, capitalist, territorial governor of Montana. *By* Paul Chrisler Phillips. *pp. 402—403.*

Hay, Charles Augustus (1821—1893), Lutheran clergyman. *By* George Harvey Genzmer. *p. 429.*

Hazelius, Ernest Lewis (1777—1853), Lutheran clergyman. *By* George Harvey Genzmer. *pp. 474—475.*

Heckewelder, John Gottlieb Ernestus (1743—1823), missionary of the renewed Unitas Fratrum or Moravian Church to the Indians of Ohio. *By* Albert G. Rau. *pp. 495—497.*

Heinz, Henry John (1844—1919), manufacturer of prepared food. *By* Asher Isaacs. *pp. 506—507.*

Helbron, Peter (1739—1816), Catholic missionary. *By* Richard J. Purcell. *pp. 510—511.*

Helffenstein, John Albert Conrad (1748 —1790), German Reformed clergyman. *By* George Harvey Genzmer. *p. 511.*

Helmuth, William Tod (1833—1902), surgeon, author. *By* Claude A. Burrett. *pp. 516—517.*

Helper, Hinton Rowan (1829—1909), author. *By* J. G. de R. Hamilton. *pp. 517—518.*

Henck, John Benjamin (1815—1903), engineer and educator. *By* Frank A. Taylor. *pp. 522—523.*

Hendel, John William (1740—1798), German Reformed clergyman. *By* Georg Harvey Genzmer. *p. 523.*

Henkel, Paul (1754—1825), Lutheran clergyman. *By* George Harvey Genzmer. *pp. 538—539.*

Herkimer, Nicholas (1728—1777), a Revolutionary officer. *By* Edmund Kimball Alden. *pp. 577—578.*

Herman, Lebrecht Frederick (1761—1848), German Reformed clergyman. *By* George Harvey Genzmer. *pp. 578—579.*

Herr, John (1781—1850), founder of the sect of Reformed Mennonites. *By* Jane Clark. *p. 584.*

Vol. IX. 1932:

Hiester, Daniel (1747—1804), farmer, business man, congressman. *By* James H. Peeling. *pp. 9—10.*

Hiester, Joseph (1752—1832), merchant, Revolutionary soldier, congressman, governor of Pennsylvania. *By* James H. Peeling. *p. 10.*

Hillegas, Michael (1729—1804), merchant, first treasurer of the United States. *By* John H. Frederick. *pp. 51—52.*

Himes, Charles Francis (1838—1918), educator and scientist. *By* John Frederick Mohler. *pp. 59—60.*

Hite, Jost (d. 1760), colonizer of the Shenandoah Valley. *By* Frank Edward Ross. *p. 80.*

Hittel, John Shertzer (1825—1901), journalist, author, statistician. *By* Herbert I. Priestley. *pp. 81—82.*

Hittel, Theodore Henry (1830—1917), writer, lawyer. *By* Herbert I. Priestley. *p. 82.*

Hoover, Charles Franklin (1865—1927), physician. *By* Allen S. Johnson. *p. 205.*

Horn, Edward Trail (1850—1915), Lutheran clergyman. *By* George Harvey Genzmer. *pp. 228—229.*

Horn, George Henry (1840—1897), entomologist, physician. *By* Leland Ossian Howard. *pp. 229—230.*

Hough, George Washington (1836—1909), astronomer. *By* Raymond S. Dugan. *p. 252.*

Hussey, Curtis Grubb (1802—1893), miner and manufacturer. *By* Frank A. Taylor. *pp. 430—431.*

Imboden, John Daniel (1823—1895), Confederate soldier, promoter of mining interests. *By* Charles Dudley Rhodes. *pp. 460—461.*

Jacobs, Michael (1808—1871), Lutheran clergyman, educator. *By* George Harvey Genzmer. *pp. 567—568.*

Vol. X. 1933:

Jordan, John Woolf (1840—1921), librarian, editor, antiquarian. *By* Joseph Jackson. *p. 215.*

Kalb, Johann (1721—1780), Revolutionary general, knovn as ,,Baron de Kalb". *By* Frank Monaghan. *pp. 253—254.*

Kauffman, Calvin Henry (1869—1931), botanist. *By* John A. Stevenson. *pp. 262—263.*

Kemper, Jackson (1789—1870), first missionary bishop of the Protestant Episcopal Church. *By* Katharine Jeanne Gallagher. *pp. 321—322.*

Kemper, James Lawson (1823—1895), Confederate soldier, governer of Virginia. *By* C. C. Pearson. *p. 322—323.*

Kemper, Reuben (d. 1827), a controversial figure on the West Florida border. *By* Isaac J. Cox. *p. 323.*

Kephart, Isaiah Lafayette (1832—1908), United Brethren clergyman, educator. *By* Walter G. Clippinger. *p. 351.*

Kline, George (c. 1757—1820), frontier newspaper editor and book publisher. *By* I eon C. Prince. *p. 444.*

Klippart, John Hancock (1823—1878), agricultural writer secretary of the Ohio State Board of Agriculture. *By* Claribel R. Barnett. *p. 445—446.*

Klipstein, Louis Frederick (1813—1878), philologist, the first American to publish works on Anglo-Saxon. *By* George Harvey Genzmer. *p. 446—447.*

Kneass, Samuel Honeyman (1806—1858), civil engineer and architect. *By* Joseph Jackson. *pp. 454—455.*

Kneass, Strickland (1821—1884), civil engineer and railroad official. *By* Joseph Jackson. *pp. 455—456.*

Kneass, William (1780—1840), engraver and die-sinker. *By* Joseph Jackson. *pp. 456—457.*

Kocherthal, Josua von (1669—1719), Lutheran clergyman, the leader of the Palatine emigration to New York. *By* George Harvey Genzmer. *p. 484.*

Kolb, Dielman (1691—1759), Mennonite preacher. *By* Dora Mae Clark. *pp. 491—492.*

Kolb, Reuben Francis (1839—1918), Alabama planter and farm leader. *By* Albert B. Moore. *p. 492.*

Krauth, Charles Philip (1797—1867), Lutheran clergyman. *By* George Harvey Genzmer. *pp. 501—502.*

Krauth, Charles Porterfield (1823—1883), Lutheran clergyman, educator and author. *By* Vergilius Ferm. *p. 523.*

Kuhn, Adam (1741—1817), physician, botanist. *By* Willis J. Jepson. *pp. 510—511.*

Kumler, Henry (1775—1854), bishop of the United Brethren in Christ. *By* Harris Elwood Staar. *pp. 511—512.*

Kurtz, Benjamin (1795—1865), Lutheran clergyman, editor. *By* George Harvey Genzmer. *p. 514.*

Vol. XI. 1933:

Leidy, Joseph (1823—1891), naturalist. *By* George P. Merrill. *pp. 150—152.*

Lemke, Peter Henry (1796—1882), Roman Catholic missionary. *By* Richard J. Purcell. *pp. 161—162.*

Lenker, John Nicholas (1858—1929), Lutheran clergyman, historian and translator. *By* J. Magnus Rohne. *pp. 169—170.*

Levering, Joseph Mortimer (1849—1908), Moravian bishop, historian. *By* Albert G. Rau. *pp. 198—199.*

Lick, James (1796—1876), philantropist. *By* Edgar E. Robinson. *p. 234.*

Lochman, John George (1773—1826), Lutheran clergyman. *By* George Harvey Genzmer. *pp. 335—336.*

Long, John Luther (1861—1927), author, dramatist. *By* Walter Prichard Eaton. *pp. 379—380.*

Loskiel, George Henry (1740—1814), bishop of the renewed Unitas Fratrum or Moravian Church. By Albert G. Rau. *p. 421.*

Loucks, Henry Langford (1846—1928), agrarian politician. By Ralph Davol. *pp. 426—427.*

Ludwig, Christopher (1720—1801), superintendent of bakers in .he Continental Army, philanthropist. By Joseph Jackson. *pp. 497—499.*

McCauley, Mary Ludwig Hays (1754—1832), Revolutionary heroine, better known as Molly Pitcher, daughter of John George Ludwig Hass. By Virginia Ronsaville. *pp. 574—575.*

Vol. XII. 1933:

Mayer, Alfred Marshall (1836—1897), physicist. By Franklin de R. Furman. *p. 448.*

Mayer, Brantz (1809—1879), lawyer. author. By Joseph L. Wheeler. *p. 449.*

Mayer, Lewis (1783—1849), German Reformed clergyman. By George Harvey Genzmer. *pp. 451—452.*

Mayer, Philip Frederick (1781—1858), Lutheran clergyman. By George Harvey Genzmer. *p. 452.*

Melsheimer, Friedrich Valentin (1749—1814), Lutheran clergyman, entomologist. By George Harvey Genzmer. *pp. 518—519.*

Mettauer, John Peter (1787—1875), physician and surgeon. By Louise Fontaine Catterell. *pp. 585—586.*

Miller, George (1774—1816), Evangelical preacher. By George Harvey Genzmer. *p. 625.*

Miller, Henry (1800—1874), pioneer Kentucky physician. By James M. Phalen. *p. 626.*

Miller, John Franklin (1831—1886), United States senator. By Robert Glass Cleland. *p. 630—631.*

Miller, John Henry (1702—1782), printer, editor, and publisher. By Joseph Jackson. *pp. 631—632.*

Miller, John Peter (1709—1796), German Reformed clergyman, later head of the Ephrata Community of Seventh Day Baptists. By George Harvey Genzmer. *p. 632.*

Miller, Samuel (1820—1901), horticulturist. By R. H. Sudds. *p. 637.*

Miller, Samuel Freeman (1816—1890), associate justice of the United States Supreme Court. By Charles Fairman. *pp. 637—640.*

Miller, Warner (1838—1918), paper manufacturer and United States senator. By W. Freeman Galpin. *p. 641.*

Vol. XIII. 1934:

Muhlenberg, Frederick Augustus (1818—1901), Lutheran clergyman, teacher, college president. By George Harvey Genzmer. *pp. 306—307.*

Muhlenberg, Frederick Augustus Conrad (1750—1801), Lutheran clergyman, politician, first speaker of the federal House of Representatives. By George Harvey Genzmer. *pp. 30—308.*

Mühlenberg, Gotthilf Henry Ernest (1753—1815), Lutheran clergyman, botanist. By George Harvey Genzmer. *pp. 308—309.*

Mühlenberg, Henry Augustus Philip (1782—1844), Lutheran clergyman, politician, diplomat. By George Harvey Genzmer. *p. 309—310.*

Mühlenberg, Henry Melchior (1711—1787), Lutheran clergyman. By George Harvey Genzmer. *pp. 310—311.*

Mühlenberg, John Peter Gabriel (1746—1807), Lutheran clergyman, Revolutionary soldier, politician. By George Harvey Genzmer. *pp. 311—313.*

Mühlenberg, William Augustus (1796—1877), Episcopal clergyman. By George Harvey Genzmer. *pp. 313—314.*

Newcomer, Christian (1749—1830), one of the founders of the Church of the United Brethren in Christ. By Frances Bates. *pp. 455—456.*

Nitschmann, David (1696-1772), bishop of the Reneved Unitas Fratrum or Moravian Church. By Albert G. Rau. *pp. 529—530.*

Oberholtzer, Sara Louisa Vickers (1841—1930), author, leader in movement for school savings. By Anna Lane Lingelbach. *p. 607.*

Oemler, Arminius (1827—1897), physician, agriculturist, and promotor of the oyster industry in Georgia. By Claribel R. Barnett. *pp. 629—630.*

Vol. XIV. 1934:

Orth, Godlove Stein (1817—1882), politician, congressman. By Joe L. Norris. *pp. 60—61.*

Otterbein, Philip William (1726—1813), German Reformed clergyman, founder of the Church of the United Brethren in Christ. By George Harvey Genzmer. *pp. 107—108.*

Otto, Bodo (1711—1787), senior surgeon of the Continental Army. By J. Bennett Nolan. *pp. 108—109.*

Otto, John Conrad (1774—1844), physician. By E. B. Krumbhaar. *pp. 109—110.*

Otto, William Tod (1816—1905), jurist, assistant secretary of the interior, United States Supreme Court reporter. By Joe L. Norris. *p. 110.*

Pastorius, Francis Daniel (1651—1720), lawyer, author, founder of Germantown, Pa. By George Harvey Genzmer. *pp. 290—291.*

Peffer, William Alfred (1831—1912), journalist, senator from Kansas. By Raymond C. Miller. *p. 393.*

Studebaker, Clement (1831—1901), manufacturer of wagons and carriages. *By*
Russel H. Anderson. *pp. 180—181.*

Swank, James Moore (1832—1914), statistician, historian, executive secretary of
the American Iron and Steel Association.
By Albert T. Volwiler. *pp. 236—237.*

Switzler, William Franklin (1819—1906),
journalist, historian, and politician. *By*
Irwing Dilliard. *pp. 254—255.*

Tanneberger, David (1728—1804), organ
builder. *By* George Harvey Genzmer.
pp. 294—295

Teusler, Rudolf Bolling (1876—1934),
surgeon, founder of St. Luke's Hospital
Tokyo. *By* Kenneth S. Latourette. *pp.
383—384.*

Tome, Jacob (1810—1898), merchant,
banker, and philanthropist. *By.* Curtis
W. Garrison. *pp. 577—578.*

Vol. XIX. 1936:

Tutwiler, Henry (1807—1884), Alabama
educator. *By* Hallie Farmer. *pp. 76—77.*

Tutwiler, Julia Strudwick (1841—1916),
educator, social reformer. *By* Hallie
Farmer. *pp. 77—78.*

Tyson, James (1841—1919), physician
and teacher. *By* Francis R. Packard.
p. 103.

Tyson, Job Roberts (1803—1858), law
lawyer, congressman, historical writer.
By Roy F. Nichols. *pp. 103—104.*

Tyson, Stuart Lawrence (1873—1932),
Protestant Episcopal clergyman. *By*
John Haynes Holmes. *pp. 105—106.*

Unangst, Erias (1824—1903), Lutheran
missionary. *By* Samuel G. Hefelbower.
p. 108.

Updegraff, David Brainard (1830—1894),
Quaker preacher, evangelist, editor. *By*
Rufus M. Jonas. *p. 120.*

Valentine, Milton (1825—1906), Lutheran
theologian, educator. *By* Luther Allan
Weigle. *pp. 141—142.*

Wagner, Clinton (1837—1914), laryngo-
logist. *By* D. Bryson Delavan. *pp. 311
—312.*

Wagner, Webster (1817—1882), manufacturer of sleeping cars. *By* Carl W.
Mitman. *pp. 312—313.*

Wagner, William (1796—1885), merchant
philanthropist. *By* Joseph Jackson.
pp. 313—314.

Wanamaker, John (1838—1922), merchant. *By* Joseph J. Senturia. *pp. 407
—409.*

Wanamaker, Lewis Rodman (1863—
1928), merchant. *By* Joseph J. Senturia. *pp. 409—410.*

Wanamaker, Reuben Melville (1866—
1924), jurist. *By* Alonzo H. Tuttle.
pp. 410—411.

Weber, Henry Adam (1845—1912),
chemist, purefood reformer. *By* C. A.
Browne. *pp. 582—583.*

Weidner, Revere Franklin (1851—1915),
Lutheran theologian. *By* John O. Evjen.
pp. 606—607.

Weiser, Johann Conrad (1696—1760),
Indian agent. *By* Carl Bridenbaugh.
pp. 614—615.

Weitzel, Godfrey (1835—1884), soldier,
engineer. *By* Oliver L. Spaulding, Jr.
pp. 616—617.

Wenner, George Unangst (1844—1934).
By Samuel G. Hefelbower. *p. 653.*

Vol. XX. 1936:

Wernwag, Lewis (1769—1843), pioneer
bridge builder. *By* Burr Arthur Robinson. *pp. 2—3.*

Wetzel, Lewis (1764—1808 ?), Indian
fighter. *By* Leland D. Baldwin. *pp. 24
—25.*

Widener, Harry Elkins (1885—1912),
collector of rare books. *By* Charles
K. Bolton. *pp. 184—185.*

Widener, Peter Arrell Brown (1834—
1915), financier and philanthropist. *By*
Hobert S. Perry. *pp. 185—186.*

Winebrenner, John (1797—1860), clergyman, founder of the General Eldership
of the Churches of God in North America.
By George Harvey Genzmer. *pp. 384—
385.*

Winkler, Edwin Theodore (1823—1883),
Baptist clergyman, editor, and writer.
By Rufus W. Weaver. *p. 389.*

Wirt, William (1772—1834), attorney
general of the United States. *By* Thomas
P. Abernethy. *pp. 418—421.*

Wise, John (1808—1879), balloonist.
By Alexander Klemin. *pp. 428—429.*

Wisner, Henry (1720—1790), member
of the Continental Congress, powder
manufacturer. *By* Edna L. Jacobsen.
pp. 431—432.

Wistar, Caspar (1696—1752), manufacturer of glass. *By* Rhea Mansfield
Knittle. *pp. 432—433.*

Wistar, Caspar (1761—1818), physician.
By Francis R. Packard. *pp. 433—
434.*

Wister, Sarah (1761—1804), diarist.
By Anna Lane Lingelbach. *pp. 434
—435.*

Wolf, George (1777—1840) congressman
from Pennsylvania, governor. *By* Asa
Earl Martin. *pp. 446—447.*

Wolfe, Catharine Lorillard (1828—1887),
philanthropist, art patron. *By* William
Bristol Shaw. *pp. 449—450.*

Wolfe, John David (1792—1872), merchant and philanthropist. *By* William
Bristol Shaw. *p. 451.*

Wolle, John Frederick (1863—1933),
organist, composer and conductor of the
Bach Choir. *By* Raymond Walters. *pp.
453—454.*

Wurtz, Henry (1828—1910), chemist and
editor. *By* C. A. Browne. *pp. 571—572.*

Bibliographien

Bibliographical Papers

Allgemeine

General

American Historical Association: Annual report of the American Historical Association for the year 1884. *New York, N. Y. & London: G. P. Putnam's Sons 1885. — ff. [Title varies]; since 1890: Washington, D. C.: Government Printing Office.* [7764

Channing, Edw. - Hart, A. Bushnell - Turner, Fr. J.: Guide to the study and reading of American history. *By . . . Revised and augmented edition. Boston and London: Guin and Co. 1912. pp. XVI, 650.* [7765

[Dahlmann - Waitz]: Dahlmann - Waitz: Quellenkunde der Deutschen Geschichte. *Herausgegeben im Auftrage des Kuratoriums der Gesellschaft Jahresberichte für deutsche Geschichte. 9. Auflage. Herausgegeben von* Hermann **Haering**. *2 Bde. Leipzig: K. F. Koehler 1931. XL, 992 S.; (2), 993—1292 S.* [7766

Eberhardt, Fritz: Amerika-Literatur. *Die wichtigsten seit 1900 in deutscher Sprache erschienenen Werke über Amerika. Bearbeitet und mit Charakteristiken versehen von . . . Leipzig: Verlag von Koehler & Volckmar A.-G. & Co. 1926. 335 S.*

= *Koehler & Volckmars Literaturführer Bd. VII.* [7766a

Edwards, Everett E.: A bibliography of the history of agriculture in the United States. *Washington, D. C.: United States Government Printing Office. 1930. pp. IV, 307.*

= *United States Department of Agriculture. Miscellaneous Publications. No. 84.* [7767

Mai, Richard: Auslanddeutsche Quellenkunde 1924—1933. *Von . . . in Verbindung mit dem Volksbund für das Deutschtum im Ausland herausgegeben von Dr. Emil Clemens Scherer, Leiter des Reichsverbandes für die Katholischen Auslanddeutschen. Berlin: Weidmannsche Buchhandlung 1936. XVI, 504 S.*

[Nordamerika. Vereinigte Staaten S. 353 —368; Kanada S. 369—371.] [7767a

Mode, Peter G.: Source book and bibliography guide for American church history. *Menasha, Wis.: The Collegiate Press George Banta Publishing Co. 1921. pp. XXIV, 735.*

[Pennsylvania in the colonial period. = *Chapter IX. pp. 149—186.]* [7768

Besondere

Special

Beers, Henry Putney: Pennsylvania bibliographies. *Compiled by . . . In: Pennsylvania History. Official organ of the Pennsylvania Historical Association. Vol. II Philadelphia, Pa. 1934. pp. 104—108; 178—182.*

[General p. 104; Local p. 105; Colonial pp. 106—107; Miscellaneous pp. 107— 108; Printed source materials pp. 178— 180; Bibliographies of manuscripts pp. 180—182.] [7769

Aurand, A. Monroe, jr.: A bibliography: Notes and Queries, Historical, Bibliographical and Genealogical, Relating Chiefly to Interior Pennsylvania, 1878 —1900: The works of Dr. William Henry Egle. *Harrisburg, Pa.: The Aurand Press 1934. pp. 64.* [7770

Bausman, Lottie M.: A bibliography of Lancaster County, Pa. 1745—1912. *Publication of the Pennsylvania Federation of Historical Societies. Philadelphia, Pa.*

Patterson & White Co. 1916. pp. IV, 460. [7771

Bender, Harold S.: Two centuries of American Mennonite literature. A bibliography of Mennonitica Americana. 1727 —1927. *In: The Mennonite Quarterly Review. Vol. I. Goshen, Ind. 1927. No. 1. pp. 34—53; No. 2. pp. 46—72; No. 4. pp. 61—79; Vol. II. 1928. No. 1. pp. 16 —55; No. 2. pp. 124—150; No. 3. pp. 206—224.*
Revised reprint: . . . 1727—1928. Goshen, Ind.: Goshen Printery 1929. pp. XII, (2), 181, ill.
= Studies in Anabaptist and Mennonite History . . . Published by the Mennonite Historical Society. Goshen College, Goshen, Ind., No. 1. [7772

Croll, P. C.: Lebanon County, Pa. imprints and bibliography. *In: Papers read before the Lebanon County Historical Society. Vol. IV. 1906—1909. Lebanon, Pa. 1909. pp. 153—199.* [7773

Cronau Rudolf: Die Quellen zur Geschichte des deutschen Elements in den Vereinigten Staaten. *In: Drei Jahrhunderte deutschen Lebens in Amerika. Eine Geschichte der Deutschen in den Vereinigten Staaten. Berlin 1909 [= Nr. 34]. S. 613 —632; 2. Aufl. 1924. S. 664—683.* [7773a

Deutsche Gesellschaft von Pennsylvanien. Archiv: Liste der vom Archivcommittee seit 1867 gesammelten Bücher. *(Nach der Zeit des Erscheinens geordnet.) In: 108ter Jahresbericht der Deutschen Gesellschaft von Pennsylvanien, für das Jahr 1872. Philadelphia, Pa.: G. P. Lippe 1873. S. 32—38.* [7774

Drury, A. W.: The Historical Society. *[Catalogue of the historical literature concerning the United Brethren Church in Christ being in possession of the Historical Society, the library of Bonebrake Seminary.] In: The Religious Telescope. Vol. 98, no. 7. Dayton, O. Febr. 13, 1932. pp. 7—8.* [7775

Faust, Albert Bernhardt: Bibliography. List of works on the Germans in the United States. *In: ,,The German element in the United States. By A. B. Faust. Vol. II. Boston, Mass. and New York, N. Y. 1909 [= no. 42]. pp. 479—562; Additional bibliography-material see: Second edition. New York, N. Y. 1927. Appendix to both vols. In: Vol. II. pp. 607— 722.* [7776
— ,,German"; (bibliography). *In: The Cambridge History of American Litera-*

ture. Edited by William Peterfield Treut, John Erskine, Stuart P. Sherman, Carl van Doren. Vol. IV. ,,Later American literature: part III." New York, N. Y.: G. P. Putnam's Sons 1921. Part of the chapter XXXI. ,,Non English writings. I. German, French, Yiddish." pp. 572— 590; Bibliography. pp. 813—820. [7777

Flory, John S.: Literary activity of the German Baptist Brethren in the eighteenth century. Elgin, Ill.: Brethren Publishing House. 1908. pp. XII, 335. *[Bibliography. pp. 291—327.]* [7778
— Literary activities of the Brethren in the nineteenth century. *In: Yearbook of the Church of the Brethren. 1919. Elgin, Ill. 1919. pp. 39—45.* [7779
— Our literary activity in the twentieth century. *In: The Gospel Messenger. Vol. LXXIII, no. 38. Elgin, Ill.: Brethren Publishing House 1924. pp. 598— 599.* [7780

Frick, W. K.: Notes on the Penna-German literature. 5 installments, dated May 31, 1887. *In: The Mühlenberg Monthly. Allentown, Pa. Vol. IV, no. 10. June, 1887; Vol. V, no. 2. Oct., 1887; no. 6. Feb., 1888; no. 8. April, 1888; no. 10. June, 1888.*
[Bibliography: 3rd to 5th installment.] [7781

Goebel, J.: Geschichte des Auslanddeutschtum. Vereinigte Staaten von Nordamerika. *In: Jahresberichte für deutsche Geschichte. Herausgegeben von A. Brackmann und Fritz Hartung. Jg. III, 1927. Leipzig 1929. S. 732—735. Fortgesetzt von F. Schönemann in: Jg. V, 1929. Leipzig 1931. S. 706—713; Jg. VIII, 1932. Leipzig 1934. S. 700—713.* [7781a

Helbig, Richard E.: German-American genealogies, chiefly Pennsylvanian, found in the New York Public Library. *In: The Pennsylvania-German. Vol. VII. Lebanon, Pa. 1906. pp. 303—307.* [7782

Hildeburn, Charles R.: List of the publications issued in Pennsylvania, 1685 to 1759. *Philadelphia, Pa.: Collins 1882. pp. 40.* [7783
— A century of printing. The issues of the press in Pennsylvania. 1685—1784. *Philadelphia, Pa.: Press of Matlack & Harvey 1885/86. 2 vols. Vol. I. 1685— 1763. pp. XV, 392; Vol. II. 1764—1784. pp. 516.* [7784

Hinke, William John: Bibliography of the Reformed Church of the United States.

Appendix to the separate prints of „The Reformed Church in Pennsylvania" by J. H. Dubbs. Lancaster, Pa.: The New Era Printing Co. 1902. = Part X. „A narrative and critical history", prepared at the request of the Pennsylvania-German Society [= no. 1486]. pp. 341—380; also issued separately.   [7785

Hinke, William John: The sources of Reformed church history in Pennsylvania. *In: The Reformed Church Review. Vol. XXIV.* Philadelphia, Pa. 1920. pp. 251—264.
                                      [7785a

Kriebel, Howard W.: Philadelphia prints in Schwenckfelder Historical Library, [not listed in: The first century of German printing in America, 1728—1830. By O. Seidensticker. *Philadelphia, Pa. 1893 (= no. 7802)]. In: The Perkiomen Region. Vol. IX, no. 2. Pennsburg, Pa. 1931.* pp. 42—48.   [7786

L.[äugin], Th.[eodore]: Das Schrifttum über Badener im Ausland. *Von der Badischen Landesbibliothek in Karlsruhe. In: Der Auslanddeutsche. Halbmonatsschrift für Auslanddeutschtum und Auslandkunde. Mitteilungen des Deutschen Ausland-Instituts, Stuttgart. Bd. VI, Nr. 12. Stuttgart 1923.* S. 339—342.   [7787

Library of Congress, Division of Bibliography: A list of works relating to the Germans in the United States. *Compiled under the direction of* A. P. C. Griffin. *Washington, D. C.: Government Printing Office. 1904.* pp. (1), 5—32.   [7788
— List of references on the Pennsylvania Germans. *December 8, 1921. Typewritten.* pp. 14. = Selected list of references No. 603.
[*At Library of Congress, Washington, D. C.*]   [7789

Long, Harriet Catherine: The Pennsylvania-Germans; a select bibliography, submitted in partial fulfillment of the requirements for the degree of B. L. S. *New York State Library School 1910. Lititz, Pa. 1910.* pp. 19.
Reprint: A select bibliography. [„A list of the more truly representative books on the Pennsylvania-Germans".] Submitted in partial fulfillment of the requirements for the degree of B. L. S. *New York State Library School 1910. In: The Pennsylvania-German. Vol. XI. Lititz, Pa. 1910.* pp. 460—476.   [7790

Losch, Philipp: Bibliographie des Subsidienwesens, insbesondere des hessischen mit besonderer Berücksichtigung der Hessen in Amerika. *In: Soldatenhandel. Von Philipp Losch. Kassel 1933 [= Nr. 2904].* S. 61—110.   [7790a

McCreary, Nancy H.: Pennsylvania literature of the colonial period. *In: The Pennsylvania Magazine of History and Biography. Vol. LII. Philadelphia, Pa. 1928.* pp. 289—316.
[Bibliography: pp. 313—316.] [7791

Morris, John G.: The literature of the Lutheran Church in the United States. *(Delivered by appointment of the Historical Society of the Evangelical Lutheran Church, at the meeting of the General Synod, at York, Pa., May 7, 1864.) In: The Evangelical Review. Vol. XV. Gettysburg, Pa. 1864.* pp. 416—428. [7792
— Sources of information on the history of the Lutheran Church in America. *In: The Lutheran Church Review. Vol. XIV. Philadelphia, Pa. 1895.* pp. 165—186.
                                      [7793
— List of books relating to the Germans in America. *Read before the German Historical Society, Nov. 8th, 1887. In: Eighth and Tenth Annual Report of the Society for the History of the Germans in Maryland. Baltimore Md. 1896.* pp. 53—60.   [7794

O'Callaghan, E. B.: A list of editions of the Holy Scriptions and parts thereof printed in America previous to 1860: with introduction and biographical notes. *Albany, N. Y.: Munsell & Rowland 1861.* pp. LIV, (6), 415, ill. with facsimiles.   [7795

Pennsylvania History Club: Publications of the Pennsylvania History Club. *Vol. I. A contribution to Pennsylvania historical bibliography. Philadelphia, Pa.: 1300 Locust Street, Febr., 1909.* pp. 58. [7796

Keyser, N. H.: Fiction dealing with Pennsylvania-Germans. *(List of works of fiction relating to the Pennsylvania-Germans.) In: The Pennsylvania-German. Vol. VII. Lebanon, Pa. 1906.* p. 272. [7797

Reichard, Harry Hess: Pennsylvania-German dialect writings and their writers. *Lancaster, Pa.: The New Era Printing Co. 1918. = Part XXVIII. „A narrative and critical history", prepared at the request of the Pennsylvania-German Society. In: The Pennsylvania German Society. Proceedings and Addresses . . . 1915. Vol. XXVI. Lancaster, Pa. 1918. Separate pagination.* pp. XI, 13—400, ill. [Bibliography. pp. 321—400.] [7798

Rosengarten, J. G.: See nos. 7836—7839.

Sachse, Julius Friedrich: Title pages of books and pamphlets that influenced German emigration to Pennsylvania. *Reproduced in fac-simile for the Pennsylvania-German Society. Philadelphia, Pa. 1897. = Appendix of the editor's book: The Fatherland (1450—1700). ... In: The Pennsylvania-German Society. Procceedings and Addresses. Vol. VII. Reading, Pa. 1897. pp. 201—256.* [7800

Seidensticker, Oswald: Deutsch-amerikanische Bibliographie bis zum Schlusse des letzten Jahrhunderts. *In: Der Deutsche Pionier. Jg. IX. Cincinnati, O. 1877—1878. S. 178—183; 241—245; 264—268; 324—328; 348—351; Jg. X. 1878—1879. S. 22—28; 62—66; 94—101; 133—136; 158—161; 194—199; 224—230; 264—270; 309—316; 374; 384—389; 422—429; 466—472. Nachtrag. Jg. XII. 1880—81. S. 220—224.* [7801

— The first century of German printing in America 1728—1830. *Preceeded by a notice of the literary work of F. D. Pastorius. Published by the German-Pionier-Verein of Philadelphia. Philadelphia, Pa.: Schaefer & Koradi 1893. pp. X, 253, (1), fac-simile.*

[Supplements see nos. 7786, 7804, 7806]. [7802

Sower, Charles G.: The Sower publications. *(A complete list of the publications of both the two Christopher Sowers, father and son, taken from the Sower chart). In: The Pennsylvania-German. Vol. II. Lebanon, Pa. 1901. pp. 89—93.* [7803

Stapleton, A.: Researches in the first century of printing in America 1728—1830. *(Issues of the German press omitted in: The first century of German printing in America, 1728—1830. By O. Seidensticker. Philadelphia, Pa. 1893 [= no. 7802]. In: The Pennsylvania-German. Vol. V. Lebanon, Pa. 1904. pp. 81—89; p. 183; pp. 262—263.* [7804

Warrington, James: A bibliography of church music books issued in Pennsylvania, with annotations. *In: The Penn Germania. Vol. I. = Old series, vol. XIII. Lititz, Pa. 1912. pp. 170—177; 262—268; 371—374; 460—465; 627—631; 755—759.* [7805

Wayland, John W.: „Literary activities and associations" of the Shenandoah Co., Va. — „Henkel press bibliography." *In: A history of Shenandoah County, Va. By John W. Wayland. Strasburg, Va. 1927 [= no. 5626]. pp. 481—497.*

[Gives a number of items which are not listed in: The first century of German printing in America 1728—1830. By O. Seidensticker. Philadelphia, Pa. 1893 (= no. 7802).] [7806

Publications by Lutherans in the United States. *In: The Evangelical Review. Vol. VIII. Gettysburg, Pa. 1856—57. pp. 264—284.* [7807

List of publications by Lutherans in the United States. *In: The Evangelical Review. Vol. XII. Gettysburg, Pa. 1860—61. pp. 542—574.* [7808

Steiner, Bernard C.: Descriptions of Maryland. *Baltimore, Md.: The Johns Hopkins Press 1904. pp. 94. = Johns Hopkins University Studies in Historical and Political Science. Series XXII, nos. 11—12.*

[A bibliography. 1526—1903.] [7809

Cappon, Lester Jesse: Bibliography of Virginia history since 1865. *By ... Under the direction of Dumas Malone. Charlottesville, Va.: The Michie Co. 1930. pp. XVIII, 900. = The University of Virginia Institute for Research in the Social Sciences Institute Monograph, no. 5.* [7810

Swem, Earl G.: A bibliography of Virginia. *3 parts. Richmond, Va.: Davis Bottom, Superintendent of Public Printing 1916—1919.*

Part I: Containing the titles of books in the Virginia State Library which relate to Virginia and Virginians, the titles of those books written by Virginians, and those printed in Virginia ... Richmond, Va. 1916. pp. (2), 37—767. = Bulletin Virginia State Library. Vol. VIII, nos. 2, 3, 4. April, July, Oct., 1915;

Part II: Containing titles of the printed official documents of the commonwealth, 1776—1916. Richmond, Va. 1917. pp. X, 1404. = Bulletin Virginia State Library. Vol. X, nos. 1—4. Jan.—Oct., 1917;

Part III: The acts and the journals of the General Assembly of the colony, 1619—1776. Richmond, Va. 1919. pp. 5—71. = Bulletin of the State Library. Vol. XII, nos. 1, 2. Jan., April, 1919. [7811

[Stewart, Robert Arminstead]: Index to printed Virginia genealogies including key and bibliography. *Richmond, Va.: Old Dominion Press 1930. pp. 265.* [7812

Weeks, Stephen B.: A bibliography of the historical literature of North Carolina. *Cambridge: Harward University 1895. pp. 78.* [7813

38*

Inhaltsverzeichnisse und Register zu Zeitschriften

Indexes to periodicals

Haldy, Gertrude Hensel and **Worner, William Frederic:** Index of authors whose papers and addresses have appeared in volumes I to XXXV of the proceedings. *[= Papers and Addresses"] of the Lancaster County Historical Society. Prepared by . . . In: Papers and Addresses read before the Lancaster County Historical Society. Vol. XXXVI, no. 1. Lancaster, Pa. 1932. pp. 1—38.* [7814

[McAlarney, M. W.]: Notes and queries, *[historical, biographical and genealogical. Edited by W. H. Egle. 12 vols. Harrisburg, Pa. 1894—1901 (= no. 3156)].* Table of contents. *Published by . . . Harrisburg, Pa. [s. d.] pp. 40. [See also no. 7770]* [7815

Stein, Thos. S.: Index to the first eight volumes of the publications of *[= ,,Papers read before"]* the Lebanon County Historical Society. *Introduction read before the Society, Jan. 25, 1924. pp. 55.* [7816

Leading articles of the Pennsylvania-German. Volumes I—XII, and of the Penn Germania. Volumes XIII—XV, January, 1900 to December, 1914. *In: The Penn Germania. Vol. III. = Old series, vol. XV. Cleona, Pa. 1914. pp. 249—256.* [7817

Descriptive list of the publications of the Pennsylvania-German Society. July, 1914. *Philadelphia, Pa. 1914. pp. 14; New print. Norristown, Pa. 1929. pp. 19.* [7818

Publications of the Pennsylvania-German Society. A descriptive list. *In: The Pennsylvania-German Society. Proceedings and Addresses. Vol. XXXIV. Lancaster, Pa. 1929. pp. 113—130.* [7819

Index to the Lutheran Quarterly. Vol. I to XL, 1890—1910 and of its predecessor The Evangelical Review. Vol. I to XXI, 1849 to 1870, *covering a period of 61 years making it the oldest Lutheran Theological magazine in America. Gettysburg, Pa.: Gettysburg Compiler Print. pp. 64.* [7820

Index to the Lutheran Quarterly for 50 years from 1871—1920. *[s. l. 1921] pp. 52.* [7821

Gedruckte Führer über Manuskript-Material
Printed Guides to Manuscript Material

Vereinigte Staaten
United States

Allison, William Henry: Inventory of unpublished material for American religious history in Protestant church archives and other repositories. *Washington, D. C.: Published by the Carnegie Institution of Washington — Baltimore, Md.: The Lord Baltimore Press 1910. pp. VII, 254.*
= *Carnegie Institution of Washington. Publication no. 137.* [7822

Godcharles, Frederic A.: The collection of the issues of the German presses, charter, treaties, etc. at the Pennsylvania State Library. *Address. In: The Pennsylvania — German Society. Proceedings and Addresses at Harrisburg, Pa., Oct. 18, 1929. Vol. XL. Norristown, Pa. 1932. pp. 11—14.* [7823

Hasse, Adelaide Rosalie: Index of economic material in documents of the states of the United States; Pennsylvania, 1790 —1904. *Prepared for the Department of Economics and Sociology of the Carnegie Institution. 1 vol. in 3 parts. [Washington, D. C.] Carnegie Institution of Washington 1919—1922.*
= *Carnegie Institution of Washington. Publication no. 85.* [7824

Henry, James: Moravian manuscript literature. *In: Transactions of the Moravian Historical Society. Vol. IV, 1891—1895. Nazareth, Pa. 1895. pp. 15—25.* [7825

Hulbert, Archer Butler: The Moravian records. *[„A rough catalogue of the manuscripts preserved in the archives of the Moravian Church and Malin Library".] In: Ohio Archaeological and Historical Quarterly. Vol. XVIII. Columbus, O. 1909. pp. 199—226, ill.* [7826

Mode, Peter: Source book and bibliographical guide for American church history. *Menasha, Wis.: The Collegiate Press George Banta Publishing Company 1921. pp. XXIV, 735.*
[„Pennsylvania in the colonial period" = Chapter IX. pp. 149—186.] [7827

Spofford, Ernest: Some of the manuscript resources of the Historical Society of Pennsylvania. *In: Pennsylvania History. Official organ of the Pennsylvania Historical Association. Vol. I Philadelphia, Pa. 1934. pp. 88—97.* [7828

Vosburgh, Royden Woodward: Early New York church records. A report and digest of the records. Transcribed by The New York Genealogical and Biographical Society, 1913—1917. *In: The New York Genealogical Biographical Record. Vol. XLIX. New York, N. Y. 1918. pp. 11—16.*
[Includes a number of Evangelical Lutheran and (German Reformed church records.] [7829

Europäisches Festland
Continental Europe

de Boer, L. P.: The archives of the Netherlands and their importance for American genealogy. *In: The National Genealogical Society Quarterly. Vol. XVI, no. 3. Washington, D. C. 1928. pp. 33—37.* [7830

Faust, Albert B.: Guide to the materials for American history in Swiss and Austrian archives. *Washington, D. C.: Published by the Carnegie Institution of Washington — Baltimore, Md.: The Lord Baltimore Press 1916. pp. VII, 299.*

= *Carnegie Institution of Washington, D. C. Publication no. 220. Papers of the Department of Historical Research.* [7831

Faust, Albert B.: Unpublished documents on emigration from the archives of Switzerland. *In: Deutsch-Amerikanische Geschichtsblätter. Jahrbuch der Deutsch-Amerikanischen Historischen Gesellschaft von Illinois. Jg. 1818—1919. Vol. XVIII—XIX. Chicago, Ill. 1920. pp. 9—68.* [7832

Kraeling, Carl H.: In quest of Muhlenbergiana. *In: The Lutheran Quarterly. Vol. II. Gettysburg and Philadelphia, Pa. 1929. pp. 180—189.* [7833

Learned, Marion Dexter: Guide to the manuscript materials relating to American history in German state archives. *Washington, D. C.: Published by the Carnegie Institution of Washington — Baltimore, Md.: The Lord Baltimore Press 1912. pp. VII, 352. = Carnegie Institution of Washington, D. C. Publication no. 150. Papers of the Department of Historical Research.* [7834

Leland, Waldo G.: Guide to materials for American history in the libraries and archives of Paris. *Vol. I. Libraries Washington, D. C.: Carnegie Institution of Washington 1932. pp. XI, 343. = Carnegie Institution of Washington Publication no. 392.* [7835

Paulmann, . . .: Hessische Regimentstagebücher meist aus dem amerikanischen Feldzug [in der Landesbibliothek zu Kassel]. *In: Nachrichten der Gesellschaft für Familienkunde in Kurhessen und Waldeck. Jg. III. Kassel 1928. S. 28— 30.* [7835a

Rosengarten, J. G.: Sources of history. A paper read before the German American Historical Society of New York and the Pionier-Verein of Philadelphia. *Philadelphia, Pa.:Press of Wm. F. Fell & Co. 1892. pp. 32.* [relative to the Hessian troops in the War of the Revolution.] [7836

— American history from German archives. (Read April 6, 1900.) *In: Proceedings of the American Philosophical Society, held at Philadephia for promoting useful knowledge. Vol. XXXIX. Philadelphia, Pa. 1900. pp. 129—154; 638—639.* [No. 1—4 are relating especially to the Hessian troops in the War of the Revolution.] [7837

Rosengarten, J. G.: American history from German archives with reference to the German soldiers in the Revolution and Franklin's visit to Germany. *Lancaster, Pa.: New Era Printing Co. 1904. = Part XIII. „A narrative and critical history", prepared at the request of the Pennsylvania-German Society. In: The Pennsylvania-German Society. Proceedings and Addresses . . . 1902. Vol. XIII. Lancaster, Pa. 1904. Separate pagination. pp. VII, 93, ill., maps.* [7838

— German archives as sources of German-American history. *Paper read before the Pennsylvania-German Society, October, 1907. In: German American Annals. New series, vol. V. Philadelphia, Pa. 1907. pp. 357—369.* [7839

England

Andrews, Charles M. and **Davenport, Francis G.:** Guide to the manuscript materials for the history of the United States to 1783, in the British Museum, in minor London archives and in the libraries of Oxford and Cambridge. *Washington, D. C.: Published by the Carnegie Institution of Washington 1908. pp. . . . = Carnegie Institution of Washington. Publication no. 90.* [7840

Andrews, Charles M.: List of commissions, instructions, and additional instructions issued to the Royal Governors and others in America. *In: Annual Report of the American Historical Association for the year 1911. Vol. I. Washington, D. C. 1913. pp. 395—528.* [7841

— List of reports and representations of the Plantation Councils, 1660—1674, the Lords of Trade, 1675—1696, and the Board of Trade, 1696—1782, in the Public Record Office. *In: Annual Report of the American Historical Association for the year 1913. Vol. I. Washington, D. C. 1915. pp. 321—406.* [7842

— Guide to the materials for American history, to 1783, in the Public Record Office of Great Britain. *2 vols. Washington, D. C.: Published by the Carnegie Institution of Washington, D. C. 1912— 1914. Vol. I. The state papers. Washington, D. C. 1912. pp. XI, 346; Vol. II. Department and miscellaneous papers. Washington, D. C. 1914. pp. VIII, 427. = Carnegie Institution of Washington. Publication no. 90 A. Vol. I & II.* [7843

Kucynski, V. Fr.: Catalogue of papers relating to Pennsylvania and Delaware, deposited at the State Paper Office, London. *In: Memoirs of the Historical Society of Pennsylvania. Vol. IV. — Part II. Philadelphia, Pa. 1850. pp. 225—385.* [7844

Great Britain, Board of Trade: Calender of state papers, colonial series. America and West Indies 1704—1705, preserved in the Public Record Office. *Edited by* Cecil Headlam. *London: Printed under the authority of His Majestys Stationary Office 1916. pp. XL, 807; . . . 1706—1708. June. . . London 1916. pp. LVIII, 871.* [7845

— Journal of the Commissioners for Trade and Plantations from April, 1704, to February, 1708—09, preserved in the Public Record Office. *Issued by the*

authority of the Lords Commissioners of His Majesty's Treasury under the direction of the Master of the Rolls. London: Published by His Majesty's Stationary Office 1920. pp. VI, 641; . . . Febr. 1708—1709 to March 1714—1715 . . . *London 1925. pp. V, 680; . . .* March 1714—1715 to Oct. 1718—1719 . . . *London 1924. pp. IV, 488; . . .* Nov. 1718 to Dec. 1722 . . . *London 1925. pp. IV,* 435; . . . Jan. 1722—1723 to Dec. 1728 . . . *London 1928. pp. IV, 481; . . .* Jan. 1728—1729 to Dec. 1734 . . . *London 1928. pp. IV, 464; . . .* Jan. 1734—1735 to Dec. 1741 . . . *London 1930. pp. IV, 447 . . .* Jan. 1741—1742 to Dec. 1749 . . . *London 1931. pp. IV, 510; . . .* Jan. 1749—1750 to Dec. 1753 . . . *London 1932. pp. IV,* 503; . . . Jan. 1754 to Dec. 1758 . . . *London 1933. pp. IV, 473.* [7846

Deutschländische Forschungsstellen und Gesellschaften für Sippenkunde

German Genealogical Institutions and Societies

Reichsstelle für Sippenforschung, Berlin NW 7, Schiffbauerdamm 26.

Volksbund der deutschen sippenkundlichen Vereine (B. S. V.), Berlin NW 7, Schiffbauerdamm 26.

Hauptstelle für auslanddeutsche Sippenkunde beim Deutschen Ausland-Institut, Stuttgart, Haus des Deutschtums.

Zentralstelle für Deutsche Personen- und Familiengeschichte, Leipzig, Deutscher Platz. (Organ: **Familiengeschichtliche Blätter**, Leipzig.)

Verein Herold, Berlin W 8, Kronenstr. 4—5 II. (Organ: **Familiengeschichtliche Blätter**, Leipzig.)

Deutscher Roland, Verein für deutschvölkische Sippenkunde e. V., Charlottenburg 5, Kaiserdamm 9. (Organ: **Der Deutsche Roland**, Berlin.)

Westdeutsche Gesellschaft für Familienkunde e. V., Köln a. Rh., Postfach 55. (Organ: **Mitteilungen der Westdeutschen Gesellschaft für Familienkunde**, Köln.)

Zentralstelle für Niedersächsische Familienkunde, Hamburg 3, Holstenwall (Museum). (Organ: **Zeitschrift für Niedersächsische Familienkunde**, Hamburg.)

Sammlungen und Kataloge

Collections and Catalogues

Aurand, Ammon Monroe: Catalog of Pennsylvanica *(new and second hand)*. A bibliography of the „Keystone State". *(Listing more than 1000 items)* . . . *Harrisburg, Pa.: The Aurand Press 1928. pp. 64.* [7847
— Historical: Bibliographical: Reminiscent. A Pennsylvania German library or, the pleasures of „riding" a hobby. *Harrisburg, Pa.: Privately printed: The Aurand Press 1930. pp. 5—61.* [7848
Boekenoogen, J. G.: Catalogus der werken over de doops gezinden en hunne geschiedenis aanwezig in de bibliotheek der Vereenigde Doopsgezinde Gemeente te Amsterdam. *Amsterdam: J. H. de Bussy 1919. pp. X, 357.* [7849
Drury, A. W.: The Historical Society. Catalogue of the historical literature concerning the United Brethren Church in Christ *being in possession of the Historical Society, the library of Bonebrake Seminary, or the Publishing House, Dayton, O. In: The Religious Telescope. Vol. XCVIII, no. 7. Dayton, O., Febr. 13, 1932. pp. 7—8.* [7850
Horsch, John: Catalogue of the Mennonite Historical Library in Scottdale, Pa. *Scottdale, Pa.: Mennonite Publishing House 1929. pp. (1), (2), 9—88.* [7851
[Morris, John George]: Catalogue of the Lutheran Historical Society's collection of books, pamphlets, manuscripts, photographs, etc., *deposited in the Theological Seminary at Gettysburg, Pa. Philadelphia, Pa.: Lutheran Publishing House. 1890.* [7852
[Weber, Christoph]: Das Deutschtum im Ausland. *Eine systematische Zusammenstellung der im Gesamtkatalog der Preußischen wissenschaftlichen Bibliotheken verzeichneten Schriften. 1900—1923. Berlin: Preußische Staatsbibliothek 1925. X, 168 S.*
[Nord-Amerika. Vereinigte Staaten. pp. 103—112.] [7853
List of books contained in the library of the Society for the History of the Germans in Maryland. *Alphabetically arranged according to subjects and authors. In: Eighth — Tenth Annual Report of the Society for the History of the Germans in Maryland. Baltimore, Md. 1896. Appendix. pp. 24;* Supplementary list of books in our library. *In: Fifteenth . . . 1900—1901. pp. 55—60.* [7854
A list of books in the library of the Historical Society of Schuylkill County, Pa. *In: Publications of the Historical Society of Schuylkill County. Vol. IV. Pottsville, Pa. 1912. pp. 93—114.* [7855
Henkels, Stan V.: The extraordinary (-valuable, -extensive) library of Hon. **Samuel W. Pennypacker,** governor of Pennsylvania. *8 vols. Philadelphia, Pa. 1905—1909. = Book Auction Rooms of Davis & Harvey, Philadelphia, 1112 Walnut Street. Catalogue no. 943. Part 1—8. Compiled and sale conducted by Stan V. Henkels.*
Part I : Embracing books printed by Benjamin Franklin, books from the library of Benjamin Franklin, letters written by Benjamin Franklin and by his son Wm. Franklin, books relating to Benjamin Franklin . . . etc., etc. pp. V, 90; 27, ill.;
Part II : . . . embraces his unique collection of personal association books, which includes books once owned by great personages, and manuscript commonplace books, journals and diaries of eminent Americans of colonial and Revolutionary times . . . pp. IV, 123, ill.;
Part III : Embracing his unique collection of books relating to the history of Pennsylvania from its inception to the present time, including many that are unique, as well as many so rare as to be almost unique being the fruits of untiring research for the last forty years in the history of his native state. Gathered from the great libraries that have been dispersed during that period in Europe and America and from the sources also his unique collection of magazines, neswpapers and other periodicals, published in Pennsyl-

vania and elswhere . . . pp. (1), 174, ill.;

Part IV: Embracing his important collection of books relating to general American history. Including many that are of the greatest rarity. Being the fruits of untiring research for the last forty years in American colonial history, the history of the Revolution, state, county and town history, Indian history, etc. etc., also a valuable collection of American genealogies. pp. IV, 166.;

Part V: Embracing his extraordinary collection of books relating to the Quakers, including the first book printed in New York. The most complete collection in existence of the publications of Christopher Sower, of Germantown. His unique and extensive collection of the publications from the presses of the inland towns of Pennsylvania . . . pp. VII, 176, ill.;

Part VI: Embracing many important autograph letters and historical documents relating to Pennsylvania in colonial times and the Revolution . . . pp. IV, 57, ill.;

Part VII: Embracing the most complete collection of the issues of the Press of Robert Bell, the pioneer publisher of Philadelphia, and of the press established by the Dunkers at Ephrata, Pennsylvania. Many unique and excessively rare Bradford imprints; early American almanacs:

Early Philadelphia and miscellaneous American imprints; early school books and juveniles . . . pp. (IV) 181, ill.;

Part VIII: — Conclusion: Embracing a large collection of books and pamphlets relating to the University of Pennsylvania, including an unique collection of medical thesis. Many important works in bibliography and catalogues . . . Miscellaneous books, embracing much American, works relating to the Palatines and Mennonites, first editions of American authors, English county histories . . . pp. (3), 112.
[7856

Executors' sale (Oct. 26 a. 27, 1920). Estate of **Samuel W. Pennypacker,** deceased. *Rare books and manuscripts, autographs, also rare paintings by Benjamin West, and other historical portraits. The collection of the late Hon. Samuel W. Pennypacker. Philadelphia, Pa.: Samuel T. Freman & Co. 1920. pp. 103.* [7857

Americana from three Virginia libraries. The late Gen. John E. **Roller** of Harrisonburg, Va.; Judge Wm. J. Robertson of Charlottesville, Va.; Gen. James Breckinridge of Botetourt County, Va. *To be sold Monday, Tuesday evenings, October twenty-ninth, thirtieth at eight-fifteen. New York, N. Y.: The Andersons Galleries [Mitchell Kennerley] 1923. pp. (4), 75.* [7858

Autoren-Register

Index of Authors

Panabaker, D. N. 5850, 5851, 5868, 7248.
Pancoast, Mary E. 5086.
Panse, Karl 204.
Papet, von . . . 2974 q, 2974 r.
Pargellis, Stanley M. 215 p.
Parker, Amelia Campbell 2975 a.
Parker, Cartlandt 6481 c.
Parkins, A. E. 3202.
Parkinson, Sarah Wodds 3820.
Parr, Amos A. 6551.
Parsons, J. Cox 5004.
Parsons, Luther C. 4672.
Parthemore, E. W. S. 1153, 1154, 1831, 3882—3902, 4146, 4367—4373, 5266, 6181, 6238, 6241, 6285, 6361, 6453, 6736, 6794, 6882, 6918, 7171, 7226, 7344, 7404, 7405, 7475, 7578, 7684, 7700, 7704.
Parton James 560.
Paschall, T.[homas] 3308, 3310.
Pastorius, Franz Daniel [Francis Daniel] 219—221, 223—226, 228—232, 237, 267, 3310, 3435, 3437—3437 b, 3443, 5115.
Patridge, Francis D. 781.
Pattee, William S. 747.
Patterson, Mrs. Lindsay 5756.
Patterson, William D. 736.
Pattison, Robert Emory 3016.
Paul, Alwin 2887 g.
Paullin, Charles O. 28.
Paulmann, . . . 2945, 7835 a.
Pausch, George 2975 g.
Paxon, Henry D. 2574.
Paxson, Isaac 5175—5177.
Peachey, Samuel W. 1015, 4539, 6190.
Pearce, Stewart 4521.
Pearce, Thomas 5852.
Pearson, C. C. 7308 b.
Pekari, Matthew Anthony 1910.
Pell, George P. 6392.
Pendleton, Wm. C. 5642.
Penn, William 129, 216—218, 3308, 3310, 3312—3316.
Pennypacker, Isaac R. 884.
Pennypacker, Samuel Whitaker [S. W.] 268, 278, 356—361, 933, 2054—2057, 2314, 2475, 3043, 3049, 3056, 3174—3176, 3193, 3308, 3781, 3783, 4673—4676, 4994, 5078, 5088—5091, 6283, 6290, 6345, 7153, 7181, 7183, 7185, 7261.
Pepper, William 2374.
Pershing, Edgar Jamison 7194.

Perry, William Stevens 3276.
Peter, P. A. 1393.
Peter, W. K. 7199.
Peters, Hermann 2973 g.
Peters, Richard 2329, 2686.
Petersen, Carl 93.
Petersen, Charles J. 2882 b.
Petersen Magnus 3329.
Pettengill, . . . 2974 g.
Pettengill, Ray W. 2945 c.
Peyster, John Watts de 2713, 6630.
Peyton, J. Lewis 5597.
Pfatteicher, E. P. 4995.
Pfautz, John Eby 7202.
Pfeifer, Gottfried 7 a.
Pfister, Ferdinand 2907, 2932, 2932 a.
Pfister, H. v. 2933—2933 e, 2934 c, 2970 m.
Pflueger, O. E. 1293.
Pflug, Ferd. 2971 g.
Pfohl, J. K.[enneth] 5745, 7482.
Phelps, E. J. 4147, 4148.
Phifer, Charles H. 7204.
Pickens, Wiley M. 5728.
Pickeral, J. Julian 5607.
Pierce, Lorne A. 5818.
Pine, John B. 6186.
Pittnam, Thomas M. 5654.
Planer, Oskar 2871 f.
Pleasants, Henry 3782.
Plumb, Henry Blackman 4522.
Plummer, Wilbur 3203.
Pohlman, H. 736 a.
Poole, . . . 2886 s.
Popp, Stephan 2973 d.
Porter, Kenneth Wiggins 561.
Porter, Thomas Conrad 2439, 6260.
Post, Frederick 3237.
Poten, B. 2883 g.
Potter, Alonzo 2372.
Poucher, J. Wilson 484.
Pound, Arthur 3275.
Povemire, H. M. 5901.
Powell, Henry Fletcher 5408.
Powell, Lyman P 5505.
Powers, Fred Perry 5092.
Pratt, W. S. 6631 a.
Precht, Victor 214 u, 542.
Prechtel, George 5479.
Preser, Carl 2934—2934 d.
Prettyman, William 1965.
Price, D. E. 1100, 1101.
Prince, B. F. 5902, 5903.
Prince, Benjamin F. 5931.
Printz, Johan 3310.
Prinzinger, A. 698.
Proctor, John Glagett 6653.
Proctor, Joseph 4677.
Prottengeier 2476.
Proud, Robert 3177.

Prowell, George R. 2974 n, 2974 o, 5267—5269, 7013, 7014.
Pullinger, Herbert 5093.
Purple, Edwin R. 215 q.
Putnam, J. 2970.
Pyle, Howard 1155.

Quinter, J. 1097.
Quinter, Mary N. 7217.
Quirk, John F. 6421.

R., 2995.
R., Cl. D. 2936.
R., H. 3903.
R., J. 2935.
R., W. F. 3904, 3905.
Race, Henry 604.
Raddatz, C. F. 5440.
Räber, Johann 5950.
Rahn, George 2724.
Raine, Friederich 5465.
Rainsford, Charles 2913.
Ramsauer, John 3422, 5721.
Ramsey, Alfred 2477.
Ranck, Henry H.[averstick] 3305, 4374, 6153.
Ranck, Samuel H. 2377.
Rand, James Hall 5659.
Randell, E. O. 1728, 5967.
Randolph, Howard S. F. [H. S. F.] 468, 6760.
Rapp, E. M. 3641.
Rarick, Ralph G. 5980.
Raschen, J. T. L. 166, 2188.
Rath, G. vom 3504.
Rath, Myron O. 4494.
Rattermann, H. A. 94, 95, 129 a, 377, 574, 615, 628, 630, 659, 672, 673, 699, 700, 737, 1156, 1618, 1807, 1933 a, 2058, 2059, 2103, 2104, 2107, 2511, 2806—2808, 2851, 2855, 2862, 2908, 2973, 2992, 2993, 5093 a—c, 5783, 5788—5791, 5904—5907 a, 6203, 6246 a, 6617 a, 6795 a, 6922, 6934 a, 6978, 7255, 7315, 7750, 7751.
Ratzel, Friedrich 18 a, 96, 2973 f.
Rau, Albert G. 1642, 4843, 4900.
Rau, Robert 4844, 4901, 4902.
Rauch, Christian Henry 1514, 1521.
Rauch, Edward H. [E. H.] 1966, 1967, 1994, 3010.
Rauck, Geo. H. 4149.
Raumer, Fred 7536.
Raumer, Kurt von 167.
Rausch, Christian Henry 3415.
Rawle, William [Brooke] 3229, 4950.
Raymond, Eleanor 2246.

Familiennamen-Register

Index of Surnames